BEGINNING SHAREPOINT® 2010

BEGINNING

SharePoint® 2010

BEGINNING
SharePoint® 2010
BUILDING BUSINESS SOLUTIONS WITH SHAREPOINT

Amanda Perran

Shane Perran

Jennifer Mason

Laura Rogers

Wiley Publishing, Inc.

Beginning SharePoint® 2010: Building Business Solutions with SharePoint

Published by
Wiley Publishing, Inc.
10475 Crosspoint Boulevard
Indianapolis, IN 46256
www.wiley.com

ISBN: 978-0-470-61789-2

ISBN: 978-1-118-02191-0 (ebk)

ISBN: 978-1-118-02190-3 (ebk)

ISBN: 978-1-118-02288-7 (ebk)

Manufactured in the United States of America

10 9 8 7 6 5 4 3 2 1

For general information on our other products and services please contact our Customer Care Department within the United States at (877) 762-2974, outside the United States at (317) 572-3993 or fax (317) 572-4002.

Wiley also publishes its books in a variety of electronic formats. Some content that appears in print may not be available in electronic books.

Library of Congress Control Number: 2001012345

For Dylan... May you stay forever young!

—Amanda and Shane Perran

For Dr. Metzgar, thanks for being that teacher who I will never forget because the lessons you taught are so applicable to my everyday life.

—Jennifer Mason

For Charlotte and Kristen, you are the most wonderful and sweet little girls, and I love you with all my heart.

—Laura Derbes Rogers

CREDITS

ACQUISITIONS EDITOR
Paul Reese

SENIOR PROJECT EDITOR
Adaobi Obi Tulton

TECHNICAL EDITORS
Martin Reid
Charlie Lee

PRODUCTION EDITOR
Daniel Scribner

COPY EDITOR
Foxxe Editorial Services

EDITORIAL DIRECTOR
Robyn B. Siesky

EDITORIAL MANAGER
Mary Beth Wakefield

FREELANCER EDITORIAL MANAGER
Rosemarie Graham

ASSOCIATE DIRECTOR OF MARKETING
David Mayhew

PRODUCTION MANAGER
Tim Tate

VICE PRESIDENT AND EXECUTIVE GROUP PUBLISHER
Richard Swadley

VICE PRESIDENT AND EXECUTIVE PUBLISHER
Barry Pruett

ASSOCIATE PUBLISHER
Jim Minatel

PROJECT COORDINATOR, COVER
Katie Crocker

PROOFREADER
Word One, New York

INDEXER
Robert Swanson

COVER DESIGNER
Michael E. Trent

COVER IMAGE
© Trevor Fisher/istockphoto.com

ABOUT THE AUTHORS

AMANDA PERRAN is a Microsoft Most Valuable Professional for Microsoft SharePoint Server located in St. John's, Newfoundland and Labrador. She has been working as a consultant and trainer with SharePoint since the release of the first version of the product in 2001. Amanda is a regular speaker and presenter at user group meetings, webcasts, and Microsoft events on topics such as Microsoft SharePoint, InfoPath, and Project Server. She is the co-founder of SharePoint Nation, `www.sharepointnation.org`, which is a virtual user group for SharePoint. You can follow her on Twitter as *@amandaperran*.

SHANE PERRAN is a Microsoft Most Valuable Professional for Microsoft SharePoint Server located in St. John's, Newfoundland and Labrador. He has been designing online user experiences for over 15 years. His strong passion for visual presentation, web standards, and usability has paved the way for a successful transition into the SharePoint Products and Technologies space where, over the past seven years, Shane has become highly involved and recognized in the SharePoint customization space. He is the co-founder of SharePoint Nation, `www.sharepointnation.org`, which is a virtual user group for SharePoint. Shane's SharePoint Customization Blog at `www.graphicalwonder.com` is a popular stop for customization enthusiasts across the globe. You can follow Shane on Twitter as *@shaneperran*.

JENNIFER MASON has dedicated the last seven years to working with SharePoint. She started out as an intern focused on SharePoint and eventually began working as a full-time SharePoint consultant. She is currently working as a Senior SharePoint Consultant with the team at SharePoint911. Her focus has been on strategy, project planning, project management, governance, and best practices for implementing business solutions using SharePoint Technologies. She has worked with a range of companies at different points in the life cycles of their SharePoint implementation. She is passionate about SharePoint, and loves using the out-of-the-box features to bring immediate ROI to the organization. Jennifer is involved in the SharePoint community and is one of the founding members of the Columbus Ohio SharePoint Users Group (BuckeyeSPUG). You can learn more about Jennifer by viewing her blog at `http://sharepoint911.com/blogs/jennifer`. You can follow Jennifer on Twitter as *@jennifermason*.

LAURA DERBES ROGERS is a Senior SharePoint Consultant at SharePoint911. Her background is in server administration, and she has been an MCSE for 11 years, working in SharePoint for the last 6 years. She is enthusiastic about accomplishing business solutions in SharePoint by using the out-of-the-box capabilities without writing code. She specializes and trains others in SharePoint workflows, data view web parts, and InfoPath. Laura is a regular speaker at several different SharePoint conferences, loves sharing ideas on her SharePoint blog at `http://sharepoint911.com/blogs/laura`, and has recorded a set of screencasts about data view web parts. Laura is a graduate of Louisiana State University, and currently resides in Birmingham, Alabama with her husband, Chris, and two lovely daughters. You can follow Laura on Twitter as *@WonderLaura*.

ABOUT THE TECHNICAL EDITORS

MARTIN WP REID is a systems analyst at the Queen's University of Belfast, one of the leading U.K. universities. In addition to administrating large SharePoint systems, Martin is particularly interested in SharePoint as an end-user tool to help information workers get the job done without having to wade through technical manuals. Martin is currently working on a 30,000 user SharePoint 2007 system. Martin has authored several technical books, including *Microsoft SharePoint 2007 for Office 2007 Users*, published by Wrox. He has been a technical editor on many technical books for Wiley.

CHARLIE LEE is a SharePoint Subject Matter Expert working for Capgemini UK. He also runs a web application development consultancy specializing in SharePoint services and contributes to the SharePoint community whenever he can. He has a wealth of experience with real-life issues with WSS 3.0, MOSS 2007, SharePoint Foundation, and Server 2010. He lives and works in the U.K. with his beautiful wife and two amazing children.

ACKNOWLEDGMENTS

IT IS COMMON FOR AUTHORS to thank their spouses or partners for their understanding and support during the book-writing process. In our case, this was a project by a husband-and-wife team, which meant that the late nights, deadlines, and missed holidays were spent together, side by side, for better or worse. Of course, we would have it no other way.

We would like to thank our families for their love, support, and encouragement throughout this book and all the other challenges and surprises that life can bring.

We are excited to have Jennifer Mason and Laura Derbes Rogers join us on this book. It is an honor and a pleasure to share a title with such talented individuals. We are so happy to have you each onboard with us for this book and look forward to any future opportunities to work together again.

As always, we would like to thank Jim Minatel for introducing us to the Wrox team so many years ago. Thank you to Paul Reese for spearheading this project and for always keeping things moving along. Thank you to Adaobi Obi Tulton for your constant grace under pressure and excellent editing skills. It was an extreme pleasure to work with you on this project and we hope our paths cross again. Thank you to Martin Reid and Jeri Freedman for your diligence and attention to detail throughout the editing process. Each of your talents contributed significantly to this project and we are so very grateful to each of you.

Finally, to Dylan. Thank you for constantly being that light at the end of the tunnel and helping to always keep life in perspective.

—Amanda and Shane Perran

WRITING A TECHNICAL BOOK has been a longtime dream of mine. It is one of the things that I have always had on my "list" of things I had wanted to accomplish throughout my career. Along the way, so many different people have invested in my future and I wouldn't be who I am without their influences.

First, I would like to thank my family for investing so much into my education and supporting me through many different changes and moves. Mom and Dad — I wouldn't be what I am today without you and I am blessed to have you in my life. Bob and Jane — thanks so much for being my "other parents"; your support means more than I could ever thank you for!

Dr. Metzgar, thanks so much for all the encouragement, knowledge, wisdom, and friendship you gave me while I was at Liberty. You taught me so many things that I can honestly say I still apply on a daily basis. I definitely wouldn't be here without your support and investment.

Shane and Nicola — you two might be the best people in the world to work for! Thanks so much for all you have done for me. I don't think it would be possible to work with a better group of people than the ones I work with at SharePoint911. I thank each of them for all the support they give me.

Laura, Shane, and Amanda, this is has been a great experience and I am honored to have written alongside you. I am looking forward to working together again on future projects.

Finally, I would like to thank the team at Wrox that helped bring this project together. Paul Reese for inviting me to join this project and Adaobi Obi Tulton for all the hard work you have done to get this book ready to go. You have shown great patience and understanding, which has been appreciated! Thanks also to Martin Reid and Jeri Freedman for all your efforts throughout the editing process. I hope that we will all be able to work together again in the future.

—Jennifer Mason

WORKING ON THIS BOOK has been quite an experience, and there are several people who I would like to thank. The major influencers in my life exist on both the personal and the professional sides.

First of all, my husband, Chris, has been amazing and supportive. His sarcasm and wit have always kept me laughing despite any book-deadline stresses. Speaking of family, I thank my daughters for always been so loving, smart, delightful, and happy. I love my sweeties! Thanks to my parents, Greg and Caroline, who have always been encouraging and supportive, and to my artist brother, Clark, and his family.

Thank you so much to Jennifer Mason for being a brilliant and driven businesswoman and friend, and thanks to Shane and Amanda Perran for being so inspiring to work with. Thanks for including me in this endeavor; it has been amazing. You three are such outstanding SharePoint gurus, and I sincerely look forward to spending more time with you and joining you in any future endeavors that may arise.

Of course, I would also like to extend my thanks to the Wrox team, especially Paul Reese and Adaobi Obi Tulton. It has been a pleasure working with all of you on this adventure of a book. I think you all have been wonderful and professional, and I hope that we cross paths again soon.

Lastly, I would like to thank those of you in my life who have been part of the path that I have taken to become a SharePoint professional, in chronological order. Thanks, Susan Cargile, for assigning me the task of first installing SharePoint in 2004. Who knew, right? Bill English, Brett Lonsdale, and Mark Miller, you have been major influences on me and the direction that my career has gone. Last, but certainly not least, I'd like to thank Shane Young and all of my colleagues at SharePoint911. You all are family to me, and I truly enjoy working with you. The personalities in this company are awesome, and we always have so much fun together.

—Laura Derbes Rogers

CONTENTS

INTRODUCTION

MICROSOFT SHAREPOINT SERVER 2010 has improved and changed dramatically over previous versions of the product. The capabilities of the platform have expanded greatly, with significant enhancements made to the Web Content Management, Social Media, Business Connectivity, and Records Management features of the platform. However, the value of this tool to an enterprise will depend primarily on the ability of individuals in the organization to understand the features and capabilities of the platform and effectively map those to specific business requirements.

This book is designed to mentor and coach business and technical leaders in an organization on the use and configuration of SharePoint to address critical information management problems. It gives detailed descriptions and illustrations of the product's functionality and also includes realistic usage scenarios to provide contextual relevance and a personalized learning experience to the reader.

WHO THIS BOOK IS FOR

The mission of this book is to provide extensive knowledge to information workers and site managers that will empower them to become SharePoint Application champions in their organizations. This book should be the premiere handbook of any active or aspiring SharePoint expert.

To complete the exercises in this book, you should have a basic comfort level using Microsoft Office client applications to create content, and a general understanding of how to interact with a website through the browser. This book is intended as a starting point for any SharePoint 2010 user, whether that user has never used SharePoint before or has some familiarity with a previous version and just wants to understand the differences with the new release.

WHAT THIS BOOK COVERS

SharePoint 2010 represents the latest release of Microsoft's portal and collaborative technology platform. This book covers in detail many of the features of Microsoft SharePoint Server 2010 that will assist you in creating an effective collaboration, content management, business intelligence, business process, or social media solution for your organization. It addresses core functionality that has existed in SharePoint within previous versions as well as new concepts that have been introduced in this latest release.

HOW THIS BOOK IS STRUCTURED

This book covers the essential elements of using and configuring SharePoint 2010 as an effective tool for business. Each chapter focuses on a dedicated topic and provides hands-on exercises to assist with your learning experience. The following is a short summary of each chapter of this book.

- **Chapter 1: Getting Started with Microsoft SharePoint Server 2010** — This chapter serves as an introduction to SharePoint and lays the foundation for important terminology and concepts explored in the following chapters of the book.
- **Chapter 2: Working with SharePoint Lists** — This chapter introduces one of the core mechanisms for sharing and organizing content in a SharePoint site. You will review what lists are and how they are used, and then explore the various templates that exist in SharePoint 2010.
- **Chapter 3: Working with SharePoint Libraries** — After reviewing some of the fundamental concepts relating to lists, the chapter introduces the other major storage mechanism in SharePoint, known as libraries. This chapter discusses some of the various templates that exist for libraries.
- **Chapter 4: Managing and Customizing SharePoint Lists and Libraries** — SharePoint templates for lists and libraries provide a great starting point for collaboration and information sharing. This chapter shows how you can extend these base templates to address an organization's specific requirements for a collaborative site or information management tool.
- **Chapter 5: Working with Workflow** — This chapter discusses the templates that SharePoint provides for workflow, and demonstrates how to create custom workflow solutions using the SharePoint Designer application.
- **Chapter 6: Working with Content Types** — Most organizations have information and documents, which often utilize consistent templates, processes, and policies each time they are created. Therefore, SharePoint has content types, which allow an organization to package templates and information to ensure that reusable components are rolled out in the organization to enforce consistency and ease of use. This chapter demonstrates what content types are and explores how they can be used through some hands-on examples.
- **Chapter 7: Working with Web Parts** — Web parts are an important element in SharePoint because they enable teams to present information on their sites to users in many different ways. This chapter explores the various groups of web parts that exist in SharePoint 2010, and gives examples on how specific types of web parts can be configured and used to present information in a desired manner.
- **Chapter 8: SharePoint Sites and Workspaces** — The fundamental components of any SharePoint environment are the sites and workspaces that it contains. These collaborative work areas contain all the components discussed in previous sections and represent how each of those items comes together to provide an effective environment for collaboration, communication, and document management. In this chapter, topics such as site templates and features are covered.
- **Chapter 9: SharePoint Branding and User Experience** — Many organizations wish to change the look and feel of SharePoint to suit their specific corporate brand. This chapter explores

the various options for changing the look and feel of a SharePoint environment as well as best practices for enhancing and improving user experience.

- **Chapter 10: Managing User Permissions and Security** — Effective management of users is of ultimate importance to any information system. The two primary tiers of effective user management include securing content and personalizing information on the portal. This chapter explains in simple terms how to effectively secure a SharePoint environment at the site level, the list or library level, and down to the unique content items stored on a SharePoint site. In addition, the chapter gives an introduction to personalization to ensure that readers understand how to effectively target information to users in a portal.
- **Chapter 11: Personalization and Social Networking** — Social networking has been an area of major enhancement in SharePoint 2010. In this chapter, you will learn how to make the most of the social networking tools that exist in SharePoint such as My Sites, tags, blogs, wikis, and ratings.
- **Chapter 12: Forms Management** — Microsoft InfoPath is the ideal companion to SharePoint for many business solutions. This chapter introduces readers to creating simple business applications using Microsoft InfoPath, including creating template parts, creating flexible form interfaces, and connecting to business data.
- **Chapter 13: Web Content Management** — This chapter provides an overview of the web content management capabilities of the system, including the use of publishing sites and features, the automatic provisioning of multilingual content through variations, and the creation of custom page templates known as page layouts.
- **Chapter 14: Records Management** — This chapter provides an overview of and introduction to the establishment of a records management practice in your organization using SharePoint 2010. The chapter covers topics including term sets, archive-based records management features, as well as in-place records management features.
- **Chapter 15: Business Connectivity Services** — This chapter introduces the concept of business connectivity services, explaining important concepts such as security, external content types, and working with business data.
- **Chapter 16: Business Intelligence and Insights** — This chapter demonstrates how to improve the overall decision making of an organization by providing access to important information, utilizing browser-based worksheets and visual indicators of performance information, and building personalized interactive dashboards.
- **Chapter 17: Working with Search** — An information system is only useful to an organization if stakeholders can easily access and locate the information it contains. This chapter discusses the search engine capabilities of the SharePoint platform, including methods that improve the search experience through the use of effective queries, configurations, and analytics.
- **Chapter 18: Implementing a Governance Framework** — This chapter explores the definition of governance as well as the effective steps and best practices toward designing a governance framework for your organization.

WHAT YOU NEED TO USE THIS BOOK

To effectively complete the examples in this book, you should have access to a Microsoft SharePoint Server 2010 environment or site collection and have administrative rights to the server. If you do not have administrative rights, your server administrator may have to assist you with some exercises in this book.

You should also have a client computer running either Windows 7 or Windows Vista along with Microsoft Office 2010 Professional or Professional Plus, SharePoint Designer 2010 and SharePoint Workspace 2010. While many exercises can be completed with earlier versions of Office, certain exercises related to workflow, forms, and Excel Services are dependent on features only available in the Professional versions of 2010.

CONVENTIONS

To help you get the most from the text and keep track of what's happening, we've used a number of conventions throughout the book.

TRY IT OUT

The *Try It Out* is an exercise you should work through, following the text in the book.

1. It usually consists of a set of steps.
2. Each step has a number.
3. Follow the steps through with your copy of the database.

How It Works

After each *Try It Out*, the example will be explained in detail.

WARNING *Boxes with a warning icon like this one hold important, not-to-be-forgotten information that is directly relevant to the surrounding text.*

NOTE *The pencil icon indicates notes, tips, hints, tricks, or asides to the current discussion.*

As for styles in the text:

- We *italicize* new terms and important words when we introduce them.
- We show keyboard strokes like this: Ctrl+A.
- We show file names and URLs within the text like so: `persistence.properties`.

NOTE *Because many books have similar titles, you may find it easiest to search by ISBN; this book's ISBN is 978-0-470-61789-2.*

ERRATA

We make every effort to ensure that there are no errors in the text. However, no one is perfect, and mistakes do occur. If you find an error in one of our books, like a spelling mistake or instructions that do not lead to the intended results, we would be very grateful for your feedback. By sending in errata, you may save another reader hours of frustration, and at the same time, you will be helping us provide even higher-quality information.

To find the errata page for this book, go to `www.wrox.com` and locate the title using the Search box or one of the title lists. Then, on the book details page, click the Book Errata link. On this page, you can view all errata that have been submitted for this book and posted by Wrox editors. A complete book list, including links to each book's errata, is also available at `www.wrox.com/misc-pages/booklist.shtml`.

If you don't spot "your" error on the Book Errata page, go to `www.wrox.com/contact/techsupport.shtml` and complete the form there to send us the error you have found. We'll check the information and, if appropriate, post a message to the book's errata page and fix the problem in subsequent editions of the book.

P2P.WROX.COM

For author and peer discussion, join the P2P forums at `p2p.wrox.com`. The forums are a web-based system for you to post messages relating to Wrox books and related technologies and interact with other readers and technology users. The forums offer a subscription feature to email you topics of interest of your choosing when new posts are made to the forums. Wrox authors, editors, other industry experts, and your fellow readers are present on these forums.

At `http://p2p.wrox.com`, you will find a number of different forums that will help you, not only as you read this book, but also as you develop your own applications. To join the forums, just follow these steps:

1. Go to `p2p.wrox.com` and click the Register link.
2. Read the terms of use and click Agree.
3. Complete the required information to join, as well as any optional information you wish to provide, and click Submit.
4. You will receive an email with information describing how to verify your account and complete the joining process.

NOTE *You can read messages in the forums without joining P2P, but in order to post your own messages, you must join.*

Once you join, you can post new messages and respond to messages other users post. You can read messages at any time on the web. If you would like to have new messages from a particular forum emailed to you, click the Subscribe to this Forum icon by the forum name in the forum listing.

For more information about how to use the Wrox P2P, be sure to read the P2P FAQs for answers to questions about how the forum software works, as well as many common questions specific to P2P and Wrox books. To read the FAQs, click the FAQ link on any P2P page.

1

Getting Started with Microsoft SharePoint Server 2010

WHAT YOU WILL LEARN IN THIS CHAPTER:

- The differences between SharePoint Foundation 2010 and SharePoint Server 2010
- Common usage scenarios for SharePoint Foundation 2010 and SharePoint Server 2010
- An overview of important SharePoint concepts and features

The goal of this book is to provide you with the knowledge to set you on the way to becoming a SharePoint master. An important part of understanding how best to manage and utilize SharePoint Server from either a developer or IT pro perspective is first to understand the core capabilities of the product and how they can be extended to meet your organization's business needs. Along those lines, this chapter introduces you to the new and exciting features and capabilities of Microsoft SharePoint Server 2010. With it, you will learn how to put the platform to work for your organization to create scalable business solutions with and without the use of custom code. In this chapter, you learn about the following topics and concepts:

INTRODUCING SHAREPOINT

Before getting started on the technical tasks associated with managing and working with SharePoint content, it is important to understand the purpose of all common usage scenarios for the technology.

Organizational stakeholders often suffer from what's been termed as information overload. Because computers play such an integral part in any business, not surprisingly, more and more of the information that is created, consumed, and shared in an organization is digital. The more business that you conduct and the more successful your business becomes, the more information you have to manage. Usually, you have some form of document for just about every process and transaction that plays out during the day-to-day operations of your company. From proposals to legal documents, from sales receipts to human resources policies, the amount of information required for a company to function is staggering.

To manage your information overload, SharePoint offers tools with which you can build business applications to better store, share, and manage digital information. With it, you can create lists, libraries, and websites for your various company teams to help run your business processes more efficiently. By locating your organization's important business data in a single location, it becomes much easier and intuitive for users to find the right information when they need it rather than searching through disparate locations such as email, computer hard drives, or file shares.

What Is Portal Technology?

A corporate portal is a gateway through which members can access business information and, if set up properly, should be the first place an employee goes to access anything of importance. Portals differ from regular websites in that they are customized specifically around business processes. In SharePoint, a portal may actually consist of numerous websites, with information stored either directly on those sites or in other systems, such as file shares, business applications, or a regular Internet website. This allows SharePoint to be the central location users may visit to find information regardless of its actual storage location. Because making informed business decisions is key to becoming and remaining successful, it's important that the information you place on a portal be secure, up to date, and easily accessible. Because a business's marketplace may span the globe, an organization also needs to have the information that reflects the needs of employees from multiple specific regions.

As an example, consider a new employee who has just joined an organization. In addition to learning her new job responsibilities, this employee must quickly get up to speed on the various company processes and policies. A good portal should provide all the company reference and policy information that the employee needs to review, as well as links to all the information systems and websites that employee needs to do her job. Information should be stored in easy-to-browse locations, based on subject or topic. In situations where the location of a document or information is not obvious, the employee should be able to type words into a search box and receive suggestions. The employee should also be able to share information with others. In many ways, a good portal should act as a table of contents for all the information and websites related to an organization or topic.

Why Does an Organization Invest in Portal Technology?

The following list provides just a few of the reasons why many enterprise organizations opt to invest in portal technologies:

- The adoption of the web and web-related technologies makes portal technologies an obvious choice. Because portal technologies are web-based, decision makers can access important information via the Internet regardless of where they are located.
- Portal technologies allow information workers to handle day-to-day tasks from a single starting point, whereas previously things were spread out across multiple places and applications.

- With important regulatory initiatives, such as the Sarbanes-Oxley Act, organizations are using portal technologies to ensure an accurate audit trail is kept on important documents and that business processes remain compliant.
- The file-share-based approach previously used to store most information was highly dependent on the habits and practices of the person creating it. Portal technologies store and share information based on the organizational structure, making them intuitive to use for everyone in the organization. This structure translates into productivity boosts because workers can more easily locate and retrieve information.
- Portal technologies, such as SharePoint, scale with an organization, offering a model that will grow as your company grows.
- While the typical business portal product incorporates many common business practices, your organizational needs may dictate a customized process. Because SharePoint offers an extensible infrastructure, you can build custom solutions. Custom solutions may be created with or without the use of code.
- Although a company may be tempted by the latest and greatest information management system, most organizations still have legacy systems and data sources such as file shares, databases or business applications. You can massage portal technologies so that they integrate with these systems, allowing easier data mining or migration.
- Much of today's digital information is created and managed using the Microsoft Office system. SharePoint, as a portal technology, integrates seamlessly with that system's tools, allowing you to create, store, manage, and collaborate on this information from a single location.

WHAT IS SHAREPOINT 2010?

SharePoint 2010 is an extensible and scalable web-based platform consisting of tools and technologies that support the collaboration and sharing of information within teams, throughout the enterprise and on the web. The total package is a platform on which you can build business applications to help you better store, share, and manage digital information within your organization. Because you can build with or without code, the package empowers the average business user to create, deploy, and manage team websites, without depending on skilled resources, such as systems administrators or developers. Using lists, libraries, and web parts, you can transform team websites into business applications built specifically around making your organization's business processes more efficient.

SharePoint 2010 is composed of two primary components:

- SharePoint Foundation 2010 is the free product that focuses specifically on the features and functionality related to content storage, team collaboration, and document control.
- SharePoint Server 2010 is the enterprise portal technology that includes all the features and functionality of SharePoint Foundation 2010, as well as more advanced capabilities related to business intelligence, search, content management, and data connectivity. For the purposes of this book, we have chosen to focus specifically on the capabilities of SharePoint Server 2010. In some cases, there will be overlap and features described in this book will also be available within the Foundation version of the product.

COMPARING SHAREPOINT FOUNDATION AND SHAREPOINT SERVER

Many organizations struggle with understanding which of the SharePoint products is most appropriate for their needs. The following sections identify some differences between the editions and usage scenarios for each. While this book has been written specifically to review features and functionality from the perspective of SharePoint Server, the following section discusses some comparisons between SharePoint Foundation and SharePoint Server. To start you off, you should remember the following:

- SharePoint Foundation 2010, previously known as Windows SharePoint Services, contains the core document management and collaboration platform features. With Foundation, the average information user can build web-based business applications without the need for technical resources or code. Because Foundation is available free with the Windows Server system, it has become a very popular collaborative tool for teams. This is largely because of the templates and existing site modules, which allow users to add documents, images, and information via a simple form rather than by using code. Users can create a new site based on an existing template in just a few seconds. SharePoint Foundation is tightly integrated with Microsoft Office applications such as Word, Excel, PowerPoint, Access and Outlook, so users can create and share content using a familiar, comfortable environment.
- SharePoint Server 2010 is the nexus of Microsoft collaborative and portal technologies. It can accelerate the adoption of business process management, content management, and business intelligence across the intranet, extranet, and Internet. SharePoint Server 2010 delivers the tools to create, publish, and manage web-based content from a cohesive environment. SharePoint Server 2010 also offers the tools to automatically aggregate content from the SharePoint team sites, rolling up content from multiple sources to a central location, making information management even easier.

SharePoint Foundation Primary Benefits

The primary features of SharePoint Foundation revolve around document management and collaboration. The following sections outline the major features of the platform that have been responsible for its wide adoption in businesses.

- **Effective document and task collaboration:** Team websites offer access to information in a central location as well as the following capabilities:
  - Workspaces for teams to share documents and information, coordinate schedules and tasks, and participate in forum-like discussions. These workspaces can be used by team members to share information regardless of their physical proximity or boundaries. Because of the use of user interface elements, such as the Ribbon, navigation within the workspace is familiar and easy to use for most business users.
  - Libraries provide a better document creation and management environment. Libraries can be configured to ensure that a document is checked out before editing, track a document's revision history, or allow users to collaborate on its review and approval.

- Role-based security settings ensure that sensitive information is secure and available only to select individuals.
- Advanced task-tracking lists and alert systems keep users updated on current and upcoming tasks.
- Templates for creating wikis and blogs allow you to share information across your organization quickly and easily.

- **Reduced implementation and deployment resources:** Because SharePoint Foundation is available to Windows Server customers as a free download, implementation time and cost are greatly reduced, resulting in the following benefits:
  - Deploying team collaboration sites is easy, so organizations can free up skilled resources, and focus on more important and complex tasks.
  - Users can immediately create and apply professional-looking site themes directly from within their browser.
  - Customized workspaces have prebuilt application templates for most common business processes, such as workflows.
  - Because SharePoint Foundation offers seamless integration with the Microsoft Office system, employees can use common applications, such as Microsoft Word, to create and manage documents, without the need for expensive training or process changes.
- **Better control of your organization's important business data:** SharePoint Foundation offers the following features for data and information management and security:
  - Enhanced browser and command-line-based administrative controls allow you to perform site provisioning, content management, support, and backup. Subsequently, a business can become more efficient and reduce costs.
  - Using advanced administrative features, IT can set the parameters under which business units can provision sites and allow access, ensuring that all units fall within an acceptable security policy.
  - The Recycle Bin item retrieval and document versioning capabilities provide a safe storage environment.
- **Embrace the web for collaboration:** By extending and customizing SharePoint Foundation, you can:
  - Create collaborative websites complete with document libraries that act as central repositories for creating, managing, and sharing documents with your team.
  - Create, connect, and customize a set of business applications specific to scaling your organizational needs.
  - Take advantage of SharePoint Designer 2010 to create reusable workflows and connect to external data systems, as well as customize and brand your team sites and applications.

In short, SharePoint Foundation represents the core content storage and collaboration features of SharePoint 2010. It is the ideal edition for teams and small organizations looking to improve on their ability to work with one another in a secure, easy-to-use collaborative workspace.

SHAREPOINT FOUNDATION USAGE EXAMPLE

The fictional organization Rossco Tech Consulting offers professional services and technology mentoring to startup companies. The following scenario outlines Rossco's experience with SharePoint 2010, beginning with SharePoint Foundation 2010 and later expanding to SharePoint Server 2010.

Because so much of Rossco's business revolves around process documentation, having a central repository with which to manage information surrounding projects is imperative. Because Rossco was using Windows Server, SharePoint Foundation became the obvious and most cost-efficient foundation on which to build solutions to manage their projects.

Planning

To identify what improvements they needed to make to enhance efficiency, the company asked team leads about the problems they were encountering when collaborating within their respective teams. From these results, the company identified the common issues each team shared and created a site hierarchy that best represented the organization's corporate culture and business processes. Because the organization consisted of only three divisions (Finance, Marketing, and Operations), they opted for a single collection of sites: a main site for the organization as a whole and three subsites, one for each division.

Because each division followed similar processes for most projects, the company could use SharePoint's template system to create a single "project" site template that all teams could use to create a collaborative project location. The sites created from this template would then have the following features:

- A document library to create, store, and organize any documents related to the project
- A contact list to store and organize important contacts involved with the project
- A task list to coordinate important tasks for team members involved with the project
- An issue-tracking list to highlight any potential project concerns

The template was created and then saved in a central site template gallery, where each division could use it to generate a new site for each project.

Because Rossco had invested heavily in the creation of its corporate identity, it was imperative that this brand be carried over within the sites. Using a combination of the built-in theme functionality and free downloadable application templates, Rossco transformed the default SharePoint environment into a more familiar, corporate-branded interface.

Moving from Plan to Practice

After defining the organizational structure via team sites on the intranet, it was time to for Rossco Tech Consulting to put their hard work and planning into real-world practice. As teams began to understand the tools that they now had available, the following practices started to drive more efficient operations within the organization:

- Projects were quickly defined via sites created using the project site template. This allowed teams to set up a central environment in which to create, store, and share information about a particular project with the entire organization in just seconds.
- Appointments and important deadlines were created and tracked from a single shared calendar on the project site that everyone on a team could easily view.
- Contact information was added to a central location so that team members could easily contact one another and other key partners or stakeholders for the project.
- Important project documents were moved to the document repository of their respective project sites where changes became easier to track and security became more manageable.
- Users began to create email alerts on the task and issues lists, ensuring that tasks and issues were dealt with in a timely manner.
- As each division began defining its role in important projects, executives realized that they now had a bird's-eye view of operations within the organization, which was met with great enthusiasm.

SharePoint Server Primary Benefits

SharePoint Server provides a set of enterprise tools that connect people, processes, and information in a central location. The following list outlines some of the more common benefits of using SharePoint Server.

- **Enterprise content management:** Business users prefer to use familiar applications, such as email, Microsoft Office, or their web browser to create, publish, and manage content within the enterprise. Built-in tools make it easy to:
  - Control document access logging using detailed audit reports.
  - Centrally create, store, and manage documents using built-in document library settings to define multistage approval and retention policies.
  - Manage web content using page layouts and master pages to create reusable templates and variations to control multilingual content.

- Reduce the need for manual data entry with electronic web-based or InfoPath client-based forms.
- Improve the organization and structure of stored content through an in-depth classification system.

- **Monitor key business activities:** Using SharePoint Server, you can effectively manage and monitor business events across your organization to:
  - Manage critical business data through business intelligence portals using dashboard capabilities, key performance indicators, chart web parts, and PerformancePoint features.
  - Quickly connect people with information by using enterprise search. Use the Search Center to find people and information in your SharePoint environment and external business systems.
  - Access important business information stored in external business systems in real-time right from the browser, using advanced features such as the Business Connectivity Services, external lists, and Excel Services.
  - Aggregate information from a wide variety of SharePoint sites onto a single page to provide a personalized rollup of relevant information based on customizable criteria.
- **Social networking and personalization:** Enjoy the benefits of a single platform for connecting stakeholders throughout your organization.
  - Enhance relationships between employees, customers, and partners through direct connections, information sharing, and portal communications.
  - Store important business information related to individuals within your organization as part of a searchable and customizable user profile allowing business users to find expertise quickly and easily.
  - Increase the visible relevance of information through keyword tagging, notes, and ratings that are applied to content throughout the system.

ANOTHER SHAREPOINT SERVER USAGE EXAMPLE

Organizations commonly use Microsoft SharePoint Server 2010 in scenarios where users must track and maintain operations via multiple mini-portals and business applications within the same main infrastructure. Users can then gather the important data from all units up to a central location.

A common scenario where you might see Microsoft SharePoint Server 2010 is a software support company. This section again presents the fictional company, Rossco Tech Consulting, to show how Microsoft SharePoint Server 2010 can be used effectively by an organization that has outgrown the capabilities of SharePoint Foundation and requires more advanced features and functionality. Rossco Tech Consulting has expanded operations to support a major software manufacturer.

This means providing English-, French-, and German-speaking customers with an Internet support portal where they can access up-to-the-minute information on the manufacturer's various software offerings.

Planning

While performing a needs analysis, the following factors were major contributors in Rossco's decision to use Microsoft SharePoint Server 2010 as the platform on which to build its customer support portal:

- The portal must accommodate multiple products from a central Internet-facing location. Each product has its own unique support materials.
- The portal must serve up content in multiple languages, although the original content will be created in English and then translated.
- For legal reasons, support documentation must be published via a strict approval process, involving several individuals in the organization.
- The portal must accommodate speedy publishing of up-to-date information on emerging products.
- Additional documentation exists beyond what is stored in the SharePoint sites. This content must be indexed and accessible via the SharePoint search interface.
- Specific reporting requirements exist for dashboard scorecards on progress related to specific requirements, as well as the aggregation of information from multiple sources on a single page.

Moving from Plan to Practice

With the planning needs in mind, Rossco set out to plan and implement a Microsoft SharePoint Server 2010 solution. The following section outlines the company's experience.

- **Internet-facing sites in SharePoint Server 2010:** Because users will access a major part of the portal via the Internet, they created the initial site collection with a special publishing feature available only in SharePoint 2010. This makes it possible to publish content through an automated and scheduled process from an internal and secured location to an external anonymous Internet-facing site. No technical skills are required for publishing this content, so Rossco can empower business users directly with the creation and publishing of web content, which cuts down considerably on the duration of updates to the website.
- **Multilingual design:** Because the portal needed to service three languages, the company used Variations, a feature that helps create a site hierarchy for each language. This feature simplifies the management of content in multiple languages by creating a source site and a site for each language.

- **Content creation:** After creating the main subsites, the product teams created intuitively named lists and libraries (introduced later in this chapter) and added important documents and information. Making use of built-in features such as content types, site columns, and views, they created and presented the data more efficiently. To ensure that the portal was in line with the corporate brand, the portal was customized. Using the master pages feature, they created custom style sheets, page layouts, and content types to remodel the look and feel of the portal. This transformed the original site with its generic SharePoint look into an easy-to-use support interface. Using page layouts, they were able to empower key business users with no programming knowledge to create and publish branded web content such as newsletters and product updates.
- **Automating operations:** Taking advantage of SharePoint's workflow features, Rossco created a strict content approval process that routed documents from approver to approver before finally publishing them to the Internet-facing portal.
- **Content aggregation:** Using built-in web parts, such as the Content Query web part, Rossco could gather the most sought-after and important information in its subsites and funnel this information to the Internet-facing portal where users had quick and easy access to support information for multiple products at a glance.

SHAREPOINT COMPONENTS OVERVIEW

Microsoft SharePoint Server includes a number of components and elements that are key to the effective use of the system and will be very important concepts to master as you progress through this book. Although each of these items is addressed in detail in later chapters, the following sections offer a brief overview.

The Ribbon

The Ribbon is a new tool within SharePoint aimed at making management and navigation activities much easier than the traditional menu-based system that was available in previous versions of the tool. The Ribbon was originally introduced in Microsoft Office client applications such as Word, Excel or PowerPoint in 2007. The goal of the Ribbon is to provide a simpler user experience when interacting with the site. Small icons are used rather than text to give a quicker visual indication of the setting you may be seeking. In addition, as you select various objects on a page, the Ribbon will adjust itself to display tabs that may be of interest to you based on your selection. An example of the Ribbon can be seen in Figure 1-1. In the image, because a media web part is selected on the page, the Ribbon is displaying options that relate to managing the media web part.

SharePoint Lists

The *list* is a fundamental component of SharePoint Products and Technologies. A list is a storage location for a group of items. Items can be defined as any object that you are tracking information about. To create an item, you must fill out a form that describes the item. The data from this form is then stored in a list. For example, you may have a list in SharePoint to track customer orders. Each customer order would be added to the list through the completion of the form. The form provides a controlled manner to collect information in a structured manner to ensure that all information tracked about customers is the same. Each customer order is considered an item. A list can have many items. However, an item may only belong to a single list.

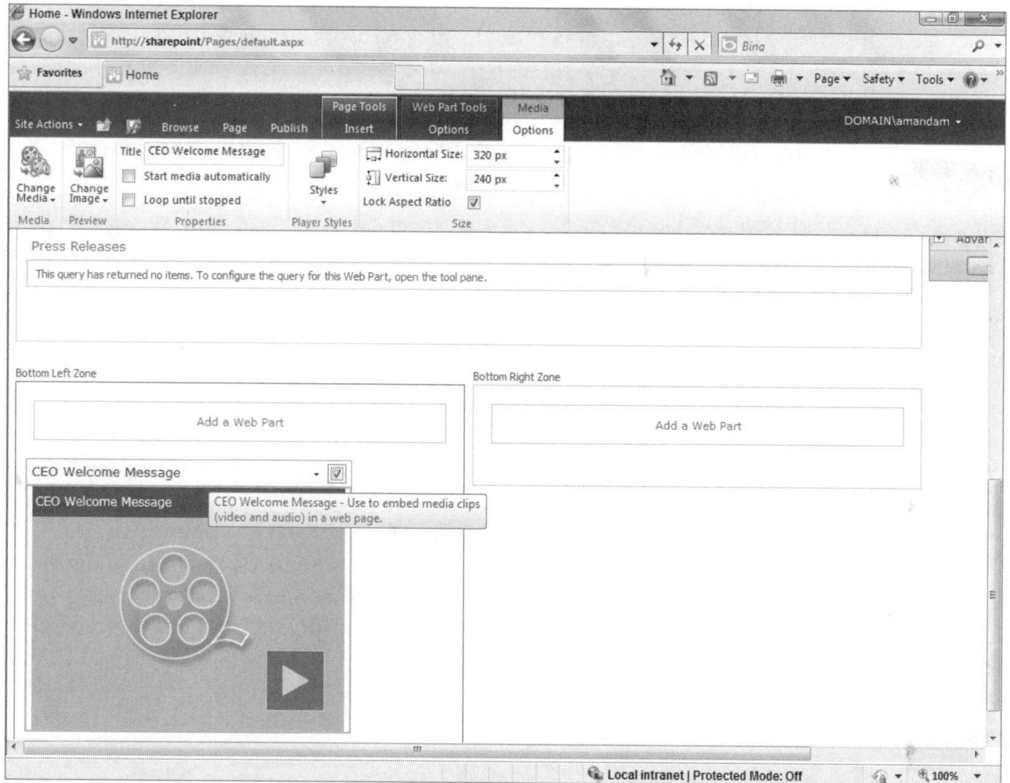

FIGURE 1-1

Although advanced and dynamic, SharePoint lists are easy to create, requiring absolutely no code, special development skills, or tools. In the past, such lists took time to create and required using an application and hiring a developer or having a user with technical skills. By using SharePoint, users most familiar with the information-tracking and -sharing needs of the organization can create the tools they need.

You can use lists to store virtually any type of information. The most commonly used list types are Contacts, Tasks, Issues, Announcements, and Calendar. You can create other lists for just about any usage scenario to track and share information related to a single item. Chapters 2 and 4 examine the common list templates and how you can extend them to meet your team's goals and objectives.

SharePoint Libraries

Libraries are much like lists with one major difference: their intended content. Whereas lists store information about items such as events, contacts, or announcements, libraries store documents. You can think of libraries as superfolders that help users find files faster and easier than ever through the use of special properties or keywords such as *status*, *owner*, or *due date*. Once you add a number of properties to documents, you can create special views or reports to filter, sort, and organize documents based on those properties.

Through SharePoint-specific technologies, such as content types, document libraries can now manage multiple types of files and templates from a single library, making it possible to quickly create and manage common document types such as those from Microsoft Office Word or Excel right from the browser. Chapters 3 and 4 explain how you can use document libraries within your SharePoint sites and further customize them to meet your team's needs.

Web Parts

When you create a list or library, SharePoint automatically generates a corresponding web part that you can later add to a web part page. You can think of *web parts* as mini-applications or modules that display information on a page or perform a special function. Web parts can perform any number of functions, from allowing a user to add custom text and images to a web page without using Hypertext Markup Language (HTML) code, to displaying a financial report based on information stored in a completely separate application.

While many common business web parts come with SharePoint, the model is extensible, and you can create custom web parts to accommodate the specific needs of your organization. You store web parts in a *web part gallery*, and you place them on a web page by dragging and dropping them into an appropriately marked *web part zone* or *content area*. Users can reuse, move, and customize web parts on multiple pages. For example, you can place a small module on the page to display the weather and have each division in your organization decide whether and where to display it on their site. Chapter 7 examines the various types of web parts that are available in SharePoint and discusses common usage scenarios for each primary category.

Workflow

A *workflow* automates a business process by breaking it into a set of steps that users must take to complete a specific business activity, such as approving content or routing a document from one location to another. Automation eliminates manual tasks and reduces the chance of data entry errors or documents getting lost in the system.

A workflow can be as simple or complex as your organization's needs. They can be very rigid and clearly defined or offer a greater level of flexibility and decision making. You can use several built-in templates as a starting point for facilitating more customized processes for your organization. Templates exist in SharePoint to represent common processes that exist within collaborative scenarios such as review and approval. If users fail to respond to a task that has been assigned to them by the workflow, the system can generate email messages to remind them of these tasks once they have become overdue.

You can customize basic workflow templates directly from within a SharePoint list or library to facilitate a process, such as giving approval, responding to a request for feedback, or signing a document. You can also design more specialized and complex workflows using SharePoint Designer 2010 or Visual Studio 2010. You will learn more about the various alternatives for participating in and creating workflows in Chapter 5.

Content Types

A *content type* represents a group of informational items in your organization that share common settings. They allow you to manage multiple types of information from a single location. You can associate content types with a document library, for example, to manage multiple file types, such as Word, PowerPoint, and Excel documents. Content types can also manage multiple templates of the same document type such as a Sales Presentation or Customer Order. As you associate a content type with a document library or list, it appears in the library's or list's New Document drop-down menu, as shown in the Figure 1-2.

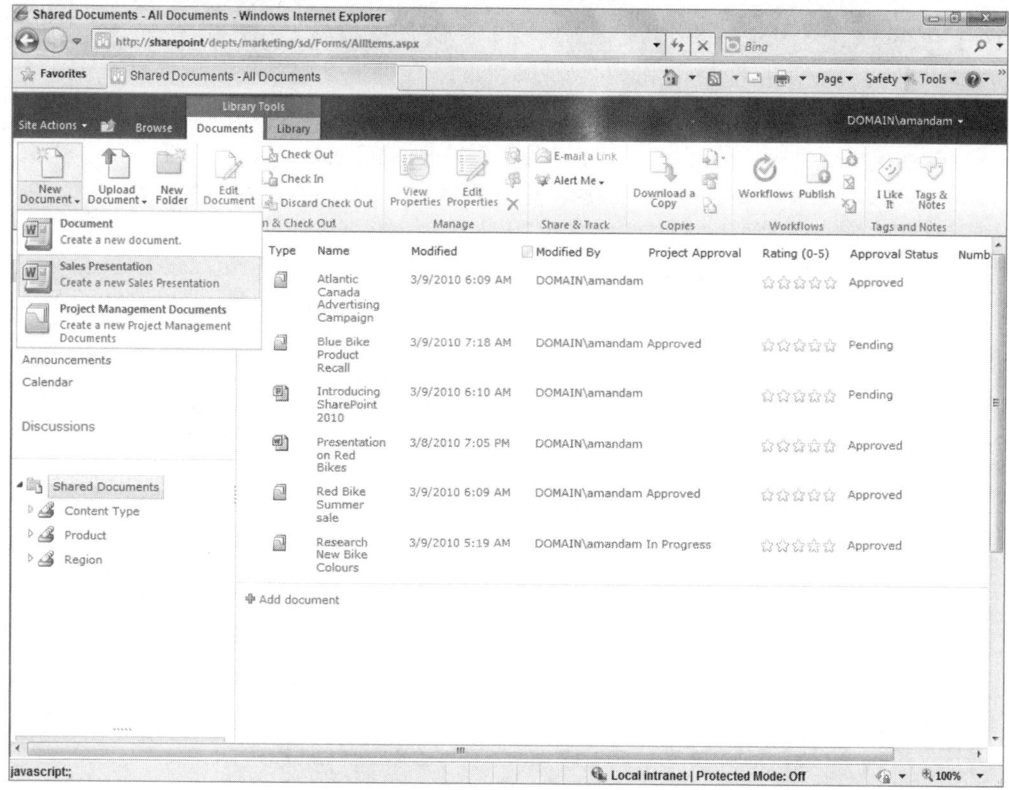

FIGURE 1-2

Content types make extensive use of global properties known as *site columns*, which means you can associate metadata, which is descriptive information, with your item to more easily find it. *Columns* are properties that help define an item; you use them similarly to the way you can use a field in a form. For example, for a task list, the field value for describing when an item is due is a column, used much like a field is for identifying who is responsible for completing a task. Content types make use of site columns because they, too, can be associated with multiple lists or libraries across a number of sites.

A more advanced use of content types involves templates known as *page layouts*, which you use to publish only certain types of content on your site. For example, you can create a newsletter article content type so that the web pages reflect your content, in this instance a column for the title, another for the date, and a third for main text body. You can create page layouts via the browser or using SharePoint Designer; after creation, they become available in the Site Actions menu under the Create Pages option as page templates. Content types are introduced and explored in Chapter 6.

Sites, Workspaces, and Site Collections

Both the terms *sites* and *workspaces*, and the term *site collections* refer to SharePoint sites. These websites, which you can create using available SharePoint templates, are also called *team collaboration sites*, and they store and share information using web parts, lists, and libraries as their various components. The following list explains how they differ:

- **Sites:** These share information in the form of list items and documents within a team or organization. Sites come in a variety of templates. Each template contains a unique set of lists, libraries, and pages. The template you select depends highly on which template most closely matches your needs.
- **Workspaces:** These are more specific to an important document, such as an annual report, on which a team collaborates, or to a significant event, such as a gala or annual business meeting.
- **Site collections:** These are a group of sites and/or workspaces that form a hierarchy with a single top-level website with a collection of subsites, and another level of subsites below it. Figure 1-3 shows a graphical representation of a site collection.

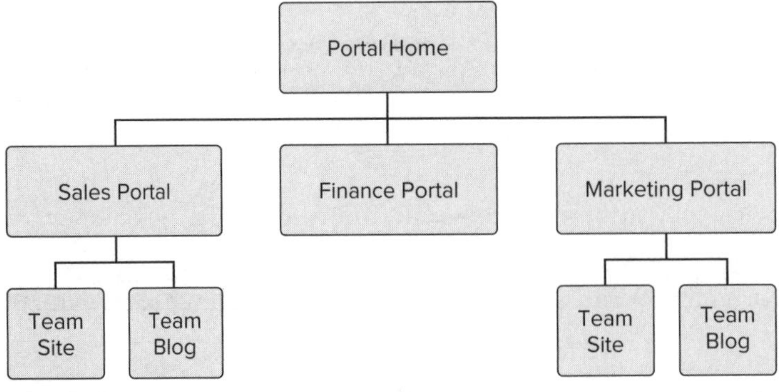

FIGURE 1-3

In the first exercise for this book, you create a new site collection based on the Collaboration Portal template, which will be known in all future exercises as the Corporate Intranet site. If you do not have the ability to create a new site collection within your SharePoint environment, you may ask your system administrator to complete this task for you and specify that your account is a site collection administrator account. Ideally, you should have a unique site collection to complete the exercises in this book; this will give you the most flexibility and a complete learning experience. If for some reason, you are unable to get your own site collection, you will still be able to complete the exercises, but you may need to complete some additional steps in certain cases.

TRY IT OUT Create a Site Collection

When learning an application such as SharePoint, it is a good idea to create an area where you can perform exercises without impacting existing environments or users. You select the Publishing Portal template because it closely matches the requirements of most organizations for an intranet site. From this site, you can create many of the content elements such as lists, libraries, and workflows that are required for the next four chapters.

To create a new site collection, you must visit the Central Administration site of your SharePoint environment. If you are unsure what the address for this site is, you should contact your system administrator or the person who installed SharePoint. You may also access the Central Administration site by logging directly into the server and selecting SharePoint 2010 Central Administration from the Microsoft SharePoint 2010 Products option on the Programs menu.

1. Log into the SharePoint Central Administration site for your server farm.
2. Select Create Site Collections from the Application Management group of links.
3. The first item in your list of things to identify is the web application on which you will create the site. Make sure that the web application you select is the correct application. If it is not, you can click the down arrow to the right of the selected web application and click Change Web Application.

> **NOTE** *Typically, you create most SharePoint sites under the web application that is hosted on port 80 so that end users do not have to see a port number in the address of their sites. For example, a web address of* `http://servername` *is much nicer than* `http://servername:32124`. *If you are unsure which application to select, ask your system administrator or the person who installed SharePoint.*

4. To create a site collection, you must provide a title, description, and URL for the site. Name the site **Corporate Intranet Site**, and enter the following description:

   Collaborative portal for practicing exercises within the Beginning SharePoint 2010 book.

5. For URL name, select /sites/ from the drop-down menu and enter **intranet** in the blank field to the right of the drop-down, as shown in Figure 1-4.

> **NOTE** *If no other sites exist in your web application, you can also create your intranet portal site at the root of the web (example:* `http://servername`*). Only one site collection can exist at the root of a website.*

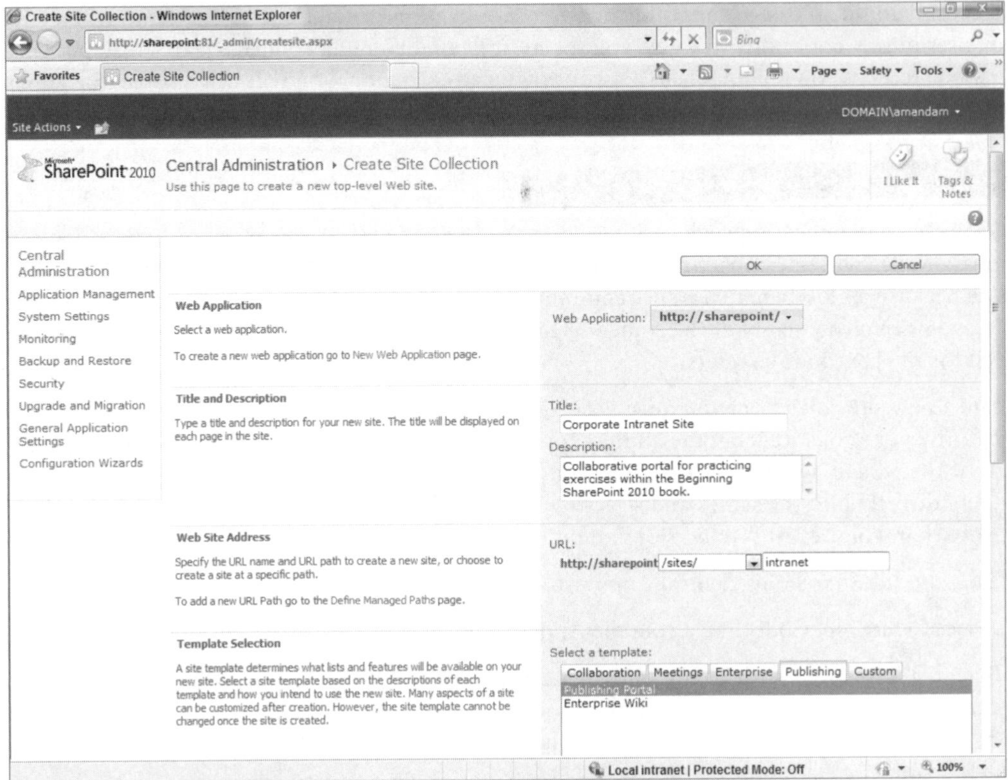

FIGURE 1-4

6. You have a variety of choices for the site template. As described earlier, each template has a unique blend of lists, libraries, and pages. The optimal template for a corporate intranet is the Publishing Portal template. Select that template from the Publishing tab (because it is a publishing site).
7. Enter your own name as the primary site collection administrator.

> ***NOTE*** *If you are having another user create this site collection on your behalf, you should request that your name be entered in the Secondary Site Collection Administrator field.*

8. Click OK. The process for creating your site takes a few minutes. After it is completed, you are redirected to a page advising you that the process has completed successfully, and a URL will be displayed for you to select to visit your site, as shown in Figure 1-5.

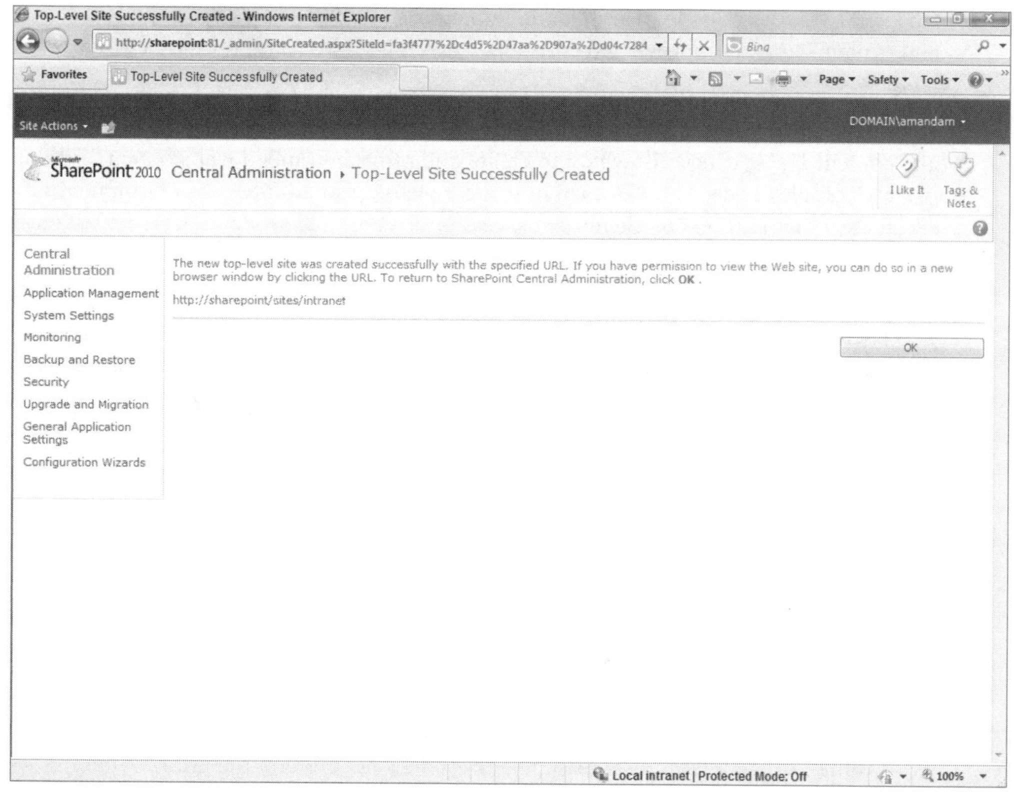

FIGURE 1-5

Enterprise Features

So far, you have examined SharePoint's basic features; however, you've yet to discover the components called *enterprise features*, so named because they often represent the functionality that large enterprises require and demand from their collaborative applications. These features also highlight some of the key differences between SharePoint Foundation and SharePoint Server.

- **Form Services:** *InfoPath* is a forms creation and completion application that is in an important part of the Microsoft Office system. *InfoPath Form Services* makes Microsoft Office InfoPath forms available via the web browser so that you can easily collect and access data, while eliminating the requirement for client applications. Chapter 12 gives more information on the use of InfoPath with SharePoint and Form Services.
- **Search:** The search feature connects you with the information, people, and processes you need to make informed business decisions. The search capabilities of SharePoint Server 2010 have been greatly improved over previous versions based on more relevant results, product enhancements, and an improved user interface for drilling down further into search results.

Chapter 17 shows how the search feature accesses multiple systems via a single search engine, and explains how to improve and customize search interfaces and result relevancy.

- **Web content management:** SharePoint Server supports web content creation and publishing for the Internet. Publishing features range from a content approval workflow to page layouts and content types, which allow you to create and publish branded web content without writing any complex code. You can then host these websites in an Internet environment or on an extranet so that partners or clients can access information. SharePoint Server 2010 has been greatly improved over its predecessor, being far more standard compliant and robust as a publishing platform. Chapter 13 shows you how to create and manage web content.
- **Excel Services and PerformancePoint Services:** Microsoft Excel's popularity means many organizations support thousands of spreadsheets full of business information. *Excel Services* lets you work with important data in real time using only the browser. You can publish interactive pivot tables, charts, and spreadsheets to a large audience, while protecting your formulas and calculations. Users are given "view-only" rights, which only allows them to see the browser-based version of a report. In addition, Microsoft SharePoint Server now features the Business Intelligence and Scorecard tools of PerformancePoint. This allows for far more robust and complex dashboards and reports along with specialized charts and analytical tools. Chapter 16 covers the options for integrating business intelligence and reporting into your portal.
- **Business Connectivity Services:** Although SharePoint may be your central application, your organization may have legacy business applications. Business Connectivity Services (BCS) allows you to connect to these external data sources and display business data via web parts, user profiles, or SharePoint lists. Although BCS does not contain the information from these systems, it acts as the virtual bridge between the alternate system and the user. Chapter 12 discusses BCS, as well as practical methods for accessing information via the various business data components, such as web parts and list columns.
- **Social networking and computing:** A major area of investment in SharePoint Server 2010 has been social networking, personalization services, and tagging. Features such as ratings and tagging provide a less structured approach to classification of content but truly help drive user adoption and relevance of content within the system. Many business users have become accustomed to these features in many of the online portals they use outside of the business world. For example, you may have purchased this book by visiting an online book retailer. From this retailer's site, you may have reviewed ratings that other readers left to describe the content of the book. Subsequently, you may also choose to rate your own personal experience in an effort to provide feedback for other potential buyers. This concept also works extremely well in the business world. As users rate content and provide comments or notes related to specific topics, it helps other users understand the content's relevance and subsequently reduces much of the time required to find the right content.
- **Records management:** SharePoint Server 2010 provides excellent support for the management of content throughout its entire lifecycle. This includes features such as auditing of content access, review and disposal of expired content, and the creation of multistage retention policies and file plans. Depending on the type of organization you work within, records

management may be something that has existed for years or it may be a new concept. Whatever your situation, Chapter 14 will take you through the effective usage and configuration of SharePoint Server 2010 as a records management system.

SUMMARY

This chapter provided basic knowledge about the features available in Microsoft Office SharePoint Server 2010 and how you can use them to service enterprise-level organizations, drive more efficient business processes, and connect people with the information required to make informed business decisions. After reading this chapter, you should also better understand how Microsoft SharePoint Server 2010 differs from SharePoint Foundation 2010. You should also better understand the core components of SharePoint Server 2010 including lists, libraries, content types, sites and workspaces, and workflow.

EXERCISES

1. What is the difference between a site and a site collection?
2. Your manager informs you that the organization is currently reviewing the need for a corporate portal. List two reasons that justify why organizations invest in portal technologies.
3. True or false: You must deploy Microsoft Foundation 2010 and Microsoft SharePoint Server 2010 together.

▶ WHAT YOU LEARNED IN THIS CHAPTER

TOPIC	KEY CONCEPTS
What is SharePoint?	SharePoint 2010 is an extensible and scalable web-based platform consisting of tools and technologies that support the collaboration and sharing of information within teams, throughout the enterprise, and on the web.
What is the Ribbon?	The Ribbon is a new tool within SharePoint aimed at making management and navigation activities much easier than the traditional menu-based system that was available in previous versions of the tool. The Ribbon was originally introduced in Microsoft Office client applications such as Word, Excel or PowerPoint in 2007.
The Difference Between a Site and a Site Collection	A site is a single location that stores lists and libraries related to a common subject. A site collection represents a group of sites that share common configurations and settings.

2

Working with SharePoint Lists

WHAT YOU WILL LEARN IN THIS CHAPTER:

- What a SharePoint list is
- How you can use lists
- The type of information that you can store in lists
- The primary activities available within the Ribbon for interacting with lists
- A breakdown of the various default list templates that SharePoint offers
- A hands-on discussion on how you can work with lists to create and view information

This chapter reviews a very important concept in SharePoint, lists, which you use throughout SharePoint to store and display information. By gaining a solid understanding of how they work early in this book, you can construct highly effective business applications and solutions in later chapters of the book by combining multiple lists with other important SharePoint components.

This chapter focuses mainly on working with the basic features and functionality of lists. In Chapter 4, you learn how to customize and manage lists to create working environments that suit your specific business requirements and needs.

UNDERSTANDING LIST ELEMENTS

Lists have items, columns, and views. Items and columns correspond to the rows and columns that you see on a grid layout in a spreadsheet. Views present list data in a friendlier format that acts very similarly to a report.

- **Items:** An item is a row in a list. For example, for a list that stores information on customers, each customer may have a unique item in the list, which is also called the customer row or customer record.
- **Columns:** A column is a field in a list. You may also see columns referred to as metadata, which is really a descriptive piece of information related to the item. In the case of a customer item in a list, the phone number, physical address, mailing address, and email address would be columns that describe the customer.
- **Views:** A single list can have multiple views. You create a view to address a user's informational needs relating to list data. A view displays a subset of information from the list, for example, customers who have been added during a specific time period. You may also create a view to show all information on a list but have items displayed in a predefined order.

DISCOVERING SHAREPOINT LIST COLUMN TYPES

SharePoint lists can have the following types of information stored in columns:

- **Single Line of Text:** Possibly the most common, because it stores a variety of formats, such as the item's title, names, phone numbers, email addresses, and virtually anything else that you can enter into a single-line textbox.
- **Multiple Lines of Text:** Occasionally, this type of column is useful because it stores larger amounts of information, such as a customer's billing address or background information on the customer. For this column type, you can select whether the information should contain plain, rich, or enhanced text elements, such as bold, italic, pictures, or tables. You can expand this column as you add text to it or you can select how many lines in the box to display initially. When you use this field to collect information from users, it is a good idea to determine the number of lines to display so that users will know how much content is expected from them.
- **Choice:** When gathering information on an item, you can offer users a selection of values or answers from which to choose. Using the example of a customer list, you may want to find out what type of services the customer purchases from you. If your organization only provides a fixed number of key services, it makes sense to present the user this set of choices to ensure that the field always contains valid information. When creating a choice column, you can choose whether to have the choices appear in a drop-down list, as radio buttons, or as checkboxes. For checkboxes, the user may select more than one item. Alternatively, you can have users fill in their own choices if their item does not appear in the list. This is known as allowing "fill-in choices."
- **Number:** You commonly need to associate numerical information with an item so that you can later perform calculations on the information stored in it. You can configure number columns to store numbers that fall within a specific range or percentage values.
- **Currency:** This is similar to the number column but specifically displays financial or monetary values. You can select what type of currency to display and the appropriate format based on region such as $123,000.00 for the United States or £123,000.00 for the United Kingdom.

- **Date and Time:** You typically have a list containing dates or times. This might include when an organization first became a customer or the last time it purchased a product. Date columns allow users to enter the date information directly into a textbox or select the date from an easy-to-use calendar tool. When configuring a date column, you can control whether to allow only dates or dates with times. You can also select a default value for the date, including a special setting that detects "Today's Date" as the user is filling out the item.
- **Lookup:** As your SharePoint environment expands, you may have many lists containing important information about things such as projects, products, and employees. In some cases, you need to take information from one list and associate it with information from another. In the example of the customers list, you may have a listing of projects that display the name of the customer for which the project is being completed. Because your customers list will contain that information, it makes sense to have a column in the projects list that displays the names of all the customers. Lookup columns encourage users to store information in a single location rather than duplicate items throughout the organization. New in SharePoint 2010 is the ability to select an item in a lookup column and have additional fields related to that item displayed in the list. For example, when selecting a customer within your projects list, the name of the key contact for that customer and an associated phone number will also be associated with the list item.
- **Yes/No:** This checkbox column indicates whether an item matches a specific criterion. In the case of the customers list, you may create a yes/no column named Active. If the customer is active, you select the checkbox. In the customer in not active, then the checkbox remains blank.
- **Person or Group:** Users can select people or groups from the site's membership source (for example, Active Directory) and associate them with items in a list. In the customer's list example, you may use this column type to associate an account manager with a customer. Optionally, you can include a display picture along with the account manager's name.
- **Hyperlink or Picture:** You can use this column type to allow users to enter a web address into a list item to create a hyperlink or display an image located at the source location. In the customer list example, you can use this type of column to display the company's website address or the company's logo.
- **Calculated:** Rather than have users manually enter information, you may want to calculate values based on other columns within the list. For this type of column, you can select the names of other columns from the list and identify relationships and formulas. For example, you may have a calculated value that displays how many years the customer has been a client of the organization based on other information in the customer record. You can then select a format for the column.
- **External Data:** In some cases, you may want to associate business data from an external business application with your list items. For example, you may have a listing of all products in a sales database and instead of recreating it in SharePoint, you can connect to it and reuse that information. Using an External Data column, you can associate a products list with your list so that, as you define customers, you can also select which products the customer typically purchases.

***NOTE** For more information on SharePoint's capabilities for interacting with business data stored in applications other than SharePoint, see Chapter 15.*

- **Managed Metadata:** In some cases within your organization, another administrative user may have already defined a set of metadata to describe important aspects of your organization. Therefore, there is no requirement for you to redefine this information yourself. In such cases, it would be more appropriate for you to create a column that connects to the managed metadata service to select the values that have been predefined by your system administrator or another user who has been empowered to configure this shared feature. Managed metadata will be described in detail within Chapter 6.
- **Audiences:** If a list has audience targeting enabled, this column type is automatically added to it. Audiences are groups of users that you define based on a set of criteria. When you use audiences on list items, the items only appear to members of the audiences associated with the item. Chapter 11 provides in-depth information on audiences and user profiles.

UNDERSTANDING THE STANDARD LIST TEMPLATES

With the basic components of a list explained, you can now look at some of the list templates that are available in SharePoint. Many of these templates address common collaborative scenarios that exist within organizations, such as tracking tasks and sharing contact and meeting information. You should think of these templates as a starting point because you can further customize them to suit the needs of any organization. More advanced techniques for customizing and managing lists are discussed in Chapter 4.

To demonstrate common collaborative scenarios that might exist in relation to the usage of lists within teams, for the remainder of this chapter, we will consider the example of using SharePoint lists for the tracking of information related to a project. Within a project, there is often a large amount of information to be tracked and many of the built-in templates can assist in providing an excellent starting point for sharing such information.

TRY IT OUT Create a Project Team Site

To get started, you will create a site that will act as a collaborative location for sharing information about a new project that is about to start, called Project Gros Morne. This is a project that will evaluate the feasibility of expanding a travel company's operations into a popular tourist location in eastern Canada.

1. From the main page of your site collection, which was created in the previous chapter, select New Site from the Site Actions menu. The Site Creation dialog will appear, as shown in Figure 2-1.

   If you do not have Silverlight installed on your computer, you may notice the display of the Site Creation Dialog is slightly different. This will be the case throughout the SharePoint administrative interface. Therefore, it is recommended that you install the Silverlight plugin to ensure an optimal user experience. It can be accessed from the Microsoft site located at `www.microsoft.com/silverlight`.

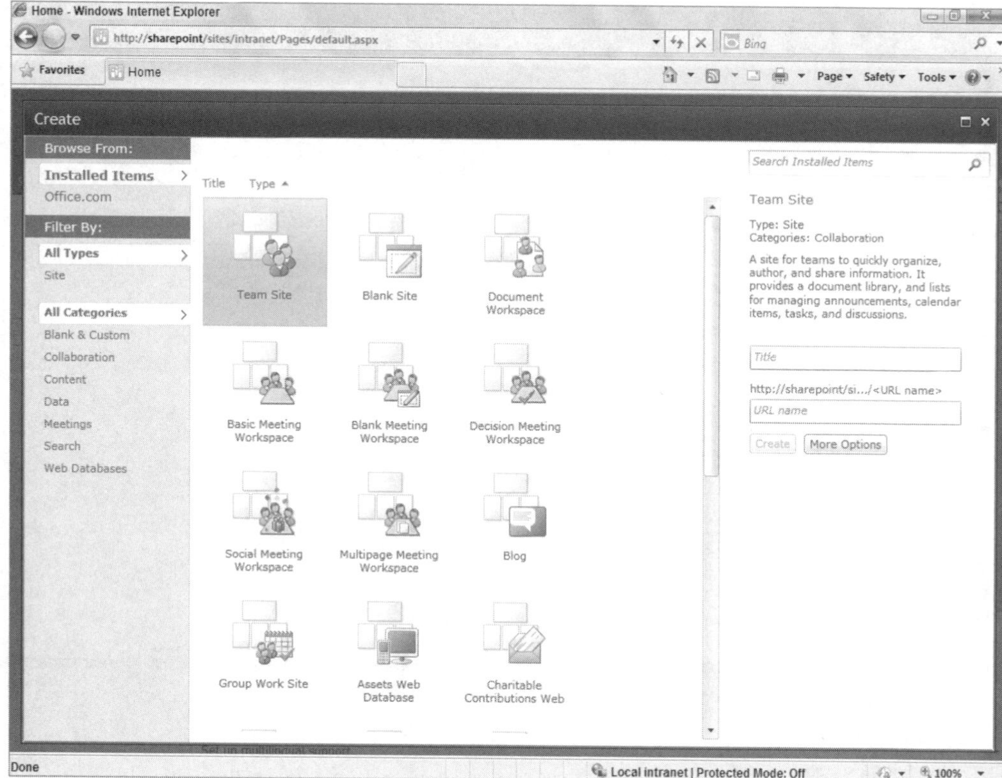

FIGURE 2-1

2. Select the Team Site template from the template list.

> ***NOTE*** *If you created a site in Chapter 1 based on the Publishing Portal template, you may be required to enable the creation of subsites based on any site template in order to complete this exercise. This is done by going to the main page of your intranet site collection, selecting Site Settings from the Site Actions menu and selecting Page layouts and site templates from the Look and Feel Group of links. You will then need to enable the Subsites so you can use any site template option within the Subsite Templates section of the page. Then you must click OK to save your changes. Now you will be able to create a subsite using any template from your intranet site.*

3. Click the More Options button. The window will refresh to provide a listing of fields as shown in Figure 2-2.

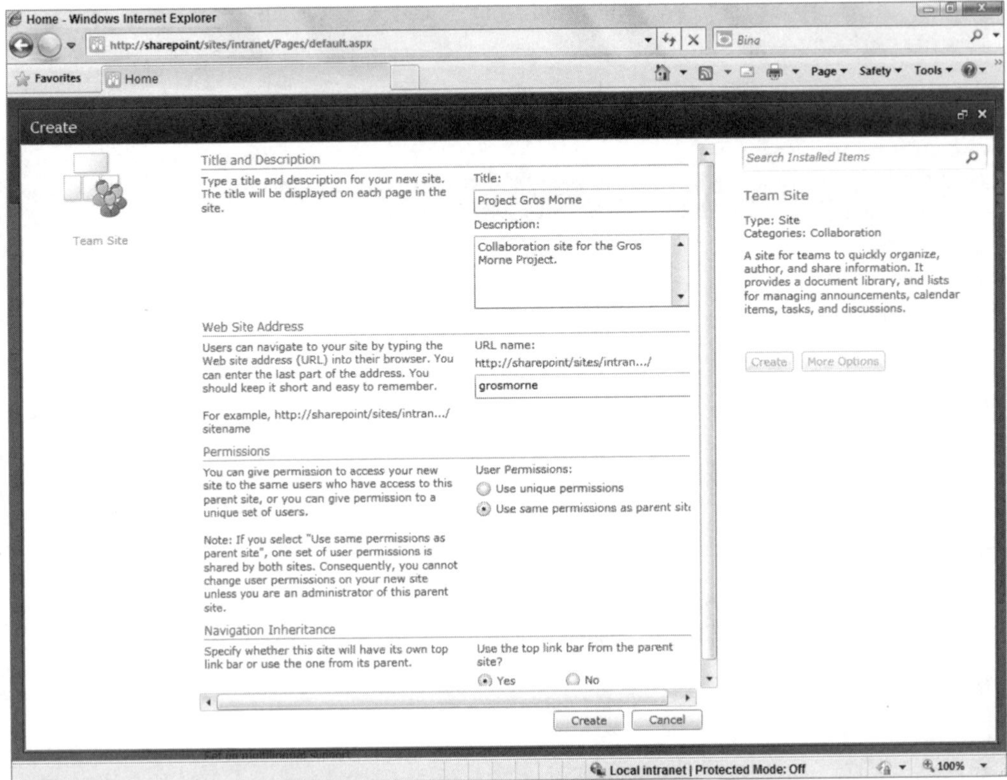

FIGURE 2-2

4. Complete the fields shown in Figure 2-2 using the information in the following table.

FIELD	VALUE
Title	Project Gros Morne
Description	Collaboration site for the Gros Morne Project
Web Site Address	grosmorne
Permissions	Use same permissions as parent site
Navigation Inheritance	Yes

5. Click Create. The site creation process will start, and upon its completion you will be redirected to the main page of your new site.

How It Works

Users with the appropriate privileges have the ability to create sites for projects, initiatives, or any other collaborative scenarios simply by completing a form to specify a template, site title, description, and URL. In the exercise above, you selected the Team Site template because it contains many of the lists that you would like to use for tracking your project.

When creating the site, you selected the option to use the top link bar from the parent site. This ensures that as users visit your site, they will see the same top-level navigation links that they saw when on the previous site. This can sometimes be considered a best practice, as users typically find it easier to navigate across multiple sites if the primary navigation stays consistent. This administrative option was available to you when you selected the More Options button in step 3. If you had not selected the More Options button, you would not have been able to specify that you wanted to use the top link bar and, by default, the site would have been created with its own unique top navigation. This setting can be changed after the site has been created by visiting the Settings page for the site and changing the navigational settings. This activity will be covered in Chapter 8.

Understanding the Contacts List

Within a project team, you commonly need to share contact information. This may be the contact information of team members but may also include contact information of other key stakeholders such as customers, vendors, partners or industry experts. SharePoint provides a very easy-to-use interface just for this purpose that you can create via a template. It's known as a contacts list. Rather than team members storing contact information of key stakeholders within individual address books, team members add contacts to a list on a SharePoint site so that the information becomes available to everyone.

A contacts list has the columns shown in the following table. However, as is the case with any list, you can create or delete columns at any time. The Last Name column is considered the title column, and you cannot remove it from the list. You may rename it if you like, however.

COLUMN NAME	COLUMN TYPE
Last Name (required)	Single Line of Text
First Name	Single Line of Text
Full Name	Single Line of Text
E-mail Address	Single Line of Text
Company	Single Line of Text
Job Title	Single Line of Text
Business Phone	Single Line of Text
Home Phone	Single Line of Text
Mobile Phone	Single Line of Text
Fax Number	Single Line of Text
Address	Multiple Lines of Text
City	Single Line of Text

continues

(continued)

COLUMN NAME	COLUMN TYPE
State/Province	Single Line of Text
ZIP/Postal Code	Single Line of Text
Country/Region	Single Line of Text
Web Page	Hyperlink or picture
Notes	Multiple Lines of Text

Adding an item to a contacts list is quite easy and can be done using one of the following methods.

- **Click New from the Ribbon:** You can click this button, shown in Figure 2-3, and then enter all the details for the list manually using a form.

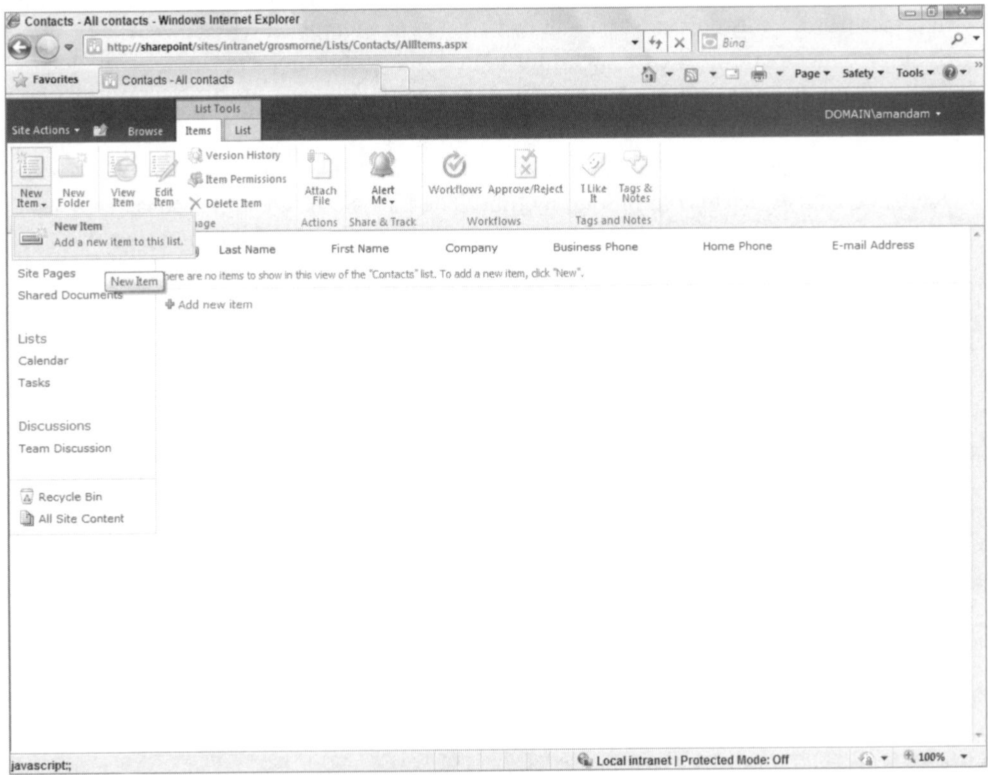

FIGURE 2-3

- **Synchronize data using an offline client application:** Contact lists can be updated using either Microsoft Outlook, SharePoint Workspace, or Microsoft Access. The methods for each are described later in this chapter within the Try It Out exercises.

The contacts list features only one view upon creation:

- **All Contacts:** This standard list view displays all items (in groups of 30) in the list sorted by Last Name. Site visitors can access it either from the list itself or a web part related to the list.

Understanding the Announcements List

Virtually every team needs to track news related to important events and activities. Instead of sending distracting direct email messages to team members, you can use the announcements list to drive members to your site to look for the latest information on key activities and events. Using the announcement list template, site managers can alert team members of key events and milestones related to their business activities, without having to adopt a more formalized news-publishing feature.

When you create an announcements list, it contains the columns shown in the following table. However, you can add more columns or remove unwanted ones. Because the Title column is considered a required column, you cannot remove it from the list.

COLUMN NAME	COLUMN TYPE	COLUMN DESCRIPTION
Title (required)	Single Line of Text	Generally, this column is used to store the headline of the announcement you are creating.
Body	Multiple Lines of Text	This column is typically used to feature the details of the announcement you are creating. It supports enhanced text with formatting, pictures, and tables by default.
Expires	Date and Time	In cases where an announcement should not appear within certain views after a specific date, the expires column can be used. Views can then be configured to only show items where the expiry date is blank or occurs in the future.
Created By	Person or Group	This is a system-generated value that displays the name of the user who originally created the announcement.
Modified By	Person or Group	This is a system-generated value that displays the name of the user who last modified the announcement.

The announcements list features two standard views upon creation:

- **All Items:** This standard list view displays all items (in groups of 30) in the list sorted by their creation date. Site visitors can access it either from the list itself or a web part related to the list.
- **Summary:** The announcement list web part uses this view to display the item title followed by a segment of the story and the author's name. This view displays the latest stories for which the expiry date has not been specified or has not passed. There is no way to edit the properties or behavior of this view.

Understanding the Tasks List

An important requirement when running a project is having the ability to effectively monitor and track task progress. SharePoint includes a list template designed specifically around the management of tasks. Using this list, you can create tasks for team members and email notifications will be automatically sent to the assigned parties containing details of the assignment. A task list features the ability to be connected to Microsoft Outlook, which allows users to view, create, and update tasks within a SharePoint list directly from within Microsoft Outlook. In addition, you can export information from a task list directly into a Microsoft project plan. This allows team leads or project managers to create a task list for the initial activities related to a project within their SharePoint team site, which can later be promoted into a more formal project plan when the project becomes more defined or complex. Similarly, team leads or project managers can synchronize existing Microsoft Project plans with a SharePoint task list. This is an activity we will review later in this chapter in a Try It Out exercise.

When you create a task list, it has the columns listed in the following table; however, you can add more columns at any time. Because the Title column is required, you cannot remove it from the list.

COLUMN NAME	COLUMN TYPE	COLUMN DESCRIPTION
Title (required)	Single Line of Text	This column is typically used to provide a name for the task. This name will be displayed in web parts to allow users to easily identify it from others.
Priority	Choice	This column is used to associate a priority level with tasks to allow users to easily identify which tasks they should resolve first. Like all other columns, this column can be customized to reflect priority values that would be relevant to your organization.
Status	Choice	This column is used to track the status of the task. Applying a status value allows your team to stay informed about how the task is progressing by visiting the list.
% Complete	Number	This column is used to track the progress of the task. Applying a % complete allows your team to stay informed about how the task is progressing by visiting the list.
Assigned To	Person or Group	This column is used to select a team member who has been assigned to complete the task. By default, only a single team member can be assigned to a task. However, the settings for this column can be modified to allow multiple users to be assigned to a single task. This customization is covered in Chapter 4.
Description	Multiple Lines of Text	This column is the location where details of the task should be included, such as the original request as well as any notes on how the task is progressing.

COLUMN NAME	COLUMN TYPE	COLUMN DESCRIPTION
Start Date	Date and Time	The start date is a column used to identify when the task is scheduled to start.
Due Date	Date and Time	The due date is a column used to identify when the task is scheduled to be completed.
Predecessors	Lookup	The Predecessors column helps team members easily identify which tasks must be completed before the task in question can be worked on or resolved.

The tasks list features the following standard views upon creation:

- **All Tasks:** This view displays all items (in groups of 30) in the list sorted by their creation date.
- **My Tasks:** This personalized view of items is a good default view for team members because it displays the tasks that have been assigned to the current user.
- **Due Today:** This view features a filtered list of tasks that have a specified due date equal to the current date. This may be an effective view to display within a web part on the main page of the site so that team members are aware of the key activities that should be taking place at a given time.
- **Active Tasks:** As your task list expands, you need to differentiate between completed tasks and those still in progress. You don't have to remove or delete completed tasks because you may need to refer back to them later. Instead, you can filter out completed tasks and only display active ones. The Active Tasks view only displays items where status is not equal to completed.
- **By Assigned To:** As a team leader or manager, you may need to view the assignments of all team members to pinpoint available resources and the progress of key initiatives. This view shows the task sorted by the person assigned to it, as well as task's status.
- **By My Groups:** This is very similar to the By Assigned To view. However, it only displays tasks assigned to groups. Items appear by the group name to which they are assigned.

Understanding the Project Tasks List

The project tasks list is very similar in structure and behavior to the tasks list in the last section. It has the same columns and most of the same views, as well as a special view, called the Project Tasks view. A project task is a Gantt view that displays a bar for each task indicating status and expected timeline. An example of this view is shown in Figure 2-4.

You can add this view to other list types. SharePoint creates it automatically with the project tasks list to give you a head start in creating visually attractive work breakdown structures that you can apply to just about any project.

Like tasks lists, the project tasks list features Microsoft Outlook and Microsoft Project integration, as well as targeted email notifications based on new assignments. However, you cannot associate a project tasks list with a workflow activity. Therefore, users who want to have Gantt chart views of workflow information are advised to use the standard tasks list and create a custom Gantt view.

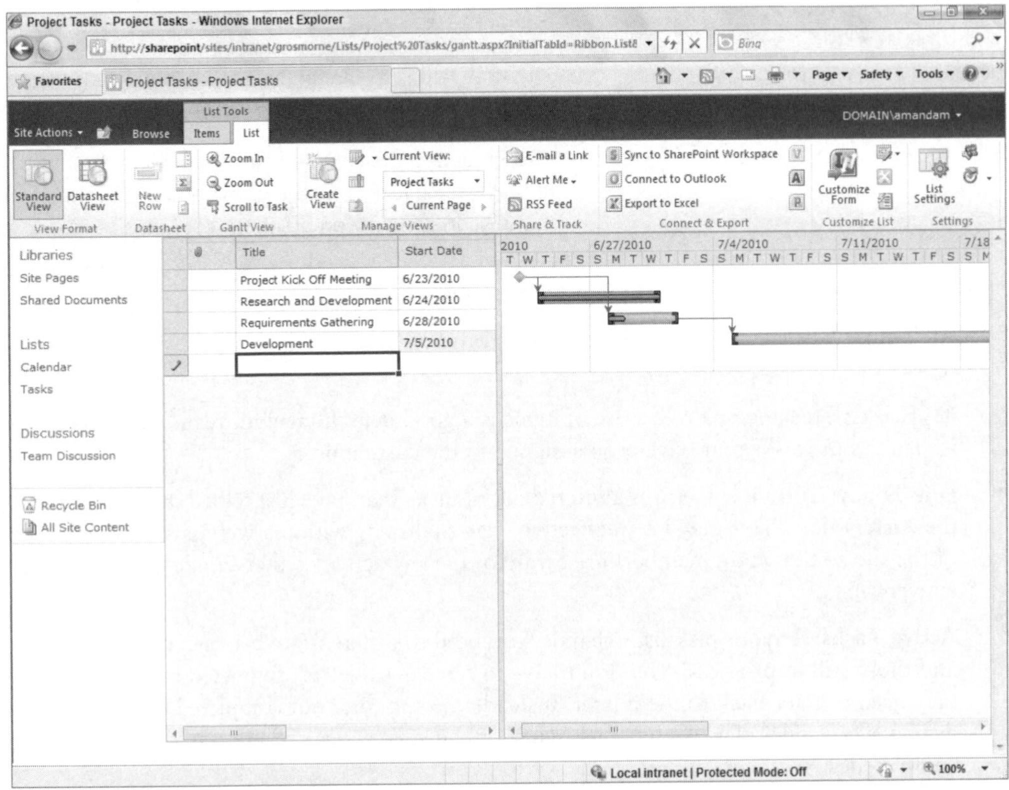

FIGURE 2-4

More information on customizing lists in this manner is described in Chapter 4.

Understanding the Issues List

Unfortunately, it's not uncommon for unexpected issues to arise when you conduct business or run a project. An *issue* is an event that requires resolution. In a software environment, this may be a bug that someone discovered in the software. In a shipping company, this may be a transportation delay because of a snowstorm. Because issues can have a huge impact on business operations and the success of an initiative, it is important to effectively track and resolve them. The SharePoint list template for issues provides an easy-to-use method for doing so.

As with the Tasks and Project Tasks list templates, you may export information from an issues list to Microsoft Access, Excel, Project, and SharePoint Workspace. In addition, information from an issues list can be exported to Microsoft Visio. An example of this will be explored within this chapter in an upcoming Try It Out.

While the issues list template does support the offline synchronization features of certain Microsoft client applications, there is no default support for Microsoft Outlook integration.

By default, an issues list contains the columns shown in the following table, but you can add columns to meet your needs. Because the Title column is considered the required column, you cannot remove it from the list.

COLUMN NAME	COLUMN TYPE	COLUMN DESCRIPTION
Title (required)	Single Line of Text	This column is typically used to provide a name for the issue. This name will be displayed in web parts to allow users to easily identify it and differentiate it from others.
Assigned To	Person or Group	This column is used to select a team member who has been assigned to complete the issue. By default, only a single team member can be assigned to an issue. However, the settings for this column can be modified to allow multiple users to be assigned to a single issue. This customization is covered within Chapter 4.
Issue Status	Choice	This column is used to track the status of the issue. Applying a status value allows your team to stay informed about how the resolution of the issue is progressing by visiting the list.
Priority	Choice	This column is used to associate a priority level with issues to allow users to easily identify which issues they should resolve first. Like all other columns, this column can be customized to reflect priority values that are relevant to your organization.
Description	Multiples Lines of Text	This column is the location where details of the issue should be included. Clearly documenting the details on an issue allows team members to better identify an approach for resolution.
Category	Choice	This column is an optional column that is meant to be customized to include relevant categories for issues. Assigning an appropriate category to each issue allows team members to more easily identify which items are related, and the list remains easy to manage as it expands.
Due Date	Date and Time	The due date is a column used to identify when the issue is scheduled to be completed.
Related Issues	Lookup	Because sometimes you cannot resolve one issue until you find resolution for another issue, the issues list has built-in functionality for tracking related items.
Comments	Multiple Lines of Text	The Comments column of an issues list timestamps and labels each entry that team members make over the duration of the issue. This provides excellent insight into the progress of a specific item.

Understanding the Calendar List

Having a shared calendar that all team members can access improves the communication of important information, such as availability, deadlines, and progress. The Calendar list template offers a variety of views and features that make the tracking and viewing of date-based information easy within team-based environments.

When you create a calendar list, it contains the columns shown in the following table. You can add or remove columns at any time, but you cannot remove the default columns: Title, Start Time, and End Time.

COLUMN NAME	COLUMN TYPE	COLUMN DESCRIPTION
Title (required)	Single Line of Text	This column is typically used to provide a name for an event. This name will be displayed in web parts to allow users to easily identify it and differentiate it from others.
Location	Single Line of Text	This column is used to identify the location of the event.
Start Time (required)	Date and Time	This column is used to identify the starting time of the event. The values selected here will determine where the event is displayed within the calendar-based views of the list.
End Time (required)	Date and Time	This column is used to identify the end time of the event. The values selected here will determine where the event is displayed within the calendar-based views of the list.
Description	Multiple Lines of Text	This column is used to provide details of the event.
Category	Choice	The category column may be used to help provide classification of the different events. This list contains many common event types but can be configured to suit your organization's specific requirements.
All Day Event	Checkbox	Similar to an event created in Microsoft Outlook, an event in SharePoint can be specified as an All Day Event. When an event is designated as All Day, the ability to select hourly time values for Start and End Time are disabled.
Recurrence	Checkbox (Special)	This special setting allows you to set a recurring schedule on an event. For example, if your team has a weekly status meeting, you can set up recurrence on a single event rather than creating a new event for each week.

COLUMN NAME	COLUMN TYPE	COLUMN DESCRIPTION
Workspace	Checkbox (Special)	Your event or special day may require a website specifically created for the event. This website, called a workspace, tracks information and documents related to the event. For example, an upcoming training session workspace may have registration forms and handout materials that a team works on in preparation for the session. When you select this checkbox and save the item, you are redirected to a site creation page where you name the site and select a meeting workspace template.

Calendar lists may be connected to Microsoft Outlook or Access. When you connect with either of these two applications, information will be synchronized between the SharePoint list and a local copy within the application. In addition, information from a SharePoint calendar list may be exported to Microsoft Excel.

The calendar list features three standard views upon creation:

- **Calendar:** This view displays all list information in a month, week, and day calendar format, as shown in Figure 2-5. Users can switch between month, week, and day views of the list items or select a specific date to view all items for the selected day.

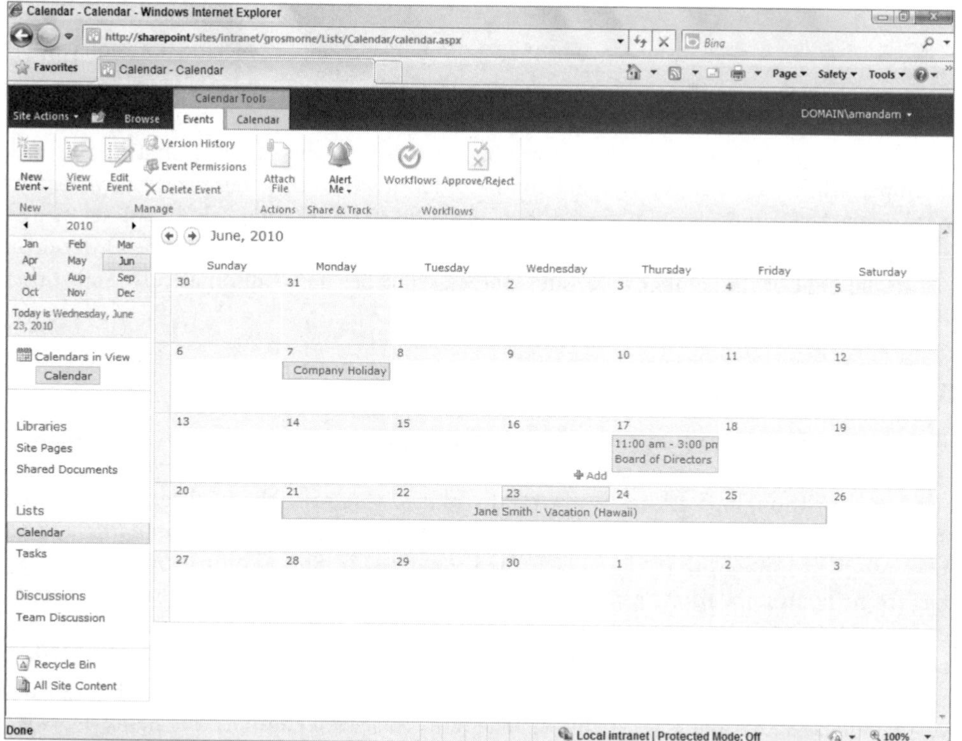

FIGURE 2-5

- **All Items:** This standard list view displays all items (in groups of 30) of the list sorted by their creation date.
- **Current Events:** This list view filters out items that have taken place in the past and displays upcoming items in the order that they will take place.

Understanding the Links List

Commonly, working on a project or initiative requires a team to set up website links to share with one another, for example links to third-party information sources. SharePoint provides a list template that makes it easy to share links with team members. Upon creation, the links list has the columns listed in the following table; however, you can add more columns later. The URL column is considered a required column and, therefore, you cannot remove it from the list.

COLUMN NAME	COLUMN TYPE	COLUMN DESCRIPTION
URL (Required)	Hyperlink or Picture	When adding a new link item to a list, you must specify a URL along with a description. The description gives your URL a title so that the full web address does not display in the list views. When you specify the URL, you can click a link that tests the address to confirm that it is a valid location. You should test your address before you publish it to all your team members.
Notes	Multiples Lines of Text	You may choose to include notes on why you feel this link is useful to other team members.

You can change the link order in case you have a reason to display links in a specific order. For example, while you can list most links in the order in which they were created, you may need to ensure that the company's public website is listed first. You accomplish this by selecting Change Order from the Actions menu, shown in Figure 2-6, and selecting 1 from the Order drop-down list to the right of the company website address. All other items automatically adjust their position based on your selection.

Understanding Discussion Lists

Because team members may be collaborating on projects from different geographic locations and have different working schedules, having an effective mode of electronic communication is critical. Although email has traditionally played this role, the proliferation of email messages within organizations often results in employees spending more time filtering and sorting through their inboxes than they can afford. As a result, SharePoint provides a more passive electronic communication. A threaded discussion allows an author to post a message, and others to reply to that message through the web interface. Because all the communication occurs on the website, team members can stay informed about decision-making processes without directly participating in a specific thread. In addition, as you will learn in Chapter 17, all this content can be indexed and made accessible via the built-in search engine. This helps provide a long-term knowledge center for users to search for answers to commonly asked questions prior to initiating a new discussion.

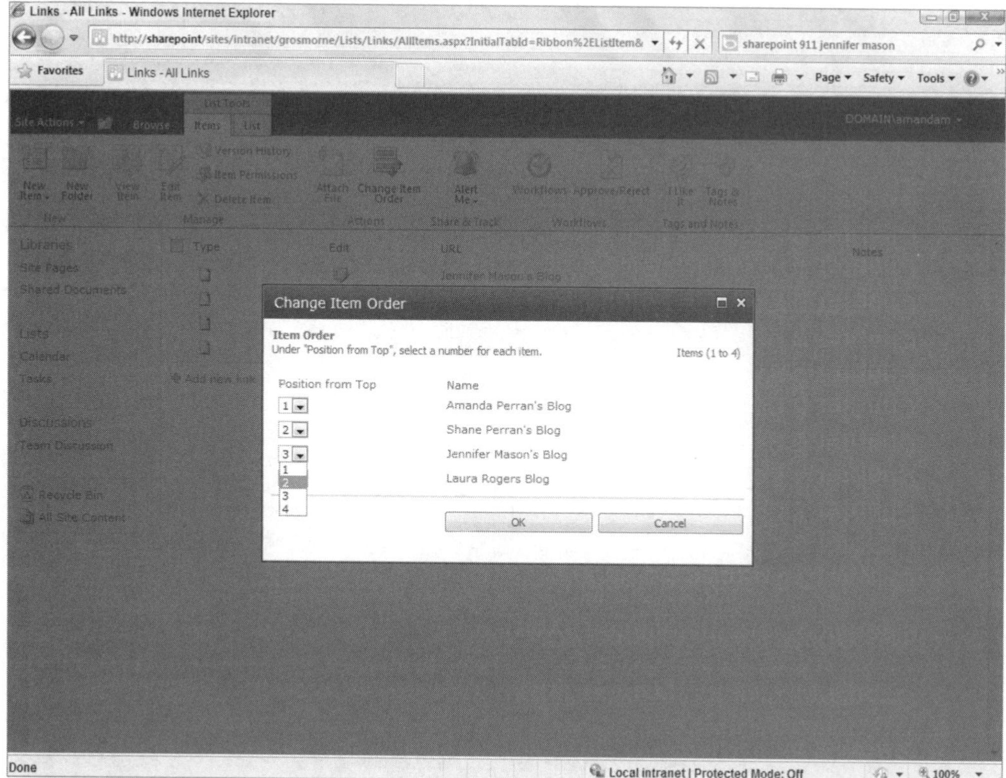

FIGURE 2-6

The discussion board list initially has the columns shown in the following table; however, you can add more columns. Because the Subject column is considered to be required, you cannot remove it from the list.

COLUMN NAME	COLUMN TYPE	COLUMN DESCRIPTION
Subject (required)	Single Line of Text	Similar to an email subject, this column will provide high-level information that describes the topic of the discussion.
Body	Multiple Lines of Text	This column will contain the message that is being shared between team members and is similar to the body of an email message.

In addition to these columns, there are three unique views associated with a discussion list. The subjects view shown in Figure 2-7 are all discussions that are available within the list, whereas the threaded and flat views offer methods for viewing the individual discussions related to a single subject.

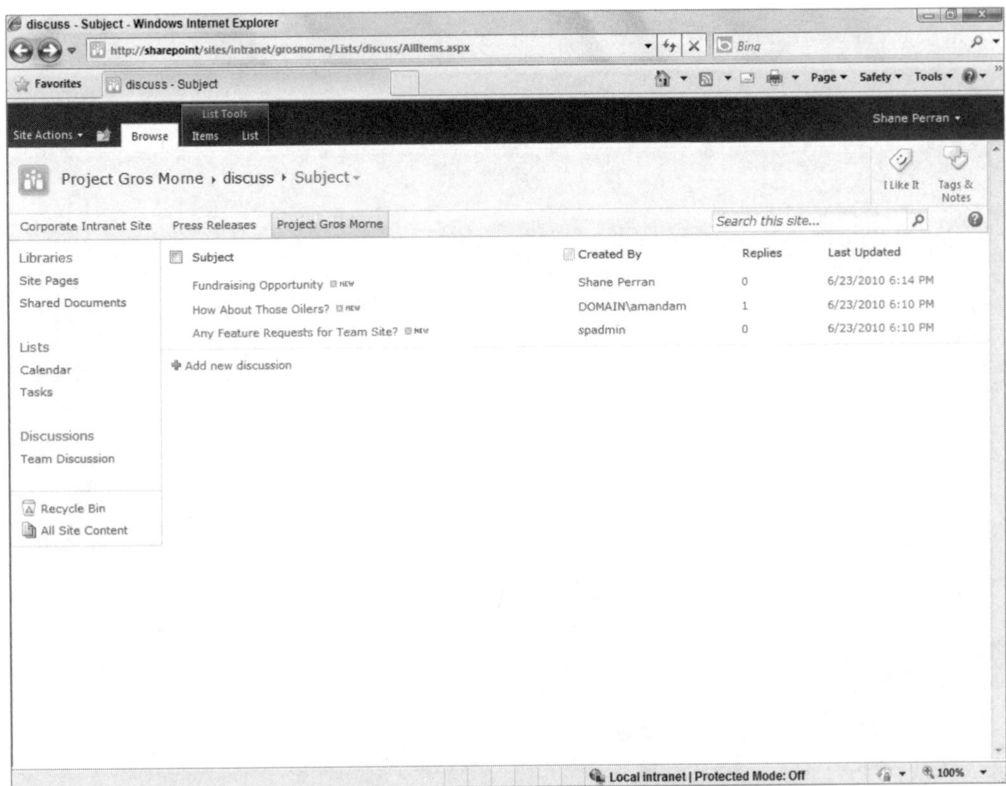

FIGURE 2-7

For team members who prefer to control their communications from an email client, you can connect to Outlook in this list template. Clicking Connect to Outlook from the Actions menu of a discussion list allows team members to view a new folder specifically for discussion in their Outlook SharePoint lists. Users can make new posts and send replies from Outlook in the very same way that they create a new email message. However, instead of sending a message directly to someone's inbox, the message is posted to a central location where everybody can share the information. Figure 2-8 shows an example of a discussion board list item in Flat view. This view is available by clicking a discussion subject.

Exploring Survey Lists

In most organizations, you need to collect information from users on specific programs and events. SharePoint provides a great tool for conducting surveys via the survey list template. This template can be highly customized to deliver dynamic surveys to an organization. All data is submitted back to the list and can be viewed in a graphical format or exported to a spreadsheet for additional processing. Figure 2-9 is an example of the graphical format of survey results that is available with every survey.

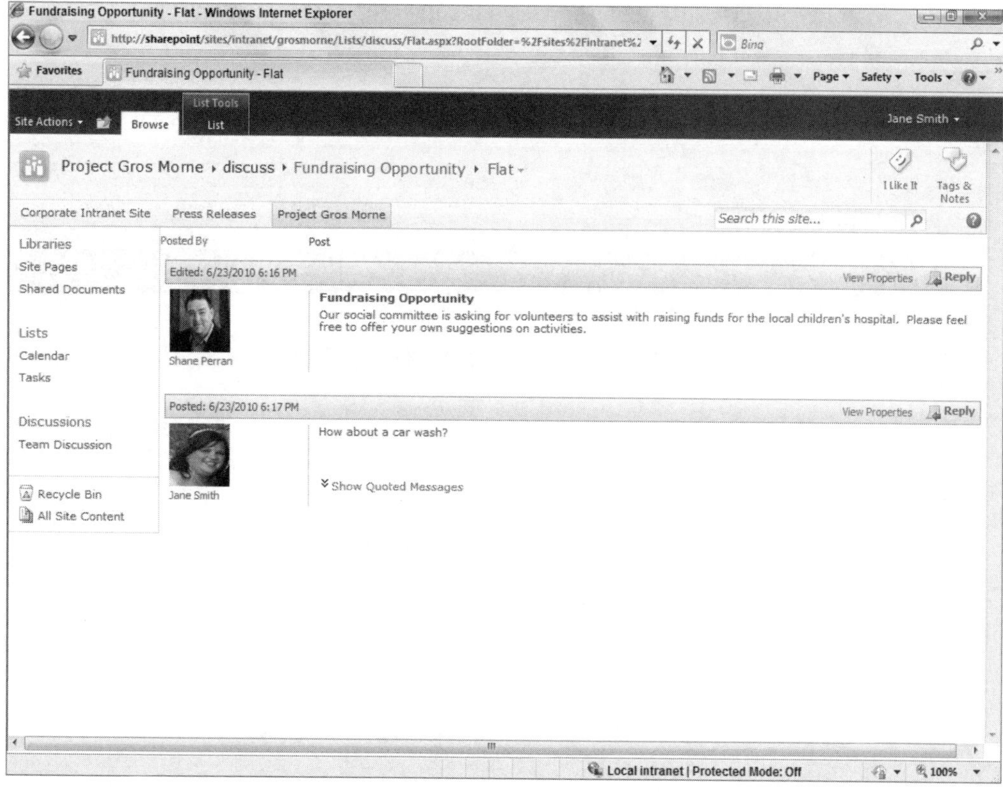

FIGURE 2-8

Creating questions in a SharePoint survey is similar to creating columns, with the exception that no default (required) columns exist. Instead, the author must complete a wizard type interface to create the questions required for the survey.

In a SharePoint survey list, you can create the question types shown in the following list:

- Single line of text
- Multiple lines of text
- Choice (menu to choose from)
- Rating Scale (a matrix of choices or a Likert scale)
- Number (1, 1.0, 100)
- Currency ($, ¥, €)
- Date and Time
- Lookup (information already on this site)
- Yes/No (checkbox)
- Person or Group

- Page Separator (inserts a page break into your survey)
- External Data
- Managed Metadata

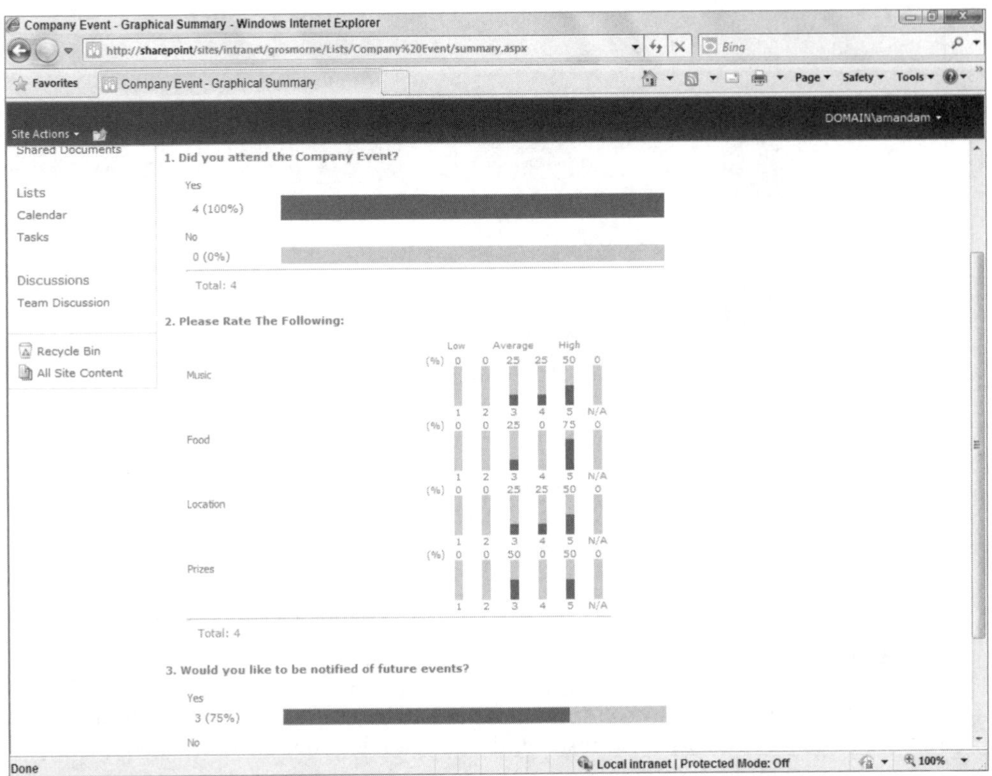

FIGURE 2-9

The survey list template has a unique feature that allows you to create page separators and rating scales to improve a survey form's usability and design. Once you create questions, you can add branching logic to improve the flow of questions and ensure that you're only asking users to answer questions relevant to them. For example, if a question asks if the user has attended the company social, you can insert branching logic to ensure that, if the user selects no, she can skip questions that focus on the company social and redirect her to the next relevant question.

Understanding the Status List

The status list template was previously known as the key performance indicator (KPI) list in SharePoint Server 2007 and is a specialized list template for tracking progress toward organizational goals and objectives. Because this feature is related to the business intelligence features of SharePoint Server 2010, it will be explored in detail in Chapter 16.

Understanding the External List

External lists are a new feature within SharePoint 2010 that support the viewing and interaction of external business data from within a SharePoint list. As this list template is dependent upon the Business Connectivity Services features of SharePoint, we will explore it in detail in Chapter 15.

WORKING WITH LISTS

Now that you know the various lists that are available in SharePoint, you need an understanding of how you can interact and work with lists to gain the insight you require from a SharePoint site and the information it contains.

Working with List Content

In the next two examples, you learn how to add content to a list, as well as make updates to existing content within a list. Because SharePoint lists are only useful if they contain information, it is very important that you understand how to update them effectively.

In SharePoint, a variety of list templates can store just about any type of information or data. In the following example, you walk through the steps of creating a new list item in an existing announcements list. However, the same steps apply regardless of the list template you use. Therefore, we recommend that you repeat these exercises using the different list templates within the Project Team Site you created earlier within this chapter.

TRY IT OUT Adding a New Item to a List

Your boss has requested that you create a news story announcing the launch of the new project. Rather than creating this story as an email message and potentially distracting your team members from more important and time-sensitive activities, you choose to create an announcement on your newly created team site.

1. From the main page of your Project Gros Morne site, expand the Site Actions menu and select View All Site Content. You will be redirected to a page listing all lists and libraries that exist within the current site.
2. Click on the Announcements link. This will bring you to the Announcements list.
3. At the top of the page, click on the Items tab within the List Tools menu. This will display the List Items Ribbon menu associated with the announcements list, as shown in Figure 2-10. From this menu, you may create new announcements or interact with existing announcements, along with accessing more advanced features that will be covered later in this book.
4. Click the New Item menu option. This will launch a form for you to complete to specify the details of your announcement.
5. Complete the form using the following details.

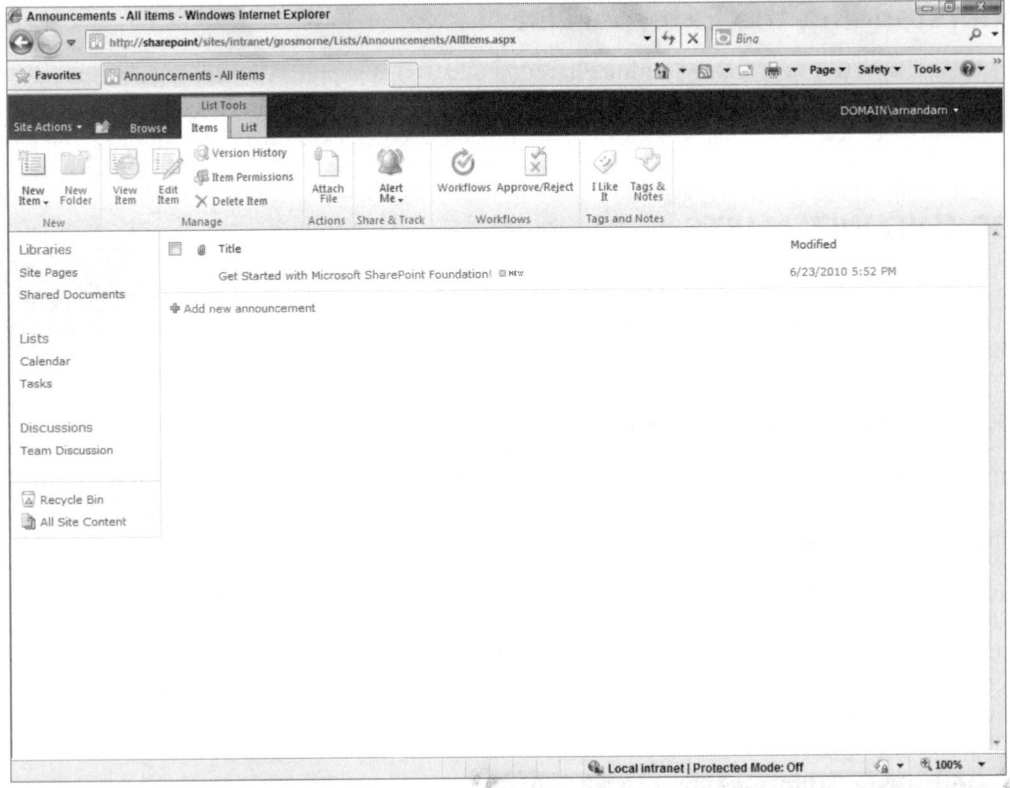

FIGURE 2-10

COLUMN	VALUE
Title	New Project Launched
Body	We are excited to annonce the launch of our new project. This project will last approximately 12 months and will focus on the exploration of a National Park located in Newfoundland and Labrador for a suitable location for a company office.
Expires	Enter a date 12 months in the future.

6. Click on the Spelling menu item. If you entered the details as specified in the preceding table, you will notice that one spelling error has been found.
7. Click OK to view the details. You should see that the word "annonce" is underlined in red, as shown in Figure 2-11.
8. Click on the word using your right mouse button. A listing of suggested words will appear.
9. Select the first choice: announce. The text of your announcement body will be updated to feature the correct spelling.

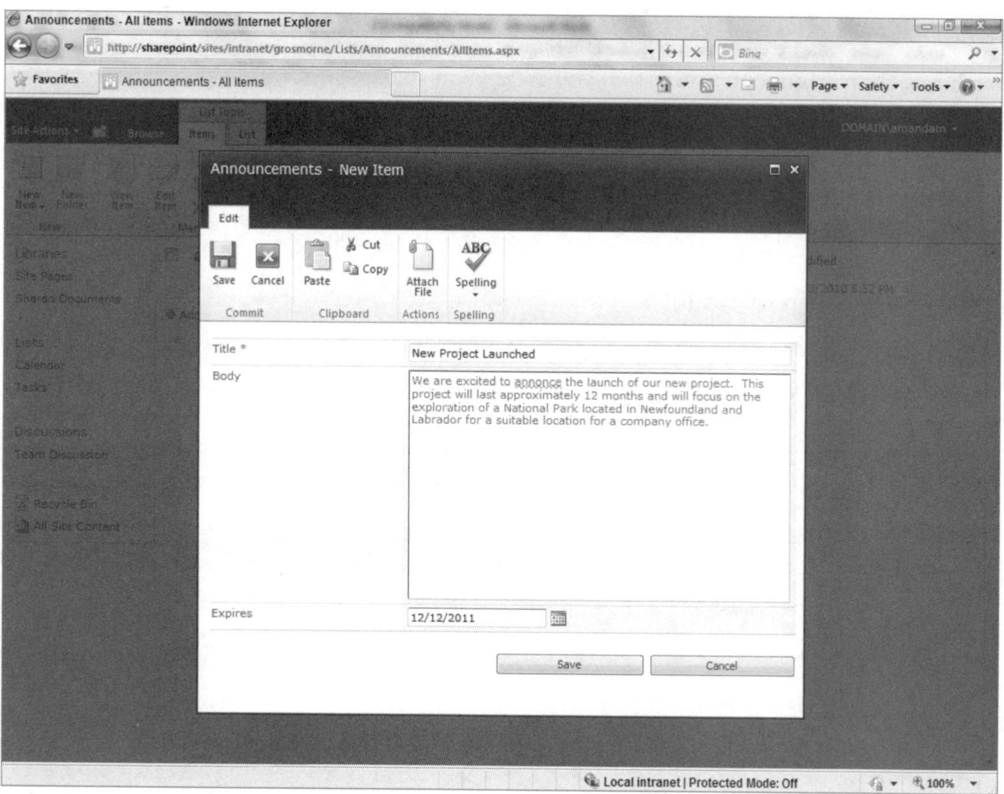

FIGURE 2-11

10. Click Save to complete the creation of your new announcement. You will be returned to the list, and your new announcement will appear on the screen with a new icon.

How It Works

In the preceding example, you navigated to the announcements list of your project site to create a new entry related to the launch of a new project. The announcement list is an excellent location for content such as this, which does not require an immediate response or action from readers. Quite often in organizations, messages such as this are sent via email. Using an announcements list, team members can receive their updates on topics at times that are more convenient for them. When you specify an expiration date for your entry, it will only be displayed in the Summary view until that date. Other views can be configured for filtering based on the Expires column as well. We will cover the creation of custom views in Chapter 4.

When navigating to the announcements list, you selected View All Site Content from the Site Actions menu. This option will allow you to access all lists and libraries on the site. In some cases, a list may have been created but not have been added to the side navigation. Therefore, you must access it using the View All Site Content option.

TRY IT OUT Editing an Existing Item in a List

Upon reading the new announcement that you created on your project team site, you realize it would have been useful to also include details related to how others can become involved. Therefore, you must update the announcement to include additional details.

1. From the main page of your project site, select the All Site Content link from the side navigation. This is an alternate method to access the page containing links to all lists and libraries on the site.
2. Select your announcements list.
3. Select the checkbox to the left of your New Project Launched announcement.
4. Select the Edit Item option from the Ribbon as shown in Figure 2-12.

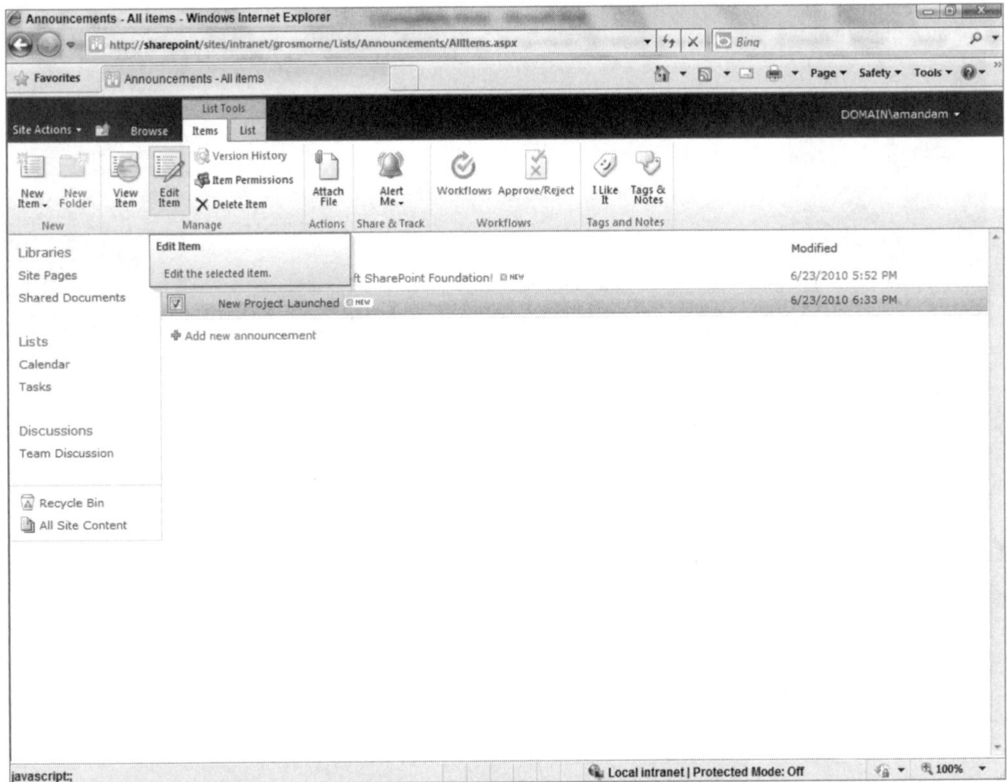

FIGURE 2-12

5. Within the Body column, add the following text:

   To become involved in this project, please contact Aaron Murphy, the Project Manager at aaron.murphy@discovernl.com.

6. Click Save.

Now when team members view your announcement, they will see your latest changes.

The previous two examples focused on creating and editing items in an announcements list. However, you can use the steps to create new items on all lists. It is highly recommended that you take some time to enter items in the other lists templates that exist on your Project Team Site before completing additional exercises.

TRY IT OUT Create a New List

When you created your Project Team Site earlier in the chapter, the site contained certain lists by default. In some situations, you may need to add additional lists to your site that utilize other templates or meet your specific requirements. In this example, you will create a new list based on the Project Tasks template. This list will be used for tracking team assignments and monitoring progress throughout the project.

1. From the main page of your Project Gros Morne site, expand the Site Actions menu and select the More Options menu item.
2. Select Filter by List, as shown in Figure 2-13.

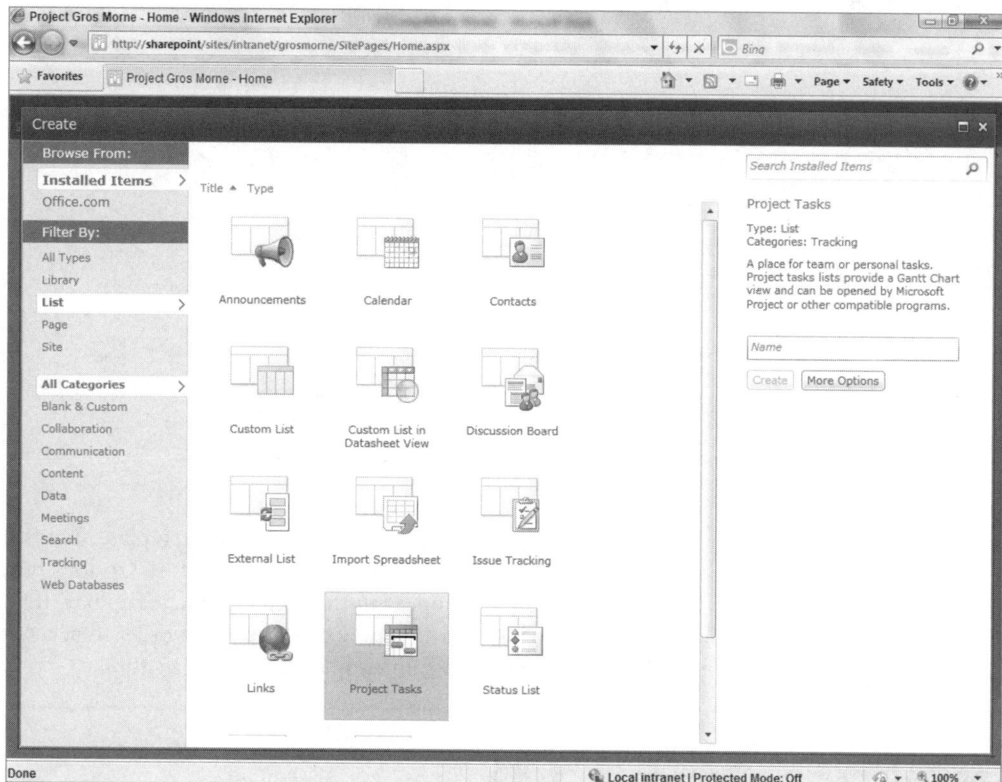

FIGURE 2-13

3. Select the Project Tasks item.
4. Enter **Workplan** as the name of your list.
5. Select the More Options button.

6. Ensure that Yes is selected to Display the list on the Quick Launch Toolbar.
7. Click the Create button.
8. The new list will be created, and you will be redirected to its location as shown in Figure 2-14.

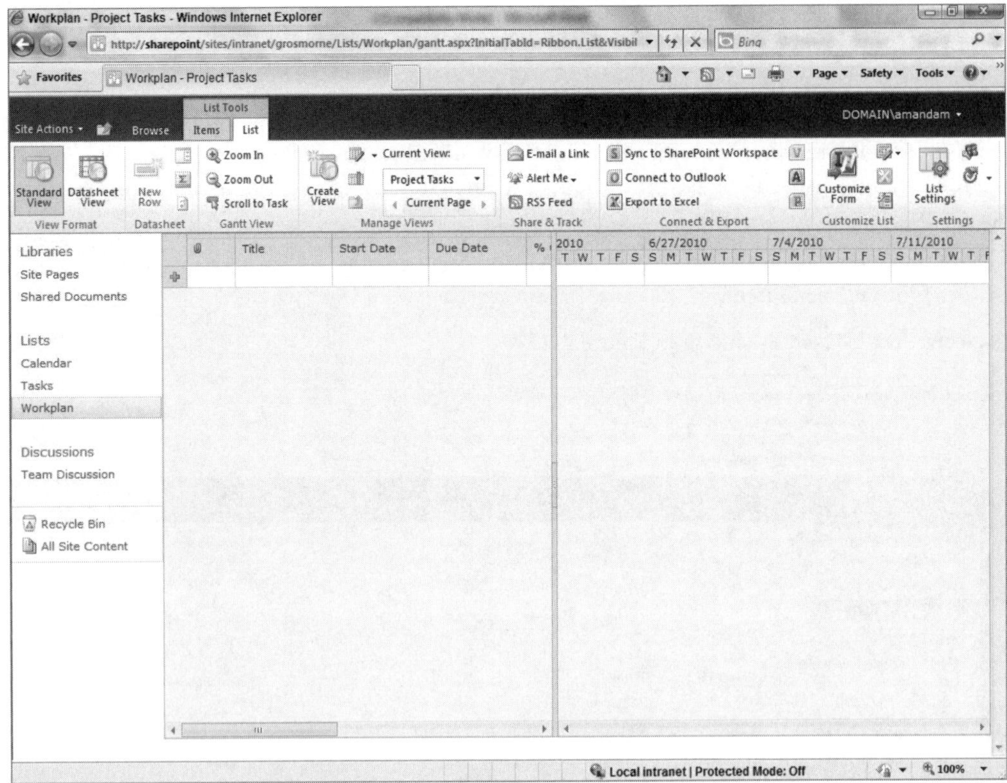

FIGURE 2-14

How It Works

In this example, you created a new list on your site based upon the Project Tasks template. This same process can be used for creating any list on your site. In step 5, you selected the More Options button, which allowed you to determine whether the list should appear in the Quick Launch Toolbar. If you selected No, team members would be required to visit the All Site Content page in order to access my list. However, selecting Yes means the link will appear conveniently in the side navigation.

TRY IT OUT Edit Items in a Gantt View

1. From the main page of your Project Gros Morne site, select the Workplan link from the side navigation to access the Project Tasks list created in the previous Try It Out.
2. You may notice that the presentation of this list is slightly different from that of the lists previously explored in the chapter. In the middle of your screen, you will notice a view divider bar. Hover

near the middle of the bar, as shown in Figure 2-15, to highlight the area on the bar that you can click and drag to the right.

3. Drag the bar to the right so that all columns are displayed in the left-hand panel of the view as shown in Figure 2-16.

4. Update the list by clicking within the table cells of each column on the left side to create the following tasks.

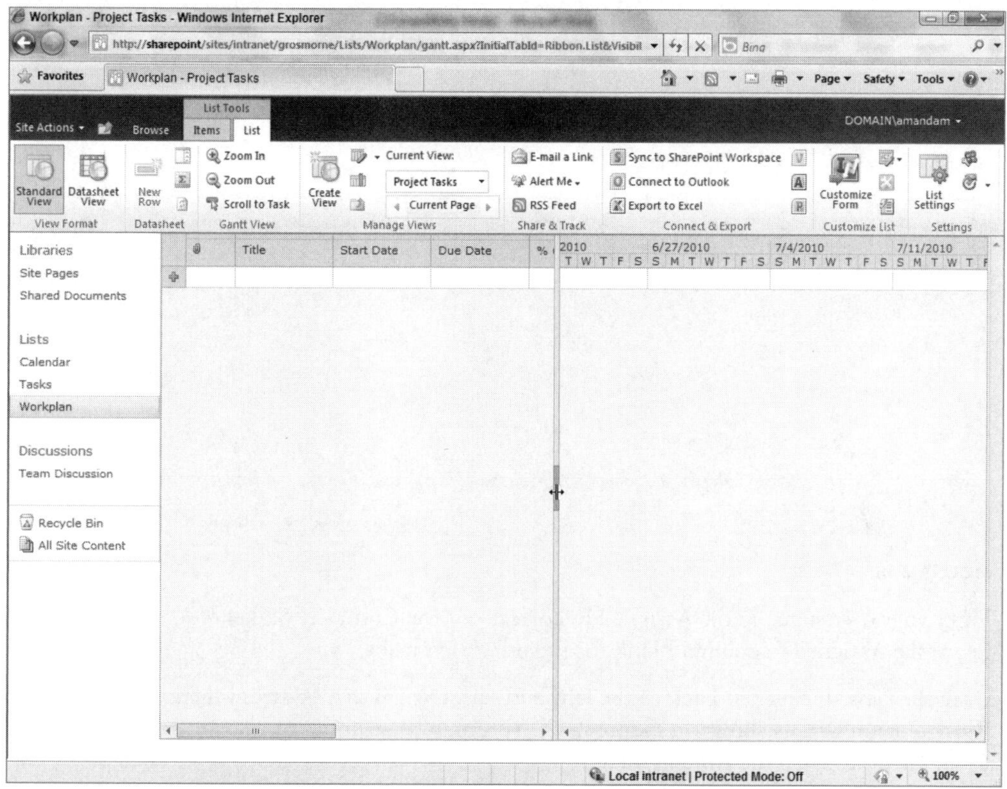

FIGURE 2-15

TITLE	START DATE	DUE DATE	% COMPLETE	TASK STATUS	PREDECESSORS
Project Kickoff Meeting	January 3, 2011	January 3, 2011	100	Completed	
Complete Stakeholder Interviews	January 4, 2011	January 11, 2011	50	In Progress	Project Kickoff Meeting
Create Requirements Document	January 12, 2011	January 26, 2011	0	Not Started	Complete Stakeholder Interviews

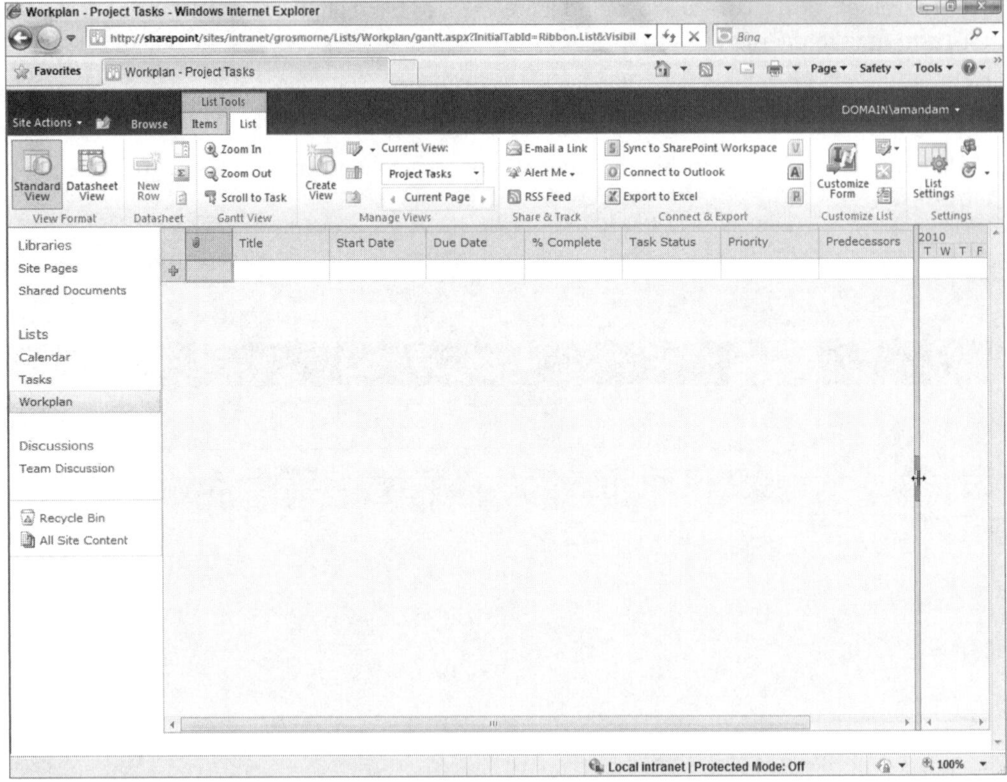

FIGURE 2-16

5. Enter your own name in the Assigned to column for the Complete Stakeholder Interviews task. Leave the Assigned to column blank for the other two tasks.

6. Drag the view divider bar back to the left, and select Scroll to Task from the List Tab within the Ribbon menu bar, as shown in Figure 2-17. You may be required to also zoom out or zoom in using the buttons on the Ribbon menu.

   You will now see a graphical representation of your task schedule displayed in the right-hand portion of your view.

How it Works

The Project Tasks list is configured to have a Gantt view as the default view type. This specialized view is helpful for viewing date-based information in a format that clearly indicates the schedule and dependencies of tasks. You will notice that lines are drawn between tasks to indicate relationships where one task has been defined as a predecessor of another. In addition, you will notice that the Complete Stakeholder Interviews task is partially filled with a black line to indicate that it is 50% complete. This helps ensure that team members can easily identify the status of the various tasks that are assigned to them.

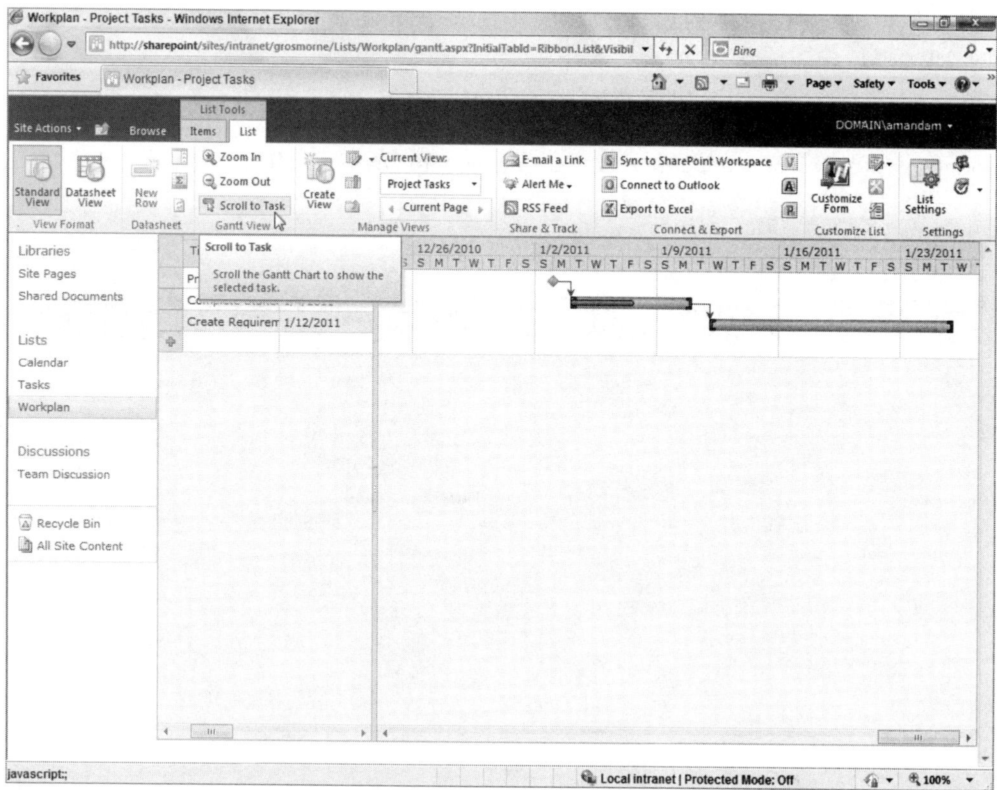

FIGURE 2-17

TRY IT OUT Change the View of a List

1. From your Workplan list, select the List tab on the Ribbon.
2. Expand the Current View drop-down, and select My Tasks as shown in Figure 2-18.
3. The page will refresh, and you will notice that a new view of the list appears that displays only the task for which you have been assigned.

How It Works

As you add more and more data to SharePoint lists, it is important that you have methods to organize and access the information in a timely and effective manner. In the previous example, if you accessed a task list on a popular team site, you could have hundreds or even thousands of list items. With such a large amount of information, it's very difficult to quickly identify relevant items in the list. However, through custom views, you create filters that look at the column data and return items that meet specific criteria.

In the example shown, you selected the My Tasks view. This view has a filter that only displays items assigned to the current user. The view uses a special property called [me], which identifies the current user and displays only items that have that user's name in the Assigned To column.

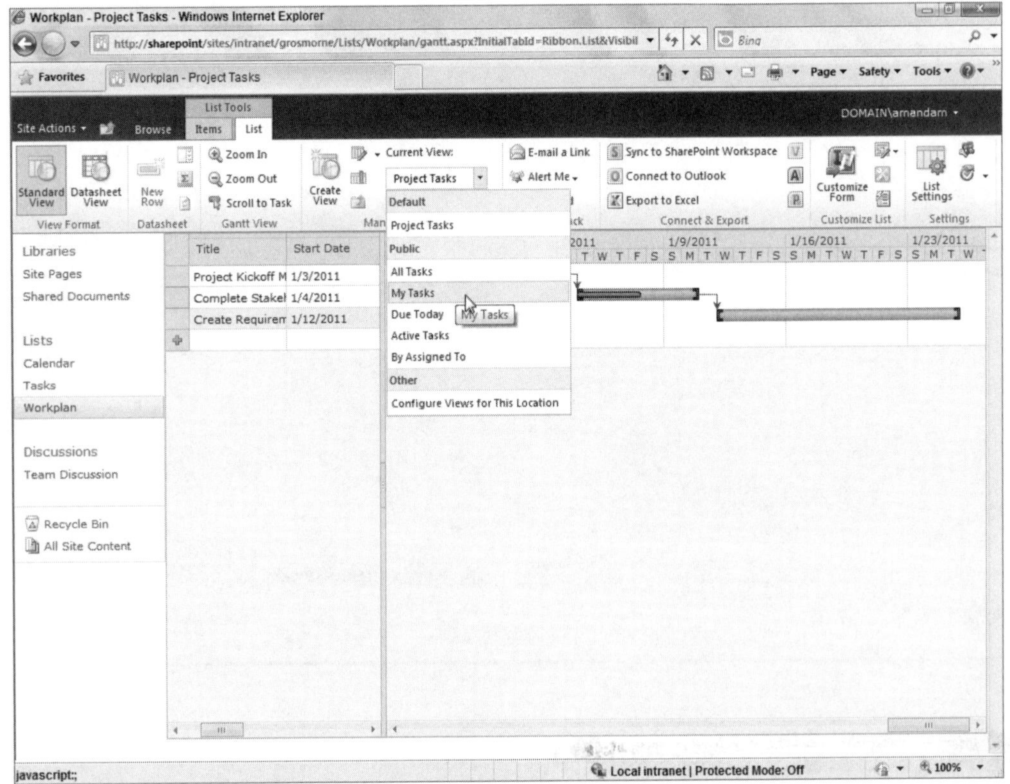

FIGURE 2-18

TRY IT OUT Export List Items to Excel

1. From your Workplan list, select the List tab on the Ribbon.
2. Expand the Current View drop-down and select All Tasks. The view will refresh, and all three tasks will be visible in the listing.
3. Select the List tab on the Ribbon menu once again.
4. Select the option to Export to Excel, as shown in Figure 2-19.

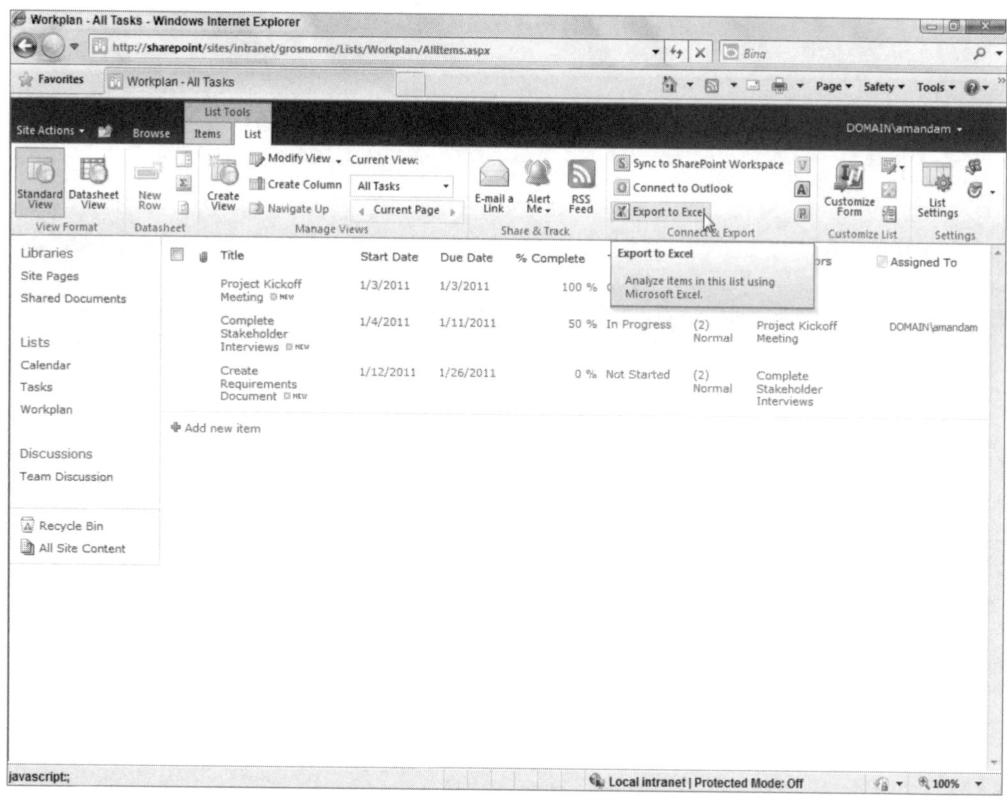

FIGURE 2-19

5. A file download box will appear asking you to Open, Save, or Cancel. Select the Open option.
6. Microsoft Excel will open on your desktop, and you will likely receive a security warning. Click the Enable button.
7. A spreadsheet will open, containing the information from your SharePoint list, as shown in Figure 2-20.

How It Works

SharePoint is a fantastic collaborative environment for storing up-to-date information in a centralized store. Editing lists is very similar to editing information in Excel, especially if you are using a datasheet view, but in Excel you can do certain things that are impossible on the browser, such as advanced calculations, data analysis, what-if analysis, and complex rich formatting. However, you can have the best of both the SharePoint and the Excel worlds; you can create custom views on large amounts of data to filter and only display relevant information. Then, through the Export to Spreadsheet functionality views of list data, you can move data into Excel worksheets to share information or run further analysis.

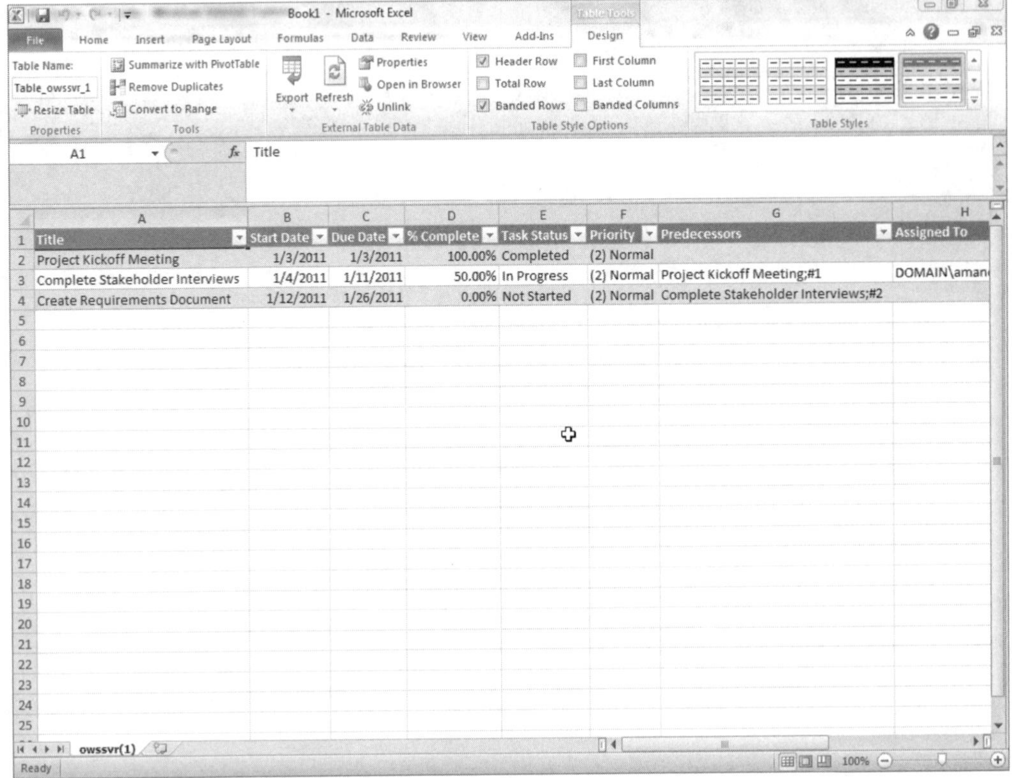

FIGURE 2-20

TRY IT OUT Subscribe to an Alert

When you work with SharePoint lists, you may want to be notified of changed or added content because receiving this information via an email is less time-consuming than physically visiting every SharePoint site to manually check for new content. SharePoint offers a special Alerts feature, to which you can subscribe and from which you can create lists to keep aware of changes.

Creating alerts allows team members to stay up to date on the changes to a SharePoint list or library in a manner that is appropriate to their unique work preferences or to receive immediate notifications on items that are of high relevance to them. For example, if you are responsible for responding to trouble tickets submitted to a list, you'll likely want notification as soon as an item is created or edited. However, you may only select a weekly summary report for another list that tracks menu choices for the cafeteria.

1. From the main page of your Project Gros Morne site, select the Workplan link from the side navigation.
2. Select the List tab on the Ribbon menu.
3. Select the Alert Me item from the menu. A small menu will appear.
4. Select the Set alert on this list option from the menu, as shown in Figure 2-21.

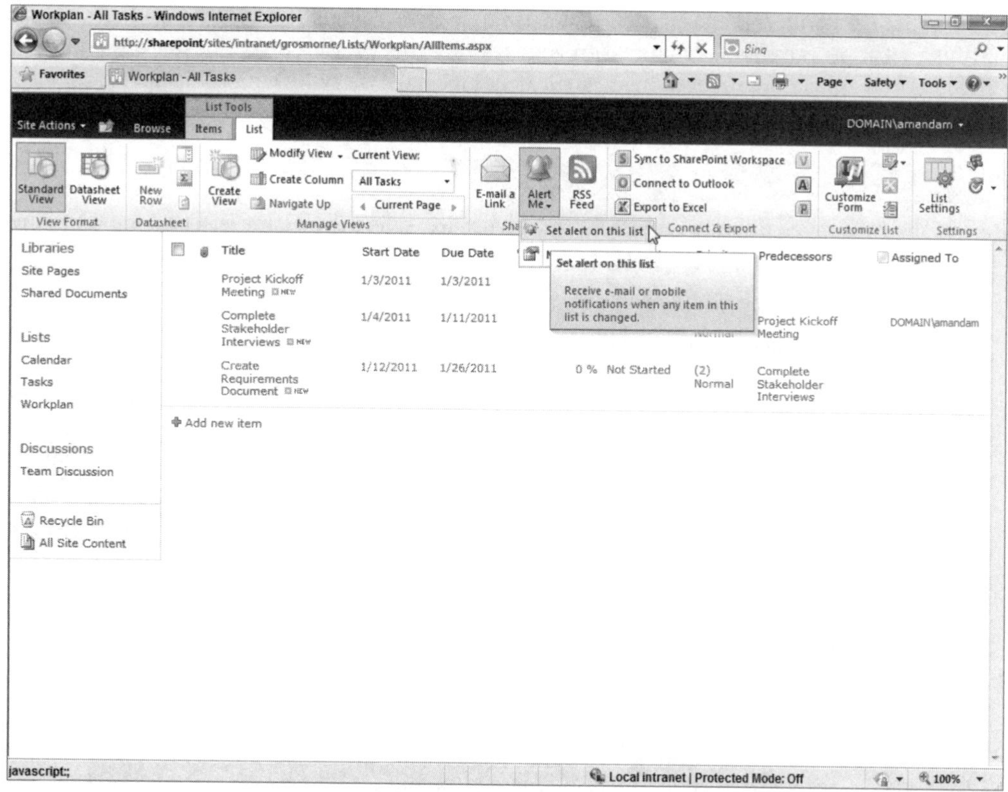

FIGURE 2-21

5. A New Alert window will appear. Enter the following settings for your new alert.

SETTING	VALUE
Alert Title	Workplan Task Updated By Team Member
Send Alerts To	Your Name
Delivery Method	Email
Change Type	Existing items are modified
Send Alerts for These Changes	Someone else changes an item
When to Send Alerts	Send a daily summary

6. Click OK.

How It Works

In the preceding example, you created an alert on the Workplan list so that you would be notified whenever a team member other than yourself makes a change to an existing task. You chose to receive your alert via email. Changing the Alert Title to an informative value allows you to easily distinguish the type of update you are receiving as it appears in your inbox, since the Alert Title will be the subject of the email message that is sent. By selecting a daily summary, you can choose which hour of the day you wish to receive the alert. As a project manager, you may wish to receive a single report at the end of each business day outlining what progress has been made on your team's tasks for the current business day. This may be more effective and efficient than receiving a single email message every time a task is updated.

TRY IT OUT Create a Threaded Discussion

1. From the main page of your Project Gros Morne site, select the Team Discussion link from the side navigation.
2. Click the Add new discussion link.
3. Enter the following details for your discussion topic.

COLUMN	VALUE
Subject	SharePoint Works Great for Projects!
Body	I really like that we can update our project team site directly from the browser and share our progress as we move towards our final goal.

4. Click Save.
5. Your new discussion topic will appear as shown in Figure 2-22.

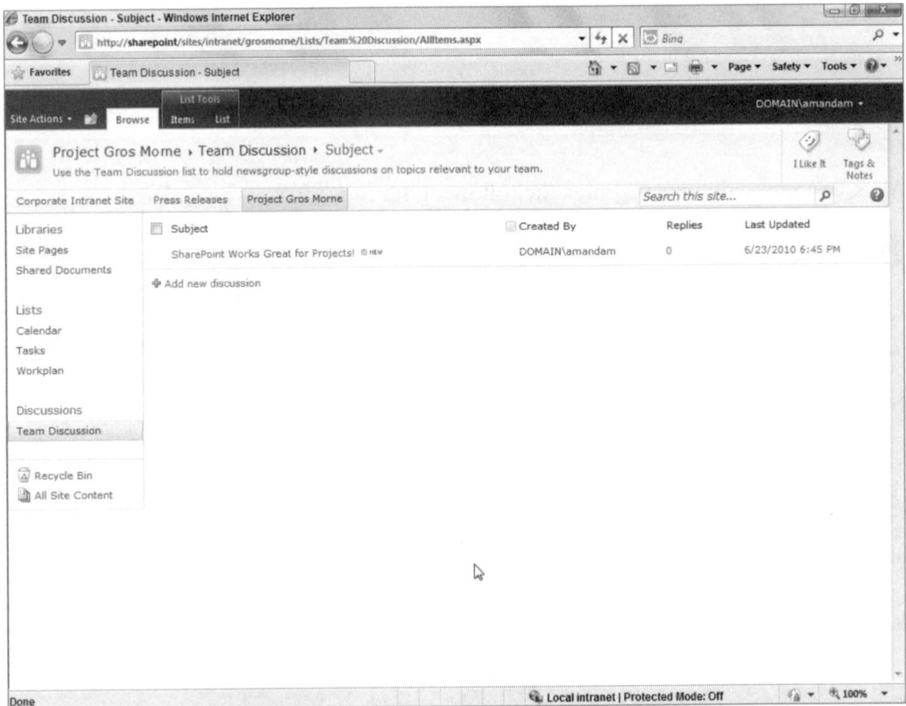

FIGURE 2-22

Now that your new discussion topic has been added to the site, other team members may come to the site and reply to your post.

TRY IT OUT Connect a List to Outlook

For many team members, Microsoft Outlook is an application that is open on their computer continuously throughout the day. It is an application that many people are familiar with and, therefore, it can be a great tool for updating information on your SharePoint site. If you use Outlook 2010, you can connect specific lists to your profile so that information stored within the list is available as a folder in Outlook. This means that you can work directly on list items through Outlook and the application automatically synchronizes your changes with the list when you reconnect. This keeps the SharePoint list information up to date, even when you are away from the office or disconnected from the network. If a conflict exists, you receive a notification and you have a choice on how you want to resolve the conflict.

1. From the main page of your Project Gros Morne site, select the Team Discussion link from the side navigation.
2. Select the List Tab from the Ribbon.
3. Select the Connect to Outlook option from the Connect & Export group.
4. You will receive a security prompt to ensure that you wish to allow the website to open the application from your computer. Click Allow.
5. Outlook will open, and you will receive an additional prompt to confirm that you wish to Connect that SharePoint Discussion Board to Outlook. Click Yes.
6. Outlook will now connect to the SharePoint list and download the existing discussions so that they can be viewed and accessed directly from Outlook, as shown in Figure 2-23.

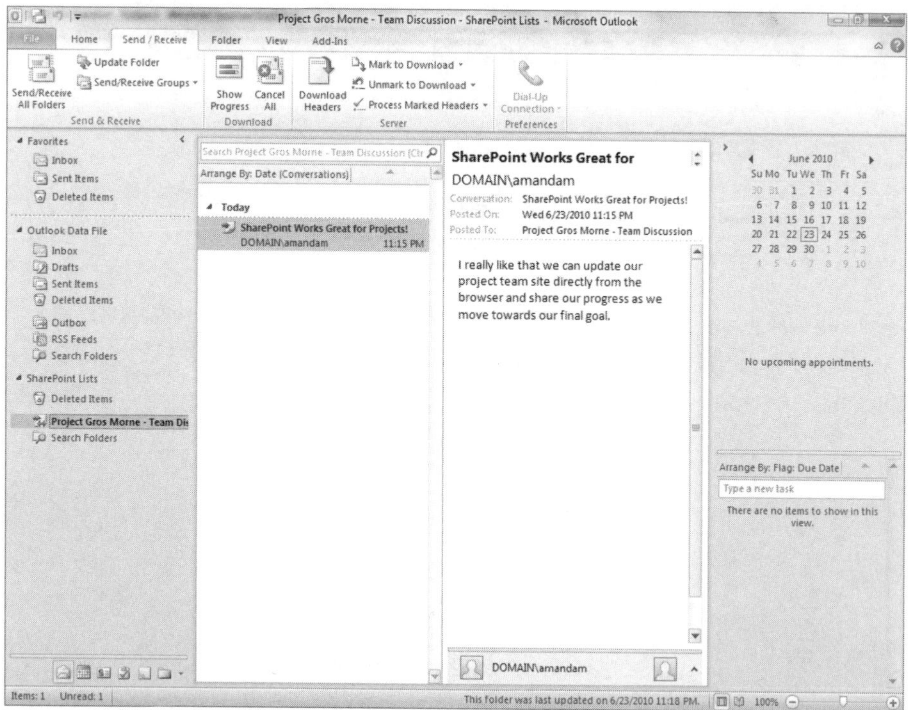

FIGURE 2-23

TRY IT OUT Reply to an Existing Discussion from Outlook

Outlook supports a two-way synchronization of content. This means that, in addition to receiving updates within Outlook from the SharePoint list, team members can submit updates to the SharePoint list from Outlook. In this example, you will reply to your previously created discussion topic from within Outlook.

1. Open Microsoft Outlook.
2. From the Mail tab, select your Team Discussion list from the SharePoint Lists, as shown previously in Figure 2-23.
3. Select the SharePoint Works Great for Projects Message.
4. Click the Post Reply button from the Home tab on the Ribbon.
5. Enter the following for your reply:

    SharePoint is great and it supports updates to lists such as Discussion Boards, Tasks, Contacts and Calendars directly from within Outlook.

6. Click Post.

When you return to your team site, you will notice that, in just a few moments, your new reply will appear with the Team Discussion list, as shown in Figure 2-24.

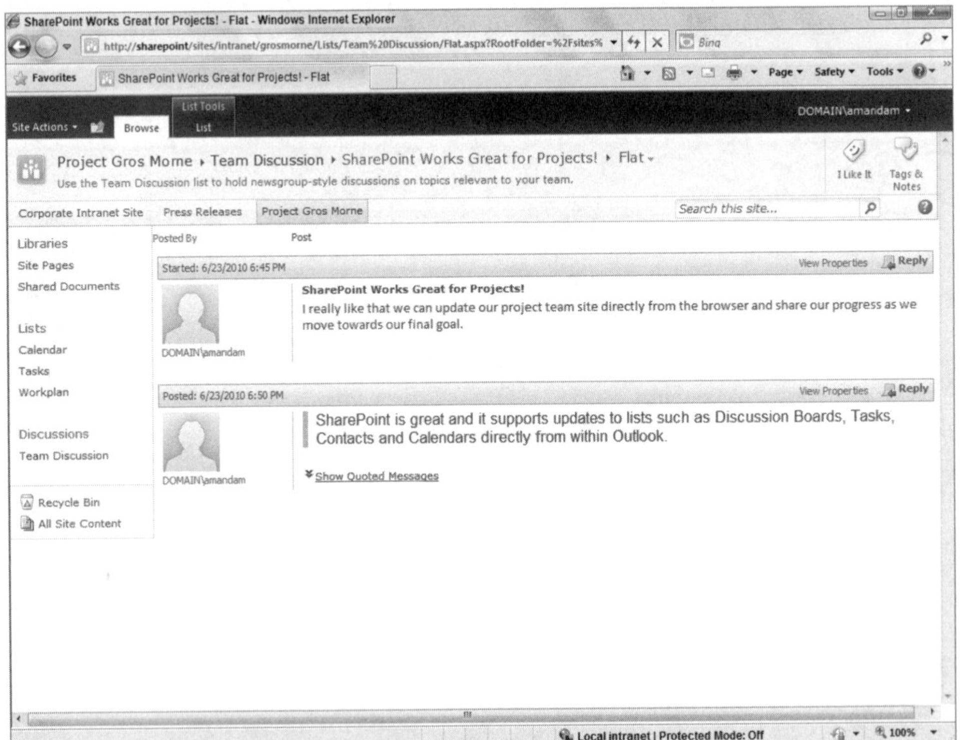

FIGURE 2-24

SUMMARY

In this chapter, you learned about the basic content storage mechanism in SharePoint, called lists. Lists allow you to collect information on a SharePoint site and share it with other team members in a manner that is easy to update and maintain. You learned the following:

- Lists contain columns of data that describe an item. Columns can contain information in a variety of formats, such as single line of text, multiple lines of text, date, or numerical data.
- You can link some lists such as tasks, project tasks, discussion boards, contacts, and a calendar to Microsoft Outlook to allow users to update and create new content on the SharePoint site directly from their email client. This is convenient for those users who are less familiar and comfortable in a web environment, but very much at ease when they work with their email program.
- By linking lists to Outlook, you can create an offline store that you can synchronize with later when the SharePoint site is available.
- You can link some list templates with an Access database. This also creates an offline store and provides a rich reporting environment for users on data that is stored on the SharePoint site.
- SharePoint has a variety of list templates that you can use to create task assignments, and perform event management and issue tracking. You can use these templates exactly as they are created, or you can customize them by creating custom views or columns.
- You can subscribe to information that is stored within lists via alerts, which are customizable email notifications that you can define directly from the List toolbar menu.
- When you need to share information stored on a SharePoint site with stakeholders who do not have access to the physical environment, you can export certain SharePoint list views into Excel spreadsheets or Visio diagrams and save the data offline for further analysis or sharing.

This chapter focused mainly on lists basics, describing the various functionality and features. In Chapter 4, you learn how to customize and manage lists to create working environments that suit your specific business requirements and needs.

EXERCISES

1. If you wanted to receive an email notification every time a new item was added to a list, how would you do that?
2. Describe the difference between a lookup column and a choice column.
3. Describe how you would send a report of information stored in a list to a partner outside your organization who did not have access to your SharePoint list.
4. What are the differences between a tasks list and a projects task list?
5. True or false: You can allow users to skip specific questions based on their responses to specific survey questions.

▸ WHAT YOU LEARNED IN THIS CHAPTER

TOPIC	KEY CONCEPTS
The core elements of a list	Lists have items, columns, and views. Items and columns correspond to the rows and columns that you see on a grid layout in a spreadsheet. Views present list data in a friendlier format that acts very similarly to a report.
What is an alert?	An alert is a subscription you can create on a list to be notified via email or text message based on activities that occur within the list such as new items added and existing items edited or deleted.
The standard types of lists	In this chapter you learned about the different types of lists that can be created in SharePoint including Tasks, Project Tasks, Threaded Discussions, Calendar, Status, Contacts, Issues, Announcements, Survey, and External Lists.

3

Working with Libraries

WHAT YOU WILL LEARN IN THIS CHAPTER:

- The key activities related to a document library such as the creation, uploading, and updating of files
- The core functionality available related to tracking unique versions of files
- Features available within the various library templates in SharePoint 2010

In this chapter, you discover the magic behind document collaboration: the document library. Document libraries allow you to create, store, manage, and collaborate on documents. SharePoint has a variety of library templates, each designed to allow maximum efficiency when you work with particular types of documents. This chapter discusses the major elements of a document library and steps you through some of the different library templates and how you can use them to manage the documents crucial to business operations.

In Chapter 4, you will learn how to configure the properties and features of a document library to fit your business needs. This chapter focuses on interacting with document libraries that have been previously created or configured.

UNDERSTANDING LIBRARIES AND DOCUMENTS

If you want to, you can think of a document library as a Windows file folder but better. Like folders, libraries act as document storage, but they also store the document's metadata or version history (more about these a little later), which folders do not. Also, Windows file folders lend themselves to user personalization in that they may stay on a user's drive or be labeled differently from another user's folder, which leads to inefficiency. You don't encounter this in libraries, which act as central stores, shared across an organization or team. SharePoint also offers collaboration features that go well beyond the traditional file-sharing techniques that you may have used in the past. Also, because SharePoint stores lists and libraries in a database rather than the file system, it is arguably more secure, more efficient, and enables more sophisticated document workflow and content management scenarios. Users are only able to see files that they have been granted access to which only exposes relevant files to their role and improves the ease by which information can be found.

NOTE *While we often refer to the storage of documents in SharePoint libraries, it is important to know that you can store a variety of file types, including presentations, images, forms, and spreadsheets. You can store virtually any file type in a SharePoint library as long as the file type has not been added to the Blocked File Types listing.*

MANAGING BLOCKED FILE TYPES

You can view the listing of blocked file types for your SharePoint environment by visiting the SharePoint Central Administration site for your server farm. Once there, you can find a link to view blocked file types, under the Security group of links.

You can remove items from this list to allow users to upload files of that type to SharePoint libraries within a web application; however, you should be very careful not to allow certain executables or file types that may cause security risks or performance issues. It is recommended that you speak with someone familiar with managing security within your network before removing a file type from this list. As a general rule, this list should not be modified unless a well-justified business case exists.

Administrators may allow users more or less flexibility for managing certain file types within their personal sites versus their collaborative sites. This may include blocking certain media file formats in the MySites application that may typically be used within the various departmental and team sites for training or reference.

- **Metadata information:** Document libraries have metadata columns for attaching information, such as document owner or status, to the document and, thus, tailoring it to your corporate practices. Metadata is useful for running searches on documents, which you learn more about in Chapter 17. Users with appropriate permissions can quickly and easily create extra metadata columns to describe the contents of a library. In fact, SharePoint document libraries offer many of the same features of lists that you explored in Chapter 2, such as rows, columns, and views.
- **Document protection:** Documents in libraries are protected by a check-in and check-out feature, which ensures that only one user at a time can edit a document. Later in this chapter, you learn about the various methods available for working with documents in this manner.
- **Document history:** Libraries keep a document audit trail, known as version history. This feature allows you to easily and quickly revert to a previously saved version of the document, directly from the browser. The version history feature will track changes that are made to the document's content as well as its metadata. Depending on which site template you are using, this feature may need to be enabled prior to its availability for use. The process for doing so is described later in this chapter.

- **Major and minor versions:** While both lists and libraries support versioning of information, document libraries support minor and major versions. Major versions are published files that are accessible to all site users, whereas the minor versions are files in a draft state that typically only a document's author or members of an approver's group can access.

On the surface, a document library view page, shown in Figure 3-1, looks very similar to a list with a few additions, including:

- **Upload button:** Located on the Ribbon, this button supports the uploading of single or multiple files to the library.
- **Open with Explorer button:** Located on theRibbon, clicking this button will open the library in a Windows Explorer type folder. Using this option, you can drag and drop files into folders, delete multiple files at once, and create new folders the same way you would when interacting with a standard Windows file folder. This feature requires the use of Internet Explorer 7.0 or later.
- **Copies:** Unique to the document library, this section of buttons provides you with the ability to interact with the document by downloading a copy of it, sending it to another location, creating a document workspace, or managing copies of the file within the system. We will cover these actions later in this chapter.

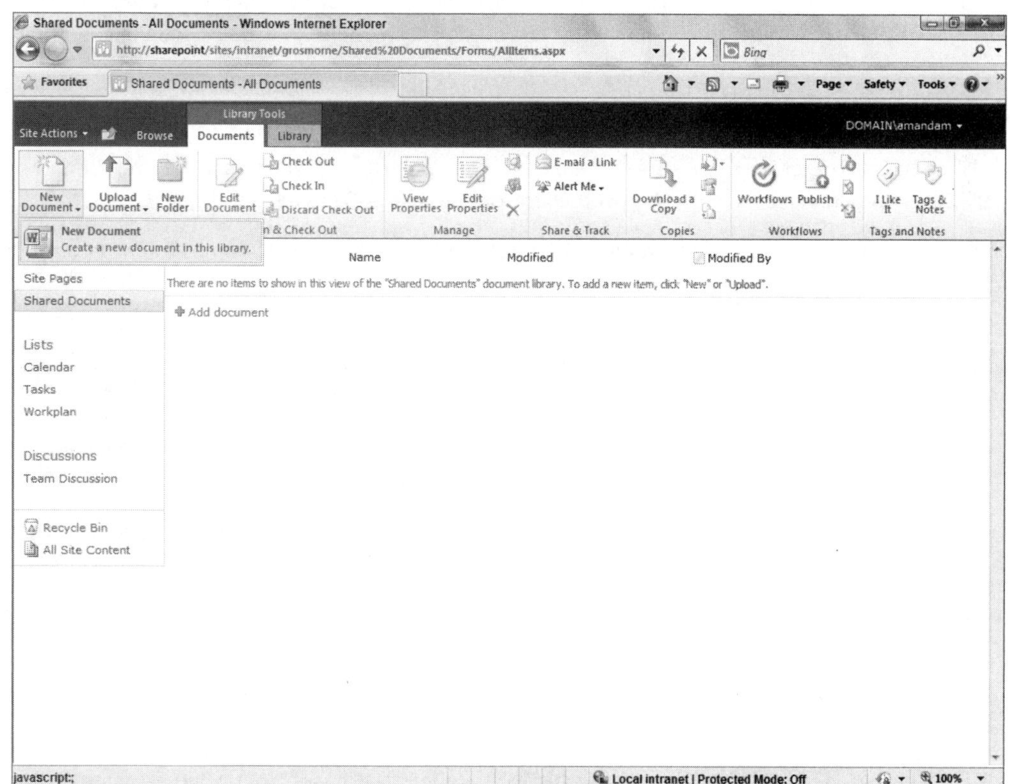

FIGURE 3-1

Creating and Managing Documents in a Library

Both employees and organizations benefit from SharePoint libraries. Organizations commonly roll out SharePoint to help ensure that documents are stored in a secure system where access, versioning, templates, columns, and content are controlled. From a user's perspective, creating and managing documents in a library is a simple process. You start by creating a document that is based on the latest version of a template. You can also easily upload single or multiple files to a location that is shared by other members of your team.

This section has a series of Try It Outs that walk you through many of the actions available within document libraries. Before you start, however, you need to understand the various document templates, shown in the following table, that can be created by clicking the New button within a document library. The obvious purpose of these templates is to start with blank document or files; however, you can also create custom templates that help your company to maintain a consistent look and feel for common document types. For example, you can have a sales proposal presentation template that contains important elements, such as your company's name, logo, and website information on every slide. Associating this template with the sales team document library allows an account manager to launch a presentation containing these elements with a single click.

TEMPLATE	PURPOSE
None	This option will disable the New Document button within the Ribbon of your library. Users will only be able to upload documents to the library.
Microsoft Office Word 97-2003 Document	Creates a blank Word document compatible with versions of Microsoft Office prior to the 2007 release.
Microsoft Office Excel 97-2003 Spreadsheet	Creates a blank Excel spreadsheet compatible with versions of Microsoft Office prior to the 2007 release.
Microsoft Office PowerPoint 97-2003 Presentation	Creates a blank PowerPoint presentation compatible with versions of Microsoft Office prior to the 2007 release.
Microsoft Office Word Document	Creates a new Word document using the new file formats. Supported only by Microsoft Office 2007 or later.
Microsoft Office Excel Spreadsheet	Creates a new Excel spreadsheet using the new file formats. Supported only by Microsoft Office 2007 or later.
Microsoft Office PowerPoint Presentation	Creates a new PowerPoint presentation using the new file formats. Supported only by Microsoft Office 2007 or later.
Microsoft Office OneNote Section	Creates a new OneNote section using the new file formats. Supported only by Microsoft Office 2007 or later.
Microsoft Office SharePoint Designer Web page	Creates a standard web page that you can edit using SharePoint Designer.
Basic Page	Creates a blank SharePoint web page containing a content editor web part to allow them to add text and basic HTML to the page.

Web Part Page	Creates a blank SharePoint web page with a series of web part zones to support the addition and configuration of multiple web parts in a desired layout.

TRY IT OUT Create a New Document from a Document Library

You can create new documents while working in applications, such as Microsoft Office Word, and then save them to a SharePoint site, or you can create them within SharePoint by selecting the New button from within a document library. By default, each document library has a single blank Word document template associated with it. You are presented with this template as a starting point to create your document. This is the case for any standard document library that you create in a SharePoint site, unless the site manager specifies otherwise or uploads a custom template.

1. From the main page of your Project Team Site created in Chapter 2, select the Shared Documents link from the side navigation bar.

NOTE *If you did not complete the exercises in Chapter 2, you may complete the exercises by creating a site based upon the Team Site template. If you require the steps to create a site, please review the first exercise in Chapter 2.*

2. Click the Documents tab from the Ribbon to display the available options for creating or interacting with documents in this document library.
3. Expand the New Document menu item as shown previously in Figure 3-1, and select the option to create a new document. A new blank Word document will open.

NOTE *While it is possible to just click on the New Document menu item, it is recommended that you always expand the menu to see what options are available. In Chapter 6, we will be exploring a way to allow the creation of multiple document types from a single library.*

4. A new blank document will open within Microsoft Word. Enter the following text in your document.

    This is a new document for my project. Even though I am using SharePoint to store and manage my files, I can still create and update the content from Microsoft applications such as Word the same way I have in the past.

5. From the File menu, select Save.
6. You will be prompted to enter a filename for the document. Notice that the save location is automatically recognized as the library that you initiated the document from. Enter **My Project Document** as the filename and click the Save button.
7. Close the Microsoft Word application.

When you return to the document library, you can refresh your browser window or click the F5 button and you will see that your file is now there. This file can now be shared with team members for collaboration purposes.

TRY IT OUT Upload a New Document

With SharePoint, uploading previously created documents is done as frequently as creating new ones. The following example guides you through the process of uploading a document from your personal computer or network share to a SharePoint document library.

Imagine that you are the project manager for the Gros Morne project, and you want to upload a recently created project plan to the team library. In the previous Try It Out, you created a new document from a library. However, you may want to share or manage documents created outside of the SharePoint environment. To accommodate this common situation, SharePoint document libraries support the uploading of content to the library from another location.

In this exercise, you browse to the location of a project plan called `GrosMorneProject.mpp`, which is available as part of this chapter's resources, and upload it to the Shared Documents library.

1. Return to the Shared Documents library of your team site, as shown in the last Try It Out.
2. Click the Documents tab on the Ribbon.
3. Expand the Upload Document menu item, and select the option to Upload Document. An Upload Document prompt will appear, as shown in Figure 3-2.
4. From the Upload Document prompt, select Browse. The Choose File dialog box appears.
5. Browse to the location of the `GrosMorneProject.mpp` file from your Chapter resources, and select Open, as shown in Figure 3-3.
6. Click the OK button. You will be returned to the document library where you will see the project plan within the document library.

How It Works

When you upload in step 4, you are presented with a standard file-open dialog box from which you can navigate to and select the file. After selecting your file and clicking OK, your document is transferred to the document library and, if applicable, you are prompted to enter any metadata that your document library requires. When uploading the file, you may have noticed the checkbox in Figure 3-2 to add the file as a new version to existing files. By selecting this box, any files that exist in the library that contain the same file name will be overwritten by the newly uploaded file. If version history is enabled in the library, the previous version of the file will be accessible through the version history.

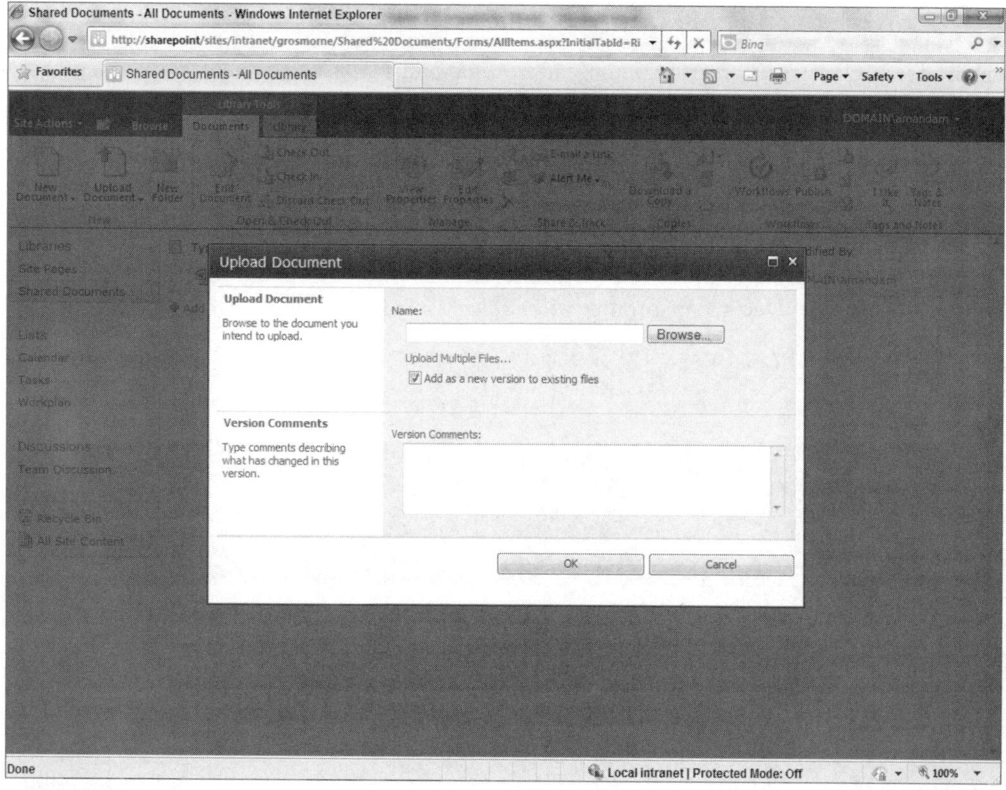

FIGURE 3-2

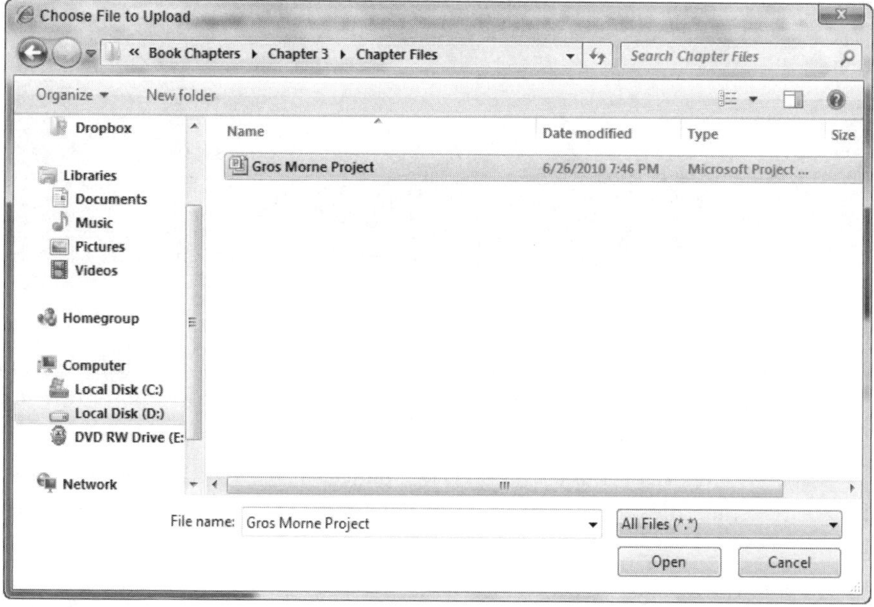

FIGURE 3-3

TRY IT OUT Upload Multiple Documents to a Document Library

The previous Try It Out works great if you only need to upload a single document to the document library. In the next example, we will review the process for uploading multiple files at once.

1. From the main page of your project team site, select the Shared Documents link from the side navigation bar.
2. Click the Documents tab on the Ribbon.
3. Expand the Upload Document menu item and select the option to Upload Multiple Documents. The Upload Multiple Documents prompt will appear as shown in Figure 3-4.

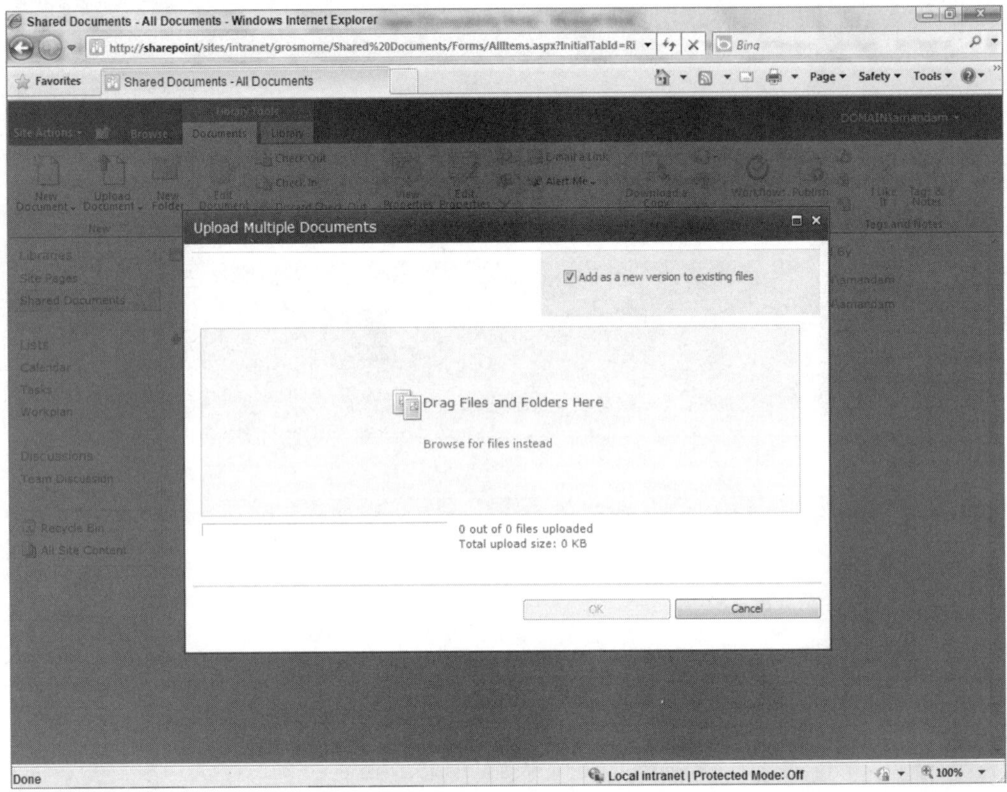

FIGURE 3-4

4. When uploading multiple files, you may drag and drop your files directly into the shaded area or click Browse for files instead hyperlink. In this example, you will click the hyperlink to browse to the location of the resources for this chapter.
5. Select the Project Charter, GrosMorneProject, and Project Budget files from the chapter resources and click Open. To select multiple files at once, you can hold down the Ctrl key while selecting each file.
6. Click OK to upload your documents.
7. Your progress will be displayed as shown in Figure 3-5. Click Done to complete the process.

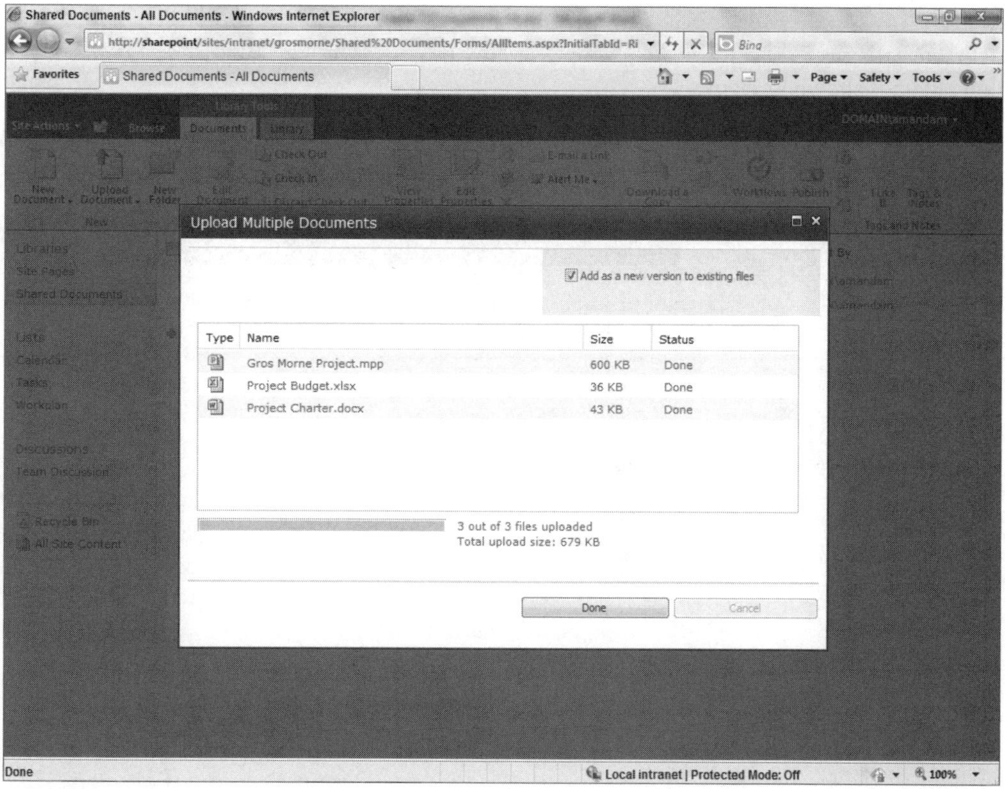

FIGURE 3-5

The default setting when you upload multiple files is to overwrite any files that already have the same name. You can change this by deselecting the Overwrite Existing Files checkbox. If you do wish to overwrite the existing files with a new version of the file, you leave the file selected. As a result, the project plan uploaded in the last Try It Out is overwritten by the copy you upload in this exercise.

TRY IT OUT Edit a Document Library View in Datasheet Mode

One important thing to remember when uploading files in bulk is that you are not prompted to complete the metadata for each item. Incomplete metadata can negatively impact searches that users perform to locate your documents. If you have to meet a deadline and can't fill in metadata information during the upload, remember to return to the library afterward and do so. The most efficient way to update multiple items at once is to use the Edit in Datasheet command. This command, which is shown in the following steps, allows you to update document metadata in a manner similar to updating a spreadsheet in Excel.

1. From the main page of your project team site, select the Shared Documents link from the side navigation bar.
2. Select the Library tab from the Ribbon.

3. Select the Datasheet view.

4. Update columns as necessary. An example of how this could look in a customized library with metadata is shown in Figure 3-6.

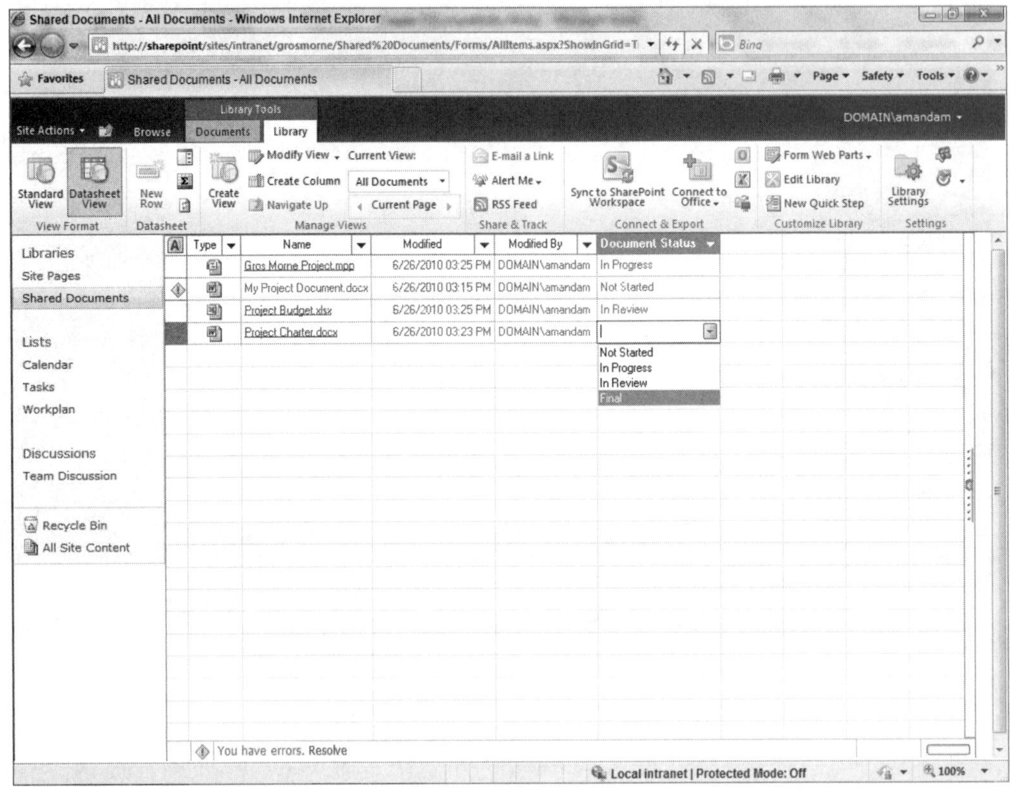

FIGURE 3-6

***NOTE** We will review adding metadata to lists and libraries in Chapter 4. On your current team site, you may not have any metadata available yet to update.*

5. When changes are complete, you can click Standard View from the Library tab of the Ribbon to return to the original view.

How It Works

In this example, you temporarily changed a standard document library view to a datasheet view. This allows updates to be made to the metadata associated with all documents within your document library. Editing a datasheet view is very similar to completing information within a spreadsheet application and is, therefore, ideal for occasions where a team member must update metadata in bulk. While you can create views that are always in datasheet mode, you can edit any standard list view in datasheet mode as shown here.

You now know how to create documents within your libraries as well as how to upload documents and update the metadata associated with them. Next is to understand how to update documents that are already in a library.

Updating and Sharing Documents

Your document's lifecycle will probably require you to perform updates and edits over time. You can quickly open and edit any document inside its document library via either of the following methods:

- **Via the contextual menu:** Hover over an item in a library to expose a contextual menu and then select the down arrow. Select Edit in Microsoft Word (or other application if applicable) from the list of menu options, as shown in Figure 3-7. You have several other options, such as Edit Properties, which edits the metadata, or View Properties, where you can view additional information associated with the document.

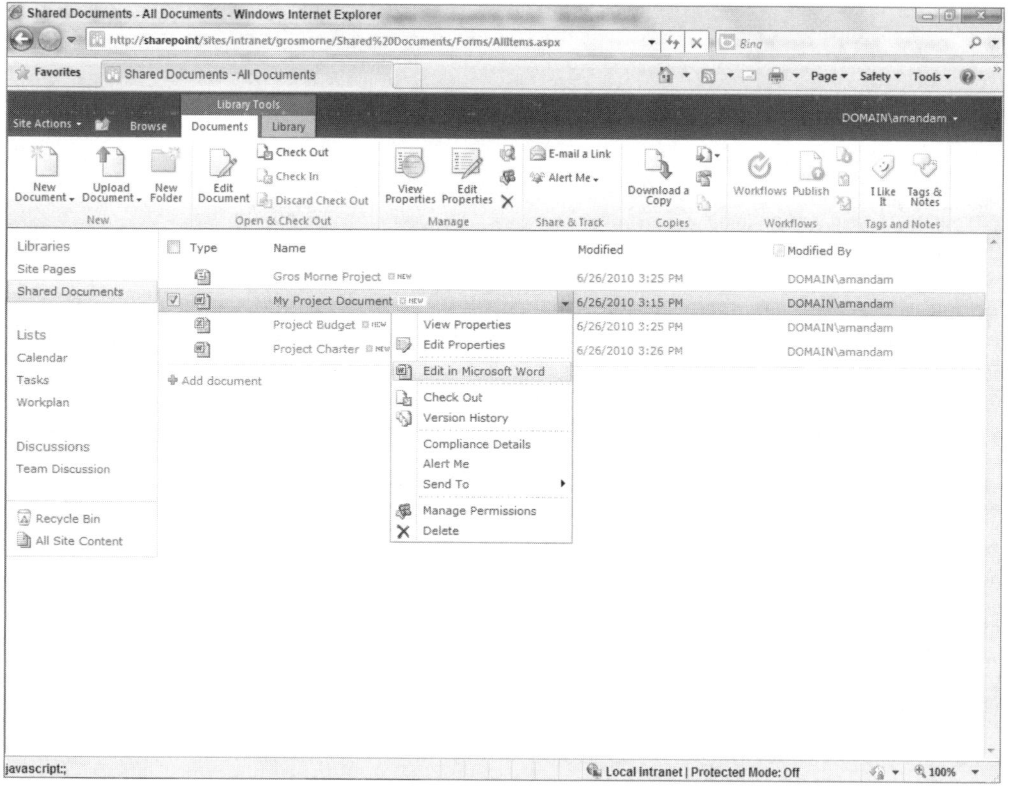

FIGURE 3-7

- Select an item in a document library and click the Edit Document item from the Ribbon as shown in Figure 3-8. The associated application opens so you can begin editing.

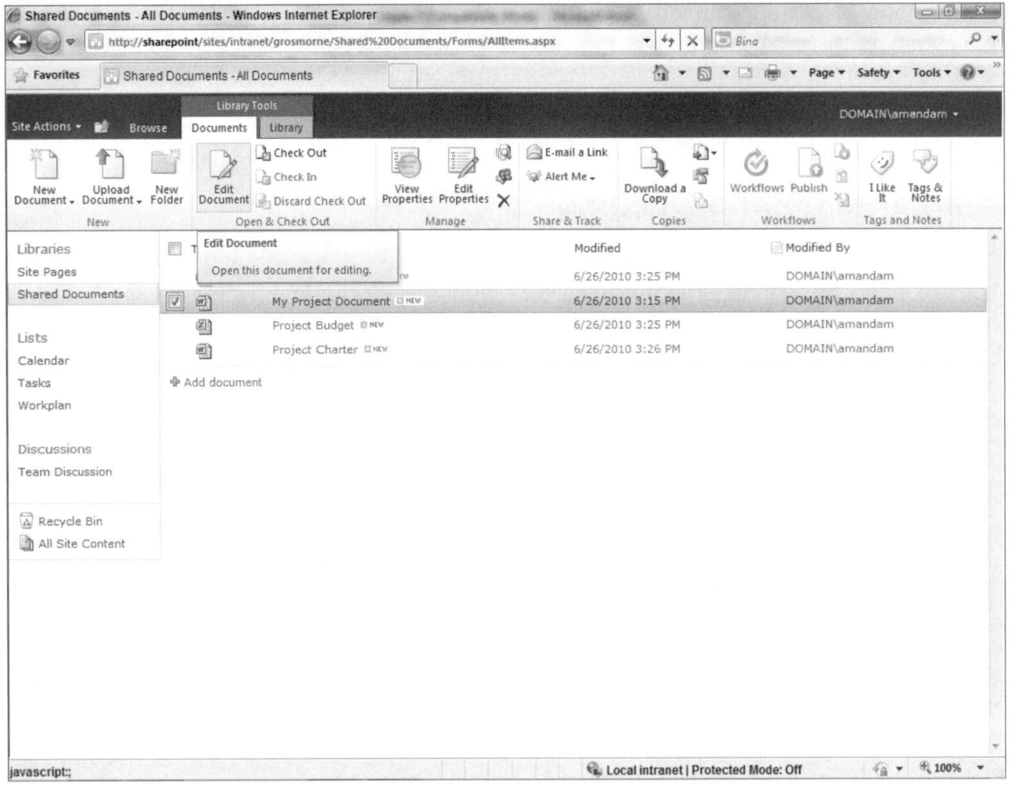

FIGURE 3-8

Obviously, the collaborating often requires that people work on the same document; however, this can lead to version conflict. For example, if you work on a document but leave the office for an extended period of time, another user can make changes to your document that conflict with your version or upload an older version of the document that could lead to confusion or lost work. When you resume your work, you definitely will notice changes but not necessarily know why or how the document was changed.

To minimize frustration, instead of directly editing the document via the contextual menu or from the document library, you can select the Check In/Check Out options beforehand. Checking out a document locks it so that others can view the last published version but cannot edit it or upload a version of the document, until you check the document back in.

The next three Try It Outs cover how to check out and check in a document, either from the SharePoint library or from an Office application, such as Word. The Check In/Check Out feature has the added benefit of allowing you to work offline while the file is in the checked-out stage. This means you can perform changes away from the office and these changes will be placed in the library when you check the document back in. In the last Try It Out, you learn how to send your colleagues notification so that they're aware of the changes you've made to a document.

NOTE *SharePoint's Check In/Check Out feature is controlled as part of library versioning. To configure and customize the settings for this feature, see Chapter 4.*

TRY IT OUT Check Out a Document

Checking out a document greatly reduces the chances of version conflicts because only one person can make changes to the document at a time. When a document is checked out, only the user who checked it out can edit the document. The following example shows you how to check out an item from a document library.

1. From the main page of your project team site, select the Shared Documents link from the side navigation bar.

2. Select the checkbox to the left of My Project Document. This will select the file and enable specific features that will be available for interacting with this document on the Ribbon.

3. Select the Check Out option from the Documents tab of the Ribbon. You receive a message informing you that you are about to check out a document, as shown in Figure 3-9.

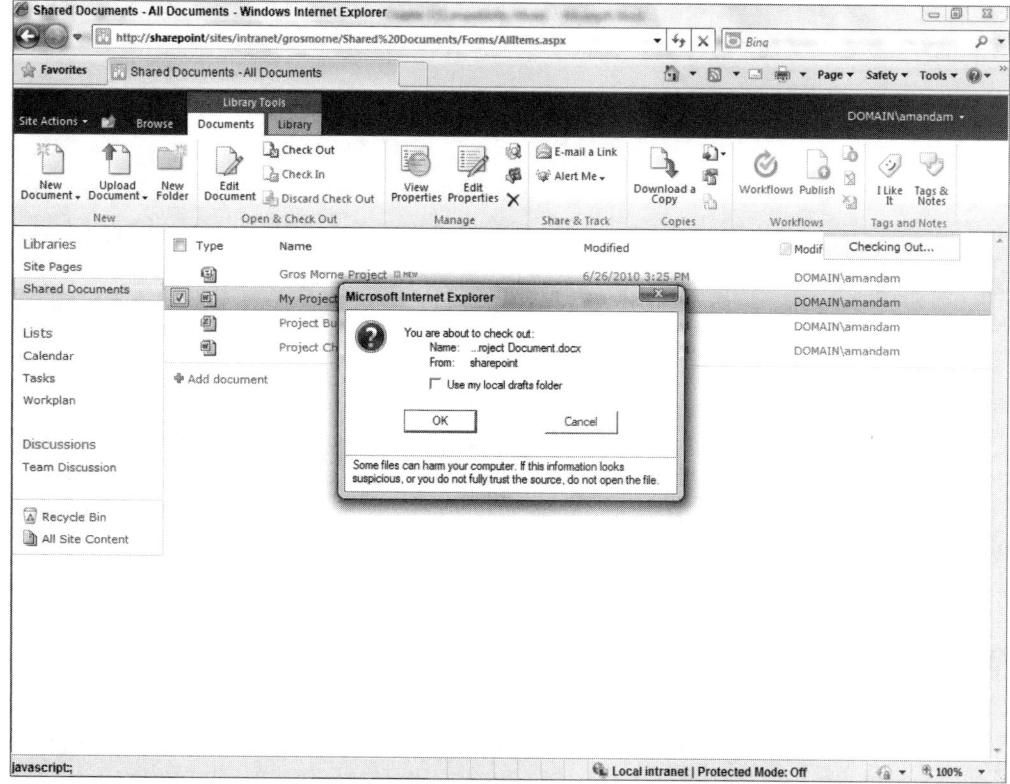

FIGURE 3-9

4. Do not select the Use my local drafts folder checkbox.

5. Click OK to check the document out. The document icon to the left of the document name changes to a document with a green arrow next to it, as shown in Figure 3-10.

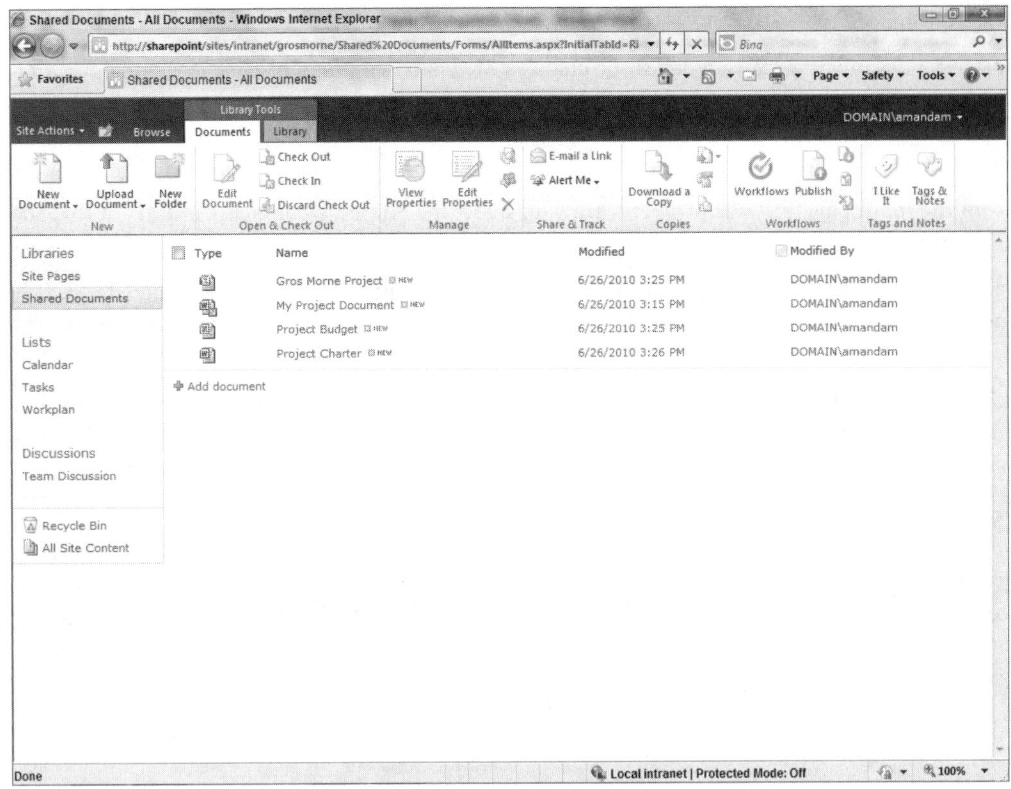

FIGURE 3-10

How It Works

When you check a document out from a library, it becomes locked and reserved to you for editing. Other members of your team may still open the file; however, they will be unable to make changes to it. When other team members view the document, they will not see the changes you are making until the document has been checked into the library again.

TRY IT OUT Check In a Document

After you make changes to your checked-out document, you need to check it back in. This creates a new version, complete with your changes, and makes the document available for others to check out. The check-in process is very similar to the check-out process, but you have the additional option of checking in changes while keeping the document checked out. This means that others can see changes you've made so far but that you can continue working on the document. It is best practice to include comments when checking a document in so that others understand what changes you made. Comments are visible in the version history, which makes tracking down problems easier in the future. The following steps show this process:

1. From the Shared Documents library, select the checkbox to the left of My Project Document.

2. Select the Check In option from the Documents tab of the Ribbon. You receive a message informing you that you are about to check in a document, as shown in Figure 3-11.

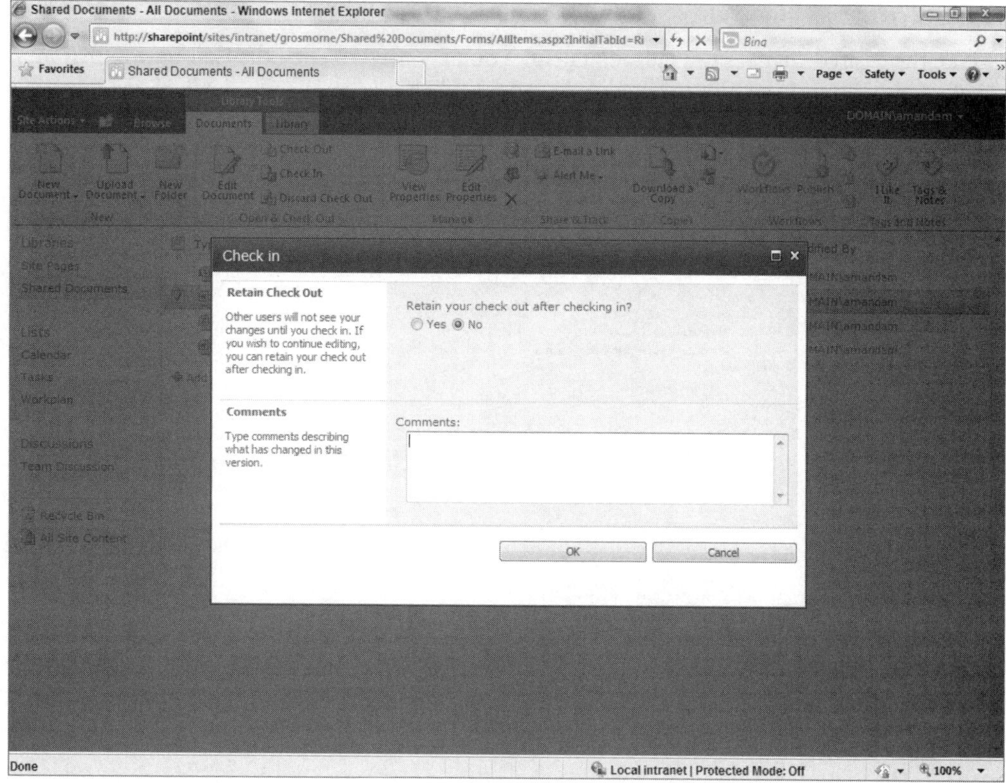

FIGURE 3-11

3. Select No for the option to Retain your check out after checking in. This is the default selection.
4. Enter notes into the comments field to describe the changes you made to the document.
5. Click OK to complete the check-in process.

TRY IT OUT Check In a Document from a Microsoft Office Application

If you are editing a document with Microsoft Office Word, instead of saving your changes, closing the document, going back to the browser and checking in your document, you can check the document back in straight from the application to cut out some steps. This functionality is only available in Microsoft Office 2007 client applications or later. All other applications and previous versions of Microsoft Office require you to check in the document using the SharePoint interface via the browser.

The following steps show you how to check in a document using Word, but they are similar to when you would check in a document in Excel or PowerPoint. Before you perform these steps, you should check out the My Project Document from your Shared Documents library following the steps described in a previous Try It Out. Checking a document in using the Microsoft Office Word client application has the same effect as checking it in via the browser (shown in the last Try It Out).

1. From the Shared Documents library, select the checkbox to the left of My Project Document.
2. Select the Edit Document option from the Documents tab of the Ribbon.
3. You will receive a prompt to confirm that you wish to open the document. Click OK to continue.
4. Make the desired changes to your document. You may need to click the Edit button that appears at the top of your document to enable edit mode. When it is complete, switch to the File tab of the Ribbon, as shown in Figure 3-12.

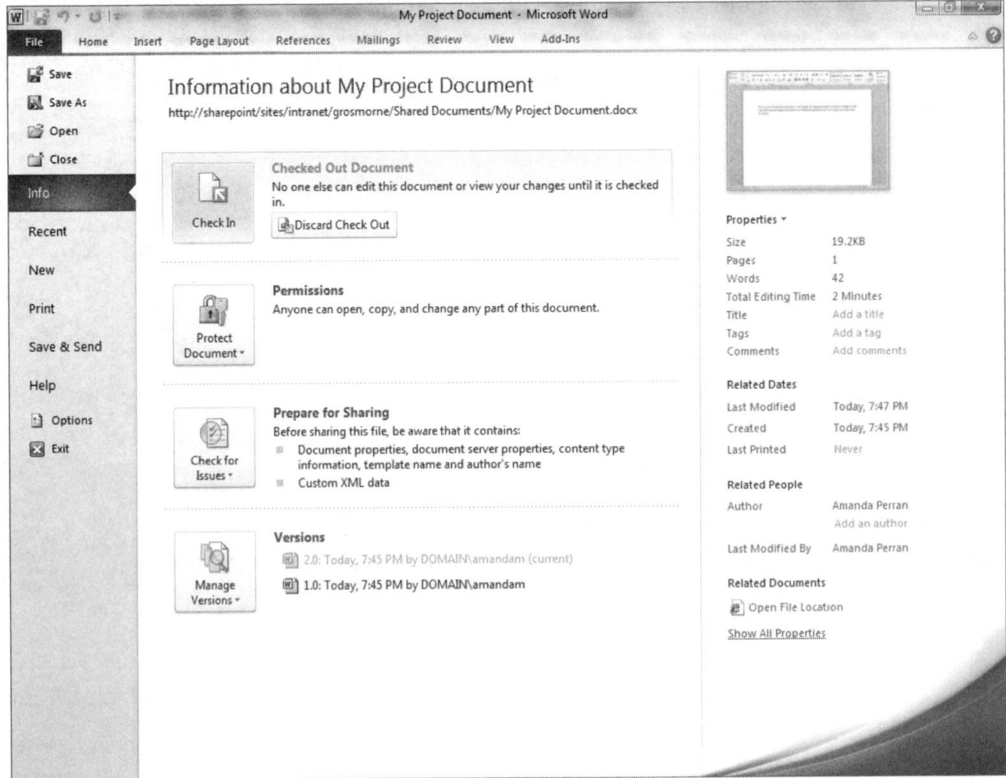

FIGURE 3-12

5. Click the Check In option.
6. Enter comments describing the changes made to the document, and click OK.
7. Close the document. Your file is now checked back into the library, and your latest changes are available to members of your team.

TRY IT OUT Work Offline on a SharePoint Document

To this point, the Try It Outs in this section have dealt with checking a document in or out and working with it on a computer that is connected to a network. As mentioned previously, you have the option of checking out a document and working offline by saving it to your local drafts folder, which is automatically created the first time you check out and save a document. SharePoint creates a physical copy that you can edit away from the office. When you check a document back in via the browser or through Microsoft Word using the steps shown in the previous Try It Outs, the offline copy of the document is synchronized with and uploaded to the document library so that your changes become available to team members.

NOTE *SharePoint 2010 has multiple methods for working offline with content, including connecting a list library to Microsoft Outlook as shown in Chapter 2 or connecting to an entire library or site using Microsoft SharePoint Workspace. We will review connecting a document library in SharePoint workspace in the next Try It Out.*

1. From the Shared Documents library, select the checkbox to the left of My Project Document.
2. Select the Check Out option from the Documents tab of the Ribbon. You receive a message informing you that you are about to check out a document.
3. Select the Use my local drafts folder checkbox.
4. Click OK to check the document out. The document is downloaded to a SharePoint Drafts folder located within the Documents folder of your computer, as shown in Figure 3-13.

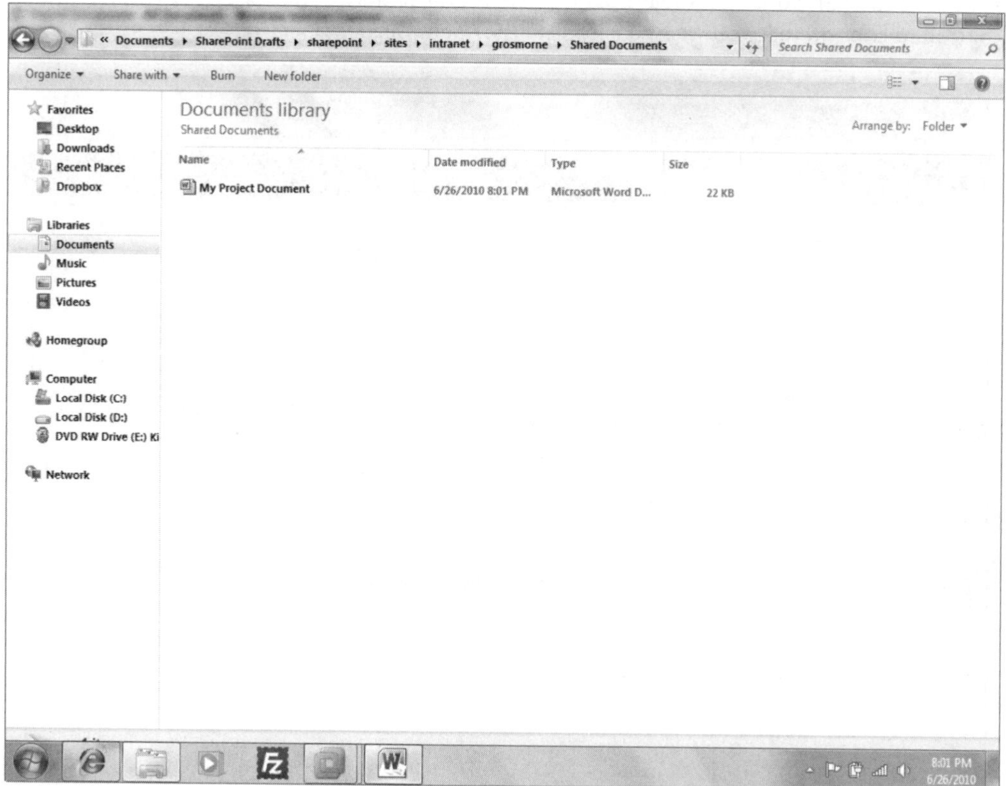

FIGURE 3-13

TRY IT OUT Connect to a Document Library with SharePoint Workspace

In addition to the method described previously for working offline on a single document, you may elect to connect an entire library to your computer through Microsoft SharePoint Workspace, a client application that synchronizes with SharePoint. In the following example, you will connect your Shared Documents library from your project team site to SharePoint Workspace.

> **NOTE** *You must have the SharePoint Workspace client installed on your computer to complete this exercise.*

1. From the Shared Documents library, click the Library tab on the Ribbon.
2. Select the Sync to SharePoint Workspace menu option. The SharePoint Workspace application will open.

> **NOTE** *If this is the first time you are using SharePoint Workspace, you will be required to create a new account. This process will just take a few minutes, and you will be asked to provide your name and email address.*

3. The sync to SharePoint workspace dialog will appear as shown in Figure 3-14. Click the OK button to confirm that you wish to complete the operations.

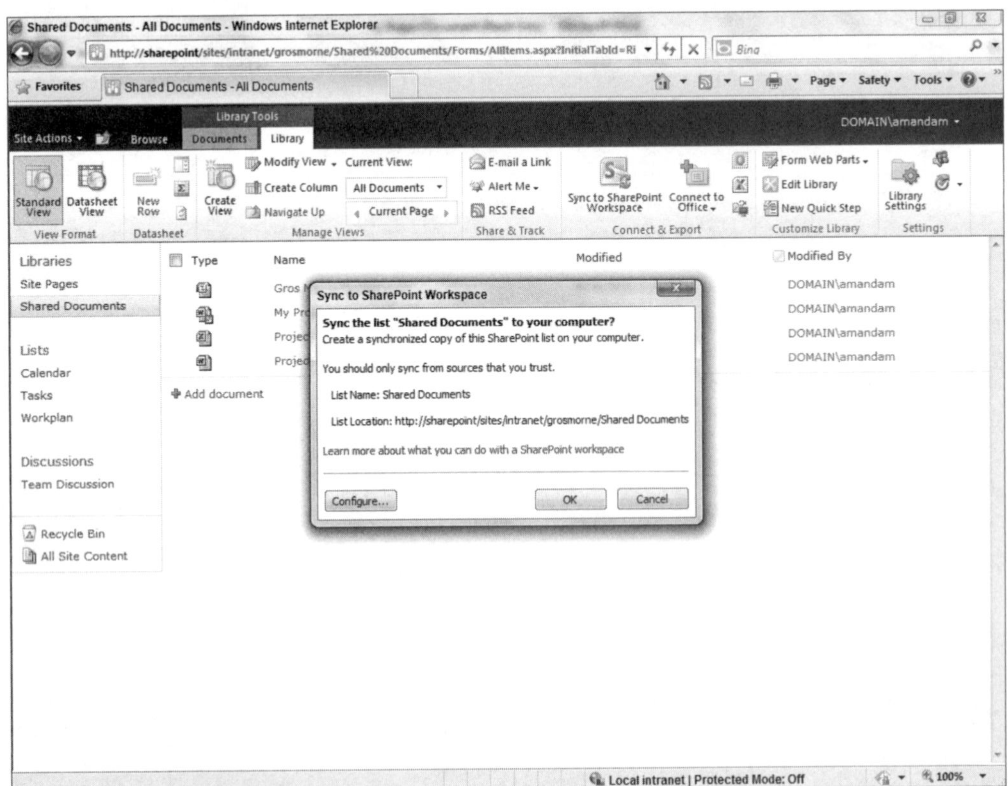

FIGURE 3-14

4. A synchronization window will appear showing the progress as documents are downloaded from your library for the first time. When the operation has completed, click the Open Workspace link.

5. SharePoint Workspace will launch a window displaying all the documents from your document library, as shown in Figure 3-15.

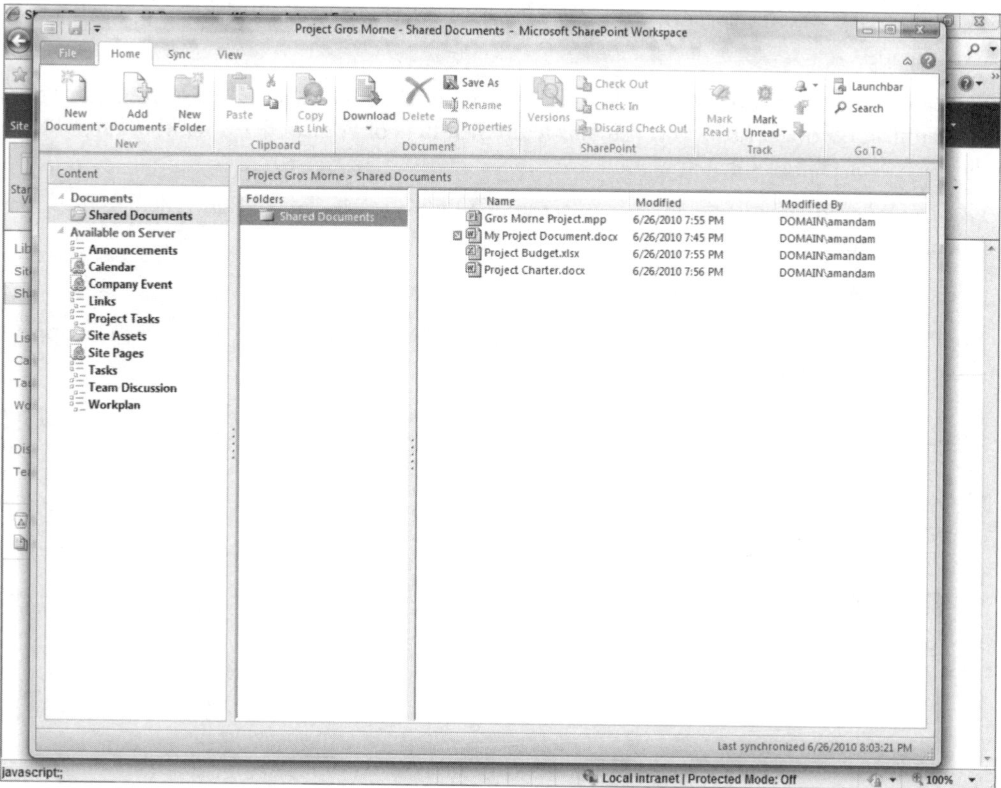

FIGURE 3-15

How It Works

Once a document library has been synchronized with SharePoint Workspace, you will have the ability to interact and edit the documents as if you were in the browser. Activities such as Checking Out, Checking In and Editing a Document are available within the SharePoint Workspace Ribbon. In addition, new files can be created and added using this application. You may make these changes remotely while not connected to the network and changes will be automatically synchronized back to the SharePoint document library the next time you launch the application while connected to the network.

You may notice in Figure 3-15, that other lists and libraries from your site are listed in the side panel. You may also right-click on each of these to open the lists or libraries from the site within SharePoint Workspace or the browser.

TRY IT OUT Send an Email Link of a Document to Others

After uploading or updating a document, you commonly want to share your changes with other team members so that they may review, collaborate, or make their own changes. In the past, this involved opening your email, writing a detailed message to your coworkers informing them of your intention to share a document, attaching the document, and finally sending it. Unfortunately, attaching a document can lead to duplicate files because team members tend to save versions of the document from the email message to their desktop or local drive. This, of course, makes change management and document control very difficult.

SharePoint bypasses this confusion by allowing you to send an email with a link that directs colleagues to your document on the library. This informs team members of your updates without removing the file from the document management system.

1. From the Shared Documents library, select your My Project Document file and click the Documents tab of the Ribbon.
2. Select the Email a Link menu option.
3. Your email client will launch. A prepopulated email with a link to your document will appear, as shown in Figure 3-16.

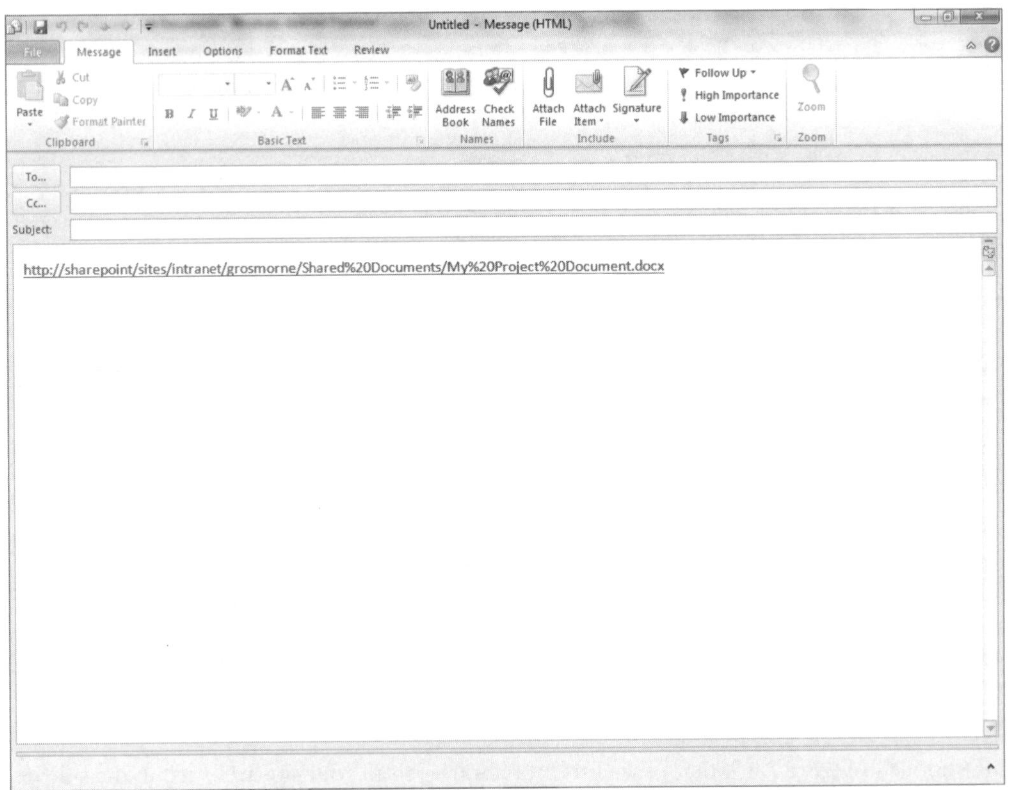

FIGURE 3-16

4. Fill in the email addresses to which you want to send the link.
5. Fill in the subject and a brief message.
6. Click Send.

Review Document Version History

Imagine working all night on a document and saving your changes to your team's collaborative location, only to have a team member overwrite your document with an older version of the document. For a collaborative team, multiple versions of a single document or overwritten files can translate into lost work and frustration. That's why most organizations implement a document audit trail, which helps users understand when changes were made and why. SharePoint's Version History option allows you to view this trail as well as restore previous versions if you catch errors or omissions in the active version. If versions after a certain date are in doubt, you can restore the document to point where you know the information is accurate and relevant. In addition, having a version history can help organizations identify exactly what a document looked like at an exact point in time.

In the upcoming exercises, you learn how to enable version history tracking on a library and how to view the version history related to a document and optionally restore a previous version of a document as the active version.

NOTE *In Chapter 4, you will learn how you can customize version history settings of a document library.*

TRY IT OUT Enable Version History Tracking on a Document Library

Some libraries may now have version history tracking enabled upon creation. Therefore, a user with permissions to manage the list will be required to enable this setting. In the case of the Gros Morne Project site, because it was created based on the Team Site template, the Shared Documents library must be configured to track version history.

1. From the Shared Documents library, click the Library tab on the Ribbon.
2. Select the Library Settings menu option. You will be redirected to a page where all the settings related to the Shared Documents library are managed.

NOTE *We will explore the settings displayed on this page in greater detail in Chapter 4.*

3. Select the Versioning settings link. The Version settings page will appear.
4. Select the option to Create major versions, as shown in Figure 3-17.

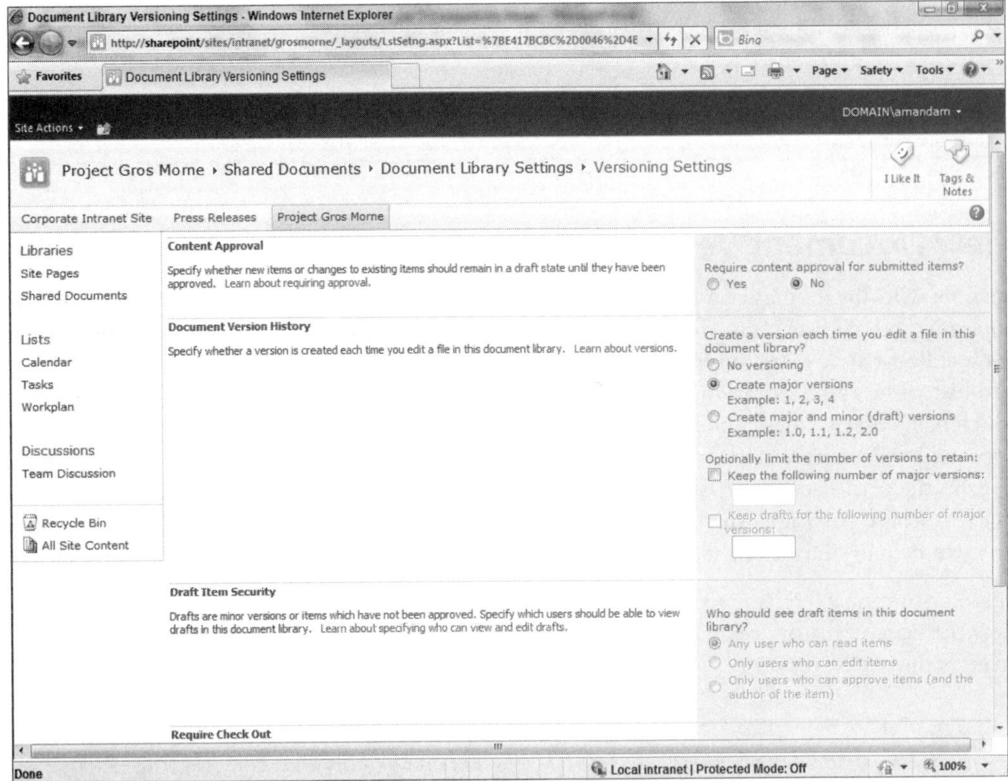

FIGURE 3-17

5. Click OK. You will be returned to the Shared Documents library settings page. Click Shared Documents from the side navigation or breadcrumb menu to return to the library.

Now that your library has been configured to track version history, it is recommended that you make multiple edits to your My Project Document file and add comments upon check in prior to completing the next exercise.

TRY IT OUT Review a Document's Version History

SharePoint updates a document's version history each time a user changes or saves the document. Imagine that while you were away from the office someone made changes to your document that you either were not satisfied with or wanted clarification on. You can visit the version history of the document and review the various versions and associated comments to determine what changes were made. In addition, you may find it useful to review versions of a document to find out what information was published and is available to users of the SharePoint site or via the File tab of the Ribbon menu of your document.

1. From the Shared Documents library, click the Documents tab of the Ribbon.
2. Select your My Project Document file.

3. Select the Version History option from the Document tab of the Ribbon. The Version History window will appear as shown in Figure 3-18.

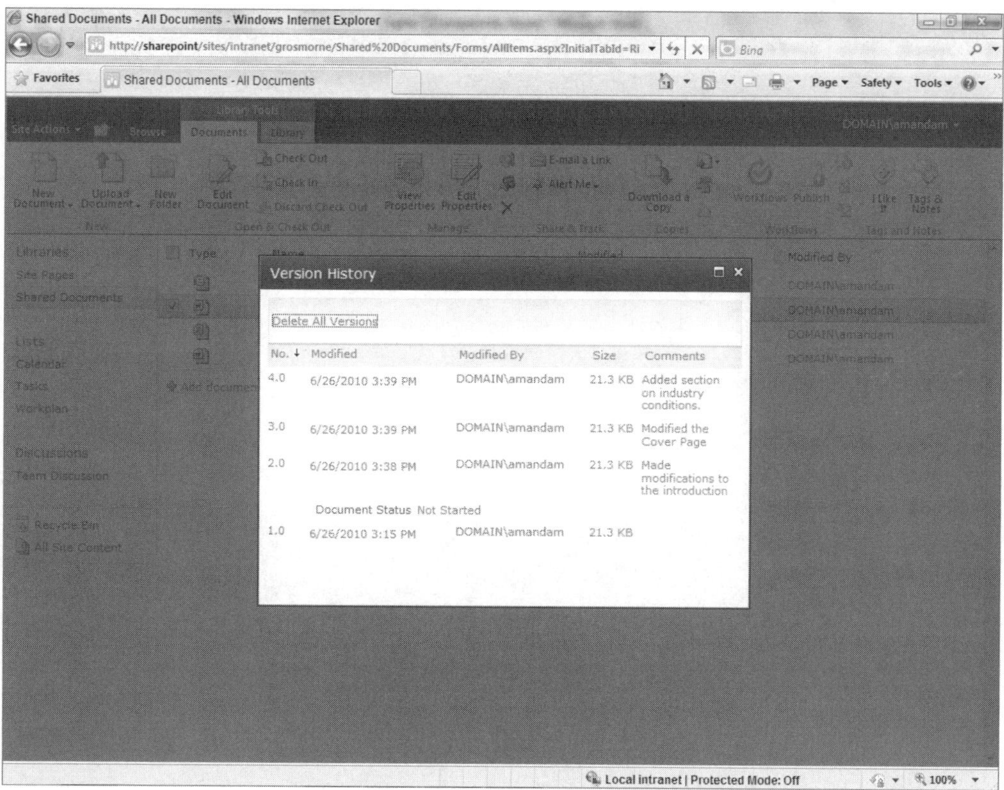

FIGURE 3-18

4. Click on the date and time of a version to preview it. The version of the document will open for you to review in the associated application.

TRY IT OUT Restore a Previous Version of a Document

When multiple team members work on a document, on occasion they may need to revert to a previous version of the document. This may be necessary because unwanted changes were made or just to perform a what-if analysis to see how changes impact a report. With SharePoint, you can easily follow a document's entire version history and, if need be, restore a previous version of the document by following these steps.

1. From your My Project Document's Version History window, hover over a previous version to expose the actions menu, as shown in Figure 3-19.

2. Select the Restore option from the menu. You are prompted with a message informing you that you are about to replace the current version of the document with the one you have selected.

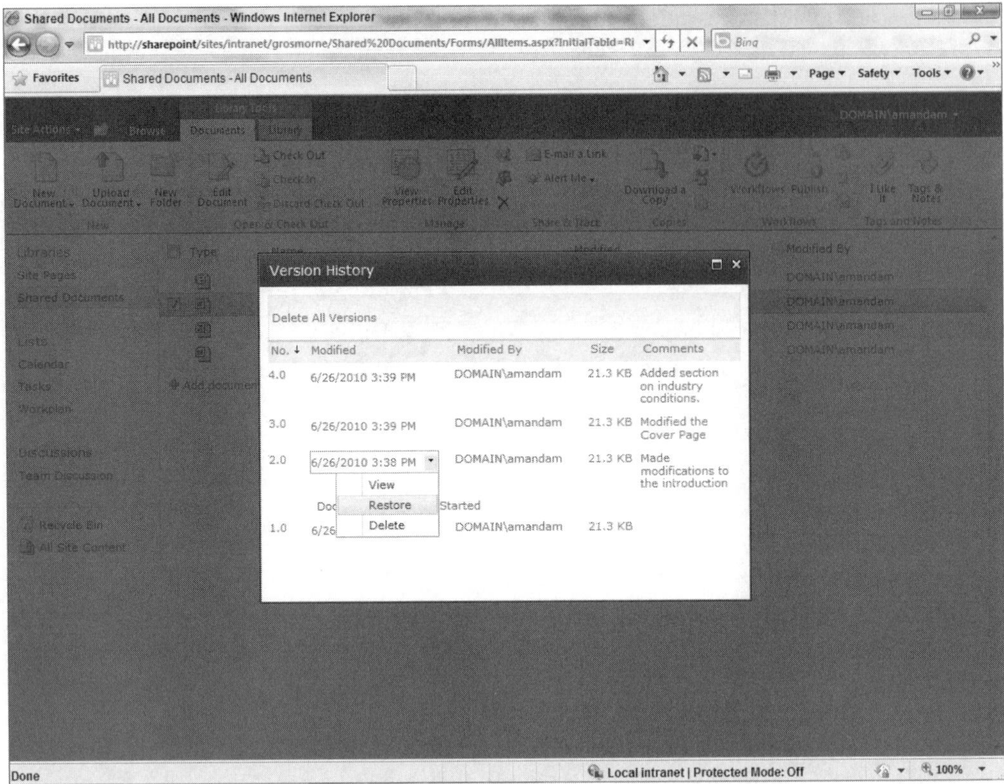

FIGURE 3-19

3. Click OK.

How It Works

When you restore a previous version of a document, the document reverts to reflect that state of the document, and it becomes the new current version of the document. The restoration of a document does not overwrite or delete previous versions. Instead, it creates a completely new version within the library. For example, if you view a listing of a document's versions, you may see that there are five versions of the document. If you were to restore version 2.0, then a new version would be created called 6.0. All previous versions would remain unaffected.

UNDERSTANDING SHAREPOINT LIBRARY TEMPLATES

So far this chapter has generically referred to libraries as document libraries. However, SharePoint actually has various library types, just as it has multiple varieties of lists. Libraries are generally defined by what you place in them. Once you create your library from the appropriate template, you can have others access the library and add content to it. Chapter 4 shows how to create and customize new lists and libraries; however, in this section, you learn about the features and functions of each so that you select the proper library for your team. The SharePoint library templates are described in the following list:

- **Document libraries:** This library stores the majority of documents and files in a SharePoint site and is the most common type of document library created.
- **Form libraries:** You use this template to create libraries that store InfoPath form data and templates. You may use this to store submitted forms, such as purchase requests or status reports created using the Microsoft InfoPath client application or Forms Services.

  We will review this library and InfoPath in greater detail in Chapter 12.
- **Wiki page libraries:** You use this kind of library for wiki pages, which are collaborative web pages that teams use to share information in a highly interactive and less structured environment. This is perfect for storing a knowledge base or FAQ section.
- **Picture libraries:** This library is for sharing photos and images in a collaborative environment. This library uses columns and properties to define images, and has special thumbnail views of the stored files. It's ideal for storing team member photos or your company's logos.
- **Asset libraries:** This library is for sharing rich media assets such as images, audio, and video. When an asset library is created, it is preconfigured with metadata and settings required for sharing rich media files.
- **Slide libraries:** You use this library to share PowerPoint presentation slides. Users can upload slides to the library so that other users can browse for slides and use them in new presentations. This template works well for teams that are responsible for creating presentations and want a central gallery from which to select the latest slides and information.
- **Data connection libraries:** These libraries store trusted data connection information that link SharePoint with documents created using InfoPath or Excel. We will explore this library type further in Chapters 12 and 16.
- **Report library:** This specialized template creates libraries that store spreadsheets and dashboards as part of the business intelligence capabilities of SharePoint Server 2010. You would use this template to create a location for reporting that would allow business managers to publish spreadsheets to others that could be viewed via the browser and that would hide any protected information from users. This type of library will be discussed in Chapter 16 along with business intelligence, because this template type is specific to that feature of SharePoint.

Document Libraries

Document libraries can store just about any kind of file and are at the center of SharePoint's file-sharing and collaboration features. The anatomy of a document library is very similar to a list and includes the following elements:

- **File Item:** From Chapter 2, you know that the primary element of a list is an item. Likewise, the primary element of a document library is a file. Most organizations collaborate using

Microsoft Office documents (Word, Excel, and PowerPoint) or other common formats, such as PDF, HTML, or JPEG. Document libraries support just about any file type, assuming that an administrator has not explicitly blocked it.

- **Columns:** The column types available for lists are also available for document libraries. Depending on what template you select, certain columns may already be created for you. Most libraries share a common set of columns; however, special templates, such as the image library and assets library, contain additional columns such as image size and copyright. You can create additional columns at any time if you have the appropriate rights to the site.

NOTE *You can find out how to add new columns to a library in Chapter 4.*

- **Views:** Similar to lists, document libraries display their items in views. The default view for a document library is the All Documents view, which shows all documents stored within the library in groups of 30 in the following columns:
    - **Document Type:** Displays an icon representing the document's file type.
    - **Name:** The file name of the document.
    - **Modified:** The date and time the document was last modified.
    - **Modified By:** The name of the user that last modified the document linked directly to their user profile or MySite.

NOTE *Users with the appropriate rights can create custom views at any time. This activity will be explored in Chapter 4.*

TRY IT OUT Open a Document Library in Windows Explorer

In addition to the All Documents view, you can open a document library in Windows Explorer via the Ribbon. This allows you to interact with your library with the usual Windows behaviors, including dragging and dropping content. In the following example, you open a Shared Documents library in Windows Explorer and create a new folder within it called Project Documentation. Instead of creating a new folder and uploading the documents via the SharePoint browser interface, you open the document library in a Windows Explorer view and create a new folder. You then move the existing files into the folder in the same manner you would if you were working in a folder on your computer.

1. From the main page of your team site, click the Shared Documents link on the side navigation bar.
2. Click the Library tab on the Ribbon.
3. Select the Open with Explorer menu option.

4. A new window opens listing the entire contents of your Shared Documents library in a Windows Explorer view, as shown in Figure 3-20. Right-click the window and create a new folder called Project Documentation.

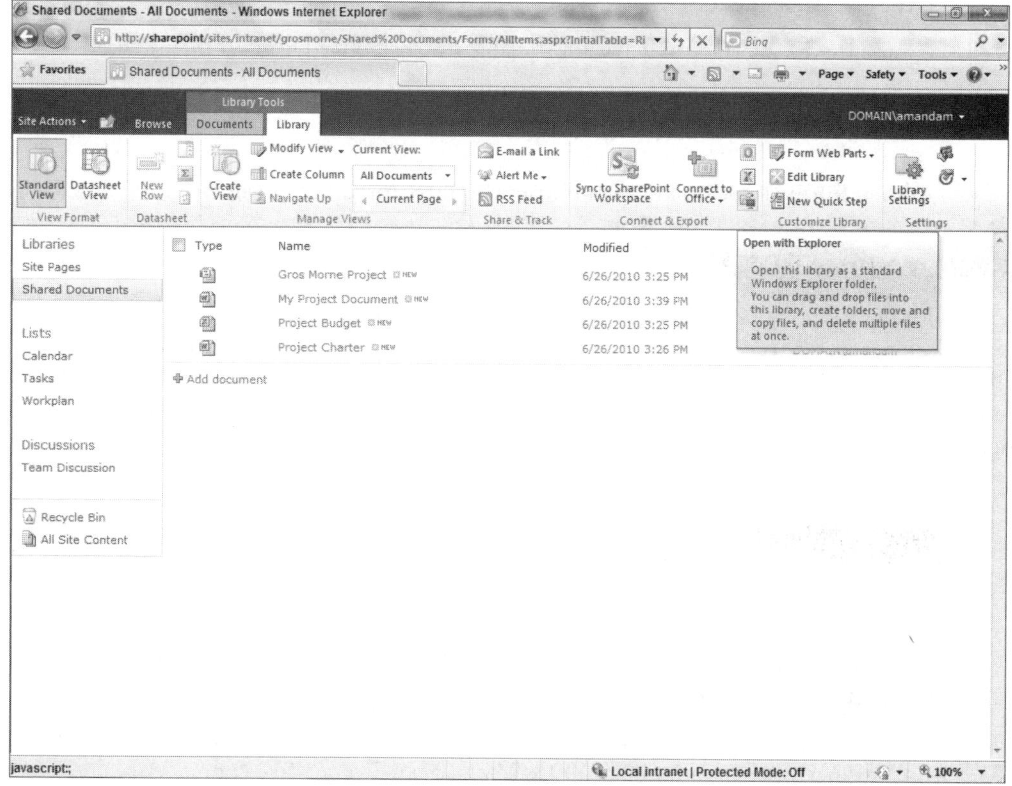

FIGURE 3-20

5. Select the files you have created in the Shared Documents library and drag them into the Project Documentation folder.

Form Libraries

Form libraries are special types of libraries that store InfoPath forms. *Microsoft InfoPath* is an application that allows you to collect and share data via highly customizable electronic forms. You can use this application to create form templates that reflect their data collection needs without requiring code or special development skills. The application makes it very easy for business users to craft an electronic form that suits their needs by dragging and dropping form elements onto a page. Users can complete InfoPath forms using either the InfoPath application or via the browser using the Enterprise Edition of SharePoint Server 2010.

You can promote data stored in InfoPath forms to the library so that you display the data in views. This gives you more advanced reporting options on the data contained in multiple forms. You might find it advantageous, for example, to create an InfoPath form to collect data from your portal users instead of using standard list functionality because with InfoPath, you can do the following:

- Connect to external data sources such as databases, SharePoint lists, or web services to either retrieve or submit data
- Customize the interface in ways not possible using standard lists via the browser
- Use code to extend forms to provide additional functionality and enhancements related to more complex data calculations or routing

We will explore InfoPath forms and the libraries they are stored in in Chapter 12.

Wiki Page Libraries

With wikis, a very popular collaborative tool for group sharing and editing content, you can add, edit, or remove web page content in an open and informal manner without following a restrictive editing or approval process. Users can edit wikis using SharePoint's built-in content editor without knowing a special language. Because of the informality and lack of restriction, wiki pages are a more inviting way for team members to record their experiences and goals.

WHAT'S A WIKI?

A wiki article or website is a site where users can freely expand or change the published content, often without registration requirements. Wiki, named for a Hawaiian term meaning "fast," is a popular method for sharing information in a quick and easy-to-use format.

A good example of a wiki is the Wikipedia project (see `www.wikipedia.org`), which formerly began in January 2001. Wikipedia delivers a free content encyclopedia to which anyone can contribute. The website has grown to become one of the largest content libraries in existence, serving up millions articles, if you're just counting the English ones.

SharePoint has an option for creating either an entire site to act as a wiki or just a wiki document library within a site:

- **A wiki site:** Useful for a technical support team's knowledge base or a training department's tips and tricks documentation. Any collaborative site in SharePoint can be transitioned into a wiki site using a special feature that transforms the main page of the site into a wiki page. We will review wiki sites further in Chapter 8.
- **A wiki document library:** Provides collaboration tool for planning and sharing ideas around specific operational events. This is illustrated in the next Try It Out.

The next two Try It Outs show how to create a wiki document library as well as how to create a new wiki page.

TRY IT OUT Create a Wiki Library

In this example, you create a wiki document library in your site to brainstorm for ideas for your project. The wiki page library has special features that allow you to share and publish wiki content pages within a single location. Team members can create these pages around a specific topic or set of topics.

1. From the main page of your team site, select the All Site Content link from the side navigation bar.
2. Click Create. A window will appear listing the various templates available to create lists and libraries from.
3. Filter the listing by selecting the Library link from the left side of the window.
4. Select Wiki Page Library from the list of Library types, as shown in Figure 3-21.

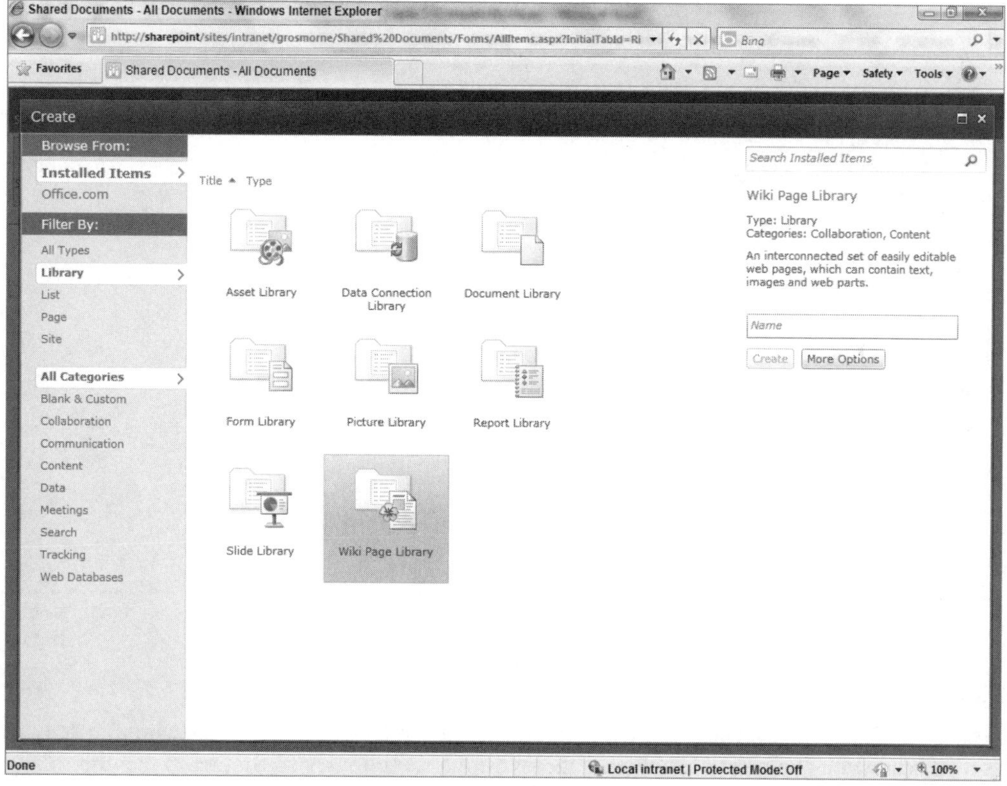

FIGURE 3-21

5. Click the More Options button.
6. Enter a name and description for the library. For this example, enter Project Wiki for the name and the following for the description:

   This wiki will be used to track information related to initial planning around scope, milestones, and timelines related to the Gros Morne project.

7. Click Yes to display the library on the site's Quick Launch navigation bar.
8. Click Create. The wiki library will be created and you will be redirected to the home wiki page, as shown in Figure 3-22.

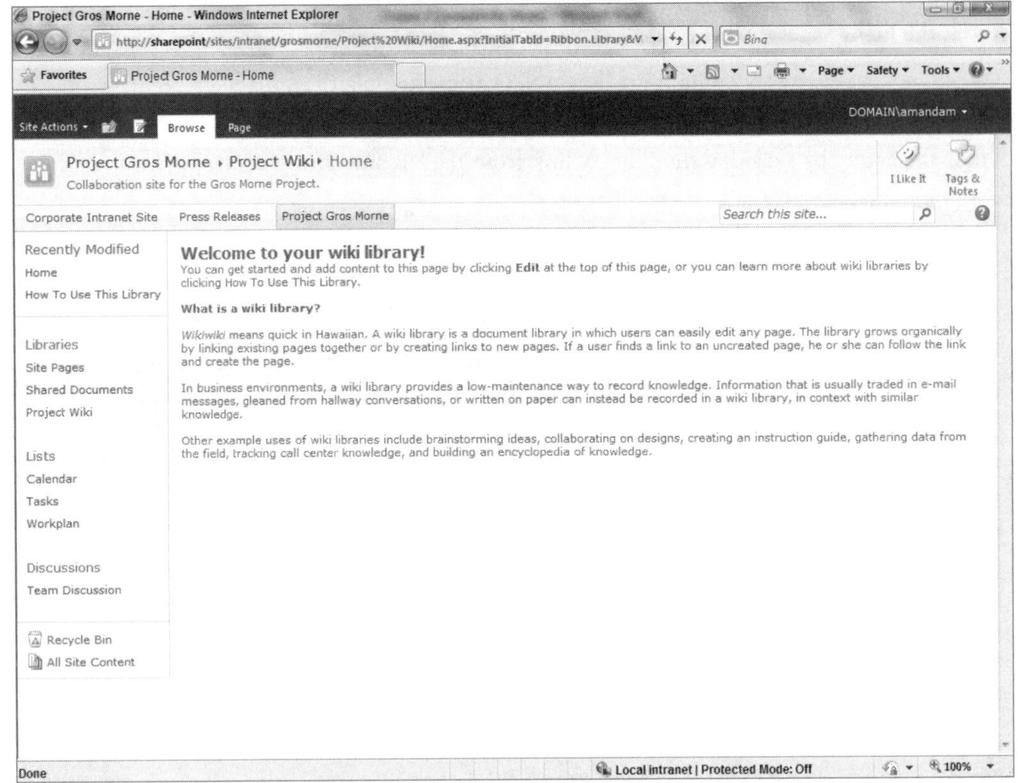

FIGURE 3-22

TRY IT OUT Create a Wiki Page

In addition to editing existing content, users can create new pages. The following example demonstrates how easily you can create new wiki pages within a wiki library so that team members can share information about what they have learned regarding a common topic, such as a new technology (SharePoint). In addition, members can leave notes on topics they would like to learn more about as an invitation for others to provide content.

1. From the main page of your team site, select Project Wiki from the side navigation bar.
2. Select the Page tab of the Ribbon.

3. Click the Edit menu option.
4. Remove the existing content from the page and add a Welcome to Your Project Wiki heading.
5. Below the welcome message, type the words **Project Ideas** between two square brackets on each side of the phrase, as shown in Figure 3-23.

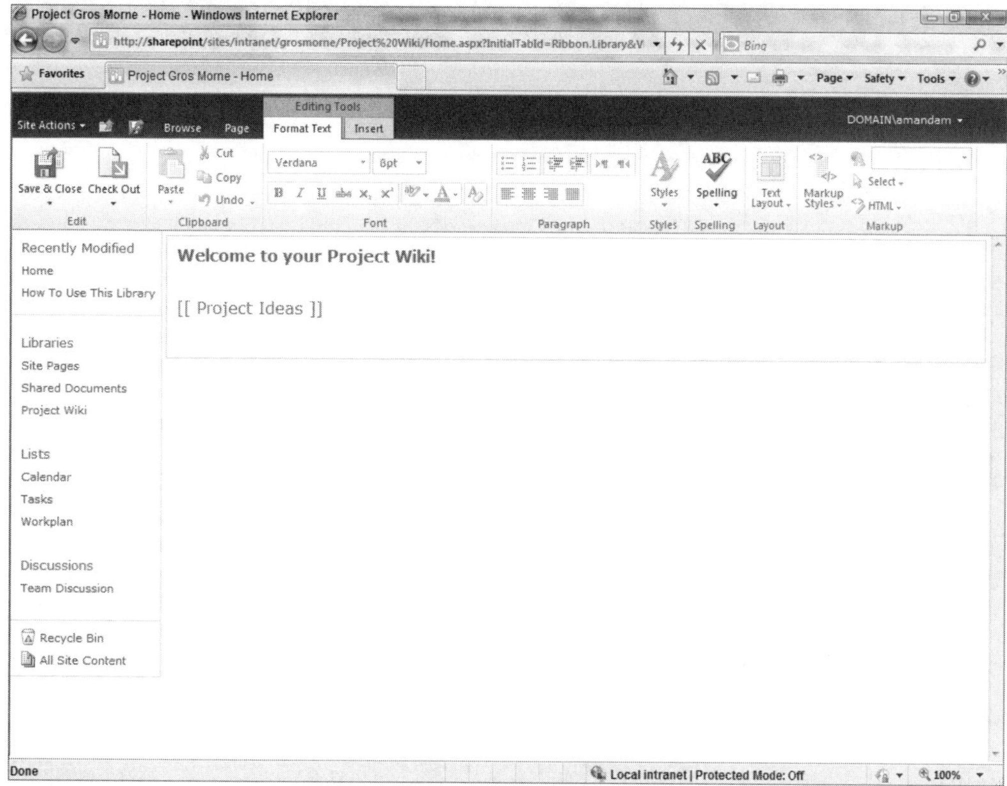

FIGURE 3-23

6. Click the Save and Close menu option.
7. The page will refresh and the Project Ideas phrase will be displayed as a link with a dashed line underneath as shown in Figure 3-24. Click the link.
8. A dialog will appear stating that the page does not exist. Click Create to create the new page in the wiki page library.
9. You will be redirected to your new page. Add content as necessary, and when you have finished, add the word **home** in between the double brackets shown at the bottom of the page in Figure 3-23.
10. Click the Save and Close menu option.

11. When the page refreshes, you will see that the word home now appears as a link and by clicking it, you can return to the home page of your wiki library.

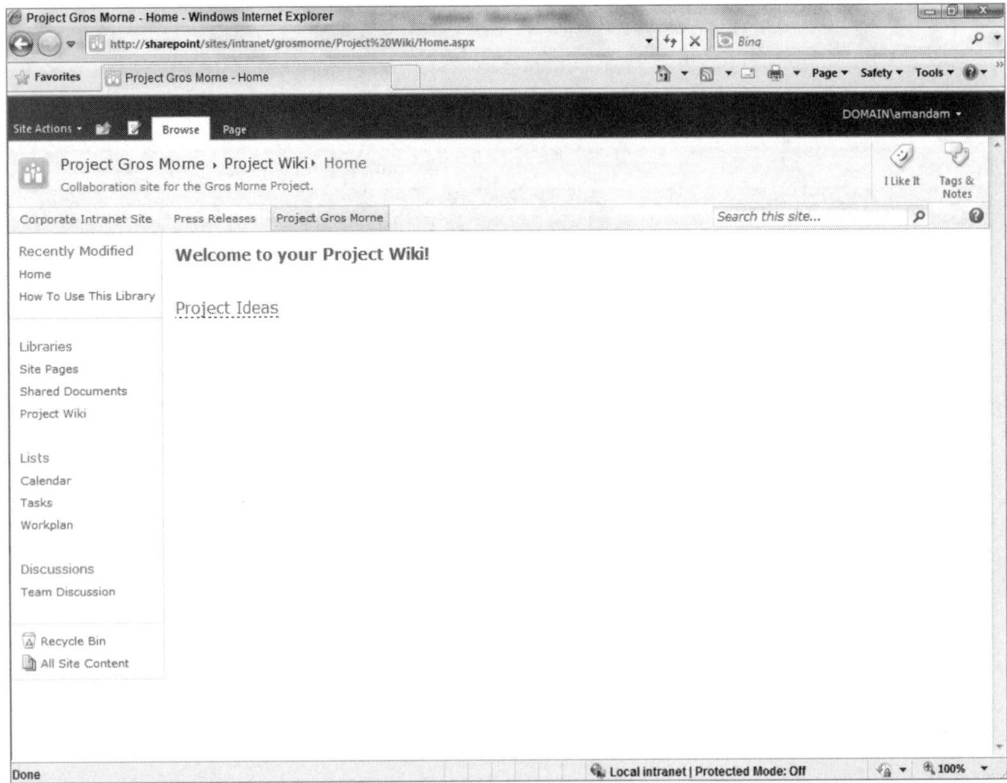

FIGURE 3-24

How It Works

Wiki pages are both easy to edit and simple to create. New pages can be created on the fly by putting the name of the page in between double square brackets as follows:

[[page name]]

To link to an existing page, the same technique can be used by placing the name of the existing page between the square brackets.

Picture Libraries

Although document libraries can store just about any file type, in some cases it's better to have a library that caters to a specific file format. Such is the case with the Picture Library template, which efficiently displays pictures and images because it includes a thumbnail preview feature. This is an invaluable feature for locating the correct image in a large collection of images.

This next series of Try It Outs demonstrates the features that make the Picture library unique. In the first Try It Out, you create a picture library using the Picture Library template. In the second Try It Out, you upload pictures into the newly created library to simulate a person sharing images with his or her team. In doing so, you will see first-hand the unique commands it offers in its menu. These commands are listed in the following table.

MENU ITEM	DESCRIPTION
Edit	Edits the selected images in a compatible editing tool
Delete	Deletes the selected images from the picture library
Download	Downloads all selected images to the user's computer
Send To	Inserts pictures into an email or document
View Slide Show	Opens a new window displaying a slide show of images within library

In the third Try It Out, you act as someone taking images from the library. You download files and see the picture library's unique options. When you download a file, you can change the size of your image. You can also change its format to one of the following:

- JPEG Interchange Format (JPEG)
- Tagged Image Format (TIF)
- Windows Bitmap (BMP)
- Graphic Interchange Format (GIF)
- Portable Network Graphic (PNG)

You can also apply one of three subviews of a primary view. These subviews are:

- **Details:** This updates metadata associated with a file stored in a picture library.
- **Thumbnails:** You can use this to preview images in a thumbnail type view.
- **Filmstrip:** This view previews a larger version of the image within the browser window.

TRY IT OUT Create a Picture Library

1. From the main page of your team site, click the All Site Content link from the side navigation bar.
2. Click Create. A window will appear listing the various templates available to create lists and libraries from.
3. Filter the listing by clicking the Library link on the left side of the window.
4. Select Picture Library from the list of Library types.
5. Enter **Project Pictures** for the Library name.

6. Click Create. The picture library will be created, and you will be redirected to the default view of the library, as shown in Figure 3-25.

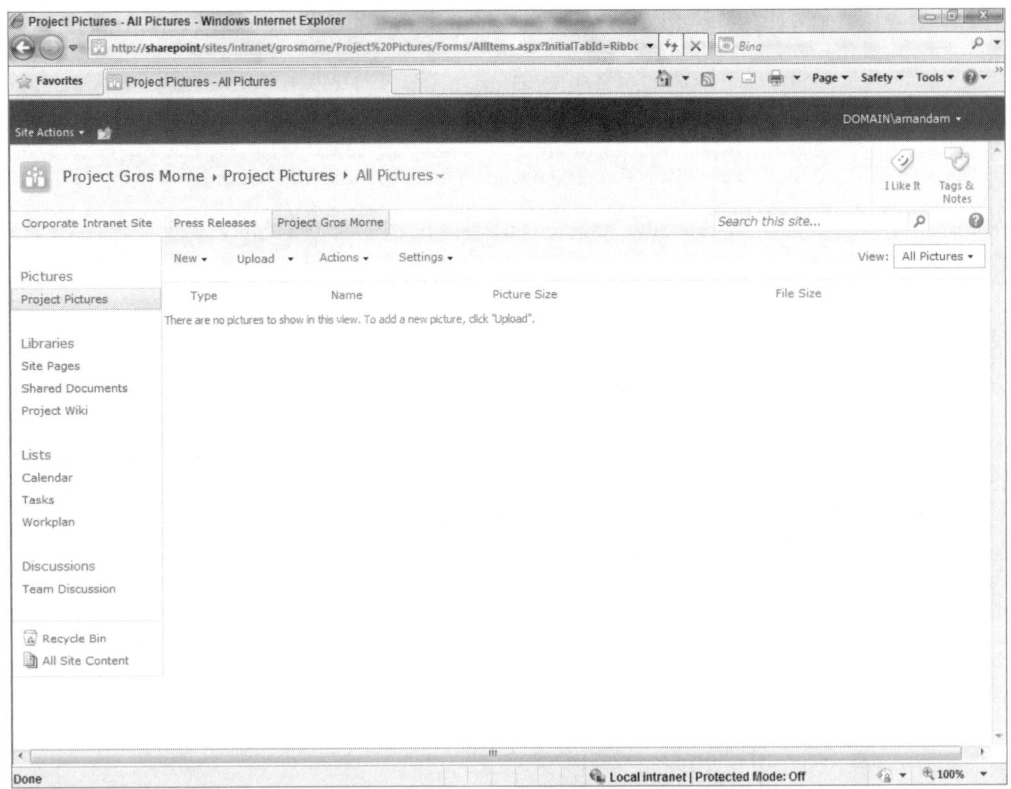

FIGURE 3-25

TRY IT OUT Upload Multiple Images to a Picture Library

When you uploaded the files in the Try It Out "Upload Multiple Documents to a Document Library," you used the browser interface. The interface you use in this Try It Out has unique functionality for managing images. You can either upload web-optimized versions of the images or upload the files in their original format. Once the files are uploaded, you can return to your library to view the images.

To identify the differences between the Picture template and the standard document library, the following steps have you upload some images into the newly created library.

1. From the Project Pictures library, select Upload Multiple Pictures from the Upload toolbar menu. The Microsoft Office Picture Manager opens, as shown in Figure 3-26

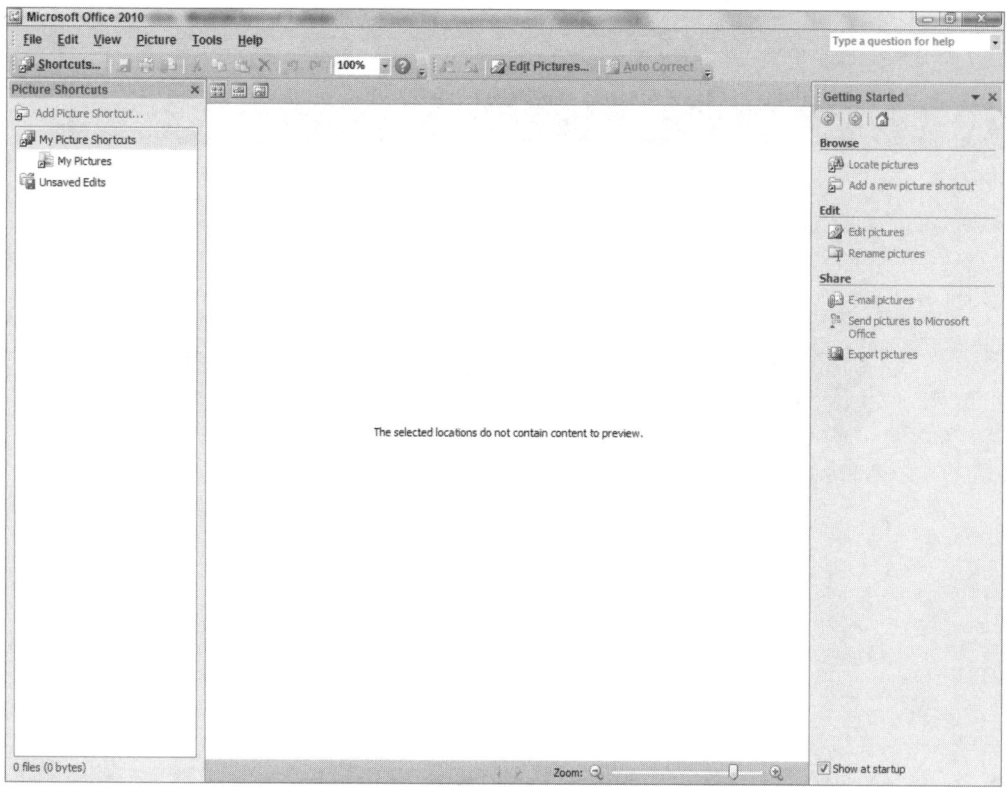

FIGURE 3-26

2. Select Add Picture Shortcut, and browse to the Project Images folder you downloaded as part of this chapter's resource materials.
3. When the correct folder is selected, click the Add button.
4. Select all the images from the folder. You can select multiple items by holding down the Ctrl button while you select items.
5. Click the Upload and Close button located at the bottom of the application window.
6. The Office Picture Manager application will close. Select the Go Back to "Project Pictures" link to return to your image library.

How It Works

Although this library may look like all other document libraries you've created so far in this chapter, take a close look at the Actions menu shown in Figure 3-27. On this menu, you will notice the links described in the table at the beginning of this section. Take some time to interact with each of the actions to become familiar with what they can do.

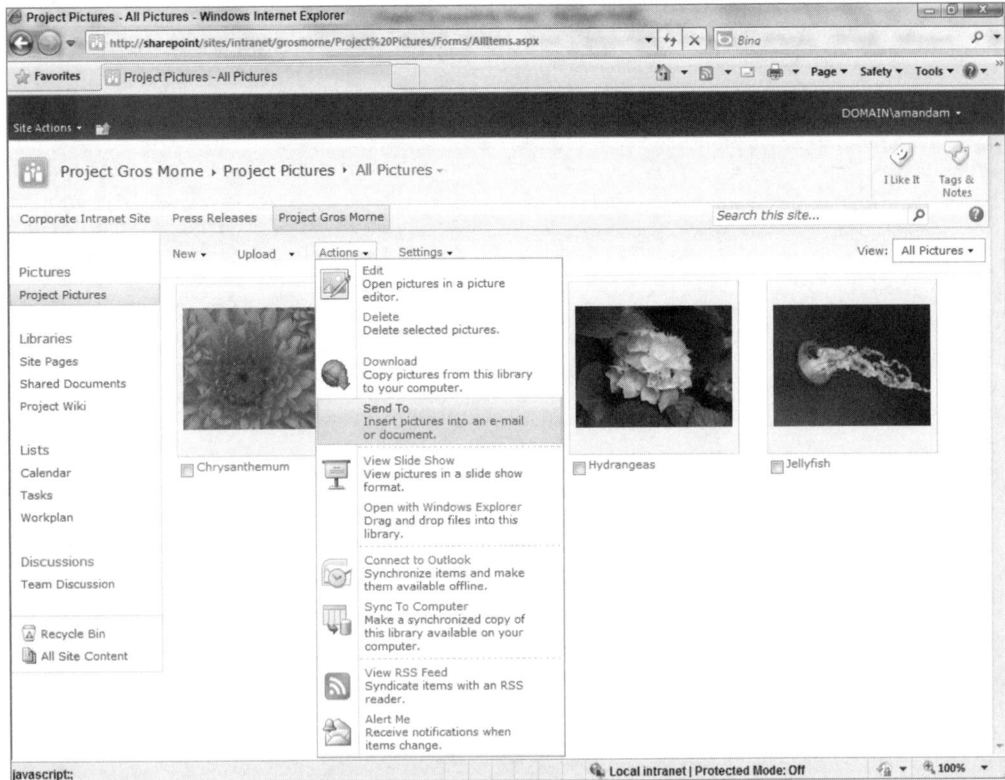

FIGURE 3-27

TRY IT OUT Download Pictures from a Picture Library

To demonstrate how the various picture library menu items work, the next example shows you how to select multiple images from a picture library for downloading. In the previous Try It Out, files in the SharePoint library were in the JPEG format. However, when you select the advanced download options in this Try It Out, you can change the format of the downloaded images. You could have kept the file in its original format or you could have selected another format. The various formats were discussed in the introduction to this section. In addition, you can select a different size for the files and send them to a document instead of downloading them directly as files to your computer. Finally, you can apply subviews to the primary view of your download.

1. From the Project Pictures library, select the first two images in the list.
2. Select the Download option from the Actions menu. You will be redirected to a page displaying the selected files, as shown in Figure 3-28.
3. Click the set advanced download options link.

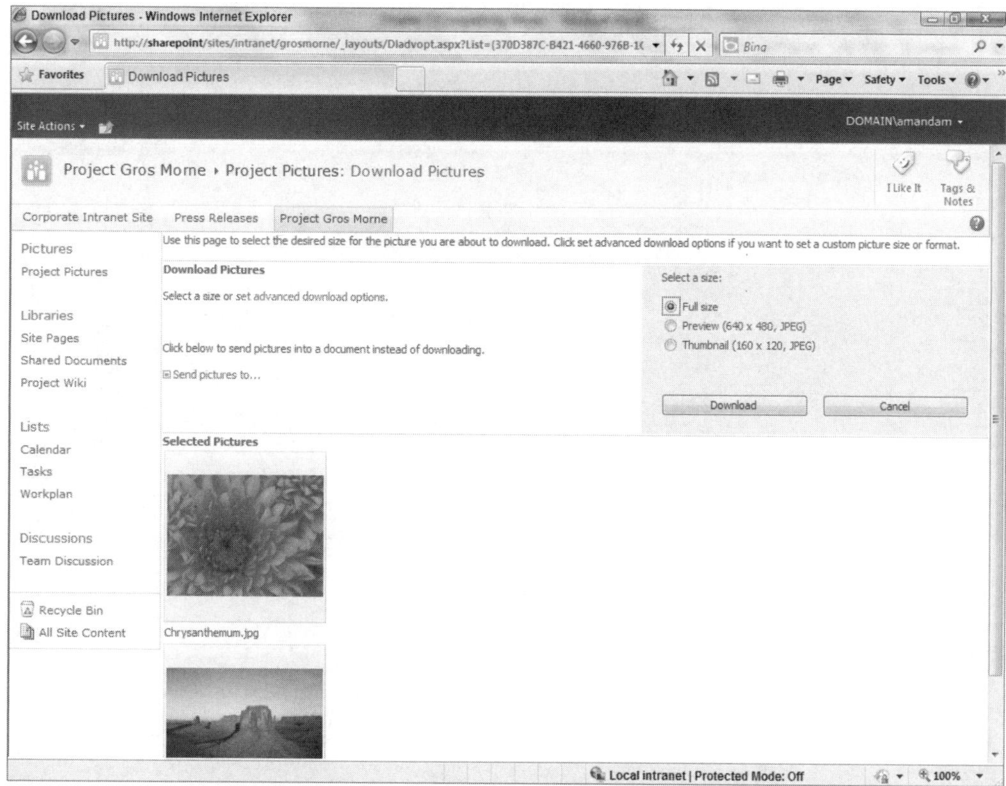

FIGURE 3-28

4. From the File Format drop-down menu, select Graphic Interchange Format (*.gif).
5. For the picture size, select custom width and height and specify 640 x 480. This may already be the default value.
6. Click the Download button. The Download Pictures window, shown in Figure 3-29, appears, prompting you for a location for the images.
7. Select a folder on your computer to store the files in.
8. Check the checkbox to rename the pictures in the new location and enter a name for the picture. For this example, you can enter **Gros Morne** for the name.
9. Click Save.
10. To apply subviews to a primary view, hover your cursor over the All Pictures view in the View Selection box and click Details to update the metadata associated with the image, click Thumbnails to see a preview of the image, as shown in Figure 3-30, or click Filmstrip to preview a larger version of the image in the browser window, as shown in Figure 3-31.

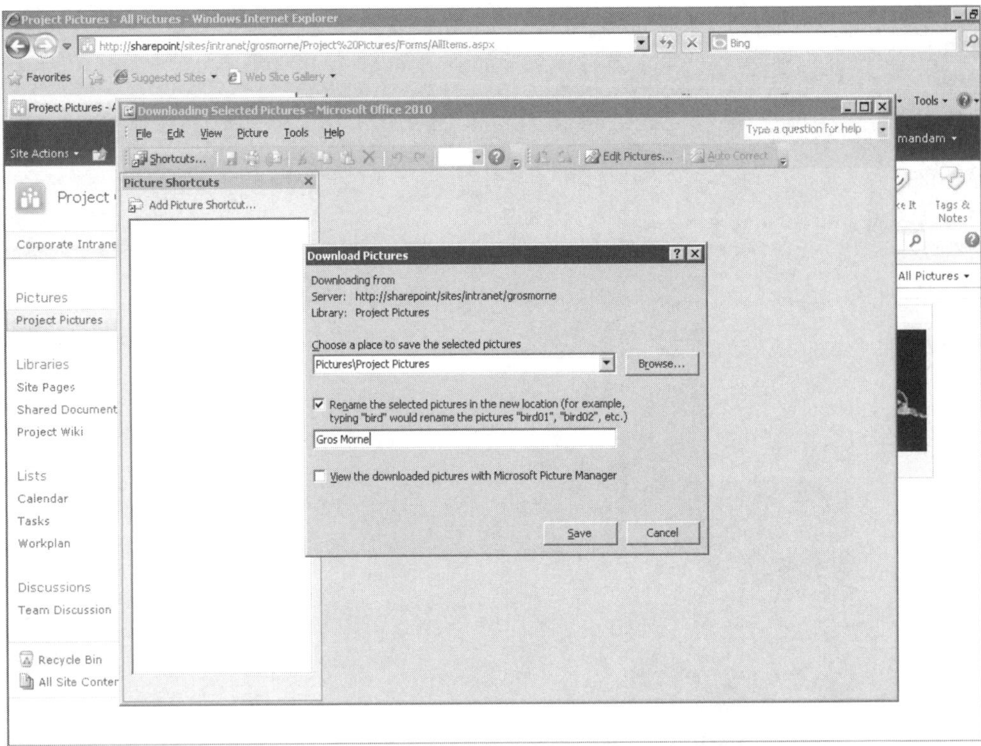

FIGURE 3-29

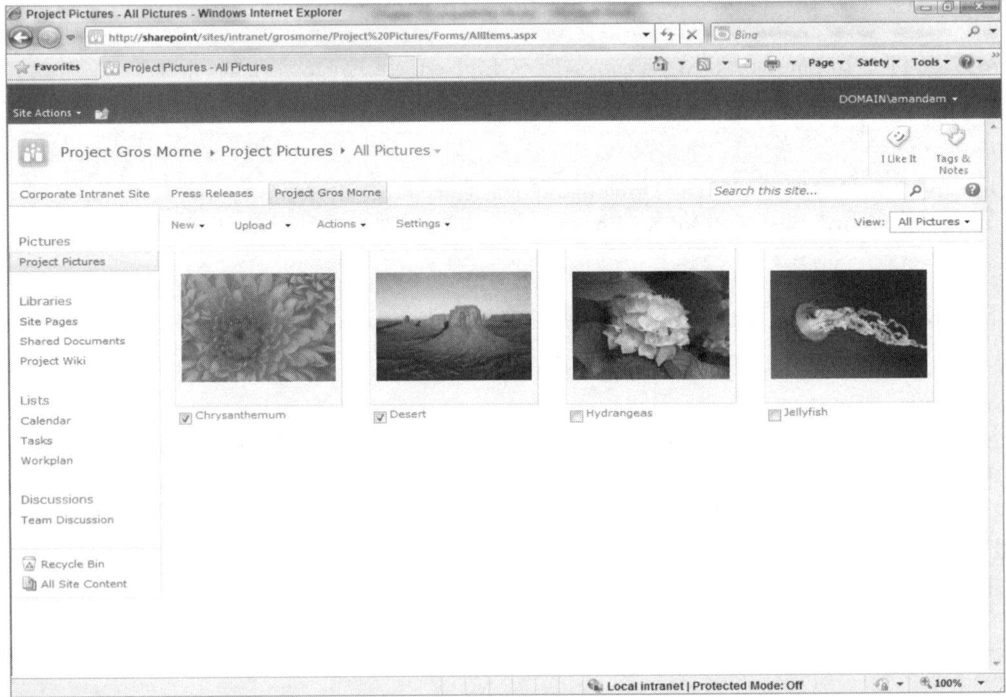

FIGURE 3-30

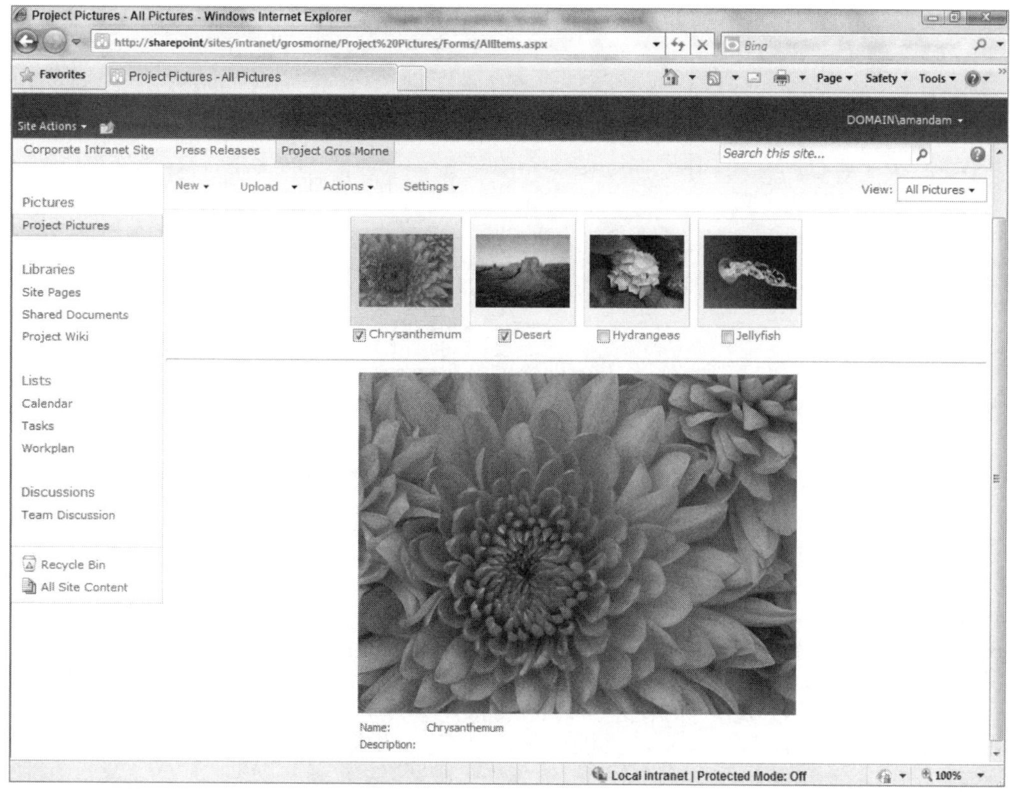

FIGURE 3-31

Data Connection Libraries

Microsoft Office applications, such as Excel and InfoPath, have great built-in support for data connectivity to external sources such as databases, web services, and even SharePoint sites. Traditionally, this meant that you managed data connections on an individual usage basis. Therefore, every time you connected to the data source, you needed to define the connection within the file or settings. This often made it very cumbersome to embed external data into files and subsequently make changes to the data source or file. For example, it might seem logical to use a SharePoint customer list in your InfoPath forms any time that you wanted to display a listing of customer names. To do this, however, you would need to create a data connection within your form template each time you wanted to include customer information.

If you later decided to move your SharePoint list to another location or add new columns, in order to have the changes updated within your InfoPath form, you would have to go back into each form template and update the settings.

Data connection libraries solve the cumbersome connection dilemma of how to deal with past versions by allowing you to create data connection files. These Universal Data Connection (UDC) files contain all the connection settings applicable to the data source and usage scenario. Therefore, instead of specifying the connection settings in each of your form templates, you save the connection settings as a file and have your form templates point directly to this file, as shown in Figure 3-32. When you do this, making changes to a single file updates multiple templates.

Form Template 1

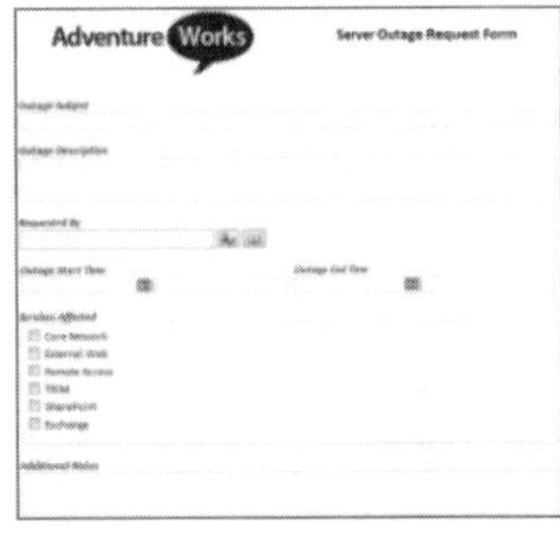

Form Template 2

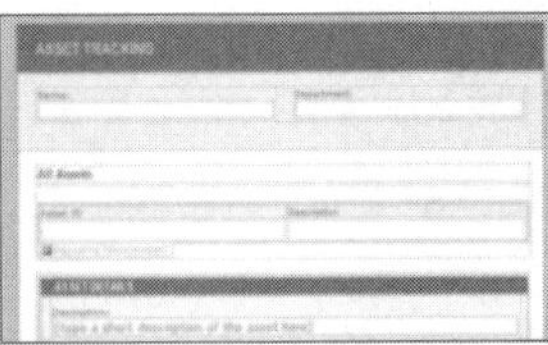

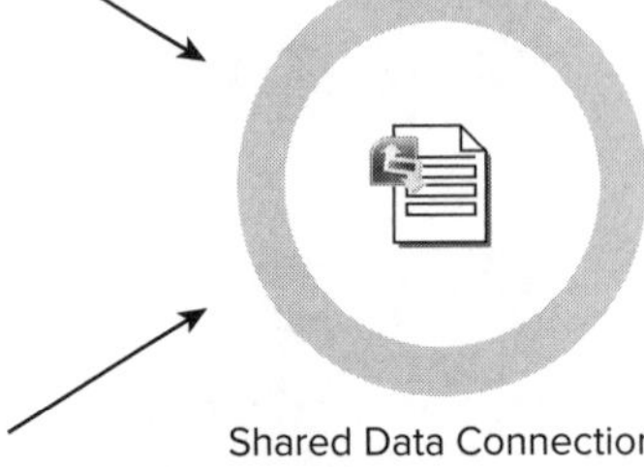

Shared Data Connection

FIGURE 3-32

NOTE *In Chapters 12 and 16, you work in greater detail with data connections. These chapters have specific examples of how beneficial data connection files can be and how you can store them centrally in a data connection library.*

Slide Libraries

Because PowerPoint presentations are a common way for members of an organization to communicate, companies generally produce, deliver, and store presentations in large quantities. Unfortunately, the sheer quantity can cause the following issues:

- **Duplicated work:** Because individuals are seldom aware of a fellow colleague's work, there is very little reuse of information.
- **Outdated material:** Duplicated material across many locations means that an individual is more likely to grab an outdated presentation or present the wrong version of a presentation. This can lead to miscommunication of objectives or performance.
- **Inconsistent presentation:** Depending who creates a presentation and what their interpretation of the content is, an organization may encounter company-wide inconsistencies in how data is presented to customers, partners, and other important stakeholders.

For these reasons, many organizations try to standardize how information is presented. SharePoint offers a unique method for consolidating presentation information that encourages users to share slide content.

The slide library template in SharePoint allows authors to upload slides to a library where other team members can view them. The following Try It Outs show you how to address these issues and, by doing so, help reduce duplicate efforts while protecting the quality and integrity of your organization's presentations. First, you learn how to upload a presentation to a slide library. You next create a new presentation in the library, and then update a presentation to incorporate corrections to a source slide.

TRY IT OUT Create a Slide Library

1. From the main page of your team site, click the All Site Content link from the side navigation bar.
2. Click Create. A window will appear, listing the various templates available to create lists and libraries from.
3. Filter the listing by clicking the Library link on the left side of the window.
4. Select Slide Library from the list of Library types.
5. Click Create.
6. Enter Project Slides for the Library name and the following text for the description:

   A consolidated library containing all presentation content related to our project.

7. Click Yes to create a version each time you edit a file in this slide library.
8. Click Create. Your new library will be created, and you will be redirected to the default view, as shown in Figure 3-33.

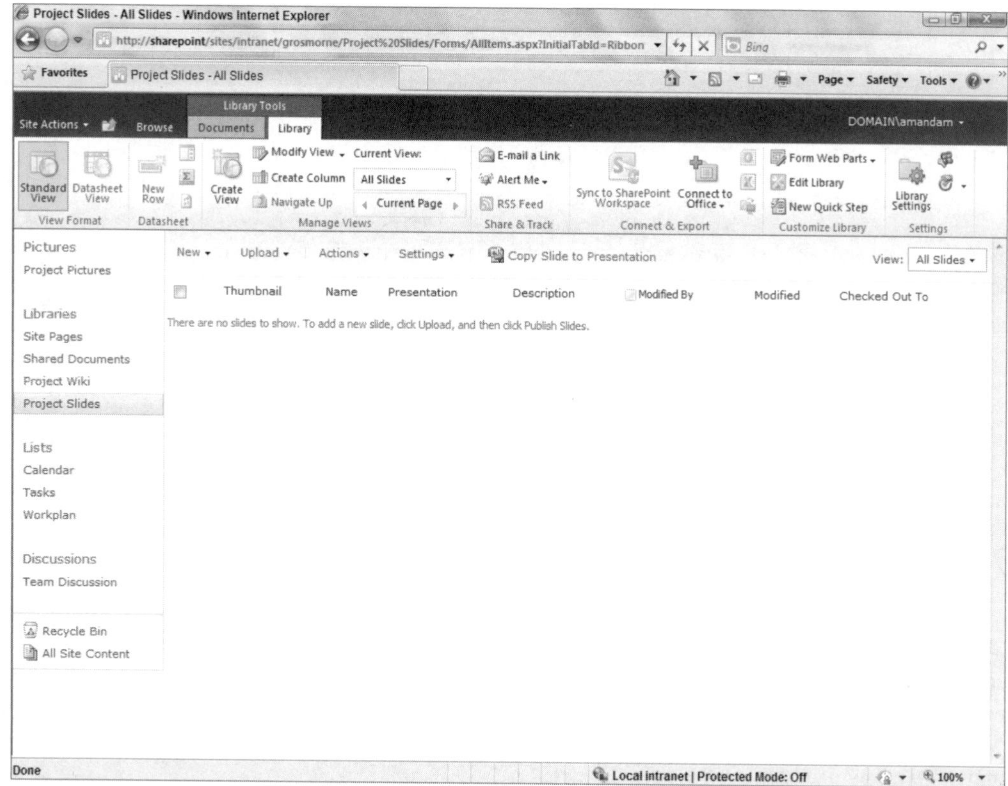

FIGURE 3-33

TRY IT OUT Upload a Presentation to a Slide Library

In the following example, you upload a presentation to a slide library so that it can be converted to individual slides that other team members can use.

1. From the Project Slides library, select Publish Slides from the Upload Menu.
2. Locate the presentation named "2010-2011Project Objectives" from the downloaded resources for this chapter (these are located on `www.wrox.com`), and click Open. The PowerPoint application will open. A publishing window, shown on Figure 3-34, lists all the slides available for upload from the selected presentation.

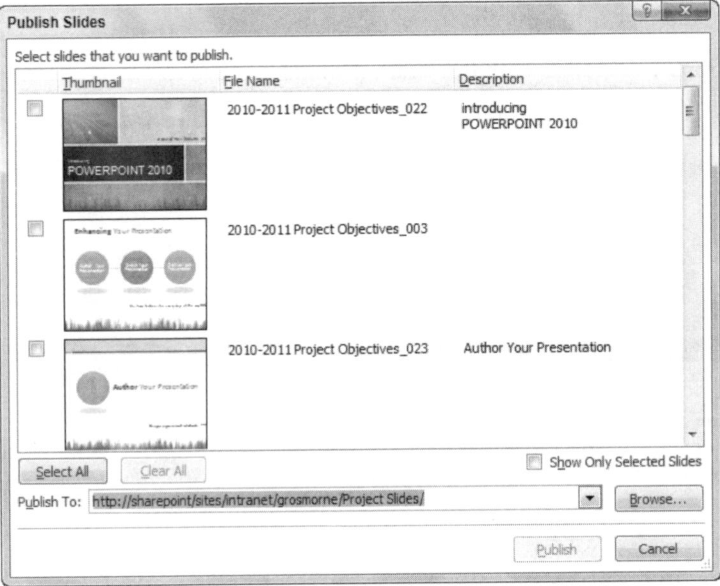

FIGURE 3-34

3. Click the Select All button and click the Publish button.
4. Your slides will be published to the Project Slides library, and when the process is complete will look similar to Figure 3-35.

How It Works

This process is noticeably different from uploading a standard document to a document library because slide libraries can accept individual slides rather than a complete presentation. Although this exercise had you upload all the slides in a presentation, the interface that appeared in step 2 during the upload process allows you to select individual slides. Once you click the Publish button in step 3, a status bar indicates where you are in the upload process. Depending on how many slides you've selected, this process may take a few minutes.

While each slide of the presentation contains a metadata field from the original presentation, you can treat them as individual files. In fact, the next example shows you how to create a new presentation based on slides in your library.

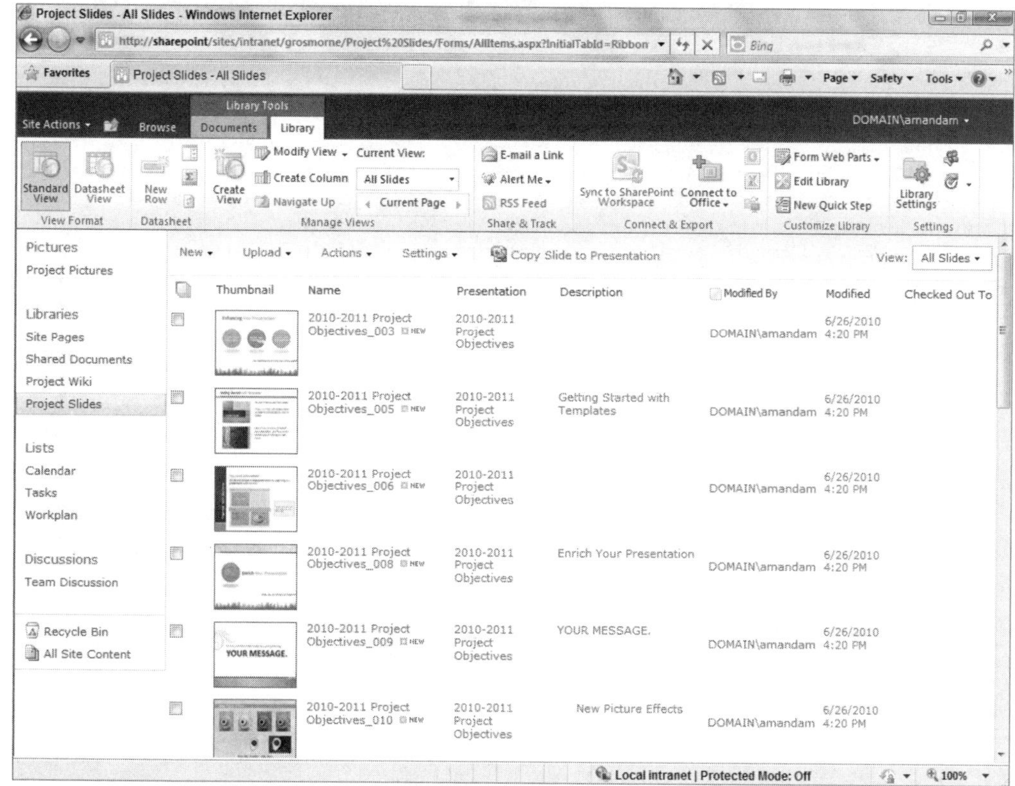

FIGURE 3-35

TRY IT OUT Create a Presentation from a Slide Library

You can create a new presentation using slides from multiple presentations. This example shows how to create a new presentation based on the slides available in a slide library. In addition to creating a new presentation, you can add slides to an existing presentation. This is ideal for a situation where you are creating a new presentation and you want to add a slide to represent content that has been used previously in a presentation or perhaps want to present content from a standardized slide.

1. From the Project Slides library, select the first, second, and third slides from the library's All Slides view, as shown in Figure 3-36.

2. Click the Copy Slide to Presentation toolbar button.

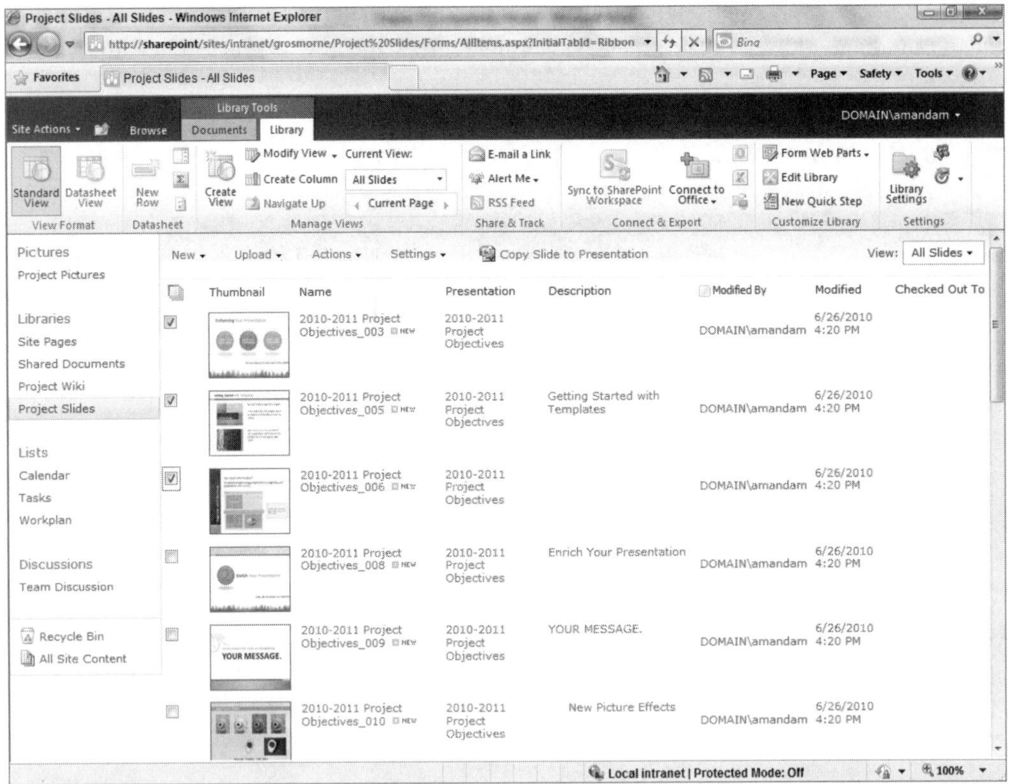

FIGURE 3-36

3. Select Copy to a New Presentation.
4. Select Keep Source Presentation Format. This will retain the formatting and background styles of your existing presentation.
5. Select the Tell me when this slide changes option, as shown in Figure 3-37.
6. Click the OK button. A new presentation will open in PowerPoint, containing the slides you had selected.

How It Works

In Step 5, you selected the Tell me when this slide changes option, which means that you are notified whenever someone updates the source slides. Keeping slides connected to the library ensures that presentations always contain the most relevant and updated information. However, synchronization is not automatic. This is actually good because you never want to change the content of an important document without first reviewing the changes or consider the impact. Also, for archiving reasons, you may want to view a presentation as it was presented, and you have no need for updated data once a presentation is made. For example, if you plan to give a presentation discussing a team's performance over a period of time, you may want to know when source slides are updated in the library, but once you deliver the presentation, there is no need to change the content.

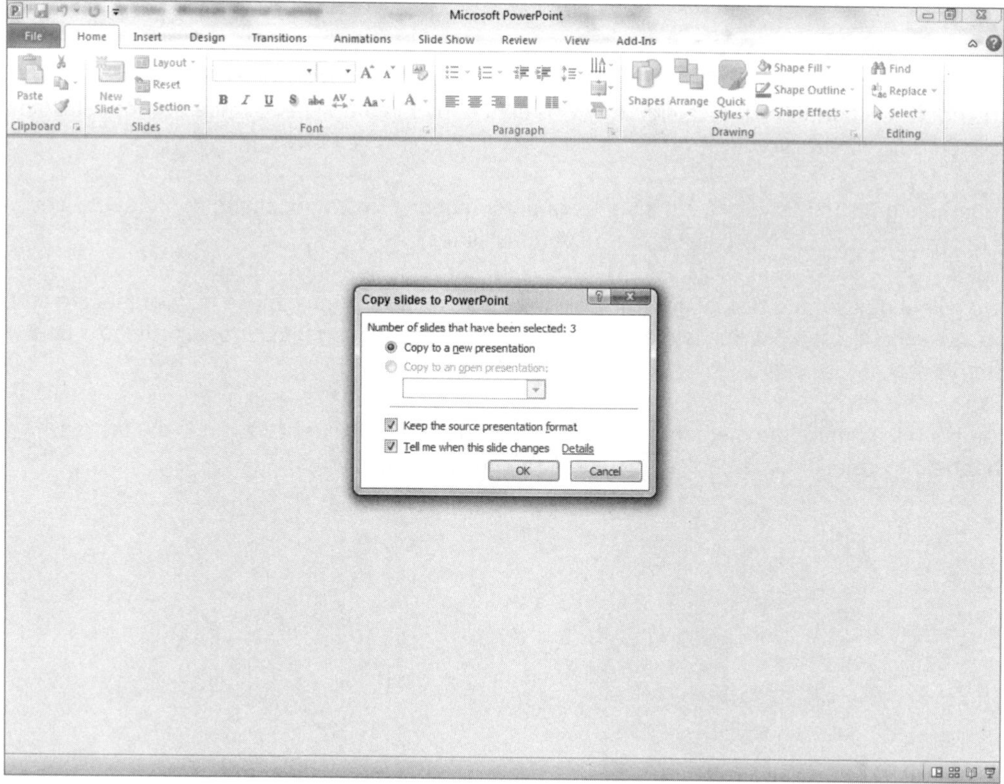

FIGURE 3-37

SUMMARY

This chapter discussed document collaboration in a team environment and then detailed the benefits and pitfalls arising from managing a single document with multiple editors. Things to remember about this chapter:

- SharePoint's library feature enables you to create, store, and manage your documents from a central location.
  - Document libraries let you track a variety of different types of information. It is the most common type of SharePoint library.
  - SharePoint also offers you libraries that are for a specific type of file or information and has templates to create these libraries, including InfoPath form data, images and pictures, Excel spreadsheets for browser-based reporting and dashboards, data connection files, and media and presentation slides.
  - Throughout this chapter, you looked at the ways that a user can interact with document libraries and the content within them. In Chapter 4, you will take a deeper look at customizing libraries along with lists to suit specific needs your organization might have.

EXERCISES

1. Your project manager informs you that the version of the document you submitted for approval was not correct and that the version that was sent earlier in the week is more appropriate. How do you remedy the situation?

2. Your manager assigns your team a series of presentations for an upcoming conference. How can your team most efficiently collaborate on various slides?

3. You've been given the task of archiving an old document. Currently, these documents are stored in a common file share. What is the best method of mass-copying these documents to a document library?

4. You need to change the metadata information for multiple documents. What is the fastest way to change the metadata of a particular column for multiple documents?

▶ WHAT YOU LEARNED IN THIS CHAPTER

TOPIC	KEY CONCEPTS
What is a Document Library?	A document library is a location for storing files in SharePoint. You can store a number of file types including Microsoft Office files, PDFs, Images or Data Connection files.
The Different Library Templates	There are a number of templates available for libraries in SharePoint including Form Libraries, Slide Libraries, Picture Libraries and Asset Libraries.
The Benefits of Version History	Version history is a feature in SharePoint that allows you to store all previous copies of a document within a single location in an organized fashion. This allows you to easily retrieve and restore previous versions of a file at any time.

Managing and Customizing Lists and Libraries

WHAT YOU WILL LEARN IN THIS CHAPTER:

- Specific reasons for customizing a SharePoint list or library
- Best practices for creating business elements
- Examples of working with list-centric columns and site columns
- The various types of views available in SharePoint and best practices related to creating them
- Working with list and document templates

The previous two chapters discussed how to use lists and libraries in their most basic format. SharePoint has some great templates that will address the most common collaborative scenarios; however, your information and sharing needs may require something different. In such cases, you can customize lists, libraries, and associated components so that they better address those needs. When you customize SharePoint to more closely reflect business practices and processes, users can focus on their jobs instead of working harder or around an ill-fitting tool. This chapter shows you how to customize both lists and libraries. Many of the examples use the term list to describe both lists and libraries because anything that you can do to a list, you can also apply to a document library.

After reading this chapter, you should feel comfortable taking a specific list or library template and customizing it to suit your specific needs. You should also understand the steps and value associated with adding your custom list to the central list of templates so that teams and users can benefit from your customization efforts.

CREATING AN ENVIRONMENT THAT REFLECTS YOUR BUSINESS

Information is not very useful if it is disorganized and hard to find. Traditionally, electronic documents are stored in a file system consisting of folders and subfolders, often many levels deep. In computer lingo, this is often called a *tree structure*. You create the document tree according to your needs or whims, and then you share it with your associates. However, they may not understand your organizational approach and so may have difficulty finding documents in your folder structure. For example, you may have a folder for each city in your territory, and within each city folder, folders for your customers in that city. In each customer folder, you store project specifications, statements of work, proposals, project status reports, and other documents related to that customer. What if an associate simply wants a list of the current project status reports for all of your customers, however? This is pretty hard to get because status reports are scattered throughout your folder structure.

This example shows the major limitation of using the file system to share documents: Because you only have one way to organize and categorize information, you must develop a system in advance that is useful for everyone, and that usually results in a compromise that no one wants. Further, once you choose a folder structure, it may become both difficult to change and difficult to teach to others.

With SharePoint, you can associate a great deal of information with documents by using standard and custom list columns. For example, you can customize a library to attach the information shown in the following table to each document.

COLUMN NAME	COLUMN TYPE	VALUES
Document Status	Choice	Not Started In Progress In Review Final Draft
Client	Lookup	Look up to title column from Clients list
Project	Lookup	Look up to title column from Projects list
Project Type	Lookup	Look up to title column from a Project Categories list
Due Date	Date and time	[*due date*]
Assigned to	People or group	[*person or group*]
Owner	People or group	[*owner*]

With standard file shares, it's impossible to store this information and have it easily associated with a specific document. However, with SharePoint, you simply add columns to the document library. By capturing the appropriate information, your associates can search and view the document library in the ways they prefer. For example, one colleague might search for projects by client, while another might search by author. Through the use of metadata and views, you can create reusable reports to allow your colleagues to find information more efficiently.

Once you recognize trends in how your team searches for documents, you can create custom views to match the most popular search criteria. For example, if users frequently search for documents assigned to them for review, you can create a view that displays a list of documents that have been assigned to the current user, and you can even sort the list in the order in which they are due. With custom columns and views, SharePoint takes you out of the restricted world of file sharing and into a multidimensional world where each of your associates can see your documents in the most appropriate way.

BEST PRACTICES FOR BUILDING A DYNAMIC SYSTEM FOR MANAGING CONTENT

In this section, you learn the best practices that ensure your SharePoint site offers the maximum value to your organization based on the customizations that you implement. This is an important consideration because the right customizations can make your site user-friendly and efficient, while the wrong ones can make data entry burdensome and can cause user confusion.

Ensure Your Changes Add Value

When you design an information system for your team to use for sharing and managing content, remember that your changes should add value; changes should make the system easier to use and the information simple and intuitive to find.

You can identify what adds value by familiarizing yourself with the information goals of team members and site users:

- Hold meetings or send questionnaires to gather information on users' frustration points.
- From these discussions, create a list of problems that you need to address.
- Rank and prioritize the list based on the number of people who are affected and the productivity impact they experience because of the issues.
- Look at how SharePoint lists and libraries can improve the situation. For example, if people have a difficult time finding documents created during a specific timeframe, you can create views that filter and sort documents based on when they were completed.

Follow Similar Processes and Practices

When you create additional columns and views to your lists, follow similar rules in each situation. The more consistency you create within the environment, the more unified and intuitive the experience will be for the users:

- A column that describes the status of a list item or document should offer the user consistent choices. If you use a certain set of status values for one list or library, use the same for all other lists and libraries. Do not use values such as "Not Started," "In Progress," and "In Review" in one location and then use completely different values to represent the same type of information elsewhere.

- If you start creating custom views, offer some level of standardization, such as consistent ordering and sorting of columns based on the type of information you're presenting.

Provide Guides and Descriptions

Have you ever been asked to complete a task without a receiving a clear explanation of what was required of you? If so, then you probably understand how frustrating completing forms and column values in SharePoint can be for your users if you do not offer good descriptions and guidelines for defining specific items. If users are unsure about what information you are asking for, they are highly likely to provide less than optimal information. Giving users clear direction will result in them entering the information you want into the system. It is always a good practice to use the description field when creating custom columns in SharePoint.

WORKING WITH COLUMNS

A column is an element of information that describes an item on a SharePoint site. In some cases, the item may be an event, a company, or a task; in other cases, it may be a document, a web page, or a business form. In SharePoint, any content stored in a list or library is considered an item. No matter what the actual item is, columns provide a great way to further define and organize information beyond what is available via titles or folders.

Defining information effectively is a key reason you use SharePoint. Therefore, you may need to add new columns to define the various list and library items. For example, you can add a column to track document status to a document library so that users can easily identify a document's current state strictly by looking at its properties rather than making an assumption or asking the author directly. This is called a list-centric column, and you will learn to create one in the next Try It Out.

You may hear people describe columns as metadata or properties of an item. As described in Chapter 2, metadata is essentially information about information. In the case of a document, metadata is information that describes the document, such as its status, owner, or due date. A single document might have multiple metadata values because quite often there are many things to describe about a document. When you design or change an information environment, you should understand what content is stored within the site and what people will need to know about it.

TRY IT OUT Create a Column

In this example, you create a column for a project documentation library so that business users can track the status of project-related documents, such as user manuals, planning documents and training presentations. Because you do not want users to enter just any value for status, you provide a list of common choices. This example assumes that you require a choice column that allows you to specify the release status of documents in a document library as Alpha, Beta, or Final Release. A choice column, one of several column types, gives users a list of values from which to select and presents them in a drop-down menu. The remaining column types are discussed in the next section.

You will continue to work within the Project Team site created within the first Try It Out in Chapter 2. If you did not complete this exercise, it is recommended that you quickly return to that example and create a site, based upon the Team Site template, called “Gros Morne Project.”

1. From the main page of your Project Gros Morne site, select Shared Documents from the side navigation bar.
2. Select the Library tab from the Ribbon.
3. From the Manage Views section of the Library tab, select Create Column. The Create Column window will appear as shown in Figure 4-1.

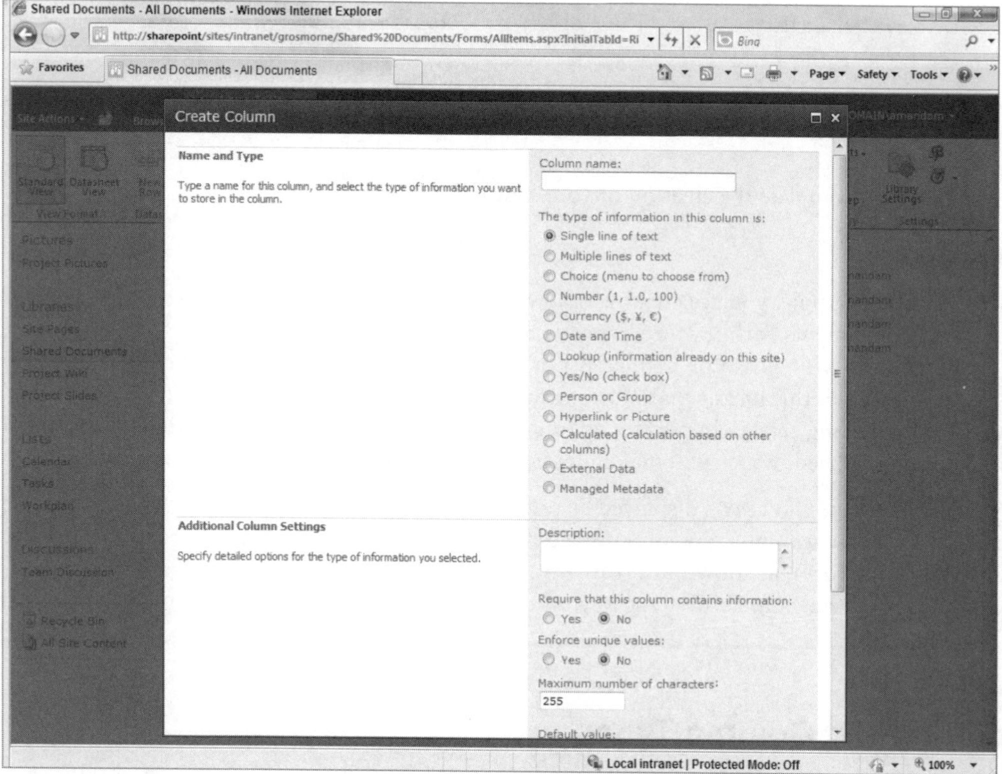

FIGURE 4-1

4. Enter the following properties for your column:

PROPERTY	VALUE
Column Name	Release Status
The type of information that is in this column	Choice (menu to choose from)
Description	This column contains the current release stage of the document.

continues

(continued)

PROPERTY	VALUE
Require that this column contains information	Yes
Enforce Unique Values	No
Type each choice on a separate line	Alpha Beta Final
Display choices using	Radio Buttons
Allow Fill-in Choices	No
Default Value	Alpha

5. Click OK to complete the creation of your new column.

How It Works

In the preceding example, you are creating a new column that will appear whenever users are uploading or editing documents within your shared documents library. Because you selected the Choice column type, the users will have a predefined list of values to select from. You specified that the column required information; this means that a user cannot check a document into the library unless this value is specified. By making certain important columns required, you can help ensure that all documents have this value specified, which will make it easier for users to locate the files within the library.

You specified that the choices be displayed as radio buttons. This will ensure that, as users complete the metadata form when uploading or editing a file, they will see what the available values to select are directly within the form, as shown in Figure 4-2. This is a suitable choice when you have just a few values. If you have a large number of items in your selection list, a drop-down menu may be more suitable.

Exploring List Column Types

Chapter 2 discussed the different types of data that you can store in a column at a high level. This section looks even more deeply at the types of columns you can have in SharePoint, and discusses some of the various customization options that exist with them. In the "Create a Column" Try It Out you just completed, you selected a Choice column type to collect information from a radio button control, but you have other options at your disposal. At the end of this section, the "Change the Order of Columns on a List" Try It Out shows you how to reorder the columns of a list to make them more user-friendly.

Single Line of Text

Virtually every list starts with the Single Line of Text column type, possibly the most commonly used within SharePoint lists, as its primary or title column. When creating a Single Line of Text column, you have very few options for customization, as you can see from Figure 4-3. However, you can select whether the column is required or optional. You can also limit the number of characters that a user can enter to prevent users from entering unnecessary data in a column. There is also the option to specify a default value, which users can enter manually or which you can allow SharePoint to calculate.

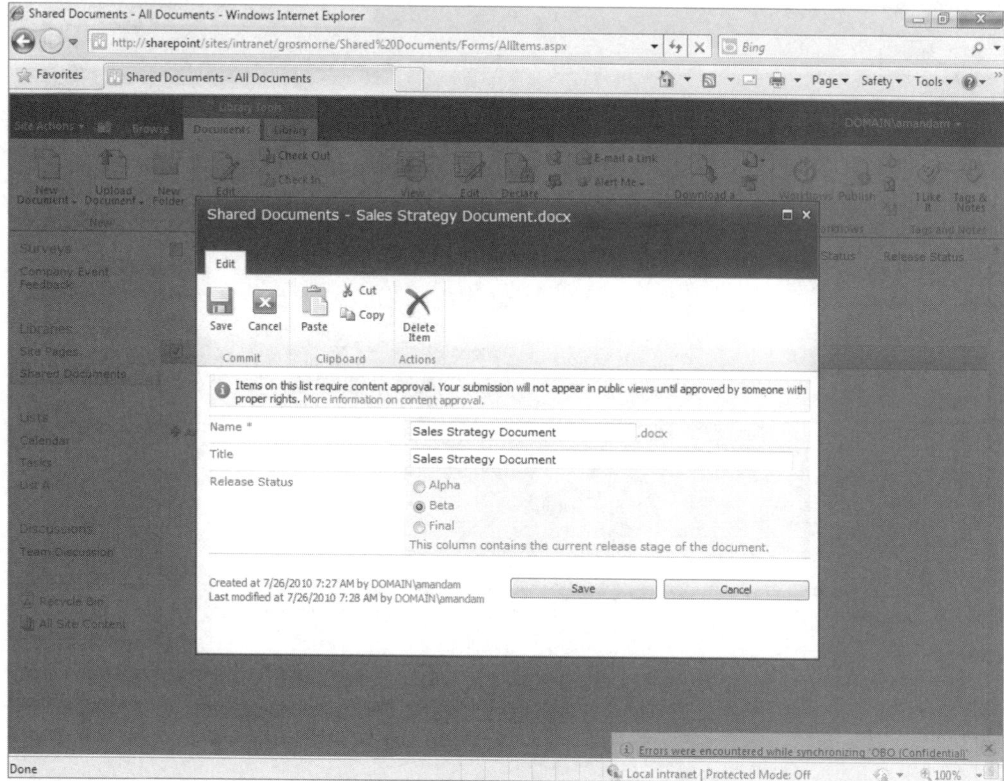

FIGURE 4-2

The final customization option is to apply Column Validation formulas to help ensure that as users specify values, they adhere to specific rules such as number of characters or other business logic that may apply.

Multiple Lines of Text

A Multiple Lines of Text column type has multiple configuration options, shown in Figure 4-4. As with other columns, you can specify whether the column is required and enter a description that tells users what information to complete.

Because this column allows a variable amount of text, you can specify how many lines the field should display when users complete the information. You should give users plenty of space for situations where you expect them to enter a great deal of data; the size gives users a visual cue of how much information you want them to enter. For example, if the column is for a mailing address, three or four lines should be acceptable. However, if the column is for background information on a customer, you may want to provide at least 25.

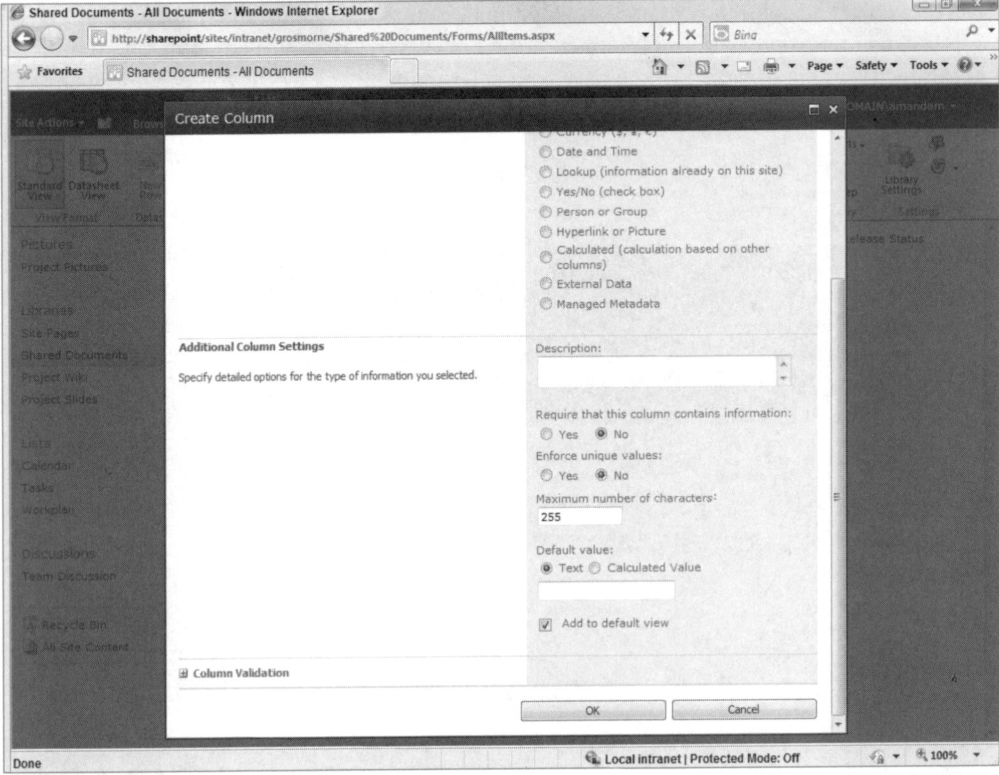

FIGURE 4-3

The Multiple Lines of Text has more advanced formatting options than most other columns, including the following:

- **Plain Text:** Most appropriate for scenarios where no special formatting is required, such as in the example of a mailing address.
- **Rich Text:** Users can format the text using the Rich Text Editor, which is ideal when users input a larger amount of text that doesn't have specially formatted elements, such as tables or pictures but may require some formatting and text alignment. You select this for notes and comments related to an item.
- **Enhanced Text:** Allows your users to add images, tables, and hyperlink elements to the column via the Advanced List Text Editor. This format is ideal for article body columns in an announcements list or employee biography content columns.

Choice

The Choice column allows a site manager to define a list of values from which a user can select, as shown in Figure 4-5. As with other columns, you can specify whether the column is required and enter a description that serves as an aid to users as they complete the information.

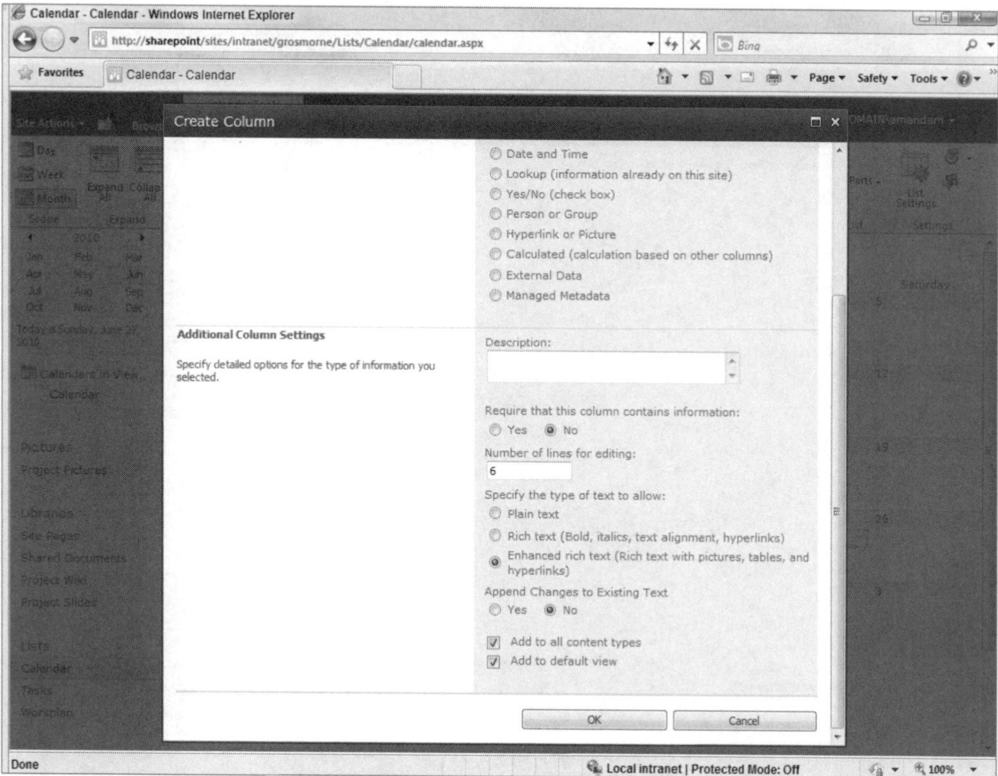

FIGURE 4-4

You enter all values by placing each value on a separate line. Users see this as a drop-down list, a set of radio buttons, or a series of checkboxes. A drop-down list or set of radio buttons means users can only select one option, while checkboxes allow them to select more than one item from the list of values. You can also specify whether users can fill in their own item if an appropriate value does not appear in the list, which is great if you want users to enter exceptional values. For example, you may have a survey list that collects information on preferences for the next company social. You may offer a set list of locations and then have an option that allows users to enter suggestions for a location.

As with the Single Line of Text, you can also include a default value from the list of choices or have the default value calculated. In cases where you are making a choice column a required field for a list, it's best not to specify a default value because users may accidentally forget to specify the value and the default selected item is then saved. By not specifying a default value, you can enforce the selection of an item, which ensures the information entered into the list is accurate. For example, if you are required to give users a choice of whether information is confidential or public in a list or library, it would not be wise to set either choice as the default value because you would want the user to think about their selection and pick the right option.

Similarly to the Single Line of Text column type, the Choice column type supports Column Validation.

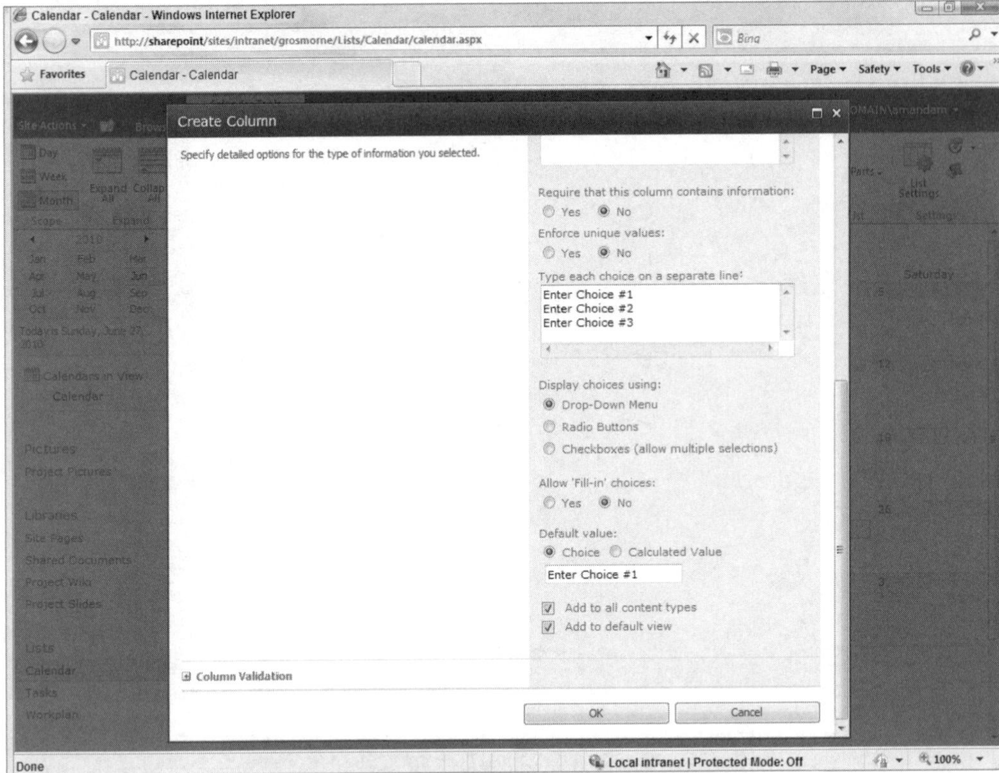

FIGURE 4-5

Number

A Number column has pretty simple customization options, as shown in Figure 4-6, but is extremely useful in many lists because it's helpful for calculations or reporting.

You can make a Number column either required or optional. You may specify an allowed range of numbers that users can enter. For example, if you have a column to represent a user's rating of an item, you can have a minimum value of 1 and a maximum of 10. You can also configure a column to display a specific number of decimal places or percentage value regardless of the format a person uses to enter the information. As with some of the previous examples, you may select a default or calculated value for your column as well as configure column validation rules.

Currency

A Currency column has the same customization options as the Number column type with one addition, as shown in Figure 4-7.

The Currency column enables a user to specify the regional format in which the data displays, such as $150,000.00 for the United States or £150,000.00 for the United Kingdom. There is no direct link between the regional setting and currency exchange rates.

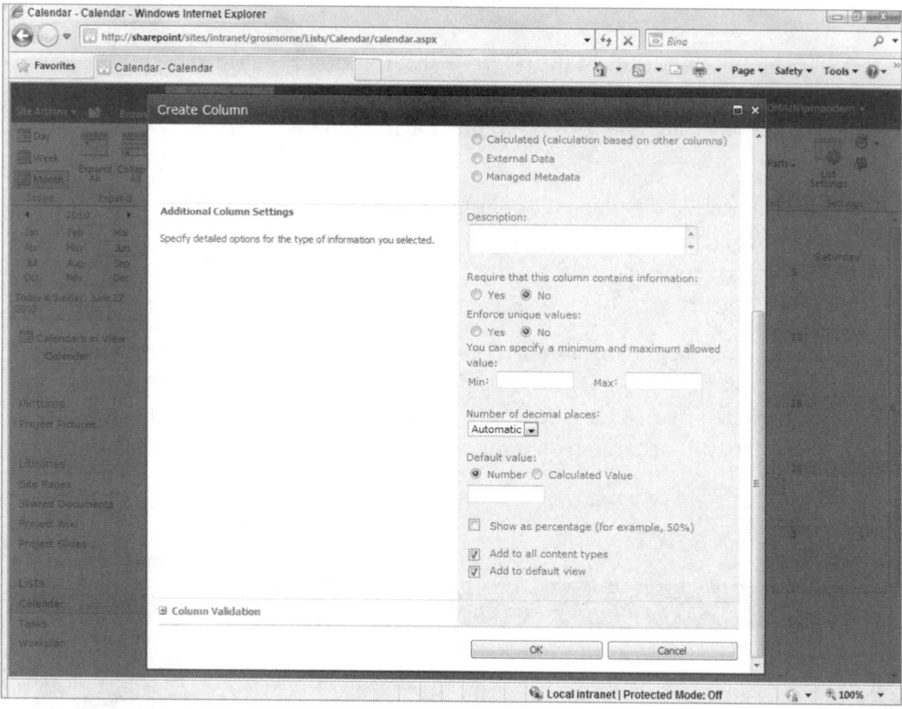

FIGURE 4-6

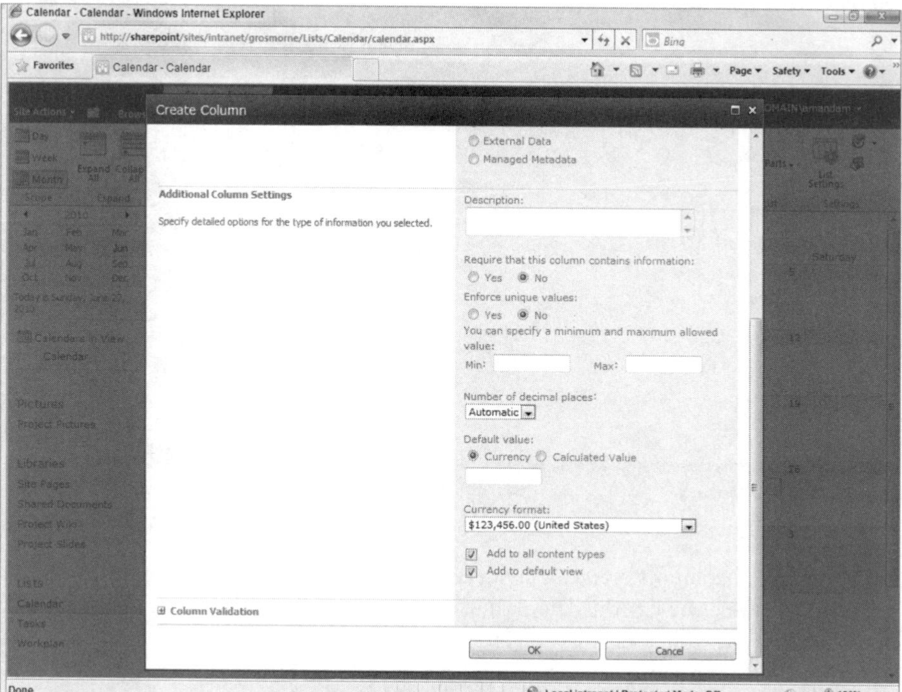

FIGURE 4-7

Date and Time

You may need to add columns containing date and time information because many of the items you track in a list have some level of time relevance, such as a due date, start date, finish date, or completion date. In fact, every list has Date and Time columns for tracking when an item was created or last modified.

Beyond the options that determine whether this column is required and that add a description, you can have the column display as only a date or a time value. Time values are particularly useful if you intend to display your list information in a daily calendar view or if you define details on events, such as meetings or appointments.

You also have a few choices for displaying a default value such as no value, the current date, or a specific date, as shown in Figure 4-8. So, if you have a list where users submit requests, you can select Today's Date as the default value for a column called "Request Date." This reduces the amount of user entry and lets you accurately determine when a user submitted a request.

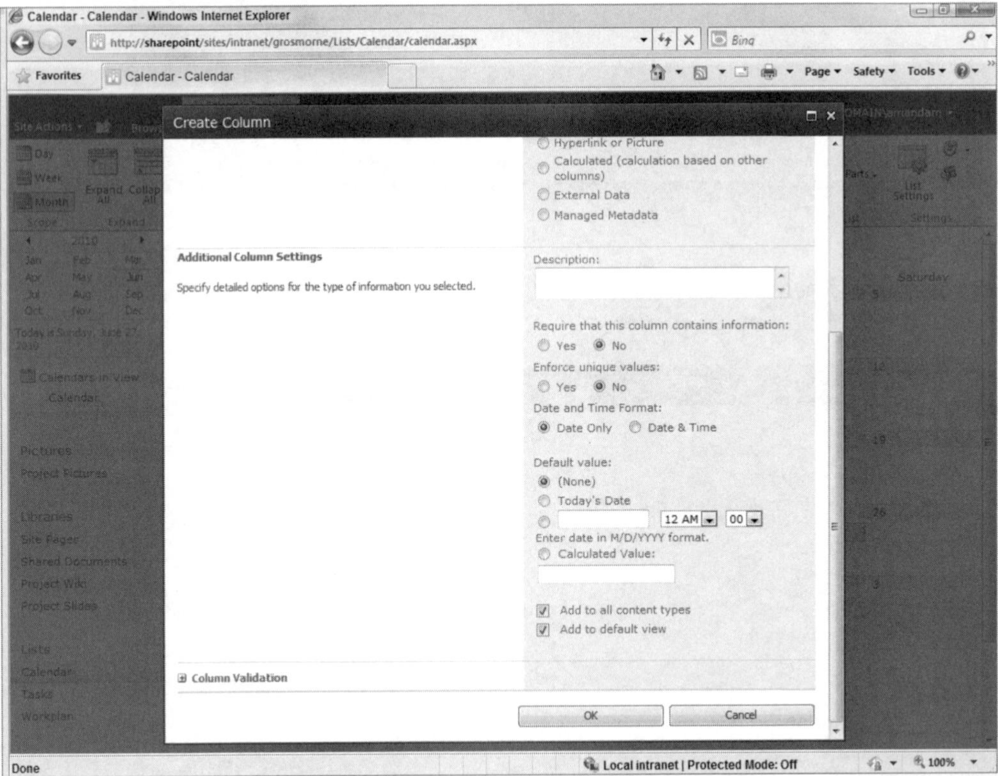

FIGURE 4-8

As with previously described columns, you can create a calculated value for a date column. This is useful if you are setting a value such as the default due date for an item. In that case, you may select the default value as [today] + 7, which sets the value to a week past the current date. As with some of the previous examples, you may configure column validation rules on a Date and Time column.

Lookup

A Lookup column is very similar to a Choice column because it supplies users with a set of predefined values for a column. The advantage is that you can point it to another list on the site and, thus, create more dynamic list values. This is better than storing all the values as a static property of the column because users update the list as part of normal business operations. For example, if you have a customer list, it's unrealistic for a site manager to constantly log in and change a list column's properties each time a company acquires a new customer. Instead, you can have this column point to a centralized customer list that those closest to the business operations can maintain. The new customer's name would then automatically appear as a value in the column as soon as the centralized customer list is updated. In addition to selecting the list and column that the Lookup column uses to display data, site managers can configure the column so that users can select multiple values for a list, as shown in Figure 4-9.

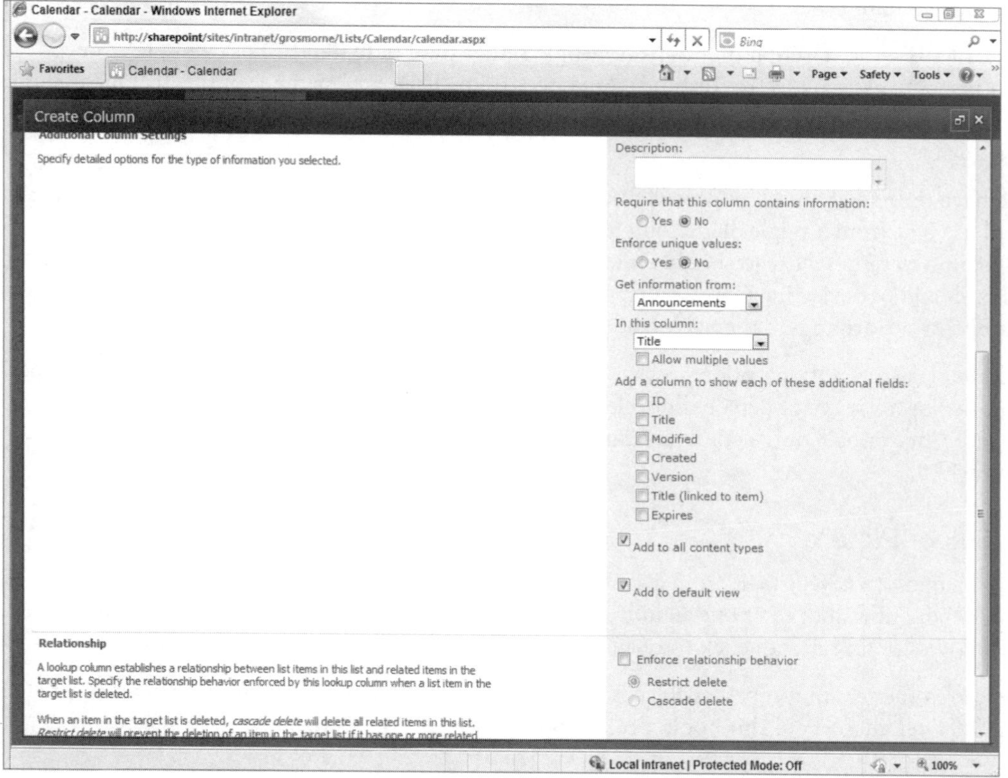

FIGURE 4-9

Another powerful feature of the Lookup list is that site managers can configure the list to display additional properties of the item that was selected within the list. As an example, if a user selects Customer XYZ, the customer's address and phone number may also be displayed within the list item along with the customer's name. The site manager may also elect to have customer data deleted from the list if the customer is removed from the system or restrict the deletion in to preserve the original data.

Yes/No

A Yes/No column type is essentially a checkbox column that defines whether an item meets a specific criteria item. For example, this type of column can designate whether an item is displayed on the main page of a SharePoint site, or whether an item is active. The primary configuration option when defining a Yes/No column is determining whether the default value should be selected or unselected.

Person or Group

The Person or Group column is ideal for assigning ownership of an item or personalizing the display of data to users of a list. Besides the usual determination of whether to make the column required or to add a description, you have the option of selecting multiple items, which allows you to assign a single task to multiple people. In fact, for a tasks list, the Assigned To column is based on the Person or Group column type.

You can allow the selection of groups of people rather than individuals. For example, you can create a task and assign it to the Technical Support group. Then any member of the Technical Support group can complete the request rather than rely on users to specify which technician should complete the task.

You have the added option of defining whether a person from this column is drawn from the list of all users or from a single SharePoint group, which is useful if you want to have an Assigned To column to represent who should review the document next. Because only those with approval rights should be reviewing items, it may make sense to specify that only members of the Approvers SharePoint site group be assigned to the column.

Your final customization option involves how the information is displayed. You can have the person identified by a variety of personal profile properties, including display name, email address, and job title. An example of the configuration options for the Person or Group column type is shown in Figure 4-10.

Hyperlink or Picture

This column offers very little from a customization perspective beyond specifying whether the item is required, but it does offer one significant attribute. You can format the URL of the item as either a web address that users can click to open or as a picture that is displayed as a thumbnail.

There are other column types, such as Audiences and Business Data, which are covered in greater detail in later chapters of this book. See Chapters 9 and 12 for details.

Calculated (Calculation Based on other Columns)

This special column type allows a site manager to define a formula that will automatically determine the value of a column without requiring a user's input. This formula can be based upon other columns within the list. An example of such a formula is [Items Sold] x [Price], which would calculate the total revenue associated with a list item that represents a customer sale. As shown in Figure 4-11, the available columns to reference in your formula are displayed for your ease of use.

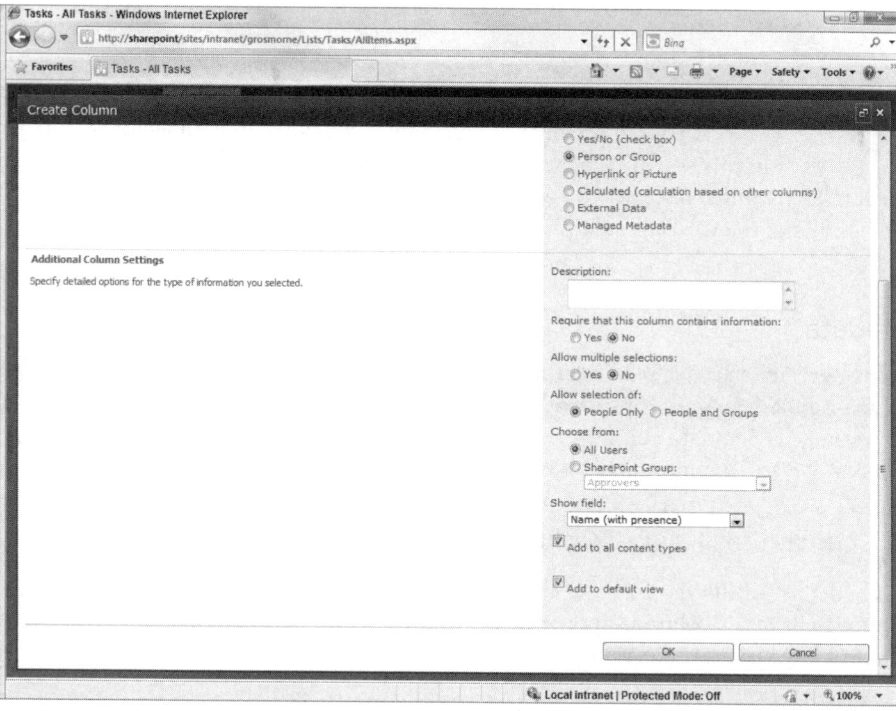

FIGURE 4-10

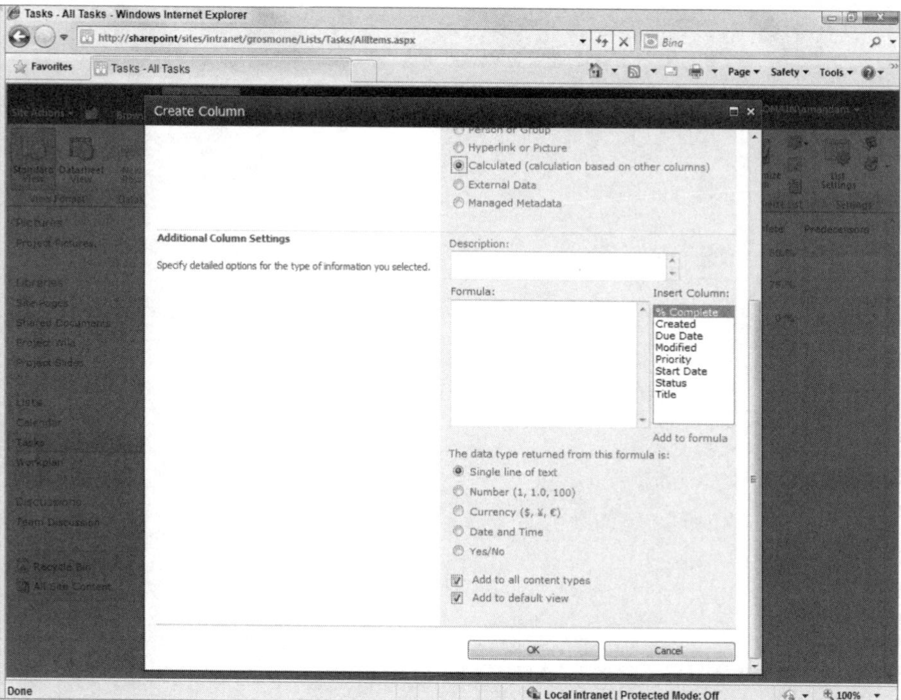

FIGURE 4-11

External Data

Based upon the Business Connectivity Services feature of SharePoint Server, the External Data column type allows a site manager to reference an external business system as the lookup location for a column's values. For example, if your company has a customer relationship management system, all customer data may exist in this system. Therefore, it would not make sense to export and replicate that information in SharePoint. Instead, you could create a column that looks up that external business system and points to the Customer database for its values. We will explore this feature further in Chapter 15.

Managed Metadata

New features in SharePoint Server 2010 are the Managed Metadata column type and Term Store. These features help provide a more robust and centrally managed metadata system than standard column types. Managed Metadata columns can support hierarchical information as well as large volumes of choices. We will explore this feature further in Chapter 14.

TRY IT OUT Change the Order of Columns on a List

Once you have defined a list or library with the columns you wish to track, you may at times realize that you would prefer to have the columns appear in a form in a slightly different order. Figure 4-12 displays the new item form for a standard Project Tasks list.

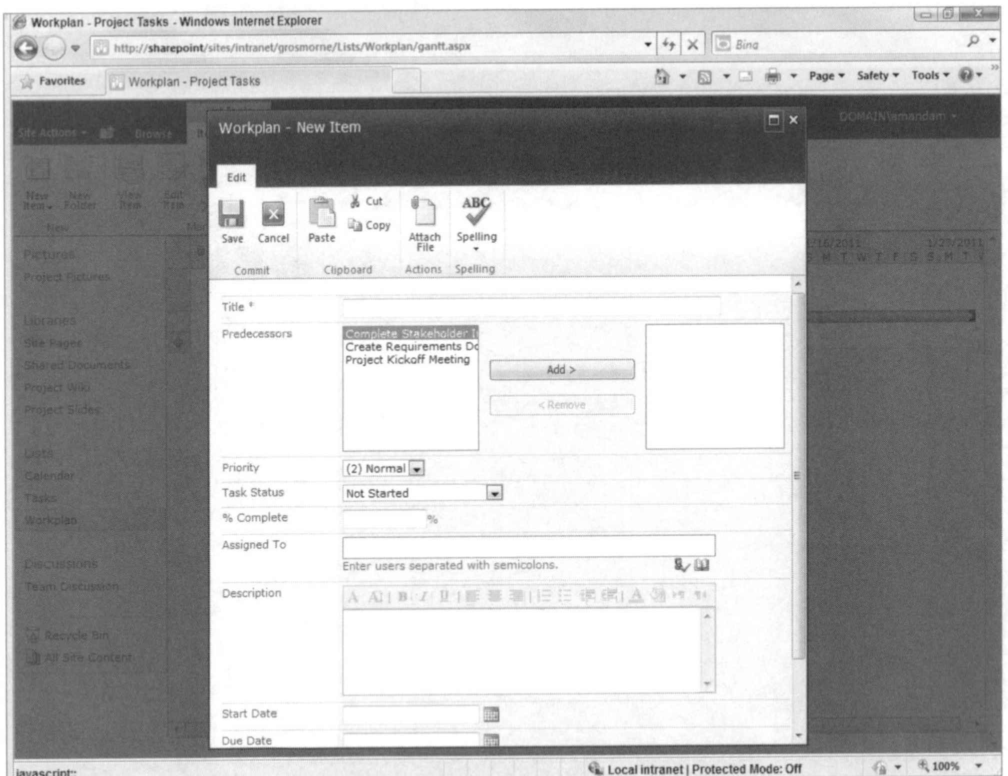

FIGURE 4-12

After reviewing the form, you decide that it would be more appropriate to move the location of the Assigned To column to just below the title. The following steps in this Try It Out can be repeated on any list or library type.

1. From the main page of your Project Gros Morne site, select Workplan from the side navigation bar.

NOTE *If you did not complete all the exercises in Chapter 2, this exercise can be performed using any standard Project Tasks list.*

2. Select the List tab from the Ribbon.
3. Select the List Settings menu option. You will be redirected to the List Settings page.
4. Scroll to the Content Types section of the page. Select the Task content type.
5. Select the Column Order link. You will be redirected to the Column Order page as shown in Figure 4-13.

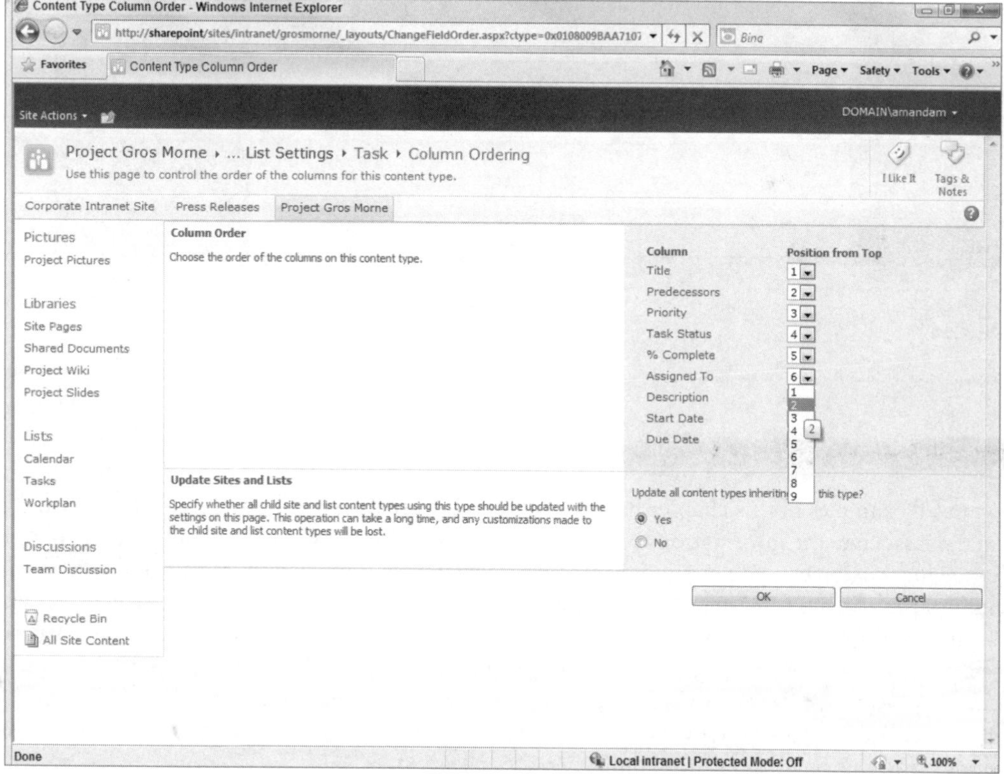

FIGURE 4-13

6. Change the Position from Top value for the Assigned To column from 6 to 2.
7. Click OK.

By changing the Column Order, users will now see the order as displayed in Figure 4-14 when filling out a new item within the Workplan list.

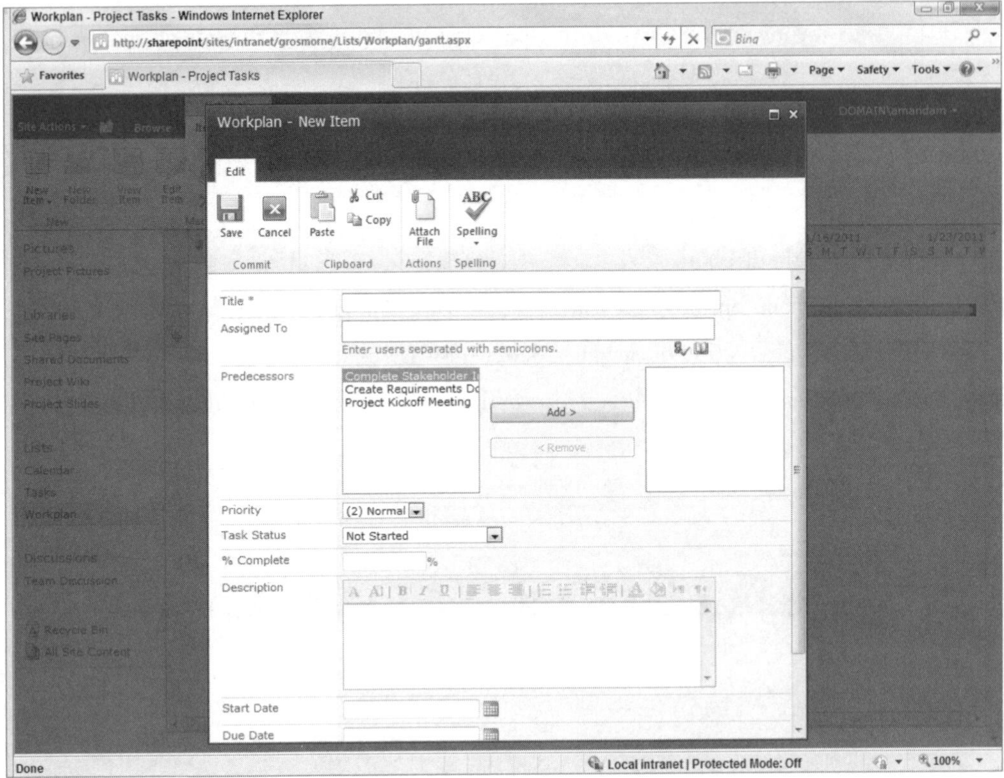

FIGURE 4-14

What Are Site Columns?

So far, all examples in this chapter have been limited to creating a column for a list or library, but you can associate the information for a single list with multiple lists. For example, for a column that defines customers, you commonly associate a customer's name with items from multiple lists and libraries. Because the steps for creating a suitable customer list are somewhat time-consuming, it's inefficient to reproduce the column in each list where you want to associate client information. Instead, you can create what is known as a site column, which makes a column available to all sites and subsites. Generally speaking, if many lists will use your column at all levels of a corporate intranet or portal, you should create it at the top-level site of a site collection. This makes the site column available on all sites throughout the site collection.

A site column may only be relevant to a specific division or team. In that case, you may want to only create the column on the divisional site itself. It will still be available to all lists within that site and all sites below it; however, it will not be listed under the Available Site columns for the other subsites within the site collection.

> **NOTE** *It's important to consider where to place site columns in order to ensure that the organization gets optimal use of this shared feature. This will be discussed later in Chapter 6.*

The next two Try It Outs show you how to create a site column as well as how to add a site column to a list.

TRY IT OUT Create a Site Column

In the "Create a Column" Try It Out, you learned how to create a list-centric column. This Try It Out walks you through creating a site column within the central gallery of columns so that it can later be used by multiple lists with a site and its subsites. For this example, you create the site column that holds all the regions in which an organization has a presence. Because you want to ensure that your column is available to the maximum number of sites in your intranet, you create it at the very top level of your site collection.

1. From the top-level site of your site collection (the site created in Chapter 1 called Corporate Intranet Site), select Site Settings from the Site Actions menu. You will be redirected to the Site Settings page for the site collection, as shown in Figure 4-15.

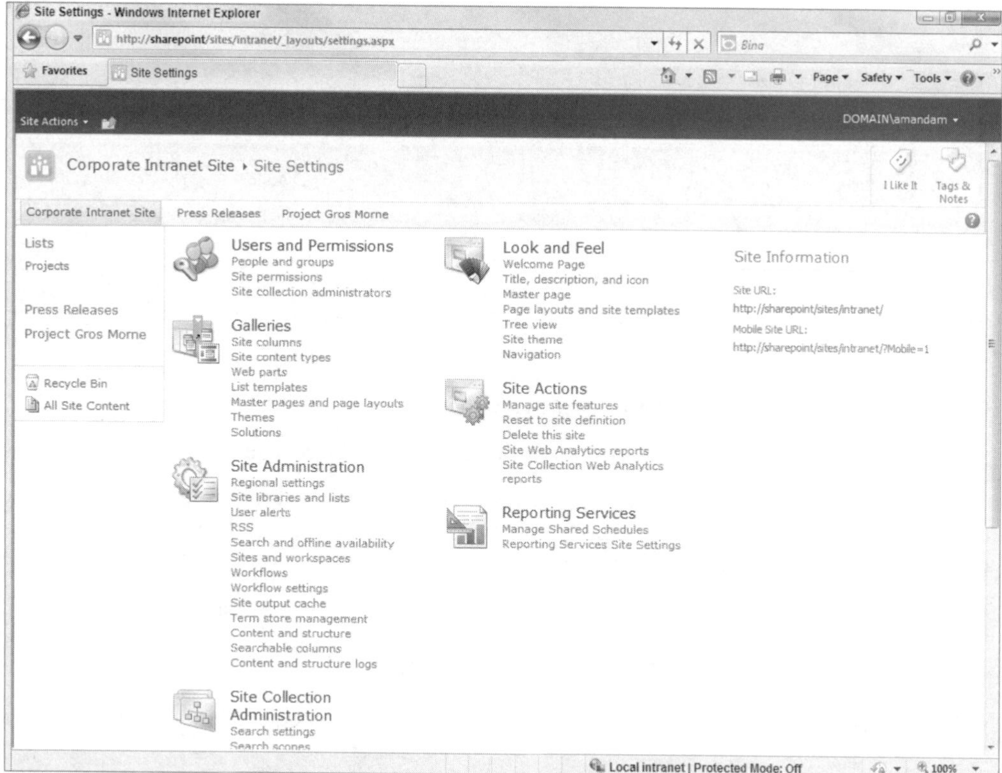

FIGURE 4-15

2. Select the Site columns option from the Galleries section. SharePoint presents you with a wide range of preexisting site columns, which are good starting points. It is always a good practice to search this listing to ensure that a similar column does not already exist.

3. Click Create from the toolbar. The Create Column window will appear as shown in Figure 4-16. You may notice some differences in this window over Figure 4-1. We will discuss these differences within the How It Works following this exercise.

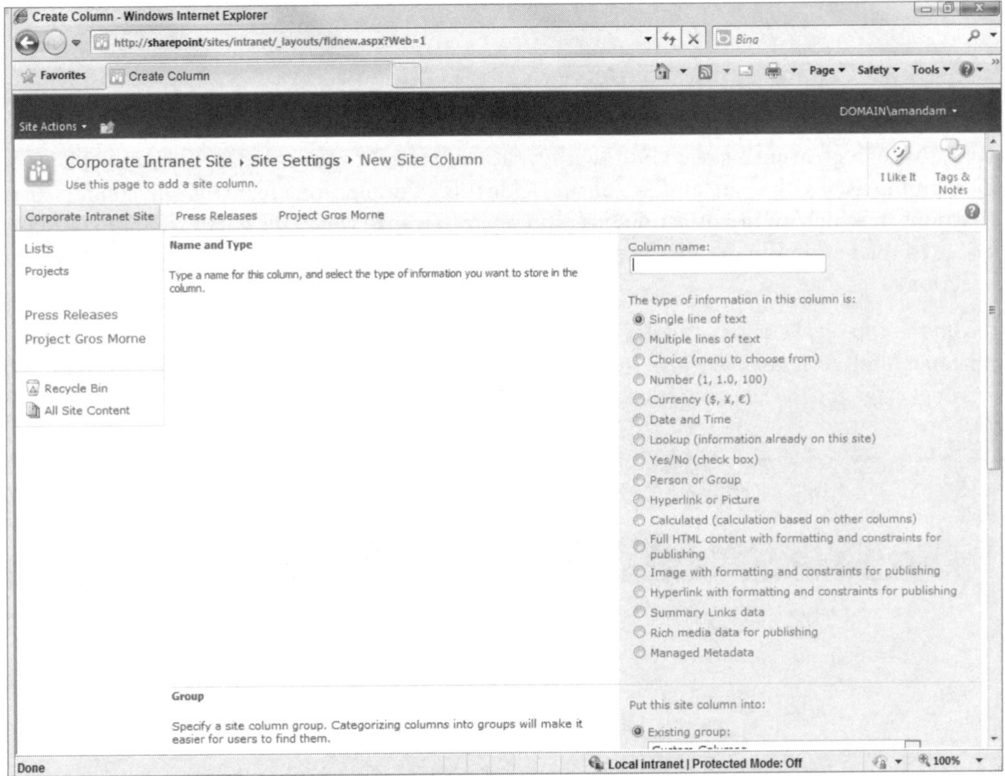

FIGURE 4-16

4. Give the site column a name. This example uses the name Corporate Regions.

5. Select the Choice (menu to choose from) option as the type of information in this column.

6. To better organize your site columns, you can choose a group for your Site Column. You can create a custom group for your custom Site Columns. To do this, select New Group, and type **Corporate Columns** in the field provided.

7. In the Additional Column Settings section, enter the following properties:

PROPERTY	VALUE
Description	This is a list of regions in which your organization has offices.
Require that this column contains information	Yes

PROPERTY	VALUE
Enforce Unique Values	No
Type each choice on a separate line	Canada United States Europe Asia Africa
Display Choices using	Drop-Down Menu
Allow "Fill-in" Choices	No
Default Value	Leave this field blank

8. Click OK. Your Site Column is now available to share and use across all lists and libraries throughout your site collection.

How It Works

Now, when users add a list item that is utilizing this site column, they are required to select a region from this list of choices. If you want update the region choices available in your site column, you can return to the site column gallery to edit your column. In addition to the previous selection options, you also see a new checkbox that allows you to update all lists and libraries using this site column, so that they include your changes.

Thus, you can update a large number of lists to accommodate a change in your organization from one single location. As you accumulate more and more lists and libraries, this valuable feature becomes more powerful and offers great time savings.

You may have noticed that the Create Column screen for the site column you created in the previous example offered additional choices for column type. These included:

- Full HTML content with formatting and constraints for publishing
- Image with formatting and constraints for publishing
- Hyperlink with formatting and constraints for publishing
- Summary Links data
- Rich media data for publishing

These columns are for the Publishing capabilities of SharePoint Server, which will be explored as part of Chapter 13. In addition, you will notice that you cannot create site columns based on External data. This option is only available on list-centric columns.

TRY IT OUT Add a Site Column to a List

The previous example guided you through creating a new site column. You can now use this site column on any list or library in your site collection. This saves you the time and energy required to recreate list-centric columns. The following example guides you through the process of attaching a site column to a list or library. Instead of creating a column on the list from scratch, you add an existing site column to the list. The steps for doing so are considerably easier, and future updates to the column properties can be streamlined and rolled out to all lists from a single location.

As you add site columns to a list, they become fields that users are required to fill out as they add list items. Most organizations like to enforce a standard set of required items that users must complete on lists and libraries, such as Owner or Status. Based on this methodology, an organization can create a site column for each type of information it wants to enforce and then reuse this column on all lists and libraries throughout the site collection. This greatly reduces the amount of maintenance.

1. From the main page of your Project Gros Morne site, select the Shared Documents library from the side navigation.
2. Click the Library tab on the Ribbon.
3. Select the Library Settings menu option. You will be redirected to the Library Settings page.
4. Scroll to the Columns section of the page.
5. Select the option to Add from existing site columns. You will be redirected to the Add Columns from Site Columns page, as shown in Figure 4-17.

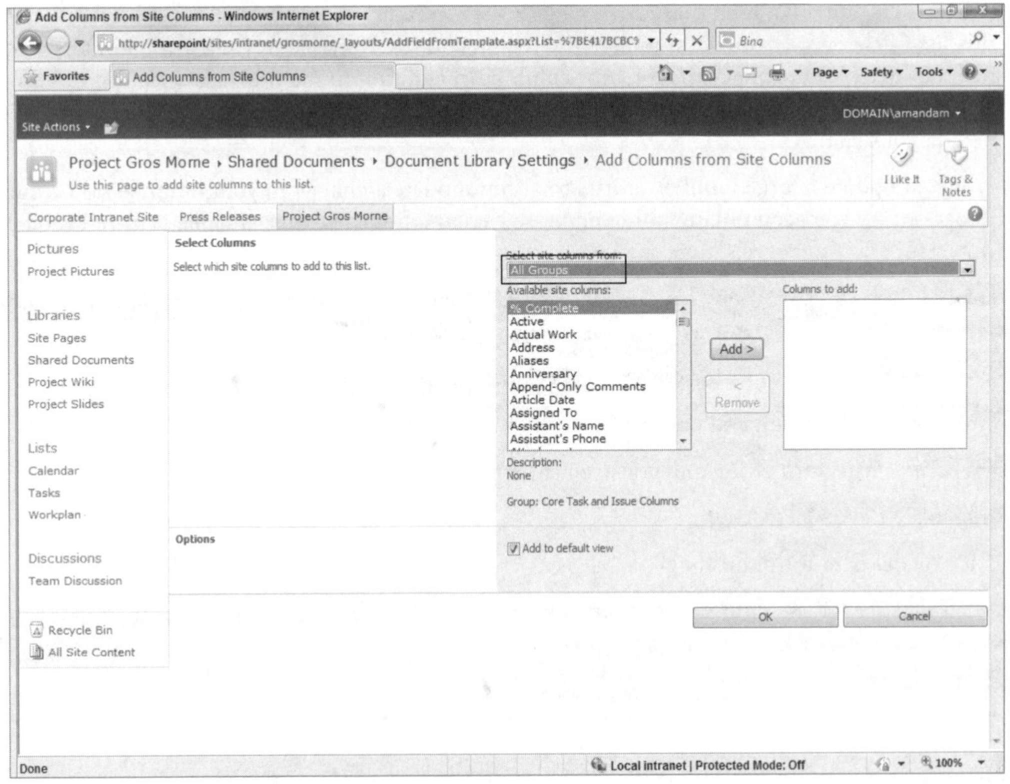

FIGURE 4-17

6. Select the Corporate Columns group from the "Select site columns from" drop-down.

7. Select the Region field and click the Add button.
8. Click OK.

Now when you edit the properties of an existing file within the Shared Documents library, you will see the Region column appear as a required value.

When to Use a List-Centric Column versus a Site Column

Now that you can create list-centric columns and site columns, it's important to understand when to use each. Although it's tempting to create a site column for everything and thus make it accessible to everyone, remember the following:

- **List-centric columns:** Some column types are only relevant for a specific list and only clutter the site column gallery for all other users and usage scenarios. For example, a software development team's issue list may have a column that tracks whether a client called about an application bug or feature request and that column isn't appropriate for any other list or site. Or, a column may contain important data that should not be shared with the entire organization, such as manually entered items or data from an external business system. In either of these cases, it's more appropriate to create a column that is attached to a single list.
- **Site columns:** These are more appropriate for information that you want to associate a column with multiple lists. You would use a site column to ensure that there is consistency in how a column is configured. Because you create the column once and it's placed in a central gallery for others to reuse, you save time and effort.

NOTE *Global elements, such as workflow templates and content types also use site columns. This is discussed in later chapters of this book.*

CREATING AND CUSTOMIZING VIEWS

In Chapters 2 and 3, you read how both lists and libraries can contain views. A *view* basically displays the information about a list in different ways. Some views display all the items in the list, while others show specific items based on their properties or metadata values. Every list has at least one view, and SharePoint 2010 offers six view types: standard, datasheet, calendar, Gantt, Access, and SharePoint Designer. You can customize these SharePoint views to quickly find relevant information. Imagine opening the telephone book and having it display only the numbers that are relevant to you. That's the type of flexibility you have with a custom view. The following examples guide you through the basics of setting up the views available with SharePoint.

This section goes deeper into what views are. You learn the different types of views as well as how to use them effectively:

- You start by setting up the standard view. The Try It Out that accompanies this section also shows how to select a view, once you create it. The method for displaying a view is the same regardless of the type of view that you create. Therefore, the rest of this chapter assumes that you'll use one of these methods whenever you select a view for a list.

- You then work your way through setting up a Gantt, calendar, and datasheet view as well as how to create a view based on an existing view. All these views are configured directly through your browser.
- You learn how to work with an Access view, which essentially lets you combine the best aspects of SharePoint and Microsoft Access.
- You will learn how to create a SharePoint Designer view, which allows for more flexible choices in how data is presented.

Working with the Standard View

Because the standard view is the most common view type and because it has so many elements, this section details those elements. You then get an opportunity to create a standard view in a Try It Out.

- **View Name:** The name that is displayed in a drop-down menu of views associated with each list. When specifying a view name, be specific so that users can clearly identify the unique nature of each view. For example, "Grouped By Status" communicates that all items are grouped together based on their status values. It is also recommended that you be concise with your naming, as longer names will not fit into the view drop-down as easily as shorter names.
- **Default View Selection:** Defines the default view for a list. This view appears first whenever a user visits the specific list or library.
- **View Audience:** When you create a view, you can make it either a personal or public view. A personal view is only available to its creator in the drop-down list of views. However, it does not have any specific security applied to it. Personal views are ideal if your list is for administration purposes and of no value to others. All users can see a shared view in the View selection drop-down associated with a list.
- **Column Selection:** You must select which columns are displayed in your view and specify their relative positions from the left. When you specify the position of a single column, all other columns automatically adjust their position.
- **Sort Order:** You can select up to two columns by which items in the list are sorted. Sort order can either be ascending (A to Z) or descending (Z to A).
- **Filter:** You can customize a view by defining the items that are displayed, based on specific column values or properties. You first select a column from the drop-down list and specify a rule so that only items that meet your criteria are displayed in the view. You can add up to 10 filter rules for a single view.
- **Inline Editing:** You can specify whether an edit icon should be displayed within each row of the view. This makes it easier for a user to quickly update an item that exists within a

list. When you click on the Edit Icon, any editable fields within the view will be enabled. An example of this is displayed within Figure 4-18.

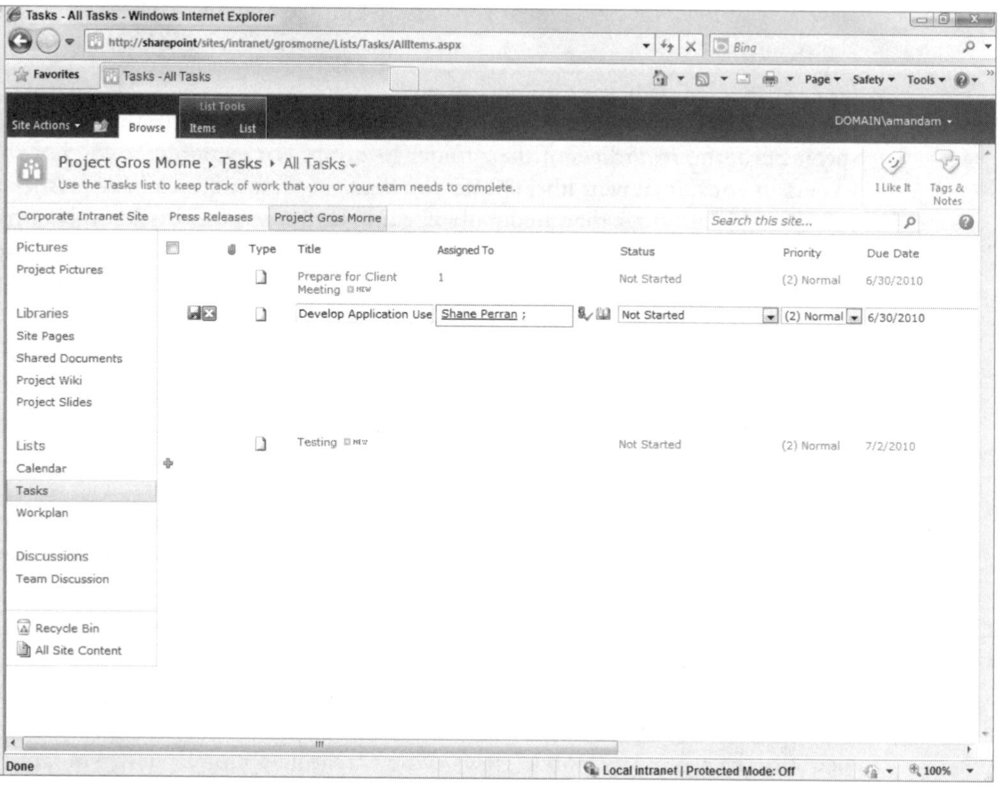

FIGURE 4-18

- **Tabular View:** You can specify whether checkboxes should be enabled on the view. When you allow checkboxes on a view, users can select multiple items to perform bulk actions such as Delete or Check Out.
- **Group By:** Because views can quite often contain a large amount of information, SharePoint allows you to group up to two columns of similar items together. The first column acts as a parent item and the second as a child of the parent. For example, you can group a task list by "Project" and then by "Assigned To." This allows users to see a report of all tasks grouped first by the project name and then by each person to whom the tasks are assigned.
- **Totals:** For numerical columns, it's beneficial to display total values for all your items. These might be the sum, average, or standard deviation of all items in a view or group. For other columns, the total value is useful to display the number of items in a view or group by selecting Count.

- **Style:** Depending on your presentation requirements, you can select a style for your view. For example, you may select "Newsletter, No Lines" for a plain view of items in a list, or "Boxed" to display items in a series of rectangular boxes. Take a few minutes to try out each view style so that you can familiarize yourself with the options that are the most appropriate choice for your views.
- **Folders:** In a list or library, folders organize items or documents. However, you may not want to show folders for a particular view. Instead, you can show items that meet specific criteria, regardless of their folder location. For example, if you have 10 layers of folders in your document library and you want to view all documents associated with a specific project, rather than manually clicking through the various levels of folders, you can create a custom view that displays items with no folders that gives a complete listing of all documents that meet your criteria in a single level. No additional clicks are required.
- **Item Limit:** For performance reasons, you commonly may only want to display a specific number of items; for example, it's not very efficient to display 10,000 documents in a single view, but groups of 30 may be more beneficial. In fact, the all items view for most lists display items in groups of 30 by default. In other cases, you may want to limit the number of items to a goal number and display them to meet a criterion. For example, you may want to show the last 25 documents that have been added to a library. You first sort the view by either the created or modified date in descending order. You then specify the limit for the view to be 25 items.
- **Mobile:** When creating or editing a view, you can select whether it is enabled for mobile access. A mobile view is one that is suitable for access from a device such as a cell phone or PDA. Many of the user interface elements, such as tables and images that would typically be seen via a standard browser, are left out of these views. Only views that are public views can be created as mobile views. When creating a mobile view, you are given an option to limit the number of items that are displayed. Because mobile devices typically have smaller screens, it is recommended that you use a smaller value. By default, this value is 3.

TRY IT OUT Create a Standard View

By sorting, filtering, and grouping the columns of metadata, SharePoint can display the contents of a list in a personalized way, one that is directly relevant to the information you want to see. This is particularly useful when you have lists shared across an organization, or when you have large lists. For this Try It Out, you will sort items in the project tasks list by their due date so that items appear in the order in which they need to be responded to. In addition, you create the view with a special filter that will only display items assigned to the current user.

1. From the main page of your Project Gros Morne site, select the Workplan list from the side navigation.
2. Click the List tab on the Ribbon.
3. Select the Create View menu option. You will be redirected to the Create View page, where a choice of view types will be displayed, as shown in Figure 4-19.
4. Select Standard View. The page will refresh to display options relevant to a standard view.

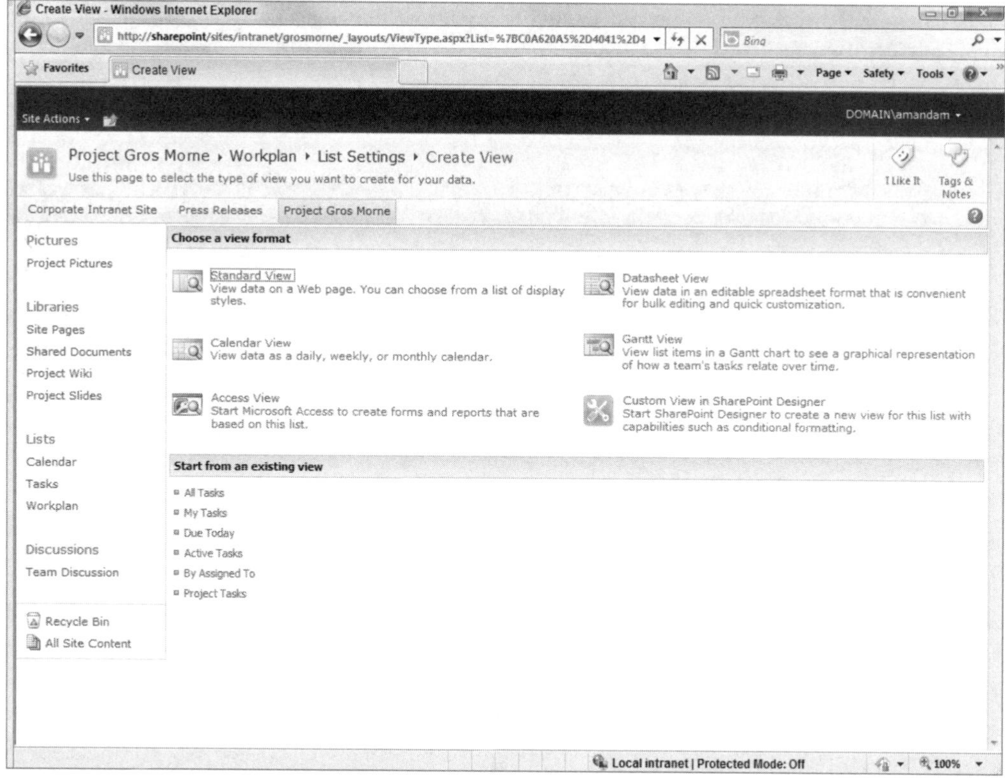

FIGURE 4-19

5. Define the view as follows:

VIEW PROPERTY	VALUE
View Name	My Upcoming Tasks
Make this the default view	No
View Audience	Create a Public View
Columns	Attachments Title (linked to item with edit menu) Start Date Due Date % Complete
Sort	Due Date (Show items in ascending order)
Filter (Show Items only when the following values are true)	Assigned to is equal to [me]
Inline Editing	Enabled

6. Click the OK button. You will be redirected to a page displaying your new view, as shown in Figure 4-20.

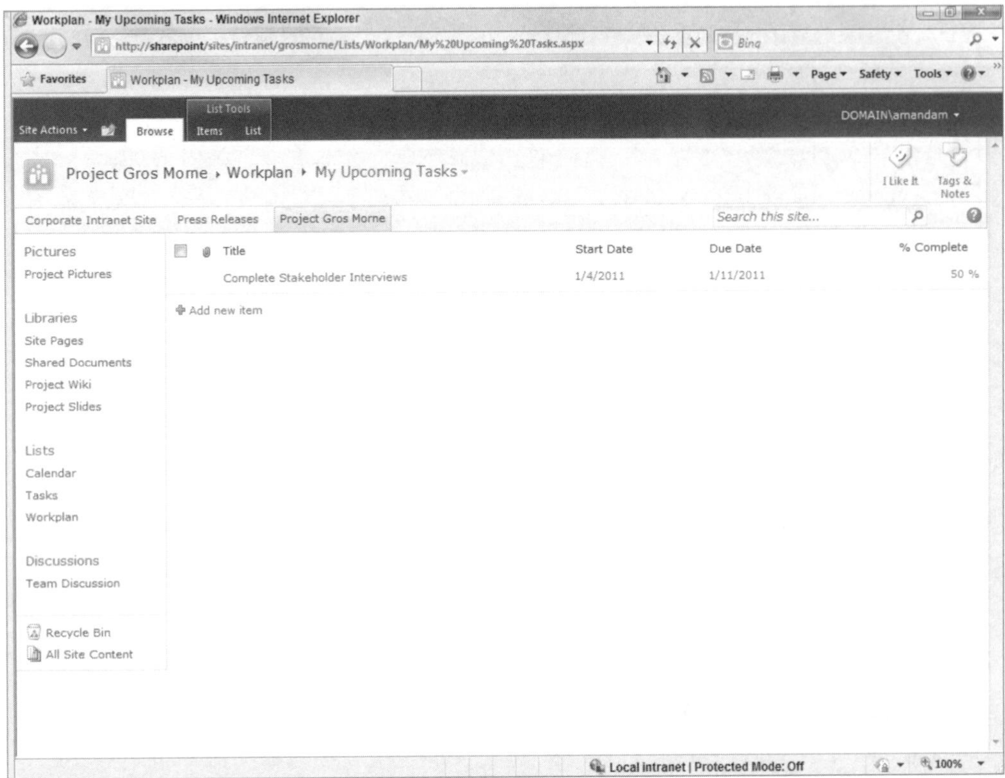

FIGURE 4-20

How It Works

In the preceding example, you created a custom view that only displayed items assigned to the current user. This was achieved by using a special property on the filter, known as [me] on the Assigned to column. Whenever a column is of the Person or Group type, you can personalize the view by using the [me] property and only the items in the list where the current user's name is selected within the Person or Group field will be displayed. In addition to filtering the view, you specified a sort order that displays items according to their due date. This is practical since users will see the items that are due the soonest at the very top of their list. This results in a sense of priority for the items that must be completed first.

Setting Up a Gantt, Calendar, or Datasheet View

This section deals with setting up three specialized views that SharePoint has to offer:

➤ **Gantt view:** This view displays a graphical representation of tasks and how they are progressing over time. It gives you a clear picture of how a project or task is evolving at a glance, and helps you easily identity bottlenecks in the process. We explored this view as it was associated with the Project Tasks within Chapter 2. However, this view type can be used on any list or library type as long as there is date-based information to reference. For many small teams, the Gantt chart view is the ideal solution for managing and reporting a project. This particular view is a big hit with project and resource managers who need to track how tasks are evolving and give updated status reports to an executive team.

- **Calendar view:** Allows you to create a daily, weekly, or monthly view of your data. We reviewed this view in Chapter 2 as it was associated with the Calendar list type. However, a calendar view can be created on any list or library.
- **Datasheet view:** This view gives you a spreadsheet-like view of your data, very similar to an Excel spreadsheet. This view is particularly useful when you want to customize multiple columns of data. We explored updating a datasheet view in Chapter 3.

In addition to showing you how to set up these views, this section also has a Try It Out that shows you how to create a view based on an existing view. This is particularly useful when you have columns that are similar but with slightly different requirements.

TRY IT OUT Create a Gantt View

When configuring a Gantt view, you must select a start and end date. Based on this elapsed time and the percentage of the task complete, SharePoint can calculate a graphical representation of how things are progressing. The following steps enable you to get starting using the Gantt view.

1. From the main page of your project team site, select the Tasks list from the side navigation bar.
2. Select the Create View menu option from the List tab of the Ribbon.
3. Select the Gantt View type. You will be redirected to the Create View page.
4. Define the view as follows:

VIEW PROPERTY	VALUE
View Name	Task Tracking
Make this the default view	No
View Audience	Create a Public View
Columns	Attachments Title (linked to item with edit menu) Start Date Due Date % Complete

5. For the Gantt Columns section, which appears as shown in Figure 4-21, enter the values as follows:

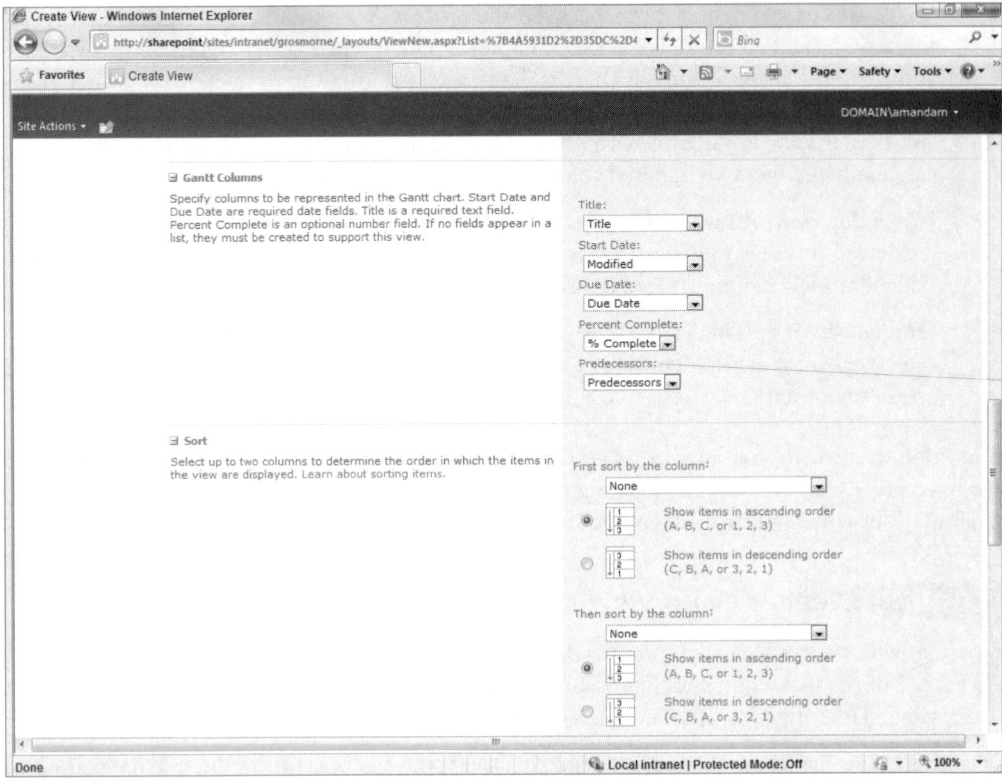

FIGURE 4-21

GANTT COLUMN	VALUE
Title	Title
Start Date	Start Date
Due Date	Due Date
Percent Complete	% Complete
Predecessors	Predecessors

6. Click the OK button to complete the view. You will be directed to a page displaying the new view.

TRY IT OUT Create a Calendar View

This view allows you to move back and forth between months, add tasks to your calendar, and even connect your calendar to Outlook, a familiar interface for managing calendars. The following steps walk you through setting up the calendar view on your Tasks list.

1. From your Tasks list, select the Create View option from the Ribbon.
2. Select the Calendar View type.

3. Define the view as follows:

VIEW PROPERTY	VALUE
View Name	Task Calendar
Make this the default view	No
View Audience	Create a Public View
Time Interval (Begin)	Start Date
Time Interval (End)	Due Date
Month View Title	Title
Week View Title	Title
Week View Sub Heading	% Complete
Day View Title	Title
Day View Sub Heading	% Complete
Default Scope	Week

4. Click OK to complete the view. You will be directed to a page displaying the new view. An example is shown in Figure 4-22.

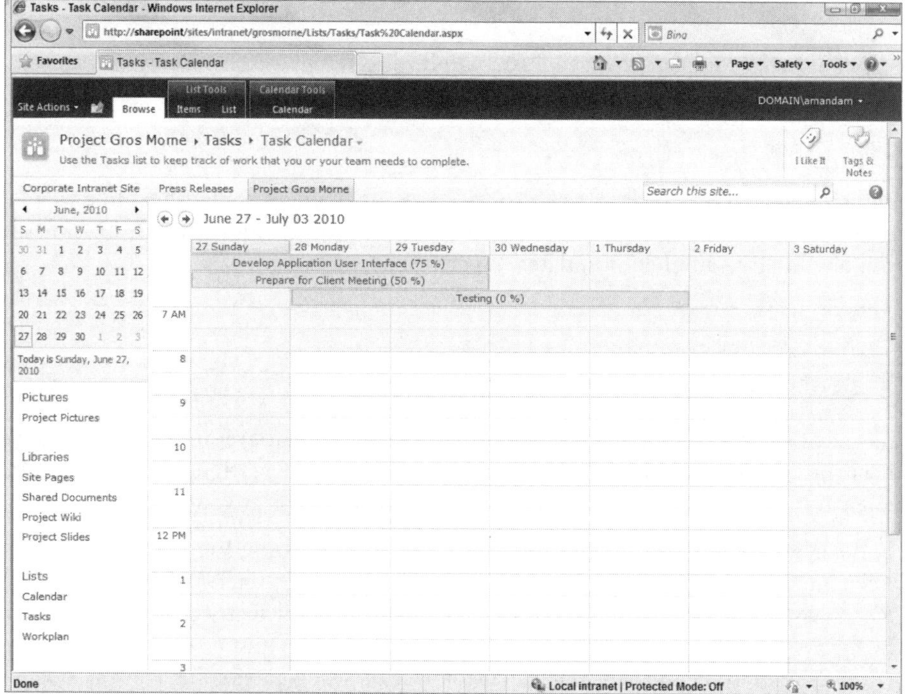

FIGURE 4-22

TRY IT OUT Create a Datasheet View

The datasheet view gives you a spreadsheet view much like Excel but allows for much easier and faster mass updates and data customization.

1. From your Tasks list, select the Create View option from the Ribbon.
2. Select the Datasheet View type.
3. Define the view as follows:

VIEW PROPERTY	VALUE
View Name	Task Datasheet
Make this the default view	No
View Audience	Create a Public View
Columns	Attachments Type Title Assigned To Status Priority Due Date % Complete

4. Click the OK button to complete the view. You will be directed to a page displaying the new view. An example is shown in Figure 4-23.

How It Works

After creating and selecting your datasheet view, you are presented with a spreadsheet-like view of your list's data. With this view, you can update multiple columns at the same time. This is a big timesaver, particularly if you have a large number of updates to perform.

TRY IT OUT Create a View Based on an Existing View

In some situations, a single list or library may contain multiple views that are similar but have slight differences to meet specific information requirements. Instead of creating each new view from scratch, you can use a particular view as a starting point and slightly alter it to meet your needs.

Each time you add a new view to a list, it appears in the Start from Existing View section in the Create View window. Selecting one of these views generates a view based on the filtering, sorting, and metadata columns of the existing view. This saves you time and helps you efficiently customize views to meet your needs. By creating a starting point, you can reuse this view to minimize your efforts for all remaining views for the list. You can also think of customization using an existing view as a way to create structure because it acts as a template for displaying common components.

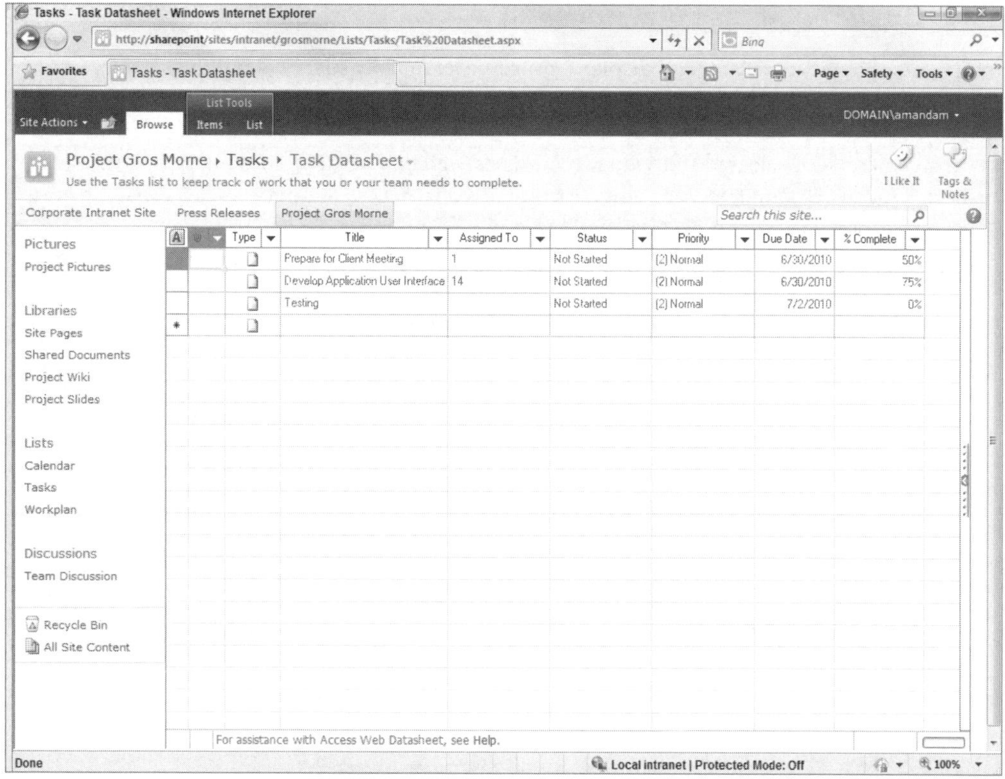

FIGURE 4-23

1. From your Tasks list, select the Create View option from the Ribbon.
2. Below the listed view types is the Start from Existing View heading with any views currently available for your list. Select an existing view from which to start building your custom view. For this example, select the Tasks Tracking view.
3. You will then need to specify a view name as well as define any unique properties of the view that did not exist in the previous view. For example, select the option to Filter based on tasks that are assigned to the current user using the method described in "Create a Standard View."
4. Click OK to complete the view.

Working with Access Views

SharePoint offers some great functionality for working with Microsoft Access. As discussed in Chapter 2, you can now link many of the lists in SharePoint to an Access database. This makes offline data available and allows you to synchronize data. In addition, Access provides reports and forms that are not available using a browser. By creating an Access view for a list, you gain all the advantages of Access's reporting functionality as well as having information stored in a central secured online store such as SharePoint.

TRY IT OUT Create an Access View for a List

In this example, you give the interface that displays your SharePoint lists more flexibility and options by creating an Access view. To do so, you export data from the list to an Access database, which creates a more advanced view for entering and updating the data. This example uses the Split Form view so that users can see details of selected individual records as well as update items simply by typing into the datasheet. Once you complete your edits, a copy of your Access database is saved back to the SharePoint site so that other users can access the created views and reports.

1. From your Tasks list, select the Create View option from the Ribbon.
2. Select the Access View type. Access will open on your computer.
3. You will be prompted for a save location for the views. Select a location on your local computer.
4. You will then be asked to specify the type of view that you wish to create. Select the Split Form view type, as shown in Figure 4-24.

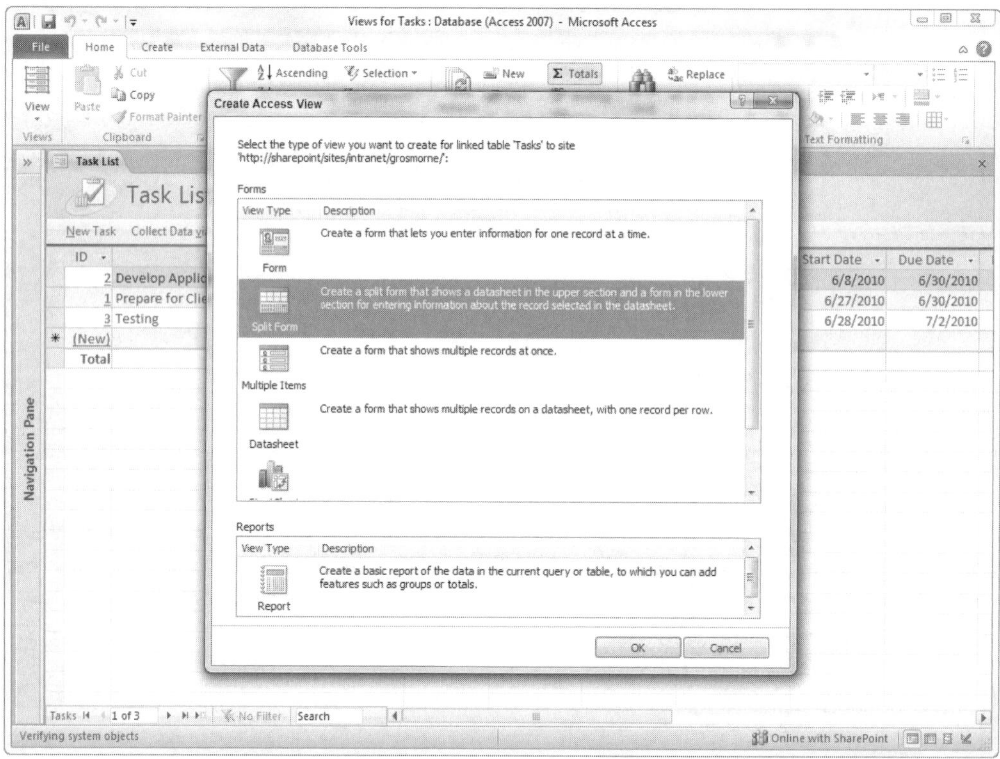

FIGURE 4-24

5. Click OK. An Access view opens with a single item list view form and a datasheet view. You can enter data into the datasheet view or form view.

6. When you finish entering or viewing your data, click the Publish to SharePoint Site button just below the top menu bar of the Access application, as shown in Figure 4-25. If this is your first time saving the Access database back to SharePoint, you are requested to identify a save location for the database.

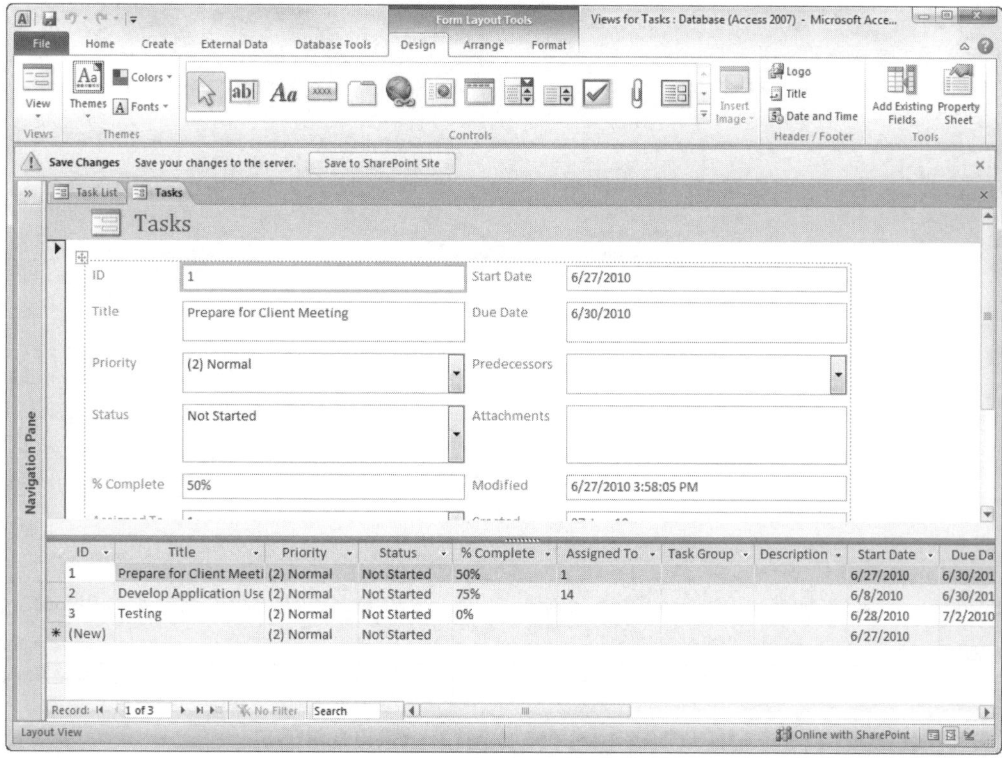

FIGURE 4-25

TRY IT OUT Select a View from a List

In the previous examples, you have created a number of custom views. In this example, you will select a view that you have created from your Task list. This same process will apply for switching views on all list types.

1. From your Tasks list, click the List tab on the Ribbon.
2. Expand the drop-down below Current View in the Manage Views section, as shown in Figure 4-26.
3. Select the view of your choice. The page will be refreshed and your selected view will be displayed.

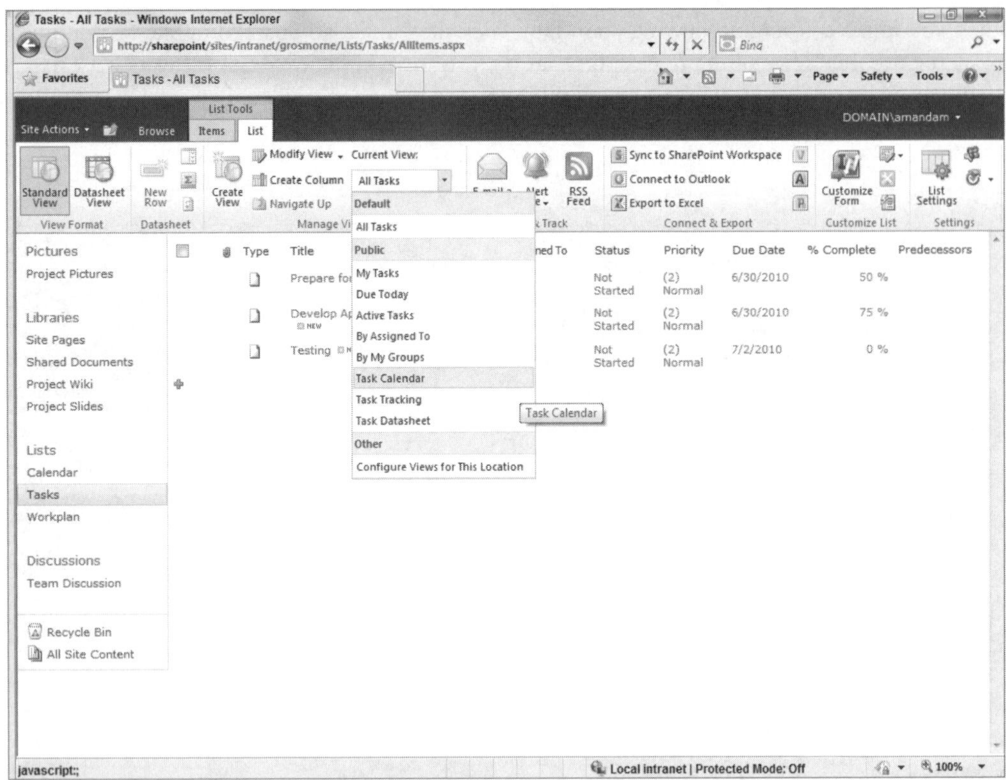

FIGURE 4-26

WORKING WITH CUSTOM LISTS AND LIBRARIES

Chapter 2 detailed the various SharePoint list templates, which are ideal for creating a list that you want to modify or customize to suit your team's or your individual needs. However, you may need to create a list where no existing template can serve as a starting point. This, of course, involves creating a custom list and defining all the columns and views from scratch. This section first introduces all the basic skills you need to create a custom list, including how to create a list and then finally how to make that list a template so that you don't have to repeat work.

Once you have list customization basics under your belt, you learn about versioning items in SharePoint so that you can modify either list items or documents, and save each updated item as a specific version. Certain customization options are unique to document library environments and do not apply to a list in exactly the same way. Finally, you will learn how associate a custom document template with a library. This helps standardize the documents that your company uses to create various memos, procedures, and processes.

Custom List Basics

As you create a column within a list or library, think about what information users need about the item or how they may need to view the item. For example, if you are responsible for creating a centralized listing of projects, you may ask users the following questions:

- What are the active projects on which the organization is working?
- Are the projects running on a schedule?
- Who are the primary contacts or project managers associated with each project?
- What is the project background, and what are the primary deliverables from the project team?
- Who is the client for whom the project is being completed?

Using the information from these questions, you can accurately create a custom list featuring the appropriate columns and views. In cases where you intend to have multiple lists for the same subject matter within an organization, you should plan the details out in the beginning, create the list, and then save the list as a template for reuse by others. This reduces the amount of repetitive work you or your team will need to perform.

The following series of Try It Outs illustrate how to work with a custom list or library. In the first Try It Out, you create a custom list with specific columns to track a project. The second Try It Out shows you how to save the list or library as a template so that others can use your work. Finally, in the last Try It Out, you see how to save the template to a gallery so that others can view and use it.

TRY IT OUT Create a Custom List

In this example, you create a custom list to represent all the projects for an organization. Based on your meetings with Project Management Office (PMO), you determine that you must implement a project list containing the columns for the project status, due date, project manager, project summary, and client. To effectively track project information, the PMO must have this information on active projects. Clicking the project name should make more detailed information on the summary available.

To meet these requirements, you create a list based on the Custom List template, which has just a single column, called Title. To this, you must add five list-centric columns. In real life, you might want to make some of these site columns so that other lists and sites could use these columns. However, for simplicity's sake, the example uses the list column model.

Next, you create a custom view on your list based on the information requirements of your stakeholders. Because the PMO requested a listing of all active projects, you will create a filtered view to show projects with a project status value of In Progress. You will then include information that is concise enough for the user to consume easily to gain a high-level understanding of the project, which in this case is the Project Manager, Client, and Due Date. Because the information in the Project Summary tends to be lengthy, you omit it from the initial view.

1. From the main page of your Corporate Intranet Site, select the More Options item from the Site Actions menu. The Create window will appear.
2. Select the Lists filter from the left side of the window and select Custom List.
3. Select the More Options button.
4. Enter Projects for the list name and provide a description.
5. Select Yes for display on the Quick Launch Toolbar.
6. Click the Create button to continue. Your list is created with a single column for title.

7. From the List tab of the Ribbon, select List Settings.
8. From the Columns section, select the Create Column link. The Create Column window appears, similar to what is shown in Figure 4-1.
9. Enter the following details for your column:

PROPERTY	DETAILS
Name	Project Status
Column Type	Choice
Description	Please specify the current status of your project
Require That This Column Contains Information	Yes
Choice Values	Not Started In Progress Complete Halted
Display Choices Using	Radio buttons
Default Value	Leave blank

10. Click OK to create your column.
11. Create another column using the same steps described previously based on the following settings:

PROPERTY	DETAILS
Name	Project Due Date
Column Type	Date and time
Description	Please enter the date your project is scheduled to be complete.
Require That This Column Contains Information	Yes
Date and Time Format	Date only
Default Value	(none)

12. Click OK to create your column.
13. Create another column using the same steps described previously based on the following settings:

PROPERTY	DETAILS
Name	Project Manager
Column Type	Person or group

PROPERTY	DETAILS
Description	Please specify the project manager for this project.
Require That This Column Contains Information	Yes
Allow Multiple Sections	No
Allow Selection of	People only
Choose From	All users
Show Field	Name (with presence)

14. Click OK to create your column.
15. Create another column using the same steps described previously based on the following settings:

PROPERTY	DETAILS
Name	Project Summary
Column Type	Multiple Lines of Text
Description	Describe the project by providing some background information and outlining the deliverables.
Require That This Column Contains Information	Yes
Number of lines for editing	25
Type of text to allow	Enhanced Rich Text
Append Changes to Existing Text	No

16. Click OK to create your column.
17. Create another column using the same steps described previously based on the following settings:

PROPERTY	DETAILS
Name	Client
Column Type	Choice
Description	Specify the client's name
Require That This Column Contains Information	Yes
Choice Values	Customer A Customer B Customer C

continues

(continued)

PROPERTY	DETAILS
Display Choices Using	Drop-down menu
Default Value	Leave blank

18. Click OK to create your column.
19. From the Views section, click the link to create a new view.
20. Select Standard View.
21. Specify the following details for your view:

PROPERTY	DETAILS
View Name	Active Projects
Audience	Create a Public View
Display Columns and Order	Select to display the columns in the following order: Attachments Title (linked to item with Edit menu) Project Manager Project Due Date Client
Sort	Project Due Date
Filter	Show items when Project Status is equal to In Progress
Group By	None

22. Click OK to create your view.

TRY IT OUT Save a List as a Template

Once your list is complete, members of your organization can use it. You may even want to save the list as a template so that other teams can use it as a starting point in the future rather than repeating all the steps you took to create this list in the last Try It Out. Follow these steps to save a list or library as a template.

1. From your Projects list created in the previous Try It Out, select List Settings from the Lists tab of the Ribbon. You will be redirected to the Lists Settings page.

2. From the Permissions and Management group of links, select the option to Save list as template. The Save as Template page will appear as shown in Figure 4-27.

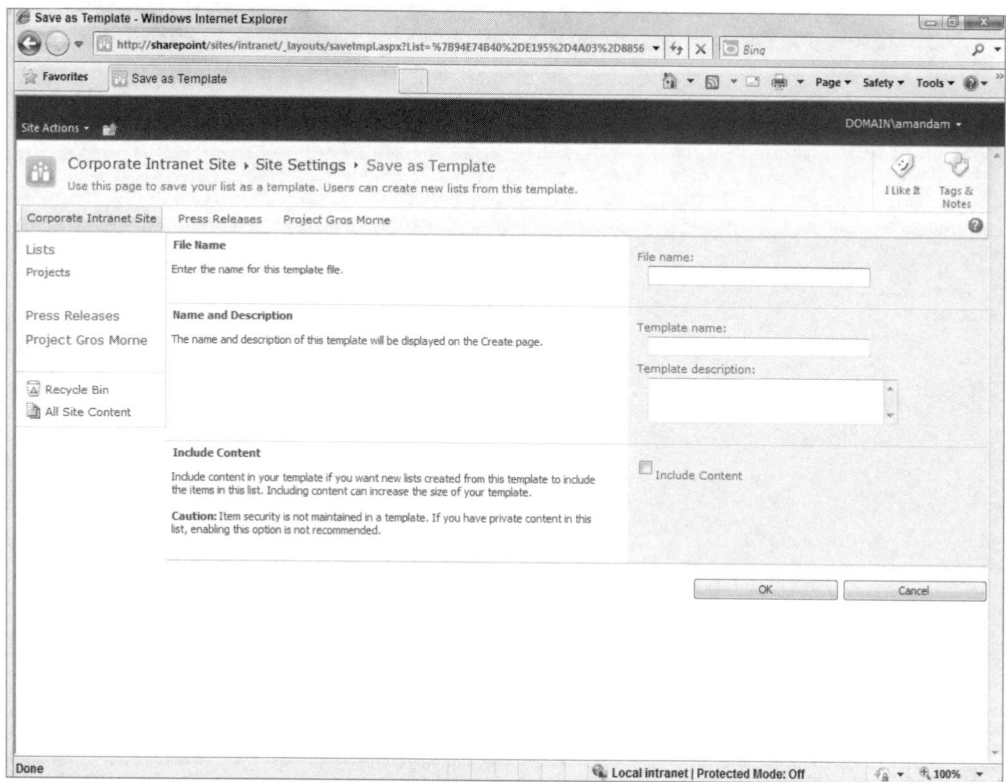

FIGURE 4-27

3. Complete the templates properties as follows:

PROPERTY	VALUE
File name	Projects
Template name	Project Listing
Template description	Centralized list template for tracking project status. Includes Active Projects view.
Include Content	Do not select

4. Click OK to create your template. You will receive a message confirming that the operation has completed successfully. Your template will be saved in the central list gallery for your site collection. The list will now appear to users when creating new lists on the list creation page, as shown in Figure 4-28.

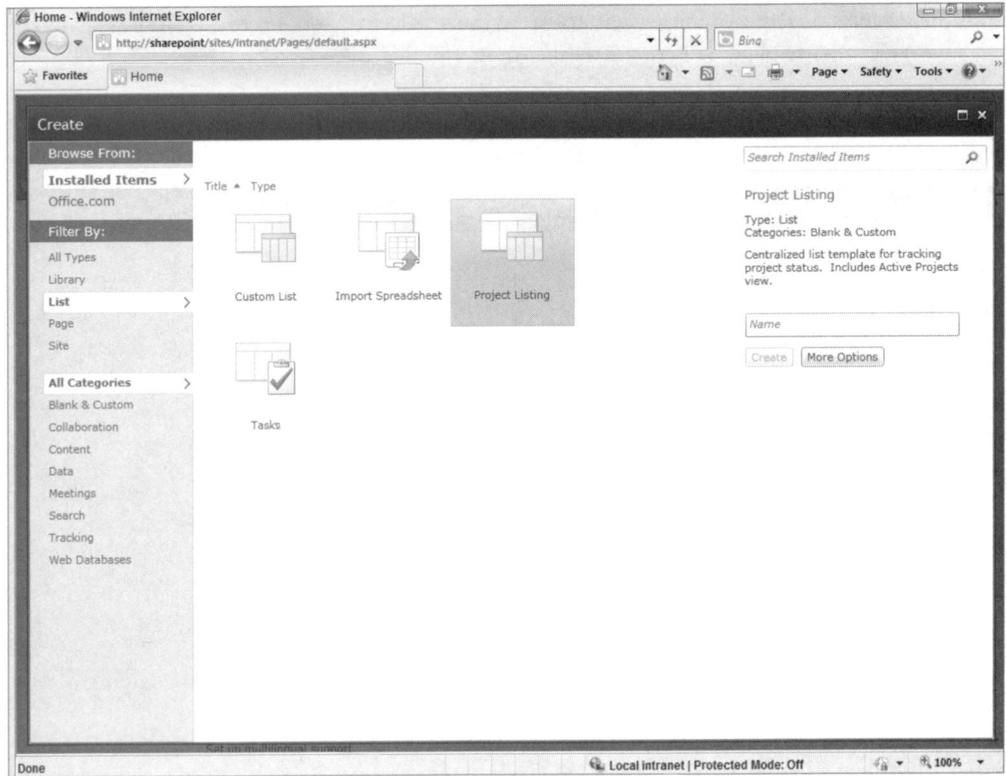

FIGURE 4-28

Managing Version Control

As briefly explored in Chapter 3, items in SharePoint can be *versioned*. This means that as you modify either list items or documents, SharePoint saves each iteration as a specific version. This allows users to revisit a previous version of an item or even to track how something changes over time. To make this functionality available, you must enable versioning on the list or library.

Certain customization options are unique to a document library environment and do not apply in exactly the same way to a list. In Chapter 3, when you enabled the document version history creation on the *library*, you had the following choices for how to store the versions:

- **Major version:** This is considered the same as a published version of a document. Over the life of a key organizational document, a site admin is more concerned with a previous major version of a document rather than the minor versions that show specific iterations of the document's creation or modification. You can limit the number of major versions that are retained. This is useful, particularly for libraries, where documents are fairly large in size and change very seldom.

- **Minor version:** This is an iteration of the document while in draft mode. This is helpful for scenarios where many people must do work on a document before it is published to the entire organization. Each time a user works on the document and saves it, SharePoint creates a new minor version. However, for long-term editing purposes, the minor versions are not as relevant.
- **Check in and check out:** Instead of making this feature optional for users, you can require that all documents be checked out before users can edit them. This provides a greater level of control in the editing process.

You can enable versions on lists as well as document libraries. However in a list, there is no concept of major and minor versions.

Managing Document Templates

When you create a document library, you are asked to select the document template that will be associated with the library by default. An example of this is shown later in Figure 4-29. This association does not affect what type of documents you can store in a library but instead determines the type of file that is created when a user clicks the New button on the Document Library toolbar. The choice of templates to select from includes:

- None
- Microsoft Word 97-2003 document
- Microsoft Excel 97-2003 spreadsheet
- Microsoft PowerPoint 97-2003 presentation
- Microsoft Word document
- Microsoft Excel document
- Microsoft PowerPoint presentation
- Microsoft OneNote 2010 Notebook
- Microsoft SharePoint Designer Web page
- Basic page
- Web Part page

When customizing a SharePoint site, the goal is to implement elements that encourage reuse and standardization. If you want to use a document library to store sales presentations, it's a good idea to associate the standard organizational template for sales presentations with the library so that the New button generates a blank presentation that users can then customize and use for their own purposes.

In cases where you have a document, such as a Word file containing your company's logo or letterhead, you may want to use that as the default document template. Another common example is an Excel spreadsheet containing the fields and calculations needed for a report that users often create when in the document library.

You have three ways to associate a custom document template with a document library:

- **Edit the template directly and save the changes:** This is most appropriate where an existing template already exists. However, it's not practical if you already have a standard organizational template available.
- **Upload the template to a specific location and change the URL:** In this case, you change the URL for the document library template to point to the new location. This is appropriate if you have a single location with multiple templates already, or you may want to have the document template associated with more than one document library. This method is explored in the next Try It Out.
- **Give your template the filename of template.doc and upload it to the Forms folder of the document library:** When you do this, you are prompted to overwrite the existing template. This is suitable for situations where you have an existing template, but you only want to associate it with a single document library.
- **Create a custom content type and associate your template with the content type:** This is a preferred method in many scenarios. which we will review in detail in Chapter 6.

TRY IT OUT Associate a Custom Document Template with a Library by Changing the URL

1. From the main page of the Project Gros Morne site, select All Site Content from the side navigation.
2. Click on the Site Assets link.
3. Click the Add document link. The Upload Document dialog appears.
4. Click the Browse button and navigate to the location of the resource files for this chapter.
5. When the `AWTemplate.docx` file is selected, click OK to complete the upload. You will be returned to the Site Assets library where your file will be listed.
6. Right-click on the AWTemplate file, as shown in Figure 4-29, and select the Copy Shortcut link.
7. Click on the Shared Documents library from the side navigation bar.
8. Select Library Settings from the Ribbon.
9. Select the Advanced Settings link. You will be redirected to the Advanced Settings page, as shown in Figure 4-30.
10. Update the Template URL field by clearing out the current value and pasting (Ctrl+V) the URL you copied in step 6.
11. Click OK.
12. Return to the shared documents library and create a new document using the method described in Chapter 3. You will notice that the file will open with a customized template.

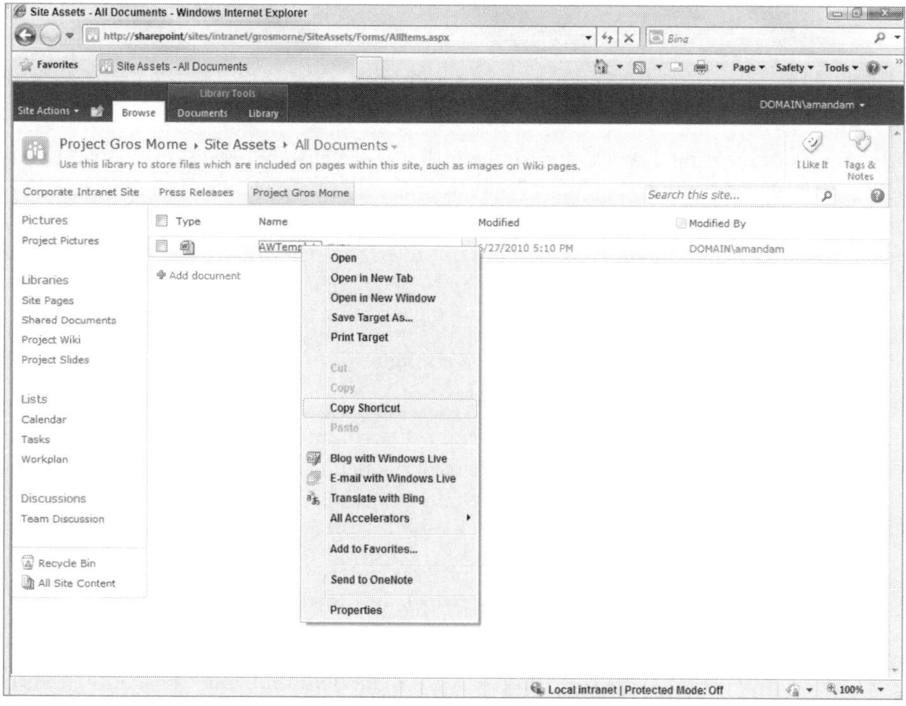

FIGURE 4-29

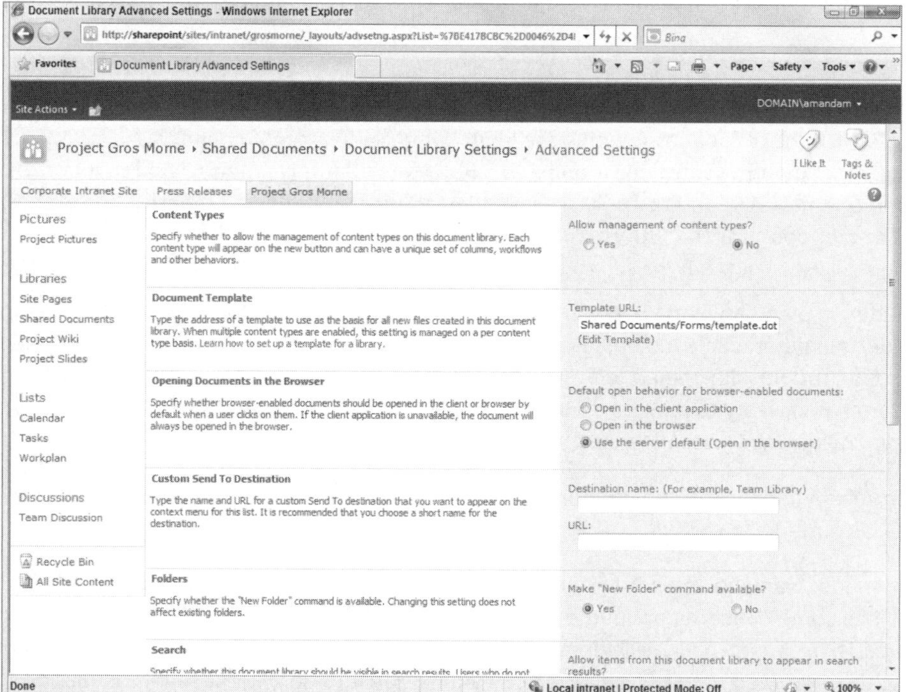

FIGURE 4-30

SUMMARY

This chapter discussed how to customize column types and views that are associated with lists and libraries. From it, you learned the following:

- The advantages of creating a work environment that more closely reflects the users' actual business activities. By customizing SharePoint to operate in accordance with common business processes, users can focus more on their specific work duties rather than on technology. However, it is always important to remember not to overcustomize. You should only implement changes that offer value to the business and operational environment.
- The types of columns that you can create in SharePoint and their specific configuration alternatives. Understanding what is possible from a configuration perspective is a key element in recognizing the appropriate customization approach.
- The difference between a list-centric column and a site column. Unlike list-centric columns that you must manually create on every single list in which they appear, site columns are stored in a central gallery on a SharePoint site and are available for use on all lists and libraries of the current site and each site below it.
- The various view types in SharePoint and the process for creating each. This included some special view types in SharePoint, such as the Gantt view and Access views, which help provide a greater level of presentation to a standard SharePoint list.
- The importance of working with your stakeholders to gain an understanding of their specific needs for information on specific subject areas. You then discovered how you can take all the concepts covered in this chapter to create a completely customized list in SharePoint, composed of multiple custom columns and a custom view that can address those needs.

EXERCISES

You've just been assigned the task of customizing the SharePoint site for your company's sales team. The team has struggled with having a central location in which to store all information related to its various opportunities, contacts, meetings, and tasks. It has had a SharePoint site for a few months; however, the team has expressed some concerns that information is too difficult to find. The following exercises focus on ways in which you need to develop the site to become a more useful tool for the sales team.

1. After conducting a planning workshop with some members of the sales team, you determine that while the sales manager wants to see all information stored in a single location, the actual sales team members struggle with seeing too much information. As a result, it takes sales team members longer than necessary to look up contact phone numbers. The sales team prefers to only see contacts from their own region. What can you do to make both groups happy?

2. Whenever a salesperson views the central list of contacts, he/she wants to see specific contacts that he/she has added. How would you accomplish that?

3. The sales manager wants to see a list of all opportunities that are in the pipeline for his staff. Because he has some concerns about the length of time certain sales staff members are taking to close their leads, he wants to visually identify leads that have the longest duration from initial point of contact to the expected date of sale. What can you suggest to help address this situation?

▶ WHAT YOU LEARNED IN THIS CHAPTER

TOPIC	KEY CONCEPTS
What is a Site Column?	A site column is a column that is defined within a central gallery and may be used within multiple lists or libraries.
The difference between major and minor versions	A major version is considered to be a published release of a document whereas minor versions typically represent a draft.
The different types of views	There are six different types of views that exist within SharePoint 2010. These include a Standard View, Datasheet View, Gantt View, Calendar View, Access View and SharePoint Designer View.

5

Working with Workflow

WHAT YOU WILL LEARN IN THIS CHAPTER:

- The definition of workflows, and basic workflow concepts
- A demonstration of out-of-the-box workflows
- How to create powerful custom workflows using SharePoint Designer 2010
- How tasks and workflow history are used in workflows
- How Office clients software such as InfoPath and Visio can be integrated with SharePoint 2010 workflows
- Troubleshooting steps and basic workflow administration processes

Business processes exist within all companies. These processes not only consist of computer interactions, but more importantly they are between individuals. SharePoint brings processes together with tasks and the people who are part of these day-to-day interactions.

Workflows are used in order to automate business processes, promoting a more efficient work experience. When they have been defined and created in SharePoint, automated workflows save time, lessen confusion, and save money.

UNDERSTANDING WORKFLOW

Before delving into the details of how to use workflows in SharePoint 2010, it is important to have a basic understanding of some of the terminology and the components that workflows are composed of. This section will introduce you to the basic building blocks of workflows. Business users can use logic to create their own applications and processes, without having to know a single line of code.

Initiating Workflows

There are four different methods you can use to start workflows, which is referred to as initiation. The first three are available options within the user interface during workflow creation, and the fourth is available from within Information Management Policy settings. Each workflow can be set up to use one or multiple methods of initiation.

- **On Creation:** The workflow is started only once, when a new item is created.
- **On Change:** The workflow is started each time an item is edited.
- **Manual Initiation:** The workflow is started manually. This entails a user clicking a Start button. The out-of-the-box workflows specify that the user who manually starts the workflow must have Edit Item permissions, and there is an option to increase the security by opting to Require Manage Lists Permissions to start the workflow.
- **Information Management Policies:** When workflows are associated with content types, information management policies can be set up at the site or library content type level. When a retention policy is defined, it can be set to initiate a workflow, relative to a date column. To set up a workflow to only be initiated based on a policy, none of the other initiation types needs to be selected. Retention policies can even be configured as repeating, if there is a need to start a workflow every 30 days.

Initiation Forms

When a workflow is set up to be started manually, it uses an initiation form. The person who makes the workflow can create predefined fields to be filled out by the person who manually starts the workflow (the initiator). When workflows are *automatically* initiated on creation or on change, there is no prompt to fill out a form.

Steps

Steps in a workflow define the order in which processes are supposed to happen. Each step can contain conditions and actions. Arrange the steps in the order in which the process should take place.

Conditions and Actions

Conditions can be thought of as rules. According to conditions that are set up, specified actions take place. Conditions are not a required component in a workflow. Actions *without* conditions in front of them will take place every time the workflow is initiated.

If the first condition is not met, then the next condition is checked. This type of logic requires an Else-If branch. When a condition is reached, and that condition is true, then its actions take place. If you've ever created rules in Microsoft Outlook, then the basic concept is similar.

Workflow Associations

Each time a workflow is created, it is associated with *something* in SharePoint. To associate a workflow is to attach it to something. Lists, libraries, content types, and even sites are all things that workflows can be associated with.

- **Content Workflows:** Content workflows are associated with specific content in SharePoint, such as a specific list or library. These are also referred to as list workflows.
- **Site Workflows:** Site workflows are not connected to any particular list or library, and these types of workflows are usually initiated manually. On a SharePoint site, click View All Site Content on the left side of the screen. The Site Workflows button is next to the Create button.
- **Reusable Workflows:** Similar to site workflows, these types of workflows are not bound to any specific list when they are initially created. Reusable workflows are created to be used multiple times and can be reused on different sites. These workflows can be connected to different lists and libraries. When a reusable workflow is created in SharePoint Designer, there is an option to pick a base content type to limit the workflow to. All content types or one particular one may be selected, such as "Announcement."

WORKING WITH WORKFLOW TEMPLATES

In SharePoint Server 2010 Enterprise, there are some very useful built-in workflows. These workflows address some common needs, such as "Approval." Workflow templates are meant to be used in a wide range of scenarios. In the previous version of SharePoint, these out-of-the-box workflows were not modifiable, but in SharePoint 2010 they can be edited and customized using SharePoint Designer 2010. In this section, you will learn about each of these workflow templates and how they are used.

NOTE *Several of the out-of-the-box workflows discussed in this chapter are only available as features in SharePoint. At the top level of a site collection, on the site settings page, click Site Collection Features. The feature called Workflows includes several of the most common workflows. Other useful workflow-related features are Three-State Workflow, Disposition Approval, and Publishing Approval Workflow. Once the features are activated, the workflows will become available within the sites.*

By default, libraries in SharePoint do not have any workflows associated with them. In the document library settings, click Workflow Settings and then Add a workflow to begin the process of associating a workflow with the library. Multiple workflows can be associated with any given list or library.

When a workflow is selected on the Add a Workflow page, it should be given a name that is applicable to its function. For example, if the documents in the library are company policies needing approval, the workflow could be named "Policy Approval."

Approval Workflow

Approval workflows are the most commonly used types of workflows in SharePoint, which is a good reason to have a useful base template. The out-of-the-box workflow called "Approval — SharePoint 2010" is easy to set up and is applicable in basic scenarios, such as when a document needs to be approved by a list of people.

The following table describes the fields to fill out when setting up an approval workflow:

FIELD NAME	FIELD TYPE	DESCRIPTION
Approvers	Person (multiple)	Pick one or more people or groups of people who will be in charge of approving the document.
Order	Choice	Choose from One at a time (serial) or All at once (parallel).
Expand Groups	Checkbox	This applies when a group of people is selected among the approvers, such as a distribution list in Active Directory. When this box is not checked, each group will be assigned one task.
Request	Text	This text will be included in the email that is automatically sent to each approver.
Due Date for All Tasks	Date	This is the final date by which all approvals must be completed. Optional.
Duration Per Task	Number	The amount of time in duration units until each assigned task is due. Optional.
Duration Units	Choice	Choose days, weeks, or months in which the task must be completed.
CC	Person	Send someone else a copy of this workflow email.
End on First Rejection	Checkbox	If any approver rejects the document, the document is marked as rejected and the workflow is stopped.
End on Document Change	Checkbox	If someone changes the original document to be approved, the document is rejected and the workflow is automatically stopped.
Enable Content Approval	Checkbox	This applies if the Document Library Settings, Versioning Settings, or Content Approval is set to Yes. If this box is checked, the workflow approval becomes seamless with the library's content approval.

TRY IT OUT Using the Approval — SharePoint 2010 Workflow

In this Try It Out, you will learn how to use the out-of-the-box Approval Workflow in SharePoint 2010. The example used here is of a company's policy management system. The company policies are documents stored in a document library in SharePoint. Each time a new policy is added, it must go through an approval process before becoming publicly visible. The pending version will be made available to only those who are approving and editing policies.

1. On your SharePoint site, click Site Actions and choose New Document Library.
2. Name the library "Policies," and click the Create button.

3. In the Ribbon's Library tab, click Library Settings.
4. In the General Settings section, click Versioning Settings.
5. In the Content Approval section, under Require content approval for submitted items, choose Yes.
6. In the Draft Item Security section, change the setting called Who Should See Draft Items in This Document Library to "Only users who can edit items."
7. Click OK.
8. Still in the Library Settings, under the Permissions and Management section, click Workflow Settings.
9. Pick the workflow called "Approval — SharePoint 2010," and name it "Policy Approval." In the Start Options section, check the box next to "Start this workflow when an item is created." Click Next.
10. In the Assign To box, type the names of two different colleagues, separated by a semicolon. Leave the default order of "One at a time (Serial)."
11. In the Request box, type **"Please review this document, and approve if applicable."** Set the duration to two days. Figure 5-1 shows an example of what this screen looks like so far.

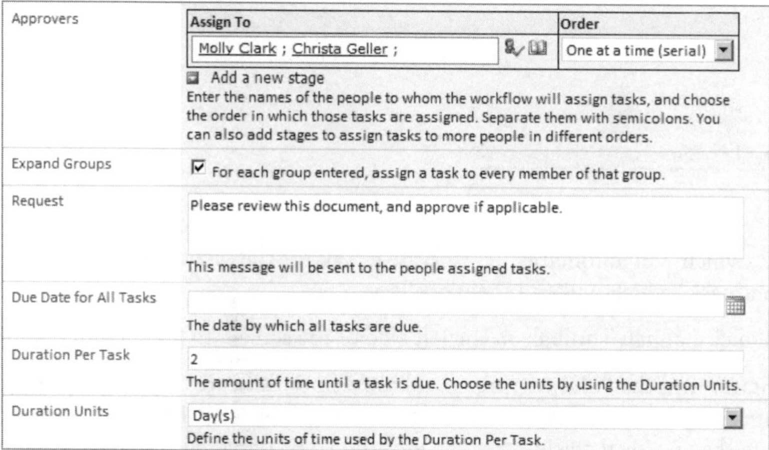

FIGURE 5-1

12. Check the box to Enable Content Approval, and click Save.
13. In the breadcrumb trail at the top of the screen, click Policies.
14. Click Add Document, to add a new company policy to the document library. As soon as the document is created in the library, the Policy Approval workflow will automatically run.
15. The first time a workflow runs, a new column is automatically added to the default view of the library. In this case, the column is called Policy Approval. This column contains a link on each row, representing workflows that have run on each item. The Policy Approval workflow is currently in progress, so click the In Progress link next to the new document that was uploaded, to see the workflow status information.

16. A couple of emails were automatically sent when the workflow started. The initiator of the workflow received an email with details about the approvers, with links to the document and the workflow status page. The first approver also received an email letting them know that a task was assigned to them, with the steps included and what is expected of them. In the tasks section of the workflow status page, click the name of the task that was assigned to the first approver, which is shown in Figure 5-2.

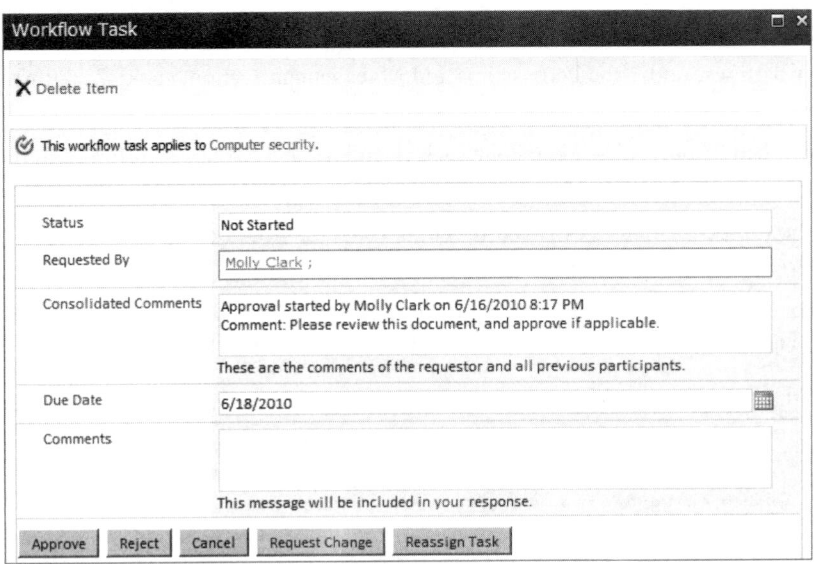

FIGURE 5-2

17. Approve the first task, which will automatically generate a task for the second approver. Go ahead and approve the second task, which will end the workflow.

18. Click Policies in the Quick Launch Toolbar on the left side of the screen, to go back to the library.

Notice that the Approval Status and the Policy Approval columns both indicate that they are Approved. The Approval Status pertains to the Content Approval setting in step 5. At step 12, you set the workflow to automatically update the approval status after the workflow is completed. Again, the content approval setting is used in conjunction with the approval workflow, so that the draft (unapproved) version is not visible to site users until after it has become approved.

How It Works

Approvers, Order and Groups Explained

When the workflow is first created, there is a section for approver names, the type of order of the workflow, and an Expand Groups checkbox. Each of these options will now be more thoroughly explained, with Figure 5-3 as an example.

- **Assign To:** This box can contain one or more individuals and groups. The groups can be Active Directory or SharePoint groups.

- **Order:** The order can be parallel or serial. When serial is selected, the order of the names in the Assign To box is important. The workflow tasks will be assigned one at a time to each of those people (or groups), in the order in which they are typed into the box. With parallel, the order of names in the Assign To box is not important.
- **Expand Groups:** When groups are "expanded," tasks are automatically assigned to each individual in the group. When the box is unchecked, and groups are not expanded, this will cause the workflow to assign only one task per group. Figure 5-4 shows the Claim Task button that shows in the top-left corner of a task when it is assigned to a group that is not expanded. This means that one person in the group can claim the task before they approve or reject it. This lets others in the group know that the task is being worked on.

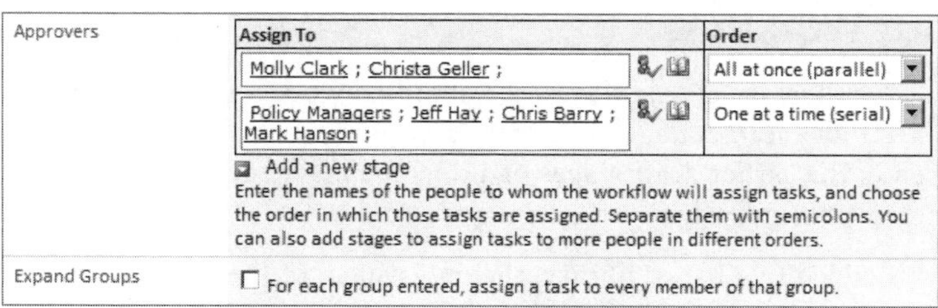

FIGURE 5-3

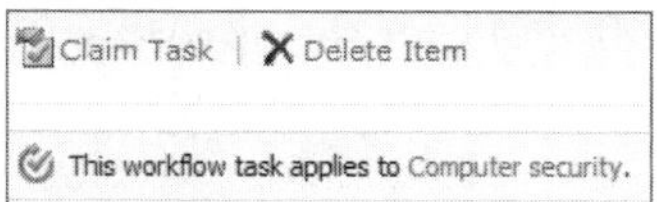

FIGURE 5-4

Approval Workflow Tasks

In the preceding example, a document was approved, but in reality there are different variations besides unanimous approval. When tasks are assigned to approvers, there are other options available besides approval. Each of the additional Task button options will now be described:

- **Reject:** Rejecting an item does not always halt the workflow. When the workflow is created, the End on First Rejection box must be checked in order to cause this behavior.
- **Cancel:** This simply closes the task window. The task still needs to be approved or rejected.
- **Request Change:** When the approver reads the item needing approval and decides that some edits need to be made, they can click Request Change. When a change is requested, several options are presented, such as the individual assigned to make the change and the duration that they have to complete it.
- **Reassign Task:** Use this button when a task needs to be delegated. When a task is reassigned to someone else, that new person is then responsible for approving or rejecting the document and completing their own task.

There is also a new Publishing Approval Workflow. When this workflow is set up, the list of approvers is assigned, which will apply to every file in that library. When users manually initiate the workflow, they are not prompted to select or change the list of approvers.

Disposition Approval Workflow

The Disposition Approval workflow is meant to be used in order to ensure that SharePoint does not become cluttered with documents that are no longer needed. The disposition approval process entails simply choosing whether a document should be deleted or not. If a document is to be deleted, optionally select a checkbox to indicate if a copy of the item's metadata should be retained in the audit log.

Collect Feedback Workflow

The collect feedback workflow is very similar to the approval workflow. The main difference is that this workflow is not meant to act as a document approval process. Typically, the feedback process would happen in the earlier draft stages of a document's lifecycle. Start this workflow when feedback from multiple individuals or groups is desired.

When this workflow is added to a list or library, the only aspect of the interface that is different from that of the approval workflow, is the fact that there are no options to End on First Rejection or Enable Content Approval. Assign this workflow to reviewers in parallel, so that they can all review the document simultaneously. Workflow participants will have the opportunity to type feedback comments in the tasks that are assigned to them, and will not see Approve and Reject buttons.

Three-State Workflow

The Three-State workflow is a bit more complex than the approval and collect feedback workflows. This workflow entails three stages, and the ability to further customize the way that tasks are assigned and emails are sent. A choice column with at least three choices must exist in the list or library with which this workflow is utilized.

When this workflow is added to a list or library, there is a plethora of settings to fill in. Each of the three states of the workflow consists of settings for tasks, due dates, and emails.

NOTE *When adding the Approval or Collect Feedback workflow to a library, the name of the new workflow is the only required field. All of the fields such as approvers and due date can be left blank if so desired. At the point when a workflow is manually initiated, the fields can be filled in by the workflow initiator. This means that all documents in a library do not need to have the same set of approvers, and can be assigned individually. If a workflow is set up in a library's workflow settings with no approvers added, and that workflow is initiated on create or on change, the workflow will automatically be rejected, since there are no built-in approvers.*

Collect Signatures Workflow

The Collect Signatures workflow can only be initiated from within Microsoft Word or Excel. It collects official signatures on documents, and once they are added, any document changes will render them invalid.

TRY IT OUT Using the Collect Signatures Workflow

In this Try It Out, you will create a Collect Signatures workflow on the previously created policies library. This document has two levels of approval, which are manager and division director. Each of these individuals will be assigned a task to sign the SharePoint document.

1. In the "Policies" Library Settings, under the Permissions and Management section, click Workflow Settings.
2. Pick the workflow called "Collect Signatures — SharePoint 2010," and name it "Policy Signatures." In the Start Options section, only put a checkbox next to "Allow this workflow to be manually started by an authenticated user with edit item permissions." Click Next.
3. Click Save.
4. In a Word document, click the Insert tab in the Ribbon, and choose Signature Line. Click OK on the informational message.
5. Type a suggested signer's title as "Manager," check the box to Allow the signer to add comments in the Sign dialog. Click OK.
6. Repeat steps 4 and 5 to create a second signature box for "Division Director."
7. In Word, click the File menu, and choose Save & Send on the left side.
8. In the Workflows section, click Policy Signatures. Click Start Workflow.
9. In the Signers box, type two of your colleague's names. In a production environment, these would be the actual names of the manager and Division Director who are responsible for signing the document. Click Start.
10. In the Tasks list on the SharePoint site, open the new task titled "This document requires your signature." Click the link to the document at the top of the task screen. The document does not need to be opened as editable in order to be signed. It can be in Read-only mode. The top of the document will have a yellow View Signatures button, as shown in Figure 5-5.

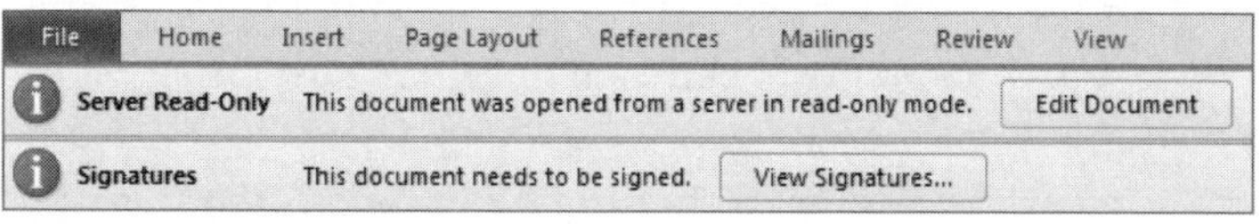

FIGURE 5-5

11. Click the View Signatures button, which will open a new pane on the right side of the screen called Signatures, with all requested signatures listed.

12. Click the drop-down box on manager, and choose Sign. Click OK to the informational message. Type the first signer's name, or optionally click Select Image, to upload a scanned image of the signature from your computer. Click the Sign button. The message shown in Figure 5-6 will be displayed, and you can click OK.

FIGURE 5-6

13. Repeat steps 10 through 12 for the Division Director approval.

Now the document has been officially approved by all signers, and if the document is ever changed, the signatures become invalid. Also, see that the signatures include the name of the logged in user who clicked the Sign button, so that in addition to typing their own name, their official login name and the date are automatically recorded in the signature.

In addition to filling out the signature within the document or spreadsheet, each signer much complete their assigned task by opening it and clicking the Sign button to indicated that their part is done.

Web Analytics Workflows

The Web Analytics workflows are the only out-of-the-box site-level workflows. All of the other workflows are meant to be associated with a list or library. Web analytics are numbers that tell the metrics related to site visits and searches. If you are interested in how popular a site is, or how people are finding it, web analytics are a great way stay informed. Some of the types of metrics for alerts and reports are listed here:

- Page views
- Unique visitors
- Referrers
- Search queries
- Storage usage
- Top browsers

The two kinds of workflows are web analytics alerts and web analytics reports.

***NOTE** The site collection feature called* Advanced Web Analytics *must be activated in order to be able to use the Web Analytics workflows.*

Web Analytics Alerts

The web analytics alerts allow you to define thresholds. When the threshold is reached, an email alert is sent. Pick a scope of the whole site collection or just the current site, and select a metric and comparison. The conditions to choose from are shown in Figure 5-7.

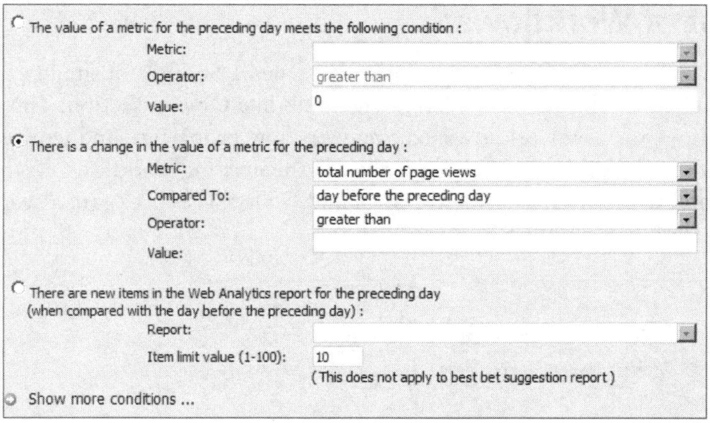

The value of a metric for the preceding day meets the following condition :
Metric:
Operator: greater than
Value: 0

There is a change in the value of a metric for the preceding day :
Metric: total number of page views
Compared To: day before the preceding day
Operator: greater than
Value:

There are new items in the Web Analytics report for the preceding day (when compared with the day before the preceding day) :
Report:
Item limit value (1-100): 10
(This does not apply to best bet suggestion report)

Show more conditions ...

FIGURE 5-7

Notice that there are options to look at the absolute value of a metric, view a comparison of a day or week before, or receive a list of daily new items that exist in the web analytics report, such as any new top referrers.

Web Analytics Reports

Web analytics reports are generated either daily or weekly, have set start and end dates, and are scoped to either the site collection or current site. Put check marks next to all of the different types of metrics to report on.

CREATING CUSTOM WORKFLOW SOLUTIONS

When the built-in workflow templates are not enough and business solutions and processes need to be more customized, SharePoint Designer workflows are the way to go. The easy user interface in SharePoint Designer lets you create your own rules-based declarative workflows.

Custom workflows can also be created with Visual Studio 2010, and these are even more flexible and scalable than the ones in SharePoint Designer. These types of workflows are created by developers, and are tested and then installed in the production environment.

In this section, you will get an in-depth understanding of how to get around in the SharePoint Designer interface and create custom workflows. SharePoint Designer 2010 is a free application that you can obtain from Microsoft's download site.

WARNING *When the top-level site (root of the site collection) is opened in SharePoint Designer, be careful with the out-of-the-box workflow templates. Changes made at this level do propagate down to every subsite. If it is necessary to change an out-of-the-box workflow, the best practice is to click Copy & Modify. Make changes to the copy instead of the original and then publish it.*

Getting around the List of Workflows

The first thing to get familiar with is the workflow design interface. Open a SharePoint site in SharePoint Designer 2010, and click Workflows in the left navigation's Site Objects section. The contextual Ribbon contains options for new workflows, editing workflow properties, and workflow management. The main content section of the page displays a list of the existing workflows on the site. By default, the out-of-the-box workflows, such as Approval and Collect Feedback, are already listed. The workflow Ribbon is shown in Figure 5-8.

FIGURE 5-8

New

Use these buttons to create new workflows. These options were discussed in the "Workflow Associations" section earlier in this chapter.

Edit

Select an existing workflow's row in the list of workflows, and use these buttons to access that workflow's settings, edit the workflow itself, or delete it.

Manage

This section pertains to the management of workflows and their associations. These buttons are related to how each workflow is associated with lists and content types, and the options in this section all allow you to take action on the workflow as a whole.

- **Save as Template:** This option is only available for reusable workflows. Save the selected workflow to the Site Assets of the current site. Go to the site's Site Assets library to find the saved template as a WSP solution file.
- **Copy and Modify:** This option is only available for reusable workflows. It allows you to create a duplicate copy of the workflow, which can then be modified.
- **Import from Visio:** Create a SharePoint workflow flowchart in Microsoft Visio 2010, and import the diagram into SharePoint, to create a workflow based from it. More about Visio and workflows will be covered in the section of this chapter "Office Client Integration."
- **Export to Visio:** All types of workflows, except for site workflows, can be exported to become Visio Workflow Interchange (VWI) files.
- **Associate to List:** Only available to reusable workflows, this button shows a drop-down list of the lists on the site that can be associated with the workflow. Clicking a list name creates the association. If a workflow has been created to be associated with a certain content type, only the lists of that same content type will be displayed as options to choose from.

- **Associate to Content Type:** This button is also only available when a reusable workflow is selected. Pick a site content type to associate the workflow with. Every list on the site that contains that content type will then have that workflow associated with it.

Getting around the Workflow Settings

For existing workflows, there are several configuration options within that workflow's settings page. Figure 5-9 shows the contextual Ribbon options.

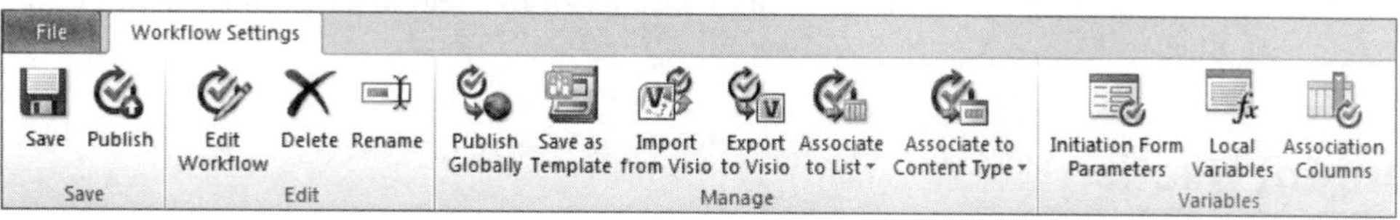

FIGURE 5-9

Save

Now in SharePoint Designer 2010, workflows can be saved before being published. This is an improvement, because if a workflow isn't ready to go into production, and needs to be completed later, it can be saved without having to publish it and go live. Making a workflow available on the site or library is now a two-step process. Save the workflow and then publish it.

Edit

Edit the workflow itself, by setting up the order of the steps, conditions, and actions. The workflow can also be deleted or renamed from here.

Manage

The Publish Globally button allows you to make the workflow reusable on every site in the current site collection, making it visible to all users. This is only available for reusable workflows. The other options here were covered on the previous page.

Variables

Variables are values that exist in a workflow only during the time that the workflow is running. For example, if a new list item is created via workflow, the ID of that item is automatically returned to the workflow as a variable. This ID can be utilized later in the workflow, in cases where data needs to be obtained *from*, or sent *to* the other list. Once the workflow is finished, this variable does not exist anymore.

- **Initiation Form Parameters:** When a workflow is manually initiated, the initiation form parameters are the fields that the user fills out when they start the workflow. The association parameters are collected when a reusable workflow is attached to a list. For each parameter that is added on this screen, choose the field type, and whether it is to be collected during initiation, association, or both. Read more about this subject later in this chapter in the section called "Variables and Parameters."

- **Local Variables:** This is a list of all of the variables that exist in the workflow. Each variable has a type, such as string, number, or date.
- **Association Columns:** In workflows, association columns are those that are created by the workflow, within the associated list. This concept is especially useful in reusable workflows, and these types of columns are not available in site workflows. When a workflow is utilized in multiple lists on various sites, there may be certain columns that are an important part of the workflow's functionality. Create these as association columns to ensure that they exist on each list or library where the workflow is run. During creation, they can be selected from existing site columns (best practice), or they can be created as columns within the associated list.

The Content Section

The options on the main content section of the page differ depending on the type of workflow.

Workflow Information

The workflow information is basic data such as the name and description of the workflow. Some of these basics will vary according to the type of workflow. Simply click on the name or description to edit them. Figure 5-10 shows an example of the Workflow Information section for a list workflow.

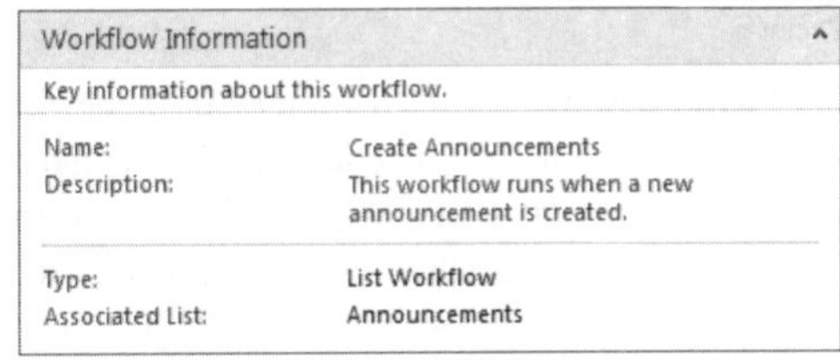

FIGURE 5-10

- **Name:** Descriptive naming of workflows is important not only for you as the workflow's creator but also for the workflow initiator as well. The name should give you a quick indication of what the workflow does and what it is associated with. For workflows that automatically run when items are created or changed, the end users won't see the names. As the administrator, you will see the list of workflow names when administrating the workflows. In the preceding example, the workflow has been named "Create Announcements," since it runs each time a new announcement is created.
- **Description:** When workflows are manually initiated, this description will be displayed to end users along with the workflow name. Describe to the user why they would run this workflow.
- **Type:** This is the workflow type, such as List Workflow, Site Workflow, or Reusable Workflow.
- **Associated List:** List workflows will display the name of the associated list.
- **Content Type:** Reusable workflows will display the name of the content type that they are associated with.

Customization

This section contains quick links to open the associated list, associated task or history lists, or edit the current workflow. Reusable workflows show only an Edit Workflow link here.

Settings

A task list and history list can be selected here. If tasks are assigned anywhere within the workflow, this is where they will be created. Reusable workflows do not give these options.

The Show workflow visualization checkbox on status page is a great new feature in SharePoint 2010. Check this box in order to see a Visio diagram that displays the current workflow when viewing the workflow status page.

Start Options

Determine when the workflow will be initiated by checking the appropriate boxes here in the Start Options. All or any one of the options can be selected. Choose for the workflow to run manually, on item creation, or when an item is changed. By default, when a workflow is created, it is only set to be manually started. For a list workflow, when the workflow can be manually started, there is an additional checkbox, Require Manage List permissions, which means that only users with that permission level or higher on the list will be able to initiate the workflow. Reusable workflows use the opposite syntax than list workflows. With these, all start options are available by default, and each box can be checked to *disable* that option.

NOTE *The default behavior of manual workflows is that only users with contribute permissions or higher will have the ability to start a workflow. In the start options section, the manage list permissions were mentioned, but you may have noticed that this is not a permission level. Manage Lists is a type of permission that can be granted within a permission level. By default, Design, Manage Hierarchy, and Full Control have this ability. You can read more about custom permission levels and security in Chapter 10.*

Forms

This section contains the list of InfoPath forms that are used in the current workflow. When a workflow has manual initiation turned on, the first time it is published, this form will be generated. Read more about InfoPath in workflows in the section of this chapter called "Office Client Integration."

Editing a Workflow

The Workflow Editor is the meat and potatoes of the workflow. This is where most of your work is done. Figure 5-11 shows the Ribbon commands available, which will now be explained.

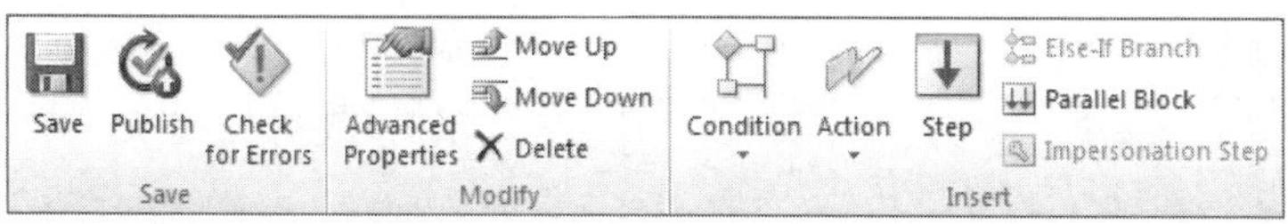

FIGURE 5-11

- **Check for Errors:** Click this button to check the logic in the workflow, to make sure that it makes sense and will run correctly.
- **Advanced Properties:** Each condition and action in the workflow has advanced properties for further configuration. Select the name of the condition or action, and click this button to modify the properties. They are different depending on what kind of item is selected.
- **Move Up and Down:** Rearrange the pieces of the workflow by selecting one and clicking the Move Up or Move Down buttons.
- **Step:** A step is the next group of conditions and actions that is to take place in the workflow's sequence. Use descriptive names for the steps, as documentation of your process.
- **Else-If Branch:** If a certain condition is met, then several actions can be added under that condition, but *otherwise* what needs to happen if the condition is not met? Insert an else-if branch to define processes this way. If there are no conditions in a workflow, this button will be disabled.
- **Parallel Block:** When several actions need to take place at the exact same time, and not in sequence, insert a parallel block, and place the actions inside of it. Do not use a parallel block if any its actions rely on something that took place in a previous action in the block.

Conditions

There are several conditions available, depending on which type of workflow is being created. Multiple conditions can be selected, and the workflow can be set up to look at ALL or ANY of them. As shown in Figure 5-12, when conditions are set, the "and" link can be toggled to "or."

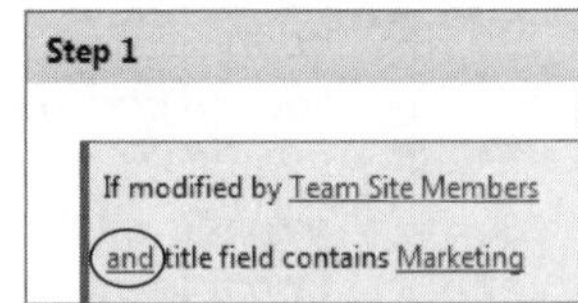

FIGURE 5-12

The following table contains a list of conditions, with their descriptions, along with the types of workflows in which they are available. There are additional conditions related to item permissions, which are covered separately in the section that follows, called "Impersonation Step."

CONDITION NAME	TYPE OF WORKFLOW	DESCRIPTION
If any value equals value	All Workflows	Compare any two fields to each other, from any list or library on the site. When fields from other lists are selected, a matching field must be selected in the "Find the List Item" section.
If current item field equals value	List and Reusable Workflows	Pick a field in the current list, and compare it to another value in the current list, workflow content/ variables, or to an item in another list.
Created by a specific person	List and Reusable Workflows	Pick a person from groups on the site, from within the list (Workflow Lookup), or simply "User who cre- ated current item."
Created in a specific date span	List and Reusable Workflows	Pick two dates as the beginning and end of the span, from date fields in the list, or by typing specific dates.

CONDITION NAME	TYPE OF WORKFLOW	DESCRIPTION
Modified by a specific person	List and Reusable Workflows	Pick a person from groups on the site, from within the list (Workflow Lookup), or simply "User who created current item."
Modified in a specific date span	List and Reusable Workflows	Pick two dates as the beginning and end of the span, from date fields in the list, or by typing specific dates.
Person is a valid SharePoint user	All Workflows	This condition ensures that the person selected is not anonymous. This condition is commonly used to look at the "User who created current item."
The file size in a specific range of kilobytes	All workflow types. Only libraries, not lists	The size of the current file is between two different specific numbers.
The file type is a specific type	All workflow types. Only libraries, not lists	Type the extension name of a specific file type.
Title field contains keywords	List and Reusable Workflows	Look at the title field of the current list. This condition *is* case sensitive.

Actions

Whether or not any conditions exist in a workflow, actions are the activities that happen when a workflow is triggered. In this section, each action will be described, with some examples included. There are additional actions related to item permissions, which are covered separately in the section that follows, called "Impersonation Step."

Core Actions

The core actions are the most commonly used actions in SharePoint Designer workflows.

- **Add Time to Date:** Do a calculation that adds time to a date field. Pick from minutes, hours, days, months, or years, and obtain a variable that contains this new calculation.
- **Convert Word Doc to PDF:** This action can only be used on Microsoft Word documents in libraries. Insert a URL in this action as the location of the library where the new PDF file should be sent. If the file is to be created in the current library, select the field called "URL Path."

NOTE *The conversion of Word Documents to PDF files relies on a service application in central administration called Word Automation Services, which can be managed by your server administrator. This service contains settings such as supported file formats and the frequency with which to start conversions (which is one minute by default).*

- **Do Calculation:** Perform calculations between two different number columns, or manually typed numbers. Calculations that can be done are addition, subtraction, division, multiplication, or mod. The answer is set as a variable in the workflow.
- **Log to History List:** This is an important action, and should be used often. This action logs information to the workflow history regarding what is going on during the workflow. It is a best practice, especially when troubleshooting, to create these actions after each step and action that happens in the workflow. When the workflow status is being viewed, this logged information will let you see what has taken place so far. Without any "Log to History List" actions in a workflow, it will often run and show as "Completed" without any further detailed information.
- **Pause for Duration:** Put the workflow on hold for a certain number of days, hours or minutes. Each of the number fields in this step can be manually typed, or they can be selected from existing number fields.
- **Pause until Date:** Put the workflow on hold until a specific date, or until the value of a date column.
- **Send an Email:** Send a custom email to recipients. Pick recipients from members of the site or from values within fields. The subject and body of the email can contain manually typed text in combination with fields inserted from a list. Hyperlinks can also be inserted into the body of the email, with fully customizable links and text.
- **Send Document to Repository:** This action is only available in library workflows, not lists. Submit a file using either Copy, Move, or Move and leave a link. Pick a destination router and type an explanation.
- **Set Time Portion of Date/Time Field:** Pick a date field, and select the exact time that should exist as the time portion of that field, and the new date/time becomes a variable in the workflow.
- **Set Workflow Status:** Choose to set the workflow status to Approved, Rejected, or Canceled.
- **Set Workflow Variable:** Create a new workflow variable, and set it to a certain value. Select from a list of existing variables or create a new one. The value of the variable can be set as the exact value from a field, or the string builder can be used to create a custom one.
- **Stop Workflow:** Stop the workflow and do not proceed to the next action or step. There is a box to type the text that is to be displayed in the workflow history when this happens.

Document Set Actions

The Document Set actions only apply to document sets, which can only be created in document libraries. You can read more about the concept of document sets in Chapter 6. The workflow interface *will* allow you to create Document Set actions in any list or library workflow, but they will not work on anything but a document set.

- **Capture a Version of the Document Set:** Pick whether to capture the last major or the latest minor version of all the documents in the set. Also, type in a comment that will show in the version history list. Versioning for the library must be turned on in order for this action to work.

- **Send Document Set to Repository:** Choose to copy, move, or move and Leave a Link. The document is then sent to the destination content organizer.
- **Set Content Approval Status for the Document Set:** When content approval is turned on for the library, this action can set the approval status to Approved, Pending, or Rejected, with additional comments.
- **Start Document Set Approval Process:** Content approval is found in the library settings under Versioning settings.

List Actions

The title of this section of actions is a bit misleading. List actions can be performed on both lists and libraries.

- **Check-In Item:** Since list items do not have the check-in/out capability, checking items in and out through a workflow will only apply to items in libraries. The item will be set as checked in by the user who is currently running the workflow.
- **Check-Out Item:** The item will be set as checked out by the user who is currently running the workflow.
- **Copy List Item:** When copying an item from one list to another, it helps if the lists contain the same content type. For example, copying a task from one task list to another task list will be successful. Only the common site columns will be copied when one list type is copied to a different list type. For example, when copying a task to an announcements list, only the Title field will be copied, since none of the other columns are the same between the two types of lists.
- **Create List Item:** In contrast to the Copy List Item action, this action allows for more granular creation of an item in another list or library. Select a destination list or library in the current List drop-down box, and then pick each field in the list one at a time to set what the value needs to be. Figure 5-13 shows the creation of a new list item in a calendar. By default, since the Title, Start Time, and End Time are required fields in the list, they each have asterisks next to them. The values in the Field column are in the calendar, and the values in the Value column can be either manually typed in or selected from list values or workflow variables.

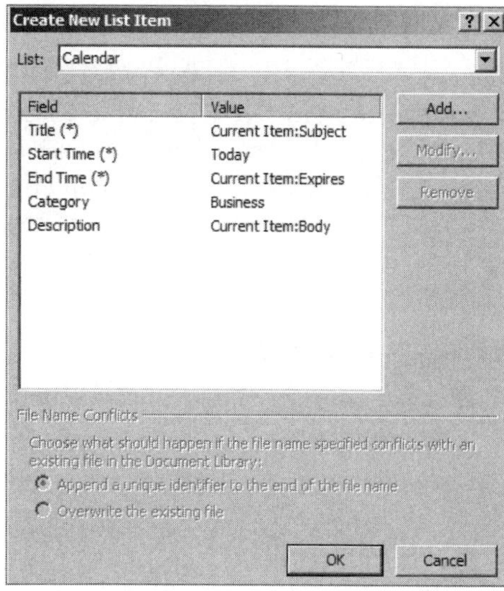

FIGURE 5-13

- **Declare Record:** Use this action in a Records Center site, in order to declare the current item as a record. The site collection feature called "In Place Records Management" needs to be activated in order to declare records.

- **Delete Drafts:** Only available in library workflows, not lists. This action simply deletes all drafts (minor versions) of the current item.
- **Delete Item:** Deletes an item in a list or library.
- **Delete Previous Versions:** Only available in library workflows, not lists. Deletes all previous versions of the current item.
- **Discard Check Out Item:** When a checked out item is discarded, this means that the changes made during the current check out are lost.
- **Set Content Approval Status:** When content approval is turned on in the library's versioning settings, this action allows the content approval status to be set to Approved, Pending, or Rejected. This is not available in site workflows.
- **Set Field in Current Item:** Set the value of any field in the current list to a certain value. This value can be taken from any other field in any list in the current site, or workflow variables or context. This action is not available in site workflows.
- **Undeclare Record:** When records management is used, this action undeclares the current item as a record. This is not available in site workflows.
- **Update List Item:** Compared to the Create List Item action, which creates a new item, this action finds an already existing item, and modifies it. The interface is similar to that of the Create List Item action, but there is an additional section that is required, called Find the List Item. To find the correct list item to update, a field in the target list must match up with a workflow variable or other list value, so that a join is defined between the updated list and the current list.
- **Wait for Change in Document Check-Out Status:** Only available in library workflows, not lists. Wait for the current document to be one of the following: Checked-Out, Checked-In, Unlocked by document editor, or Discarded.
- **Wait for Field Change in Current Item:** Pick a field in the current list and define what to wait for. The workflow will pause until the item is changed and the field matches what has been defined here. Once the condition is met, the workflow proceeds to the next action. Depending on what type of field is selected, there will be different options available here. This action is not available in site workflows

Relational Actions

There is only one relational action, in which information about the current user is being related in the workflow.

- **Lookup Manager of a User:** Pick a user, and that user's manager name will be set as a variable in the current workflow. Hint: Use "As String" in the Return Field As drop-down box for the person lookups.

Task Actions

The assignment of tasks plays a huge role in many workflows; therefore, there are several different methods that can be used to assign tasks from within the Workflow Designer. The first three task actions are compared in the following table. For each of these actions that will take place, the workflow waits until the task or tasks are completed before moving on to the next action. Each task that is created will contain a Complete Task button for the assignee to click.

ACTION	RETURNS TASK ID AS VARIABLE	ASSIGN TO MULTIPLE GROUPS AND USERS	DESCRIPTION
Assign a Form to a Group	No	Yes	Define task title and fields for the assignee to fill out.
Assign a To-do Item	No	Yes	Define a task title.
Collect Data from a User	Yes	No	Define task title and fields to be filled out.

Figure 5-14 shows the interface in Assign a Form to a Group and Assign a To-do Item when multiple users are selected for task assignment. The person who created the current item, the person who modified the current item, and the SharePoint group called Approvers will all be assigned tasks to complete. On the left side of the screen, users who have never visited the site will not be listed, but they can still be added by manually typing their names in the Type a Name or E-mail Address box.

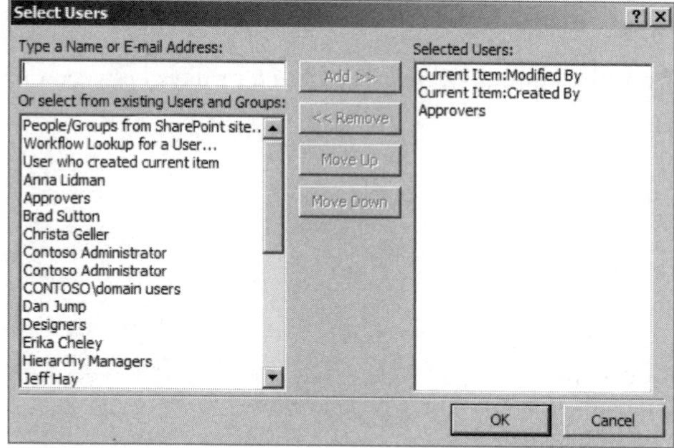

FIGURE 5-14

New to SharePoint 2010 are three customizable task processes that exist as actions in a workflow. These processes are workflows within a workflow, each with its own custom interface to set up task process options. Read more about the Task Process Designer in the section called "Workflow Tasks and History."

- **Start Approval Process:** This action is designed as a standard approval workflow, which can be customized according to your business requirements. The assignees will approve or reject the item that is assigned to them.
- **Start Feedback Process:** This process is the basis for the out-of-the-box "Collect Feedback" workflow. The only task outcome is for the assignee to mark the task as Completed.
- **Start Custom Task Process:** This action contains a blank template of some standard task workflow steps.

Utility Actions

The new utility actions allow granular control over how strings are structured. If you are familiar with Excel functions such as LEFT, RIGHT, and MID, these utilities will be easy to understand. For each of these actions, the data that is extracted becomes a workflow variable.

- **Extract Substring from End of String:** Define the number of characters needed from the end (right) of a specified field.
- **Extract Substring from Start of String:** Define the number of characters needed from the beginning (left) of a specified field.
- **Extract Substring from Index of String:** Set the number of characters at which to start copying the data from a field. Starting at that number, the value of the rest of the field will be obtained.
- **Extract Substring of String from Index with Length:** This one is similar to the previous action, except that instead of grabbing the rest of the field's value starting with a character number, this action lets you start at a certain character number, and only obtain a defined number of characters from that point.
- **Find Interval Between Dates:** Find out the number of minutes, hours, or days between one date and another.

Impersonation Steps

In SharePoint Designer workflows, impersonation steps are created when workflows need to write to lists or libraries that the person running the workflow does not necessarily have access to. Impersonation steps run as the person who created the workflow, which is typically a site manager/owner who has a higher level of permissions than most other site users. By default, when a new workflow is created, there is a single step called "Step 1," and when the cursor is placed inside of step 1, notice that the Impersonation Step button in the ribbon is grayed out. Click the cursor outside of Step 1, so that the orange blinking line shows below it, as seen in Figure 5-15, and notice that the Impersonation Step button is not disabled anymore.

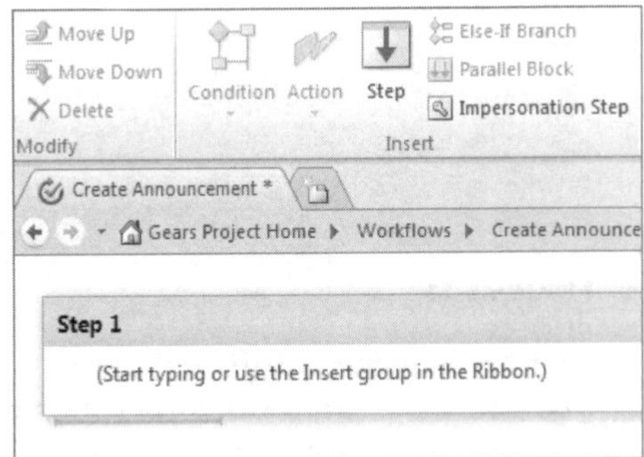

FIGURE 5-15

Click the Impersonation Step button to add this type of step to the workflow. The following table shows a list of impersonation workflow conditions.

CONDITION NAME	DESCRIPTION
Check list item permission levels	Pick one or more individuals or groups, choose one or more permission levels, and choose the current list or another on the site.
Check list item permissions	Pick one or more individuals or groups, choose permissions, and choose the current list or another on the site.

Figure 5-16 shows an impersonation condition.

If permissions for Workflow Context:Current User are at least Contribute on item in Current Item

FIGURE 5-16

Impersonation Steps also contain a set of actions that do not exist in non-impersonation steps. The following are the impersonation actions, which are located in the List Actions section.

- **Add List Item Permissions:** Pick one or more users, and select the permission levels that will be granted to them on a list item. These permissions are simply added to the already existing ones.
- **Inherit List Item Parent Permissions:** When items in a list have been set up with permissions that are unique to the permissions defined at the list level, this action resets the permissions on the item to inherit from the parent (list or library) again.
- **Remove List Item Permissions:** The name of this action is a bit misleading. From the sound of it, this action would remove *all* permissions from the item. This is not the case. A list of specific users and permissions must be defined.
- **Replace List Item Permissions:** This action is very powerful, in that it completely removes all permissions on a list item, and replaces them with the list of users and permission levels that you define.

Custom Ribbon Buttons

In the previous version of the product, there was a commonly asked question about starting workflows. "Why does it take so many clicks to initiate a workflow? Can't I just click a button there on the item?" This issue has been addressed in SharePoint 2010, with the ability to create Custom Actions in SharePoint Designer 2010. This is not done from within the workflows, but from within the Lists and Libraries.

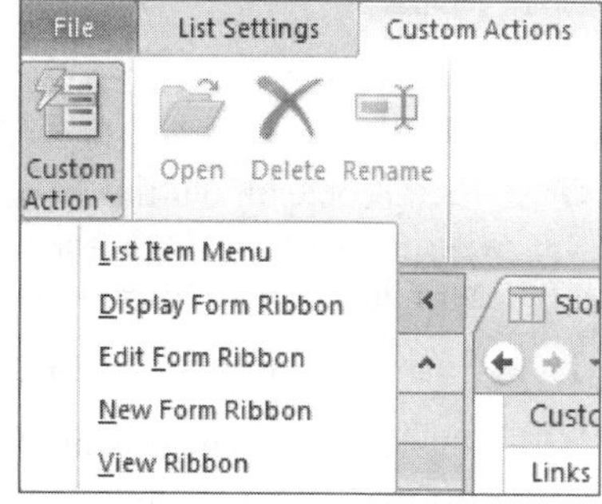

FIGURE 5-17

In SharePoint Designer, click Lists & Libraries on the left, and click the name of a list. Click inside of the Custom Actions section at the bottom right. A new Custom Actions section of the Ribbon will appear. The Custom Actions button is a drop-down box, shown in Figure 5-17.

Click the name of the location that you would like this new button to appear. After the name and description have been typed, choose the Initiate Workflow option, and pick the name of a workflow from the drop-down box. Only workflows that are associated with the list will be displayed here.

Variables and Parameters

Variables and parameters are values that are used within a workflow. Parameters are values that are filled in on an initiation form by a user when the workflow is being manually started. Variables are values that exist within the workflow only while it is running, and were defined earlier in the chapter in the section called "Variables." As you work through the next example, the meaning of a variable will become more clear within the context of the workflow.

TRY IT OUT Creating a SharePoint Designer Workflow

In this Try It Out example, you will learn how to create your own custom SharePoint Designer workflow from beginning to end. The scenario is a very simple company store, where employees can have items delivered to their office. The store site will consist of a library of items and an order list. The workflow will be used to calculate the total cost of an item when it is ordered. This workflow is going to consist of two actions as follows:

- Multiply item quantity by the price
- Use the result of the calculation to set the total cost.

1. On your SharePoint site, create a custom list called "Store Items."
2. Create a new currency column in the list called "Price."
3. Create several sample items in this list, each with a title and price.
4. Create a new custom list on the site called "Store Orders."
5. In the Store Orders list, create new columns as defined in the following table.

COLUMN NAME	COLUMN TYPE	DETAILS
Store Item	Lookup	Get information from the Store Items list, in the Title column.
Quantity	Number	Zero decimal places.
Total Cost	Currency	Two decimal places.

6. When people fill out the Store Orders list, the workflow will run when an item is created, which will automatically fill in the total cost. Therefore, the title and total cost can be hidden from the user filling out the form. In the Store Orders List Settings, click Advanced Settings.
7. In the Content Types section, change Allow management of content types to Yes. Click OK.
8. Now that the management of content types is turned on, form fields can be set as hidden. In the Content Types section in the middle of the list settings page, click the "Item" content type.

9. Change Title and Total Cost to Hidden, as shown in Figure 5-18. Note that even though certain fields have been hidden from the forms that users fill out, these columns are still shown in the default view of the list.

Columns			
Name	Type	Status	Source
Title	Single line of text	Hidden	Item
Store Item	Lookup	Optional	
Quantity	Number	Optional	
Total Cost	Currency	Hidden	

FIGURE 5-18

10. Click the name of the All Items view in the Ribbon at the top of the list. Choose Modify this view.

11. Uncheck the box next to the title column. Make sure that the boxes *are* checked next to quantity, store item, total cost, and created by. Click OK.

12. Now it's time to create the workflow. Still on the Store Items list, click the List tab in the Ribbon.

13. Click the Workflow drop-down box at the top right. Choose Create a Workflow in SharePoint Designer.

NOTE *SharePoint Designer 2010 workflows can also be accessed this way: Click Start, choose All Programs ⇨ SharePoint ⇨ Microsoft SharePoint Designer 2010. Click to Open Site, and use the full URL to your site. Once the site is opened in SharePoint Designer, click Workflows on the left.*

14. The SharePoint Designer 2010 application will run, and a Create List Workflow screen will pop up. Name the workflow "Create Store Order," and type the description of "This workflow is used to process new orders in the company store." Click OK.

15. The Workflow Editor is now shown. Before adding any actions, the workflow needs to be set up to run each time an item is created. In the breadcrumb trail shown in Figure 5-19, click Create Store Order, This shows the workflow's main information screen.

FIGURE 5-19

16. In the Start Options section, put a checkbox next to Start workflow automatically when an item is created. Uncheck the option to Allow this workflow to be manually started.

17. Click Save at the top left.

18. In the Customization section, click Edit Workflow.

19. The editor is shown with a blank "Step 1," with a blinking orange line inside of it. Click the Action button in the Ribbon, which shows a list of all of the available actions. In the Core Actions section, choose Do Calculation. This empty action is shown in Figure 5-20.

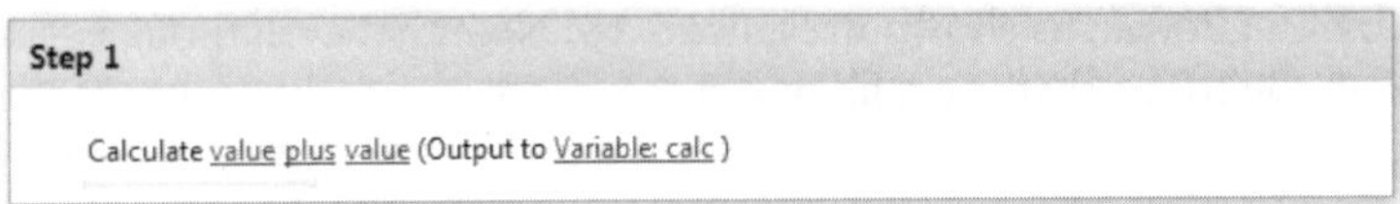

FIGURE 5–20

20. Each of the underlined text items is configurable. Click on the first word "value," and click the function button (fx). Select the Quantity field from the Current Item, as shown in Figure 5-21. Click OK.

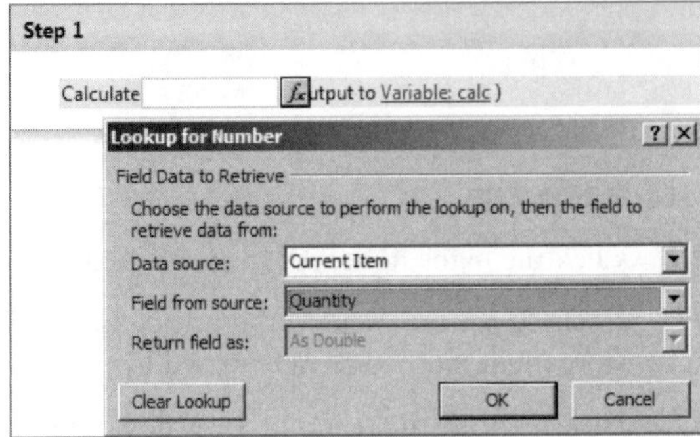

FIGURE 5-21

21. Click the word "plus," and change it to "multiply by." Click the second underlined word "value." This is where the workflow gets fancy, because the cost of the item will be looked up from another list.

22. Change the Data Source to the Store Items list. In Field from source, select Price.

23. Since the source was changed to another list, a new section will appear in the bottom of the dialog box, called Find the List Item. In the Field drop-down, select ID.

24. For the Value, click the Function button and choose the Store Item field from the Current Item.

25. The Return field as box is new to SharePoint 2010. Select "Lookup ID (as Integer)." Click OK. These dialog boxes are shown in Figure 5-22.

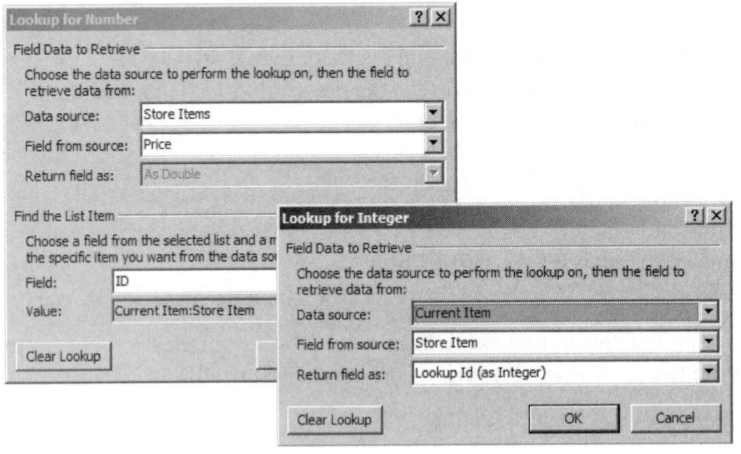

FIGURE 5-22

***NOTE** It is important to understand at this point that when looking up the price for the item that is being ordered, the "Store Item" that the user selects in the lookup field is being matched with the ID of the item in the Store Items list. Every SharePoint list and library has a built-in field called ID that is always unique. When one list contains a Lookup column to another list, the selected item's ID is what is actually stored in the lookup field. In workflows, when using the Find the List Item section to match one list to another, it is not required that ID fields are used, but these are simply preferable since they are guaranteed to be unique.*

26. After you have clicked OK on both dialog boxes, back on the workflow edit screen, click the name of the Variable: calc. It's a good practice to give good descriptive names to workflow variables, instead of using the generic default ones. Click Create a new variable.
27. Name the new variable "Total Cost Calculation," with a type of Number. Click OK.
28. The next step is to add a second action to occur after the first "Do Calculation" action. Click underneath the first action in order to see the orange blinking line.
29. Click the Action button in the Ribbon and choose Set Field in Current Item.
30. Click the word "field," and choose the Total Cost field.
31. Click the word "value," and click the Function button. Change the Data source to Workflow Variables and Parameters.
32. In the Field from source box, choose the name of the variable that was just defined: "Total Cost Calculation."
33. Click OK. Figure 5-23 shows what the whole workflow looks like at this point.

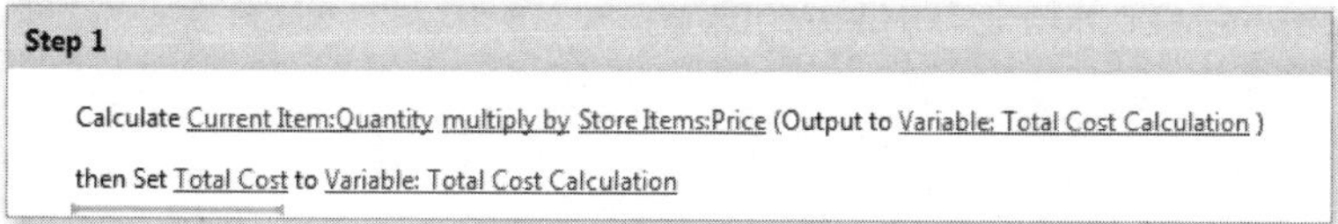

FIGURE 5-23

34. Click the Save button at the top left, and then click the Publish button (leave the workflow screen open after publishing).
35. On the store orders list in the browser, click Add New Item. Add a new item in the list. Pick an item and quantity, and click Save. This new item form is shown in Figure 5-24.

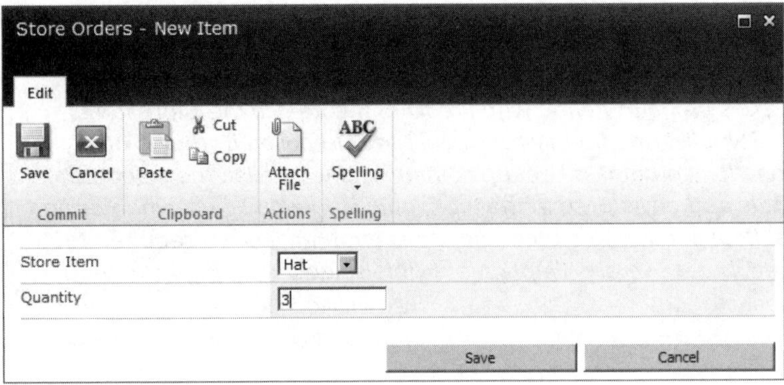

FIGURE 5-24

There are a few things to notice after the workflow has run for the first time. The Total Cost column has been filled out, and there is a new column in the list with the same name as the workflow. Since the workflow completed successfully, you can click the word Completed, to see the workflow history (which is empty). There are just two more things to do, so go back over to the workflow in SharePoint Designer.

36. Since there was no information on the workflow status screen that was viewed when you clicked "Completed," it's time to add some log information. After the last action in the workflow, add a new action called Log to History List. Add two of these.

37. Type information to log. Click "this message" on each of the items, to fill them in as follows:
    - Total cost has been calculated.
    - The total cost field has been filled in.

38. The goal here is to insert log history information after every step in the workflow for informational and documentation purposes. Click the drop-down box on each of the new actions, and click Move Action Up, so that the workflow looks like Figure 5-25.

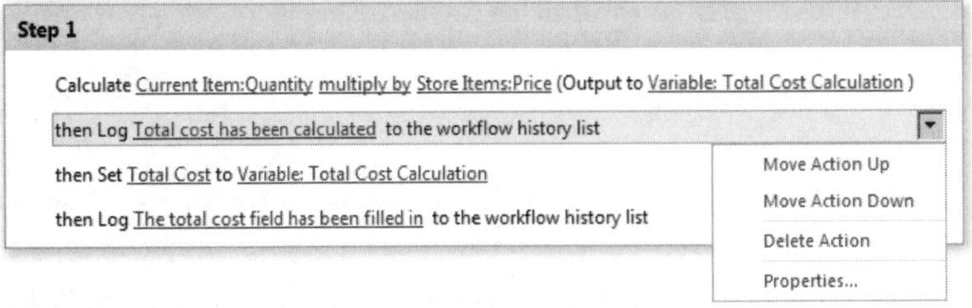

FIGURE 5-25

39. Save and Publish the workflow.

40. Back on the Store Orders list, click Add New Item to Add a new item in the list. Pick an item and quantity, and click Save.

Congratulations, you have finished creating your first SharePoint Designer 2010 workflow. When a new store order item is first saved, the Create Store Order column will probably show as In Progress. Refresh the web page to see the workflow shown as Completed. Click Completed to look at the Workflow

Status page. Notice that the Workflow History section contains the text that you created in the Log to History List actions.

WARNING *When logged into SharePoint as the "System Account" (the SharePoint administrator), workflows may not run as they should. If you have a problem where a workflow will not automatically run when a new item is created or changed, it could be because of the account that you are logged in as. Look at the top-right corner of the SharePoint page in the browser where it says the name of the current logged-in user. If this says "System Account," try logging in as a regular user account instead, and run the workflow again.*

Sending Emails

Emails are one of the most common actions in workflows, and are also heavily customizable. The interface for workflow email creation has been changed a lot from the previous version of the product. There is already an easy alternative, which is to create alerts on all SharePoint lists and libraries. Sometimes these canned alerts are not enough. Create workflow emails when they need to be more specific and customized.

TRY IT OUT Creating a Workflow Email

In the previous Try It Out, you created a workflow in order to calculate a total and set information in a field. In this Try It Out, you will add on to the "Create Store Order" workflow by adding an email action to let the recipient know the details of his or her order, and that it was received.

1. In SharePoint Designer 2010, open the workflow that was created in the previous Try It Out section. Click Edit Workflow.
2. Inside of Step 1, put the cursor directly under the last action, and add a new Action to Send an Email.
3. Click the text "these users" to bring up the Define E-mail Message interface.
4. Click the address book icon next to the To box, choose "User who created current item," click the Add button and click OK.
5. Click the ellipsis button next to the Subject box. This lets you create a string that combines free-form text with values from the form.
6. Fill in the String Builder as shown in Figure 5-26. The Add or Change Lookup button at the bottom of the String Builder is used to insert the Store Item text into the string. Click OK on both dialog boxes.

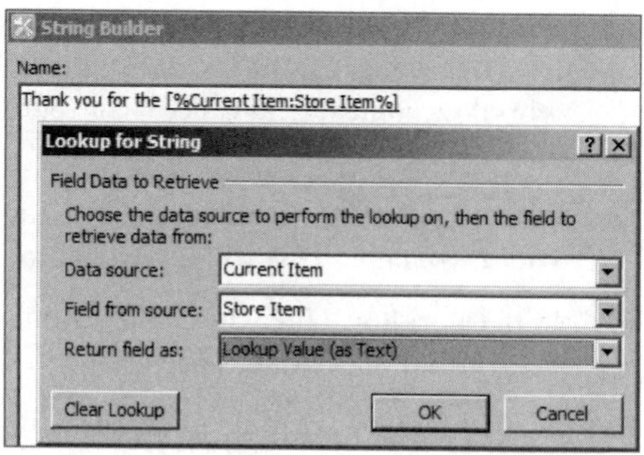

FIGURE 5-26

7. The body of the email can contain some "Thank You" text, and optionally details about the order, such as the item, price, quantity, and total. Use the Add or Change lookup button to add each field's value.

8. The Price is the tricky field, since that value is a lookup to an item in another list. Figure 5-27 shows an example of the email message, with the Price lookup interface displayed. See the earlier note that explains the concept of creating lookups to other lists.

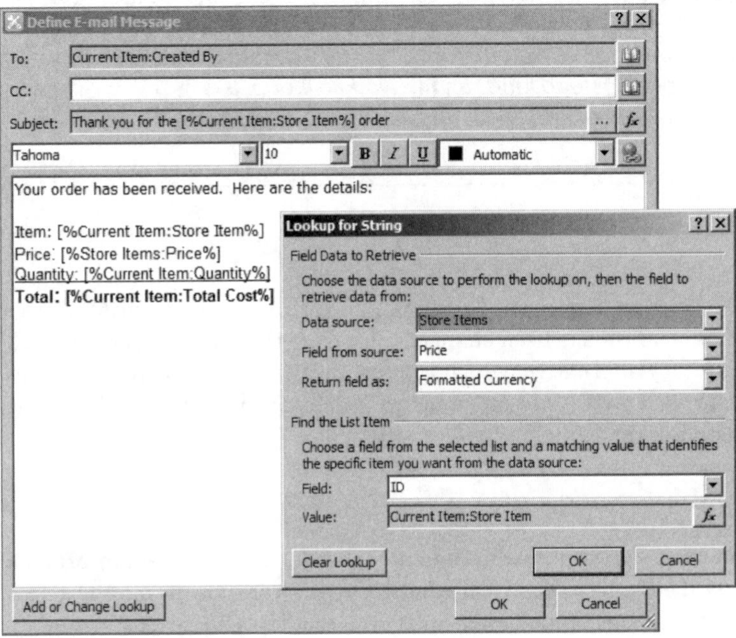

FIGURE 5-27

9. The last thing to add to the email is a link for the email recipient to open the order in SharePoint. Put the cursor at the end of the email, and click the hyperlink icon to insert a hyperlink.

10. For the Text to display, type: Click to view order.

11. For the address, the URL cannot be a relative URL, and must be absolute. SharePoint 2010 has new values that can be inserted, called "Workflow Context." Figure 5-28 shows how to insert the workflow context field called "Current Item URL." Click OK and then click OK again to save the email.

12. Click to select the Email action, and click the Advanced Properties button. In the BCC box, add your own name. This will allow you to receive a blind copy of each email. Click OK.

13. In the workflow, after the email action, add another Log to History List action, with the message "Confirmation email has been sent."

Test the workflow by creating a new order in the Store Orders list. You will receive the email about the item you ordered, with a link that takes you back to that list item.

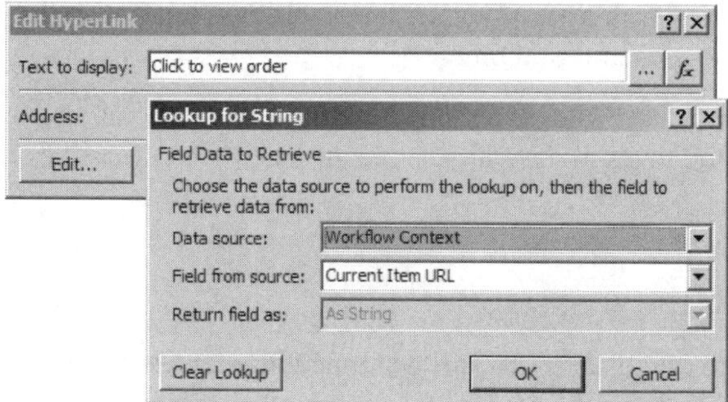

FIGURE 5-28

WORKFLOW TASKS AND HISTORY

When workflows are created on lists and libraries, the Tasks and Workflow History lists are two secondary lists that the workflow utilizes. Every workflow doesn't necessarily make use of a Task list, but every workflow does write to a Workflow History list.

Tasks

So far in this chapter, you may have noticed that the use of tasks in SharePoint workflows is substantial. Assigning tasks to workflow participants gives you the ability to allocate accountability to individuals. Knowing that you can rely on workflows not only to assign tasks as part of defined business processes but also to automatically follow up with individuals, allows you to become more efficient in your day-to-day work.

When tasks are assigned using workflow actions, they look a bit different from tasks that are normally created in a SharePoint task list. This is because workflows automatically add new content types to task lists, and they also make use of InfoPath as a custom form interface.

NOTE *In SharePoint 2010, there is a new ability to restrict users from reading and editing tasks that are not their own. There are three new workflow task actions called Start Approval Process, Start Custom Task Process, and Start Feedback Process. When any of these is added to a workflow, click the name of it to access its customization settings. In the Settings section, check the box called "Only allow task recipients and process owners to read and edit workflow tasks."*

Task Process Designer

There is a new feature in SharePoint Server 2010 called the Task Process Designer. It is basically like inserting a workflow *inside* of any workflow that you create. This mini-workflow not only contains conditions and actions that take place regarding task assignment in the workflow, but it also has easy interfaces to create additional task form fields and outcomes.

When these task processes are used, the associated tasks perform follow-up actions by automatically sending reminder emails to assignees when due dates arrive. This is one of many functionalities that are built into these processes.

TRY IT OUT Creating Task Processes

In the previous Try It Out, a workflow was created and set up to run when new items are ordered in a store. The last action that was added was an email notification to the person who ordered the item. Next, tasks must be assigned so that the order gets shipped out. In this example, the Processor Group is a SharePoint group containing those in charge of processing the order, and the Shipper Group contains those in charge of shipping it out. In this Try It Out, you'll learn how to use the new Task Process Designer to assign tasks.

1. Create two new SharePoint groups on the site, called Processor Group and Shipper Group.
2. Open the previously created workflow called "Create Store Order" in SharePoint Designer.
3. Click Edit Workflow.
4. Immediately below the last action in the workflow, insert a new action called Start Feedback Process.
5. Click on the word Feedback in the action, which will take you to the Task Process Designer.
6. Click the Name box in the Task Information section, and change the name to "New Order Placed."
7. In the Outcomes section on the right, there is one outcome called Completed. There are three columns in this section, called Sequence, Name, and Task Form Button. Click on the value in the Task Form Button column, and change it to say "Mark Completed."
8. Click the Save button, and click Return to the workflow.
9. In the same action in the workflow, click the blue link "these users." This lets you define who will be assigned the tasks.
10. For the participants, select the Processor Group and then the Shipper Group. Use the Add button to move each group to the right. These are SharePoint groups on the site. *For testing purposes, it is okay to insert two individuals' names instead of groups here*. Leave the order as "One at a time (serial)."
11. Click the ellipsis icon next to the title box, to elicit the String Builder.
12. The task title should be "New Store Order;" use the Add or Change Lookup button to insert the ID field from the current item. This ID field is unique to each order that is placed.
13. In the Instructions box, type "**Please perform your role in the new order process.**"
14. Set the Duration per Task to 3 days. This screen is shown in Figure 5-29. Click OK.
15. Save the workflow, and click Publish.

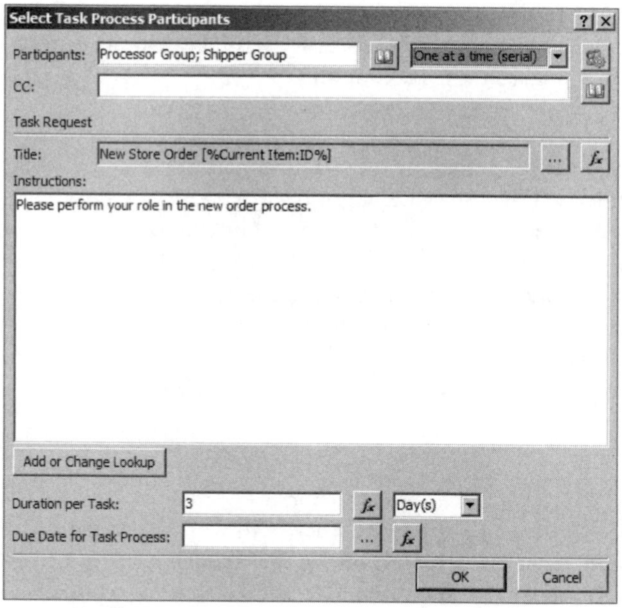

FIGURE 5-29

Try it out now by adding a new item to the Store Items list. A few seconds after you create the new item, a task will be created. In the Store Items list, click the In Progress link in the Create Store Order column. In the Tasks section of the Workflow Status page, click the title of the task that was created. The task is shown in Figure 5-30.

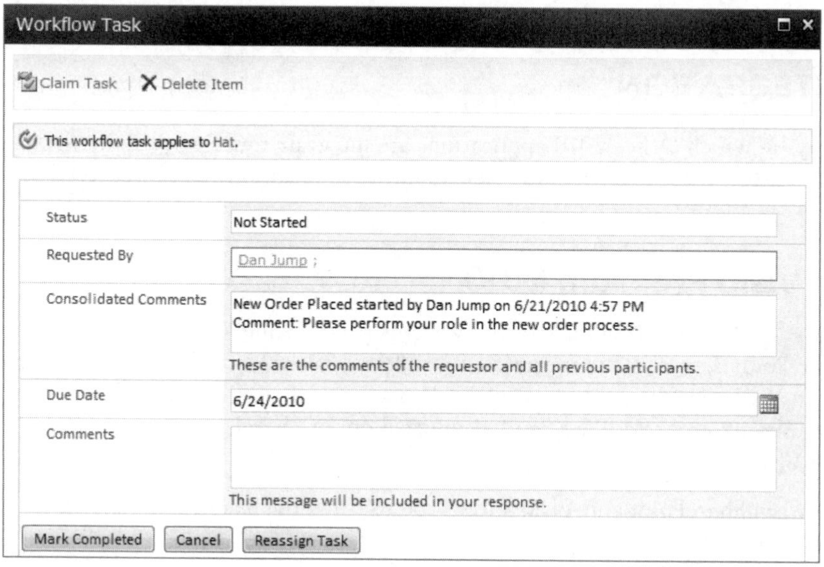

FIGURE 5-30

Notice that the button at the bottom of the task is called "Mark Completed," which was modified by you in the Outcomes section of the Task Process Designer. Site users who are not administrators, and who are not involved in this workflow will not see these tasks at all.

> When assigning tasks, sending emails, or performing any other action in a workflow that involves people, it is recommended that SharePoint groups or variables be used instead of individuals. For example, if a file needs to be approved by the company's CEO, even though there is only one, create a SharePoint group called CEO. Put that one person in the group. In the workflow, send an email to the group. When groups are used, people can easily be added and removed from them, so that the workflow itself does not need to be modified.

History

On every SharePoint site, there is a built-in list called "Workflow History." All workflows that run on the site are logged in this list, which also includes all errors. Knowing that there is a history log and where it lives gives you a good basis of understanding when it comes to workflow status screens and troubleshooting. The location of the workflow history list is:

`http://your_site_url/lists/workflow%20history`

This list is automatically sorted in ascending by Date Occurred order, but just as with any list, you can create your own views for sorting and filtering purposes. The data in the workflow history does seem a bit cryptic, since it makes use of unique IDs for lists and workflows, but it is a good reference sometimes.

OFFICE CLIENT INTEGRATION

There are several new ways in which Office 2010 applications are integrated with SharePoint Server 2010. Visio 2010, InfoPath 2010, and the Back Stage view in Office applications will be covered in this section.

Visualization With Visio Premium 2010

SharePoint workflows can now be visualized on Workflow Status pages, using Visio Premium 2010 and Visio Services in SharePoint Server 2010 Enterprise. Workflow flowcharts can also be created by business process owners in Visio, imported into SharePoint Designer, and published as a functioning workflow. Lastly, existing SharePoint workflows can be exported out of SharePoint Designer and imported to be viewed in Visio 2010 Premium.

This tight integration between SharePoint and Visio allows you to bring the business users into the world of workflow creation. Now, the requirements-gathering process can be made a bit easier because end users or project managers can bring you a diagram of the envisioned process. You, as the workflow's creator, can import their diagram straight into SharePoint!

TRY IT OUT Visio 2010 Workflow Creation

In this Try It Out, you will create a very simple workflow and import it into SharePoint. The goal of the workflow is to look at who created a document and send an approval task to that person's manager for them to approve that document.

1. Open Visio 2010 Premium, and on the New screen, click Flowchart from the Template Categories.
2. On the Choose a Template screen, click Microsoft SharePoint Workflow.
3. Click the Create button on the right.
4. The SharePoint Workflow shapes are shown in the Shapes panel on the left. Drag the following SharePoint Workflow shapes onto the page, in a row:
    - Start
    - Lookup manager of a user
    - Start approval process
    - Terminate
5. Click the Connector icon in the Ribbon, and drag a line between each action, moving from left to right.
6. Each of these shapes can now be described. Double-click on each shape and modify the existing text, to make it more descriptive. The workflow is shown in Figure 5-31.

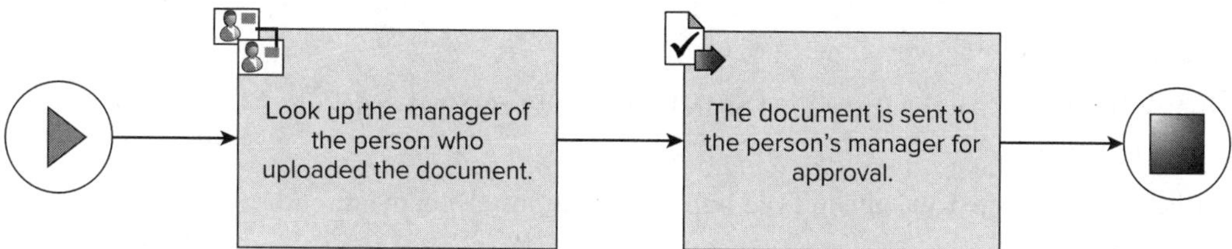

FIGURE 5-31

7. On the Process tab in Visio, click the Check Diagram button, and verify that no issues were found.
8. On the Process tab, click the Export button. Name the file "Manager Approval" and save it to your desktop.
9. In SharePoint Designer, click the Workflows section on the left. Click the Import from Visio button in the Ribbon.
10. Browse to the saved file on your desktop, and click Open. Click Next.

11. The workflow name should be Manager Approval. Select Reusable Workflow, and choose the Document content type. Click Finish.
12. The workflow actions are displayed on the screen, with the underlined words needing to be configured. Next to Find Manager of, click "this user." Choose User who created current item, and click OK.
13. In the output to "manager" drop-down box, click Create a new variable, name it Manager and click OK.
14. Next to Start Approval process, click "this item," and click OK.
15. Click "these users." Next to the participants box, click the Address book icon. Double-click Workflow Lookup for a User.
16. Enter the following information:

FIELD	VALUE
Data source	Workflow Variables and Parameters
Field from source	Variable: Manager
Return field as	As String

17. Click OK, and then click OK again.
18. On the Select Task Process Participants screen, type the title **Approve New Document.** Click OK.
19. Save the workflow. Click the Workflow Settings button. Check the box next to Show workflow visualization on status page.
20. Save and Publish the workflow.
21. Click Workflows on the left side of SharePoint Designer. Single-click the Manager Approval workflow row to select it.
22. Click the Associate to Content Type button, and choose Document.
23. The Add a Workflow screen will come up in the browser. Click OK.

Now this new Manager Approval is associated with every library that uses the Document content type, which is the default content type for all document libraries. Click the drop-down box on any document on the site, choose Workflows, and click Manager Approval. On the initiation screen, click the Start button. This workflow looks up the initiator's Manager, and assigns a task to that person. This task is created in the default Tasks list on the site.

WORKFLOW DESCRIPTIVE TEXT

When workflows are created in Visio, text can be added to each action, as workflow documentation. In Step 6 of the previous Try It Out, you added descriptive text to each shape in the diagram. Notice that after the workflow has been imported into Visio, this text is displayed in gray above each action in the workflow, as shown in Figure 5-32.

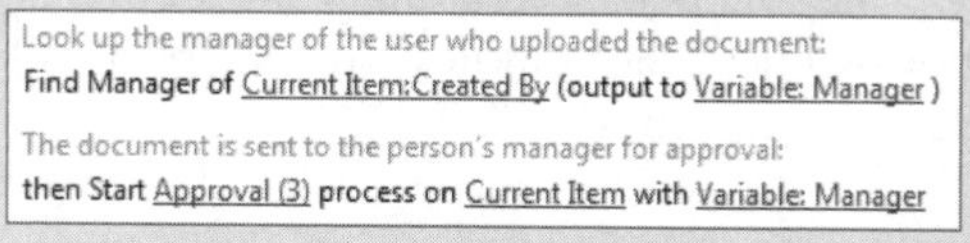

Look up the manager of the user who uploaded the document:
Find Manager of Current Item:Created By (output to Variable: Manager)
The document is sent to the person's manager for approval:
then Start Approval (3) process on Current Item with Variable: Manager

FIGURE 5-32

In the workflow's settings, if you select the box next to Show workflow visualization on status page, this diagram will also contain the descriptive text. These descriptions cannot be added from within SharePoint Designer.

InfoPath Forms and Workflows

A part of the Microsoft Office Suite of applications, InfoPath is used for the creation and filling out of forms. The ability for business users to easily create and customize their own forms is very powerful. With InfoPath, no programming knowledge is required, and the interface and form publishing processes are simple and familiar. Within workflows, InfoPath is most commonly used in tasks and initiation forms.

- **Task Forms:** When tasks are assigned from within workflows, custom forms are automatically generated by SharePoint Designer as the user interface for these tasks.
- **Initiation Forms:** The initiation form is the page that the workflow starts on when it is manually initiated. If there are no initiation form parameters, an initiation form will only consist of Start and Cancel buttons, but it is still an InfoPath form that can be modified.

The Workflow Settings page in SharePoint Designer has a section called Forms. Click a form name here to open it in InfoPath, modify it, and publish it back to the workflow. For example, modify a default plain initiation form to add a nice title, colors, and some descriptive text to it.

Workflows in the Back Stage View

Another way that workflows are integrated with Office is within the new Back Stage view that exists in Office 2010. This screen is seen when you click the File button at the top left. When a document library has workflows that are configured to be manually initiated, they can be started from within their native Office application. In Office, click the File menu, and click the Save & Send tab on the left side. In the Workflows section, click the name of the workflow you would like to start, and click the Start Workflow button on the right. When the initiation form pops up, click Start.

WORKFLOW ADMINISTRATION

The administration, management, and troubleshooting of workflows is an important part of the job of the workflow creator. In this section, the workflow status screen will be explained, along with topics such as workflow deletion and even workflow reporting.

Workflow Status

When a workflow is in progress and after it has completed, there is a workflow status screen that can be viewed. Each time a new workflow is run for the first time on a list or library, a new column is automatically added to the default view of the list. The column name is the name of the workflow. This column contains status text of the workflow, such as In Progress or Completed. This status text is a link to the Workflow Status page for that workflow, specific to that list item. The following are the sections of the workflow status screen.

Workflow Information

This section shows basic facts about who started the workflow, when, and what the status is.

In the workflow's settings in SharePoint Designer, when the "Show workflow visualization on status page" box is checked, a full Visio diagram is displayed on the workflow status page. Check marks indicate steps in the workflow that have already taken place.

Also, below the workflow visualization are some additional actions that may be taken. These are Add or update approvers of Approval, Cancel all Approval tasks, and Update active tasks of Approval. These options do not exist in every workflow by default, but they *do* exist in the out-of-the-box ones such as Approval and Collect Feedback.

There is a link here called Terminate this workflow now. This is very useful when it comes to errors. When a workflow gets stuck, terminate the workflow, so that it can be modified, published, and tried again.

Tasks

This is a list of all of the tasks that have taken place so far, or are currently in progress. Information about each task and assignee is listed, along with the outcome such as "Approved." Click any task's name to open it.

Workflow History

This section contains a list of everything that happens in the workflow, including any errors. When out-of-the-box workflows are used, they output some pretty detailed information, but when you create workflows from scratch, it is up to you to use the Log to Workflow History action to create this data.

View Workflow Reports

A link in the Workflow History section, the View Workflow Reports button allows you to quickly generate an Excel file with information about a workflow. For each workflow, there is an Activity Duration Report and a Cancellation & Error Report. Click the name of a report, select a location, and an Excel file will be generated and placed in that location.

There is another way to get to the reports. In SharePoint Designer's Lists and Libraries screen, click the name of a list or library that has a workflow associated with it. Put the cursor in the Workflows section of the List Settings page and a Workflows tab will show in the Ribbon. Click View Workflow Reports.

Editing Workflows

In the Creating Custom Workflow Solutions section of this chapter, you learned how to edit workflows within SharePoint Designer 2010. There are also some edits that can be made from within the browser when reusable workflows are used. In a document library, in the Library tab of the Ribbon, click the Workflow Settings button. The settings of reusable workflows, such as "Approval — SharePoint 2010," can be modified from this screen by clicking their names.

Deleting Workflows

Workflows can easily be deleted from within SharePoint Designer by selecting the name of the workflow and clicking the delete button. This *removes it* from all lists and libraries that it is associated with, which was *not* the case in SharePoint 2007.

Go to a SharePoint list with a workflow, such as the Store Orders list that was created in a previous Try It Out. In the List Settings, click Workflow Settings. This screen is shown in Figure 5-33.

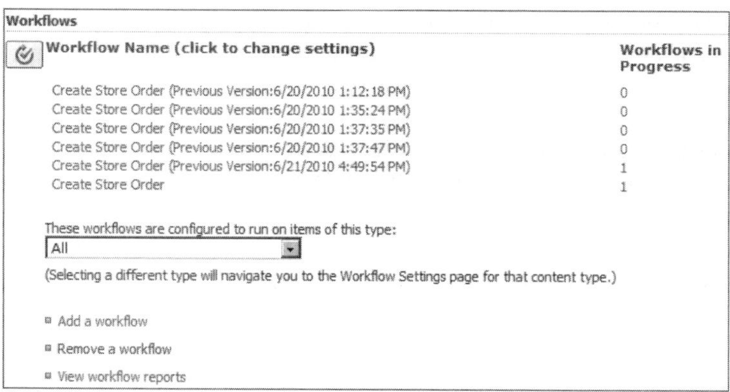

FIGURE 5-33

Notice that there are many different versions listed of the same workflow. Each time it was modified and published, a new version was placed in this list. The Workflows in Progress column shows you that a couple of these workflows are currently running. When you click the Remove a workflow link, you can safely remove any of the workflows that are previous versions and are not currently running. The only workflows to be careful about are the ones that are currently in progress. In this example, go back to the list and sort the Create Store Order column to see those items. Click the In Progress link to see each workflow's status page. If you have determined that it is okay, click Terminate this workflow now.

To temporarily unpublish a workflow without deleting it, remove it from the list on the Workflow Settings screen in the browser. The next time you click the Publish button in SharePoint Designer, the workflow will be associated with the list again.

When it comes to Site Workflows, go to Site Settings, and click Workflow Settings. The list of Site Workflows will be shown here, with the same type of interface for adding or removing workflows.

SUMMARY

SharePoint Workflows are fundamental in the creation of automated business processes, and in making jobs and tasks more efficient. This chapter has supplied you with introductory information about out-of-the-box and custom workflows, so that you can effortlessly create and configure your own. Not only have workflow basics been described, but you have learned how to get around in SharePoint Designer, and practiced creating workflows from scratch.

EXERCISES

1. The marketing department has a custom picture library approval status workflow. They would like to see a Visio diagram of a live flowchart that shows the steps of the workflow, and what activity has taken place. What setting do you recommend that they use?

2. Each document in the company policies library needs to go through a strenuous collaboration and approval process. When the workflow is kicked off, it first needs to be sent to everyone in the taxation department for review and feedback. After the feedback is collected, the approval process should automatically begin. How do you recommend they configure the out-of-the-box approval workflow in the browser?

3. The personnel department has an approval workflow that needs to be strictly locked down so that members of the process cannot see each other's assigned tasks. Which action do you recommend that they use in their custom SharePoint Designer workflow?

4. Sue Ellen has added the content approval status action to her custom workflow, but she is baffled at why this action does not seem to be doing its job. What list setting do you recommend that Sue Ellen modify?

5. Bob is attempting to manually start his workflow called "Policy Approval," but he does not see it in the "Start a New Workflow" section of the workflows page for that item. He has verified that the workflow is allowed to be manually started, and it has been published. Where can you look to troubleshoot his problem?

▸ WHAT YOU LEARNED IN THIS CHAPTER

TOPIC	KEY CONCEPTS
What is a workflow?	Business processes are everywhere, and workflows are how we automate them.
What are common workflow terms?	Workflow terminology was covered, because it is important to know concepts like conditions and actions, and the logical steps involved.
Out-of-the-box workflows	The out-of-the-box workflow templates were covered in detail. A content approval workflow and a collection signatures workflow were both created.
SharePoint Designer 2010 workflows	SharePoint Designer 2010 workflows were introduced, and you learned how to get around in the interface.
Tasks and history list	The integral concepts of workflow tasks and history lists were covered. These types of lists are a large part of the inner workings of SharePoint workflows.
Office 2010 integration	Microsoft Office 2010 client integration was discussed, with regard to the applications that are involved in workflows. Visio and InfoPath allow you to add nice visuals to forms and processes.
Workflow troubleshooting	Workflow administration concepts were discussed. When workflows go wrong, it is extremely important to know how to dig in, find the problem, and even terminate a workflow if necessary.

6

Working with Content Types

WHAT YOU WILL LEARN IN THIS CHAPTER:

- What a content type is and why it is such an important part of SharePoint
- What the various content types you can create are
- How to create the major content types
- Best practices for creating and managing content types for your organization

Thus far, this book has discussed components that can help you organize information in a SharePoint site. You should now know how to create lists and libraries, and assign metadata values to content items. You should also know how to associate business processes with lists and libraries so that you can track, review, and approve items in a consistent and automatic manner. Using this functionality in your work environment means that you spend more time doing actual work, rather than trying to locate information in disorganized filing systems.

This chapter takes the concepts discussed thus far and brings them together to create an information management package that ties to your content. After reading this chapter, you should feel comfortable creating content types suitable for efficiently managing the information that is vital to your organization.

CONTENT TYPES OVERVIEW

A *content type* represents a group of informational items in your organization that share common properties such as meeting minutes. You can define these properties, which include name, description, and a grouping category, to meet your business needs. In addition, you can adjust the properties associated with templates, workflow, site columns, and information policies as well as the settings for the document information panel. You can change these properties at any time and optionally apply those changes to your entire environment.

NOTE *For more on the various Content properties and what they do, see the section "The Anatomy of a Content Type."*

SharePoint offers several content types that provide solid foundations for all future content types. You can select one of these content types, and use it to create your content type in the central gallery, where you can then apply it to multiple lists and libraries throughout a site collection. By creating new content types, you can apply rules and properties to customize information and tie it to your business activities. Once you define your content type, you can create a new item by selecting the appropriate template from a drop-down menu presented by the New Document command on your list or library's Ribbon (see Figure 6-1). This chapter discusses the various elements of a content type as well as some of the configuration and customization alternatives of the most common content types.

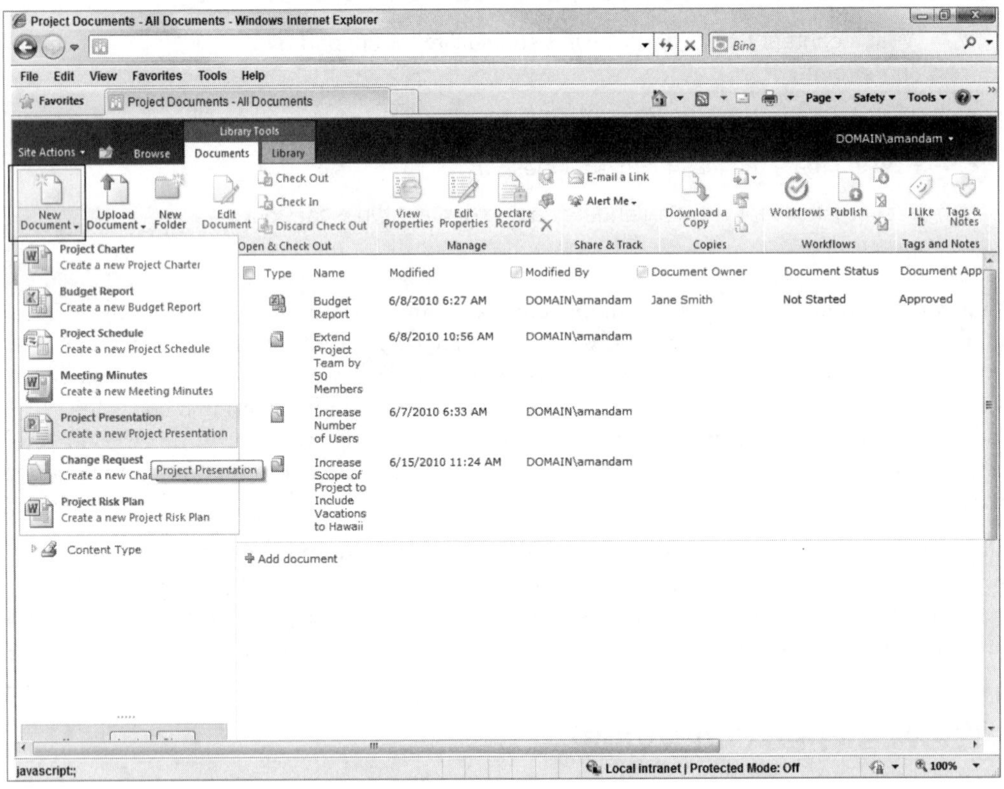

FIGURE 6-1

KNOWING WHERE TO CREATE CUSTOM CONTENT TYPES

It's important where you create a custom content type in the site hierarchy. If you plan to use it throughout your organization in many sites, you should store it in the content type gallery of the top-level site. For more specialized content, you might create content types that will apply to a specific site and its subsites. Figure 6-2 displays a site hierarchy. In this example, a content type created at the top-level site (Portal Home) would be available for use within every site in the site collection. However, a content type that was created on the Marketing site would only be available for use on the Marketing site and the team sites below it. It is important to create your content types at the appropriate location in the site collection, as they cannot be moved once they have been created.

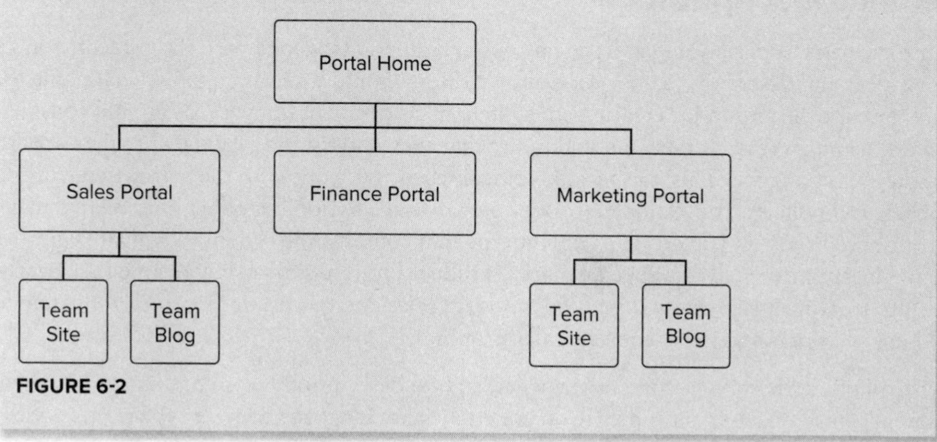

FIGURE 6-2

When you create a content type, you must select a parent from which it will automatically inherit any existing settings for a template, workflow, or metadata columns. You should consider the content types you need for your organization and then identify any relations they may have with each other or inheritances that they share so that you can place similar content types into groups. Using the same parent for each of these content types means you can filter based on the parent and include information from all child content types. For example, to manage your workflow, you may need a general purchase request form that will manage the approval process for new purchases within each division. You can create a standard purchase request content type and then create each divisional content type using it as the template. All metadata and the form template will become associated with each divisional content type automatically; however, you can define a unique workflow process for each child content type to allow different departmental managers to approve requests. You can easily update the form; because each divisional content type is based on the same parent, edits to the parent are copied down into each child.

THE ANATOMY OF A CONTENT TYPE

The magic of SharePoint is making its various pieces fit your business situation, and nowhere is that more evident than in content types. Content types all have properties, the basic ones being the name, description, and grouping category. In addition, you have properties associated with templates, workflow, site columns, and policy management as well as settings for the document information panel. You can define and redefine these properties to fit your business situations, but to do that, you need an understanding of the how to work with them. For example, you can change a content type's name to reflect a change in process, but it's important for you to make the name consistent and intuitive when you redefine it. In this section, you learn about the various content type properties and how to work with them.

Name and Description

Because the name is displayed on all the buttons and labels associated with the content, you should assign a clear and descriptive name. For example, users should intuitively know what name to select when they click the button for creating a new item in a document library. You should consider who will work with this content type and make sure that they understand exactly what they are creating when they select a name. This is especially critical when you work with the automated workflows, templates, and policies. For example, if your company sells multiple product lines related to aerospace and transportation, and you create a content type that contains the proposal template, approval process, and metadata related to a specific marine product line, consider using a name that clearly defines which product line it is associated with. Naming it "sales document" or "marine product documents" would not be as appropriate as "marine sales proposal."

As with all other SharePoint content elements, a good description helps communicate the purpose and intended use of a content type. If you concisely state what the content type is, users can more easily fill in information, modify settings, or select a content type for inclusion with a list or library.

Parent Content Type

You must define hierarchical relationships between two content types. In SharePoint, the *parent content type* defines the properties for a child content type, which, in turn, inherits all the parent's properties. For example, going back to the marine sales proposals scenario, you can create a new content type called "Marine Documents," which has specific site columns and metadata that you want to apply to all marine-related documents. By basing all Marine Sales Proposals on the Marine Document content type, they will inherit the existing properties of the parent—in this case, Marine Sales Proposals. Likewise, if you later need to add a new site column to all marine content types, you simply add columns to the Marine Documents parent content type to automatically have them added to the children of the content type. Once you create a content type, you cannot change its parent. Therefore, it is strongly recommended that you plan your content types carefully and work out the logistics of the hierarchy on paper before starting to define your content types in SharePoint.

Group

You can organize your various customized content types by grouping them. As you create or edit a content type, you must specify a group name either by selecting an existing group name or by creating a custom group. Instituting some standards for groups provides a solid base for expanding and organizing content types as you create them. For example, using the Marine Sales Proposals as an example, it may be appropriate to associate the content type with a custom group called "Marine Sales Documents" that can store all content types related to the marine product line.

Template

In many organizations, standard templates are used for business documents. Content types can be associated with these templates to improve the functionality and information flow within SharePoint and to make document libraries, for example, more useful to you. When you associate document templates with a content type, you can better control the quality of the data that you collect. You can base the template on a variety of file formats, including Word documents, Excel spreadsheets, InfoPath forms, and custom web pages. You can either upload a custom template to the content type, or you can point to a template stored at another location. If you want to point to an existing template, be sure that all members using the content type can access the location of the template. For example, if you create a sales proposal content type and a document template for sales proposals already exists on the sales team site, make sure that the people who will create content based on your newly created content type have access to that sales team site.

For Microsoft Office files, such as Word and Excel, updating or changing the document template associated with a content type has no effect on items that users have already created and that are stored in the document library. This is because of the way these files relate to a template. In Word, a document template is primarily only relevant for the initial creation of the document. However, for content types based on InfoPath or publishing templates such as page layouts, changing the template associated with the content type updates the existing documents to display the information as detailed in the template. This will become clearer when you explore those content types in greater detail later in this book.

Chapter 4 discussed how you can associate custom document templates with a document library. This association means that users can automatically generate documents based on that template by clicking the New Item button for a document library. With content types, you now have more than one item in the New Item menu, which gives you a single document repository in which to store several different types of information and simplify how people access materials.

To show you how to create and specify some of the reviewed properties of content types, this section presents two Try It Outs. In the first, you see how to create a new content type, and in the second, you see how to edit one of the content types that SharePoint has to offer to suit your needs by specifying a template.

TRY IT OUT Create a New Content Type

You need to manage your company's sales proposals in a more organized fashion as well as provide more automated support to the sales team during the proposal-creation stage. This includes giving them access to a standard proposal template as well as an automated review and approval workflow process. To reach your goal, you must first create the initial shell of the content type, which you can later modify to include elements such as templates, standard metadata, and workflow processes. In this Try It Out, you will create a company document content type based on the document parent content type and place it in a group. Then, you will create a second content type that inherits from that content type.

1. From the top level of your site collection, select Site Settings from the Site Actions menu. The Site Settings page appears.

2. Under the Galleries group, select Site Content Types. The Site Content Types page will appear listing all content types available within the site collection.
3. Click Create. The New Site Content Type screen appears, as shown in Figure 6-3.

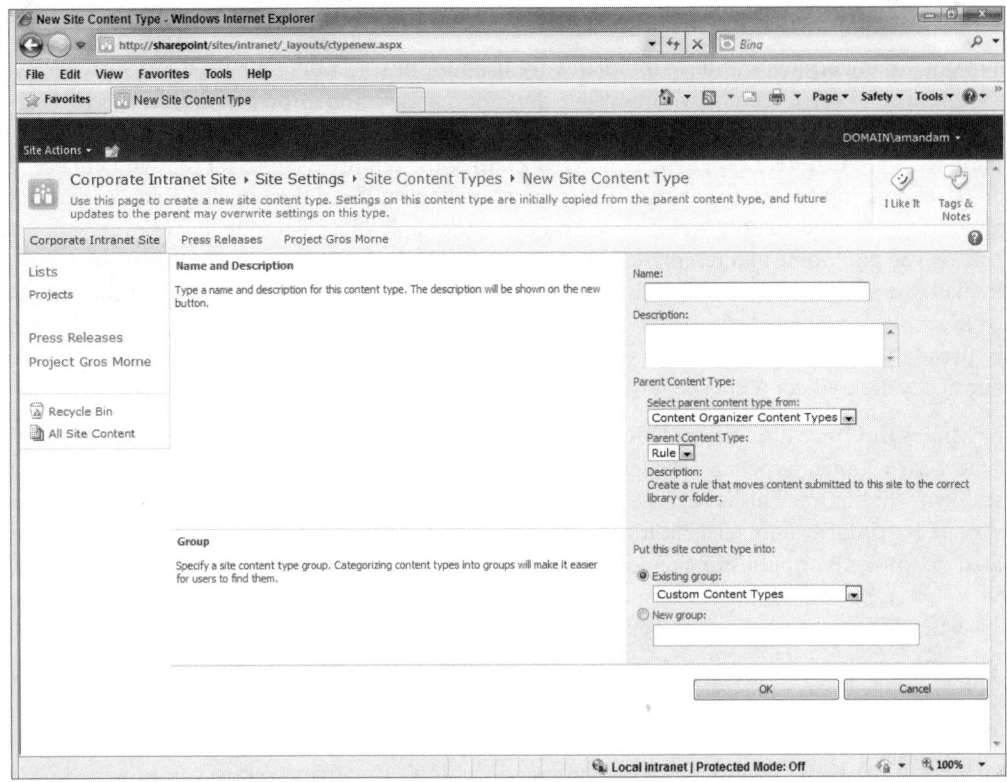

FIGURE 6-3

4. Define your new content type as follows:

PROPERTY	VALUE
Name	AW Document
Description	AdventureWorks Standard Document
Select Parent Content Type From	Document Content Types
Parent Content Type	Document
Put this Content Type into (New Group)	Company Documents

5. Click OK. You will be redirected to the administration page for the new content type as shown in Figure 6-4. From this page, you will be able to manage the properties of the content type such as metadata, workflow settings, and template.
6. From the breadcrumb navigational menu, return to the Site Settings page of your site.

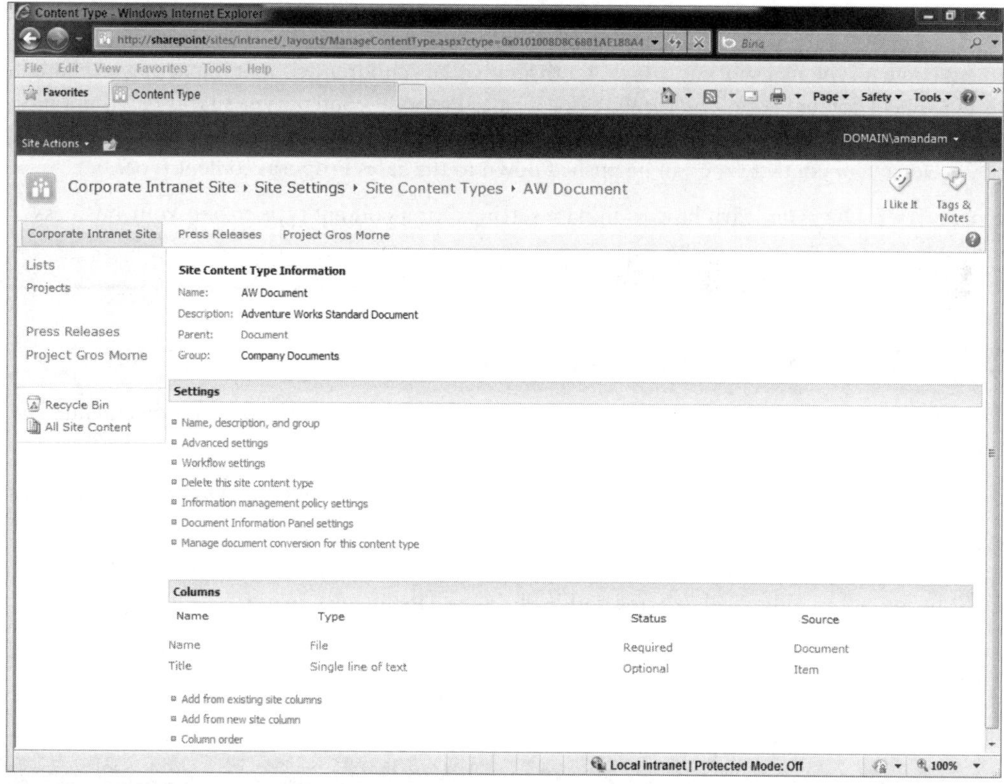

FIGURE 6-4

7. Select Site Content Types.
8. Click Create.
9. Define your new content type as follows:

PROPERTY	VALUE
Name	Sales Proposal
Description	AdventureWorks Sales Proposal
Select Parent Content Type From	Company Documents
Parent Content Type	AW Document
Put this Content Type into (New Group)	Sales Documents

10. Click OK.

How It Works

In this Try It Out, you created two custom content types. The AW Document content type is the base document content type for your organization. You created it from the default system content type of

Document. It is good practice to always create at least one custom content type that will act as the parent for all other custom content types in your organization. This will allow you to apply settings to the AW Document content type that will cascade down through all its children without impacting or changing the default Document content type. You then created a Sales Proposal content type that is based upon the AW Document content type. Therefore, any custom settings related to template, metadata, or workflow applied to the AW Document content type can be pushed down to the Sales Proposal content type.

In the next Try It Out, you learn how to update settings for a content type to suit your business requirements.

TRY IT OUT Edit and Existing Content Type

1. From the top level of your site collection, select Site Settings from the Site Actions menu. The Site Settings page appears.
2. Under the Galleries group, select Site Content Types. The Site Content Types page will appear listing all content types available within the site collection.
3. Select Sales Documents from the Show Group drop-down as shown in Figure 6-5. The content type will be filtered to only display items within the Sales Documents group.

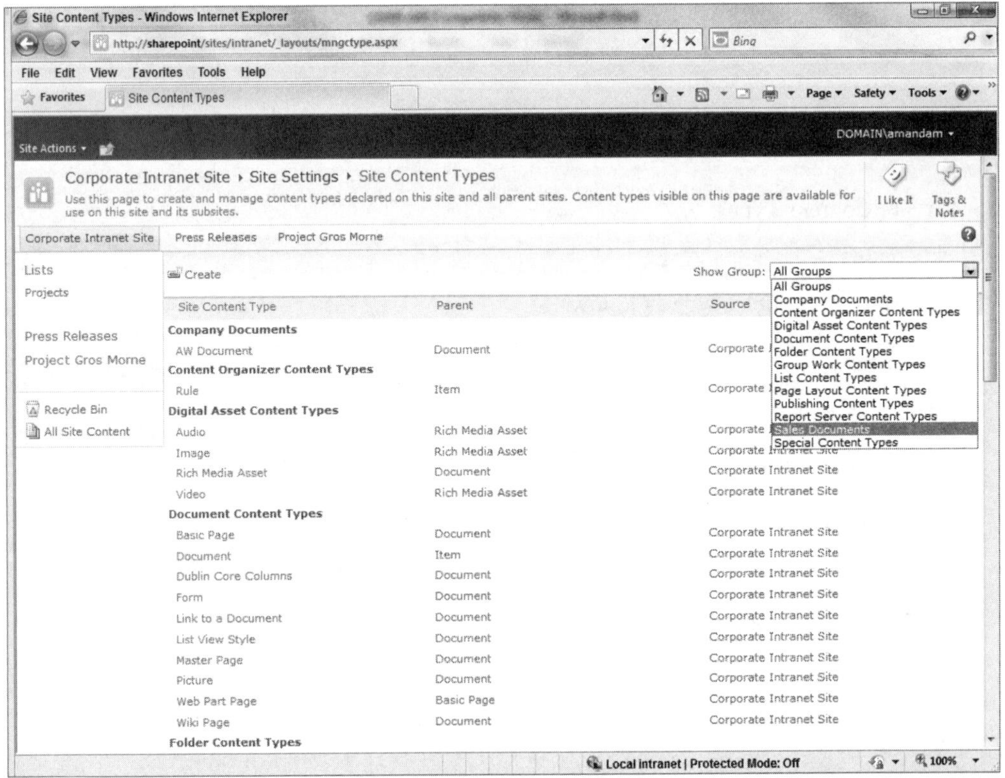

FIGURE 6-5

4. Select the Sales Proposal content type created from the previous exercise.
5. Select the Advanced Settings link.
6. Select the option to Upload a new document template.
7. Click the Browse button.
8. Locate the Proposal `Template.docx` file from this chapter's resource files and click Open.
9. Click OK. The page will refresh, and you will be returned to the Sales Proposal content type administration page.

How It Works

In steps 4–9, you specified a custom document template for your Sales Proposal content type. This means that whenever users create a New document based on the Sales Proposal content type, the document you specified will open based on the associated document template. This helps address a common challenge in many organizations, whereby users have difficulty locating the latest version of a template when creating new documents.

Workflow

Creating important documents often requires the creator to follow an equally important business process. This process ensures that everyone involved in the collaboration activity is doing their part and communicating properly. When people follow processes without the aid of automated tool, they often encounter or create roadblocks because of distractions and other duties. For example, if a sales manager completes an important sales proposal and sends it to a colleague or supervisor for feedback with an email notification, that colleague may not immediately respond because of another task or emergency and, as a result, the request gets buried in an inbox or lost in the shuffle. This is a common situation because many people struggle to keep up with email and daily responsibilities. Unfortunately, this means missed deadlines, frustration between team members, and missed opportunities, and it may ultimately impact the overall operations of the company.

By assigning a workflow template with a content type, you can define a realistic series of tasks with built-in reminders for a specific business activity so that workers can focus on their duties. For example, in the previous scenario, whenever a salesperson creates a sales proposal, he or she can send it to the sales team or a supervisor for feedback with tasks and deadlines automatically created so that the request for feedback is less likely to be lost. Even if the sales team supervisor does forget the task, the system will send reminder messages to the supervisor until the task is complete. This means that the salesperson doesn't have to follow up on the task.

Depending on the parent content type you select when you define your custom content type, you may already have workflows enabled. If these workflow processes do not apply, you can remove them, but be careful not to remove a workflow that is important to the operations of a specific content type. By updating the workflow settings of a parent, you can optionally update any content types that are inheriting from that content type.

Adding a custom workflow to a content type is a fairly simple process and similar to adding a workflow to a document library or list as described in Chapter 5. The advantage here, however, is that you typically only have to define the process once, and it is then applied to multiple document libraries that utilize that content type. If you add multiple content types to a single library, each content type can have its own unique workflow or set of processes that are independent of the others.

TRY IT OUT Define a Workflow for a Content Type

To better track approvals related to sales proposals, you have decided to configure a workflow on the Sales Proposal content type that tracks the approval process of each proposal that is added to the library.

1. From the Sales Proposal content type administration page, select Workflow settings. You will be redirected to the Workflow Settings page.
2. Select the Add a Workflow link. You will be redirected to the Add a Workflow page.
3. Select the Approval - SharePoint 2010 template, as shown in Figure 6-6.

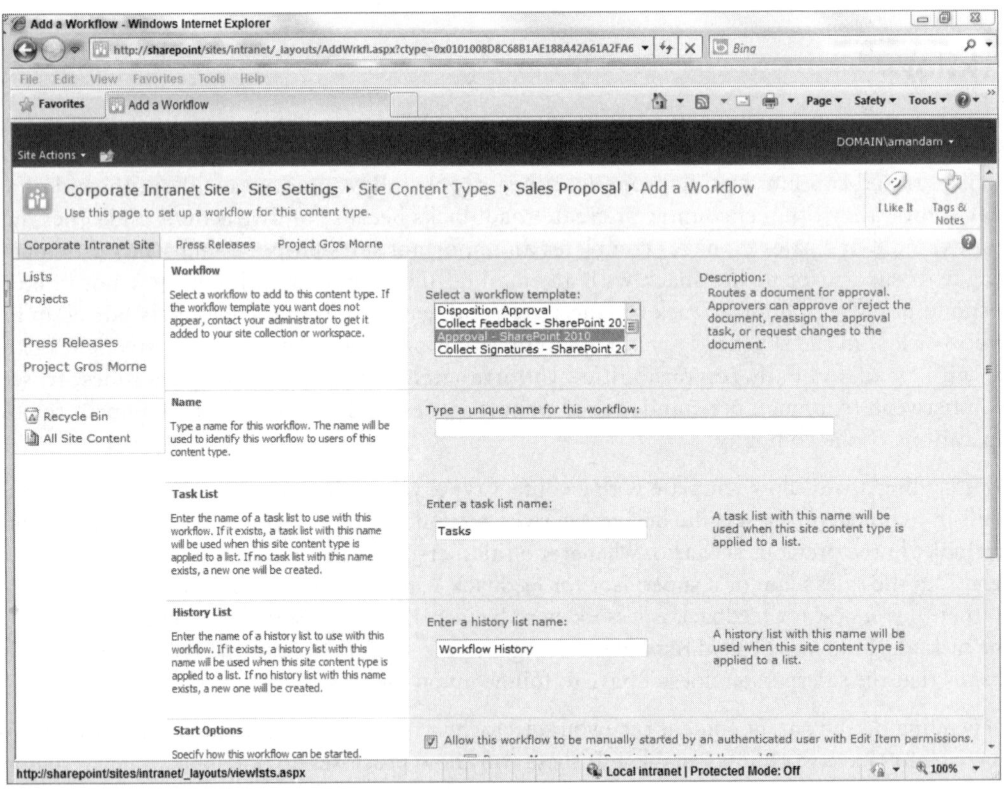

FIGURE 6-6

4. Specify the details as follows for the new workflow:

PROPERTY	VALUE
Name	Sales Proposal Approval
Task List	Tasks
History List	Workflow History
Start Options	Start this workflow when a new item is created.
Update List and Site Content Types	Yes

5. Click the Next button to enter the remaining workflow details.

6. Enter the following details for the remaining properties:

PROPERTY	VALUE
Approvers	Assign To: Enter your own name Order: One at a time (serial)
Expand Groups	Deselect
Request	The following sales proposal has been added to the library. Please review it and provide an approval decision.
Duration Per Task	2
Duration Units	Day(s)
End on First Rejection	Select
End on Document Change	Select

7. Click Save. You will be returned to the Workflow Settings page, as shown in Figure 6-7.

How It Works

The workflow activity you created will launch whenever a new item is created based on that content type, and a task will be created for you because you selected your own name as an approver for the serial workflow. The due date for the task will be two days from the point the document is created. If you do not complete the task by the assigned date, you will receive a reminder. Because you selected the option to end on first rejection, the workflow will end if you reject the item. Similarly, if the document is changed after the workflow has launched, the workflow will be canceled.

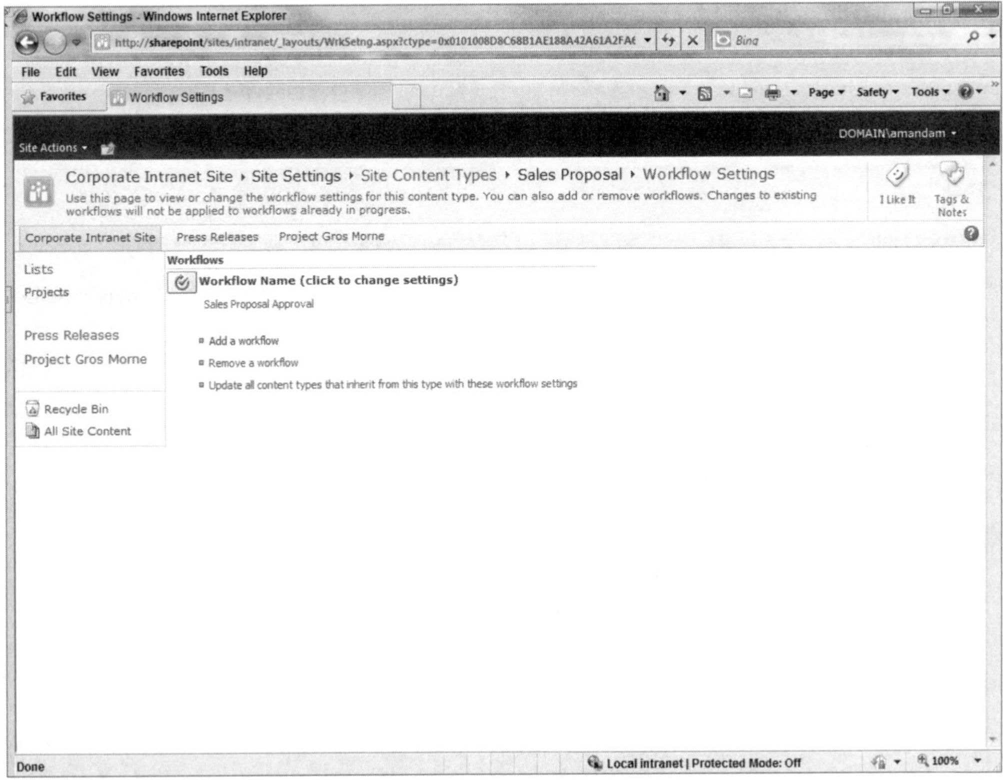

FIGURE 6-7

Site Columns

In Chapter 4, you learned about the importance of site columns when creating standard metadata properties for lists and libraries. To recap, site columns are stored in a central gallery on each site, and any list or library can use them on the same site or any site below it. Site columns provide standardization and ease of use when you want to share important information across multiple lists, libraries, or sites.

Site columns are also very important in content types. Because content types are created and stored in a central gallery, all associated components must be centralized as well. Therefore, you can only associate site columns with a content type. When you add a content type to a library, the required site columns are automatically associated with that library for use by the content type. You can create custom views on the columns and web parts, such as the content query web part, and you can apply advanced filtering.

NOTE *Web parts are explained in Chapter 7.*

Remember the following when working with site columns:

- When defining metadata for a content type, you can use existing site columns or create new site columns directly from the Content Type Settings page. When you use existing site columns, you are redirected to a site column selection page.
- By using the Group Selection drop-down, you can filter the list of site columns to a more manageable size. This is why group names are very important, and why you should make them intuitive when you create site columns.
- Once you select the site columns you want, you click the Add button to move them from the left-hand listbox to the right-hand listbox.
- You can remove an item you may have added accidentally by selecting it from the box on the right and clicking the Remove button.
- You can update all content types that inherit from the current content type with the new columns you selected. For example, if you have a content type called Human Resources Document that is the parent to the other content types Policies and Procedures and Vacation Request Form, and you select the Yes option in the Update List and Site Content Types section for a site column called Division that is added to the Human Resources Document, it will also be added to Policies and Procedures and Vacation Request Form content types.

You can also create a new site column as you create a content type. Even though you're creating the site column from the administration interface of the specific content type, SharePoint still adds it to the central gallery of the site, making it available to other content types, lists, and libraries on the current site and sites below it.

TRY IT OUT Add a Site Column to a Content Type

To better track the owner of each sales proposal, you decide it would be a good idea to add a column to the Sales Proposal content type to track the account manager who is assigned to the specific opportunity.

1. From the Sales Proposal content type administration page, select Add from new site column from the Columns section.
2. Enter the details for your new column as follows:

PROPERTY	VALUE
Column Name	Account Manager
The type of information in this column is	Person or Group
Group	Sales Related
Description	Enter the account manager for this opportunity.
Allow Multiple Sections	No
Allow Selection of	People Only
Show Field	Name (with picture)

3. Click OK to save your column. You will be returned to the Content Type Administration page, and your new column will appear in the column listing.

TRY IT OUT Add a Site Column to a Parent Content Type

You have decided that, for every document that is created within your organization, you wish to track its confidentiality rating. It would not be realistic to manually update every single library with this column nor would it be practical to manually add the column to each content type. Therefore, you decide instead to create a column called Confidentiality Rating to the content type AW Document, since all other document-based content types in your organization will inherit from that content type. Therefore, all existing and new content types will be created with that column.

1. From the AW Document content type administration page, select Add from new site column from the Columns section.
2. Enter the details for your new column as follows:

PROPERTY	VALUE
Column Name	Confidentiality Rating
The type of information in this column is	Choice
Group	Corporate Classification
Description	Please select the appropriate confidentiality rating for this document.
Type each choice on a separate line	Private - Internal Private - Team Public
Display Choices Using	Radio Buttons
Allow "Fill-in" Choices	No
Default Value	Blank

3. Click OK to save your column. You will be returned to the Content Type Administration page and your new column will appear in the column listing. You will also notice that by visiting the Sales Proposal content type, the new column will appear in the listing, as shown in Figure 6-8.

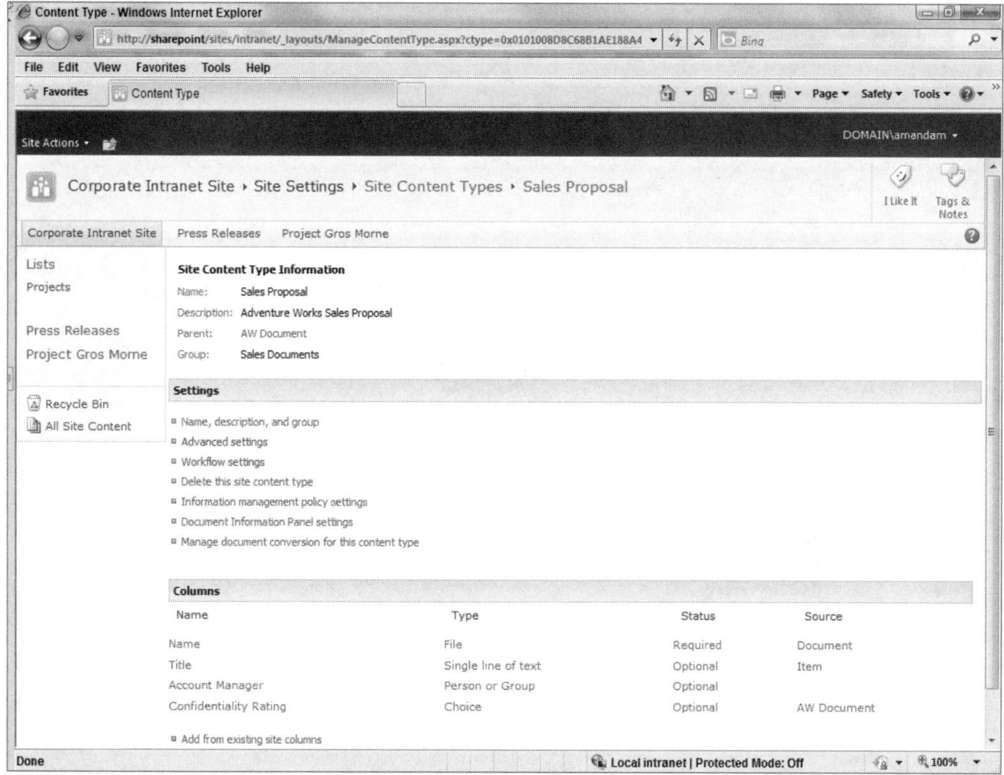

FIGURE 6-8

Document Information Panel Settings

Whenever you are saving a file in a Microsoft application such a Word or Excel, you will notice a form appear at the top of the application containing all the columns that are associated with the content type or library you are saving to. This is the *document information panel*, which asks you to complete metadata, as shown in Figure 6-9, and which is the subject of the next Try It Out.

If you desire, you may modify the document information panel for a content type. We will review the process for doing this in the following Try It Out.

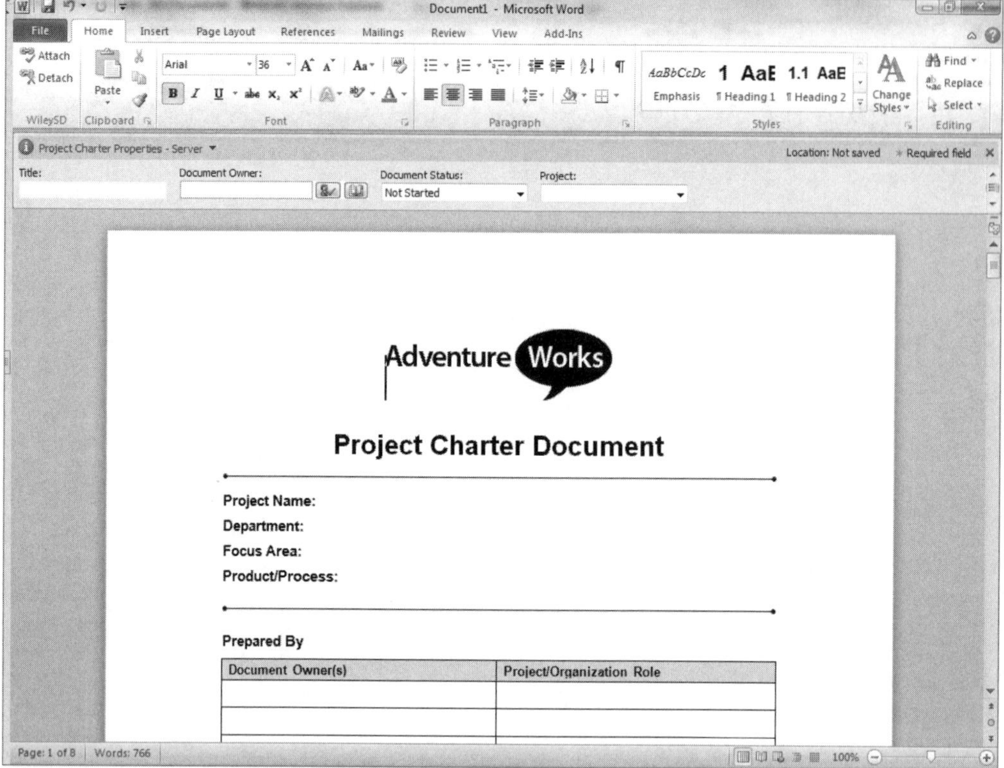

FIGURE 6-9

TRY IT OUT Edit the Document Information Panel of a Content Type

1. From the Sales Proposal content type administration page, select the Document Information Panel settings link.
2. Select the Create a New Custom Template link. Microsoft InfoPath Designer 2010 will open. A dialog message will appear as shown in Figure 6-10; click the Finish button. The document information panel will appear.
3. Select to the left of the Title field and click the Return button on your keyboard to insert a space above the three fields.
4. Select the blank row above the fields and select the Insert tab from the Ribbon menu.
5. Select the Picture button and browse to the location of this chapter's resources to locate the `awlogo.png` file.
6. Click the Insert button. Your logo should now appear above the three fields as shown in Figure 6-11.

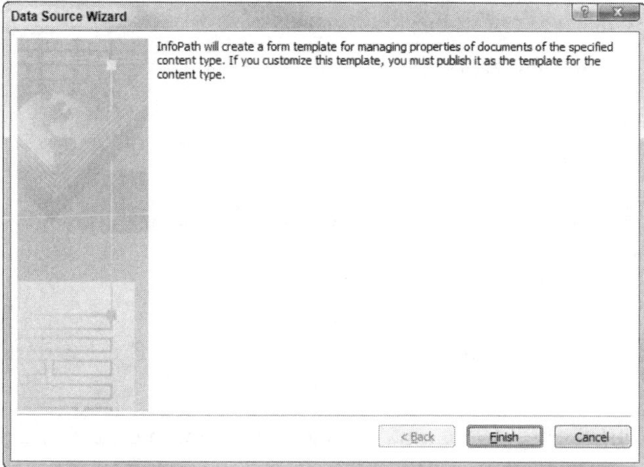

FIGURE 6-10

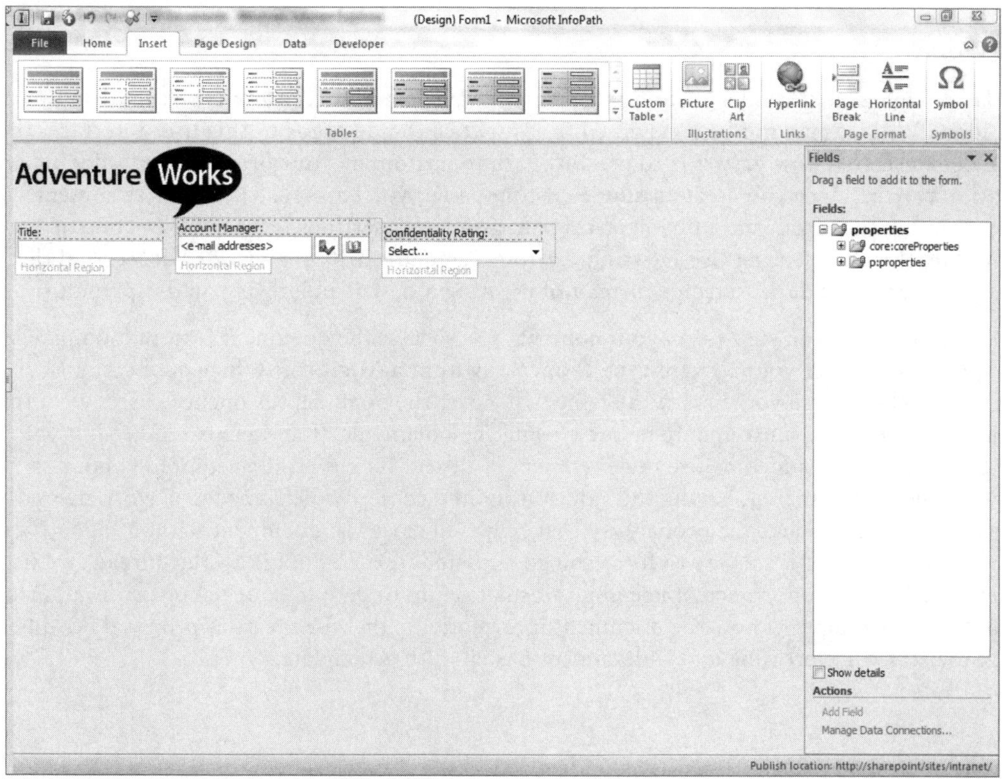

FIGURE 6-11

7. Click the Publish button on the File tab of the Ribbon menu.
8. Select the Document Information Panel publish option.
9. You will be prompted to save the form template. Click OK.
10. Save the file to your chapter resources using the same proposal form.
11. The Publishing Wizard will display a final verification page listing details for the form. Click the Publish button to complete the process.
12. Click the Close button.
13. You will be returned to a page with a link to return to the Document Information Panel settings page. Click the link.
14. Select the checkbox to Always show Document Information Panel on document open and initial save for this content type.
15. Click OK.

How It Works

In this Try It Out, you created a custom information panel for your content type that displays a custom logo. While it may not be considered best practice to add logos to this user interface, this example demonstrated how easy it is to use InfoPath to customize your organization's document information panels. Once you create a single custom panel, you can reuse it for other content types by pointing to it from the Document Information Panel settings of your other content types. You would do this by selecting Use Existing Custom Template (URL, UNC, or URN) from the Document Information Panel settings instead of creating a new template as you did previously.

You enabled a checkbox in step 14 on your content type so that the document information panel always appears whenever your content type is opened within a Microsoft Office application such as Word or Excel. Because you display the panel whenever the document is opened, users treat the panel as a form that they must update before closing the document. If an item is required, it will have to be completed or added before the document is closed. However, if a required column is already specified but outdated, having the values front and center while someone is working on the document should help reduce the probability that they will close the document without updating the latest information. There is no way to force someone to update a column if a value already exists, so communicating the importance of keeping information up to date to your team is still important. Figure 6-12 is an example of how the document information panel for the sales proposal document will look to users when creating a new document based on that template.

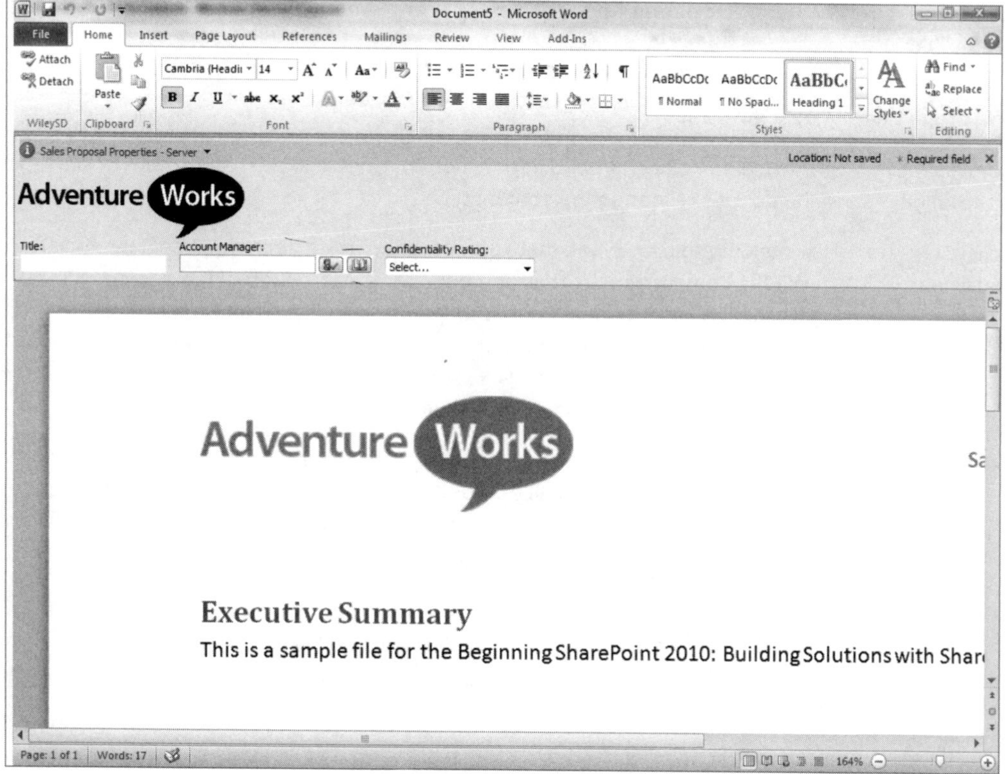

FIGURE 6-12

Information Management Policies

Another great feature of content types is how you can define certain policies and behaviors around how they are managed. Because content of a specific type quite often has the same requirements for retention and management, it is beneficial to define a set of policies around a content type and have those inherited by all documents that are created from it. While it is possible to define information management policies on a library, it is often a better practice to define the policy based on the content type so that you can have specific rules for each type of content that can be reused throughout your organization in a consistent manner.

You can configure the items in relation to a content type's information policies as listed in the following table:

POLICY SETTING	DESCRIPTION
Administrative Description	Provide some background information to users who are responsible for managing the policies related to the content type.
Policy Statement	A customizable message that appears when users open documents associated with the content type. A message bar appears at the top of the document in an Information Management Policy box. Users can click a Details button to view all the details related to the policy message. By using a policy statement, content type owners can ensure that users have all the information they need concerning the important policies related to specific content.
Retention	Allows you to control the life span of specific types of content. You can configure content types to automatically be deleted after a certain time based on a document property. Alternatively, you can launch a workflow that gives the user a final chance to review the document before it is archived or deleted.
Auditing	If you enable auditing on a content type, the following activities related to documents associated with the content type are tracked: ➤ Opening or downloading documents, viewing items in lists, or viewing item properties ➤ Editing items ➤ Checking out or checking in items ➤ Moving or copying items to another location in the site
Barcodes	This automatically inserts an auto-generated barcode into documents of a specific content type. You can also prompt users to insert barcodes when they use specific Microsoft Office client applications.
Labels	Ensures that important properties or messages are printed with documents related to a specific content type, such as a confidential or a specific noncalculated document property. Content type owners can customize the presentation of the label by choosing font formatting and size.

We will review information management policies in detail in Chapter 14 when we look at the records management features of SharePoint.

Document Conversion

If the document conversion feature is enabled on your web server, you can configure rules for each content type that support the files being automatically converted to an alternate file type such as a web page or image file. This feature will be reviewed as part of Chapter 13 when we review the web content management features of SharePoint.

BASE CONTENT TYPES

SharePoint offers a repertoire of content types that address basic business needs. These are organized into groups according to their purpose. This section details each of these built-in content groups and types.

Business Intelligence Content Types

SharePoint offers powerful features that organize, track, and display data from a variety of sources so that you can monitor the status of your business. This section discusses the business intelligence content types, and Chapter 16 describes the useful set of business reporting tools included in this latest version of SharePoint. The content types in the following table are available as part of the Business Intelligence group. The indicator types contain columns that collect business intelligence information from a data source so that it can be presented as a key performance indicator (KPI) or in a report. By creating a new content type based on one of these base content types, you can augment the information that is gathered by default. You can also customize the dashboard and report types to meet your needs.

CONTENT TYPE	PARENT	DESCRIPTION
Excel-Based Status Indicator	Common Indicator Columns	A key performance indicator based on information stored within an Excel workbook. This type of indicator can be created from the Status list template.
Fixed-Value-Based Status Indicator	Common Indicator Columns	A key performance indicator based on information entered manually into a list item. This type of indicator can be created from the Status list template.
Report	Document	An Excel document page for the browser-based display of spreadsheet information.
SharePoint List-Based Status Indicator	Common Indicator Columns	A key performance indicator based on information stored within a SharePoint list. This type of indicator can be created from the Status list template.
SQL Server Analysis Services-Based Status Indicator	Common Indicator Columns	A key performance indicator based on information stored within SQL Server Analysis Services. This type of indicator can be created from the Status list template.
Web Part Page with Status List	Document	A preconfigured web part page with an associated Status List. This page can be further configured to provide an informative dashboard page to business stakeholders.

Content Organizer Content Types

Only one content type exists within the Content Organizer group, and it is tied primarily to the records management capabilities of SharePoint; however, it can be utilized in collaborative scenarios as well. We will explore this content type in Chapter 14.

CONTENT TYPE	PARENT	DESCRIPTION
Rule	Item	A list item content type for configuring rules related to the routing of documents to appropriate library locations.

Document Content Types

You will probably use the document types frequently in your SharePoint sites because the typical site functions as a document repository and viewing system for your team. The following document types are built into SharePoint, many of which will be explored throughout this book.

CONTENT TYPE	PARENT	DESCRIPTION
Basic Page	Document	Standard web page containing location for sharing text-based information.
Document	Item	Standard base content type for the storage of documents in SharePoint.
Dublin Core Columns	Document	Based on the Document content type but contains many standard columns to conform to the requirements for the popular classification system known as Dublin Core.
Form	Document	Based on the Document content type and is specifically designed to support the use of InfoPath. See Chapter 12 for more information on this content type.
Link to a Document	Document	In some cases, a document may be stored in one location and linked from another library. This content type helps support such scenarios by creating a record or row in a document library that references the document located in the other location.
List View Style	Document	System content type for the definition of list view styles.
Master Page	Document	Content type for the definition of master pages. See Chapter 9 for more information on this content type.
Picture	Document	Based on the document content type and is the primary content type associated with a picture library.
Web Part Page	Basic Page	A web page with a number of web part zones for the use of web parts. These web pages can come in a variety of layouts and templates.
Wiki Page	Document	A web page for use within a wiki library.

Document Set Content Types

Only one content type exists within the Document Set group. The Document Set content type is a specialized content type that supports the management of a group of documents.

CONTENT TYPE	PARENT	DESCRIPTION
Document Set	Document Collection Folder	Specialized content type for the grouping and management of related files as a single entity.

When defining a document set, you associated one or more content types that can be created within the set as well as define specific templates or content that can exist within the document set folder when it is created. In the next two Try It Outs, you will enable the use of Document Set content types on your site collection and then define a Document Set for managing the sign-up process for new customers.

TRY IT OUT Enable Document Sets on a Site Collection

1. From the top level of your site collection, select Site Settings from the Site Actions menu. The Site Settings page appears.
2. Select the Site Collection Features link from the Site Collection Administration group of links. You will be redirected to a page listing all features available within the site collection.

NOTE *If you do not see that group, you are not listed as a Site Collection Administrator of the site and you will need to work with your system administrator to be added to this group or to complete this exercise.*

3. Select the Activate button associated with the Document Sets feature. The page will refresh and the feature will now appear as Active, as shown in Figure 6-13.

How It Works

SharePoint supports a wide range of functionality. Each site template is configured with certain features enabled while others are inactive until a user with appropriate privileges activates the feature for use. Once the feature is activated, the functionality it represents becomes enabled within the site or site collection. In the above example, the document sets' functionality was not available until you selected the Activate button. Now when you visit the Site Content Types gallery, you will be able to create Document Set content types.

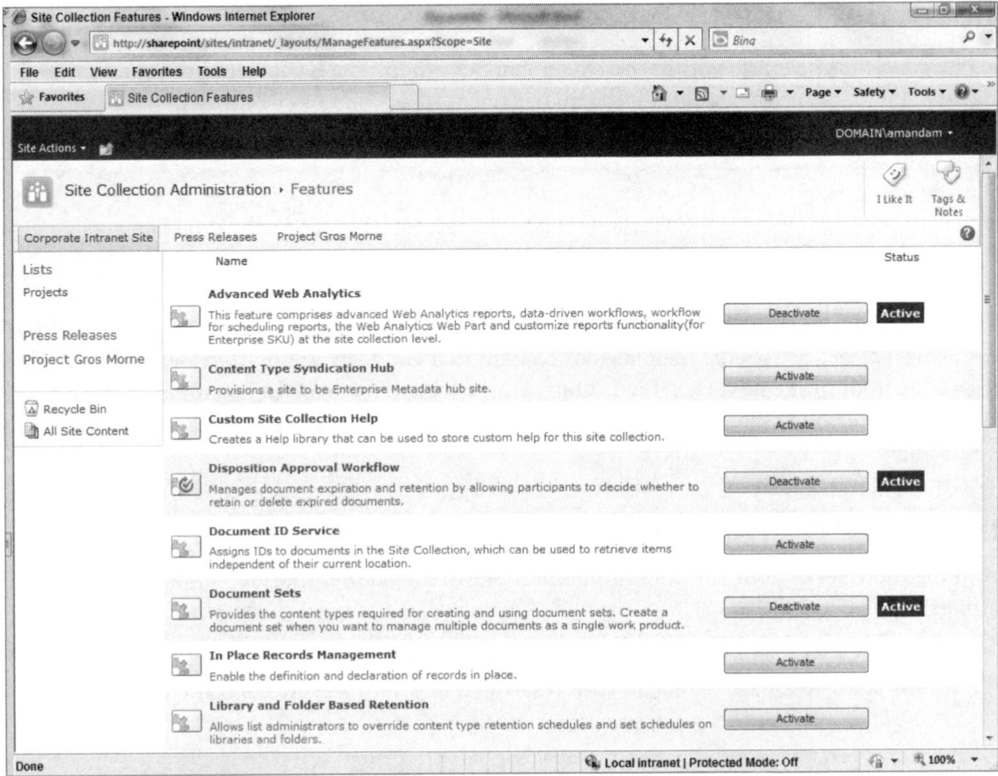

FIGURE 6-13

TRY IT OUT Create a Document Set

1. From the top level of your site collection, select Site Settings from the Site Actions menu. The Site Settings page appears.
2. Under the Galleries group, select Site Content Types. The Site Content Types page will appear listing all content types available within the site collection.
3. Click the Create button.
4. Create the content type using the following settings:

PROPERTY	VALUE
Name	New Customer
Description	Package for Creating a New Customer
Select Parent Content Type From	Document Set Content Types

PROPERTY	VALUE
Parent Content Type	Document Set
Put this Content Type into (New Group)	Sales Documents

5. Click OK. You will be redirected to the New Customer Content Type administration page.
6. Select the Document Set settings link. You will be directed to a specialized administration page for Document Set content types as shown in Figure 6-14.

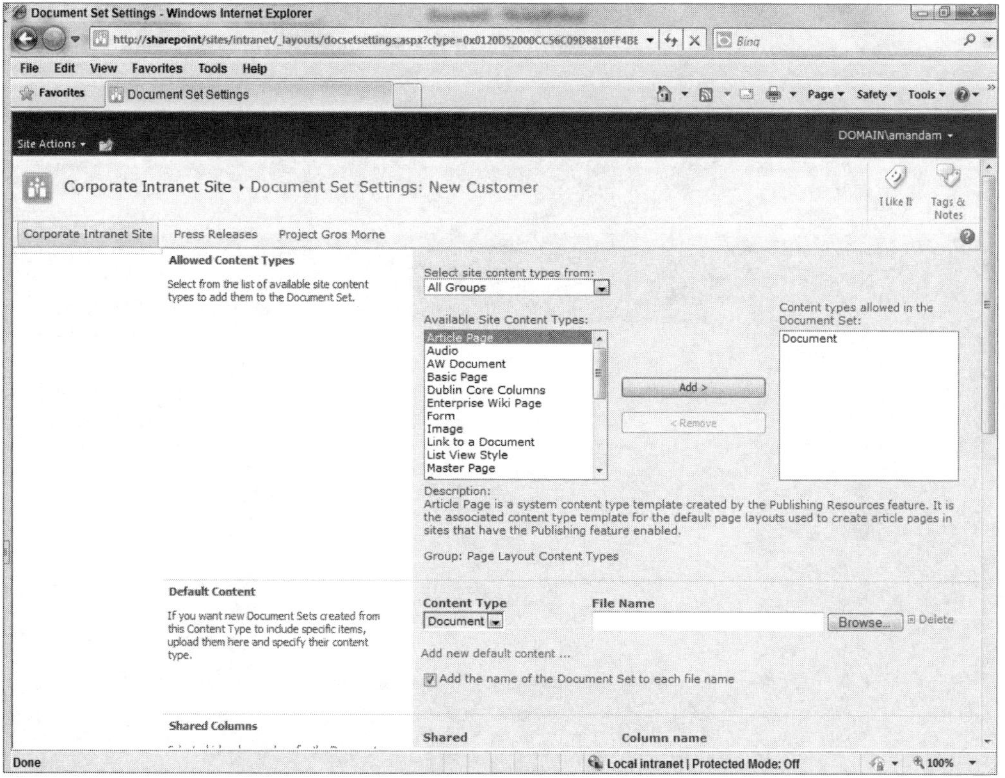

FIGURE 6-14

7. Select the content types that you wish to allow users to utilize when creating a new customer. In this example, you will select AW Document and Sales Proposal.
8. In the Default Content section, click the Delete button next to the Browse... button. This will remove the Document content type from this library.
9. Select Add new default content link.
10. Select Sales Proposal as the content type, and upload the Proposal Template from this chapter's resource files.

11. Return to the Allowed Content Types section, and remove Document from the allowed listing.
12. Scroll to the bottom of the page, and click OK.

How It Works

In this example, you created a new Document Set content type for new customers. Whenever a user selects this content type from the new document option of the Ribbon menu, a window will appear, as shown in Figure 6-15. Users will define the details of the new customer and then be redirected to a details page list for the document set. From this details page, users can create new documents based upon the allowed content types as well as fill in documents such as the Proposal Template that exists already upon creation, as shown in Figure 6-16.

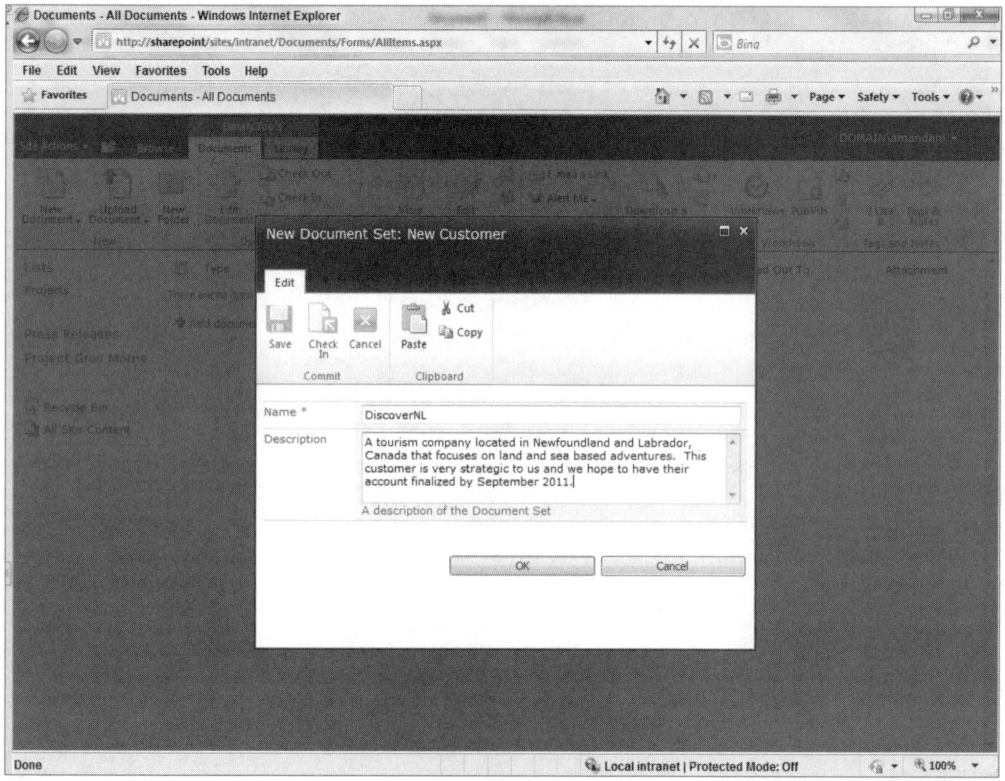

FIGURE 6-15

There is also a specific Ribbon menu tab for Documents Sets, as shown in Figure 6-17. From this menu, users can edit properties, manage permissions, or capture version history of the entire set of documents. In addition, workflows can be launched based upon the available workflows that have been assigned to the content type. For example, account managers may run an approval workflow once all documentation related to the new customer is complete so that the sales manager can approve the new customer.

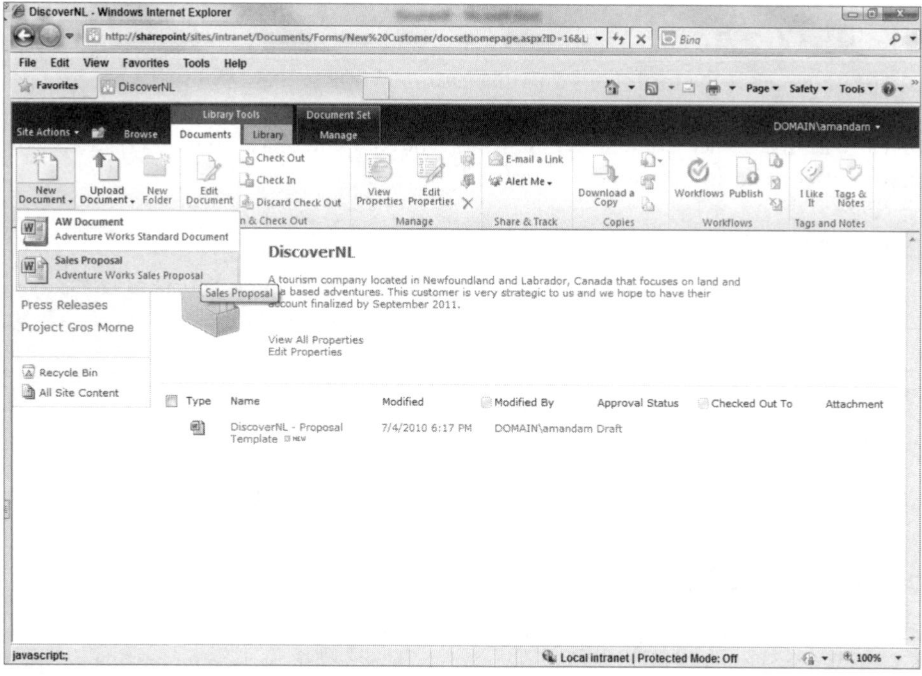

FIGURE 6-16

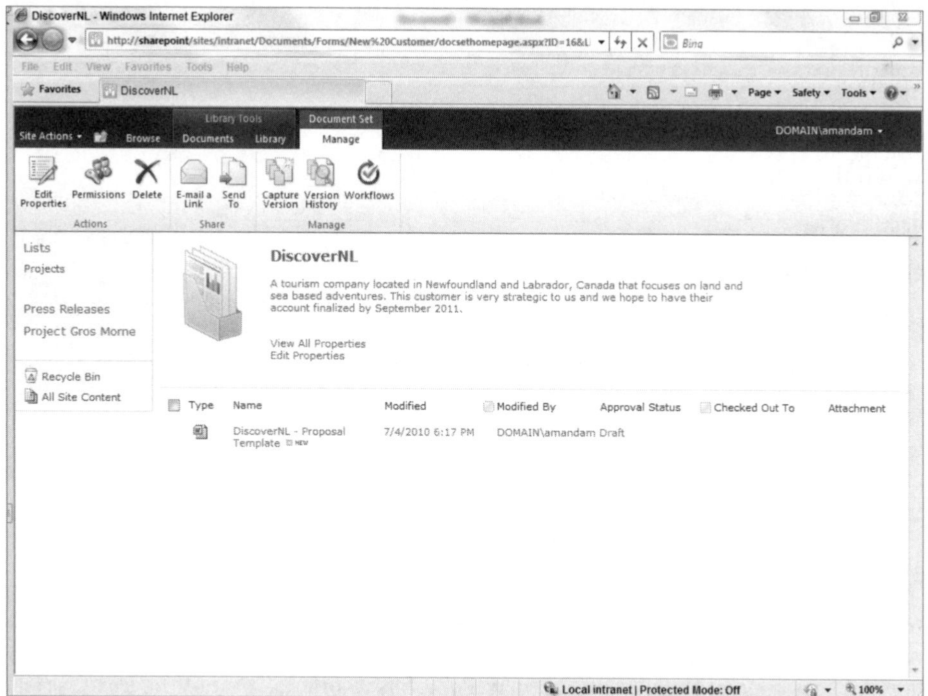

FIGURE 6-17

Folder Content Types

You use this type of content type for folders and discussion boards in SharePoint. Because individual discussions in SharePoint are stored within folders, it is appropriate that the base content type be affiliated with the Folder Content Types group. The following base content types are what SharePoint has to offer as part of the Folder Content Types group.

CONTENT TYPE	PARENT	DESCRIPTION
Folder	Item	Specialized folder that supports columns and metadata like any other element stored within a list or library.
Discussion	Folder	This content type is associated with a discussion list, which was discussed in Chapter 2.
Summary Task	Folder	This content type is associated with the tasks and project tasks lists, which were discussed in Chapter 2.

Group Work Content Types

The Group Work content types are a set of specialized content types associated with lists available within the Group Work Site template. This site template is designed to be a collaborative location for sharing data between team members of subjects such as whereabouts, phone calls, assignments, and schedules. The content types associated with this group all inherit from the Item content type and are as follows:

- Circulation
- Holiday
- New Word
- Official Notice
- Phone Call Memo
- Resource
- Resource Groups
- Timecard
- Users
- What's New Notification

List Content Types

An important SharePoint feature is the capability to easily create and store information in lists. Lists can hold any type of information, from a simple To-Do list, to a more complex resource-tracking list. The following base content types are what SharePoint has to offer as part of the List Content Types group.

CONTENT TYPE	PARENT	DESCRIPTION
Announcement	Item	Based on the Item content type and used for tracking simple news updates for a team. This content type is associated with an announcements list, which was covered in Chapter 2.
Comment	Item	Based on an Item content type and contains the columns required to post responses to blog articles. Blogs will be covered in Chapter 8.
Contact	Item	Based on an Item content type and contains the columns required to share contact information. This content type is associated with the contacts list, which was covered in Chapter 2.
East Asia Contact	Item	Very similar to the Contact content type but contains special columns related to phonetic information. We do not cover this content type in this book.
Event	Item	Based on the Item content type and used for tracking date-based information such as appointments, meetings and events. This content type is associated with a calendar list, which was covered in Chapter 2.
Issue	Item	Contains columns for tracking problems that may arise within a collaborative or work environment. This content type is associated with the issues list, which was covered in Chapter 2.
Item	System	A parent content type of the Document content type and many list items. It is created by default with a single column for Title.
Link	Item	Based on the Item content type and used for hyperlink references to sites or documents. This content type is associated with a links list, which was covered in Chapter 2.
Message	Item	Based on the Item content type and is used for storing replies associated with Discussion Topics. This content type is associated with a discussion board list, which was covered in Chapter 2.
Post	Item	Based on an Item content type and contains the columns required to post articles within a blog. Blogs will be covered in Chapter 8.
Reservations	Event	This content type contains information related to the group calendar list.
Schedule	Event	This content type contains information related to the group calendar list.
Schedule and Reservations	Event	This content type contains information related to the group calendar list.
Task	Item	Based on an Item content type and contains the columns required to share task information. This content type is associated with the tasks list, which was covered in Chapter 2.

Page Layout Content Types

One of the most significant advancements of SharePoint over the past few versions has been its advancement as a web content management system. This great functionality allows users to create content for a site directly from the browser without having any special web development knowledge or skills.

Most sites have unique types of pages. For example, you might have a main page, a generic subpage, and a newsletter page. Each of these page types, in turn, has specific content elements that make it unique to the site. For example, the Newsletter page likely has a Title, Newsletter Body, and Published Date. A Page Layout content type defines these unique content elements by attaching site columns to your content type. You can later use this content type to create a Page Layout, which is a special type of template page that users can use to create new pages in a site. The following base content types are what SharePoint has to offer as part of the Page Layout Content Types group.

CONTENT TYPE	PARENT	DESCRIPTION
Article Page	Page	Contains many of the common properties that a page should have, including elements used for publishing such as scheduling date and others that are used for content display such as page content.
Enterprise Wiki Page	Page	Enterprise Wiki Page is the default content type for the Enterprise Wiki site template. It provides a basic content area as well as ratings and categories.
Project Page	Enterprise Wiki Page	Project Page is a content type included with the Enterprise Wiki site template. It provides some basic information to describe a project, including a project status and a contact name.
Redirect Page	Page	Redirect Page is a content type associated with a specialized page template that supports the definition of a URL that will redirect visitors automatically to the described location.
Welcome Page	Page	Contains a number of columns for the displaying and publishing of content.

PerformancePoint Content Types

The PerformancePoint content types are utilized by the business intelligence features of SharePoint Server 2010. They will be discussed in detail in Chapter 16. These content types are used for the display of reporting information such as Dashboards, key performance indicators, and Reports. The PerformancePoint content types include the following:

- PerformancePoint Dashboard
- PerformancePoint Data Source
- PerformancePoint Filter
- PerformancePoint Indicator

- PerformancePoint KPI
- PerformancePoint Report
- PerformancePoint Scorecard

Publishing Content Types

Another web content management-related content type group in SharePoint Server is Publishing content types. The base publishing content types provide the structure for all major web publishing components. The following base content types are available as part of the Publishing content types group.

CONTENT TYPE	PARENT	DESCRIPTION
Page	System Page	Page is a system content type template created by the Publishing Resources feature. The column templates from Page will be added to all pages libraries created by the Publishing feature.
Page Layout	System Page Layout	Page Layout is a system content type template created by the Publishing Resources feature. All page layouts will have the column templates from Page Layout added.
Publishing Master Page	System Master Page	Master Page is a system content type template created by the Publishing Resources feature. All master pages will have the column templates from Master Page added.

Special Content Types

The Special content type group allows users to upload documents regardless of content type to a library. It offers no special customization characteristics and is intended for use in situations where the content type is unknown or not important.

MANAGING CONTENT TYPES

An important aspect of managing a SharePoint site or environment is to understand how to combine and manage the information that a team or group shares. In this section, you discover some of the common management tasks that ensure that users in your organization can easily share and use your content types.

Enabling Content Type Management on a Library

In order for content types to be used within a SharePoint document library, the library must first be configured to utilize content types. We will review this process in the next Try It Out. While we will review the steps for enabling content types on a document library, the same steps apply to configuring a list to utilize content types.

TRY IT OUT Enable Content Types on a Library

1. From the document library you wish to configure, select Library Settings from the Library tab of the Ribbon menu.
2. Select the Advanced Settings link. You will be redirected to the Advanced Settings page as shown in Figure 6-18.

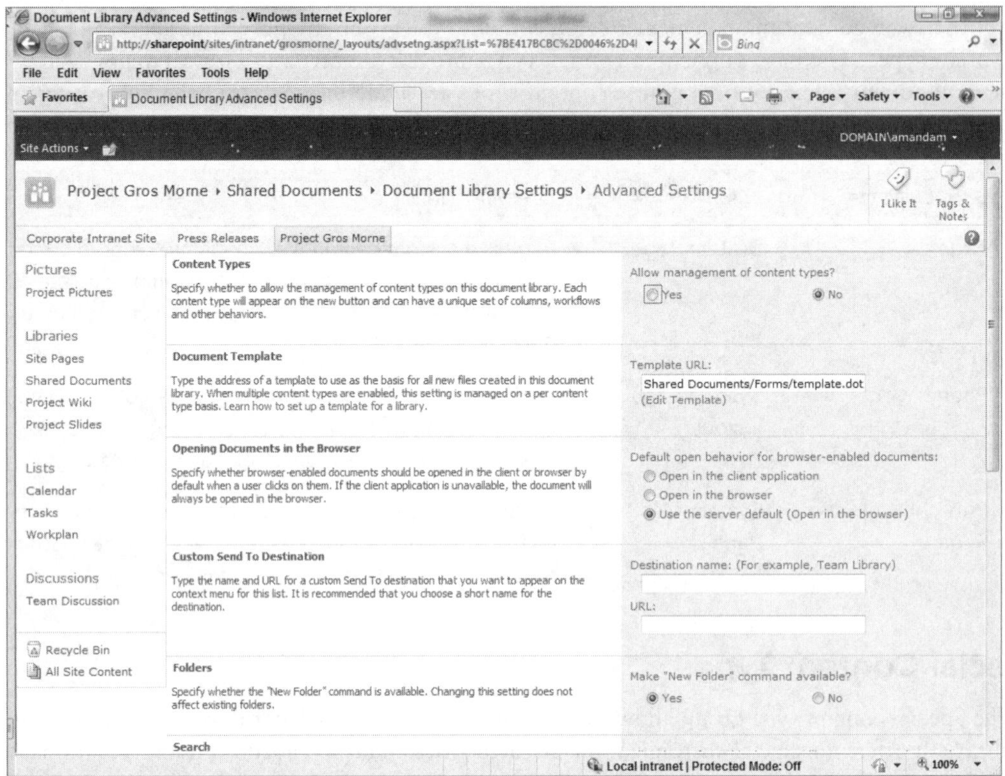

FIGURE 6-18

3. Select Yes for the Allow management of content types option.
4. Scroll to the bottom of the page, and click OK.

How It Works

Once you enable the management of content types from a list or library, you will notice that a Content Types section will appear on the administration page for that list or library, as shown in Figure 6-19. From this section, users can add or remove content types for use within the library.

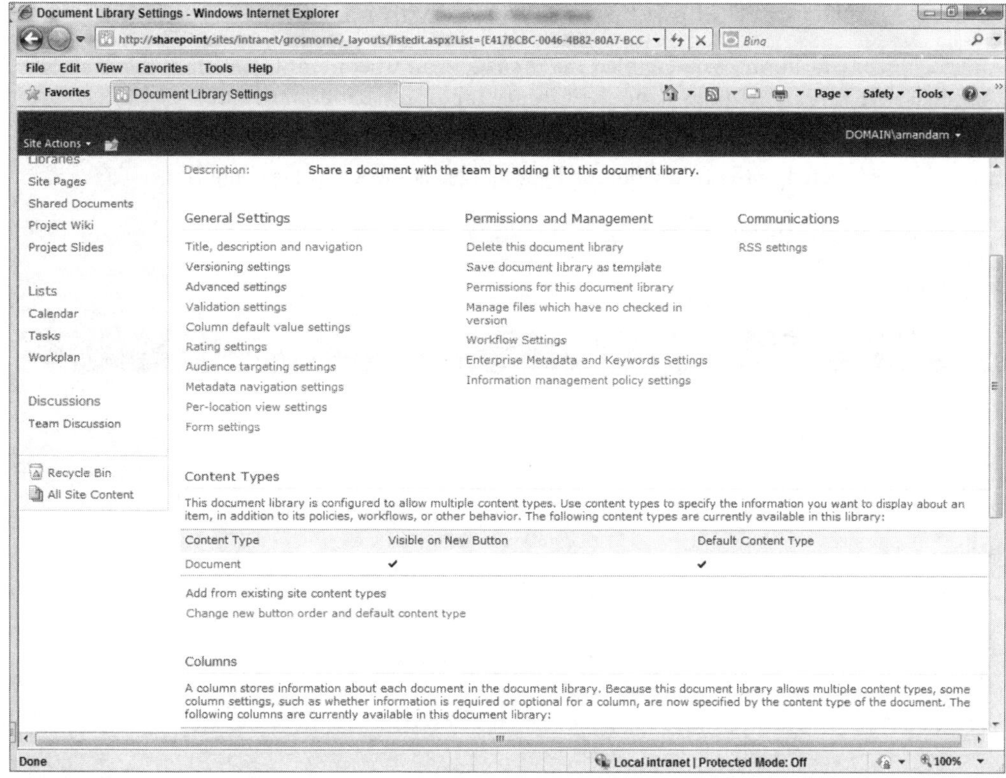

FIGURE 6-19

Managing Multiple Content Types in a Library

Today's business world often requires working with various types of content, which means managing many document templates, business processes, and information policies. Using the standard configuration of a document library, you can only associate a single document template with a document library, so you would require a large number of document libraries just to accommodate unique document templates and classification requirements. By associating multiple content types with a document library (shown in the next Try It Out), however, you can freely manage all important information from a single location. These can be different types of templates using the same format, or completely different applications such as Microsoft Office Excel, InfoPath, PowerPoint, or Word. This means that you can save a tremendous amount of time because you can edit and share multiple types of documents from the same location.

TRY IT OUT Associate Multiple Content Types with a Library

1. From the document library you enabled the management of content types on in the previous example, select Library Settings from the Library tab of the Ribbon menu.
2. From the Content Types section of the page, select the Add from existing site content types link. You will be redirected to the Add Content Types page, as shown in Figure 6-20.

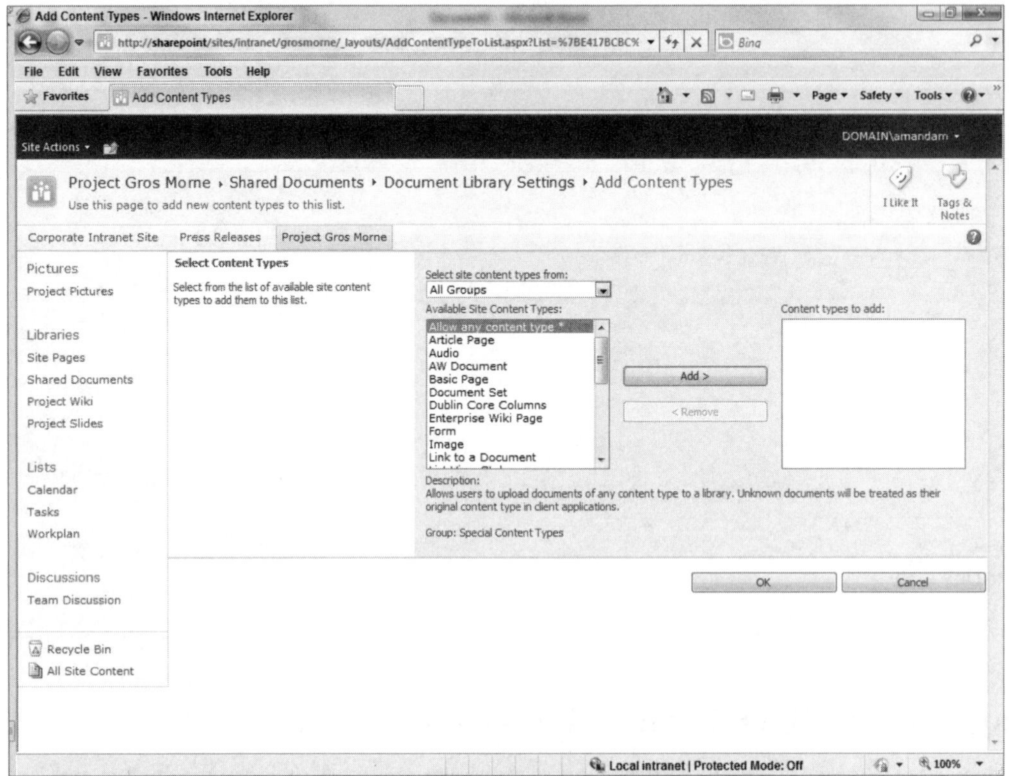

FIGURE 6-20

3. Select the Sales Documents group from the drop-down menu. The content types associated with that group will appear. Add the Sales Proposal and New Customer content types.
4. Click OK. You will be returned to the Library Settings page.

How It Works

When you associate multiple content types with a document library, they become available in the drop-down menu of the New item on your document library toolbar, where you can select the type of document you want to create. For example, you might have a content type for Sales Proposals associated with a Microsoft Office Word template and a New Customer Document Set content type, as shown in Figure 6-21.

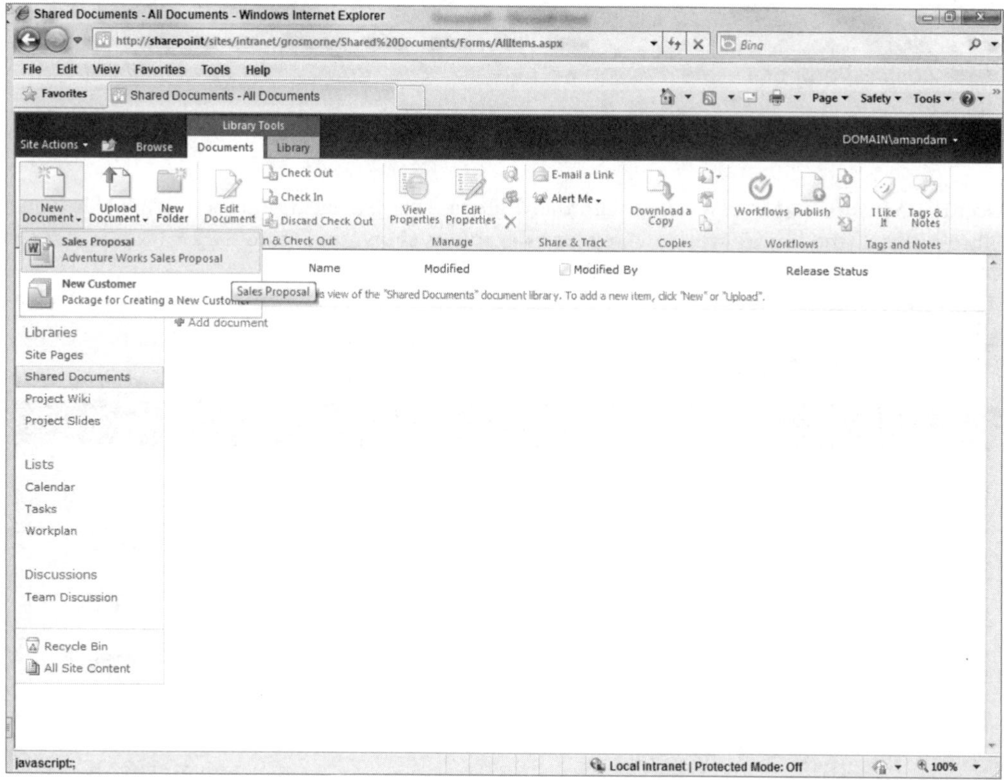

FIGURE 6-21

Managing Content Types across Site Collections

Once you have defined your content types for a single site collection, you may wish to make them available to other site collections. To do this, you must first enable your site collection to be an Enterprise Metadata hub site. This is done by managing the Site Collection Features settings of your site. We will review this process in the next Try It Out.

TRY IT OUT Configure Your Site Collection to Be a Content Type Syndication Hub

1. From the top level of your site collection, select Site Settings from the Site Actions menu. The Site Settings page appears.
2. Click the Site Collection Features link from the Site Collection Administration group of links. You will be redirected to a page listing all features available within the site collection.

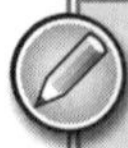

> **NOTE** *If you do not see that group, you are not listed as a Site Collection Administrator of the site and you will need to work with your system administrator to be added to this group or to complete this exercise.*

3. Select the Activate button associated with the Content Type Syndication Hub feature. The page will refresh and the feature will now appear as Active as shown in Figure 6-22.

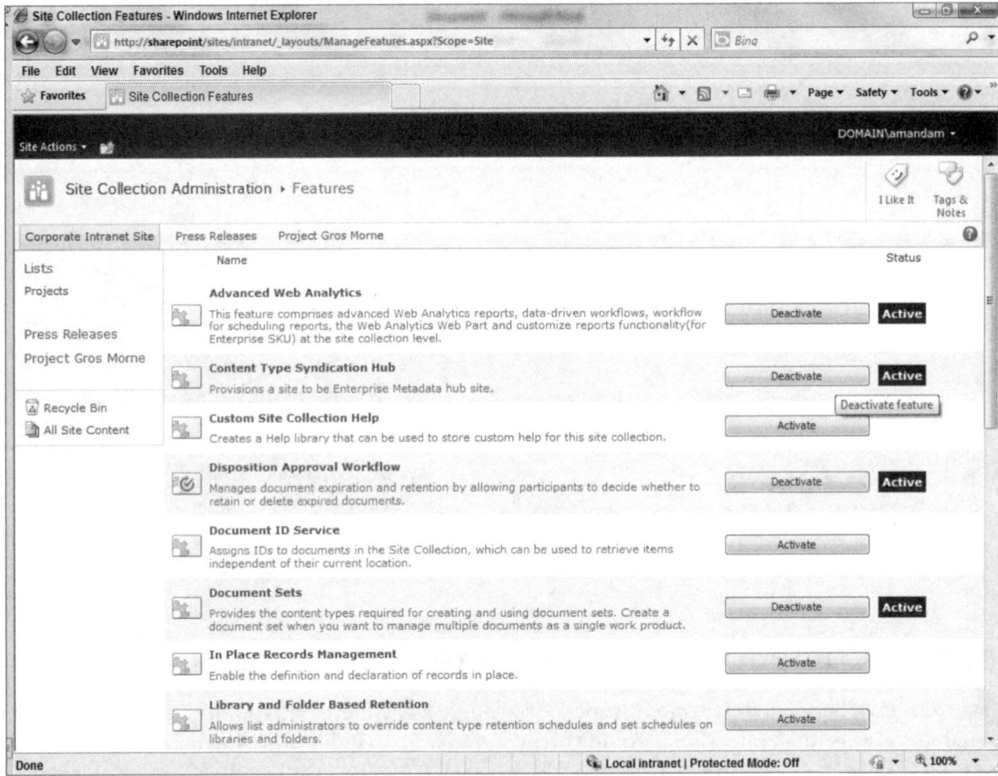

FIGURE 6-22

How It Works

Once your site collection is configured to be a content type syndication hub, the administration page of each content type will now display a new option to support the publishing of that content type to other web applications or site collections, as shown in Figure 6-23

To complete the configuration of the content type syndication hub, you must change additional settings related to the Managed Metadata Service Application. Because the management of service applications is outside of the core scope of this chapter, detailed instructions for completing this process are included in Appendix A of this book. If you are not an administrator of your SharePoint farm, you may require additional assistance from a member of that group to complete the exercise.

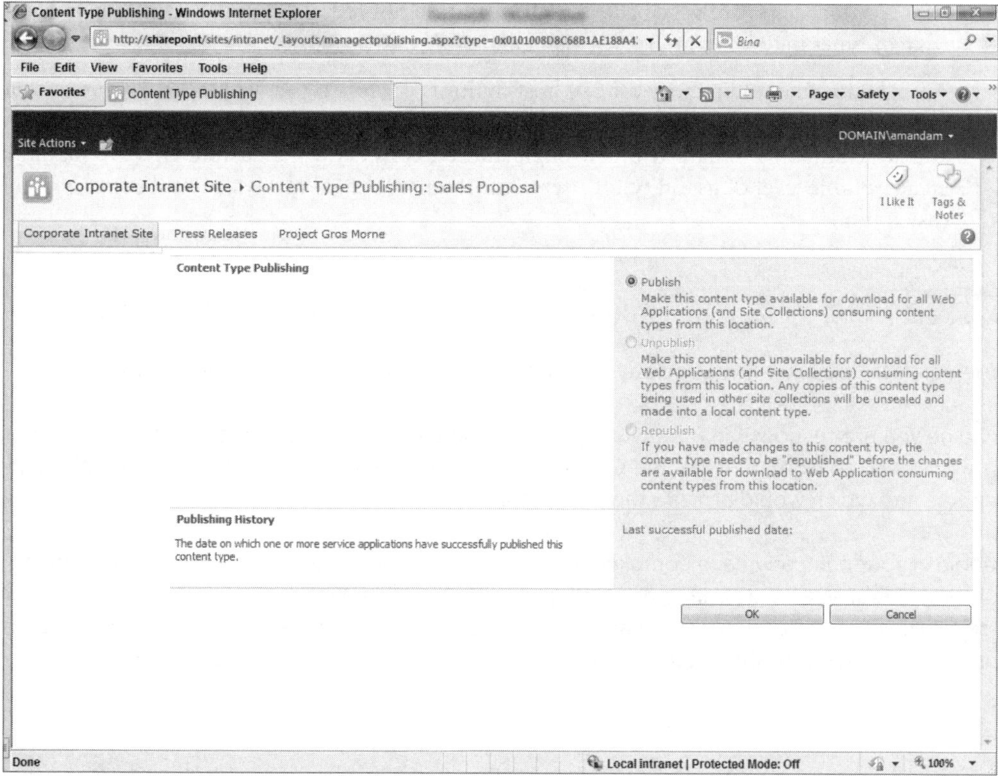

FIGURE 6-23

SUMMARY

This chapter discussed the very important SharePoint 2007 feature known as content types. Content types allow you to package and manage elements such as templates, workflow processes, policies, and metadata columns as a single reusable component. You can then associate these components with list and libraries throughout a site collection. Users can then make edits centrally to the site content type gallery, and all existing content types can be updated with the changes. After reading this chapter, you should know the following:

- The default groups of content types include: Business Intelligence, Document, Folder, List, Page Layout, Publishing, and Special content types.
- Every new content type must have a parent content type from which it inherits its settings. You can extend the parent content type to suit your business requirements.
- You can associate a content type with a custom template, workflow processes, and site columns. You can also create information management policies to control what information is displayed when an item is opened or printed. In addition, you can configure rules to determine when it must expire.

- Some content types are very basic in nature and do not require configuration; however, other content types may be more heavily regulated and controlled.
- A single document library or list can host multiple content types. This allows users to work from a single repository for related content. However, when managing multiple content types and large amounts of data within a single library, consider using custom views to maintain an acceptable level of usability for users. Information should always be well organized and easy to find.

EXERCISES

1. True or false: You can only associate one document template with a document library.
2. Imagine you are responsible for ensuring that all documents created and printed within your organization have the words Private and Confidential on them. What are your options for making this happen, and which would provide the best results?
3. People in your company have complained that recent job postings are being published on the corporate intranet website with typos and grammatical errors. Your management team demands a certain level of professionalism in any content that division members post. What are some steps you can take to ensure that future job postings are reviewed prior to publishing them?

▶ WHAT YOU LEARNED IN THIS CHAPTER

TOPIC	KEY CONCEPTS
What is a content type	A content type represents a type of information in your organization that shares common properties such as a template, workflow, site columns, and information policies.
What is a parent content type	Content types are organized in a hierarchy and each new content type must have a parent from which it inherited the basic properties.
What are the base content types	The base content types in SharePoint include Business Intelligence, Content Organizer, Document, Document Sets, Folders, Group Work, List, PerformancePoint, Page Layout, Publishing, and Special Content Types.

7

Working with Web Parts

WHAT YOU WILL LEARN IN THIS CHAPTER:

- What web parts are
- How to add and configure web parts
- How to use out-of-the-box web parts
- How to create custom web parts

Web parts are elements of a SharePoint page that display data and provide their own functionalities. Web parts are modular, which means that they can individually be added, removed, and even rearranged, in order to customize the way the content is displayed. Web parts are the basic building blocks on SharePoint pages, and one of the best ways in which targeted information can be made available to business users.

When making the decision as to which web parts to add to a page, think about the information on the site that will be the most dynamic, interesting or relevant to the site's users.

USING WEB PARTS

Before delving into descriptions of each out-of-the-box web part, it is important to have an understanding of some web part fundamentals. In this section, you will learn not only how to add a web part to a page but also how to configure or delete it. You will also learn the process for importing and exporting web parts, and even for connecting them to each other.

Adding a Web Part to a Page

Multiple web parts can be added to any SharePoint page, using the new contextual Ribbon interface at the top of the page. Web parts are added to web part zones on the page. Web part zones are predefined areas of a page, which are laid out in a specific manner. Web parts can be moved between zones, hidden within the page or completely closed. When a SharePoint site is created, depending on what site template is selected, there will be a different web part zone layout, and even a different way to add web parts to a page. In SharePoint 2010, wiki pages and web part pages have different interfaces, so each of these will now be explained.

Wiki Pages

SharePoint wiki pages are pages that allow for not only the insertion of web parts, but allow for free-form rich text to be typed directly on the page and formatted as desired. When a new site is created, and the Team Site template is selected (for example), the home page of the team site is a wiki page. When web parts and images are added to a page, they are simply dropped into this rich text area.

Web Part Pages

Web part pages are different from wiki pages in that they do not contain free-form rich text areas. These pages simply consist of one or more web part zones in which web parts can be added in a vertical stack. When a new site is created, and the document workspace template is selected (for example), the home page of the site is a web part page by default.

CHANGING A HOME PAGE FROM A WEB PART PAGE TO A WIKI PAGE

In the section about web part pages, it was mentioned that a document workspace is one of the types of site templates that has a web part page as a home page. To change any site's home page to a wiki page, click Site Actions and choose Site Settings. Click Manage Site Features and activate the Wiki Page Home Page feature.

Figure 7-1 displays the pane for adding a web part to a page.

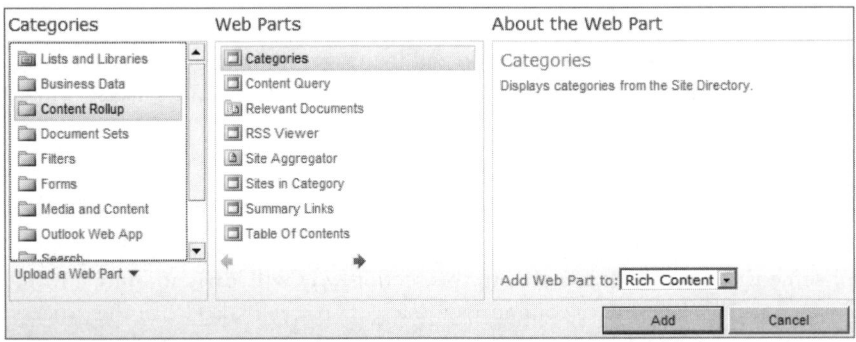

FIGURE 7-1

TRY IT OUT Adding a Web Part to a Page

In this Try It Out, you will go through the steps of adding a web part to a page. In many of the remaining activities in this chapter, different web parts will be added to pages, so this procedure is important to understand.

1. On your home page, click Site Actions, and choose Edit Page.
2. This step is where there are differences between web part and wiki pages.
   - If the page is a web part page, you will see sections on the page that have Add a Web Part sections. Click Add a Web Part.
   - If the page is a wiki page, the Ribbon at the top of the page will have a tab that says Editing Tools. Click the Insert tab in this section, and click the Web Part button.
3. A new pane is now displayed at the top of the page. The Categories section shows a list of folders that are the web part categories. The Web Parts section shows the list of web parts that exist in the category that is selected on the left. The About the Web Part section displays a short description of the currently selected web part, along with a drop-down box to select the web part zone in which the web part is to be inserted. Explore the web parts by clicking through the categories and looking at the lists of web parts in each category.
4. In the Lists and Libraries category of web parts, select the Announcements web part, and click the Add button on the right.

Now that the web part has been added to the page, it can be moved around from zone to zone by clicking the title part of the web part, and dragging it around the page.

Configuring a Web Part

Each web part that has been added to a page can be customized to change settings or its look and feel. The Web Part tool pane is where most configurations will be accomplished. The Web Part properties in this tool pane will vary between different types of web parts, but there is a standard set of options that are standard across web parts. In this section, each of the standard web part settings will be covered and described.

To configure a web part, the logged-in user must have at least a permission level of Designer. Hover your mouse over the top-right corner of any web part to see a small black triangle. Click this triangle to display a drop-down box. Choose Edit Web Part to elicit the Web Part tool pane, which will show on the right side of the page.

NOTE *When the page is in edit mode, there will be more choices in the drop-down box in the corner of the web part. Click Site Actions and Edit Page to switch to edit mode.*

Figure 7-2 shows an example of a web part drop-down box when the page is in edit mode.

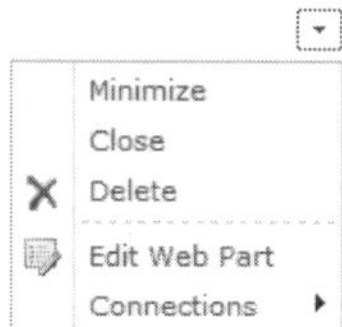

FIGURE 7-2

The following standard settings exist in the web part tool pane properties of every web part. The name and description of each property are listed.

Appearance

The Appearance section is used to set up the size and the way that the frame of the web part looks. The following table lists the options available in the Appearance section of the Web Part tool pane. The chrome is the frame, or the box around the web part, and this section allows you to choose the way it looks.

NAME	DESCRIPTION
Title	This is the title that displays in the top of the frame of the web part. For list (and library) web parts, by default the title is the name of the list. Note that changing the web part title does not change the actual name of the list. This can be done in the list settings, in the Title, Description and Navigation section.
Height	The height of the web part, in a selectable measurement, such as pixels or inches.
Width	The width of a web part, in a selectable measurement.
Chrome State	The options are minimized and normal, with normal being the default.
Chrome Type	These options consist of various combinations of the title and border of the web part. When "none" is selected, neither a title nor a border will be displayed.

Figure 7-3 shows some of the appearance options, and the way they apply to the look of a web part.

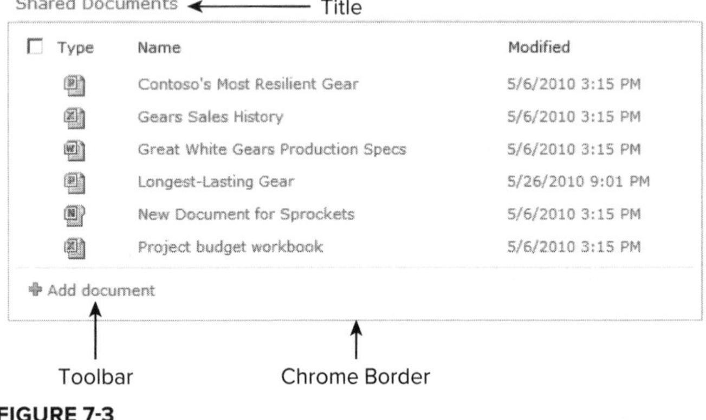

FIGURE 7-3

Layout

The layout is how the web part looks, relative to the rest of the page and the other web parts.

NAME	DESCRIPTION
Hidden	Hide the web part. This web part can only be seen by the page designer, while the page is in edit mode. This option is sometimes useful for testing purposes, or in cases where the web part contains code or script and does not need to be displayed. When working in a wiki page, this is not configurable.
Direction	Right to left or left to right.

NAME	DESCRIPTION
Zone	Pick which web part zone to put the web part in. This is not configurable in wiki pages.
Zone Index	Type the number of the zone index. This is the order in which the web parts are displayed within the web part zone. Typing a "1" here will bring the web part to the top of the page. This can optionally be used instead of dragging web parts with the mouse. This is also not configurable in wiki pages.

Advanced

The main consideration for this section is that each site member will have options available for modifying the way a page is displayed personally, even though they do not have Designer permission on the page. Figure 7-4 shows the drop-down box at the top-right corner of a web part, as seen by a site member.

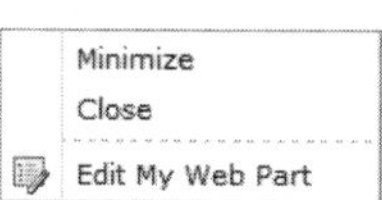

FIGURE 7-4

The Advanced Options allow the page designer to restrict some of the ways that site members can modify the way the page looks to them.

NAME	DESCRIPTION
Allow Minimize	Uncheck this box to disallow the option to minimize the web part.
Allow Close	Uncheck this box to disallow the option to close the web part. Not available on wiki pages.
Allow Hide	Uncheck this box to disallow other page designers from checking the box in the layout options that changes the web part to hidden. Not available on wiki pages.
Allow Zone Change	Site members will not be able to put the page in edit mode and rearrange web parts using their mouse, but they will be able to click Edit My Web Part to open the Web Part tool pane. When Allow Zone Change is unchecked, the site members will not have the ability to change zone information for a web part. This option is not available on wiki pages.
Allow Connections	Uncheck this to disallow creating connections from this web part to other web parts on the page.
Allow Editing in Personal View	Uncheck this to disable the Edit My Web Part button from site members.
Title URL	When the title of the web part is clicked, this is the URL that you will navigate to.
Description	When you hover over the web part title with your mouse, this description is shown as the tooltip.
Help URL	If there is a specific page that you have created, for users to obtain help regarding this web part, enter the URL to that page here. When a URL exists here, there will be a new option called Help, available to users when they click the web part's drop-down box.

continues

(continued)

NAME	DESCRIPTION
Help Mode	Choose from modal, modeless, or navigate. When the Help button is clicked, the help page pops up in a new window. This option allows you to configure the behavior of that new window.
Catalog Icon Image URL	This is the image that represents this web part.
Title Icon Image URL	This icon is displayed next to the title of the web part. By default, there is no icon in this location.
Import Error Message	Type the error message that you would like to be displayed if there is ever an error importing the web part.
Target Audiences	Pick the target audience of people who you would like to see this web part. By default, this setting is blank, and the web part is shown to everyone who visits the page. Pick from global audiences, distribution/security groups, or SharePoint groups. Audience targeting is not a substitute for security but is used in order to personalize the way that the page is viewed, according to whom the viewer is. Show the most relevant information to any audience.
Export Mode	This only appears in the properties for web parts that are exportable. Choose from Do Not Allow, Non-sensitive data only, or Export all data.

Removing Web Parts

There are two different ways to remove a web part from a page, closing it or deleting it. It is important to know the difference between these methods, so that page performance does not suffer because of bad practices. Click Site Actions and Edit Page in order to see the close and delete options in the drop-down box in the top-right corner of each web part on a web part page.

NOTE *The ability to close a web part without deleting it is not available on a wiki page. This can only be done on a web part page.*

- **Close a Web Part:** When a web part is closed, it is temporarily removed from the page but is placed in a "Closed Web Parts" category in the list of web part categories on the site, and it can be added back at any time. When many closed web parts exist on a page, it can affect the page load performance. Closing a web part is usually not necessary but is done in cases where the web part and its configuration need to be saved for later, but not displayed on the page.
- **Delete a Web Part:** Deleting a web part permanently removes it from the page. It is a good practice to get in the habit of deleting web parts instead of closing them, unless it is absolutely necessary to close one and use it later.

The Web Part Checkbox

Most anything that needs to be done to configure a standard web part has already been covered in this section, but just as in many places in SharePoint, there are multiple ways to accomplish the same goal. New in SharePoint 2010 is a small checkbox at the top-right corner of every web part. Checking this box when the page is in edit mode opens the Web Part Tools/Options Ribbon at the top of the page, as shown in Figure 7-5.

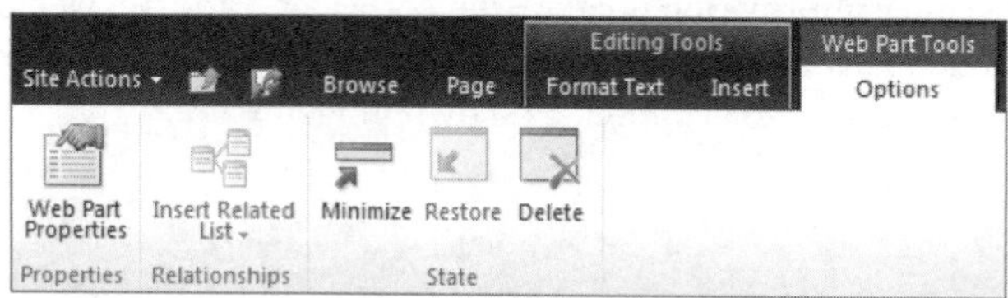

FIGURE 7-5

- **Web Part Properties:** Opens up the Web Part tool pane.
- **Minimize and Restore:** Minimizes or restores the web part, which is the same as the Chrome State in the Appearance options.
- **Delete:** Permanently deletes the web part.
- **Insert Related List:** Any list can have one or more lookup columns that look up information in another list on the site. Once this lookup field exists, these two lists are considered to be related lists. This button allows you to quickly add a second list that is related with a lookup *to* the currently selected list. The two web parts are then automatically connected. If there is no other list on the site that is related to the current list, this button will be disabled. There will be more information about web part connections in the section in this chapter called "Connect Web Parts."

Exporting and Importing Web Parts

Some types of web parts can be imported and exported, which is a way of saving a web part and its settings, and adding it to another page. List View (list and library) web parts cannot be exported, but most other types can. When in edit mode, click the drop-down box at the top right of a web part, to see if Export is listed as an option. When the Export button is clicked, you will be prompted to save the web part to your computer. Pick a location on your computer to save the web part to.

Saved web parts can be imported to be displayed on a page. When adding a web part to a page, as shown in Figure 7-1, notice that in the bottom left there is an Upload a Web Part button. Click this button, and then browse to the location on your computer where the web part file exists. Click the Upload button. The next time you click to insert a web part, there is a new category on the right, called Imported Web Parts, which is where the new web part can be selected and inserted on the page.

What if you want this customized web part to always be displayed when you click to insert a web part? Take a look at the "The Web Part Gallery" section toward the end of this chapter.

Connect Web Parts

Some web parts on a page can be connected to each other to allow for passing of filters or parameters from one web part to another. When web parts on a page contain columns with common data in them, they can be connected. An example of common data that can be connected, is a list that contains a lookup column to another list on the site. It is not required that the connected lists contain a lookup column, as long as the data columns being connected contain the same type of information, such as a number or text. The web part that sends the filter information is called the "provider," and the web part that gets filtered is referred to as the "consumer." When a page is in edit mode, click the drop-down box in the top-right corner of a web part to see the Connections option, as shown in Figure 7-2.

TRY IT OUT Connecting Web Parts

In this Try It Out, you will learn how to connect two web parts to each other. This example will entail creating tasks on the site, and setting up each task so that it is associated with a specific document in a document library. Multiple tasks can be created and associated with any one document. You will then create an interface on the page so that site users can click one document and automatically see the list of tasks associated with that document.

1. On your SharePoint site, click Site Actions and choose More Options. On the Create screen, click Tasks as the type of list. In the Name box on the right side, type "Tasks Test" and click Create.
2. On the same site, click Site Actions, and choose New Document Library. Name the library "Library Test" and click Create.
3. Upload several example documents to the library, and be sure to fill out the Title column for each one.
4. On the Quick Launch Toolbar on the left, click the Tasks Test to go back to the Task list. In the Ribbon at the top of the page, click the List tab.
5. In the Manage Views section of the Ribbon, click the Create Column button. Fill out the Create Column screen as follows:

FIELD NAME	DATA
Column Name	Document
Type of information	Lookup
Get information from	Select Library Test from the drop-down list
In this column	Select Title from the drop-down list

6. Leave all other fields at the default, and click OK.
7. In the Tasks Test list, create a few sample tasks in the list, fill out the various fields, and for each task, pick the name of a document in the Document drop-down box. Now the relationship has been created between tasks and documents, so the web part connection can be created.

8. On the home page of your site, follow the instructions in the "Try It Out: Adding a Web Part to a Page" to add the Tasks Test and the Library Test to the page.
9. Open the Web Part properties of the Library Test web part, and in the drop-down in the top corner of the web part, choose Connections. In the fly-out, choose Send Row of Data To, and choose Tasks Test.
10. On the Choose Connection box that pops up, leave the default of Connection Type: Get Filter Values From, and click Configure.
11. On the Configure Connection tab that is shown in Figure 7-6, choose Title as the Provider, and Document as the Consumer. Click Finish.
12. Click the Save button at the top left of the page, to save your page changes.

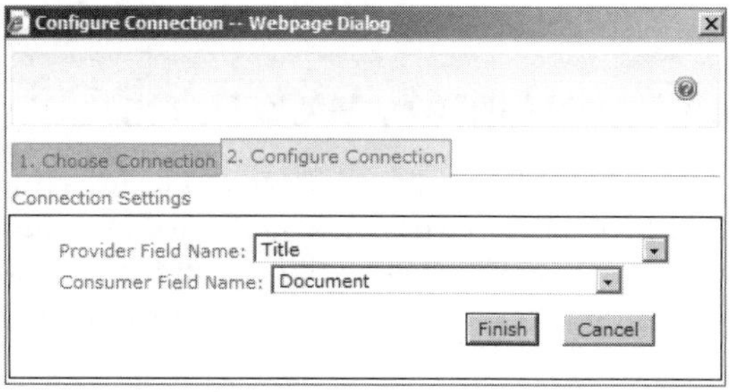

Configure Connection -- Webpage Dialog

1. Choose Connection | 2. Configure Connection

Connection Settings

Provider Field Name: Title

Consumer Field Name: Document

Finish Cancel

FIGURE 7-6

The web parts are now connected! The Title of the document in the Library Test is the provider. The Document is the lookup field that you created in the Tasks Test list, which looks up to the Title column, and it is the consumer. Each time you click the gray double arrow next to a document, the task list will be filtered to show only tasks associated with that document, as shown in Figure 7-7.

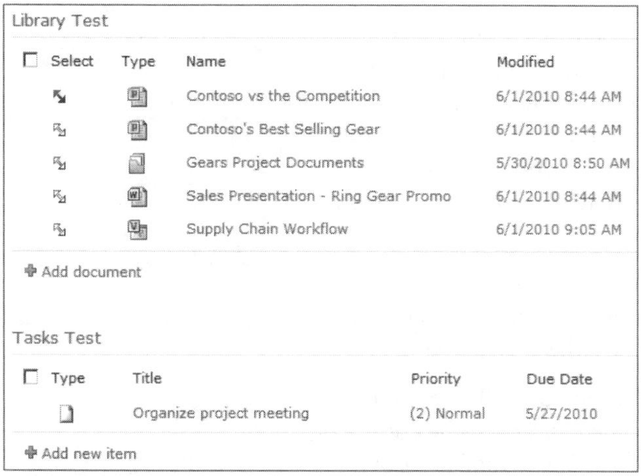

Library Test

Select	Type	Name	Modified
		Contoso vs the Competition	6/1/2010 8:44 AM
		Contoso's Best Selling Gear	6/1/2010 8:44 AM
		Gears Project Documents	5/30/2010 8:50 AM
		Sales Presentation - Ring Gear Promo	6/1/2010 8:44 AM
		Supply Chain Workflow	6/1/2010 9:05 AM

Add document

Tasks Test

Type	Title	Priority	Due Date
	Organize project meeting	(2) Normal	5/27/2010

Add new item

FIGURE 7-7

To remove a web part connection, follow step 9 above, and then click the Remove Connection button on the Configure Connection screen. Sometimes it is necessary to temporarily remove connections in order to make changes to the filter web part configurations.

ABOUT THE OUT-OF-THE-BOX WEB PARTS

There are so many web parts that already exist in SharePoint, that they can be used for most everything that needs to be accomplished on a SharePoint page. On one end of the spectrum, programmers can save themselves a lot of development time by learning what SharePoint can already do. On the other end of the spectrum, site managers and end users can decrease the use of IT resources to accomplish some simple "web page development" that does not involve the use of any custom code.

List and Library Web Parts

Any SharePoint list or library can be inserted onto a page as a web part, and these are referred to as List View web parts. As you learned in Chapter 4, views are simply different ways of looking at the same data. Whether working with lists or libraries, this web part is referred to as "list view," and the term "lists" in this section refers to both lists and libraries.

Web Part Views

We define the way data will be displayed in a list web part by selecting columns and setting up grouping, sorting and filtering. Learn more about views in Chapter 2, "Working With SharePoint Lists."

Web Part Tool Pane

The Web Part tool pane is displayed on the right side of the page when configuring Web Part properties. At the top-right corner of every web part, there is a small arrow, which opens a drop-down box. In this drop-down list, click Edit Web Part in order to view the Web Part tool pane. As shown in Figure 7-8, there are several sections of settings to configure. The focus here is on the options that are unique to list view web parts.

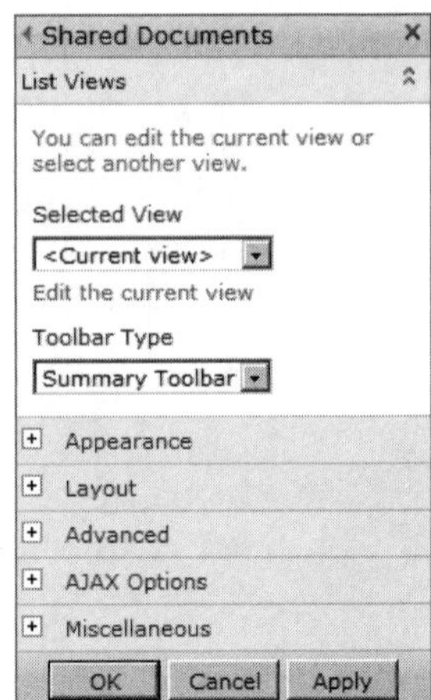

FIGURE 7-8

The List Views section of the Web Part tool pane contains a drop-down box called Selected View. Any existing view can be selected, or an ad hoc view can be created by clicking Edit the current view.

The Toolbar Type contains three options. The Summary Toolbar only displays an Add new Item or Add new Document button at the bottom of the Web Part, and it is the same as Full Toolbar. Show Toolbar displays the standard toolbar that you normally see when you go to the home page of a list or library. No Toolbar obviously removes all toolbars.

TRY IT OUT Using the List View Web Part

In this Try It Out, you will learn the steps and the principles behind adding and modifying List View web parts on a page. In this scenario, you will create a task list, take a look at its default views, and then display an existing view in a web part on your home page. You will then modify the web part view.

1. Go to the Tasks Test list that was created in the Connect Web Parts section of this chapter.

2. In some of the tasks, edit them to put your own name in the Assigned To column.
3. At the top of the screen, the View drop-down box will say All Tasks because that is the default view. Click this view name, and choose the My Tasks view. Notice that this view only displays items that are assigned to you, the logged-in user.
4. In the breadcrumb trail at the top of the page, click to go back to the home page of the site.
5. Click Site Actions, and choose Edit Page.
6. In the Ribbon at the top of the screen, in the orange Editing Tools section, click the Insert tab.
7. Click the Web Part button, and a new pane will be displayed across the top of the page, with lists of all of the web parts that can be inserted. This is shown in Figure 7-9.

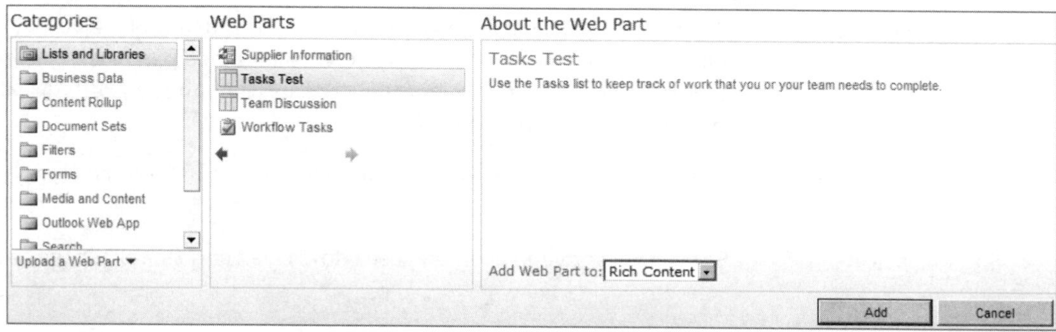

FIGURE 7-9

8. By default, the Lists and Libraries section on the left is selected. Scroll to the right, using the dark gray arrows in the Web Parts section, click to select the Tasks Test list, and click the Add button.
9. The task list is now displayed as a web part on the page. At the top right of the web part, click the arrow drop-down and choose Edit Web Part.
10. In the Selected View drop-down box in the Web Part Tool Pane, choose the My Tasks view.
11. An informational message will pop up. It states that switching to a different view removes changes you have made to this view. This means that, since the web part "current view" is not one of the saved views in the list, any view changes that have been made in this web part will be lost when a new view is selected.
12. At the bottom of the pane, click the Apply button.
13. Notice that the web part now displays only tasks assigned to you. This view in the web part is now disconnected from the My Tasks view in the list, and changes made here will not affect that view. In the Web Part tool pane, click Edit current view, so that a couple of tweaks can be made.
14. On the View Settings page, only put check marks next to the columns called Title and Due Date. In the Sort section, pick the Due Date column, and choose ascending order. In the Item Limit section, type a number **3** as the item limit. Click OK.

The My Tasks view has now been customized to take up less space on the home page, by decreasing the number of displayed columns and displaying fewer items in the view. When viewing the home page, users will now see the list of their three upcoming tasks.

AJAX

AJAX is short for asynchronous JavaScript and XML. It allows for data to be retrieved from the server asynchronously. This means users do not have to refresh the browser to see changes that others may have made to data that is shown on the page in the web part. The web part's information will be refreshed in the background without interfering with the display, behavior, or other web parts on the existing page. The following are the AJAX options available for list web parts and data view web parts. In this context, asynchronous means that the content in the web part will be loaded independently of the other web parts on the page.

This table lists the options available for AJAX, per web part.

NAME	DESCRIPTION
Enable Asynchronous Load	When the page loads, this web part loads independently of the others. An example of the use of this option is when one web part must retrieve a large amount of data (list items) to be displayed. An animated GIF will indicate that the data is loading.
Enable Asynchronous Update	This checkbox allows any of the below checkboxes to be configured.
Show Manual Refresh Button	Select this in order to allow end users to click a button to refresh the data.
Enable Asynchronous Automatic Refresh	When a user navigates to the page and leaves it open in the browser all day, live data will continue to be displayed without having to use F5 to refresh the browser page.
Automatic Refreshing Interval (seconds)	When Enable Asynchronous Automatic Refresh is selected, type the number interval of seconds at which the automatic refresh needs to happen.

NOTE *When "Show manual refresh button" or "Enable Asynchronous Automatic Refresh" options are checked, the checkbox for "Enable asynchronous update" will also automatically be selected when the Web Part properties are saved.*

Miscellaneous

NAME	DESCRIPTION
Sample Data	If the list is empty, sample data can be displayed while testing the web part.
XSL Link	This is the URL to an XSL style sheet that contains display settings for the web part.

NAME	DESCRIPTION
Enable Data View Caching	Cache the data view.
Data View Caching Time-out (seconds)	If caching is enabled, set the time in seconds that the data should be cached.
Send first row to connected web parts when page loads	When web part connections are used, when this option is enabled on the provider web part, the first row of the web part will be sent to the consumer, as the default filter.

Business Data Web Parts

This category of web parts displays data from SharePoint or other line-of-business systems. In this context, business data can consist of charts, graphs, key performance indicators, and even Visio diagrams.

Chart Web Part

The Chart web part is an extremely customizable web part that displays charts based on data existing in one of the following locations:

- **A SharePoint list:** Connect to any list not only in the current site but anywhere in the current site collection.
- **The Business Data Catalog:** Connect to external content types, for example, other databases such as SQL, and other line-of-business systems.
- **Excel Services:** Connect to data that exists in a spreadsheet that exists in a library on the site.
- **Another web part:** Connect to another web part on the same page.

This web part consists of easy wizards for connecting to data and customizing the way the chart looks. Once the data connection has been set up, there is an Advanced Properties interface in which the chart's look and feel can be granularly customized.

TRY IT OUT Using the Chart Web Part

In this Try It Out, you will go through the steps of configuring the Chart web part to display data in a SharePoint list. First, you will create a simple list with regional sales data, which the chart will be based on. Once the example data exists, you will insert a chart on the front page of your SharePoint site.

1. At the top-left corner of the site, click Site Actions and choose More Options.
2. Choose Custom List as the type, name the list Regional Sales, and click Create.
3. Now that the list has been created, in the List tab of the Ribbon, click List Settings.
4. In the Columns section, click the name of the Title column, and change the name of the column to "Region" instead of "Title."

5. In the Columns section, click Create column. Call this new column "Amount," and choose Currency as the type of information in this column. Click OK.

6. In the breadcrumb trail at the top of the page, click Regional Sales, so that you can start adding items to this example list.

7. Click the Add new item button, and you will add four items, as shown in the following table.

REGION	AMOUNT
North	800
South	500
East	1000
West	400

8. Now that the list contains some data, the Chart web part can be added to the page. Navigate to the home page of the site, click Site Actions, and click Edit Page. Add the Chart web part to the page, and a standard chart with blue bars is displayed as the default.

9. Click Data & Appearance, in the middle of the web part, to get to the Data Connection & Chart Appearance Wizards screen shown in Figure 7-10. If a message pops up warning about saving changes to the web page, click OK.

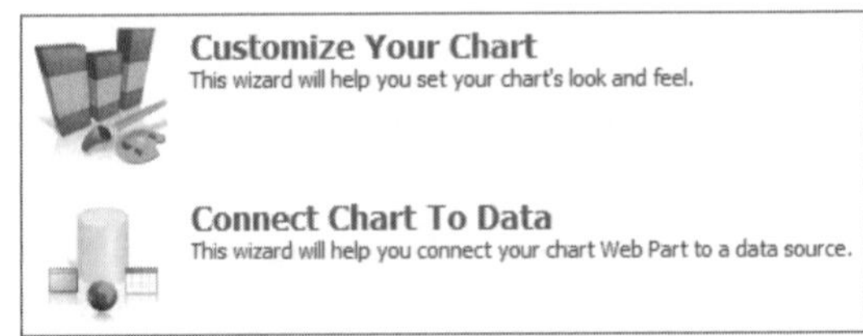
Customize Your Chart
This wizard will help you set your chart's look and feel.
Connect Chart To Data
This wizard will help you connect your chart Web Part to a data source.

FIGURE 7-10

10. Click Connect Chart to Data.

11. On the Choose a Data Source screen, choose Connect to a List. Click Next.

12. In the Site drop-down box, choose the name of the site in which the lists exists. In this example, it will be the name of the site in which the Regional Sales list was created at Step 2. Then, in the List drop-down box, choose the Regional Sales list. Note that this web part can be configured to display list information from any site in the site collection. Click Next.

13. The Filter Data screen gives you the option of creating a data filter. Click the plus next to Filter Data, which expands the section to show the interface for creating filters. No filters will be created in this example, so click Next.

14. At Step 4, Bind Chart to Data, explore this page by clicking the plus sign next to each section to view all available chart options. Make no changes, and click the Finish button.

15. The Chart web part is now displayed on the page, still with the standard blue bars. Next, click Data & Appearance again, and this time click Customize Your Chart.

16. On the Select Chart Type screen that is shown in Figure 7-11, select the Bar chart type and the 3D Chart Types tab. Click Next.

17. Notice that there is an Auto Preview displayed on the right side of the screen from this point on in the wizard, so that changes can be previewed in real time. Change the theme to your favorite color and click Next.

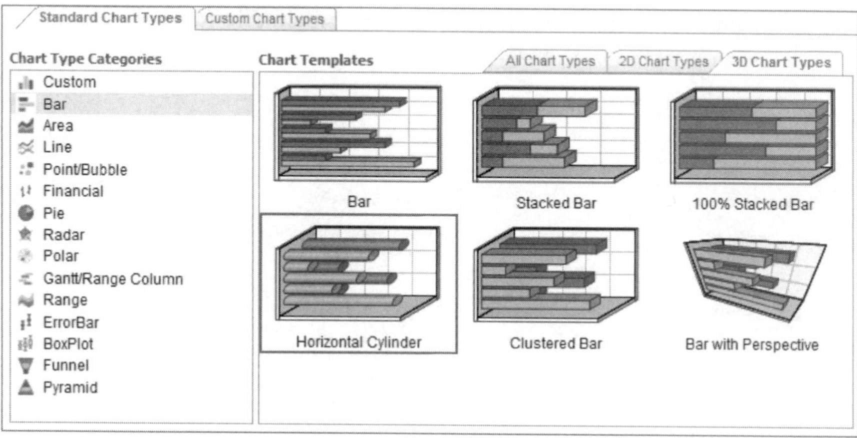

FIGURE 7-11

18. Explore the Chart Element Properties screen by clicking each of the tabs across the top, which contain options for Title and Legend, Axes and Grid Lines, Data Labels and Markers, and Hyperlinks and tooltips. Click Finish.

Figure 7-12 shows an example of what the final 3D chart looks like.

After a chart has been created, if further customization is needed, click the Advanced Properties button. This advanced Chart Properties interface allows for granular changes to be made to the different aspects of the chart.

Chart web parts can also be exported and then imported to other sites or site collections. By default, the ability to export the web part is disabled. To enable the ability to export, in the Web Part tool pane's advanced section, change the Export Mode option to Export all data. Charts that display data from external content types or Excel Services can even be imported onto sites in other site collections.

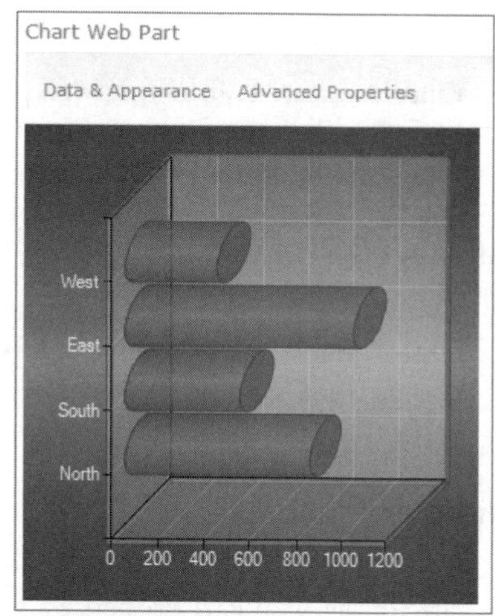

FIGURE 7-12

Excel Web Access

The Excel Web Access web part allows for the display of a spreadsheet or portion of a spreadsheet on a page. When planning for these types of web parts, the location of the site or specific document library must be added to the list of trusted locations in the Excel Service Application in Central Administration. A spreadsheet can be published to Excel Services from within Excel. On the File menu, choose the Save & Send tab on the left, and select Save to SharePoint. As shown in Figure 7-13, click the Publish Options towards the top right of this screen.

This Publish Options screen is quite useful, because it allows for granular selection of components of a spreadsheet to be published, such as sheets, charts, and ranges. This screen also allows for the creation of parameters, which are useful in creating spreadsheet interactivity, and in connecting to other web parts on the page.

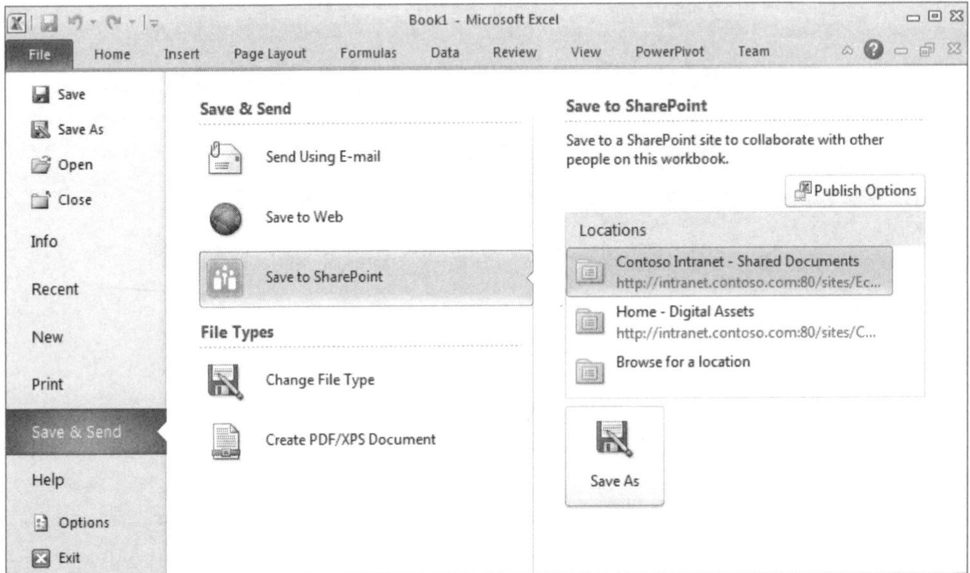

FIGURE 7-13

Once an Excel Web Access web part is added to a page, the Web Part tool pane contains a multitude of configuration options. Select the spreadsheet that is to be displayed, and optionally type the name of one range, chart, or table in the Named Item box.

Status List

The Status List web part displays key performance indicators from an existing Status List in SharePoint. Once a Status List has been created, indicators can be created to view data values compared to goals. In the Web Part properties, pick an existing Status List anywhere in the current site collection.

Indicator Details

The Indicator Details web part displays a single selected indicator from within a Status List on the site. In the Web Part properties, select a Status List in the current site collection and a specific indicator in that Status List.

TRY IT OUT Using the Status List Web Part

In this Try It Out, you will learn how configure the Status List web part. A prerequisite before getting started is to create and populate the Regional Sales list, following the instruction steps one through seven from "Try It Out: Using the Chart Web Part." The goal in this example is to display indicators that allow management to quickly determine which regions are doing well in their sales figures.

1. Click Site Actions and choose More Options. Choose Status List, name the list Status List Test, and click Create.

2. In the list's New drop-down box, choose SharePoint List-based Status Indicator.
3. Fill in the fields on the New Item screen, based on the following table, and click OK.

FIELD	VALUE
Name	Regional Sales
List URL	Click the orange icon, select the Regional Sales list, and click OK.
Value Calculation	Calculation using all list items in the view. Choose Average (in the calculation drop-down box) of Amount (in the drop-down box of number fields in the list)
Display [green]	1,000
Display [yellow]	500

4. On the home page of the site, click to insert a web part. In the Business Data section, choose the Status List web part and add it to the page.
5. Open the Web Part tool pane. In the Indicator List box, select the Status List Test. Configure the rest of the Web Part properties as indicated in the following table, and click OK.

FIELD	VALUE
Show only Status icon	Yes
Display multiple indicators columns	Yes
Status Indicator	Regional Sales
Column or dimension	Region
Members to display	Click the filter icon and select all four regions.

The regional sales data is now displayed, simply represented by indicator icons. These icons are based on the goal values of 1,000 and 500 in the indicator properties. The resulting web part is shown in Figure 7-14.

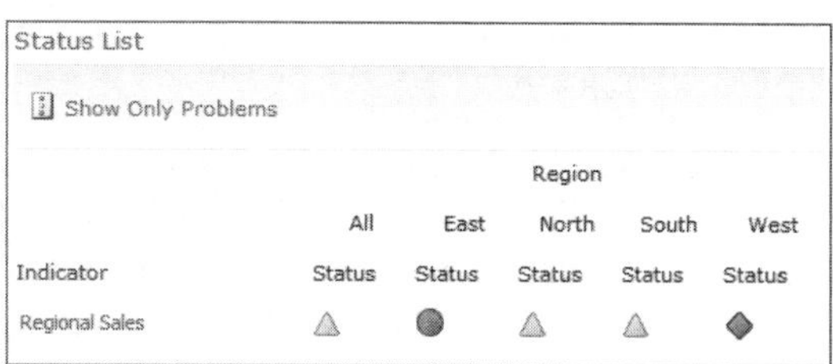

FIGURE 7-14

Visio Web Access

The Visio Web Access web part displays a Visio diagram on a page. Visio is an Office Suite application that allows for the creation of advanced visuals such as charts, diagrams, flowcharts, and even network diagrams and floor plans. When working in Visio, files can be saved as Web Drawing (VDW) files. In the properties of the Visio Web Access web part, an existing VDW file is selected for display. Additional settings can be configured, such as the toolbar and drawing interactivity.

More Business Data Web Parts

There are several more web parts in the list, that all start with "Business Data." These web parts will be covered in Chapter 15.

Content Rollup Web Parts

The main thing that all of the Content Rollup web parts have in common is the fact that they can all display information from other sites, or from multiple sites. Each of these web parts works in a different manner, and they are all useful in their own unique way.

Content Query

The Content Query web part is used in order to display content from multiple sites in one rolled-up view, and it is only available on sites in which the SharePoint Server Publishing Infrastructure feature has been enabled. The settings of this web part have two main sections, called Query and Presentation, which allow you to configure the type of data to roll up and in what manner to present it.

> **COLUMN SELECTION IN THE CONTENT QUERY WEB PART**
>
> When using the Content Query web part, it is important to know that the columns available for sorting, grouping, and filtering are only site columns. In planning to use this web part, think about the columns that will be utilized in the Web Part Settings. If nondefault columns will be used, then set up lists to use site columns instead of creating the columns at the list level. That way all of the needed columns will be available in the web part.

Query

- **Content Type:** Pick any one content type to roll up, or keep the default of "All Content Types."
- **Audience Targeting:** Each list and library has an audience targeting setting that can be turned on. Each item in that list can then be targeted to an audience. When those lists are displayed in this web part, and this setting is selected, site visitors will only see items in this web part that are targeted to them. Check the box Include items that are not targeted, if you would like untargeted items to be displayed.
- **Additional Filters:** Up to three filters can be created to narrow down the content that is displayed. Only site columns are available to choose from.

Presentation

- **Grouping and Sorting:** Pick from site columns to group or sort by.
- **Styles:** Choose predefined styles for groups and items.

- **Fields to Display:** Type the names of the site columns to be displayed, separated by semicolons.
- **Feed:** Check this box to include an RSS feed icon and link in the corner of the web part.

TRY IT OUT Using the Content Query Web Part

In this Try It Out, you will learn about this powerful web part that allows you to display information from multiple locations. This web part is only available on sites that have the SharePoint Server Publishing feature activated. For the source of the content query, pick the whole site collection, a particular site, or an individual list. The list types to choose from will be familiar, because these are seen on the Create screen for new lists and libraries. The content types to choose from can also be seen in Site Settings ⇨ Content Types.

1. First of all, the publishing feature needs to be enabled at the site collection level. At the top-level site of a new site collection, click Site Actions and choose Site Settings.
2. In the Site Collection Administration section, click Site collection features.
3. Next to SharePoint Server Publishing Infrastructure, click the Activate button.
4. Navigate to the home page of the site where this web part will be added. Click Site Actions and choose Edit Page.
5. Look at the Ribbon at the top of the screen, and in the Editing Tools section, click the Insert tab.
6. Click the Web Part button in the Ribbon, take a look at the Categories section on the left side of the screen, and click the Content Rollup category.
7. Click to select the Content Query web part, and in the Add Web Part drop-down box choose the location on the page in which you would like to insert the web part. Click the Add button.
8. In the top-right corner of this web part, click the small arrow that is a drop-down box. Choose Edit Web Part.
9. The Web Part tool pane is now displayed on the right side of the screen. In the Query section, fill out the settings according to the following table, and click OK.

FIELD	VALUE
Source	Show items from all sites in this site collection
Show items from this list type	Posts
Group items by	<Site>, Ascending
Sort items by	Created, Descending
Group style	Banded
Item style	Title and description
Fields to Display: Link	Nothing, leave it blank

continues

(continued)

FIELD	VALUE
Fields to Display: Title	Title
Fields to Display: Description	Created By
Enable feed for this web part	checked
Feed Title	Consolidated Blogs
Feed Description	This is a consolidated feed of all of the blogs in the site collection.

An example of what the end result could look like is shown in Figure 7-15.

The 15 most recent blog posts are displayed, grouped by the name of the blog site. The name of the person who created each item is displayed under its title. Click the orange RSS Feed icon at the bottom right in order to view or subscribe to this list of blogs as a single RSS feed.

FIGURE 7-15

Relevant Documents

The Relevant Documents web part displays all site documents that are relevant to the current logged-in user. The Data section of the Web Part properties contains several configuration options, as shown in Figure 7-16.

Relevant Documents rolls up information from all libraries on the site, and automatically displays only the most recent ones in the order that they were modified, descending. This web part is only available on sites that have the publishing feature enabled.

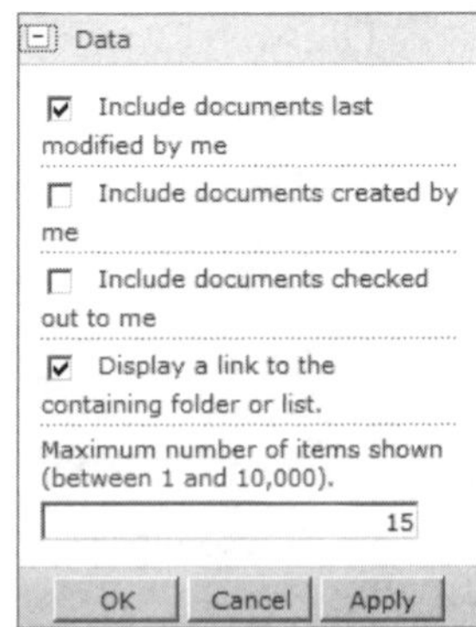

FIGURE 7-16

RSS Viewer

Similar to the Content Query web part, the RSS Viewer web part is only available on publishing sites. This web part is used in order to view an RSS feed of content that exists either inside or outside of SharePoint. Within the Web Part tool pane, enter the URL of the existing RSS feed, and choose a Refresh Time (in minutes) and a Feed Limit. The feed limit is the number of most recent items to be displayed from the feed. It is important to think about how often the content changes in the RSS feed, so that the refresh time may be configured accordingly. It would be a waste of resources to configure a refresh time of 120 minutes for content that is only updated once a week.

Summary Links

The Summary Links web part allows you to add a list of links to the page. The Summary Links web part is only available when the publishing features are enabled on the site. Each time a new link is added, there are several configuration options, such as the ability to set the link to open in a new window. Click the Configure Styles and Layout button to pick group and item styles.

Web Analytics

The Web Analytics web part is a great way to display the site's most popular content. Each time this web part is added to a page, it can be configured to display one of the following:

- **Most Viewed Content:** Pick a scope, such as the current site collection or site, and this web part will display the list of items that have been clicked on the most.
- **Most Frequent Site Search Queries:** In the search box on the site, when users click "This Site:..." as their scope, this is considered a site search.
- **Most Frequent Search Center Queries:** When searches are performed on "All Sites," or performed from within the Search Center on the site, these are considered Search Center queries. When this option is selected, a drop-down box will be available, from which to pick all search scopes or a specific one.

For more information about searches and scopes, read Chapter 17.

TRY IT OUT Using the Web Analytics Web Part

In this Try It Out, you will learn a way to display a site's most popular content in a web part.

1. Use the steps you learned in "Try It Out: Adding a Web Part to a Page" to add the Web Analytics web part to the site home page.
2. Fill out the Web Part properties according to the following table.

FIELD NAME	SELECTION
Information to Display	Most Viewed Content
Site Scope	This Site and Subsites
Period	Preceding 180 Days
Item Limit	5

3. Check the boxes next to Show Frequency, Show Popularity Rank, Show Popularity Rank Trend, and Enable RSS Feed. Click Apply.
4. Notice that the web part now displays the top-five most popular items on the site, with a number in parentheses next to each one, indicating the number of clicks in the last 180 days (frequency).
5. In the Web Part properties, put a checkbox next to Enable User Department Filtering and click OK.

The Web Analytics web part has now been configured to display the most popular content, and users have the ability to pick a Department from the drop-down box to see a top-five list of the most popular content viewed by users in a particular department!

WSRP Viewer

WSRP stands for Web Services for Remote Portlets. The WSRP Viewer web part displays portals from websites that use WSRP 1.1. WSRP is an older network protocol specification that allows you to use presentation-oriented web services created by developers, and display that data inside of SharePoint. This would be used in situations where the organization has other intranet applications which need to be leveraged inside of SharePoint.

XML Viewer

The XML Viewer web part displays a selected XML file. It transforms XML data using XSL and displays the results. Enter the XML or XSL into their respective editors, or link to already existing XML or XSL files.

Table of Contents

This web part displays a table of contents consisting of sites, lists and libraries. By default, this web part displays two child levels below the current site, as shown in Figure 7-17.

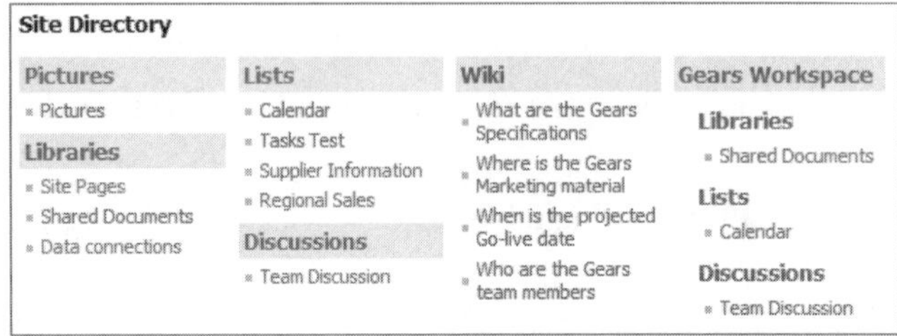

FIGURE 7-17

The Web Part properties tool pane allows for further configuration. There are options to change the site level to start on, the number of levels deep to display, and columns, styles, and sort options.

Document Set Web Parts

There is a set of web parts called Documents, and most of these pertain to Document Sets. Document Sets are a new feature in SharePoint 2010, in which you can group together similar files, and they exist as a content type in a document library. When the name of the Document Set is clicked, you are taken to a special page that acts as a welcome page for the Document Set, which is shown in Figure 7-18, and it consists of the two web parts called Document Set Contents and Document Set Properties. Use these web parts in situations where the detailed information about a document set needs to be displayed outside of the context of the Document Set welcome page.

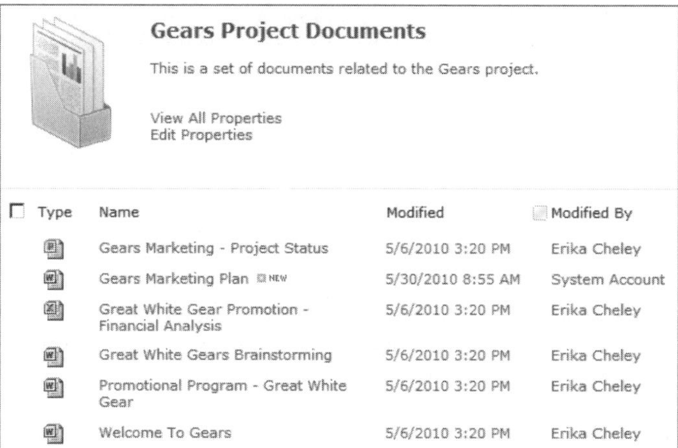

Gears Project Documents
This is a set of documents related to the Gears project.
View All Properties
Edit Properties
Type
Name
Modified
Modified By
Gears Marketing - Project Status
5/6/2010 3:20 PM
Erika Cheley
Gears Marketing Plan NEW
5/30/2010 8:55 AM
System Account
Great White Gear Promotion - Financial Analysis
5/6/2010 3:20 PM
Erika Cheley
Great White Gears Brainstorming
5/6/2010 3:20 PM
Erika Cheley
Promotional Program - Great White Gear
5/6/2010 3:20 PM
Erika Cheley
Welcome To Gears
5/6/2010 3:20 PM
Erika Cheley

FIGURE 7-18

Document Set Contents

The Document Set Contents web part is similar to a list view web part, but it displays only files that exist in the current Document Set.

Document Set Properties

The Document Set Properties web part displays pertinent information about the current Document Set, such as the title and description.

Document ID

The Document ID web part exists in the category of Document Set web parts, but is not necessarily related to Document Sets. There is a site collection feature that can be enabled, called Document ID Service. When documents have this unique ID, the Document ID web part is used to quickly type in the ID of a document to open up that file. This web part simply consists of a text box and a button to open the file.

Media and Content Web Parts

The media and content web parts are added in order to make a SharePoint page visually appealing. Inserting media such as images and video is a good way to grab the attention of site visitors.

Content Editor

The Content Editor web part is a freeform and very versatile web part. Once it has been added to a page, click "Click here to add new content" in the body of the web part. This is where most of the web part configuration is done, which is a lot different from previous versions of SharePoint. When the cursor is in the body of the web part, an Editing Tools tab will show in the Ribbon, as seen in Figure 7-19. Type and edit rich text, or click the HTML button to directly edit the HTML source of the web part.

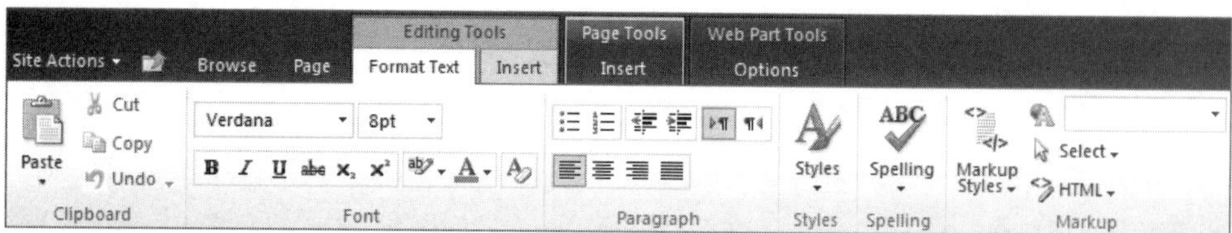

FIGURE 7-19

Image Viewer

This web part allows for the display of a single image on the page. Before an image can be displayed using this web part, it must exist either somewhere on the Internet, where it can be referenced from, or on the SharePoint site. If the document does not exist online yet, create a Picture Library on the site and upload the image to it. The URL to the image can be pasted into the Image Link box in the Web Part properties. Note that visitors to the page must also have at least read-only access to the image in order for it to be displayed properly to those people.

Besides using the Image Viewer web part, there is another way to insert images onto a page, which is new to SharePoint 2010. When a page is in edit mode, on the Insert tab in the Ribbon, click the Image button. On a Web Part Page, this action is identical to placing the Image Viewer web part on a page. Alternately on a wiki page, clicking to insert an image will prompt with three choices: From Computer, From Address, or From SharePoint.

Media Web Part

Display streaming media in the Media web part. Now in SharePoint 2010, the steps for inserting media files on a page are simple and intuitive. Media files consist of movie files, such as those of the type *.WMV, or audio files such as *.MP3 or *.MP4. The follow is a list of the web part settings:

- **Change Media:** Insert a media file that exists on your computer, on SharePoint, or at an address (URL of a website).
- **Change Picture:** Insert a picture that exists on your computer, on SharePoint, or at an address (URL of a website). This picture will be displayed as the default view of the web part when the page is loaded.
- **Title:** Create a descriptive title for the media. This title is displayed on the web part and at the top of the media file while it is playing.
- **Start media automatically:** The media will immediately start playing when each user arrives at the site. It is recommended that this setting be used minimally, in order to conserve network bandwidth.
- **Loop until stopped:** When the movie is played, it will continue to play over and over again until it is manually stopped.
- **Styles:** There are two different styles that can be applied to the media player, dark or light. This relates to the shading of the Play button on the web part and the frame.
- **Size:** Configure the size of the media player on the screen by setting up the height and width in number of pixels.

TRY IT OUT Using the Media Web Part

In this Try It Out, you will learn the steps of how to insert a WMV movie on your site, in order to display a marketing department training video.

1. On your SharePoint home page, click Site Actions and choose More Options.
2. Click Picture Library, call it "Media," and click Create.
3. Click Site Actions and choose Edit Page.
4. In the Editing Tools tab at the top of the Ribbon, click the Insert tab.
5. Click the Video and Audio button.
6. A blank Media web part will now be displayed on the page. Unlike all other web parts, most of the configuration is accomplished via the Ribbon at the top of the page as opposed to the Web Part tool pane. Click the middle of the empty Media web part in order to display the contextual Ribbon showing a Media Options tab. This tab is shown in Figure 7-20.

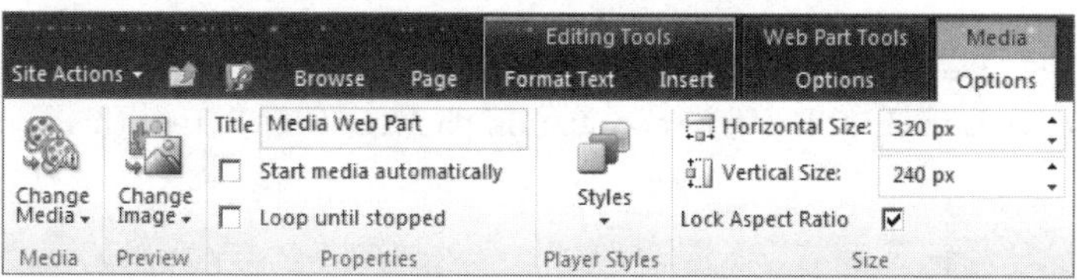

FIGURE 7-20

7. Click the Change Image button, and pick From Address. The image used in this example already exists on the server. Type the following in the Address box and click OK: **/_layouts/images/newsimage.jpg**
8. In the Title box, type **Marketing Training**.
9. For the media file, you'll need your own file on your local computer. Click the Change Media button and choose From Computer.
10. You will be prompted to upload the media file from your computer to a SharePoint library. Click the Browse button to select the media file on your computer. In the Upload To box, pick the "Media" library that you created at step two. Click OK.
11. When the screen comes up that says that the document was uploaded successfully, click the Save button.
12. At the top left of the SharePoint page, click the Save button to save the page changes.

Figure 7-21 shows the resulting Media web part. Click the play button (triangle) to watch the movie in the browser.

FIGURE 7-21

Page Viewer

The Page Viewer web part is used to display content from another place, similar to looking at another site through a small window. Types of locations that can be shown in this web part are web pages, folders, and files. The folder and file choices only apply to network shares and files on network shares.

Picture Library Slideshow

Previously known as the This Week in Pictures web part, the Picture Library Slideshow web part is perfect for displaying picture library content on any SharePoint page, in a nice visual slideshow format. The web part tool properties allow you to select a picture library from a drop-down box that contains all of the picture libraries on the current site. Configure the duration in seconds that each picture is to be shown, pick a view from the library, and show the pictures in either random or sequential order.

Silverlight Web Part

Use the Silverlight web part to display online Silverlight applications. The configuration of this web part simply entails entering the URL to the Silverlight application package (.XAP) that this application should run from.

OWA Web Parts

The Outlook Web Access web parts are mainly for use on SharePoint My Sites, and they allow a user to display information from their own Outlook account, such as email, tasks, contacts, and a calendar. Each of these web parts has a mailbox name box, where a user's email address name is typed. There is also a Mail Server Address box. On a SharePoint intranet, the mail server address is the internal URL of a mail server, such as `http://servername/exchange`, and *not* the URL that a user would go to from outside of the network, such as `https://email.contoso.com`.

WEB PART NAME	DESCRIPTION
My Calendar	Display your calendar from Outlook. Web part properties contain settings to display a daily or weekly view.
My Contacts	Display your Outlook contacts.
My Inbox	This web part allows you to display your own Outlook inbox.
My Mail Folder	Select this to display a specific folder in your mailbox.
My Tasks	Display the tasks in your Outlook task list.

Form Web Parts

The Form web parts all entail allowing end users to fill in a form inside of a web part, and the InfoPath Form web part is brand new to SharePoint 2010.

HTML Form Web Part

By default, the HTML Form web part consists of a textbox and a Go button. There is a Source Editor button in the Web Part properties, which allows the code behind the form to be modified. This web part is typically connected to another web part to send the form field information to filter another web part on the page.

InfoPath Form Web Part

The InfoPath Form web part allows you to insert any browser-based InfoPath form on a page. When a form is easily accessible to site users as a web part, it is a few clicks easier for site users to fill out the form. The Web Part properties allow you to select a form from your site collection or site. Forms that have been activated to the site collection as administrator-approved templates will be available, as well as forms that have been published to a library on the site. In SharePoint 2010, there is a new ability to convert a regular SharePoint list form to an InfoPath form. These SharePoint list forms are also available to choose from in the Web Part Properties.

TRY IT OUT Using the InfoPath Form Web Part

In this Try It Out, you will insert an InfoPath form on a page. By default, there will not be any InfoPath forms on the site, so this exercise entails creating an InfoPath form first. A prerequisite before getting started is to create and populate the Regional Sales list, following the instruction steps one through seven from "Try It Out: Using the Chart Web Part."

1. Open the Regional Sales list, and click the List tab in the Ribbon.
2. Click List Settings, and click Advanced Settings.
3. Change the Attachments setting to Disabled and click OK. Click OK on the warning message.
4. Click Regional Sales in the breadcrumb trail at the top, and choose the List tab in the Ribbon again.
5. Click the big Customize Form button.
6. Look at the form that is automatically created in InfoPath, and click the Quick Publish button at the top left (next to the Save button).
7. Click OK to the message that the form template was published successfully, and close InfoPath.
8. On the home page of the site, insert the InfoPath Form web part.
9. Open the Web Part tool pane, and in the List or Library drop-down box, choose Regional Sales.
10. In the Submit Behavior box, choose Close the Form. In the Appearance section, type **Regional Sales** as the Title. Click OK.

The resulting form is shown in Figure 7-22.

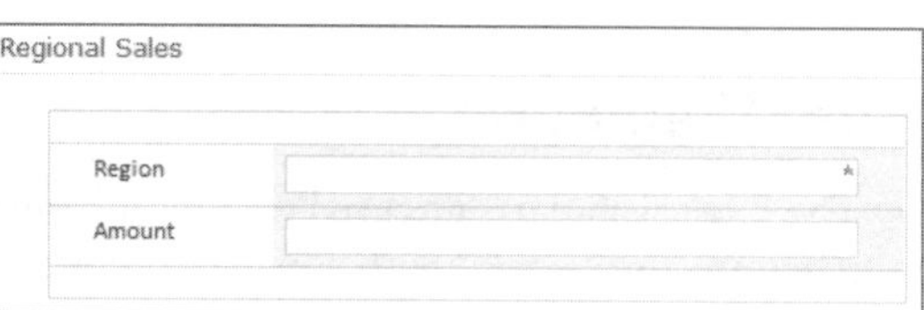

FIGURE 7-22

See that users can now fill out the form directly on the page. Also notice that there is no Submit button. Click your cursor inside of the form, and see the contextual Ribbon at the top of the page. Among other items, the Ribbon contains a large Save button that users can click once they have filled out the form.

Social Collaboration Web Parts

This category of web parts is centered around the concept of personalization in SharePoint. SharePoint users are individuals, and those individuals interact with each other not only in their day-to-day jobs but also via SharePoint. SharePoint 2010 brings together content collaboration, personal information, and communication, which are all utilized in the Social Collaboration web parts.

Contact Details

The Contact Details web part displays contact information about an individual in the organization. One good example of a use for this web part is to display information to site users, regarding whom they should contact with questions about the site. In the Web Part properties, pick a user's name from the global address list, and pick whether to display their picture and their job title. The picture of the contact comes from the user's My Site photo, and an example of this web part is shown in Figure 7-23.

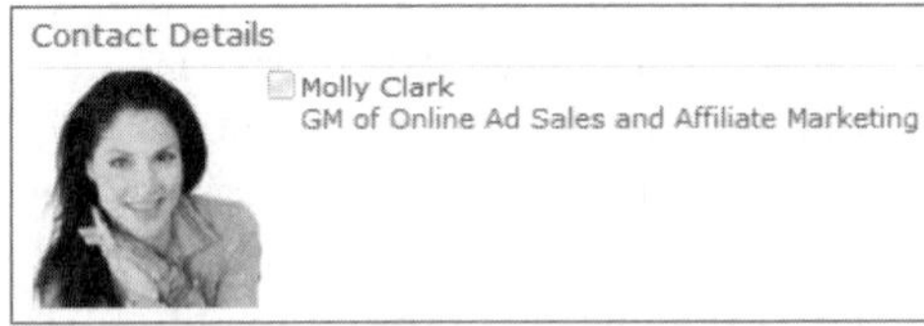

FIGURE 7-23

Site Users

When the organization uses an integrated instant messaging server, such as Office Communication Server (OCS) and Office Communicator or Windows Live Messenger are installed on the client computers, the Site Users web part can be used. Display site users in order to quickly send instant messages or email to them. Pick the maximum number of users to display, as well as a specific SharePoint group of people, such as Site Members.

User Tasks

The User Tasks web part displays tasks that are assigned to the currently logged-in user. This information comes from all task lists on the current site, where the user is in the Assigned To column.

Social Computing Web Parts

As part of the new social computing components in SharePoint, there are several new out-of-the-box web parts. These web parts, such as Note Board, Organization Browser, and Tag Cloud, will be covered in Chapter 11.

Filter Web Parts

The Filter web parts are used to filter information in other web parts on the same page. These web parts are always used with a web part connection to another web part on the page. Any one of these web parts will not be useful without a connection to another web part. Connections are *required*. For more information about web part connections, read the "Connect Web Parts" section earlier in this chapter.

***NOTE** If one of the Filter web parts has been added to a wiki page, but isn't visible when the page is in edit mode, here's a trick. On any other web part on the page, click the drop-down box in the top right, and choose Edit Web Part. Your hidden Filter web part will appear, so that you can now configure it.*

Choice Filter

In this filter, manually type in a list of choices in the Web Part properties. The site user will be presented with a filter button that allows them to pick from one of the choices. Use this web part when the items in the choice list are fairly static, compared to the SharePoint List Filter, which is used for a dynamic list of items.

SharePoint List Filter

Display a choice list of items that exist in a SharePoint list on the current site. This filter is used for dynamic data, or data that is updated fairly frequently. Select a list or library, and pick which column to display as the drop-down choices. Unfortunately, the Title column will not be available as an option in this web part.

Current User Filter

The Current User Filter web part utilizes information about the currently logged-in user, which comes from a specific profile property. This data exists in the user profile properties. Some of this information comes from the company's directory service such as Active Directory, and some of the information is entered by each user on their My Site. In the Current User Filter properties, the default property is the current user name. There is a drop-down box called SharePoint profile value for current user, in which you can select from a long list of other properties, such as Department, Manager, or Job Title.

Date Filter

The Date Filter web part consists of a date picker box. In the Web Part properties, the default value can be set to today, a specific date, or a number of days relative to today. When connecting this web part, the matching column in the consumer web part must be a date column.

Page Field Filter

The Page Field Filter web part can only be used on a wiki page. This web part filters data using column information from the page library in which the current Wiki Page exists.

Query String (URL) Filter

The Query String (URL) Filter uses information from the URL of the current page. For example, the URL to the default view of a task list might look something like this:

```
http://intranet.contoso.com/Lists/Tasks/AllItems.aspx
```

Once this web part has been added to the task list's allitems.aspx page, the URL with a query string would have a question mark in it, followed by the name of the filter, as in the following example URL:

```
http://intranet.contoso.com/Lists/Tasks/AllItems.aspx?Status=Completed
```

In this example, "Status" has been set as the parameter, and a web part connection has been created to send the query string to the status column in the Tasks web part on the page. The result is a list of items filtered by only tasks that are complete.

Text Filter

The most simple of the Filter web parts, the Text Filter is simply a freeform textbox. The filter text must exactly match the column that is to be filtered, and no wildcards are allowed.

SQL Server Analysis Services Filter

This filter uses a SQL Analysis Services cube. Before using this web part, a data connection to a cube must be created in a Data Connection library. Within the Web Part properties, select the dimension and hierarchy of the cube.

Filter Actions

The Filter Actions web part is used in conjunction with another Filter web part on the same page. Use this web part to allow users to save their favorite filters. Once a user has set a filter to a certain value and saved it, that same filter will be applied next time that user visits the site.

TRY IT OUT Using the Filter Web Parts

In this Try It Out, you will learn how to insert Filter web parts on a page and configure them to send information to a Consumer web part. In this example, the goal is to display a list of tasks on the site to filter by a department name. Users will be able to switch the filter to view another department's tasks. The two web parts that will be used are the SharePoint List Filter and the Tasks Test list that you created in "Try It Out: Connecting Web Parts."

1. Click Site Actions, choose More Options, and choose Custom List. Name the list "Departments" and click Create.
2. In the List tab of the Ribbon, click Create Column. For the column name, call it "Department," change Enforce Unique Values to Yes, and click OK.
3. Click List Settings, and in the Columns section click the name of the Title column. Change "Require that this column contains information" to No. Click OK.
4. In the breadcrumb trail at the top of the screen, click Departments.
5. Add two new items to the list, with simply "IT" and "Marketing" as each Department name. Again, you are not using the Title column at all because the SharePoint List Filter web part will not recognize it.
6. Click the Tasks Test list on the left side of the page, and click the List tab in the Ribbon. Click the Create Column button.

7. Fill in the following information when creating the new column, and click OK:

FIELD	VALUE
Column Name	Department
The type of information in this column	Lookup
Get information from	Departments
In this column	Department

8. In the example tasks in the list, edit each item and pick a department to associate with it.
9. On the home page of the site, add two web parts, the Tasks Test list, and then the SharePoint List Filter.
10. Open the Web Part tool pane for the SharePoint List Filter. The List box allows you to click the orange icon on the right in order to select the departments list on the site.
11. Configure the web part as shown in Figure 7-24, and click Apply.
12. In the drop-down box in the corner of the SharePoint List Filter, click Connections. In the fly-out, choose Send Filter Values To, and choose Tasks Test.
13. In the Choose Connection box that pops up, click Configure.
14. In the Consumer Field Name drop-down box, choose Department and click Finish.
15. Save the page.

The end result is a filter in which users can select a department, which then filters the tasks list to only show tasks associated with that department name. In the Departments list, unique values were enforced, so that the same department will not ever be listed twice.

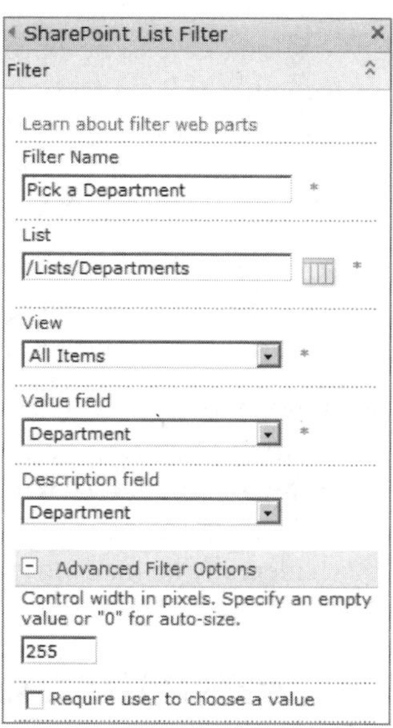

FIGURE 7-24

TESTING FILTER WEB PARTS

In some cases, it is not always apparent exactly what data will be provided from the Filter web part. There is an easy way that these web parts can be tested to see exactly what the filter information will be. Add your provider web part (such as the Current User Filter) to the page, and also add the Text Filter web part. Configure your provider web part as needed, and then create a web part connection to Send Default Value To ⇨ Text Filter. Once the page is saved, the results of the filter will be displayed in the Text Filter web part.

Search Web Parts

Search web parts exist on search pages in a Search Center site, and are covered in Chapter 17.

XSLT LIST VIEW WEB PARTS

The XSLT web part was previously known as the Data View web part or the Data Form web part. This flexible web part can be used to display and aggregate information from various sources. Your company may have data dispersed on multiple systems in addition to SharePoint. With the functionality leveraged by XSLT List View web parts in SharePoint 2010, there is the potential to have a singular repository accessible by the end users. Data of interest can be displayed all in one place — SharePoint.

As custom as this web part is inherently, you don't need to know any development language, and you don't have to be a programmer to create XSLT List View web parts. Web part creation is accomplished in a friendly user interface, using a free program called SharePoint Designer 2010. Not only can you create these types of web parts to extend the look and functionality of regular list views, but you can create views of data in other external systems, also. These systems include databases, web services, XML files, and linked data sources.

Why create these custom web parts? Have you ever run into a situation where a regular list view didn't quite achieve the requirements for a site? This is where the XSLT List View web part steps in to allow you to take it to the next level. Create conditional formatting; create custom buttons in the Ribbon, and even modify the "no matching items" message.

Creating an XSLT List View web part is as simple as opening up your site in SharePoint Designer, opening a list, and clicking the New button to create a new view. When working in these web parts it is a good practice to click the View tab and choose Zoom to Contents. This way, changes cannot accidentally be made to the other areas of the page, such as the navigation.

THE WEB PART GALLERY

The web part gallery exists on every site collection and is the master location that all web parts are stored. These files are either .DWP or .WEBPART files. On the Site Settings page at the top level of the site collection, in the Galleries section, click Web Parts. Explore this list by clicking the Edit button on different rows to see some of the settings. Notice the Title field, which will help you to recognize the names of some of the web parts. Also, see that the Group field indicates which category the web part will be displayed in when inserting it on a page.

Exporting and Importing web parts was covered earlier in this chapter, and it was mentioned that a web part can be imported to a gallery instead of just one page. When it is determined that a web part should be available on all sites and it has been tested on different sites in a site collection, it can be uploaded to the gallery and categorized. On the Documents tab in the Ribbon, click the Upload Document button, and upload the file to the gallery. It will then be available on all sites in the site collection.

SUMMARY

Web parts are fundamental to the way SharePoint pages display content, and to how people who visit your site will perceive it. This chapter has supplied you with a plethora of introductory information so that you can effortlessly add and configure web parts on your site. Not only have web parts fundamentals been described, but you have also learned about each of the out-of-the-box web parts and even tried some of them out.

EXERCISES

1. Some users visit one particular document library on a regular basis, and they claim that it is very important that they are aware as soon as a change is made in the library. They have set up email alerts to be notified but would also like the document library on the page to also automatically stay updated, so that they don't have to refresh the browser to see changes. How can you make this happen?

2. The marketing manager has spent a lot of time configuring a Chart web part that is based on data in an external content type. He would like to save this web part and put a copy of it on a site in another site collection. How would he accomplish this?

3. The Human Resources department has its own Team Site for collaboration. Members of the site would like to quickly see a list of all documents that they are working on, no matter which library the files exist in. Which web part can accomplish this most easily?

4. The company picnic happened last week, and the picnic photos have been uploaded to a picture library on the site, along with all of the pictures from other past events. How can you display only the picnic pictures in a pretty slideshow view on your site?

5. There is an announcement list on the site that really only pertains to IT managers. Without involving security or permissions, how do you display these announcements on a page so that only the SharePoint group of IT Managers can see the web part?

▶ WHAT YOU LEARNED IN THIS CHAPTER

TOPIC	KEY CONCEPTS
Description of web parts	Web parts are modular, and can be added to pages on SharePoint sites in order to display pertinent content to site users.
Adding web parts	Understanding the steps for adding a web part to a page are crucial in this chapter, because these steps are used in every "Try It Out" section.
Configuring web parts	When configuring web parts, there are some settings that are standard across all of them. Some settings are unique, depending on the type of web part.
Export and Import web parts	Some types of web parts can be exported from one page, and imported to be displayed on another page, usually to save time in configuring another web part.
Connect web parts	Web parts can be connected to each other to allow for the passing of filter information or parameters.
List View web parts	List and library web parts automatically exist for every list and library on the site.
Business Data web parts	These give us different ways of viewing and analyzing business data, whether it be inside or outside of SharePoint.
Content rollup web parts	Display data from multiple locations, or from another location besides the current site.
Document Set web parts	Some are used in document sets, and one is used in conjunction with the Document ID Service.
Media and Content web parts	In general, these can display media on a page, such as pictures or video.
Outlook Web Access web parts	These are used on My Sites, and show each user their own Outlook information.
Form web parts	Allow site users to fill out and submit forms directly on the page, which saves them time and clicks.
Social Collaboration web parts	Most of these will be covered in Chapter 11, but several of the legacy ones were described in this section.
Filter web parts	These are extremely powerful, and allow you to highly customize the interactivity of a SharePoint page. All of these require connections to other web parts.
XSLT List View web parts	These are also known as data view web parts, and can be called the Swiss Army Knife of SharePoint. They allow you to highly customize the way data is viewed. Conditional formatting is one of the major benefits of creating these versatile web parts.
Web part gallery	This exists on every site collection, and is the location where all of the web part files are stored.

Sites and Workspaces

WHAT YOU WILL LEARN IN THIS CHAPTER:

- The differences between site collections and sites
- How to create a custom template based on an existing site
- How to build a site structure
- The differences between the templates provided out of the box and when each one should be used
- The benefit and value found from Meeting Workspaces

So far in the book we have covered many of the different components that can be included within a SharePoint site. We are going to dedicate this chapter to understanding the container that you are building the objects within. We are going to look at several key concepts that should help you pull all the pieces together. We will be looking at the creation process for new site collections and sites, as well as providing you the information to know when to create each one.

SITE COLLECTIONS AND SITES

Site collections and sites are the containers that you use to hold all of the content you are storing within SharePoint. A site collection can contain many sites, and each site within the site collection can contain many lists and libraries. Beyond the fact that site collections contain sites, there are specific characteristics of a site collection that should be understood. By knowing these differences, you will be better equipped to make a decision when creating new content.

Understanding the Boundaries

When you think of site collection, you should think of the term *boundary*. Whenever you create a site collection, you are in essence creating a boundary within your SharePoint farm. This boundary is a container for content and can have specific settings configured that will apply to all sites within the container. Following are some of those key settings that are applied at the site collection level:

- **Site Collection Administrator:** This configuration allows you to determine which users can have full administrative rights within the site collection.
- **Web Parts:** This gallery contains all of the web parts that can be used within the site collection. If you want to add a web part to a web (subsite), then it must be added at the site collection level.
- **List Templates:** This gallery stores all the different list templates that can be used within the site collection. Whenever you save a list as a template within the site collection, it is saved to this location.
- **Themes:** This gallery contains all of the themes that can be used within the site collection. You can configure what theme you want to use on each site; however, custom themes can only be added at the site collection level.
- **Solutions:** This gallery contains all of the custom solutions that can be used within the site collection. This includes all custom site templates. Whenever you save a site as a template, it will be stored within this Solutions gallery.
- **Workflows:** This page provides a list of all the workflows within the site collection, including their status (active, inactive).
- **Search Settings:** For each site collection, the search settings are configured at the site collection level and then are applied to all sites within the site collection. These settings include scopes, search center location, keywords, best bets, and any FAST search settings.
- **Recycle Bin:** This is the site collection recycle bin, which allows you to restore content that has been deleted within the site collection. There are both an end-user recycle bin and a recycle bin that has been created to store content that has been deleted from the end-user recycle bin.
- **Site Collection Features:** This is the location where you enable and disable site collection features. This is basically a way to allow behaviors within the site collection. If you activate features here, you are enabling sites to also activate the features.
- **Site Hierarchy:** From this location, you can view and drill down through the hierarchy of the site collection. This will show you all of the subsites created and provide you with a link to manage them (open their settings page).
- **Site Collection Navigation:** This configuration setting will allow you to enable/disable navigation within the site collection. This configuration page will also allow you to disable security trimming of the navigation and to disable/enable audiences for the site collection.
- **Audit Settings:** These settings will allow you to configure what items can be audited within the site, as well as a link to generate and review the audit reports.
- **Portal Site Connection:** This page will allow you to configure a portal connection. This connection will be displayed as the topmost link for the site. This can be configured to any link and is often used to link one site collection to another site collection. Using this approach will allow users a way to seamlessly navigate to a new location, as if it were part of the current location.

- **Site Collection Management Policies:** From this location you can import, create and configure management policies that apply to the entire site collection. An example of this is creating a retention policy for all content within the site collection.
- **Content Type Publishing:** This screen will allow you to view all of the content type hubs that are pushing data to your site collection. You will be able to force a refresh for all content types on the next update, view the error log, and view the hubs.
- **Publishing Features:** These features allow you configure the different elements of publishing, including the variations and the translatable columns.
- **Suggested Content Browser Locations:** This configuration allows you to add links to locations were you want to direct users to look when adding assets (images, media files) to their pages. Think of this as a shortcut so that they don't have to remember where the assets are located. This setting also helps reduce the possibility of the same content being uploaded multiple times.
- **SharePoint Designer Settings:** This link allows you to enable and disable certain functionality that is available in SharePoint Designer. For instance, you can allow users to create custom workflows but disable their ability to create custom master pages.
- **Visual Upgrade:** If your upgrade from 2007 takes advantage of the visual upgrade features, then this is where you can configure the site collection to use the new updated 2010 user interface.
- **Help Collections:** From this screen, you can configure what help collections are available within the site collection. By default, as new features are activated, the corresponding help collections are enabled.
- **Site Collection Analytic Reports:** This link allows you to view reports that show the usage data for the site collection.

Reviewing this list should give you an idea of the various configuration settings that are available across the site collection. These settings are configured once and then consumed by all webs within the site collection. These settings can also help you determine when you would create a site collection versus a web. For instance, you would want to create two separate site collections if you had two different teams, both of which needed to create templates and neither of which wanted to see the other team's templates. However, you could create a single site collection if you wanted all the teams to inherit the same navigation, list templates, and site templates.

So far, we have covered the different settings that you can configure at the various site levels, but we haven't really covered some of the administrative features that would play a part in determining whether to create a site collection versus a web. While it is likely that your administrators will have put procedures in place to help you determine what to create, it is also very helpful for you to understand these concepts so that you can be proactive in managing your content.

- **Site Quotas:** These are configured at the site collection level and apply a restriction to all content within the site collection. This means that you could potentially have one web within the site collection that uses all of the quota allotment. If you know the quota size at the onset you can use that to determine if you want to create a web or a new site collection.

- **Database Size:** As you are adding content to your site, it is ultimately being stored within a SQL database. While it is possible to create a dedicated database for your site collection, it is not possible to store content from your site collection across multiple databases. This means that you want to be sure to only grow your site collection to a size that is manageable at the database level. The database size recommendation for SharePoint 2010 is 200 GB; however, it is likely that your administrators have a database size that they would like to limit your site collections to. They can use quotas to help control the growth of the site collection; however, if you are aware of the limitations up front, then you can design a site structure that meets your needs as well as adheres to the guidelines created by your server administration team.

Now that you have a better understanding of the site collection boundaries, you should have most of the information needed to help determine if you should create site collections or webs. I say most, because sometimes the decision to create a site as a web is not really a black-and-white decision. In fact, it is often gray and cloudy! In many cases, you could go either way and, in many cases, whichever way you choose could potentially have an impact in one way or another. Let's review an example that shows how gray the choice can be at times. In this scenario, you have a need to collaborate on our internal projects. Here are some of the requirements:

- Each team needs to work using the approach presented by your internal Project Management Office (PMO). Each team will need to store a large amount of content, including documents and media files.
- Each team will need to have some flexibility so that they can extend the model provided by the PMO. (This means the template may contain 2–3 lists, but they need the ability to create additional lists).
- The PMO wants to create reports that roll up data from all project sites.

In this scenario, there are a few things that stick out; first you want to use a common template among the project sites, so that leads you to creating a custom template within a site collection and then creating a site for each of the project sites. This will also allow you to easily create rollups of data from within the site collection (we will be covering this later in the chapter), but what do you do to accommodate for all of the large files that each of the project sites will need? Since you know you are going to be dealing with large amounts of data, you need to consider a few things. How many projects will you be doing in the next six months, next year, or next two years? At this point, you will need to make a few decisions about how to best separate the data. Could you do several site collections and group like projects together? Could you create a site collection for each year of projects? Do you create a site collection per project? The answer to these questions is "it depends." At this point, you are really making a management decision. You will need to look at your scenario and determine the best solution for you and your team. If you decide to manage multiple site collections, then managing SQL and database sizing will be easier. If you decided to create one site collection, then you will need to be careful with your site collection size and be sure to have a plan in place, in case you end up needing to store more content. Keep in mind that each team will likely come to a different conclusion as to what solution is best for them. This is common and, as long as you are following best practices for storage and configuration, the actual hierarchy can be flexible enough to meet your specific needs.

TRY IT OUT Create a Site Collection

In the first Try It Out, you are going to be creating a site collection. To create a site collection, you need to have access to the Central Administration configuration site. If you do not have access, you will need to talk with your SharePoint administrator. It is also possible that your site administrator has configured a custom site collection creation process that allows you to create site collections without having access to Central Administration.

1. Open the Central Administration Site.
2. Select the Create Site Collections link within the Application Management grouping, as shown in the Figure 8-1.
3. Enter the following properties for the new site collection and then click OK. An example is shown in Figure 8-2.

FIGURE 8-1

- **Web Application:** Accept the default option, unless directed otherwise by your server administrator
- **Title:** Projects
- **Description:** Location to create and store all internal project information
- **URL:** /sites/projects
- **Template Selection:** Team Site
- **Primary Site Collection Administrator:** Your username
- **Quota Template:** No Quota

Web Application Select a web application. To create a new web application go to New Web Application page.	Web Application: **http://team.contoso.com/**
Title and Description Type a title and description for your new site. The title will be displayed on each page in the site.	Title: Projects Description: Location to create and store all internal project information.
Web Site Address Specify the URL name and URL path to create a new site, or choose to create a site at a specific path. To add a new URL Path go to the Define Managed Paths page.	URL: **http://team.contoso.com** /sites/
Template Selection A site template determines what lists and features will be available on your new site. Select a site template based on the descriptions of each template and how you intend to use the new site. Many aspects of a site can be customized after creation. However, the site template cannot be changed once the site is created.	Select a template: Collaboration Meetings Enterprise Publishing Custom Team Site Blank Site Document Workspace

FIGURE 8-2

***NOTE** The user that you enter as the primary site collection administrator will be the user that is notified by the system when something needs attention. This can include site access requests and quote notifications. This user will have full control to the site collection.*

4. On the Top-Level Site Successfully Created page, click the link to open the new site collection. Your site should look similar to the site in Figure 8-3.

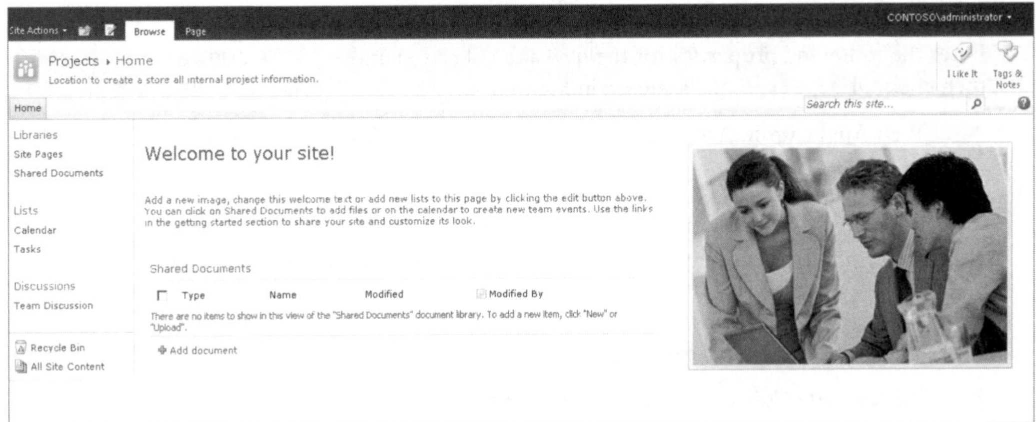

FIGURE 8-3

How It Works

When you create a site collection in Central Administration, you provide all of the details for your site collection, and then the site is provisioned for you and a link is returned.

TRY IT OUT Create a Web (Subsite)

In this Try It Out, you are going to create a web within your projects site collection. This will allow us to start to build a site hierarchy that can be used for the remaining chapter examples.

1. Open the Projects Site Collection that you created in the previous example.
2. Navigate to the Site Settings Page by selecting the Site Actions menu and the Site Settings Option.
3. In the Site Administration group, select the Sites and workspaces link, as shown in Figure 8-4.
4. Select the Create option at the top of the page, enter the following properties for the site, and then select Create. An example is shown in Figure 8-5:
    - **Title:** Project A
    - **Description:** Location to store all content for Project A

- **URL:** /sites/projects/projectA
- **Template Selection:** Team Site
- **Permissions:** Use same permissions as parent site
- **Display on the Quick Launch of the parent site?:** Yes
- **Display on the top link bar of the parent site?:** Yes
- **Use the top link bar from the parent site?:** Yes

Don't worry if you don't understand all of these configuration options at this point in the chapter. You will be working through them later in the chapter, and by the time you reach the end, you will be familiar with how they all work together.

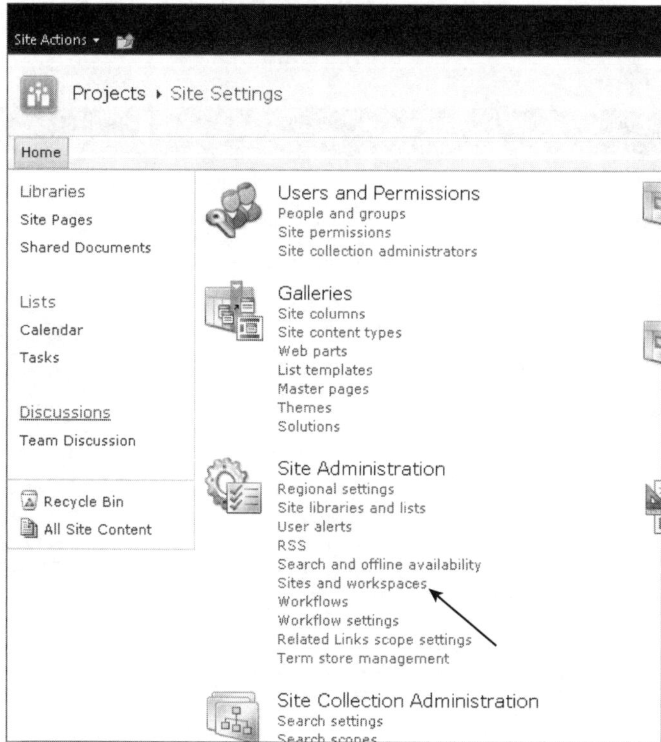

FIGURE 8-4

5. Once the web (subsite) has been created, you will be redirected to the new site. Your screen should look similar to the one displayed in Figure 8-6.

How It Works

When you enter the data for the new site, the site is created within the site collection. Since you are creating the site from within a site collection, it is created within that site collection.

Create Cancel

Title and Description

Type a title and description for your new site. The title will be displayed on each page in the site.

Title:
Project A

Description:
Location to store all content for Project A.

Web Site Address

Users can navigate to your site by typing the Web site address (URL) into their browser. You can enter the last part of the address. You should keep it short and easy to remember.

For example, http://team.contoso.com/sites/projects/*sitename*

URL name:
http://team.contoso.com/sites/projects/ projectA

Template Selection

A site template determines what lists and features will be available on your new site. Select a site template based on the descriptions of each template and how you intend to use the new site. Many aspects of a site can be customized after creation. However, the site template cannot be changed once the site is created.

Select a template:
Collaboration | Meetings | Web Databases | Enterprise
Team Site
Blank Site
Document Workspace
Blog
Group Work Site
Visio Process Repository

FIGURE 8-5

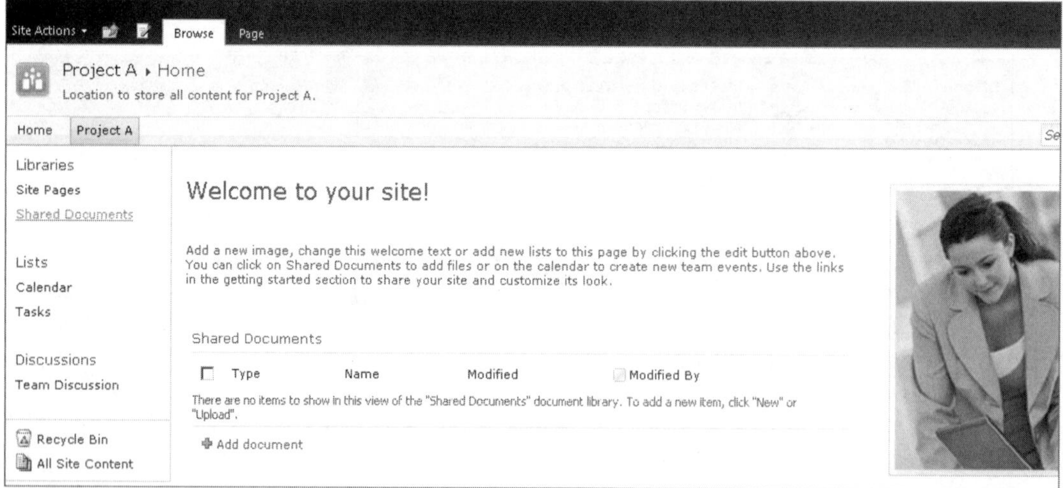

FIGURE 8-6

MANAGING SITE COLLECTIONS AND SITES

Now that you have created a site collection and a web, we are going to focus on some of the things that you can do to manage them. We are going to be covering several different areas, and it is good to remember that each of these is available based on the type of licensing that you have configured. We are going to focus on the key things that are done to manage a site, including:

- Activating/deactivating features
- Creating content

- Managing permissions
- Site analytics
- Managing navigation
- Working with themes and master pages
- Working with content across webs

These are pretty extensive topics, some of which have a chapter dedicated to them within this book. For those sections, we will cover things at a high level and tell you to refer to the other various chapters for greater detail.

NOTE *We are just getting started with site collections. If you are wondering about the progression, it will start with creating site collections and webs, adding content and configuring them, and then saving them as templates. Along the way we will also be covering all of the default templates and working with content offline. Feel free to jump around the chapter to the sections that pertain the most to your specific needs.*

Features

Features are a way within SharePoint to turn on or turn off certain functionality. Some common examples include the SharePoint Enterprise Features and SharePoint Publishing Features. By default, each of the templates provided by Microsoft has different features activated. This means that if you create a site using the Enterprise Wiki template, different features are activated by default than if you had used the Team template. This doesn't mean that you can't use the additional features, it just means that you first have to activate them. You can think of features like a light switch. When you want to see the functionality, you simply activate the feature. If you do not want to see it any longer, then you can deactivate the feature. Features can be activated at the site collection level and the web (subsite) level. When you activate features at the site collection level, you are basically allowing them to be used within the site collection. When you activate them at the web level, you are saying you want to use the feature on that site. The features can only be activated at the web level if they have been activated for the site collection.

NOTE *The publishing features come preactivated on the Publishing sites and Enterprise sites and will have an impact on how pages are created and stored, including the home page. You can still activate the publishing features on other site collections, but this will not move the home page to the pages folder. You would need to create a new home page in the pages folder and then set that page to be the home page for the site.*

TRY IT OUT Activating Site Collection Features

Throughout the remainder of the Try It Outs in this section, we will be covering some topics that include additional features to those currently activated in the test site collection that you created earlier. In this example, you will activate some additional features on the site collection.

1. Open the Projects Site Collection that you created in the previous example.
2. Navigate to the Site Settings Page by selecting the Site Actions menu and the Site Settings Option.
3. In the Site Collection Administration group, select the Site collection features link, as shown in Figure 8-7.
4. Next to the following features, select the Activate Button.
   - SharePoint Server Enterprise Site Collection features
   - SharePoint Server Publishing Infrastructure
5. Navigate back to the Site Settings page. You should notice that there are now several additional management links on this page.

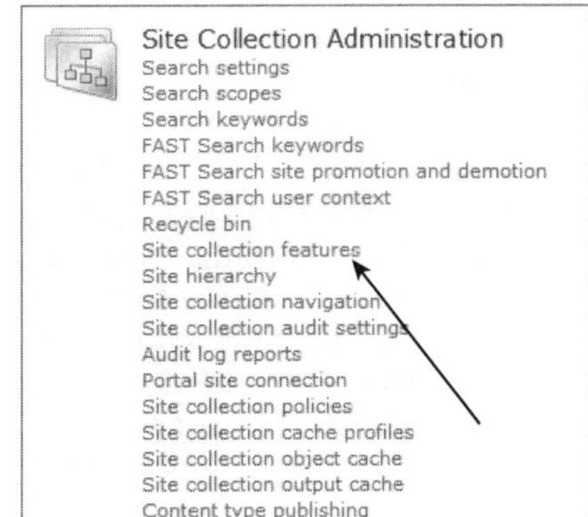

FIGURE 8-7

How It Works

When you activate the site collection features, additional lists, libraries, and web parts are made available for use within the site collection. You will notice that as you activate features, additional items become available for configuration.

Managing Content and Structure

Once a site is created, typically the first thing you need to do is to customize it to match your requirements. While Microsoft does a great job providing you with templates to get started, it is unlikely that you will be able to use the template as is without making modifications. We covered how to create lists and libraries in earlier chapters, but it is likely that you are wondering if there is an easy way to view all of the different types of content within your site. There are several different ways that you can view the content within a site collection, including those discussed in the following sections.

View All Site Content

This is a page that is accessed from the site actions menu and displays all of the lists and libraries within your site. You can also see all of the webs (subsites) within the collection; however, you can't see the webs lists and libraries.

Site Hierarchy

This link can be accessed from the root site in the site collection. It provides a view of all of the webs (subsites) in the site collection, as well as a link to easily navigate to their site settings page. An example of this page is shown in Figure 8-8.

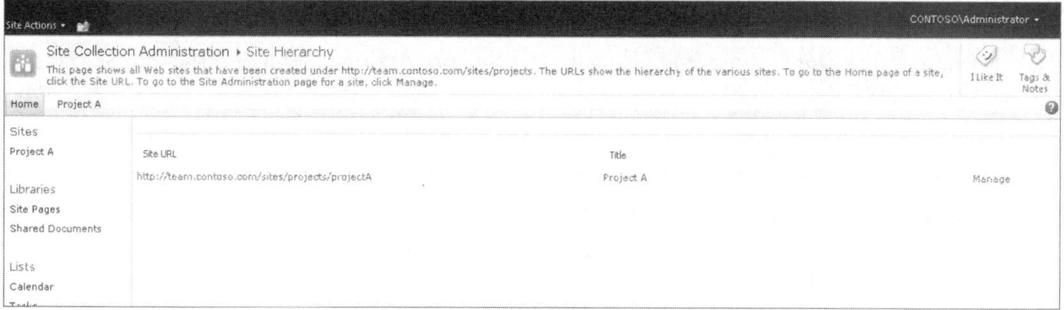

FIGURE 8-8

Site Content and Structure

When the publishing feature has been activated, an additional link is provided in the Site Administration section that allows you to see a tree view of the content within the site collection. From this view, you can easily create content, move content, and configure the content behavior (general settings, advanced settings, and permissions). This is a valuable tool that provides a quick way to work with content within the site collection. It is highly recommended that you take advantage of using this feature when creating and managing your content. An example of this page is shown in Figure 8-9.

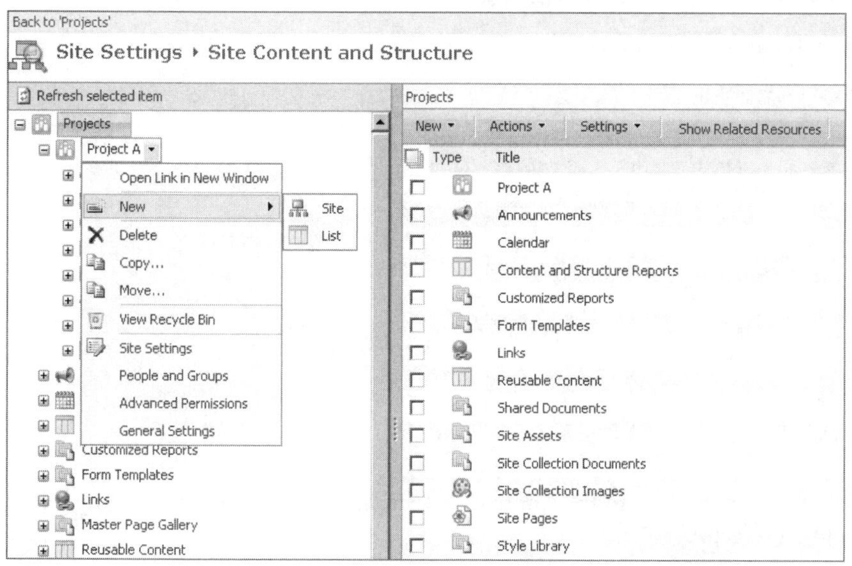

FIGURE 8-9

TRY IT OUT Create and Move a Site from the Content and Structure Page

In this example, you are going to use the Content and Structure page to create a new project site. You are going to create the site as a project site under Project A and then decide to move the site so that it is a sibling to Project A instead of a child. While it might not be common in the real world to create a site and immediately move it, it is common to move a site. So, we will just combine the two operations within one exercise.

1. Open the Projects Site Collection that was created in the previous example.
2. Navigate to the Site Settings Page by selecting the Site Actions menu and the Site Settings Option.
3. In the Site Administration group, select the Content and structure link. An example of this is shown in Figure 8-10.
4. Select the drop-down menu next to Project A. Select the arrow next to the word New and then select Site. An example of this is shown in Figure 8-11.
5. When the create page loads, enter the following properties for the site and then click Create:
    - **Title:** Project B
    - **Description:** Location to store all content for Project B.
    - **URL:** /sites/projects/projectA/projectB
    - **Template Selection:** Team Site
    - **Permissions:** Use same permissions as parent site
    - **Display on the Quick Launch of the parent site?:** Yes
    - **Use the top link bar from the parent site?:** Yes

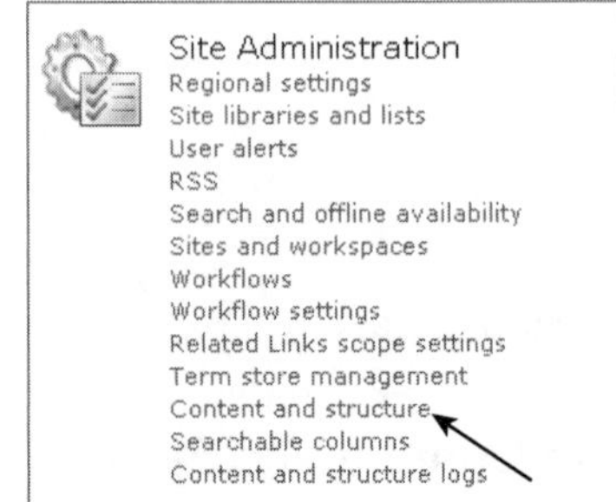

FIGURE 8-10

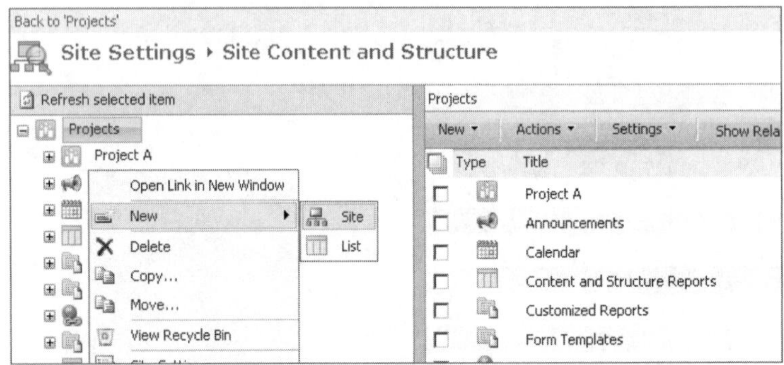

FIGURE 8-11

6. Select OK and you will be redirected to the Content and Structure page. You should now see Project B listed under Project A.
7. Now that you have the site created, you would like to move the site so that it is under projects. Remember that you could have created the site directly under projects; we are just using this as an example so that you understand the process for moving sites.

8. Select the drop-down next to Project B and select the Move option, as shown in Figure 8-12.
9. Select Projects within the Move dialog and then click OK, as shown in Figure 8-13.
10. Once the site has been moved, you will be redirected to the Content and Site Structure page. Keep in mind that this move also updates the URL of the site, so if any users had the link saved, they will need to have the updated link to access the site.

How It Works

The Content and Site Structure page gives you an easy way to quickly work with and configure the content within your site collections. As seen is this example, you can easily create content and then move content around. In the example, you moved a site from one location to another, but you should also note that you can move lists from one location to another, and you can also move list content from one list to another (providing that the lists support the same content types). This is a very powerful tool that can help you manage your site collections, and it is recommended that you spend some time exploring this tool in detail.

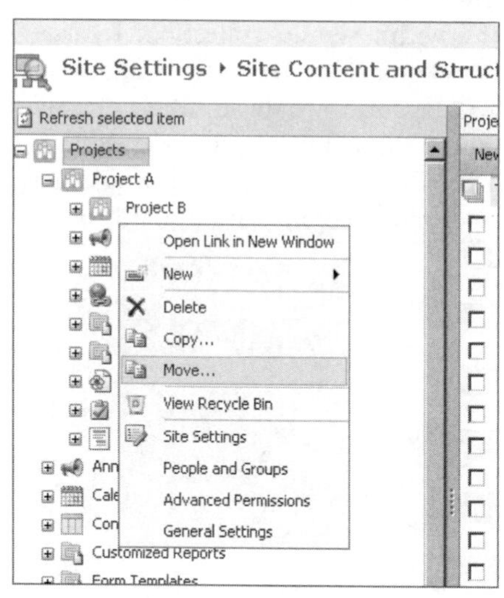

FIGURE 8-12

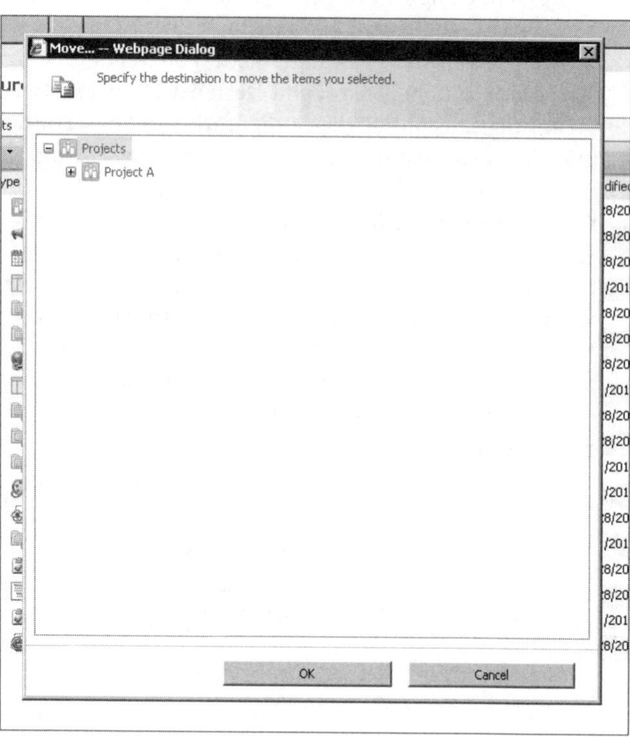

FIGURE 8-13

Managing Permissions

Since there is a whole chapter dedicated to managing permissions, we won't spend much time on it here. You will have noticed that when you create new sites, you are given the option to inherit permissions or to create unique permissions. So far, you have been inheriting permissions. Many times for subsites it is likely that you will want to inherit the permissions of the parent site. However, if you are working with a site that needs restricted permissions or a site that you aren't ready for everyone to access yet, then you will likely need to choose the option that allows for unique permissions. Keep in mind that this is something that can be reconfigured at a later date. Let's look at this example. You have a web that you want to create, but you want to first spend some time configuring and designing it before you open it up to the larger audience. In this example, you could create the web with unique permissions and then, once all of your configuration has been completed, you can go into the site and set the site to inherit the permissions of the parent site.

SharePoint Designer Settings

SharePoint Designer is a design tool that can be used to customize and configure SharePoint sites. The typical progression of SharePoint development is to start with what you can do within the browser, then what you can do within SharePoint Designer, and finally what you can do with custom code solutions. SharePoint Designer is a very powerful tool that can be leveraged to do many great things, including the configuration of SharePoint workflows. However, like any good tool, it must be monitored to ensure that it is not abused and that it is being used in a way that adheres to the governance policies in place. It is likely that you will want your designers to be able to do certain tasks in SharePoint Designer but not others. When this is the case, you can restrict their access to SharePoint Designer by using the configuration options available within the site collection. To access this configuration, go to the site settings page and select the SharePoint Designer Settings under the Site Collection Administration Group. From this screen, you will be able to enable/disable particular feature sets within SharePoint Designer. By default, you will inherit the settings configured by your farm administrator. This means that if the farm administrator has disabled settings, you would have to go to them to get them enabled again. Figure 8-14 shows the different configuration options that you have available.

FIGURE 8-14

Help Settings

You may have noticed a link at the bottom of the Site Collection Settings called Help Settings. If you click this link, you will see that you can select different help catalogs to include in the SharePoint help for the site. This means that you can enable and disable the content that users will be searching for help. As you activate features within the site collection, they will automatically be enabled within this help catalog. You can also create a custom help catalog for your users and then load the catalog with help entries. To do this, you will need to activate the Custom Site Collection Help site collection feature. Once this is activated, a Site Collection Help library will be created for you. Within this library, you can then create content that can be included within the custom catalog. Once you create the catalog, you will see it as an option to be enabled within the Help Settings. Figure 8-15 shows an example of this page, which contains the available help collections.

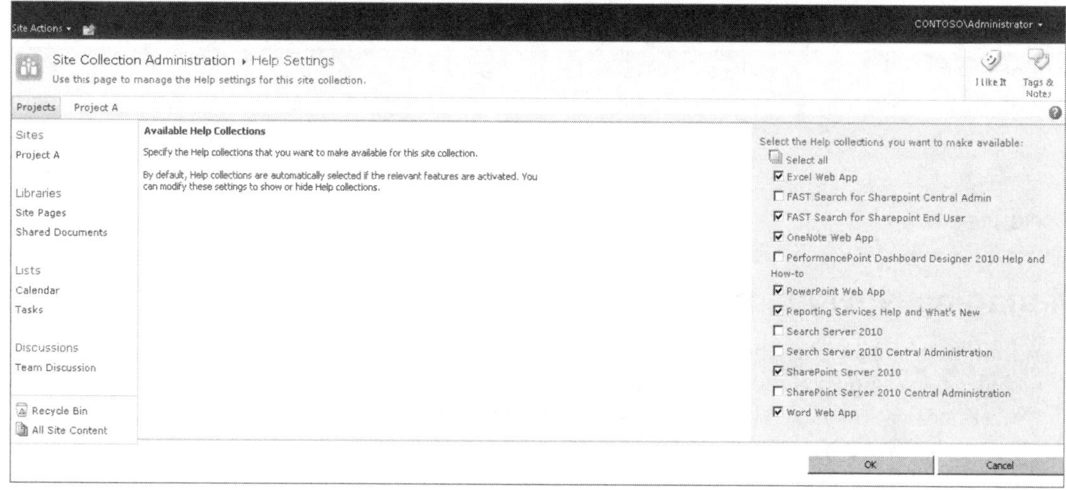

FIGURE 8-15

Site Analytics

One thing that will be important to you as you manage your sites is the ability to understand how the site is being used. Are users accessing the site consistently? When they access the site, what pages are they viewing? Having all of this information easily accessible will help you make modifications to your site that improve its usability and functionality. Out of the box, SharePoint provides several reports that provide information about the usage within the site and within the site collection. You can access these reports through the Site Web Analytics and the Site Collection Web Analytic reports in the Site Actions section of the Site Settings page. Figure 8-16 shows a sample of one of these report pages.

As you can see from this page, there are several different reports available as links in the Quick Launch toolbar. There is also a link at the top of the page that allows you to Change the Settings. Once this link is clicked, you will see several configurable options for both date and scope. You can also create alerts and reports so that you can be notified when certain criteria is met within the web analytic reports.

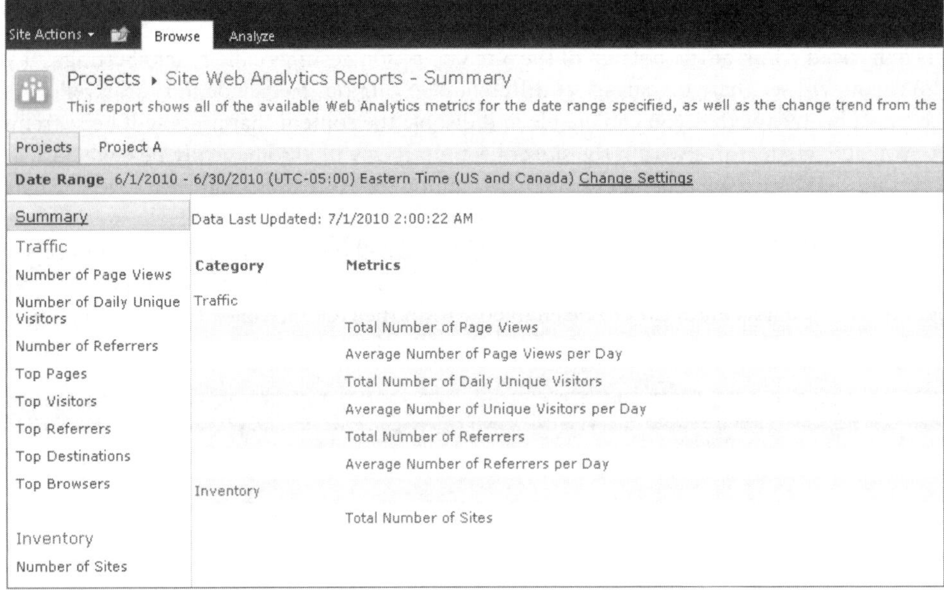

FIGURE 8-16

Managing Navigation

Within each site and site collection, you have the ability to control the navigation. Navigation includes two regions on the page, the top bar or global navigation region and the Quick Launch or Current navigation area. This is one of those areas where you will see different options based on the features that you have activated, including the names for the areas. For instance, if you only have the standard features activated, then the link to modify the navigation settings is called Top Link Bar and the navigation settings page will look something like Figure 8-17.

Site Actions
Team ▸ Site Settings ▸ Top Link Bar
Use this page to specify the links that appear in the top link bar of the site.
Home
Libraries
Site Pages
Shared Documents
Lists
Calendar
Tasks
Discussions
Team Discussion
New Navigation Link
Home

FIGURE 8-17

From this Top Link Bar management page, you will be able to modify the tabs across the top of the page. You will be able to create new links, and if you are a working from a web, you will be able to inherit the parent links. To manage the Quick Launch links, you will need to select the Quick Launch link under the Look and Feel section of the site settings page. From here, you will be able to create new content links and reorder the existing links. Figure 8-18 gives an example of this management page.

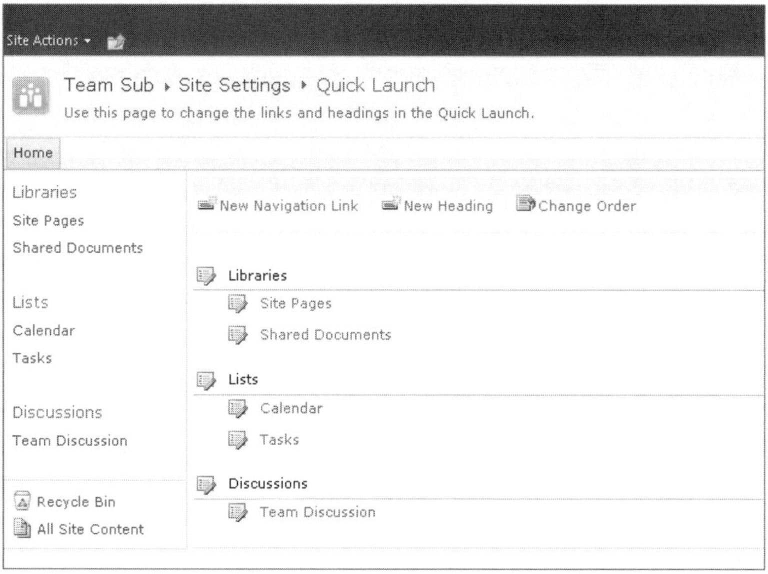

FIGURE 8-18

Once the publishing features have been activated, you will be able to manage both sets of links using the Navigation link under the Look and Feel section of the site settings page. This screen will allow you to manage both sets of links in one single location and will also allow you to configure an automatic sort order and provide an option that allows you to automatically show pages and subsites. Figure 8-19 provides a view of this management page.

When working with webs in a publishing site collection, you will notice a few additional options for inheritance. Each of these options is explained here:

- **Display the same navigation items as the parent site:** This option will only display the current navigation of the parent site. This means that if you create lists within the current site and select to add them to the Quick Launch toolbar, they will not be displayed.
- **Display the current site, the navigation items below the current site, and the current site's siblings:** This option will show the site's information as well as all the site's siblings. A site's sibling is a site that is at the same level in hierarchy as the current site. In the examples from this chapter, Project A and Project B would be considered sibling sites.
- **Display only the navigation items below the current site:** This option will only display Quick Launch content for the current site collection.

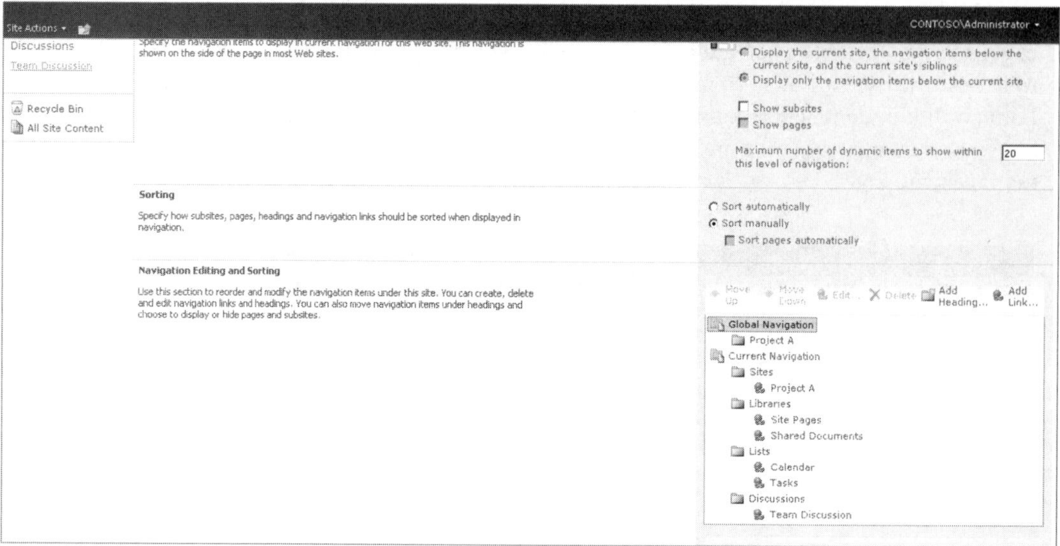

FIGURE 8-19

TRY IT OUT Modify the Navigation for the Projects Site Collection

In this Try It Out, you are going to modify the navigation settings for the Project site collection that you created in previous examples. You are going to configure the global navigation settings for the top-level site.

1. Open the Projects Site Collection that you created in the previous example.
2. Navigate to the Site Settings Page by selecting the Site Actions menu and the Site Settings Option.
3. In the Look and Feel group, select the Navigation link, as shown in Figure 8-20.

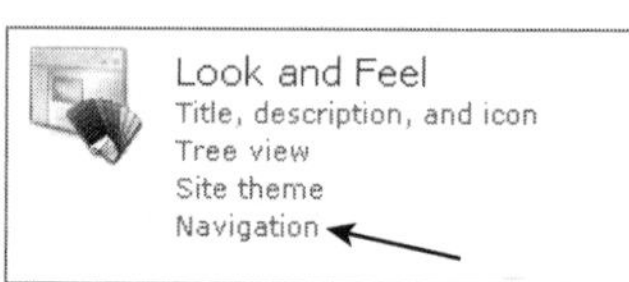

FIGURE 8-20

4. In the Global Navigation section, select the option to Show subsites. Notice that your two subsites are now listed below in the Navigation Editing and Sorting section and then click OK, as shown in Figure 8-21.

   You will also notice that Project A is listed twice. Once as a header (denoted by the folder icon) and once as a site (denoted by the site icon). This is because of the order of operations you worked through in the examples. You initially created the site without having any of the publishing features activated. Because of this, when you created Project A and selected the option to add it to the parent site's top navigation, it was created as a header. Once you have activated the publishing features, additional features are made available; however, the work

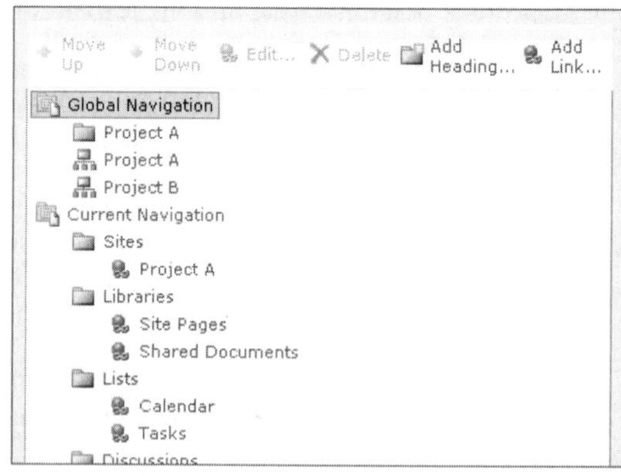

FIGURE 8-21

you have already configured is not overwritten. This is something that is important to understand because it is likely that, as you are configuring solutions within SharePoint, you will start with a certain set of features and then activate additional features as you develop your final solution. In this example, you can simply delete the header link.

5. Highlight the Project A Header link and select the Delete option. An example of this is shown in Figure 8-22.

   Now that you have modified the global navigation, you should see both project sites listed as tabs across the top of your home page. This is shown in Figure 8-23.

   All new subsites that are created will also have tabs created. If there is a certain site that you do not want to be displayed as a tab, then you can select the site in the configuration page and select the Hide option. As you can see in Figure 8-24, the Hide option is displayed in the top of the menu structure.

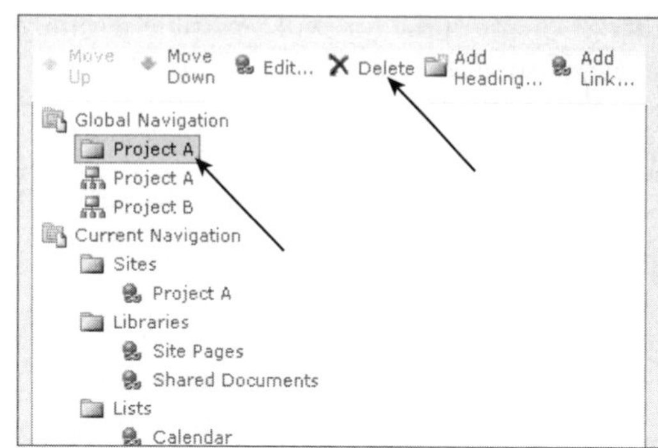

FIGURE 8-22

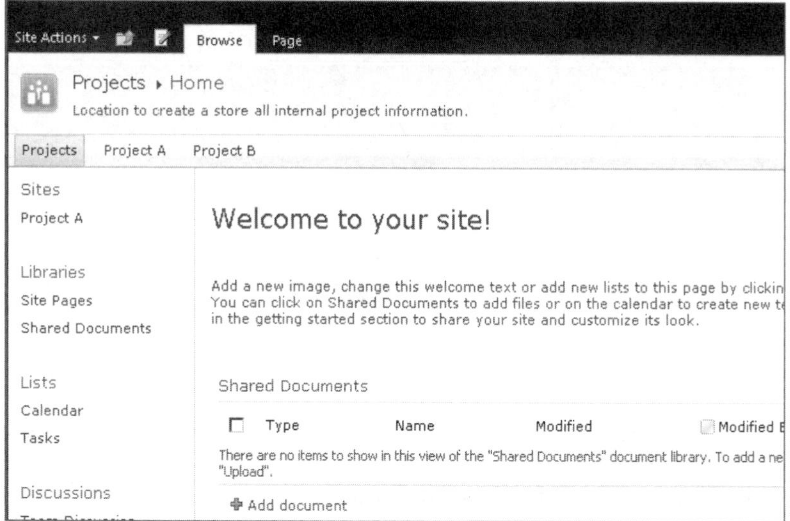

FIGURE 8-23

6. Next you will want to configure the current navigation so that the subsites are displayed. Return to the Navigations settings page, and select the subsites option under the Current Navigation options, as shown in Figure 8-25.

7. You should again notice extra links in the Current Navigation settings. There is a Header called Sites and a link called Project A. Since you are now using the publishing features, these two items can be deleted. Once you have completed deleting the items, your finished configuration should look similar to the Figure 8-26. Click OK to save your changes.

How It Works

When you choose to use the same global navigation as the parent site, you are in essence just copying the navigation structure. Whatever configuration changes made at the top will be visible within your site as well.

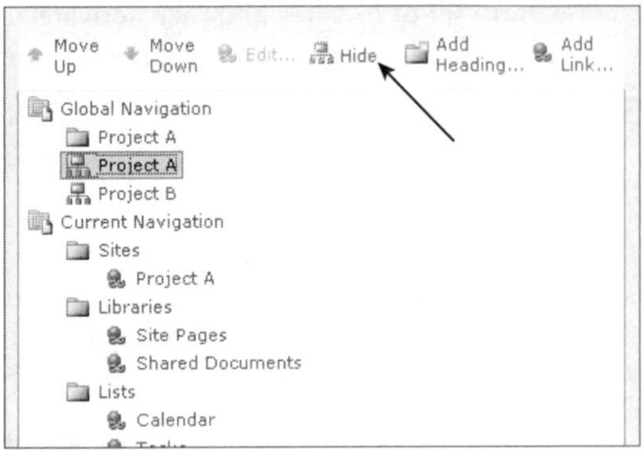

FIGURE 8-24

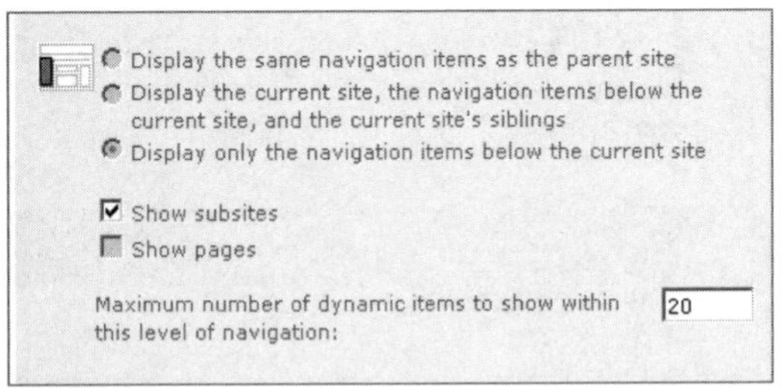

FIGURE 8-25

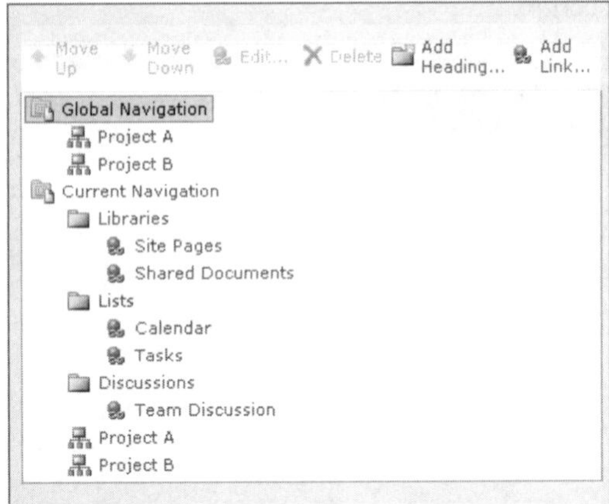

FIGURE 8-26

TRY IT OUT Modify the Current Navigation for Project A

In this Try It Out, you are going to modify the current navigation settings for the Project A site. You are going to configure the site so that both the current and sibling quick launch are displayed within the site.

1. Open the Project A Site that was created in the previous example.
2. Navigate to the Site Settings Page by selecting the Site Actions menu and the Site Settings Option.
3. In the Look and Feel group, select the Navigation link.

4. In the Current Navigation section, select the Display the current site, the navigation items below the current site and the site's siblings option, and then Click OK. An example of this is shown in Figure 8-27.

5. Once you navigate back to the Project A home page, you should see the content from the existing site, as well as the link to the sibling site, Project B. Figure 8-28 shows an example of this.

How It Works

By selecting this display for the current navigation, you are saying that you want to group your content at a high level, but list categories, and that you also want to see a link displayed on the site that will take you to all other sites that are at the same level of the site hierarchy.

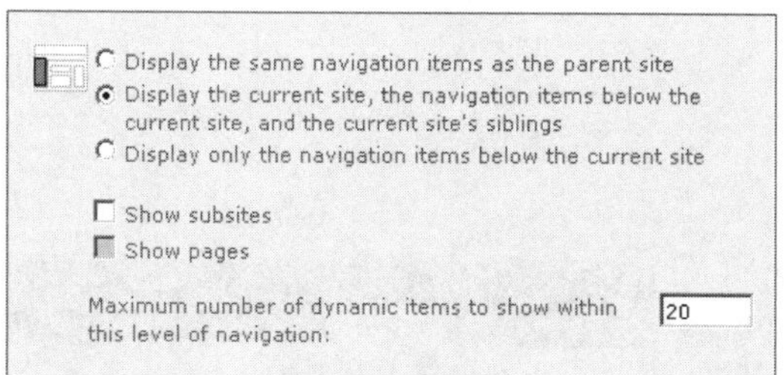

FIGURE 8-27

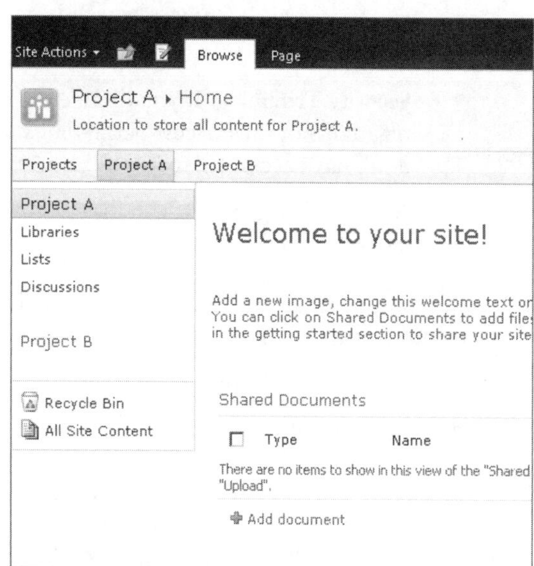

FIGURE 8-28

Things to Note about Navigation

There are few more things we should note about navigation before moving on. The first thing has to do with security trimming. Security trimming is a great SharePoint buzzword that means you only see content that you have access to. This is a great concept, and many people who want to build solutions want to take advantage of this option. One thing to note about navigation, however, is that only links generated and added to SharePoint by SharePoint are security trimmed. This means that if you add a global navigation link to a different site collection, all users will see that link, regardless of the permissions to the site. If users click on the link from within your site but don't have access to the site collection, they will be prompted for credentials. This can become very frustrating for users, especially if they are used to only seeing links that they have access to.

NOTE One option to get around the issues of unwanted items showing up in the navigation would be to instead use a redirect page. You could create a redirect page and then apply permissions to that page. That way, only a user who had access to that page would see the link in the navigation.

Another thing to note about navigation is that, in this release of the product, Microsoft has included some additional settings that let you control the overall behavior of navigation. When publishing has been activated, these settings can be accessed through the Site Collection Administration section on the site settings page. They allow you to enable or disable the following navigation options:

- **Navigation Enabled:** If you disable this option, all navigation bars will be hidden on the page.
- **Security Trimming:** If you disable this option, all navigation links will be visible to all users, regardless of their access permissions to those links. If they try to navigate to a link that they don't have access to, they will be prompted for authentication.
- **Audience Targeting:** If you disable this link, audience targeting will not be able to be used for navigation links.

The final thing that we will cover in the navigation section is a reminder to remember the small navigation options that can make a big difference:

- Portal Site Connection
- Breadcrumbs

Breadcrumbs provide a way for users to easily navigate through the tree structure that they are working within. From any level within the site structure, they can use the breadcrumbs to navigate to a different level within the site collection. An example of this is shown in Figure 8-29.

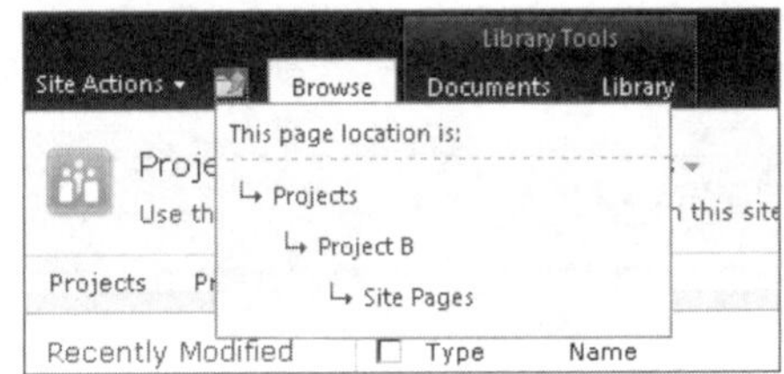

FIGURE 8-29

The Portal Site Connection is a configurable option within the Site Collection that provides a way for you to create a link as the topmost link displayed in the breadcrumbs. You configure this option from the Site Collection Administration group on the site settings page. Figures 8-30 and 8-31 show the configuration screen for this option, as well as the breadcrumb that displays the custom portal connection.

Working with Content across Sites

As you start working with site collections and sites, a question that is bound to come up is "How do I display data from one site on another site?" If the two sites exist within the same site collection, this can easily be done by using the Content Query web part (CQWP). If the two sites are not within the same site collection, then you must create a custom solution. This can be created using SharePoint Designer or by creating a custom web part.

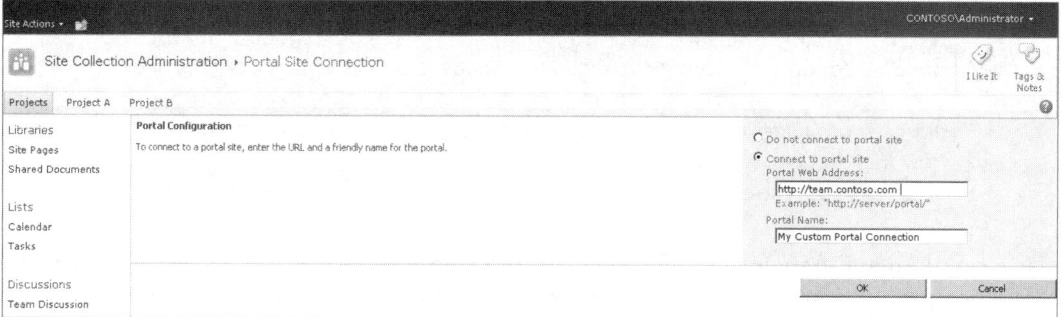

FIGURE 8-30

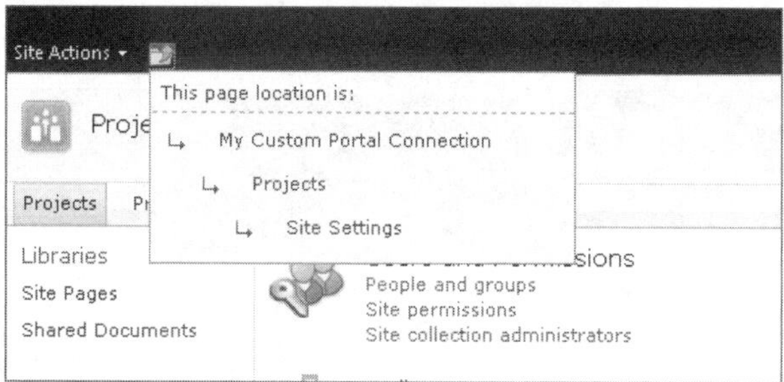

FIGURE 8-31

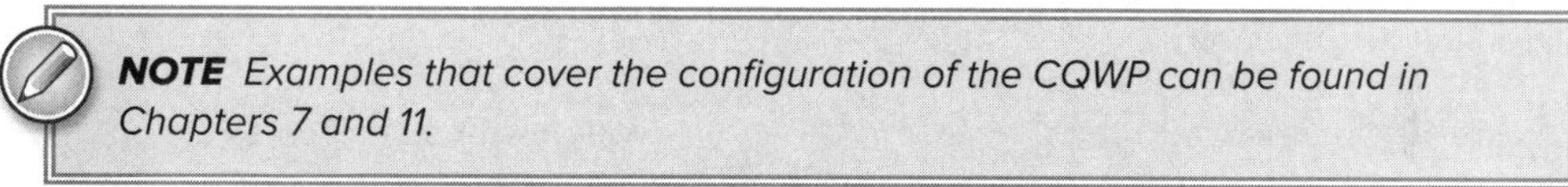

NOTE *Examples that cover the configuration of the CQWP can be found in Chapters 7 and 11.*

UNDERSTANDING THE TEMPLATES

When a site is first created, a template must be assigned to the new site. Templates are basically preconfigured sites that have certain characteristics. Some templates are designed specifically with a team process in mind; others are designed for the purpose of publishing content to the masses; and yet others are designed for the storage of data. As a solution developer, you will need to understand the templates available to you, so that you can make the best selection to get you started. There are really no right or wrong reasons when you pick a certain template over another; you just need to understand what it is you are trying to accomplish and then pick the best tool available to help you get there.

Site Collection Templates

Just as with many other things in this chapter, there is a breakdown between what templates are available for a site collection top site and the webs (subsites). We will first be covering the site collection top-level site templates. Site collections are created either from the Central Administration management site or from a custom process.

NOTE *It is likely that your organization has a process developed whereby you are able to request that new site collections be created. This process is likely very different from organization to organization, so be sure to review your governance team's site creation policies and procedures so that you can understand how this process works in your organization.*

In Central Administration, when the option to create a new site collection is selected, a template selection panel is displayed where users are able to select the type of site template they would like to use for their site. Depending on your farms licensing, there are up to five different categories of sites available, including:

- Collaboration
- Meetings
- Enterprise
- Publishing
- Custom

Collaboration Templates

The templates in the collaboration category are designed to help you create an environment where users can easily share, build, and collaborate on content. The table that follows describes the specific templates that are available:

TEMPLATE	DESCRIPTION	YOU MIGHT USE THIS WHEN...
Team Site	A site for teams to quickly organize, author, and share information. It provides a document library, and lists for managing announcements, calendar items, tasks, and discussions.	You have a team that needs to share general content. By default, several lists and libraries are preconfigured for you. A team could take this template and immediately have everything they need to get started.
Blank Site	A blank site for you to customize based on your requirements.	When none of the templates work the way you want, you can start with this blank template and build the site as you need to.
Document Workspace	A site for colleagues to work together on a document. It provides a document library for storing the primary document and supporting files, a tasks list for assigning to-do items, and a links list for resources related to the document.	This is a site that is designed to help you create a document. This would be ideal for the team that was working together to generate a final proposal. This site could store all of the supporting documentation and meeting notes that were needed in the creation of the final document.

TEMPLATE	DESCRIPTION	YOU MIGHT USE THIS WHEN...
Blog	A site for a person or team to post ideas, observations, and expertise that site visitors can comment on.	When you want to create a blog to post information. This could be used within a team, used for the entire organization, or even presented through the external website.
Group Work Site	This template provides a groupware solution that enables teams to create, organize, and share information quickly and easily. It includes Group Calendar, Circulation, Phone-Call Memo, the document library, and the other basic lists.	When you have a team that is working closely together and you want to manage their location (e.g., Out of the Office, In Office, Vacation). This template also comes preconfigured with some calendar and scheduling tools that allow you to quickly work together as a team on project calls and discussions. This template would be ideal for a fast-moving team with a high volume of content that is being shared.
Visio Process Repository	A site for teams to quickly view, share, and store Visio process diagrams. It provides a versioned document library for storing process diagrams, and lists for managing announcements, tasks, and review discussions.	When you have a team that is creating a collaborating on multiple Visio diagrams. This site collection comes preconfigured with a library and Visio content types as well as a discussion board.

Meetings Templates

The next section of templates pertains to the creation of meeting workspaces. These templates are designed specifically with meetings in mind. There is a way to track the meeting minutes, meeting issues, and meeting documents. The list below represents the different styles of templates available for the meetings:

- Basic Meeting Workspace
- Blank Meeting Workspace
- Decision Meeting Workspace
- Social Meeting Workspace
- Multipage Meeting Workspace

These templates can be configured to support single meetings or recurring meetings. You can create the template as a top-level site collection or web, but you can also create these sites from directly within a calendar list. Within the new item form in the calendar list, you will see an option to store the meeting information within a meeting workspace. If you select this option, then you will be asked to select a template to use to store your meeting minutes. Figure 8-32 shows this option within a new calendar item, and Figure 8-33 shows an example of a meeting workspace that is associated with a recurring weekly meeting.

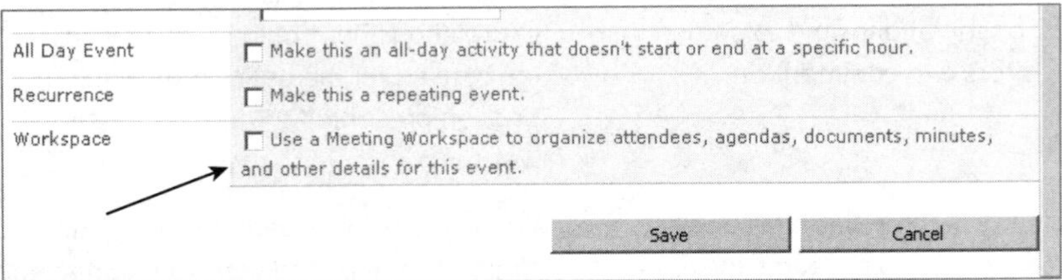

FIGURE 8-32

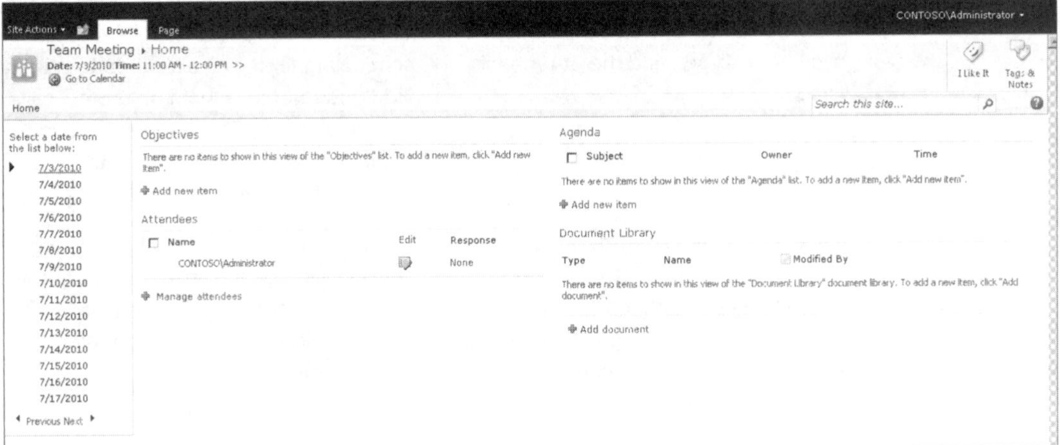

FIGURE 8-33

Enterprise Templates

The Enterprise templates provide the templates needed to implement the Enterprise features within SharePoint. Typically, these site collection templates will be used by the system administrators when they are configuring the farm. In some cases, your environment may have multiple sites collections that use these templates; however, it is likely that they will still be configured by one of the administrators. The table below describes each of the available templates.

TEMPLATE	DESCRIPTION
Document Center	A site to centrally manage documents in your enterprise.
Records Center	This template creates a site designed for records management. Records managers can configure the routing table to direct incoming files to specific locations. The site also lets you manage whether records can be deleted or modified after they are added to the repository.
PowerPoint Broadcast Side	A site used for hosting PowerPoint broadcasts. Presenters can connect to this site and create a link for remote viewers to watch a slide show in a web browser.

TEMPLATE	DESCRIPTION
Business Intelligence Center	A site for presenting the Business Intelligence Center.
Enterprise Search Center	A site for delivering the search experience. The welcome page includes a search box with two tabs: one for general searches, and another for searches for information about people. You can add and customize tabs to focus on other search scopes or result types.
My Site Host	A site used for hosting personal sites (My Sites) and the public People Profile page. This template needs to be provisioned only once per User Profile Service Application, please consult the documentation for details.
Basic Search Center	A site for delivering the search experience. The site includes pages for search results and advanced searches.
FAST Search Center	A site for delivering the FAST search experience. The welcome page includes a search box with two tabs: one for general searches and another for searches for information about people. You can add and customize tabs to focus on other search scopes or result types.

Publishing Templates

The publishing templates are templates that are preconfigured to take advantage of the rich content management features across the development of site pages. There are two different publishing templates to choose from:

- Publishing Portal
- Enterprise Wiki

These templates come configured with all of the publishing features activated and ready for use. Out of the box, they allow you to create pages from preconfigured page layouts and allow you to publish these pages through an approval workflow.

Custom Templates

The final section of templates is Custom Templates. Out of the box, only one template is included in this section:

<Select template later....>

This template allows the person creating the site to provision the site with no template selected. The first time that one of the site administrators tries to access the site, they will be presented with a set of templates that they can pick from. This allows someone to provision a site collection for a user without having to select a specific template for them.

Web (Subsite) Templates

When you are working within a site collection, the templates available for creating additional webs depend on the features that you have activated. As you activate additional features, additional templates become available. To create a new site you can select the New Site link from the Site Actions menu. Once selected, a pop-up will be displayed that shows all of the different templates available. An example of this is displayed in Figure 8-34.

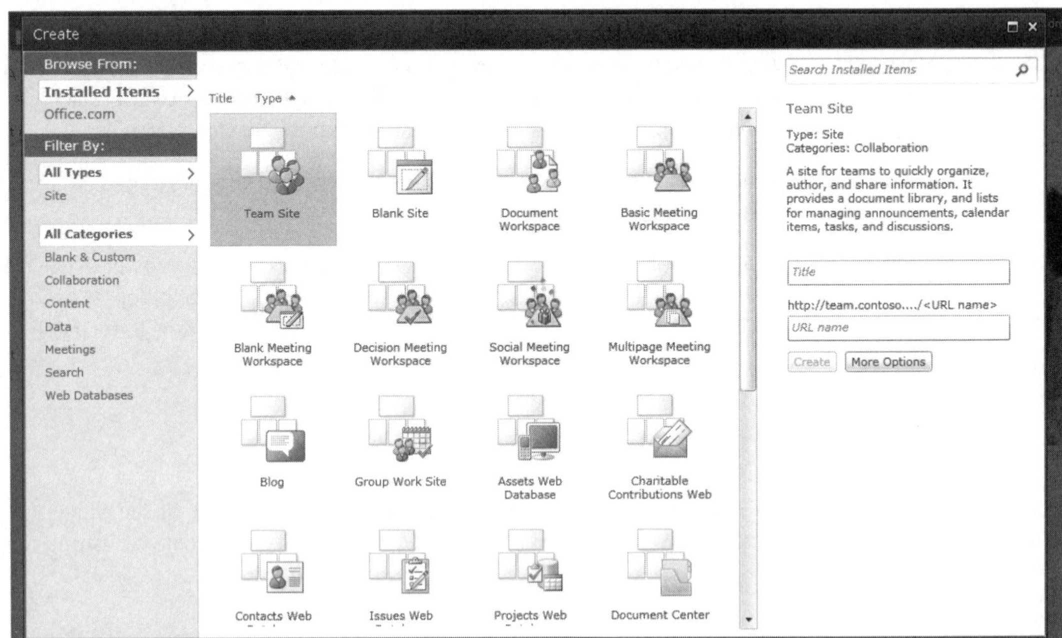

FIGURE 8-34

The listing of available templates includes many different templates in addition to the ones discussed earlier in the chapter, including the following:

- Assets Web Database
- Charitable Contributions Web Database
- Contacts Web Database
- Issues Web Database
- Projects Web Database

These templates, called Web Databases templates, are configured to be used with Access Services. When you create a site with these templates you are creating a site that contains an access database and that uses Access Services web parts to display the site data. Figure 8-35 shows an example of one of these site templates.

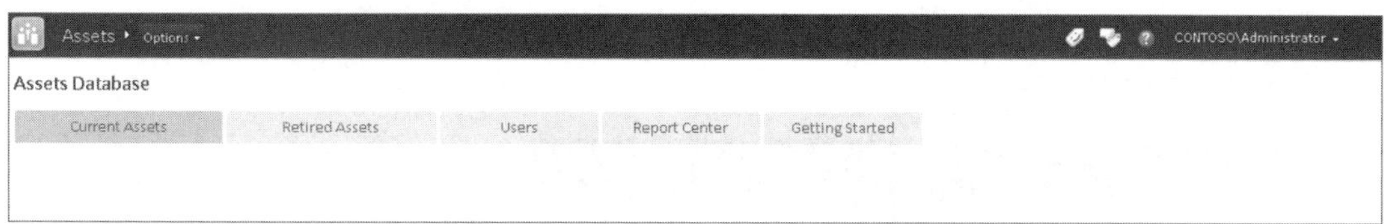

FIGURE 8-35

CREATING CUSTOM TEMPLATES

Now that we have covered the different templates available out of the box, it is time to cover the process of creating your own custom templates. A site template is basically a preconfigured site that you can use as a starting point for any new site. You start the process of creating a site template by building a site that you can use as the base template or by saving an existing site as a template. Once the site has been saved as a template, it will appear as an option for anything within the site collection that is creating a new site. When you save a site as a template you can either choose to include the content as part of the template or not include the content. There are limitations in the size of templates, so be sure that if you are planning to include content in your template that you first verify the size limitations with your governance team.

Saving a Site as a Template

The option to save a site as a template is located in the Site Settings page in the Site Actions grouping. It is important to note that you will only see the Save site as template link when the site you are working within can be saved as a template. Some sites, including those that enable publishing within the site, do not support the Save as Template option.

TRY IT OUT Save Project A Site as a Template

In this Try It Out, you are going to modify the Project A site and then save the site as a template. You are then going to create a new site called Project C that uses your new template.

1. Open the Project A Site that was created in the previous example.
2. Create a new image library within this site and upload several images to the library. If you need instructions on how to create an image library, refer to Chapter 3. Figure 8-36 is a screenshot of the library page within my Project A site.
3. Open the Site Settings page for Project Site A, and select the "Save site as template" link in the Site Actions group. An example of this is shown in Figure 8-37.
4. As shown in Figure 8-38, Enter the following information to save the site as a template, and then click OK:
    - **File name:** CustomProject
    - **Template name:** Custom Project Template

- **Template description:** This template contains the list and libraries to manage our custom projects.
- **Include Content:** Yes

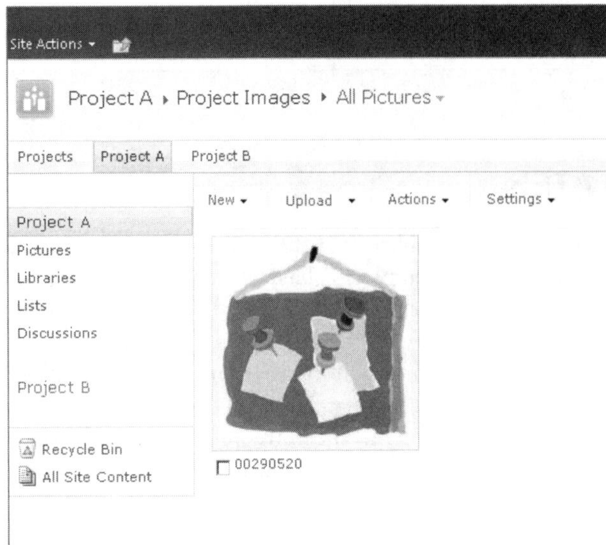

FIGURE 8-36

FIGURE 8-37

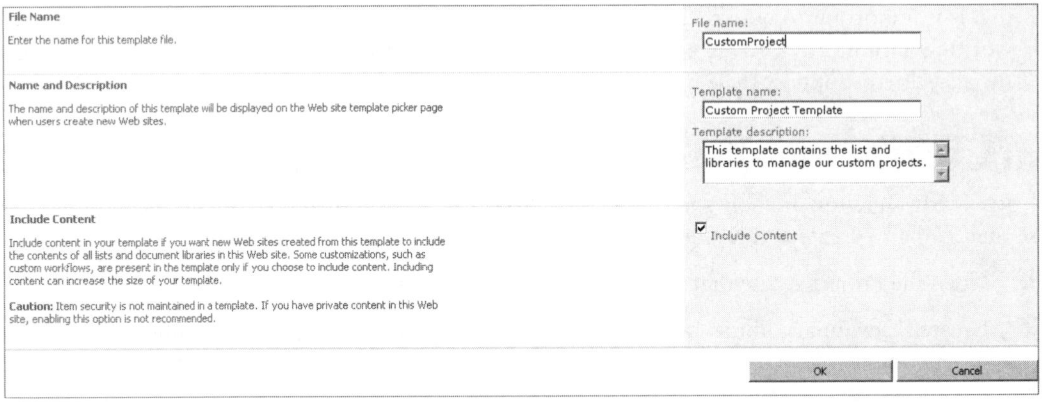

FIGURE 8-38

5. Click OK on the pop-up screen (Figure 8-39) that confirms your site template was created.
6. Open the Projects Site Collection that was created in the previous example.
7. From the Site Actions Menu, select the New Site link.
8. In the create dialog, select the Blank & Custom filter. Notice that if you select the Custom Project template, the description you entered above is displayed on the right side of the dialog. Figure 8-40 shows an example of this.

FIGURE 8-39

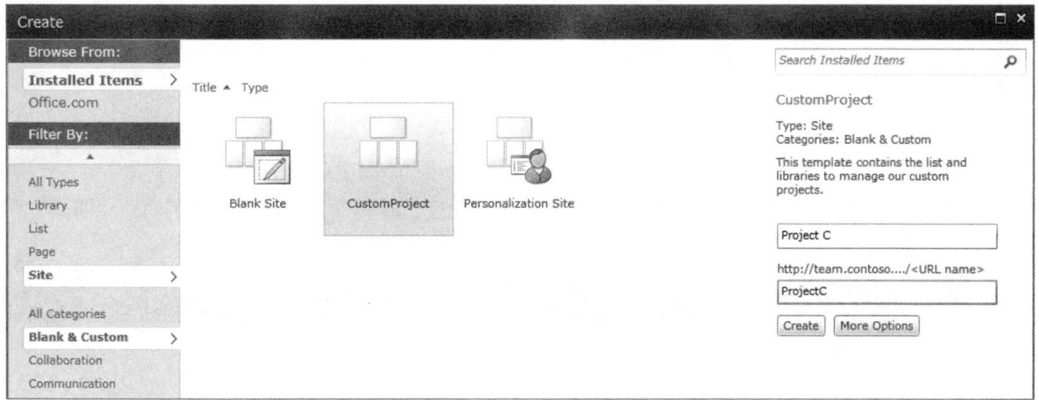

FIGURE 8-40

9. Enter the following title and URL for your new site and then select the More Options button:
   - Title: Project C
   - URL: ProjectC
10. Notice that when selecting more options we have the ability to manage permissions and to inherit navigation. We will accept the defaults and click Create, as shown in Figure 8-41.
11. Once you are redirected to the new Projects C site, you will want to verify that your template was used. To do this, you can check to see that your custom library and content are included in the site.
12. From the Project C home page, select the Pictures link in the current navigation. Notice in Figure 8-42 that your list, Project Images, is included and is showing that there is one item in the list.

How It Works

When you saved your site as a template, the configurations and content were saved to the site Solutions gallery and made available for use within the site collection. When you created a new site, the new site was based on the site within the Solutions gallery.

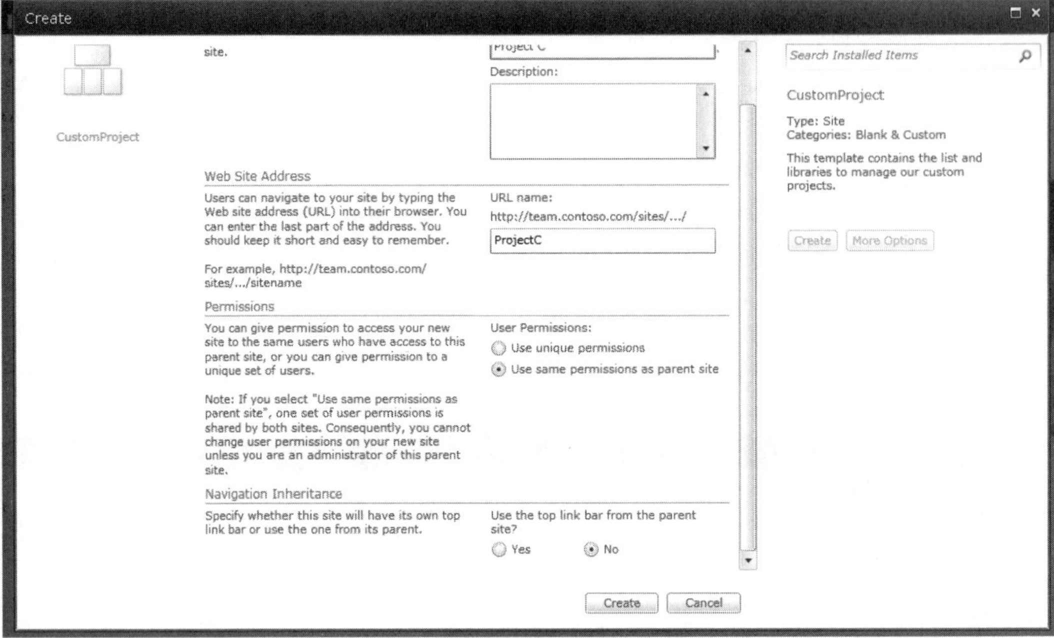

FIGURE 8-41

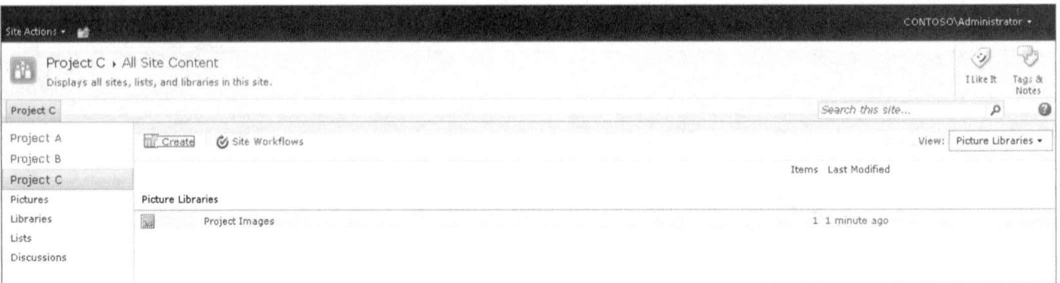

FIGURE 8-42

Moving the Template to a New Location

When a template is created it is stored as a `.wsp` file within the Solutions gallery. This gallery can be accessed through the Solutions Gallery link in the Galleries section of the Site Settings page and is shown in Figure 8-43.

This Solutions gallery is basically a list that contains solutions that are used within the site collection. Because it is a library, you are able to upload additional solutions. This means that you can move templates between different site collections simply by saving them locally and then uploading them to a different site collections Solutions gallery.

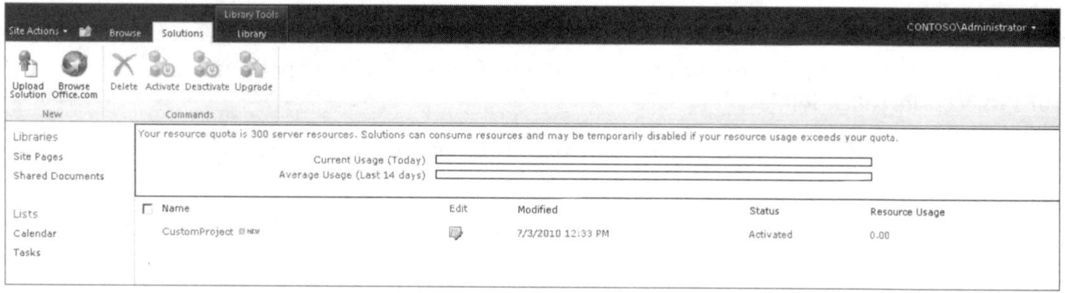

FIGURE 8-43

Creating Templates for Site Collections

One final area that I wanted to cover within the Templates section is the idea of creating a template that can be used to create new site collections. This is a question that comes up often; however, there is no solution that is available to power users to fill this request. If you have a need to use a custom template for your top-level sites, you will need to work with your system administrators and developers to determine the approach that is best for you. The approach could include several different options, including:

- Importing Global Templates
- Creating Custom Site Definitions
- Creating Custom Features

All of these topics go beyond the scope of this book; however, it is good for you to be aware of them. Your system administrators and developers should be able to work with you to determine the best approach to meet your particular requirements.

WORKING WITH CONTENT OFFLINE

One question that comes up repeatedly during the discussions about SharePoint is the need to work with your SharePoint site content offline, in a disconnected state. When the manager of sales is off-site, he still needs access to the sales dashboards, and when a team member has to spend two days traveling to get to a meeting, she will need access to the content during the travel times.

SharePoint Workspace

SharePoint Workspace provides this functionality and is available with a Microsoft Office Professional Plus license key. Users who have this client application installed will be able to connect with their SharePoint sites and download a local copy of the site. This copy will be synched with the live site on a regular basis to ensure that the content store locally remains current. When users are offline, they will be able to make changes to the content, and then that content will be synched to the live site when they are able to connect again.

TRY IT OUT Connect to a Site Using SharePoint Workspace

In this example, you are going to open the SharePoint Workspace client application and connect it to your Projects site collection.

1. From the windows start menu, open the Microsoft SharePoint Workspace 2010 client application.
2. From the Ribbon, select the SharePoint Workspace option within the New drop-down. An example of this is shown in Figure 8-44.

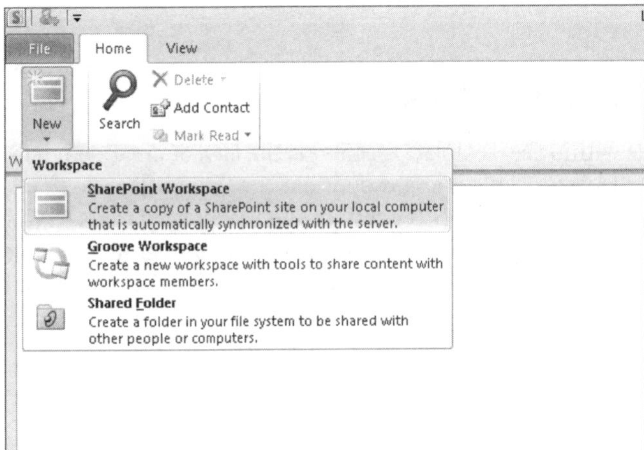

FIGURE 8-44

3. Enter the URL for your projects site collection in the dialog, and click OK, as shown in Figure 8-45.

New SharePoint Workspace

Sync to SharePoint Workspace

Create a synchronized copy of a SharePoint site on your computer.

You should only sync from sources that you trust.

Learn more about what you can do with a SharePoint workspace

Select a SharePoint Site:

Name	Location
My SharePoint Sites	

Location: http://team.contoso.com/sites/projects/

Configure... OK Cancel

FIGURE 8-45

4. A status dialog will be displayed that will display the progress of the site being created locally. When the dialog shows that progress is completed, click the Open Workspace button.

5. Select the Shared Documents library and click the Add Documents button on the Ribbon, as shown in Figure 8-46.

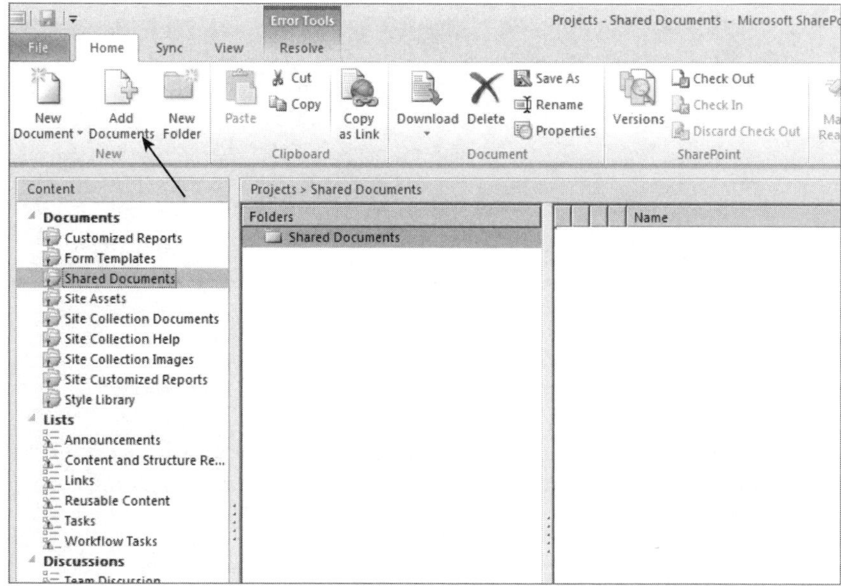

FIGURE 8-46

6. Upload any document to the library. Once you complete this action, open the site in the browser and verify the document has been added.

7. Select the Sync Ribbon toolbar, and the under the Sync menu, select the option to Sync Workspace as shown in Figure 8-47.

8. When the sync status (bottom right) shows as completed, close the client application and open the site in the browser. You should now see your document uploaded into the shared documents library. An example of this is shown in Figure 8-48.

Keep in mind that, for this demo, you remained connected to the server at all times, and you forced a manual sync. This was simply to show you the functionality. Under normal circumstances, the workspace would synch on a consistent basis.

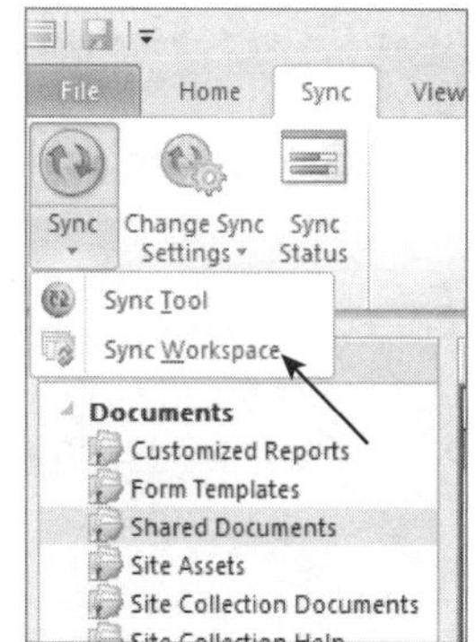

FIGURE 8-47

How It Works

When you connect a SharePoint Workspace to a SharePoint site, you are creating a local copy of the content. This copy will be synched on a regular basis with the live site so that the content remains current. Whenever you are offline, this local copy can be used to provide access to the site content. Once you are online again, the changes you made in the workspace will be synched with the live site.

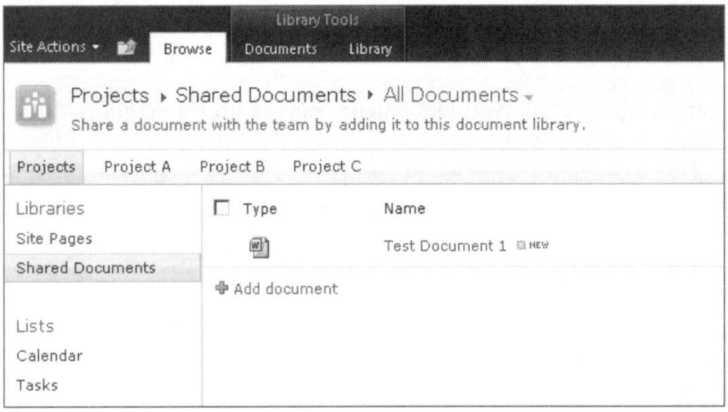

FIGURE 8-48

SUMMARY

In this chapter, you have covered many different configuration options for creating site collections and sites. After reading through this chapter, you should be familiar with the following concepts:

- The differences between sites collections and webs (subsites)
- The different templates available for use out of the box
- How to create and configure your own custom site templates
- How to work offline with site content

EXERCISES

1. Describe the differences between a site collection and site.
2. You have been asked to create a site to manage the collaboration of a small committee that meets on a regular basis. What template would be appropriate for managing this content?
3. What options do you have for working with your site offline?

▶ WHAT YOU LEARNED IN THIS CHAPTER

TOPIC	KEY CONCEPTS
Site Collections vs. Sites	These are both powerful tools used within SharePoint, but each should be used in certain circumstances and situations.
Site Templates	SharePoint provides many out-of-the-box site templates that are preconfigured for use within your environment. Sites can be created based on the templates and then customized further to meet project needs.
Custom Site Templates	If no template exists for your needs, you can create a custom template with the lists and libraries configured as you need.

Branding and the User Experience

WHAT YOU WILL LEARN IN THIS CHAPTER:

- Why organizations brand
- Best practices for enhancing the user experience
- Working with themes
- Working with master pages

In the previous two chapters, we discussed the basics of creating collaboration sites and working with web parts to extend those sites, bringing users rich features that will help them to more easily store, share, and find people, processes, and information within their organization.

In this chapter, we will delve into the world of user experience and the role branding plays in its success. More specifically, we will attempt to uncover the layers of a successful brand strategy and unleash the secrets leading to mass user adoption, the ultimate compliment and purpose of any brand.

Finally in this chapter, we will dive into a slightly more technical side of SharePoint branding, working with master pages where you will learn how to leverage this out-of-the-box feature to build a consistent user interface in tune with corporate brand standards.

WHY ORGANIZATIONS BRAND

The reasons to brand are many and may differ slightly from organization to organization, but there are a few consistent underlying motivations across the board, and that is where we will focus our attention.

Most organizations strive to build a trusted image that encompasses the core values and general purpose the organization represents. That image or brand is often broken down into a set of tools, patterns, and practices that, when combined and used consistently, build a common experience that people begin to remember, identify with, and ultimately trust.

This subliminal trust is the key to a positive user experience, which ultimately leads to user adoption. Successful user adoption means the sale of products or services in most common scenarios, but in our case things are slightly different. You are not selling a product or service; you are selling the usage tool, namely "SharePoint 2010" as a better way to work, collaborate, and communicate.

Microsoft has helped develop a trust in the SharePoint platform that having a unified infrastructure upon which to build business applications will ultimately make organizations more efficient. To make this possible, however, an organization needs to ensure that its employees adopt the tool and use it frequently to best leverage the investment. Simply deploying SharePoint (or any tool) and demanding usage by employees is not enough. This is where branding experts come in. This is why organizations brand their SharePoint portals, to ensure that the portal falls in line with other tools, patterns, and practices used across the organization. Essentially, by branding you are building a more familiar and better user experience, which will lead to greater user adoption and, ultimately, a more successful deployment. Users will become less focused on the technology aspect of the tool and see the application as an integrated portion of their business.

The payoff is more effective sharing of people, processes, and information, leading to a more efficient organization overall.

BEST PRACTICES FOR ENHANCING THE USER EXPERIENCE

As with most things there are best practices for enhancing the user experience. These best practices are the lessons learned as a result of several iterations of the SharePoint platform (2001, 2003, 2007, and now 2010). Several years of implementing different tactics and listening to the feedback from users has yielded many different points of view, but there are a few that keep coming up time and time again, and those are the practices we will focus on.

Likely the most significant best practice for enhancing user experience is one that is not specific to SharePoint but rather relates to the mentality with which you should approach most any project, and that is "KISS," or "Keep it simple, stupid." To quote Albert Einstein; "Everything should be made as simple as possible, but not simpler." This should apply to every level of your branding initiative, from your plan, to your tactics, to your execution. The simpler your roadmap, the less risk that is involved, and similarly the easier things are to use, the better experience your users will have and subsequently the faster users will adopt your tools.

Another common best practice and general rule of thumb when it comes to branding is consistency. People are creatures of habit, and few feel positive toward a lot of change in their day-to-day activities. For this reason, it is imperative that you align your branding initiatives with tools, patterns, and practices already in place. For example, if users currently store the majority of their documents in a shared folder called G-Drive, then to keep things consistent for the user, you might want to consider naming your new store, such as a SharePoint document library, G-Drive. While as a general rule, more descriptive names are better, by limiting the amount of change you are introducing to how employees do their work you will create a sense of familiarity across current practices and applications, and ultimately users will have a better experience.

Follow existing brand guidelines. Some organizations feel that because the intranet is not publicly available, all rules go out the door. Unfortunately, this could do more harm than good when it comes to user experience and, ultimately, user adoption. If your corporate color scheme is made up of blues, then stick with blues on your intranet. If your main heading fonts are Helvetica and standard copy is Verdana, then keep those also. If your users click your logo in the top left to return to the home page, then don't change that either; the more familiar the practices and processes are, the better the experience will be for the users of the system.

Stick with best practices for web design; after all, SharePoint is a web-based platform. Keep your user interface easy to navigate, and ensure you use easy-to-read typography and colors (no yellow on red!).

Less is more. Having all of your organization's information at your fingertips and presented within a single page might seem like a good idea, but it is much better to stick with the information that is important to your users and getting their job done. That way your page will not be cluttered, and you can focus on what is important.

CHANGING THE SITE LOGO

A common requirement most organizations have is to have their company logo displayed predominantly within the site's primary navigation area. Each site within SharePoint has a setting to allow site administrators to specify a custom image to be displayed in the header of their site. If you apply this setting to the top-level site within your site collection it will be applied to all subsites as well if an alternate image is not specified. We will review the process for setting the site image in the next Try It Out.

TRY IT OUT Associate a Custom Logo with Site

1. From the top-level site of your site collection, select View All Site Content from the Site Actions menu.
2. Select the Style Library.
3. Upload the `AWlogo.png` file to this library using the method described in Chapter 2 of this book.
4. Once the file is uploaded, select the file and click the Publish button on the Documents tab of the Ribbon. This will ensure that the file can be viewed by all users of the site.
5. Right-click on the awlogo file and select the Copy Shortcut option, as shown in Figure 9-1. This will add the address of the image to your clipboard.
6. Select Site Settings from the Site Actions menu.
7. Select the Title, Description, and Icon link from the Look and Feel group of links. You will be redirected to the Title, Description, and Icon page, as shown in Figure 9-2.
8. Paste the address copied in step 5 into the URL field by selecting in the field and clicking Ctrl+V.
9. Click the link below the URL field to test the URL.
10. Click OK. The page will refresh and your image will be displayed in the header of your site, as shown in Figure 9-3.

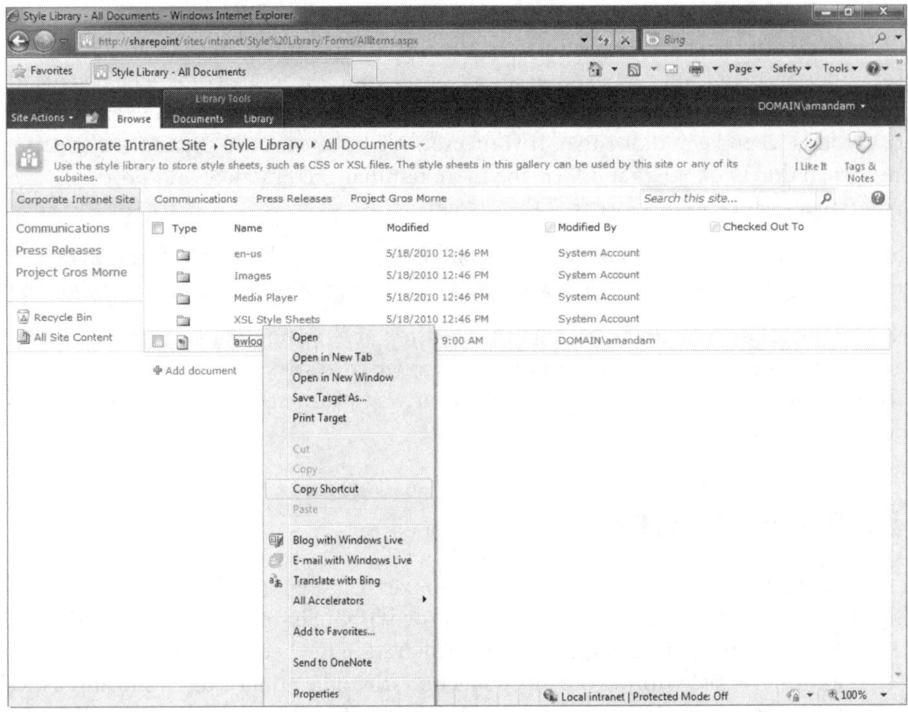

FIGURE 9-1

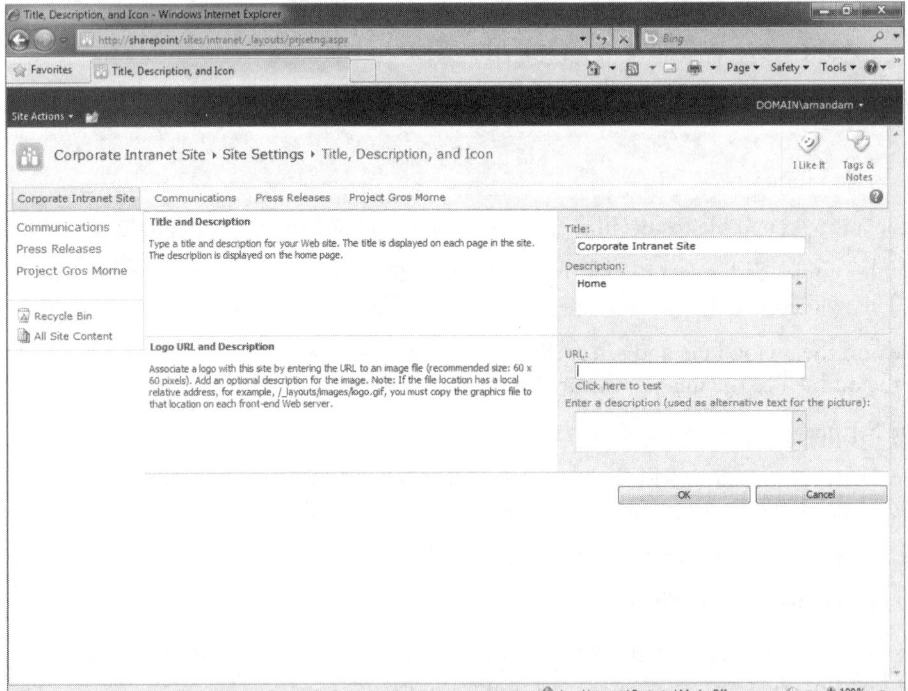

FIGURE 9-2

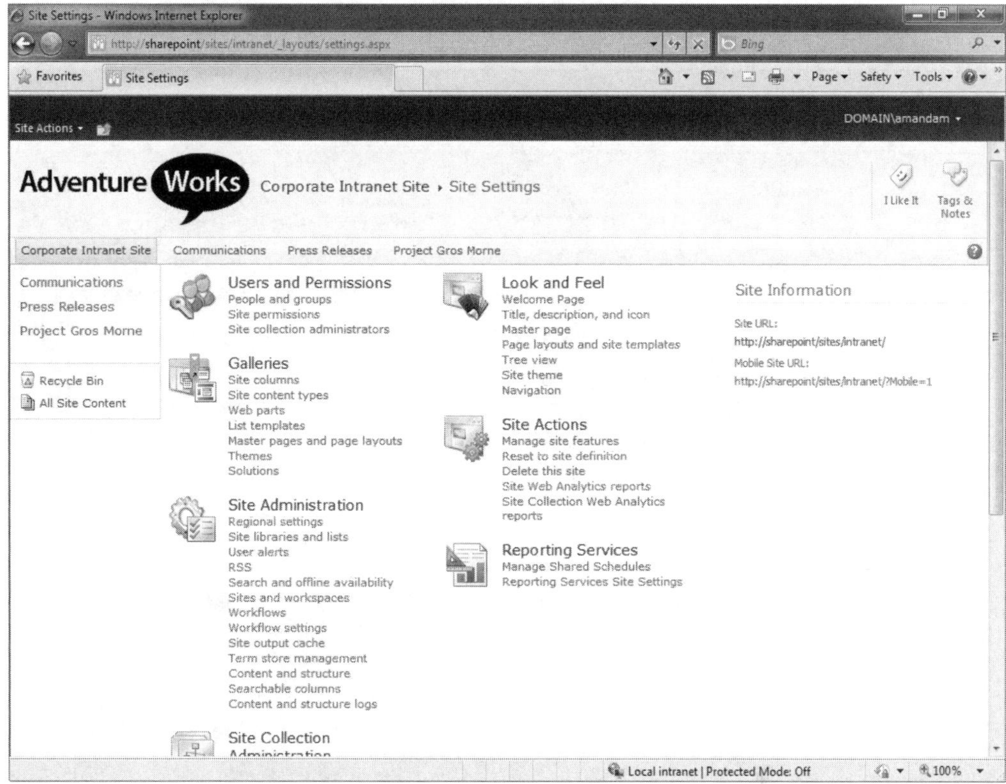

FIGURE 9-3

How It Works

When you configure your top-level site with a logo as detailed in this Try It Out, you will notice that all pages of your site and associated subsites display the image in the top-left corner of the page. Clicking on this image will return you to the home page of whatever site you are currently on. You may further customize your site logo to appear in different locations or contain a hyperlink to return you to the home page of the top-level site of the site collection by editing the master page. We will review this type of customization later in this chapter.

WORKING WITH THEMES

Themes are a feature within SharePoint that allow you to make basic color scheme and font changes to visual elements within your site. Themes have evolved in SharePoint 2010 considerably from previous versions of SharePoint. In earlier versions of SharePoint, only users who were skilled in the use of CSS were able to create or modify themes within a SharePoint environment. SharePoint 2010 offers a built-in Theme Designer tool that provides users, with the appropriate privileges, the ability to apply existing themes or create new themes to suit their own requirements. Figure 9-4 displays the Theme Designer tool that is available on each SharePoint site to site owners or designers.

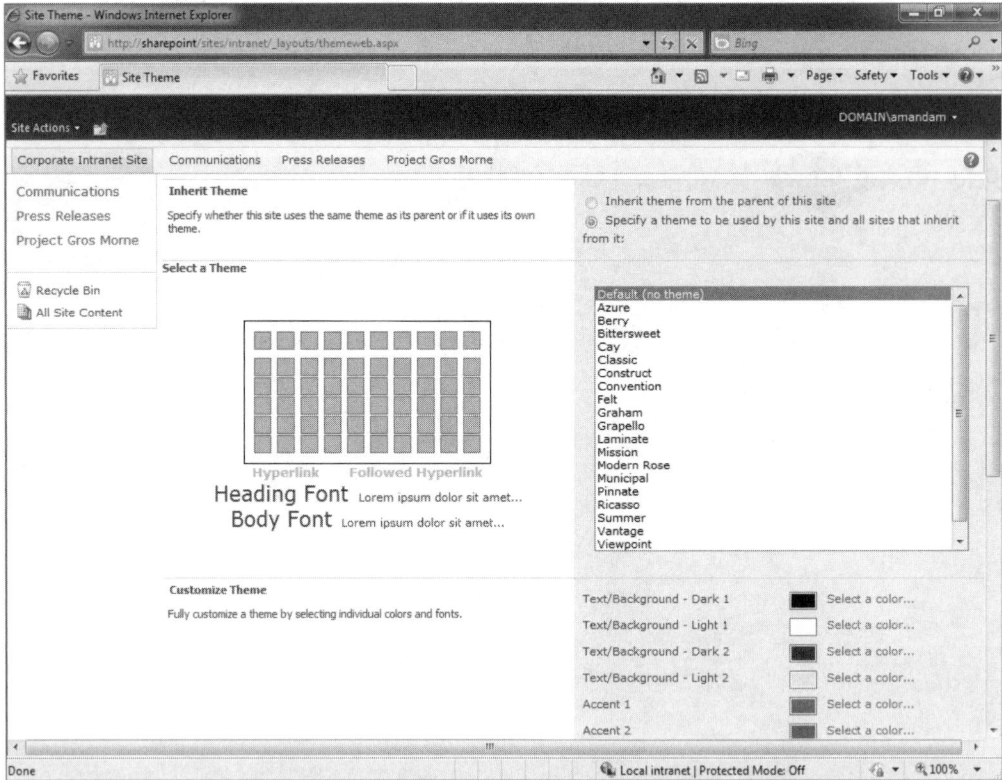

FIGURE 9-4

If you are familiar with the Theme Designer tools that were introduced as part of applications such as Microsoft PowerPoint and Word 2007, then you will likely notice some similarities. In fact, themes you create within the Microsoft client applications can be exported and reused within your SharePoint sites. This will help in scenarios where a company's color scheme has already been defined for tools such as PowerPoint. However, if you do not wish to take such an approach, you may elect to simply apply an existing theme or create a new theme in SharePoint directly, using the steps in the next Try It Out.

TRY IT OUT Apply a Theme to an Existing SharePoint Site

In this Try It Out, you will apply an out-of-the-box SharePoint theme to the Corporate Intranet site that was created in Chapter 1 of this book. If you did not complete the exercises in Chapter 1, you can follow these steps to apply a theme to any site.

1. From your Corporate Intranet site, select Site Settings from the Site Actions menu.
2. Select Site Theme from the Look and Feel group of administrative links. You will be redirected to the Theme Designer tool.
3. Select the Ricasso theme, as shown in Figure 9-5.

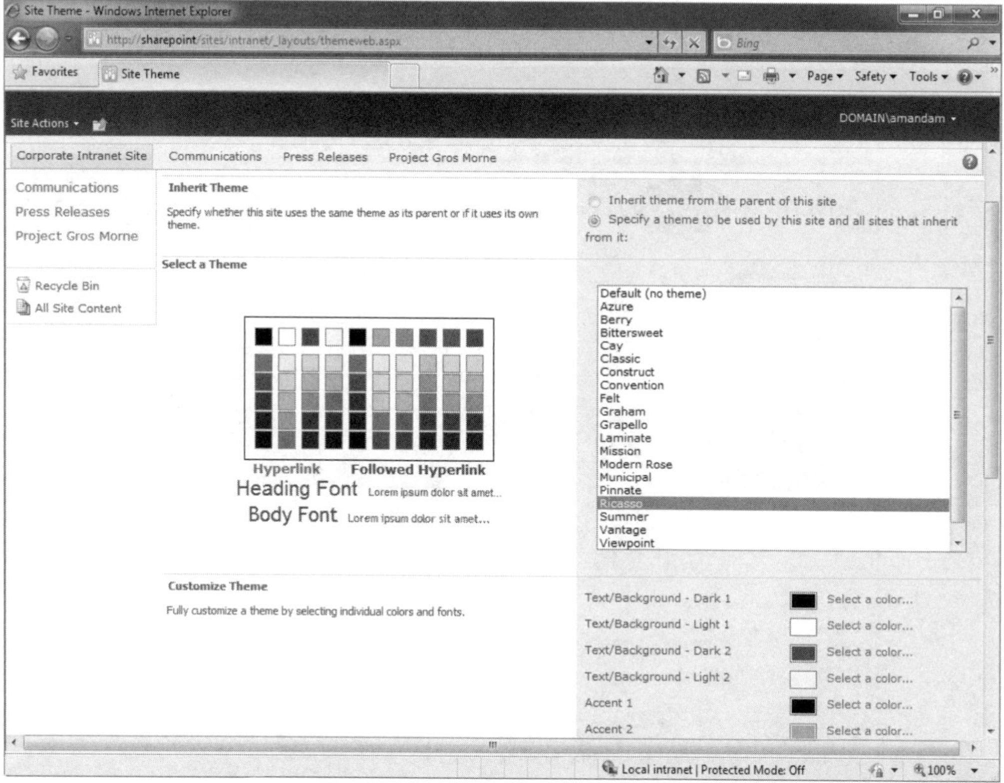

FIGURE 9-5

4. Click the Preview button. A new window will appear, as shown in Figure 9-6, displaying a preview of your site with the Ricasso theme applied.
5. Close the pop-up window.
6. Select the option to "Apply the selected theme to this site and reset all subsites to inherit this setting." You will be returned to the Site Settings page of your site, and the new theme will be applied.

How It Works

From the theme designer tool, you can select from either of the existing themes. When you select a theme, an image appears to the left, as shown in Figure 9-5, to give you a high-level preview of the theme's color scheme. However, to see exactly how your site will look with the theme you have selected applied, you selected the Preview option, which opened the site in a new window with the theme applied.

By selecting the option to apply the selected theme to the current site and reset all subsites below it, you applied the theme to more than one site. If you wish to apply the same theme to every site in your site collection, you select this setting when applying the theme to the top-level site of a site collection.

In the next Try It Out, you will customize an existing theme further to suit your specific preferences.

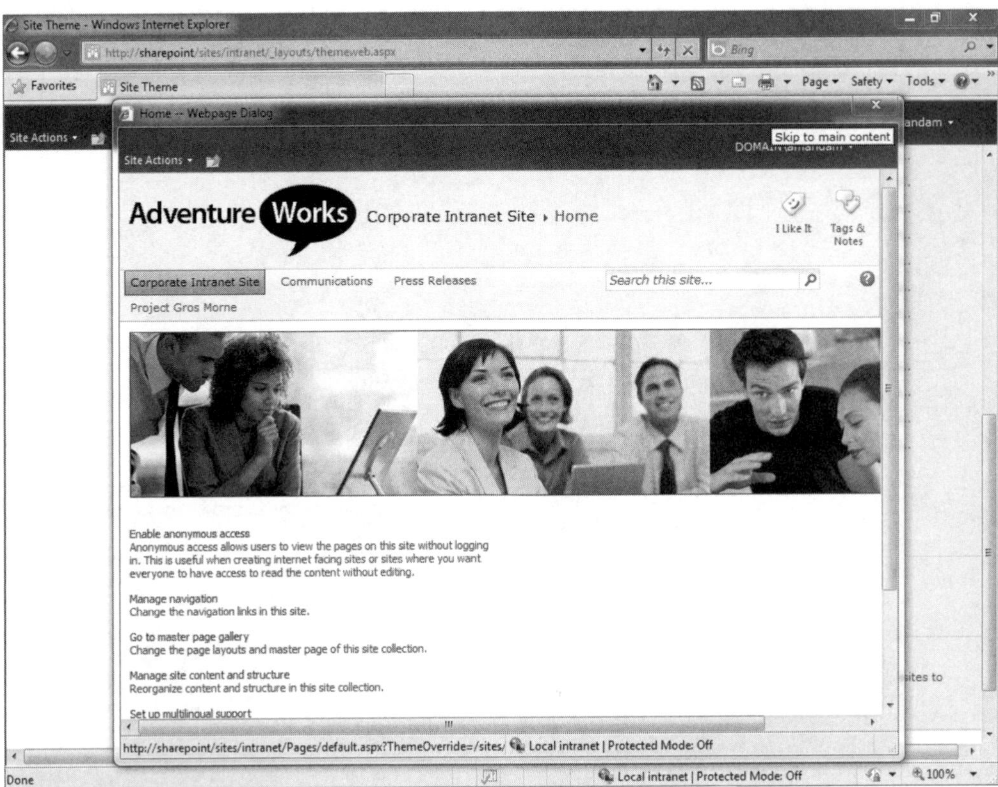

FIGURE 9-6

TRY IT OUT Customize an Existing Theme

1. From your Corporate Intranet site, select Site Settings from the Site Actions menu.
2. Select Site Theme from the Look and Feel group of administrative links. You will be redirected to the Theme Designer tool.
3. From the customize theme area of the page, select Verdana for the Heading Font and Body Font.
4. For Accent 1, click the Select a Color link. A color picker interface will open as shown in Figure 9-7.
5. Select a color of your choice from the color picker, and click OK.
6. For Accent 2, click the Select a Color link.
7. Enter #99CC00 in the New Color text box, as shown in Figure 9-8.

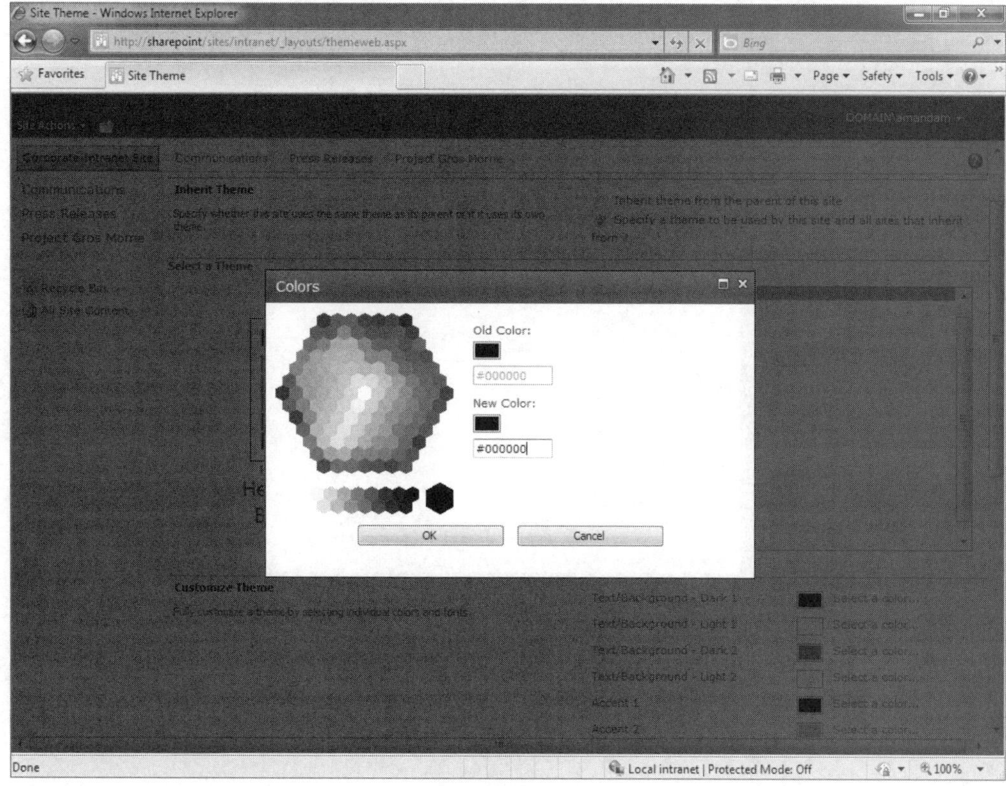

FIGURE 9-7

8. Make additional color selections as required.
9. Click the Preview button to view your site with the new theme applied.
10. Close the Preview window.
11. Select the option to "Apply the selected theme to this site only."
12. Click the Apply button.

How It Works

In this Try It Out, you started with an existing theme applied and then customized the theme to suit your needs. To change the colors of the theme, you used the built-in color selection feature. Using this feature did not require any code changes. When selecting colors, you had a choice between selecting them from the color picker or entering a hexadecimal code for a color that is not represented within the color picker.

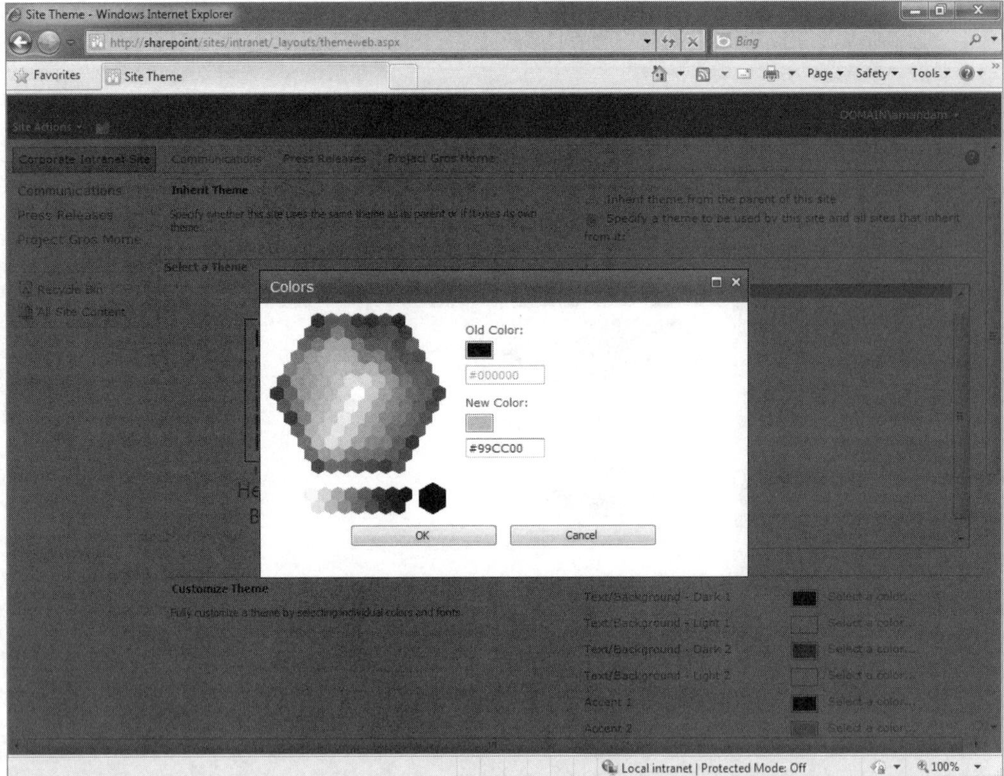

FIGURE 9-8

Tips for Success

When creating a theme, it is important to place usability and the user experience of your site's members ahead of your own personal color preferences. Just because you really like a particular color scheme and combination does not necessarily mean that the content and navigation are easily readable by others. So when designing your themes, keep these following tips in mind:

- Avoid using light text on a light background or dark text on a dark background. Text should always be very easy to read, and selecting contrasting colors is important. Most users will find it hard to read text if the chosen color does not stand out strongly from the background color that is applied to an area. This is particularly true for users who may be color blind or have a visual impairment or disability.
- If you select a custom font for either the Heading Font or Body Font, be sure to select a font that is commonly used, easy to read, and likely to be installed on the systems of users of your site. Common choices include Verdana, Arial, Tahoma, Helvetica, and Times New Roman.

- It may be difficult to identify which areas of the site are represented by the different Accent colors identified in the Theme Designer tool. Take some time to set all Accent choices to a common color such as white. Then one by one, apply a color to an Accent choice and apply the theme to the site. You should then navigate around the site to identify which areas of the site were affected by the change. This will help you easily identify which areas are affected by which changes and will subsequently allow you to make better choices when setting your theme accent colors.

When to Use Themes

Themes allow for the basic modification of site visual elements without requiring any modifications to code or knowledge of style sheets. These are intended for use in scenarios where slight changes to the visual look and feel are required without the need for advanced styling techniques such as background images or layout changes. Themes are most appropriate for shared environments and collaborative scenarios where strict brand guidelines may not exist and long-term management requirements are low. They require very little effort to create and deploy; however, there are limitations on the number of changes you can apply.

For more complicated scenarios where strict brand guidelines exist or where long-term changes must be accommodated in a well-defined and governed process, applying customizations to master pages and style sheets are recommended as it allows for more flexible and consistent changes to be applied in a unified fashion across all sites. We describe these types of customizations in detail in the following section.

WORKING WITH MASTER PAGES

Master pages are one of the most powerful tools in your arsenal when it comes to branding your portal and building a consistent user interface. Before we begin, it is important to note that this requires some basic web development knowledge, as this is a slightly more technical aspect of branding involving code.

NOTE *To edit the master pages, you will make use of SharePoint Designer 2010, a free download from Microsoft available at the following URLs:*

Download 32-Bit SharePoint Designer 2010:

`www.microsoft.com/downloads/details.aspx?displaylang=en&FamilyID=d88a1505-849b-4587-b854-a7054ee28d66`

Download 64-Bit SharePoint Designer 2010:

`www.microsoft.com/downloads/details.aspx?familyid=566D3F55-77A5-4298-BB9C-F55F096B125D&displaylang=en`

What Is a Master Page?

A master page is essentially a template that defines the chrome of your site. The chrome refers mainly to the parts of a site that are shared across all pages, items such as a top or side navigation bar or the header and footer. In a nutshell, by using master pages you can make SharePoint look less like SharePoint and more like any regular website. In fact, there is really nothing that can be done on a regular website that cannot be done in SharePoint, a common misconception.

Using master pages drastically reduces efforts associated with branding in the future, as it will allow you to make sweeping changes to the look and feel of all pages in your site by modifying a single file, the master page.

Master pages work in conjunction with another type of template called a "page layout" to produce the page that you see in the browser after clicking on a link. A page layout is to content what the master page is to the User Interface chrome. A page layout allows you to customize the look and feel of content on your page.

For example, when you click on a link called products in the navigation menu, a process takes place in the background. The master page and page layout associated with the products page merge and form a single page, `products.aspx`, which is then presented to the user. This framework gives you immense flexibility in both the chrome and the content of your website, offering true separation of your presentation from the content of your site.

The master page contains a variety of controls and placeholders. The controls remain consistent across pages and are usually used for items such as the global navigation, current navigation, and search, while the placeholders allow page layouts to inject content or controls. This is done by matching IDs with Content Place Holders in the master page with Content Controls in the page layout. For example, if you request a page that has a Content Place Holder with an `ID="productmap"`, and the page layout associated with the page you requested has a Content Control with an `ID="productmap"`, the content contained in the page layout's Content Control with the `ID="productmap"` will automatically override anything in the master page's Content Place Holder, and that is the content that will be displayed to the user. The most common example of this is the Content Place Holder in the master page with the `ID="PlaceHolderMain"`. This is where the page layout is inserted and basically means this is where all your content is inserted, as shown in Figure 9-9.

For more detailed information on working with page layouts, refer to Chapter 13.

Understanding the Relationship between Master Pages and Style Sheets

The presentation of items on a master page is controlled by a combination of XHTML and Cascading Style Sheets. Presentation refers to things such as the colors, fonts, and placement of items on a page.

By default, a file-system-based style sheet (CoreV4.CSS) is applied to new sites, but you can override this by using an out-of-the-box feature called Alternate CSS. The Alternate CSS is applied after the default style sheet and hence overrides any identical selectors (Classes and IDs). The alternate CSS, while still a style sheet, should not be confused with themes, which we discussed earlier in this chapter. Later in this chapter, you will be guided through the process of applying and editing both the master page and an alternate style sheet.

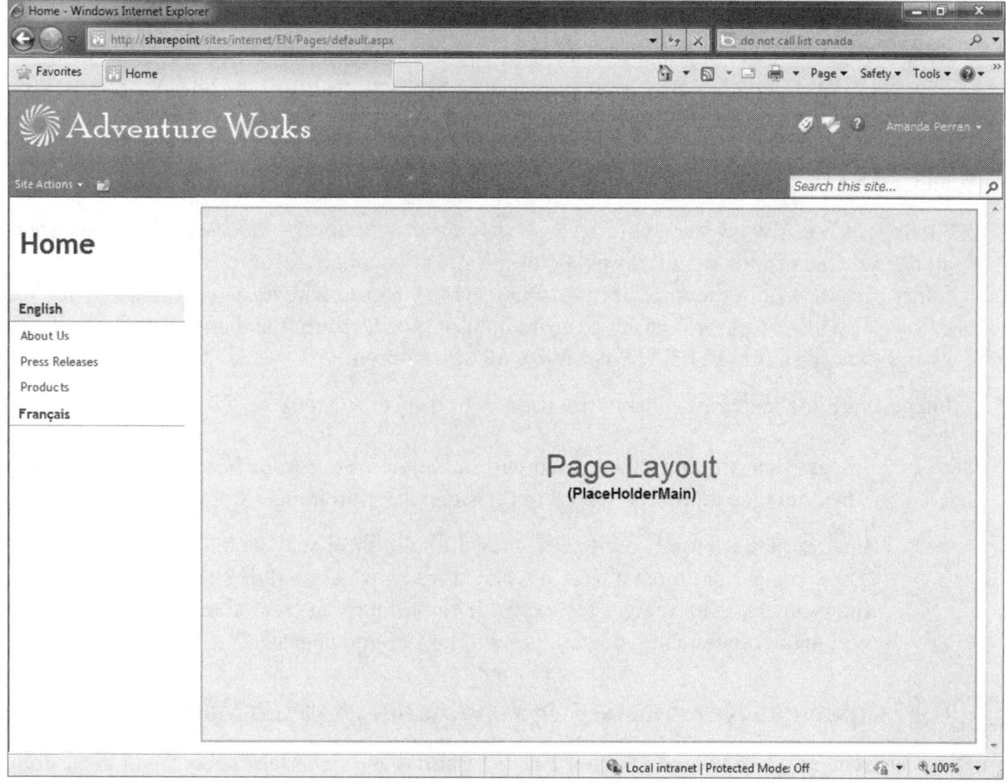

FIGURE 9-9

Best Practices for Branding SharePoint

As is the case with any project involving the modification of files and code, there are best practices to follow to mitigate any risks associated with upgrades or patches and to ensure your site is running smoothly.

There are several rules of thumb to follow when branding SharePoint. Some of the more important ones are:

- Never modify the out-of-the-box files as this can lead to complications during patches or upgrades. Instead, make a copy of a file and modify the copy.
- When modifying master pages, never remove placeholders. If you prefer not to have a certain control displayed, simply hide it using CSS or use the more common practice of hiding it at the bottom of your page in an ASP panel that is set to `HIDDEN`.
- Always store files in the correct locations. Some of the rich features of SharePoint, such as browsing to files, work better and faster when the files are in a location (or path) that is selected by default.

Some of the more common file locations you will be using are:

- **Master Pages:** Master pages (and page layouts) are stored in the Master Pages and Page Layouts gallery, which is accessible by selecting Site Settings from the Site Actions menu and Selecting Master Pages and Page Layouts from the Galleries group of links. The Master page is also accessible via the left-hand menu when editing your site in SharePoint Designer 2010 under the Master Pages folder.
- **Alternate CSS:** Always store your style sheets in the style library. In cases where you are managing multiple brands within a single collection, it is strongly recommended that you create a folder per site within the style library to house the CSS to make it easier to identify for future editing. It will also make it easier to store images specific to that site and style sheet. The style library is accessible via Site Actions, View all Site Content.
- **Images:** In most scenarios, images are used in two specific ways:
  - Images that are shared and used within content, photos, or headers, for example. These images should be stored in the site collection images library.
  - Images that are used specifically with the style sheet such as background images. These images are most effective when stored with your style sheet. It is recommended that you create an images folder inside the folder you created to store your CSS; this will make referencing your images via the CSS much easier.

TRY IT OUT Creating a New Master Page and Adding It to the Master Page Gallery

The marketing department has informed you that a new corporate look and feel is required for the company intranet. After researching the various options you have decided to have your intranet shadow your public-facing website to create a more familiar atmosphere for users and, hopefully, aid in the user adoption process. To do this, you have decided to embrace branding of a master page and alternate style sheet.

1. Before you begin, best practices dictate that you should create a copy of an existing master page rather than modifying a default. To do this, select Site Settings from the Site Actions menu. The Site Settings page appears.
2. From the Galleries group of links, select Master Pages and Page Layouts. The Master Page gallery will appear, as shown in Figure 9-10.
3. Find V4.master in the list and select it. Select Download a Copy from the Documents tab of the Ribbon.
4. Download the file to your desktop and save it as V5.master.
5. Return to the Master Page and Page Layouts gallery via your browser and select Upload Document from the Documents tab of the Ribbon.

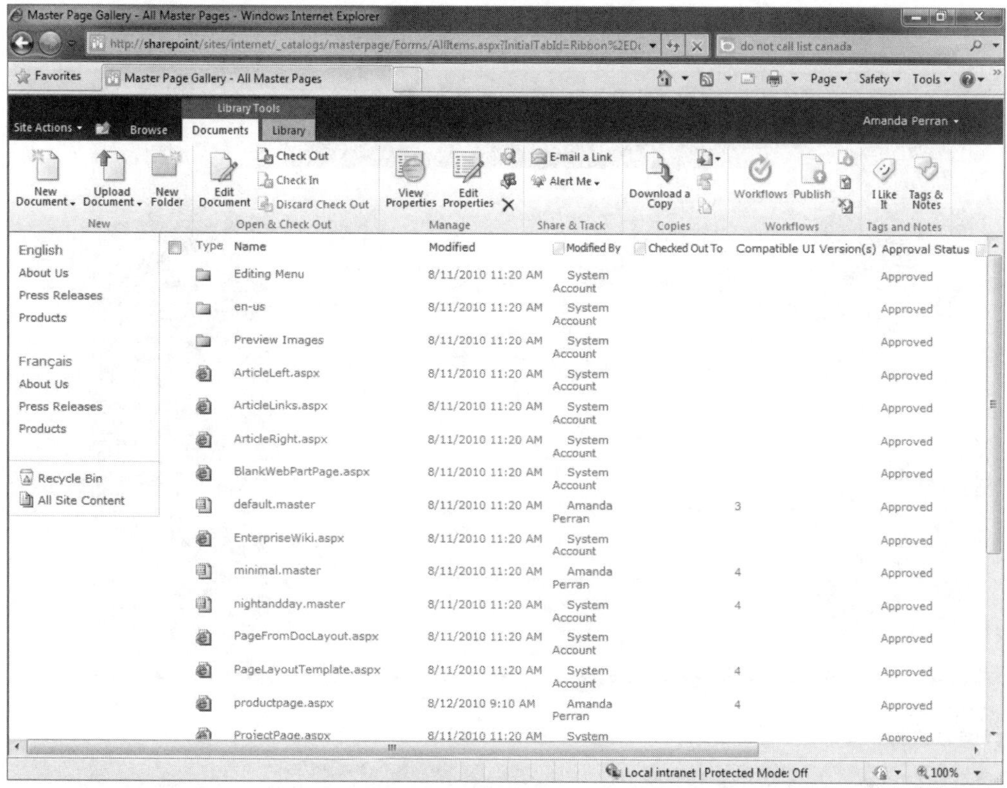

FIGURE 9-10

6. Upload V5.master, completing the metadata as shown in Figure 9-11.

7. Remember to always check in the file, publish, and approve a new major version. You can check in, publish a major version, and approve it using either the Ribbon or the drop-down menu associated with the file, as shown in Figure 9-12. You are now ready to apply your new master page to the site and begin modifying it.

How It Works

In this example, you set the stage for branding your intranet by creating a copy of an existing master page in the Master Pages and Page Layouts gallery. This master page will then be applied to your site and subsequently be accessible in SharePoint Designer 2010, where it will be modified.

This helps to ensure that the default master pages remain untouched. This is of particular importance during upgrades or patches, where the risk is highest for default file replacement.

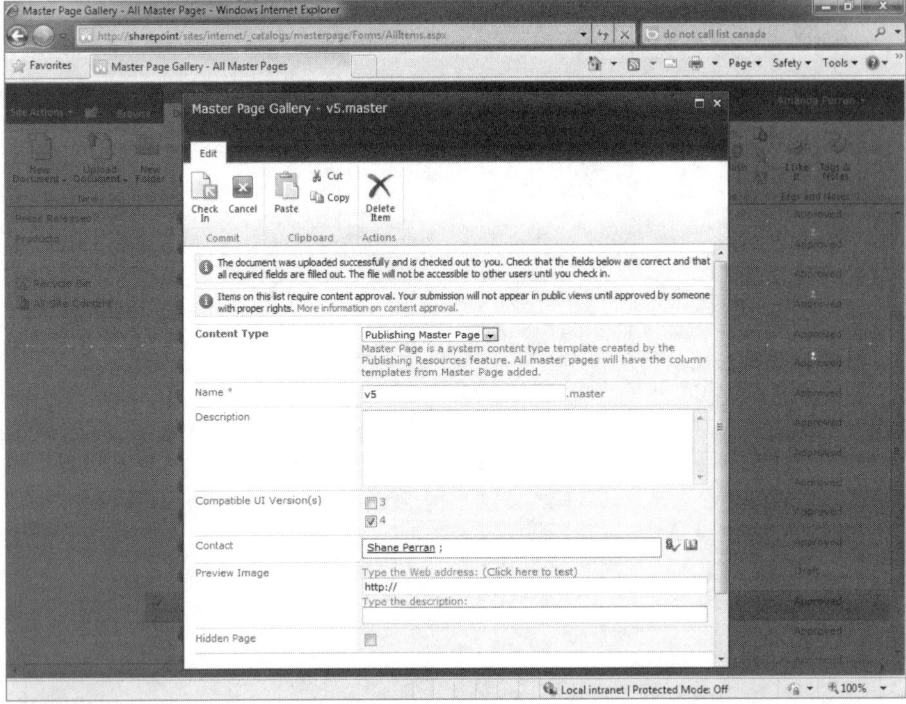

FIGURE 9-11

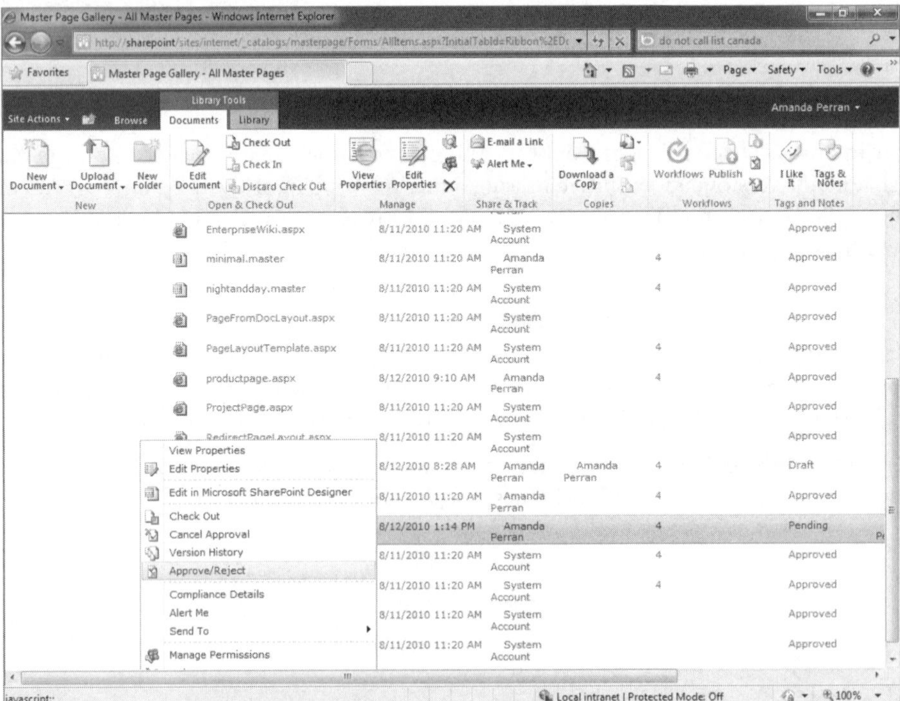

FIGURE 9-12

TRY IT OUT Creating a New Style Sheet and Adding It to the Style Library

To best separate the presentation such as layout and colors from your master page markup, you will be using a cascading style sheet. Best practices dictate that your style sheet should be stored in the style library.

1. From the top level of your site collection, select View all Site Content from the Site Actions menu. The View all Site Content page appears.
2. From the Document Libraries heading, select Style Library to enter the style libraries. The style library will appear, as shown in Figure 9-13.

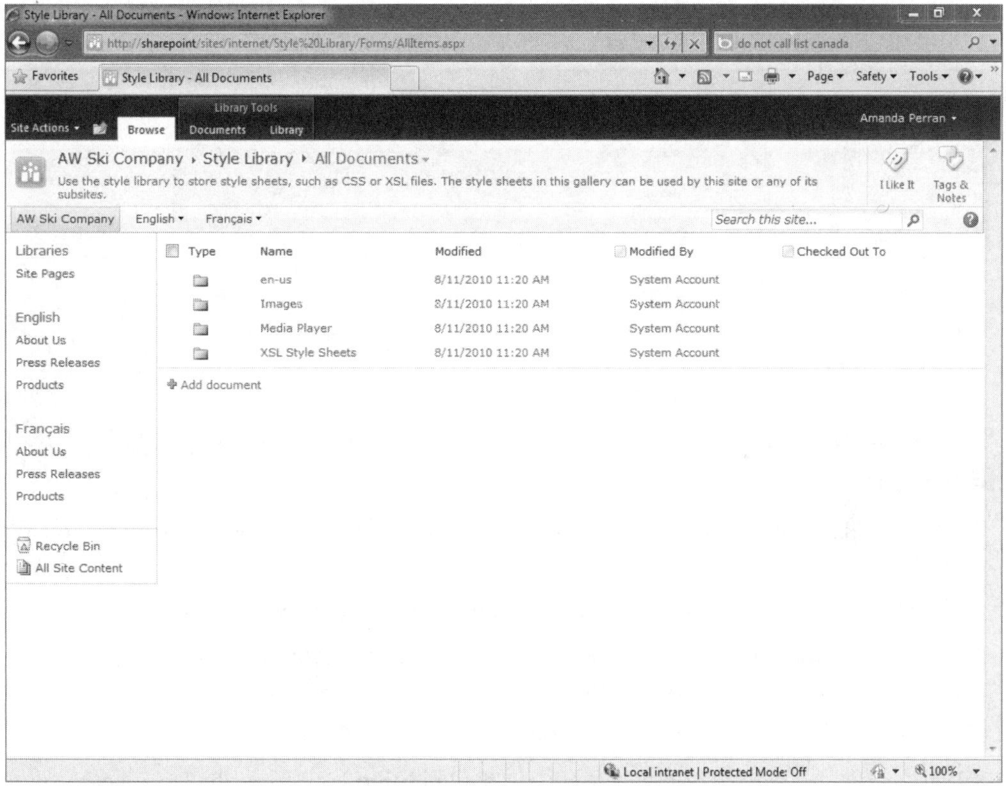

FIGURE 9-13

3. Select New Folder from the Documents tab of the Ribbon.
4. Name your new folder Contoso, and click Save.
5. Enter the Contoso folder by clicking on it in the list.
6. While inside the Contoso folder, select New Folder from the Ribbon. Name your folder Images and click Save. This is where you will store images such as backgrounds used in your CSS.
7. Using the breadcrumb navigation, as shown in Figure 9-14, return to the Contoso folder.

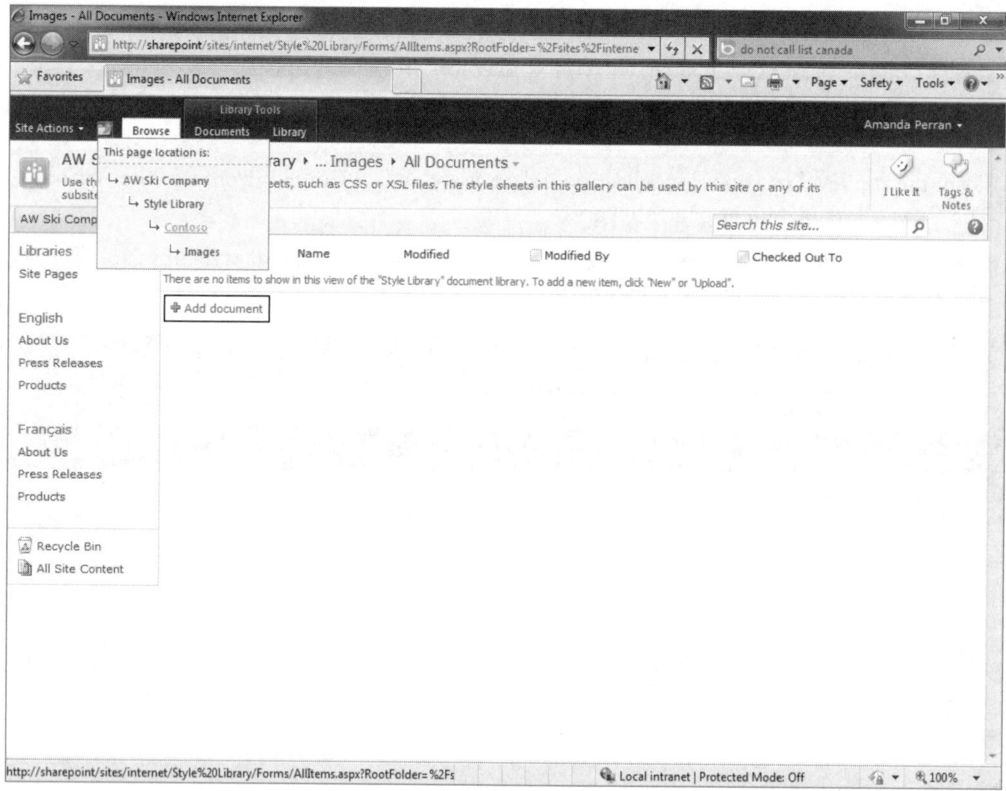

FIGURE 9-14

8. While inside the Contoso folder, select the Add document link. The Upload Document dialog appears.
9. Under Upload Document, click Browse. The Browse dialog appears.
10. Browse to the location of the materials associated with this chapter and select your `MyFirstStyles.CSS` style sheet. Click OK to upload the style sheet.
11. Select the Check In option from the Ribbon. The page will refresh.
12. Select the `MyFirstStyles.css` file, and click the Publish option from the Documents tab of the Ribbon to publish a major version of the file. This will be required for end users to see your branding styles.

How It Works

In this example, you set the stage to use the Alternate CSS feature to control the look and feel of your master page by creating a new style sheet and uploading it to the style library, where it can be applied to your site and subsequently be accessible in SharePoint Designer 2010, where it will be modified.

This helps to ensure that the default style sheet remains untouched. This is of particular importance during upgrades or patches, where the risk is highest for default file replacement.

TRY IT OUT Applying Your Master Page and Alternate Style Sheet

The master page and Alternate CSS are so closely linked that they are applied in the same place. You will commonly find yourself applying a new master page and an alternate style sheet at the same time. For that reason we have combined applying them into a single exercise.

1. From the top level of your site collection, select Site Settings from the Site Actions menu. The Site Settings page appears.
2. From the Look and Feel section, select Master Page. This is the area where you will apply both your new master page and alternate style sheet.
3. From the Site Master Page section, select V5.master from the drop-down menu, as shown in Figure 9-15.

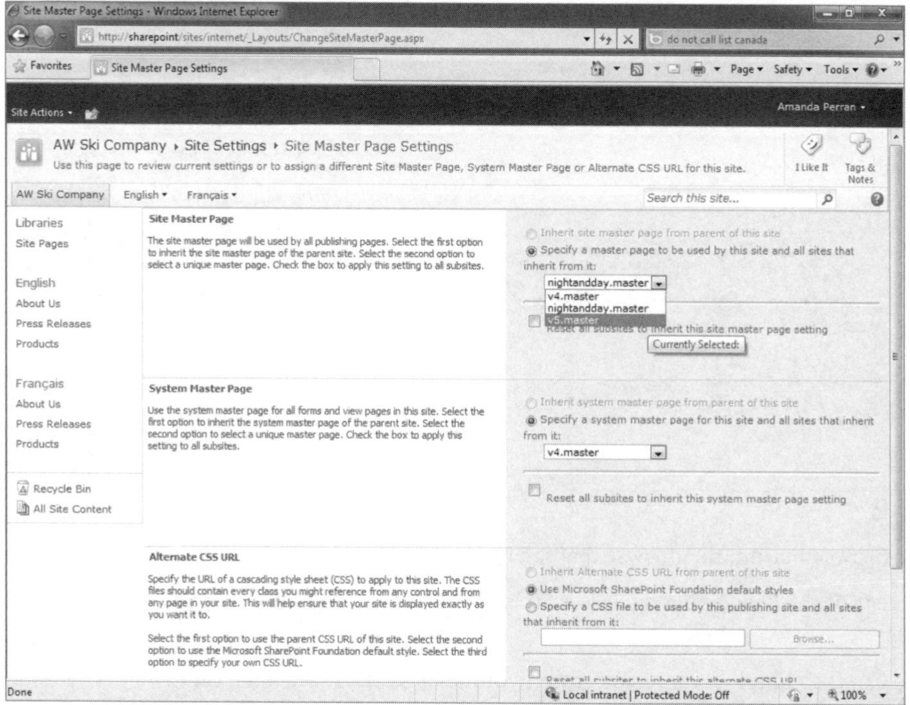

FIGURE 9-15

***NOTE** If you forgot to publish a major version and approve it when you uploaded your master page, you will receive a warning and will have to go back and do that before continuing. You can do that by selecting to the Master Page and Page Layouts section of the Site Settings area and then hovering over V5.master to expose the menu items and selecting Publish a Major Version. After publishing it, you will need to repeat the process, this time selecting Approve/Reject and finally selecting Approve from the dialog that appears. Once that process is complete, start at step 1 of this exercise again. Otherwise, continue to step 4.*

4. Select the checkbox labeled "Reset all subsites to inherit this site master page setting."

5. From the System Master Page section, select V5.master from the drop-down and select the checkbox labeled "Reset all subsites to inherit this system master page setting."

6. From the Alternate CSS URL section, select the option Select a CSS file to be used by this publishing site and all sites that inherit from it, as shown in Figure 9-16.

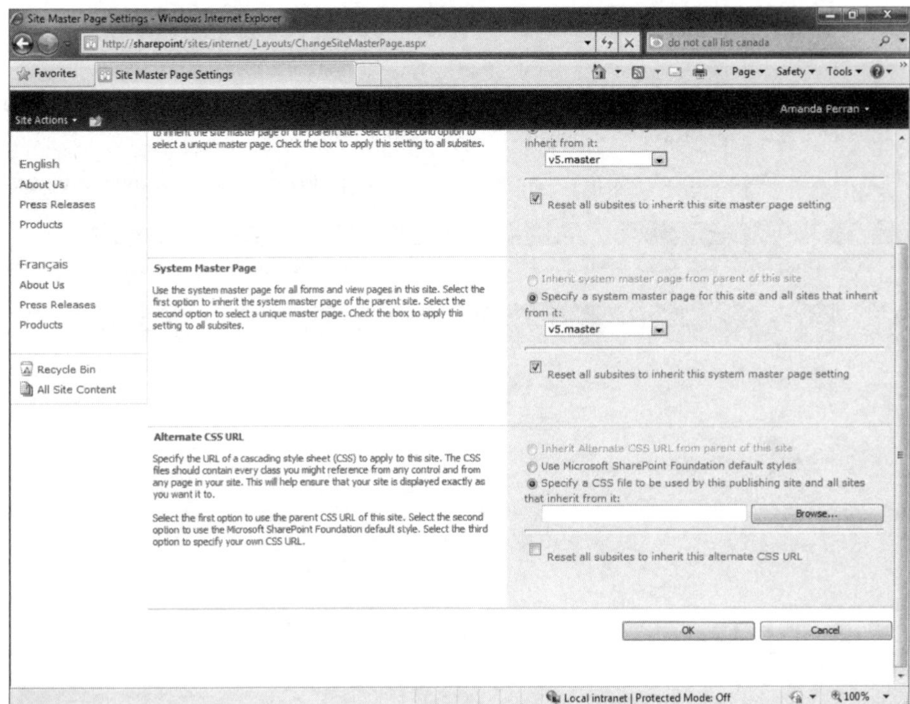

FIGURE 9-16

7. Click the Browse button; the Browse dialog appears.

8. From the left of the Browse dialog, select Style Library. The style library appears on the right of the dialog.

9. Enter the Contoso library, where you stored your style sheet, by clicking on it.

10. Select MyFirstStyles.CSS, and then select OK.

11. Select the checkbox labeled "Reset all subsites to inherit this alternate CSS URL."

12. Click OK. You have applied your master page and alternate style sheet to the site and are now ready to begin modifying the look and feel accordingly using SharePoint Designer 2010.

How It Works

In this exercise, you applied a custom master page and an alternate style sheet to a site. These files will override the default look and feel of the site, allowing you to transform the out-of-the-box SharePoint site into a vibrant intranet that is more in line with corporate brand standards used on your public-facing website. Now that you have applied the master page and style sheet, you can connect to the site using SharePoint Designer 2010 and make the changes required.

TRY IT OUT Modifying Your Custom Master Page and Alternate Style Sheet Using SharePoint Designer 2010

With the stage set as best practices would prescribe for branding your portal, you are now ready to dig into the more technical parts, dealing with the markup of the master page and style sheet. To do this, you will be connecting to your site using SharePoint Designer 2010.

1. Open SharePoint Designer 2010.
2. Under File, Sites, Select Open Site. The Open Site dialog appears.
3. Type the URL of your site in the Name area of the dialog window and click OK. SharePoint Designer 2010 will connect to your site.
4. From the left-hand menu under Site Objects, select Master Pages. The master pages library is displayed to the right.
5. Click V5.master. The V5.master options page appears, as shown in Figure 9-17.

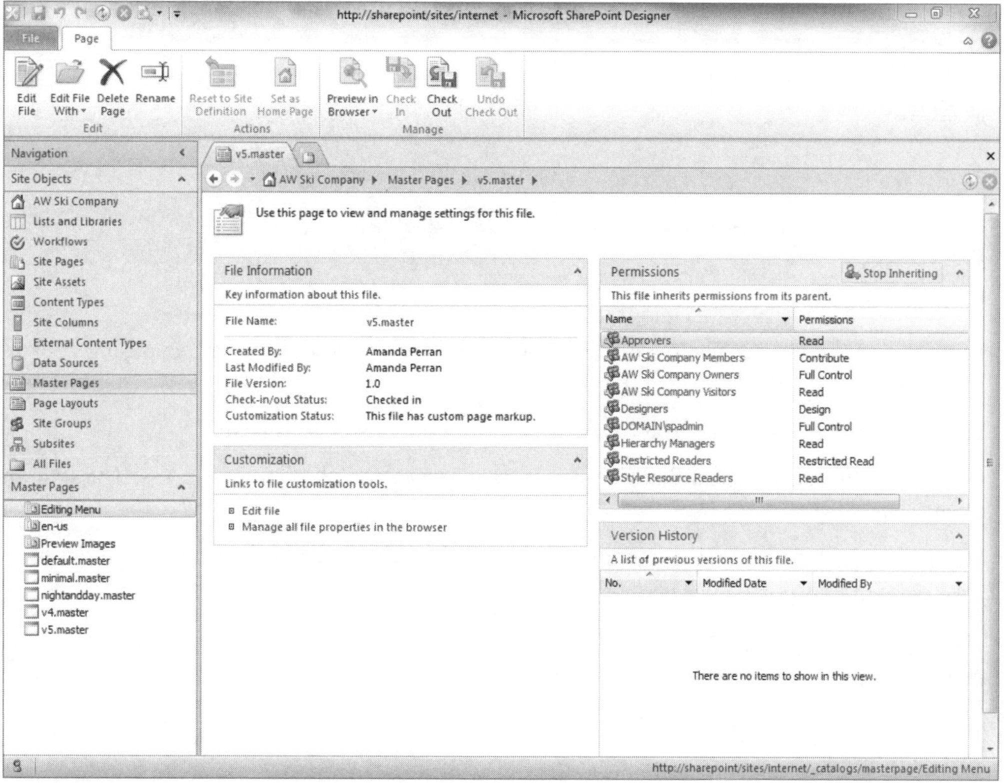

FIGURE 9-17

6. Under Customization, select Edit file. When prompted to check out, choose Yes. The master page opens, as shown in Figure 9-18.
7. Select All Files from the left-hand menu. The All Files window appears to the right.

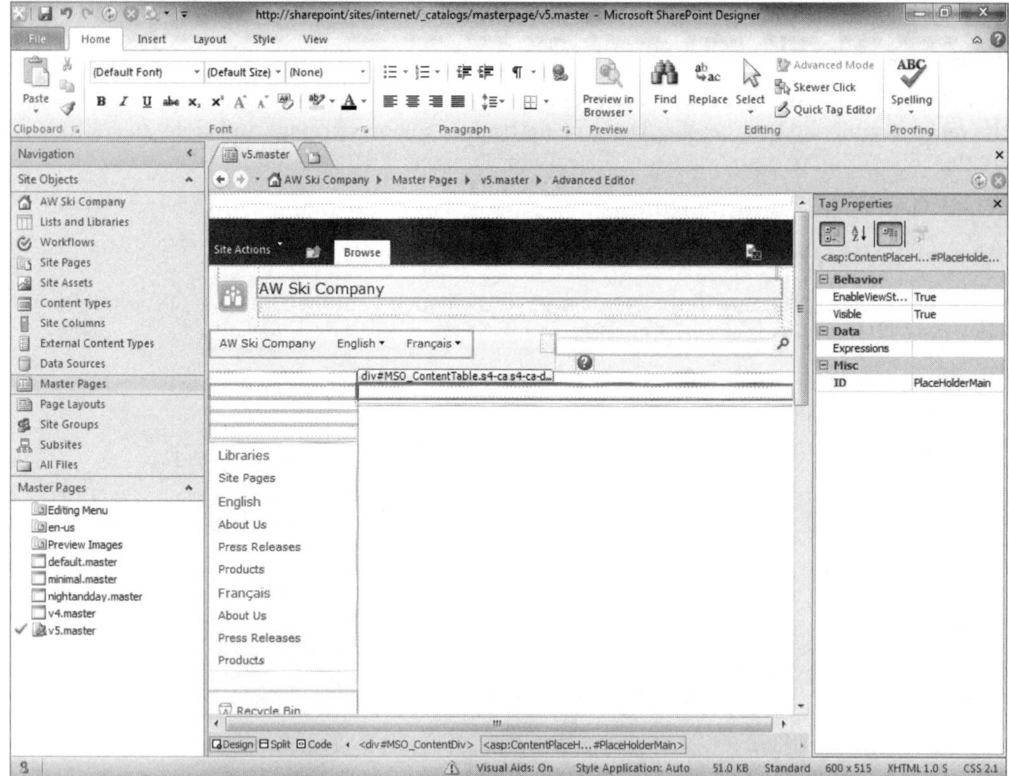

FIGURE 9-18

8. Select Style Library and then Contoso. The Contoso folder contents appear, exposing your style sheet.
9. Select `MyFirstStyles.css`. The MyFirstStyles.CSS options page appears.
10. Under Customization, select Edit File. When prompted to check out, choose Yes. The style sheet opens.
11. Select the tab at the top of the window for your style sheet, and add the following code:

```
.bluecontentarea
{
background-color:#99CCFF;
padding:20px;
}
```

12. Save your changes.
13. From the All Files location, select the Style Library and then Contoso folder, and right-click on your style sheet to expose the menu options, as shown in Figure 9-19.

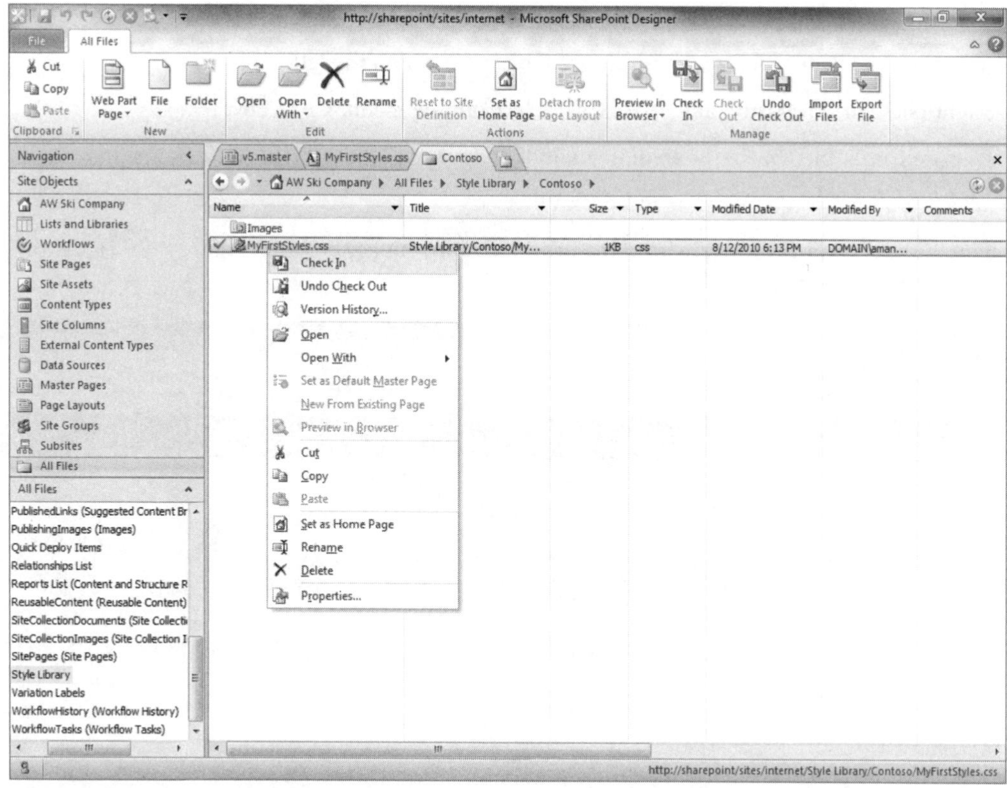

FIGURE 9-19

14. Choose Check In. The Check In dialog box appears.
15. Select Publish a Major Version, and click OK.
16. From the top tabs on the right, select V5.master. Ensure that you are in code view. The Code View tab is located at the bottom of the page; click it if you are not already in code view.
17. Locate the following code in the master page. This is where Page Layout (Content) for your page is inserted.

```
<asp:ContentPlaceHolder id="PlaceHolderMain" runat="server">
</asp:ContentPlaceHolder>
```

18. As a simple example, you will change the background of the Content area to blue. To do this, you will replace the preceding code with the following:

```
<div class="bluecontentarea">
<asp:ContentPlaceHolder id="PlaceHolderMain" runat="server">
</asp:ContentPlaceHolder>
</div>
```

19. Save the master page.
20. Select Master Pages Library from the Site Objects menu on the left.
21. Right-click on V5.master, and select Check In from the menu. Click OK.
22. Choose Check In. The Check In dialog window appears.
23. Select Publish a Major Version and click OK.
24. Finally, select Approve/Reject from the drop-down menu, as shown in Figure 9-20. This will launch the content approval interface.

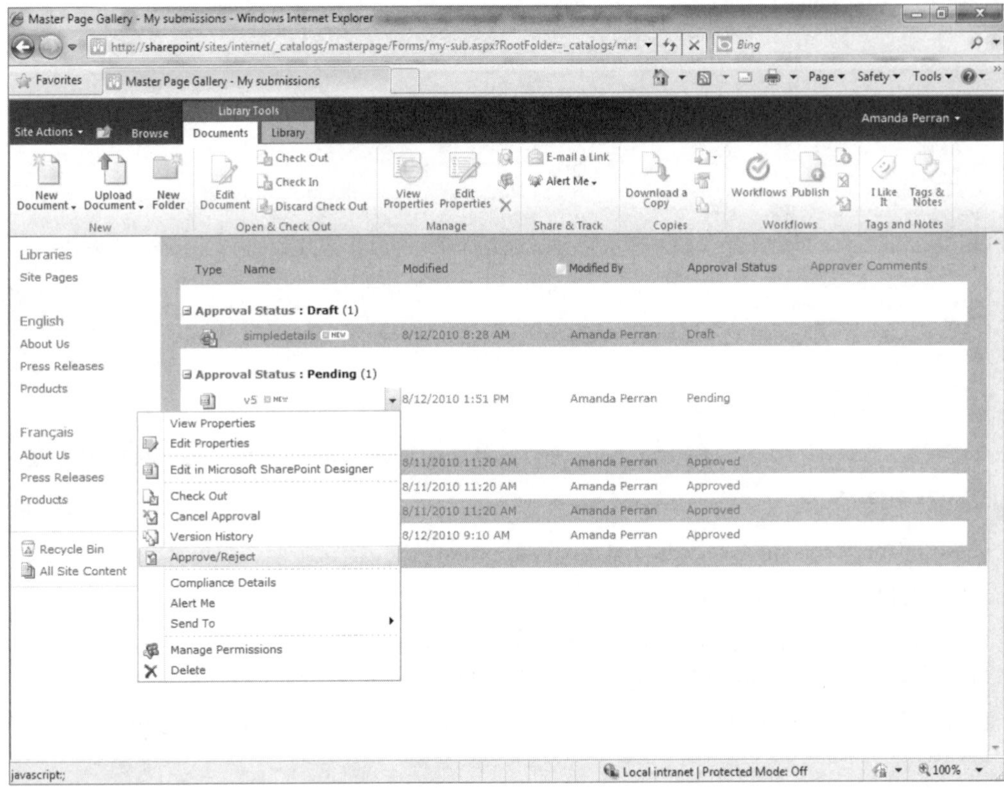

FIGURE 9-20

25. Select Approved and click OK.
26. If you view your site in the browser, you will notice that the content area has changed and now has a blue background, as shown in Figure 9-21. This is a very basic example, but it is also the basis of how you modify your style sheet and master page to create a more visually appealing site. Your design will dictate how you build your style sheet and master page.

How It Works

In this example, you connected to your site using SharePoint Designer 2010 to access the master page and style sheet that you uploaded via the browser previously. Using a combination of XHTML, CSS, and some modification of the control properties visible in the code of each control, you can completely transform your intranet site from a plain vanilla SharePoint site into a more aesthetically pleasing work of art — a site more in tune with corporate brand standards.

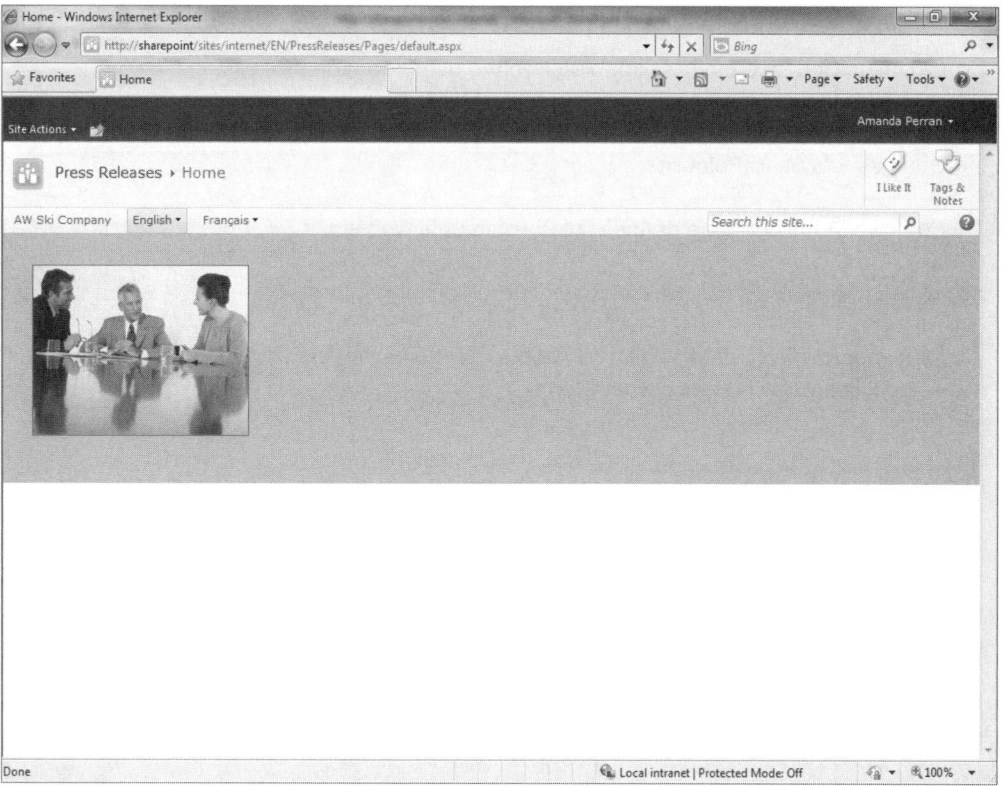

FIGURE 9-21

SUMMARY

In this chapter, you delved into the world of corporate branding and how that applies to the SharePoint world. This chapter touched on many facets of a successful brand strategy, starting with the purpose of branding, which we concluded was ultimately to drive user adoption by creating a better user experience.

After reading this chapter, you should now have a working knowledge of the following branding components:

- Best practices for branding and creating positive user experiences in SharePoint
- SharePoint themes

- Master pages and style sheets
- Using SharePoint Designer for the modification of branding related files

EXERCISES

1. Explain the importance of user experience to the user adoption process.
2. True or false: Themes and master pages require an understanding of CSS in order to apply branding changes to a SharePoint site.
3. True or false: A master page defines the chrome on a website.
4. According to best practices, where should store your style sheets?
5. Why is it important to create and modify copies of existing versions of files rather than modifying the default files when branding SharePoint?

▶ WHAT YOU LEARNED IN THIS CHAPTER

TOPIC	KEY CONCEPTS
What are Themes?	Themes allow for the basic modification of site visual elements without requiring any modifications to code or knowledge of style sheets. These are intended for use in scenarios where slight changes to the visual look and feel are required without the need for advanced styling techniques such as background images or layout changes.
What is a Master Page?	A master page is essentially a template that defines the chrome of your site. The chrome refers mainly to the parts of a site that are shared across all pages, items such as a top or side navigation bar or the header and footer. In a nutshell, by using master pages you can make SharePoint look less like SharePoint and more like any regular website.
Why Organizations Brand SharePoint	By branding you are building a more familiar and better user experience, which will lead to greater user adoption and, ultimately, a more successful deployment. Users will become less focused on the technology aspect of the tool and see the application as an integrated portion of their business.

10

User Management, Audiences, and Profiles

WHAT YOU WILL LEARN IN THIS CHAPTER:

- The difference between user access and personalization
- The different permission levels in a SharePoint site
- SharePoint site groups and the built-in ones you can use
- How to update user profile information manually and automatically
- How to create audiences based on specific memberships or profile properties
- How to target information and web parts to specific audiences

So far in this book, you've read a lot about how to work with SharePoint content and the various components you can create and customize. Unfortunately, none of your work with these topics means anything unless your users can quickly access that content, and configuring access to that information has a lot to do with how much of it there is and where it's located. Just because users have access to content does not mean that they have a requirement to see the content. It's important to evaluate the content that will be stored in your information system and determine how users will need to access and view it. You may need to do this by asking some important questions: Do you have too little information? Do you have so much information that a user can't wade through it? Where is your information located? Do you have one location in which to store information or do you have information located throughout a hierarchy? Can users easily access the information they need to perform their jobs? Is the content they view relevant to them?

After reading this chapter, you should feel comfortable planning and implementing changes to your SharePoint environment to ensure that users can access content relevant to them.

UNDERSTANDING USER ACCESS MANAGEMENT AND PERSONALIZATION

Before you learn how to manage access to any SharePoint site, you need to understand two very important concepts in SharePoint related to the users who connect to your sites:

- The difference between access management and personalization
- How users log in to a SharePoint site

Understanding these concepts helps you learn how to effectively manage a site, protect the site's integrity from users who shouldn't have access to certain information, and make the user experience as productive and problem-free as possible.

What Is the Difference between User Access Management and Personalization?

Imagine you work for a company where users from around the globe share information related to their various business activities. There are different divisions such as Sales, Marketing, Finance, and Legal. Members of a specific division can log in to their portal site and stay up to date on projects and initiatives, as well as work with others in their divisions and teams. For this to happen effectively, you must configure the SharePoint environment to support the following:

- **User access management:** These are the rules that determine what a user can do on a site. To ensure that users can only access the content they need to perform their work, you apply permissions to each divisional site. Within a specific division, users may have different roles and privileges. For example, some users only view content, while others can add or approve new content.
- **Personalization:** This ensures that content is relevant to the users of a site. You use personalization and audience features to do this. *Personalization* is allowing users to only view content that is relevant to them. You may accomplish this by providing them the ability to customize the interface to only display items that are of interest to them, or it may mean creating certain views that only display items where a person's username is displayed in a specific column, such as the Assigned to column. In some cases, you may want to target specific content elements, such as a document, list item, or web part, to members of a role. Through *audiences*, you can identify the groups of people that would find information relevant as you publish it. Perhaps in the Sales division, for example, certain promotions and sales procedures are only relevant for the North American region, and are distracting to sales personnel from the other regions. Therefore, when publishing these promotional documents, the content manager would select a North American audience.

Before you try to personalize content, it's very important that you solidify the underlying content access. With that in mind, the chapter covers user access features of SharePoint first, and then discusses audiences and other personalization features in greater detail.

How Do Users Log In to a SharePoint Site?

When users click a link or enter the web address of a SharePoint site, they are either logged in to the site automatically because they are already authenticated on the site due to the configuration of their network or they are prompted for a username and password via a dialog box or form. In some cases, there may be no need for authentication because the site is configured for anonymous access. For this chapter, you will primarily review scenarios where the user is connecting in an authenticated environment.

Once users are logged in to the site, they will only see content and user interface elements that they have been given permission to view. The content that users view and edit is determined by their SharePoint site group membership and permission levels. *Site groups* are specific roles in SharePoint that determine what a user can do within a site. Permission levels define the activities that a user or group is allowed to perform in a specified location.

NOTE *For more on the different site groups and permission levels, see the section "Working with Site Groups and Permission Levels."*

Most organizations using SharePoint in a corporate or enterprise setting, such as an intranet, will use Active Directory to manage user profiles and determine how users log in to the network, which is also known as the *authentication process*. If your organization uses Active Directory, SharePoint becomes a great browser-based tool in which to work because a user who logs in to the domain does not typically need to enter credentials again to access a SharePoint site. This is because when the system administrator configured the SharePoint server, it was added as a member of your Active Directory domain. Therefore, when you enter your username and password to connect to the network, the SharePoint environment will recognize you as a member and, therefore, not require you to specify your username and password again. In addition, SharePoint will allow you to connect to sites based on your site group membership and will retain your permissions as you access various other Windows-based systems such as file shares or printers. Most users prefer this type of experience because it can be tedious and confusing to manage both multiple usernames and passwords.

A site manager can add specific Active Directory users to a site group by typing their names or email addresses into the site membership interface. See Figure 10-1 for an example of how this can work.

However, in organizations with thousands of users, it's more realistic to add Active Directory security groups to a SharePoint site group. This not only reduces administrative overhead when you first set up a site but also means the site's membership stays up to date as new users join or leave the organization. As you add users to the Active Directory security group, they are automatically assigned to the SharePoint site group that has been associated with the security group, as shown in Figure 10-2.

The rest of this chapter looks at specific access and authentication examples based on an underlying assumption that Active Directory is the primary membership store.

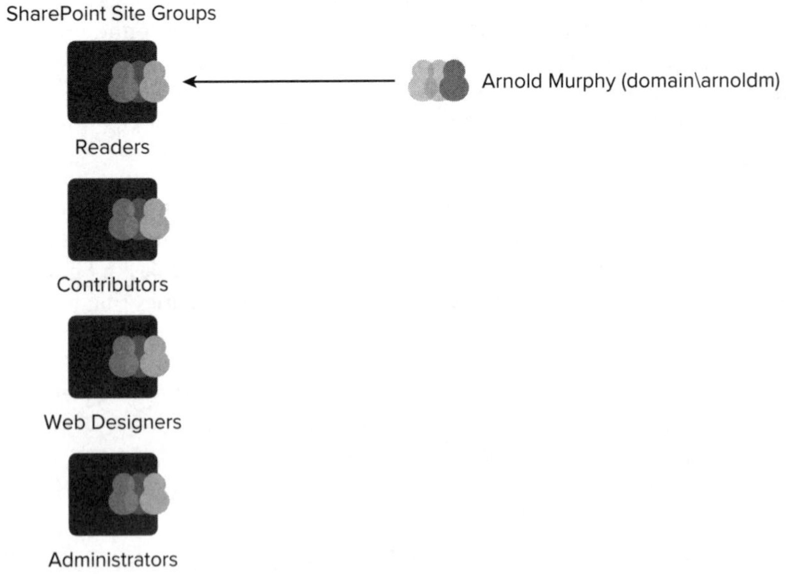

SharePoint Site Groups
Arnold Murphy (domain\arnoldm)
Readers
Contributors
Web Designers
Administrators

FIGURE 10-1

SharePoint Site Groups
Active Directory Groups
Samantha Murphy (domain\smurphy)
Readers
Sales Team Members
Melanie Perran (domain\mperran)
Contributors
Sales Team Managers
Web Designers
Creative Team
Administrators
IT Helpdesk

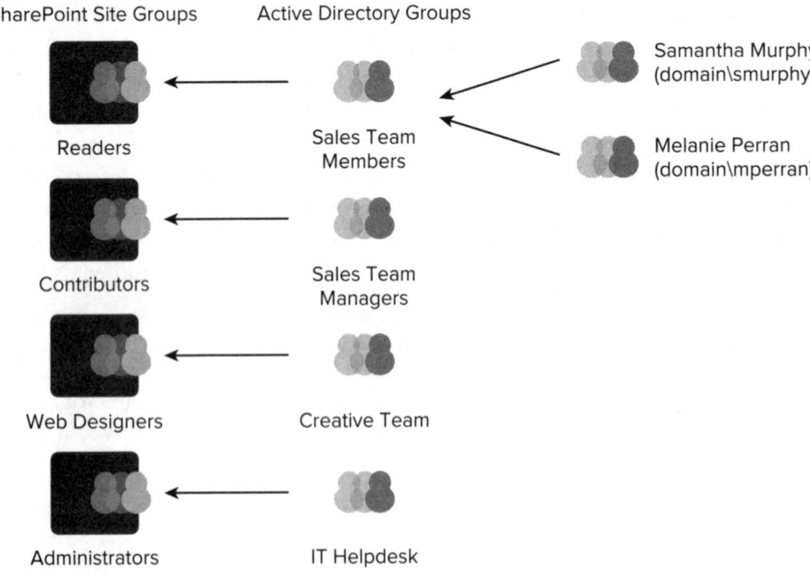

FIGURE 10-2

OTHER AUTHENTICATION METHODS

In SharePoint, you can connect your membership database to stores aside from Active Directory or Windows. In fact, because SharePoint is built on the .NET Framework, any membership provider that you can use in ASP.NET can control access to the SharePoint environment using forms-based authentication.

Although Active Directory and other membership provider services, such as a SQL Server database or custom application, provide some great benefits to SharePoint, you're not required to use them. In fact, users can log on to SharePoint sites if they have local user accounts on the server.

Although enabling forms-based authentication is beyond the scope of this book, you can use custom membership databases as well as existing non-Active Directory connections. For more information, see *Professional SharePoint 2010 Development* (Rizzo, et al, Wrox, 2010).

TRY IT OUT Sign In as a Different User

In this Try It Out, you've already logged in to a site with a user account and need to sign in as a different user with a different username and password. Depending on how your organization is using SharePoint, you may have entered login information when you first accessed the site, or you may be automatically logged in because your organization is using Active Directory.

Signing in as a different user can be helpful in scenarios where you must troubleshoot access issues for another user. It is always a helpful practice to have test user accounts configured for common user roles.

1. From the home page of your intranet site collection created in the first chapter of this book, expand the menu containing your name, as shown in Figure 10-3. This menu is known as the Personalization menu.
2. Select Sign in as Different User. A login box appears.
3. Enter the credentials of the user you want to log in as.
4. Click OK. You now see the name of the user you logged in as in the Welcome menu.

How It Works

The capability to sign in as a different user is important when you start applying special access settings or configurations to your environment and you need to validate your configurations by logging on under test user accounts. For example, if the members of the sales team group for your site should not have access to a specific document library, you can set up a test user account in the sales team group and log in as that user to confirm that the library is not accessible. Also, if you support an environment and users claim that they cannot perform a specific action or see a particular menu item, you can log in as a test user with the same access rights as that user to troubleshoot the problem.

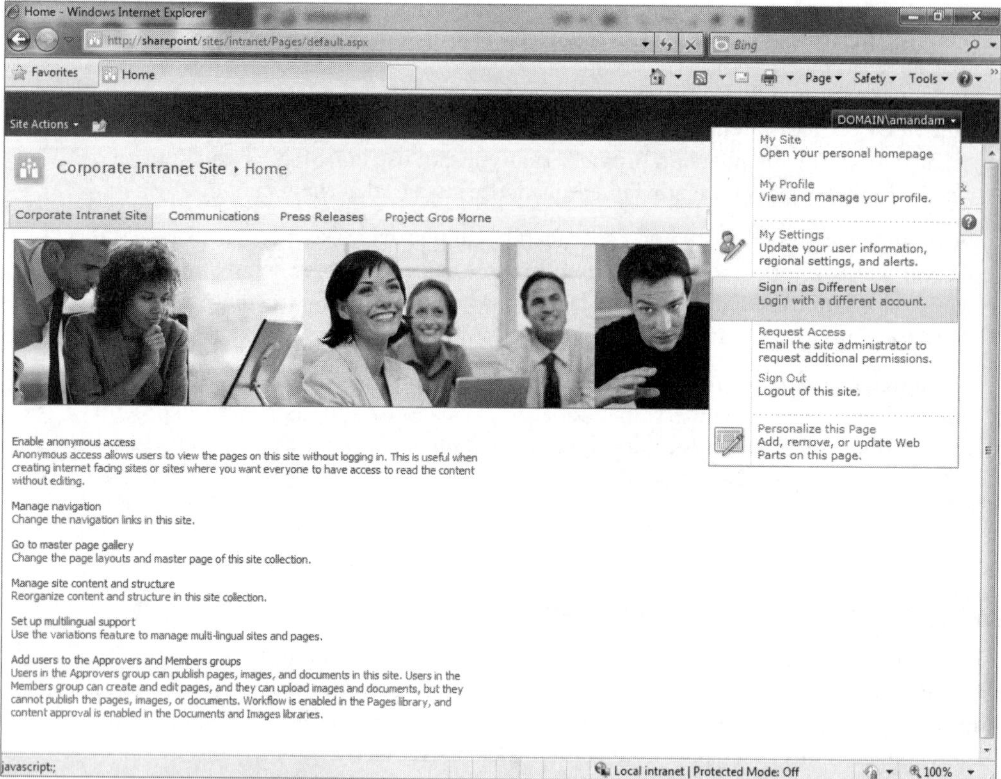

FIGURE 10-3

MANAGING ACCESS IN SHAREPOINT

As your SharePoint environment starts to become populated with important business documents, it's important to manage access properly. Users who require information to do their jobs should be able to easily locate and then access information. In cases where you have sensitive information on the portal, it's crucial that only users who have a business requirement to access it have the rights to do so. Finally, because SharePoint will become a central storage location for important business information, it is critical that this information be protected. This means locking out those who could cause harm to the system or should not have access to information.

Understanding the SharePoint Permission Levels

A *permission level* represents a set of rights that can be assigned to a user or group on a specific SharePoint object such as site, list, or document. Out of the box, several permission levels exist to reflect the most common usage scenarios of the system; however, you can create custom permission levels to meet your specific requirements.

> ***NOTE** It is not recommended to ever change the out-of-the-box permission levels; rather, create new permission levels to match your specific needs. By modifying the out-of-the-box permission levels you may run the risk of creating an environment that is difficult to identify and control exactly what rights users have.*

The table below outlines the default out-of-the-box permission levels in SharePoint 2010.

PERMISSION LEVEL	HIGH-LEVEL SUMMARY
Restricted Read	Can view pages and documents but cannot view historical versions or user permissions
Read	Can view pages and list items and download documents
Contribute	Can view, add, update, and delete list items and documents
Design	Can view, add, update, delete, approve, and customize
Approve	Can edit and approve pages, list items, and documents
Manage Hierarchy	Can create sites and edit pages, list items, and documents
Full Control	Has full control
Limited Access	Can view specific lists, document libraries, list items, folders, or documents when given permission

TRY IT OUT Create a Custom Permission Level

In certain cases, you may wish to assign a set of rights that isn't completely covered by the out-of-the-box permission levels in SharePoint. For example, you may wish to allow users to read and write, but you may not wish to allow them to delete items. Therefore, the Contribute permission level will not be suitable for your requirements. In this Try It Out, you will create a new permission level by copying the Contribute permission level and making modifications to the new permission level to suit your requirements.

1. From the top-level site of your site collection, select Site Settings from the Site Actions menu.
2. Select Site Permissions from the User and Permissions group of links. You will be redirected to the Permissions management page, as shown in Figure 10-4.
3. Select Permission Levels from the Ribbon.
4. Select the Contribute permission level. You will be redirected to a page containing the various rights and activities allowed within the Contribute permission level.
5. Scroll to the bottom of the page and click the Copy Permission Level button. A new blank permission level will be created containing the same settings as the Contribute permission level.
6. Enter Collaborate as the name for the new permission level.

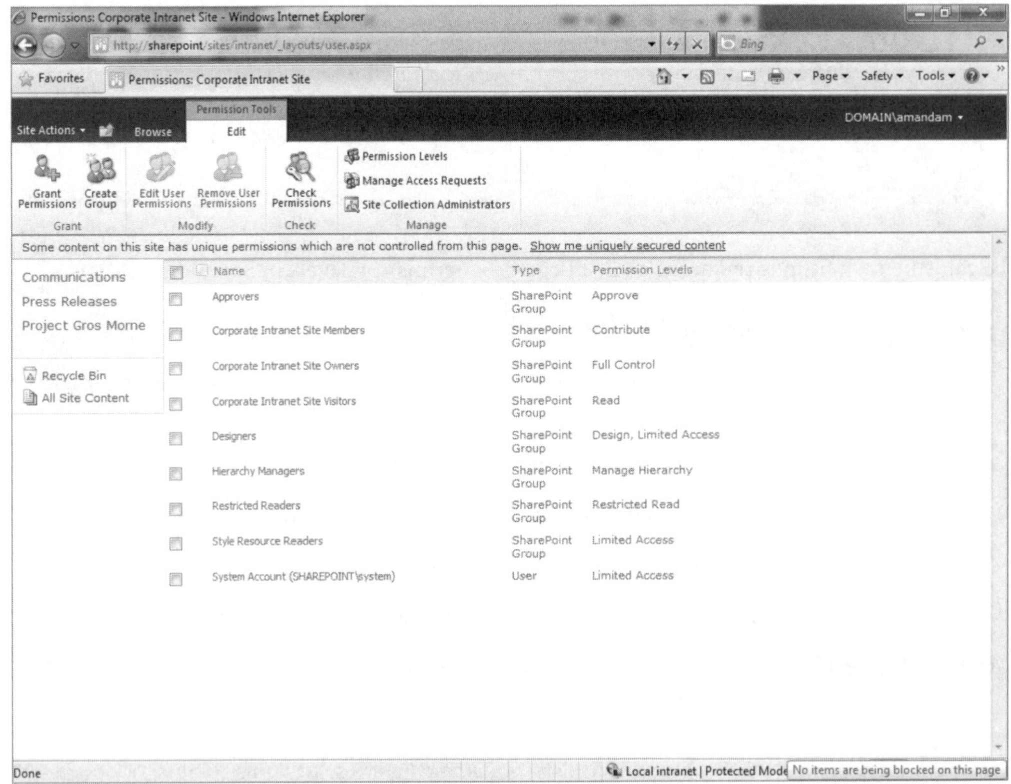

FIGURE 10-4

7. Enter the following for the description:

   Can read and write but cannot delete.

8. Deselect the options to Delete Items and Delete Versions.

9. Scroll to the bottom of the page and Click Create. Your new permission level will now be displayed within the permission level listing, as shown in Figure 10-5.

How It Works

The Contribute permission level contained rights similar to those you wished to provide the end users of your site, except for the fact it allowed users to delete items. Since you do not wish to allow users to delete documents or list items, you created a custom permission level called Collaborate. Rather than create everything from scratch, you created the Collaborate permission level from a copy of the Contribute permission level and removed the rights for deleting items and versions. Your new permission level is now available for use within your site and its subsites.

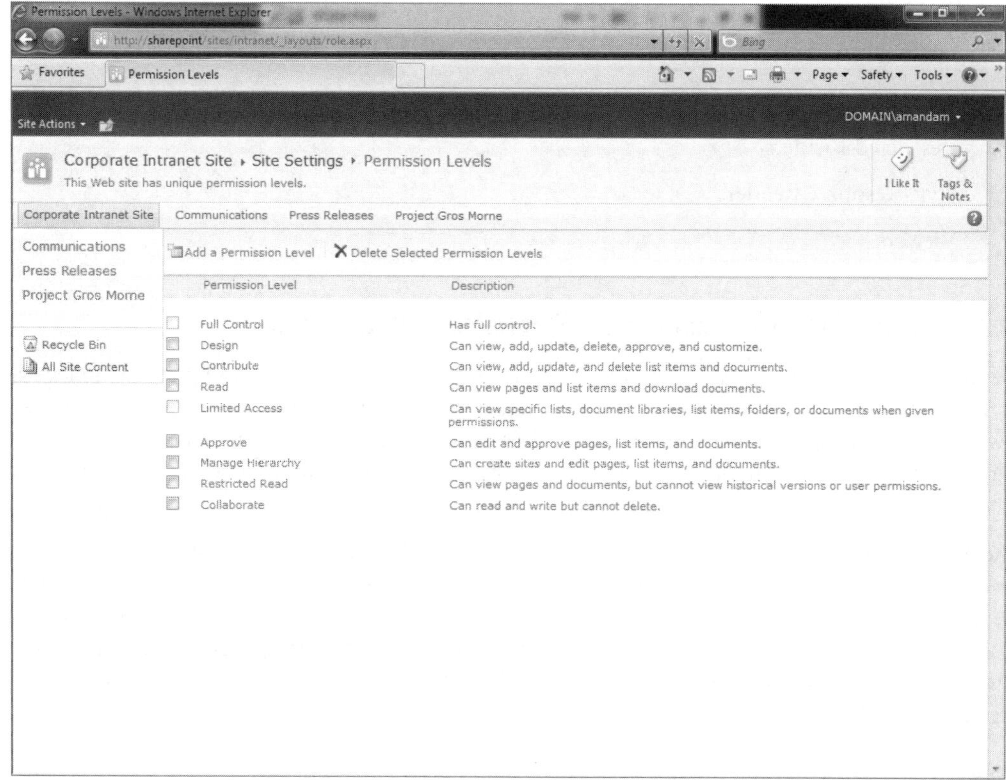

FIGURE 10-5

Understanding the SharePoint Site Groups

A SharePoint site group defines the membership of a specific role within an organization. The following list shows the different types of site groups that SharePoint has to offer out of the box. Depending on which site you create, you may notice all of these groups or a subset of them. However a better practice in real-life scenarios is to create custom groups that reflect your organization's structure.

- Approvers
- Site Members
- Site Owners
- Site Visitors

- Designers
- Hierarchy Managers
- Quick Deploy Users
- Restricted Readers
- Style Resource Readers
- Viewers

Working with Site Groups and Permission Levels

Now that you have an understanding of the various SharePoint site groups and permission levels, let's take a look at some of the ways you can manage access to the content stored with sites by working with the site groups and permission levels. This section looks at how you can create your own site groups as well as change the access rights of a user or group by changing their existing permissions. You also learn how to control how users request access changes related to your site.

In the next Try It Out, you will create a site group called Employees to represent the employees of your organization, and you will assign the newly created permission level to that group. You then add new team members to your site group. If you find later that you need to change permissions on a group or user that you've already created, or totally remove a user altogether, you learn to do so in the third and fourth Try It Outs. In the last Try It Out of the section, you find out how to enable access to a site when a user requests it.

TRY IT OUT Create a New Site Group

1. From the top-level site of your site collection, select Site Settings from the Site Actions menu.
2. Select People and Groups from the Users and Permissions group of links. You will be redirected to the Group Management area of the site. By default, you will be viewing the membership of the Site Members group.
3. Select the Groups link from the left-hand navigation menu. You will be redirected to the Groups listing page.
4. Select the option to create a New Group from the New menu of the toolbar. You will be redirected to the Create Group page, as shown in Figure 10-6.
5. Enter Employees for the name of the group.
6. Enter the following description into the About Me field for the group:

   Site group for Adventure Work employees

7. For this example, you should enter your name for the Group Owner value. However, it is a best practice to create a SharePoint Administration group and specify that group as the owner for all other SharePoint groups.
8. Retain the default configurations for Group Settings and Access Requests.

9. For the Give Group Permission to this Site section, select the Collaborate permission level. This will give all members of the Employees group collaborate access to the site.

10. Click Create.

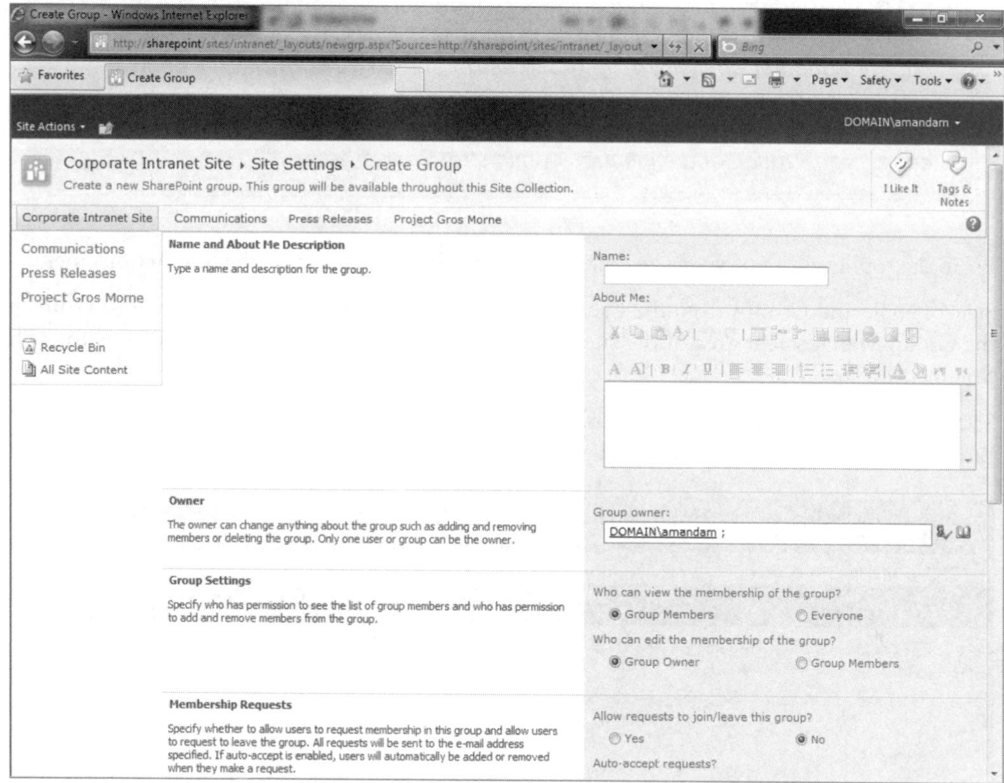

FIGURE 10-6

How It Works

When you create your group, you automatically become a member because you are the creator. The next step is to add new team members to your site groups. You do this in the next Try It Out.

TRY IT OUT Add a User to a Site Group

In this example, you will add a special group known as "Authenticated Users" to your new SharePoint site group. This will ensure that any user who has successfully authenticated to your network will have access to your intranet site. In some cases, this may not be appropriate if you have users who have access to your overall network, but you do not want to give them access to SharePoint. In such a case, it would be more appropriate to specify an Active Directory group that represents all the employees of your organization. It is good practice to plan such group membership choices with the appropriate members of your organization's security team.

NOTE *You may run into situations where the people responsible for managing a SharePoint environment may not be experts in the Active Directory group structure that another administrative group establishes. To prevent this, whenever two groups plan a new SharePoint environment or site collection, they should consult each other to ensure permissions are assigned in a way that benefits the entire organization and minimizes administrative overhead.*

1. From the top-level site of your site collection, select Site Settings from the Site Actions menu.
2. Select People and Groups from the Users and Permissions group of links. You will be redirected to the Group Management area of the site. By default, you will be viewing the membership of the Site Members group.
3. Select the Employees link from the left-hand navigation menu. You will be redirected to the Employees Membership page, as shown in Figure 10-7.

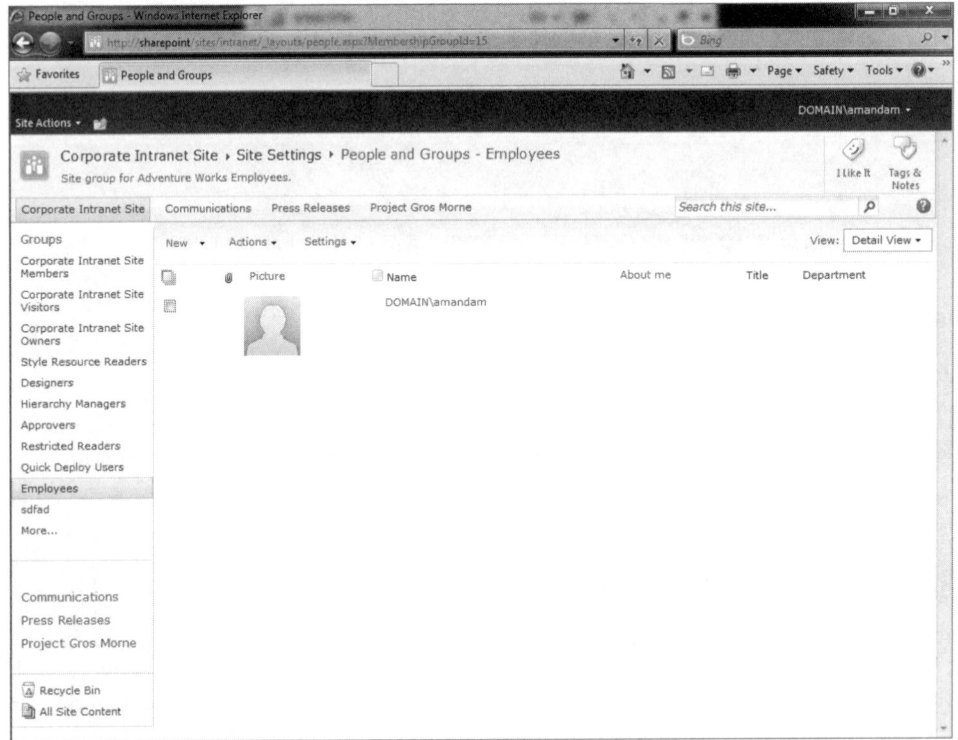

FIGURE 10-7

4. Select the option to Add Users from the New menu of the toolbar. The Grant Permissions window will appear, as shown in Figure 10-8.

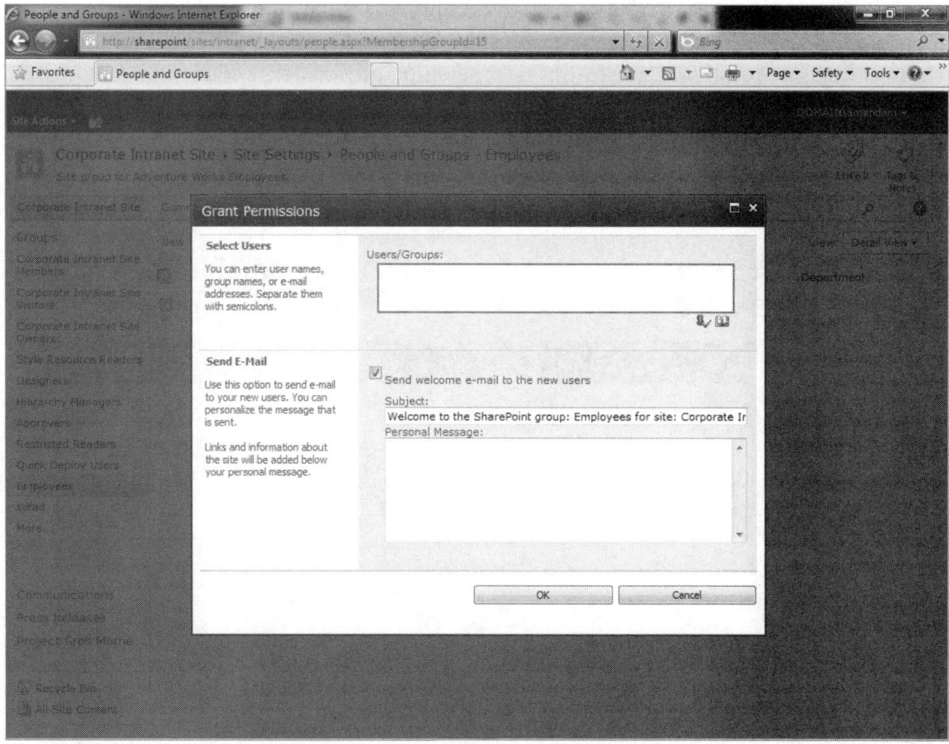

FIGURE 10-8

5. Click on the Address book icon to launch the user and group search interface.
6. Search for the term "users." You will receive a listing of results that contain the term users.
7. Select the Authenticated Users group, and click the Add button.
8. Click OK. The Authenticated Users group will now appear in the Grant Permissions window.
9. Click OK. You will be returned to the Group Membership page.

How It Works

Using the Authenticated Users group ensures that as new employees are added to the organization, they are automatically provided access to the SharePoint sites with which the Employees group has been associated. This provides a more seamless access management environment and helps standardize access across groups.

TRY IT OUT Modify the Permissions of an Existing User or Group

In some scenarios, it's necessary to change the specific rights that a single user or site group has on a site. This may be related to a direct request from a business manager, a change in requirements or perhaps because you need to grant a certain user rights to a workspace beyond what he or she currently has. This may be because the user has demonstrated exceptional skills and would make a good candidate to assume more responsibility for managing the SharePoint site. In the next example, you see the process for identifying and modifying the group membership and site permissions of a single user.

1. From the top-level site of your site collection, select Site Settings from the Site Actions menu.
2. Select Site Permissions from the Users and Permissions group of links.
3. Select the checkbox associated with the Employees group, as shown in Figure 10-9.

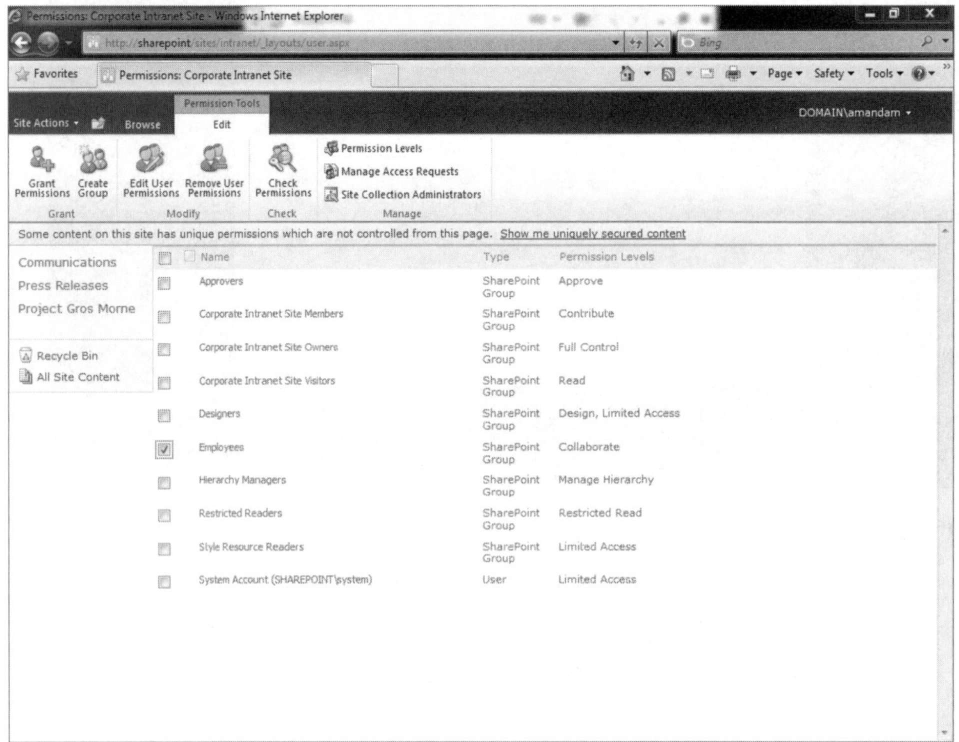

FIGURE 10-9

4. Select the Edit User Permissions option from the Ribbon.
5. Deselect the Collaborate option and select the Read permission level.
6. Click the OK button. You will be returned to the Site Permissions page, where you will see the Employees group now has Read access to the site.

How It Works

In the preceding example, you changed the permissions associated with the Employees group from Collaborate to Read. This may be because of a recent requirements change to limit the access rights of all employees and to limit the number of employees that had the ability to update information within the intranet.

TRY IT OUT Remove a User from a Group

When you created the Employees group, your username was automatically added as a member of that group. Since you are already a member of the Authenticated Users group, there is no need to also have your user account individually assigned to the group. Therefore, you will remove it from the group using the following procedure.

1. From the top-level site of your site collection, select Site Settings from the Site Actions menu.
2. Select People and Groups. You will be redirected to the Group Management area of the site. By default, you will see the membership of the Site Members group.
3. Select the Employees link from the left-hand navigation menu.
4. Select the checkbox to the left of your name from the membership listing.
5. Select the Remove Users from Group option from the Actions menu. You will receive a warning message, as shown in Figure 10-10.

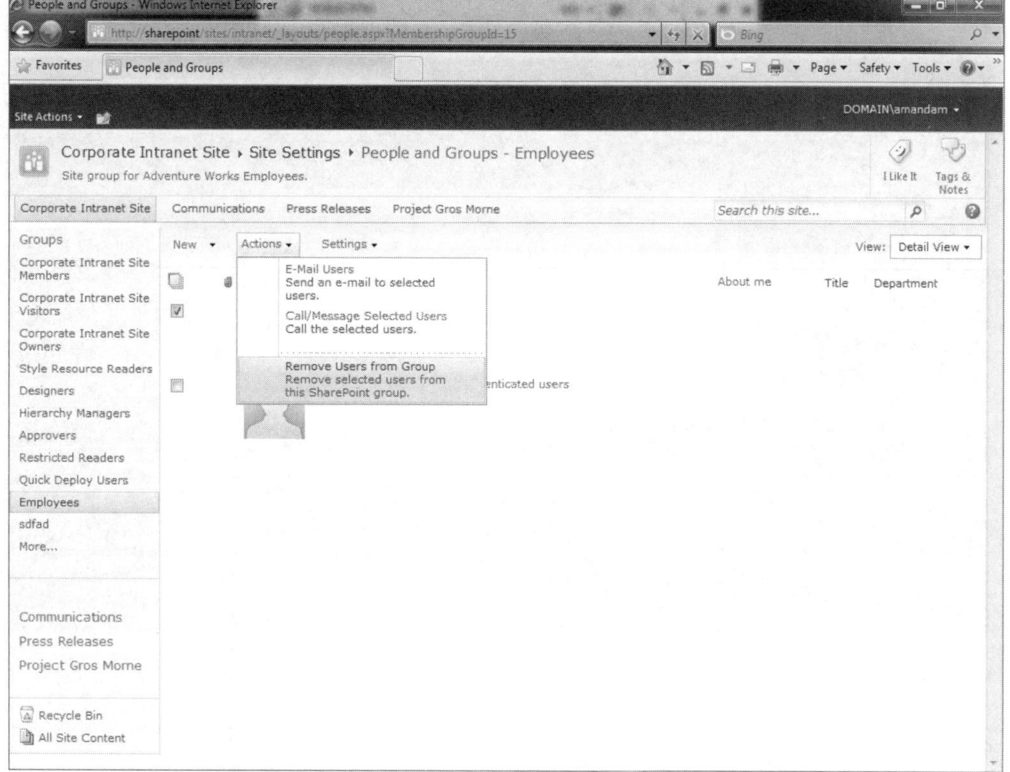

FIGURE 10-10

6. Click OK to confirm your action and complete the operation.

TRY IT OUT Enable Site Access Requests

So far, you've seen tasks that you, a site owner, can complete to assign access to team members or groups. However, certain situations may require that users request access to a site. For example, a user might click a hyperlink to a site of which he or she is not a member. SharePoint has a built-in access management feature that allows users to request access via the web interface by clicking a Request Access link.

1. From the top-level site of your site collection, select Site Settings from the Site Actions menu.
2. Select Site Permissions.
3. Select the Manage Access Requests link. A window will appear, as shown in Figure 10-11.

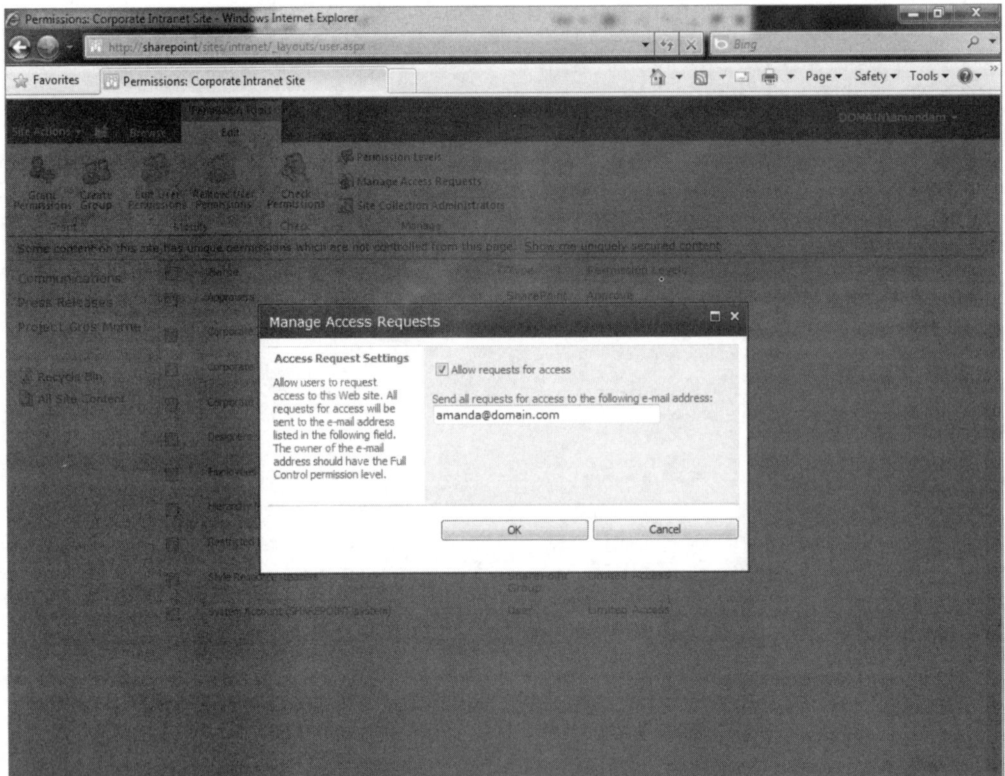

FIGURE 10-11

NOTE *If you do not see this item in the Settings menu, your server may not be configured to send email. You can change this by having your system administrator configure the outgoing email settings from the Operations tab of the SharePoint Central Administration site.*

4. Select the Allow request for access checkbox.
5. Enter the email address that all access requests should be sent to. It is good practice to use a distribution list for this address rather than a single user's email address.
6. Click OK.

How It Works

When users that do not have access to the site attempt to visit the address, they will be presented with a page similar to the one shown in Figure 10-12.

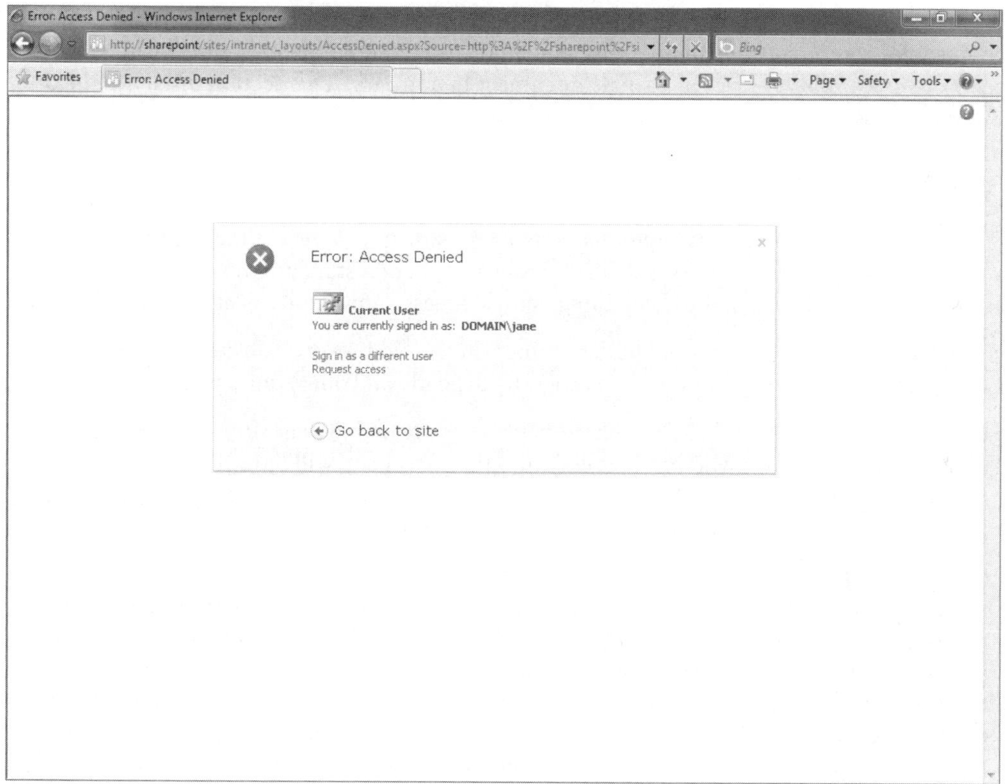

FIGURE 10-12

From this page they may request to be added to the membership of the site. This method has several benefits including:

- **Users can request access without having to access another tool or interface:** The system automatically provides all the information that is required to effectively address the request and routes the request to the appropriate individual responsible for the site. This is the person (or group of people) associated with the email address specified in the previous steps. This saves both parties valuable time and is a benefit in large organizations that use ticket-tracking systems to provide such access.

- **The user requesting access does not know who is responsible for the site:** It discourages people from going around a defined methodology and using more direct access request methods such as telephone or manual email, which could be potentially more time-consuming and distracting.

UNDERSTANDING THE DIFFERENT LEVELS OF ACCESS IN SHAREPOINT

Everything you've learned so far has been related to controlling access and rights on a SharePoint site. However, SharePoint also supports permissions management on the list and item level. This means that, while a user may contribute to his team's collaborative site, he may only be a reader for a particular document library or even a single document in a library. This section discusses the different levels of access that you can have on a SharePoint site.

Site-Level Access

Each of the examples thus far in this chapter has applied to managing access at the site level because, by default, this is the level where access is defined. From a restriction standpoint, you do not want to overcomplicate access and you want to keep things simple unless your requirements dictate otherwise.

When you work on a site level, you need to determine whether you want a subsite to inherit permissions from a parent site or not. Your decision generally depends on your requirements:

- **Inheriting permissions:** When you inherit permissions from a parent site, you create a scenario in which any user who has permission to the parent site will have the same permissions and rights on the child site. This cuts down on the tasks and effort associated with managing permissions and creates a consistent access experience for all users.
- **Creating unique permissions:** Creating a site with unique permissions will allow you to manage permissions and access to your child site, independent of the settings specified for the parent site. Therefore, a user who can add content on the parent site may not necessarily have access to the child site. Users perform different roles from site to site. This means that you'll have to spend more time setting up and managing the site, but you will have greater flexibility in meeting the access requirements of each individual team. Sometimes it's beneficial to give users greater access rights on a subsite than they have on a parent site. For example, in a sales proposal workspace, members of the sales team may be able to create lists and libraries to aid in their production of the proposal, whereas on the sales team site they may only have permissions to add content to existing lists.

TRY IT OUT Stop Inheriting Permissions from a Parent Site

You may have created a site and selected the option to inherit permissions from the parent, but at a later time, realized you needed to manage the site's permissions independently of the parent site. The following example uses the project site that you created in Chapter 2 and assumes that the site has different usage requirements than your main intranet site. You change the permissions settings on the existing site, which copies all permission settings from the parent into the project site so that you can manage them separately.

Remember that if users have permissions on the parent site and you do not want them to have access to the project site, you must remove them after breaking the inheritance because SharePoint copies the permissions, groups, and users from the parent into the child. You wouldn't have to do this if you had not selected to inherit permissions when you first created the site. In that case, once the site is created, it has a blank set of permissions, and no users of the parent have access to the site unless explicitly given access. The exception, of course, is a site collection administrator or site owner on the parent site.

NOTE *If you did not complete the exercises from Chapter 2, you can create any subsite on your site collection that inherits the permissions of parent. The same steps apply regardless of what site template you use.*

1. From the main page of the Project Gros Morne site, select Site Actions from the Site Settings menu.
2. Select Site Permissions.
3. Click the Stop Inheriting Permissions option from the Ribbon.
4. You will receive a warning message, as shown in Figure 10-13.

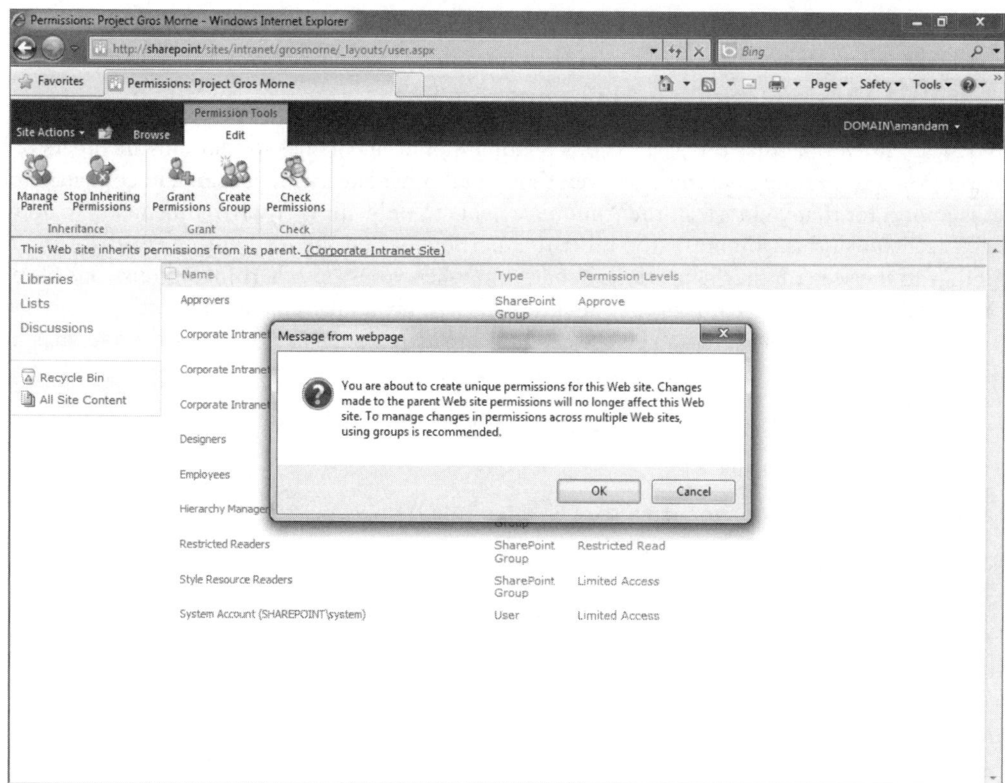

FIGURE 10-13

5. Click OK to confirm your action. The page will refresh and a yellow message bar will appear at the top of the screen, indicating that the site has unique permissions.

How It Works

Once you selected the option to stop inheriting permissions, the users, groups, and permissions from the main intranet site were copied down into the project site. You may now make additional changes such as removing groups or adding users. Any changes you make to the project site will not have any impact on the main intranet site.

List- or Library-Level Access

Sometimes a list or library on a team site requires a different set of permissions than the rest of the site. For example, a document library containing sensitive financial performance reports should not be shared with everyone who has access to the site. You could create a separate site to store this information, but it's easier to simply adjust the permissions on the library so that a subset of users can access the library. Another example is where only certain users can edit a specific list or library in which team members can only view content. For example, only a manager can create new items on an Announcements list for a team, but team members can contribute to list and libraries on the rest of the site.

TRY IT OUT Assign Unique Permissions to a List

In this Try It Out, you modify the permissions on an announcements list so that only members of the Approvers group can create new content. Even though all other site members can add content to other lists, it is important that you restrict the Announcements to only allow Approver members to add new items. To accomplish this, you must stop inheriting permissions on the Announcements list from the site. Similar to the scenario in the previous Try It Out, when you stop inheriting permissions for a list from a site, all rights are copied from the site into the list, so you must update the settings to reflect your requirements. For this exercise, you use the Project site from the last Try It Out, which has unique permissions from its parent.

1. From the main page of your Project site, select the All Site Content link from the side navigation.
2. Select the Announcements list.
3. Select the List Settings option from the List tab of the Ribbon.
4. Select the Permission for this list link. You will be redirected to the Permissions Management page for the list.
5. Click the Stop Inheriting Permissions option from the Ribbon.
6. You will receive a warning message.

7. Click OK to confirm your action. The page will refresh, and a yellow message bar will appear at the top of the screen indicating that the list has unique permissions, as shown in Figure 10-14.

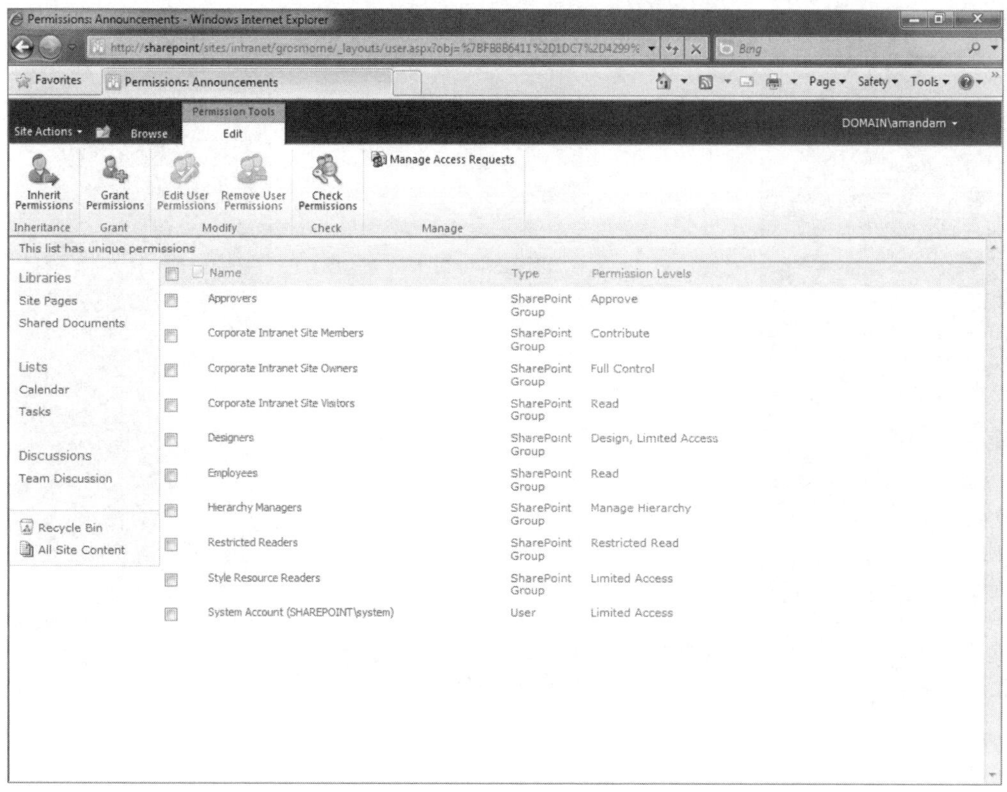

FIGURE 10-14

8. Select all groups except the Approvers group, and click the Edit User Permissions option from the Ribbon.

9. Select the Read permission level, as shown in Figure 10-15.

10. Click OK.

How It Works

When you disconnect from the permissions of the site, all rights and users are copied to the permissions scheme for the Announcements list. Therefore, you must edit the rights of each group and user so that they can only read items. You selected every group and changed their rights to Read-Only, but then deselected the Approvers group so that its members could edit content. Note that the Site Owners group or any other group with Full Control to the site can still add content, and you cannot remove this group from a specific list or library.

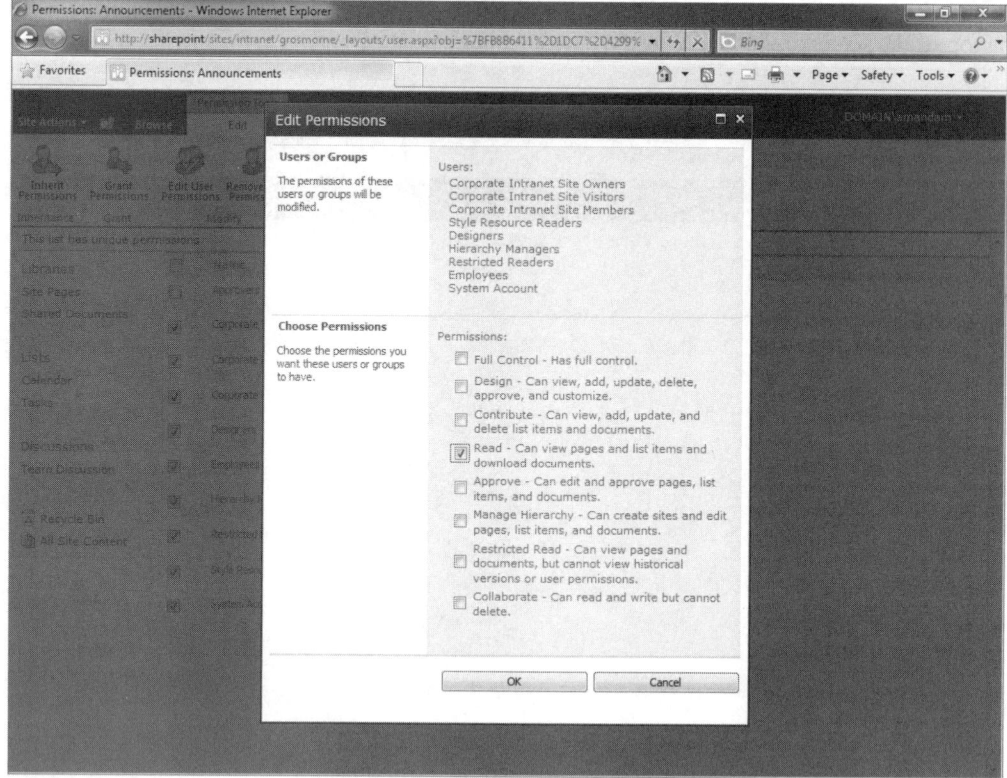

FIGURE 10-15

Item-Level Access

By default, access to an individual list item is inherited from the list or library in which it resides. However, you may need to better define this. For example, storing a policies and procedures document within a team's shared documents library means anyone can contribute to it and add contents; however, for legal reasons, only certain managers should have the right to edit it. You can restrict access to one document, even if it resides in a list or library to which everyone has access, as shown in the next Try It Out. In a second Try It Out, you learn how to limit access to a list so that users may only view or edit items that they have created themselves.

TRY IT OUT Assign Unique Permissions to a Document

In this Try It Out, you create a new document and restrict the rights so that only members of the Approvers group have the access to edit the document.

1. From the main page of the team site, select Shared Documents from the Quick Launch bar.
2. Click the New Document option from the Document tab of the Ribbon.
3. Save the document with a filename of **Team Policies and Procedures.docx.**

4. Hover over the document with your mouse and select the Manage Permissions item from the drop-down menu, as shown in Figure 10-16.

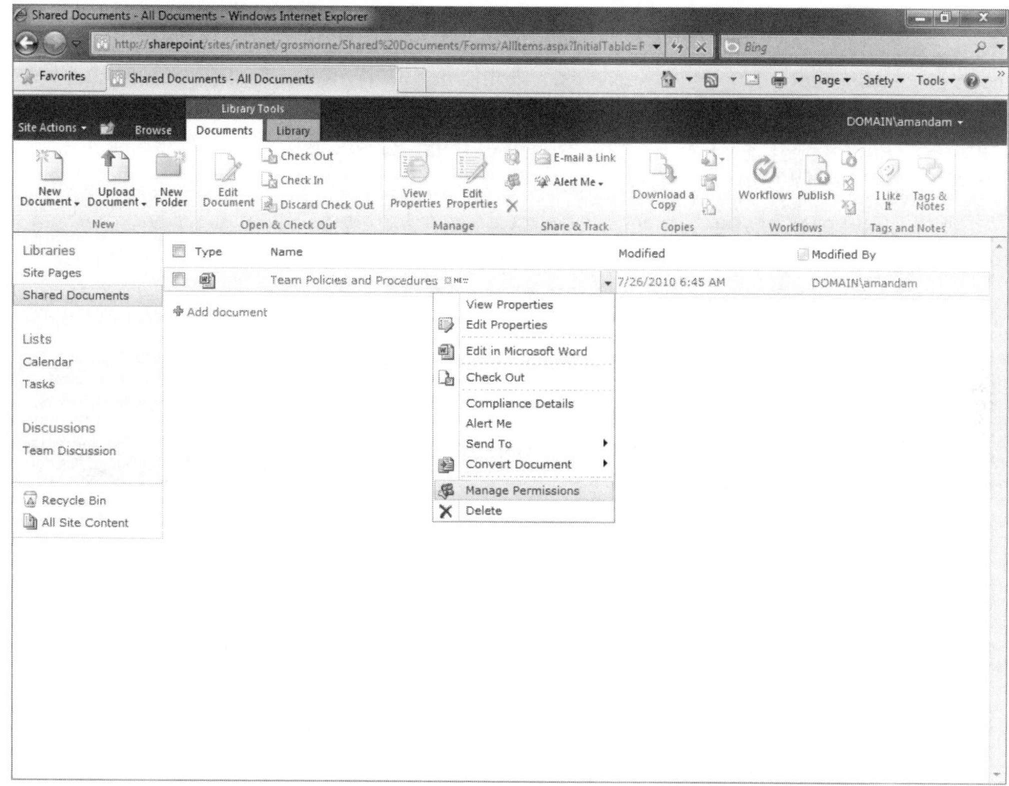

FIGURE 10-16

5. The Manage Permissions page for the document appears. Select the Stop Inheriting Permissions option from the Ribbon. The page will refresh and a yellow message bar will appear at the top of the screen indicating that the site document has unique permissions.

How It Works

In this example, you created a new document that had slightly different requirements over all other documents in the library. Rather than place it in a unique location, it's far more effective to manage the rights of this document independently of the library and make the required changes on an item-by-item basis.

NOTE *While you just learned the steps for securing items individually in your environment, you should always confirm the necessity of such configurations as the more uniquely secured items that exist within your environment, the higher degree of management and control that will be required to support them. It is highly recommended that you avoid uniquely secured items unless absolutely required by your business scenario.*

TRY IT OUT Customize Item-Level Access Rights on a List

You can uniquely apply permissions to documents or list items in the same way as in the last Try It Out. However, lists also have a unique function that allows for a site manager to determine if users can view or edit their own items or the items of others. For example, it may be helpful to allow team members to view each other's appointments. However, a user should not be allowed to edit appointments belonging to a coworker. In the following example, you modify the default settings of the Calendar list so that users can view, but not edit, a coworker's items. You can do this on SharePoint lists but not with documents stored within document libraries.

1. From the main page of your project site, select Calendar from the side navigation.
2. Select List Settings from the Calendar tab of the Ribbon.
3. Select Advanced Settings. The Advanced Settings page for the list will appear as shown in Figure 10-17.

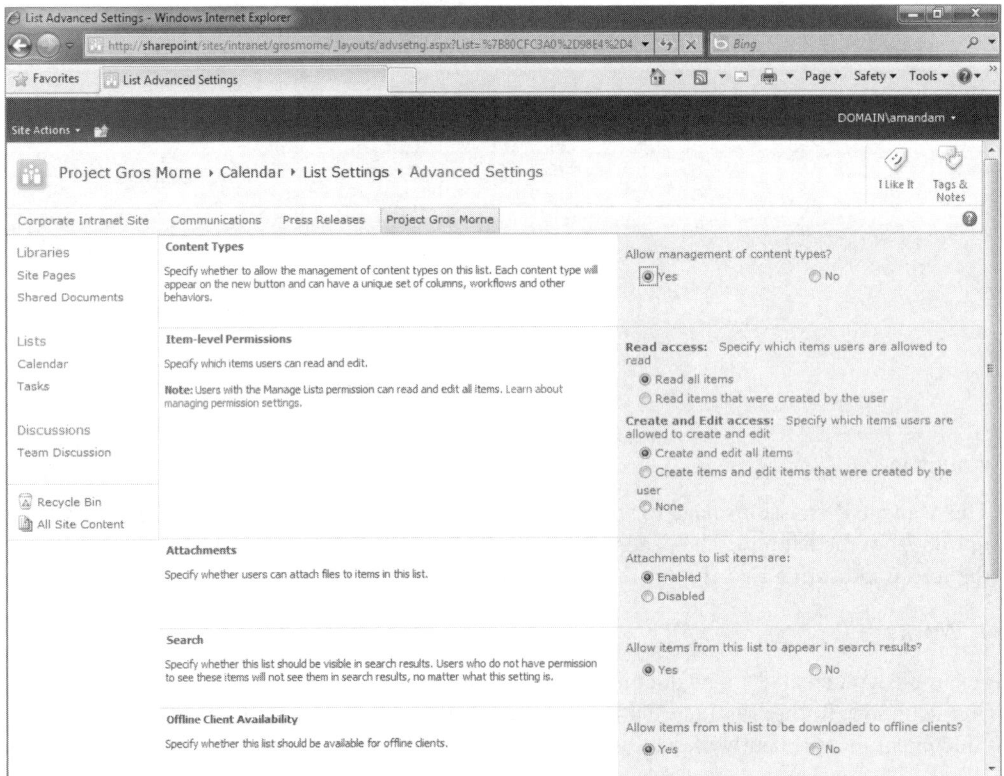

FIGURE 10-17

4. In the Item-level Permissions section, for Read access, keep the default value that users can Read all items.
5. In the Item-level Permissions section, for Create and Edit access, select the option that users can Create items and edit items that were created by the user.
6. Click OK.

UNDERSTANDING USER PROFILES

SharePoint Server has a special database that can store information about the users of the system, called the *user profile database*. This database contains properties and metadata about each user of the system in a very similar manner to that in which you can store information describing a document in a document library. User profile information is useful for storing contact information and biographies of the different users of the system for information-sharing purposes, but you can also use it for more advanced purposes, such as content targeting and personalization via audiences (discussed in a later section of this chapter).

While SharePoint can import profiles from other sources, this chapter assumes that Active Directory is your primary profile source because it is the most common identity store for organizations using this application. SharePoint maps user profile properties to common profile properties from Active Directory, including Name, Email Address, Phone Number, Manager, and Address. SharePoint can also import custom profile properties such as skills, languages, and employee ID.

In addition to importing information from Active Directory, SharePoint can obtain user information from the following sources that can augment user profiles with additional information:

- Other LDAP servers
- Business applications (through Business Connectivity Services)
- User-defined properties

Adding and Updating User Profiles

User profiles are not required for an organization to implement SharePoint; however, they allow you to personalize information, including profile information to share with coworkers. For example, each SharePoint user can create a My Site, where he or she can store personal or shared files, view organizational content, write a personal weblog, and maintain his or her own profile properties. You can create a personal site by selecting the My Site link from the personalization menu of any page or site in the portal, as shown in Figure 10-18.

Each My Site has an area known as My Profile, where users can share information about themselves. By sharing more details on personal sites and profiles, workers can get to know each other better, which helps in situations where employees work for the same company but in different buildings.

From the Public Profile page, you can view a variety of information about an employee including:

- An image of the employee
- Contact information
- Documents that the employee has shared
- Information on who the employee reports to and any other employees who report to them
- Things that the employee has in common with you based on profile properties such as languages, skills, or schools
- Tags and Notes that the user has created
- Colleagues

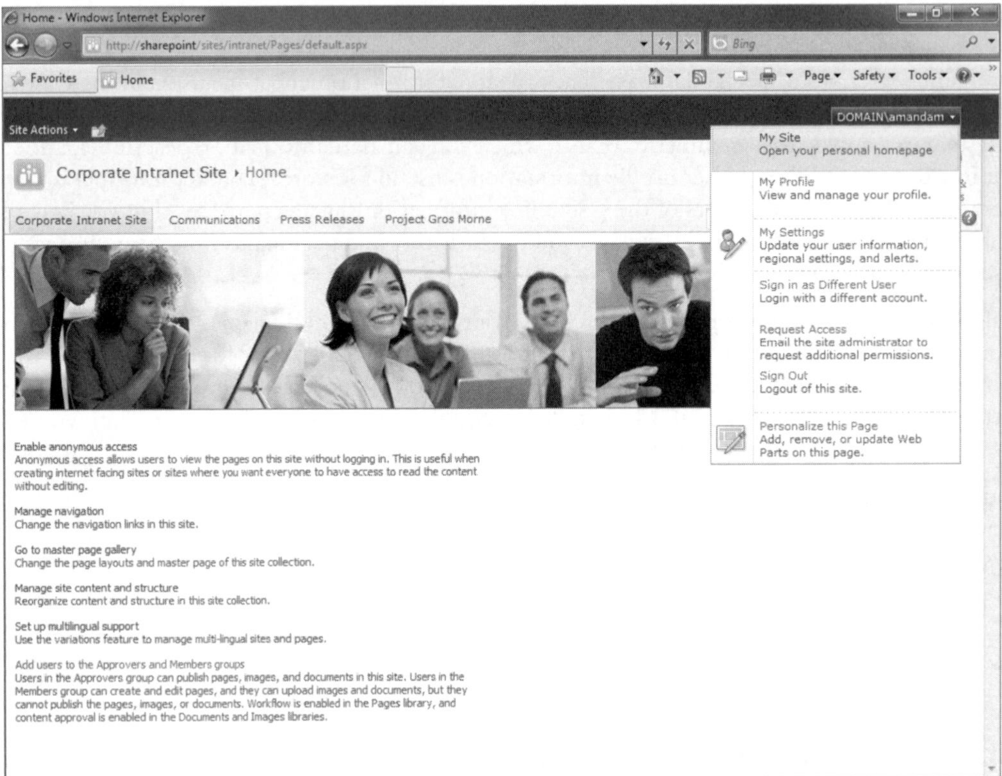

FIGURE 10-18

An example of a public profile page is shown below in Figure 10-19.

Because profile properties are indexed and searchable, you can search for a specific property and find a list of people who have that property assigned to them. For example, if you are a manager looking for a computer programmer with ASP.NET experience to build a custom web part for your SharePoint site, you can use the People search scope to search for ASP.NET to receive a list of people in your organization who have that skill. When you click their names, you are redirected to their personal site, where you can find out who their manager is (in case you want to contact the manager) and what previous projects the employees have worked on.

Although you can import some profile properties from primary membership systems such as Active Directory, users can update others themselves via their My Site. This helps keep information up to date and relevant. The server administrator decides what profile properties a user can update. A user can also select from the following choices on who can view information that is stored in specific properties:

- Everyone
- My Colleagues
- My Team
- My Manager
- Only Me

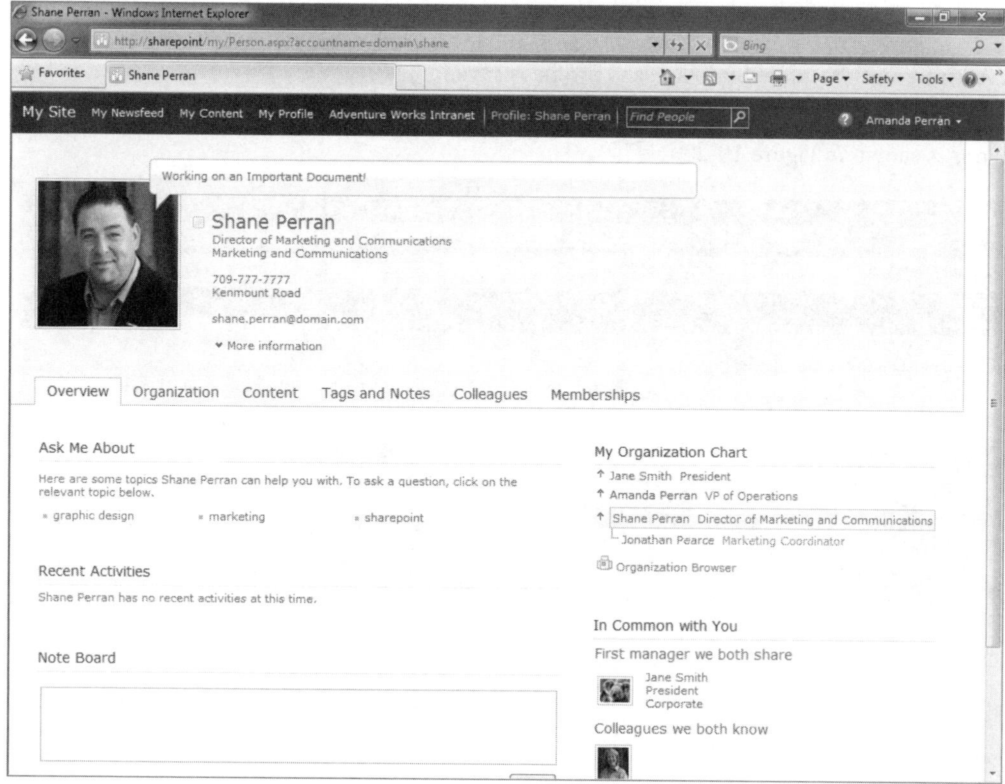

FIGURE 10-19

For example, something such as skills or schools would be shared with Everyone, while a home phone number would only be viewable by a manager. The following Try It Outs illustrate how users can update their own profile properties via their personal site. In the event you have a specific detail that you want a user to provide on the site, for example, specific professional experience, certification, or attended business seminars, you can add a new user profile property.

Many of the remaining exercises of this chapter are based on the assumption that you are working in a SharePoint Environment where the User Profile Server Application has been configured for use. Please confirm with your system administrator that this has been configured properly. While this topic is considered outside the scope of this book, details related to the configuration of this Service Application are available here: `http://technet.microsoft.com/en-us/library/ee721050.aspx`

TRY IT OUT Update a User Profile

In this Try It Out, you update all profile properties that you have access to edit, noting that you cannot edit some profile properties such as your manager or your account name. Generally, the information that you cannot edit is imported from a central directory or application dedicated to storing such information.

Updating profile properties is only a small fraction of what you can do from your personal site, but it's a great way to familiarize yourself with your personal site and will keep your personal information up to date. All information entered into a user's profile is saved.

1. From the home page of your corporate site, click the My Profile link from the Personalization menu, as shown in Figure 10-20.

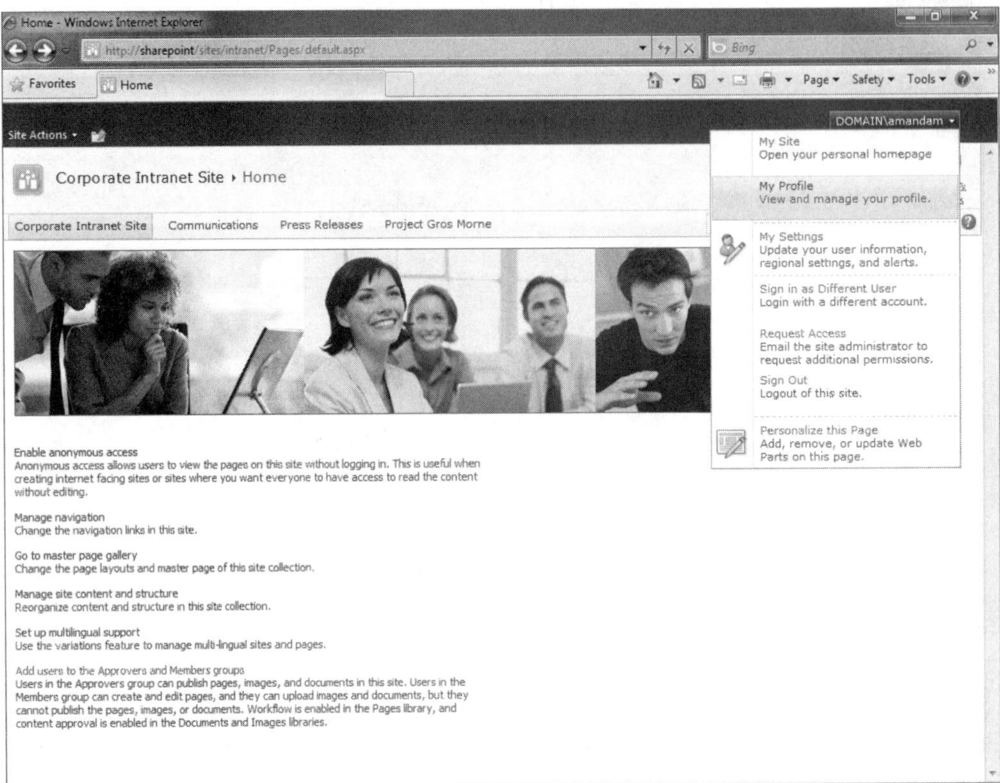

FIGURE 10-20

2. Select the Edit My Profile link. The Edit Profile page will appear.
3. Complete all missing information in your personal profile.
4. For the Home Phone field, change the Show to drop-down value to My Manager.
5. Click Save and Close.

TRY IT OUT Add a New User Profile Property

In the last Try It Out, you updated common profile properties. In addition to those properties, you can add new profile properties that users can update on their own. For example, you can add a property to allow users to specify what certifications they have attained, as the following steps show. Because users may have more than one certification, you should allow for multiple values. Because not every user may want to specify that information, you can make it optional.

1. From the main page of the Central Administration site, select the Manage service applications link.
2. Select the User Profile Service Application item from the listing, as shown in Figure 10-21, and click the Manage option from the Ribbon. You will be redirected to the Manage Profile Service page.

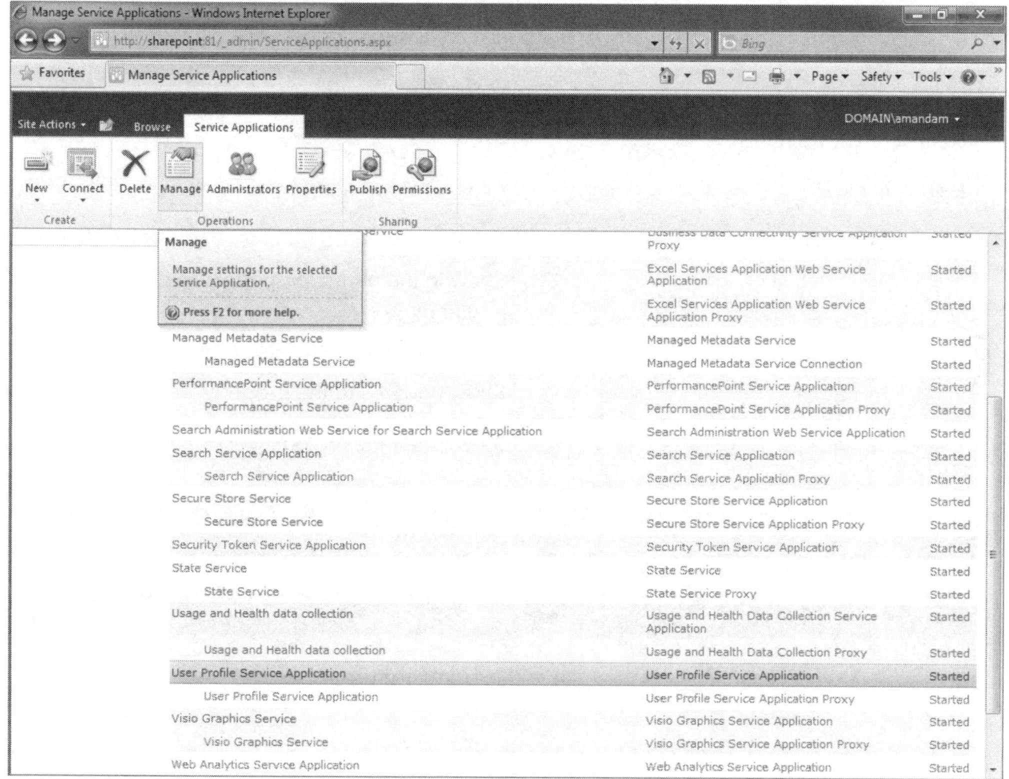

FIGURE 10-21

3. Select the Manage User Properties link.
4. Select the New Property option. The Add User Profile Property page will appear, as shown in Figure 10-22.
5. Complete the information as follows:

ITEM	VALUE
Name	Certifications
Display Name	Certifications
Type	String (MultiValue)
Length	25
Multivalue Separator	Comma: A,B,C,...

continues

(continued)

ITEM	VALUE
Sub-type of Profile	Default User Profile Subtype
Description	List any professional certifications you have received
Policy Settings	Optional
Default Privacy Setting	Everyone
Edit Settings	Allow users to edit values for this property
Display Settings	Select these three options: Show in the profile properties section of the user's profile page Show on the Edit Details page Show updates to the property in newsfeed
Search Settings	Select the Indexed box

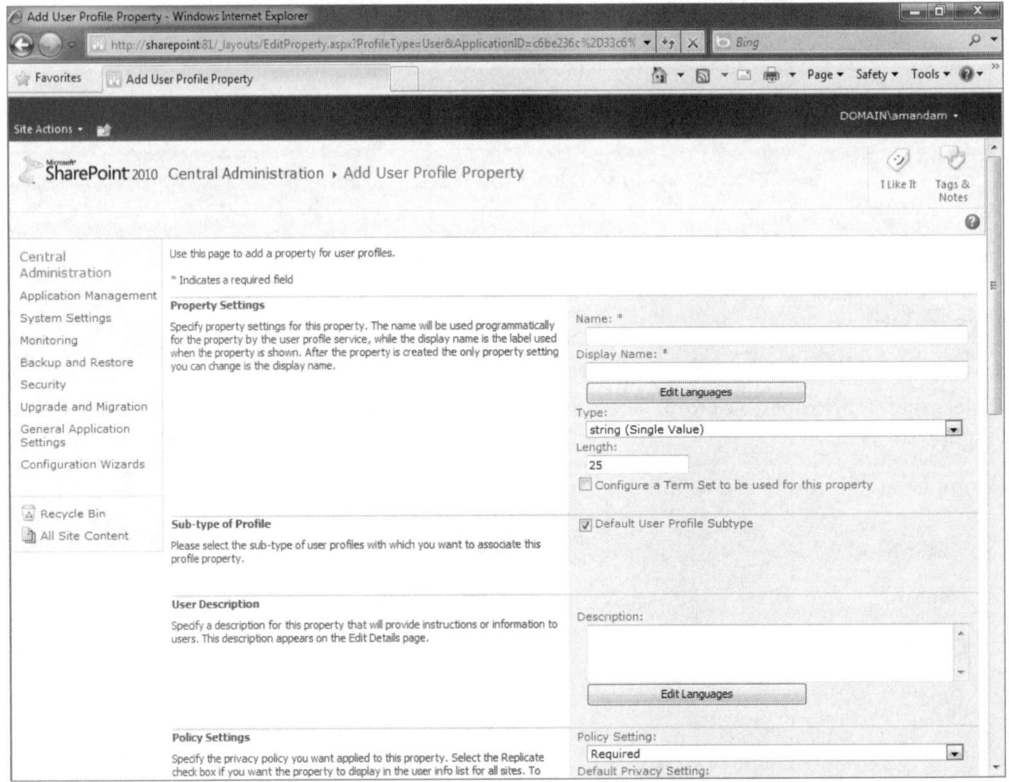

FIGURE 10-22

6. Click OK.
7. Click the My Profile link from Personalization menu.
8. Select the Edit My Profile link.
9. Scroll to the bottom until you see the custom property you created for Certifications. Update this with any certifications you have attained, and click the Save & Close button.

How It Works

In this Try It Out, you specified that the property should be indexed because this may be a value for which someone might want to search. For example, when a business manager prepares to launch a major new project for an upcoming product launch, she may want to search for someone who has a project management certification such as PMP. By searching for this item, she can find employees with this qualification and review their experience on past projects to discover who might be a perfect match to manage this new project.

Configuring Profile Updates

You import user profiles into SharePoint on a scheduled basis and can do so from single or multiple sources. In cases where you are importing profile information from more than one database, you must have a master connection, which is either Active Directory or another LDAP server and a secondary connection, which is a Business Connectivity Services application.

You configure connection synchronization settings from the Manage Profile Service page. You can access this site from the Manage Service Applications page by selecting the User Profile Service Application and clicking the Manage button from the Ribbon.

If no synchronization connection exists, you must create a new connection under the Configure Synchronization Connections link, as shown in Figure 10-23.

From the Manage User Permissions section, you may specify permissions for a variety of personalization services, such as:

- Create personal site
- Use personal features
- Use social features

WORKING WITH AUDIENCES

An *audience* is a special group to which content is targeted so that only people in that audience see it. A user becomes a part of an audience based on profile properties or membership to a distribution list or SharePoint site. Audience content targeting should not be confused with access. Just because users cannot see an item does not necessarily mean that they do not have access to the item. An audience may exist for members of an organization that work out of a certain region such as

Canada. Therefore, if you assign the audience to an announcement related to a special event taking place at the Canadian office, it will be seen only by members of that audience. The following sections give some examples of how you can use audiences.

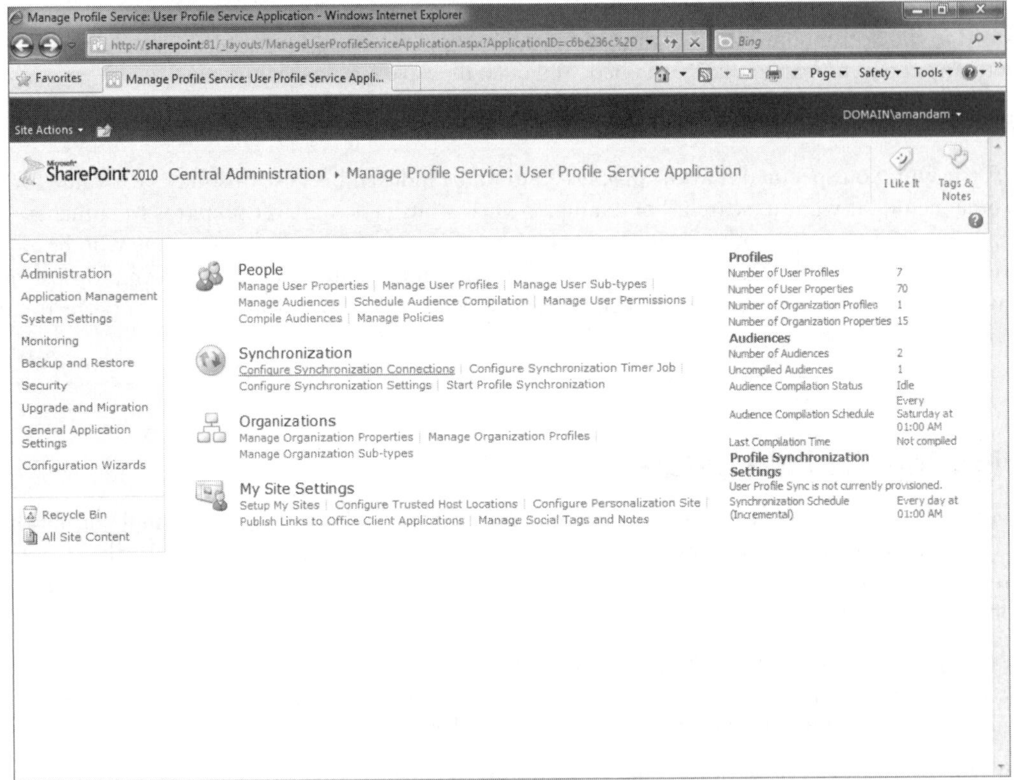

FIGURE 10-23

You can configure certain web parts such as the Content Query web part, discussed in Chapter 7, to support audience filtering. This means that when you display multiple items in a web part, users will only see those that are targeted to them. Figures 10-24 and 10-25 demonstrate examples of filtering list information by audience via a Content Query web part. Figure 10-24 is what the team site main page looks like to a member of the sales team audience, who can view the Sales Strategy document because it's targeted to their audience. Figure 10-25 shows the same site page as viewed by someone who is not a member of the sales team audience. Notice the user does not see the Sales Strategy document even though it exists in the library.

If the user who isn't in the sales team audience were to click the Shared Documents library, he or she could still see the document listed in the view, as shown in Figure 10-26. This is because the Content Query web part filters items so that they are only displayed to targeted audiences and the standard list web parts are not. All web parts, however, allow you to target the contents of an entire web part to an audience.

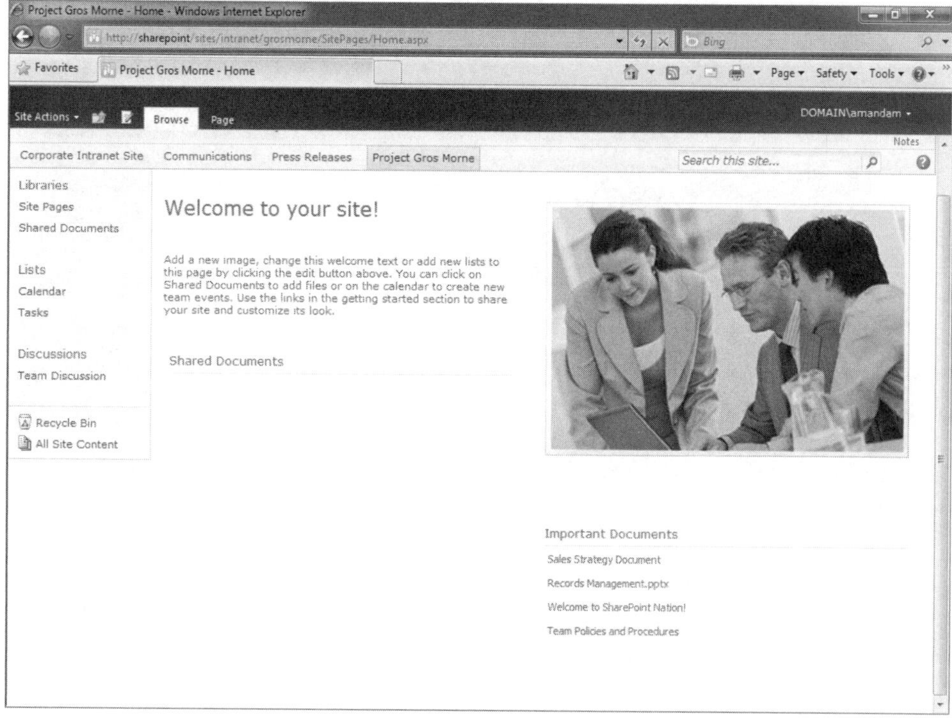

FIGURE 10-24

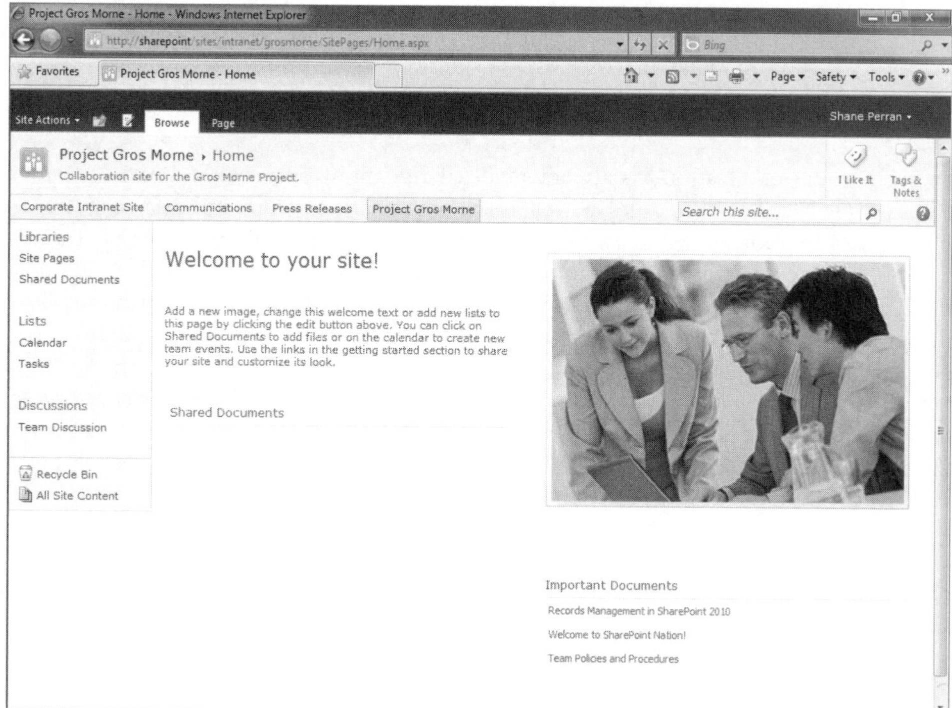

FIGURE 10-25

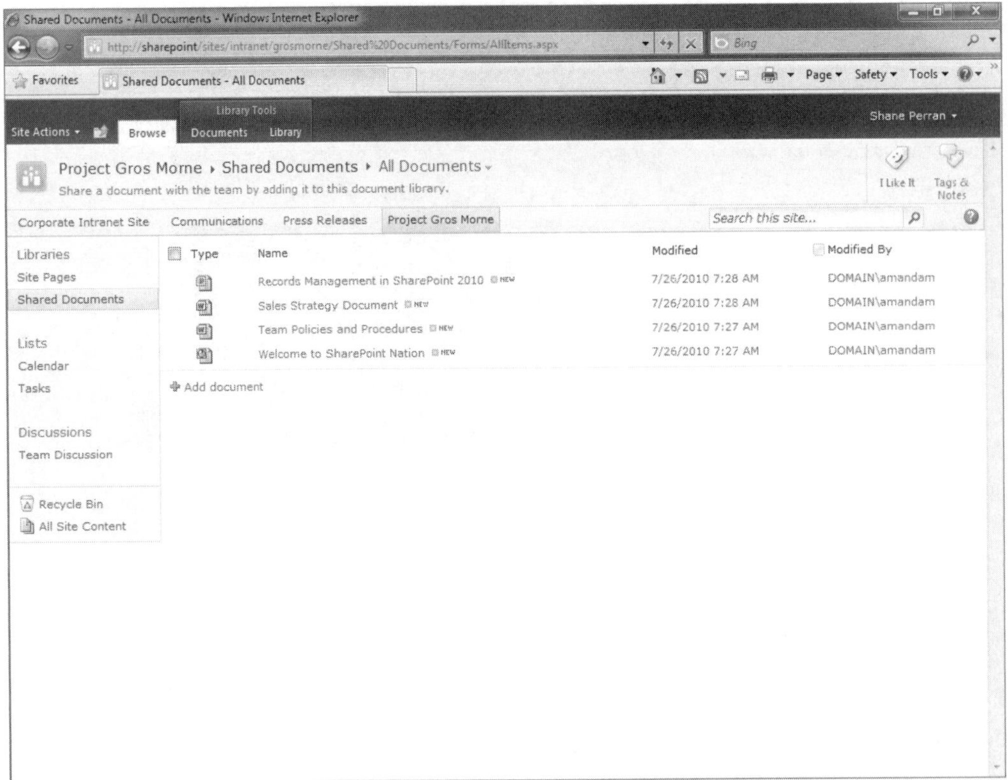

FIGURE 10-26

Membership-Based Audiences

More than likely, your organization has already made significant investments in Active Directory, which groups people based on their roles as well as the organization's communication requirements. So instead of creating audiences, which you need to manage and maintain as an extra layer in the SharePoint environment, you can take advantage of existing objects, such as Windows Distribution Lists or Security Groups. In fact, your organization probably has a distribution list on your Exchange mail server for the sales team that keeps them informed of product updates and sales promotions. You can use the distribution list as an audience and target content from the SharePoint environment directly to the audience's members. As announcements are added to the corporate portal, the audience can see and, thus, view the latest news as soon as they log on. If the organization is fairly busy and generates numerous new announcements each day, the use of audiences helps users "separate the wheat from the chaff."

The next two Try It Outs show you the process of managing a membership-based audience. The first Try It Out shows you how to target an item to a distribution list so your audience can keep up to date on new promotions and other information via a central portal page. This is useful for sales teams, who, because they travel and work remotely, have limited time and need to view content directly related to them. The next Try It Out shows you how to target specific list items, documents, or even entire web part content to an audience by creating audiences based on membership to SharePoint site groups.

TRY IT OUT Targeting a List Item to an Audience

You can target specific news and announcements to an audience. This allows members to keep up to date on new promotions and sales tactics when they visit a central portal page that contains a web part that supports the use of audiences. Other team members cannot view the announcement in this example when they visit the same page, although they still have access rights to view it if they want to. This page may contain updates for many other groups and divisions, so by effectively using audiences to target content to users based on their roles, you help ensure that content is limited to only what is relevant to users.

1. From the main page of your project site, select the View All Site Content item from the Site Actions menu.
2. Select the Announcements list.
3. Select List Settings from the List tab of the Ribbon.
4. Select Audience Targeting Settings. You will be redirected to the Modify List Audience Targeting Settings page.
5. Check the checkbox to Enable Audience Targeting.
6. Click OK.
7. Click the Announcements link from the breadcrumb navigation trail.
8. Click the Add new announcement link.
9. Enter the following information into the list item form:

COLUMN	VALUE
Title	New Sales Promotion Launched
Body	A new sales promotion has been launched that will offer customers up to 50% off the pricing of last year's product line. For more information, please contact your regional director's head office.
Expires	Select a date one month from the current date.

10. For the Target Audiences column, select the Browse button. The Select Audiences dialog appears, as shown in Figure 10-27.

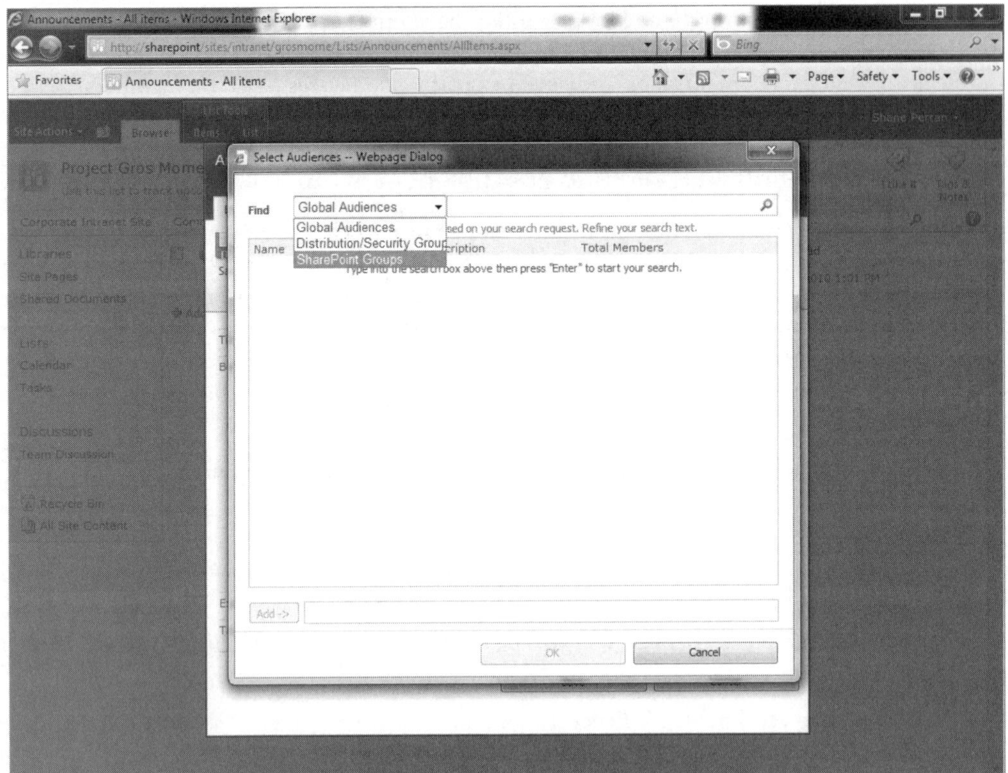

FIGURE 10-27

11. Search for and select the Approvers group from the SharePoint Groups and click the Add button.
12. Click OK to complete your audience selection.
13. Click Save to save the announcement to the list.

How It Works

Once you have configured audiences for the list, you can add a Content Query web part to the main page of your team site and query the announcements list using the method described in Chapter 7. You can then select the option to apply audience filtering, as shown in Figure 10-28.

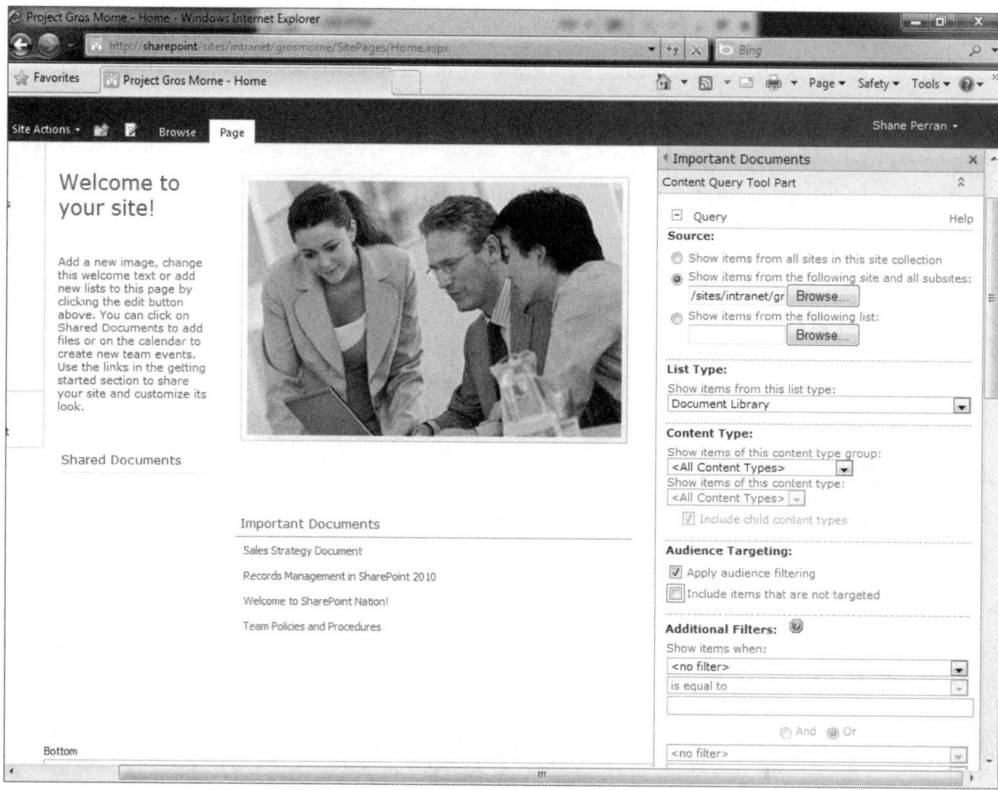

FIGURE 10-28

TRY IT OUT Target a Web Part to an Audience

You can target specific list items, documents, or even entire web part content to an audience. In this example, you target a list web part that displays items that are pending approval to the SharePoint site group responsible for approving content. If you add the web part to the main page with a listing of all pending items as the default view, Approvers are more likely to respond in a timely manner. An example of this is a web part on the main page of a site that highlights items pending approval. Because these items are relevant only to members of the Approvers group, you select this audience on the web part to ensure that only they can see the web part on the main page. While other team members can still access the documents, no action is required from them, so the web part would only be a distraction.

1. From the main page of your project site, select Shared Documents from the side navigation.
2. Select Library Settings from the Library tab of the Ribbon. You are redirected to the settings page for the document library.
3. Select Versioning Settings. You are redirected to the library's Version History Settings page.
4. Select Yes for Require Content Approval for Submitted Items.
5. Click OK.
6. Return to the main page of your site by clicking the Team Site link in the navigational breadcrumb trail.
7. Select Edit Page from the Site Actions menu.
8. Add the Shared Documents web part to the page using the method described in Chapter 7.
9. Select the Shared Documents web part, and click the Web Part Tools tab from the Ribbon.
10. Select the Web Part Properties option from the menu.
11. Change the selected view to the Approve/Reject Items view. You may receive a pop-up window warning that you may lose changes made to the view. Click OK to continue.
12. Expand the Advanced properties pane.
13. From the Target Audiences field at the very bottom of the web part pane, select the Browse button. The Select Audience dialog box appears, as shown in Figure 10-29.

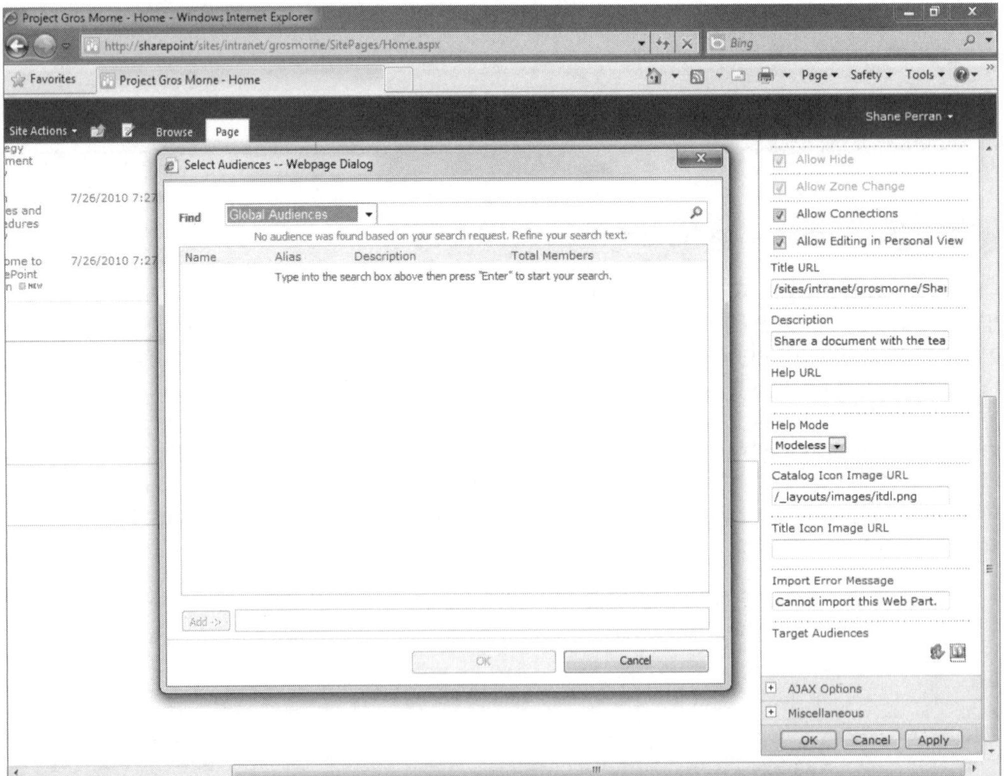

FIGURE 10-29

14. Select SharePoint Groups from the Find drop-down, enter **Approve** in the search box and click the Search icon to the right of the box that resembles a magnifying glass.
15. Select the Approvers group.
16. Click Add.
17. Click OK on the Audience selection window.
18. Click Apply, and then click OK on the web part.
19. Click Exit Edit Mode on the main page.

How It Works

In this Try It Out, the pending status of documents is of no interest to team members other than the Approvers group. To other members, it might be distracting and take up valuable real estate. Sometimes by effectively using audiences on web parts, you can fit a greater deal of content on a page, yet avoid unnecessary clutter on each user's screen by limiting the number of web parts he or she sees.

Profile Property-Based Audiences

All examples of the audience creation process so far have been based on either Active Directory or SharePoint-based groups. This chapter now discusses how audiences are created based on properties from the user profiles. When you consider that the profile can contain information not only from Active Directory (or another LDAP server) but also from other business applications, such as a human resources or financial database, you can see that the possibilities for how specifically you can target content are endless. By using personal profile properties, you can make audiences very detailed to the point of defining audiences for specific topics. For example, you can create a profile property called News and Promotions that has a value list from which users can select via their profile to identify what products they want to receive promotional updates on.

In the following example, you see how to create an audience based on the property you created earlier in the chapter for certifications in the Try It Out "Adding a New User Profile Property." If you recall, this field gives users a place to update their own certifications from their My Site. However, it is equally as possible for you to automatically update this profile property from an external system, such as Active Directory or a central human resources database.

TRY IT OUT Create an Audience Based on User Profile Information

In this Try It Out, you create a rules-based audience that checks the certifications profile property and compiles the members who have a project management certification. Because this is an audience where you expect membership changes over time, you will base membership on a profile property that you know users will keep up to date on their own, rather than manually identifying and updating membership within a specific Active Directory group, distribution list, or site group.

1. From the main page of the Central Administration site, select the Manage service applications link.
2. Select the User Profile Service Application item from the listing, and click the Manage option from the Ribbon. You will be redirected to the Manage Profile Service page.

3. Select the Manage Audiences link.
4. Select the New Audience button from the toolbar. You will be redirected to the Create Audience page, as shown in Figure 10-30.

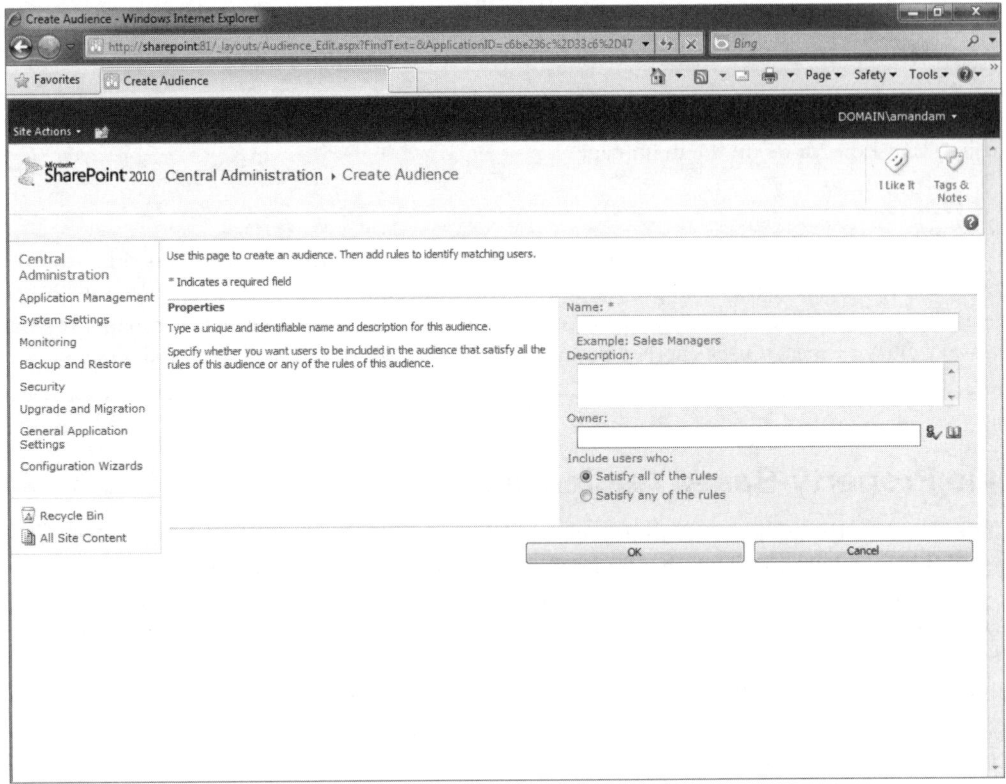

FIGURE 10-30

5. Enter a name for the audience. This example uses **Certified Project Managers.**
6. Enter a description for the audience. For this example, enter the following:

   This is an audience that represents all employees who have attained a project management professional certification.

7. Enter your own name for the owner of the audience.
8. Select the option to include users who satisfy any of the rules.
9. Click OK. The Add Audience Rule window appears, as shown in Figure 10-31.
10. Because this audience is based on a user property, select Property for Operand.
11. Select the Certifications profile property from drop-down.
12. Select Contains from the Operator selection box.
13. Enter **PMP** for value.
14. Click OK. You will be returned to the View Audience Properties page.

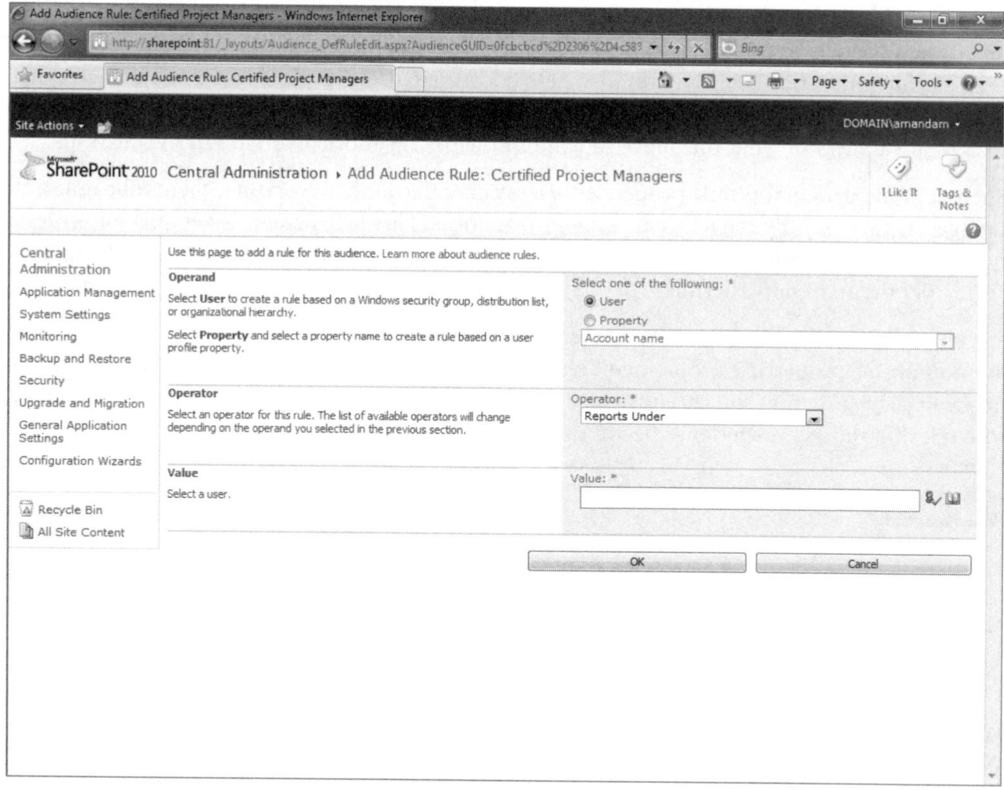

FIGURE 10-31

15. Click the Compile Audience link to complete the process. Any users who have completed their user profiles and included PMP as a certification will now be placed within the new audience. Each time the audience compiles, it will query all profiles and add or remove members based on the changes made since the last update.`

SUMMARY

This chapter discussed two important concepts related to information management: user access and personalization. User access is the way you can control who can view, edit, or create content in a SharePoint environment. You can define access on the site level, document library, or list level through permission levels and site groups. For lists, you can also define rules for what content users can read or edit at the item level.

As a general rule, you should use existing Active Directory groups and objects when you assign permissions to specific roles in a SharePoint group. In most organizations, Active Directory is kept up to date as employees change positions, leave, or are hired. By creating a relationship between Active Directory and SharePoint site groups, you automatically keep user membership current without relying on manual updates.

Personalization in SharePoint is delivered via functions such as user profiles, audiences, and My Sites. When you use personalization features, users are only exposed to content that is relevant to them. Profile properties and My Sites also help encourage users to learn more about each other and interact with one another. In many organizations, users do not connect with one another because of a lack of awareness of what they have in common with one another or who has what skills.

When defining personal profile properties, users can determine if everyone, their colleagues, their manager, teams, or only the user can view information. This helps create a network of professional and personal information sharing that is controlled and secure so that users feel comfortable sharing specific details and know that these details will only be shared with the appropriate audience.

This chapter also discussed how you can create audiences to identify groups of users who share common profile properties, group memberships, or characteristics. Once an audience is created, content from the SharePoint site can be targeted at them. The more audiences are used for content, the more relevant the user experience becomes.

EXERCISES

1. Explain the difference between a SharePoint site group and an audience.
2. True or false: By targeting content to users, you can ensure that only the right people have access to view items.
3. What are the three different types of audiences that you can create?
4. What are the different levels of access that you can control in SharePoint?
5. Explain from what source you can import user profile information.

▶ WHAT YOU LEARNED IN THIS CHAPTER

TOPIC	KEY CONCEPTS
What is a SharePoint Group?	A SharePoint group is a role defined to which users can be added. These groups can then be assigned specific rights and permissions to different elements within SharePoint.
What is a Permission level?	A permission level is a set of rights that can be assigned to a user or group in SharePoint.
What is an Audience?	An audience is a group of people that share common characteristics. Content or web parts may be targeted at specific audiences so that when members of that audience view a page, the content will be visible to them but not to users that are not members of the audience. This helps create a relevant user experience for site members as they only see information that has been targeted to their role.

11

Personalization and Social Networking

WHAT YOU WILL LEARN IN THIS CHAPTER:

- Some concepts regarding personalization and social networking, as well as how they can be beneficial in an organization
- All of the aspects of SharePoint My Sites functionality with examples
- The concepts of tagging, note boards, and ratings, as well as the new out-of-the-box web parts that are related to personalization features
- The capabilities of blogs and wikis with a side-by-side comparison
- The concept of targeting content to audiences, including the kinds of content that can be targeted, as well as how existing groups can be used as audiences

The term Web 2.0 represents a fundamental change in the Internet in the past 10 years or so, in the way we interact with applications, content, and other people. The web is now a platform for promoting a collective intelligence, and so is SharePoint 2010. The new methods of content creation and participation, such as blogs, tagging, and ratings, involve everyone in the enterprise in deeper and more meaningful ways.

In this chapter, you will learn how to make the most of the social networking tools that exist in SharePoint and how they apply to you. Also, you will be provided with several walk-through scenarios to try out.

PERSONALIZATION OVERVIEW

Personalization and social networking tools are a powerful thing to put in the hands of business users. This chapter contains information related to how to work with the new social computing features, but before we get into the technical details, what is the big picture? In the grand scheme of things, what does Web 2.0 and social computing/networking mean to the company?

Engage People

Inherently, SharePoint is a collaboration platform. You are not simply feeding read-only information to people, you are giving them their own locations to upload and edit team and project documents and much more. Engaging employees in SharePoint has been taken to a new level in SharePoint 2010. Notes, tags, and ratings can now be quickly added to content, which allows people to know that they have a hand in the creation and categorization of it. Each individual is now helping the online community in the organization by specifying which content they think has the greatest relevance and value.

Improve the Search Experience

Searching helps us find people and aggregate information. The rich and interactive search experience in SharePoint creates an environment where people can find and engage each other. When participation is encouraged, this actually improves search results, because the tags and ratings have an effect on the contents' search result ranking. Information workers typically spend a large part of their day searching for content. Getting the business community involved in tagging will shorten the amount of time that is spent searching, thus increasing company efficiency and productivity.

Knowledge Mining

Knowledge mining is the concept of using the tags inside of user profiles to mine for areas of expertise in the organization. People are encouraged to fill out their own profile information with their skills and interests, which makes experts easier to find. For example, if a manager would like to put together a team for a new project to create a company policy system, a people search for "policies" would provide a list of potential additions to the team.

The Informal Organization

In social computing, there's an organic element of self-organization, also known as a user-generated taxonomy, or folksonomy. This transcends the traditional organizational hierarchy. This informal organization lacks the rigidity of an ineffective, management-imposed organizational tree. When people in the organization come to an understanding as to the power of the social computing tools in SharePoint 2010, they will realize how much their contributions as individuals have shaped the collective information.

UNDERSTANDING MY SITES

When My Sites have been set up, each user in the organization gets their own landing page of SharePoint goings-on. This hub is where a list of the recent activities of colleagues is displayed; users can update their own personal information and store personal or shared files. My Site consists of My Newsfeed, My Content, and My Profile.

My Profile

The My Profile page is where other people can read all about you. This page contains information about skills, projects you've worked on, ways to contact you, and a list of what you've been doing in SharePoint. Figure 11-1 shows the main page of My Profile.

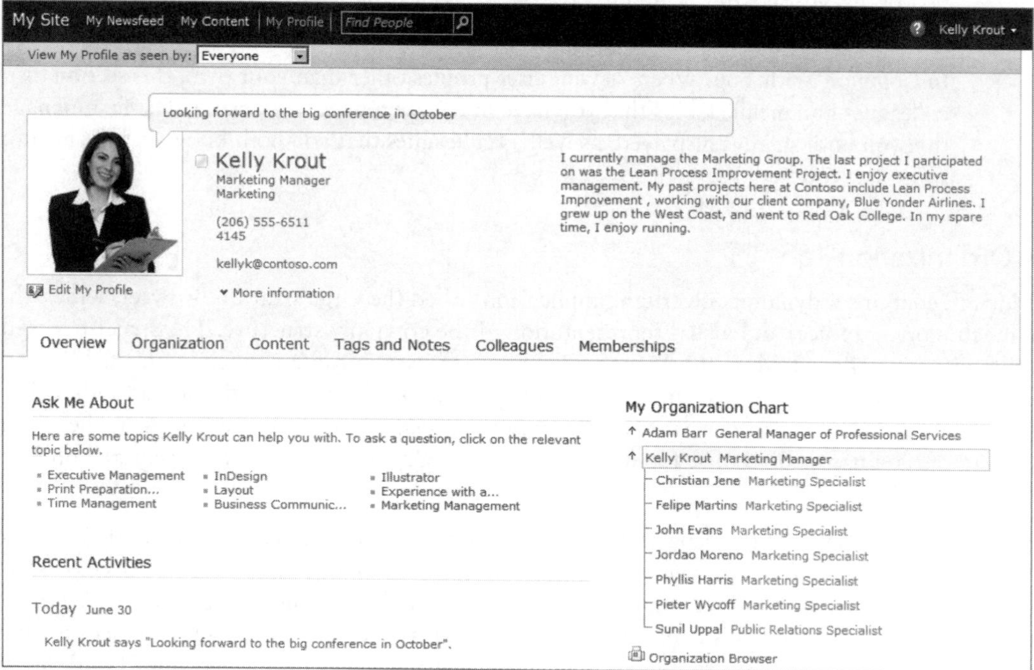

FIGURE 11-1

In the preceding example, when Kelly Krout views her own profile, this is what she sees. The top portion of the page contains basic information about how she can be contacted. SharePoint 2010 now contains status updates, also known as microblogging. The text above Kelly's name that states "Looking forward to the big conference in October" is her current status. Users can each type their own current status here, in order to quickly let others know what they are up to. This same microblogging concept may be familiar as "Status updates" on Facebook, and as "tweets" on Twitter.

The Overview Tab

The following is a list of web parts that are displayed on the Overview tab on the My Site profile.

- **Ask Me About:** These are links to topics that you want to encourage people to ask you about. When a link is clicked, such as Time Management in Figure 11-1, text is added to a new note in the Note Board on the page "Question on Time Management."
- **Recent Activities:** This is a list of your most recent activities in SharePoint. Each activity contains a link to the item, such as a document that was tagged or rated.
- **My Organization Chart:** The organization chart is a very simple, text version of the organization, including names and job titles. Click anyone's name to see their profile.
- **Note Board:** The Note Board is a location where people can publicly post notes. In the context of the My Site, this is used to post quick notes as public messages to the owner of the site. Individuals receive email messages when others post notes to their note boards.
- **In Common With You:** When viewing user profiles other than your own, this section displays colleagues and memberships that you have in common with that person. The first manager that you both share is displayed, as well as colleagues that you both know and the memberships that you both share.

The Organization Tab

This tab contains a dynamic Silverlight application called the Organization Browser, which shows a much more graphical and visual representation of the company structure. The structure itself is built automatically, based on the Manager field in each user's profile. Typically, this field is carried over to SharePoint from Active Directory (or other directory services), and is a read-only field in SharePoint profiles. The information in this organizational tree is only as accurate as the manager data in the company's directory. Figure 11-2 shows the Organization Browser, centered on Kelly Krout.

Each person's name, job title, department, and About Me information is displayed in their square. When you click from person to person in this application, the chart dynamically moves to center around the person clicked. Once someone is centered on the screen, click the person's name to see their profile page. To view this application in all its magnificence, the Silverlight browser plugin needs to be installed on client computers. Those without Silverlight should click the HTML View link at the bottom-left corner of the page.

The Content Tab

This tab is a trimmed down version of your own My Content site. Only public content is available here. By default, your blog site, Shared Documents, and Shared Pictures are visible to anyone. To learn more about the permissions settings involved in shared versus public files, read Chapter 10. Figure 11-3 shows Kelly's Content tab when viewed by someone else.

FIGURE 11-2

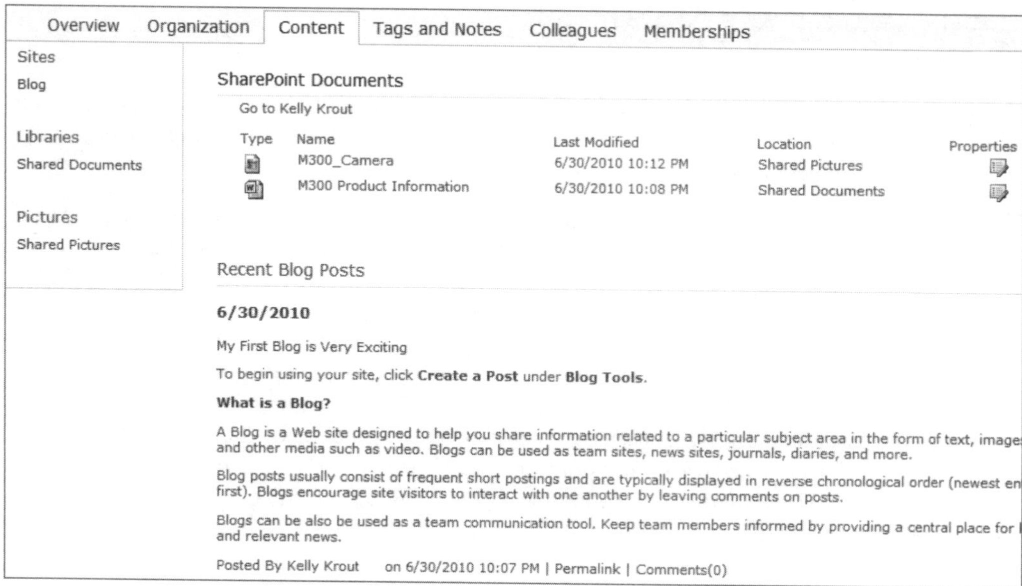

FIGURE 11-3

The Tags and Notes Tab

Your social activities within SharePoint are logged and listed on the Tags and Notes tab. Others who are interested in your work can take a look at what you have done to participate in the tagging of information, and they can see your opinions as note board notes. This tab is also utilized by each person to manage his or her own stream of activity. When viewing your own Tags and Notes tab, you will see that each item has a Delete button next to it, and you also have the ability to switch public items to private. Private items are only visible to you. Figure 11-4 shows this tab as it is seen by someone else visiting your My Site.

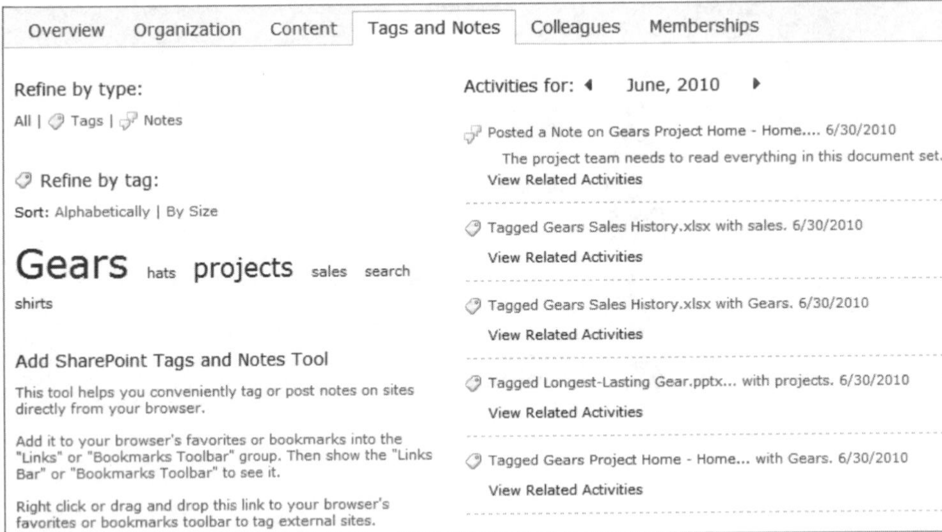

FIGURE 11-4

Narrow down the view of activities on the right by clicking the refinement links on the left. You can refine by type, such as tags or notes, and even refine by the tags themselves. A tag cloud displays all of the tags that the person has used.

There is also a section called Add SharePoint Tags and Notes Tool. This tool provides a way to tag other Internet content that is not in SharePoint, and the instructions for using it are listed on the page.

> ***NOTE*** *It is important to note that all tags and notes are ultimately managed by the SharePoint administrator, from Central Administration. In the User Profile Service Application, the administrator can perform searches by type, user, URL, date range, or keywords on the Manage Social Tags and Notes screen. The administrator can delete any content considered inappropriate.*

The Colleagues Tab

In SharePoint, colleagues are those people whose activities you are following. SharePoint assumes that you are most interested in people whom you work most closely with, so they are automatically added to your list of colleagues. Direct reports and people who have a common manager will already be on the list. This information comes into SharePoint profiles and properties from a directory service such as Active Directory, and the connection is set up by the SharePoint administrator. On this tab, colleagues can be added, edited, and removed manually. Adding a colleague to your list does *not* automatically add your name to that person's list of colleagues.

Options on this tab are:

- **Add Colleagues:** Multiple colleagues can be added at once. By default, each person that is added will receive an email notification letting them know.
- **Edit Colleagues:** Select the checkbox next to one or more people, and click the Edit Colleagues button.
- **Remove Colleagues:** Select the checkbox next to one or more colleagues, and click the Remove Colleagues button.
- **View Suggestions:** Based on emails and instant messages that have been sent, and the organizational hierarchy, colleagues will be suggested by SharePoint.

TRY IT OUT Adding a Colleague

In this Try It Out, you will pick someone in your organization who is not already in your list of colleagues and add them to the list. In the example's screenshots, the logged-in user is Kelly Krout, and she would like to add Todd Rowe as one of her colleagues. Todd is the CEO of the company, and Kelly would like to keep up on current information pertaining to him.

1. On your SharePoint home page, click your name at the top right, and in the drop-down menu choose My Profile.
2. Click the Colleagues tab in the center of the screen.
3. Click the Add Colleagues button above the Name column.
4. Fill in the new colleague information according to the following table. Figure 11-5 shows an example of this screen.

FIELD NAME	DATA
Colleagues	Your coworker
Add to My Team	Yes
Add to a Group	New Group: Executives
Show To	Everyone

5. Click OK.
6. On the Colleague Suggestions screen, click Skip.

The new addition is now displayed in the list of colleagues. Scroll down to the bottom of the page to see the new grouping called Executives, with one person listed. The groups exist purely for the purpose of organizing the list, and they are not related to security or audiences.

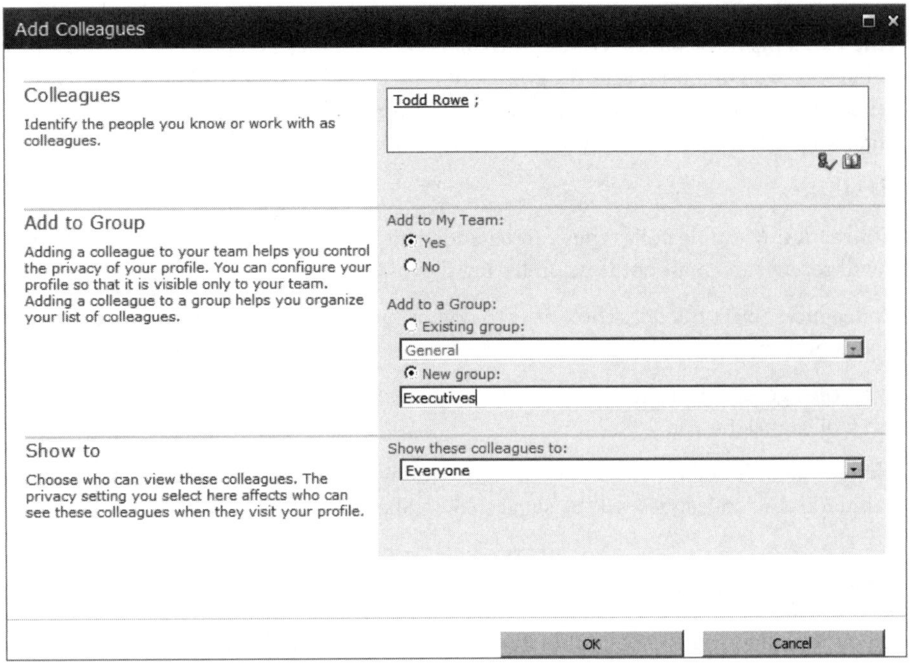

FIGURE 11-5

The Memberships Tab

This tab displays the person's group memberships, with information about each group. When someone is in the default "Members" SharePoint group on several sites, those are listed here. Also, email distribution lists are here, along with the total number of people in the group. Click any email distribution list's name to create a new email to that group. Select the checkbox next to one or more lists to modify their properties. Similarly to the way that the list of colleagues can be organized, these can be grouped and the Show To selection can be changed.

THE SHOW TO OPTION

So far in this chapter, the Show To drop-down box has been seen in a couple of different places, such as the Memberships and Colleagues tabs. Before you delve into profile editing, it is important for you to understand them. The following table describes each of these options.

SHOW TO OPTION	DESCRIPTION
Everyone	Everyone in the organization.
My Colleagues	People listed on the Colleagues tab. Self-defined.

SHOW TO OPTION	DESCRIPTION
My Team	On the colleagues tab, everyone who has a Yes in the My Team column. Self-defined.
My Manager	The person that you directly report to.
Only Me	You.

Edit My Profile

Profiles tell a lot about people, and their skills and interests. Individuals can edit their profile, and are encouraged to be thorough when it comes to Ask Me About, Projects, and Skills. Filling out a profile accurately is helpful when it comes to knowledge mining, so that when someone is searching for an expert, the right people will be found.

Figure 11-6 shows the top portion of Basic Information about Kelly Krout.

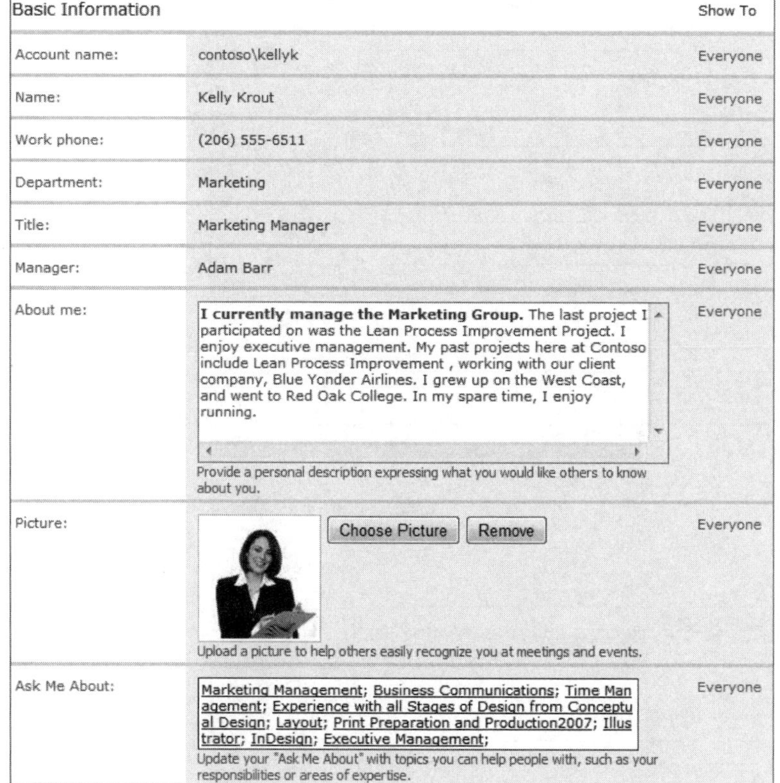

FIGURE 11-6

Some of the fields on the profile are editable, and some are not. These are called profile properties and are set up in Central Administration by the administrator. The Show To column is displayed down the right side of the page, and indicates who can see which information. Some of the Show To options are editable, and some are not.

Click the cursor inside of the About Me box to see the Format Text tab of the contextual Ribbon. The display of the information in this box can be customized to be more eye-catching, with font colors and sizes and the ability to edit the HTML code.

The Ask Me About information is an important part of making people findable in the organization. This is a list of proficiencies, and they are also tags that auto-fill as they are typed. The keywords typed here are displayed on the public profile, in the Ask Me About section of the Overview tab.

The Contact Information section of the profile lists the different methods by which you may be contacted. This screen can look different from organization to organization, because the SharePoint administrator configures the settings that determine which fields are read-only, required, or hidden. Notice that in the Show To column, some items have drop-down boxes, while other items are static. This, too is determined at the server level. Take a look at the Show To Options table in the previous section as a reference in deciding what the setting should be for each of these on your own profile. Figure 11-7 shows an example of the Contact Information section. Kelly has decided that only her manager can see her home phone number, all of her colleagues can see that she went to LSU, and everyone in the company can take a look at her past projects and skills.

Contact Information		Show To
Work e-mail:	kellyk@contoso.com	Everyone
Mobile phone:	This number will be shown on your profile. Also, it will be used for text message (SMS) alerts.	Everyone
Fax:		Everyone
Home phone:	205-555-4413	My Manager
Office:	4145	Everyone
Office Location:	Birmingham Enter your current location. (e.g. China, Tokyo, West Campus)	My Team
Time Zone:	(UTC-06:00) Central Time (US and Canada) Select the time zone for your current location. We will use this information to show the local time on your profile page.	Everyone
Assistant:		Everyone
Details		**Show To**
Past projects:	Lean Process Improvement; Provide information on previous projects, teams or groups.	Everyone
Skills:	SharePoint; Include skills used to perform your job or previous projects. (e.g. C++, Public Speaking, Design)	Everyone
Schools:	LSU; List the schools you have attended.	My Colleagues

FIGURE 11-7

All of the information that people share in profiles becomes part of SharePoint's searchable information. Social tags will be covered in detail later in this chapter, but it is important to understand that each of the words that appear as underlined are tags. These keywords are stored in a database in SharePoint, so that any other type of item in SharePoint that has been tagged with one of these words is now in a sense *related* to this individual profile. This all ties back to the concept of SharePoint 2010 as an organic and dynamic platform in the organization.

Further down the Edit My Profile page, there is a list of checkboxes within sections called Email Notifications and Activities I Am Following. The email notification options allow for granularly deciding what kinds of social activities that you would like to receive email notifications about. The Activities I Am Following checkboxes are options to narrow down the types of activities that you will see listed in your newsfeed.

NOTE *For the purpose of this book, most of the examples that have worked through will occur at the site level and on personal My Sites. If, after working through the chapter's activities, you are still looking for more in-depth administrative knowledge, it is recommended that you refer to the following SharePoint 2010 administrator book:*

Professional SharePoint 2010 Administration, Chapter 17, "Social Computing and SharePoint 2010."

My Content

Each user gets a personal site collection called My Content, which is a link in the My Site toolbar. These sites can be customized by changing the theme, adding web parts, uploading content, and adding lists and libraries.

NOTE *The first time the My Content site is created there is small button on the page called "Set as default My Site." This button is above the Shared Documents web part. To get the full integration capabilities of Office and SharePoint, click this button. One of the benefits is that a My Site link will automatically be added to the left side of the Save As and Open screens in Office applications like Excel and Word.*

Blogs

When the site is first created, there will not be a blog yet, but the right side of the page has a quick link to create one. The Create Blog button is shown in Figure 11-8.

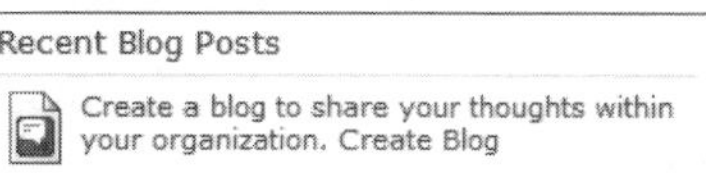

FIGURE 11-8

Shared and Personal Content

A new My Content site also contains some libraries in which to upload your own files. By default, everyone in the organization has read-only access to the Shared Documents and Shared Pictures libraries, and the Personal Documents library is only accessible to the site owner. Click Site Actions to create more libraries and lists on the site.

Web Parts

Chapter 7 covered web parts extensively. The My Content site is a great place to try out different out-of-the-box web parts, and there are even some that are made especially for this site.

TRY IT OUT Customizing the My Content Site

In this Try It Out, you'll learn how to work in your own site, add web parts, and even create your own blog. Not only is this site a great location to store files that you're editing and collaborating on, but it can be used as a learning tool for getting familiar with SharePoint.

1. From your main SharePoint home page, click your name at the top-right corner, and click My Site. In this example, Jenni Merrifield is a new employee at Contoso.
2. At the top of the My Site, click My Content. Wait while the new site is generated for the first time.
3. Click the button to Set as Default My Site. If this button is not displayed, it simply means that another site has already been set as the default My Site. Once this button is clicked, the My Site will show in the Office applications on your computer, on the Open and Save As screens, to quickly access the files on the My Site. This allows you to work on those files without necessarily opening the My Site in the browser.
4. In the Recent Blog Posts section, click Create Blog.
5. A new blog site has now been created as a subsite. On the right side, click Create a post. Fill in a Title and Body and click the Publish button.
6. Unfortunately, by default no one will be able to make comments on your blog. Click All Site Content in the Quick Launch, and click on the Comments list.
7. In the List tab in the Ribbon, click the List Permissions button on the far right.
8. Check the box next to NT AUTHORITY\Authenticated Users, and click the Edit User Permissions button. Check the box next to Contribute, and uncheck Read. Click OK.
9. Click My Content to navigate back to your top-level site.
10. Click Site Actions and choose Site Settings. In the Look and Feel section, click Site theme.
11. By default, the site has no theme. Click through the names of each of the themes to see previews. Select your favorite, and click Apply.
12. Click your own name at the top left to navigate back to your home page.
13. Click Site Actions and choose Edit Page. The page is now in edit mode.
14. Click any Add a Web Part button.
15. There is a list of Web Part categories on the left, with Recommended Items selected by default. These are the most common web parts that are used specifically on this type of site. Select My

Inbox and click the Add button. This web part is for Microsoft Exchange's Outlook Web Access (OWA) email.

16. In the new web part, click Open the tool pane.
17. For the mail server address, enter the URL of your OWA mail server. Obtain this URL by logging into OWA in another browser window, and copying the URL.
18. For the Mailbox, type your own email address. At the bottom of the Web part tool pane, click OK. Logging in to the web email may also be necessary at this point. This web part displays your email.

Explore the site further by clicking Site Actions and More Options. This gives you the ability to create different types of lists and libraries. Pick and choose which ones to share (and with whom) by setting up the permissions on each. Back on the Content tab on My Profile, notice that your new blog post is displayed, along with any files that you may have uploaded. If you have uploaded files to any other SharePoint sites that you are a member of, they will also be listed here.

My Newsfeed

Each person's newsfeed is their own stream of activities that they are following. These are things that are going on with people and topics that are of interest to the individual. Figure 11-9 shows an example of a newsfeed.

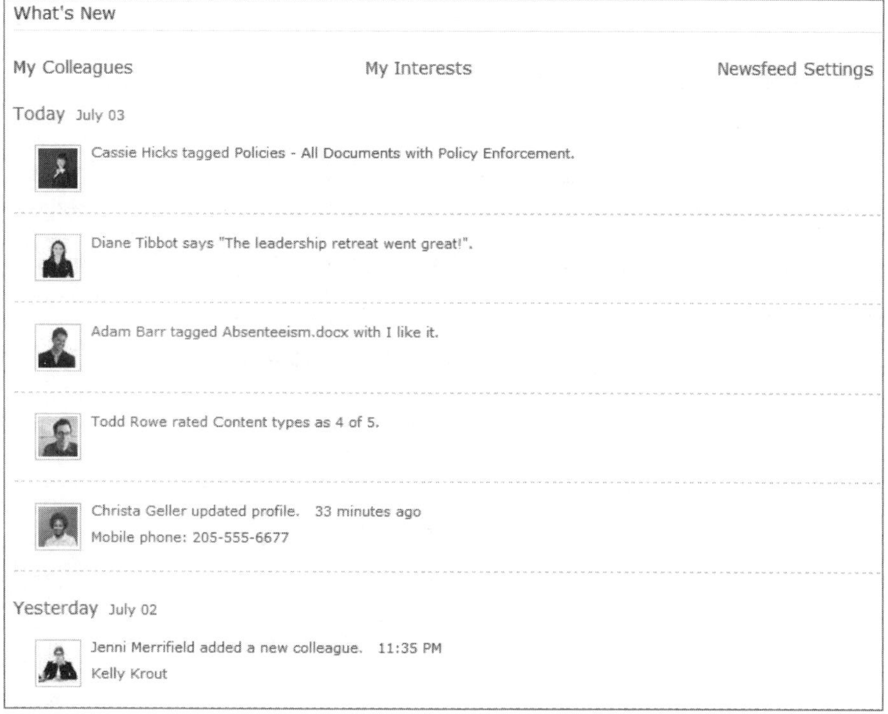

FIGURE 11-9

My Links

This hidden gem is perfect for saving favorite site locations inside or outside of SharePoint. My Links is a personal list that each user owns and manages, and is a bit hidden now in SharePoint 2010. This section will cover tasks like adding and managing links, and information about places where this list can be found. Links can also be categorized, and this is another place where the Show To box is used.

TRY IT OUT Managing My Links

In this Try It Out, you will learn how to add links to your own personal My Links list and how to utilize it the most effectively. The goal is to make the document libraries that you do the most collaboration in readily available.

1. The library that you will start with is called Policies and contains company policies that you are working on. Click on the name of this library in SharePoint.
2. In the Library tab in the contextual Ribbon, click the Connect to Office button, as shown in Figure 11-10.
3. Click Add to SharePoint Sites.
4. Click Yes to the message box called "Connect Office to your portal." Now that one library has been added, you would like to be able to access your list from within your My Site.

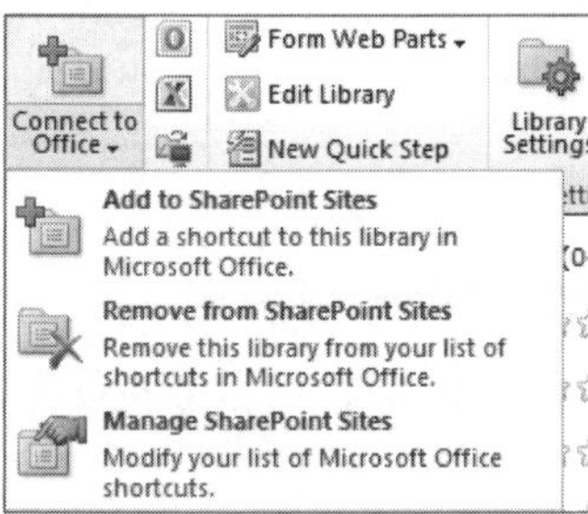

FIGURE 11-10

5. At the top right, click your name, and click My Site.
6. Click My Content to go to your own site collection.
7. Click Site Actions and choose Edit Page.
8. Click Add a Web Part, and add the My Links web part to the page.
9. Click the Stop Editing button.

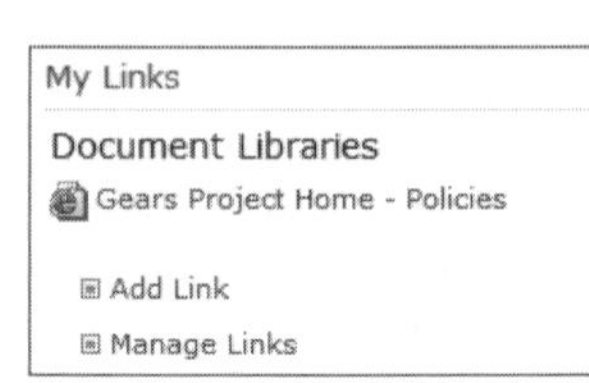

FIGURE 11-11

10. Figure 11-11 shows the My Links Web Part, with one link added so far.
11. Click the Manage Links button.
12. Click Add Link, create the new link using the values shown in the following table, and click OK.

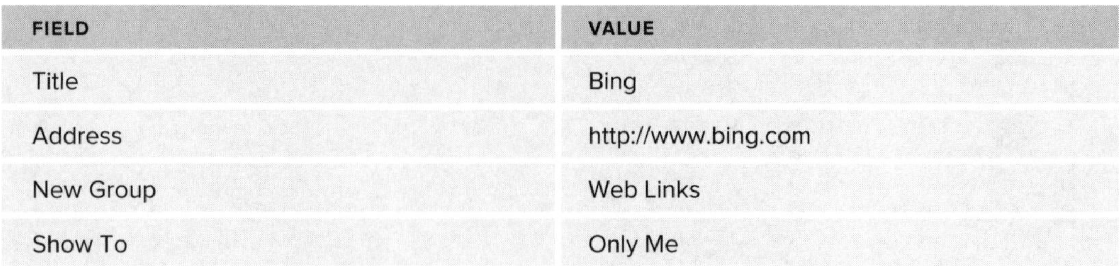

FIELD	VALUE
Title	Bing
Address	http://www.bing.com
New Group	Web Links
Show To	Only Me

13. Put a checkmark next to Bing, and click the Edit Links button.

14. Change the Title to Bing Search and click OK. The link management page will now look like Figure 11-12.

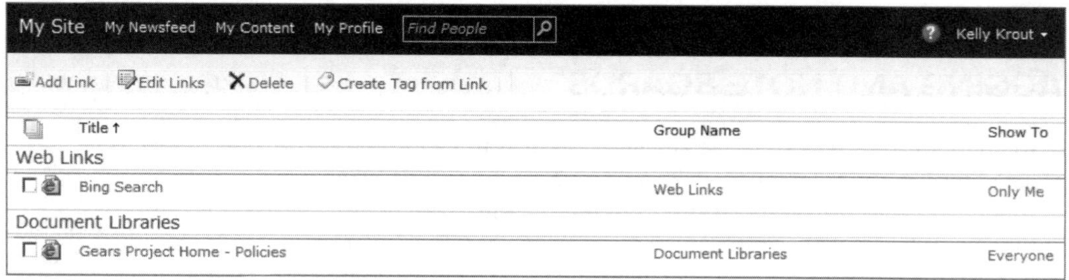

FIGURE 11-12

15. Check the box next to the document library that was added at step three, and click Create Tag from Link. A message will show on the page, letting you know that tags were successfully created from the selected links.

16. Click My Profile, and go to the Tags and Notes tab. Take a look at your two most recent activities on the right site. Each item was tagged with the text in the Group Name column for that link. Notice that since Bing Search was set up with Show To set to Only Me, the Make Private box is automatically checked.

17. Open Microsoft Word, click the File menu, and choose Save & Send on the left side. Notice that the library that was added at step 3 is now listed under Locations on the right side, along with My Site. Also, sites that you are in the Members group of will be displayed under Locations, as shown in Figure 11-13.

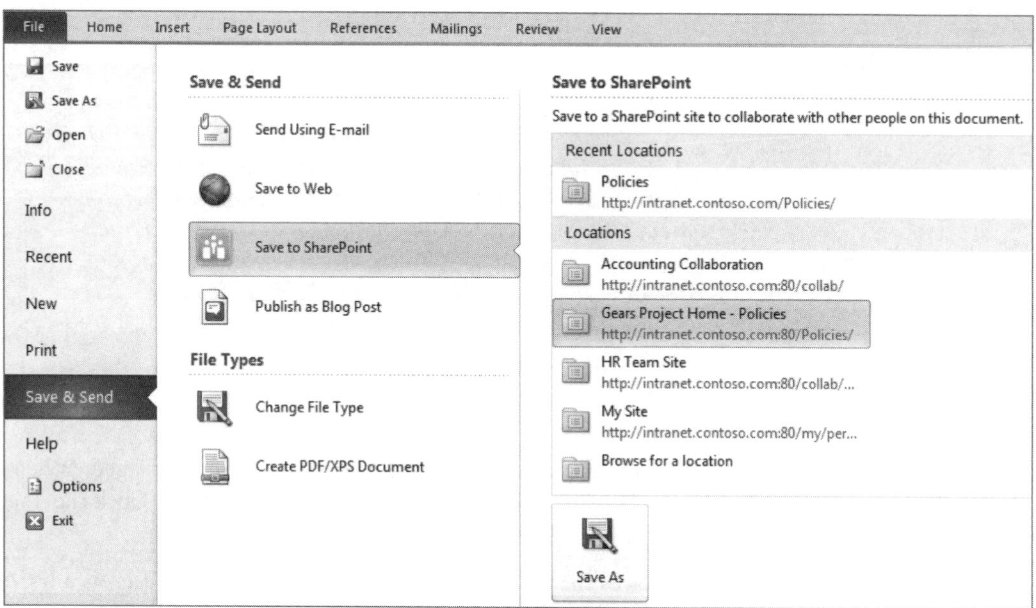

FIGURE 11-13

You have now seen how to create and manage My Links, and how they are available not only within SharePoint but also in the Office applications that you work in every day.

TAGGING AND NOTE BOARDS

To tag objects in SharePoint is to assign keywords to them. The tags that are associated with any given item allow it to be found more readily when people in the organization perform searches that contain that tag. Note boards are areas where public comments can be posted about any given item. Participating in tagging and note boards is part of being an active member of the online community in your organization. In SharePoint 2010, everyone who visits the sites is encouraged to tag and make notes, which makes the experience organic and dynamic. Figure 11-14 shows the buttons that are used.

FIGURE 11-14

Where can you add tags and notes? Pretty much everywhere! The following is a list of some of the objects that you can tag.

- Pages
- Lists and Libraries
- Documents
- List Items
- Blogs
- Wikis
- Images
- Tag Profiles

NOTE *When working with libraries, the Tags & Notes buttons will not be available unless they have been turned on in the library settings. The owner of the library can click Document Library settings, and choose Enterprise Metadata and Keywords Settings. Check the box called Add Enterprise Keywords (a one-way operation), and check the box called Metadata Publishing. Click OK.*

Tagging

This section describes the tagging interface, as well as how tags are used and managed. When the I Like It button is clicked, this simply adds a tag called "I Like It" to that object. Click the Tags & Notes button to see the screen shown in Figure 11-15.

The title portion of the screen contains the name of the object being tagged. My Tags is a list of tags that the current user has added, and below it the Suggested Tags have already been added by other people. Recent Activities shows both tags and notes on the current item. Anyone can click the

Private checkbox to set their own tags on that item to be visible only to themselves. When a new tag is added, click the Save button.

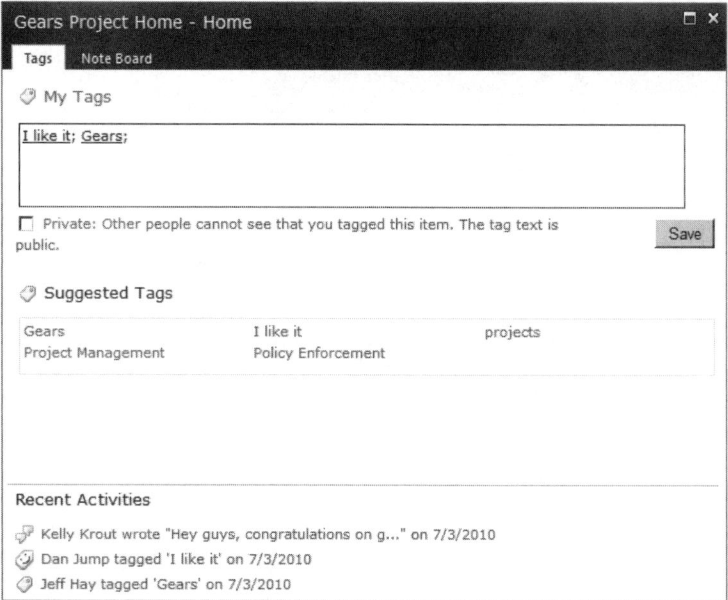

FIGURE 11-15

Any of the items in the Suggested Tags can be clicked to take further action. If that tag has not already been added to My Tags, there is an option to Add to My Tags. Each tag also has a tag profile, which will be covered in the next section.

Tag Profiles

Every tag in the organization exists in a database on the server and can be managed by administrators in the Term Store Management Tool. There is also a tag profile to represent each tag. The tag profile is a page where the tag information is displayed, as well as a list of every time the tag was used, and a note board just for that tag. The tag description, categorization, and synonyms have been set up by the administrator. Figure 11-16 is an example of a Tag Profile for a tag called "Customers - NDA."

The Get Connected section is a great tool for staying tuned in to all of the activities related to the tag.

- **Follow this tag in My Newsfeed:** Click this button to add this tag to the list of interests in your profile. Tags that a user is interested in will be displayed on their Newsfeed.
- **Add to "Ask Me About" in My Profile:** Add this tag to your own profile's Ask Me About section.
- **View people who are following this tag:** Click this button to go to a search results page that displays all people who have this tag listed in their profile as responsibilities OR interests.

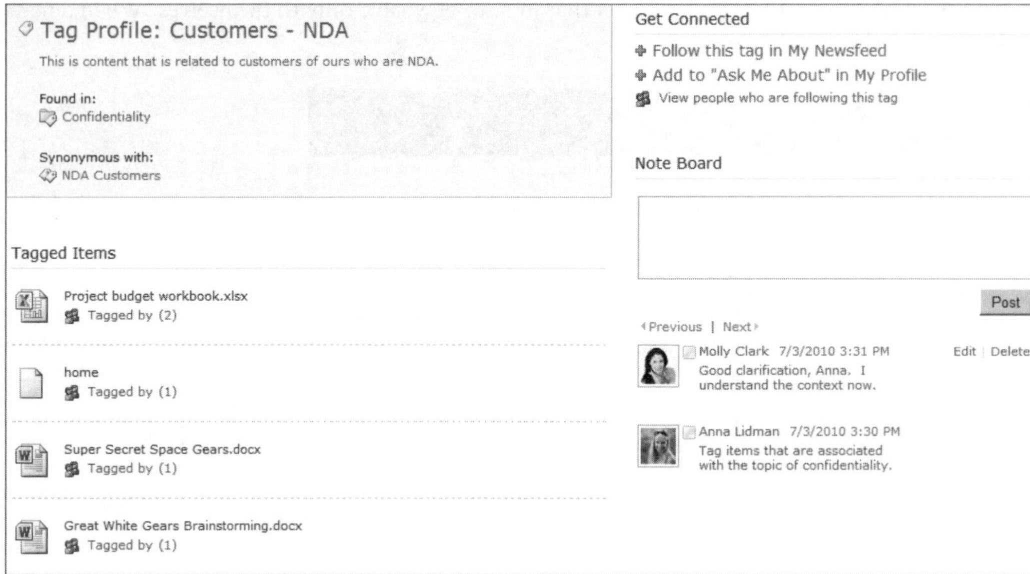

FIGURE 11-16

Note Boards

Use note boards to make quick public notes about any object in SharePoint. In the example in Figure 11-17, Anna Lidman is the currently logged-in user. Notice that Anna only has the ability to Edit or Delete her own notes, not those of others. Writing on a note board in SharePoint can be likened to posting to a "wall" on the Facebook website.

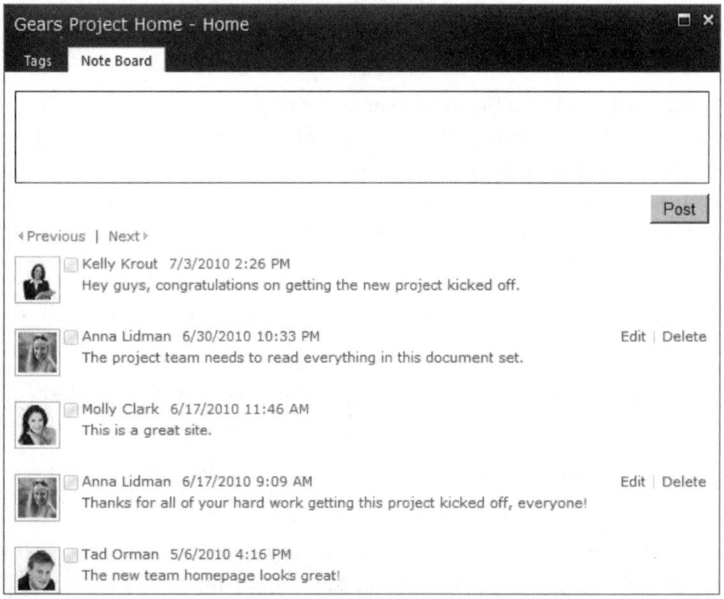

Gears Project Home - Home

Tags | Note Board

Post

Previous | Next

Kelly Krout 7/3/2010 2:26 PM
Hey guys, congratulations on getting the new project kicked off.

Anna Lidman 6/30/2010 10:33 PM — Edit | Delete
The project team needs to read everything in this document set.

Molly Clark 6/17/2010 11:46 AM
This is a great site.

Anna Lidman 6/17/2010 9:09 AM — Edit | Delete
Thanks for all of your hard work getting this project kicked off, everyone!

Tad Orman 5/6/2010 4:16 PM
The new team homepage looks great!

FIGURE 11-17

TRY IT OUT Creating Tags and Notes

In this Try It Out, you will participate in SharePoint social computing by creating new tags and notes on several different objects in a SharePoint site. The prerequisite is that you already have a document library, with some files in it.

Follow these steps to create tags and notes in SharePoint.

1. Navigate to your SharePoint site's home page.
2. At the top right, click the Tags & Notes button.
3. Type the words **Test Tag**. Type the letters slowly, and notice that a list of similar word suggestions will be displayed underneath them, as shown in Figure 11-18. If the SharePoint server is brand new, there may not be any suggestions yet, since the database of tags starts out empty.

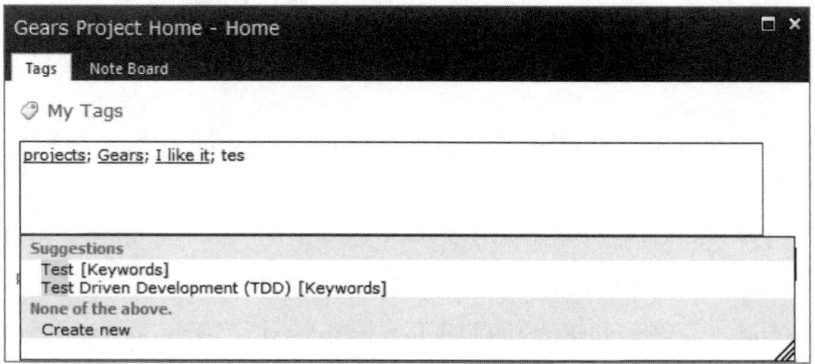

FIGURE 11-18

4. After Test Tag is typed, click Save. An underline will be displayed under the word, and it will be listed in the Suggested Tags section.
5. Click the Note Board tab at the top.
6. Type the following: **This is a test note.**
7. Click Post. See that the new note is added to the top of the list of notes in the bottom part of the window.
8. Click the X at the top-right corner to exit.
9. Click on the name of a document library, such as Shared Documents, which will take you to that library's page.
10. Click the Library tab in the Ribbon, and click the Library Settings button.
11. Click Enterprise Metadata and Keywords Settings.
12. Check both boxes to add enterprise keywords and to turn on Metadata Publishing. Click OK.
13. Click the name of the library at the breadcrumb trail at the top of the page to get back to the library's main view. Click the I Like It button at the top right.
14. Select the row of one of the files in the library by clicking somewhere in the row (but not on the name of it, which would open the file). A selected file is displayed in Figure 11-19.

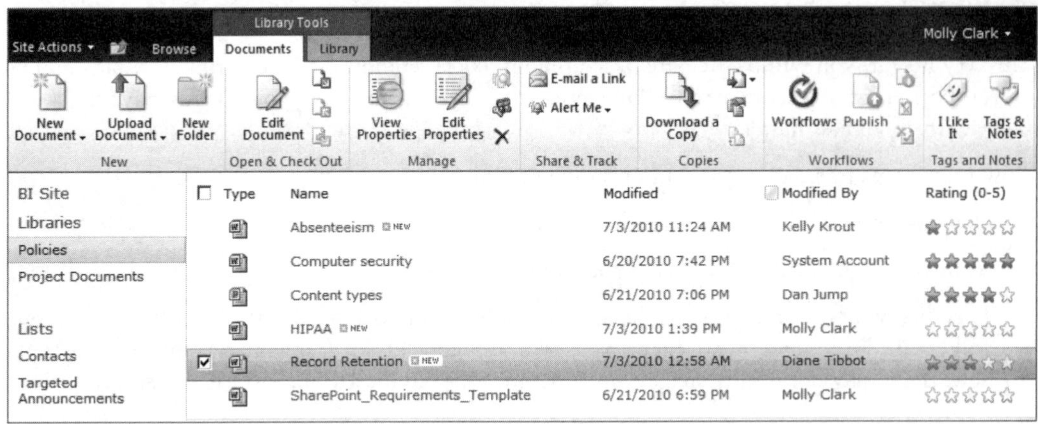

FIGURE 11-19

15. Click Tags & Notes.
16. Type your own tag that is relevant to the content of the selected file, post a Note Board note, and close the Tags & Notes screen.
17. Click your own name at the top right, and click My Profile.
18. Click the Tags & Notes tab to see your recent activity.
19. Delete the last few test tags and notes by clicking the Delete button next to each one on the right side of the page.

Now that you've started participating in the continuously developing taxonomy of your own SharePoint environment, just keep going. Why stop now? Remember that tagging lists and list items works the same way as with libraries, but there is no pesky list level setting to enable in advance. Another thing to keep in mind is that when meaningful tags are associated with objects, this helps people find the item more quickly when searches are performed. Words that exist as tags on an item take precedence over the words that exist inside of the document, for searching.

MANAGE CONTENT RATING

A new feature of SharePoint 2010 is the ability to rate items on a scale of one to five. Content rating is yet another mechanism for engaging all of the SharePoint users to participate on their sites, even if it simply involves clicking a star to quickly rate an item. Ratings can be used for any kind of list items, documents, and even wiki pages. When items are rated, this helps in determining their relevancy. SharePoint users will tend to lean more toward referencing documents that have more stars than to the ones with fewer, and the higher-rated items will be returned first in search results.

The settings page for any list or library has a link called Rating settings, as shown in Figure 11-20. This page describes what rating settings entails, with Yes and No radio buttons.

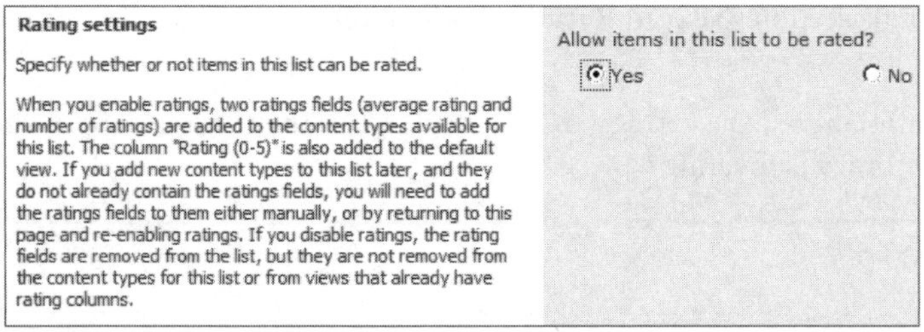

Rating settings

Specify whether or not items in this list can be rated.

When you enable ratings, two ratings fields (average rating and number of ratings) are added to the content types available for this list. The column "Rating (0-5)" is also added to the default view. If you add new content types to this list later, and they do not already contain the ratings fields, you will need to add the ratings fields to them either manually, or by returning to this page and re-enabling ratings. If you disable ratings, the rating fields are removed from the list, but they are not removed from the content types for this list or from views that already have rating columns.

Allow items in this list to be rated?

(•) Yes ( ) No

FIGURE 11-20

TRY IT OUT Content Rating

In this Try It Out, content rating will be used in a document library, and you will see the ratings in action. The prerequisite is that the document library has several items in it for rating.

1. In the Library tab of your document library, click Library Settings.
2. Click Rating settings, change the setting to Yes, and click OK.
3. A new column called Rating has been added to the default view of the library. Rate items in the library by clicking one of the stars next to each. When you hover your mouse over the set of stars for each item, a tooltip will let you know if you have already rated it and what that rating number is, or it will say "My Rating: not rated yet." Figure 11-21 shows a library of items that several people have already rated. When the logged-in user rates items for the first time, the stars appear yellow because they are new. The blue-star ratings already existed.

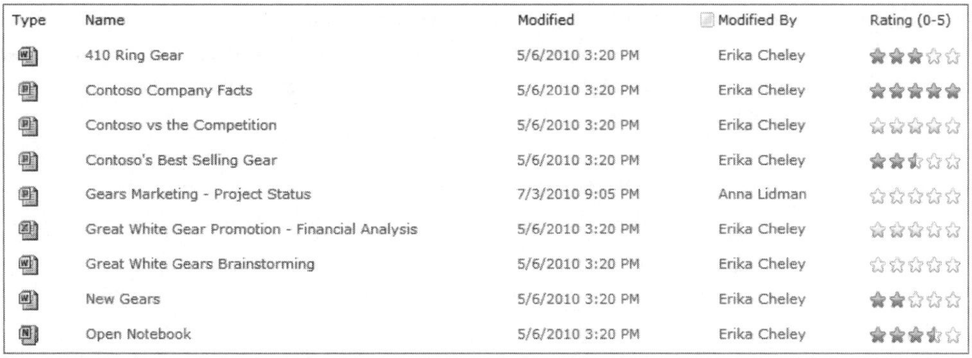

Type	Name	Modified	Modified By	Rating (0-5)
	410 Ring Gear	5/6/2010 3:20 PM	Erika Cheley	
	Contoso Company Facts	5/6/2010 3:20 PM	Erika Cheley	
	Contoso vs the Competition	5/6/2010 3:20 PM	Erika Cheley	
	Contoso's Best Selling Gear	5/6/2010 3:20 PM	Erika Cheley	
	Gears Marketing - Project Status	7/3/2010 9:05 PM	Anna Lidman	
	Great White Gear Promotion - Financial Analysis	5/6/2010 3:20 PM	Erika Cheley	
	Great White Gears Brainstorming	5/6/2010 3:20 PM	Erika Cheley	
	New Gears	5/6/2010 3:20 PM	Erika Cheley	
	Open Notebook	5/6/2010 3:20 PM	Erika Cheley	

FIGURE 11-21

4. The newly rated items will only appear in yellow for a few minutes. Refresh the page to see all stars in blue. When multiple people have rated an item, the star that is displayed is an average rating, which is why some appear as half-stars.
5. At the top of the document library, click the name of the current view, such as "All Documents," and choose Modify This View.
6. Put a checkmark next to the Number of Ratings column.

7. Scroll down and expand the Totals section. Next to Rating, choose Average, and click OK at the bottom of the page.

The page now displays more information about the ratings, and the average at the top lets people know how valuable the information in the library is, overall.

> **NOTE** *It may take a while for newly added ratings to appear as blue stars next to the items that were rated. New ratings depend on a timer job on the server called the "User Profile Service Application - Social Rating Synchronization Job," which runs hourly by default.*

SOCIAL COMPUTING WEB PARTS

There are several out-of-box web parts that make use of the SharePoint 2010 social computing features. These web parts can be added to any page, and add a dynamic aspect to the page. Chapter 7 has detailed information about how to work with web parts and about more of the out-of-box ones.

Tag Cloud

A tag cloud is a visual representation of a set of tags on a site. The tags are displayed by size, with the most frequently used tags being the largest. When this web part is added to a page, by default it only shows the current user's tags. The web part properties contain a setting called Show Tags, and it can be changed to show tags by all users. Figure 11-22 shows an example of a tag cloud web part.

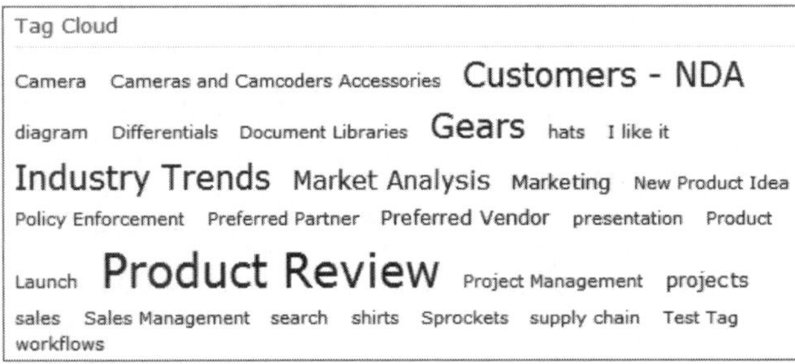

FIGURE 11-22

Click on the name of any tag to go to its tag profile.

Organization Browser

The organization browser is the same Silverlight web part that is seen on the Organization tab of the user profile. It can be inserted on any page and will automatically show the organization centered on the currently logged-in user. The only setting in this web part is to optionally change it to show the HTML view only.

Note Board

The Note Board web part contains the same note board interface that is seen when clicking Tags & Notes at the top right of any page. This web part simply brings the notes themselves to the surface of the page. Figure 11-23 shows the configurable settings in the web part property tool pane.

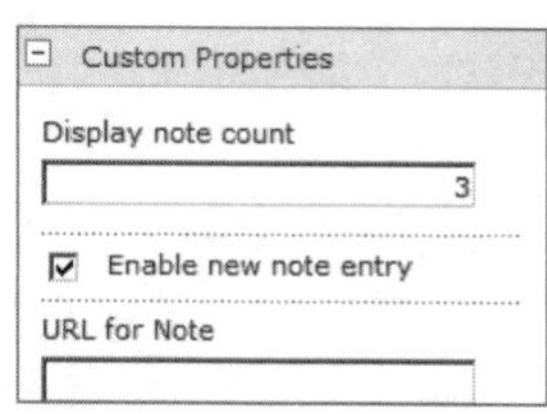

FIGURE 11-23

The note count is the number of the most recent notes that are displayed, and the new note entry box is the big text box where new notes can be typed. Unchecking the Enable New Note entry frees up some real estate on the page, and new notes can still be added by clicking Tags & Notes at the top right. By default, this web part displays notes related to the current page, but a different URL can be entered in the URL for Note box if you would like to display the notes for any other object. For example, enter the URL to a document library to display that library's notes.

PEOPLE SEARCH

The information in each person's user profile is searchable in SharePoint 2010, with a greatly improved rich user interface and refinement panel. The more information that exists in the profiles, the more dynamic the people search experience will be. Figure 11-24 shows an example of a people results page. In this example, the currently logged-in user is Kelly Krout, and the search that was performed was "marketing manager."

The words in the search term are shown in bold on the page, where they appear in each person's profile. Since Kelly is the one performing the search, and her own name also came up in her search, there is an extra box called Help people find me. This lets Kelly know how many searches have led to her and the keywords that were used in the searches.

Down the left side of the screen, the refinement panel allows for quickly drilling down to narrow the search. These sections listed are properties in the users' profiles, such as interests, past projects, and schools.

Detailed contact information is listed about each person, along with quick links to add that person as a colleague or browse the organizational chart. Click the By *Username* link to see a list of recent documents and files that the person has worked on.

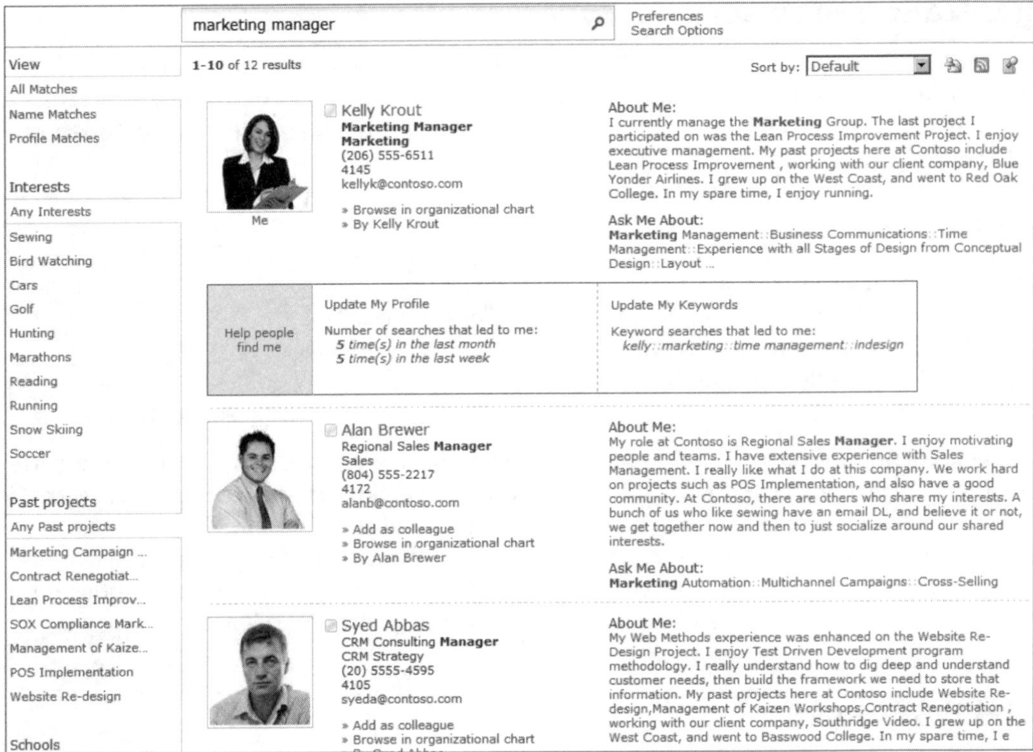

FIGURE 11-24

BLOGS AND WIKIS

When the Internet began, it was mostly composed of static HTML pages, and web page creation required knowledge of code languages. In the past 10 years or so, the web has evolved to become a much more interactive experience, and it has become easy for everyone to become participants. Now, people are collaborating, discussing, and forming online communities around topics. These collaborations can combine data, content, images and multimedia from multiple sources to create personalized experiences.

Blogs

A blog is a personal journal written on the web, originally called a "web log." Blogs can be written about any topic, ranging from daily life to information about a particular product, to opinions on politics. Within SharePoint in the enterprise, blogs are usually of a business-related nature. Here are a few blog concepts to be familiar with:

- **Blog posts:** Using the concept of a blog being a journal, blog posts are the individual journal entries.

- **Comments:** Blog readers may enter their own input about each blog post, for a running commentary.
- **Blog site:** The blog site is the SharePoint site in which the blog posts and comments reside.
- **Blog account:** The account comprises the URL to the blog site and the associated user login information.

TRY IT OUT Creating Blog Posts in Microsoft Word

Not only can blog entries be created from within the browser, but this can be done from Word as well. In this Try It Out, you will post an entry to your own blog, using Word.

1. From any SharePoint site, click your own name at the top right of the page, and choose My Site. Click My Content at the top of the My Site page.
2. If a blog site has not been created yet, click Create Blog on the right side. If it already exists, click the title of the web part Recent Blog Posts.
3. On the right side, click Launch Blog Program to Post.
4. Microsoft Word will start with a prompt to create a New SharePoint Blog Account. The URL of your blog site will already be listed. Click OK, and click Yes to the informational message.
5. On the Account registration successful screen, click OK.
6. Click the text that says [Enter Post Title Here], and type **This Is My Blog Post from Word**
7. Put the cursor below the horizontal line and type **This is the body of the post.**
8. Go to the next line and click the Insert tab in the Ribbon. Select a picture from your hard drive and click Insert.
9. On the Blog Post tab, click the Insert Category button, and choose Personal in the Category drop-down box.
10. Click the Publish button at the top left, and if prompted, authenticate yourself with your username and password.
11. Go back to the browser window and press the F5 key on the keyboard to refresh the page in order to see the latest post; an example is shown in Figure 11-25.
12. Click Manage comments on the right side.
13. In the List tab in the Ribbon, click Alert Me, and choose Set alert on this list. Modify the alert settings as needed and click OK to receive email alerts when people add comments to your blog.

The blog has been posted and placed into the Personal category. Click any category on the left side to filter by the items in that category. Images that are placed into blog posts and published with Word automatically are placed in a Picture Library on the site, called "Photos." Click Site Actions and Edit Page in order to personalize the About this blog section on the right. To edit the blog post in the browser, click the name of the post, then click the Edit this page link on the page next to the post title.

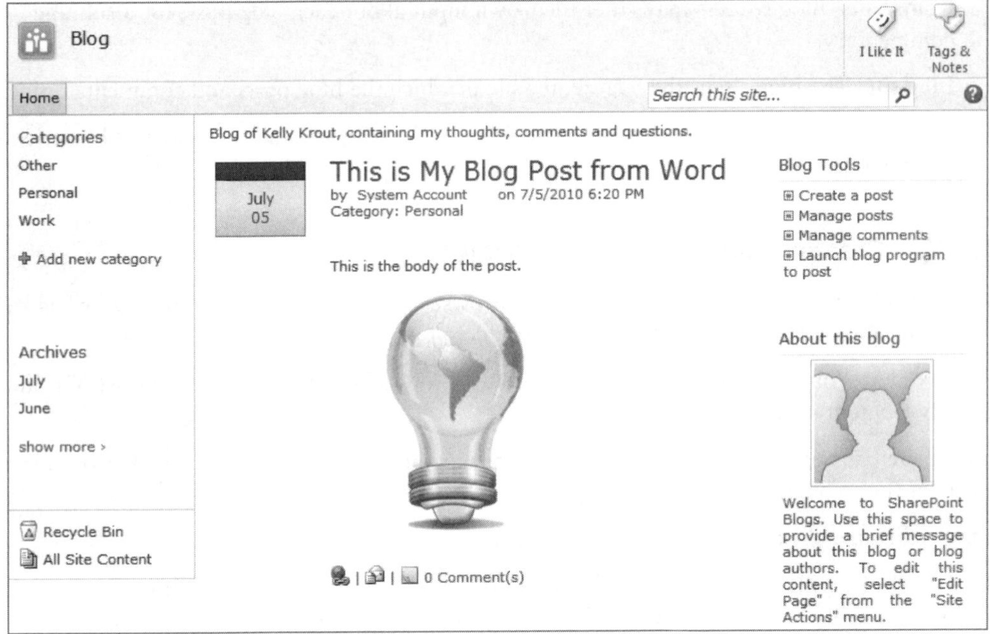

FIGURE 11-25

Wikis

"Wiki-wiki" is the Hawaiian word for quick. Wiki pages are web pages that can be quickly edited by typing directly into the browser. Use wikis to maintain a knowledge base, obtain community input on a topic, or simply to take personal notes.

Here are the major differences between blogs and wikis:

- A blog is a whole site, whereas a wiki can be a wiki site or simply a wiki library on an already existing site.
- Comments can be made on blogs, not wikis.
- This table lists the items that can be inserted into a blog versus a wiki:

TYPE OF ITEM TO INSERT	BLOG	WIKI
Table	Yes	Yes
Picture	Yes	Yes
Video and Audio	No	Yes
Link	Yes	Yes
Upload File	Yes	Yes

TYPE OF ITEM TO INSERT	BLOG	WIKI
Reusable Content	No	Yes
Web Part	No	Yes

***NOTE** Team sites in SharePoint 2010 have a new feature called a Wiki Page Home Page. This means that the whole home page itself is a wiki page onto which images and text can be added directly to the page. The familiar buttons to Add a Web Part do not exist on these types of pages. Inserting a web part or anything else, is done from the Insert tab in the Ribbon. Here's how you can turn off the wiki page if necessary. Click Site Actions, choose Site Settings, and in the Site Actions section, click Manage site features. Click the Deactivate button next to the Wiki Page Home Page feature.*

TRY IT OUT Creating a Wiki Site

In this Try It Out, you will create a new wiki site and two new wiki pages. The interface for text formatting and inserting items will also be used.

1. On your SharePoint site, click Site Actions, and click New Site.
2. In the list of different site templates to choose from, click Enterprise Wiki. On the right, type **Test Wiki** as the title and **testwiki** as the URL. Click Create.
3. Click the Page tab in the Ribbon and choose View All Pages.
4. On the Library tab in the Ribbon, click Library Settings, and in the Columns section click Wiki Categories.
5. In the Term Set Settings, choose an existing term set. Under "Site Collection - the name of your site collection," Click Wiki Categories and click OK.
6. Click Pages in the breadcrumb trail at the top of the page.
7. Click the Documents tab in the Ribbon and click the New Document button.
8. For the Title, type Test Wiki, and click Create.
9. In the list of pages, click the name of the new Test Wiki.
10. Click the Edit this page link.
11. Type some text about the joys of learning SharePoint 2010, and use the Format Text tab to change the colors and fonts.
12. Click the Insert tab and choose the Picture button. Click From Computer.
13. Browse to an image on your hard drive and Upload it to the Images library. Click OK.

14. When the image properties box comes up, click Save.
15. Notice that when the image is selected, the contextual Ribbon shows a Picture Tools Design tab with design options for the picture. Click the Save & Close button.

A wiki site has been created, and your first wiki page has been published. The formatting and inserting interfaces are easy to use. Any wiki page can be set as the default for the page by clicking Make Homepage on the Page tab in the Ribbon. The ability to add ratings is turned on by default for wikis.

UNDERSTANDING AUDIENCES

In SharePoint, audiences are used in order to target certain content to users, depending on information about them. Audiences are defined as groups of people who have certain attributes in common. For example, you can create a "Marketing" audience that includes everyone involved in the organization's marketing campaign. Content on a SharePoint page can be set up to be displayed to only members of a specific audience. Audience targeting is not the same as security, though. Just because an item is not targeted to a particular user, doesn't mean that the user will not be able to navigate to that item or find it in a search. Utilize targeting to personalize the page according to information about the logged-in user, so that any given person will automatically see the information that is relevant to them. In this section, you'll learn how to target content to audiences, and how to create new audiences.

Targeting Content to Audiences

In this section, you will learn about the five different ways to target content to audiences.

List Items Displayed in a Content Query Web Part

Audience targeting is an option in every list and library in SharePoint, but the content query web part is the only place that this item level targeting can be utilized. This means that items that are set up as targeted will still be displayed to everyone when they look at views of the list. Inserting the list or library as a web part on the page does not allow for the use of audiences, either.

Web Parts

Each individual web part on a page can be targeted to an audience. This helps to clean up the clutter of many web parts being presented, and helps to eliminate scrolling. Target each web part to only those users for whom the content is relevant. In the Web Part tool pane, expand the Advanced section. Target Audiences is the last option in this section, and the names of the audiences can be filled in here. Read more about Web Parts in Chapter 7.

Web Part Pages

Web part pages can only be targeted if audience targeting is enabled for the page library. In the library's settings, on the Audience targeting settings screen, check the box to Enable audience targeting. Each page's settings will have a box to fill in the names of the target audiences. In the site's navigation settings, when the Show Pages checkbox is selected, the pages that are displayed in navigation will be visible only to their target audiences.

Navigation Links

When new links are manually created in the site's navigation settings, each link can be targeted to an audience. On the Navigation Settings page, click Add Heading or Add Link to see the page where the link's audience can be selected, as shown in Figure 11-26.

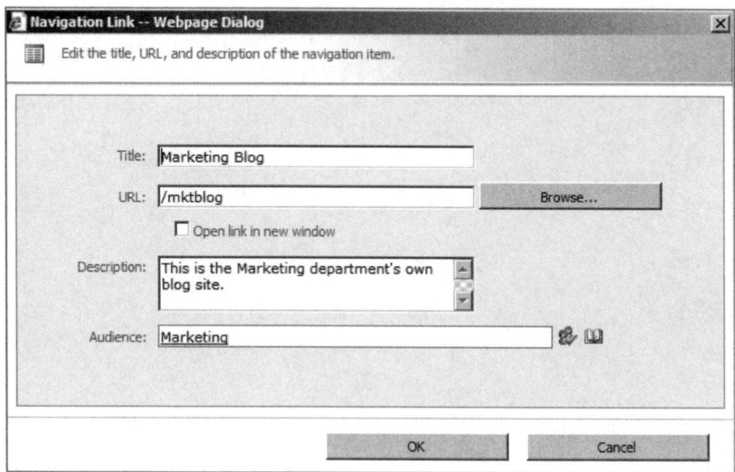

FIGURE 11-26

NOTE *Remember that, aside from any audience targeting, navigation items will automatically be security trimmed. This means that if you don't have access to a site, list, or library, you won't see it in the navigation.*

Personalization Site Links

Personalization Site Links are created by a SharePoint administrator and are links that are only displayed in the top navigation of personal sites, such as My Site and My Content. Use these types of links in order to target links to specific groups of people. Although an owner's name is required for each link, it is not tied to any type of security. The owner's name is used purely for informational purposes. In Central Administration, under a service application called the User Profile Service Application, click Configure Personalization Site to create these links.

Publish Links to Office Client Applications

Also in the User Profile Service Application, these types of links can be created for use in Microsoft Office applications such as Word and Excel. When links are created here, users in the target audiences will see their links in Office when viewing the Open or the Save As screens.

There is a way to create and define audiences at a global level, by an administrator, but this is not required in order to make use of audiences. Active Directory or SharePoint groups can be used as audiences. The following table compares the different methods of targeting content to show what kinds of audiences can be utilized with each one. This is useful when determining when it may or may not be necessary to elicit the help of the SharePoint Administrator.

METHOD	GLOBAL AUDIENCE	DISTRIBUTION/ SECURITY GROUP	SHAREPOINT GROUP
List Items displayed in a Content Query Web Part	Yes	Yes	Yes
Web Parts	Yes	Yes	Yes
Web Part Pages	Yes	Yes	Yes
Navigation Links	Yes	Yes	Yes
Personalization Site Links	Yes	No	No
Publish Links to Office Client Applications	Yes	No	No

TRY IT OUT Using Audiences

In this Try It Out, the example is a company intranet home page where announcements are added frequently. The goal is to target each announcement so that it is only visible on the home page to the pertinent audience. With audience target announcements and the content query web part, the home page will appear personalized to each user who views the page. The content query web part will not easily display the formatting that exists in an announcements list, so one of the first things that will be done will be to change the way that the text is formatted inside of the announcements. This will also give the web part a more cohesive appearance. Groups called Marketing and Accounting will be created as a demonstration, but many different audiences can be created in your real-world scenario.

1. Create two SharePoint groups on the site: Accounting and Marketing. Put yourself in one group, and another test user in the other group. When each group is created, leave all of the default settings.
2. Click Site Actions and choose More Options. For the list type, select Announcements. Name the list Targeted Announcements and click Create.
3. In the List tab at the top of the screen, click the List Settings button.
4. In the columns section of the List Settings page, click the name of the Body column.
5. On the Change Column screen, under Specify the type of text to allow, choose Plain text, and click OK.
6. On the List Settings page, click Audience targeting settings.

7. On the Modify List Audience Targeting Settings page, put a checkmark next to Enable Audience Targeting. Click OK.

8. Click the name of the list Targeted Announcements in the breadcrumb trail at the top of the page. Use the Add New Announcement button to add several new announcements, as shown in the following table:

TITLE	BODY	TARGET AUDIENCES
Test 1 To Marketing	There are new company shirts now available to members of our department.	Marketing
Test 1 To Accounting	Remember to turn in the monthly figures by Friday.	Accounting
Test 2 To Marketing	You all did an outstanding job reaching the targeted marketing goals this month.	Marketing
Test 2 to Accounting	Welcome to our new Controller, Jeff Hays.	Accounting
Test To Both Groups	Marketing and Accounting groups will both see this.	Marketing; Accounting
Test No Audience	The company picnic was a great success. Thanks to all who participated.	

9. After the six items have been created, navigate back to the home page of the site.

10. Click Site Actions and choose Edit Page.

11. On the Insert tab in the Ribbon, click Web Part.

12. In the Content Rollup category on the left, click the Content Query Web Part, and add it to the page.

13. Click to select the new web part on the page, and in the Web Part Tools Options tab in the Ribbon, click Web Part Properties.

14. In the Source section, select Show items from the following list, and choose the Targeted Announcements list. Note that this section also allows you to view every announcement in the site collection, if the first option were selected.

15. In the Audience Targeting section shown in Figure 11-27, check both boxes:

    - **Apply audience filtering:** If this box is not checked, all audiences that have been set on the items will be ignored.
    - **Include items that are not targeted:** Any items that have an empty Target Audiences box will still be displayed, such as the "Test No Audience" item that was created in the preceding table.

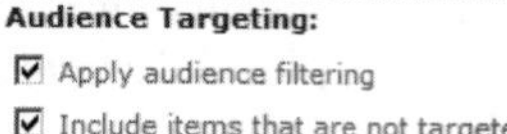

FIGURE 11-27

16. Expand the Presentation section and take a look at the Styles. Click the Item style drop-down box and change it to Title and Description.

17. In the Description box, type the name of the field Body. This part of the tool pane is shown in Figure 11-28.

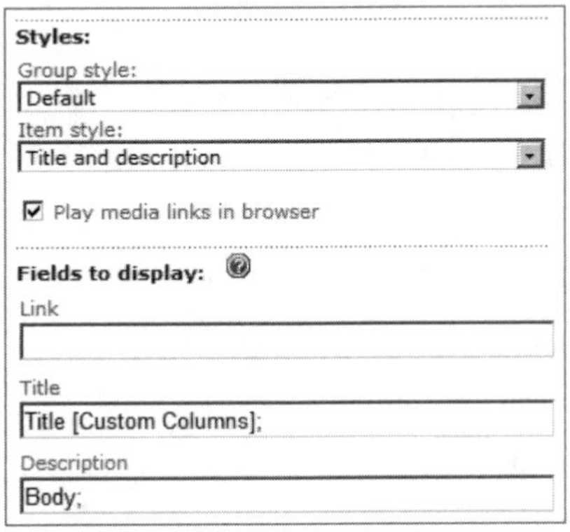

Styles:
Group style:
Default
Item style:
Title and description
Play media links in browser
Fields to display:
Link
Title
Title [Custom Columns];
Description
Body;

FIGURE 11-28

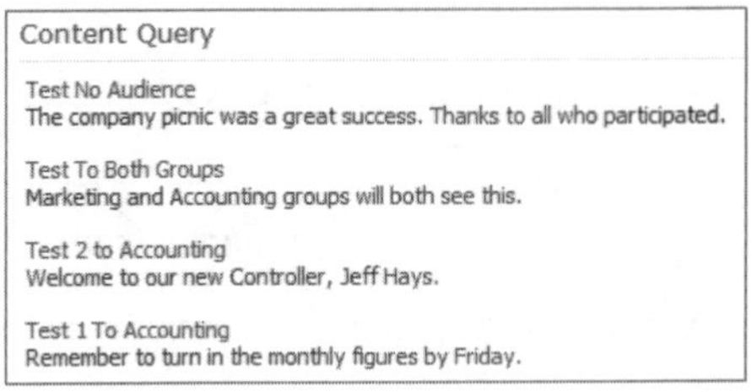

Content Query
Test No Audience
The company picnic was a great success. Thanks to all who participated.
Test To Both Groups
Marketing and Accounting groups will both see this.
Test 2 to Accounting
Welcome to our new Controller, Jeff Hays.
Test 1 To Accounting
Remember to turn in the monthly figures by Friday.

FIGURE 11-29

18. At the bottom of the tool pane, click OK.

The resulting web part displays only the items that have been targeted to you. You will see four items in total: the two that were targeted to the group that your account is a member of, the item targeted to both groups, and the item that had no target audience. The final result is shown in Figure 11-29.

Creating Audiences

SharePoint Administrators can create global audiences, which are rules-based. These are created from within Central Administration and can be applied to any of the types of targeted content. Use these types of audiences when a SharePoint Group or Distribution list is not sufficient for defining the list of users who should exist in an audience.

ADMINISTRATING GLOBAL AUDIENCES

If you are not a SharePoint administrator and would like to create global audiences, you can request to be given explicit permissions for managing audiences. If you are an administrator: In Central Administration, click Manage Service Applications. Click to select the row of the User Profile Service Application. In the Ribbon, click the Administrators button. Type the user's name in the Account box and click Add. Click to select the name of that user, and put a checkmark next to Manage Audiences. Click OK.

Creating global audiences is a matter of first defining the group of people and then creating a set of rules to pull them into the audience. Audiences are composed of properties and rules; after they are assembled, they must be all be compiled on one schedule.

Audience Properties

The audience properties consist of a name, description, and owner's name. The owner's name is used for documentation purposes only and is not related to any type of permissions. There is also a very important choice to be made, called Include users who, where there are two options. Choose "Satisfy all of the rules" in a case where the audience is very specific. Choose "Satisfy any of the rules" in situations where the audience should include as many users as possible.

Audience Rules

Many rules can be added to any audience. Each time a new rule is created, there are two different types of rules to choose from, which are referred to as *operands*. The User operand lets you select either the name of the person that the user reports to, or the name of a directory group or distribution list that they are a member of. The Property operand contains a list of many user properties, such as Department, Office, Job Title, and a host of others. In Figure 11-30, an audience called Accounting has been created. Since the audience's creator would like to encompass as many people as possible in this audience, it has been set up to include any user who satisfies *any* of the rules.

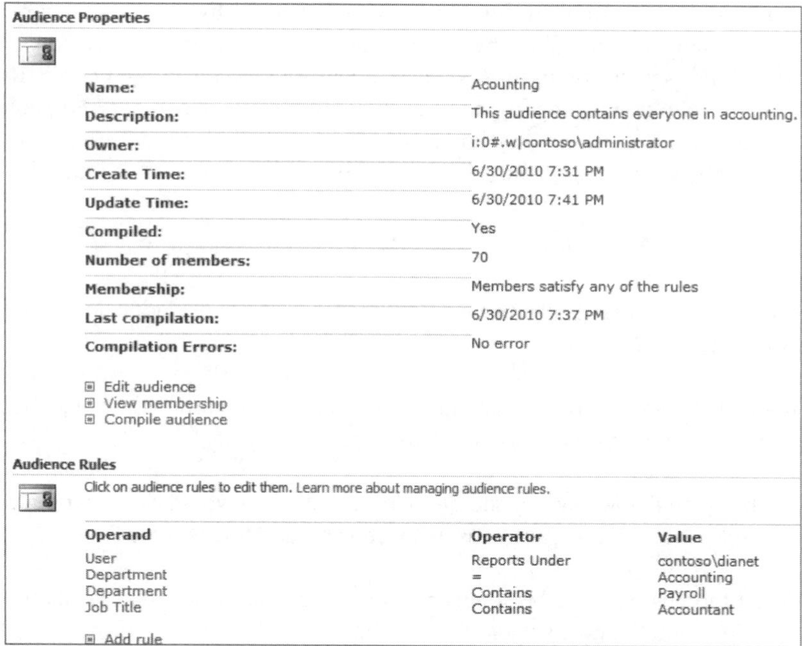

FIGURE 11-30

Audience Compilation

Set up a compilation schedule for all audiences. During a compilation, all of the users in SharePoint are examined to check to see if they meet the defined rules. In this case, if there is a new person in the Accounting department, he or she will be placed in this audience during the next compilation. The Schedule Audience Compilation link is on the User Profile Service Application screen.

THE OUTLOOK 2010 SOCIAL CONNECTOR

There is a plugin that comes with Outlook 2010, called the Social Connector. This allows you to configure Outlook to display information from the various social networks that you are a member of. The SharePoint 2010 network is included by default, but others that can be added are LinkedIn and My Space.

When a social network is added, a new contacts list is added to Outlook, importing the contacts from each network. When corresponding with these individuals, a People Pane appears at the bottom of the page. This pane contains information such as the person's picture, along with a quick list of the most recent activity associated with that person, such as emails and calendar appointments.

In Outlook 2010, click the View tab in the Ribbon, and click the People Pane button. Choose Account Settings in order to set up your list of social networks.

SUMMARY

Personalization and social networking in SharePoint 2010 are fundamental aspects of how people will share, categorize, and find information. In this chapter, you learned why these social concepts are important and how they are applied in the organization. You also learned how to go about making use of these tools as part of day-to-day work in SharePoint. The more people that get involved in social computing in your company, the easier it will be to find content and people. When people participate and feel like they are making a contribution to the community of the organization, they will not only be more efficient at their jobs, but will feel valued as individuals.

EXERCISES

1. You need to see where in the organizational chart a person named Christa Gellar fits in. How can you find that information about her?
2. Bob complains that the activity feed on his My Site has too much information, especially about ratings. How do you recommend that he change the settings?
3. Sally uses the Projects library on the Marketing site quite frequently. She would like it to be more readily available to her within the Office applications. How can she add this shortcut?
4. Todd has added the Tag Cloud web part to his team site. He wants to know if he can configure it to display the number of times each tag was used. What is the answer?
5. Management has decided that the link to My Links should be displayed in the top navigation of My Site. How can this be accomplished?

▶ WHAT YOU LEARNED IN THIS CHAPTER

TOPIC	KEY CONCEPTS
My Sites	These are used by individuals to keep up with the daily activities of people and tags that they are interested in.
My Content	These are personal site collections where files can be stored as personal or shared.
My Profile	This is an important page to fill out, so that others will know where your expertise lies.
Socially Contributing	Tagging and note boards are all over the place, which makes it extremely simple for people to contribute to the categorization of content.
Content Rating	Ratings can be turned on for any list or library, and it is a quick way to let people rate the worth of an item. These ratings can be quantified and summarized.
Web Parts	There are several out-of-box web parts related to social computing that can easily be placed on any SharePoint page.
People Search	Searching for people is a rich and dynamic experience, with detailed information being displayed about each person. The refinement panel allows quick filtering of the results page, to find the person you are looking for.
Blogs and Wikis	Blogs and wikis both offer quick ways of posting content directly to web pages in the browser, and they each have pros and cons.
Audience Targeting	Audiences in SharePoint are not used for security but do allow for content targeting of several different types of objects. SharePoint groups or distribution lists can be used for targeting in some cases, or global audiences can be created.

12

Forms Management

WHAT YOU WILL LEARN IN THIS CHAPTER:

- Information collection techniques with InfoPath 2010
- How to create an InfoPath form template
- How to create a reusable template part
- How to connect to external data using InfoPath

An important aspect of working in a business environment and collaborating with others is the collection of information. A common challenge is to identify ways to make this process more efficient and effective. One solution is to collect information in a form that contains preconfigured fields for the data you want to receive. This ensures that all the required information is collected, and it also helps consolidate information which can be used for comparison or calculations. For example, by collecting feedback from your customers on their satisfaction level with your services, you can identify trends or averages in their responses. If the average of all customer satisfaction ratings is 4.5 out of 5, and a customer submits a rating of 3 out of 5, it is easy to see that the response is below average. If all customer feedback was submitted verbally or via a less structured format such as email, it would be more difficult to compare results in a calculated manner.

Forms simplify the task of gathering important information. In Microsoft Office, you can use InfoPath Designer to create electronic forms that you can then publish to team members and others through SharePoint. InfoPath is straightforward enough that nonprogrammers can use it for a simple forms creation system, yet flexible enough for programmers to create sophisticated forms-based applications.

After reading this chapter, you should feel comfortable identifying scenarios where the use of InfoPath forms would be beneficial for your organization for the collection of information from various key stakeholders. This chapter requires that you use Microsoft InfoPath Designer 2010 for the creation of form templates. In addition, in order for users to complete forms created in InfoPath Designer, you must either design the forms to be browser compatible or the users will need to have Microsoft InfoPath Filler installed on their systems. For the majority of the exercises in this chapter, you will be creating browser-based forms.

WHAT IS INFOPATH?

InfoPath is an application that integrates with SharePoint to collect and present data. InfoPath forms are XML-based documents that you can design to help collect data in ways that the standard SharePoint interface cannot. While InfoPath can be used on its own, it truly excels as a data collection tool when combined with SharePoint. Some ways of using InfoPath within an organization include:

- **Team reports:** Team members can create weekly status reports from which the team's manager can create a single report that tracks the team's progress. This involves creating a form template that features fields related to weekly activities and publishing it to a shared location, such as the team's SharePoint site. Every week, the manager can access a special view that displays all the forms and then she can merge them into a single document. This consolidation reduces the amount of work that a manager must perform each week. She can even customize that single document to present to her own management team.
- **Data connections:** Sales people can use forms to report on customer information from a centralized database containing details on the customer and previous purchases. They can also attach a document with a record of meetings and communication with the customer so that colleagues can access this later. Again, you must create a form template and store it on a centralized team site, but this template features special data connections that display customer data directly from the database. This reduces duplicate data by eliminating the need to recreate this content in SharePoint because it already exists in the database, improves data access, and allows the sales team to make accurate decisions. With InfoPath, you can also submit information to other data systems via a web service, which means that you don't have to enter data into two separate systems.
- **Customer web forms:** Customers can visit a web page and complete an electronic form to request information on a company's products and services. The form is submitted securely to a location, and the customer is supplied with the requested information. A special feature of InfoPath, when utilized with the Enterprise version of SharePoint Server, is the ability to create forms that customers can view and edit via the browser. This eliminates the need for users to have special software on their computers.
- **Employee feedback:** A human resources department can get feedback from employees on new policies and procedures. To help control the collection of feedback, the department sends a form embedded in an Outlook email message. Employees can complete the form and send it directly back the human resources SharePoint site where the information is collected and analyzed. Employees can keep a copy of their submitted information in a folder in Microsoft Outlook for later reference.

CREATING AND CUSTOMIZING AN INFOPATH FORM

You use InfoPath in situations when you need to improve how information is shared or collected in your organization. One of the primary advantages of using InfoPath is that the interface can be made very simple and intuitive for users to add and complete information. An example of a typical InfoPath form is shown in Figure 12-1.

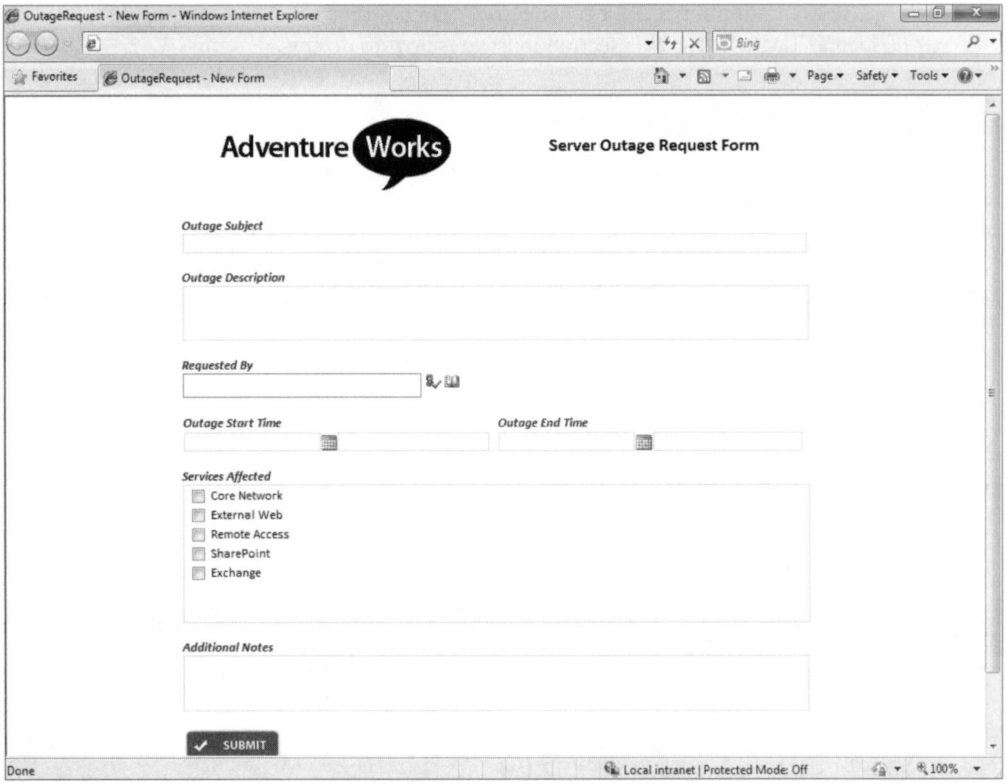

FIGURE 12-1

Before a user can complete an InfoPath form, you must start with a form template, which someone using the InfoPath Designer application creates. An InfoPath form template is a file with an `.xsn` extension. You then have to publish the template to a location where users can complete the form by adding information. Each time a user completes and saves the form, a new file is created. The data file that is created when a user completes a form has an `.xml` extensions. For example, if you take the example of the weekly status reports described in the introduction of this chapter, a single form template exists that contains all the required and optional fields that the form should contain. This form template would be published to the SharePoint site using a method similar to that described in Chapter 4 for document libraries or Chapter 6 for content types. Each team member would then click the New button on the Library toolbar to open a new instance of the form. Once the form is completed, the team member would save it to the library and create a new form data file. If there are five members on a team, then each week five new form data files are created in the library as the team members create their status reports. However, there would only be one form template file for the status reports.

To get started with using InfoPath, you must first create or design a form template. In the first Try It Out in this section, you open an existing sample template in Design view and modify a field to make it more appropriate for your organization. You can also make modifications to the form to give it a look and feel that is more appropriate for your organization. This may include adding a company logo to the various form views or adopting a color scheme that matches that of other company documents and interfaces. The second Try It Out in this section illustrates how to do this.

TRY IT OUT Creating an InfoPath Form

Using a starting point to create a form gives you more time to focus on tailoring the form to fit your needs. In this Try It Out, you modify the existing Meeting Agenda form template to include the names of staff members who typically organize your meetings. You also make this a mandatory field because, in your company, every meeting should have an identified meeting organizer. Giving users a list of values rather than a standard textbox reduces the amount of time it takes users to complete the form. The list of values also allows you to build special views in the SharePoint library so that you can filter them via the meeting organizer. For example, this allows Amanda Perran to select or create a view that only displays meetings that she organizes.

1. Open the Microsoft Office InfoPath Designer application.
2. From the New tab of the Ribbon, select Open.
3. Locate the `MeetingAgenda.xsn` form template from this chapter's materials and click Open. The form will open in design mode as shown in Figure 12-2.

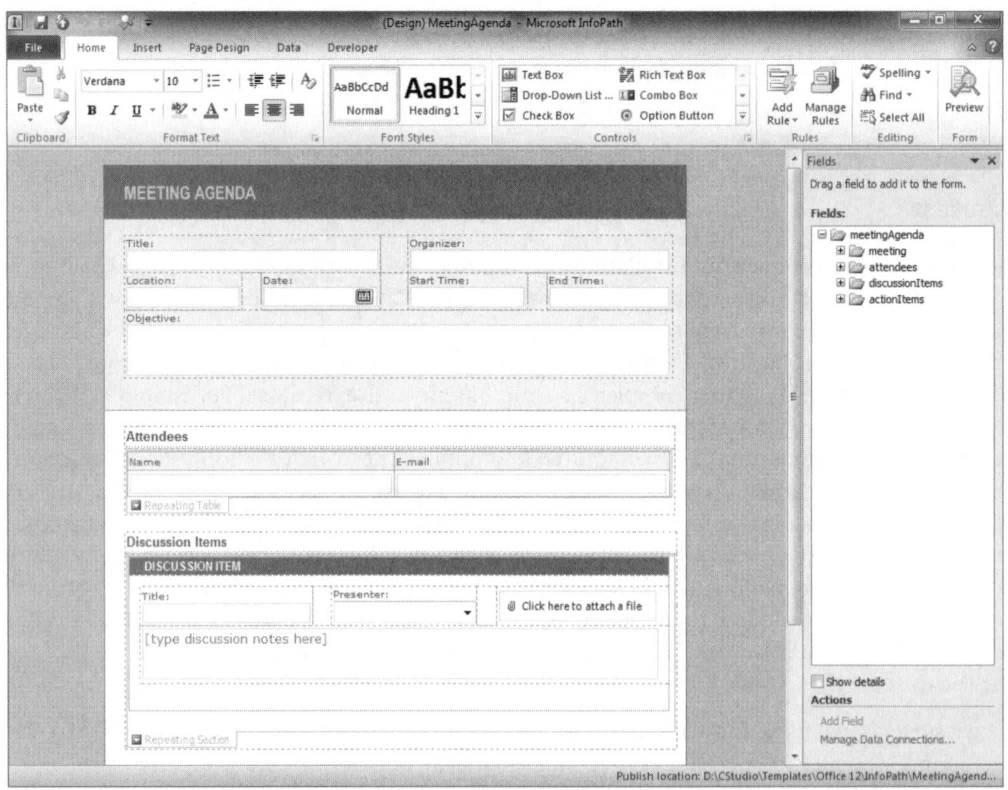

FIGURE 12-2

4. Click to select the Organizer field.

5. Right-click and select Change Control, then Drop-Down List Box from the menu, as shown in Figure 12-3. Notice that the Organizer field changes from a standard textbox to a drop-down listbox.

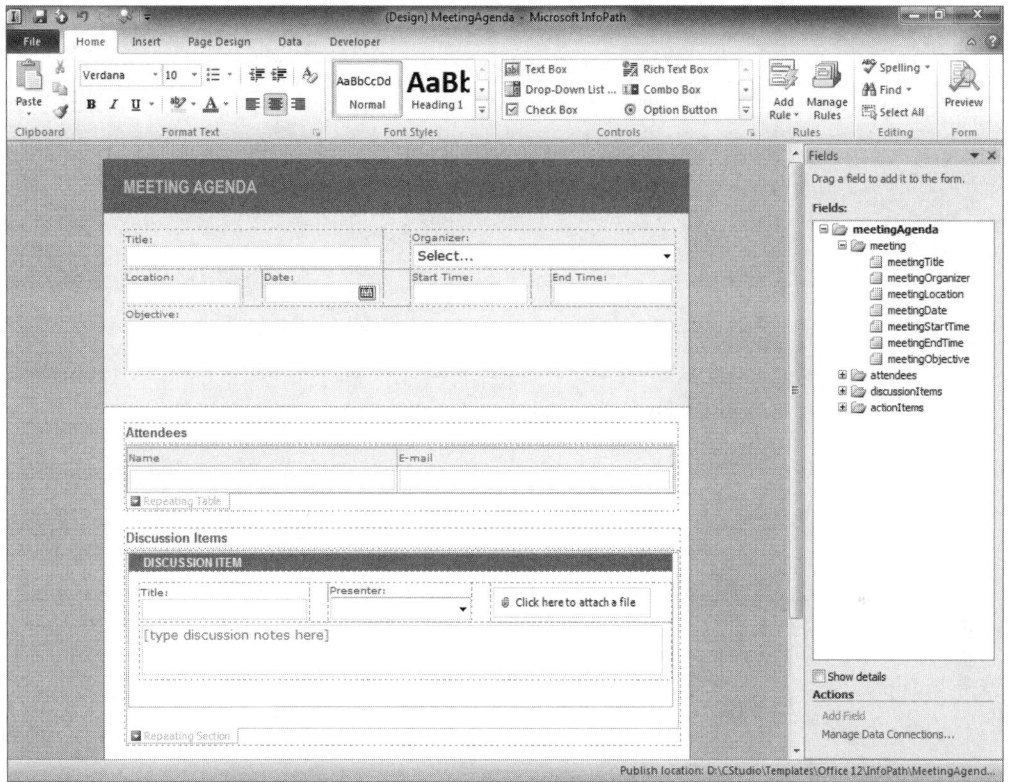

FIGURE 12-3

6. Right-click again, and this time select Drop-down List Box Properties. The Drop-Down List Box Properties dialog box appears, as shown in Figure 12-4.

7. Check the Cannot be blank checkbox under the Validation section.

8. From the List box choices section, click Add. The Add Choice dialog box appears.

9. Enter a name for the team organizer. For this example, enter **Amanda Perran** in the Value and Display Name fields. When you enter the text for the Value field first, it is automatically added to the Display Name field.

10. Click OK. You will now see Amanda Perran as a value listed in the properties of the field.

11. Repeat this process by clicking Add again and entering another team organizer. In this case, enter **Shane Perran** as a value for the drop-down, and then again enter your own name as a value.

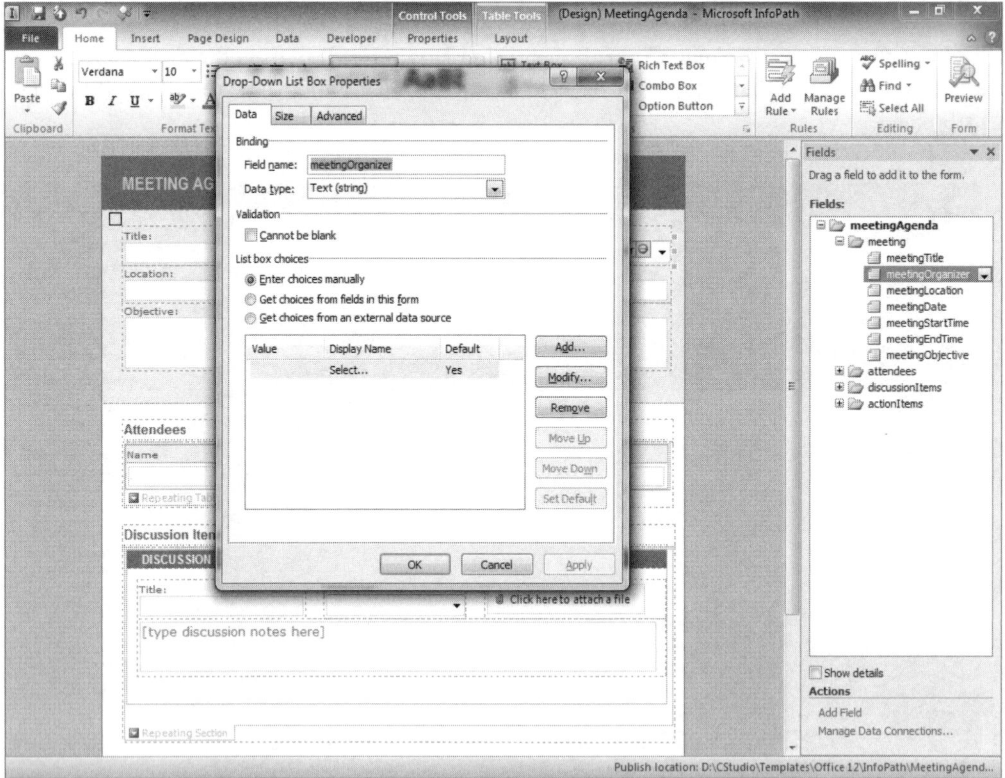

FIGURE 12-4

12. Click Apply.

13. Click OK.

14. Select Save As from the File tab of the Ribbon menu.

15. Save the file on your computer in the location containing the resource files for this chapter. Give the form template a file name of **CH12meetingagenda.xsn.**

16. Select the Preview option from the right-hand side of the Home Ribbon menu. Your form opens in preview mode, as shown in Figure 12-5.

You now see that the Organizer field is a drop-down listbox featuring the names you entered in the previous steps.

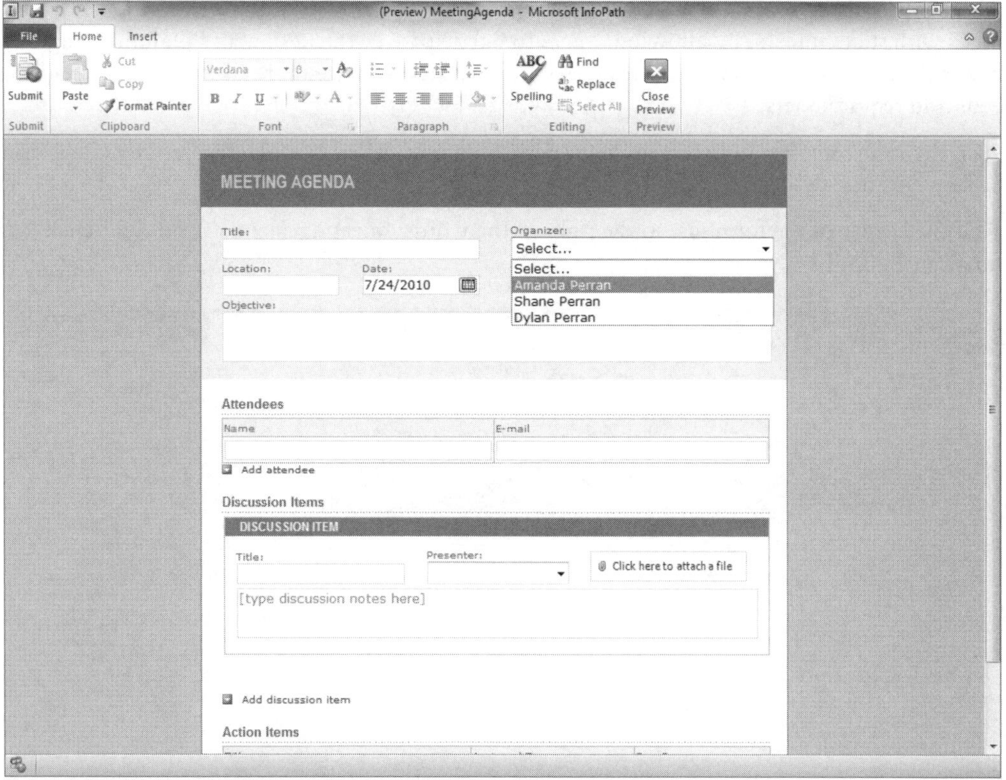

FIGURE 12-5

TRY IT OUT Customize the Look and Feel of a Form Template

In this Try It Out, you add your company's logo to the form template so that it appears whenever users view or print the form. Branding forms and document templates help create a more professional image for your forms and can help customers identify you as a company. Also, it's good to have a standardized template with a logo for conducting business activities so that people can clearly identify the official company template.

For this example, you make slight look-and-feel changes to the form template. Note that any alterations you make should be reviewed with the appropriate departments in your organization such as communications or marketing. If these departments do not exist in your organization, consider reviewing changes with stakeholders. By allowing others to participate in the design and planning stages, you can increase the probability of solid end-user adoption because you are more likely to directly address their needs and requirements.

1. Open the form template designed in the previous example called `CH12meetingagenda.xsn` using the same method described in the previous Try It Out.
2. Click the header of the form just to the right of the words "meeting agenda" and right-click, as shown in Figure 12-6.

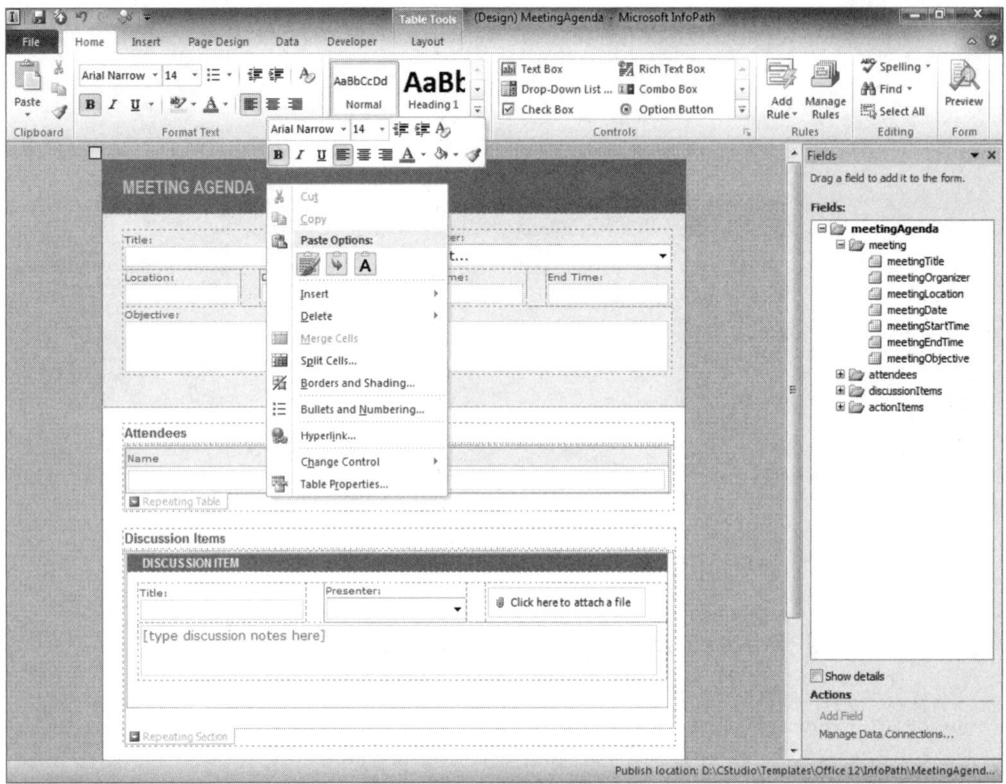

FIGURE 12-6

3. Select Borders and Shading. The Borders and Shading dialog will appear.
4. Select the Shading tab.
5. Select the light-blue color. You will notice that the background color of the heading changes to match your selection.

6. Click the header of the form just to the right of the words "meeting agenda" and right-click.
7. Select Split Cells. A dialog box appears requesting information on the format you want to create for your table.
8. Enter 2 for the number of columns, keep the value of 1 for number of rows, and click OK. The table is reformatted as specified.
9. Click in the right-hand column of the header. Select the Insert tab of the Ribbon and select the Picture option. A file selection window appears as shown in Figure 12-7.

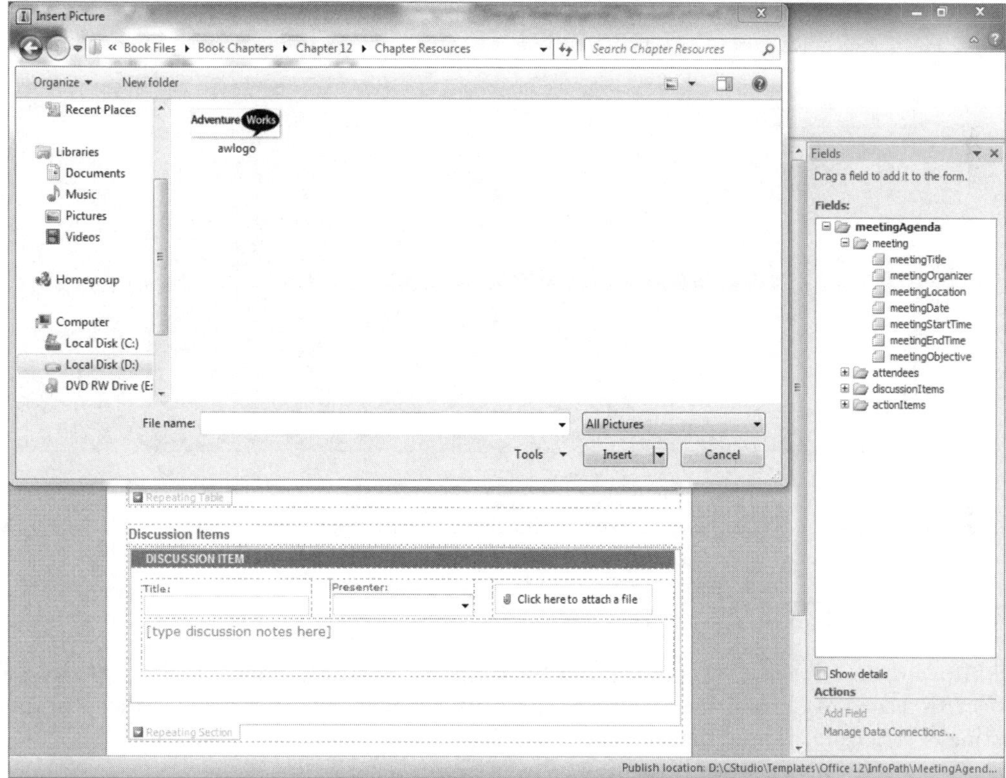

FIGURE 12-7

10. Browse to the resource files from this chapter and select `awlogo.png`.
11. Click the Insert button. The form will refresh, displaying the AdventureWorks logo, as shown in Figure 12-8.

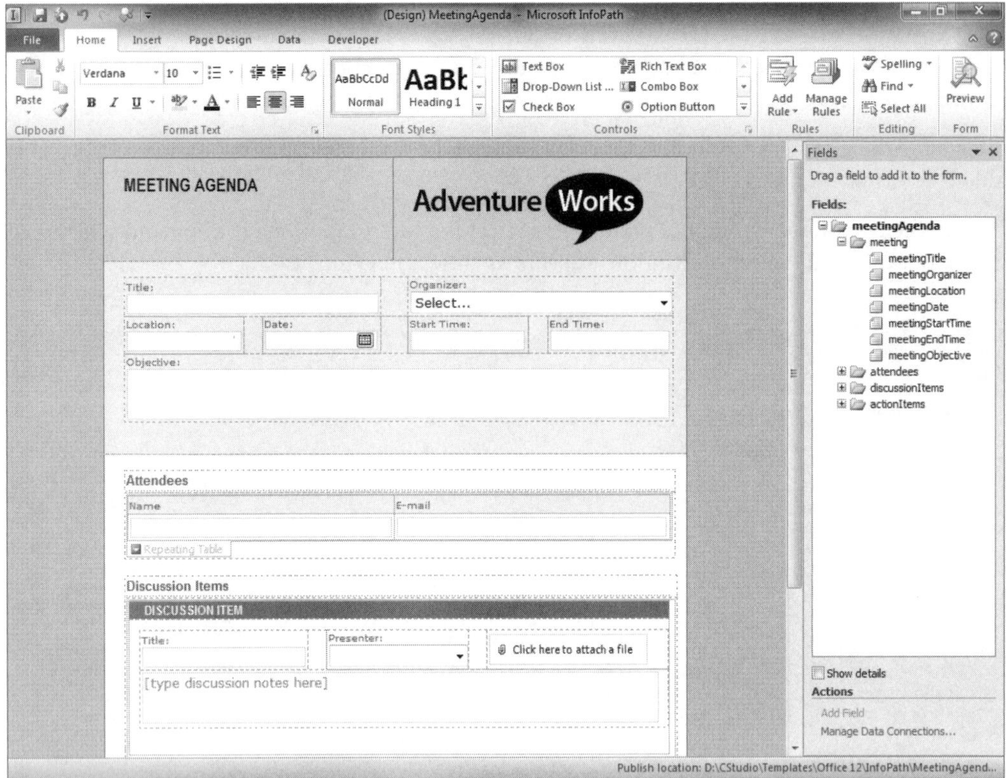

FIGURE 12-8

CORE CONCEPTS

In InfoPath, the Ribbon, shown in Figure 12-9, contains the most common design activities and concepts related to customizing or developing a form template. By clicking any of the tabs, you get a listing of actions relevant to that subject.

You start with a blank form template, and it launches with fields or controls. You may choose to apply a layout to the form. As you add controls to the form in design mode, fields automatically appear in the form's data source to support the use of these controls. The data source represents all the available fields that have been added to the form template. You can view the data source by clicking the Show Fields option on the Data tab of the Ribbon. Next, you can create various views for the form, which are similar as those discussed in Chapter 4 related to lists and libraries, but in this case they are specifically located in the form. You can basically create a set of criteria that displays your data in different ways, depending on what you want to collect or represent. You then check your design to make sure that it's compatible in the browser where it will operate. Some field types are not suitable for use in a web browser, so when creating a form for the browser, it is important to only include elements that are supported. InfoPath has a Design Checker mode that helps support you with this. Finally, you publish your form template so that others can use it and so that you can begin collecting data.

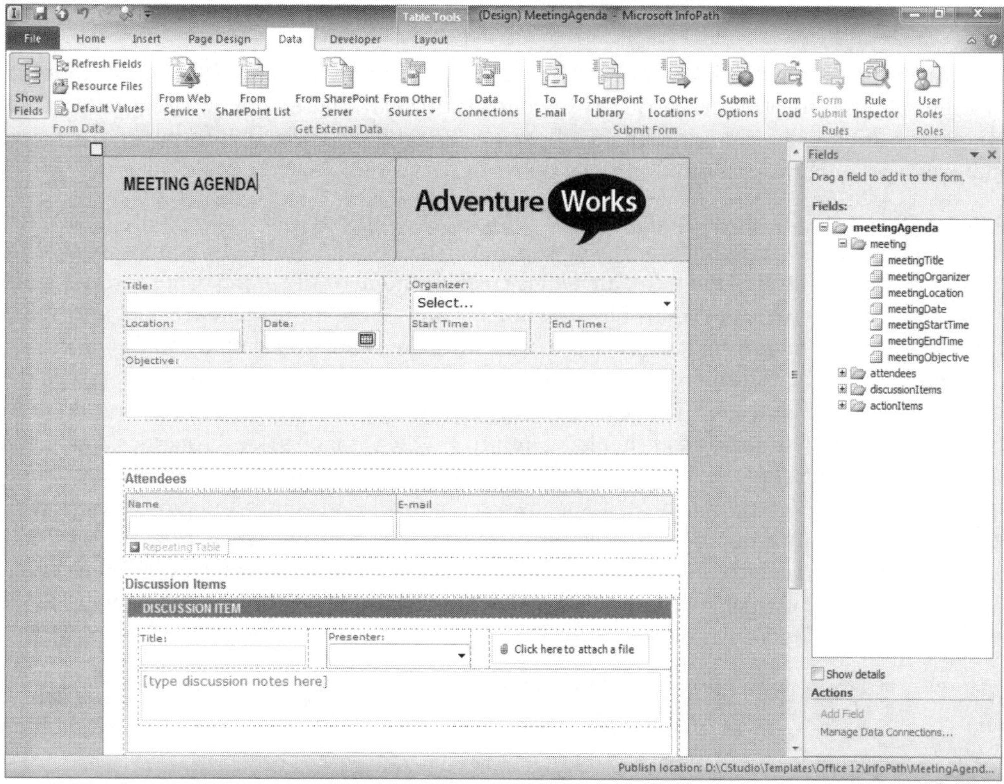

FIGURE 12-9

NOTE *To learn how to create and publish a form template, see the next section, "Working with Form Templates."*

If you are not creating your form from an existing file, you should take time to plan it out. By considering your information requirements in advance and sketching a form out on paper, you can determine what your form and data source elements should be before you even start creating the form template.

Page Design

The Page Design tab allows you to create tabular layouts in your form to control how information is presented. Quite often, in order to create a form that contains multiple columns of information, you need a table to effectively organize everything. From the Page Design tab, you can:

- Insert a predefined layout into your form template that corresponds to your need
- Create or change views
- Apply style changes or themes to your form
- Apply page settings such as margins or print settings
- Configure header and footer settings

Controls

Once you lay out a form and define its overall structure, the next step is to add the fields that the form will contain. InfoPath offers a variety of controls that can be used to effectively collect and display information in a form, including textboxes, rich text boxes, selection listboxes, data pickers, checkboxes, option buttons, buttons, and sections.

Adding controls is closely linked to creating the form's data source, which is covered in the next section. You can start with a blank form template and create the data source by adding controls to the form. As you add a control to the form, an item is created automatically in the data source to represent that control. You can add a control by selecting the area in the form where the field is to appear and clicking on the control from the Home tab of the Ribbon menu. You should name your fields as you add the controls. You can rename a field by selecting it and editing the name property in the Ribbon menu as shown in Figure 12-10 or right-clicking the field and selecting the control Properties. The name cannot contain spaces and should be intuitive. When you open the Properties dialog box, you will see other aspects of the field that you can customize, such as default values, display options, or selection values. Each type of control has its own set of unique attributes and properties. Some controls are not supported in browser-based forms and are only available when using the InfoPath Form Filler tool for the completion of forms. Therefore, when planning your forms, it is important to consider the medium by which they will be completed and the availability of specific controls to support your requirements.

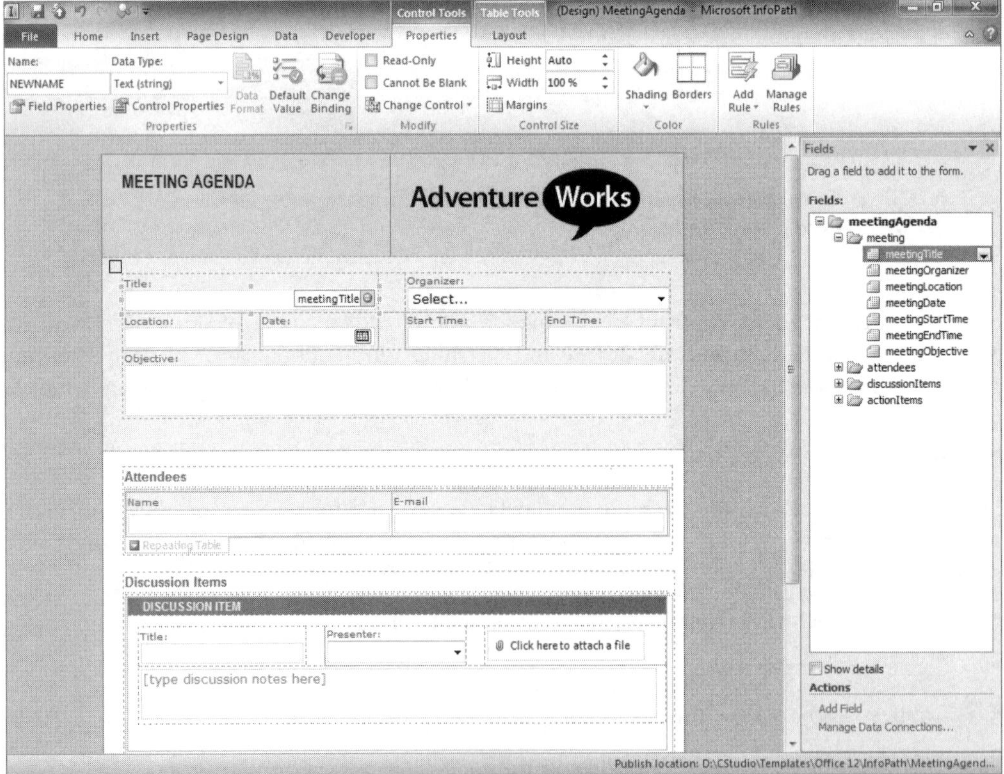

FIGURE 12-10

Textbox

A textbox can hold all sorts of information types such as Name, Phone Number, or Currency. When you edit the properties of a textbox, you can determine what format the information should be stored as by selecting the Data Type. When designing a form using this field type, you can have default values populated based on a user's selection for other fields. InfoPath also supports the use of customizable rules that allow you to perform actions such as show a dialog box message or set a field's value based on the user's selection of an item or activity within the form. You may also include placeholder text that demonstrates to a user the type of information that the field should contain or how they can complete the item. Some of the options related to the textbox control are listed in Figure 12-11, including some of the formatting and display alternatives:

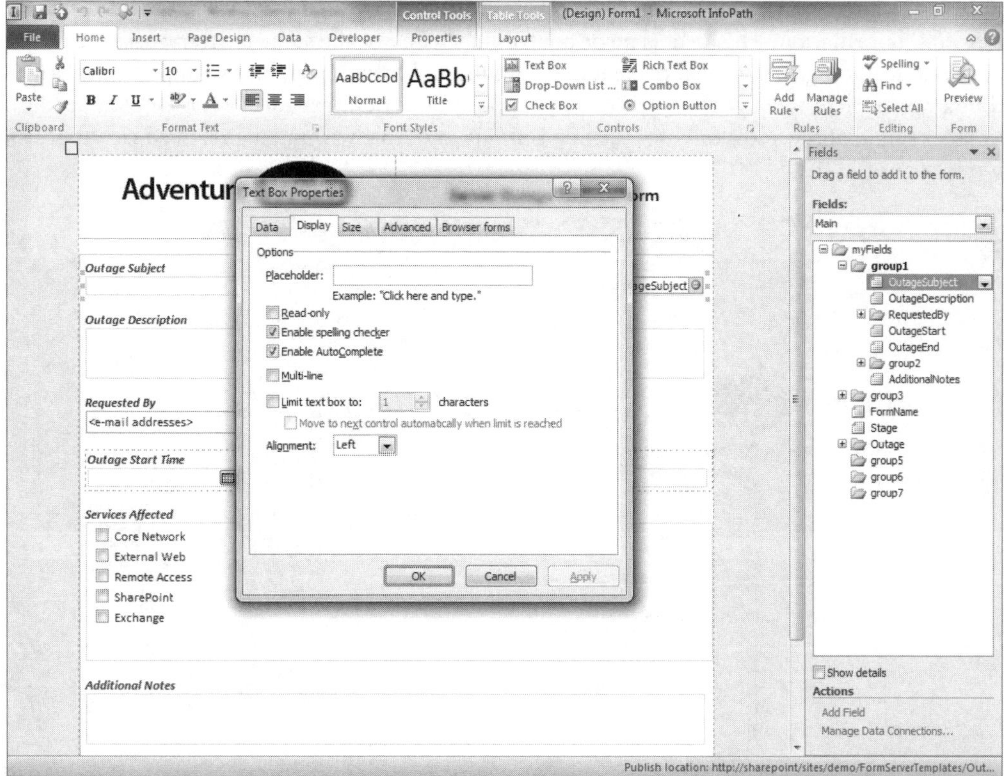

FIGURE 12-11

- **Auto Complete:** This option suggests words or phrases to a user as she is completing a form based on previously entered options. Sometimes Auto Complete can make the process for filling out a form easier for the users. However, it is not typically appropriate for forms where information entered may be of a sensitive or confidential nature.
- **Spell Check:** This enables spell checking on content stored in the field.
- **Multi-line:** By using this option, you can specify whether a textbox can include paragraph breaks or if text can wrap. This is helpful for situations where the text may exceed a single line. If you do select Multi-line, you can determine whether the control should allow scrolling or expand to display the text when it exceeds a single line.

- **Text box limit:** This option allows you to specify the number of characters a field can contain. You may use this option when accepting information, such as a phone number or Social Security number, where the number of characters is limited to a fixed number. If you enable the Multi-line option listed previously, this option will be disabled.
- **Placeholder Text:** You can use placeholder text to include suggestions in a textbox or field to represent the text a user might enter or provide instruction on how he or she should complete a field. For example, for a name field, you might have placeholder text that states "Enter Name Here." As soon as a user clicks the field, the text is erased.

Rich Text Box

You use the rich text box to collect more detailed information from a user, such as a description or background information. This field type or control has many of the same customization features as the textbox, including spell check, placeholder, conditional formatting, and wrapped text. When customizing this field type, you may choose to support basic rich text formatting or enhanced rich text. An example of the additional formatting options available within an enhanced rich text field is shown in Figure 12-12.

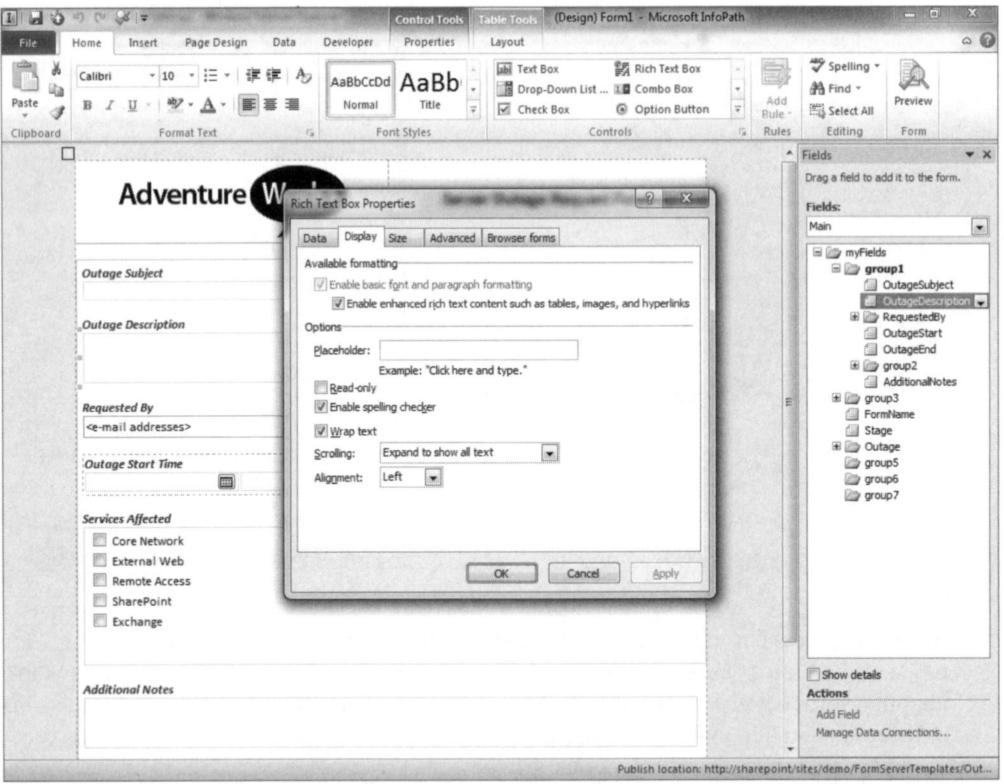

FIGURE 12-12

Selection Listboxes

Selection listbox field controls include drop-down listbox, combo box, listboxes, and multiple selection listboxes. Depending on the type of information you are collecting from your users and whether you intend to make the form available in the browser, your implementation choices may vary:

- **Drop-down listbox:** This type of box allows users to select from fixed sets of values. If there are many items, you may select a drop-down listbox to save room because it only shows one item until the user clicks a down arrow. Having too many items can negatively affect the user experience, so consider applying a filter so that only a relevant set of items are displayed based on a user's selection in another field. For example, if the user enters the United States as his country, a field for State or Province selection could be filtered to only display states because there is no requirement to display provinces.
- **Standard listbox:** This option allows users to select from a fixed set of values. The items are displayed in a listing box and are viewable all at once. This is different from the drop-down box for that reason and is typically only suitable when you have less than 10 or so values. Otherwise, the control will take up a large amount of space, and selecting from too large a set of values may be difficult for some readers.
- **Combo box:** The combo box is very similar in presentation to the drop-down listbox; however, it also allows users to enter their own values in a list. Therefore, if the item they want to select is not listed in the drop-down, they can type in their own value.
- **Multiple selection listbox:** The multiple listbox is similar to the standard listbox but contains checkboxes for each item and can also optionally allow users to enter their own values into the list. An example of a multiple selection listbox is shown in Figure 12-13.
- **Person or Group Picker:** This selection field integrates with the membership listing of your SharePoint environment to allow for the selection of users or groups through this field. By using this field type, you can link a user's profile directly within a form rather than merely just entering a textbox with their name. This field is very similar to the person or group column type that was explored in Chapter 4.
- **External Item Picker:** This selection field integrates with the Business Connectivity Services feature of SharePoint Server to allow for the selection of external business data within an InfoPath form. If an external application has been defined in SharePoint Server through the Business Connectivity Services feature, you may associate it with this field type. An example of the configuration options for defining the data source of this field type is shown in Figure 12-14. Business Connectivity Services is explored in Chapter 15 of this book.

Date Picker

This feature helps a user select a date, which is especially helpful when you have regional variations in date formats. For example, 05/06/07 can represent a completely different day in Canada than it would in the United States. An example of the Date Picker control as seen by an end user on the completed form is shown in Figure 12-15.

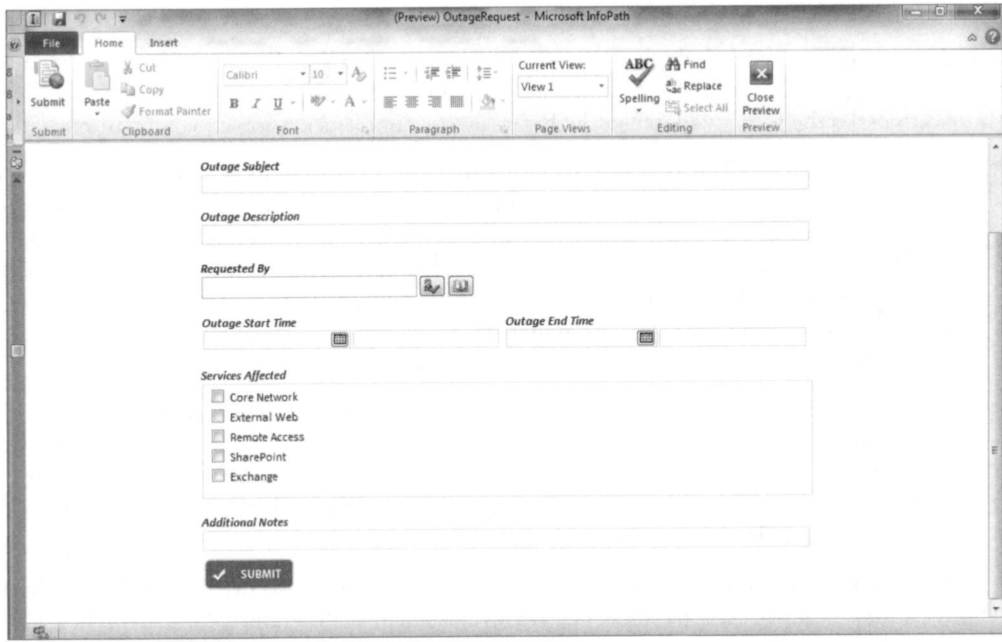

FIGURE 12-13

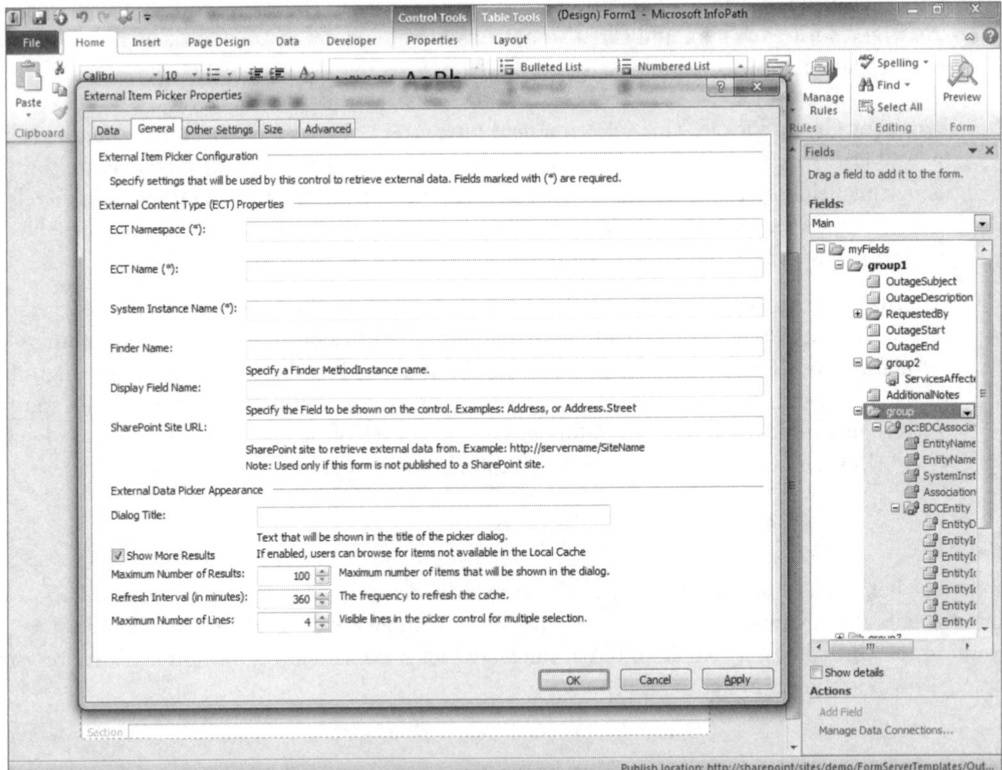

FIGURE 12-14

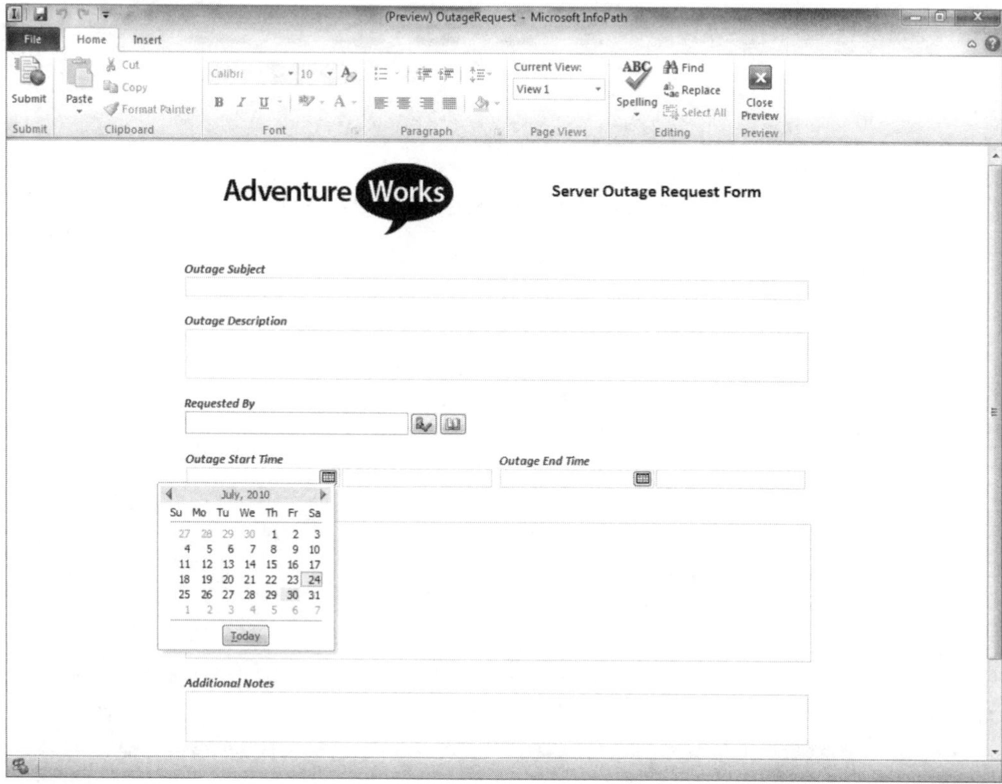

FIGURE 12-15

You can configure the Date Picker to contain certain default values including special functions, such as today (), which sets the default date to the current date of when the user is completing the form.

Checkbox

In many of the exercises in this book, you selected a checkbox to enable an option for an application. The same logic applies in a form template. You can have a single checkbox to provide a Yes or No type answer to a question. For example, if a checkbox were associated with a to-do list, a blank box would indicate that the task had not been completed, whereas a selected checkbox would be an indication that task was complete. Alternatively, you have checkboxes that allow a user to select one or more items from a group of choices, as shown in Figure 12-16. While each choice is an individual field, you can group the checkboxes in a section or table for data organization purposes.

Option Button

The Option button, sometimes referred to as a radio button, gives users a choice between items. Instead of allowing users to select more than one item, you give them a list of choices and only allow them to select one of them. In Figure 12-17, a user can only select a single size when ordering their pizza.

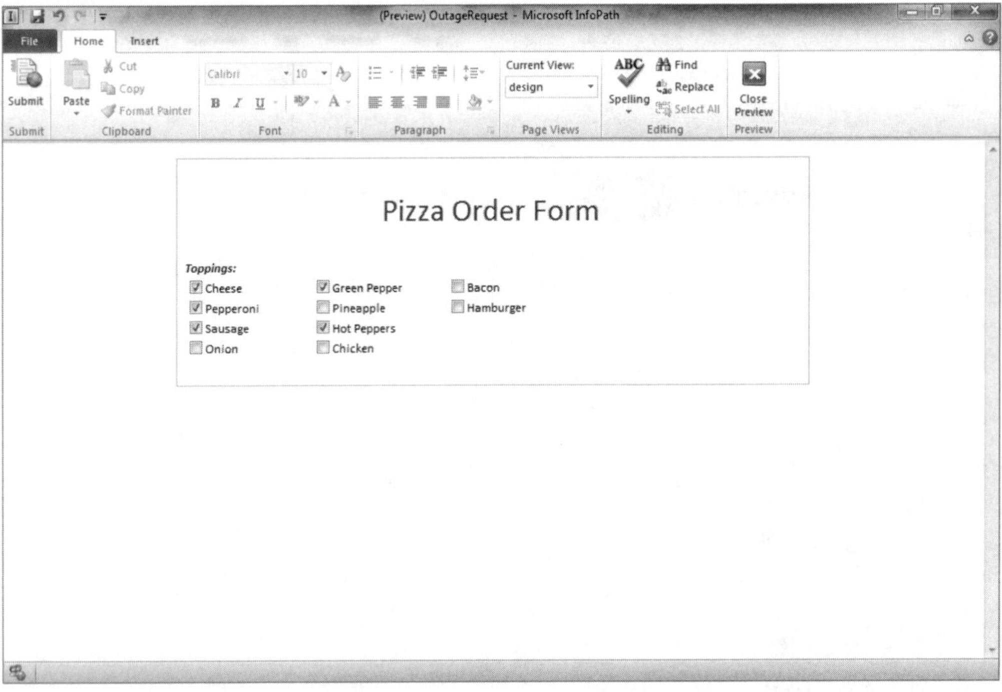

FIGURE 12-16

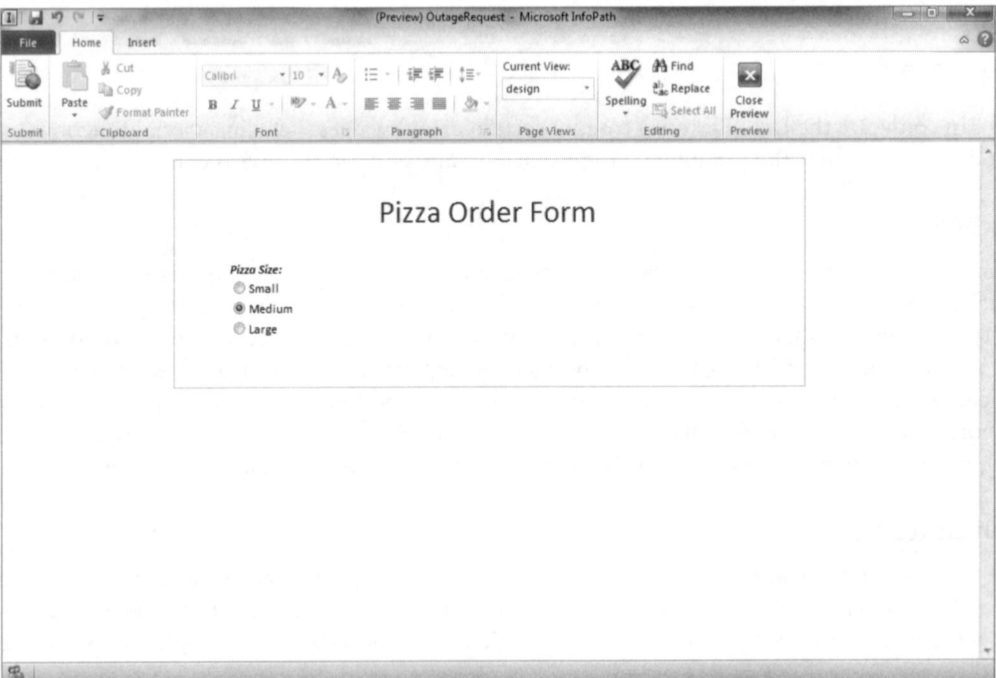

FIGURE 12-17

You select how many choices you want to give the user, and you assign each option button a unique ID that makes it easy for you to identify the user's selection.

Button

You can add a button to launch a new activity or series of rules on a form. When the user clicks the button, the activity or rule triggers. You can use buttons to launch a number of actions, including:

- Change views in a form
- Submit to a data connection
- Retrieve information from a data connection
- Launch a new form (InfoPath Form Filler Only)
- Launch a message window or display box (InfoPath Form Filler Only)
- Set the value for a field in the form
- Close a form

By implementing rules in combination with special conditions, a simple form template can become a dynamic application and drive specific business processes in a way that is very intuitive and easy to use.

Picture Button

A Picture button has the same capabilities of the button control described previously but has the additional capability of allowing the form designer to select a custom image for the presentation of the button.

Sections

Sections give elements structure and are, therefore, important when you design a form's data source and display needs. You can add, remove, or hide sections within a form template. As shown in Figure 12-18, you can select an option to have a section initially excluded from the form or added by a user. You may choose to hide a section if you want to have portions of your form only appear based on a user's response to a question. For example, if you have a set of questions in your form related to what pizza toppings a user wants on their pizza, you might choose to hide those questions if in a previous answer the user selected that he wanted to order hamburgers.

It is generally a good idea to add sections to your form templates to group information that is similar or related. You should name sections appropriately so that you can better identify a set of related fields within the form's data source.

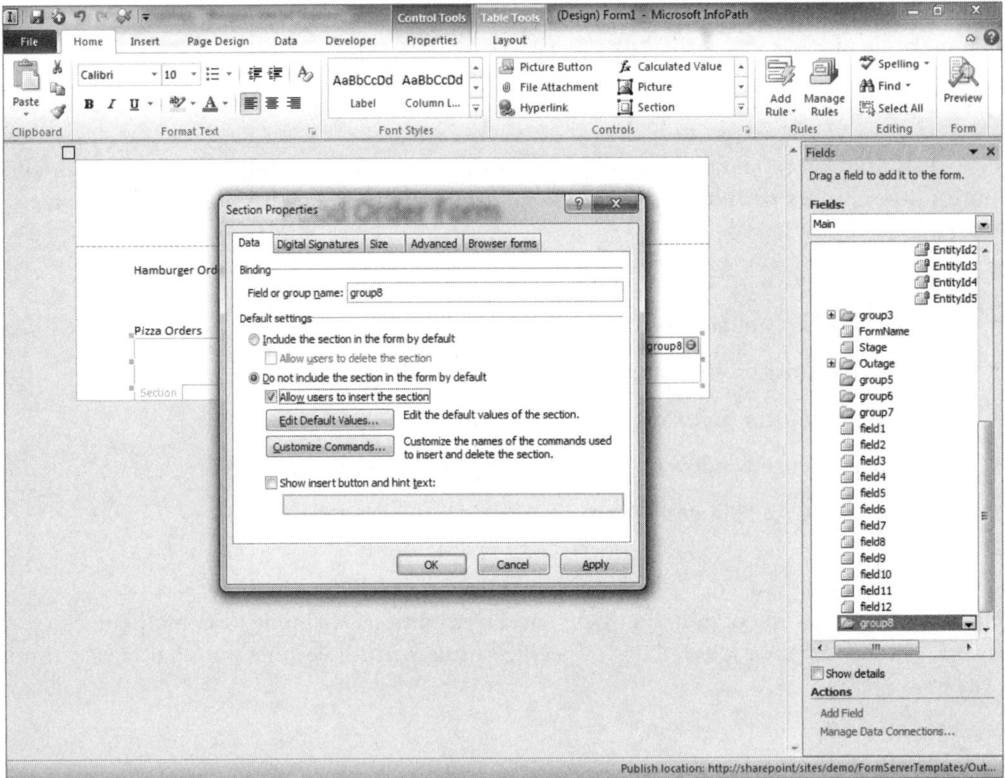

FIGURE 12-18

Other Controls

The previously listed field types are just a few of the standard controls available for use in an InfoPath form. Additional control types include:

- **Tables:** You can include tables in your form for users to complete. Each table can contain a number of fields and may include repeating rows so that users can add more information or items to the table as required.
- **Master/Detail:** In some cases, you may have two controls or sections whereby the selection in one will dictate the detail displayed in another. An example of this might be a product category list and a product details listing. If a user selects a category, the details listing should be reformatted to display only the items related to the selected category.
- **Lists:** A list can be a more informal control that allows a user to add a bulleted or numbered list in his response. You may include a list in a form that asks a user to submit ideas for a new product or accomplishments for a particular time period.
- **File Attachment:** It may be appropriate or beneficial to have a user attach a file to his form instance. This file becomes embedded in the form document and others can access it later when reviewing the form.

- **Picture:** This control allows you to create a field that will either upload and embed a picture in the form, or link to a picture stored elsewhere.
- **Ink Picture:** For users with a drawing tablet or Tablet PC, InfoPath has built-in support for Ink, which allows a user to write directly into a form with a digital pen. This field supports the drawing of an image directly within the form. This field is only supported for forms that will be completed using InfoPath Filler.
- **Hyperlink:** This control allows you to insert a hyperlink into the form whereby you can specify the link to location and display text.
- **Calculated Value:** For more advanced users, this control can be used to enter an XPath expression that can perform advanced calculations on data stored in the form. The results of the calculation are displayed in the form.
- **Vertical Label:** For design purposes, you may want to have a vertical label added to your form. This control presents the form designer with a textbox within which text can be added. This text is displayed vertically on the form. This field is supported only for forms that will be completed using InfoPath Filler.
- **Regions or Groups:** Similar to sections, regions and groups are organizational elements that can be added to pages to support fields or text.

Data Source

The primary data source of your InfoPath form is basically the skeletal information structure of your form. In order to have a field in the form, it must be tied to an element in the data source. When you create your form by adding controls, data source elements are automatically added in the primary data source for you. You can also have secondary data sources, such as external data connections that you can use to display information in the form. For example, you may have a secondary data source that is a database. You can drag information from your database onto the form and select which fields or controls should be used to display the information.

As described in the last section, the data source is very closely tied to the controls. You should name your fields as you add the controls. This will automatically update the data source. The name cannot contain spaces and should be intuitive. You can also add groups, tables, or sections in your form's data source so that you can easily track elements or items that related to one another.

The primary data source of a form can be imported based on an XML file, or generated from a data connection. The available options for creating a new form from a data connection are displayed in Figure 12-19. This approach is more advanced; a formalized data structure is imported into the form and then controls are added to the form to represent the data.

If you are not creating your data source from a data connection or XML schema file, you should take time to plan it out. Consider your information requirements, and sketch a form out on paper. By considering what some of the information requirements are in advance, you can generate a good idea on what your data elements should be before you even start creating the form template.

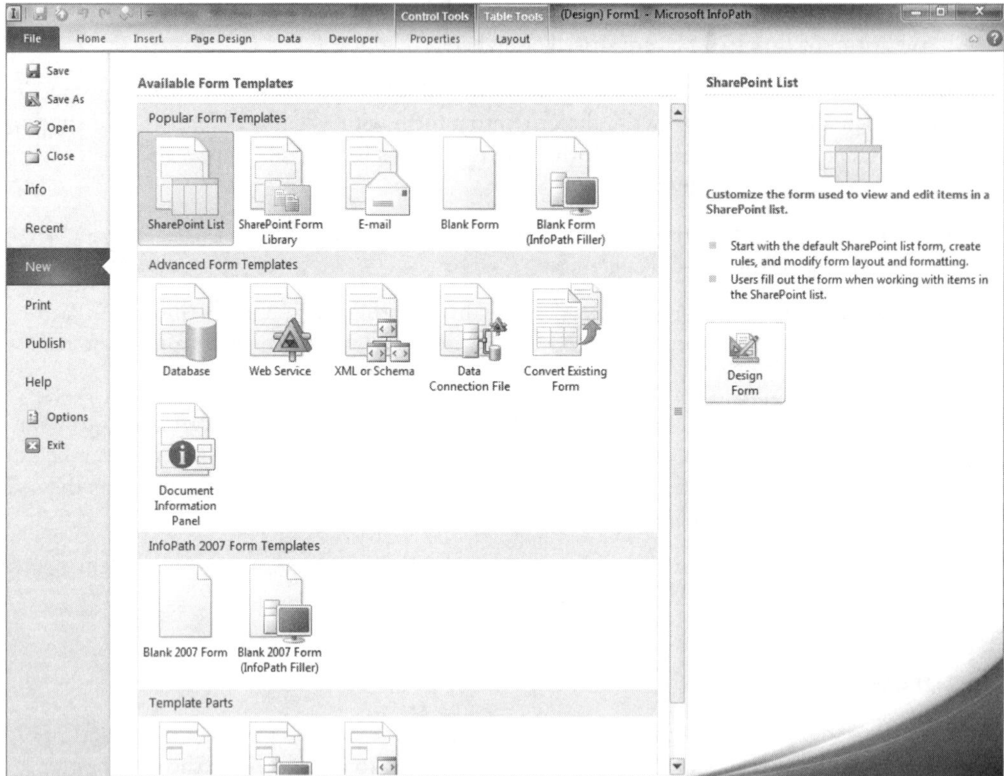

FIGURE 12-19

> **NOTE** *When you remove a control from a form's view, you do not remove the field from your data source. Views are discussed in the next section.*

In addition to the primary data source of a form template, additional data sources become available as new data connections are added to the form. An example of this can be seen in Figure 12-20.

Similar to the behavior of the primary data source, you can drag elements within a secondary data source onto the page. This can help provide some data reporting from external data sources within the form itself. You can add items either as sections or tables and then format them as required. For example, in a form template that tracks information about a customer, the primary data source of the form may contain items such as the customer's phone number, company name, and email address. And you might create a secondary data source that connects to the orders database. You can drag information from this secondary data source onto the form to show a salesperson all the products the customer has purchased.

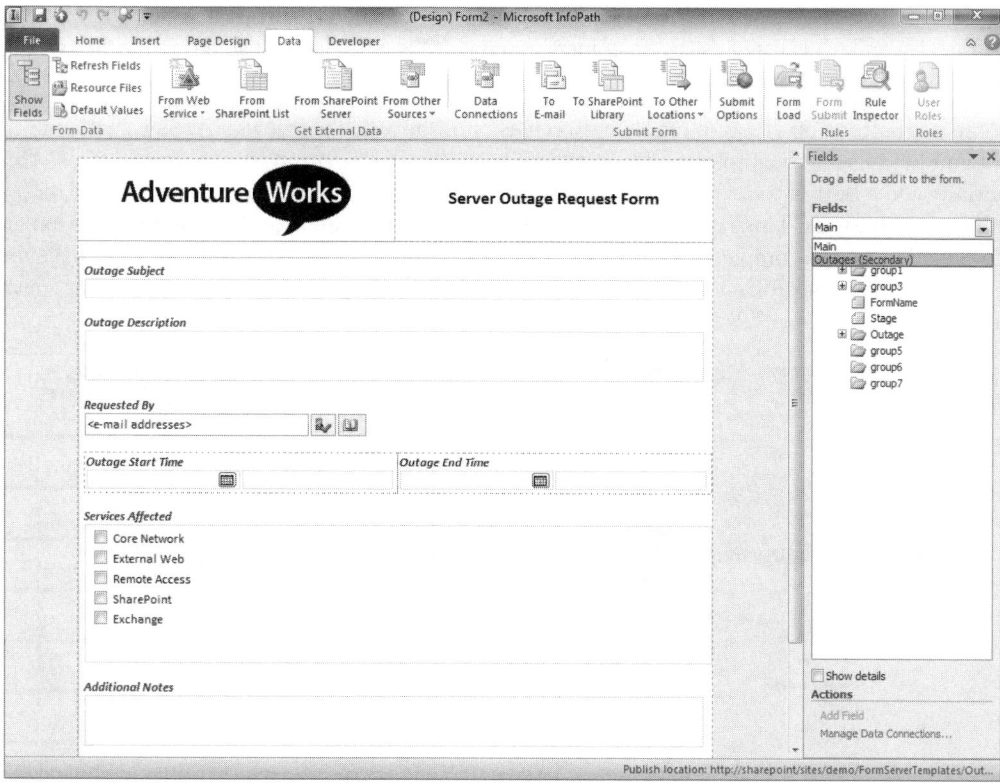

FIGURE 12-20

Views

In Chapter 4, you saw how to create custom views for lists and libraries to display different records and columns from a single data source. With InfoPath, you can also create multiple views from a single form. The views can either act as reports or pages in a form where they can represent completely unique steps related to the completion of a process. For example, you can have a form template with four different views: one for customer requests; a second that logs troubleshooting issues that an employee must resolve; a third that tracks correspondence with customer; and a final one that tracks customer's comments on the level of service they've received.

Views can be created from the Page Design tab of the Ribbon menu by selecting New View. When a view is created, it is blank. The Form Designer must drag layout elements such as tables onto the form and add controls as needed. A single field can be added to multiple views. For example, you may have a field for customer name. You can add this field to every view in your form. You can also change unique characteristics related to the presentation of the field on each view. While the data remains the same, the presentation of a field on each view can be slightly different. For example, on one page the customer's name may appear in large bold letters in Read-Only format, and on another it may appear in a drop-down box. However, the data of the field remains the same. Therefore, if "Graphical Wonder" is listed as the customer in one view, it will also be listed on all other views in that field.

You can use buttons on views to toggle between each of the available views. In some cases, multiple views and buttons can be implemented on a form to collect information from a user in steps. You essentially add a button to a view that, when selected, will launch another view using the Rules capabilities of buttons. This replicates the experience of a wizard and can help simplify the experience of the user as she completes the operation. If you don't use custom buttons, you can have users switch between various form views within the InfoPath Filler application using the Current View menu, as shown in Figure 12-21.

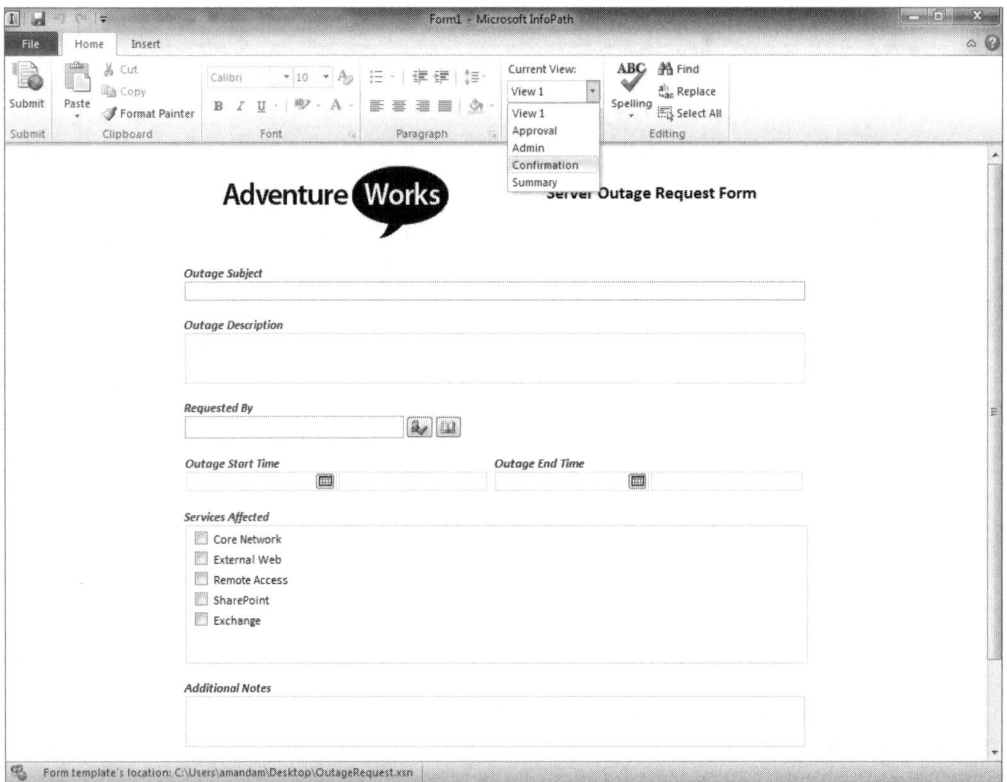

FIGURE 12-21

A similar view selector may be enabled on the toolbar of browser-based forms as shown in Figure 12-22. This is an optional setting that can be configured in the Advanced Form options that is available from the File menu.

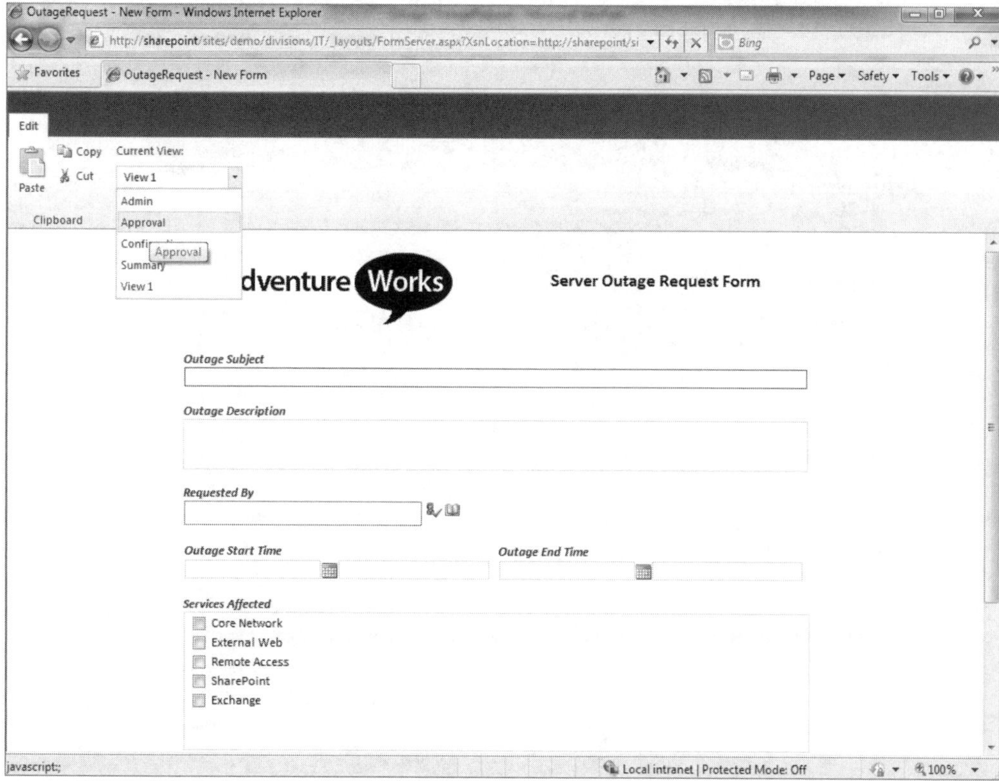

FIGURE 12-22

Design Checker

As previously stated, not all form controls are supported for use within browser-based forms. Therefore, you need to consider who the audience for your form will be and how they will access the form. If the form has to be available for use on the browser, careful consideration is required to ensure that the experience is positive. This may seem like a lot to understand if you are just getting used to creating these forms. Therefore, a Design Checker exists with the InfoPath application to guide you by highlighting anything you may have in your form that would not be compatible with the browser or previous versions of InfoPath.

If you decide that a form should be browser-compatible after you have already begun the form design process, you can change the setting by selecting the Web Browser Form within the Compatibility settings under Advanced Form Options, as shown in Figure 12-23.

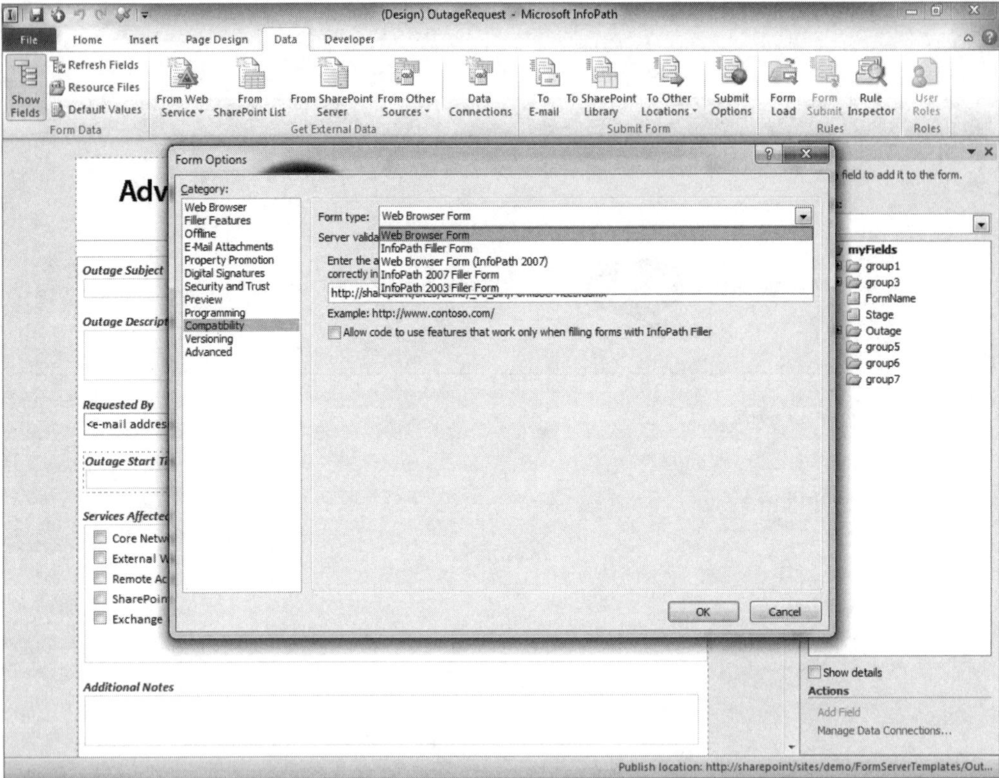

FIGURE 12-23

Another option in this same interface is a URL to test whether the form will be compatible with the destination SharePoint server. If you specify a URL, the Design Checker displays alerts and messages indicating items in your form that may affect compatibility with either the browser or older versions of the application.

Publish Form Template

You can always save a template in a location for your personal use and to edit further, but to make your form available to others, you need to publish the template to a central location. You can publish an InfoPath form template to any of the following locations:

- A SharePoint Server with Enterprise Features (supports browser-based forms or the use of InfoPath Filler)
- A SharePoint Server with Standard Features (requires InfoPath Filler)
- A SharePoint Foundation Server (requires InfoPath Filler)
- A shared network location such as a file share (requires InfoPath Filler)
- An email message to recipients (requires InfoPath Filler)

Depending on the environment in which you are working and what tools you have available, you may select any one of these options when completing the Publishing Wizard.

NOTE *The next section, "Working with Form Templates," walks you through examples of publishing an InfoPath form to a SharePoint server, including directly publishing a form to a document library, creating an InfoPath Form content type, and uploading an administrator-approved form template.*

If you publish your form template to any of these locations, you must save a local copy of the template on your computer. If later you want to make updates to the form template, you can make them to your local copy and complete the Publishing Wizard to update your form template in its shared location. However, you should be confident that no edits were performed directly on the template in its shared location. If there are edits, then you may overwrite them by publishing an older version of the form. It is a good idea to identify and define development policies and procedures related to your organization's custom InfoPath forms to ensure that such situations do not occur. Once the initial publishing process has completed, future updates can be delivered to the server using the Quick Publish feature. This republishes the form using the same settings as previously defined in the last publishing process.

WORKING WITH FORM TEMPLATES

Now that you know the design-related functions of an InfoPath form template, you can start creating some actual form templates that can help you collect and view information. This section discusses creating a new form template and then addresses some options for publishing and customizing the form to further meet the business requirements.

Designing a New Form

Before you can begin creating a new form, you need to figure out the form's requirements. This might involve gathering information from the group or sponsors who are requesting the form. However you gather the information, you should know the following:

- What types of information should the form collect?
- How should you present the information, and what special rules are there for submitting the information? For example, you should create Name and Email fields because they are required to contact employees after they submit feedback.
- How should you format the Data fields? For example, you may apply special formatting or filtering that disables a field based on a user's input in another field. This is helpful to ensure that users only have to deal with the fields they are required to complete.
- Is there additional data that is stored in an external system that should be available within your form?

Once you have the information that you need, it's time to do the actual work of creating the form template.

Although there are many steps in the next Try It Out, they represent a small portion of the steps required to create the most basic of electronic forms. In the second Try It Out of this section, you look at the functionality of InfoPath related to creating reusable template components called *template parts*.

TRY IT OUT Design a New Form Template

For this Try It Out, you first set up the layout of the form. This helps mold the canvas for how the form will look. It is also recommended that prior to opening the InfoPath application you should always sketch out how you want the form to look on a piece of paper. This is something that can be helpful for collecting feedback from your sponsors prior to starting any development work. As you see in the Try It Out, sometimes there can be many steps to even creating the most basic of forms. Therefore, it is always a good idea to have a solid roadmap before you even start.

Once the layout is defined, you begin adding controls and creating the data source. In this situation, every time you add a new control to the page, it creates a new data source field. You name the fields as you go along to keep things organized and easy to follow. This is very important as forms become more complex and large numbers of fields are created.

1. Open the Microsoft InfoPath Designer 2010 application. The new form template selection window will appear.
2. Select the option to create a blank form. On the right-hand side of the window, your selection will be displayed as shown in Figure 12-24.
3. Click the Design Form button. A blank form template will open.
4. Click in the title area and enter **Employee Feedback** for the form title.
5. Click within the second row of the form template, and select the Layout tab of the Ribbon.
6. Select the option to Split Cells. The Split Cells dialog will appear.
7. Enter 3 as the value for columns and **2** as the value for rows.
8. Click OK. Your new form layout will be displayed as shown in Figure 12-25.
9. Select within the area of the first row and column of your table and right-click to select the Table Properties menu option.
10. Select the Column tab.
11. Enter 300 **px** for the width of the left column.
12. Click the Next Column button. The middle column will be selected.
13. Enter 50 **px** for the width of the middle column.
14. Click the Next Column button. The right column will be selected.
15. Enter 300 **px** for the width of the right column.
16. Click Apply and then OK. The table properties dialog window will close, and you will be returned to your form.

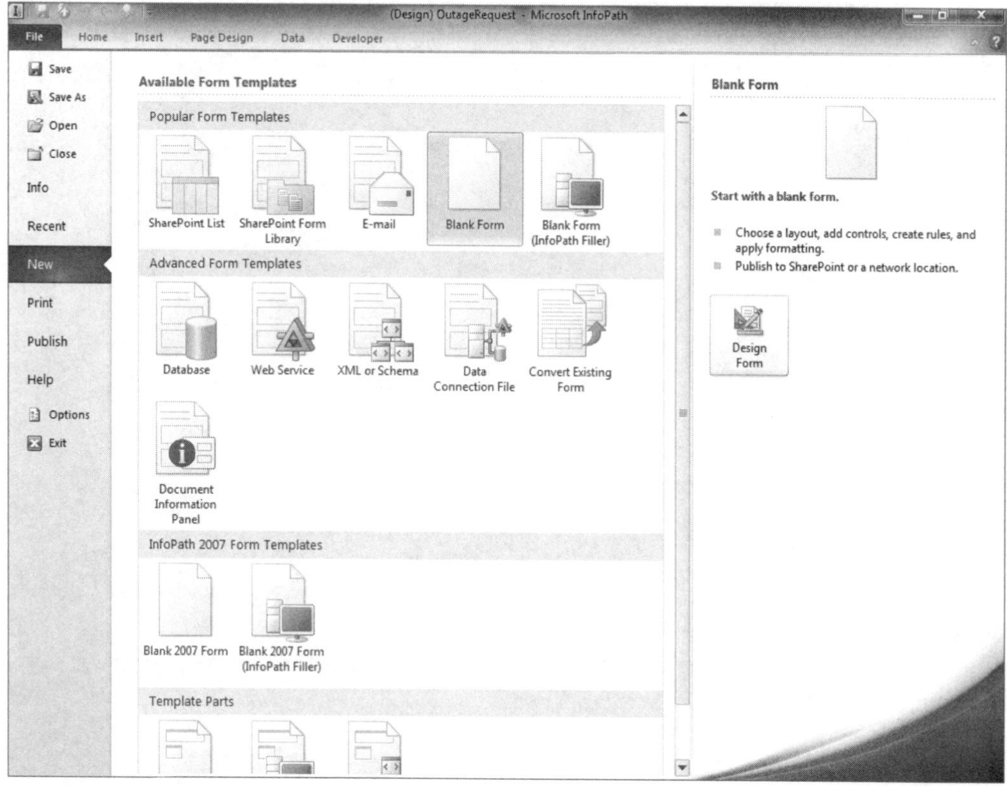

FIGURE 12-24

17. Click within the left column of the first row, and enter the words **Employee Name**.
18. From the Home tab of the Ribbon, select the Text box control. A new textbox field will appear below the Employee Name label.
19. Right-click on the field, and select the Text Box Properties option.
20. Specify EmployeeName for the field name.
21. Check the Cannot be blank setting checkbox, as shown in Figure 12-26.
22. Click Apply, then OK.
23. Click within the right column of the first row, and enter the words **Employee Email**.
24. From the Home tab of the Ribbon, select the Text Box control. A new textbox field will appear below the Employee Email label.
25. Specify EmployeeEmail for the field name.
26. Check the Cannot be blank setting checkbox.
27. Click Apply, then OK.
28. Select the last row in the table with your mouse to highlight each column.

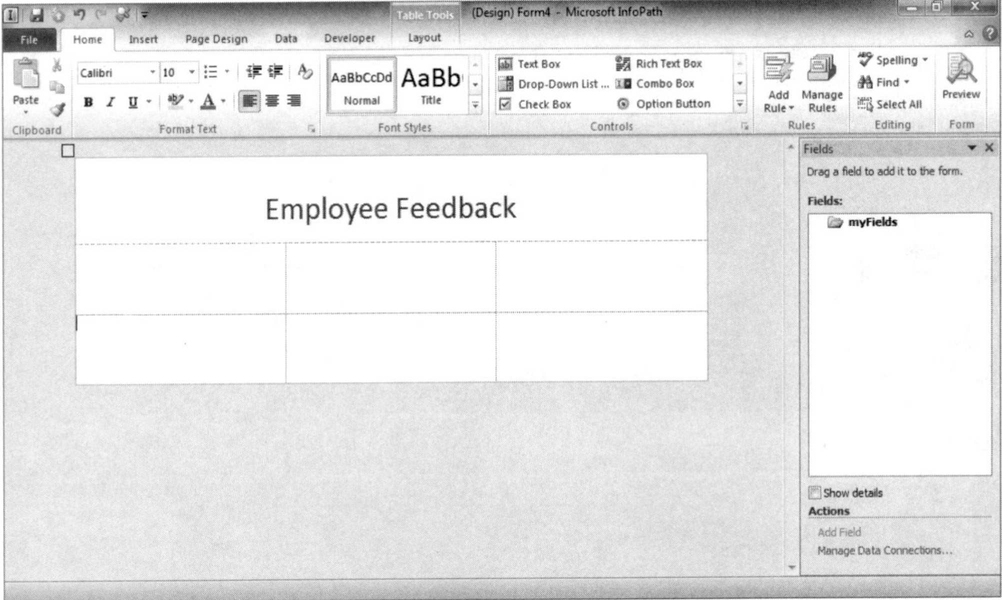

FIGURE 12-25

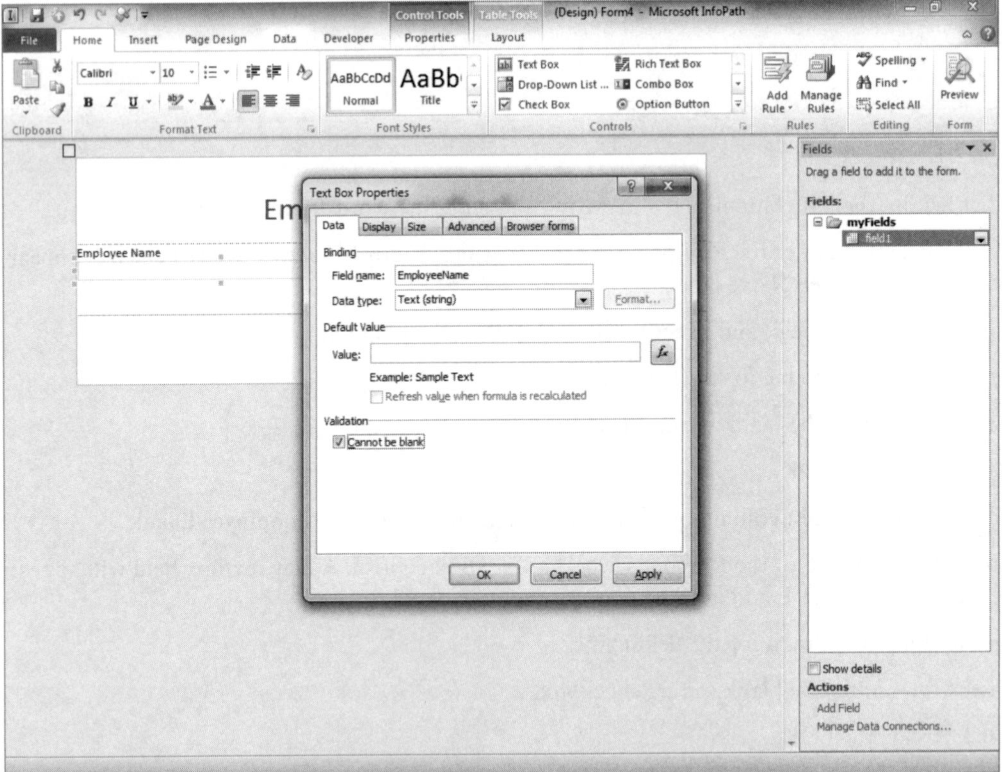

FIGURE 12-26

29. Select the merge cells option from the Layout tab of the Ribbon menu.
30. In the newly merged row, enter the text **Tell Us What You Think** and press Enter.
31. From the Home tab of the Ribbon menu, select the Rich Text box. A new field will be added to the form.
32. Select your newly created field, and click the Properties tab of the Ribbon menu.
33. Enter **EmployeeFeedback** in the name field, as shown in Figure 12-27.

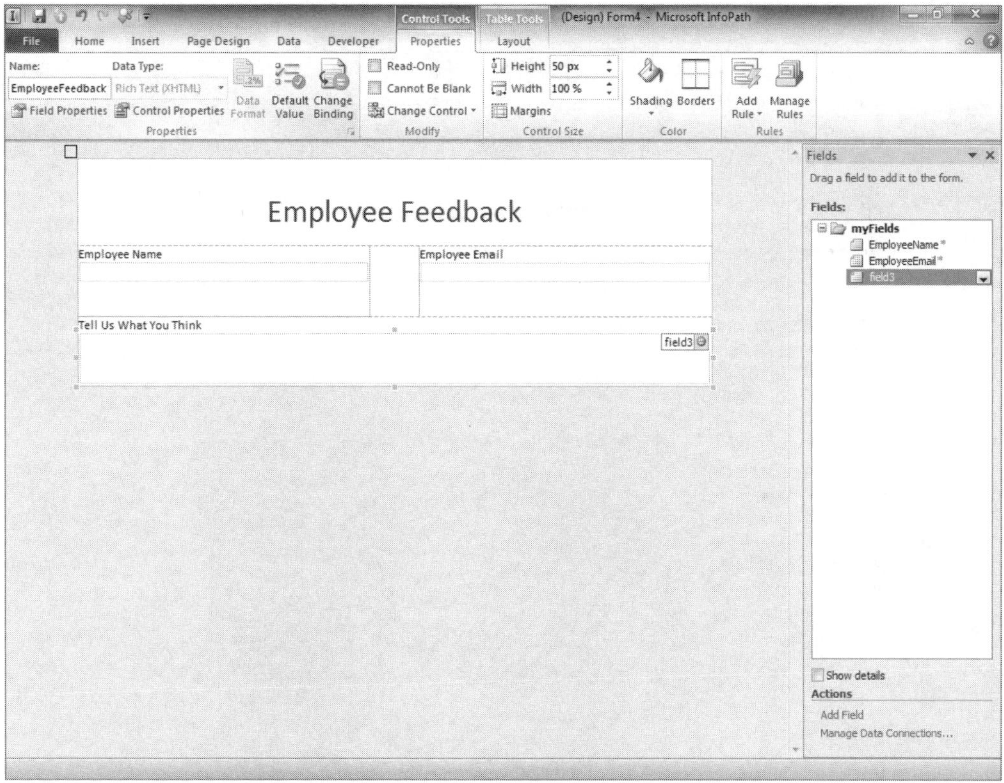

FIGURE 12-27

34. Select the Cannot be blank checkbox from the Ribbon.
35. Select the entire table within your form. This is most easily done by selecting the box that appears at the very top left of the form whenever you click within a table cell.
36. Select the Cell Padding option from Layout tab of the Ribbon menu.
37. Enter **10 px** for the Left and Right cell padding options.
38. Click the Apply the OK buttons. You will notice that the form will refresh displaying more space around each of the form fields and labels.
39. From the File tab, select the Save as button.

40. Save the form in the folder containing this chapter's resource files using the name **EmployeeFeedback.xsn.**

41. From the Home tab of the Ribbon menu, click the Preview button.

How It Works

After you finish adding fields and save the form, you preview it. Figure 12-28 demonstrates that each field has a special character within it that communicates to the user that the fields are required.

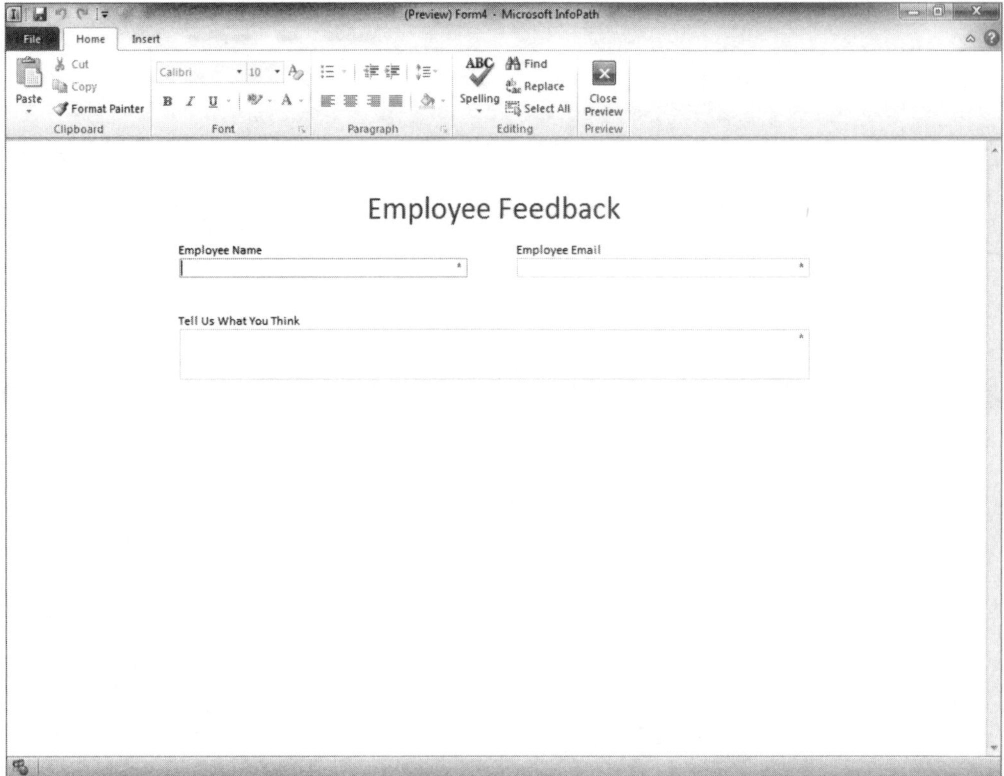

FIGURE 12-28

TRY IT OUT Create a Template Part

In the last Try It Out, you looked at the process for creating an entire form template. However, a fantastic feature in InfoPath is the ability to create reusable components called template parts. A template part is a section or group of controls that may have specific fields, data connections, or customizations that could be potentially reused across multiple form templates. For example, consider a common contact form. It generally contains a name, email address, phone number, and address. In fact, many other forms also contain this information. Therefore, it's beneficial to create template parts containing each of those items so that they can be easily added in the future to all other forms requiring those components.

1. Open the InfoPath Designer application.
2. Select the option to create a blank template part.
3. Click the Design Form button. A blank form template will appear.
4. From the Controls section from the Home tab of the Ribbon menu, select the Section control. A blank section control will appear in your form.
5. Right-click on the new section control, and select Section Properties.
6. Enter **ContactInformation** as the name of the section.
7. Click the Apply and OK buttons.
8. Insert a table and add four new textbox fields to your form, as shown in Figure 12-29, to represent the name, phone number, email address, and street address fields.

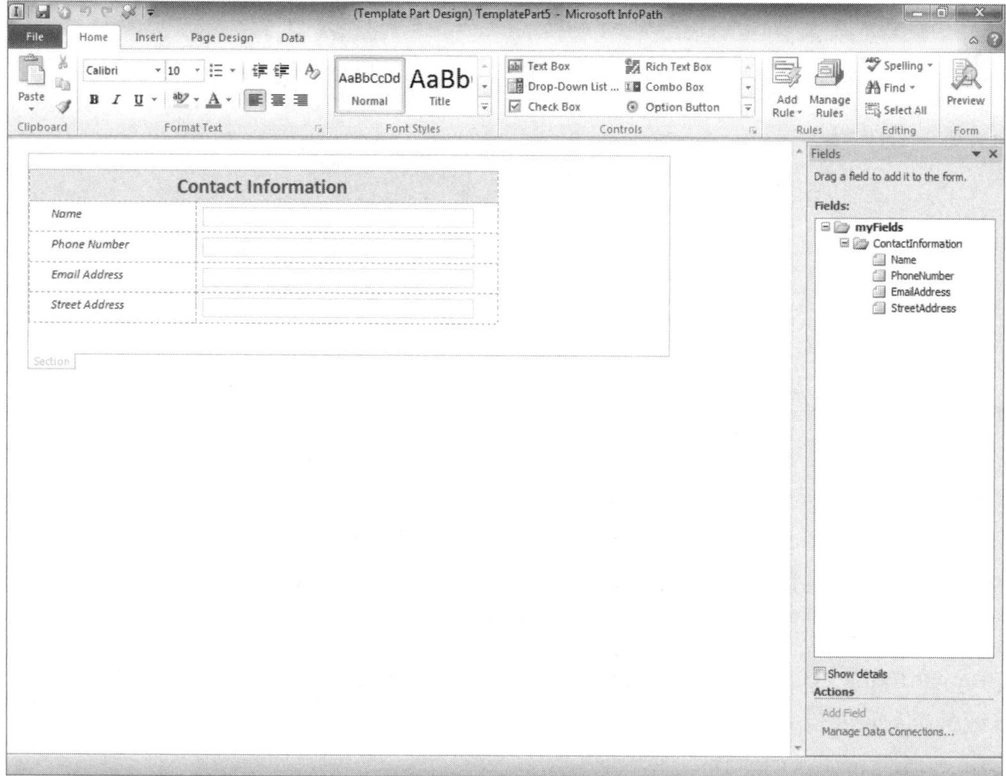

FIGURE 12-29

9. Apply your desired configuration settings to the four fields. When finished, select the Save as option from the File tab of the Ribbon.
10. Save the form using the name **ContactInfo** in the folder containing this Chapter's resources.
11. Close the form.

12. From the File tab of the Ribbon, select the option to create a New Blank Form using the same steps described in the previous Try It Out.
13. Expand the controls section of the Home menu, as shown in Figure 12-30.

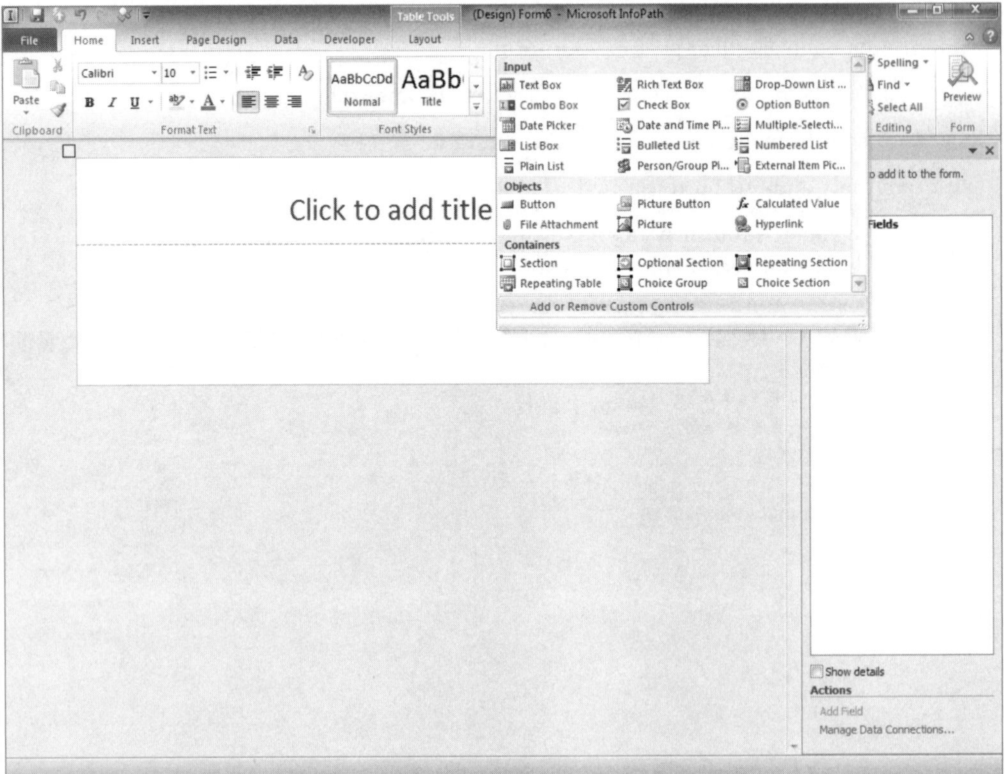

FIGURE 12-30

14. Select the option to Add or Remove Custom Controls. A dialog box will appear.
15. Click Add. The Add Custom Control Wizard will appear, as shown in Figure 12-31.
16. Select the option to add a Template Part, and click Next.
17. Browse to the location of your Contact Info Template part that was saved in step 10.
18. Click Finish.
19. Click Close.
20. Click OK.

How It Works

The custom template part that you created will now be available for use within the Controls section of the Home menu, as shown in Figure 12-32. In future scenarios where a form template calls for a combination of name, email address, phone number and street address fields, this control can be dropped onto the form.

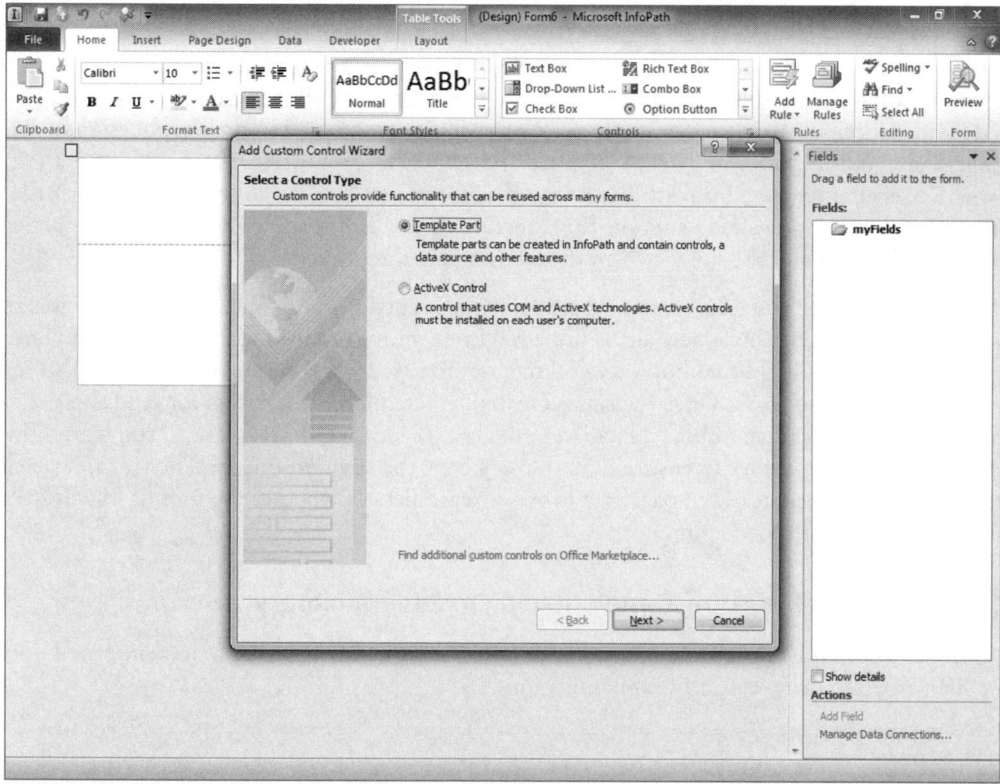

FIGURE 12-31

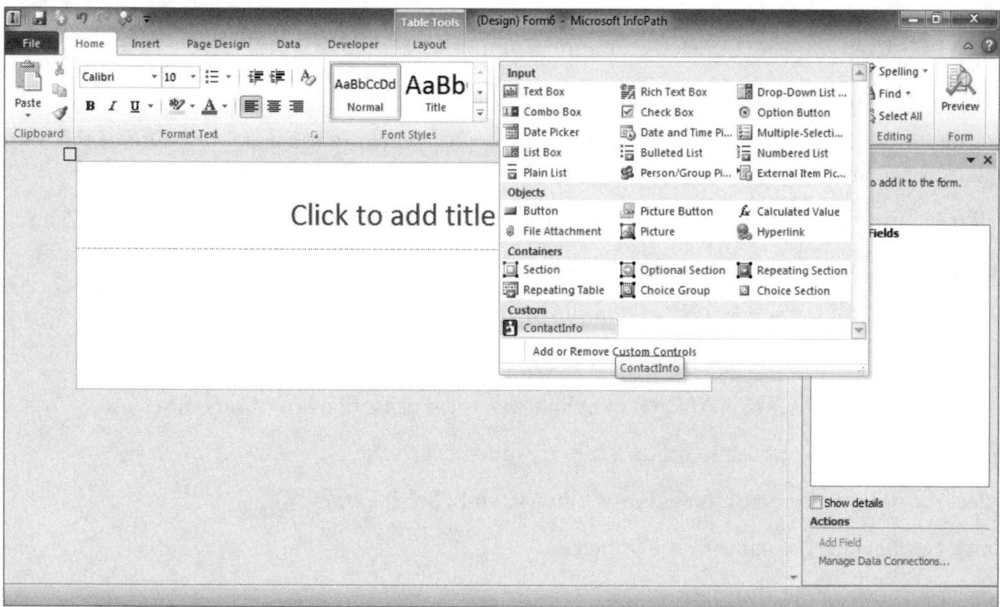

FIGURE 12-32

Publishing a Form Template to a Library

In the previous example, you created a very simple form for users to fill out to provide feedback to a communications group within an organization. Once a form template is created, it must be published to a location where users can fill it out. As previously mentioned in the introduction of this chapter, SharePoint includes support for *browser-based forms*, an Enterprise server feature that allows for users to complete InfoPath Forms via the browser so they do not require the InfoPath application. In order for a site to support this functionality, this Enterprise feature must be activated on the site collection and the site to which the form is being published.

In the next Try It Out, you create a new SharePoint site named "Communications" which uses the Blank site template. Creating a new site is not a requirement for publishing a new form template; however, because you will be adding very specific lists for use by this form, you will create a brand-new site from which to work. Once the site is created, you explore the process for publishing a form template to a document library. Finally, in the last Try It Out of this section, you learn how to configure a document library to ensure that all users have the same editing experience, and specify that the form be opened as a web page in a browser regardless of whether the user has the InfoPath application installed on their computer.

TRY IT OUT Publish a Form Template to a Document Library

1. From the Corporate Intranet Site created in Chapter 1 of this book, create a new site based upon the Blank site template, called "Communications."

NOTE *Detailed steps for creating a new site are described in the first Try it Out of Chapter 2.*

2. Open the Microsoft InfoPath Designer application.
3. Select Open from the File menu.
4. Locate the `employeefeedback.xsn` template that you created in the first Try it Out of this chapter, and click Open.
5. Select Publish from the File menu. The Publish window will appear as shown in Figure 12-33.
6. Select the option to Publish form to a SharePoint Library.
7. Enter the URL of the site you created in the first step of this Try It Out.
8. Click Next.
9. Ensure that the checkbox is selected to enable this form to be filled out using a browser.
10. Select the option to publish to a Form Library, and click Next.
11. Select the option to create a New Form Library, and click Next.
12. Enter **Feedback** as the name of the library.
13. For Description, enter the following:

    Electronic form for collecting feedback from employees on new communications web site.

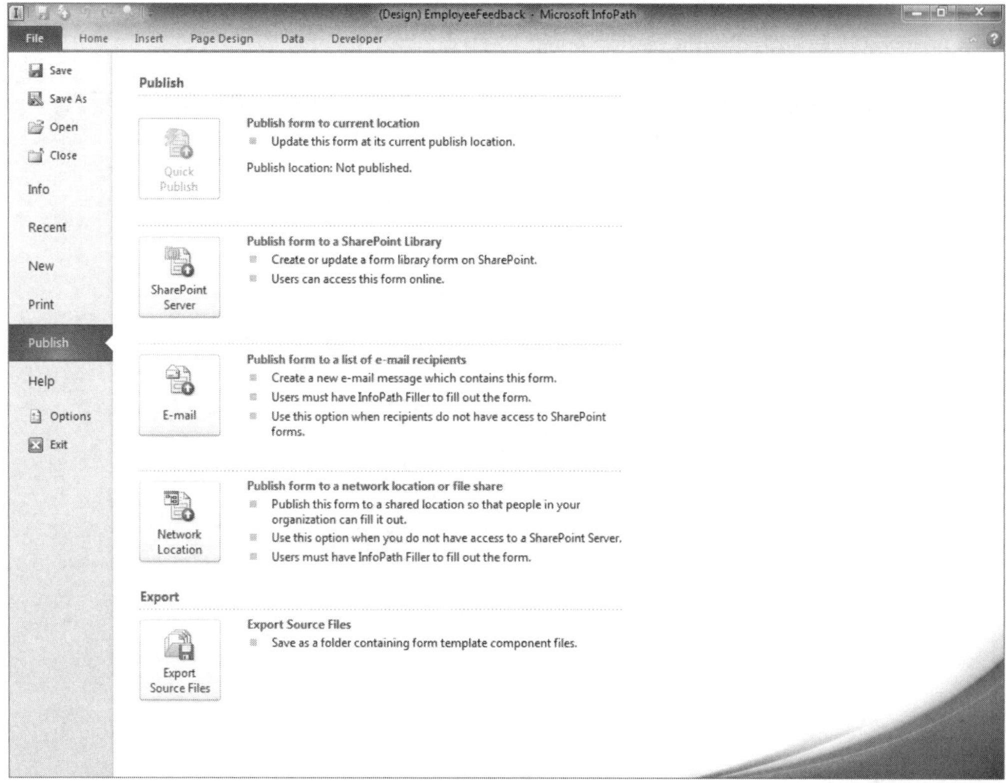

FIGURE 12-33

14. Click Next. The wizard will continue to the field selection stage of the publishing process.
15. Click Add.
16. Select the EmployeeName field from the list of fields, as shown in Figure 12-34.
17. Click OK.
18. Repeat steps 16 and 17 for the remaining fields in the form.
19. Click Next.
20. Click the Publish button. Upon the successful publishing of your form, you will receive a confirmation window containing a link to view the form within the browser and to open the form library.

How It Works

In this example, you created a new document library on the communications sites as part of the form-publishing process. This document library has the form template associated with it so that whenever a user enters the site and clicks the New button, the form is launched.

During the publishing process, you chose to promote specific fields within your form template to become columns within your document library. This allows you to see the contents of the forms in a view in the library without having to open each form individually. This makes it possible to create custom reports on data stored within a document library.

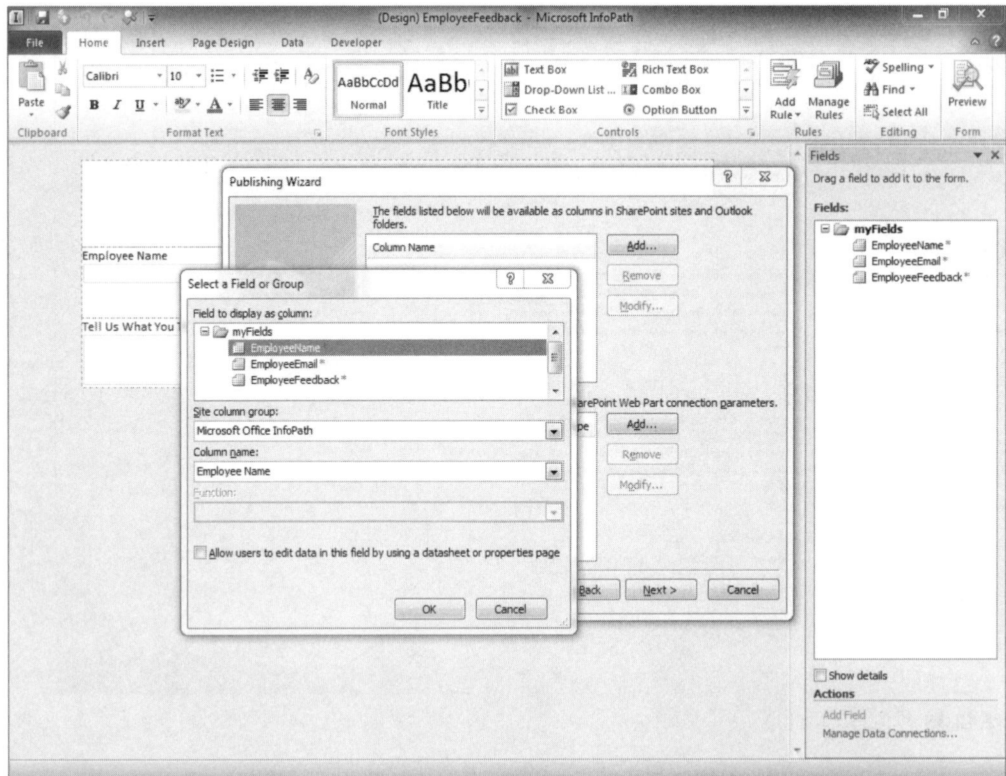

FIGURE 12-34

TRY IT OUT Force a Form to Open as a Web Page

In the next Try It Out, you will review how you can change the setting on the document library to enforce everyone to open the form within a browser. In some situations, this technique will be used to ensure that all users have a consistent experience when completing forms. As well, it helps control the interface so that only items exposed within a specific view are displayed to the user. Depending on the default settings of your server, form libraries may already be configured to open forms in the browser by default. This same process can be used to force the form to open in either the browser or the InfoPath Filler application.

1. From the main page of your communications site, click the All Site Content link.
2. Click the Feedback link to enter the document library.
3. Select the Library Settings option from the Library tab of the Ribbon.

4. Click the Advanced Settings link.

5. For the Opening Documents in the Browser value, select Open in the browser, as shown in Figure 12-35.

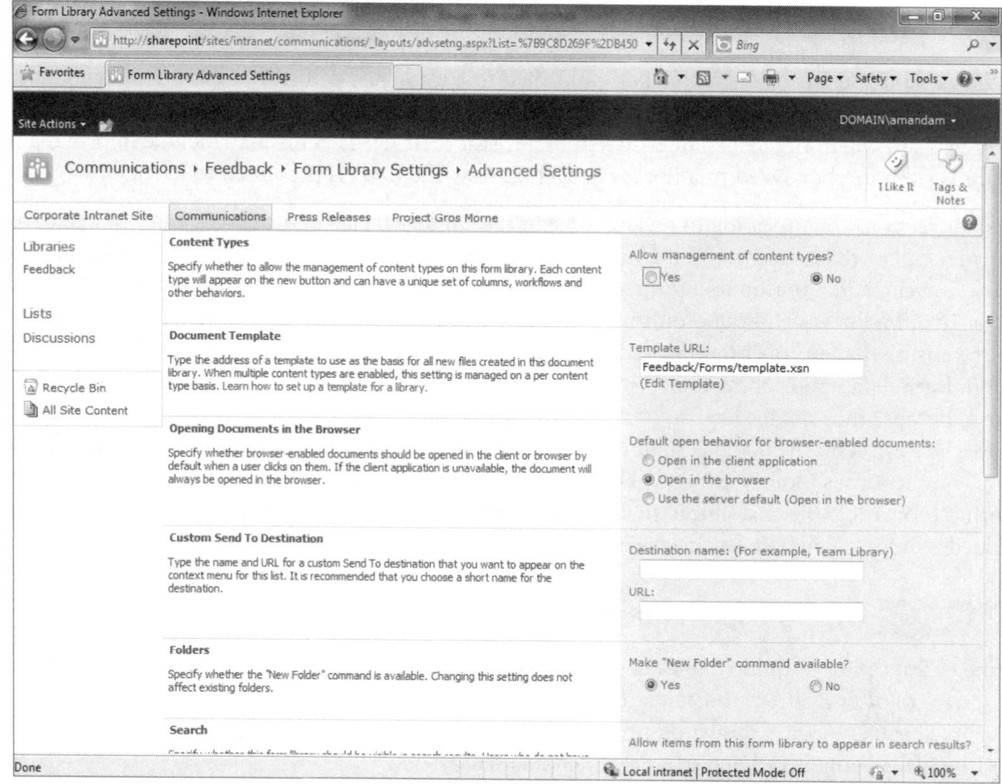

FIGURE 12-35

6. Click OK.

7. Return to the document library by clicking Feedback in the breadcrumb navigation.

8. Click the New Document option from the Document tab of the Ribbon.

How It Works

As previously described, in some situations it may be necessary to ensure that all users open a form as a web page regardless of whether or not they have the InfoPath Filler application installed. In this exercise, you modified the properties of the document library to ensure that all browser-enabled documents, including InfoPath forms, are opened in the browser.

Now that you have published your form template to the site, users can enter the site and complete the form template. When they are done, they can save the form back to the library by using the toolbar buttons. However, after giving the matter some consideration, you have decided that it would be nice to add a Submit button to the form, which will save the document back to the library and name it automatically. This is the subject of the next section.

CUSTOMIZING A FORM TEMPLATE

Once a template has been created and published to a library, it can still be edited and enhanced to further address business needs. As a form designer, you should consult with business users to identify ways in which the form can evolve to better suit their needs. This may include improving how data is submitted or saved to a library as well as how the form is presented to users.

In this section, you are going to review some of the enhancements and changes you can make to a form template that might make it a more effective tool for a team. In the first Try It Out, you look at how you can add a button to a form as well as a submit a data connection that will save the form to a destination library without requiring a user to select Save As from the File menu. These approaches helps ensure that a proper naming scheme is followed for saved forms because the name can be derived from form data upon submission. As well, it makes the user experience better for those completing the form because they do not have to bother with understanding the details of where and how they should save the form. Once you add a Submit button, there may no longer be a need to expose the Save buttons on the form's toolbar to users. Therefore, in the next Try It Out of this section, you learn how the form's toolbar can be customized to suit your needs. You then look at how a data connection can be added to a form template to retrieve information from another content source.

TRY IT OUT Add a Submit Button to a Form Template

In some cases, rather than having users select Save As and manually name their form file, it's more appropriate to offer a Submit button at the bottom of the form that users can select when they complete the form. This makes the submission process easier because the users do not have to be concerned with where the file is being saved and what the filename will be.

In this exercise, you edit the Employee Feedback form to include a Submit button that will save the file to your library and automatically generate a name based on information stored within the form.

1. Open the Microsoft InfoPath Designer application.
2. Select Open from the File menu.
3. Locate the `employeefeedback.xsn` template that you created in the first Try it Out of this chapter, and click Open.
4. Add some space to the bottom of your form by selecting to the right of the Employee Feedback control and pressing Enter twice.
5. Add the button control from the Controls section of the Home Ribbon.
6. Select the button and select the Control Tools Ribbon. The Properties tab of the Control Tools Ribbon will appear, as shown in Figure 12-36.

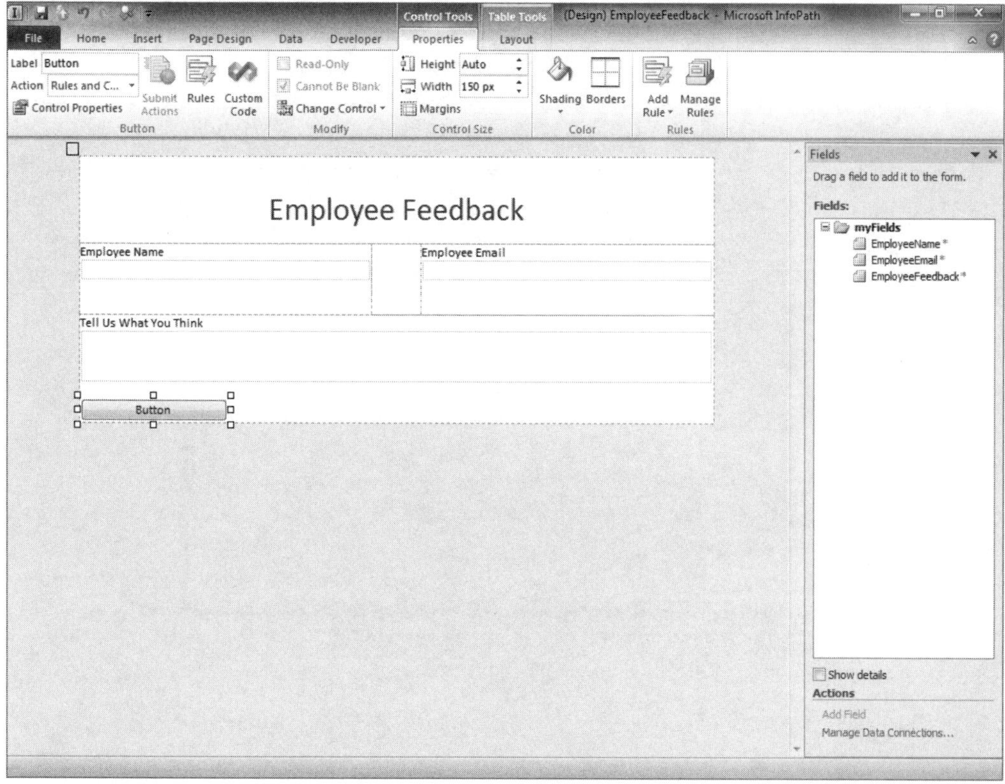

FIGURE 12-36

7. Enter **Submit** in the Label field.
8. From the Action drop-down, select Submit. The Submit Options window will appear.
9. Select the option to allow users to submit the form. The submit options will become enabled.
10. Select the option to Send form data to a single destination and select SharePoint document library from the associated drop-down menu.
11. Click Add. The Data Connection Wizard will appear.
12. Enter the URL for the document library you created for feedback forms. If you are unsure of the exact URL, visit the document library and copy the URL. Be sure to only include the URL of the library and to remove the portion of the URL that includes the text "Forms/AllItems.aspx" or similar text. An example is shown in Figure 12-37.
13. For the Filename field, click the *fx* button to the right of the field.
14. Enter the following into the Formula field, as shown in Figure 12-37.

    concat(EmployeeName, " - ", now())

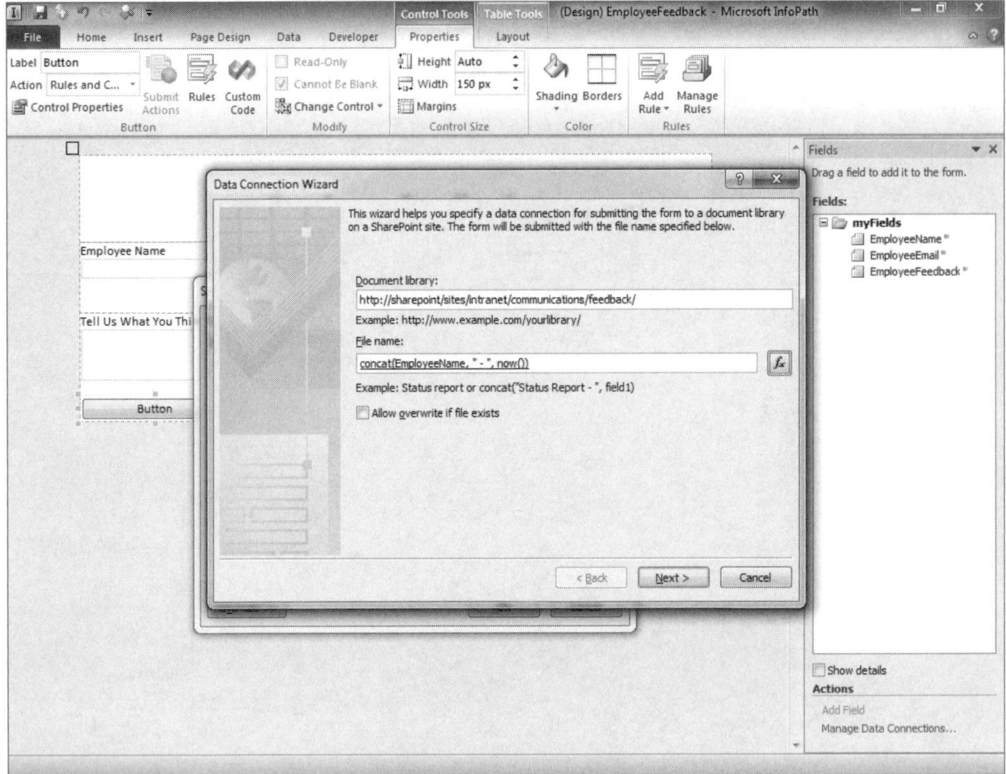

FIGURE 12-37

15. Check the checkbox Allow overwrite if file exists.
16. Click Next.
17. Click Finish.
18. Click OK.
19. Click the Preview button from the Home tab of the Ribbon.
20. Complete the form with sample data, and click the Submit button.
21. Return to the Feedback library of your Communications site, and you should see a form successfully submitted to the library, as shown in Figure 12-38.

How It Works

In this example, you made a modification to the form template to allow users to more easily submit their changes to the document library. Previously, you had to rely on users to click the Save As button from the toolbar or menu. From that point, users were required to name the file on their own. This could lead to major inconsistencies in naming practices and the ability to easily identify specific differences between forms.

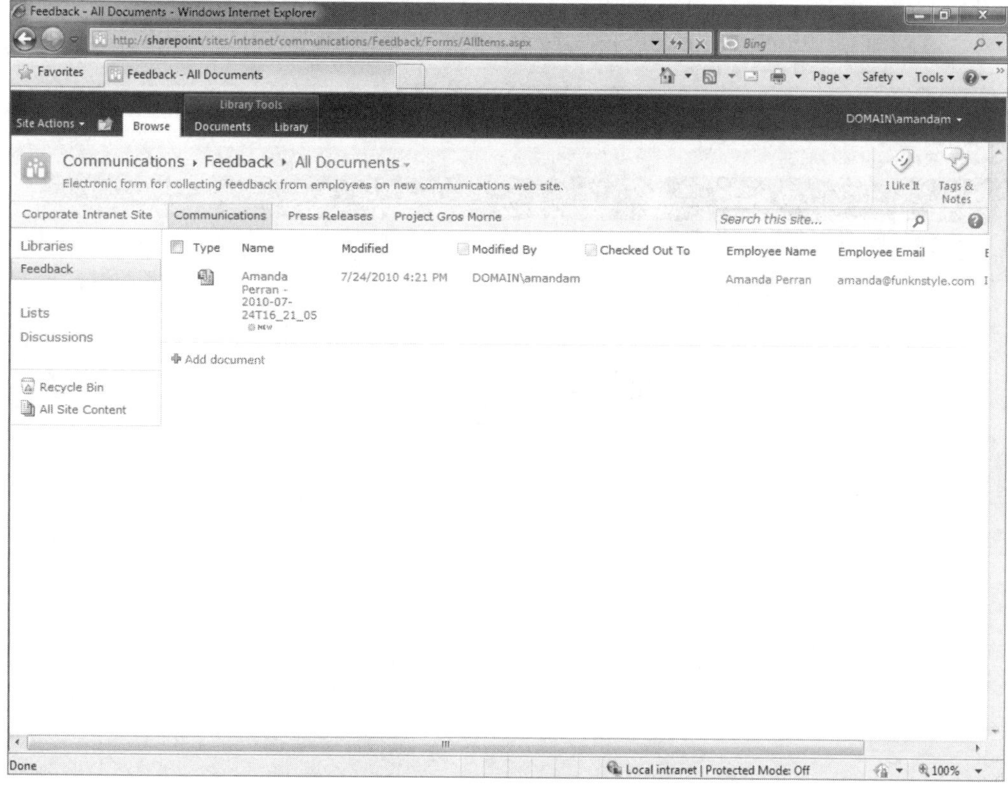

FIGURE 12-38

You implemented a Submit button on the form. There were a number of different methods you could use to submit the form, including the use of Web Services or email. However, in this situation, because all completed forms are being saved to the same document library you are using to launch the form, it makes sense to use the Submit to Document Library option.

In addition to specifying where you can submit a form, you can also select how the form should be named and whether items with the same name should be overwritten, along with what actions take place once the form is submitted. In this situation, you chose to name the forms based on the name of the employee submitting the form in addition to a special set of characters known as now(), which define the exact time the form was submitted. While this does not create a visually appealing filename, you can be sure that it will be very easy to identify who submitted each form, and you can ensure that filenames will be unique. You also determined that if a file was updated and resubmitted, then the existing form record should be overwritten rather than creating a completely new record.

TRY IT OUT Customize the Browser-Based Form Toolbar

Typically, once such an update is made to a local copy of the form template, the changes should be immediately published to the SharePoint document library again. However, there is still another set of changes that need to be made to the form to make it more usable and intuitive. In Figure 12-39, you see a screenshot of what the form looks like in its current form.

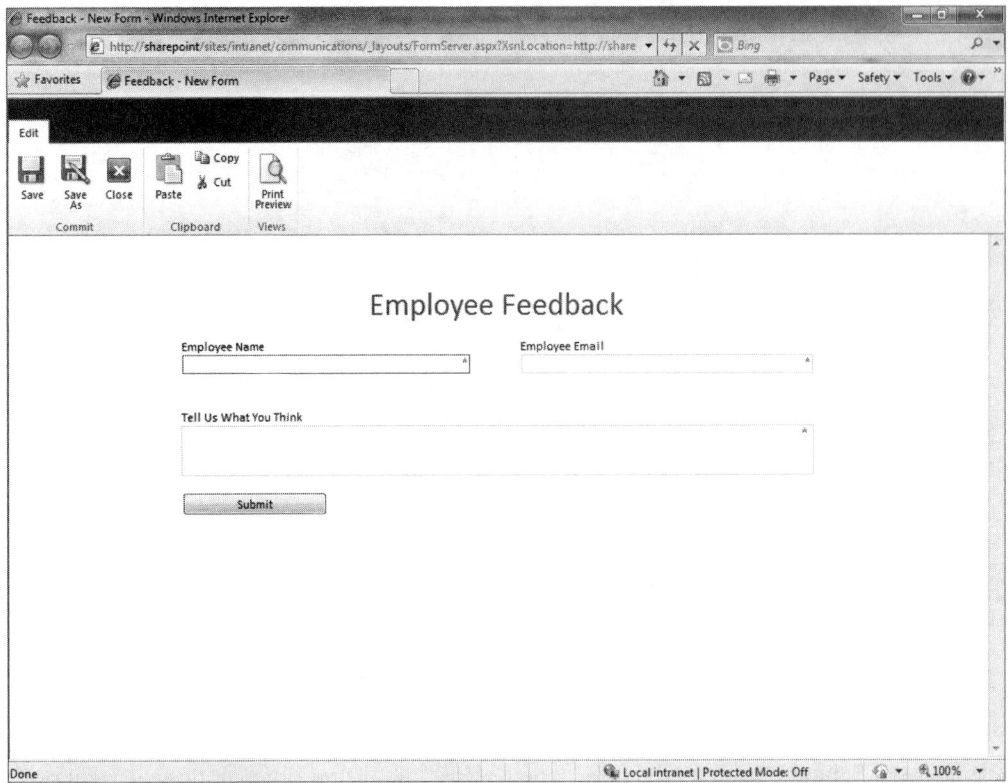

FIGURE 12-39

The users now have to choose between the custom Submit button, a Save button, and a Save As button. This can lead to some users choosing to save their forms using their own naming structure, and thereby eliminates any benefits associated with a standardized naming scheme that has been introduced with the custom button. Most importantly, for a very simple form you are offering users far too many choices. This leads to confusion and possibly even frustration. So in this example, you customize the toolbar that is automatically added to the browser-based forms to only display the Print View option because this is something that users might find useful. In addition, because your form is fairly simple and small, you will remove the Footer toolbar because you don't need it in this form.

1. Return to your local copy of the Employee Feedback template featuring the changes implemented in the previous example.
2. Select Form Options from the File tab of the Ribbon. The Form Options will appear, as shown in Figure 12-40.
3. Select the option to Show toolbar at the top of the form.
4. Unselect all commands except Print Preview.
5. Click OK.

6. From the File tab of the Ribbon menu, select the Quick Publish option. You will receive a message confirming the operation has completed successfully once the form has been published.

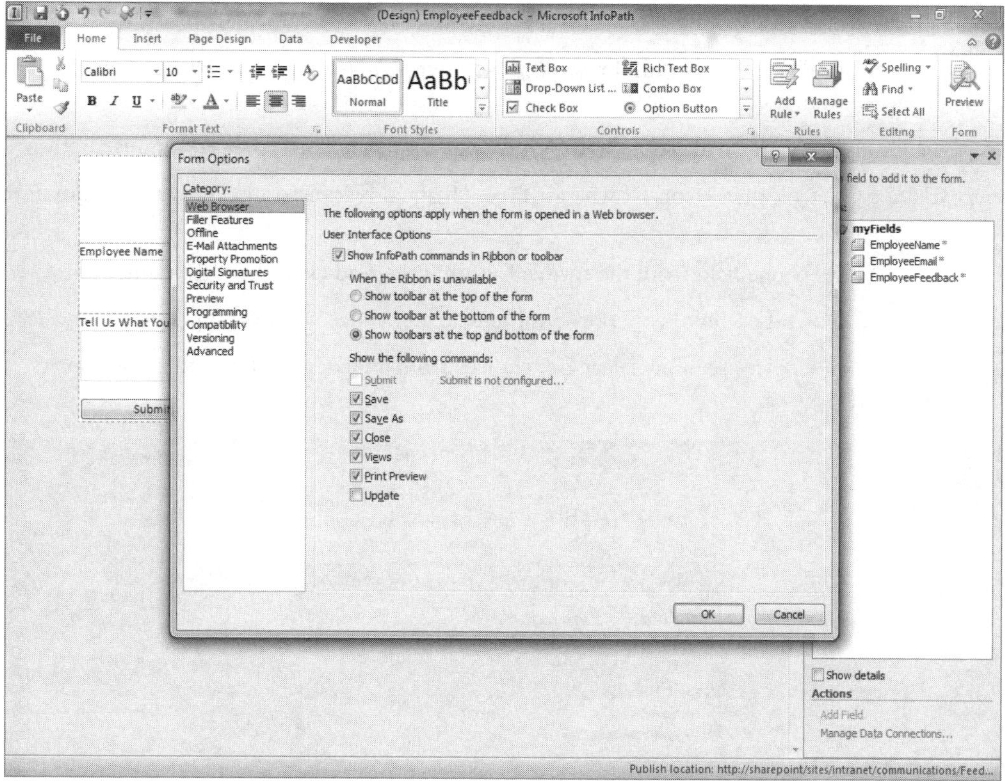

FIGURE 12-40

How It Works

In this example, you used the Form Options menu to customize what commands are displayed in a toolbar when users view the form via the browser. You did this to simplify the interface so that users can easily identify what they should select when it comes time for them to submit their information to the site. As in most cases, it is far more important for users to focus on the information they are submitting rather than the steps they are taking to submit it. Once your changes were complete, you used the Quick Publish option in InfoPath to republish your changes to the previously published location.

TRY IT OUT Add a Data Connection to a Form Template

So far, you have reviewed how to create a custom template that supports browser-based viewing and editing. You created a data connection in the form template to allow for the form to be submitted to the document library using a standardized naming scheme. However, you can also use data connections to display information in a form from an external data source, such as a database, web service, or SharePoint site.

In this example, you discover how data entry can be made easier by allowing information to be pulled directly from a central source. For this example, you will use the user information list from your site collection. If for some reason you are unable to query that list, you can create a custom list on your site containing a field for Employee Name and Work Email Address and use that list as a data source.

1. Return to your local copy of the Employee Feedback template featuring the changes implemented in the previous example.
2. Select the EmployeeName field from the form's Design view, and click the right mouse button.
3. Select Change Control, then Drop-Down List Box. The field is transformed into a drop-down listbox.
4. Select the employeeName field from the form's Design view, and click the right mouse button.
5. Select the Drop-Down List Box Properties option. The properties window appears.
6. From the List Box Choices section, select Get choices from an external data source option, as shown in Figure 12-41.

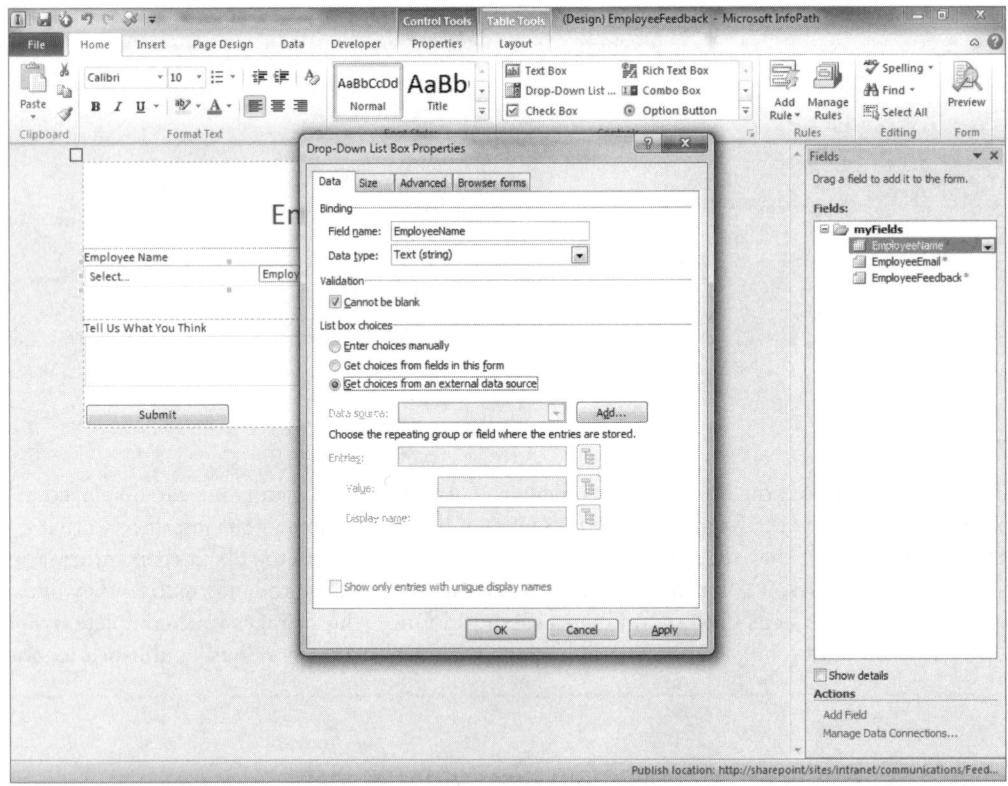

FIGURE 12-41

7. Click Add to launch the Data Connection Creation Wizard.
8. Select the Create a New Connection To option button, and select Receive Data.
9. Click Next.

10. Select SharePoint List or Library, and click Next.
11. Enter the URL of the top-level site of your site collection. A listing of all lists in that site is returned.
12. Select the User Information list.
13. Click Next.
14. Select the Name and Work Email fields, and click Next.
15. Select the checkbox to store a copy of the data in the form template.
16. Click Next.
17. Retain the default settings for the data connection name and synchronization settings.
18. Click Finish.
19. Click the button to the right of the Entries field.
20. Expand the groups and select the Name field, as shown in Figure 12-42.

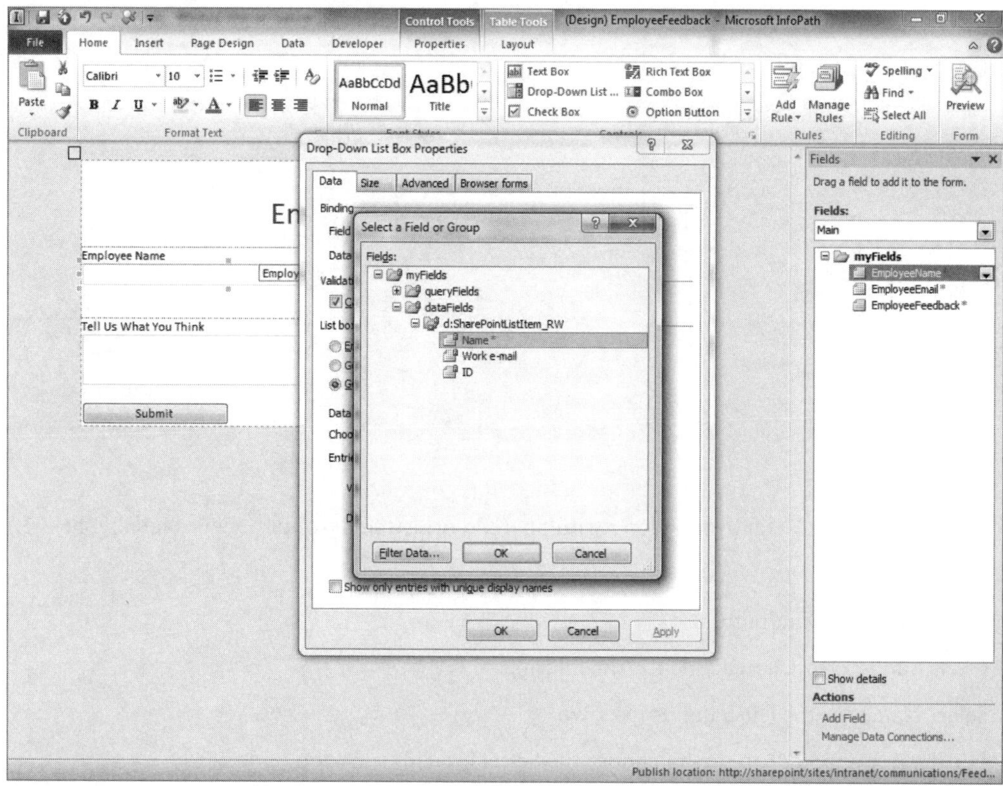

FIGURE 12-42

21. Click OK.
22. Click the Apply button, then OK.
23. Right-click on the EmployeeEmail field and select Text Box Properties.

24. Select the *fx* button to the right of the Value field.
25. Click the Insert Field or Group button.
26. From the Data Source drop-down, select User Information List (Secondary), as shown in Figure 12-43.

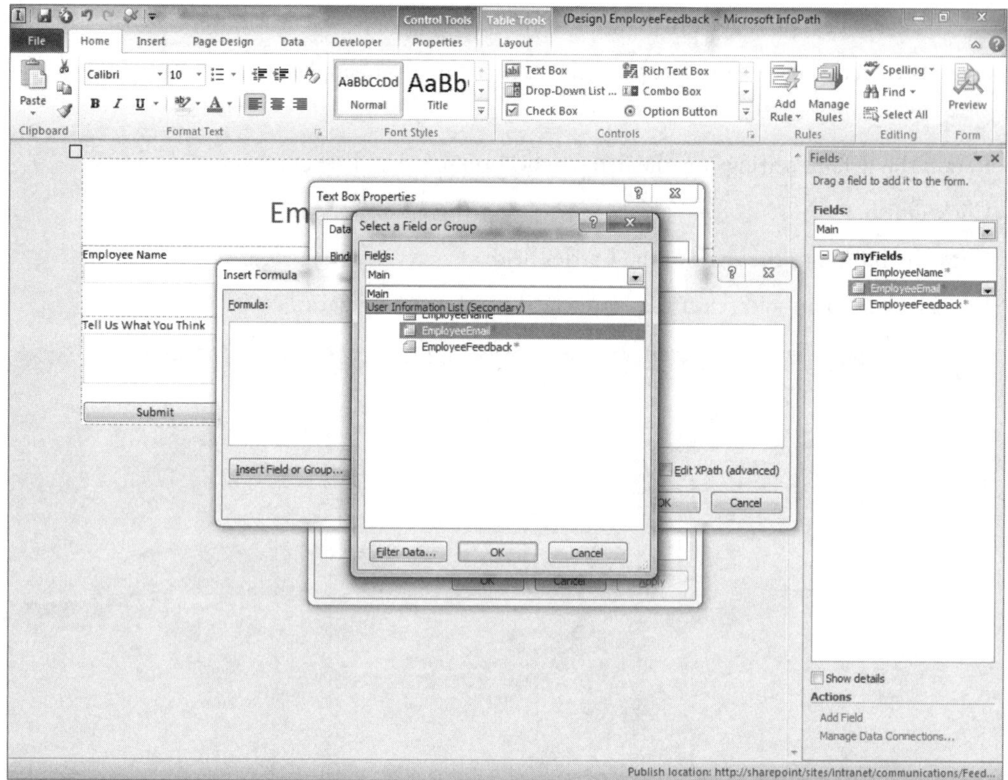

FIGURE 12-43

27. Expand the Data Fields group along with SharePointListItem group to view available fields.
28. Select the work_e-mail field.
29. Click the Filter Data button.
30. Click Add to create a new rule for the filtering.
31. Select Name for the left-hand drop-down.
32. For the right-hand drop-down, choose the Select a Field or Group option.
33. Change the data source back to Main and select EmployeeName, as shown in Figure 12-44.
34. Click OK on all open windows to commit changes.
35. Click the Save button on the File tab to ensure that your changes are committed to the template.

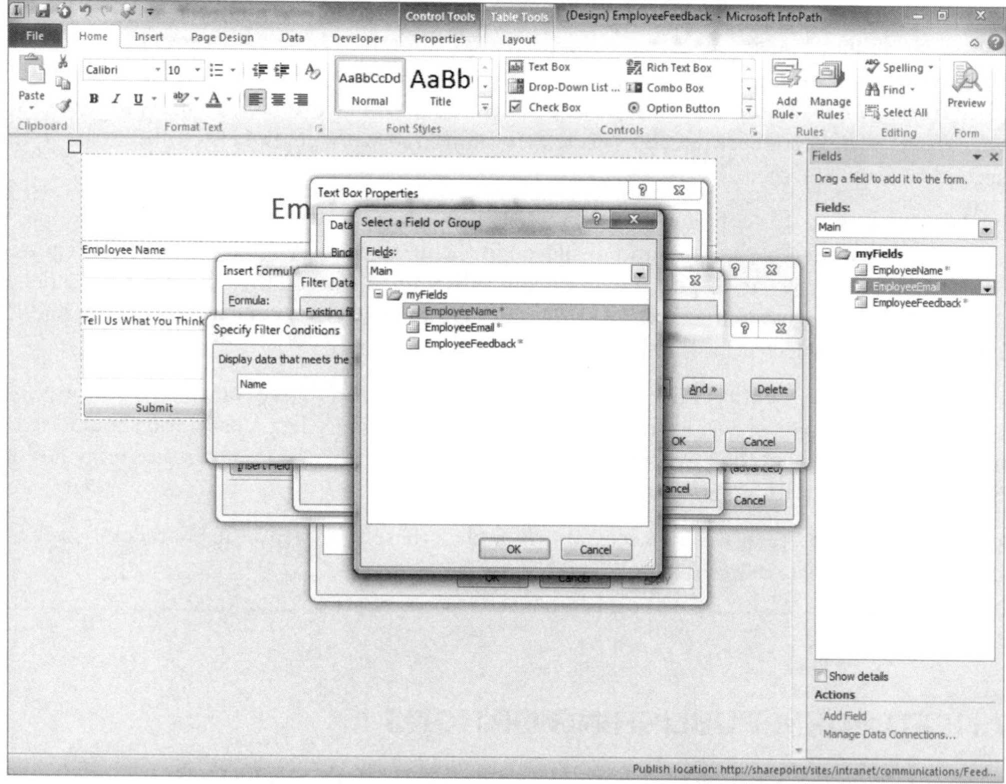

FIGURE 12-44

How It Works

When you first created your feedback form, you allowed users to enter whatever they wanted into the User Name field. As a result, you had mixed results because sometimes users would enter their first name and not their last, or enter their employee user ID, or, in a rush, would make a typo or misspell their name. This makes reporting on the data difficult. Instead of allowing users to enter their name in a textbox, you decided to let them select their name from a drop-down list of choices. In addition, rather than manually maintaining this list of users, you can draw the value list from an external data source. In this case, it made sense to look up the users who were members of the SharePoint intranet site because these were the users you would be collecting information from directly.

In addition to a requirement to standardize the data that was being entered for name, you recognized a need to reduce and simplify the data entry experience of users as they were completing the form. For example, it seemed somewhat ridiculous to some users to specify their email address because they were logged in to the network as registered users. Therefore, the organization should already have an email address associated with them. You did not want to just strictly remove the field because your goal might be to later email all users who complete the form. Therefore, you decided that it would be useful to retain the Email Address field but have its value auto-populated based on the selection of a user's name.

Therefore, you added a new data connection to the form template that looked up the user information list of the site collection. You specified that the information contained in this list should be available within the form itself. This allows you to open and interact with the external data when you are offline or detached from the network. A cached local copy of the data will be available to users to while they are offline. From the data connection, you selected the name and work email fields to be added to the form's secondary data source.

Once the data connection was configured, you connected the drop-down listbox to the data connection. By default, all names are returned and displayed in the drop-down listbox. However, if required, with additional filtering you can display only a certain subset of users. You then configured the default value of your email address to be the email address specified for the user on the team site who had the same name as the value selected for EmployeeName within the form.

When you click the Preview button after making the changes, you should see the names of users from your communications site displayed in the drop-down listbox. As you select a user, you should see that user's email address appear in the Email Address field of the form. If you do not, the user may not have a specified email address within her SharePoint user profile.

Once you finish your updates, it will be necessary to publish these changes to the SharePoint server again to update the template associated with the library.

ADVANCED FORM-PUBLISHING OPTIONS

In the section "Publishing a Form Template to a Library," you learned how a form template is published to a single document library. This approach is suitable for scenarios where a form is only required in a single location and where multiple groups or sites do not reuse the form. However, you may need to make a form template available to multiple sites in a site collection or multiple site collections. In each of these cases, you can choose one of the advanced form publishing options.

For scenarios where you want to publish a form template to multiple sites or libraries in the same site collection, the optimal publishing choice is to publish as a Content Type. In Chapter 6, you learned how content types can be associated with multiple libraries and locations in a single site collection. In the first Try It Out of this section, you publish your employee feedback form template as a content type so that it can be added to multiple libraries. Because the data connection is added to submit your form to a central location, you do not have to worry about users saving the form data in multiple locations.

In some situations, you may have a single form template that you want to make available in multiple site collections. In this case, you would choose to upload your template as an Administrator-Approved form template via the Central Administration site. From there, form templates can be activated to site collections from one central location. This method is also the only supported choice for advanced form templates containing custom code or highly complex data connections. In the second Try It Out of this section, you walk through the process of uploading a form template to the Central Administration site and activating it out to a site collection.

TRY IT OUT Publish a Form Template as a Content Type

You now know how to publish a form template directly to a SharePoint document library. The next step to look at is the process for creating a content type by publishing a form template. For this example, you use the Feedback form created in the previous section. However, you open it in Design view and choose a different publishing location and type. You will publish the form template as a content type so that you can deploy it to multiple sites in the site collection.

1. Open the Feedback Form template within InfoPath Designer.
2. From the File tab, select the Publish option.
3. Select SharePoint Server from the list of Publish choices.
4. Because you have previously published this form, an existing URL may already exist. Remove it and enter the URL of your corporate intranet portal (example: http://servername), and click Next.
5. Check the Enable the Form to Be Filled Out by Using a Browser checkbox.
6. Select Site Content Type (Advanced).
7. Click Next.
8. Select the Create a new content type option, as shown in Figure 12-45.

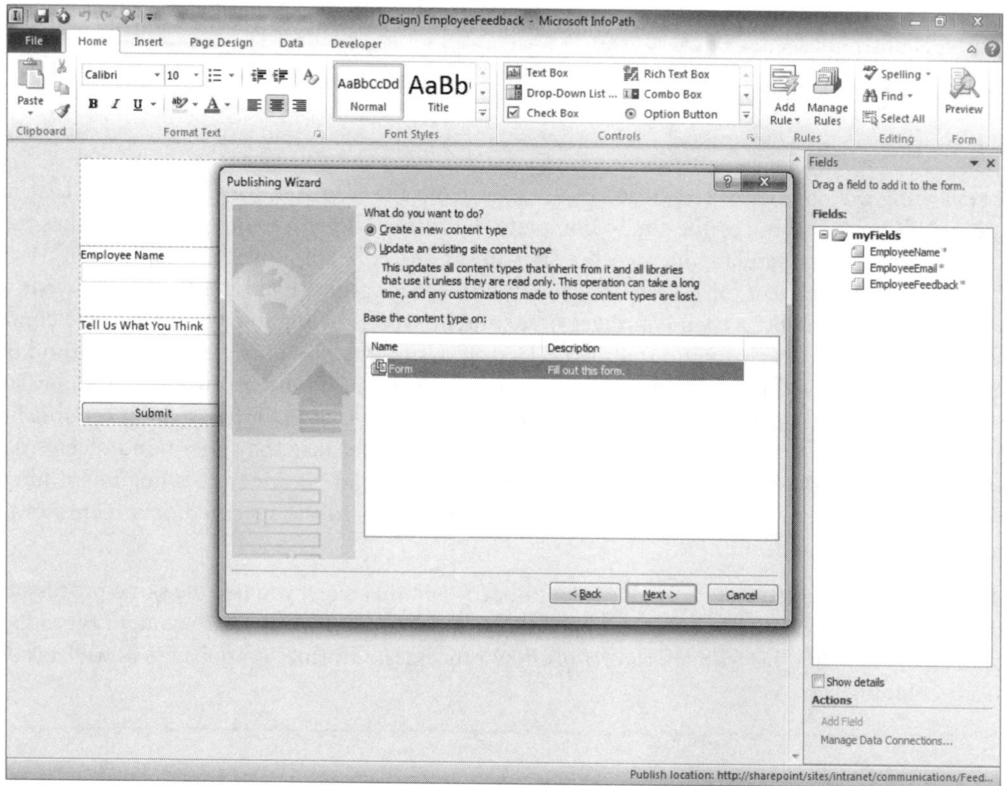

FIGURE 12-45

9. Click Next.
10. For the name of the content type, specify **Employee Feedback Form** and enter the following for the description:

    This content type is an electronic form for collecting feedback from employees on various communication methods and promotions. All content submitted using this content type will be directed to the communications site.

11. Click Next.
12. Click the Browse button to specify a location where the form template can be stored within the site collection.
13. Select the Form Templates document library, and click Open.
14. Enter the name in the Filename field as **employeefeedback.xsn**.
15. Click Save.
16. Click Next.
17. Verify that the appropriate fields have been selected to be promoted as columns to document libraries within the site collection, and click Next.
18. Click the Publish button. You will receive a confirmation indicating that the form template was successfully published.
19. Click Close to complete the wizard.

How It Works

After reviewing the number of responses you receive from the feedback form, you notice that not enough people were coming to the site to complete the form. Therefore, you decide it makes more sense to push the form template out to other sites in the site collection because quite often users are more inclined to complete a form from their own workspace rather than take the time to visit other workspaces. One of the primary advantages of a content type is being able to add a single content type to multiple locations throughout a site collection. Using the previously explored method of publishing directly to a document library, the form template could only be pushed out and associated with a single library. There would be no way to add it to other libraries without republishing it manually in a series of redundant and unrelated processes. Because the submit and receive data connections are still associated with the form, even if the template is added to a document library in another site, completed forms will still be submitted directly to the specified document library on the communications team site.

To add the InfoPath content type to a document library on other sites, you use the same process as was explored in Chapter 4. Similarly, you can apply all the same features available to content types to this form template including the association of workflow processes, information policies, as well as additional site columns.

TRY IT OUT Publish a Form Template as an Administrator-Approved Template

You may have a single form template that you are required to share with users across multiple site collections or a form template that was created using advanced development techniques and custom code. For each of these situations, you are required to use the Administrator-Approved Upload technique as described in this example. The example shows how to publish a form template to an administrative area of the portal so that it can be activated and published to multiple site collections. You typically use this method for complex forms that contain custom code, use advanced functionality, or must be created as content types across more than one site collection. In this example, you use one of the sample forms available with InfoPath to keep things simple, but recognize that this is the method most commonly used for custom-developed complex forms.

1. Open the Feedback Form template within InfoPath Designer.
2. From the File tab, select the Publish option.
3. Select SharePoint Server from the list of Publish choices.
4. Enter the URL of your corporate intranet portal (example: http://servername), and click Next.
5. Check Enable the Form to Be Filled Out by Using a Browser checkbox.
6. Select Administrator-approved form template (Advanced).
7. Save the file locally to the folder containing all resource files for this chapter. Name the file **feedbackformtemplate.xsn**. Click Next.
8. Select any fields from the form that you want displayed in document libraries as columns, and click Next.
9. Click the Publish button. You will receive a confirmation indicating that the form template was successfully published.
10. Click Close to complete the wizard.
11. Go to the Central Administration site for your SharePoint server. If you do not have access to this site, you will require assistance from your server administrator to complete this exercise.
12. Select the General Application Settings link.
13. Select Upload Form Template from the InfoPath Forms Services group, as shown in Figure 12-46. The Upload Form Template page appears.
14. Browse to the location where you saved the `feedbackformtemplate.xsn` template in Step 8. Select the form and click Open. You are returned to the Upload Form Template page.
15. Click the Upload button. You receive a success message.
16. Click OK.
17. The final step in this process is to activate the form template in a site collection. Hover over the form's name in the list of form templates and select Activate to a Site Collection from the drop-down menu, as shown in Figure 12-47.

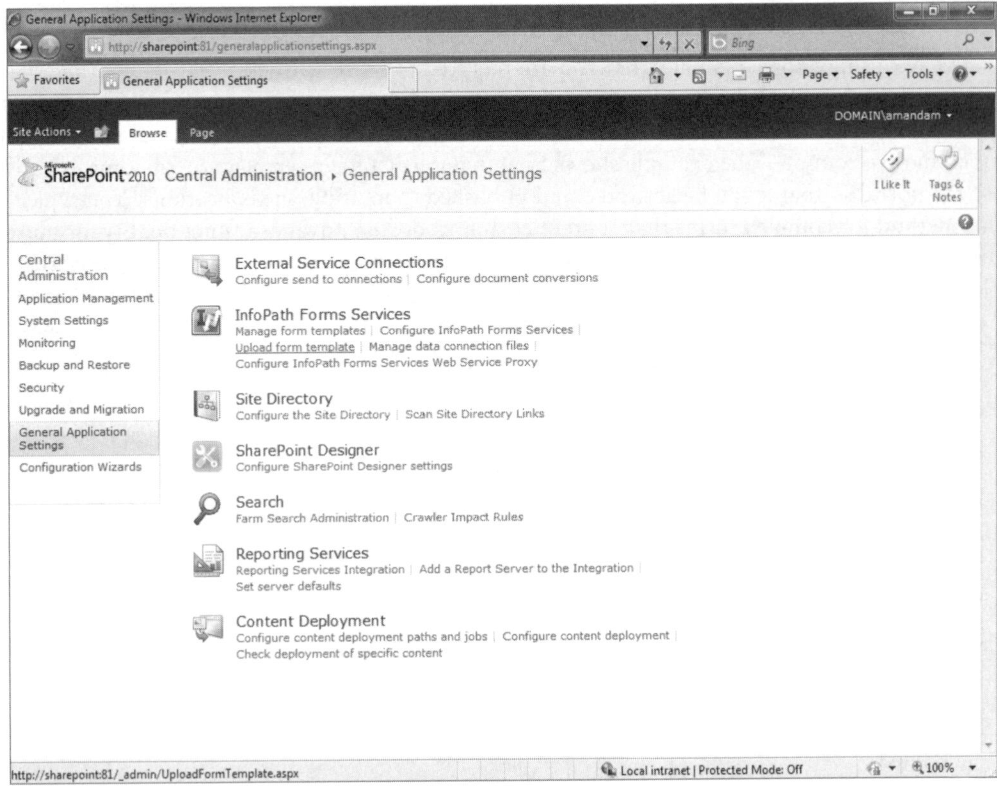

FIGURE 12-46

18. Select your Corporate intranet site collection as the Activation Location. You may need to change the default value to do this.

19. Click OK.

How It Works

In this exercise, to publish the form template, you first had to save it locally as is required for publishing all form templates. Next, you defined where you want to publish the template. You then had to save the form a second time. The most common reason for this second save is that in many organizations, the person creating the form is not necessarily the person with the rights to perform the upload operation. Instead, the form's creator saves the form template to a shared location on the network where a server farm administrator can access the form and complete the operation.

Once you completed the Publishing Wizard, the form was prepped for uploading. However, the upload had to take place from the SharePoint Central Administration site. From there, the form template was uploaded from the shared location. Once it was uploaded, it was then activated in the site collections where you intend to use the form. The activation process created a content type within the site collection using the Microsoft Office InfoPath group name.

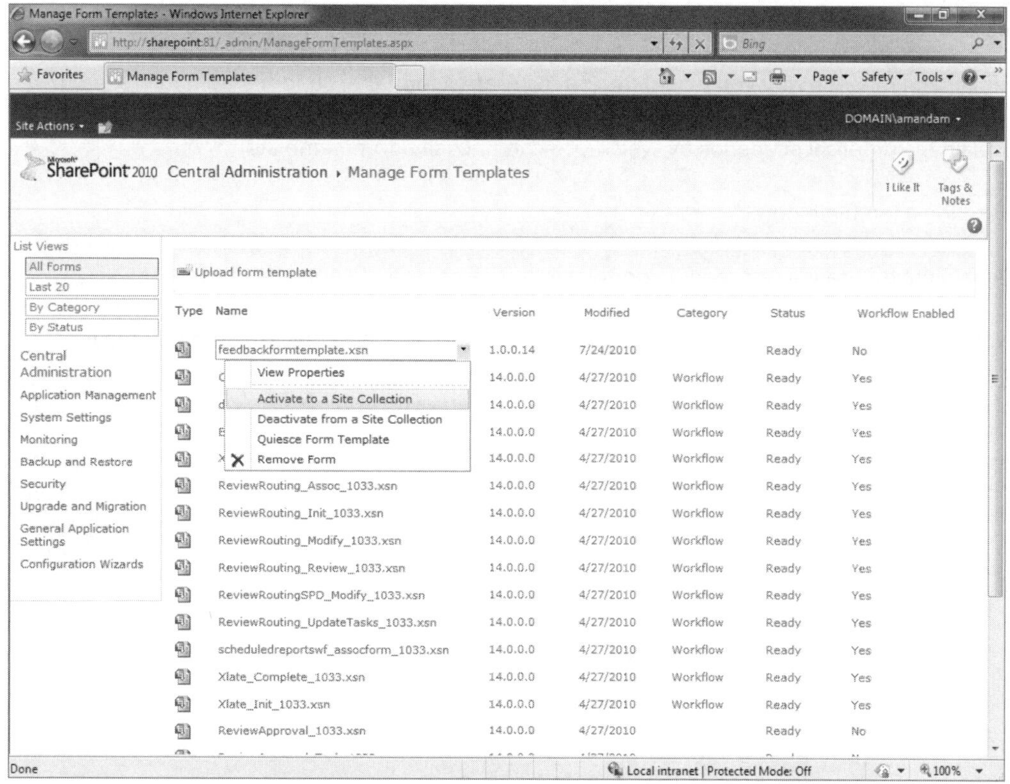

FIGURE 12-47

SUMMARY

This chapter discussed how a Microsoft Office application for creating electronic forms can be used and integrated with SharePoint, using InfoPath Forms Services.

You looked at how InfoPath has evolved since its last release, including support for browser editing and viewing of form data, as well as enhanced support for external data connections and controls.

You learned about the various design-level tasks and elements associated with an InfoPath form, including its layout, controls, data source, design check, and publishing functions. You saw some of the standard controls you can add to a form, as well as what some of the publishing possibilities are for a form template.

This chapter offered several step-by-step examples showing how to create form templates and use them within SharePoint. After reading this chapter, you should feel comfortable planning, designing, and developing InfoPath form templates that can map directly to specific business activities within your organization and improve the efficiency and effectiveness of collecting information from users.

EXERCISES

1. Explain the reasons why you would decide to create a form that supports editing in the browser.

2. Explain the different scenarios by which you can publish a form template.

3. Describe a template part.

4. Explain the difference between a control and a data source element.

5. True or false: InfoPath cannot submit to a data connection. It can only retrieve information.

▶ WHAT YOU LEARNED IN THIS CHAPTER

TOPIC	KEY CONCEPTS
What is InfoPath?	*InfoPath* is an application that integrates with SharePoint to collect and present data. InfoPath is comprised of two tools. InfoPath Forms Designer, which is the tool used to create form templates, and InfoPath Forms Filler, which is a tool that is used to complete InfoPath Forms.
The difference between a form template and a form data file	An InfoPath Form Template is designed and published to a shared location by a forms designer. It has an .xsn file extension. An InfoPath data file is created when a user completes a form and has an .xml file extension.
What is a template part?	A template part is a reusable portion of an InfoPath form that is designed once and can then be easily added to future form templates with little to no effort.

13

Getting Started with Web Content Management

WHAT YOU WILL LEARN IN THIS CHAPTER:

- What is web content management?
- How to use sharePoint to publish web content in a single or multiple languages
- How to create custom page layouts and templates

With more and more business activities taking place online, web content management (WCM) has become increasingly important for businesses. WCM is the process of creating and managing web content either on the Internet or an intranet. Where possible, a good web content management system should support a variety of information and provide tools to users for updating this content with minimal effort.

In the past, a major roadblock to managing web content has been the lack of effective tools, which meant relying on expensive, labor-intensive, and time-consuming processes. You don't have these roadblocks using a web content management system such as SharePoint, however. In this chapter, you take a look at WCM and how SharePoint 2010 can make business teams and processes more efficient.

WEB CONTENT MANAGEMENT

A traditional challenge in many organizations has been the reliance of business users on technical teams to publish new content and to improve communication with stakeholders on the web. SharePoint 2010 makes business users more independent in their content publishing activities, which empowers them to more effectively publish up-to-date information and communicate with their target audience through their website.

So, how can WCM work in your situation? If your company headquarters is in one part of the world, with support teams in other locations, your employees can still collaborate by accessing a company website, regardless of location. Website content owners create lists and libraries and supply employees with the materials they need to perform their day-to-day duties. Managers can create and update a tasks list that outlines what the team needs to do and who is responsible. Teams everywhere can log in to the portal and instantly access important information or even create it for someone in another country. Employees can create email alerts on the important lists and libraries so that colleagues are instantly notified of new or changed content. Specifically, SharePoint has the following features for managing and publishing content:

- **Page layouts and master pages:** Enforce consistency across your website and ensure that all new pages that are created follow your corporate brand.
- **Creating web pages from the browser:** Allows users without knowledge of HTML code to create web pages that inherit the site's look and feel.
- **Workflows:** Automate the process of publishing or approving content. For example, you might create content for a website and then send it through a workflow system where it is approved and finally published to your website.
- **Content versioning:** Ensures that you are always using the most up-to-date versions of your documents and allows you to restore to a previous version by keeping an electronic paper trail as the document evolves.
- **Reporting dashboards:** This is a great way to get a high-level overview of your content.
- **Check in/check out:** Ensures that multiple people are working on the same up-to-date content so that you can check out and in your documents during editing.

PUBLISHING FEATURES OVERVIEW

Publishing refers to the act of creating content such as a new page in your site or modifying content such as a block of text or a picture. By using built-in publishing tools explained throughout this chapter, you can quickly and easily modify your web content without the need for code. With SharePoint's Publishing feature, you can publish web content for pages and run content approval workflows directly from the browser or use tools like the Enhanced Text Editor to edit text right on the page. SharePoint has various templates, such as the Publishing Portal, that have the Publishing feature already enabled. However, you can enable the Publishing feature on a regular team site, such as a blank site, at any time to give it the publishing capabilities.

Creating a Publishing Portal

If you are planning to create a site that is going to be highly customized and feature many pages of content, you may select the Publishing Portal as the site template for your site collection. You can only select this template as a top-level site within a site collection. In the next Try It Out, you create a Publishing Portal that acts as a sample site for the remainder of this chapter.

TRY IT OUT Create a Publishing Portal Site

In this example, you create a new site collection that acts as a host for your company's public Internet site. This site contains news articles and company information pages, as well as information on various ski products and services in multiple languages. In the past, creating a public-facing Internet site required in-depth knowledge of HTML and other related technologies.

To create a new site collection, you must visit the Central Administration site of your SharePoint environment. If you are unsure what the address for this site is, you should contact your system administrator or the person who installed SharePoint. You may also access the Central Administration site by logging directly in to the server and selecting SharePoint 2010 Central Administration from the Microsoft SharePoint 2010 Products option on the Programs menu.

1. Log in to the SharePoint Central Administration site for your server farm.
2. Select Create Site Collections from the Application Management group of links.
3. The first item in your list of things to identify is the web application on which you will create the site. Make sure that the web application you select is the correct application. If it is not, you can click the down arrow to the right of the selected web application and click Change Web Application.
4. You must provide a title, description, and URL for the site. Name the site **AW Ski Company**, and enter the following description:

   Corporate Website for AW Ski Company

5. For the Web Site Address name, select /sites/ from the drop-down menu and enter **internet** in the blank field to the right of the drop-down, as shown in Figure 13-1.
6. Select the Publishing Portal template from the Publishing tab.
7. Enter your own name as the primary site collection administrator.
8. Click OK. The process for creating your site takes a few minutes. After it is completed, you are redirected to a page advising you that the process has completed successfully, and a URL will be displayed for you to select to visit your site, as shown in Figure 13-2.

How It Works

A publishing portal is created with many of the initial lists and libraries that you will need to get started on your website. Figure 13-3 shows an example of how the Internet site will look upon creation.

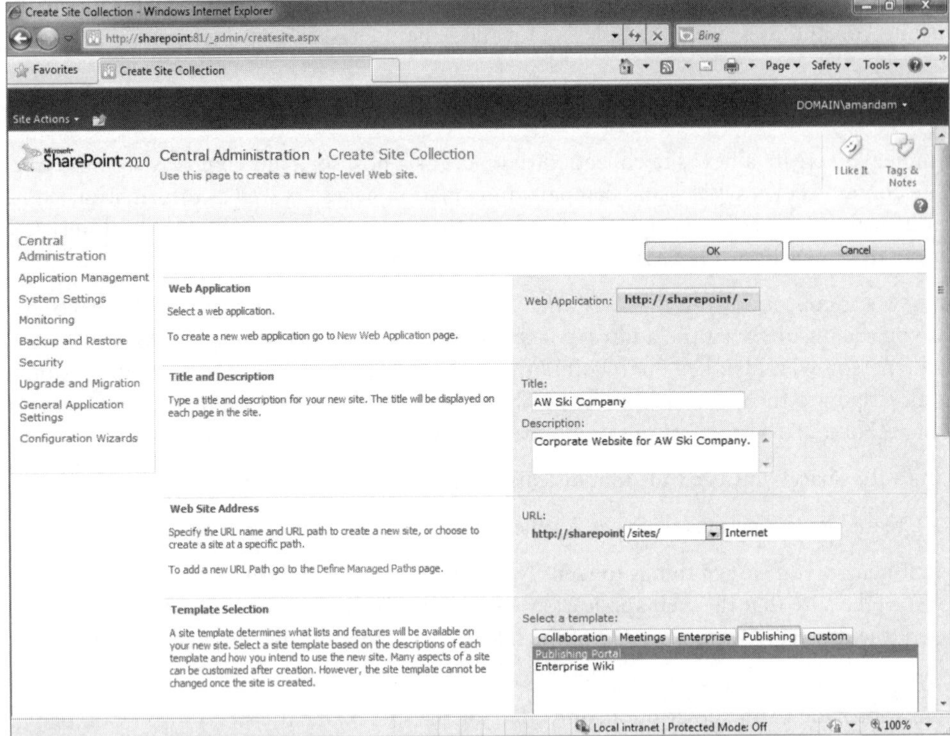

FIGURE 13-1

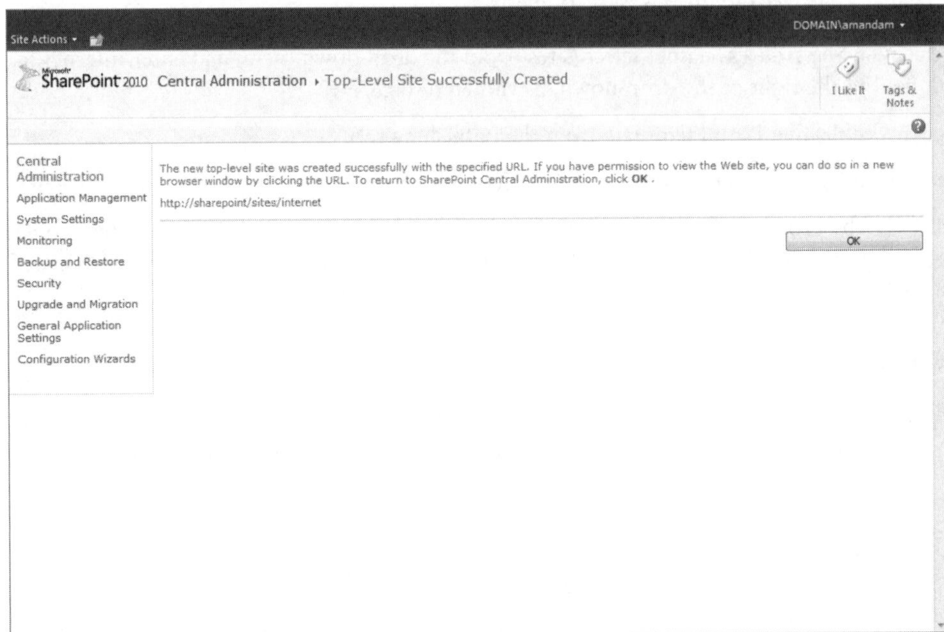

FIGURE 13-2

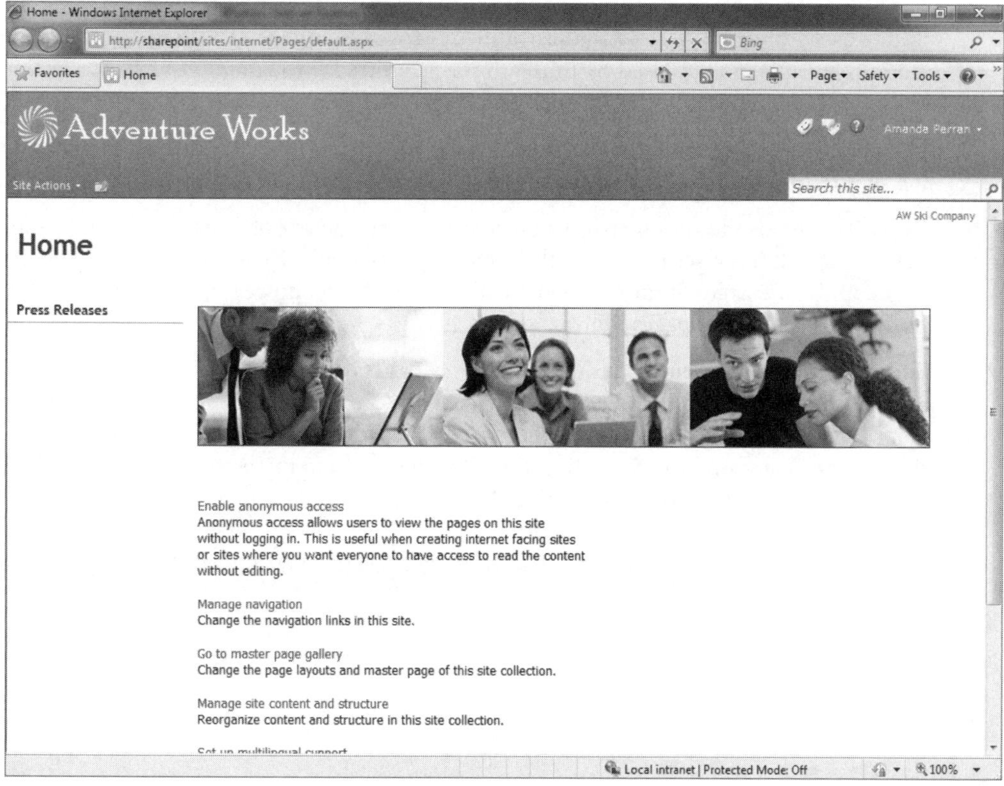

FIGURE 13-3

The Publishing Portal's Lists and Libraries

As mentioned in the last Try It Out, a publishing portal comes with lists and libraries to get you started, including the ones shown in the following list. In addition to these lists, the site collection contains two subsites for Press Releases and Search. You can create new subsites to represent the various sections of your company website. So, although you may think of a company website as a single site, in fact, it contains multiple subsites. As you create each subsite, the navigation updates to reflect your changes. The navigation controls allow visitors to your site to browse the various sections in a seamless and intuitive manner that does not make them feel as though are actually visiting multiple sites.

- **Customized Reports:** This document library has the templates to create Web Analytics custom reports for the site collection.
- **Documents:** This library stores documents and files to which your website's various content pages link. You can add columns, content types, or views to suit your specific requirements. By default, this library has versioning and content approval enabled, as well as columns for the publishing start and end dates. A version of this library is created in each publishing subsite for files and documents unique to that site.

- **Form Templates:** Chapter 12 discussed how to publish InfoPath Form templates to a site collection as a Content Type or Administrator Approved Template. This is a useful location for storing central templates used by InfoPath forms utilized throughout your site collection.
- **Images:** This system-generated library stores images for display in the current site that has versioning and content approval enabled. A version of this library is created in each publishing subsite for images unique to the site.
- **Pages:** This holds the various pages you create for the content of your website, including the default page. It has a series of special content types that allow you to create site content and pages. Only one pages library can exist within a single site; however, each subsite will have its own version of this pages library.
- **Site Collection Documents:** This document library acts as a centralized store for documents and files that are required and accessed throughout the site collection. Various publishing controls, such as the Enhanced Text Editor or Publishing hyperlink, can access documents in this library. You can select Site Collection Documents from the left menu when editing either of these controls, as shown in Figure 13-4.

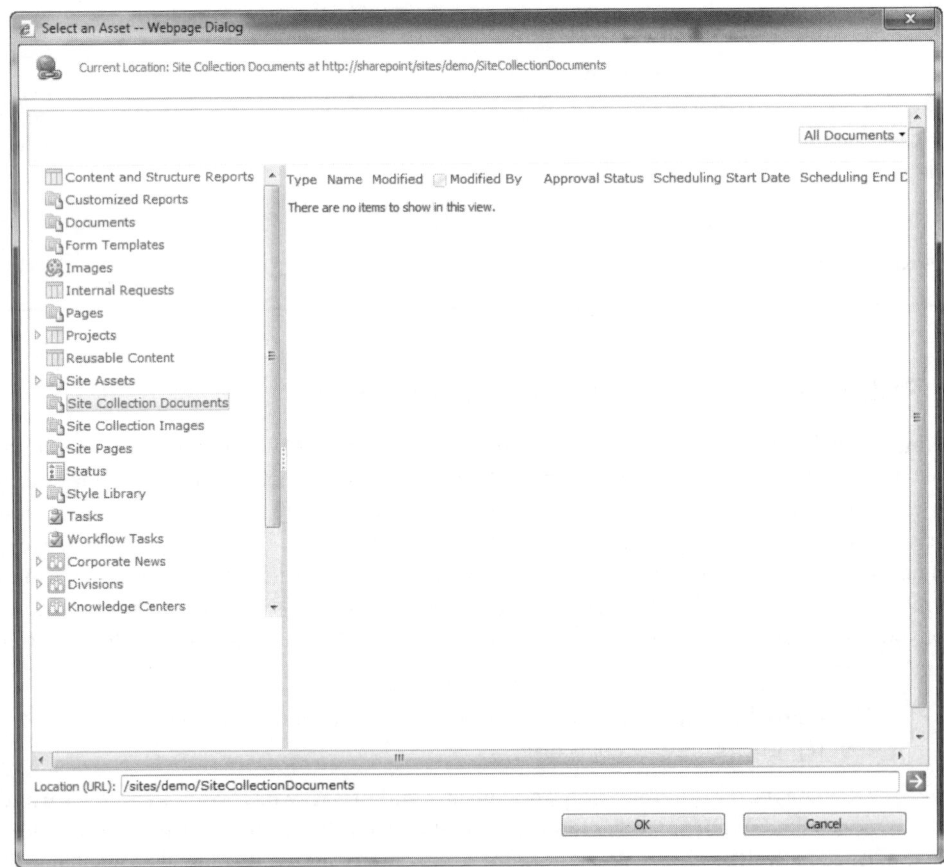

FIGURE 13-4

- **Site Collection Images:** This document library stores the images that a site collection requires. Like the site collection documents library, this is available directly via the interface when you use the various image publishing controls.
- **Style Library:** This system-generated library contains many of the style elements that your site requires, including custom XSL styles and CSS files; however, you can also add your own style sheets, which you can reference from within the site collection. It is considered a best practice to store any of the branding files related to your site within this library.
- **Content and Structure Reports:** This system list contains special queries within each list item that help to generate the reports available on a publishing site from the Manage Content and Structure section of the site. Reports are helpful for identifying tasks and content that exists throughout the publishing site collection. An example of such a report is shown in Figure 13-5.

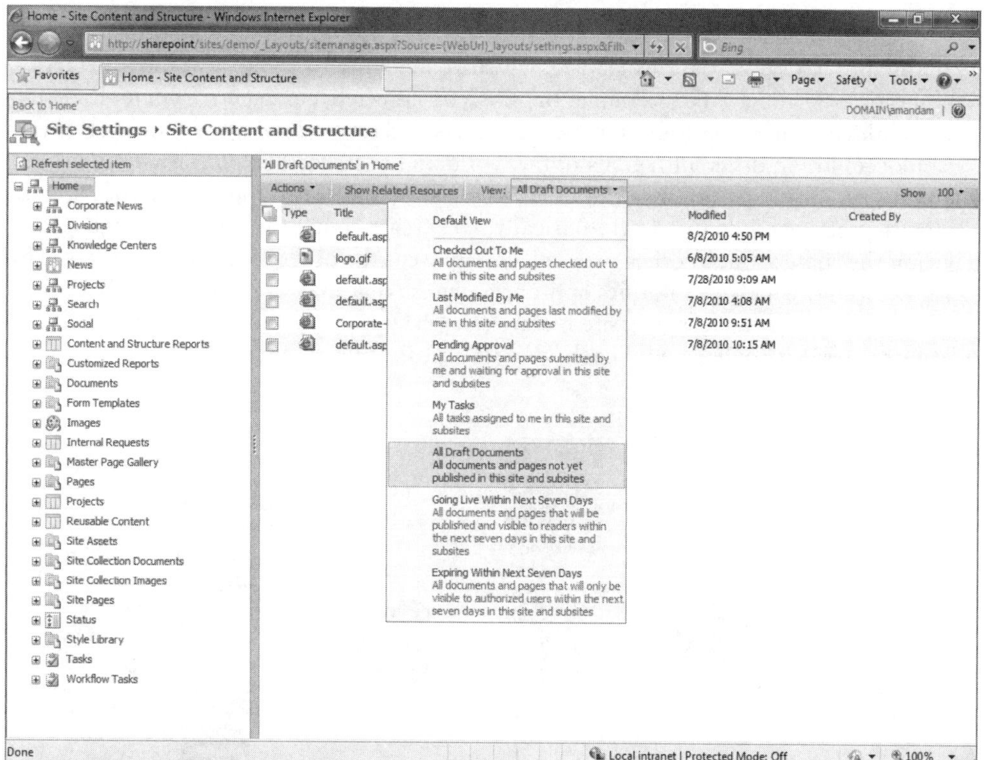

FIGURE 13-5

- **Reusable Content:** You may need to display content in multiple web parts or locations that are pulled from a single centralized source. This system-generated list contains content that you can display within specific web parts. You can opt to link it back to the source so that as content updates in the list, the areas within the site that are using this content will also automatically be updated.

- **Workflow Tasks:** This system-generated task list tracks the workflow tasks that are created as a result of the various publishing workflows.

In addition to the seamless navigation experience that SharePoint offers users between sites, it also has support for creating portals in multiple languages. In the next section, you see how to take a company website and configure it so that content users can view it in multiple languages.

WORKING WITH VARIATIONS

When you design an Internet-facing website or corporate intranet, you may need to present it in multiple languages. This may simply mean providing users access to documents in multiple languages, or you may need all your content, including web pages and interface elements, in multiple languages. In the latter case, if your content is in one language, such as English, you must translate documents into other languages, but the system should support and manage this process.

SharePoint has the Variations feature, which you can use to create a website hierarchy for content in multiple languages. For example, the site may be where customers from multiple languages can view information about the company's products and services, or a corporate intranet site where employees live in different regions of the world and need access to information in their primary languages. Although Variations does not actually translate the content for you, it starts a workflow that helps you do this work. Basically, you create content in a source language and then provision the content out to other sites, which represent the other required languages. This happens via workflow, which also notifies appropriate users that they are required to perform the translations. Figure 13-6 represents a site hierarchy with support for English and French versions of the website. Besides English and French, Variations can support any other languages, such as Spanish, Japanese, and German.

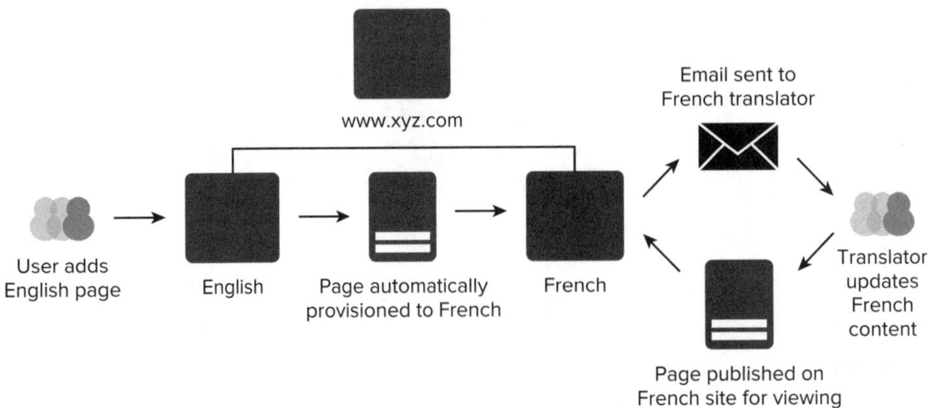

FIGURE 13-6

In this section, you learn how Variations work, including how to enable this feature. You then learn how to create labels for each language on your site, and then how to manage the workflow so that you have all the pieces you need for a working site with multiple language pages.

How Do Variations Work?

After login, the version of the site that users see is determined by their preferred language setting in their browser, as shown in Figure 13-7. If, for some reason, a user has a requirement to change the site language to something other than his or her default language, he or she may do so using the global navigation or a language selection control. If that page does not exist or is not published yet, the user is directed to the next page in the site hierarchy, which is typically the parent page.

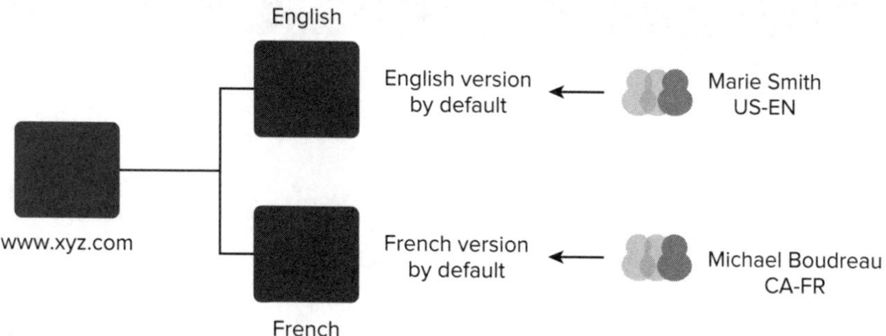

FIGURE 13-7

For a site to become available in multiple languages, you must first enable the Publishing feature. By default, the Publishing Portal has this feature enabled. Enabling variations on a Publishing site, site collection is fairly simple in comparison to the benefit and functionality it provides an organization. In the next example, you configure a site collection to support this feature. You use the Ski Company site for this example.

TRY IT OUT Enable Variations on a Site Collection

Your ski company has customers throughout the United States and Canada, which means you need content in both English and French. To do this, you enable the Variations feature. Because this functionality applies to the entire site collection, you enable this feature from the Site Collection Administration page.

The Variation Settings window has several options. In this example, you start your variations at the root of your site collection, subsequently making English your main language variation, then you opt to automate the creation of pages for other languages. This means that if you create a new page on the English site, a new page is automatically created in the French site. You then select to recreate any deleted target pages when you republish the source page. You also opt to have web part modifications made in one site carry over into the second site. Whether you decide to update web parts has to do with the level of web part customization you plan to do between languages. For example, if you want unique views available on a product's web part for each language, you may opt not to update web parts so that the English web part doesn't overwrite changes you want on the French web part. Finally, you choose to send an email when variation pages have been updated, and choose to share resources with the source variation rather than creating new copies.

1. From the main page of your AW Ski Company site collection created in the first Try It Out of this chapter, select Site Settings from the Site Actions menu.

2. From the Site Collection Administration set of links, select Variations.
3. Enter a "/" for the Variation Home field, as shown in Figure 13-8. This indicates that the Variations feature should be enabled at the root of the site collection.

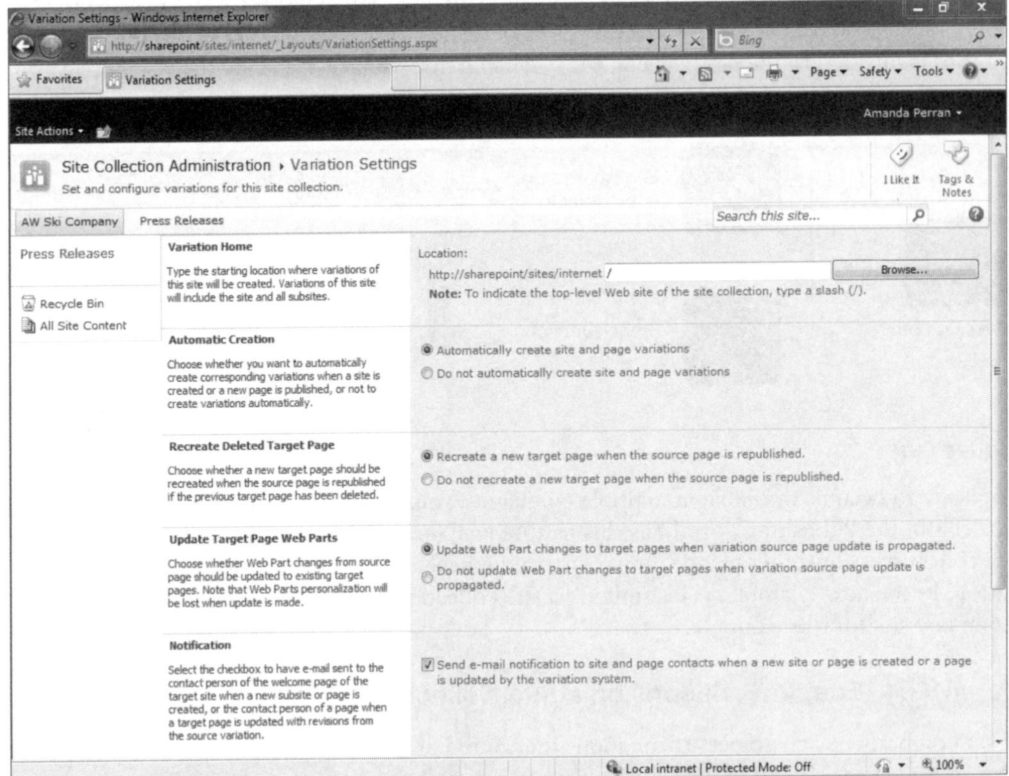

FIGURE 13-8

4. Select the option to Automatically create site and page variations. This setting is likely already selected by default.
5. Select the option to Recreate a new target page when the source page is republished. This setting is likely already selected by default.
6. Select the Do not update Web Part changes to target pages when variation source page update is propagated option for Update Target Page Web Parts.
7. Select the checkbox to send an email notification to site and page contacts when a new site or page is created or a page is updated by the Variation system. This setting is likely already selected by default.
8. Select the option to Reference existing resources.
9. Click OK. The variations feature will be enabled, and you will be redirected to the Site Settings page of your site.

How It Works

The variations feature is enabled for your site collection with the options you selected in this exercise. Once you enable Variations, the next step is to create labels to represent the sites for the various languages you want to support. This is the subject of the next section of the chapter.

Understanding Labels

In Variations, you create a label for each language you want to represent within the site collection. The label defines the language of the site, the display name, the locale, as well as the hierarchy and source hierarchy.

- **Label name and description:** These values are for organizational purposes only. It is important to be descriptive when entering a description for your label so that it is clearly understood by all site administrators.
- **Display Name:** You next define the display name for each site hierarchy. This is the name as it displays in the navigation menu. You generally make the display name the name of the language as it would appear to native speakers, so that they can recognize it and select it. For example, for the French display name, you enter **Français**, which is the word for "French" in the French language. This is particularly helpful for viewing the structure of the site in reports such as the Manage Content and Structure Report shown in Figure 13-9.

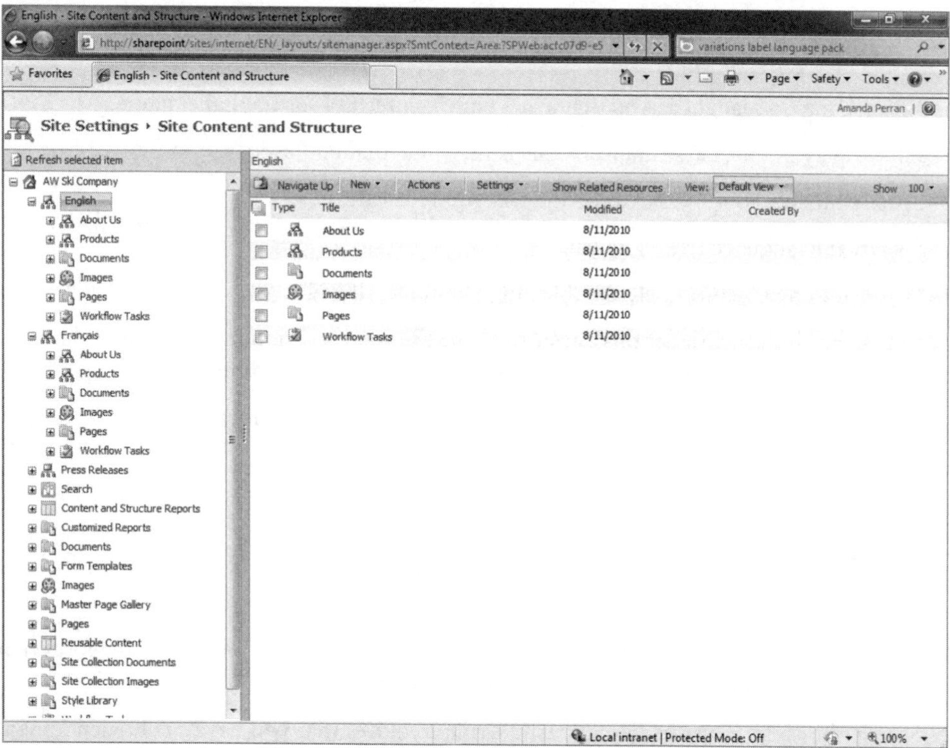

FIGURE 13-9

- **Locale:** This further tailors your site to reflect the nuances in variations on the same language. For example, you can define whether your French-speaking audience is French Canadian or from France. Likewise, you can distinguish between an English speaker from the United States and a speaker from Great Britain.
- **Hierarchy Creation:** For each language you want to represent on your website, a subhierarchy is created below the root site.
- **Source Variation:** You must choose the main language for your variations. This will be the initial language in which all content is created before translation and should be based on the majority of your user's first language.

TRY IT OUT Create Labels for Each Language

In this example, you create labels for each of the languages in which you want your Ski Company site to be available. Each label represents a major language, which in turn represents a unique site hierarchy containing all the elements related to that language. In this example, you make the Ski Company site available in both English and French, but you can expand into other languages later by adding additional labels.

1. Return to the site settings page of your site collection. You may already be there after completing the previous exercise.
2. Select Variation Labels from the Site Collection Administration links.
3. Click the New Label button from the toolbar. The Create Variation Label window appears, as shown in Figure 13-10.
4. Because the first language you define is English, enter **EN** for the Label name.
5. For Display Name, enter **English**. This is the value that end users see on the site.
6. Specify the locale of the site to be English (United States).
7. Specify the language to be English.
8. For Hierarchy Creation, select Publishing Sites and All Pages.
9. Check the checkbox to Set this variation to be the source variation. A message window appears to advise you that this action cannot be undone. Click OK to continue.
10. For Publishing Site Template, select Publishing Site with Workflow, as shown in Figure 13-11.
11. Click OK.
12. Select New Label from toolbar once more.
13. Enter **FR** for the Label Name.
14. For Display Name, enter **Français**.
15. Specify the locale of the site to be French (Canada). You do this because you expect that many of the French visitors to your site are French Canadian.
16. Specify the language to be French. This setting requires that you have the French Language Pack installed on your server. If you do not have the French Language Pack installed, your new label will be automatically created in English.

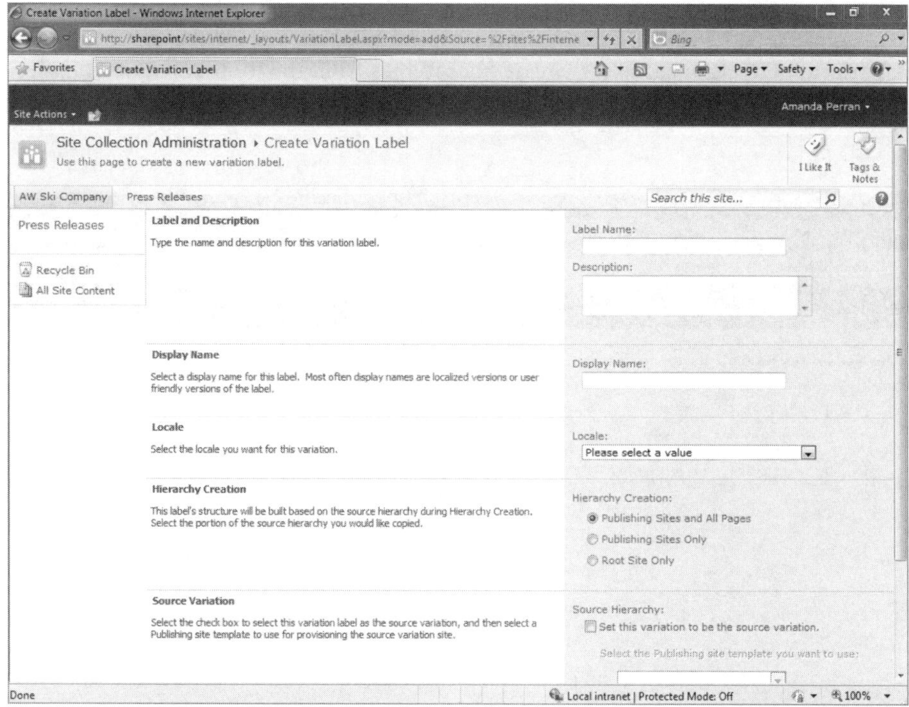

FIGURE 13-10

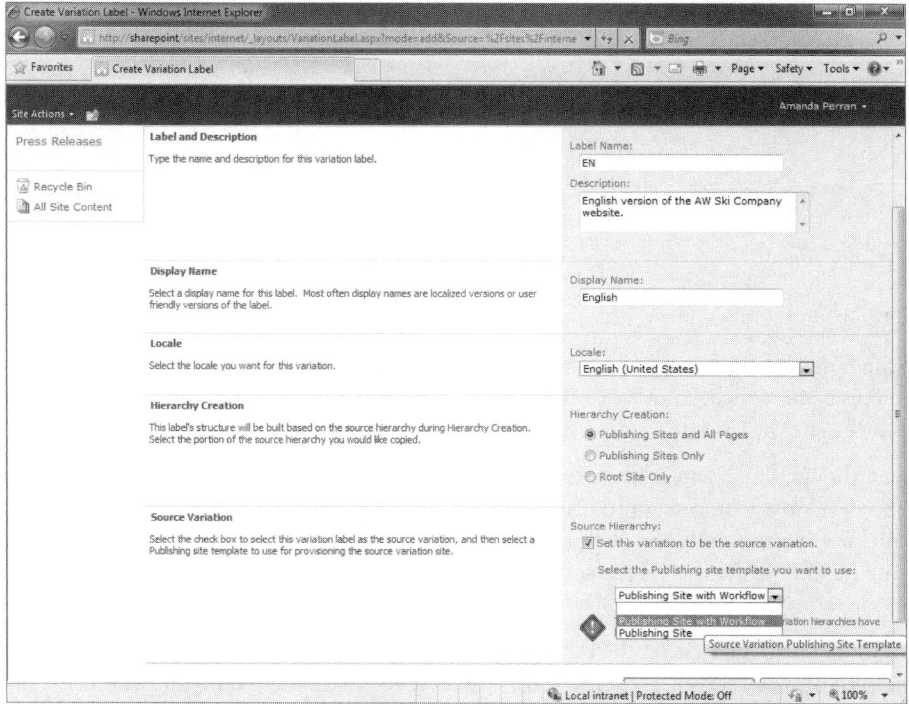

FIGURE 13-11

17. Click OK.

18. From the Variation Labels page, select Create Hierarchies from the toolbar. Upon completion, a message window will appear stating that the variation hierarchy will be created, as shown in Figure 13-12.

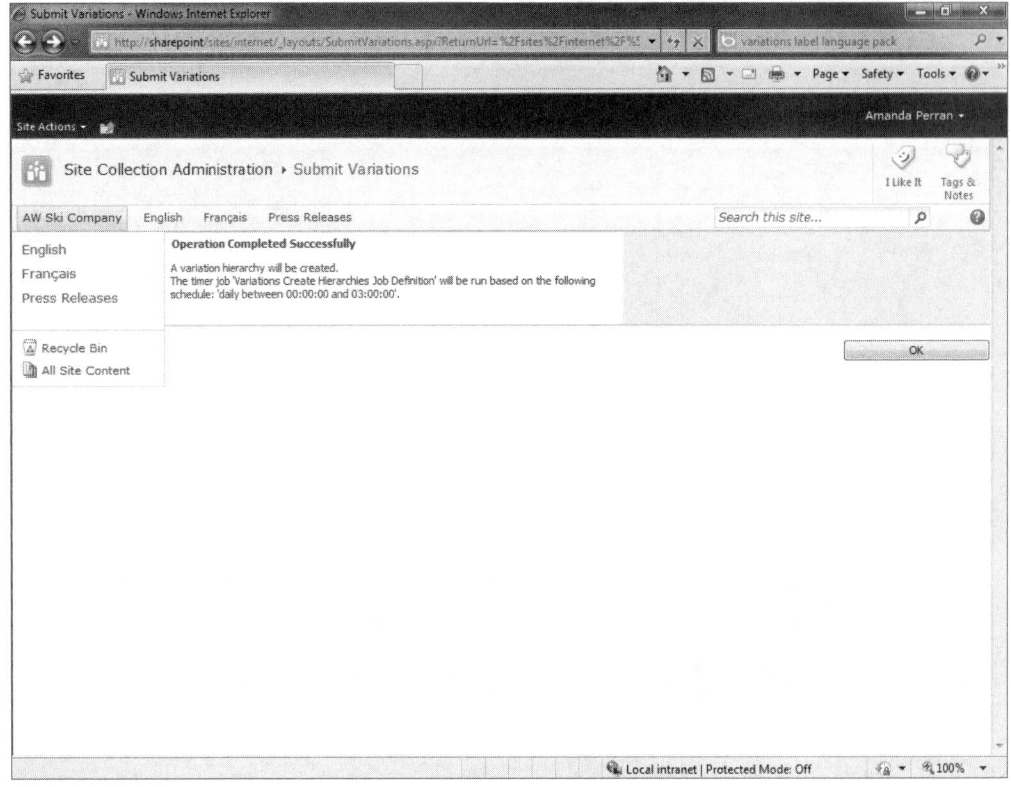

FIGURE 13-12

How It Works

Depending on the language preference that a user has set in the browser, a user is taken to the site with the appropriate language, which, in this example, is English. If a user defines a language preference that does not exist on the site, he or she is redirected to the source language.

In this example, although you created labels for two languages, you can still add new languages later. So, if you were to develop a requirement to offer the Ski Company website in Spanish, you could do so by creating a label for Spanish and then clicking the Create Site Hierarchies button again. Any content contained in your English site, which is the source site, would be copied into the Spanish site and queued for translation.

The hierarchy will be created based on the configuration of the Variations Create Hierarchies Job Definition Timer job on your server. By default, this job is scheduled to run daily; however, it can be updated from the Central Administration site to run more frequently as required or set to run on demand, as shown in Figure 13-13.

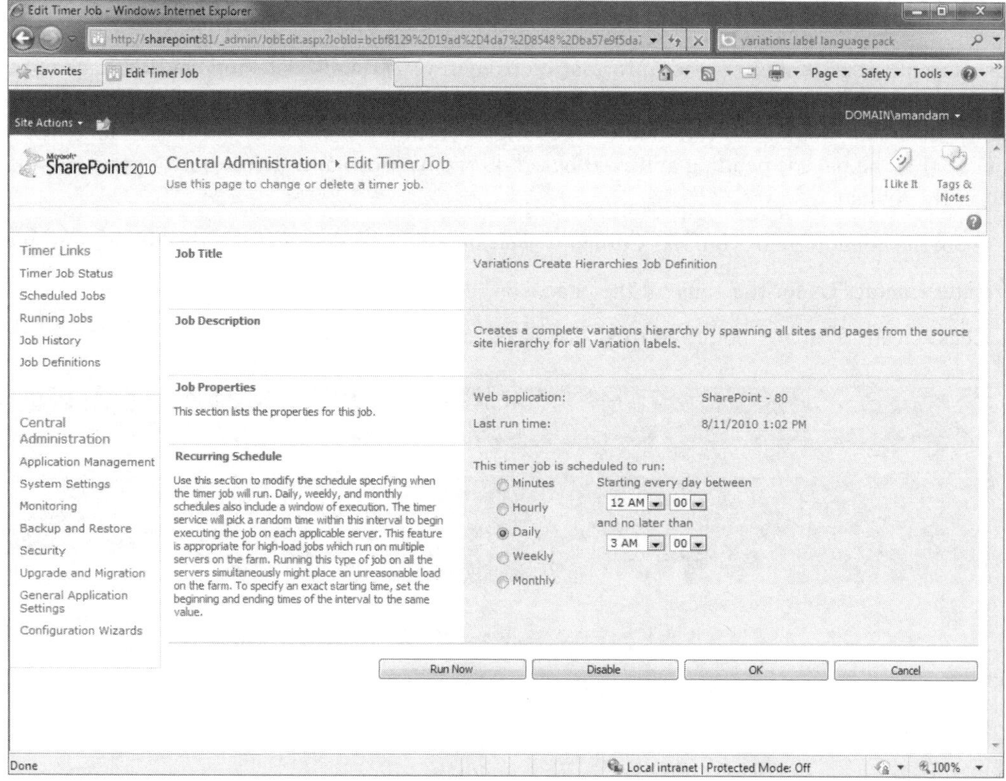

FIGURE 13-13

Managing Translation Workflows

To ensure that pages are translated into the required language of the destination sites as they are created, you can tie your site to a special workflow. As the last section showed, pages are automatically created in the language of the source site. The process works something like this: you create content for the source language page. When you check the page in, this automatically launches an approval process. The group that is to approve the page is automatically notified and a task is assigned in their task list. When the source language page is approved, Variations automatically creates the pages for other languages, and email notifications are sent to translators notifying them that new content has been added to their sites. They translate the page to the appropriate language and, upon checking in the page, start a second approval process.

This section features three Try It Outs that show you the inner workings of the workflow. In the first Try It Out, you create a new page in the source site, which is English. The page is created in the French site, and both sites go through the content editing and approval stages. In the second Try It Out, you create the site's hierarchy by adding a series of subsites that reflect the two main sections of the website: About Us and Products.

Finally, in the third Try It Out, you move the Press Releases site from the root structure of the site into the English version of your site. Once you do this, SharePoint automatically creates a French version of the Press Releases site, just as it did with the Products, About Us, and Custom Contact page from the first and second Try It Outs.

TRY IT OUT Create a New Page in the Source Site

In this example, you create a contact information page in your English site and check it back in to the system to launch an approval workflow. Because you are a member of the Approvers group, you would normally receive an email notification and task assignment, but for the sake of this example, you can clearly see that the page is pending approval based on the Approve and Reject buttons that are displayed in the toolbar.

1. From the home page of your Ski Company website, select New Page from the Site Actions menu.
2. Enter **Contact Us** for the name of the page.
3. Click Create. You are redirected to an empty page, as shown in Figure 13-14.

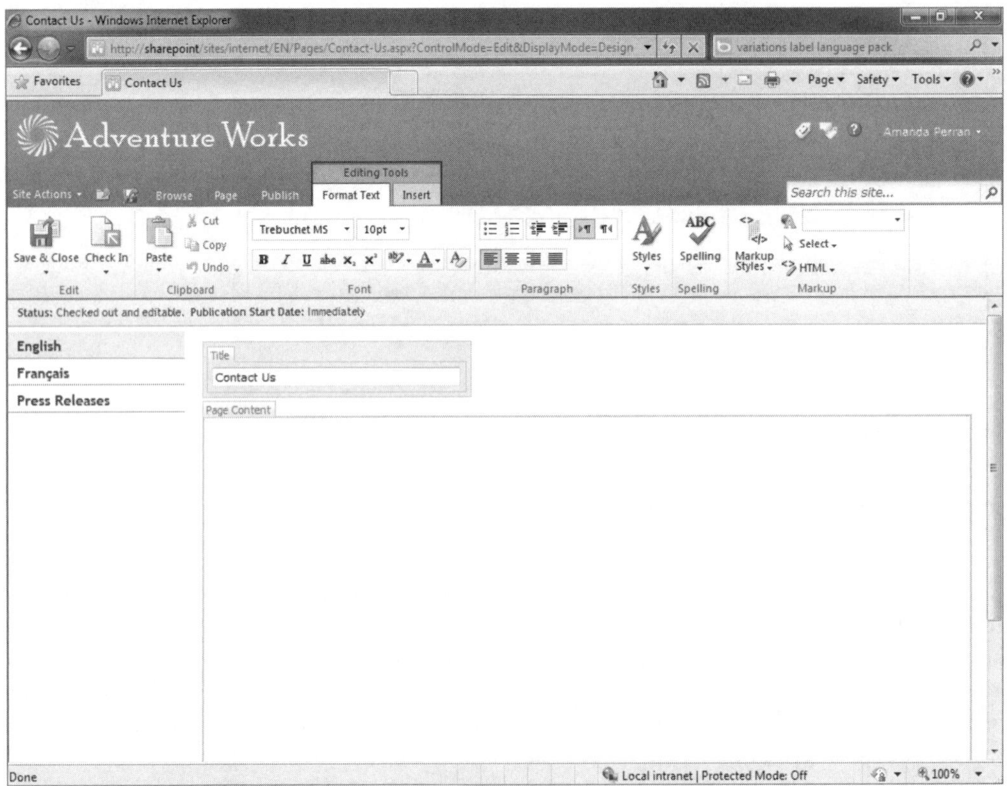

FIGURE 13-14

4. From the page tab of the Ribbon, expand the Page Layout option and select Image on Right. The page will reformat to display a layout containing a Page Image control on the right, as shown in Figure 13-15.
5. Enter some content into the page using the various controls and select Check In from the Ribbon.
6. Add some comments, as these will be useful to yourself and others later when reviewing the page's version history, as discussed in Chapter 3.

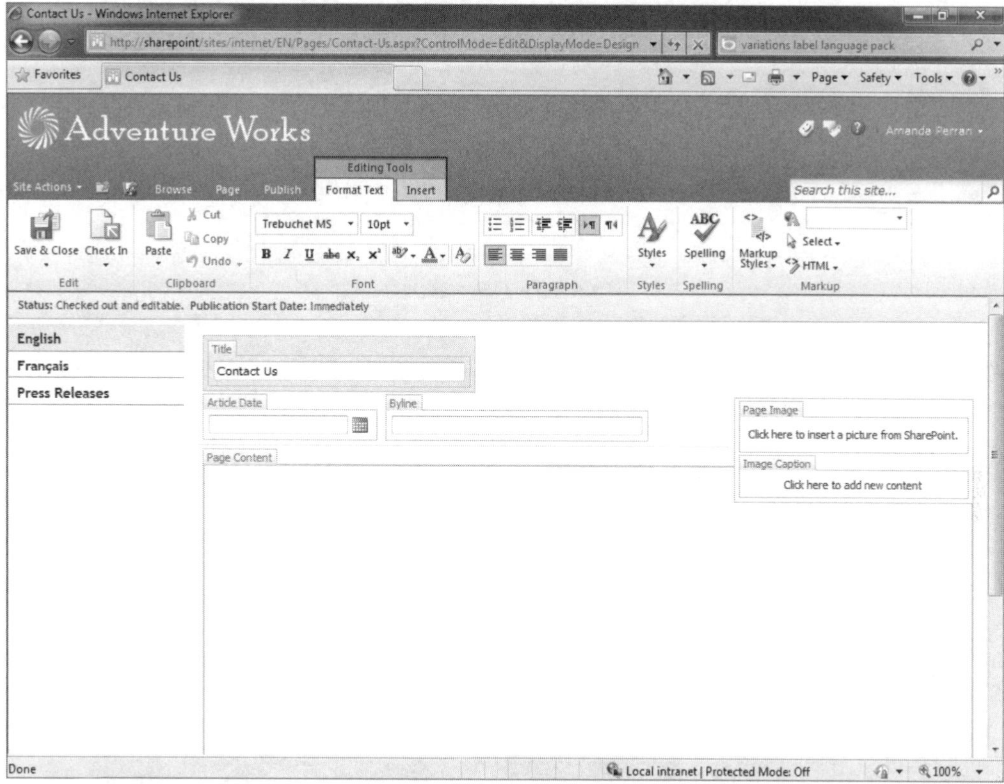

FIGURE 13-15

7. Click the Continue button.
8. From the Publish tab of the Ribbon, select the Submit button. A workflow form will appear, as shown in Figure 13-16.
9. Enter details to describe your workflow, including Request and Duration per Task, and click the Start button.
10. Click Approve from the Publish tab. You will be redirected to the workflow approval form.
11. Add comments related to your approval of the page, and click the Approve button.

How It Works

Once the workflow has run, a yellow bar will appear at the top of the page, as shown in Figure 13-17, indicating that the page is waiting for approval.

The workflow was automatically assigned to the built-in Approvers group. Upon approval of the English page, the French page for Contact Us will be created, and content owners from the French site receive email notifications. This process may take a few minutes, depending on the configuration of your server. They can then edit a draft page that the system creates, and then publish the page. Content approval workflows are also launched for this page, and the approvers of this page are notified.

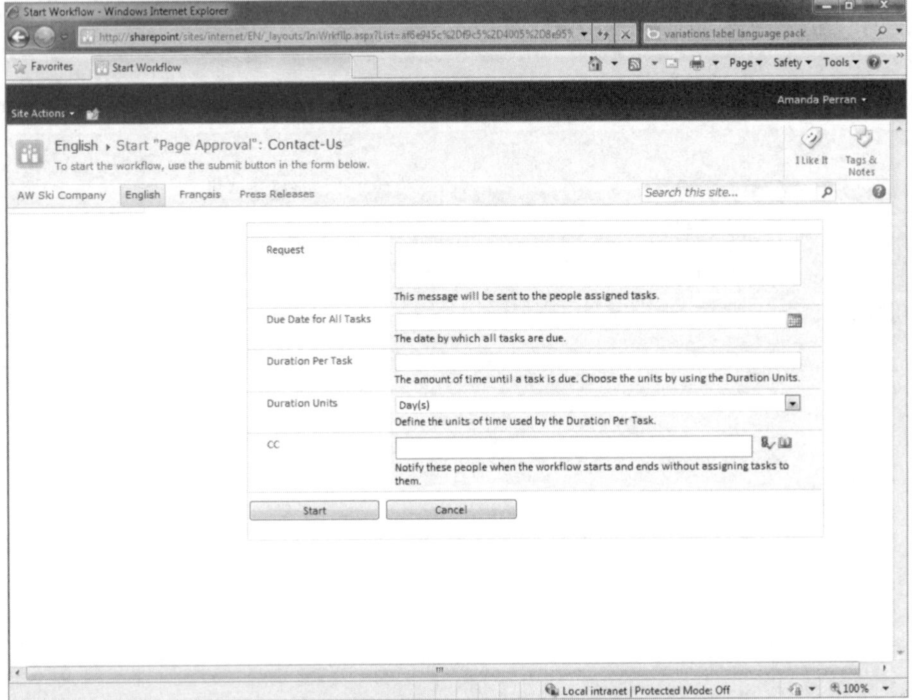

FIGURE 13-16

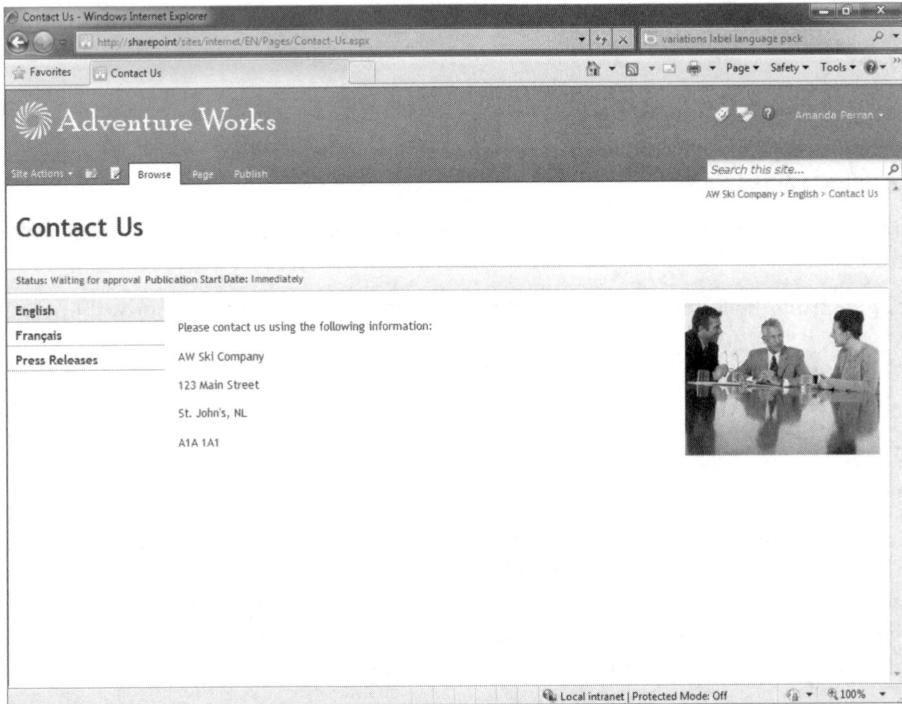

FIGURE 13-17

TRY IT OUT Create a Site Hierarchy of Publishing Sites

In this example, you walk through the steps of creating two subsites for your publishing site collection. For the first site, you use the Create Site command from the Site Actions menu, which is the easiest way to create a single site from within a publishing site. Notice that this option along with several others on the Site Actions menu did not exist in the previous examples when you worked on sites without the Publishing feature enabled.

Because you need to create multiple subsites, you should use the Manage Content and Structure interface, shown in this example. From this interface, you can activate many administrative functions such as copying or moving a site, or creating new content. In addition, you can manage security or content across multiple sites very conveniently from this section. The Manage Content and Structure window, shown in Figure 13-14, provides a good visual diagram of the entire site collection and its various content elements.

1. From the main page of your AW Ski Settings website, select Manage Content and Structure from the Site Actions menu.
2. Expand the menu associated with the English site and select the option to create a New Site, as shown in Figure 13-18.

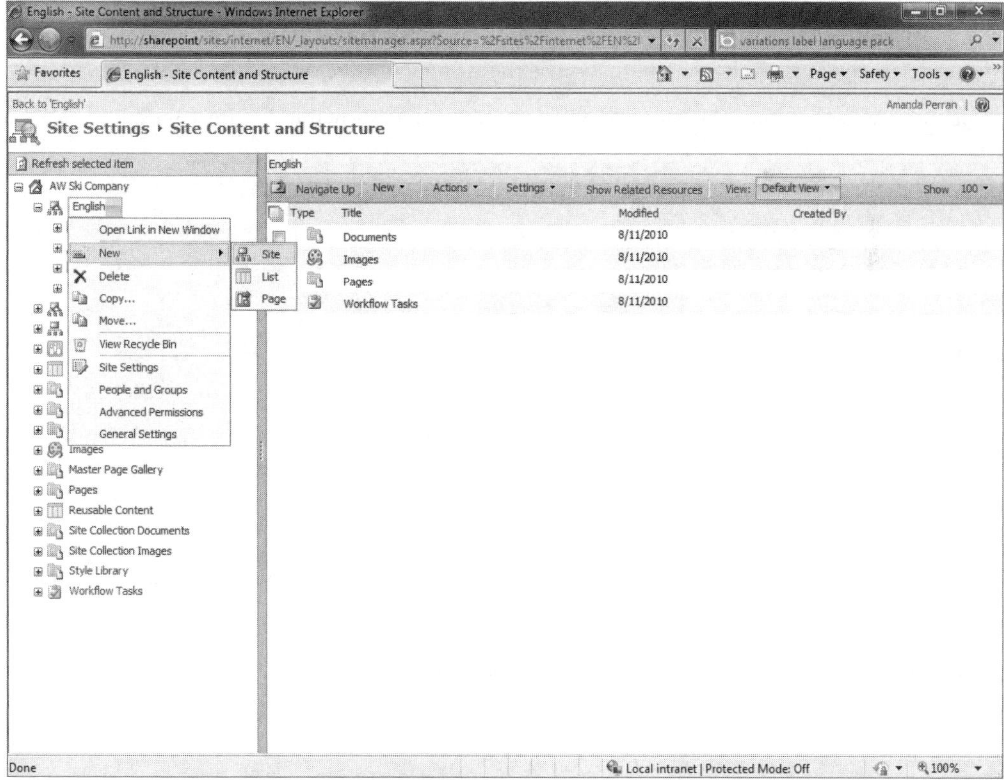

FIGURE 13-18

3. Enter a title and URL for the site. For this example, enter **About Us** for the title and **aboutus** for the URL.
4. Select the Publishing Site with Workflow template.

5. Select the option to use the same permissions as the parent site.
6. Select the Yes option for Use the Top Link Bar from the Parent Site.
7. Click Create.
8. Repeat steps 2 through 6, but this time, enter **Products** for the Title and **products** for the URL Name in step 3.

How It Works

As you create the new sites, these sites are also created in the French version of your site based upon the configured schedule of your server. The manage Content and Structure view will clearly outline the hierarchy of your site, including the multilingual branches.

TRY IT OUT Move a Site within a Site Collection

From the Manage Content and Structure section, you can perform many administrative functions such as moving sites. In this example, you move the Press Releases site under the English site hierarchy.

1. From the home page of your Ski Company website, select Site Actions then Manage Content and Structure. The Site Content and Structure window appears.
2. Hover over the Press Releases site to expose the Administrative drop-down menu.
3. Select the Move option. The Move Site dialog appears, as shown in Figure 13-19.

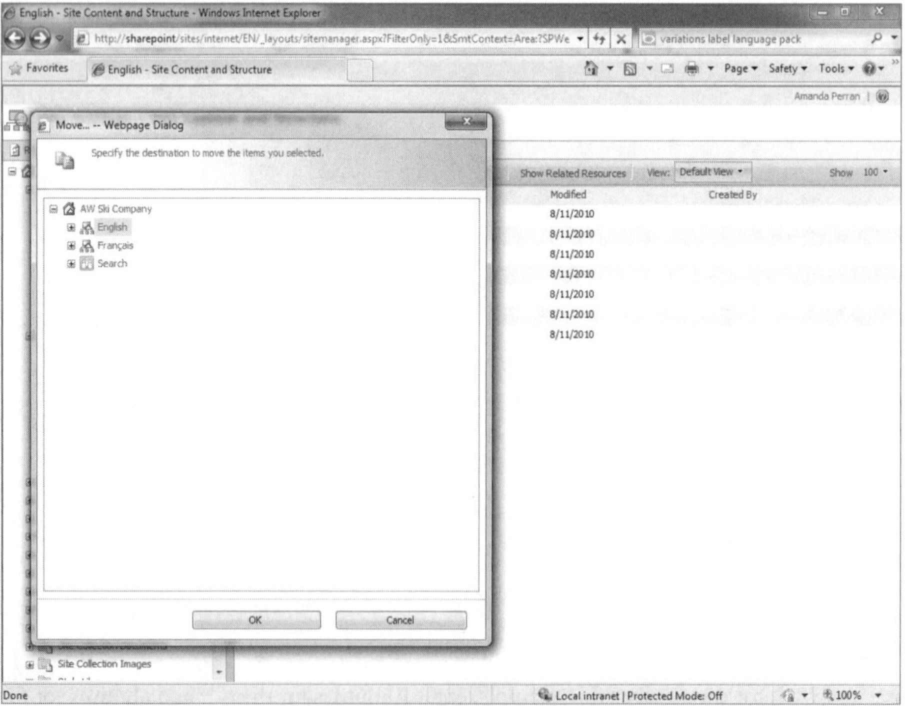

FIGURE 13-19

4. Select the English site.
5. Click OK.

How It Works

Because Variations is enabled, moving the site triggers the creation of the Press Releases site under the French hierarchy. At this point, French content translators can go into the French version of the site and rename pages and update content to reflect the appropriate language. Figure 13-20 shows how the site hierarchy looks with the creation of the additional subsites in both languages.

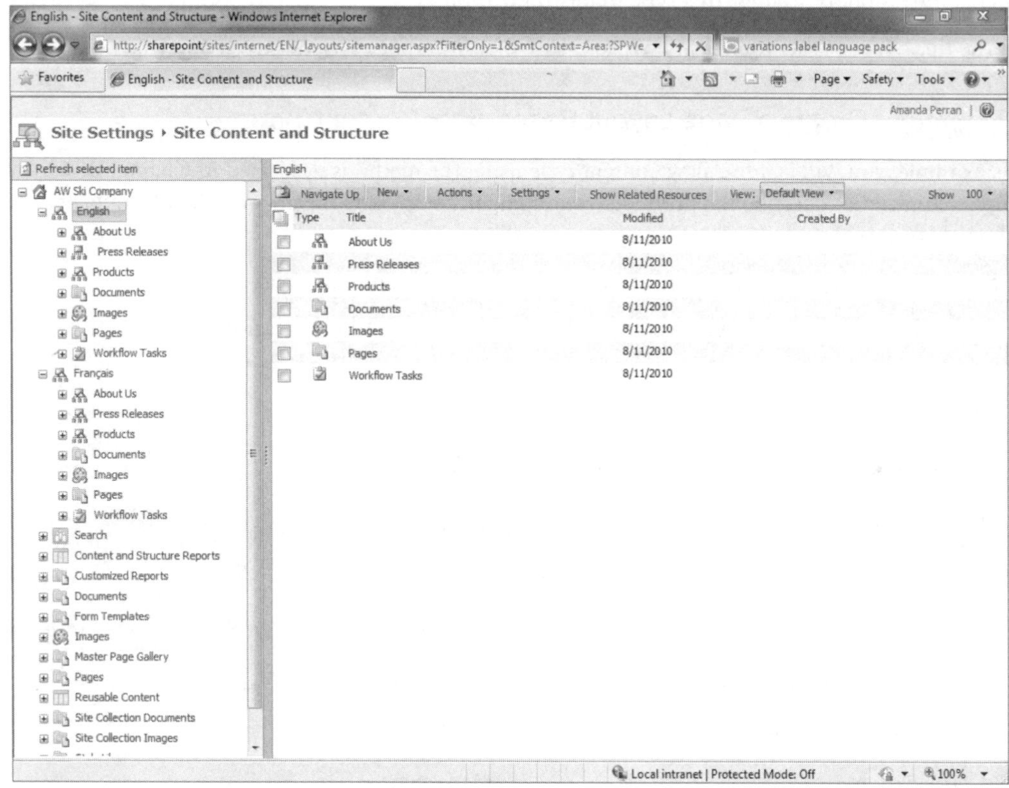

FIGURE 13-20

PAGE LAYOUTS AND CONTENT TYPES

Page layouts control the type of content that can be created on a page as well as where and how that content is displayed. Page layouts are built on content types, which were discussed in Chapter 6. A *content type* has one or more metadata columns associated with it, and these metadata columns ultimately control the type of information associated with that particular content type, things such as rich HTML fields or images. You can also place web part zones on the page to allow for web part placement.

You define page layouts either through Microsoft Office SharePoint Designer 2010 or via the browser. By default, when you use the browser method, which is described in the first Try It Out in this section, the controls are all added to the page from the top down, stacked one after another, with little control over how the various controls on the page are presented or positioned.

When you require full control over the layout of the page, you can use SharePoint Designer 2010 to create the page layout. If you are comfortable editing a page in SharePoint Designer, you can get started by following the steps in the second Try It Out in this section.

Because SharePoint Designer 2010 is required, it's recommended that only experienced web developers or professionals attempt this type of customization.

In the final Try It Out, you learn how to create a custom page based on your new layout.

TRY IT OUT Create a Page Layout Based on a Content Type

In this example, you will create a new content type using the methods described in Chapter 6, which includes columns that describe the products your company sells. You create a Product Details page layout based on this content type.

1. Select Site Settings from the English site of your AW Ski Company site collection.
2. Select Go to top-level site settings from the Site Collection Administration section.
3. Select Site Content Types.
4. Click Create.
5. Create your content type with the following settings:

PROPERTY	VALUE
Name	Product Details
Description	Information page on AW Ski Company Products
Select Parent Content Type From	Page Layout Content Types
Parent Content Type	Article Page
New Group	Marketing

6. Click Create.
7. Create site columns within your content type based on the following:

COLUMN NAME	COLUMN TYPE
Product Name	Single Line of Text
Product Category	Choice
Product Description	Full HTML content with formatting and constraints for publishing

COLUMN NAME	COLUMN TYPE
Product Image	Image with formatting and constraints for publishing
Promo Video	Rich media data for publishing

8. Click on each of the following columns and change the Column Setting to Hidden. These columns will not be required in your page layout.
   - Page Content
   - Page Image
   - Contact
   - Contact E-Mail Address
   - Contact Name
   - Contact Picture
   - Byline
   - Article Date
9. Return to the Site Settings page for your site.
10. From the Galleries section, select Master Pages and Page Layouts.
11. Select New Page Layout from the Ribbon, as shown in Figure 13-21.

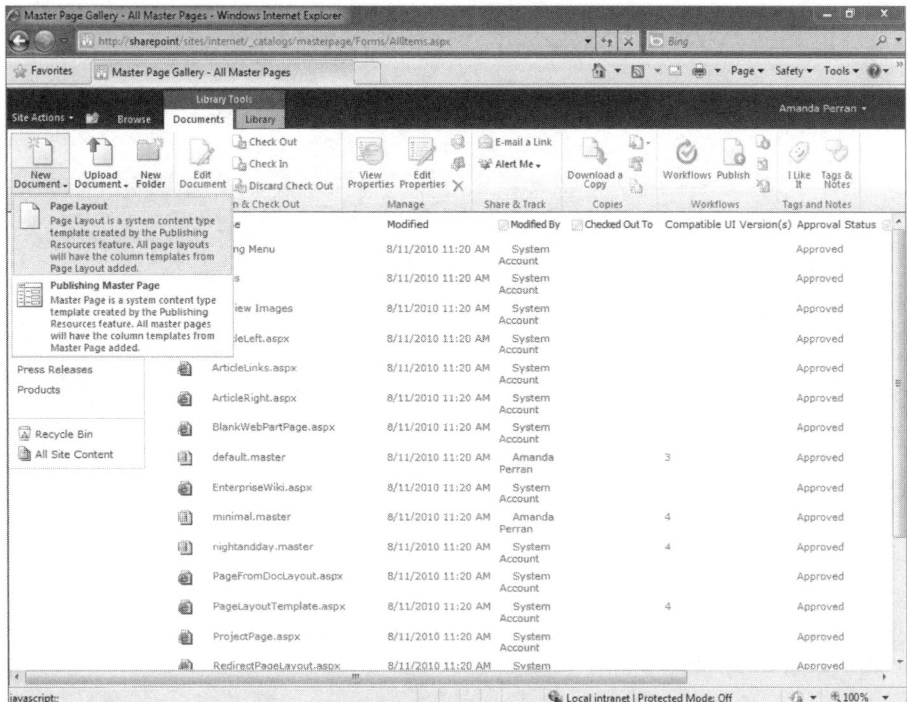

FIGURE 13-21

12. You must first associate your page layout with a content type. The columns defined in your content type become the content allowed on the page. In the Content Type group, select Marketing. Any custom content type groups you may have created become accessible in the menu.
13. Select Product Details for the Content Type Name.
14. In the Page Layout Title and Description section, enter **simpledetails** in the URL Name field.
15. In the Title field, enter **Simple Product Details Page**.
16. In the Description field, enter Simplified product details page for demonstrating how to create a page layout through the browser.
17. Select EN and FR, and click the Add button for the Variations Labels field as shown in Figure 13-22.

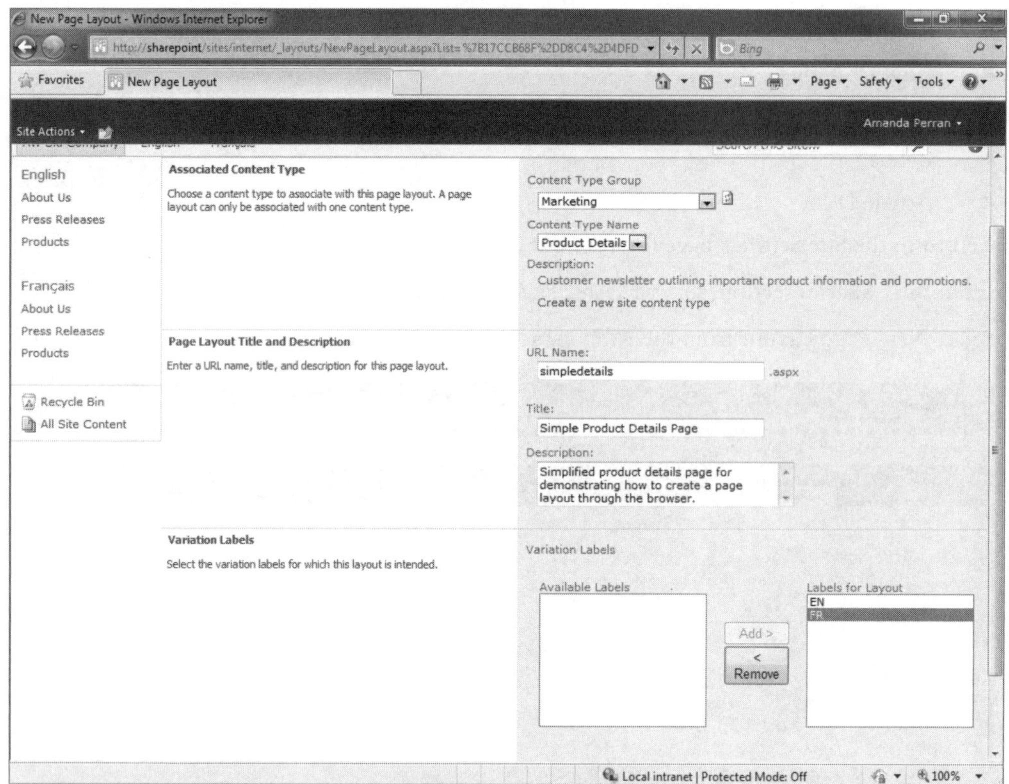

FIGURE 13-22

18. Click OK.

How It Works

Once you have created a page layout, it becomes visible in the list of Layouts on the Create Page window. You can view this list by clicking New Page from the Ribbon of the Pages library of your site. The New Page is shown in Figure 13-23.

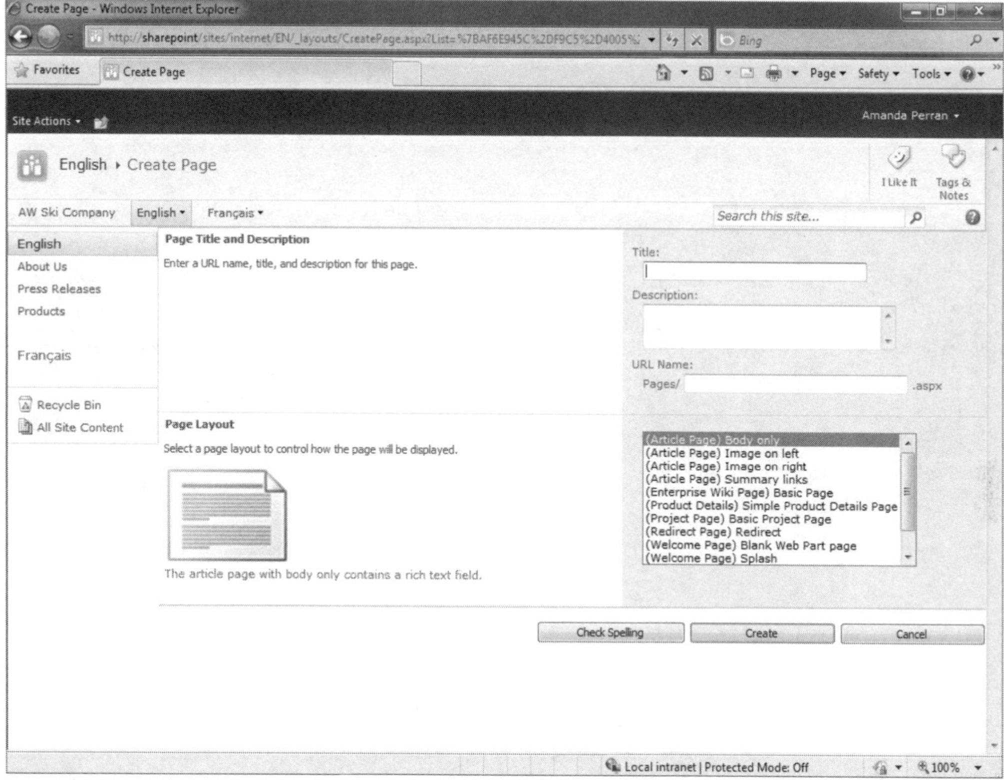

FIGURE 13-23

TRY IT OUT Create a Page Layout Using SharePoint Designer 2010

Page layouts set the stage for the type of content you want to allow on a particular page. For example, you might allow someone to place an image and description on a page. These pieces of content are actually columns in the content type on which you built your page layout. These columns are accessible in SharePoint Designer as content controls in the SharePoint Controls section of the Ribbon.

Using SharePoint Designer, you can place content controls on the page by selecting them from the Controls to be added to the page where you want to display them. It is important to note that the content controls should be placed inside the placeholder labeled PlaceHolderMain.

1. In SharePoint Designer 2010, open your AW Ski Company website.
2. Select Page Layouts from the left-hand navigation.
3. Click the New Page Layout option from the Ribbon menu. A dialog will appear, as shown in Figure 13-24.
4. From the Content Type group drop-down, select Marketing.

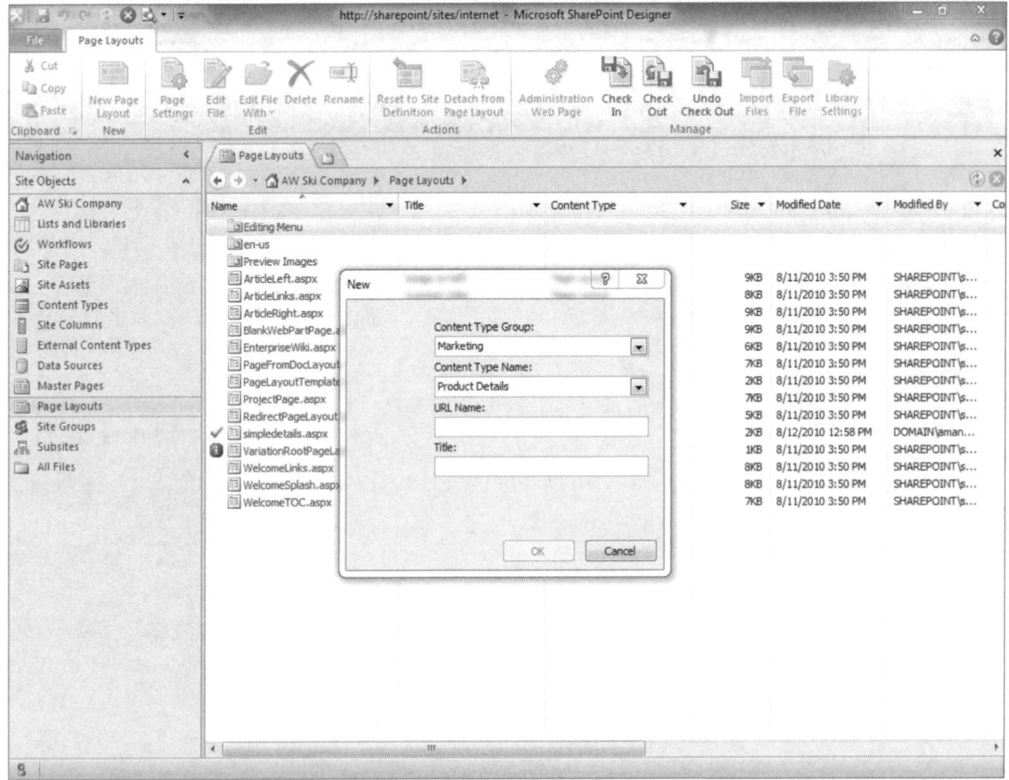

FIGURE 13-24

5. From the Content Type Name, select Product Details.
6. In the URL Name field, enter **productpage**.
7. In the Title field, enter **Product Details Page.**
8. Click OK.
9. Your page layout should open for editing. What you have just done is create a blank page layout ready for customization.
10. Enter code view by selecting code at the bottom of the editing window, locate the PlaceHolderMain tag. This is the main content area of the page where you want to make any layout changes, as well as accept particular types of content.
11. Add the following table code between the PlaceHolderMain tags. This is the area where you allow content to be created.

```
<table width="100%">
<tr>
<td valign="top"></td>
<td valign="top"></td>
</tr>
```

```
<tr>
<td valign="top"></td>
<td valign="top"></td>
</tr>
<tr>
<td valign="top"></td>
<td valign="top"></td>
</tr>
</table>
```

12. When you create a content type, you attach metadata columns to the content type. These columns are the content you place in your page layout that ultimately becomes the content that the users will add to the page. These columns are visible from the Insert tab of the Ribbon, as shown in Figure 13-25. It is recommended that you select the Show Toolbox link at the bottom of the menu to add the Toolbox to the right-hand panel of your screen.

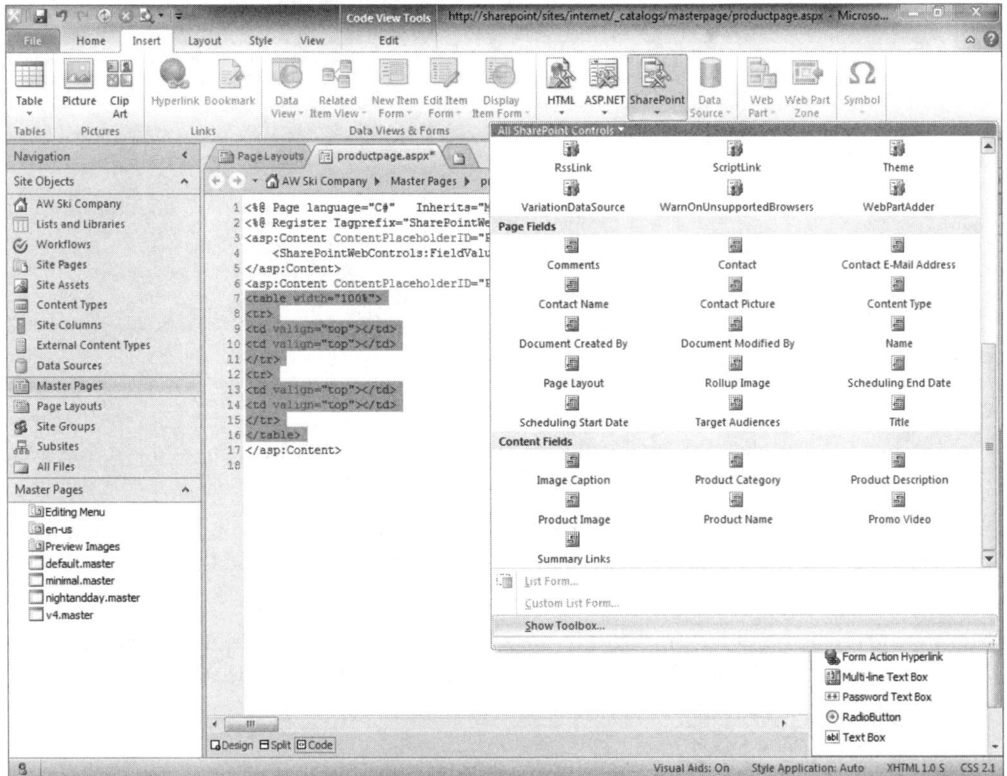

FIGURE 13-25

13. Switch to Design mode by selecting the Design tab at the bottom of the editing window. Select the first column within the first row in the table you created. From the Toolbox, locate Content Fields, right-click the Product Name field, and select Insert to add it to the selected cell of the table, as shown in Figure 13-26.

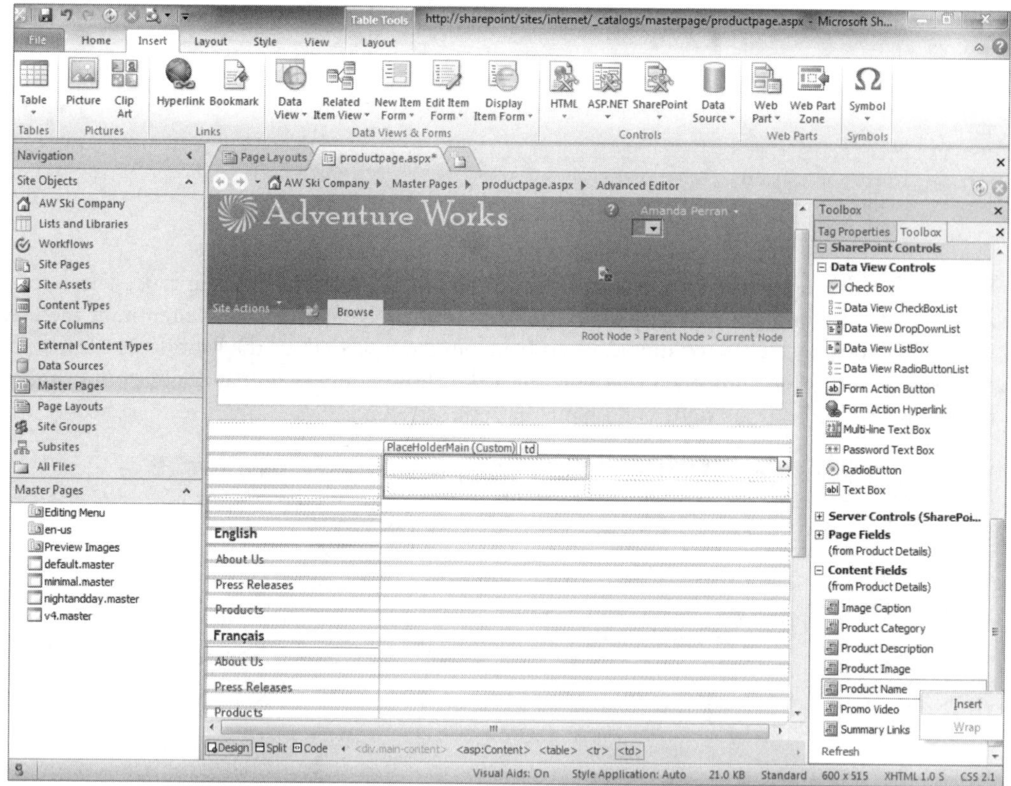

FIGURE 13-26

14. Select the First column of the second row in the table you created. From the Toolbox, locate Content Fields, right-click the Product Description field, and select Insert to add it to the selected cell of the table.

15. Select the second column of the second row in the table you created. From the Toolbox, locate Content Fields, right-click the Product Image field, and select Insert to add it to the selected cell of the table.

16. Select the first column of the third row in the table you created. From the Toolbox, locate Content Fields, right-click the Promo Video field, and select Insert to add it to the selected cell of the table.

17. Save and close the page layout.

18. Page layouts are located under source control, and you need to check them out for editing, and check them in and publish them when they are final. From the Page Layouts tab of SharePoint Designer, right-click productpage.aspx and choose Check In.

19. Select Publish a Major Version, and click OK. Select Yes for content approval when prompted.

20. Hover over the productdetails.aspx file, which is currently pending, and select Approve/Reject from the drop-down menu.

21. Select Approved and then click OK.

How It Works

You can now put your page layouts to work by creating new pages based on these layouts. To create a new page, you must specify a page layout. By selecting the product details page that you just created, you generate a page to which you can add a title and page content, just as you specified in the page layout. See Figure 13-26.

TRY IT OUT Create a Page Using a Custom Page Layout

As shown previously in Figures 13-15 and 13-23, you may select from a number of page layouts when creating a page. However, the page layouts that are available for selection can be limited by the site administrator. In this example, you will configure your Products site to allow the use of your Product Details page layout only to create new pages. You will then create a new page on the site using the Product Details page layout.

1. Select Site Settings from the Products subsite of the English site of your AW Ski Company site collection.
2. Select Page Layouts and Site Templates from the Look and Feel section. The Page Layout and Site Template Settings page will appear, as shown in Figure 13-27.

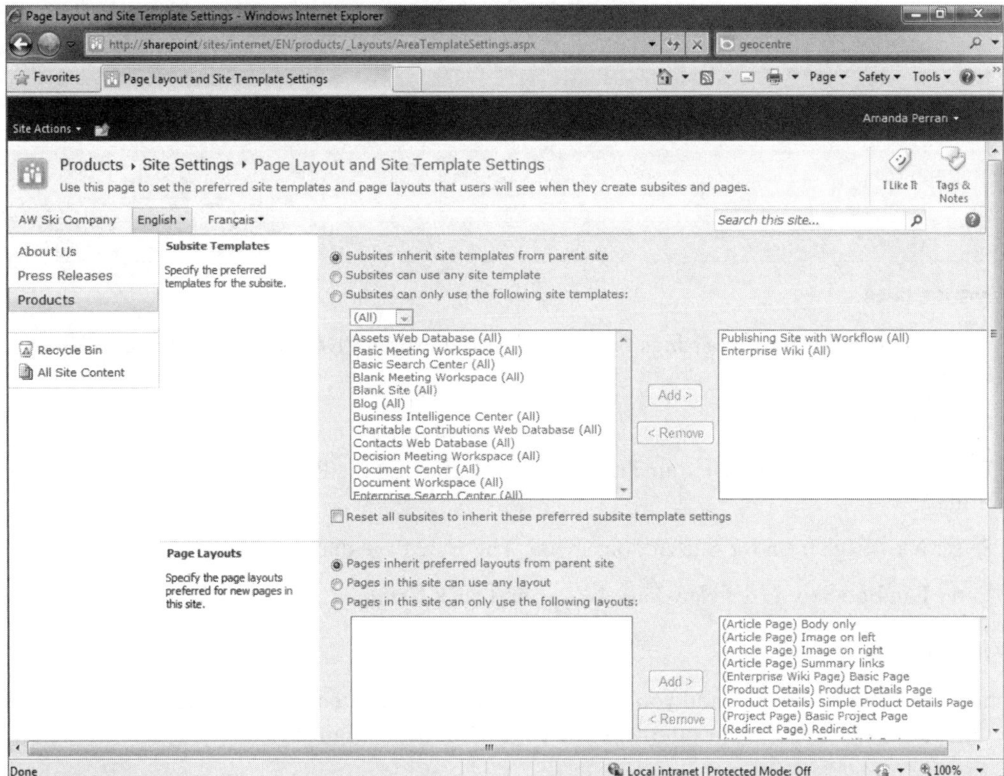

FIGURE 13-27

3. From the Page Layouts section of the screen, select the Pages in this site can only use the following layouts option, and remove all layouts from the right-hand side, except the Product Details Page, as shown in Figure 13-28.

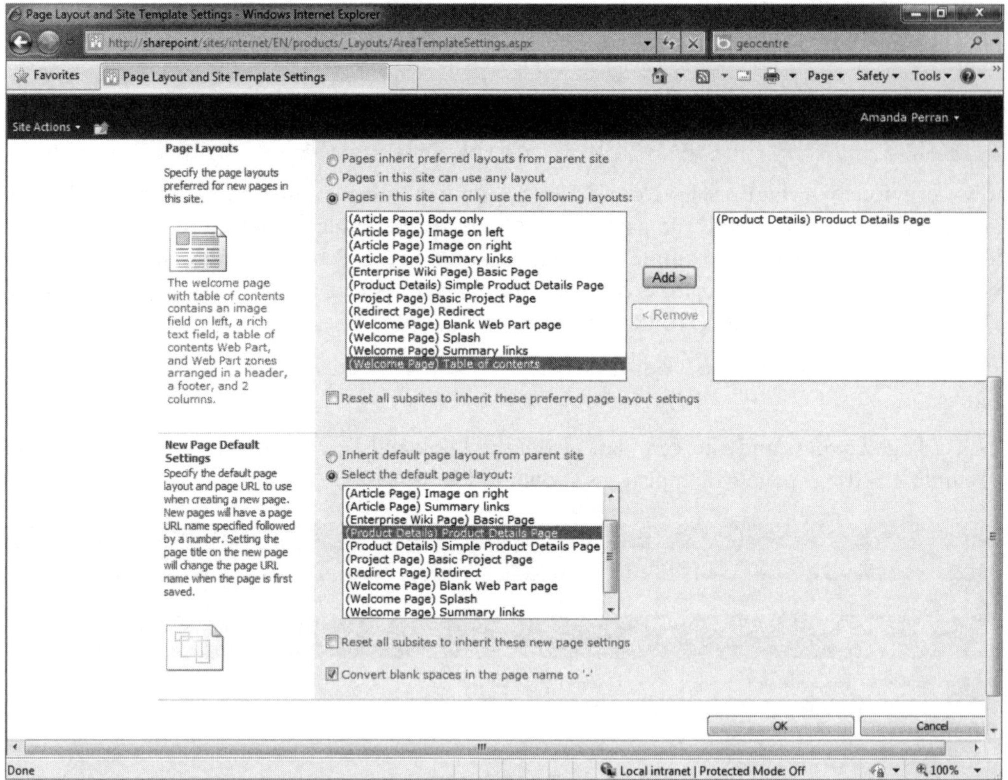

FIGURE 13-28

4. In the New Page Default Settings section, select the Product Details Page as the default page layout.
5. Click OK.
6. Return to the main page of your Products site by clicking the Products link in the breadcrumb trail.
7. Select New Page from the Site Actions menu. The New Page dialog will appear.
8. Enter **Bamboo Skis** as the New Page Name, and click Create.

How It Works

Your new page will be created, and you will be able to specify content in the associated content areas as defined in your page layout. An example of the page is shown in Figure 13-29.

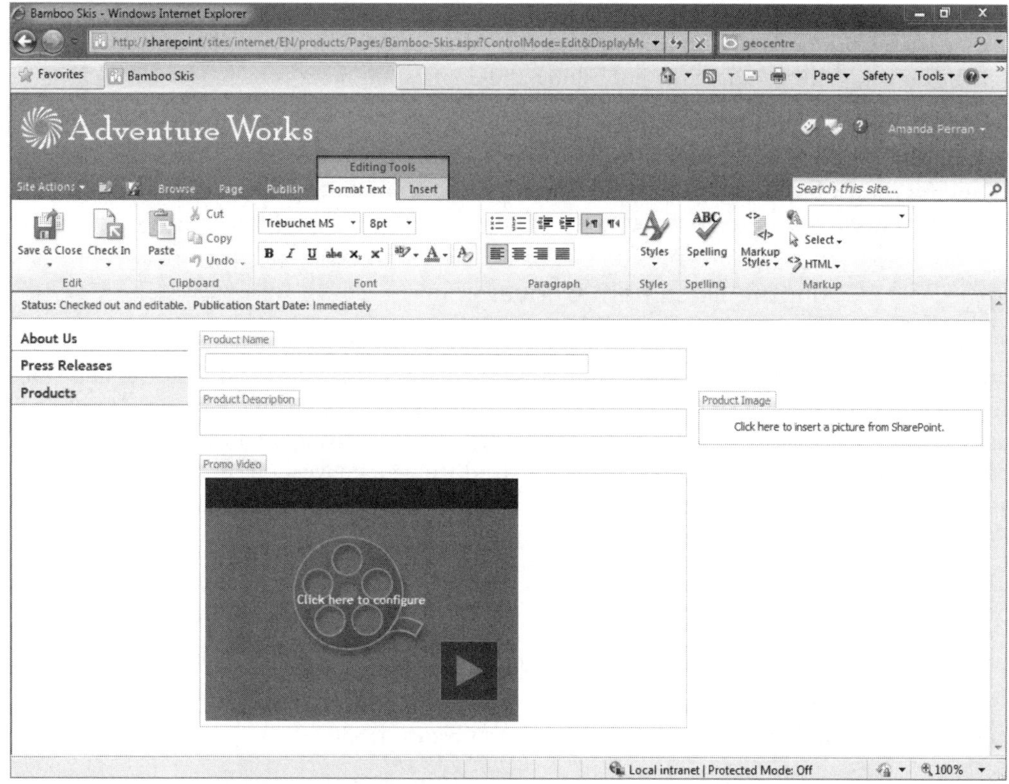

FIGURE 13-29

UNDERSTANDING DOCUMENT CONVERSION

Many organizations create and store a great deal of information in popular file formats, such as Word or InfoPath. Because the information already exists in a format with which users are familiar, it does not always make sense to repeat the authoring process when this content needs to go on a website. Instead, it's faster to create web content directly from these files. Further, if you present this content within the corporate website, you would want to maintain the corporate look and feel. SharePoint supports a document conversion feature that allows users to create web pages of content directly from specific file types. SharePoint supports document conversion for the following formats:

- An InfoPath form to a web page
- A Word document to a web page
- A Word document with macros to a web page
- An XML document to a web page

In addition, developers can write their own converters and install them. This becomes relevant only if you have a large amount of data in files on your SharePoint server that you want to make available as web content, while avoiding the publishing and duplication processes.

Before you can convert a document, which you do directly from the document libraries, you must first configure this service and then enable the feature via the Central Administration site, which are the subjects of the first and second Try It Outs in this section. In the third Try It Out, you learn how to convert a document into a web page.

TRY IT OUT Configure Document Conversion

In this example, you learn how a server farm administrator enables document conversion. You start this process by visiting the Central Administration site to ensure that the Load Balancer and Document Conversion services are enabled on the server. You then visit the Document Conversion Configuration page and select the settings required to enable the service. These settings control which server acts as the load balancer server and the interval by which the document conversion timer job runs. In this example, four document converters have been installed on the system, and you can configure each of these to define maximum file size, time-out length, and maximum retries.

1. From the Central Administration site of your SharePoint environment, select Application Management.
2. Select the Manage Services on Server link from the Service Applications group.
3. Click the Start link for the Document Conversions Load Balancer Service. The page will refresh and the service will appear as started, as shown in Figure 13-30.

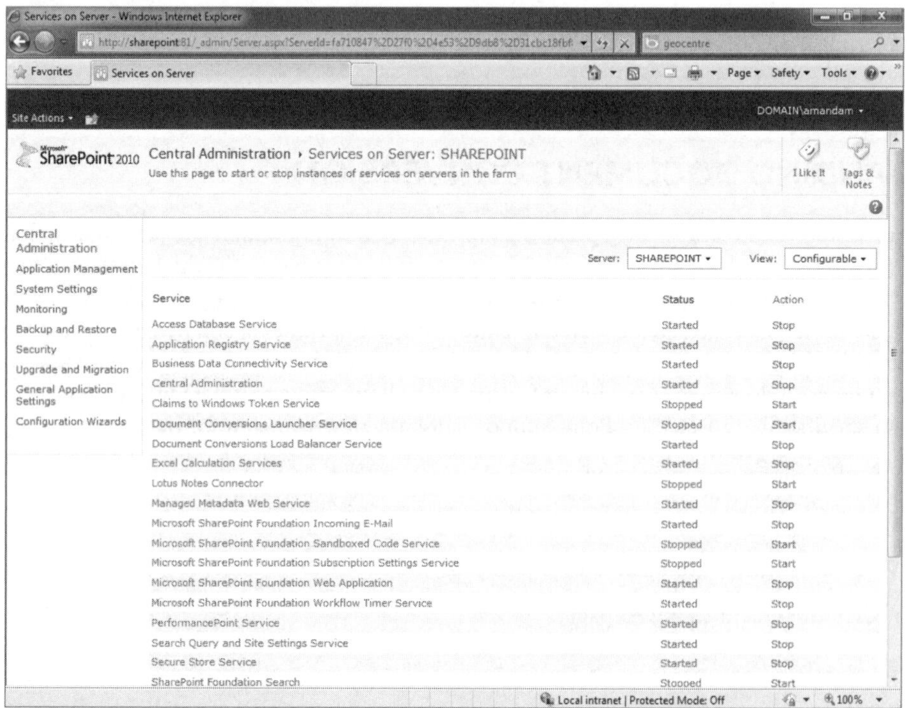

FIGURE 13-30

4. Click the Start link for the Document Conversions Launcher Service.
5. Select the server you want to use for the launch server as well as the load balancer server, and click OK.
6. Select General Application Settings from the left-hand navigation.
7. Select Configure Document Conversions. The Configure Document Conversions window appears, as shown in Figure 13-31.

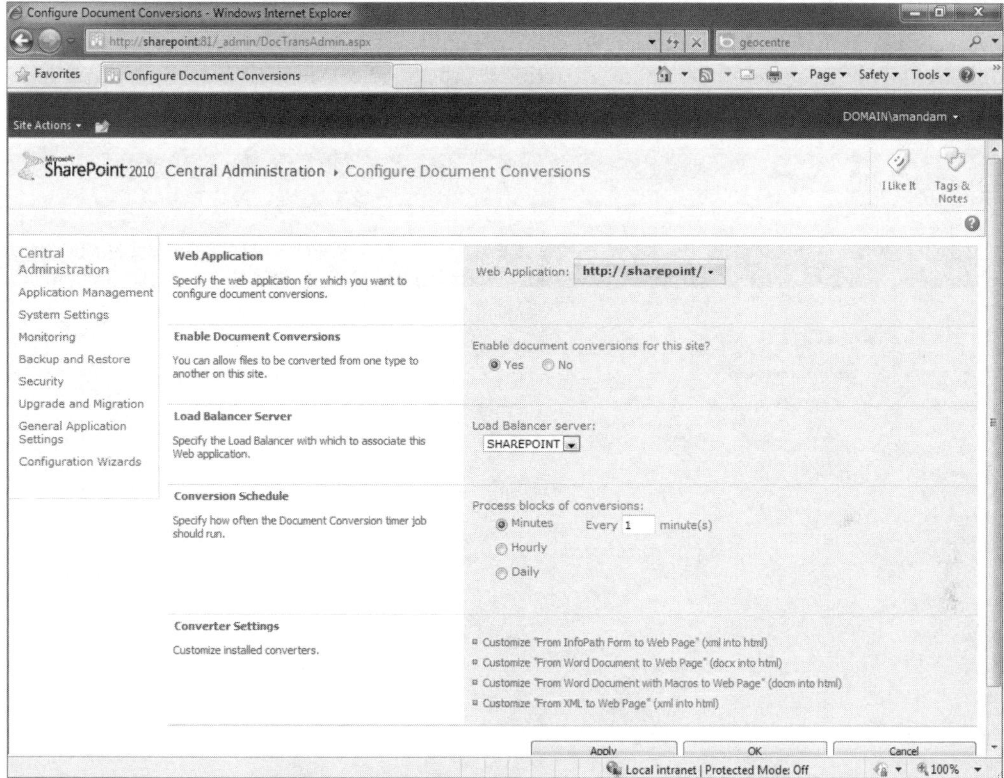

FIGURE 13-31

8. Select the appropriate web application from the list. In many cases, the web application you will be working with will be hosted on port 80. Confirm with your server administrator if you are unsure.
9. Select Yes for Enable Document Conversions for This Site.
10. Select the server that will act as the load balancer server. Depending on the type of configuration of your server farm, the server name may be already populated in the drop-down box.
11. Specify an appropriate interval for the document conversion process to run. Depending on your requirements, your selection here may vary. For an environment that anticipates many documents being converted on a regular basis, the interval may be more frequent. For an environment with few documents and a requirement to ensure optimal performance, the timer job may run less frequently and perhaps be scheduled on a daily basis for when the server does not anticipate a great deal of load.

12. Select the hyperlink for the From Word Document to Web Page.
13. Change the time-out length to 240 seconds.
14. Click OK.
15. Click Apply.
16. Click OK.

How It Works

Once you configure the service on the server, you can enable it on specific content types so that it's available to users in document libraries as an action on the Send to Menu of a document, as shown in Figure 13-32.

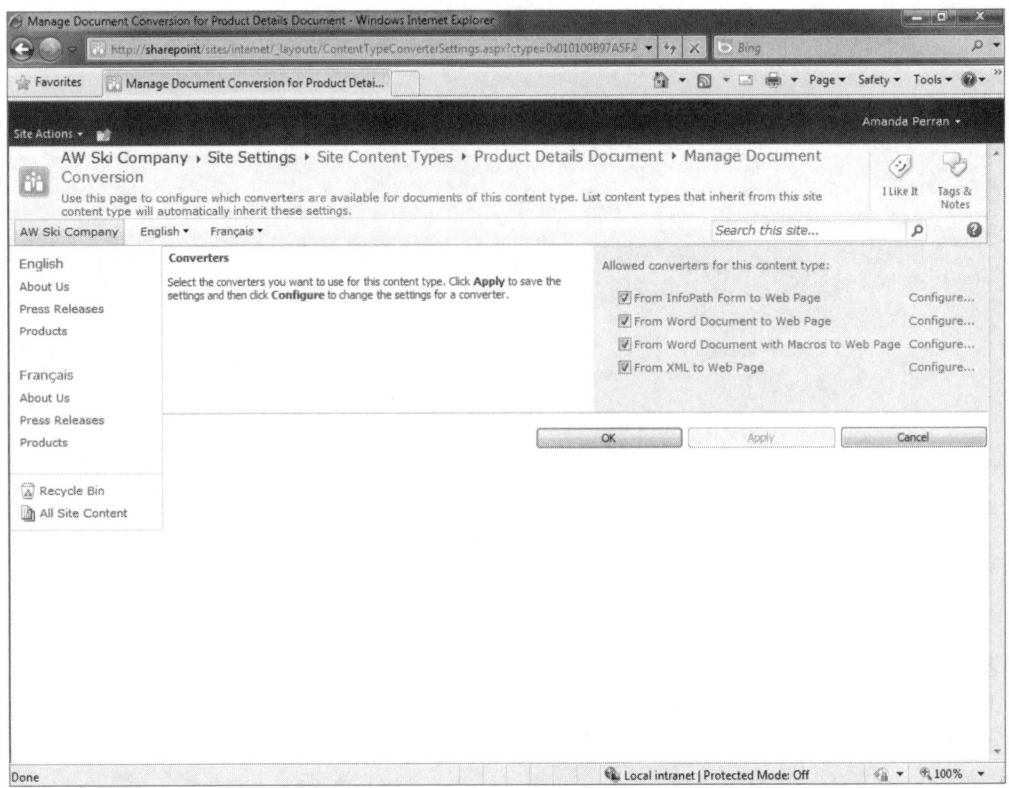

FIGURE 13-32

TRY IT OUT Enable Document Conversion on a Content Type

In this example, you configure document conversion on a content type so that users can convert a Word document for your ski company to a web page. The users have a Word document template that they've been using for years to fill out on the company's various products, and it keeps information current. These users have exceptional skills with Word, but very little web publishing or coding skills. By converting the Word document to web content, you allow them to keep their familiar tool while converting content to the company's unique look and feel for the web.

1. Select Site Settings from the English site of your AW Ski Company site collection.
2. Select Go to top level site settings from the Site Collection Administration section.
3. Select Site Content Types.
4. Click the Create button from the toolbar. The New Site Content Type window appears.
5. Type a name for the content type. For this example, enter **Product Details Document**.
6. Select Document as the parent content type from the Documents Content Types group.
7. Enter a group name for the content type. This group name helps organize your content types. For this example, select Marketing.
8. Click OK. You are returned to the Site Content Type administration page.
9. Click the Advanced Settings link.
10. Select upload a new document template, and click Browse to locate the file ski product information.docx from the resources outlined for this chapter.
11. Click OK. You are returned to the Site Content Type administration page.
12. Select Manage Document Conversion for This Content Type. The Manage Document Conversion for Product Details window appears, as shown earlier in Figure 13-32.
13. Unselect all checkboxes except the one for the conversion of a Word Document to a Web page.
14. Click Apply.
15. Click the Configure link to the right of the Word Document to a Web page item. You will be redirected to the Configure Document Conversion Settings page, as shown in Figure 13-33.
16. Select Define Unique Settings for This Content Type.
17. Select the Product Details Page layout from the page layout drop-down menu.
18. For field for Converted Document Contents, select Product Description.
19. For the Location section, select the checkbox to set a default site for creating pages. Because the content you are creating is related to the products site, you need to create all pages there. Click the Browse button to open the Choose Site Dialog, as shown in Figure 13-34, then click the Products site and click OK.
20. Keep the default setting for processing, which is Create Pages One at a Time, and Take Users to the Page Once It Is Created.
21. Click OK.
22. From the Products site, select View All Site Content from the Site Actions menu.
23. Select the Documents library.

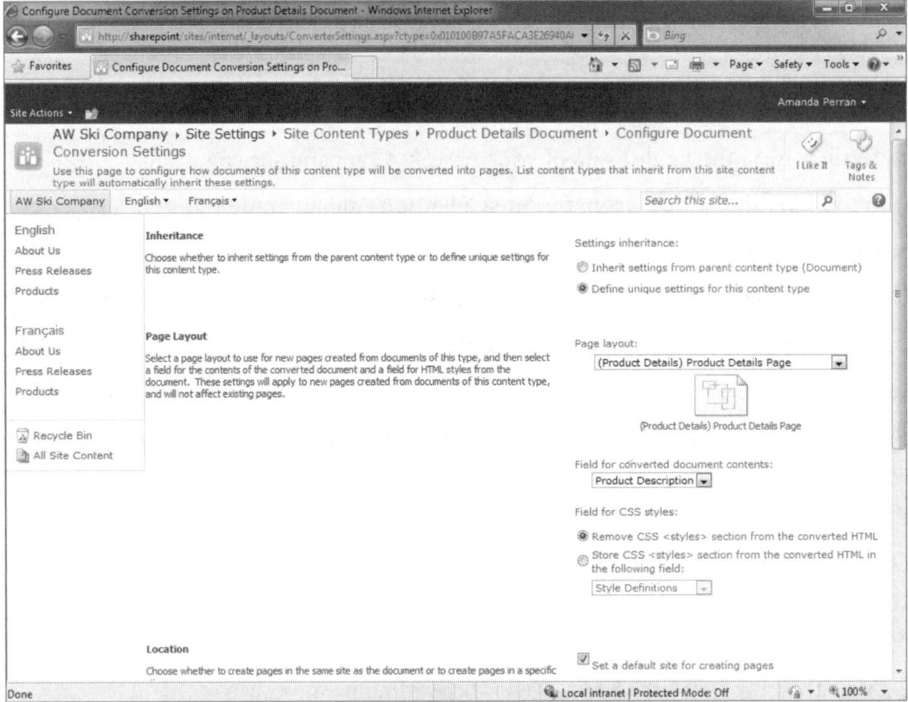

FIGURE 13-33

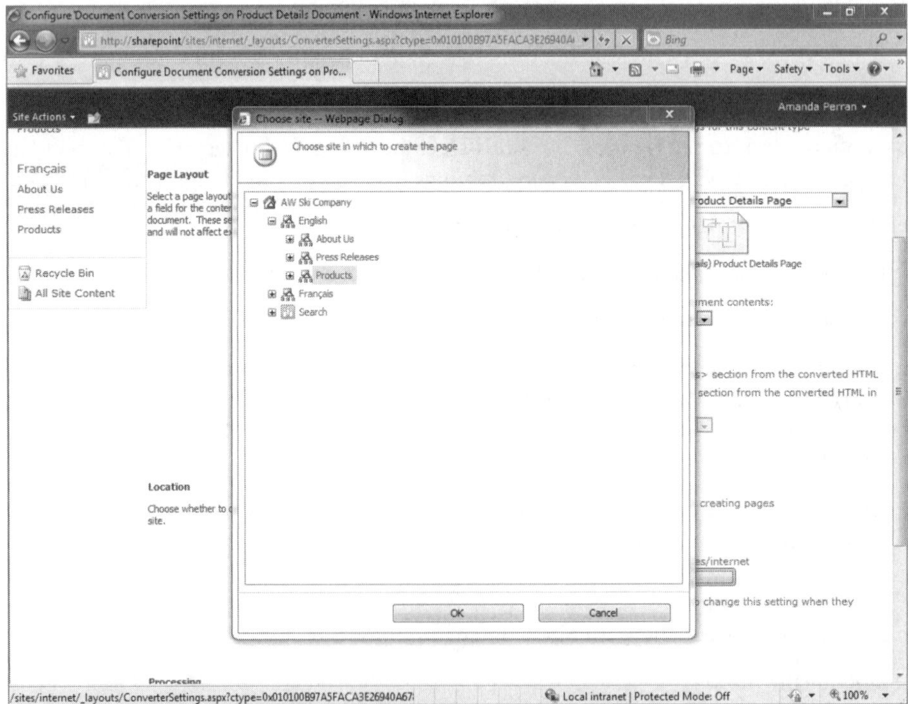

FIGURE 13-34

24. Select Library Settings from the Ribbon.
25. Select Advanced Settings.
26. Select Yes to allow management of content types.
27. Click OK.
28. Select the Add from Existing Site Content Types option.
29. Select Marketing from the Groups drop-down.
30. Select the Product Details Document content type, and click the Add button to add your content type to the library.
31. Click OK.

How It Works

In step 19, you specified that the newly created web pages should be published to the Products Site Pages library regardless of where the documents themselves exist. This means that users can create their content in a collaborative area or other area where they have access, and have the pages automatically go to the appropriate site. Because you define the document conversion process at the content-type level, it's convenient for a site administrator to determine the publishing location based on the type of content that is being created; the users creating the content don't have to be concerned with this.

TRY IT OUT Convert a Document to a Web Page

This example shows you how to convert a document to a web page. This involves creating a document from a document library based on a content type, following the same procedure covered in Chapter 6. Once you create the content, you then convert it to a web page that you can publish to a site.

1. From the main page of your Products website, select View All Site Content from the Site Actions menu.
2. Select the Documents library.
3. Select New Product Details Document from the toolbar.
4. Fill in the details for your new product as follows:

DOCUMENT SECTION	DETAILS
Product Description	These revolutionary new skis are the latest innovation in cross-country and downhill skiing. Using these skis, you will be able to cover miles of trail without feeling like you left the comfort of your living room.
Price	$1999 USD

5. Save the file as **APJ Bamboo Skis.docx**.
6. Close the document, and check it in as a major version of the document using the process reviewed in Chapter 3.

7. Return to the document library. Hover over the document to expose the menu.
8. Select Convert Document from Word Document to Web Page, as shown in Figure 13-35.

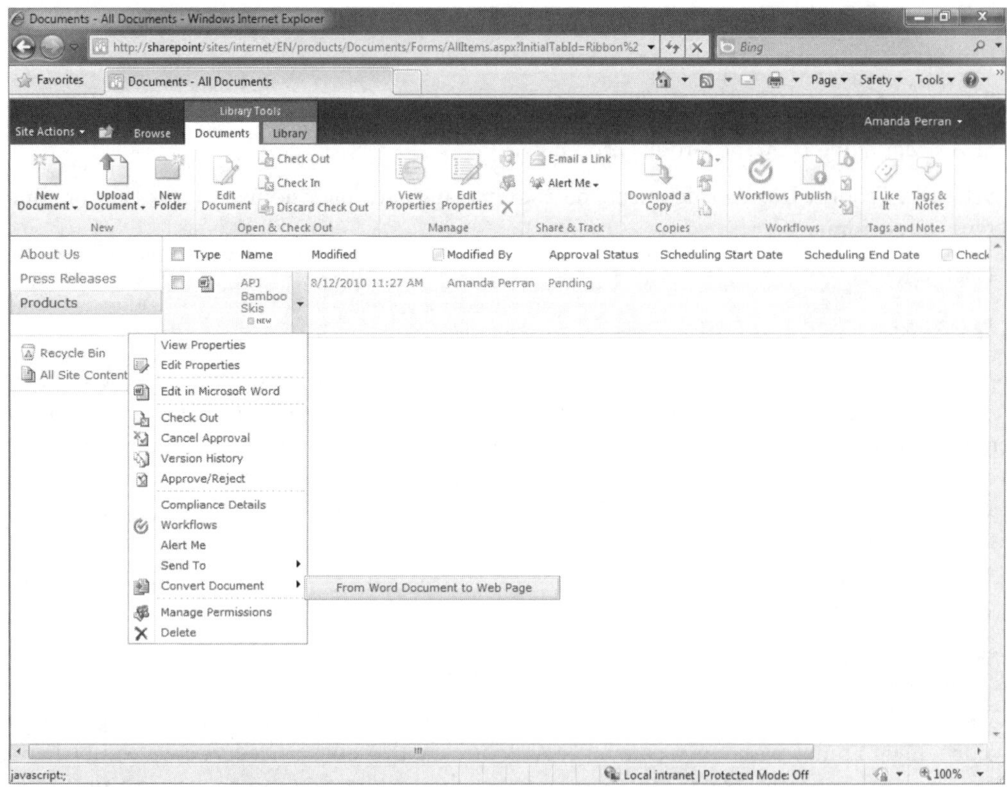

FIGURE 13-35

9. Enter a title for the web page. For this example, enter **APJ Bamboo Skis**.
10. Select the Create This Page for Me Now, and Take Me to the Page When It Is Created option.
11. Click Create.

How It Works

Notice how the page automatically appears in the navigation control of the site, and how the URL illustrates how the page is stored in the Pages library of the Products site, even though the original document is located at the top level of the site collection in the site collection documents library.

ENABLING PUBLISHING ON A TEAM SITE

So far, the examples in this chapter have worked with the Publishing Portal site template. This is primarily because this template contains many of the components and elements you need to create a web-facing site. However, you may need to make use of publishing features within a standard team site or workspace, and to do so means you have to enable the Publishing feature. Switching on the publishing features means you can transform any team site into a publishing site, complete with content approval workflow and new lists and libraries.

TRY IT OUT Enable the Publishing Feature on a Team Site

In this example, you have a team site that your ski company is using to create content and track progress across various initiatives. However, to track team announcements and news, you decide to enable the Publishing feature on the site. To do this, you visit the Site Settings page for the site and select Activate for the Publishing feature.

When you enable the Publishing feature on a collaborative site, such as a team site or a blank site, you can no longer save that site as a template. This is something you should be aware of before making the choice to enable specific features or functionality on existing sites.

1. From the SharePoint Central Administration site, create a new site collection from the Application Management section using the Team Site template called "Ski Team Site."
2. From the main page of your new team site, select Site Settings from the Site Actions menu.
3. Select Site Collection Features from the Site Collection Administration links.
4. Click the Activate button next to the SharePoint Server Publishing Infrastructure feature.
5. Return to the Site Settings page of your site.
6. Select Site Features from Site Administration links.
7. Click the Activate button next to the SharePoint Server Publishing feature.

How It Works

When you enable the publishing feature, this creates new lists and libraries, automatically adds content approval workflow, and expands the Site Actions menu so that you can create pages.

SUMMARY

As your business publishes more and more content online, you need tools to efficiently accomplish this task. This chapter covers one of the core features of SharePoint Server known as web content management (WCM). Using the WCM, users can perform tasks that once required the expertise of a skilled programmer. From this chapter, you learned the following:

- You can use publishing features to create web content without any web programming skills.
- Using content types, you can fully control what content a user creates. These content types can be attached to lists, document libraries, and even web pages.
- You can create page layouts based on content types. While content type controls the type of content that you can have on the page, the page layout itself can be customized to position and style the content. Users can later create content or pages in the site based on these page layouts.

- Doing business internationally means having sites that are in multiple languages. SharePoint can help you set up different calendars and local settings in various languages using Variations, regional settings, resource files, and language packs.

EXERCISES

1. Your manager informs you that you have been selected to create a website for the communications department on the new SharePoint Server. The main requirement is to have the site allow nontechnical employees in the communications division to publish product information that can be viewed as a web page. What do you do?

2. True or false: you can enable the Publishing feature after you create a team site.

3. The sales manager says a recent sale requires the implementation of an externally facing customer support portal in two languages, English and French. How do you proceed?

4. True or false: you only add controls to your page layouts that support text and rich text. You must use web parts for the display of rich media.

▸ WHAT YOU LEARNED IN THIS CHAPTER

TOPIC	KEY CONCEPTS
What is web content management?	Web content management features allow business users or content publishers to create web content for a site without the requirement for custom code or HTML knowledge. This may include the creation of web pages or the publishing of images or video.
What does Variations do?	Variations is a feature available within SharePoint to support scenarios where multiple sites may exist around a common topic but have slight differences, such as language. A change in content in one site can then be automatically copied to the other sites.
What is a page layout?	Page layouts are web page templates that contain specific content fields pre-configured and laid out on a page so that they can be completed by a content publisher.

14

Records Management

WHAT YOU WILL LEARN IN THIS CHAPTER:

- The essential components of a records management solution
- How to create a file plan
- How to create a classification plan
- About records declaration
  - Using the archival approach
  - Using the in-place records approach
- How to use records retention and disposition
- How to use holds

As the amount of paper and digital information continues to increase within our organizations, the effective retention, organization, and disposal of this information becomes more and more critical. Records management is becoming a larger area of focus for many organizations today. SharePoint Server 2010 provides multiple features to assist organizations with their records management requirements whether they are just getting started or have a highly defined and well-governed records management practice.

WHAT IS RECORDS MANAGEMENT?

Records management is the practice of organizing and maintaining documents within an organization based on a series of predetermined rules. These rules control things such as where files are stored, how long they are retained, how they should be disposed of, and who is responsible for these files. An organization may practice records management for either operational or regulatory purposes. This chapter will provide you with a greater insight into the activities that are related to implementing a records management solution within your organization.

Getting Started with Records Management

If you are new to records management, you may be wondering about how you should approach the establishment of a records management practice or solution for your organization. It is important to be specific to your organization's needs when devising a plan. While some fundamental elements are consistent across most organizations, records management is not a one-size-fits-all concept. Following is a high-level listing of the key elements of a records management solution.

Key Roles and Responsibilities

It is important to clearly identify the key roles and responsibilities related to your records management implementation. Typically, this will include records administrators who are the key managers and enforcers of your records management strategy. Members of this group are closely familiar with the rules and regulations within your organization related to records declaration, retention, and disposal. They are responsible for managing and maintaining the file and classification plan as well as ensuring that these items evolve as the organization changes and develops. These members must have the buy-in and support of the organization's decision makers in order to define, implement, and govern the policies appropriately to ensure the successful adoption of the practice.

In addition to the records administrators, it is important to clearly understand and communicate the involvement of standard end users of the system. How should they be involved in the identification and declaration of records? Should they be empowered to classify content and identify the appropriate stage at which a document becomes an official record or should such stages be identified automatically by the system independent of the involvement of the end users of the system? Should end users be allowed to view or edit a document once it has been declared an official record?

Finally, you must consider the involvement of the technical system administrators of your solution in the management and configuration of various technical aspects of the system. What level of access should they be given to the records within the system?

These are questions that you must consider and clearly answer as part of the planning stage of your records management implementation. While some similarities exist across organizations, the answers to the preceding questions should be based on the specific needs of your organization based on its size, the maturity of its information management processes, regulatory or legal requirements, and the complexity of the organization's structure and information.

The File Plan

A core element of every records management solution is the identification, planning, and subsequent creation of a file plan. The file plan typically includes information such as:

- The categories of documents that exist within the organization. Examples may include Sales, Marketing, Human Resources, and so forth. Depending on the complexity of the organization, there may be multiple layers of categories and subcategories.
- The individuals or groups responsible for the governance of each category of documents.

- The types of documents that exist within each category. Examples within the Human Resources category may include Personnel Records, Forms, Policies, and so forth.
- The location of the records associated with a specific category. This location may be a library or folder within the solution or it may refer to a physical storage location for paper records.
- Details of the regulatory or organizational rules related to how long the records should be stored within the system (retention) or when they should be removed from the system and whether they should be deleted or moved to another location (disposal).
- Details related to when an item should be considered a record and any associated restrictions that should be placed on the item at that point. For example, in some organizations, once an item has been declared a record, it should no longer be available for editing or deletion by users of the system. In other organizations, a document is a record as soon as it has been created.

It may seem overwhelming to address these aspects of a records management plan, if you have not yet begun the process. In fact, it does require a significant amount of planning and effort. However, a key strategy to effectively executing the development of your file plan is taking an iterative approach to planning and including key stakeholders within your organization in the process. The file plan is not something that should be created by a single member of a technology team but rather should be a joint effort between the appropriate experts within the business.

When identifying the categories, subcategories, and associated document types within an organization, it is helpful to create a mind map or hierarchy diagram to assist with the visualization of such information. A sample of how this may look is provided in Figure 14-1.

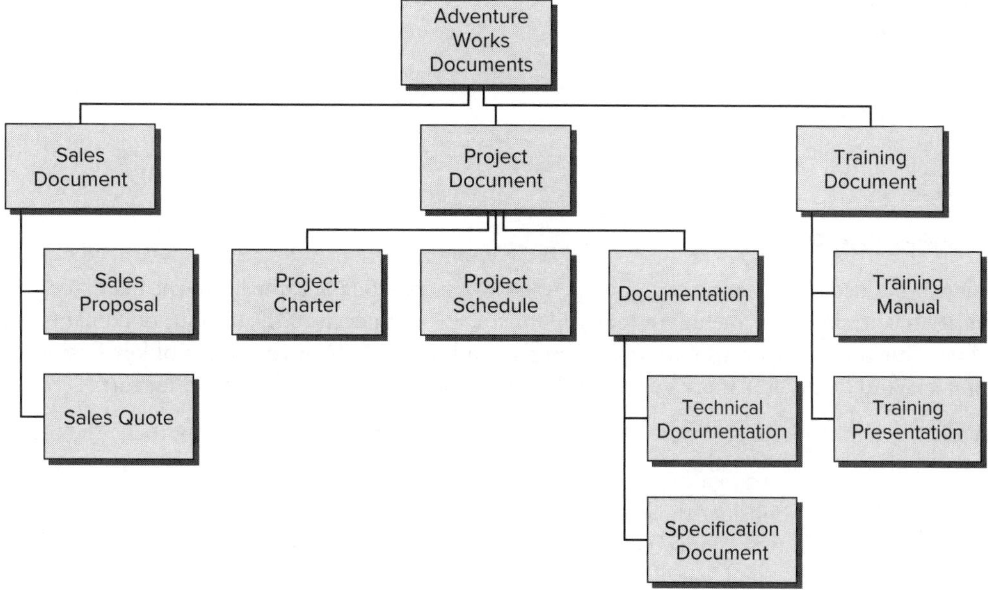

FIGURE 14-1

It may take multiple iterations and revisions to get a final listing. Once you have effectively identified all categories and subcategories, you would typically then assign a unique identifier to each and begin planning for the storage location for each. It is important to be flexible enough to accommodate changes over time, while still providing the appropriate level of detail to suit your requirements today. Figure 14-2 is an example of a document library that has been configured to represent a single category of documents with subfolders to represent the associated subcategories.

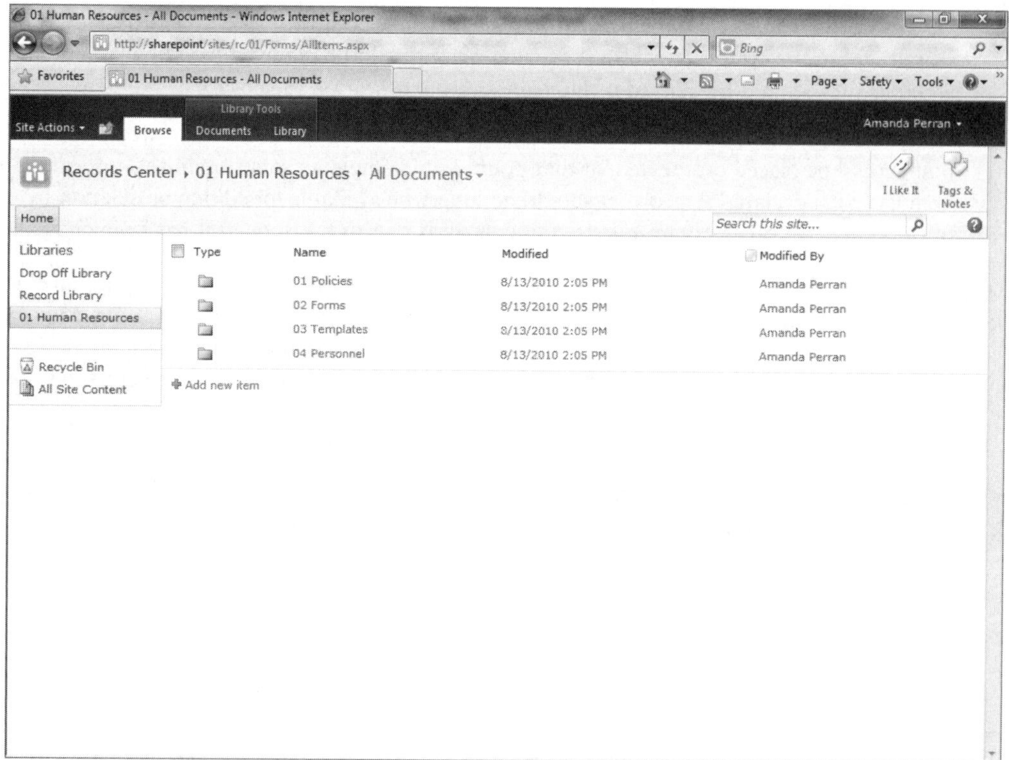

FIGURE 14-2

The Classification Plan

Once you have identified the various document types within your organization, the next step will be to identify the attributes or metadata that you must track with each of the various documents within that type. This process is once again quite iterative and requires the involvement of key business stakeholders and decision makers to ensure that the appropriate level of detail is captured.

When identifying attributes for your various document types, it is important to approach the process from two angles:

- First, you must consider the high-level attributes that must be tracked against every type of document in the organization. This may include properties such as Document ID, Department, or Confidentiality Level.

- You must then review each of the various document types to identify the attributes that are specific to that type of information. Once you have completed a review of each individual document type, you should compare and analyze the various attributes to identify those that are common or can be combined for maximum efficiency in maintenance.

It is important when identifying the properties that are required for your records management solution to not over-classify items to the point where tracking the values for properties related to documents becomes tedious for end users. It is important to identify an appropriate balance between the benefit that will be received from tracking certain items with the effort required from content authors to ensure the properties are up to date and accurate.

You may start to recall at this point concepts covered in Chapter 6 of this book, known as Content Types and Site Columns. When we refer to document types, there is an inherent relationship with content types, and when we refer to classification plans and attributes, there is a relationship with site columns. The goal is to define your document types and classification attributes down to a level that will translate into the creation of content types and site columns to support these requirements. Figure 14-3 demonstrates an example of the attributes required for individual document types. This can then become an outline for how your content type must be configured within the solution.

Title	Category	Attributes
Sales Proposal	Sales Documents	Title Client Sales Lead Document Status Document Owner Submission Date
Sales Quote	Sales Documents	Title Client Sales Lead Document Status Document Owner Submission Date
Sales Contract	Sales Documents	Title Client Sales Lead Approval Status Document Owner Signature Date

FIGURE 14-3

Figure 14-4 demonstrates how each individual attribute can be defined. This can then become an outline for how your site column can be configured within the solution.

Site Column	Type	Group	Required	Configuration Notes
Approval Status	Choice	Sales Documents	Yes	Value List: Pending Submission In Review Approved Display as: Radio Buttons Allow Fill in: No Default Value: None

FIGURE 14-4

IMPLEMENTING A CLASSIFICATION PLAN

SharePoint 2010 offers a new feature known as the Managed Metadata Service and an associated concept known as the Term Store. These new features provide great new functionality related to the creation of structured classification plans in SharePoint.

Using the Managed Metadata Service and Term Store, attributes may be defined once centrally within the entire solution and then reused throughout the organization in multiple site collections. Attributes are defined as term sets. A term set is created either directly within the system through the browser or imported from a file. Several benefits of the term set feature include:

- Term sets support the definition of metadata as a hierarchy. This is a major improvement over standard choice columns in SharePoint, which only support one level of information.
- Unique users or groups can be defined as Owners of a specific term set and subsequently empowered to manage the values associated with a single term set.
- Synonyms can be provided for individual terms. This makes it easier for end users to specify an attribute using their own wording; however, a suggestion will be provided for the appropriate wording. An example of the interface available for defining synonyms is shown in Figure 14-5.
- Terms may be added, reorganized, merged, or deprecated over time to address the changing needs of the organization.
- Unstructured terms or keywords may be promoted to structured values over time based on their usage within the system.
- Term sets are shared across the system and may be used within multiple site collections.

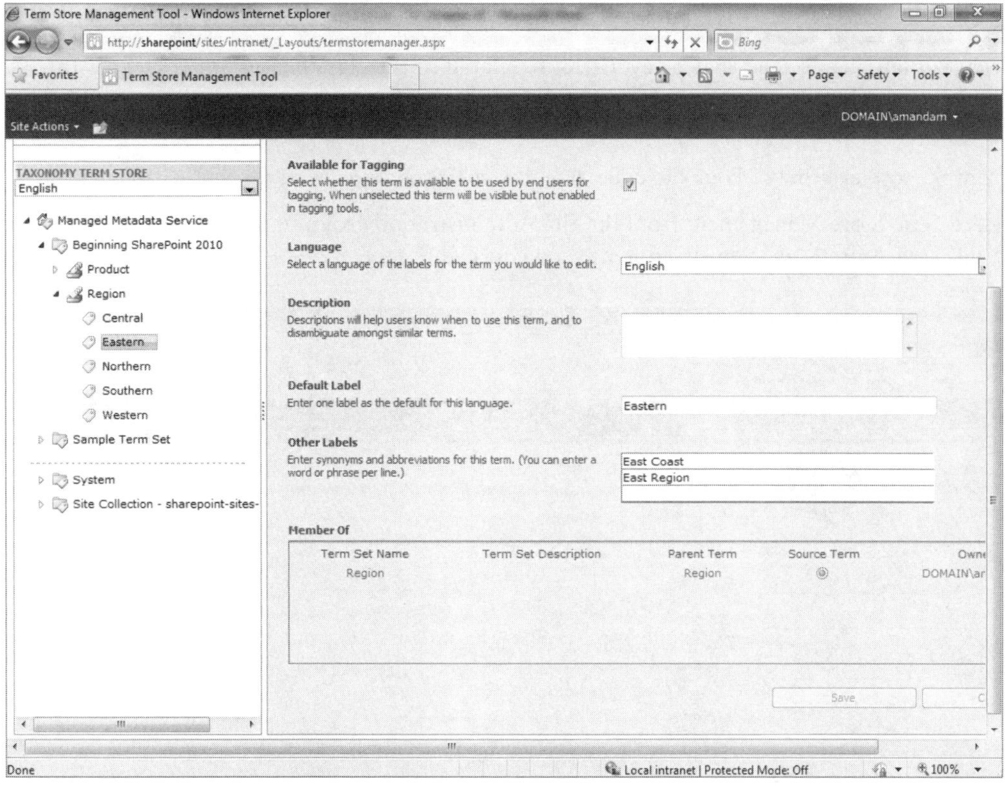

FIGURE 14-5

Working with Managed Metadata

In the next few exercises, you will gain some experience working with the Managed Metadata Service and creating custom term sets within the Term Store. You will start by creating a simple term set directly through the browser. Then you will create a more advanced hierarchy of terms by importing a term set via a custom `.csv` file. Finally, you will create a site column based on the Managed Metadata Service and point it to your custom term set, which was created in the second example.

NOTE *In order to complete these exercises, it is assumed that you have been given the appropriate permissions to access the Term Store and Managed Metadata Service. If you cannot access these interfaces, please see your system administrator regarding being given full access to the Term Store via the Managed Metadata Service Application.*

You can modify the permissions of the Term Store and Managed Metadata Service by going to the Central Administration site, selecting Application Management, and then Manage Service Applications. Select the Managed Metadata Service Application, and click the Permissions option from the menu.

TRY IT OUT Create a Term Set Manually

Your organization has decided that a key attribute related to the classification of content is the region it was created in. In this example, you will create a custom term set in the Term Store called "Region."

1. From the top-level site of your site collection, select Site Settings from the Site Actions menu.
2. Select Term Store Management from the Site Administration group of links. You will be redirected to the Term Store Management Tool, as shown in Figure 14-6.

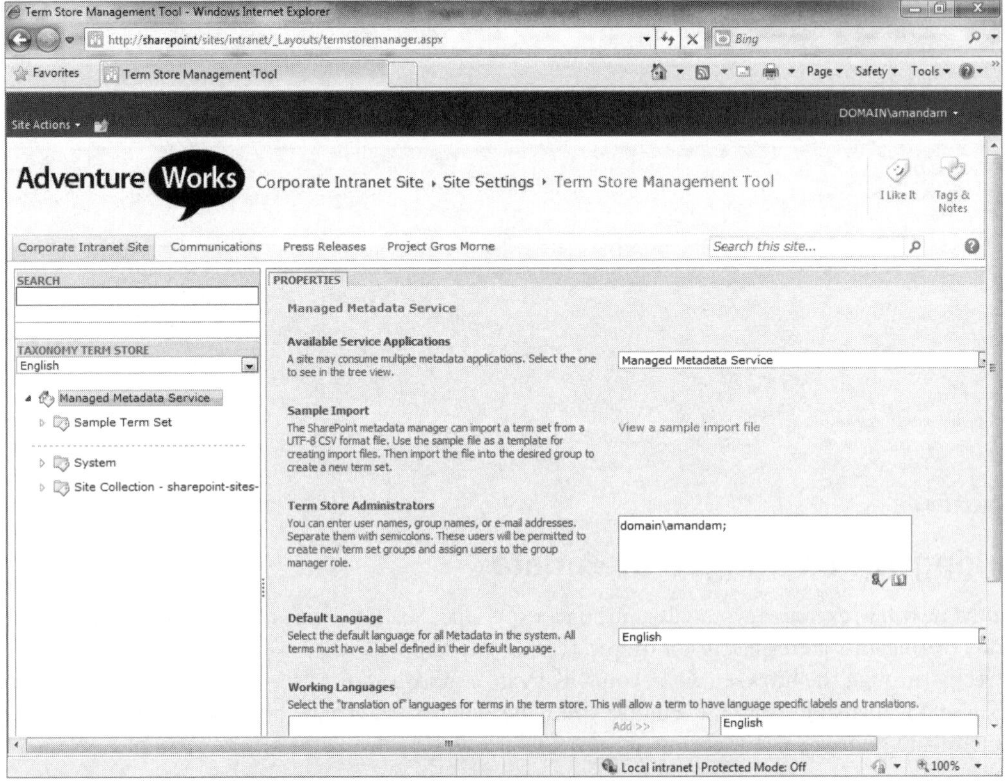

FIGURE 14-6

3. Hover over the Managed Metadata Service item in the left-hand panel and select the arrow that appears on the right-hand side to expand the menu, as shown in Figure 14-7.
4. Create a New Group called **Beginning SharePoint 2010**.
5. Expand the menu associated with your new group, and select the New Term Set option.
6. A new branch is added to your hierarchy. Enter **Region** as the name of your term set. The page will refresh to display the available settings for your term set, as shown in Figure 14-8.
7. Expand the menu associated with the Region term set, and select the Create Term option.
8. Enter **Eastern** as your term.

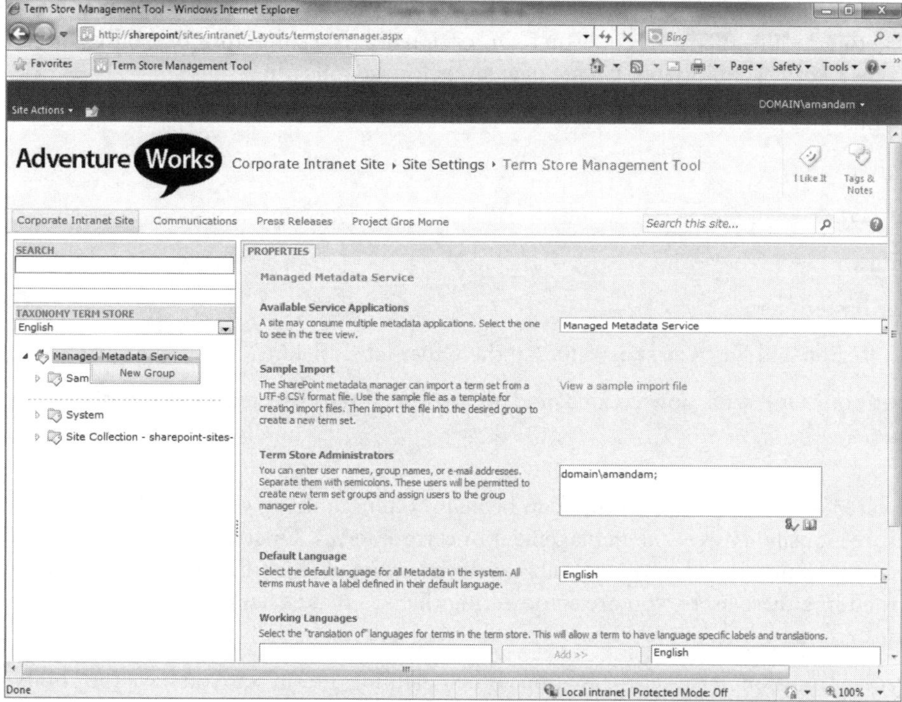

FIGURE 14-7

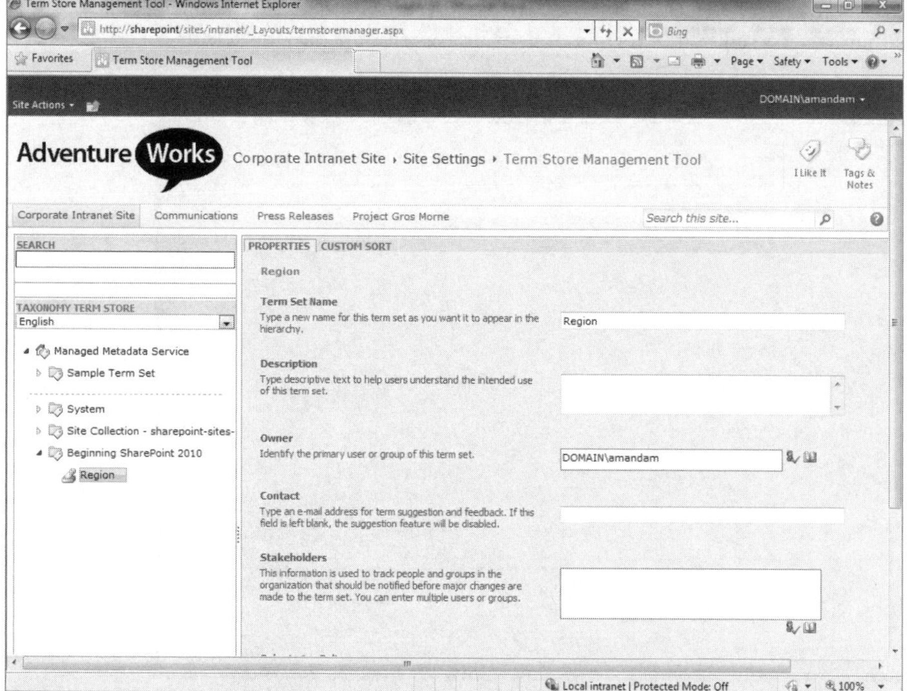

FIGURE 14-8

9. After you finish typing **Eastern**, you may hit Enter on your keyboard and a placeholder for a new term will automatically appear in the listing. Or, optionally, you can return to the Region term set and select the Create Term option. Create new terms for the following:
    - Central
    - Western
    - Northern
    - Southern
10. Select your Eastern term.
11. Enter **East Region** and **East Coast** as values in the Other labels field.
12. Click Save. Your term set is now created, and all associated settings have been saved.

How It Works

To start, you created a custom group. Groups can be helpful in organizing your various terms as well as for delegating responsibility over the management of certain terms. Once the group was created, you could have specified details related to the description of the group or identified group managers and contributors. By adding these users, you are empowering them to make changes related to the terms stored within this group.

You then created your custom term set for Region. When defining a term set, you have the ability to identify stakeholders that should be notified before changes are made to a term set. You may also specify whether a specific term set is open or closed. If a term set is open, users may add new values to the term set through the managed metadata interface as shown in Figure 14-9. If a term set is closed, then only the values that are entered by the term manager or contributor may be selected.

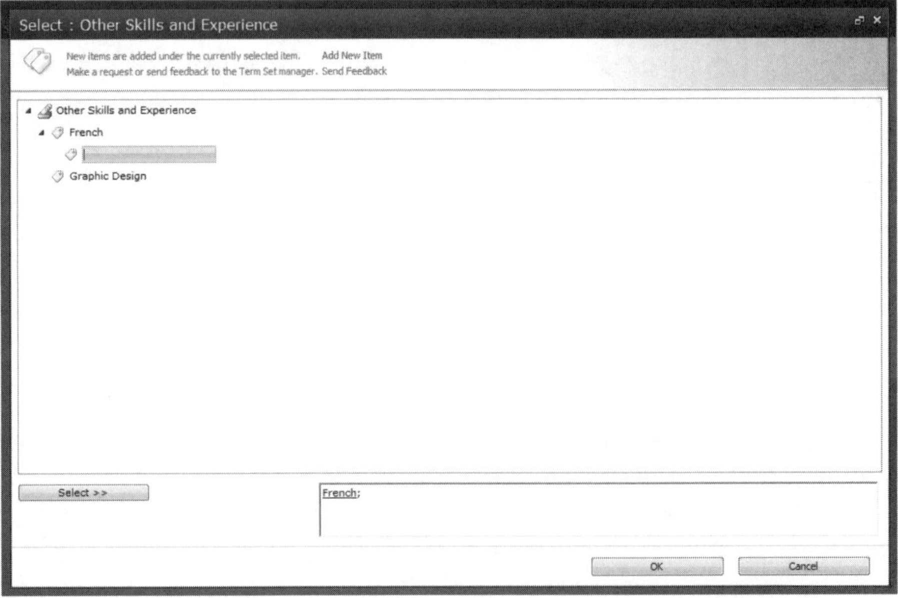

FIGURE 14-9

Finally, before completing the configuration of your term set, you updated the Eastern value with two additional synonyms that may be entered by end users of the system instead of the predefined value.

TRY IT OUT Create a Term Set Using an Import File

In addition to region, another key attribute related to the classification of content in your organization is product name. Because products are categorized in groups, you will create a term set that utilizes a hierarchy of values. While this hierarchy could be created manually using the steps outlined in the previous Try It Out, you will generate the values by importing a file. This is a more effective method for creating large or complex term sets.

1. From the top-level site of your site collection, select Site Settings from the Site Actions menu.
2. Select Term Store Management from the Site Administration group of links.
3. Expand the menu associated with your Beginning SharePoint 2010 group, and select the Import Term Set option, as shown in Figure 14-10.

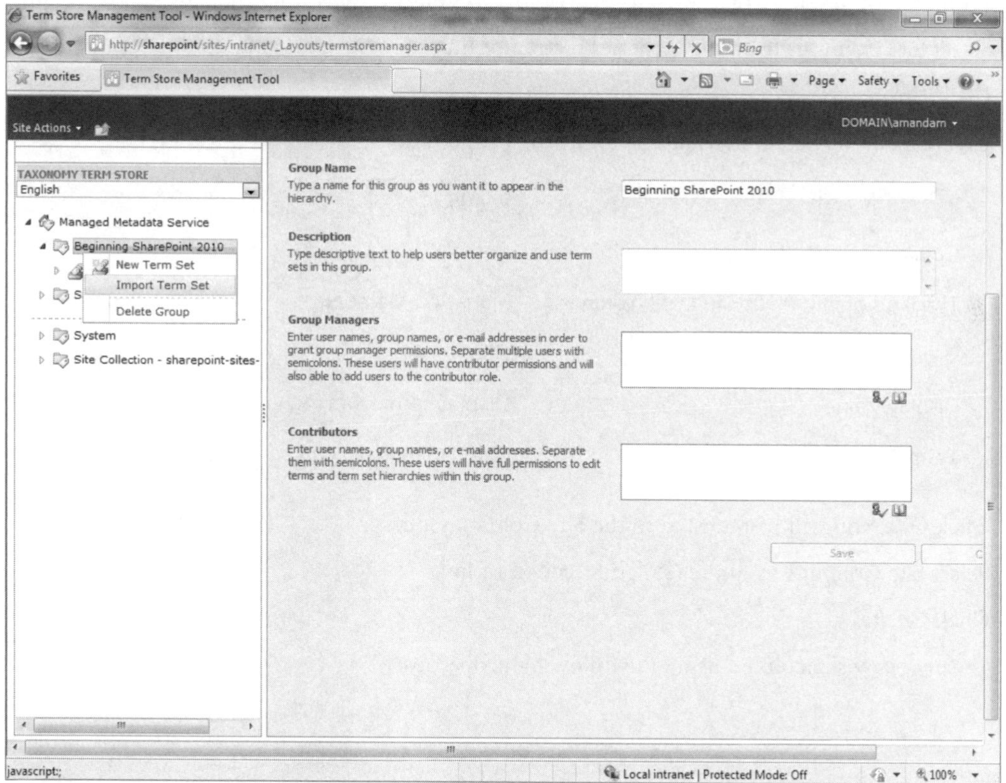

FIGURE 14-10

4. The Term Set Import dialog will appear. Browse to the location of this chapter's resource files and select `products.csv`.
5. Click OK.

How It Works

Once the file import is complete, your new term set will be created with all associated properties. Depending on the size of your import file, this process may take anywhere from a few seconds to a few minutes. Term sets can support a large number of values and complex hierarchies; however, it is recommended that you not try to exceed more than 5000 values within a single term set. Values higher than this may have an adverse impact on the performance of the system. In fact, from a user experience perspective, it is recommended that you avoid such high numbers, as it will be tedious for the end users to navigate such a large list within the managed metadata selection interface or metadata navigation interface.

TRY IT OUT Create a Site Column Based on Managed Metadata

In this example, you will create two new site columns based on the custom term sets you defined in the previous two Try It Outs. You will then create a custom content type that utilizes these site columns using the same methods described in Chapter 6.

1. From the top-level site of your site collection, select Site Settings from the Site Actions menu.
2. Select Site Columns from the Galleries section of links.
3. Click Create.
4. Create a new site column using the following properties:

PROPERTY	VALUE
Column Name	Region
The type of information in this column is:	Managed Metadata
Group (New Group)	Chapter 14
Display Value	Display term label in the field
Term Set Values	Use a managed term set (Select the Region Term Set).

5. Click OK. You will be returned to the Site Column Gallery.
6. Select Site Columns from the Galleries section of links.
7. Click Create.
8. Create a new site column using the following properties:

PROPERTY	VALUE
Column Name	Product
The type of information in this column is:	Managed Metadata
Group (New Group)	Chapter 14
Display Value	Display the entire path to the term in the field
Term Set Values	Use a managed term set (Select the Product Term Set)

9. Click OK. You will be returned to the Site Column Gallery.
10. Select Site Settings from the Site Actions menu.
11. Select Site Content Types from the Galleries group of links.
12. Click Create.
13. Create the content type using the following settings:

PROPERTY	VALUE
Content Type Name	Sales Contract
Select parent content type from:	Document Content Types
Parent content type	Document
Group (New Group)	Chapter 14

14. Click OK. You will be redirected to the administration page for your new content type.
15. Select the option to add from existing site columns.
16. Select the Chapter 14 group and add both the Region and Product columns.
17. Click OK.

How It Works

Once your new content type is created, it can be added to document libraries throughout your site collection. Users will be able to specify the metadata when uploading new sales contracts using the Managed Metadata selection interface. Figure 14-11 is an example of the Products column as it would appear to end users of the solution when specifying a product to be associated with a sales contract.

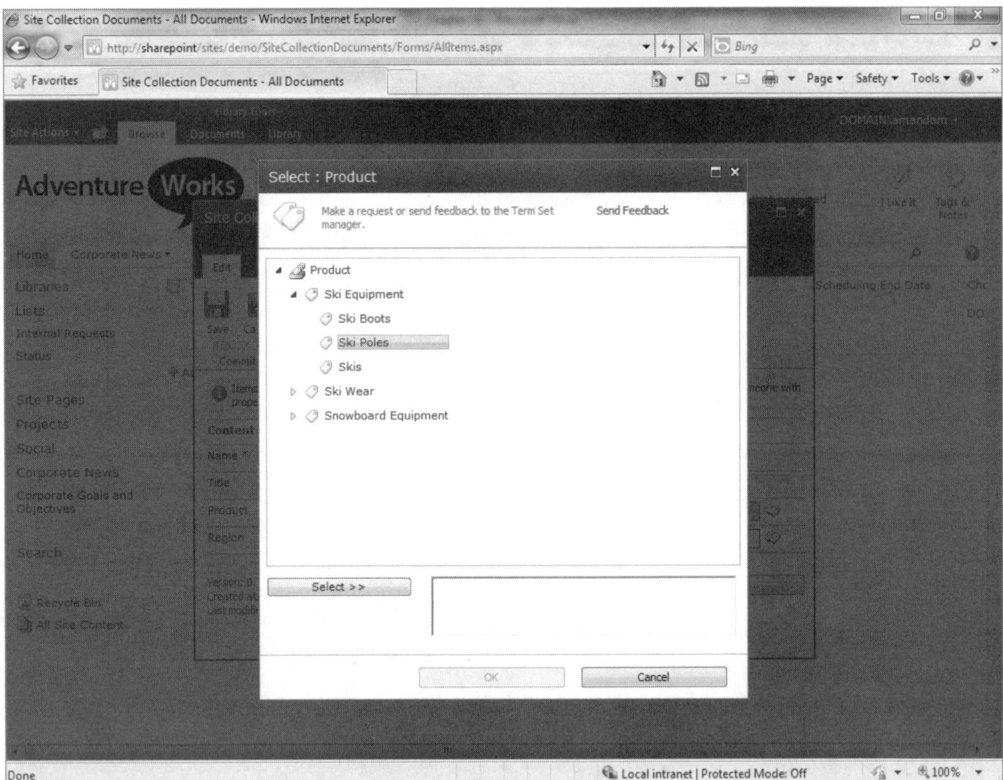

FIGURE 14-11

THE RECORDS REPOSITORY

An important aspect of any records management is, of course, the repository in which all records will be stored. Due to the flexibility of SharePoint as a records management platform, a number of options exist related to how the repository is configured and structured.

Archive Approach

A common approach to records management is to submit a record to a Records Repository once it has been recognized as an official record. This record submission, also referred to as Records Declaration, can be either a manual or automated process. When a file is declared as a record, it is either copied or moved to a Records Repository, often referred to as a Records Center. Within the

Records Center the file can be either queued for manual filing by a records manager or it may be automatically moved to the correct location within the file place based on its metadata or properties. The feature that controls the automatic filing of records based on properties is known as the Content Organizer.

In the upcoming exercises, you will create a new site collection that will act as your Records Repository. You will then configure an external connection to this Records Repository so that users can submit documents to it. In the third Try It Out of this section, you will configure the Content Organizer to move content based on specific attributes. Finally, in the fourth Try It Out you will submit a document to the Records Repository from a collaborative site in a different site collection.

TRY IT OUT Create a Records Center

1. Log into the Central Administration site for your SharePoint environment.
2. Select the Application Management link.
3. Select the Create Site Collections link.
4. The first item in your list of things to identify is the web application on which you will create the Records Center. Make sure that the web application you select is the correct application. If it is not, you can click the down arrow to the right of the selected web application and click Change Web Application.
5. You must provide a title, description, and URL for the site. Name the site **Records Center**, and enter the following description:

    Official Records Repository
6. For Web Site Address name, select /sites/ from the drop-down menu and enter **rc** in the blank field to the right of the drop-down.
7. Select the Records Center template from the Enterprise tab.
8. Enter your own name as the primary site collection administrator.
9. Click OK. The process for creating your site takes a few minutes. After it is completed, you are redirected to a page advising you that the process has completed successfully, and a URL will be displayed for you to select to visit your site.

How It Works

Depending on your requirements, you may elect to have the Records Center be a site within an existing site collection, a separate site collection, or a completely separate web application. Your decision should be based upon security, scalability, and integration requirements. In this example, we selected a separate site collection. Once your Records Center has been created, it will look similar to Figure 14-12.

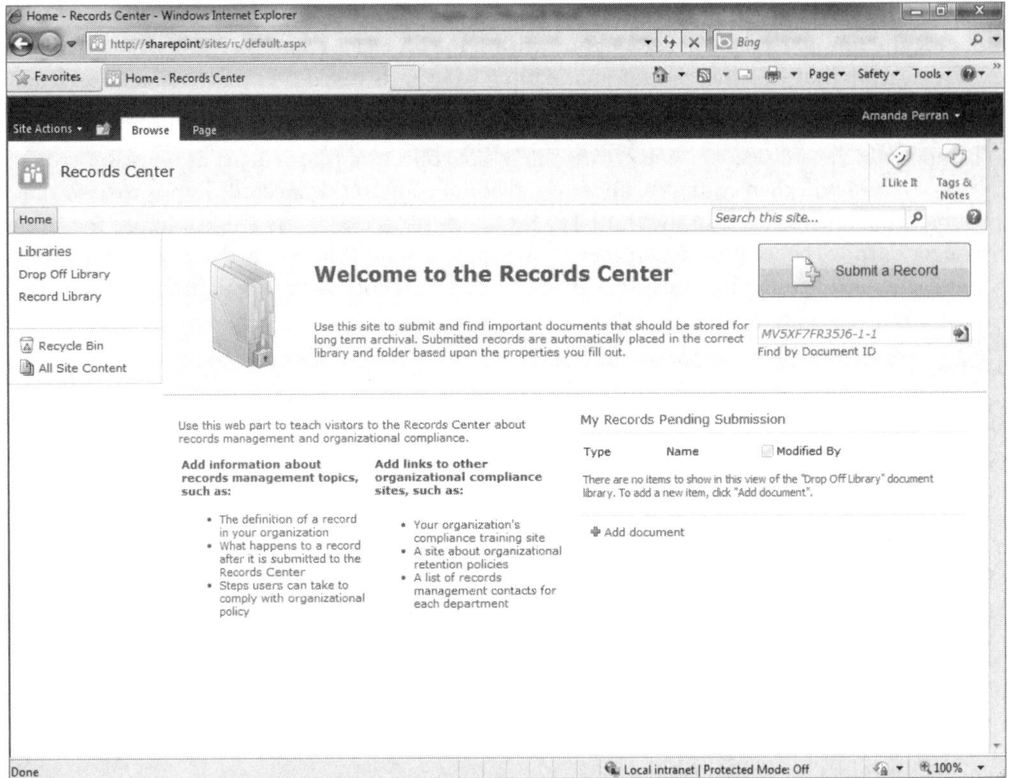

FIGURE 14-12

TRY IT OUT Define a Records Connection

1. Log in to the Central Administration site for your SharePoint environment.
2. Select the General Application Settings link.
3. Select the Configure Send to Connections link. You will be redirected to a page where you can define connections that will be available to users from within a document library.
4. Select the correct web application.
5. Select New Connection as shown in Figure 14-13.
6. Enter **Records Center** as the Display Name.
7. Enter the URL of the Records Center web service. Based on the naming convention used in the previous Try It Out, you should enter something similar to `http://servername/sites/rc/._vti_bin/officialfile.asmx`. Be sure to keep the portion of the URL that contains `/_vti_bin/officialfile.asmx`, as it is required.
8. For Send to Action, select Move and Leave a Link.
9. Click the Add a Connection button.

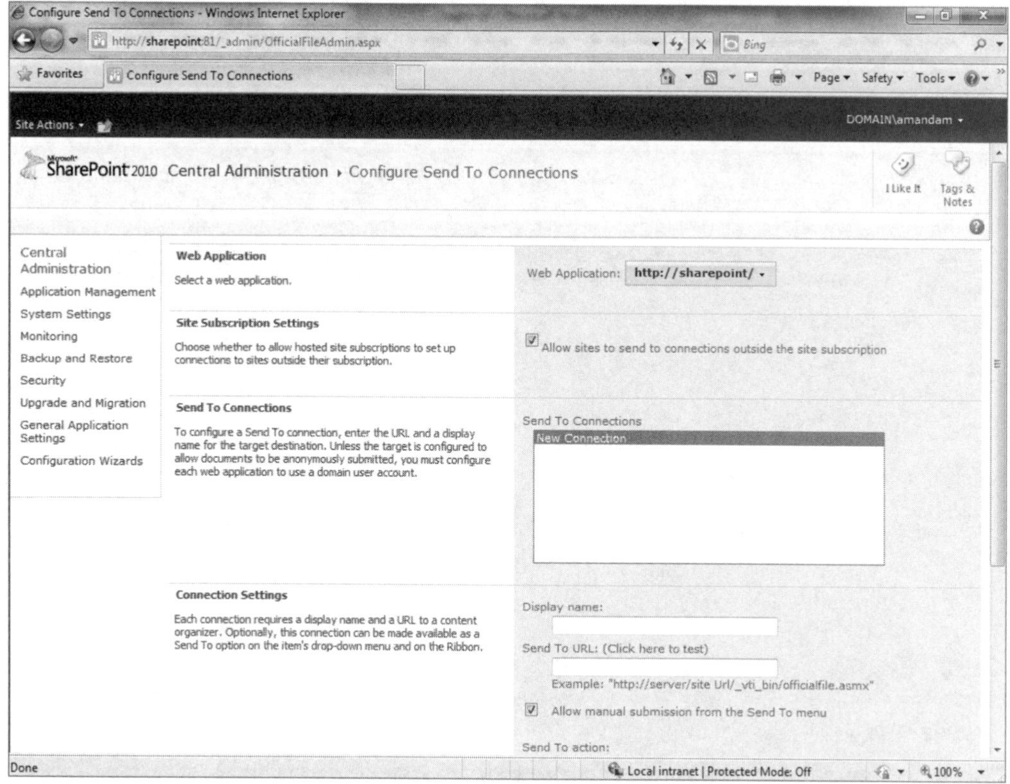

FIGURE 14-13

10. Click OK.

How It Works

In this example we created a Send to Connection. A Send to Connection is a location that will appear in document libraries whenever a user has a file selected, as shown in Figure 14-14.

By making this connection available, users can now select files in a collaborative site and manually declare them as records by selecting Send to Records Center.

For Send to Action we had a choice of Copy, Move, or Move and Leave a Link. By selecting Copy, a duplicate of the file would be copied into the Records Center. This normally is not a best practice but could be beneficial for cases where a separate Records Center existed for each legal case an organization was involved with. Then copies of important documents could be added to each case site without impacting the existing collaborative environment. The Move option will remove the file from the collaborative site and place it into the Records Center. This is effective for archival purposes but will limit standard user access to the file from the collaborative location. In our case we selected Move and Leave a Link, which will move the file into the Records Center and supply a link to the Records Center location. When a user clicks on the link they will be redirected to a page similar to Figure 14-15 that describes that the file has been moved with a link to its new location.

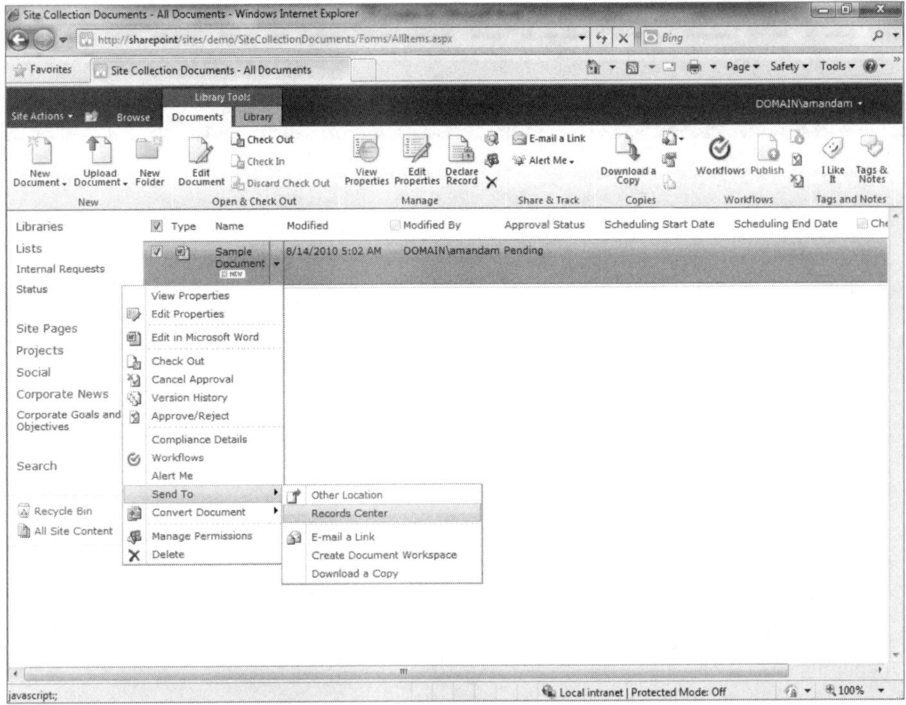

FIGURE 14-14

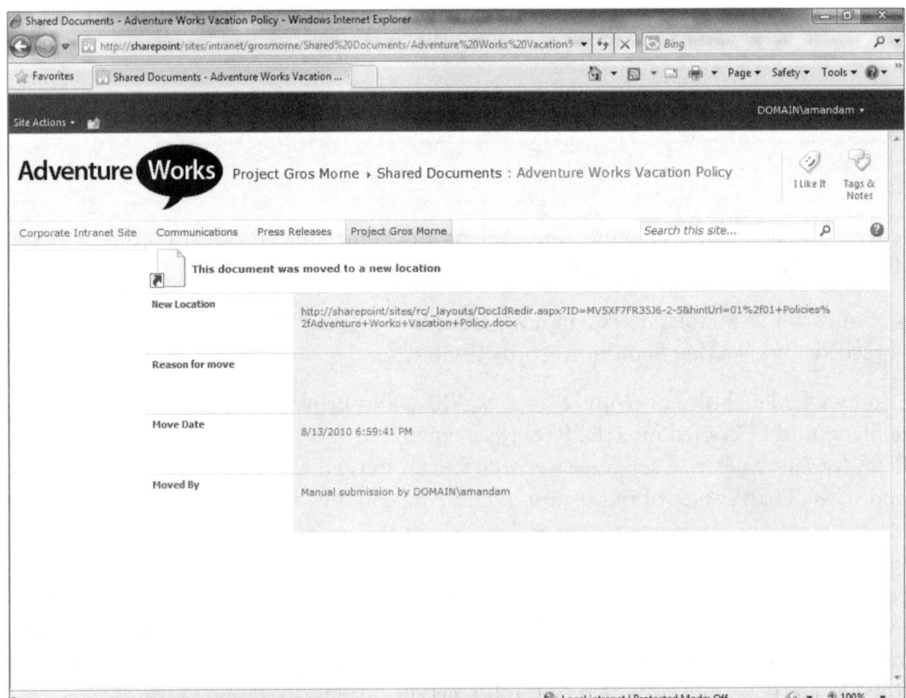

FIGURE 14-15

TRY IT OUT Configure a Records Center Site

1. From the Records Center site created in the first Try It Out of this section, select Manage Records Center from the Site Actions menu. You will be redirected to a specialized page designed to assist in the configuration of a Records Center site as shown in Figure 14-16.

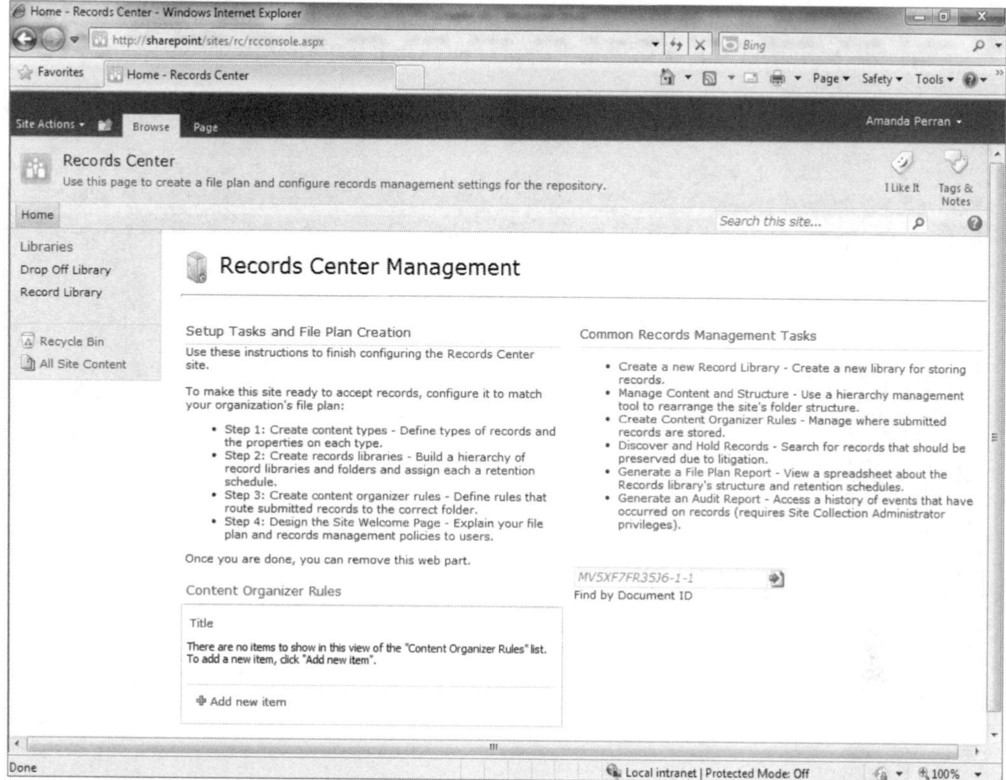

FIGURE 14-16

2. Select the link to Create Record Libraries. You will be redirected to a page listing the various templates for lists and libraries.
3. Select the Records library template.
4. Enter **01** as the Name.
5. Click Create.
6. Click on Library Settings from the Library tab of the Ribbon.
7. Select the Title, Description and Navigation link.
8. Change the name of the library to **01 Human Resources**.
9. Create New Folders in the library with the following names:

    - 01 Policies
    - 02 Forms

- 03 Template
- 04 Personnel

10. Select the Manage Records Center link from the Site Actions menu.
11. Select the link to Create Content Organizer Rules. You will be redirected to the Content Organizer Rules list.
12. Click the Add New Item link. A form will appear as shown in Figure 14-17.

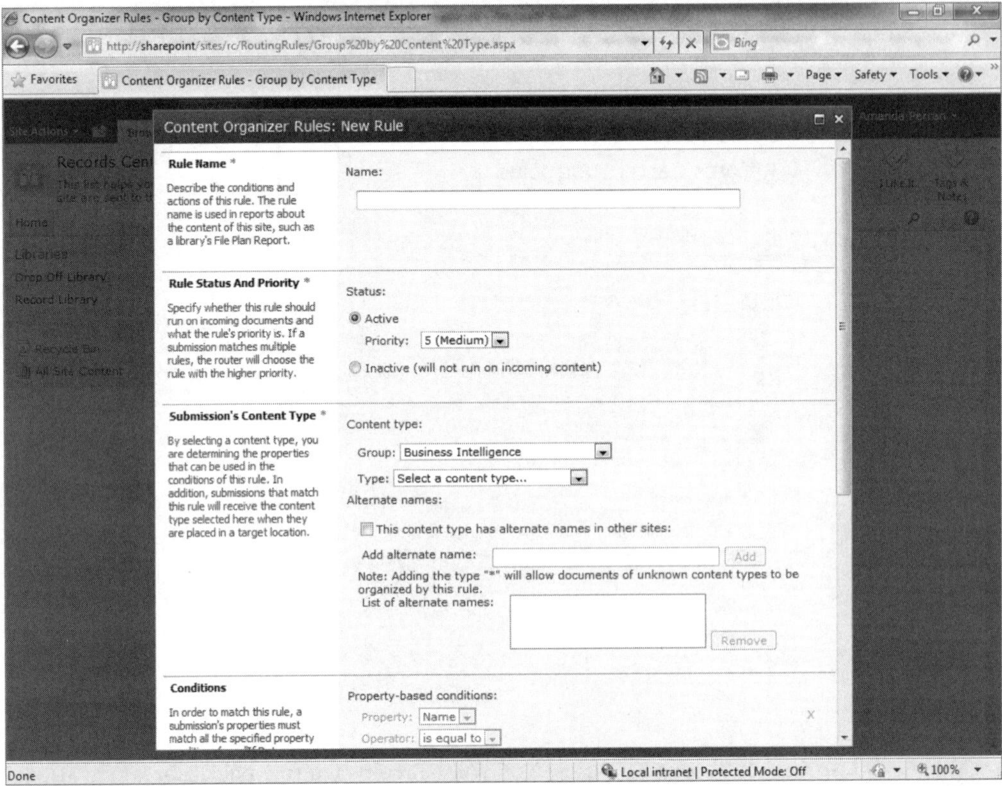

FIGURE 14-17

13. Define your rule based on the following properties:

PROPERTY	VALUE
Name	0101 Policy
Status	Active
Content Type (Group)	Document Content Types
Content Type (Type)	Document

PROPERTY	VALUE
Property Based Conditions	Title Contains all of Policy
Target Location	/sites/rc/01/01 Policies (Browse to the location of the 01 Policies folder within the 01 Human Resource library)

14. Click OK.

How It Works

In this example, you started to create the file plan for your Records Center by creating a library for human resources files. When a list or library is first created, the URL is the value that is entered for Name. However, if the list or library is renamed later, it will still retain the original value that was entered as the name for its URL. Because 01 was chosen as the unique identifier for the Human Resources category of documents, you named the library 01 upon initial creation and then later renamed it 01 Human Resources. This ensures that the path to the Human Resources library is a simple URL.

Once the Human Resources library was created, you added subfolders to the library to reflect the structure of the file plan. You then created a content organizer rule that will intersect any files that are added to the Records Center and review the properties to determine where the destination location in the Records Center should be. In this example, you selected that any document with "policy" in the title should be routed to the HR library's Policy folder. This rule, while easy to create for demonstration purposes, may not be a practical solution for real life and, therefore, it is recommended that you base your rules on more discreet properties, such as content type and other uniquely identifying metadata.

TRY IT OUT Submit a Document to a Records Center

In this example, you will submit a document from a collaborative location to the Records Center defined in the previous example.

1. From any collaborative site in your SharePoint environment, upload the Vacation Policy document that is included in this chapter's resources.
2. Select the file in the library.
3. Select the Send to Records Center item from the Ribbon as shown in Figure 14-18.
4. You will receive a warning dialog advising you that you are about to move the file and create a link. Click OK.

How It Works

The file will now be moved to the Records Center. This operation may take a few moments, but when it is complete a confirmation message will appear, as shown in Figure 14-19.

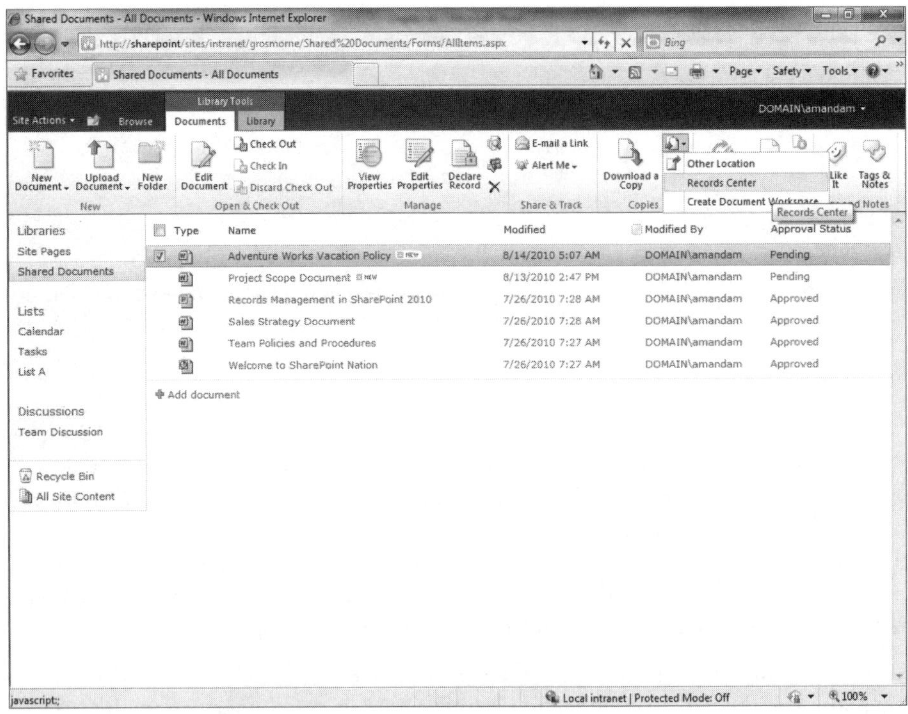

FIGURE 14-18

FIGURE 14-19

If you visit the Records Center, you will notice that the file has been automatically placed into the Policies folder of the Human Resources library as defined in the content organizer rule you created in the previous example. Similarly, if you were to return to the library from which you sent the file originally, you would notice that clicking on the link to the file would redirect you to a page similar to the one previously shown in Figure 14-15. An icon will appear on the link in the library similar to that shown in Figure 14-20.

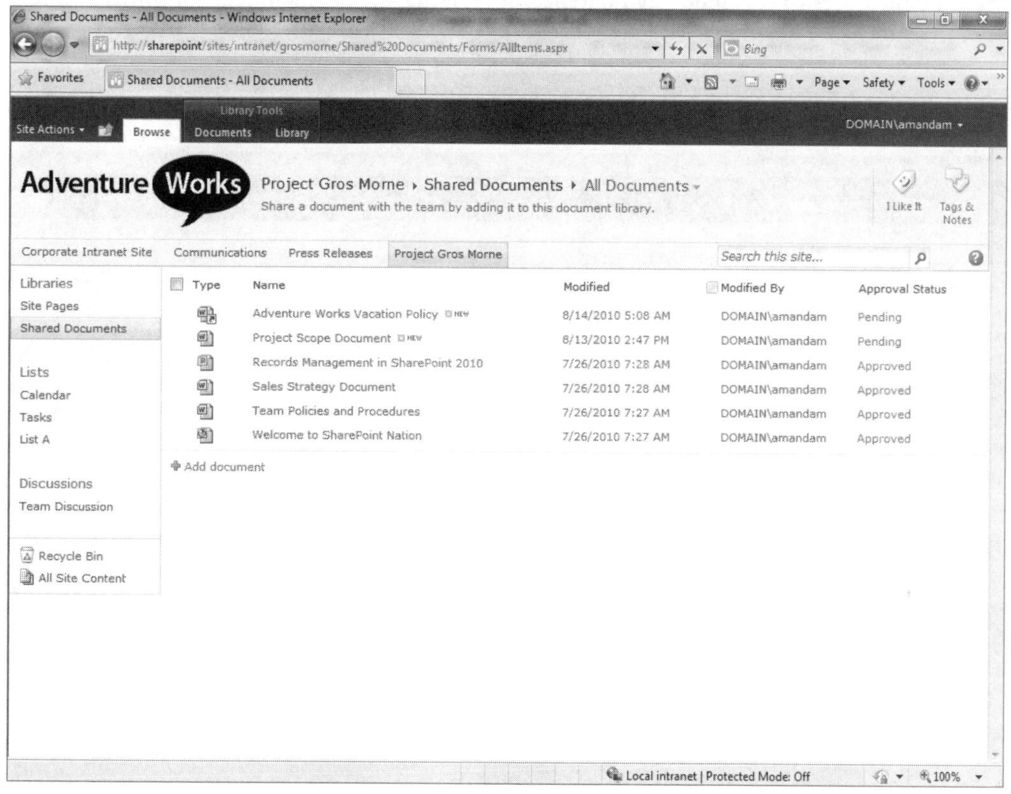

FIGURE 14-20

In-Place Approach

Previously in SharePoint and in many other applications, records management activities were managed separately from collaborative activities. As a result, there was often a great risk of certain documents "falling between the cracks" and not being properly submitted to the Records Repository. SharePoint 2010 includes a feature called In Place Records Management. This feature allows teams to declare records while collaborating in their standard environment. The records are not moved from the system but instead are stored within the same library with a visual indicator, as shown in Figure 14-21.

When an item is declared as an in-place record, restrictions can still be put in place to disable the editing capabilities of users, as well as the ability to delete items. However, the file stays in the library it was originally created in, which can be helpful for teams that may have a requirement to access the file after it has been declared a record. An example of this is a collaborative project site. The project scope document is created at the start of the project and approved by a client. Once the scope document has been approved, it is automatically (or manually) declared a record. The file is then locked for editing and deletion; however, it will continue to exist in the document library, along with all other project documents, throughout the duration of the project. This allows team members to continuously reference the original scope document for informational purposes.

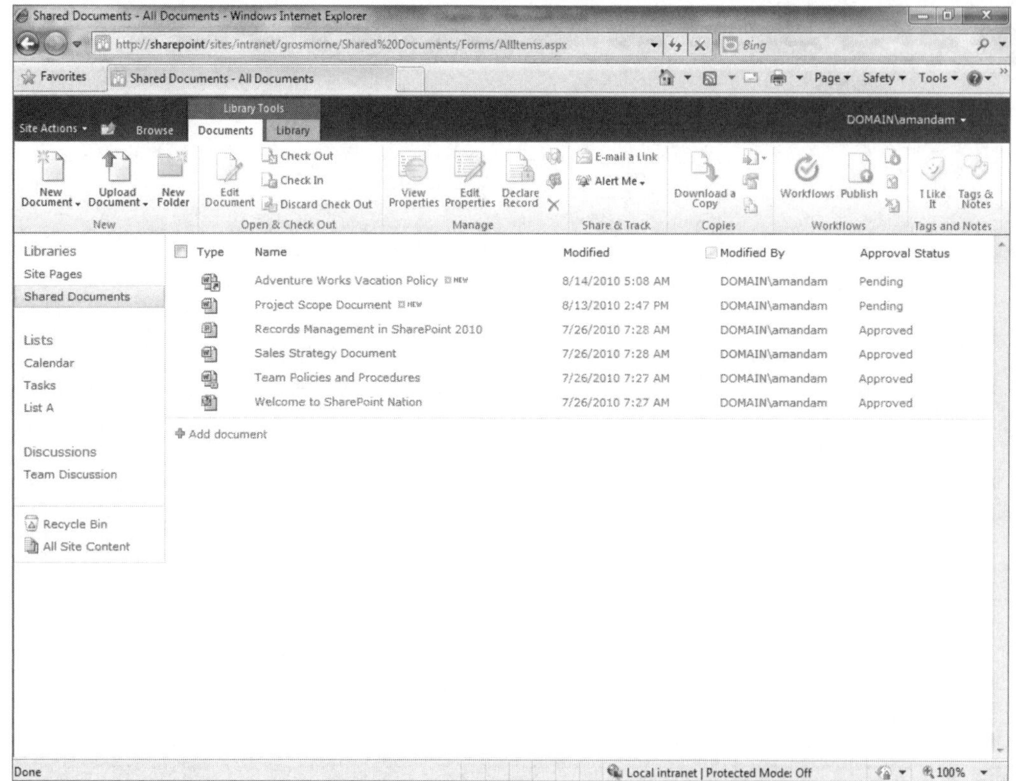

FIGURE 14-21

By default, the In Place Records Management feature is not enabled on a collaborative site. Therefore, it must be enabled. You will explore how this is done in the next Try It Out.

TRY IT OUT Activate the In Place Records Management Feature

1. From the top-level site of your site collection, select Site Settings from the Site Actions menu.
2. Select Site Collection Features from the Site Collection Administration group of links. You will be redirected to the Site Collection Features page, shown in Figure 14-22.
3. Click the Activate button next to the In Place Records Management item.

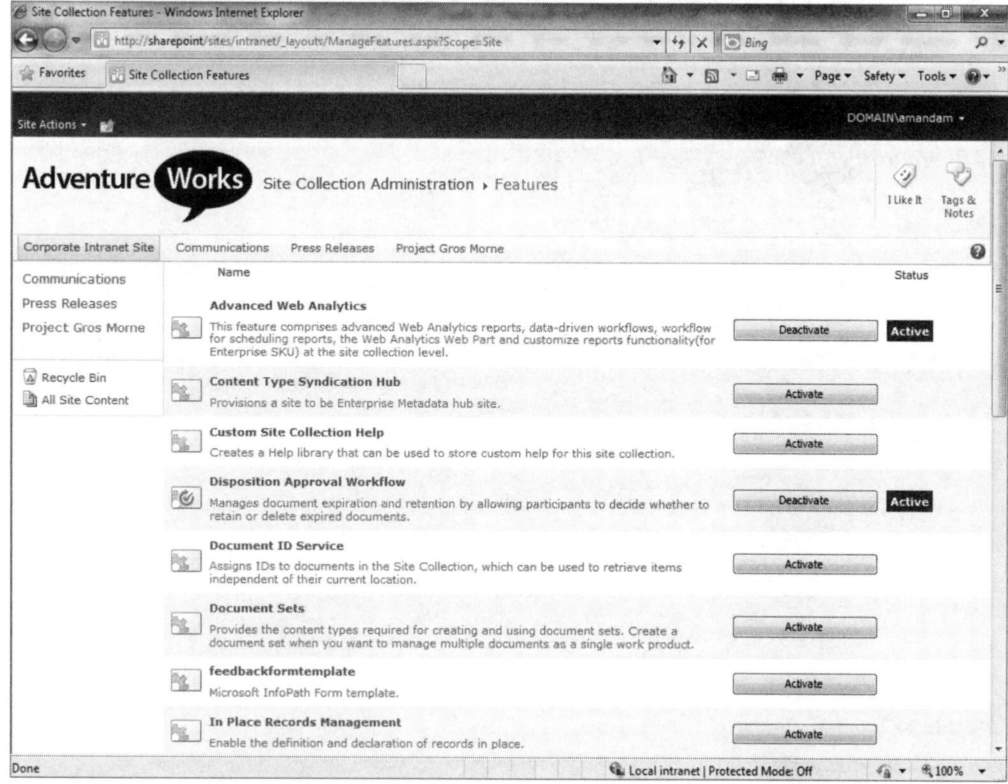

FIGURE 14-22

TRY IT OUT Modify Records Declaration Settings on Site Collection

1. From the top-level site of your site collection, select Site Settings from the Site Actions menu. For this example, you are using the intranet site collection created in Chapter 1.
2. Select the Records Declaration Settings link. You will be redirected to the Records Declaration Settings page, shown in Figure 14-23.
3. For Records Restrictions, select the option to Block Edit and Delete. This may be the default setting in your environment.
4. For Records Declaration Availability, select the Available in all Locations by Default option.
5. Click OK.

How It Works

Now that you have enabled the In Place Records Management feature on your site collection and configured the Records Declaration settings, each library in the site collection will support the declaration of records from the Ribbon, as shown in Figure 14-24.

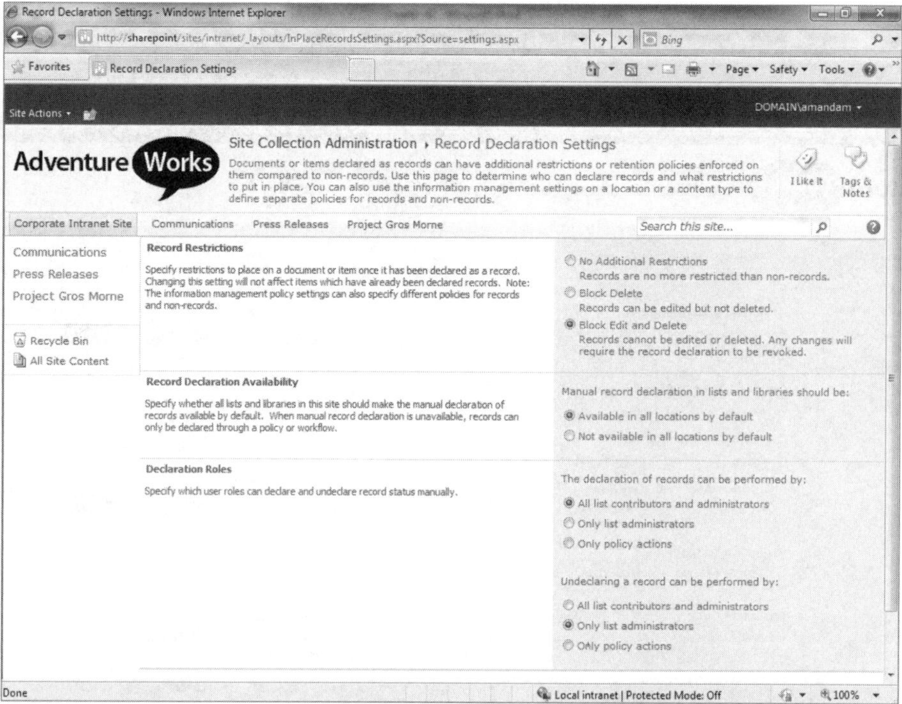

FIGURE 14-23

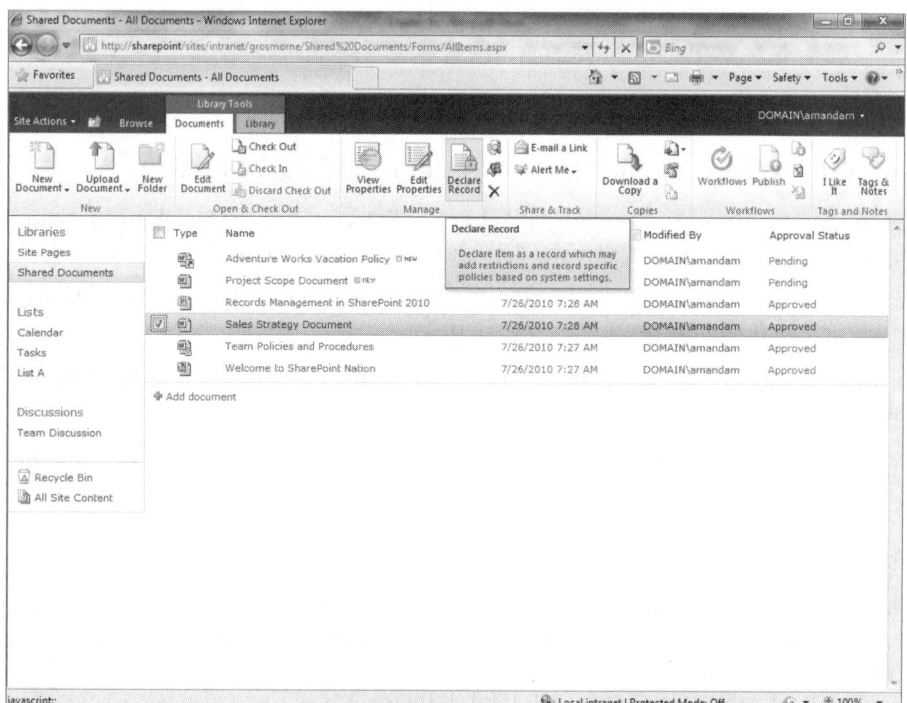

FIGURE 14-24

In step 3, you selected the option to Block Edit and Delete once a file has been declared a record. As a result, these options will be grayed out from the Ribbon whenever a file has been declared as a record. You could also identify the roles in your organization that have the ability to declare a record as undeclared within your site collection. In this exercise you went with the default setting.

TRY IT OUT Declare an In Place Record

1. From a collaborative site in your intranet site collection, upload the Project Scope Document from this chapter's resource files.
2. Select the file in the library.
3. Select the Declare Record option from the Documents tab of the Ribbon, as shown in Figure 14-25.

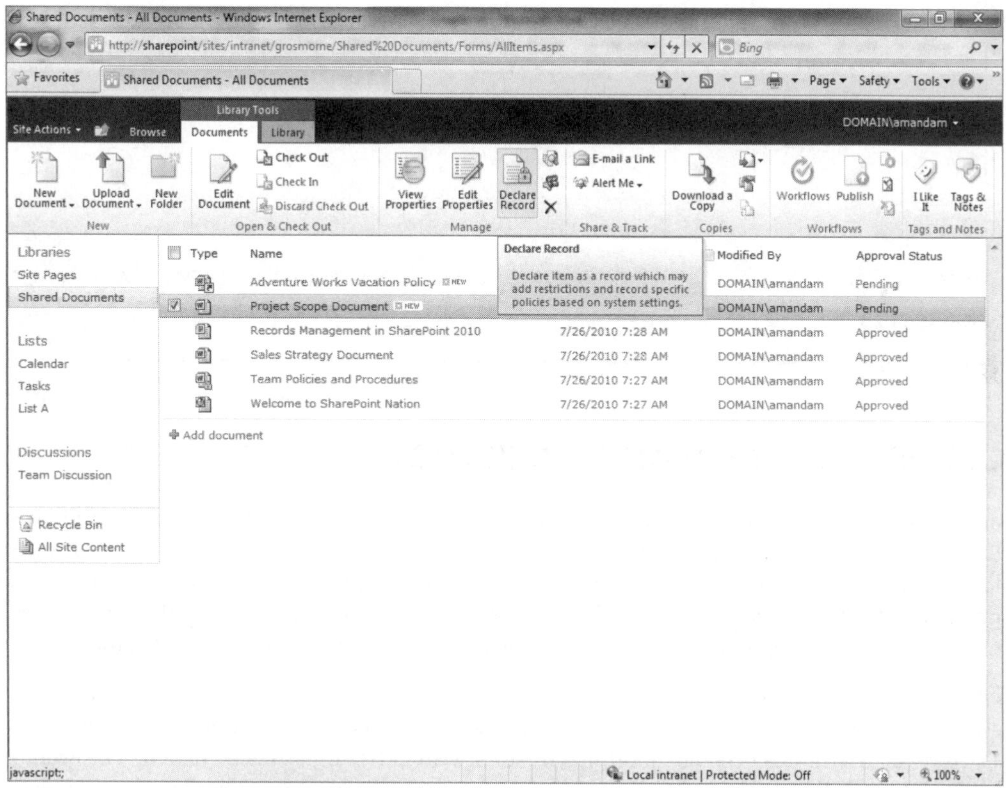

FIGURE 14-25

How It Works

Once the file has been declared a record, you will notice that the Edit and Delete buttons are disabled when the file is selected, as shown in Figure 14-26.

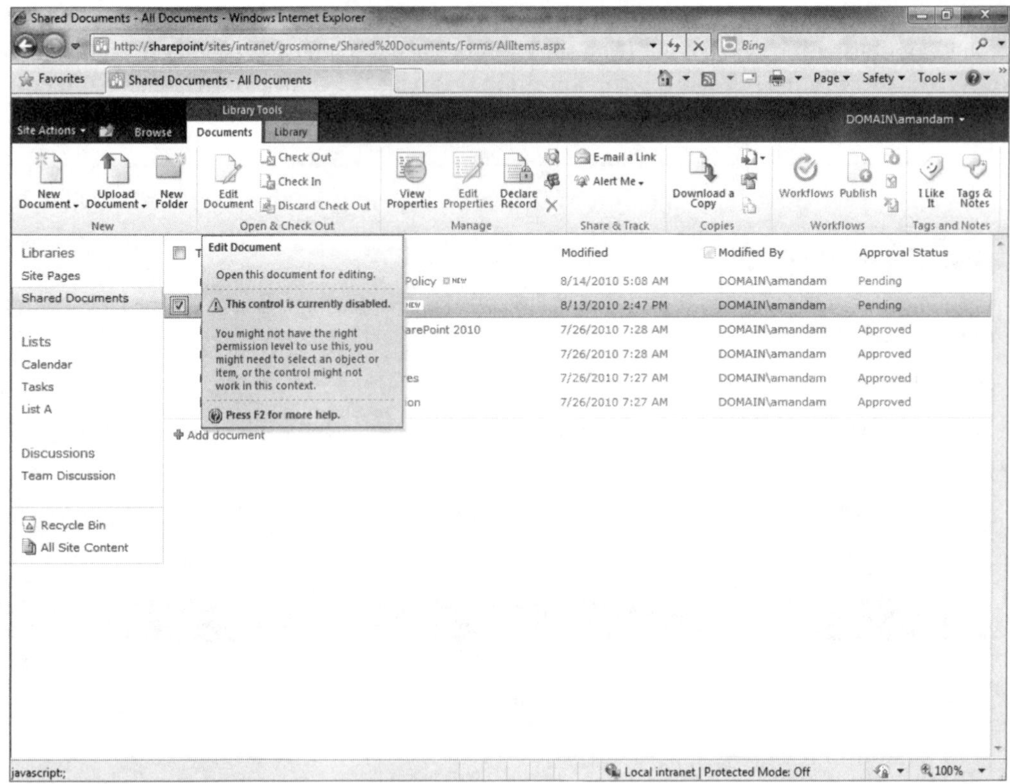

FIGURE 14-26

RECORDS RETENTION AND EXPIRATION

Another important aspect of records management is the determination and management of how long records should be retained before they are removed from the system. In many organizations, there may be regulatory reasons for this determination. In other organizations, the decision may be more operations based. SharePoint supports the definition of multistage retention schedules for records and nonrecords. These schedules can be applied according to content type or physical location.

When defining a retention schedule, you must identify an event that must occur to initiate the actions that will follow. An event can be defined using date-based properties of the document, such as two years after it has been last modified or seven years after it has been created. The event may also be determined according to a programmatic formula that has been installed on the server.

Once a schedule has been set for an event, an action can be identified that will take place after that event has occurred. These actions may include one of the following options:

- **Move to recycle bin:** This delete activity provides a "soft delete," which can be undone by a user with appropriate privileges.

- **Permanently delete:** This delete activity represents an action that cannot be undone. The intent is to remove the document from the system without any opportunity for review or reconsideration. In many cases, this action is selected for regulatory reasons.
- **Transfer to another location:** In some cases, once an event has occurred, the file should be added to a new location. This may result in the file being copied, moved, or moved with a link. A logical scenario for this action would be to remove the file from the collaborative location where it was created and add it to a records repository.
- **Start a workflow:** In some cases, further review or consideration is required before the appropriate action for a file can be determined. Therefore, you may elect to have a review workflow launched to determine if the file should be deleted from the system or moved to an alternate location.
- **Skip to next stage:** For a particular stage, there may be no specific activity other than to move to the next stage of the life cycle for the document.
- **Delete previous drafts:** This activity will remove all minor versions of a document. This may be relative for cases where it is not necessary to keep all draft versions after a certain period, and since it is unlikely for the document to be updated further, it is logical to conserve on disk space and purge all pervious draft versions. All major versions of the document will still be retained.
- **Delete all previous versions:** This activity will remove all versions, including major and minor versions.

In the next two Try It Outs, you will create retention schedules for a content type as well as a physical location. In the final Try It Out for this section, you will review the compliance details of a document for which a retention schedule has been defined.

TRY IT OUT Create a Retention Schedule for a Content Type

In this exercise, you will create a retention schedule for the Sales Contract content type created earlier in this chapter.

1. From the top-level site of your site collection, select Site Settings from the Site Actions menu.
2. Select Site Content Types from the Galleries section.
3. Select the Sales Contract content type.
4. From the Content Type Administration page, select Information Management Policy Settings. You will be redirected to the Edit Policy page, as shown in Figure 14-27.
5. Select the checkbox to Enable Retention. The retention options for this content type will be displayed.
6. Under the Non Records section, select the Add a Retention Stage option. A Retention Stage properties window will appear, as shown in Figure 14-28.
7. Select the option to create the event based on a date property.
8. Select Modified as the date from the drop-down and enter **5 years** in the textbox.

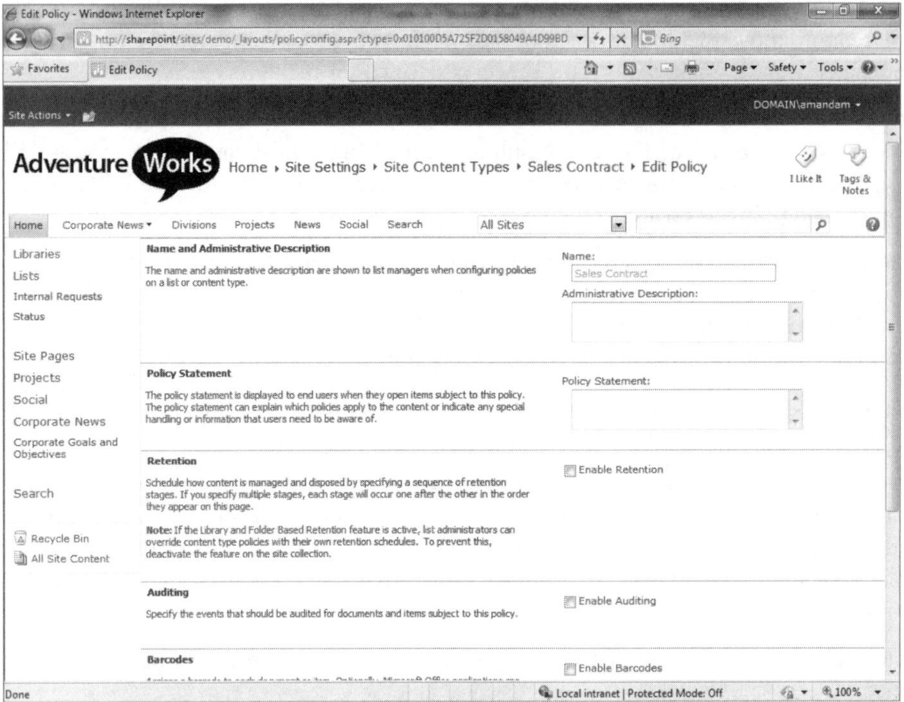

FIGURE 14-27

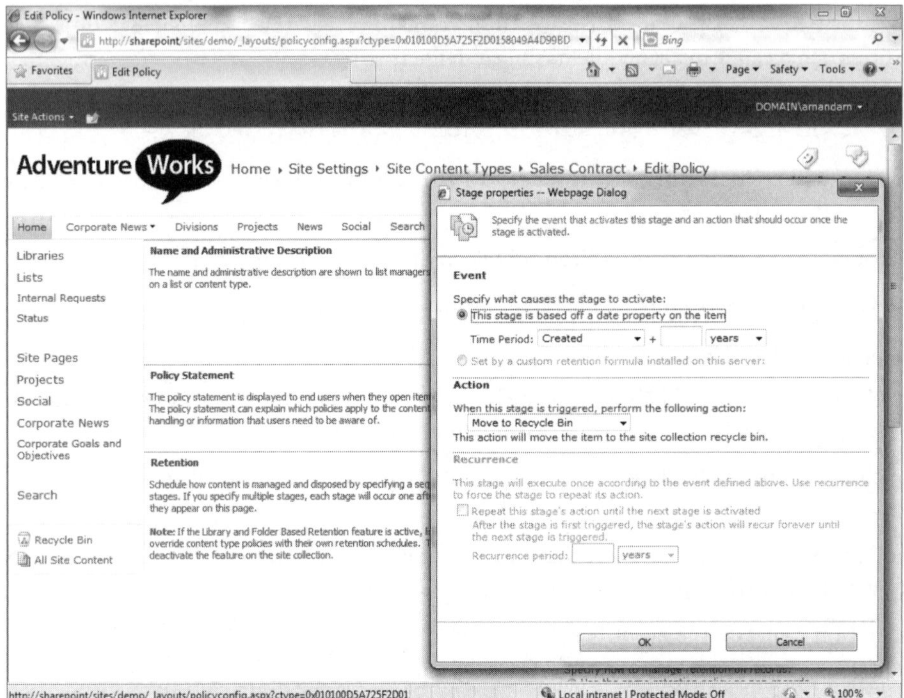

FIGURE 14-28

9. Select the Move to the Recycle Bin action.
10. From the Records section of the Retention Policy page, select the Add a Retention Stage option.
11. Select Declared Record as the date from the drop-down and enter **3 years** in the textbox.
12. Select the Transfer to Another Location action.
13. For Type of Transfer, select Move and Leave a Link, as shown in Figure 14-29.

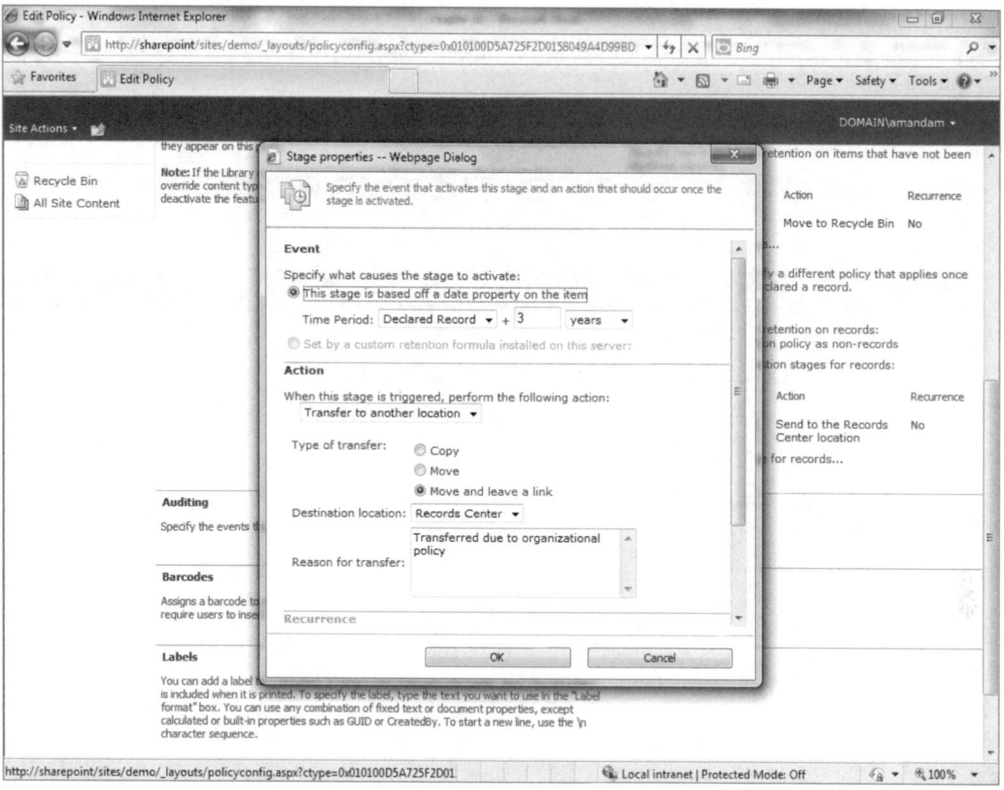

FIGURE 14-29

14. For Destination Location, select Records Center.
15. Click OK.
16. Click OK on the Edit Policy page.

How It Works

When you enabled retention for the content type, you had the option to define unique rules for non-records and records. If you had enabled this feature, your document would have had a unique retention schedule up until the point where it was declared a record. This is a way of ensuring that proper expiration and handling rules are applied to nonrecords within your system as well as records. In this example, you selected the option that nonrecords should be deleted five years after they have been modified. If a document is declared a record, then it should be moved from the collaborative location where it is stored to the Records Center after three years. Once it is in the Records Center, it will be managed by the retention schedule defined for that location.

TRY IT OUT Create a Retention Schedule for a Library

1. From the main page of the Records Center site collection that you created in a previous exercise, select the 01 Human Resources library.
2. Select Library Settings from the Library tab of the Ribbon.
3. Select Information Management Policy Settings. You will be redirected to the Policy Settings page for the library, as shown in Figure 14-30.

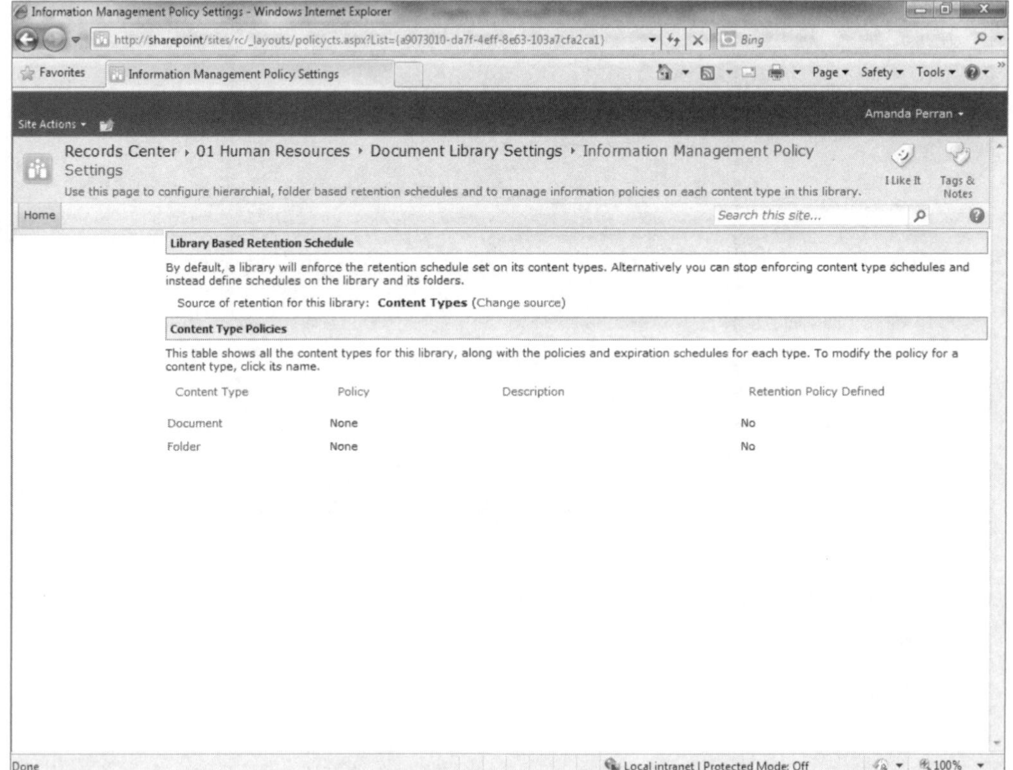

FIGURE 14-30

4. You should notice that at the top of the page, the retention source for the library is listed as Content Types. Select the Change Source link.
5. Select Libraries and Folders as the source of retention.
6. You will receive a warning message. Click OK to accept it.

7. Click the Add a Retention Stage link.
8. Define the rule that states seven years after the file has been declared a record, it should be permanently deleted. The settings for this rule are displayed in Figure 14-31.

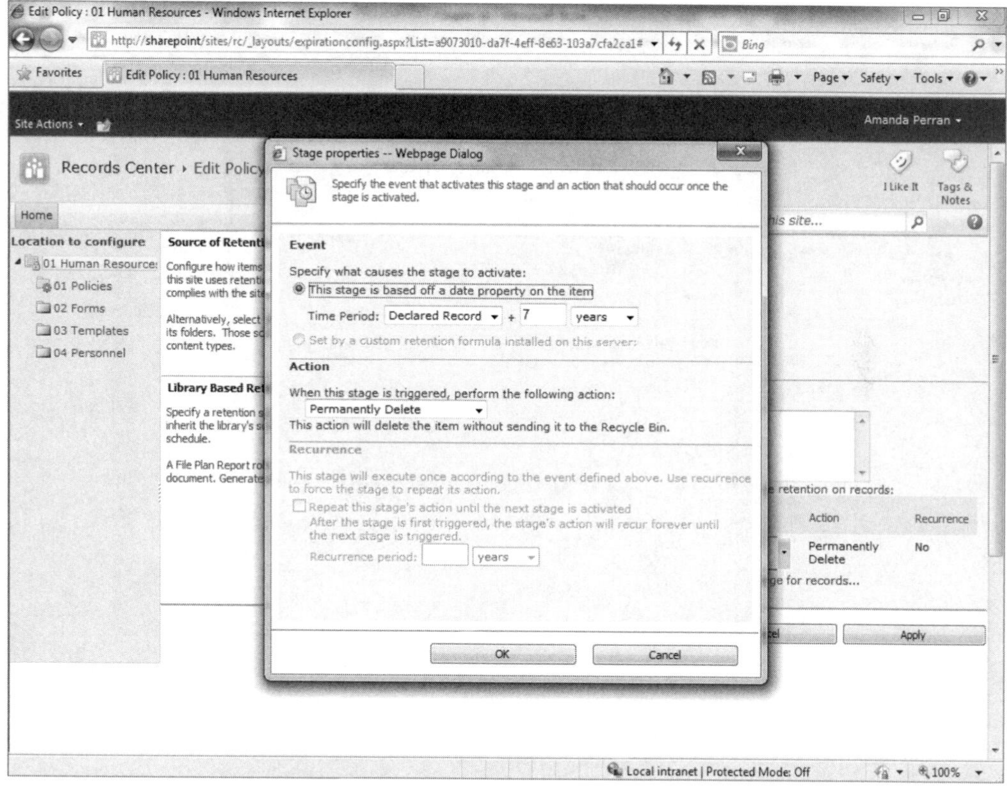

FIGURE 14-31

9. Click OK to save the rule.
10. Click Apply, then OK to save the settings for the library.

How It Works

In this example, you created a retention schedule for a library that was independent of content type. This is a relevant scenario in cases where a formalized file plan exists and content is organized and grouped according to properties such as retention and expiration requirements. In this case, you defined the rule that seven years after a file has been declared a record, it should be permanently deleted. This rule will apply to all folders and documents in the library by default. However, you will review in the next example how an individual folder may have a unique retention schedule defined that will override that of the library.

TRY IT OUT Create a Retention Schedule for a Folder

1. From the 01 Human Resources library of your site, expand the Policies folder menu and select Compliance Details. The Compliance Details report will appear for the folder, as shown in Figure 14-32.

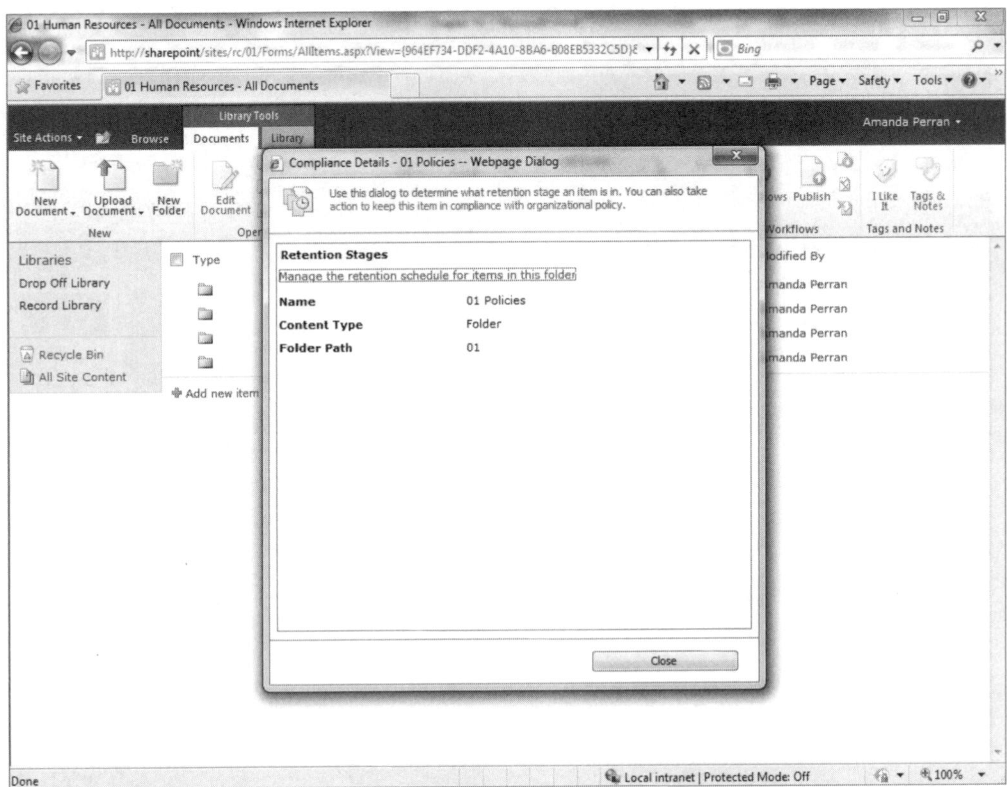

FIGURE 14-32

2. Select the Manage Retention Schedule for Items in this Folder link. You will be redirected to the Folder Based Retention Schedule page.
3. Select the Define Retention Stages link.
4. Select the Add a Retention Stage for Records link.
5. Define the rule that states five years after the file has been declared a record, it should be permanently deleted.
6. Click OK to save the rule.
7. Click Apply, then OK to save the settings on the folder.

How It Works

In this example you created a retention schedule for the Policies folder that was unique from that of the Human Resources library. In this case, files in the Policies folder will be deleted five years after they are declared a record, versus the seven year rule that exists for the library.

TRY IT OUT View Compliance Details for a Document

1. From the 01 Human Resources library of your site, select the Policies folder.
2. Expand the menu associated with the Adventure Works Vacation Policy document and select Compliance Details. The Compliance Details report for the document will appear, as shown in Figure 14-33.

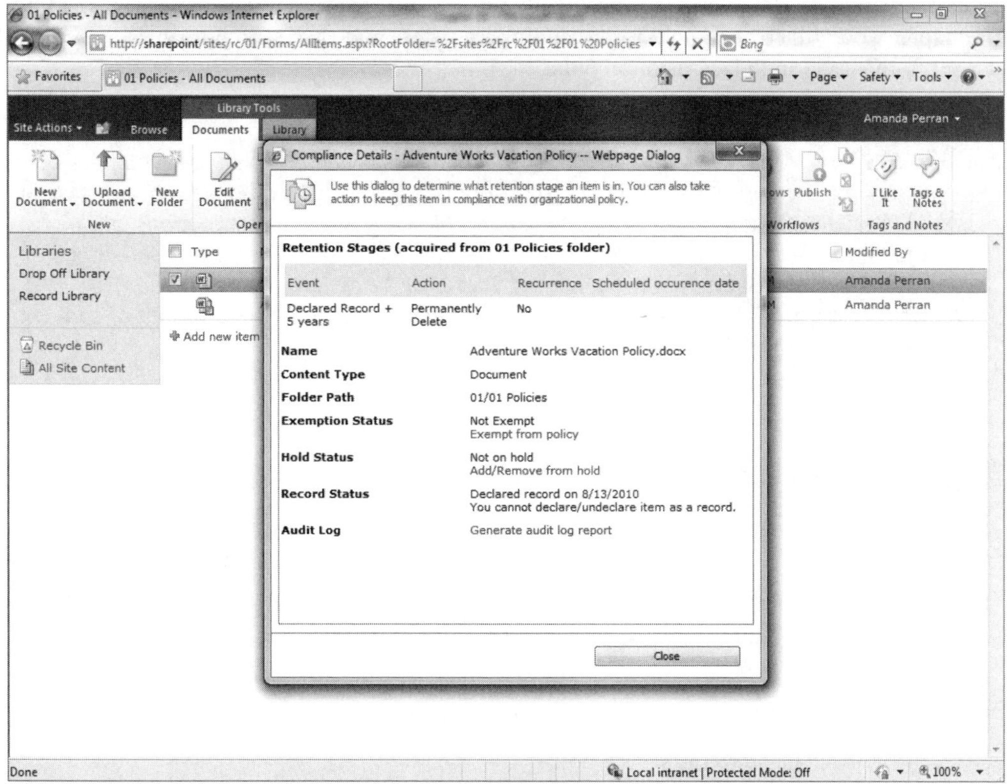

FIGURE 14-33

How It Works

In this example, you can see that the Adventure Works document is scheduled to expire five years after it is declared a record. You can also view the date that the file was declared a record. In Figure 14-33, the file was declared a record on August 13, 2010. You can also perform activities such as generating an audit log report to view details of how the file has been accessed.

HOLDS

In certain cases, an organization may be involved in legal proceedings or regulatory reviews that require the collection of evidence or documentation related to a specific topic or subject. In these situations, it is critical that important documents be accessible to stakeholders involved in the proceedings or investigation. As a result, it may be appropriate to place holds on the records, which will temporarily exempt the files from any retention or expiration policies that have been defined for them. If a record's expiration date passes while it is on hold, it will not expire. However, once the file is removed from the hold, all normal policies will resume, and the file will be queued for expiration according the defined policy.

A key aspect of adding a document to a hold is searching for and locating the file. This is done through a search interface designed specifically for the Holds feature. In the final few Try It Outs of this chapter, you will create a hold for a pending legal case and then search for files that might be relevant to this case and place them on hold.

NOTE *In order to complete the next Try It Out, it is recommended that you perform an incremental crawl of your SharePoint content. You can do this by going to the Central Administration site, selecting Manage Service Applications, clicking on the Search Service Application, selecting Content Sources, and selecting Start Incremental Crawl from the Local SharePoint sites drop-down menu. This activity may take several minutes to complete, depending on the amount of content in your SharePoint environment.*

TRY IT OUT Place Files on Hold

1. From the main page of the Records Center, select Manage Records Center from the Site Actions menu.
2. From the Common Records Management Tasks web part, select the Discover and Hold Records option. You will be redirected to the Search and Add to Hold page, as shown in Figure 14-34.
3. You may select any site collection you wish on which to perform your search. For this exercise, you will retain the default setting to search the Records Center for items.
4. Enter the word **Policy** into the search box.
5. Click the Preview Results button. A new window will appear, as shown in Figure 14-35, showing items in your site collection that contain the word "policy."
6. Close the results window.
7. Select the Keep in Place and Add to Hold Directly option.
8. Select the Add a New Hold option. A new window will appear, as shown in Figure 14-36.
9. Enter the details of the hold as follows:

PROPERTY	VALUE
Title	Policy Review Hearing
Description	Legal Case of Employee #12345 vs. Adventure Works
Managed By	Enter your own name

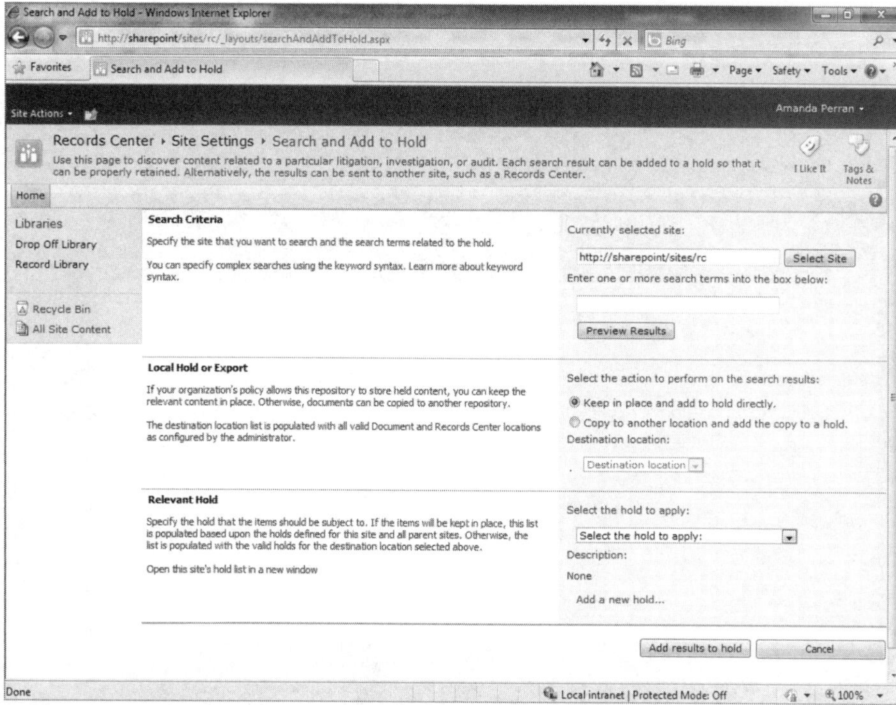

FIGURE 14-34

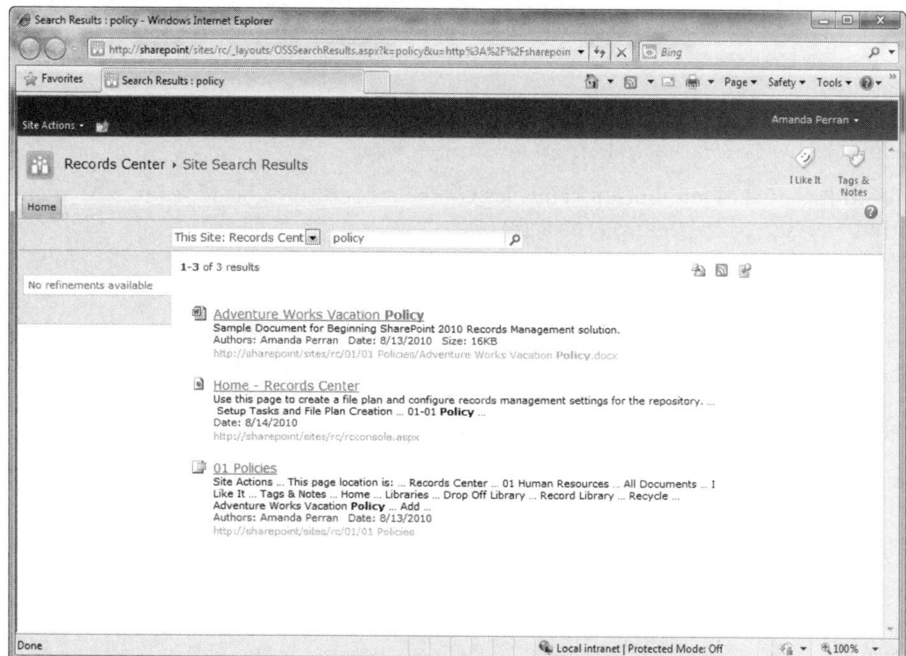

FIGURE 14-35

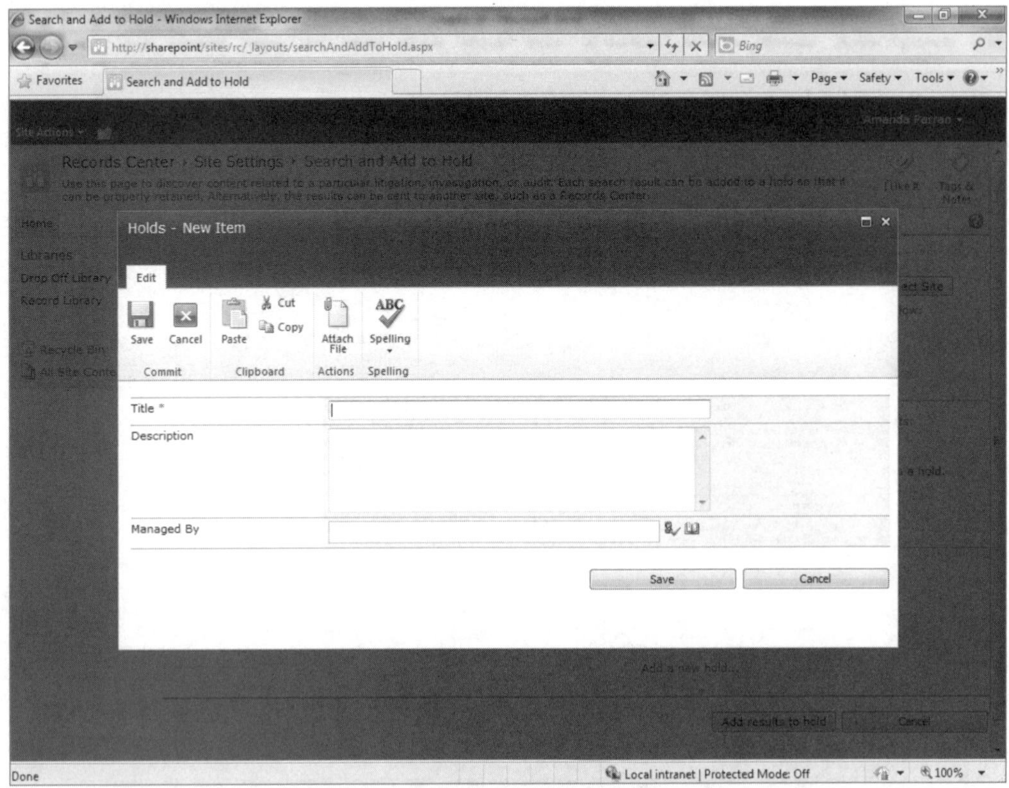

FIGURE 14-36

10. Click Save.
11. Select the Policy Review Hearing hold from the drop-down.
12. Click the Add Results to Hold button. The files will be scheduled to be added to a hold and a confirmation message will appear on the screen.

How It Works

There is a scheduled job on your server that will process all pending hold requests. Once the hold has been placed on the records, items within that hold are exempt from their standard retention schedules. Figure 14-37 is an example of the Compliance Details report for the Adventure Works Vacation Policy document, which has now been placed on hold.

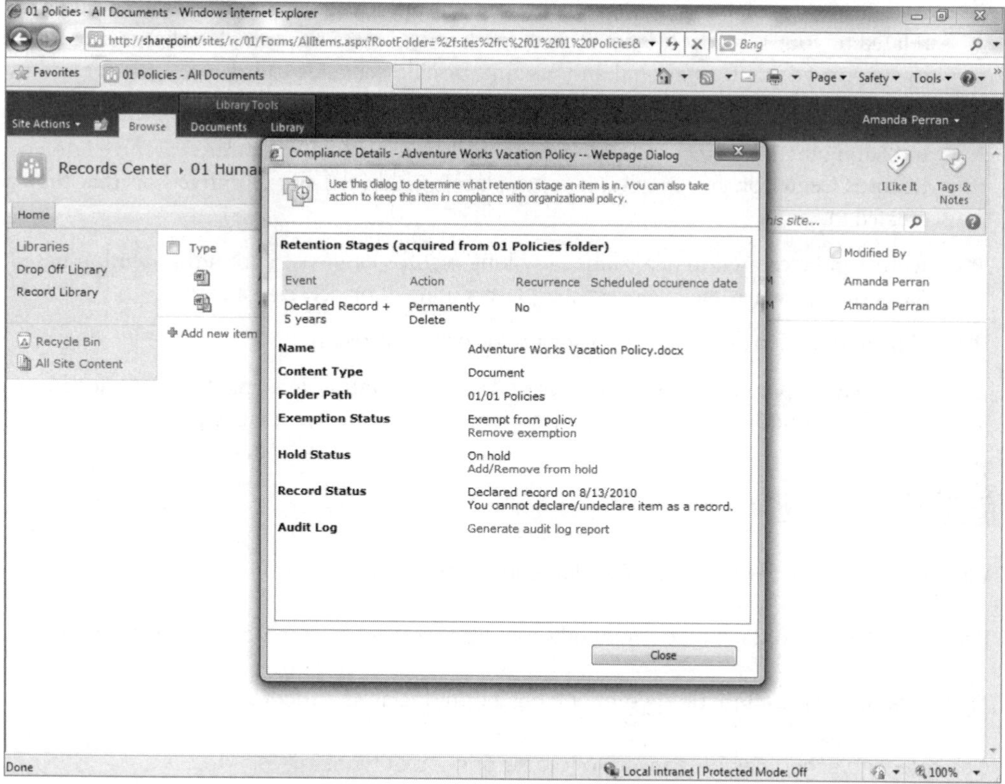

FIGURE 14-37

SUMMARY

In this chapter, you learned the fundamental elements of creating a records management solution in SharePoint 2010. After reading this chapter, you should have a complete understanding of the following:

- The importance of identifying roles and responsibilities related to your records management implementation.
- A file plan is a critical element of your records management solution that outlines the categories and types of documents that exist within your organization. Developing a detailed file plan is an important step that must take place prior to configuring any technical elements of SharePoint.

- A classification plan is a detailed listing of all properties and attributes that should exist related to your records. It is important to identify a classification plan that is detailed enough to support your informational and organizational needs but still manageable for end users to populate and maintain.
- In SharePoint 2010, records may be managed separately in a dedicated archive known as the Records Center or they may remain "in place" within the collaborative sites that they were created in.
- Rules can be created to determine how long records can exist within the solution based on dates such as when they were created, last modified, or declared a record.
- Unique retention rules may exist for nonrecords and records.
- Files may be placed on hold for investigative or regulatory reasons. If a file is added to a hold, it cannot be removed from the system until the hold is removed.

EXERCISES

1. What is the difference between a file plan and a classification plan?
2. How is in-place records management different from archive-based records management?
3. True or false: A file cannot be deleted if it has been declared a record.
4. Can retention schedules be applied to folders or content types?

▶ WHAT YOU LEARNED IN THIS CHAPTER

TOPIC	KEY CONCEPTS
What is Records Management?	Records management is the practice of organizing and maintaining documents within an organization based on a series of predetermined rules. These rules control things such as where files are stored, how long they are retained, how they should be disposed of, and who is responsible for these files.
What is a Hold?	In regulatory or legal cases, it is critical that important documents be accessible to stakeholders involved in the proceedings or investigation. As a result, it may be appropriate to place holds on the records, which will temporarily exempt the files from any retention or expiration policies that have been defined for them.
What is the Difference between Archive and In Place Records Management?	Archive-based records management focuses on the movement or copying of a file to a centralized location where all records are stored. In-place records management focuses on retaining the record within the same repository it has been created and stored in along with all other documents that relate to the same topic or subject.

15

Business Connectivity Services

WHAT YOU WILL LEARN IN THIS CHAPTER:

- How to configure a BCS Application
- How to use BCS with SharePoint 2010
- How to work with BCS as a SharePoint administrator
- How to develop custom solutions for BCS

Business Connectivity Services (BCS) is all about using SharePoint to connect the isolated silos of data in your company. What kind of data exists in any given organization? There are payroll and personnel systems, patient databases in healthcare, customer and vendor databases, and sales and inventory systems. The list goes on and on. These different types of databases can be seen as separate islands of information, but with SharePoint 2010 and the BCS, they can all be brought into one interface. External content types (ECTs) are new in SharePoint 2010, and they allow for the exposure of data from external systems, such as databases and Web Services, into SharePoint. There is a new type of list called an external list, which has the appearance of a regular SharePoint list, but is really a web interface directly to the external data. Compared to the read-only nature of the SharePoint 2007 Business Data Catalog, the new BCS not only allows viewing of the external data, but also provides the ability to insert, update, and delete data. All of this can be done out-of-box, in an easy user interface, without having to write any custom code! Figure 15-1 shows a high-level diagram of BCS, featuring some ways that SharePoint interfaces with external data sources.

The ability to have one point of interaction with various business systems within SharePoint and Office applications has the potential to drastically increase work efficiency. Instead of having disparate systems and various logins, business users will be able to go to a single place to access these systems, and that is SharePoint.

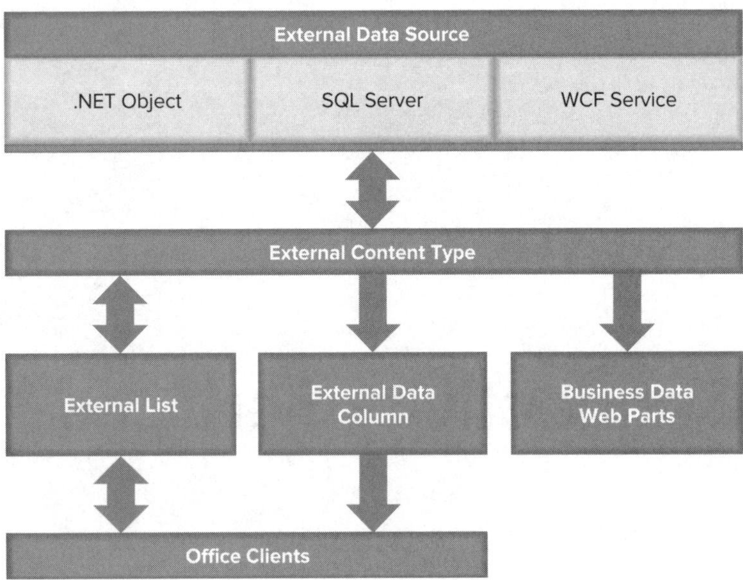

FIGURE 15-1

CONFIGURING A BCS APPLICATION

When creating and configuring a BCS application, there are several factors to take into consideration before beginning. The main factor, and the most complicated one, is security. Once the decision has been made regarding which method or combination of authentication methods will be used, the easy part is the creation of the external content type. Creating an application sounds like something that only developers would do, but in the case of the BCS, that is not necessarily true. In this section, we will go over a high-level list of some security and authentication options, and then show examples of how to go about creating an external content type and external list from scratch.

Security Considerations

When working with Business Connectivity Services, the security options are quite varied and complex. The concepts of database security and authentication are out of the scope of this book, but here is a high-level list of several levels to consider when setting up user access to the BCS data:

- **Database security:** Grant end users permission directly on the databases that they will be using in the ECTs.
- **External content type permissions:** In the Service Application in Central Administration, permissions can be granted per ECT, as shown in Figure 15-2.
- **Operations:** When the ECT is created, a database table is selected, and the operations are created. These are referred to as CRUD (create, read, update, delete). There is the ability to

create all of these operations in an ECT, but it is not required. Pick and choose specific operations that you want to allow, if necessary.

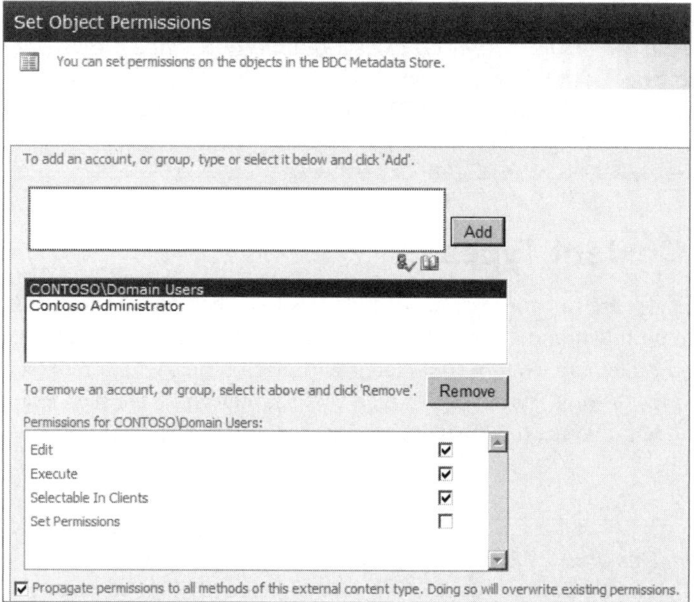

FIGURE 15-2

- **SharePoint list permissions:** This does not apply to the ECT, only to the external list. Use permissions on one of these lists in the same manner as with any other SharePoint list or library.
- **Impersonation:** When creating an ECT, and the database connection is being added, there is a prompt called SQL Server Connection, as shown in Figure 15-3. Instead of giving the end users direct access to the database, an impersonation can be created and used, via an Application ID from the Secure Store Service Application.

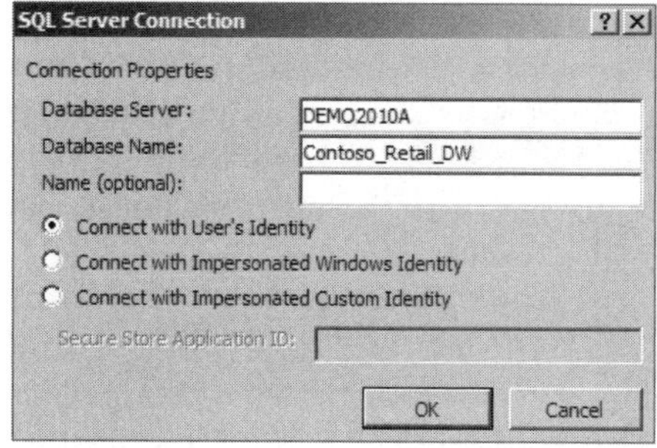

FIGURE 15-3

- **BCS Identity:** There is one more, lesser-known method of authentication. Using the BCS Identity allows the connection to Revert To Self, which means that it uses the BCS service identity to connect to the data. With this method, secure store target applications need not be created.

Of these multiple levels, the strictest level of security will always apply. For example, if users do not have access to the external content type, and they are given "Full Control" SharePoint permissions, they will still not have any access to that list. For more information about BCS security and authentication options, refer this TechNet site: `http://technet.microsoft.com/en-us/library/ee661743.aspx`.

WARNING *When logged-in users have direct access to the database that is used in the ECT, their credentials need to be passed all the way from their Windows login to SharePoint, and then from SharePoint to the back-end system where the BCS data lives. This is referred to as a double-hop, since the identity has to be passed twice. If the organization is going to grant users access to the back-end data and use this method, then NTLM authentication in SharePoint will not be sufficient, and Kerberos will have to be implemented.*

Creating External Content Types

External content types (ECTs) are the cornerstone of Business Connectivity Services. Think of each ECT as equivalent to a table in a database. Several ECTs can be created to represent multiple tables in the database, and tables can even be associated with each other, which represents the same concept as table relationships or joins. After you've read this chapter and have seen examples of how ECTs are used within SharePoint, the business reasons for utilizing the new BCS will become apparent.

NOTE *SharePoint Designer 2010 is a free desktop application and can be obtained from Microsoft's download site here:* `http://bit.ly/SPD2010-32`. *Chapter 5 showed how to use SharePoint Designer to create custom workflows with no code.*

TRY IT OUT Creating an External Content Type

In the demonstrations in this chapter, we will be using an example set of SQL data that can be downloaded from Microsoft's site here:

`http://bit.ly/ContosoBIdemo`

This database example is for the retail industry, and is called Contoso_Retail_DW. The download page contains the instructions for downloading, extracting, and installing the database on a SQL Server. In this Try It Out, you will learn how to create an external content type in SharePoint Designer.

1. Open SharePoint Designer 2010, and open your SharePoint site.
2. Click External Content Types in the list of Site Objects on the left side of the screen. If you have access to any other ECTs that have been created in the farm, you will see them here.
3. At the top of the screen, in the New section of the Ribbon, click the External Content Type button.
4. Click the Name, and change it from New External Content Type to **Sales**, as shown in Figure 15-4.
5. Click the link that says "Click here to discover external data sources and define operations," which is shown at the bottom of Figure 15-4.

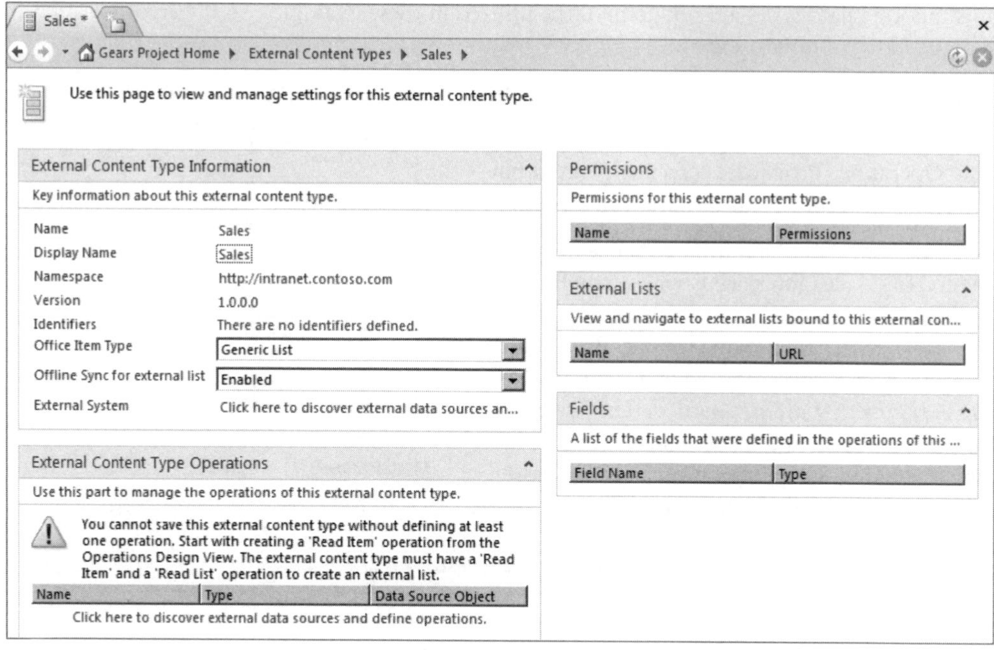

FIGURE 15-4

6. Click the Add Connection button, as shown in Figure 15-5.

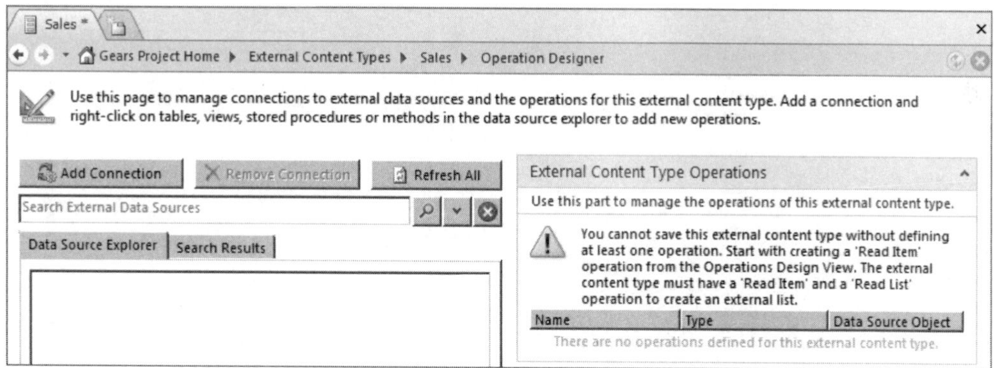

FIGURE 15-5

7. For the Data Source Type, choose SQL Server, and click OK.

8. In the SQL Server Connection box, type the name of your SQL server and the name of the example database that you preinstalled, which is Contoso_Retail_DW, as Database Name. Leave the authentication option as Connect with User's Identity, and click OK.

9. Click the plus icon next to the name of the data source, to expand it so that all of the tables are displayed. If there is an error called Cannot Complete Refresh, click OK. The tables that have

unsupported data types are not going to be utilized in these examples, so the error is irrelevant. The expanded list of tables is shown in Figure 15-6.

10. Right-click on the table called FactSales, and click Create All Operations.

11. The Operations Properties screen explains what all of the different operations are. Click Next.

12. The Parameters configuration screen is shown in Figure 15-7. This interface is where you have the ability to granularly define which fields from the table will be pulled into SharePoint. By default, all fields have a check next to them, but you can uncheck any that are not needed. The Errors and Warnings section at the bottom is helpful in letting you know what issues need to be addressed before moving on to the next step. We will address each of the errors as we proceed.

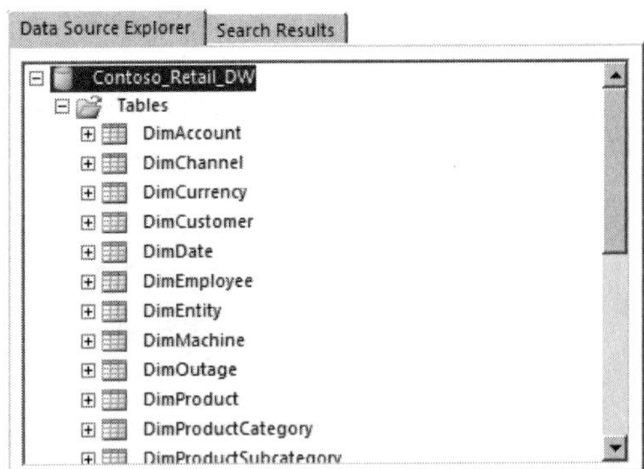

FIGURE 15-6

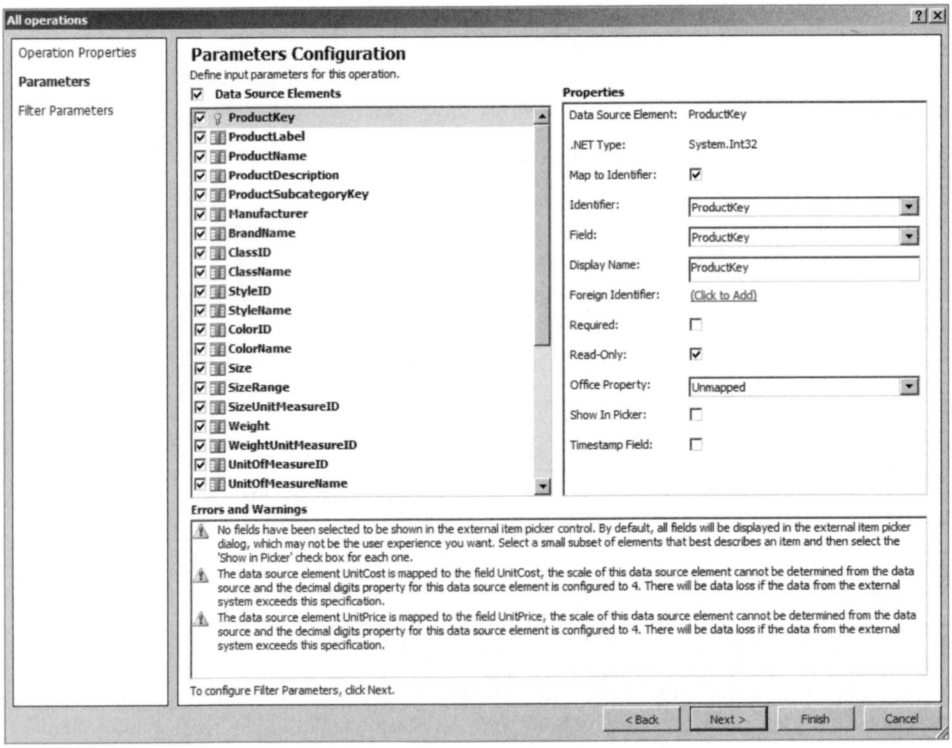

FIGURE 15-7

13. This is the first error: "No fields have been selected to be shown in the external item picker control. By default, all fields will be displayed in the external item picker dialog, which may not be the user experience you want. Select a small subset of elements that best describes an item and then select the 'Show in Picker' checkbox for each one."

    What does this mean to you? By default, every single column in the FactSales table will be available in the external item picker, which may not be the outcome you desire. There is a checkbox on the right side of the screen in Figure 15-7, called Show In Picker. For each data source element that you select on the left, you can check this checkbox to indicate if you would like to use it in SharePoint. In this demonstration, check Show In Picker next to the following fields: StoreKey, UnitCost, SalesQuantity, and TotalCost. We will cover more information about the external item picker later on in the section called "Using the External Data Column."

14. The rest of the warnings are the same and are related to the currency fields: "The data source element UnitCost is mapped to the field UnitCost, the scale of this data source element cannot be determined from the data source and the decimal digits property for this data source element is configured to 4. There will be data loss if the data from the external system exceeds this specification."

    What does this mean? If these fields contain more than four decimal places in the backend system, SharePoint won't recognize those. In this example, you are not worried about the number of decimal places and can ignore those warnings.

15. The names of the columns aren't really friendly names, so you have the ability to change the display name of each column. Click the name of the SalesKey field on the left, and in the Display Name box on the right, change it to **Sales Key** (with a space in between). Do the same thing for each of the other fields, by changing each display name to two separate words where needed. This change is simply cosmetic.

16. Click on the last field on the left, called UpdateDate. Check the Timestamp Field box on the right. Checking this box signifies that this field represents the last time the item was modified, which is significant when performing searches.

17. Click Next.

18. The Filter Parameters Configuration screen has a warning that says: "It is strongly recommended to add a filter of type 'Limit' for this operation type. Without a limit filter, this operation may result in large result sets."

    This is the screen where you configure any needed filters on the data. For example, you could filter out sales from a store that is no longer open, or customers who are no longer active. The only filter that we will focus on in this example is the limit filter. This is important because if the data is brought into SharePoint with thousands of items in the list with filter, it could severely impact the performance of the server. You will create a limit filter of 100 items, which simply means that only 100 items will be pulled from the database at a time.

19. On the right side in the Properties, next to the word Filter, click the blue link that says (Click to Add). This screen is shown in Figure 15-8.

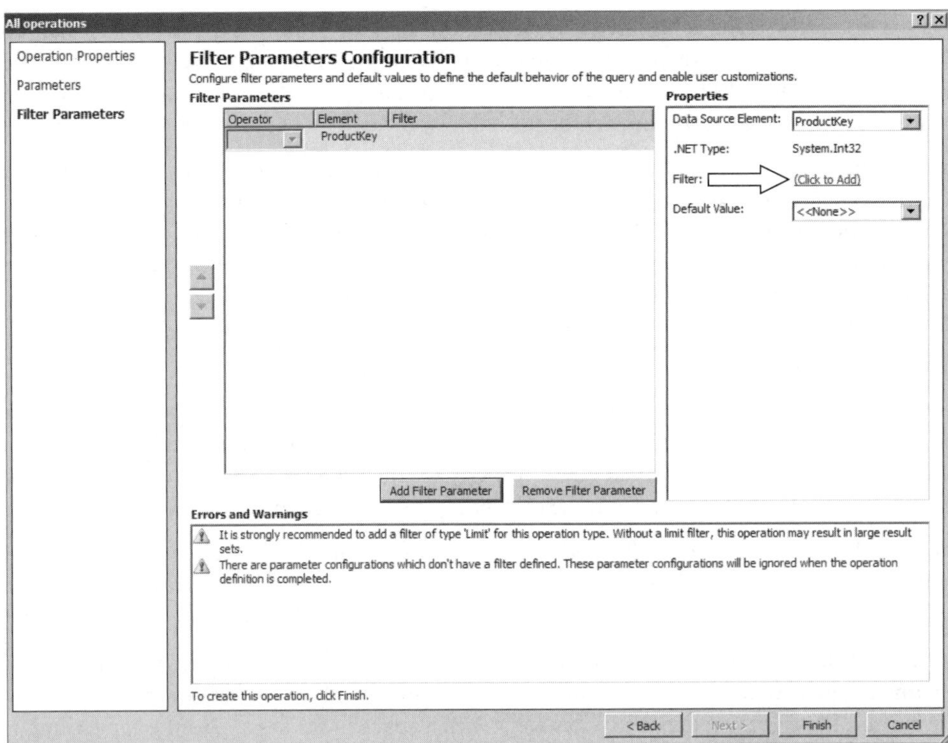

FIGURE 15-8

20. On the Filter Configuration screen shown in Figure 15-9, pick the Limit as the Filter Type, and SalesKey as the Filter Field. Click OK.

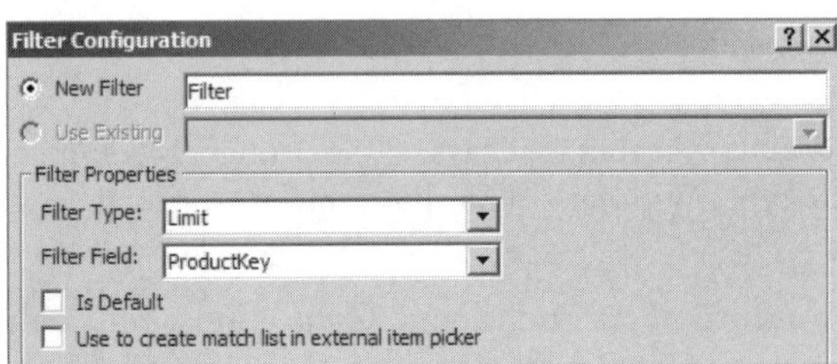

FIGURE 15-9

21. In the Properties section on the right, enter 100 as the Default Value, as seen in Figure 15-10.

22. Click Finish.

23. Click Save at the top-left corner of SharePoint Designer.

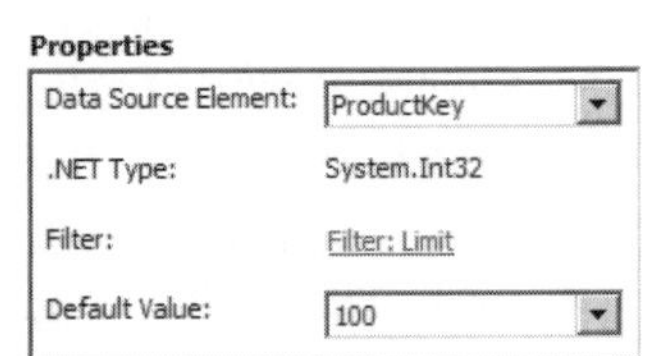

FIGURE 15-10

The external content type has now been created. This will be used in many of the other examples in this chapter.

WARNING *The person who created the external content type in SharePoint Designer still may not necessarily have access to it. Work with your SharePoint administrator to set up the permissions correctly in the Business Data Connectivity Service application. After the ECT has been created, the Summary view will look something like Figure 15-11.*

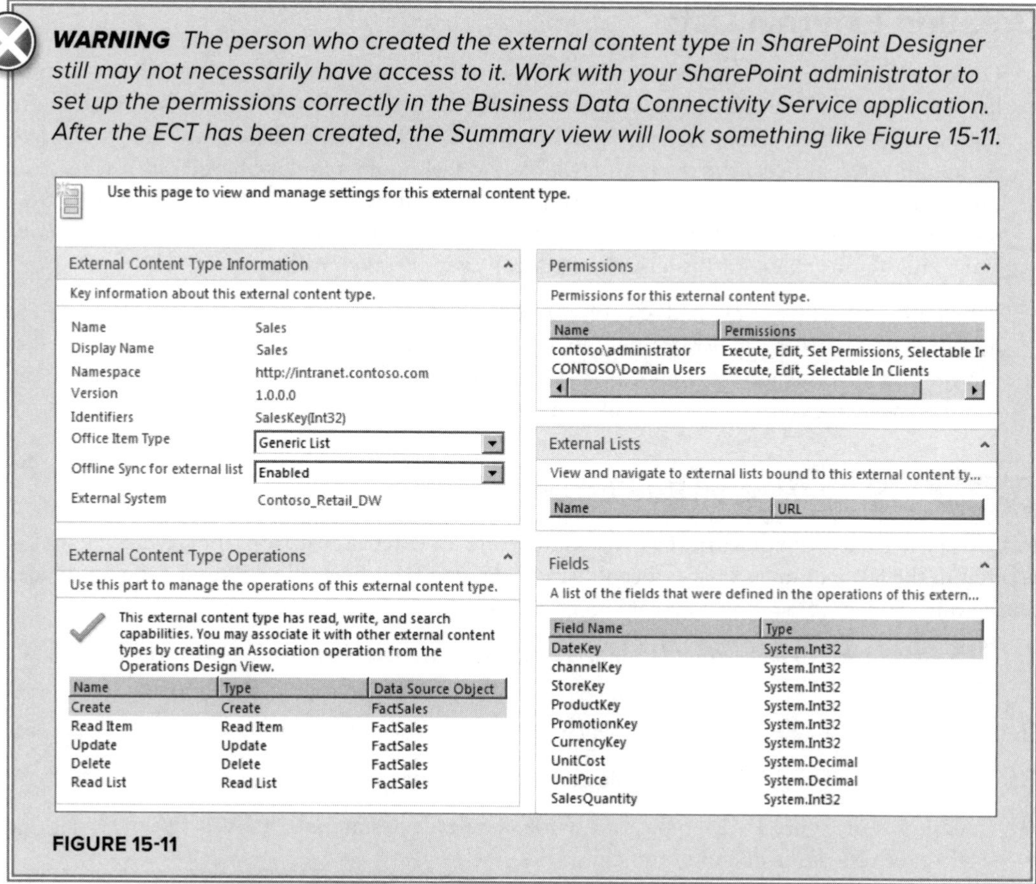

FIGURE 15-11

Notice that there is a Permissions section on the right but no interface to modify them. The administrator who has access to Central Administration can carry out the following steps, in order to modify the list of permissions:

1. In Central Administration, click Manage service applications.
2. Click Business Data Connectivity Service.
3. The Set Metadata Store Permissions button at the top can be used to set up the default permissions that will exist each time a new ECT is created. This can be determined by the administrator.
4. Click the checkbox next to the Sales item in the list, and click the Set Object Permissions button in the Ribbon.
5. This screen is where the permissions can be set up for the Sales external content type that you created.
6. Click the View drop-down box in the Ribbon, and choose External Systems. Check the permissions to the back-end data source Contoso_Retail_DW, and modify them if necessary.

Creating External Lists

Once the ECT has been created, the next step is to create an External List, which is a SharePoint list that directly interfaces to the back-end database data. This list data is not stored in SharePoint but remains in the external system, with SharePoint as the front-end web interface to the live data. Although external lists have the familiar look and feel of any regular SharePoint list, there are a few things that are not included, such as versioning, check in/out, workflows, and content types. Not only are these lists wonderful because they have that familiar user interface, but also, as you will learn later in this chapter, this business data can even be taken offline.

When an external list is created, its columns come from the external content type, and cannot be modified from within the list settings. Views can be created, in order to display the desired columns, but the columns themselves cannot be changed, added, or removed. There is a one-to-one relationship between an external content type and its external list.

TRY IT OUT Creating an External List

In this Try It Out, you will learn the process to create an external list from the Sales ECT that was created in the last example. This external list of sales can then be used in several different places in SharePoint. Follow these steps to create an external list.

1. Open your site in SharePoint Designer, and click External Content Types on the left side of the screen.
2. Click the name of the Sales ECT, which will display its summary view.
3. In the Ribbon, click the Create Lists & Form button, as shown in Figure 15-12.

FIGURE 15-12

4. As shown in Figure 15-13, type a list name of **Sales**, enter an optional description, leave the rest of the defaults, and click OK.

   Notice that there is a checkbox option to create an InfoPath form. As you learned in Chapter 12, InfoPath can now be used as the interface to any SharePoint list. This includes external lists, and this decision does not need to be made immediately. The InfoPath form can be created later, if desired, simply by clicking the Create Lists & Form button again.

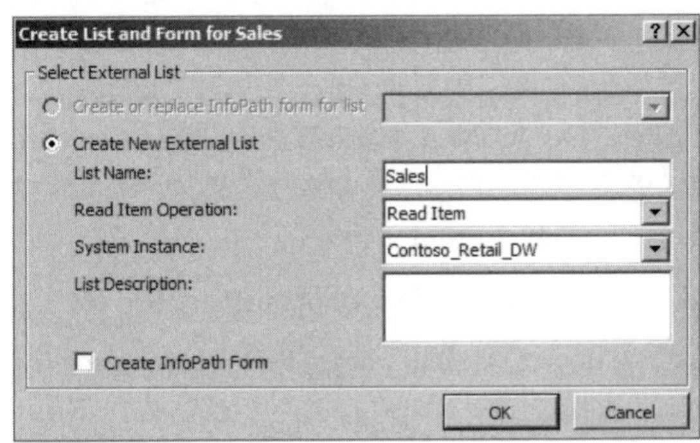

FIGURE 15-13

5. The External Lists section on the right side of the page now contains one item, called Sales. Click that item, and click the Go To List button in the Ribbon.
6. Take a look at the Sales list information page, and then click the Preview in Browser button in the Ribbon.
7. See that all of the columns in the SQL database are now displayed as a SharePoint list!

Explore the new list by clicking on any item to look at the detail view of it, edit an item, and sort or filter. New views can also be created, just as with any list.

Understanding Profile Pages

A *profile page* is a page in SharePoint that displays detailed information about a single item in a database table. It is simply an item detail page. This web part page can be customized by changing the theme and even adding other web parts such as a company logo. The profile page is not related to the external list that has been created. These pages are typically used with the Business Data web parts, which will be covered later in this chapter.

Before the first profile page can be created, several criteria must exist, as follows:

- A SharePoint site must be created by an administrator as the dedicated location for all profile pages.
- The administrator must grant at least Design permissions to anyone who will be creating or updating profile pages.
- Business users who will be viewing the business data must be granted read permission on this site.
- In Central Administration, in the Business Connectivity Service application, the administrator sets the URL of the dedicated site that has been created. To do this, in the Ribbon, click the Configure button in the Profile Pages section, check the box to Enable Profile Page Creation, paste the URL, and click OK.

FIGURE 15-14

Once the above criteria have been met, profile pages may be created for any ECT. Open any ECT in SharePoint Designer, and click the Create Profile Page in the Ribbon, as shown in Figure 15-14. Note that an external list for the ECT is not required in order to use a profile page.

Profile pages are also important if the BCS data will be searchable. Searching BCS data will be covered later in this chapter; just keep in mind that when BCS results are discovered, the search results page will include the link to the profile page of the found item. Figure 15-15 shows an example of a profile page for the "Stores" external content type.

Stores

StoreKey:	4
SalesTerritoryKey:	3
StoreName:	Contoso Bellevue Store
StoreDescription:	Contoso Bellevue Store
Status:	On
OpenDate:	3/1/2004 12:00 AM
StateProvinceName:	Washington
CityName:	Bellevue
ZipCode:	97001
StorePhone:	612-555-0100
StoreFax:	612-555-0100
AddressLine2:	West Lake Hills shopping mall
UpdateDate:	7/1/2009 12:00 AM

FIGURE 15-15

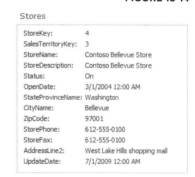

Understanding Associations

In the BCS, associations can be created in order to join two tables by a common field. This concept can be likened to creating relationships in Microsoft Access and other database programs. Use associations when a field in one external table needs to look up (join) to a field in another table.

The interface to create associations can be found on the Operations Design View of any ECT. For an association to be created, more than one ECT needs to exist. First of all, define the names of the fields to be associated with each other. For example, the Sales table has a field called Store Key, which can be associated with the Store Key field in the database's table called Stores. There can be many items in the Sales table related to any one item in the Stores table. With this relationship, each sale that takes place in the company can be linked with a specific store. When associations have been created, this allows for very rich and interactive BCS web part interfaces to be created. Figure 15-16 shows an example of two related (associated) tables.

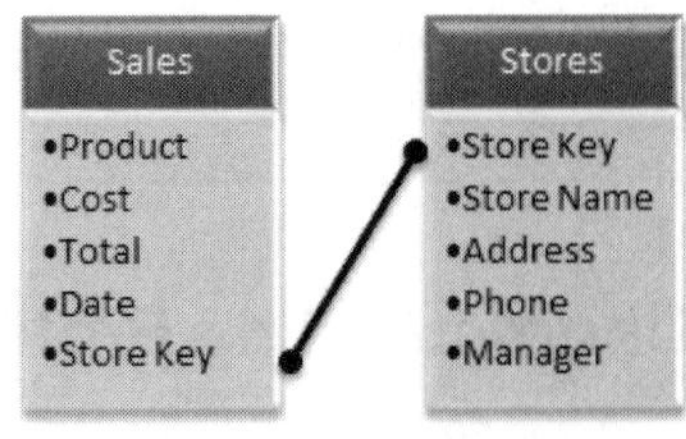

FIGURE 15-16

After the association has been created, generate a profile page for the Stores ECT. This new profile page not only will contain details about one store record but also will automatically include a connected web part with the list of sales transactions that have occurred for that store.

Understanding Business Data Actions

Business Data Actions can be created for each ECT and are best described as different links that can be clicked from within the ECT. These are actions that can be carried out in relation to the currently displayed ECT detail item. For example, create business data actions in order to link directly to the edit page for an item, or to navigate to a page that contains web parts that are filtered by certain query string parameters.

Business Data Actions are only created by an administrator from within the ECT in Central Administration. In the Business Data Connectivity Service application, click the name of any ECT to see its detailed information page. This configuration screen contains the list of existing actions, and the Ribbon has buttons that allow for the creation, modification, and deletion of any of them. Figure 15-17 displays the default View Profile action that exists in an ECT.

Name Type a name for the action.	Action Name View Profile
URL Type the URL to navigate to when you click on the action. If you want the URL to vary depending on the item to which it applies, add one or more parameters, then assign a property to each parameter below. Type a number in braces such as {0} where you want to insert a parameter in the URL.	Navigate To This URL http://lcaweb.contoso.com:80/BCSPROI Example: http://example.com/edit.aspx?id={0} Launch the action in a new Web browser window (applies to External Data Web Parts only): Yes No
URL Parameters Assign a property to each parameter in the URL.	Parameter Property 0 SalesKey [Identifier] Remove Add Parameter
Icon Choose an icon to display next to the action.	No icon Standard icon Delete The image at this URL /_layouts/1033/images/viewprof.gif
Default action Select the check box if you want this to be the default action.	Default action

FIGURE 15-17

The following is a list of the fields to fill out when creating a new action:

- **Action Name:** This is the text that is displayed on the Action button.
- **URL:** The URL will always include a query string parameter, just like the "Example" text that is displayed in the URL box.
- **URL Parameters:** Since the URL will need to include a query string, the URL parameters must be defined in order to match each parameter with a field in the data source. In this example, the SalesKey is the parameter, so when `"SalesKey=a value"` is included in the URL, the number is equivalent to a specific sales item. Where the brackets {0} are inserted into the URL will be the location of the SalesKey.
- **Icon:** This is the icon that will represent this action, and it will be displayed on the button next to the action name. Use a URL to an image. The example includes a URL pointing to a location on the SharePoint server.
- **Default action:** Check this box to indicate if this should be the default in the list of Actions.

WORKING WITH BCS

Once external content types and external lists have been created, there are several different ways that they can be utilized within SharePoint. BCS data can be taken offline using Outlook or SharePoint Workspace, and interactive interfaces to the data can be created using the BCS web parts. There are many possibilities for the creation of custom business solutions, all without needing to write any code.

Accessing BCS Data from Outlook 2010

There are certain types of SharePoint lists that can be connected to Outlook and taken offline. These lists are Contacts, Tasks, Calendars, and Discussion Boards. The ECT that was created at the beginning of this chapter was created as the default Generic List, which is the equivalent of a custom list in SharePoint, and cannot be connected to Outlook. Now, with Business Connectivity Services, each ECT can be created as one of the following list types:

- **Generic List:** Custom list, cannot be connected to Outlook
- **Appointment:** Can be connected as an Outlook Calendar
- **Contact:** Can be connected as Outlook Contacts
- **Task:** Can be connected as Outlook Tasks
- **Post:** Can be connected as a Discussion Board in Outlook 2010

The ability for business users to work on database data offline is quite powerful. Think about systems such as those used in customer relationship management (CRM) and the ability to use those contact lists or filtered subsets of them in daily activities within Outlook.

TRY IT OUT Connect to BCS Data in Outlook

In this Try It Out, you will learn how to create an ECT as a SharePoint list of contacts, and then connect it to Outlook. When ECTs are created as an Office Item Type other than Generic List, there is an interface to map the database information to fields that exist for that item type. In this example, an ECT will be created from a list of stores in SQL, and table fields will be mapped to pertinent contact fields. When the list of the company's stores is readily accessible to business users, they will always have the current updated information at their fingertips and will not have to rely on lists sent around in email, or spreadsheets that are occasionally updated.

1. Open SharePoint Designer 2010, and open your SharePoint site.
2. Click External Content Types in the list of Site Objects on the left side of the screen.
3. At the top of the screen, in the New section of the Ribbon, click the External Content Type button.
4. Click the Name, and change it from New External Content Type to **Stores**.
5. Select the Office Item Type of Contacts, as shown in Figure 15-18, and leave the default Offline Sync for external list as Enabled. When a list is enabled for offline sync, it can then be used within Outlook and SharePoint Workspace and taken offline.
6. Click the link that says "Click here to discover external data sources and define operations."

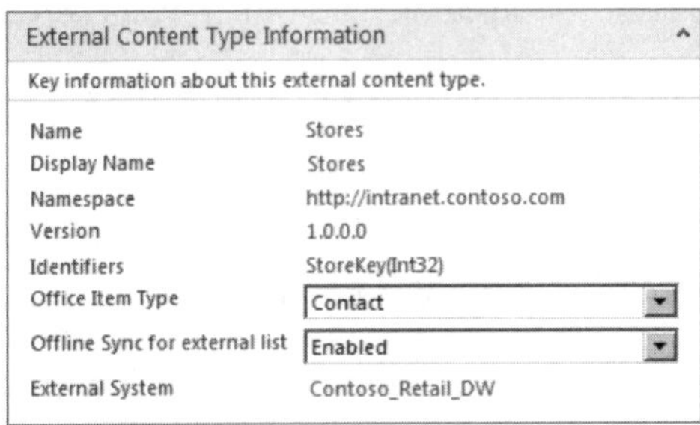

FIGURE 15-18

7. Since an ECT was already created in the first Try It Out, the Contoso_Retail_DW database will already be displayed in the Data Source Explorer, with the list of tables already expanded.
8. Right-click on the table called DimStore, and click Create All Operations.
9. The Operations Properties screen explains what all of the different operations are. Click Next.
10. This Parameters Configuration interface is where you granularly map table fields to SharePoint contact fields. Uncheck the box called Data Source Elements at the top of the screen, so that all of the element checkboxes are unchecked. You will only add the necessary ones, as indicated in the following table. This table also lists the field to select in the Office Property drop-down box for each field.

FIELD NAME	OFFICE PROPERTY	OTHER CHECKBOXES
StoreKey	Custom Property	Map To Identifier Read Only
SalesTerritoryKey	Custom Property	
StoreName	Full Name	Show in Picker

FIELD NAME	OFFICE PROPERTY	OTHER CHECKBOXES
StoreDescription	File As	
Status	Office Location	
OpenDate	Creation Time	
StateProvinceName	Business Address State	Show in Picker
CityName	Business Address City	Show in Picker
ZipCode	Business Address Postal Code	Show in Picker
StorePhone	Business Telephone Number	Show in Picker
StoreFax	Business Fax Number	Show in Picker
AddressLine2	BusinessAddressStreet	
UpdateDate	Custom Property	Timestamp Field

11. After all of the fields have been configured as indicated in the preceding table, there will be no more errors or warnings. Click Next.
12. Click Add Filter Parameter.
13. Click the (Click to Add) link on the right.
14. Change the Filter Type to Limit, and click OK.
15. For the Default Value, type 100, and click Finish.
16. Click Save at the top left.
17. Click the Create Lists and Form button on the Ribbon.
18. Click the Create Profile Page button on the Ribbon.
19. Click the Go To List button on the Ribbon, and then click the F12 key to open the list in the browser.
20. Now that the list has been created as a SharePoint contact list, it can be connected to Outlook. In the browser, click the List tab in the Ribbon, and click the Connect To Outlook button.
21. The first time you connect an external list to Outlook, an Outlook add-in called the Business Connectivity Services add-in will be installed. If a screen called the Microsoft Office Customization Installer pops up, click the Install button.

The Stores database table is now a contacts list in Outlook! There will be a new section in the Navigation Pane on the left side of Outlook, called SharePoint External Lists, with the new contact list listed. Figure 15-19 shows the Stores as seen in Outlook.

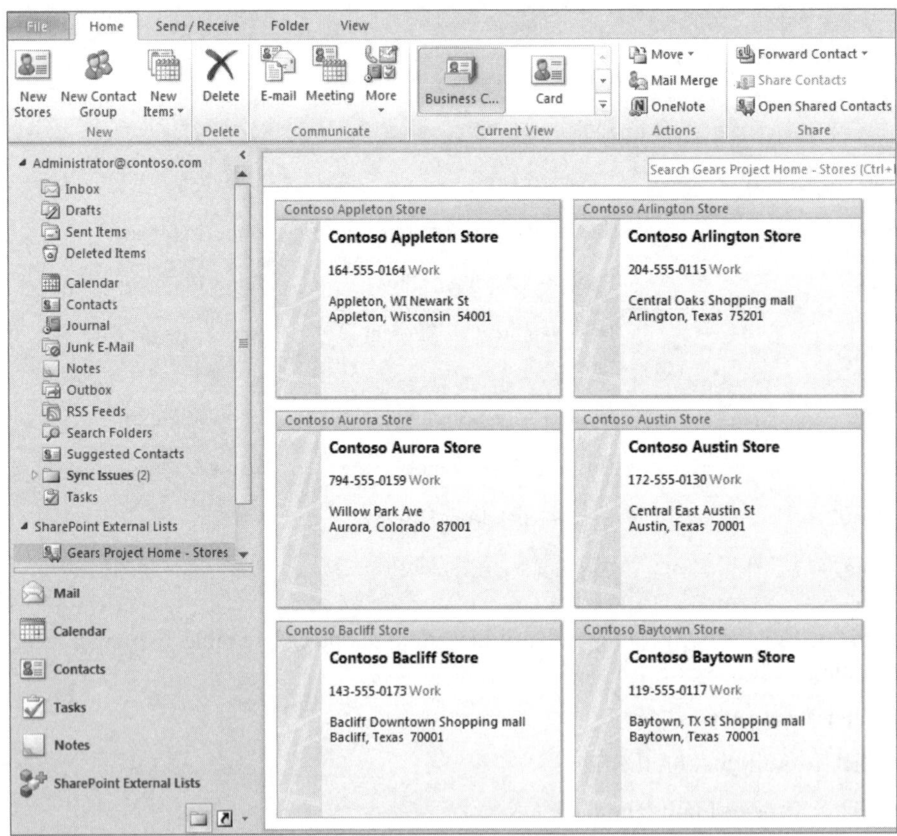

FIGURE 15-19

Using BCS Associations

Earlier in this chapter, a high-level explanation of associations was given. In this section, you will learn how to create them, and why. This section contains more information about the context in which associations are created, and the effects of existing associations on web parts.

TRY IT OUT Creating an Association

In this Try It Out, you will learn how to create a new association between two ECTs. In previous demonstrations, you have conveniently created two content types that happen to have a common "lookup" field. You have a Stores table, and a Sales table, with a common field called StoreKey. For each record in the Stores table, there are multiple records in the Sales table. Follow these steps in order to create an association with the Stores ECT from within the Sales ECT.

1. In SharePoint Designer, open your site, go to the list of External Content Types, and click to open the Sales ECT.
2. Click the Operations Design View button on the Ribbon.

3. This is the screen where CRUD (create, read, update, and delete) operations can be performed, allowing data to be added, edited, or removed. Right-click the FactSales table in the Data Source Explorer, and choose New Association, as shown in Figure 15-20.

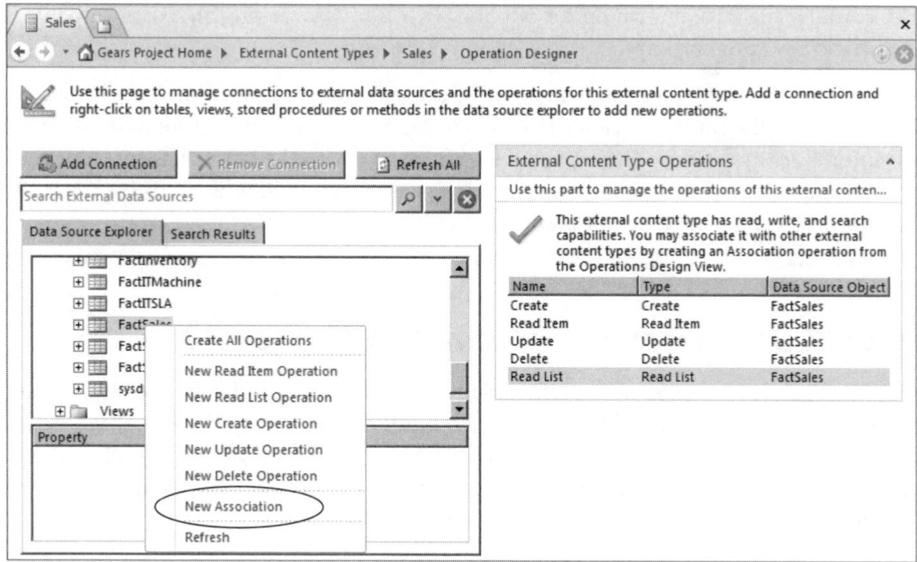

FIGURE 15-20

4. Click the Browse button, select the name of the Stores ECT, and click OK.

5. The section in the middle of the Association Properties page that is used to map the identifiers is already filled in with the matching field in this case, which is StoreKey. Click Next.

6. On the Input Parameters Configuration screen, click on the StoreKey field on the left, and check the Map to Identifier checkbox, as shown in Figure 15-21. Click Next.

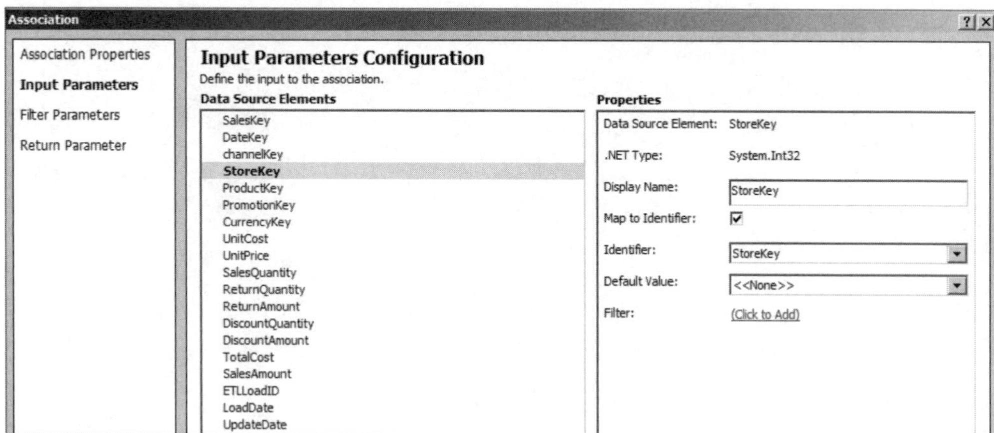

FIGURE 15-21

7. Add a limit filter, using the same steps as in steps 20 through 22 when the ECT was created. Click Next.

8. The Report Parameter Configuration can be left with the defaults. Optionally, select the name of each data source element to change the display name or configure other options. Click Finish.
9. Click Save.
10. Click the Create Profile Page button on the Ribbon. If you're overwriting an existing profile page, it's okay to click Yes at the prompt.

Now that the association has been created, it will not be apparent until the BCS web parts are used, especially when looking at the Business Data item. When a specific store detail is viewed, all of that store's sales are automatically displayed on the profile page along with the store. This profile page is also seen when the BCS data is displayed in SharePoint search results. You will get to see the result of the association creation in the section entitled "Using the BCS Web Parts."

Accessing BCS Data from SharePoint Workspace 2010

SharePoint Workspace 2010 is part of the Office Suite of applications and is used to take SharePoint data offline. Business users who travel frequently or remote workers who have less reliable network connections will find this tool invaluable. Not only can SharePoint lists and libraries be taken offline and changes synchronized when you're back on the network, but now the BCS allows you to take external lists offline to work on them from wherever you are.

SharePoint custom lists, and external lists that are created as Generic Lists, cannot be taken offline in Outlook, but they *can* be taken offline and synchronized using SharePoint Workspace. Figure 15-22 shows an external list as viewed from within SharePoint Workspace.

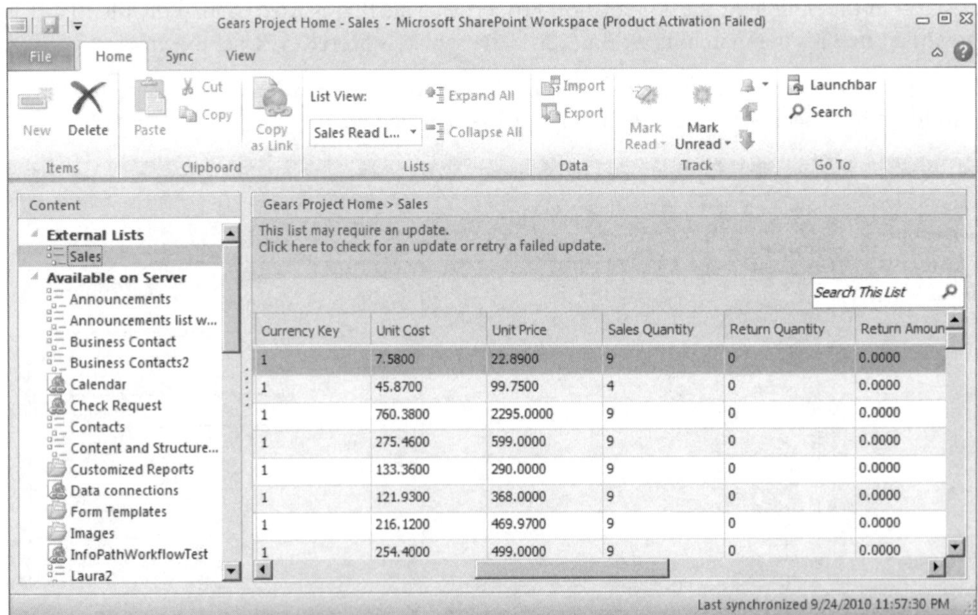

FIGURE 15-22

Using the BCS Web Parts

There are several out-of-the-box web parts that can be used in order to display data from ECTs. Inherently, these web parts are *not* related to the external lists at all, and are only associated with ECTs. In other words, externals lists do not need to exist in order to make use of these web parts.

Business Data List

Use this web part to display a list of data from a single ECT. The information is shown as a table on the page. The web part settings allow for the selection of an existing ECT in the Type box.

There is a drop-down box called View, where an existing view may be selected. Since these web parts are not related to external lists, any views that have been created at the list level will not be shown here. This list of "views" is really the list of Read List Operations that have been defined in the ECT.

TRY IT OUT Using the Business Data List Web Part

In this Try It Out, you will learn how to use the Business Data List web part. Not only will you practice inserting it on the page, but you will also learn about the capabilities of the View drop-down box, for filtering information. First, you will walk through adding this web part to a page, and then you will add a new "view" in the ECT. Once this new "view" (read list operation) has been created, it will be available as an option in the web part properties.

1. Pick a page on your SharePoint site with which to test these web parts. Click Site Actions and choose Edit Page.
2. Click to insert a web part on the page. In the list of web part categories on the left, click Business Data. Click the Business Data web part, and click the Add button.

NOTE *For more information and instructions on how to add a web part to a page, please refer to Chapter 7.*

3. Now that the empty Business Data List web part has been added to the page, click the link to Open the tool pane.
4. You will use the Stores ECT that you created earlier in this chapter. There are two buttons next to the Type box in the Web Part tool pane, as shown in Figure 15-23. Type the name, or pick the Stores ECT from the list.
5. At the bottom of the web part tool pane, click OK.
6. Notice that by default, the web part is extremely wide, as it displays all of the columns from the ECT. Click the Edit View button at the top right of the web part, as shown in Figure 15-24, so that the list of displayed columns may be modified.

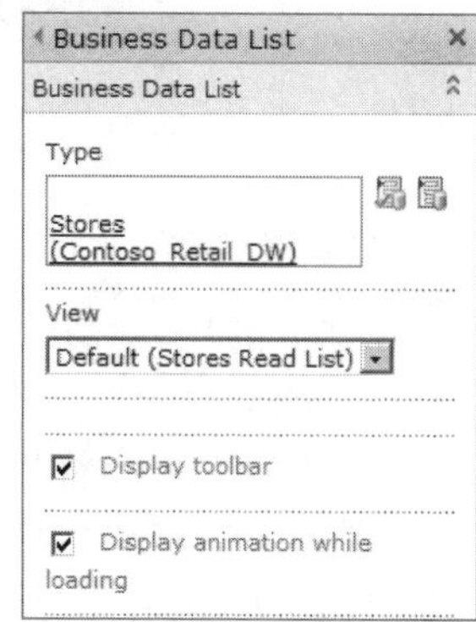

FIGURE 15-23

7. On the Edit View screen, deselect several columns in order to make the web part more narrow, and click the Title radio button next to Store Name. Click OK.

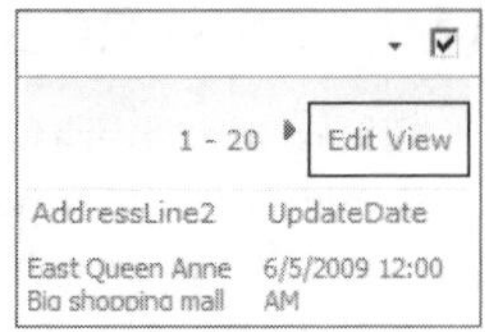

FIGURE 15-24

8. The next step is to add a new read list operation to the ECT. We want people to be able to quickly filter by a full or partial city name. Open the site in SharePoint Designer, and click External Content Types on the left.
9. Click to open the Stores ECT.
10. In the Ribbon, click the Operations Design View button.
11. In the Data Source Explorer pane, right-click the DimStore table, and click New Read List Operation.
12. Enter **Field Filter** as the Operation Name *and* the Operation Display Name. Click Next.
13. Click the Add Filter Parameter button.
14. As the Data Source Element, choose CityName from the drop-down box. Click the (Click to Add) link next to Filter.
15. On the Filter Configuration box, enter **City** as the Filter Name in the box called New Filter, and the Filter Type is Wildcard, as seen in Figure 15-25. Click OK.
16. In the Properties pane on the left, change the Default Value to <<Null>>.

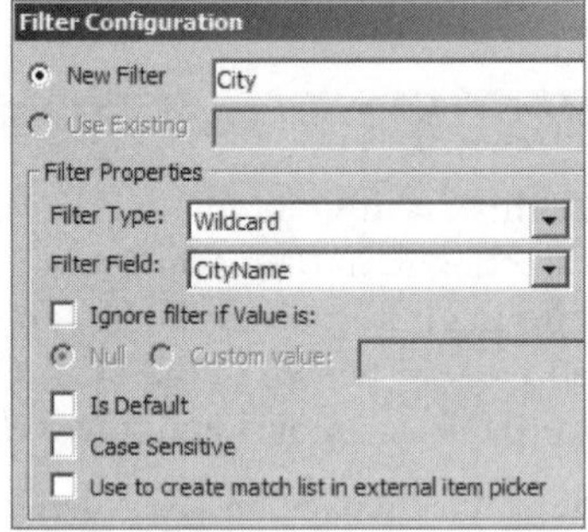

FIGURE 15-25

17. Click the Add a Filter Parameter button.
18. Click the (Click to Add) link next to Filter. Change the Filter Type to Limit and click OK.
19. Type **100** as the default value. The Filter Parameters Configuration screen is shown in Figure 15-26.

Filter Parameters Configuration
Configure filter parameters and default values to define the default behavior of the query and enable user customizations.

Filter Parameters

Operator	Element	Filter
	CityName	City: Wildcard
TOP	StoreKey	Filter: Limit

Properties

Data Source Element: CityName
.NET Type: System.String
Filter: City: Wildcard
Default Value: <<Null>>

FIGURE 15-26

20. Click Next.
21. Configure the Data Source Elements in the same manner as in step 10 of the earlier Try It Out, "Connect to BCS Data in Outlook." Click Finish.
22. Click Save at the top left, to save the ECT.
23. In the browser, look at the page where the Business Data List web part was added. Refresh the page, and then open up the Web Part tool pane. In the View drop-down box, notice that the new view, called Field Filter, is now an option. Select Field Filter and click OK.

The web part now has a new option at the top, which allows for a query to be done on the city name, as shown in Figure 15-27.

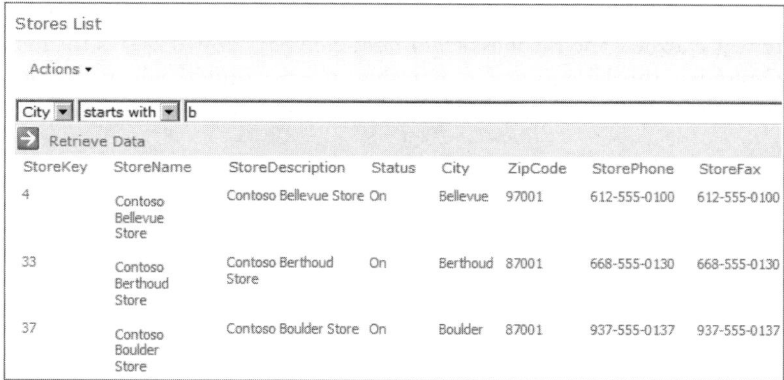

FIGURE 15-27

Try out this City filter by using different operations in the drop-down box, to see the way that the results are retrieved. If multiple fields need to be added in addition to City, you would repeat steps 13 through 16 for each additional field. Also, remember the BCS association that you created? Click the name of any store in the list to see its profile page, and notice that all the store's associated sales are listed on the page.

Business Data Item

This web part displays a single item from an ECT. The Web Part tool pane has settings to select the external content type and then optionally pick a specific list item. There is also a button to pick the fields that need to be displayed, as well as a button to select actions. The Item field does not have to be filled in, because the item to be displayed can be passed to this web part using a web part connection. Web part connections were covered in detail in Chapter 7.

TRY IT OUT The Business Data Item Web Part

In this Try It Out, you add the Business Data Item web part to the same page as the Business Data List web part. A web part connection will then be created between the two web parts, so that when an item in the list is clicked, the detailed information about that item will be displayed in the Business Data Item web part.

1. On the page where you added the Business Data List, click to add a new web part, and insert the Business Data Item web part on the same page.
2. In the Business Data Item Web Part tool pane, select Stores in the Type box. Leave the Item box blank.
3. Under Fields, click the Choose button. Take a look at the list of fields, and see that you can deselect items and rearrange them vertically. Click OK.
4. The next step is to create the web part connection. With the page in edit mode, click the drop-down arrow at the top-right corner of the Stores List web part. Click Connections ➪ Send Selected Item To ➪ Stores.

5. Click Save and Close at the top left of the page.

Each item in the Stores list will now have a new connection filter icon next to it. In Figure 15-28, the list has been filtered to show a subset of stores, and then the connection (double arrow) icon next to the Contoso Baytown Store was clicked. The Business Data Item web part now displays the details of that store on the page. Of course, the Title of any item in the store list could be clicked to see its profile page, but with this web part connection method, you do not have to navigate away from the current page.

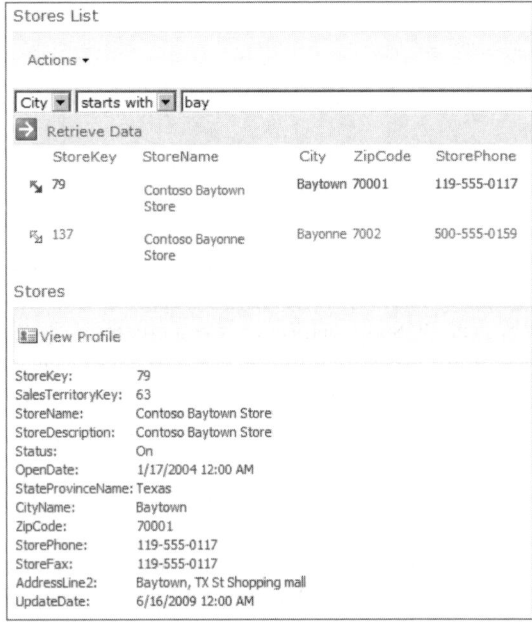

FIGURE 15-28

Business Data Actions

This web part displays a list of the actions associated with a specific external content type. It is simply a view of the links to the different actions for the ECT that is specified in the web part properties.

Business Data Connectivity Filter

This web part performs a filter using data that exists in an ECT. In the Web Part tool pane, pick an ECT. Optionally, pick a default record in the table. This web part is then meant to be connected to another web part on the page, to pass filters or parameters to it. The Business Data Connectivity Filter has no use if not connected to other web parts, using web part connections. This web part can be used to pass business data to web parts such as those that display SharePoint list or library data; it does not need to be used in conjunction with other Business Data web parts.

Business Data Item Builder

The Business Data Item Builder is used on a page in order to pass query string information from the URL to the web parts on the page. This web part automatically exists on all BCS profile pages. This web part is not seen unless the page is in edit mode, as it is only used to pass parameters and has no user interface. For example, once the profile page for the Stores ECT has been created, and an item name is clicked in a BCS web part, the URL for the profile page will have a query string. In this case, it is `"StoreKey = 4"`. The StoreKey is the unique identifier in the table. The Business Data Item Builder sees this unique StoreKey and can pass it to other web parts on the page through web part connections.

Business Data Related List

When associations have been created between external content types, they are considered "related lists." When the Business Data Related List web part is inserted on a page, it allows you to pick a list that is related to a BCS ECT that has been added to the same web part page. For example, if a page already contains a Business Data list of stores, and a Business Data Related List is inserted on the page, the only option for the source data will be the Sales ECT, since it is the only one that is related to Stores. A web part connection still needs to be created between the sales and stores web parts, to pass the filter information.

Chart Web Part

Chart web parts are new in SharePoint 2010 and were covered extensively in Chapter 7. One of the data source options that can be used is Connect to Business Data Catalog, which allows an ECT to be selected. Once the source has been selected, configure the X and Y axis and customize the way the chart appears visually. This web part was covered in detail with screenshots in Chapter 7.

Using the External Data Column

The external data column is a type of column that can be added to any list or library. Once external content types have been set up, create lookups to their data by adding external data columns.

TRY IT OUT Creating an External Data Column

Using the Stores ECT that you created in the Try It Out called "Creating an External Content Type," you will learn how to create an external data column in a document library. The scenario is a library full of company policies. Each policy can be associated with a specific company store. Once the document library has been created, you will create the lookup to the ECT.

1. On your SharePoint site, click Site Actions, and choose New Document Library.
2. In the Name box, type "Policies." Click Create.
3. Click the Add document button, and add a couple of example documents that can pose as company policies.
4. On the Library tab in the Ribbon, click the Create Column button.
5. Use the following table in order to fill out the fields on the Create Column screen, and then click OK.

FIELD	DATA
Column Name	Store
Type of information	External Data
Description	Pick a company store
External Content Type	Stores (Contoso_Retail_DW)
Select the Field to be shown	StoreName
Display the actions menu	Yes (checked)
Link this column to default action	Yes (checked)
Show each of these additional fields:	CityName, StateProvinceName, StorePhone
Add to default view	Yes (checked)

6. Hover over the name of the first document in the Policies library, and click Edit Properties.
7. In addition to the default fields like the file name and title, the new Store field will be displayed, as shown in Figure 15-29.

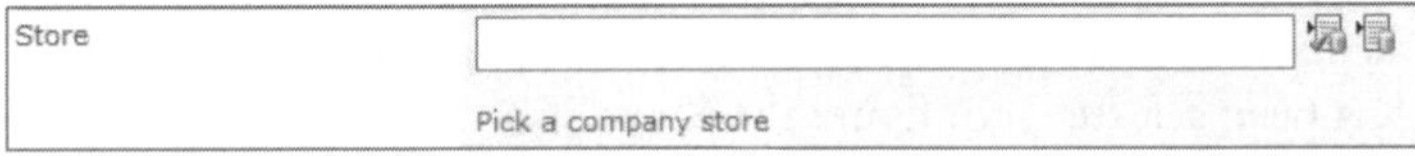

FIGURE 15-29

8. Type the name of a store, or use the item picker button on the far right in order to search for a store. Once any store has been selected, click to Save the document properties.

Notice that four of the Store table columns are shown in the document library and the row of the document you just edited displays all of the extra information about that store. Not only is the store name displayed, but the city, state, and phone number associated with that store are shown in their columns. These external data columns show live data, so that when the external system changes, the document library will automatically show that current information.

Earlier in this chapter, in the Try It Out titled "Creating an External Content Type," step 13 mentioned the checkbox for "Show in Picker." You can select this checkbox for each column of data. When you use an external column, this column is filled in for the list items, and data is looked up in the ECT. The interface for the selection of data is similar to that of the people picker control. In Figure 15-30, the field is being filled out with "Seattle"as the search term to find the correct store in the list. This interface is what is referred to as the picker, and was used in step 8 above if you clicked the item picker button.

NOTE *An external list is not required in order to use an external content type in an external data column.*

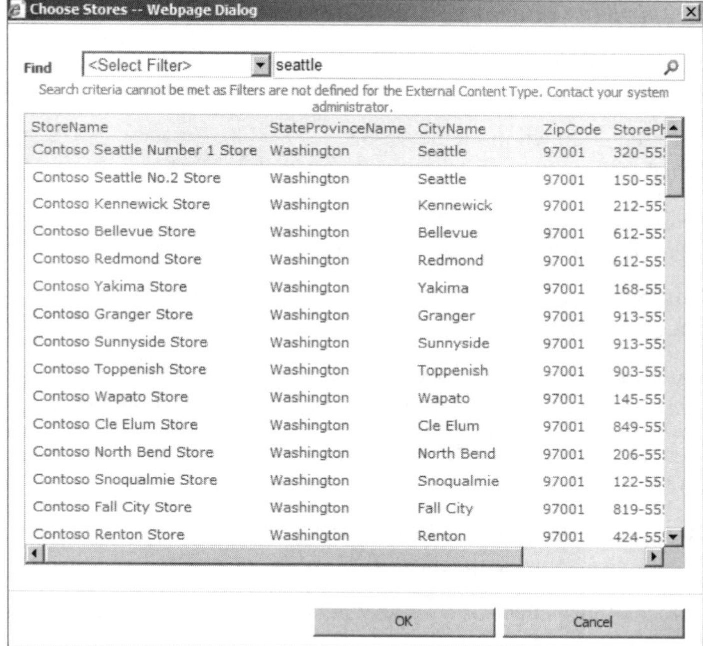

FIGURE 15-30

Using BCS Data in Office Applications

External data columns that have been created in libraries can be utilized within Office applications such as Word and Excel. The Document Information Panel and Quick Parts were first introduced in SharePoint 2007, and they still have very powerful capabilities when it comes to Office integration with SharePoint. In this section, you will learn about these points of integration, the differences, and how they can be utilized in business examples.

The Document Information Panel is a small panel that displays a document library's metadata inside of the associated Office application. All columns associated with a library are editable in this panel. Just as with any other columns, business data is also surfaced inside of the Document Information Panel.

TRY IT OUT BCS Data in Microsoft Word

In this Try It Out, you will continue with the concept of a company policy library. You added the external data column to the library in the last Try It Out, so this example will involve working with this external data from within Word 2010. If you have not uploaded a Word document to the Policies library, do so before following these steps:

1. The Document Information Panel is not necessarily going to be displayed by default, inside of the files in the library, so the first step is to set the library up to always display it. In the Library tab of the Policies library, click Library Settings.
2. In the General Settings section, click Advanced Settings.

3. Set Allow management of content types to Yes, and click OK.
4. Still on the Library Settings screen, in the Content Types section, click the name of the Document content type.
5. The Content Type Information screen is shown in Figure 15-31. Click Document Information Panel settings.
6. Check the box labeled Always show Document Information Panel on document open and initial save for this content type. Click OK.
7. Click Policies in the breadcrumb trail at the top of the screen, to navigate back to the main screen of the library.

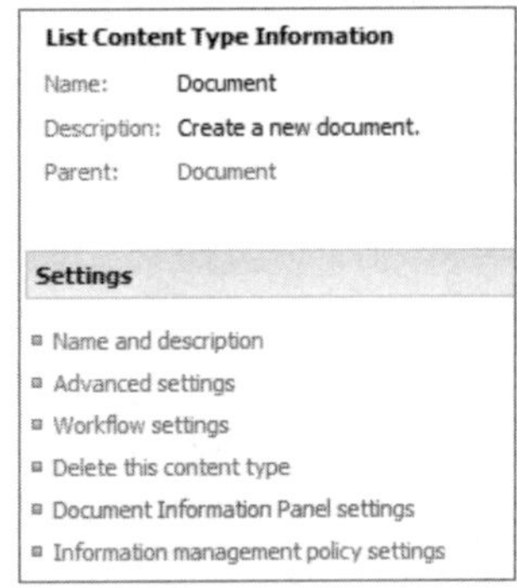

FIGURE 15-31

8. Click the Add Document button in the library, in order to upload a new document to the library. Browse to a document, double-click to select it, and upload it.
9. A screen containing editable document properties will be displayed. In the Store box, select the name of any store. Click Save.
10. Click the drop-down box on the name of the new document in the library, and select Edit in Microsoft Word. If an information message pops up, click OK.
11. Take a look at the Document Information Panel, shown in Figure 15-32. The store information fields are displayed in it.

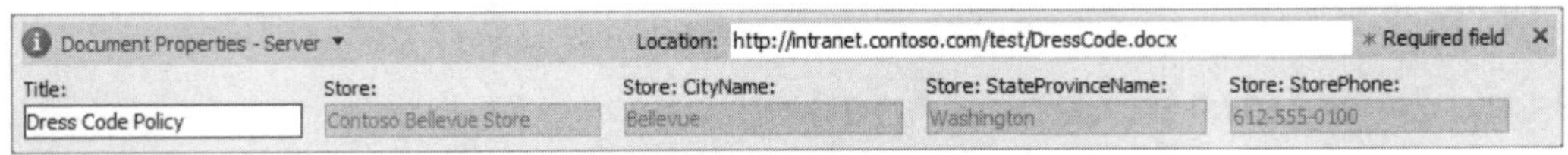

FIGURE 15-32

Now that you've seen how the external data is displayed inside a Word document, the next step is to try out the Quick Parts in Word. The Document Information Panel is limited to a read-only interface, and the information does not follow the document when it is printed or emailed out.

In the example of company policies, companies typically use a standard template, such as one with company colors or a logo. You will now learn how to quickly customize the library's document template and insert the external business data into the document.

1. On the Library tab in the Policies library, click Library Settings.
2. In the Content Types section, click the name of the Document content type.
3. Click Advanced Settings, and in the Document Template section, click the link that says (Edit Template).
4. A blank Word document is displayed. This is the template that can be customized with company colors and logo. In this simple example, we will simply insert some business data into the document. At the top of the document, type the word **Store:** and then a tab.
5. On the Insert tab in the Ribbon, click the Quick Parts button, as shown in Figure 15-33.

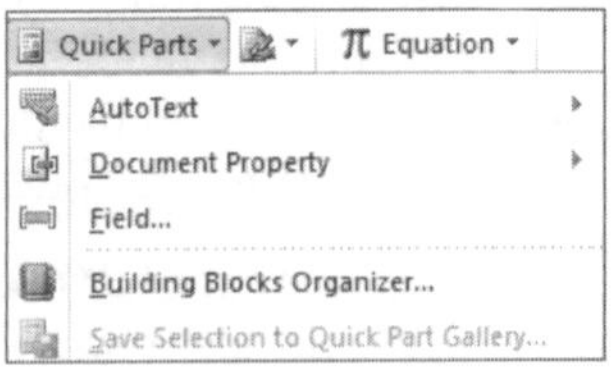

FIGURE 15-33

6. Select Document Property, and a list of all of the document's fields will fly out to the side. Notice that all of the newly added Store columns are in the list. Click Store.
7. On the next line in the document, type **City:** and a tab. Insert the Quick Part called Store:CityName.
8. Repeat step 7 for the store's state and phone number fields, so that the document looks like Figure 15-34.
9. Close the document template and click Save.
10. On the Advanced Settings screen, click OK.
11. Navigate back to the main screen of the document library, and on the Documents tab, click the New Document button.
12. In the gray Quick Part next to the word Store, use the External Data Picker to select the name of a store.

FIGURE 15-34

As soon as a store has been selected, see that the other three fields are automatically filled in with the extra data about that store. At this point, the business user would then fill in the rest of the company policy text in the body of the document, give it a title, and save it. The information in the Quick Parts will always be live data from the external system as long as this file is in the library. The document can be emailed outside of the company, and the Quick Parts will retain their information, but they will not be dynamically connected to the database anymore. Note that other fields from the document, such as the title and date, can also be inserted as Quick Parts. Figure 15-35 shows the final result of the policy document.

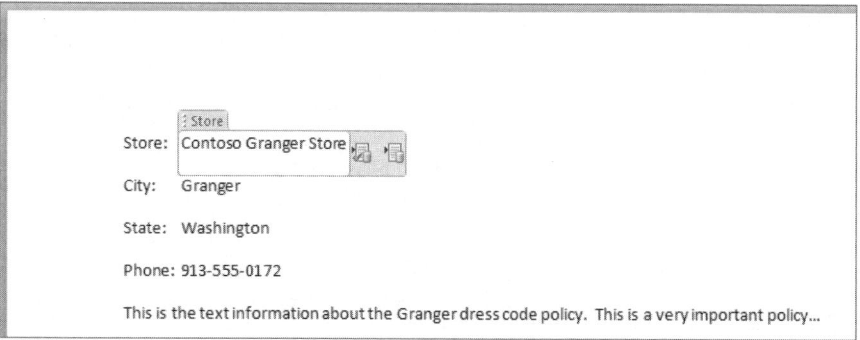

FIGURE 15-35

***NOTE** Note that in Office 2007, the document information panel will display the BCS data, but those fields are not editable from within that interface. Office 2010 will allow for both viewing and editing of these fields from within the application.*

FOR THE ADMINISTRATOR

For those who have administrator access in Central Administration, there are some additional interfaces to the BCS to note. Within the Search Service Application, there is a way to index BCS data. Also, in the User Profile Service Application, BCS data can be added as a secondary user profile data source. This section touches on topics that are pertinent to SharePoint Administrators. For information that is targeted to administrators, there is a book called *Professional SharePoint 2010 Administration* by Todd Klindt, Shane Young, and Steve Caravajal (Wrox, 2010) that goes into much more detail.

Searching BCS Data

When performing searches within SharePoint, there are several types of data that can be searched for. In addition to SharePoint sites, websites, file shares, and Exchange public folders, ECTs can be searched. This is simply another type of content source that the administrator can create in the search administration area. Once an ECT database has been added as a content source and crawled, relevant results will be included on the search results page. Just as with SharePoint results, the BCS data will be security trimmed, so that users will only see data results that they have access to.

In the search service application in Central Administration, look at the list of content sources. When a new content source is created, you can choose Line of Business Data as the content source type. This will allow for the selection of either all business data, or particular databases. Once the BCS source has been added and crawled, its items will be returned as part of regular search results. Figure 15-36 shows the creation of a new BCS content source.

Name Type a name to describe this content source.	Name: * BCS Data
Content Source Type Select what type of content will be crawled. Note: This cannot be changed after this content source is created because other settings depend on it.	Select the type of content to be crawled: SharePoint Sites Web Sites File Shares Exchange Public Folders Line of Business Data Custom Repository
External Data Source A Line of Business Data content source crawls external data sources defined in an Application Model in a Business Data Connectivity Service Application. Select whether to crawl all external data sources in the Business Data Connectivity Service Application, or include only selected external data sources. Crawl Rule: To create a crawl rule for an external data source, use the following pattern: bdc3://*ExternalDataSourceName*	Select the Business Data Connectivity Service Application: Business Data Connectivity Service Crawl all external data sources in this Business Data Connectivity Service Application Crawl selected external data source adventureworksdw Contoso_Inventory Contoso_Retail_DW SupplyChainSQL

FIGURE 15-36

Secondary User Profile Data

In situations where user profile information is stored in multiple systems and databases, it can all be brought together in SharePoint using the BCS. For example, an organization may store basic directory information about users in Active Directory. Then, their personnel information such as salary and performance information may be stored in a database that is external to SharePoint and Active Directory. As long as there is a field that exists that is unique to each user and is common between Active Directory and the other system, a new BCS connection can be created in order to bring in each user's associated information from that external source.

From within the User Profile Service Application's Configure Synchronization Connections page, once the main LDAP connection (such as Active Directory) has been created, BCS can be created as a secondary connection. When a new synchronization connection is created, pick the desired external content type. As shown in Figure 15-37, the next choice is whether the relationship is one-to-one, or one-to-many between Active Directory and the ECT. It is important that the field called Return items identified by this profile property contain a field that will match items in the two systems together.

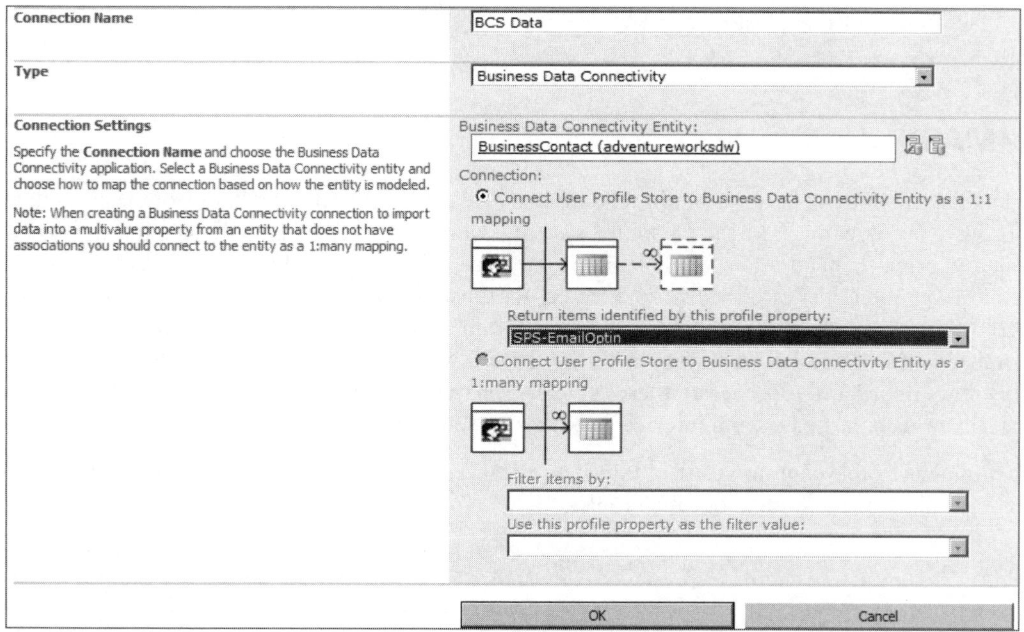

FIGURE 15-37

DEVELOPING CUSTOM SOLUTIONS FOR BCS

Custom Business Connectivity Services solutions can be developed using Visual Studio 2010. Custom development is not just for programmers, though. Custom BCS Solutions can be created as XSLT List View web parts in SharePoint Designer. These were previously referred to as Data View web parts. These custom web parts allow you to granularly format the way the information looks on the page, adding conditional formatting, grouping, sorting, and filtering.

Open your SharePoint site and external list in SharePoint Designer 2010. In the views section at the top right, click the New button to create a new XSLT list view. When the cursor is placed inside the table content in the middle of the page, a new section will appear in the contextual

Ribbon at the top, called List View Tools. This section of the Ribbon contains four tabs that contain all of the buttons that are needed for configuring the view: Options, Design, Web Part, and Table.

ADVANCED NO-CODE SOLUTIONS

Simple solutions can be put together using ECTs and external lists, without any custom code. On the other end of the spectrum, completely custom solutions can be created by developers using Visual Studio (VS) 2010. Using VS, a data source can be created as a .NET assembly. With a third-party product called BCS Meta Man, more advanced custom solutions can be created without writing any code. With this product, developers can save time by generating the BCS model and code visually, and then dig in and customize the code with VS if needed. This product allows a middle ground to be achieved, somewhere between out-of-the-box and totally custom-coded applications.

SUMMARY

Business Connectivity Services in SharePoint 2010 are the key to utilizing data from various data silos in your company. Take the personnel system, sales database, and patient accounting system, and bring them all into a single familiar interface, which is SharePoint. ECTs with external lists are web interfaces into the live back-end data. Once the proper security and authentication methods have been implemented, BCS gives you wonderful tools to make the organization much more streamlined and efficient. Use the Business Data web parts, external data columns, and even workflows in order to incorporate these typically separated islands of data into all of the familiar SharePoint web part pages and interfaces that the business users are accustomed to.

The following table contains a list of Internet references. These sites can be used in order to obtain more detailed information about BCS topics.

SITE NAME	URL
BCS Resource Center	`http://technet.microsoft.com/en-us/sharepoint/ee518675.aspx`
BCS Team Blog	`http://blogs.msdn.com/b/bcs/`
BCS Information on MSDN	`http://msdn.microsoft.com/en-us/library/ee556826(office.14).aspx`

EXERCISES

1. Chris is in the company's marketing department. He has created a custom list on the departmental SharePoint site. He would like to create a lookup column in this list, to show the list of the company's products. This data already exists in a SQL database. How can he go about creating this lookup?

2. Lori is a project manager and has created two external content types in SharePoint Designer. One ECT is a list of projects, and the other is a list of all tasks. Each task is related to one project. How can Lori create the relationship between the two lists in SharePoint?

3. Charlotte would like to use a query string in a URL and pass this information to several Business Data web parts on a page. Which out-of-the-box web part will allow her to do this?

4. The project managers have a list of project tasks in a database. They would like to be able to view and work on these tasks from within Outlook, in the familiar interface. How can they accomplish this?

5. The IT department would like to allow users to create change requests in a help desk ticketing system that exists in a SQL database. Each change request should go through an approval process before it can be entered in the database. What is a method that can be used to accomplish this?

▶ WHAT YOU LEARNED IN THIS CHAPTER

TOPIC	KEY CONCEPTS
Are development skills required?	Business Connectivity Services can be used by anyone in order to bring external systems into SharePoint. Programming knowledge is not required in order to do this.
How are people given access to BCS data?	There are several levels of security permissions and authentication to work through. This can easily be considered the most complicated part of setting up the BCS.
Profile pages	These can be created for each ECT. This is a read-only interface that simply shows a detail view of a single item in the ECT.
Associations	Can be created between multiple ECTs in the BCS. Define common fields between the tables on the Operation Design View of the external content type in SharePoint Designer.
Web parts	There is a set of Business Data web parts that can be inserted on web part pages. These web parts can display ECT data of your choosing, and can even be connected to each other to pass filters or parameters.
External data columns	Use an external data column in any SharePoint list or library, as a lookup column to data that does not exist in SharePoint.

16

Business Intelligence and Insights

WHAT YOU WILL LEARN IN THIS CHAPTER:

- The different types of business intelligence tool sets available in SharePoint
- Work with the out-of-the-box business insight features to configure charts, graphs, and spreadsheets
- Use Visio to publish content to a Visio Services web part

Business intelligence (BI) and insights are the ways that you can help provide tools that bring information directly to the users through a single interface. There are several different concepts that you will dig into throughout this chapter. We will look at how to get started and how to start bringing immediate value to the organization. In case you are just getting started with business intelligence, we will also look at ways to progressively incorporate these features into your organization. Once you have completed this chapter, you should have a good handle on the following topics:

- Defining business intelligence
- Working with Excel Services
- Using the Chart web part
- Working with Visio Services
- Working with KPI features
- Understanding PerformancePoint features

GETTING STARTED

The first step to getting started with business insights is understanding what they are and how you are planning to use them within your organization. Business insights is a very common buzz phrase, the type that your CEO will hear in a demonstration and march directly into your office explaining that you must have KPI and charts and dashboards and you need them immediately. While it is true that all of those things will bring value to the organization, it is also true that there must be a plan in place and an end goal in sight. Having charts to have charts is never going to provide any business value. Instead, having charts that solve specific business problems or that provide information to a group of users will provide value and a return on investment. So, when faced with the CEO who has been bitten by the "demo bug," be sure to help him refocus what he has seen with your organization in mind. Once you have the end goal in mind, you can then select the tools to help you get there. The following list shows some common goals or phrases that can be used to describe different scenarios that can be resolved with the business insight tools within SharePoint. This list should give you some ideas and serve as a checkpoint that you can use to verify your goals.

- Show a visual representation of the task breakdown for our project.
- Show a visual indicator of issues that are present within a project, report, or collection of data.
- Provide information to the sales team from last year's sales numbers, so that they can make decisions for this year.
- Provide a single entry point into legacy business data so that users from one single location can drill into the specific information that they need for their current tasks.

There are many different reasons to deploy insights within your environment. The key thing is that you understand your end goal and then work together with the business to provide the proper tool set to meet their specific needs. The tools available within SharePoint, specific to insights are:

- **Chart web parts:** These web parts allow you to easily create a visual representation of list data or data from Excel Services. These web parts can be added to pages to create a dashboard.
- **KPI lists and web parts:** These lists and web parts allow you to configure specific items that you want to monitor through performance indicators. As an example, you could be notified when more than one task in a task list is overdue.
- **Visio Services web part:** This web part allows you to display a Visio document directly within a web part.
- **Excel Services:** These features include web parts that allow you to display data from an Excel workbook directly within a SharePoint web part. Within this web part you can also configure parameters which allow the data to be displayed based on the selections of the user.
- **PerformancePoint:** The PerformancePoint features allow you to easily create dashboards based on date that are distributed across various enterprise systems.

Like most things in SharePoint, there is a level of progression when working with these features. If you are just getting started, it is recommended that you first start with the Chart web parts and the KPI lists. Once you are familiar with those elements, you should move on to Excel Services and

Visio Services. Finally, once you have become familiar with those elements you could begin working with the PerformancePoint features.

One final note that we should cover is the concept that working with PerformancePoint features will require the involvement of several key roles within the organization. The idea of PerformancePoint is that you are pulling data from many locations and bringing it together via dashboards and web parts. This is a great tool that can provide tremendous value to the organization. However, it is important to note that the quality of the data returned is dependent on the quality of the data that is available. Don't be surprised if part of your process of moving to a solution that utilizes PerformancePoint features also includes an element of restructuring and verifying your current data structure.

Throughout the rest of the chapter, you will be reviewing examples and learning the details of each of the components discussed above. You will start with the Chart web parts and end with PerformancePoint Services. Each section will build on various examples, which will show you how you can combine all elements together to build a solution for your users.

EXCEL SERVICES OVERVIEW

Excel Services is the tool within SharePoint that allows users to interact with Excel workbooks directly from the browser. These features allow a workbook to be published to a SharePoint library and then displayed using a collection of Excel Services web parts. These web parts allow you to build dynamic dashboards through web part connections. Before we get into the details of working with Excel Services within a SharePoint site, it would be good to cover some of the basics of Excel Services. Once you understand this basic foundation, you will be able to easily see how Excel Services can be combined to build business solutions. At the core level, Excel Services consists of the following three components:

- Excel Calculations Services
- Excel Web Access
- Excel Web Services

These three components work together to provide the overall end user experience. The Calculation Services engine is responsible for running all the calculations within the workbook. These calculations are run directly on the server without direct interaction from the users. This service is also responsible for maintaining sessions and refreshing data within each session. The web access components are the web parts that allow you to display the Excel information within SharePoint sites. These web parts also allow connections, allowing you to pass information to the web part that changes the data displayed, based on the input. Finally, there is the Web Services component. This component is new with SharePoint Server 2010 and provides an application programming interface (API) that can be used by developers that want to write custom applications to interact with the Excel workbook.

Once the workbook has been published to the SharePoint site, the site administrator can configure the web parts to display the Excel workbook. The Excel web parts can be configured to display the entire workbook or just a named region within the workbook. Once the workbook is displayed on the site, users can interact with it through preconfigured parameters. These parameters are created within Excel prior to its being published to the SharePoint site. Users will only be able to read the Excel document from the Excel web parts, but if they need to edit the content within the workbook, they can always use the Excel Office web application to make browser-based changes to the workbook.

Now that you have briefly covered the basics, you are going to work through the steps required to publish a workbook to SharePoint using Excel Services. You will start by publishing a workbook and then using a web part to display the workbook on a dashboard page. Once you have completed that, you will return to the workbook and add a named region and some parameters that you can use to filter the workbook from the dashboard. Finally, you will open the workbook using the Excel web app so that you can experience the process of users who have to edit the workbook through the browser.

Publishing an Excel Workbook

To get started, you will open an Excel workbook and then save it to a SharePoint library. When you use the Office Backstage view to save to the SharePoint library, you will see additional links for publishing options, as shown in Figure 16-1.

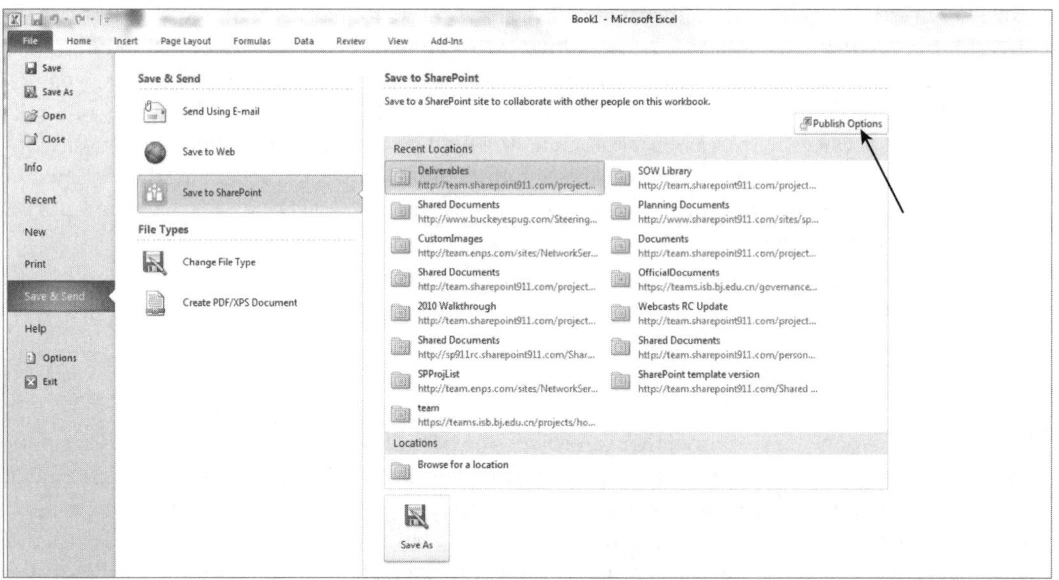

FIGURE 16-1

Since this book focuses on SharePoint, we are not going to spend a lot of time on configuring the workbook. Instead, you will use one of the Microsoft samples that comes with Excel 2010. This sample contains several pivot tables that you can use for the remainder of the examples. The first Try It Out in this chapter will be creating an Excel document based on this template.

TRY IT OUT Create a Site Using the Business Intelligence Template

The first thing that you will do in this chapter is create a site based on the Business Intelligence site template. You will do this from the Central Administration site; however, the steps can also be completed from any site that has the Enterprise Features enabled. You are creating this site collection so that you have a location to add content to for the remaining chapter demos.

1. Open the Central Administration site.
2. Select the Create Site Collections link within the Application Management grouping, as shown in Figure 16-2.

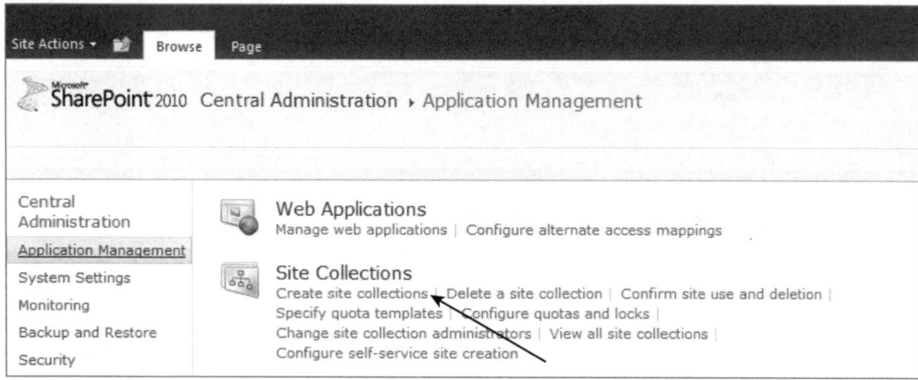

FIGURE 16-2

3. Enter the following properties for the new site collection as shown in Figure 16-3, and then click OK:

PROPERTY	VALUE
Web Application	Accept the default option, unless directed otherwise by your server administrator.
Title	Insights
Description	Location to create and store dashboards and reports.
URL	/sites/insights
Template Selection	Business Intelligence Center
Primary Site Collection Administrator	Your Username
Quota Template	No Quota

4. Click on the URL to open the new site collection. You will see that the site collection comes preconfigured with several different lists and libraries that are built to hold BI data, as shown in Figure 16-4.

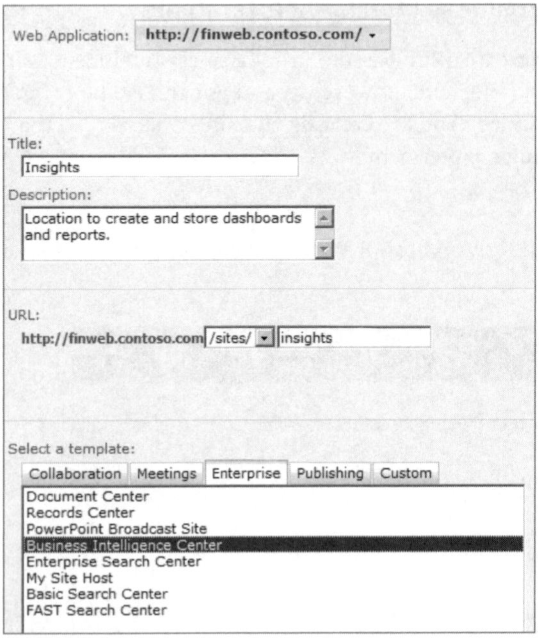

Web Application:
http://finweb.contoso.com/
Title:
Insights
Description:
Location to create and store dashboards and reports.
URL:
http://finweb.contoso.com
/sites/
insights
Select a template:
Collaboration
Meetings
Enterprise
Publishing
Custom
Document Center
Records Center
PowerPoint Broadcast Site
Business Intelligence Center
Enterprise Search Center
My Site Host
Basic Search Center
FAST Search Center

FIGURE 16-3

Site Actions
WINGTIP\Administra
Insights
I Like It
Insights
Dashboards
Data Connections
Libraries
PerformancePoint Content
Recycle Bin
All Site Content
Business Intelligence Center
The Business Intelligence Center enables you to collaborate, discover and manage the information you need to drive the business forward. With Business Intelligence, users are empowered with the right business insights enabling them to make informed decisions, and move the business forward, one activity at a time.
Monitor Key Performance
Use scorecards and status lists to track your progress towards goals more effectively. At a glance, your organization can see how it is performing and identify areas that require attention.
Build and Share Reports
Publish your Excel workbooks to SharePoint using Excel Services and let your team access and interact with their data in full fidelity. Use PerformancePoint Services analytic views to gain quick insights from your dashboards.
Create Dashboards
Use SharePoint to create rich, interactive dashboards that help you turn data into insights. Dashboard pages can include scorecards, Excel Services Reports, analytic views and other data-driven visualizations.

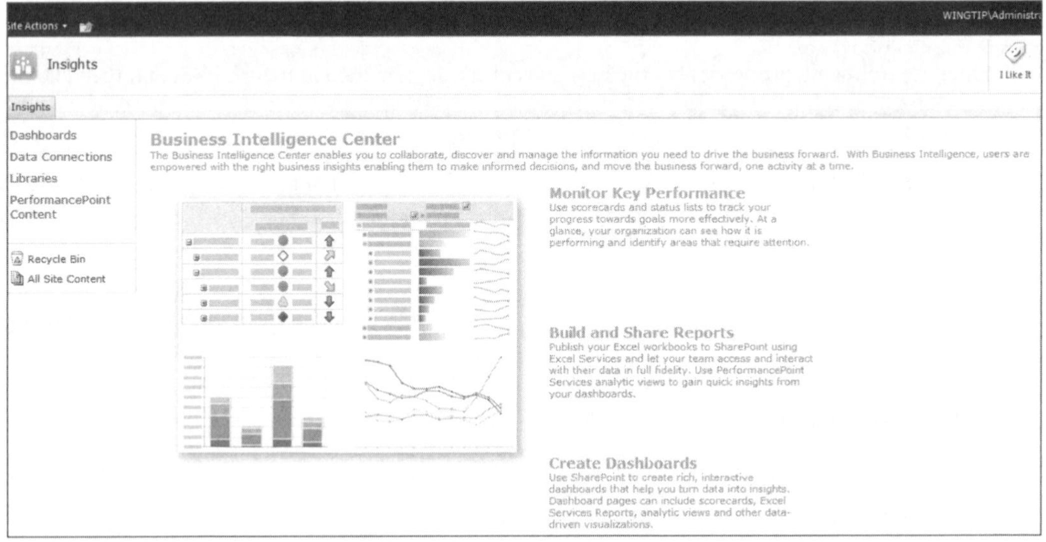

FIGURE 16-4

How It Works

When you create a site collection in Central Administration, you provide all of the details for your site collection and then the site is provisioned for you and a link is returned.

PUBLISHING TO THE BI TEMPLATE

In the example, you are publishing the Excel document to a site that was created using the BI template. This template has already been preconfigured with many of the features you will be using, including:

- Dashboards Library
- PerformancePoint Library
- Data Connections Library

We are doing this to expose you to the template; however, you could in theory publish to any team site where the publishing features have been installed and where the server administrators have marked the location as safe. If you are unsure if your site is considered a safe location for publishing, you can check with your server administrator. The steps used in the preceding example and throughout the rest of the chapter can be completed within any site collection.

TRY IT OUT Create and Publish an Excel Workbook to the SharePoint Library

In this Try It Out, you will be publishing an Excel document to the SharePoint site you created in the previous example. You will be starting in Excel and will complete the demo by viewing the published Excel document in the browser.

1. Open Excel from the Windows Start Menu.
2. Create a New Document based on the Sales Report sample template, as shown in Figures 16-5 and 16-6.
3. Once the sales template loads, take a few minutes to review the content in the document.
4. Select the File option to open the Backstage view.
5. Select the Save & Send menu option, shown in Figure 16-7, and select Save to SharePoint.
6. Select the Option to Browse for a location, and click Save As.
7. In the File Name field, enter the URL for the site collection that was created in the preceding example and press Enter. If prompted, enter your user credentials to gain access to the site collection.

8. When the site loads, double-click the Documents item to open the Documents library.

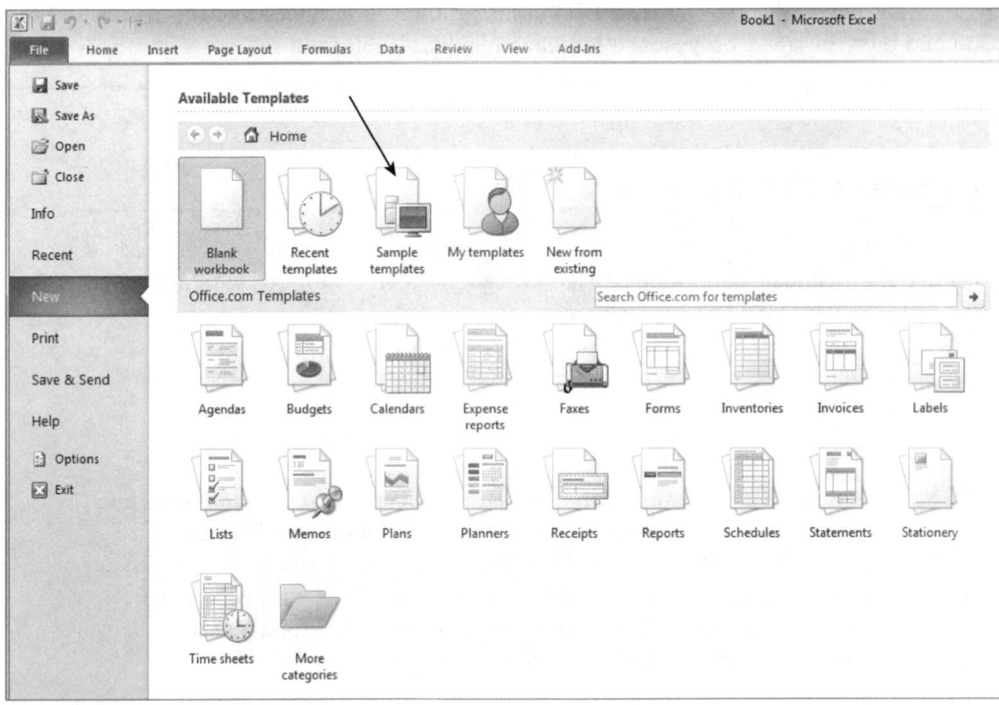

FIGURE 16-5

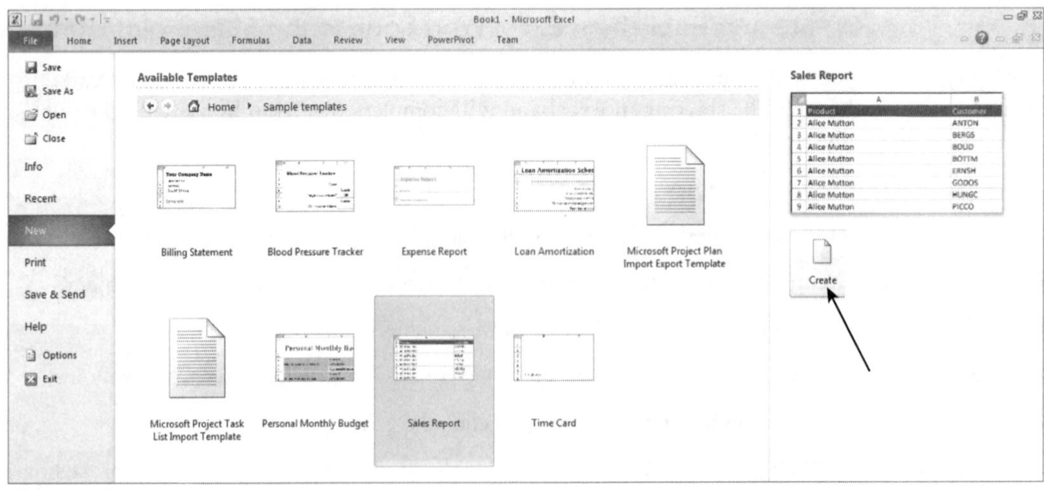

FIGURE 16-6

9. Click on "Publish Options . . ." to see the different settings you can configure for publishing. In this example, you are going to accept the default options. Select OK to close the options box.

10. Enter the file name of **Sales Report**, and click Save.

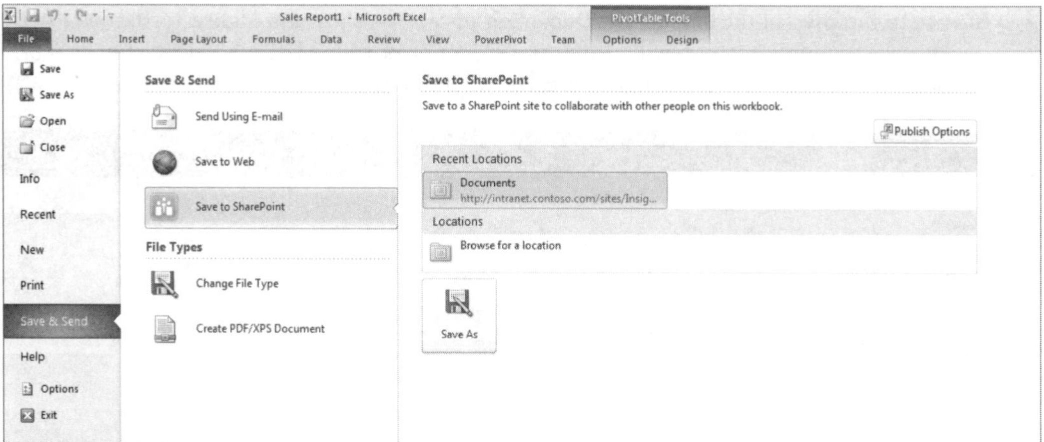

FIGURE 16-7

11. The document will be saved to SharePoint, and the browser view of the form will be opened for you to review, as shown in Figure 16-8.

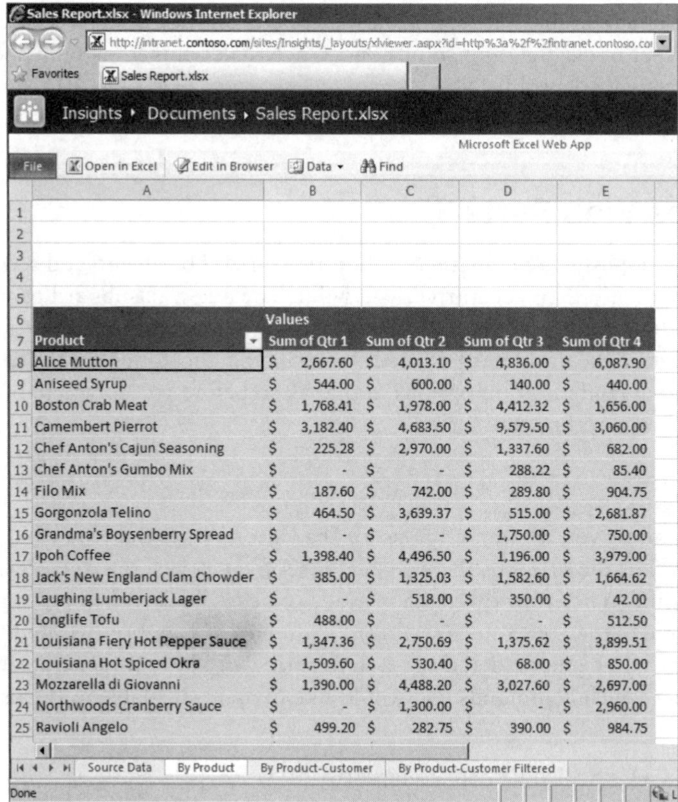

FIGURE 16-8

12. Browse to the URL of the SharePoint Document library, as shown in Figure 16-9, to verify that the document was uploaded. You will also notice a document called Excel Services Sample Workbook in your library. This is a sample that is created when the site is created.

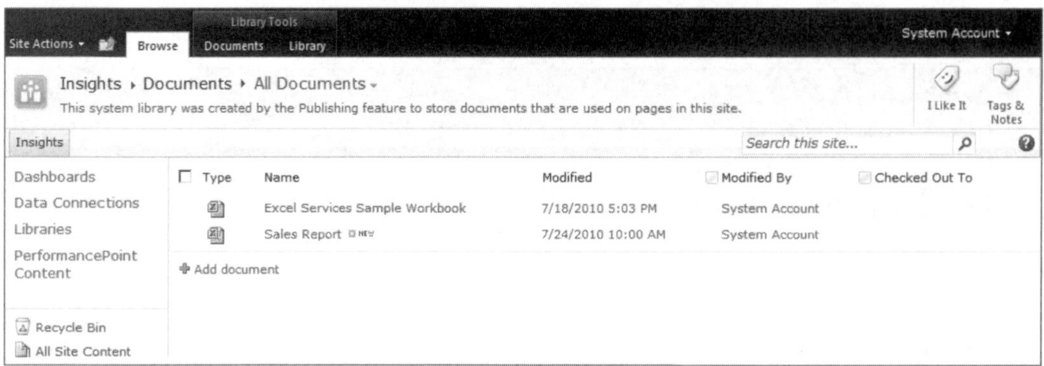

FIGURE 16-9

How It Works

When you select the option to save to SharePoint, Excel publishes the document to the SharePoint library using the configurations you set under the publish options. Once the document is published successfully, you will see a browser view displayed for you.

Using the Excel Services Web Parts

Now that you have the workbook published to a SharePoint library, you will be able to add a web part to display the workbook information. To get started, you will create a new dashboard page. A little later in the chapter we will discuss this in greater detail, but for now you are going to create it in order to get started. Once you have the dashboard created, you will add and configure the Excel workbook. There are many different configuration options available, so before you complete the examples, we will review the different options you have.

Toolbar and Title Bar

The toolbar and title bar options allow you to supply values for the various ways that you can configure the display of the web part. For the title bar, the web part is set to auto-generate the title and the link by default. If you would like to use your own title instead, you can deselect the option in this section and enter a custom title in the appearance settings. If you have this option selected, then the title in the appearance settings will be ignored and the web part title will be auto-generated. The toolbar options allow you to select which commands you would like to make available to the users and include the following options:

- Open in Excel, Download a Copy, Download a Snapshot
- Refresh Selected Connection, Refresh all Connections

- Calculate Workbook
- Named Item Drop-Down List

It is likely that each workbook you display using a web part could require a different combination of settings. By default, all the settings listed above are enabled, so if you don't want to use those features, you will need to update the configuration of your web part.

Navigation and Interactivity

The navigation and interactivity options allow you to configure how the users are able to navigate and interact with the workbook. The table that follows describes each of the different settings available for configuration.

OPTION	DESCRIPTION
Hyperlink	If enabled, users will be able to use hyperlinks from within the workbook. These hyperlinks could link to other locations in the workbook or other sites.
Workbook Interactivity	If disabled, users will not be able to interact with the workbook through the features described below. Disable this if you want a quick way to remove all interactivity.
Parameter Modification	If enabled, users will be able to modify the content using parameters.
Display Parameter Task Pane	If enabled, users will be able to access a parameter tool pane that allows them to easily switch between the worksheet parameters.
Sorting	If enabled, users will be able to sort ranges within the worksheet.
Filtering	If enabled, users will be able to filter various items within the worksheet.
All PivotTable Interactivity	If enabled, users will be able to expand and drill down through the pivot tables within the worksheet.
Periodically Refresh if Enabled in a Workbook	If enabled, the worksheet will refresh periodically. A notification will be present during a refresh.
Close Session Before Opening a New One	If enabled, the current workbook will be closed if a new one is opened. This setting is useful for performance considerations when many users are accessing the same workbook at the same time.

Standard Web Part Tool Pane Settings

The remainder of the configuration options are the standard web part properties. When working with Excel Services web parts, one of the most common web part settings used is located within the Appearance options. In many cases, you will want to manually configure the size of the web part so that your worksheet is displayed correctly on the page. Often the charts, tables, and graphs from the worksheet are larger than the default size of the web part, and when that occurs, scroll bars are displayed within the web part. To eliminate the need for the scroll bars, you can either shrink the content within Excel and republish the web part or you can configure the web part to be large enough so you don't need the scroll bars.

TRY IT OUT Create a New Dashboard

Within the Business Intelligence site template, dashboards can easily be created. These dashboards are basically web part pages that you can use to create dashboards. You are going to create a dashboard in this example so that you can have a location in which to add the Excel Services web part. Throughout the remainder of this chapter, you should refer to this exercise whenever you need to create an additional dashboard.

1. Open the site you created in this chapter's first Try It Out.
2. Select the Dashboards link in the Quick Launch Toolbar.
3. In the Documents Ribbon, select the New Document drop-down.
4. Select the New Web Part Page option, as shown in Figure 16-10.
5. Enter the following properties for the dashboard, as shown in Figure 16-11.

PROPERTY	VALUE
Name	ExcelServices
Choose a Layout Template	Header, Footer, 4 Columns, Top Row
Document Library	Customized Reports

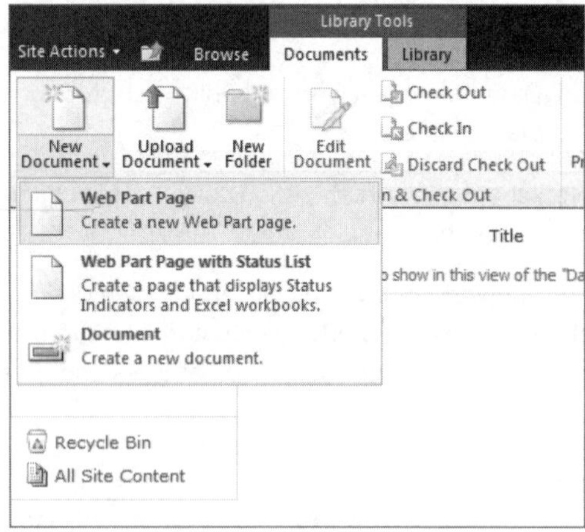

FIGURE 16-10

6. Click Create, and you will be directed to the new dashboard page, as shown in Figure 16-12.

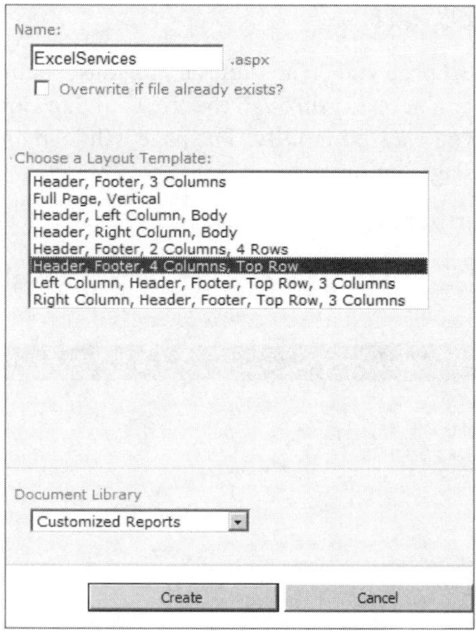

FIGURE 16-11

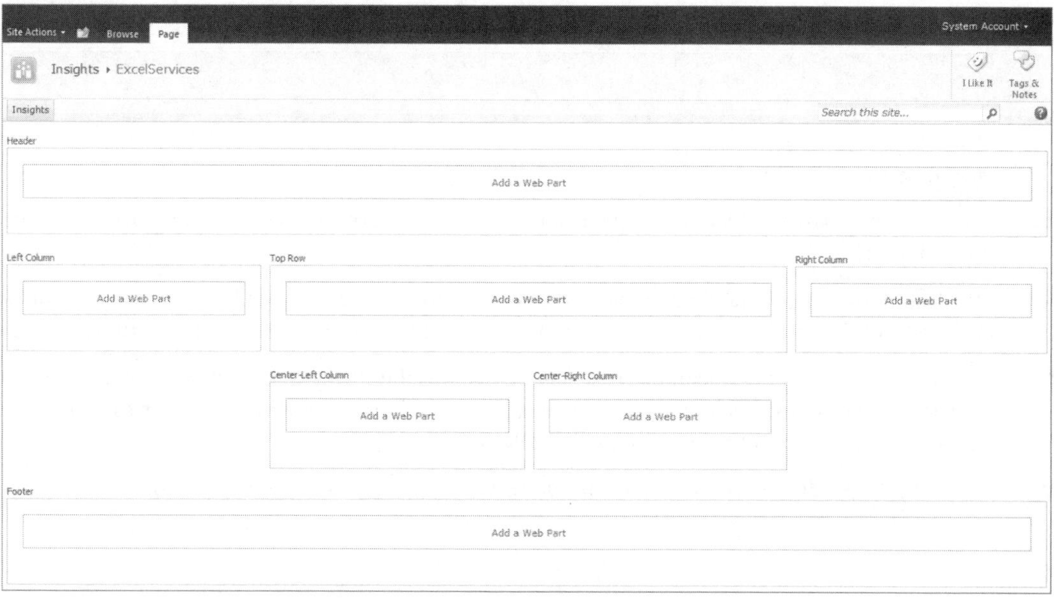

FIGURE 16-12

How It Works

A new dashboard page is created and stored in the Customized Reports library. You can access this page by accessing the library or by adding the link to the navigation.

TRY IT OUT Configure the Excel Services Web Part

In this Try It Out, you will add web parts to the dashboard page you created in the previous example. If you have already closed the page you created above, you can access it through the View all Site Content page. Once you open the library, you can select the item you want to modify. The page will load and then you can use the site actions menu to access the Edit Page option.

1. Click the Add Web Part option in any of the web part zones.
2. In the Business Data category list, select the Excel Web Access web part, as shown in Figure 16-13, and click Add.

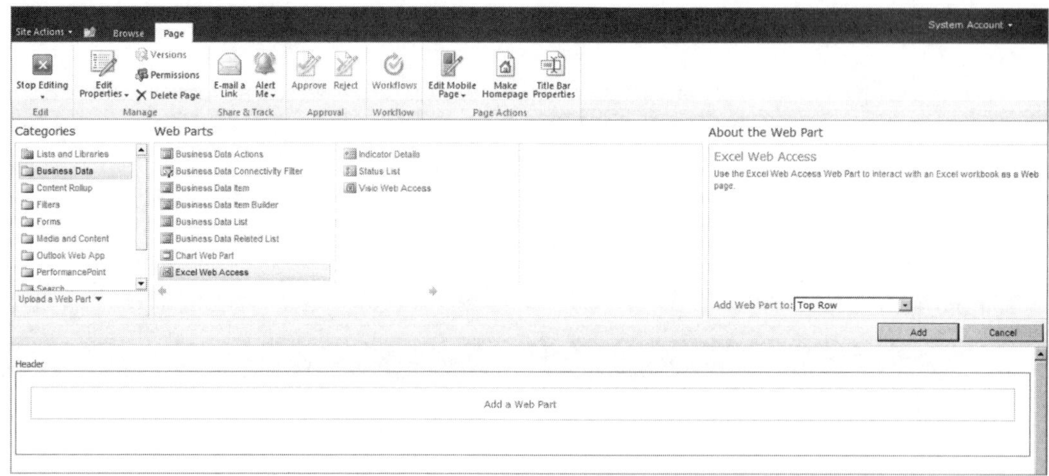

FIGURE 16-13

3. When the web part is added to the page, click the "Click here to open the tool pane" link within the web part.
4. Click the ellipse next to the Workbook field to browse for the location of the document you published in the previous example, as shown in Figure 16-14. Click OK once you have selected the document.
5. When you click OK, the document link will be displayed in the Workbook field. Notice the remaining tool pane options. Each of the options was described previously in detail. For this example, you will accept the default configuration. Click OK.
6. Select the Stop Editing option in the Ribbon to view the page as shown in Figure 16-15.

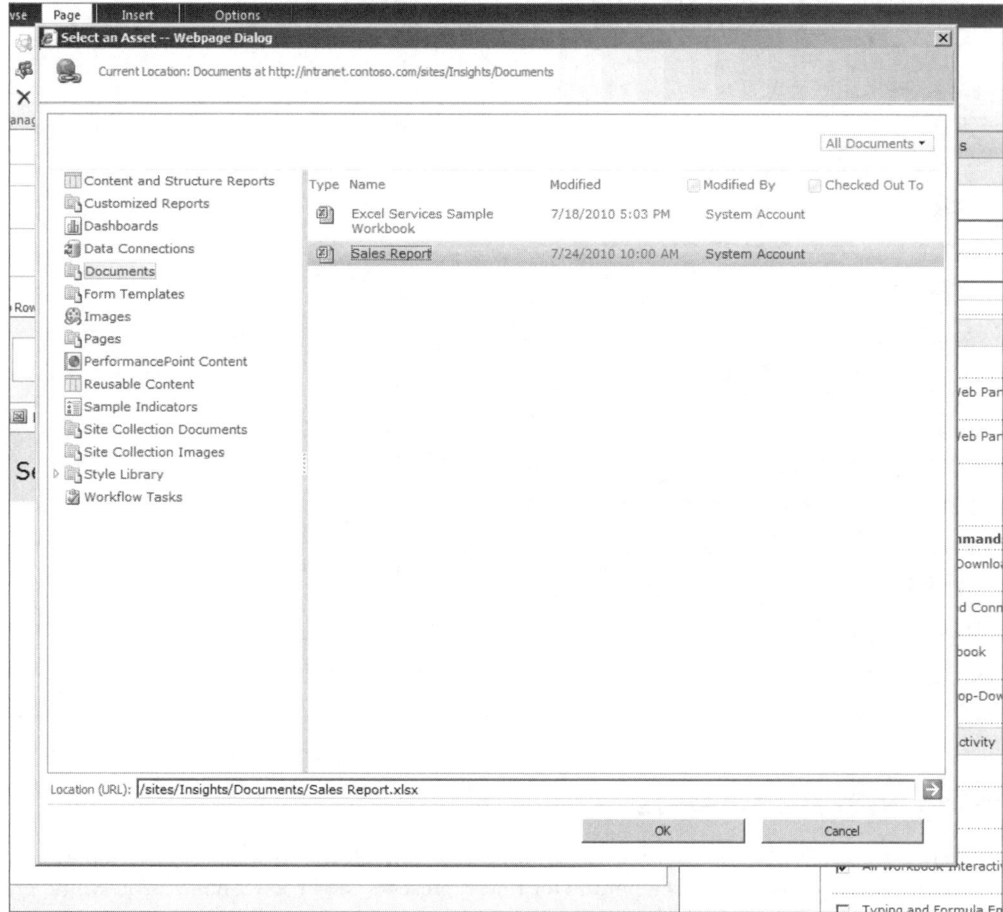

FIGURE 16-14

How It Works

The web part is configured to reference the document that you published to the site. The document's contents will be displayed within the web part and will be in sync with the data that is being published.

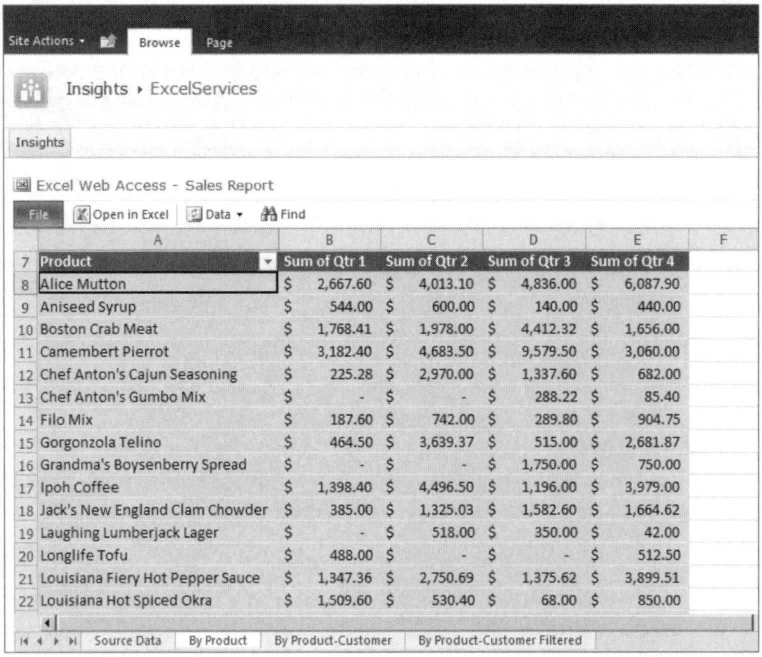

Site Actions Browse Page

Insights ▸ ExcelServices

Insights

Excel Web Access - Sales Report

File | Open in Excel | Data | Find

	A	B	C	D	E
7	Product	Sum of Qtr 1	Sum of Qtr 2	Sum of Qtr 3	Sum of Qtr 4
8	Alice Mutton	$ 2,667.60	$ 4,013.10	$ 4,836.00	$ 6,087.90
9	Aniseed Syrup	$ 544.00	$ 600.00	$ 140.00	$ 440.00
10	Boston Crab Meat	$ 1,768.41	$ 1,978.00	$ 4,412.32	$ 1,656.00
11	Camembert Pierrot	$ 3,182.40	$ 4,683.50	$ 9,579.50	$ 3,060.00
12	Chef Anton's Cajun Seasoning	$ 225.28	$ 2,970.00	$ 1,337.60	$ 682.00
13	Chef Anton's Gumbo Mix	$ -	$ -	$ 288.22	$ 85.40
14	Filo Mix	$ 187.60	$ 742.00	$ 289.80	$ 904.75
15	Gorgonzola Telino	$ 464.50	$ 3,639.37	$ 515.00	$ 2,681.87
16	Grandma's Boysenberry Spread	$ -	$ -	$ 1,750.00	$ 750.00
17	Ipoh Coffee	$ 1,398.40	$ 4,496.50	$ 1,196.00	$ 3,979.00
18	Jack's New England Clam Chowder	$ 385.00	$ 1,325.03	$ 1,582.60	$ 1,664.62
19	Laughing Lumberjack Lager	$ -	$ 518.00	$ 350.00	$ 42.00
20	Longlife Tofu	$ 488.00	$ -	$ -	$ 512.50
21	Louisiana Fiery Hot Pepper Sauce	$ 1,347.36	$ 2,750.69	$ 1,375.62	$ 3,899.51
22	Louisiana Hot Spiced Okra	$ 1,509.60	$ 530.40	$ 68.00	$ 850.00

Source Data | By Product | By Product-Customer | By Product-Customer Filtered

FIGURE 16-15

Working with Parameters

Parameters are values that are configured within the workbook that can be used to change the view of the data. An example of this is a parameter that represents the Product name. You would create and configure the parameter within the workbook. Once you have created the parameter, end users could use it to modify the display of the data within the web part. The parameters can be configured within the web part through the parameters tool pane, or they can be configured through a web part connection. In the example of a parameter based on the Product name, users could in theory select only the products that they are interested in. Once those products were selected, the Excel data would then be filtered based on the product selection.

TRY IT OUT Configure a Parameter Based on Product Name and Connect with a Filter Web Part

In this Try It Out, you are going to configure a parameter within an Excel document so that you can use a filter to modify the display of the web part. You will create a parameter within the Excel Services Sample Workbook, which is loaded to the site when the site is created.

1. Open the Documents library in the site collection you created earlier in this chapter.
2. Open the Sales Report document that you created earlier in the chapter.

3. Open the By Product Worksheet, select any cells within the table to open the PivotTable Field List.

4. Add the Customer field to the Report Filter section. This is done by selecting the Customer field and dragging it to the Report Filter box. You should notice that there is now a filter drop-down above the table that is labeled Customer, as shown in Figure 16-16. If you modify the selected value, the table will be updated based on your selection.

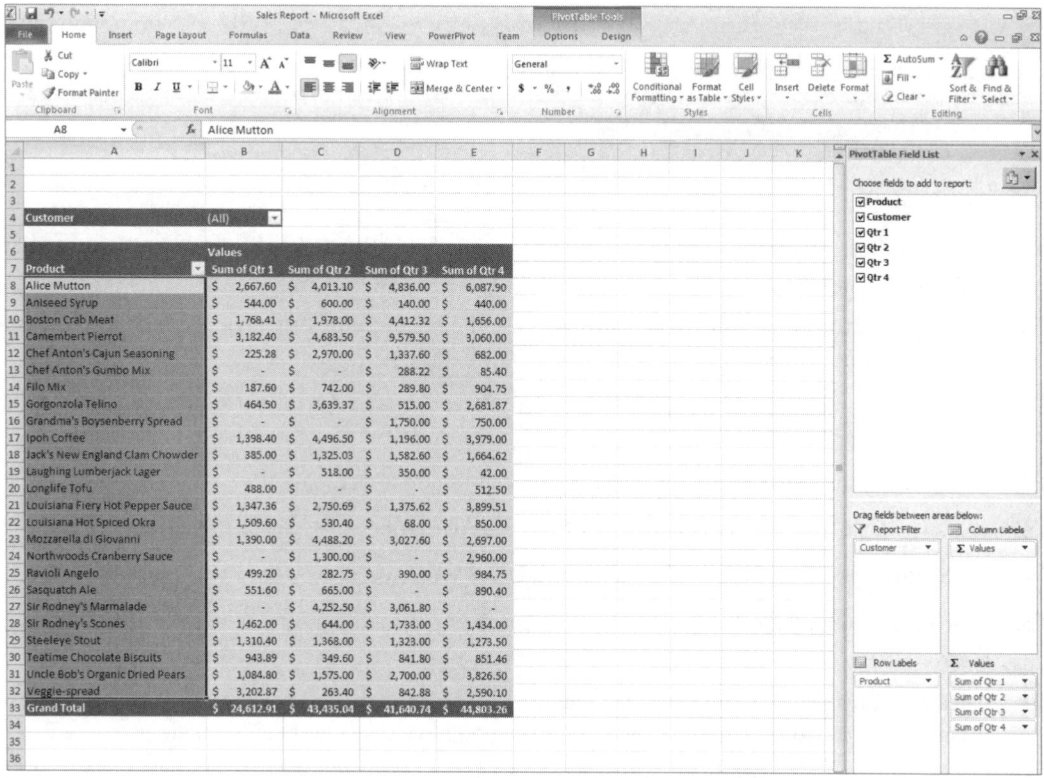

FIGURE 16-16

5. Select the cell that contains the Customer value. In the Formulas Ribbon, select the Define Name option and name the cell Customers. Click OK to save the name changes. You will notice that whenever you have that cell highlighted, the name "Customers" is displayed in the toolbar, as shown in Figure 16-17.

6. Select the file menu to open the Backstage options.

7. Select the Save & Share option and the Save to SharePoint option.

8. Since you opened the document from SharePoint, you can save the document back to the current location. You first need to update the Publish Options so that you can publish your parameter. Click the Publish Options button. In the Parameters tab, select the Add option, and select the Customers parameter. Click OK twice to save the changes. In the Show options, select the Items in the Workbook option and check all items.

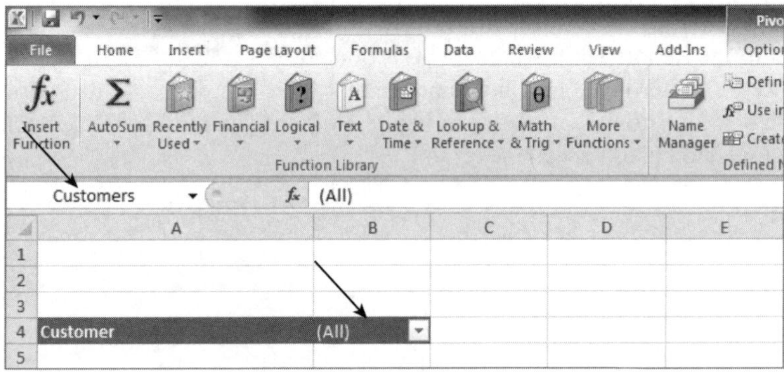

FIGURE 16-17

9. Select the Save As option, and then click Save in the Save dialog. Click Yes when prompted as to whether you want to save over the existing file.
10. Once the document appears in the browser, use the breadcrumbs to navigate back to the home page for the site collection.
11. Using the steps in the earlier Try It Out called "Create a New Dashboard," create a new dashboard called ExcelServices2.
12. When the dashboard page loads, click in any cell to add a web part.
13. Click the Add Web Part option in any of the web part zones.
14. In the Business Data category list, select the Excel Web Access web part and click Add.
15. When the web part is added to the page, select the "Click here to open the tool pane" link within the web part.
16. Click the ellipse next to the Workbook field to browse for the location of the document you published in the previous example. Click OK once you have selected the document.
17. Configure the remaining tool pane options as follows:

PROPERTY	VALUE
Named Item	By Product
Type of Toolbar	PivotTable1
Appearance	Set the height and width settings to use 7 inches.
Reaming Options	Keep the Default

18. Select the Add a Web Part link in any of the web part zones and add the Choice Filter web part from the Filters category, as shown in Figure 16-18, and click Finish.

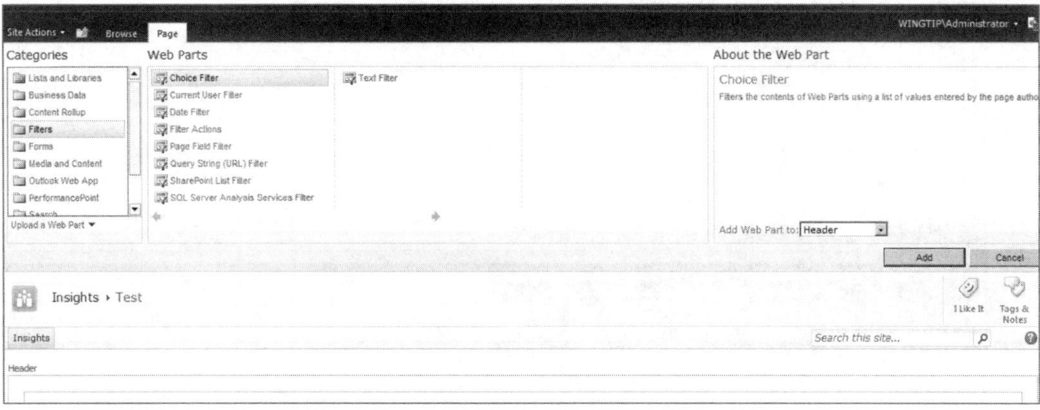

FIGURE 16-18

19. Open the Filter web part tool pane and add the customer data. This list can be obtained by copying the data from the Excel spreadsheet. Keep the remaining default options, and click OK. It is likely that, when you implement this within your organization, you will instead work with an external content list that is referencing a back-end system that stores your client data. If that is the case, then you could use the SharePoint list filter. To keep the example simple, you are going to enter the customers manually.

20. The final step is configuring the Filter web part to pass values to the Excel Document. Select the Filter web part drop-down menu and select the configuration option. Select the Send Filter Values To option and then select the Excel Web Access web part, as shown in Figure 16-19.

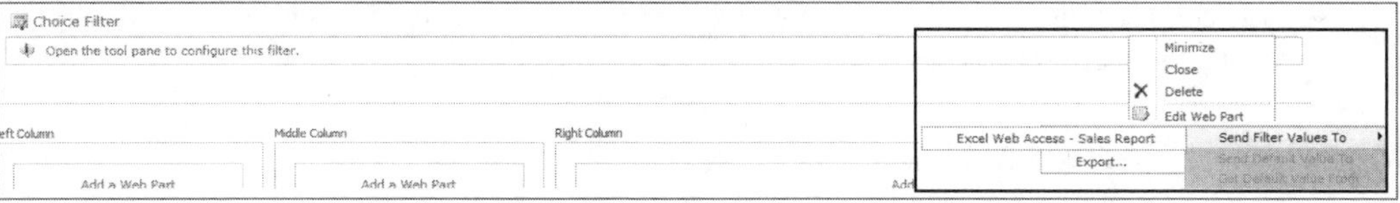

FIGURE 16-19

21. In the Configuration Wizard, set the connection type to Get Filter Values From and then click Configure. Select the Customers field for the Filtered Parameter option, and click Finish.

22. Using the Page Ribbon, select the option to Stop Editing the page.

23. Use the filter drop-down to select a client. Once you press Enter, you should notice that the values in the table were updated based on the value you selected.

How It Works

The value passed from the Filter web part acts as the parameter filter in the Excel Web Access web part. For any report that you have in Excel that used parameters for values, they can be filtered on SharePoint pages using the Filter web parts.

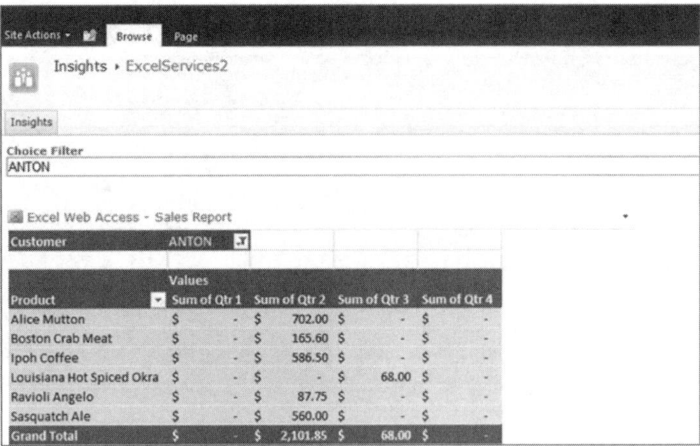

FIGURE 16-20

External Data Connections

Many times within Excel, worksheet connections are made to external data sources. These connections can be used for worksheets that are published to SharePoint, as long as the connections are stored within a trusted location. If you are planning on publishing Excel worksheets that contain connections to external data sources, then you will need to work with your administrator to ensure that all of the data connections are configured correctly for use within your environment. In most cases, the connections will need to be created in a data connection file and then stored within the farm's data connection libraries.

Managing Permissions

There are two different ways to manage permissions for the content within the worksheet. The first option is to control what content is visible on the server. This is configured during the publishing process. Any objects that you haven't selected will not be visible when the worksheet is viewed from the server. Figure 16-21 shows the configuration step from the publishing process. In this Try It Out, you are choosing to publish only two of the worksheets to the server.

If you read the fine print above, you will notice that the option applies to the server view only. If users open the workbook within the Excel client, they will have access to all the content. In most cases, this is probably not the desired result. Within SharePoint there is a way to configure permissions so that even if users open the worksheet, they only have access to the published information. This is done by using the View Item permissions. Users who have the View Item permissions will only be able to open a snapshot of the spreadsheet in the client. This snapshot will only show limited information and will prevent them from seeing the content that was not shared during the publishing process. The two lists that follow outline the different types of content that will be available within the snapshot and the types of content that will be removed from the snapshot.

- Available within a Snapshot
  - Formatting
  - Visible grid information
  - Cell values
  - Objects

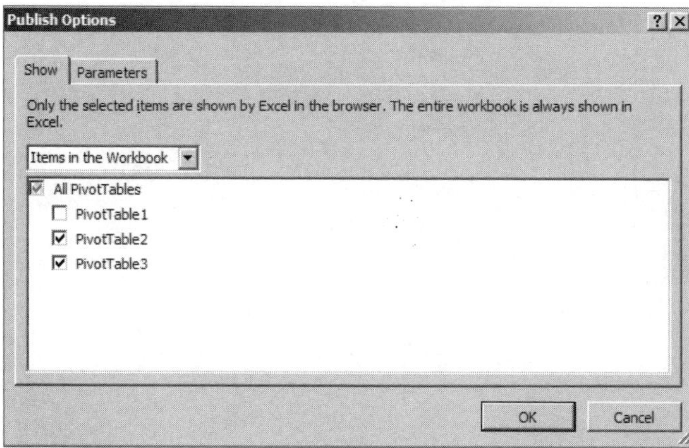

FIGURE 16-21

- Removed from a Snapshot
  - Private information
  - Conditional formatting
  - Hidden data
  - Formulas
  - Interactive data
  - Connections
  - Web-related content

CHART WEB PART

The Chart web part is a new web part that comes with SharePoint Server Enterprise. This web part can be added to any web part zone and can be configured to chart data from several different sources. When the web part is added to the page, you will have access to two different Configuration Wizards, which will walk you through the process of configuring and customizing the Chart web part. Figure 16-22 is an example of the web part that was added to the page before it has been configured. You will notice two links appear on the screen and then also in the web part drop-down menu.

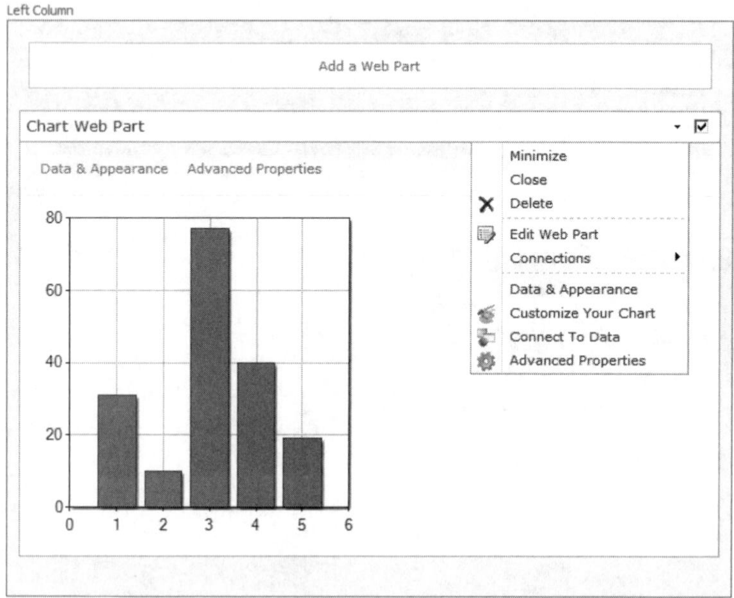

FIGURE 16-22

This web part can be configured to create reports for several different data sources, including the following:

- Web Part
- Connect to a List
- Connect to Business Data Catalog
- Connect to Excel Services

The process for configuring the web part is a four step process. You start by connecting to the data and then move through the remaining steps. At any time in the process, you can select the desired step from the Data Connection Wizard Quick Launch to modify your configurations. An example of this wizard is shown in Figure 16-23.

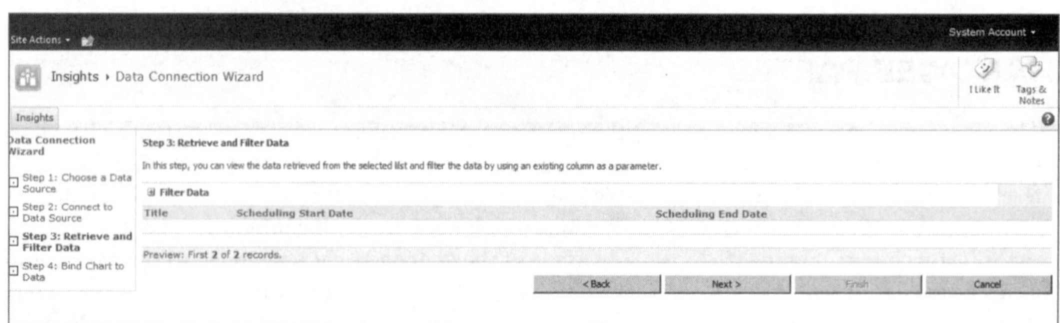

FIGURE 16-23

Once you have the data configured, you can customize the appearance of the chart using the Customize Your Chart Wizard. Within this wizard, you will be able to select the type of chart; configure the appearance, which includes the theme, height, width, and 3D properties; and modify the chart elements, which includes the chart title, legend, gridlines, data labels, and hyperlinks. An example of this wizard is shown in Figure 16-24.

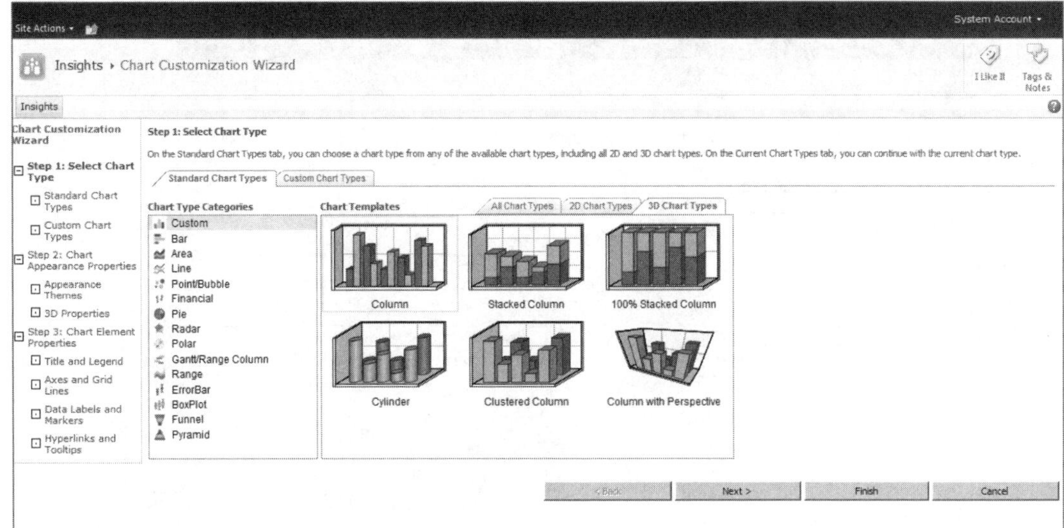

FIGURE 16-24

TRY IT OUT Use the Chart Web Part to Display Data from a SharePoint List

In this Try It Out, you are going to add a chart to the dashboard you created in the previous example. You have already added the Filter web part and the Excel Services web part. You will now add a Chart web part that will display a graph based on some list information you have stored within the site collection. You will first need to create the list and add the data. Since you have already covered how to do this in previous chapters, we won't cover it in detail. You can always refer to Chapter 3 if you need additional instructions.

1. Create a list using the Import Spreadsheet option. To import the spreadsheet, create a new document from the Sales Report template (see the previous examples if you need more details) and save it locally. Using the Import Wizard, you can point to the saved file and select the data range from the Source Data worksheet. An example of the range selection is shown in Figure 16-25.

2. Once the list is imported, it will be opened for you to review. Keep in mind that this exercise is simply to show how the configurations work. It is not likely that you would have the same type of data within your environment. You will likely have different columns and different values. Completing this exercise, however, should give you the information you need to build the charts with your data.

3. Using the steps in the previous "Create a New Dashboard" Try It Out, create a new dashboard called ChartWebPart.

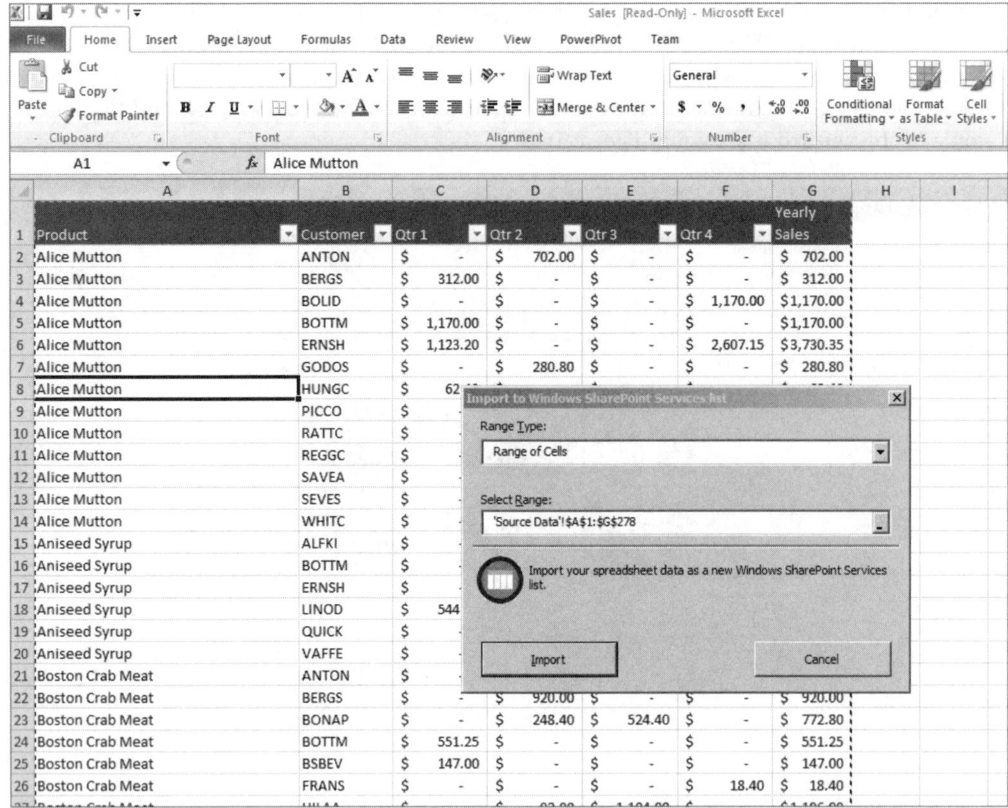

FIGURE 16-25

4. When the dashboard page loads, click in any cell to add a web part.
5. Click the Add Web Part option in any of the web part zones.
6. In the Business Data category list, select the Excel Web Access web part, and click Add.
7. When the web part is added to the page, click the Data & Appearance link within the web part.
8. Select the Connect Chart to Data option.
9. Select the Connect to a List option, and click Next.
10. Select the Sales Data list from the list drop-down option, and click Next.
11. The data from the list will load for your review. On this screen, you can also filter the data that is presented. For this example, you will filter the data based on Product. Your default value will be Alice Mutton, as shown in Figure 16-26.
12. You will now configure your chart. You are going to create a line chart with a series for each quarter. You will first start by modifying the Default series so that it has the values, as shown in Figure 16-27.

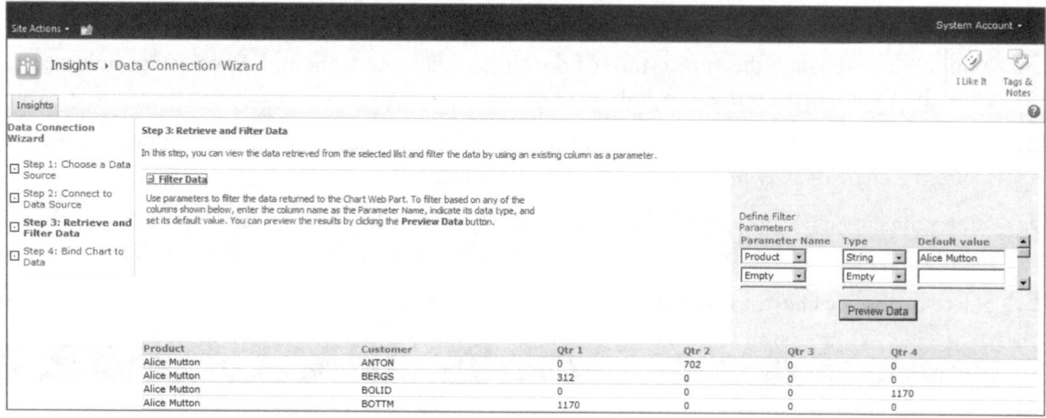

FIGURE 16-26

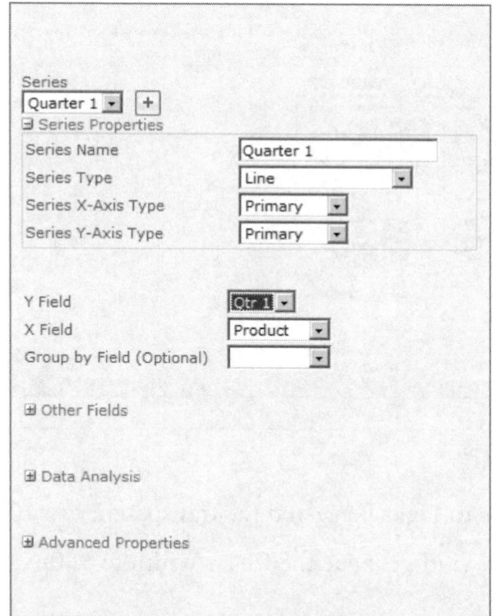

FIGURE 16-27

13. Next, you need to create the three additional series. You do this by selecting the Plus icon next to the Series drop-down. Each series should be named and given properties as shown in the following table:

NAME	SERIES TYPE	Y FIELD	X FIELD
Quarter 1	Line	Qtr 1	Product
Quarter 2	Line	Qtr 2	Product
Quarter 3	Line	Qtr 3	Product
Quarter 4	Line	Qtr 4	Product

14. Click Finish and you will see a preview of the chart.
15. You will now change the appearance of the chart. Click the Data and Appearance link again, and click the Customize Your Chart link.
16. Within this menu, you can change the appearance of your chart. For this example, you are going to make the chart display in 3D using a different theme.
17. When the customization page loads, select the Standard Chart Types tab. You will see all of the different types of charts that are available. Select the Line category and the 3D Chart Types tab.
18. Select the Spline chart, as shown in Figure 16-28, and click Next.

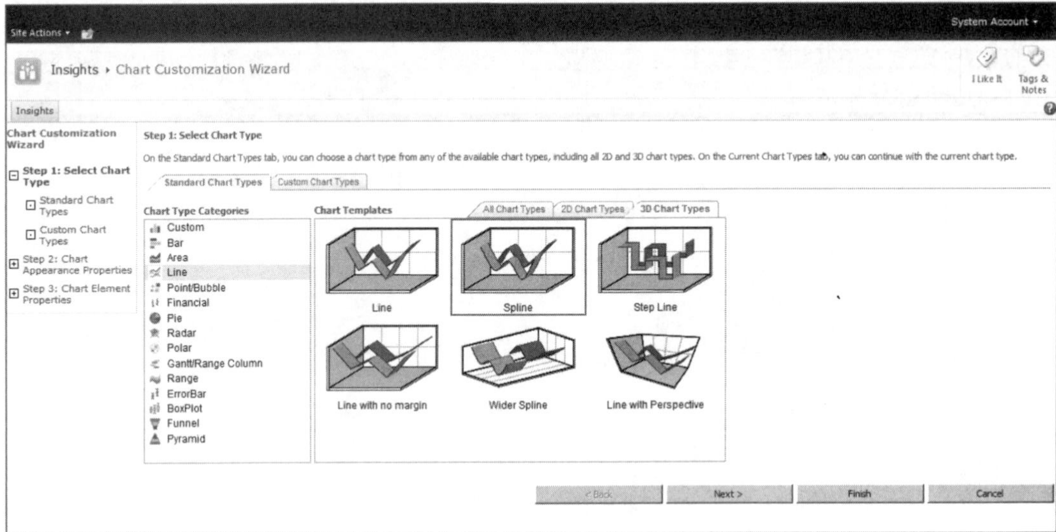

FIGURE 16-28

19. On the next configuration screen, change the theme to Light Beige and the transparency to 10%.
20. In order to give your chart some additional display width, change the Chart Width to 900px, as shown in Figure 16-29.
21. Click Finish and the updated web part page will be displayed. Select the Stop Editing option to see what the page will look like when users open the dashboard. Remember, though, that only users who have the ability to design and edit the page will see the links for Data & Appearance and Advanced Properties, as shown in Figure 16-30.

How It Works

You configured the Chart web part to pull a collection of filtered data from a SharePoint list. Using the configurations within the web part, the chart is displayed on the web page. For this Try It Out, you used only a filtered view of the product; however, you could apply additional filters to show additional views of the data.

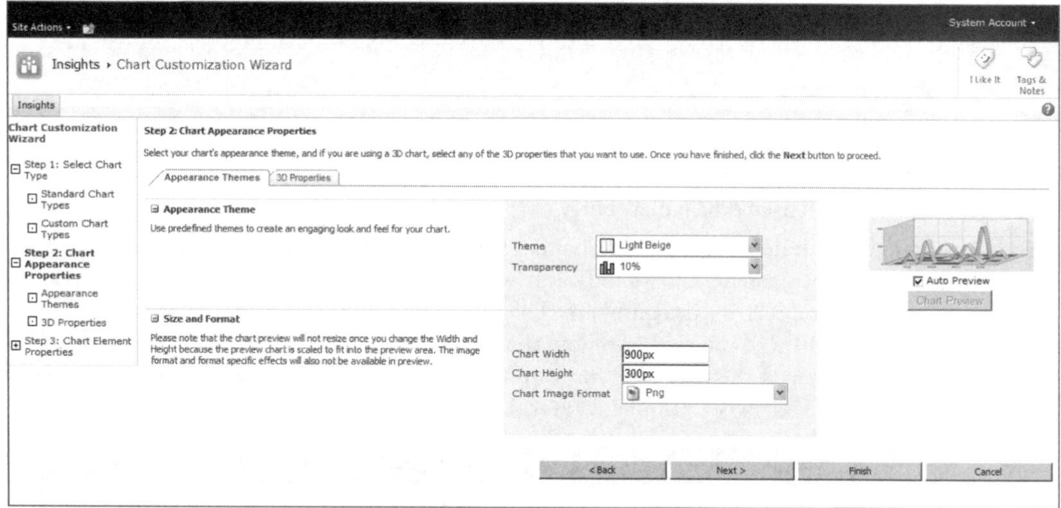

FIGURE 16-29

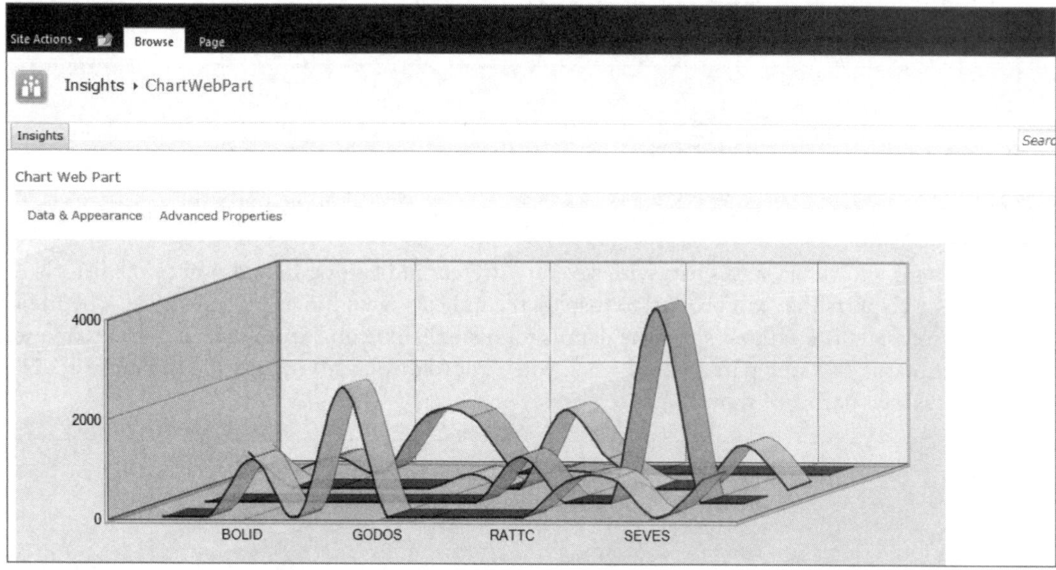

FIGURE 16-30

UNDERSTANDING STATUS LISTS

A status list in SharePoint 2010 is similar to the KPI list in SharePoint 2007. This list is populated with various status indicators that you create to produce a visual representation of the status of the data. Indicators can be created for several different types of data, including the following:

- SharePoint List
- Excel Services
- SQL Analysis Services
- Fixed Value based on Manual Entry

For each item in the indicator, a goal level and a warning level are configured. The indicator will be updated based on the content, and an indicator will be displayed based on the calculated value. An example of a common KPI is sales numbers. The indicator could be configured to display a red status until you reach 50% of the goal, a yellow status from 51%–74% and a green status for 75% and higher. Just by looking at the indicator you would have a good idea of how your sales numbers were tracking. Figure 16-31 shows a sample of several KPI indicators.

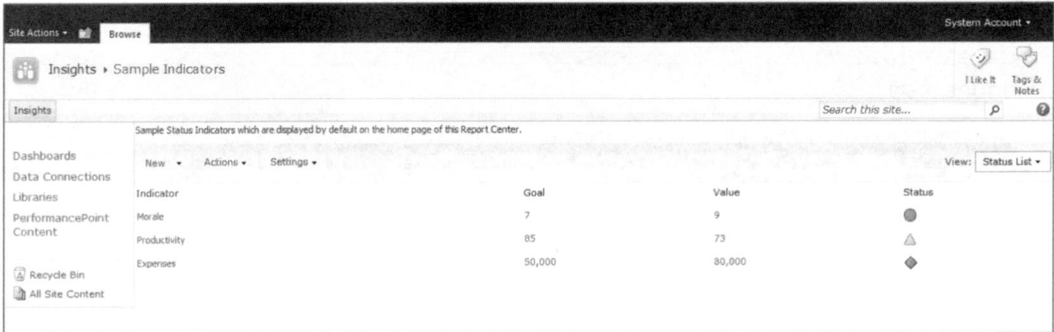

FIGURE 16-31

Figure 16-31 shows the status list, with several different indicators. In addition to the list, there are two KPI web parts that can be used to display the indicators within a web part zone. The Indicator Details web part is used to display the details for a single indicator from the list. The second web part, the Status List web part, is used when you want to display all indicators. In Figure 16-32, these two status web parts are shown.

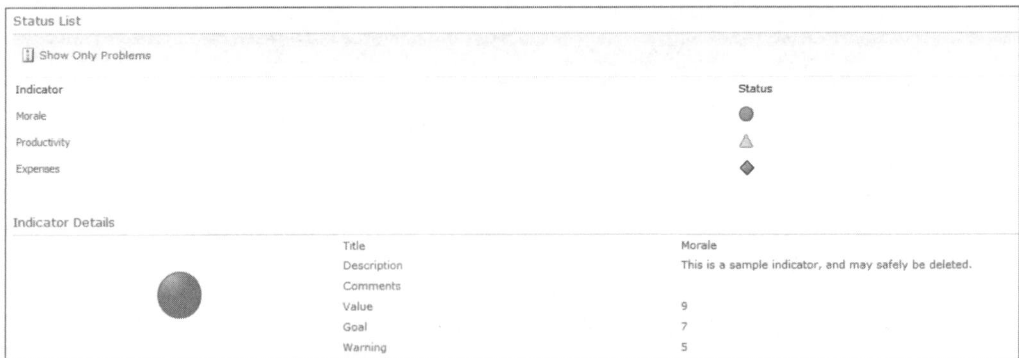

FIGURE 16-32

TRY IT OUT Create a Dashboard to Report on Sales Data

In this Try It Out, you want to monitor the average sales of Boston Crab Meat. You have noticed a trend, and you want to monitor the average sales across clients. You will create a KPI list item to monitor average sales.

1. Click Site Actions, View all Site Content, and navigate to the Sample Indicators list.
2. In the New menu, select the option to create an Indicator from a SharePoint list, as shown in Figure 16-33.

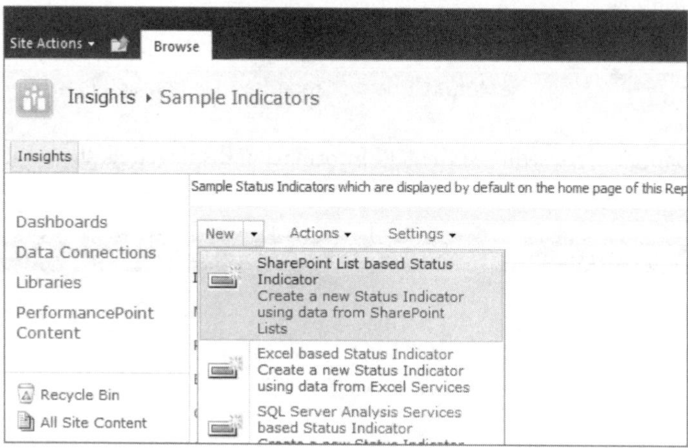

FIGURE 16-33

3. Fill in the following values for the indicator and click OK.

PROPERTY	VALUE
Name	Quarter 4 Average Sales
List URL	Click on the List icon and navigate to the Sales Data list. Doing this will populate the list URL for you.
View	All Items
Value Calculation	Average of Qtr 4
Goal	400
Warning	200

4. You will now create another dashboard page, which you will use to display the KPI. Using the steps in the earlier "Create a New Dashboard" Try It Out, create a new dashboard, called KPI.
5. When the dashboard page loads, click in any cell to add a web part.
6. Click the Add Web Part option in any of the web part zones.
7. In the Business Data category list, select the Status List web part.

8. Open the Web Part tool pane, and configure the following options:

PROPERTY	VALUE
Indicator List	Sample Indicators
Show Only Status Icon	Selected
Display Multiple Indicators Column	Selected
Status Indicator	Quarter 4 Average
Column of Dimension	Product
Member to Display	Alice Mutton; Boston Crab Meat; Camembert Pierrot

9. Click OK. The page will reload, and you will see the KPI information displayed as shown in Figure 16-34.

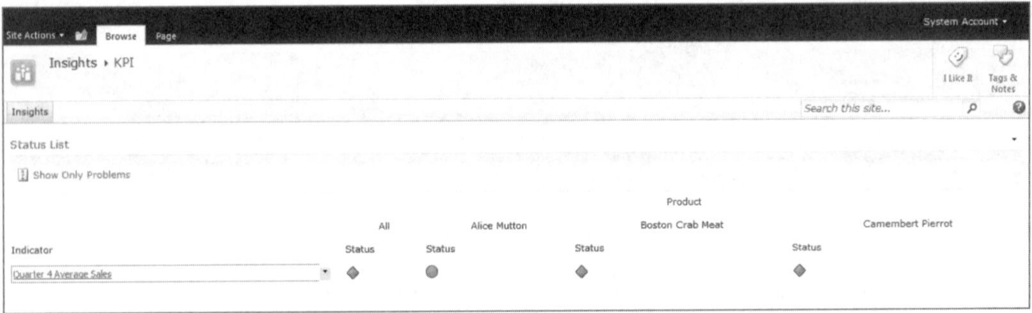

FIGURE 16-34

10. Click the Indicator title to go to the Details page.
11. Click the List link to open the Sales Data list.
12. Select the first Boston Crab Meat list item, update the Quarter 4 value to $4000 and click Save.
13. Click on the Dashboards link in the Quick Launch Toolbar, and then open the KPI dashboard. You will notice that the status of the Boston Crab Meat product is now yellow, as shown in Figure 16-35.

How It Works

The status indicator is configured to pull an average value from the Sales Data list. As the values are changed, so are the KPI indicators. The Status Indicator web part is being used to show the current KPI values, and is taking advantage of the feature to show multiple indicators in order to provide additional details about some of the products included in the average sales. This example would allow you to see a KPI value for all items in the list, as well as provide a way to monitor specific key product lines.

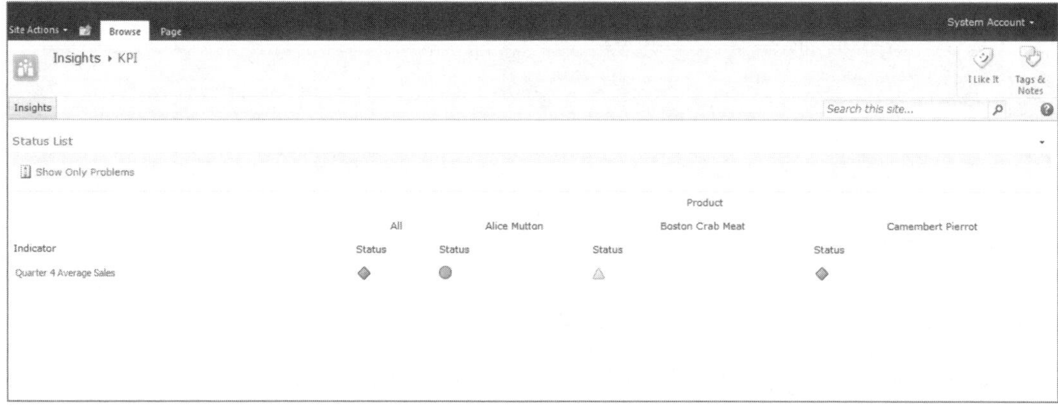

FIGURE 16-35

WORKING WITH VISIO SERVICES

Visio Services is a new service application within SharePoint that allows you to interact with data from Visio diagrams. At the base level, a Visio Web Access web part is used to display the data from a published Visio diagram. The diagrams are first created in Visio and then published to SharePoint as web drawings. The Visio web part can then be added to any web part zone within the farm that is hosting the drawings. Keep in mind that, since the document is stored in SharePoint, the document will only be rendered in the web part for users who have at least View permissions for the document. Since you can point to any document within the farm, it is possible for you to render the information in many places, while still keeping a single entry point for the data.

The Visio web part supports web part connections, which allow users to interact with the published data. Some examples of possible configurations are:

- **Master/Detail:** This can be used when you have a step process; the master could display steps 1–4, for example. As you select a shape in the master diagram, the detail diagram is updated to display the detailed information for that step.
- **SharePoint List:** When your Visio diagram is connected to a SharePoint list, you will be able to connect the diagram to the List web part and interact with the data. When you select items within the SharePoint list, the corresponding items in the diagram will be highlighted.

The connection settings are configured within the Visio Web Access web part in the Connections menu option. As you can see from Figure 16-36, the menu option provided for configuring the connection is very straightforward and easy to understand.

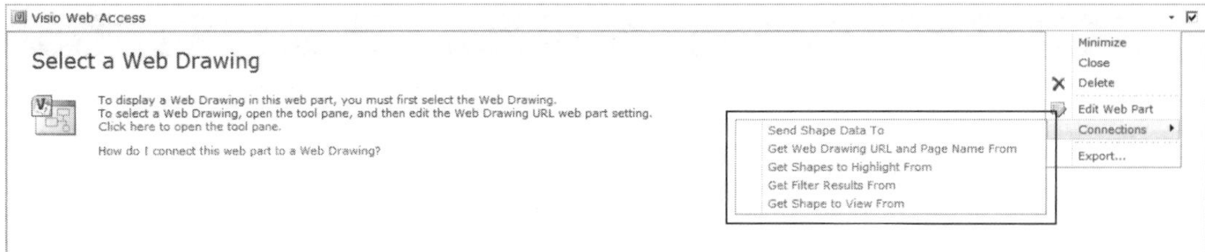

FIGURE 16-36

The table that follows describes the different connection options available, as well as an example of when you would use that particular connection.

CONNECTION TYPE	DESCRIPTION	EXAMPLE
Send Shape Data To	Send the data for the selected shape to another web part.	When you have to show diagrams in a master/detail relationship, you would send the shape data to the Details web part so that it would know what data to display.
Get Web Drawing URL and Page Name From	This connection allows you to dynamically accept the Drawing URL and Page name.	This could be used when you had a list of drawings and you wanted users to be able to easily select a drawing from a list and have the drawing displayed.
Get Shapes to Highlight From	This connection allows you to highlight shapes in the diagram. The connection will need to have the name of the shape and the color of the highlight.	This could be used if you wanted to be able to select from a list of items and have certain ones highlighted. For example, if you had a floor plan drawing and wanted to highlight all rooms that were 6 x 8.
Get Filter Results From	This connection will filter the items in the Visio diagram based on the SharePoint list contents. This connection only works when the Visio diagram is connected to the SharePoint list and the only list that can pass the connection is the List web part of the connected list.	This would highlight values that match the filtered SharePoint list. If you look again at the floor plan example, you could have a list that contains all of your information about each of the rooms. If you filtered the list based on the fireplace option, then all rooms with fireplaces would be highlighted in your web part.
Get Shape to View From	This connection allows you to change the zoom view for a specific shape.	This would be useful, for example, if you wanted to have a list of values that, when selected, would cause a new view to display that zooms in to show all of the details.

As you can see from the table, there are many different ways you can configure and connect the web parts. In the Try It Outs that follow, you will be working through several different examples. Once you complete these Try It Outs, you should have a good understanding of how these diagrams can be connected to provide valuable, dynamic information to users.

TRY IT OUT Create a Visio Services Document

The process for creating a Visio services document is the same as for creating a standard Visio document. In this Try It Out, you will upload two separate Visio files. The first one has several different pages, and the second one has only one page. Since the content is not relevant, you can use whatever Visio diagrams you have access to. If you do not have any, you can simply open Visio and create two separate diagrams with various shapes.

1. The first thing that you need to do is to create a document library in which to store your Visio documents. To do this, select the All Site Content option from the Home page, and then select the Create option. Select the document template and select More Options. Enter the following values and click Create.

PROPERTY	VALUE
Name	Diagrams
Navigation - Display on Quick Launch	No
Other options	Use the default values

2. Open the first Visio document that you want to publish to the site. Select the File option to open the Backstage view. Select the Save & Send option and the Save to SharePoint option, as shown in Figure 16-37. You should notice that this screen looks very similar to the Excel screen. Select the option to Browse for a location, and set the file type to Web Drawing.

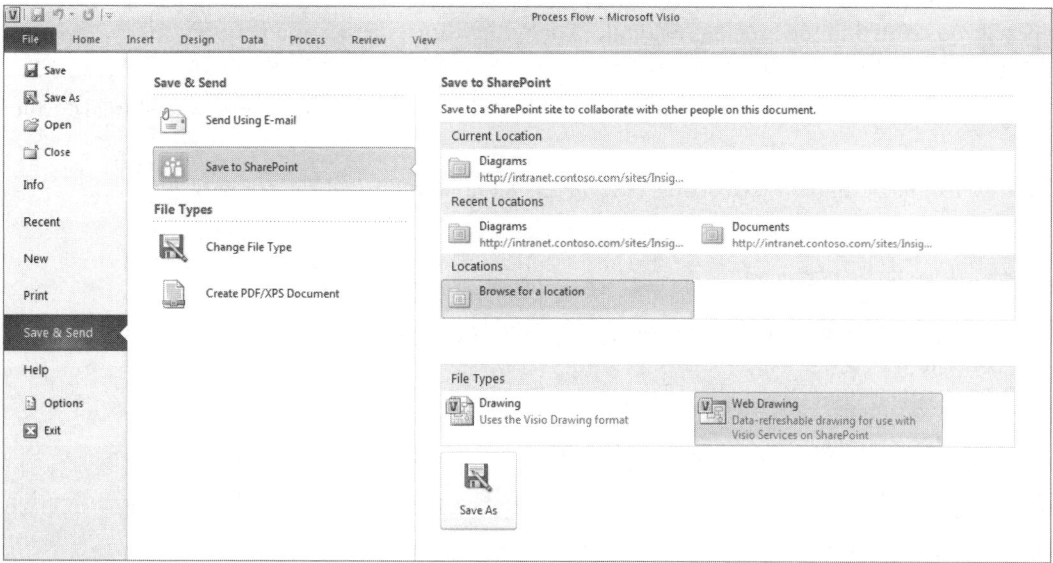

FIGURE 16-37

3. Enter the URL for the library that you created in step 1. When the library loads, enter the desired filename and click Save. When the document has finished saving, it will open in the browser for you to preview, as shown in Figure 16-38.

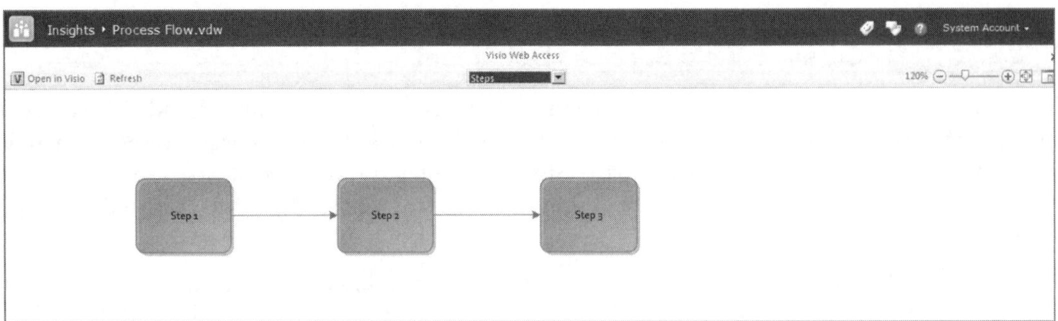

FIGURE 16-38

4. Repeat steps 2 and 3 for another Visio document. This will give you at least two different diagrams in your library.

How It Works

When you publish a document to a SharePoint site, the document is saved in a format that can be displayed within the Visio Access web part. In the next Try It Out, you will configure the web part on a dashboard page.

TRY IT OUT Connect a Visio Services Web Part to a List Web Part

In this example, you will add the Visio Web Access web part to the page and connect it to the Diagrams library you created in the previous example. You will create a connection between the two web parts so that the Visio web part will load the drawing you select in the Diagram web part.

1. Using the steps in the "Create a New Dashboard" Try It Out, create a new dashboard called Visio.
2. When the dashboard page loads, click in any Column cell to add a web part.
3. Click the Add Web Part option in any of the web part zones.
4. In the Lists & Library category list, select the Diagrams web part.
5. Select the zone next to the one you used for the Diagrams web part, and click the Add a Web Part option.
6. In the Business Data category list, select the Visio Web Access web part and select Add.
7. Select the Edit Web Part menu for the Visio web part, and click the Connections link.
8. Select the Get Web Drawing URL and Page Name option, and then click the Diagrams option.
9. In the Configure Connection dialog, select the following options and click Finish:

PROPERTY	VALUE
Provider Field Name	Document URL
Consumer Field Name	Web Drawing URL

10. Select the Stop Editing option in the Ribbon, so you can view the web part page. Notice that, as you select each of the diagrams, the Visio document being displayed is updated to match the selected diagram, as shown in Figure 16-39.

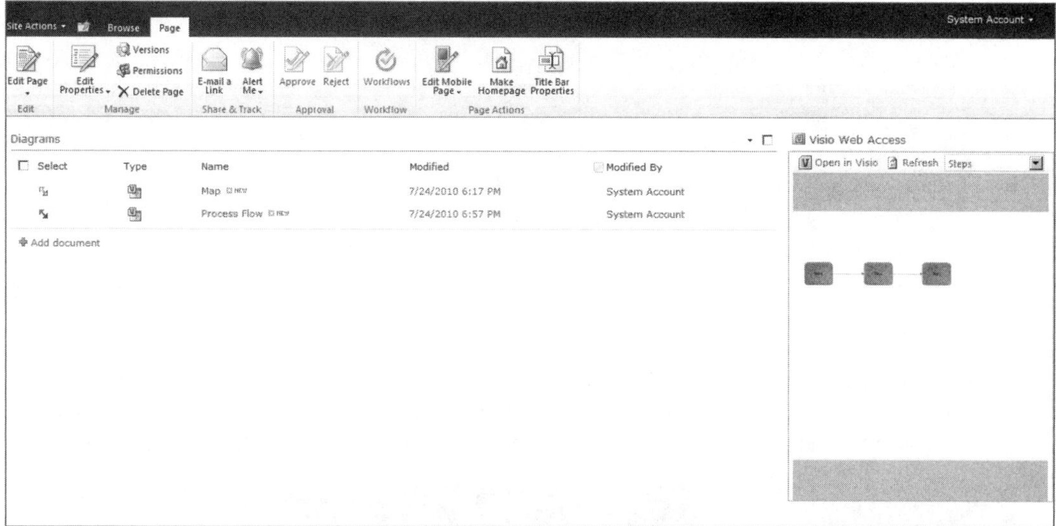

FIGURE 16-39

This is just one example of using the Visio Web Access web part. In this Try It Out, you used a web part connection to display the Visio documents. If you did not want to use a connection, you could configure the web part to display a single Visio Document by entering the Web Drawing URL within the Web Part tool pane.

How It Works

The two web parts are added to the page and a connection is built between them. The values for the Web Document URL are passed from the Diagrams List web part. Doing this allows any user to select which diagram they want to be displayed.

PERFORMANCEPOINT FEATURES

In previous versions of product releases, PerformancePoint was a standalone server product for building business intelligence reports and dashboards. With the latest release of SharePoint, the PerformancePoint features have been incorporated into SharePoint, allowing users to easily create rich reports, dashboards, scorecards, and KPIs using the Reports Builder. When the farm is configured, the SharePoint administrator will complete the process for configuring the PerformancePoint service application. Once the configuration is complete, users with the appropriate permissions will be able to incorporate the PerformancePoint content into their sites.

One of the key benefits of PerformancePoint is the ability to design and build content using the Dashboard Designer. As you can see in Figure 16-40, this design environment is similar to that of other office applications and includes the Ribbon.

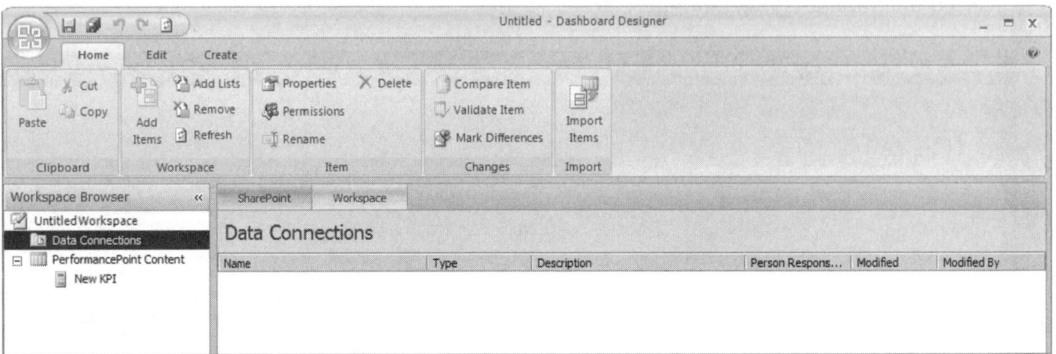

FIGURE 16-40

The Dashboard Designer can be accessed easily from any list created with the PerformancePoint content template. From within the list, the Dashboard Designer is launched whenever you create new content items. Figure 16-41 shows an example of how you would launch the dashboard.

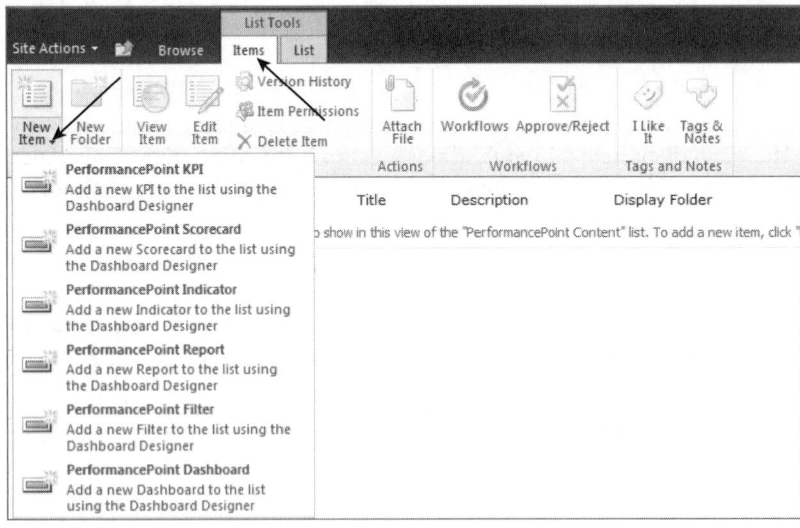

FIGURE 16-41

PerformancePoint is a very large component of reporting and business intelligence, and there is no way that a small section in a single chapter will be able to do it justice. Since most of the work done to create reports using PerformancePoint is done in the PerformancePoint Dashboard Designer, it is out of the scope of a beginning SharePoint solutions book. In the list that follows are several different links that you could reference to learn more and to gather more experience on this particular topic:

- TechNet Documentation

  Plan for PerformancePoint Services:
  `http://technet.microsoft.com/en-us/library/ee681486.aspx`

- Solution Scenario Walkthrough

  Corporate Dashboards Sales Solution:
  `http://technet.microsoft.com/en-us/bi/ff643005.aspx`

- Business Intelligence Resource Center:

  `http://technet.microsoft.com/en-us/bi/default.aspx`

GETTING STARTED

After reading this chapter, you will have been exposed to many of the different tools available to you. These are all powerful tools that, when combined, can be used to provide immediate, dynamic, and meaningful information to the users on demand. There are a few things to keep in mind, though, as you move forward with the solutions you are building. In this section, we will cover some of the things that you should be thinking about as you begin to work with these tools.

Understanding the Organization

As you begin to look at the tools available and the information you want to present to the user, it is important to also look at the user. If you have been sending out an Excel document for five years and now you want to display it on the web page, what impact will that have on your users? It is so important that you consider this. You can build the best solution ever, but if users don't understand it, then it won't provide the value that you and they need. Be sure that you talk to your users to truly understand how they are currently working with the data and then formulate a plan that will empower them to do more with SharePoint.

Walk Before You Run

Like with many things in SharePoint, insights is an area that has several levels of complexity. It is important that you understand each of these levels before you advance to the next one. This will keep you from over-customizing something when you could use the tools that are available out of the box. To get started, you could work with the tools available out of the box, such as the web parts and the KPI lists. From there you could move into working with Excel and Visio services and, finally, you could build more custom and advanced reports using the PerformancePoint Dashboard Designer. There are many different tools, and it may take some time for you to realize the best combination and configuration of tools to meet your organization's unique reporting requirements.

SUMMARY

In this chapter, we have reviewed many of the key aspects of the new insights features within SharePoint 2010. After reading this chapter, you should be familiar with and able to configure the different business intelligence components within the site, including:

- Defining business intelligence
- Working with Excel Services
- Using the Chart web part
- Working with Visio Services
- Working with KPI features
- Understanding PerformancePoint features

EXERCISES

1. What site template comes preconfigured to support business intelligence content?
2. True or false. In SharePoint 2010, Excel Services content can be edited through the browser.
3. What permission level would you need to apply so that users would only be able to open a snapshot of an Excel Services document?
4. What types of content can be configured within a KPI indicator?

▶ WHAT YOU LEARNED IN THIS CHAPTER

TOPIC	KEY CONCEPTS
Business Intelligence Features	SharePoint has many features that provide the functionality to build dynamic, rich business intelligence solutions including: Chart web part, Excel Services, Visio Services and PerformancePoint Services.
Getting Started	When getting started with building BI solutions, it is important to first understand all of the tools available. Once you have an understanding of the tools, an evaluation of your internal data should be completed to determine how the tools can be applied to your existing data. Whenever possible, take small steps to help ensure that you are getting the most benefit from the out-of-the-box tools.

17

Working with Search

WHAT YOU WILL LEARN IN THIS CHAPTER:

- Basic search
- Building search queries
- Customizing the search experience
- Customizing Search Center
- Search Service application configurations
- Search analytics

Search is a very common action among users today. When they access a website, they expect to be able to quickly and easily find the relevant content that they are looking for by searching the site. SharePoint is no exception to this concept, and your site users are going to want to be able to reliably and quickly find relevant content. The tools covered in this chapter can be combined to help you build powerful search solutions for your users.

UNDERSTANDING SHAREPOINT SEARCH

SharePoint Search comes in several different flavors, based on the version of the product that you have installed. As you move to a higher level of licensing, additional search features are available. The examples in this chapter are based on the Enterprise version of the product; however, it is good to understand the different types of search available in each of the application platforms. You learned earlier in the book about the three different versions of SharePoint: Foundation, Standard, and Enterprise. The table that follows describes the primary differences in these versions of search. Keep in mind that each version of the product includes all the features available in previous versions.

FOUNDATION SERVER	STANDARD	ENTERPRISE
Site Search	Site search	Site search
	Best bets and keywords	Standard search features
	Relevancy by number of clicks	Extensible search platform
	Managed metadata search	Business connectivity framework
	Mobile search	Thumbnails and previews
	People search	Deep refinement
	Phonetic search	Similar results
	Search connectors	
	Relevancy tuning	

As you can see, there are many search features included with the Enterprise version that can be used to enhance your experience with SharePoint. Imagine how much faster and more efficiently you will be able to work, having all your organization's knowledge available through SharePoint search. In the remainder of this chapter, we will review different ways that you can configure and manage search. We will start by reviewing several different key terms, and then, you will work through several examples of search configuration.

NOTE *In addition to the search platforms described above, there are also two additional search configurations, include Search Server and FAST Search. Search Server is often paired with Foundation Server to add additional functionality to the search features included in Foundation Server. FAST Search provides additional features to the Enterprise Search Features. To find additional information on either FAST Search or Search Server, refer to the following URL:* `http://technet.microsoft.com/en-us/enterprisesearch/default.aspx`.

Before we jump into the details, let's do a quick review of some of the common search terms. It is likely that as you start to work with search, you will run into these terms frequently. Having a solid definition of each of them will help you to understand how all the search components work together and how you can use them to help you build powerful solutions that incorporate search.

Key Terms

There are quite a few components that make up SharePoint Search; in fact, entire books have been dedicated to explaining how to best configure, manage, and use the search features of SharePoint. While this book won't go into as much detail, it will cover all the search basics and give you enough information to start using Search within your solutions. To get started, let's review some common search terms that you are likely to hear.

Content Source

A *content source* is a collection of content that is included in the search results. Content sources are created and managed within the Search Service application. Many different types of data can be included within a content source, including:

- SharePoint sites
- File shares
- Exchange public folders
- Non-SharePoint websites
- People Profiles
- Line-of-business applications
- Database content
- Content from Web Services

Server administrators are typically responsible for creating new content sources, since they are configured within the Central Administration management site. You can think of a content source as a pointer to a collection of data that you want to have returned within the search results.

IFilter

IFilters define how the content within the content sources is indexed. In order for SharePoint to understand how to read and index the files, an IFilter must be installed. The common Microsoft products such as Word, PowerPoint, and Excel will, by default, have all of the proper IFilters installed with the SharePoint installation. Typically, environments will install additional IFilters for non-Microsoft file types; a common example of this is PDF files.

Crawl Schedule

When a content source is created by a server admin, one of the configuration items is the crawl schedule. Crawling is the process that the SharePoint server uses to access the data within the content source and build the search index. The process is called crawling, and the crawl schedule refers to the frequency with which the index will be updated. The crawl schedule should be based on the frequency of the changes in the data. For example, if you had a file share location that you used to store archived project data, then you would probably not need to update the index often, because the data is archived and does not change often. On the other hand, your SharePoint sites are likely very active and dynamic and should be crawled on a very frequent basis.

Index

The index is what SharePoint uses to store the data from the content sources once it has been crawled. The index files are updated during each crawl and then made available for search queries.

Query

When you retrieve data from the index files, you will run a search query. This is often done through the entry of a search term in the search box. When you enter the search term, a query is conducted against the index files and the results that match your query are displayed.

Search Scopes

Search scopes are a way to query a subset of data within content sources. As an example, a search scope could be used to search only against the file shares or the public website. Typically, in each environment, there are several global search scopes created, and then within each SharePoint site collection, more granular search scopes are created that relate specifically to a project. Later in this chapter, we will cover search scopes in detail and will have several Try It Outs dedicated to creating and using search scopes.

Keywords and Best Bets

Keywords and best bets are a function of Search that allows you to help guide users to the content that best matches what they are looking for. Take the Holiday Calendar as an example. It is likely that many users will want to access this calendar from the intranet site. Each user will think differently, however, and will likely enter a different search term than another user. Using best bets and keywords, you can determine what the users are likely to search on and then ensure that the results you want to take them to are displayed clearly on the page.

Federated Search

Federated search provides the ability to incorporate indexes from other locations into your search results. This functionality will allow you to query multiple index locations at one time and will display the information on different web parts within the search results page.

Search Center

The Search Center is an enterprise site definition that can be used within SharePoint sites. Typically, each organization has one central Search Center site that is used for all enterprise search queries.

While the concepts covered above aren't all-inclusive, they should give you a solid understanding of the search basics. Throughout the remainder of the chapter, you will work through the search configurations. You will start by looking at search out of the box. Once you understand what to expect when a new site is created, you will look at how to customize the search experience for the site collection. This will allow you to understand the creation of custom scopes, keywords, and even customize the way that the search results look. Once you have covered things at the site collection level, you will look at some of the global search service configurations. You will be working through a lot of examples in this chapter, so it will be a good idea to take a few minutes and make sure that you have a site collection that you can use for testing. If you have been following along through the previous chapters, the Try It Outs will be based on those sites, but if you are just picking up with this chapter, it will probably be a good idea to get a site ready before proceeding. You just need to have a single site collection with several different Office documents uploaded. The Try It Outs in this chapter will be created using examples of content that has been uploaded to the site in previous chapters.

If you have not completed the previous examples, then you simply need to update your search queries to match data that currently exists within your environment.

WORKING WITH SEARCH

Now that you have gotten a brief overview of the different search terms and configuration items, you are going to dive into the search details. You are going to start with the default configuration for search when you create a new site collection, and then, you will move to the different customizations you can make so that search is configured to meet your specific needs and wants.

Basic Search

Basic search is the default configuration for a new SharePoint site collection. With a basic search, users are able to enter a search term for an item and then press Enter. When they press Enter, they will be redirected to a search results page from which they will be able to interact with the search results. Search is easy to locate on the page and contains a user prompt that says "Search this site... ." Figures 17-1 and 17-2 show examples of the basic search configuration for both a team site template and an enterprise publishing site template. You can see from the screenshots that the search is configured in a similar location and layout on each of these site templates.

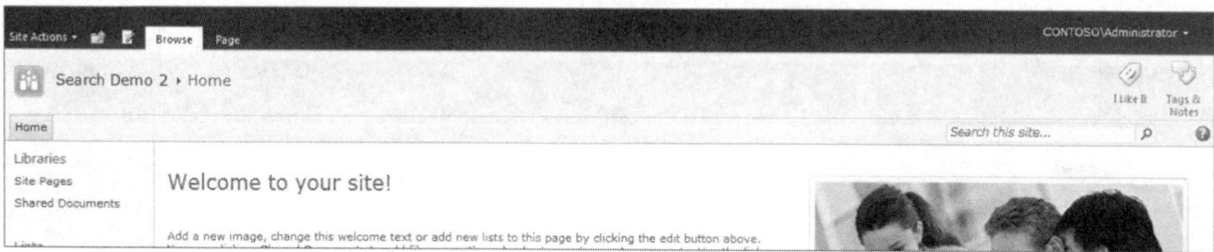

FIGURE 17-1

FIGURE 17-2

When a user adds a value to the search box and presses Enter, the value is translated into a query string that is passed to the search results page. Let's take the search term "gears" as an example. When the user enters the term "gear" into the search box and presses Enter, he or she will be redirected to the search results page, and the search results will automatically appear. If you look at the URL when you arrive at the search results page, you will notice that your search term is part of the page URL. The URL for our example is `http://team.contoso.com/sites/SearchDemo/_layouts/OSSSearchResults.aspx?k=gears&cs=This%20Site&u=http%3A%2F%2Fteam.contoso.com%2Fsites%2FSearchDemo`, and the table below describes each of the elements.

VALUE	TRANSLATION
`http://team.contoso.com/sites/SearchDemo/_layouts/OSSSearchResults.aspx`	The search results page
`k=gear`	The keyword search value
`cs=This%20Site`	The content source
`u=http%3A%2F%2Fteam.contoso.com%2Fsites%2FSearchDemo`	The source URL

Figure 17-3 shows an example of the search results page, including the URL. As you are completing different Try It Outs in this chapter, you will notice the URL for the search page will change based on the different values you configure for the search. There are many ways that you can use this knowledge as you are building different search solutions. In fact, you can even forgo the search box completely and just give users a link that contains the search URL. When users click on the URL, it will send them directly to a preconfigured search results page.

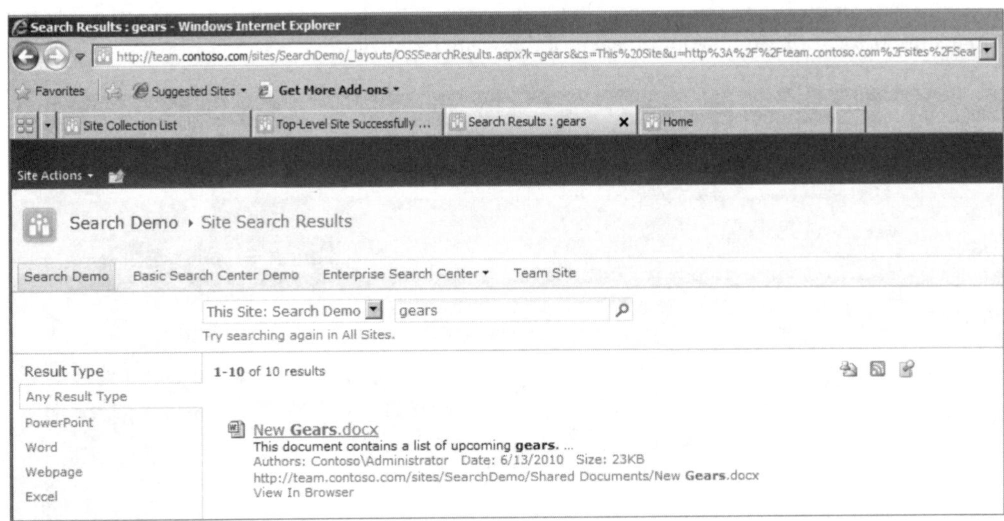

FIGURE 17-3

TRY IT OUT Perform a Basic Search

In this Try It Out, you are going to be completing a basic search. This will allow you to quickly get a feel for how search works. To get started, log in to the home page of your SharePoint site.

1. On the home page of the site, locate the search box in the upper-right corner of the page.
2. Enter the phrase **sales** into the search box shown in Figure 17-2 and press Enter. You will be redirected to the search results page, where all items that match your search criteria are displayed. An example of the results is displayed in Figure 17-3.

How It Works

For the search we conducted, we entered a search query in the search box. The search query was conducted against the search index, and everything within the This Site search scope that contained your search query was returned in the search results.

Now that you have completed a basic search query, take a few minutes and review the search results page. Across the top of the page, you can see the search term that you entered on the previous page. Across the left side of the page, you see the search refinement panel. Using this panel, you can apply additional filters to your search results. And finally, you should notice several icons to the right of the search results. These icons allow you to create an alert for the search results, view the RSS feed for the search results, and save this location so that you can search it later from Windows Explorer. It should be noted, however, that these action buttons will be dependent on internal server and client configurations, so if you don't see the same things within your environment, then you will need to work through a resolution with your farm administrator. Figure 17-4 shows an example of the search results page with each of the elements just discussed highlighted.

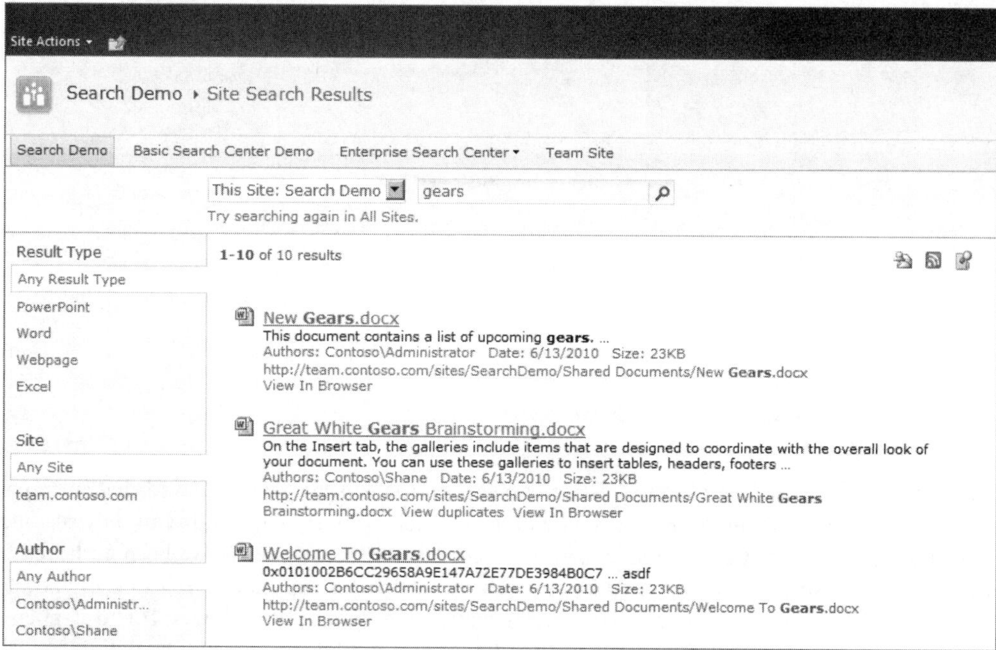

FIGURE 17-4

TRY IT OUT Use the Search Refinement Panel to Refine Search Results

In this Try It Out, you are going to use the search refinement panel to help you further narrow your search results. You will be working from the search results page from your previous exercise, so if you need to get back to the search results page, refer to the previous "Perform a Basic Search" Try It Out.

1. From the search results page, locate the refinement panel on the left of the page. An example of this is shown in Figure 17-5.
2. Select the PowerPoint filter and review the updated search results. Notice (shown in Figure 17-6) that only PowerPoint files are displayed in the search results. Also notice that your search URL now has an additional parameter for the file extension: `fileextension%3D%22pptx%22`.

FIGURE 17-5

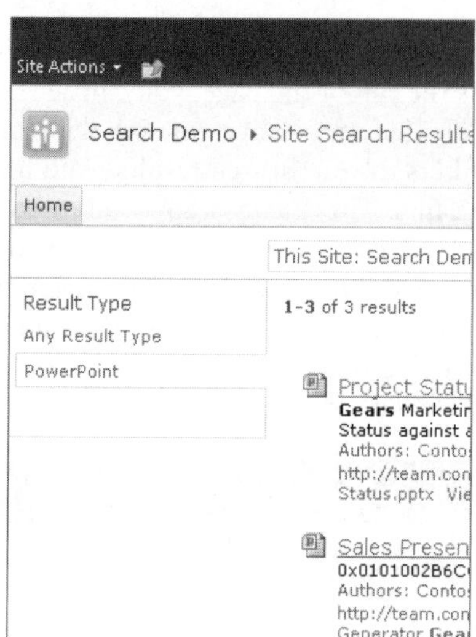

FIGURE 17-6

3. Now, you will apply a filter to limit the results based on the Author. Keep in mind that since you are working in different environments, you will have different authors listed. If you only see one author listed, this means that all documents returned in your search query have been authored by only one person. Notice that as you select the author, the other filters remain. This occurs because the current author you have selected has content that applies within those filters. If you happen to select an author that has only Word documents, the option to filter by results type will not be displayed because it is not relevant to the current search results. Also notice as you select filter options that they are outlined with a small gray box (shown in Figure 17-7). This allows you to quickly see what value you have selected for each of the categories. A value is also displayed that allows you to easily show all values for that category.

FIGURE 17-7

How It Works

The search refinement tool allows you to quickly and easily refine your search results based on common elements such as file type and author. This will allow you to quickly narrow your search results based on criteria such as "I know who worked on the presentation and I know they worked on it recently." As you select the options in the refinement panel, the values displayed in the search results are narrowed to match your selected criteria.

Search Default Settings

So far, all of the examples in this chapter have been based on the default search settings. The default settings provide a great starting point and allow users to easily search for content within their site; however, these default settings are quite limited, and if they are not customized further, then you will be missing out on many of the great features included with SharePoint Enterprise Search. The rest of this chapter will be focused on the different customizations that can be made for search.

Building Search Queries

Before you go too deeply into the details, let's take a few minutes to look at some of the features within SharePoint that you can use to build search queries. If you have ever watched someone search for something on the Internet, you have probably thought to yourself that you would have likely searched a little differently for the same thing. The truth of the matter is that we all search a little differently from each other. Some users want to use a very rich interface, and some users want to manually type in search queries. We wanted to take a little space in the chapter to let you know of some of the tools that you can use to help build effective search queries.

Boolean Search

One of the newest features in SharePoint 2010 is the ability for users to manually enter Boolean Searches from a search box. The following Boolean properties (also referred to in places as logical operators) are supported within the search entry box:

- AND
- OR
- NOT

These can be combined to form a search query. An example is `("Gear" OR "Machines") AND (title: "Presentation" OR title: "Report")`. Entering this search query would return all items that contain Gear or Machines and have Presentation or Report in the title. Keep in mind when you are using the Boolean operators that they are case-sensitive, and if they are not in all CAPS, then they will be considered part of the search phrase and not an operator.

Prefix Matching

A prefix matching search is where a user adds a * to the end of a text phrase and then the search returns all the results that start with the text the user entered before the *. An example of this would be a user searching using the query "ba*" and getting the results for bake, ball, bacon, and backpack.

LOCATION OF THE *

Keep in mind that this type of search is a prefix matching search only, so the * must come at the end of the phrase. Using the * at the beginning of the phrase is considered suffix matching and is not supported. This can often become a point of confusion for your user community if they are expecting SharePoint to fully support the wildcard search (including both prefix and suffix searching).

Phonetic People Search

One of the wonderful features in SharePoint 2010 is the ability to do a people search based on the phonetic spelling of a user's name. This is a great feature because, in many cases, it can be difficult to know the spelling of all the users' names within your organization. Using phonetic search, you can enter the search term "Neal" and you will also get results for "Neale."

Suggestions and Did You Mean?

SharePoint 2010 includes a feature that will look at users' search queries and provide them will additional suggestions in the form of a "Did you mean?" suggestion. These suggestions are created from recent search queries, a dictionary, and a custom location where you can enter your own suggestions. This feature is great because it can help users easily identify and correct any mistakes within their search query.

Customizing the Search Experience

Now that you have covered the basics of search, it is time to move to some of the different things you can do to customize your search experience. You are going to start your configurations at the site collection level. You learned earlier in the book that a site collection is the smallest boundary available in SharePoint. When you apply settings to the site collection, they affect all webs within that site collection. In this section, your changes will only affect the current site collection. Once you have worked through the various changes you can make at the site collection level, you will look at the changes you can make at the service application level. We are taking this approach because it is very likely that many readers of this book will only have access to the site collection. To access the search settings we are discussing, you will need to have full control of the site collection. The search settings are accessed through the site settings page, under the site collection heading. There are three specific configuration pages that we will discuss, search settings, search scopes, and search keywords. Figure 17-8 shows the locations of these links on the site settings page.

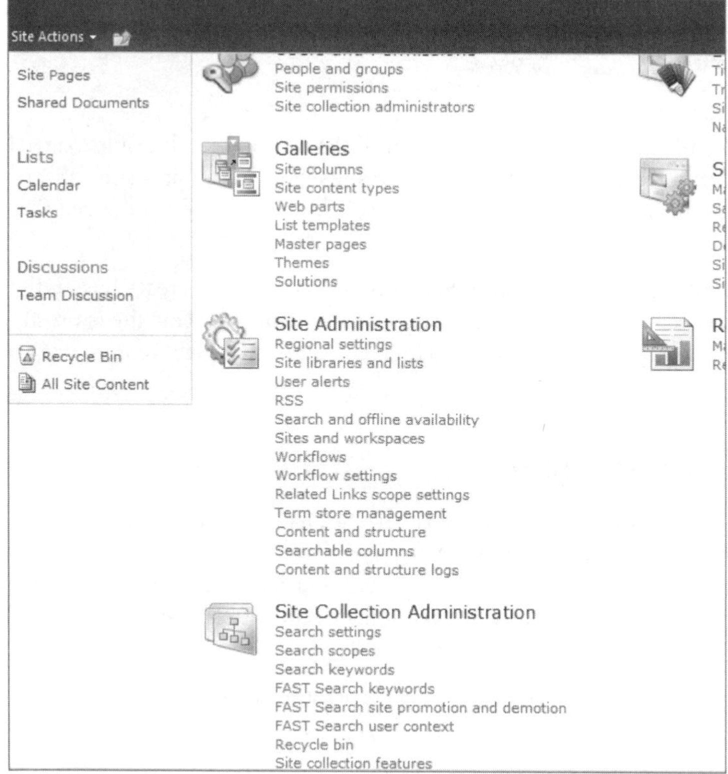

FIGURE 17-8

Search Settings

The first option displayed under the Site Collection settings is Search Settings. From this screen, you will be able to configure the behavior of searching for all sites within the site collection. There are three different settings that you can modify from this page, including enabling search scopes, defining how the scopes drop-down is configured, and determining what search results page will be used to display your search results. Before we go any further with these configuration settings, there are a few items that you need to be sure you understand. Once you understand these items, you will be able to understand the different configuration options available to you.

- **Contextual Search:** A contextual search is a search that is based on your location. It is denoted in the scopes drop-down with "This Site: [site name]" or "This List: [list name]." By default, your site is configured to use the contextual search scope of This Site for all searches. Unless you configure the site collection differently, This Site will be the only search scope used within the site collection. So far, all of the examples in this chapter have been examples of contextual searches.
- **Scopes Dropdown:** The scopes drop-down is the drop-down box located next to the search box that allows users to choose a specific scope for searching. This is not enabled by default; however, as you will see below, it can be enabled within the site collection. Figure 17-9 shows a site that has been configured to use a scopes drop-down.

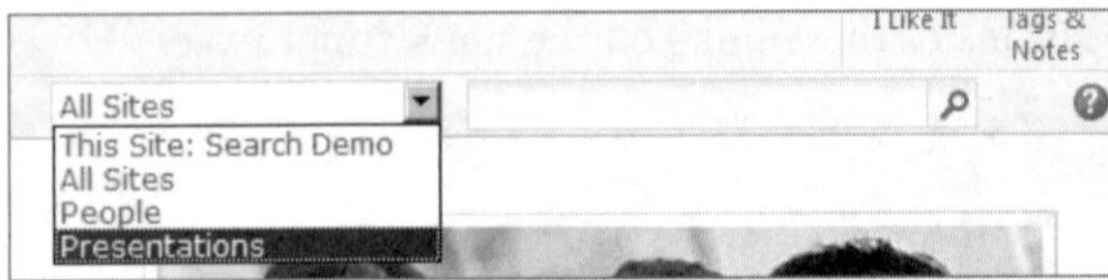

FIGURE 17-9

- **/_layouts/OSSSearchResults.aspx:** This is the location of the default search results page. This page is located on the server and is the default search results page for all new site collections. Keep in mind that since this page is stored on the server, it can't be easily customized through the browser.
- **Search Center:** A Search Center is a site within SharePoint that has been created using the Enterprise Search Center template or the Basic Search Center template. This site is preconfigured with all the Search web parts. Many of the search customizations will require you to use one of these Search Center sites.

TRY IT OUT Create a Search Center Site

Since you will need to reference a Search Center in the next Try It Out, let's take a few minutes and walk through the process for creating a Search Center site. Since you want to take full advantage of the features installed, you are going to create a Search Center using the Enterprise Search Center template. Because this is an enterprise template, it requires that you have some of the Enterprise features enabled, so enabling these features will be the first step in the process.

1. Within your site collection, access the site settings page and access the Site Collection Feature page (see Figures 17-10 and 17-11 below).

FIGURE 17-10

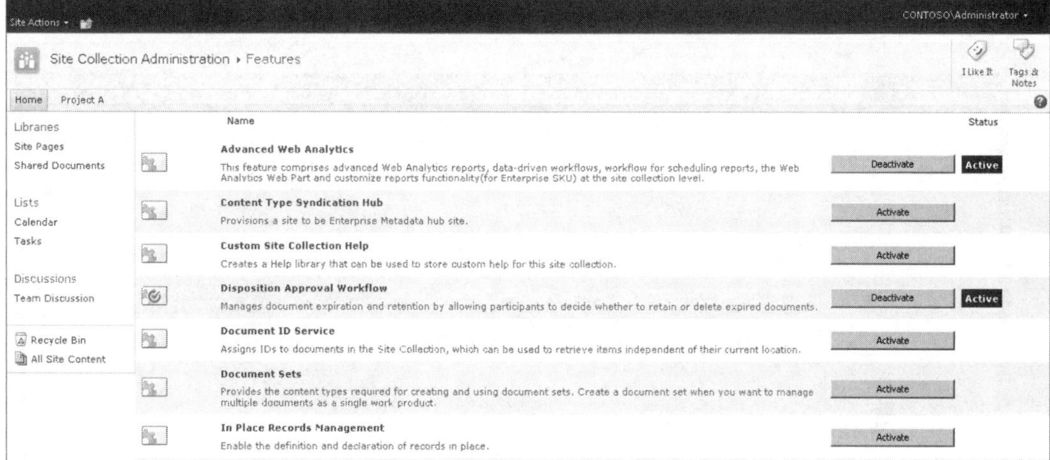

FIGURE 17-11

2. If they are not activated, activate each of the features listed below:
    - Search Server Web Parts
    - SharePoint Server Enterprise Site Collection Features
    - SharePoint Server Publishing Infrastructure
3. From the Site Actions menu, select the New Site option. Once the new site page is loaded, enter the term "Search" in the Search Installed Items textbox, as shown in Figure 17-12, and press Enter. This will allow you to filter the available templates to only show those with "search" in their title.
4. Ensure that the Enterprise Search Center is selected; enter a title and URL for the new site and click the More Options button. On the More Options screen (see Figure 17-13), select the desired configuration options. Click Create, and the new Search Center site will be created.
5. Once the new site is created, you will be redirected to the Search page (See Figure 17-14). You will be referencing this URL in future exercises, so be sure to remember the configuration settings you used while creating this site.

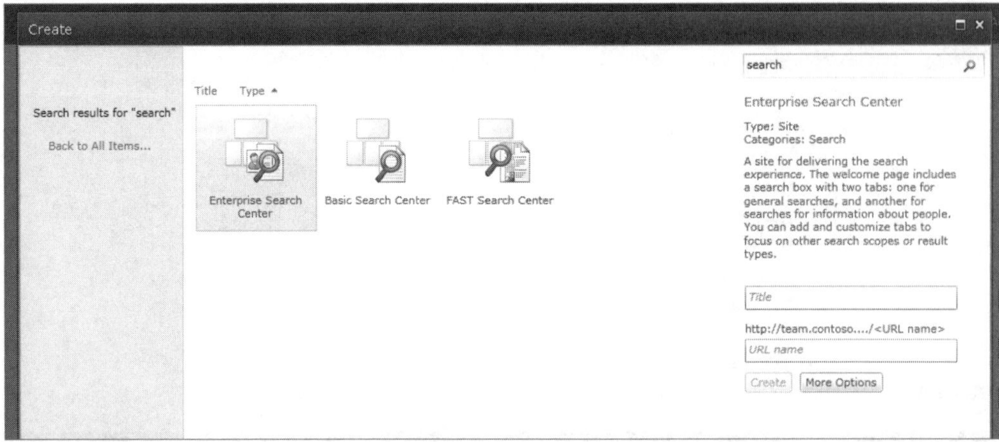

FIGURE 17-12

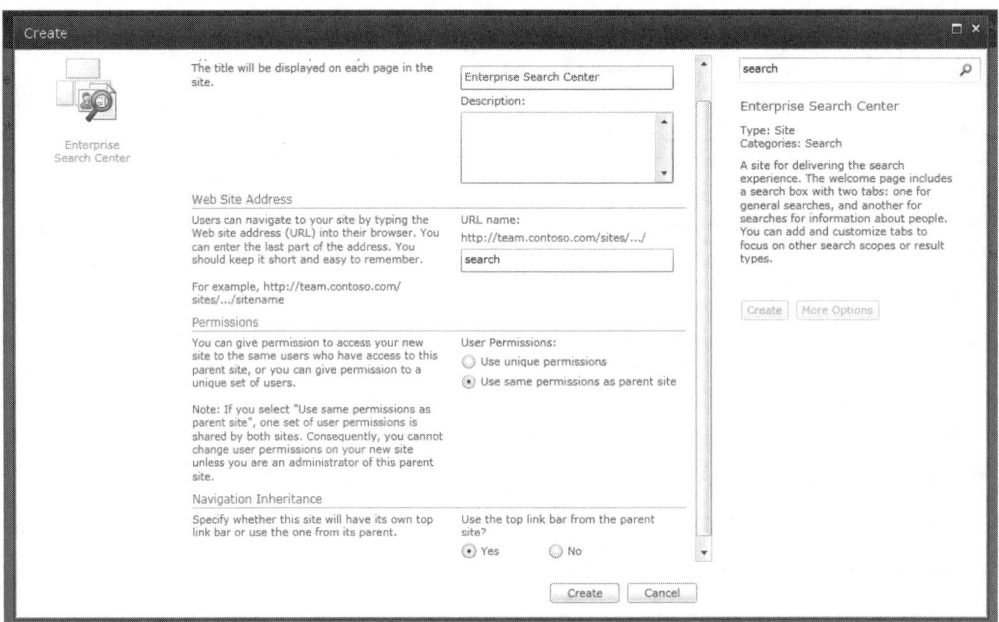

FIGURE 17-13

How It Works

The Search template is a site definition that is preconfigured with all the different web parts and lists that are needed for configuring a Search Center. Creating this site is the first step in configuring the search experience for users.

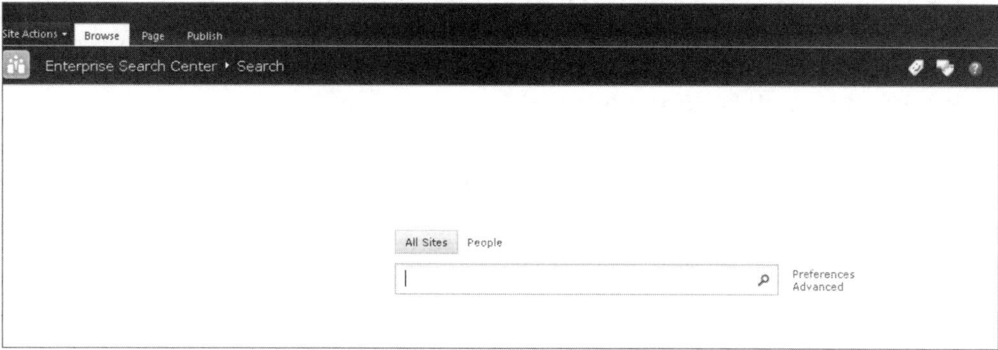

FIGURE 17-14

Now that you have created the preliminary required Search Center, you will work your way through the search configurations for the site collection. If you need to navigate back to the search settings, simply click on the Site Actions menu, then click Site Settings, and then click the Search Settings link in the Site Collection Administration group.

Site Collection Search Center

The first option for configuration determines if sites will use search scopes. You have two options available for configuration, which are described below and shown in Figure 17-15:

- Enable custom scopes (such as "All Sites") by connecting this site collection with the following Search Center:

  Do not use custom scopes. Use only contextual scopes (such as "This Site"). Display results in the Site Collection Search Results Page configured below.

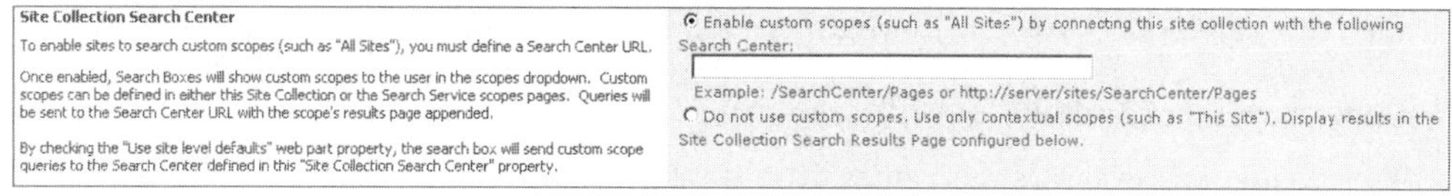

FIGURE 17-15

The first option will configure our site collection to use custom scopes. The scopes available to the site collection are configured in a different location and will be covered later in the chapter. This option is simply the option to turn them on within the site collection. By default, the scopes available with an out-of-the-box configuration are All Sites, which includes all content stored within SharePoint, and People, which includes all users stored in the Profile database. In addition to what is available out of the box, you may also see some additional scopes that have been configured within Central Administration by the Farm Administrators. When you turn the search scopes on, you are also required to provide a link to a Search Center. This Search Center will then be used for all search queries completed within the site collection.

Site Collection Search Dropdown Mode

The next configuration option will determine how the scopes you activated above will be displayed. Figure 17-16 shows the different configuration options available.

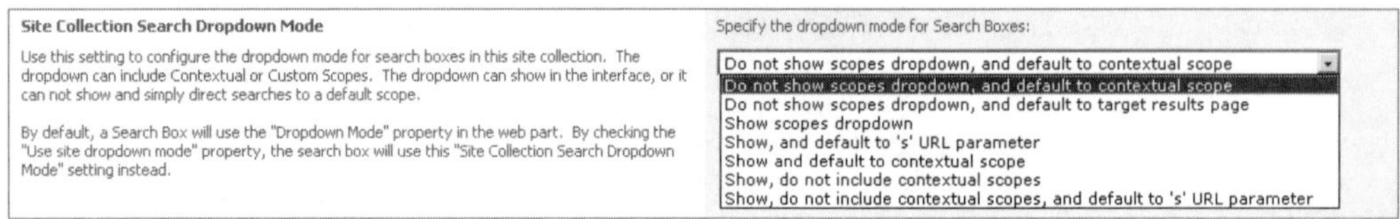

FIGURE 17-16

These options tend to be worded in a very technical nature, and often cause confusion for users who are trying to configure them for their site collection. Throughout the rest of this section, we are going to work through each of these configurations so that we can help reduce any confusion. For each grouping of configurations, an image will be added so that you can see how the display is altered.

Do not show scopes dropdown, and default to contextual scope

This is the default configuration that we have been using. No scopes drop-down is displayed and the initial search is done against the current site. An example is shown in Figure 17-17.

FIGURE 17-17

Do not show scopes dropdown, and default to target results page

For this configuration, no search drop-down is displayed and the search results are passed to the target results page. Since no scope is being specified, the results displayed will be based on the configurations of the target page. This means that if the target page is configured to return things from all scopes, then the search query you enter into this search box will return items from all scopes.

Show scopes dropdown

This configuration shows the scopes drop-down and includes all scopes configured for the site collection, including the contextual search scopes. The search scope will default to the scope configured as the default for the site collection. An example is shown in Figure 17-18.

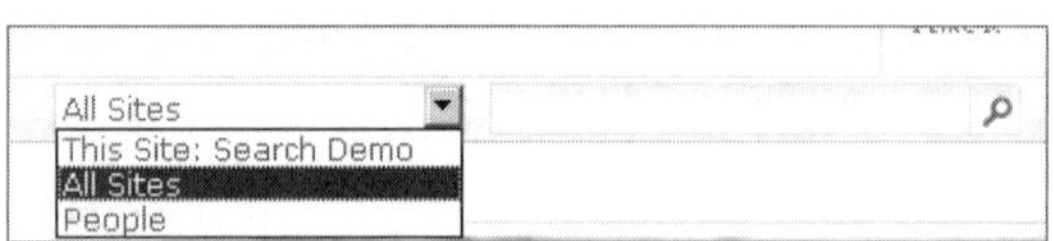

FIGURE 17-18

Show, default to 's' URL parameter

This configuration shows the scopes drop-down and includes all scopes configured for the site collection. The search scope defaults to the parameter that is passed when the site is accessed. If no "s" parameter is defined in the page URL, then the page will load with the default search scope. An example of this is shown in Figure 17-19. Notice that the URL used to access the site contains the parameter `s=People`, which causes the search scope to default to the People search scope when that link is used to access the page.

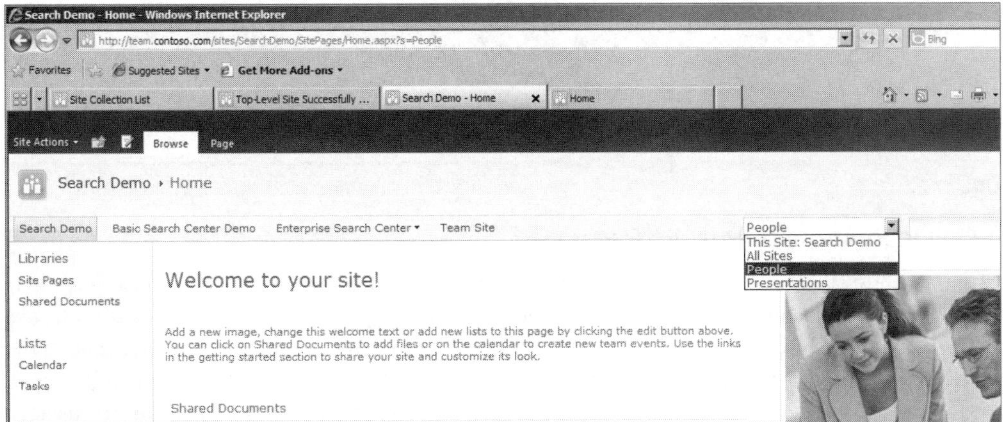

FIGURE 17-19

NOTE *While it is configurable to pass an "s" parameter to the home page, it is not likely that this scenario would be encountered often. Where this is more likely is when you are configuring Search web parts or the Search Center. As you work through the Try It Outs later in this chapter, you will see how this "s" parameter can be used to create a rich experience for end users.*

Show and default to contextual scope

This configuration option shows all of the search scopes but defaults to the contextual scope. This means that all the search scopes will be displayed for the site collection, but by default, the search will be done against the current site. Users will be able to specify a scope, but by default, they will search the current site. An example of this is shown in Figure 17-20.

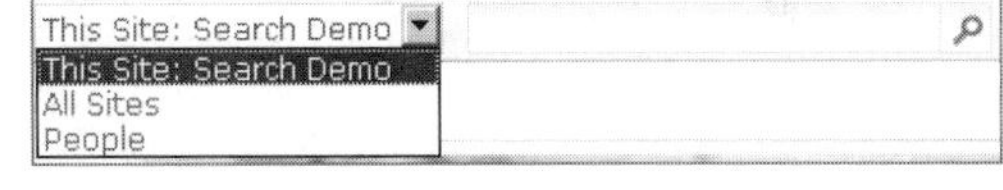

FIGURE 17-20

Show, do not include contextual scopes

This configuration option will show the scopes drop-down but will exclude all of the contextual search scopes. An example is shown in Figure 17-21.

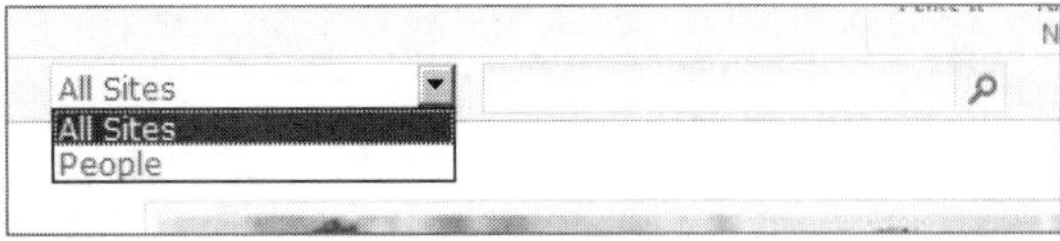

FIGURE 17-21

Show, do not include contextual scopes, and default to 's' URL parameter

This configuration option will show the scopes drop-down, exclude all of the contextual search scopes, and default the scope to the "s" parameter in the URL. An example is shown in Figure 17-22.

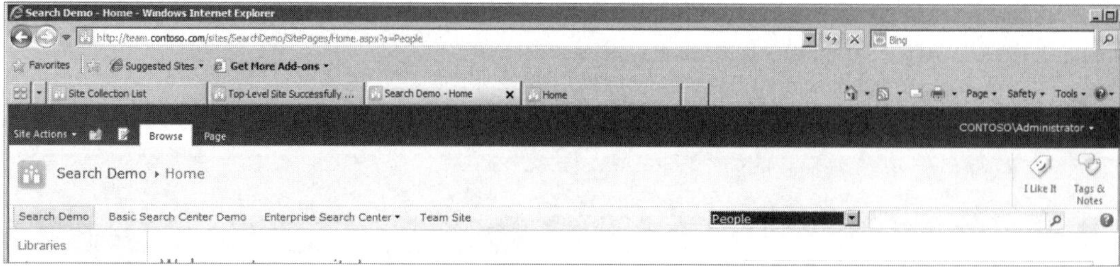

FIGURE 17-22

Site Collection Search Results Page

Our final configurable setting in Search Settings is the Site Collection Search Results Page. This is the location to which contextual searches will be sent. This page is, by default, configured to use the `/_layouts/OSSSearchResults.aspx` page. Keep in mind that, if you use a page other than the page you configured for the search scope page, your users will be taken to different results pages, depending on the scope they are using to search. This can sometimes cause confusion for users, so it is a decision that you want to be sure you think through completely before configuring the setting.

TRY IT OUT Enable and Configure Search Scopes Drop-down

In this Try It Out, you will enable the site collection to use search scopes and then configure the behavior of the search scopes.

1. Within your site collection, access the site settings page and access the Search Settings Page (as shown in Figure 17-23).

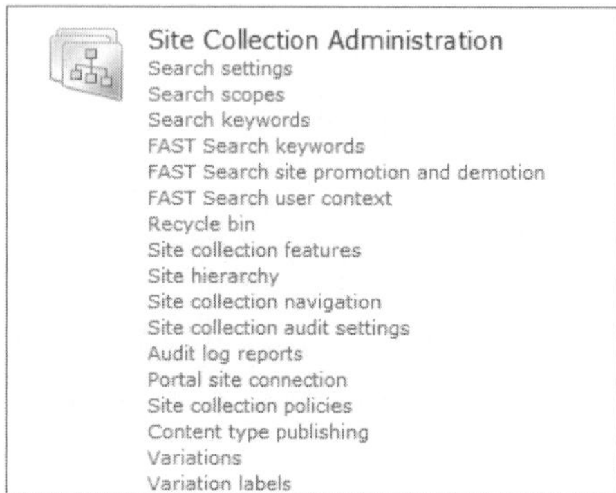

FIGURE 17-23

2. In the Site Collection Search Center configuration settings, select the option to Enable custom search scopes and then enter the URL for the Search Center created in the preceding exercise (as shown in Figure 17-24).

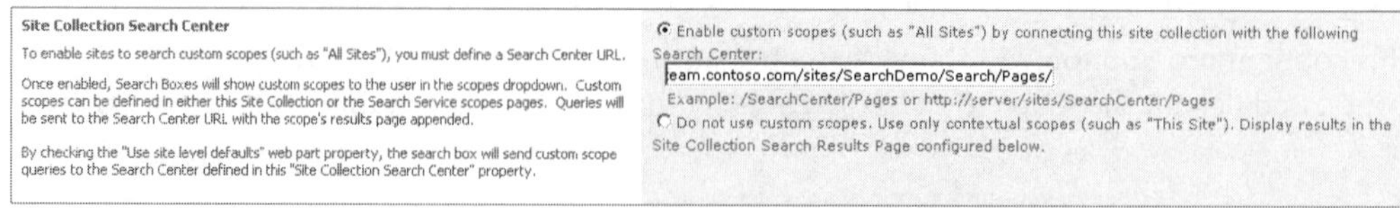

FIGURE 17-24

3. In the Site Collection Search Dropdown Mode, select the Show and default to contextual scope Search Scope. You are choosing this option because you want to allow your users to search against all site content from within your site, but you want the default search to be restricted to just the current site (as shown in Figure 17-25).

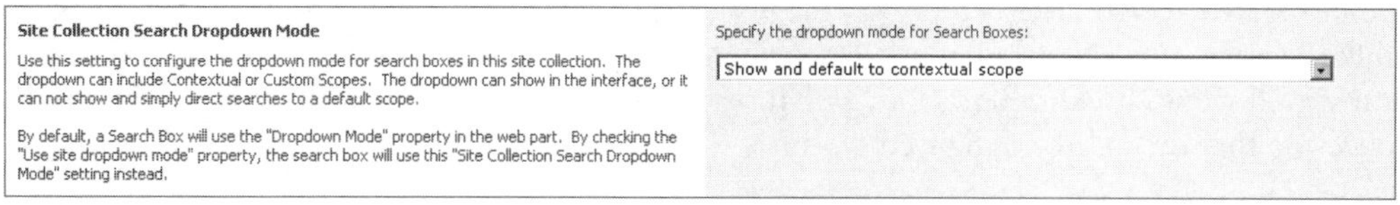

Site Collection Search Dropdown Mode

Use this setting to configure the dropdown mode for search boxes in this site collection. The dropdown can include Contextual or Custom Scopes. The dropdown can show in the interface, or it can not show and simply direct searches to a default scope.

By default, a Search Box will use the "Dropdown Mode" property in the web part. By checking the "Use site dropdown mode" property, the search box will use this "Site Collection Search Dropdown Mode" setting instead.

Specify the dropdown mode for Search Boxes:

Show and default to contextual scope

FIGURE 17-25

4. In the Site Collection Search Results Page, enter the same URL that was used for the Site Collection Search Center with `/results.aspx` added to the end of the URL. This will cause all searches, whether contextual or scope-based, to be delivered through the same Search Center (as shown in Figure 17-26).

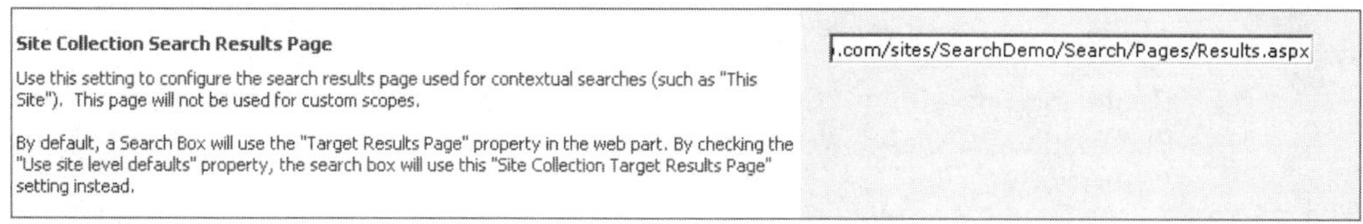

FIGURE 17-26

5. Select OK and then navigate back to the home page of the site collection. In the search area, you should now see a search scopes drop-down box, and when you complete a search, your results should be displayed in the Search Center site. You can test this by using the search term "gear" from the previous Try It Out.

6. Enter the search term **gear** in the search box, and press Enter. Notice that the search results are displayed using the site you configured in steps 2 and 4 (as shown in Figure 17-27).

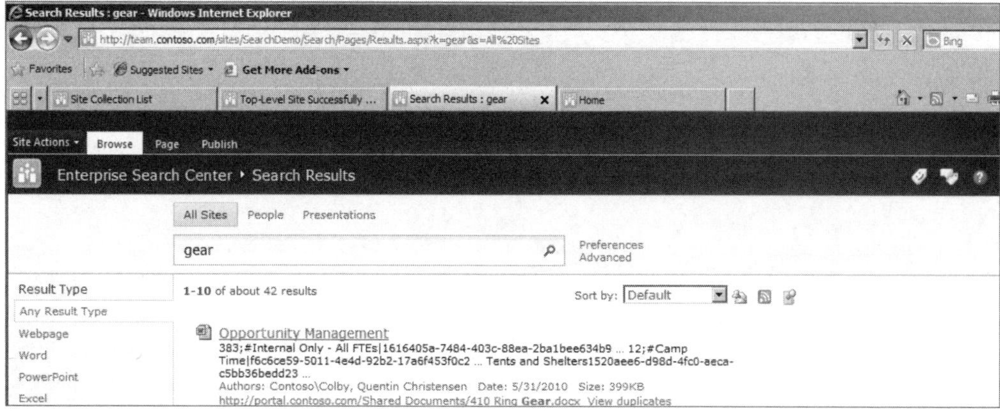

FIGURE 17-27

How It Works

As you make configuration changes to the scope settings, the search boxes within the site collection are updated to match those configurations. In this example, you configured the scopes to behave in a certain way and configured the search queries to be sent to a specific search results page.

Search Scopes

Now that you have configured the basic search settings for your site collection, you will move on to configuring custom search scopes. You defined search scopes earlier in this chapter as a way to create a subset of the index so that you were running queries only against that subset. Search scopes can be created at two different levels: global search scopes and site collection search scopes. Once a global search scope is created, it can be consumed by any site collection within the farm. Site collection search scopes are different from global search scopes in that they are limited to the specific site collection that they were configured within.

NOTE *For the purpose of this book, most of the examples that we will be working through will occur at the site collection level. At the end of this chapter, there will be an advanced search configuration section that will briefly cover some of the admin configurations. If, after working through the advanced section, you are still looking for more in-depth detail, it is recommended that you refer to the following SharePoint 2010 admin books:*

- Beginning SharePoint 2010 Administration: Windows SharePoint Foundation 2010 and Microsoft SharePoint Server 2010 *by Husman and Stahl (Wrox, 2010)*
- Professional SharePoint 2010 Administration *by Klindt, Young, and Caravajal (Wrox, 2010)*

The search scope configuration pages can be accessed from the Site Settings Page, under the Site Collection Administration option. Figure 17-28 shows the configuration screen. In the remainder of this section, you will work through the different configuration options available within this page. You will start by first creating a new scope and then conclude by modifying the different display groups.

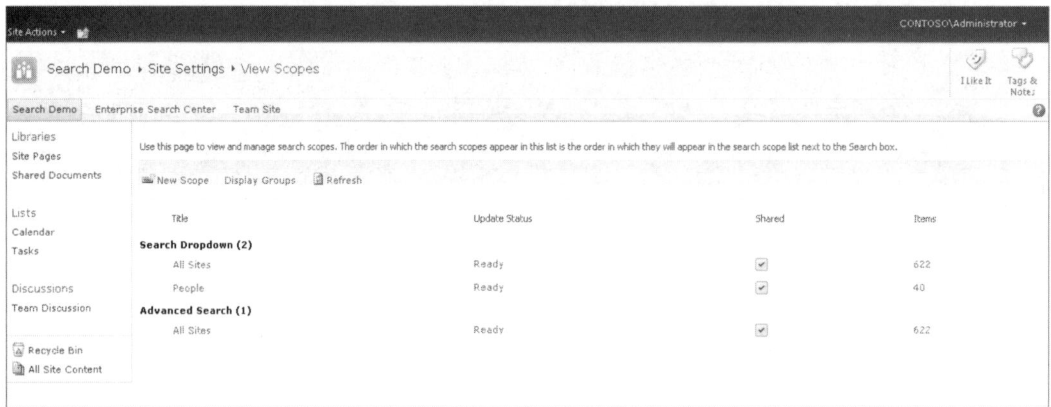

FIGURE 17-28

New Scope

The New Scope option on the configuration screen allows you to create and configure a new search scope. When you select this option, a form is generated that requires you to configure the new search scope. You start by first giving your scope a unique name. This is the name that will be displayed in the Search drop-down. You then select one of the following options for your display group:

- **Search Dropdown:** When you select this item, your search scope will be displayed within the search drop-down box.
- **Advanced Search:** When you select this item, your search scope will be displayed on the Advanced Search page.

When selecting the display group, you can select one, both, or neither. Keep in mind that, if you select neither, then users will only be able to query the search scope by manually adding the "s" parameter to the search query URL or through a custom solution. Finally, you are able to select one of two target results page options:

- **Use the default Search Results Page:** Selecting this option will use the default results page that has been configured for the site in the Search Settings.
- **Specify a different page for searching this scope:** Selecting this option will allow you to enter a specific search results page's URL.

NOTE *Keep in mind that changing the search results page here will change it for only one specific scope. While this may be the desired behavior, this may also cause confusion for your end users. Be sure to think through various use cases to make sure that the decisions you are making around these settings will not cause any undue confusion to your users.*

Figure 17-29 provides an example of a new scope configuration page where the scope will be allowed for both the Search Drop-down and the Advanced Search and where the results will be presented on the default search results page.

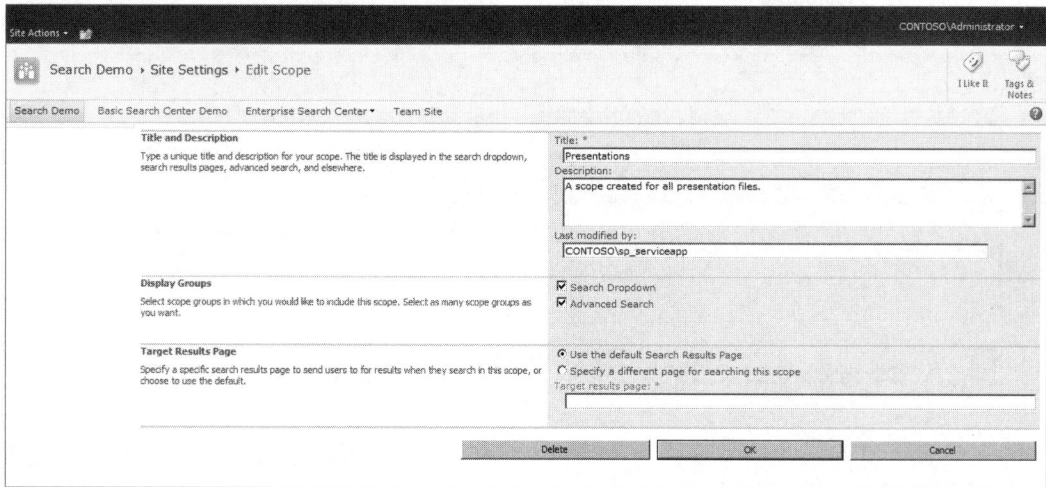

FIGURE 17-29

Once you click OK on the scope creation screen, you will be redirected to the scope settings page. You will notice that, just as in Figure 17-30, your new scope is displayed with the status of "Empty–Add Rules."

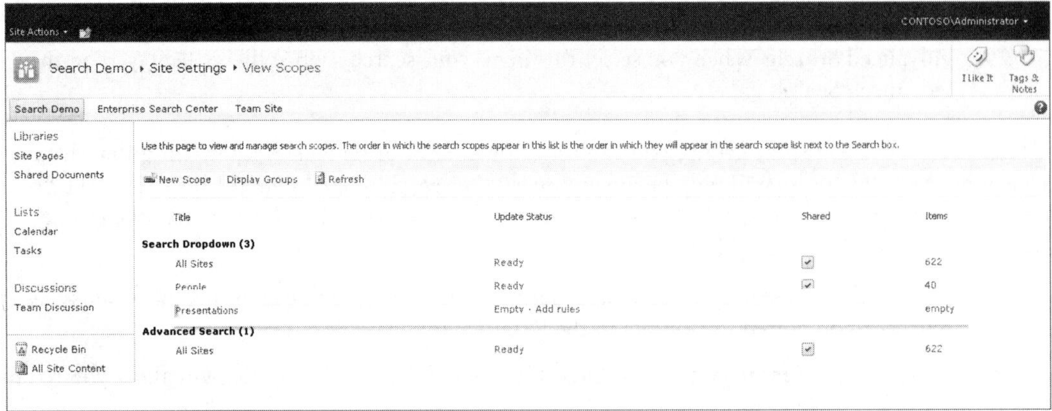

FIGURE 17-30

Rules are the guidelines that the scope uses to determine what content from the index should be included in the scope. A single scope can have many different rules within it. Rules are built one at a time and then, as the scope is compiled, all rules are executed to ensure that only the content you specify is included in the search. If you click on the Add Rules link, you will be redirected to the Rules Configuration page. On this page, there are three main configuration areas. As you select the option on the top of the page, you will be prompted for the required values to complete the form. Each of the Rule Types requires different values for configuration.

- **Web Address:** This is the URL of a specific site. When you select this option, you are required to enter a valid location for one of the following options (see Figure 17-31):
  - Folder
  - Hostname
  - Domain or Subdomain

Scope Rule Type Scope rules define what is in or not in a scope. Use different types of rules to match items in various ways	(•) Web Address (http://server/site) ( ) Property Query (Author = John Doe) ( ) All Content
Web Address Web Address scope rules can be used to create search scopes that include content in web sites, file shares, exchange public folders, or any other content in the search index that has a URL. Folder rules will include items in the folder and subfolders of the indicated path. Domain or hostname rules include all items within the specified domain or hostname.	(•) Folder: Example: http://site/subsite/folder ( ) Hostname: Example: servername ( ) Domain or subdomain: Example: office.microsoft.com
Behavior Decide how this rule should be applied to the overall scope. The scope-wide filter is used when combining the items matching all rules to determine what is in the scopes overall.	(•) Include - Any item that matches this rule will be included, unless the item is excluded by another rule ( ) Require - Every item in the scope must match this rule ( ) Exclude - Items matching this rule will be excluded from the scope
	OK Cancel

FIGURE 17-31

- **Property Query:** This is the option you select if you want to include or exclude content based on a property such as author, file extension, or creation date. When you select this option, you are required to select the property that you want to query against and then enter the value that will be used for validation. If the equation equates to true, then the rule is executed for that item (see Figure 17-32).

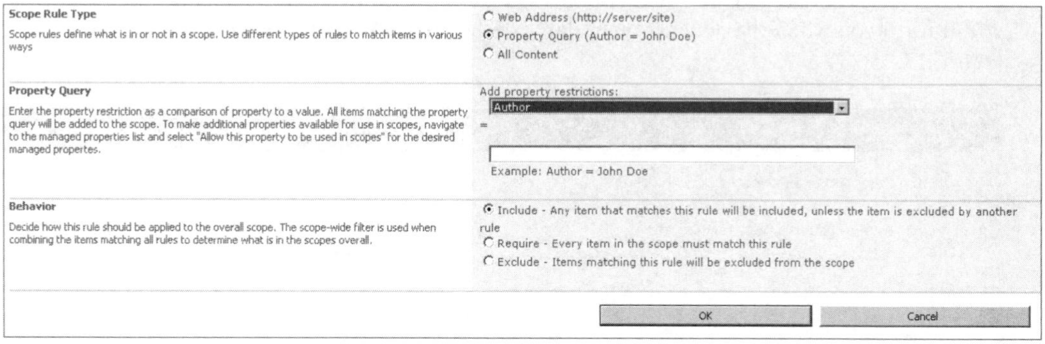

FIGURE 17-32

NOTE *The values available for selection in the scope rules are for properties that have been mapped in the search service configuration. For the purpose of this example, we are not covering how to create managed properties; you are just consuming the managed properties that have already been created within the environment.*

- **All Content:** You select this option if you want to pull content from all content sources (see Figure 17-33).

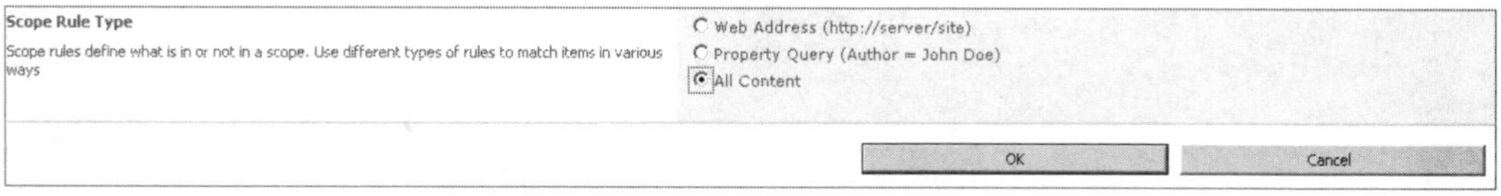

FIGURE 17-33

Rules based on a web address or a property also have a configured behavior. This scope looks at the behavior of all the created rules to determine what is included and excluded from the scope. Since you can have multiple rules, it is possible that one rule includes content, while another excludes it. There are three specific options for behavior:

- **Include:** This means that if the rule equates to true for a particular item, it will be included in the scope, as long as there is no other rule that excludes it.
- **Require:** This means that the rule must equate to true for every item in the scope.
- **Exclude:** This means that if the rule equates to true, then the item will be excluded from the scope.

Once you click OK, you are redirected to the Scope Properties and Rules page. Figure 17-34 shows an example of this page. From this page, you can configure additional rules for the scope and also modify the general scope settings. Also note that you can see a summary of the rules you created, which includes an approximate Item Count from the index. This page will also show an update status for the scope. Scopes are recompiled on a scheduled basis, which means that there will likely be a short delay between you making your changes and the scope being updated. The status line item will inform you when the next scope update is scheduled. An example of this update can be seen in Figure 17-35.

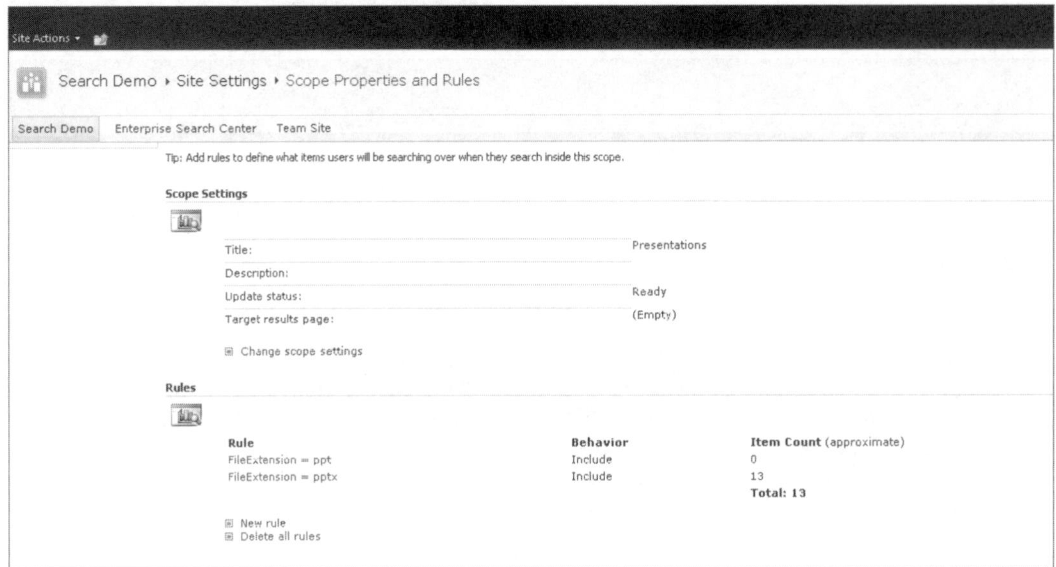

FIGURE 17-34

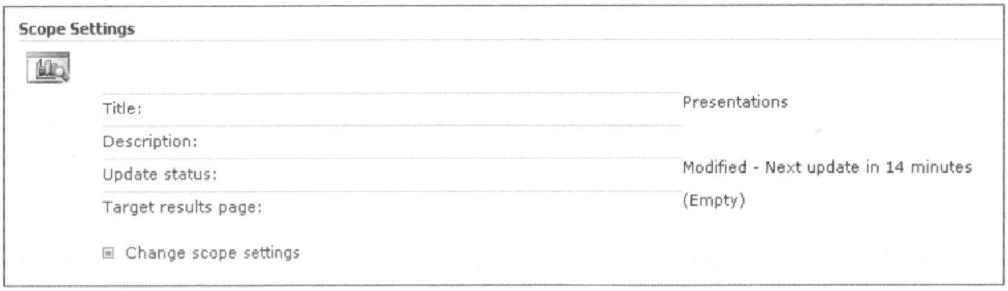

Scope Settings

Title: Presentations

Description:

Update status: Modified - Next update in 14 minutes

Target results page: (Empty)

Change scope settings

FIGURE 17-35

This page can be accessed at any time from the Scope Settings page. Once you are on this page, there is really no easy way to navigate back to the Scope Settings page. So, when you are on this page, click the Site Settings link in the breadcrumbs and then select the Scope Settings link to return the summary page.

Display Groups

There are two configurable display groups for search scopes, the search drop-down and the advanced search. So far in this chapter, we have only worked through the search drop-down. We will be covering the advanced search further in the chapter, once we get to the Search Center. Within each display group, you can configure which scopes are visible, which order they are displayed in, and which scope is the default scope for the display group. To access these settings, click on the Display Groups link on the top of the Search Scopes settings page. From this page, click on the group you would like to modify to open the configuration page. An example of this page is shown in Figure 17-36.

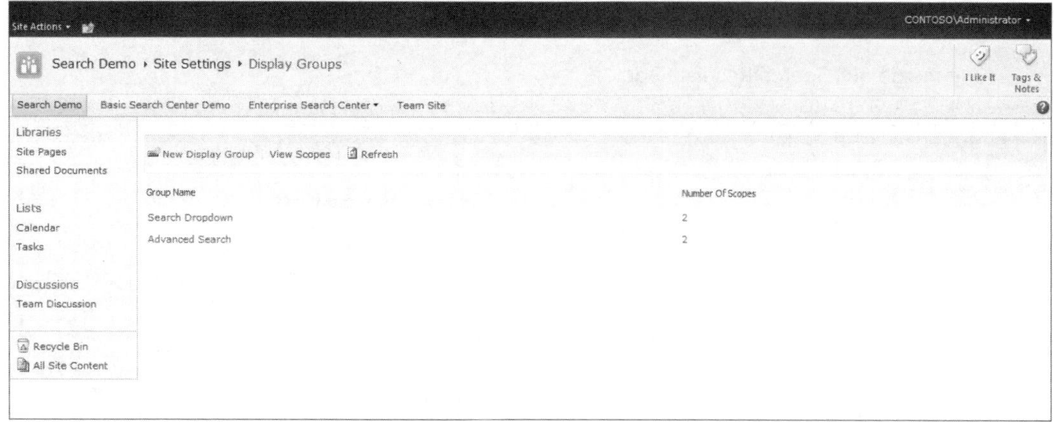

FIGURE 17-36

Refresh

You have probably noticed the link called Refresh across many of the Search Scope management pages. This link is provided as a tool to refresh the information on the page. This could be helpful if you are waiting to see when the next scope update will be. This link only needs to be used when you have the page open for an extended period, and serves the same purpose as doing a refresh within the web browser.

TRY IT OUT Create a Custom Search Scope

In this Try It Out, you will create a custom search scope. You will use the scenario of working within a sales department. Within the sales department site collection, you are storing many different presentations. You would like to create a search scope so that you can search through all presentations. There are a few ways that you could determine which documents were presentations, including the use of content types or metadata. For this example, however, you are going to base your scope requirements on the file extension. You are doing this because you know that all presentations are created in PowerPoint.

1. Within your site collection, access the site settings page and access the Search Scopes Settings Page.
2. Select the New Scope option and configure your scope with the following options (see Figure 17-37):

PROPERTY	VALUE
Title	Presentations
Description	A scope created for all presentation files

continues

(continued)

PROPERTY	VALUE
Last Modified	Leave as default
Search Drop-down	Yes
Advanced Search	Yes
Use the default Search Results Page	Yes

Title and Description
Type a unique title and description for your scope. The title is displayed in the search dropdown, search results pages, advanced search, and elsewhere.
Title: *
Presentations
Description:
A scope created for all presentation files.
Last modified by:
CONTOSO\Administrator
Display Groups
Select scope groups in which you would like to include this scope. Select as many scope groups as you want.
Search Dropdown
Advanced Search
Target Results Page
Specify a specific search results page to send users to for results when they search in this scope, or choose to use the default.
Use the default Search Results Page
Specify a different page for searching this scope
Target results page: *
OK
Cancel

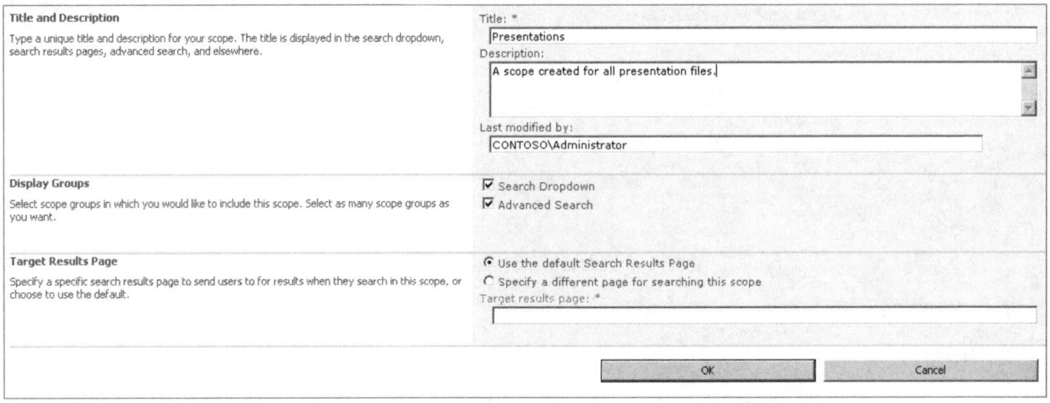

FIGURE 17-37

3. Select the Add Rule link on the View Scopes page, and configure the rule with the following properties (see Figure 17-38):

PROPERTY	VALUE
Scope Rule Type	Property Query
Property Query	FileExtension = pptx
Behavior	Include

Scope Rule Type
Scope rules define what is in or not in a scope. Use different types of rules to match items in various ways
Web Address (http://server/site)
Property Query (Author = John Doe)
All Content
Property Query
Enter the property restriction as a comparison of property to a value. All items matching the property query will be added to the scope. To make additional properties available for use in scopes, navigate to the managed properties list and select "Allow this property to be used in scopes" for the desired managed propertes.
Add property restrictions:
FileExtension
=
pptx
Example: Author = John Doe
Behavior
Decide how this rule should be applied to the overall scope. The scope-wide filter is used when combining the items matching all rules to determine what is in the scopes overall.
Include - Any item that matches this rule will be included, unless the item is excluded by another rule
Require - Every item in the scope must match this rule
Exclude - Items matching this rule will be excluded from the scope
OK
Cancel

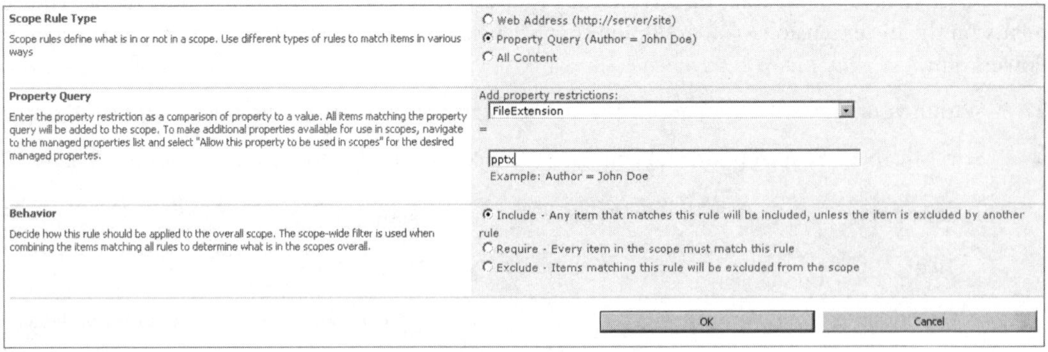

FIGURE 17-38

4. Click OK. Notice that you are redirected to the View Scopes page and that your scope status shows that you are a new scope and gives an approximate time before the next update (see Figure 17-39).

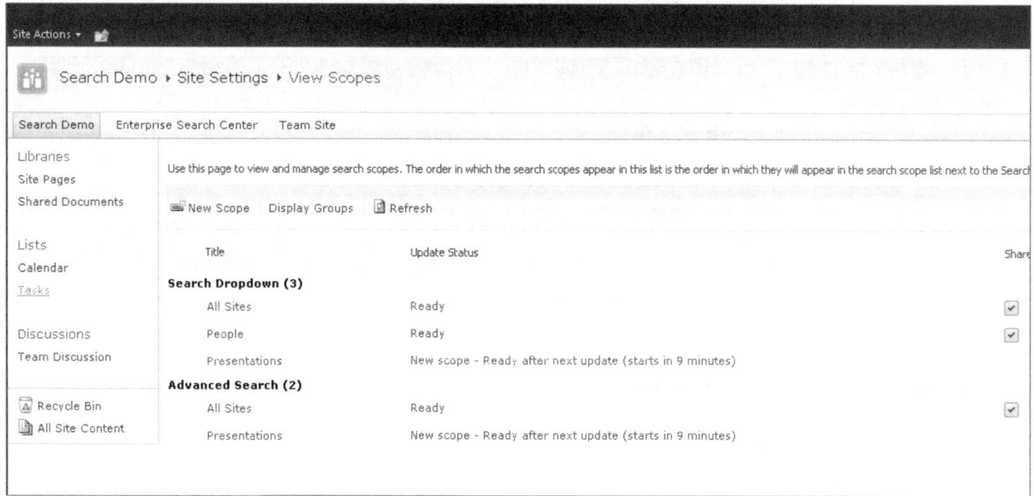

FIGURE 17-39

5. Since you know not all users are going to be using the latest version of Office, you are also going to add a rule for `.ppt` files. From the View Scopes page, click on the Presentations scope and open the Scope Properties and Rules page.

6. Click the New Rule link and configure a new rule with the following properties:

PROPERTY	VALUE
Scope Rule Type	Property Query
Property Query	FileExtension = ppt
Behavior	Include

7. Click on the Site Settings breadcrumb, and then open the Search Scope Settings page.

8. Once the status for your scope has changed to Ready, navigate back to the Site Collection home page.

9. On the home page, you should now see your new scope within the scope drop-down (see Figure 17-40).

10. Enter the search term **gear** into the search box, and press Enter. Notice that all of the search results are PowerPoint files and the search scope in the URL is set to Presentations (see Figure 17-41).

How It Works

In this Try It Out, you created a custom search scope. This scope will be compiled against all the indexes, and if the items in the index meet your scope criteria, they will be included in the scope searches. Whenever users choose to query against your scope, they will be searching only within the items that meet your criteria.

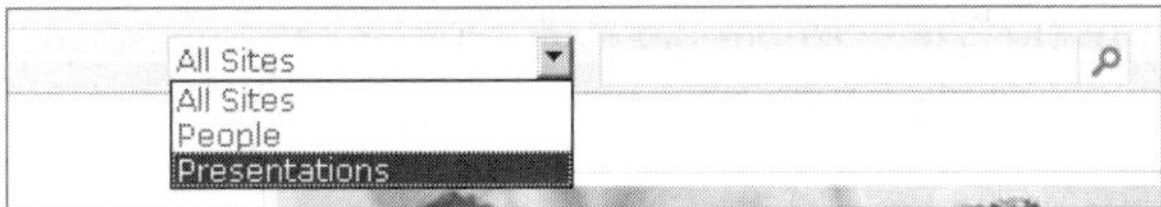

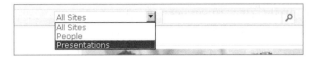

FIGURE 17-40

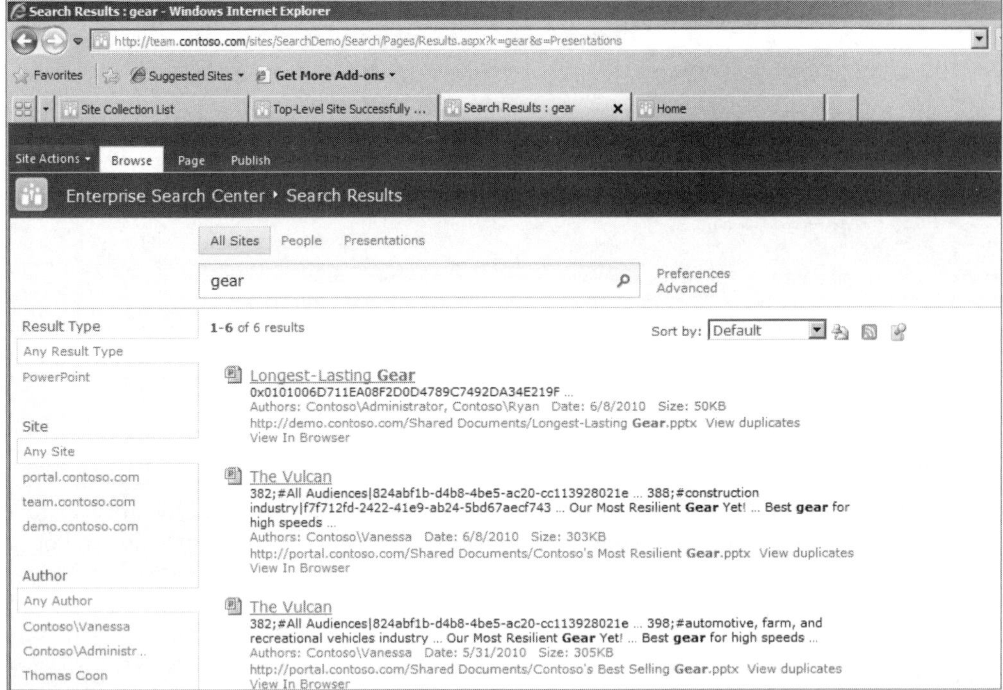

FIGURE 17-41

There is one final thing that we need to cover before moving on from search scopes, and that is the ability to make a copy of an existing search scope and save it as a new search scope. This is a great way to create a baseline scope that can be used as a template for additional scopes. The Copy command is located in the Item Control Block on the View Scopes page. When you select the Make Copy option, a new scope is created with the name "Copy of Scope." You can then access that scope and change the title and modify the rules. You will notice that, when the site is created, it is added to a Display Group called Unused Scopes. This occurs because, by default, the copy of the scope is not added to the same display groups as the scope. This allows you to update and configure the copy as needed, before adding it to one of the display groups. Figure 17-42 shows the location of the copy command, and Figure 17-43 shows the newly created search scope copy.

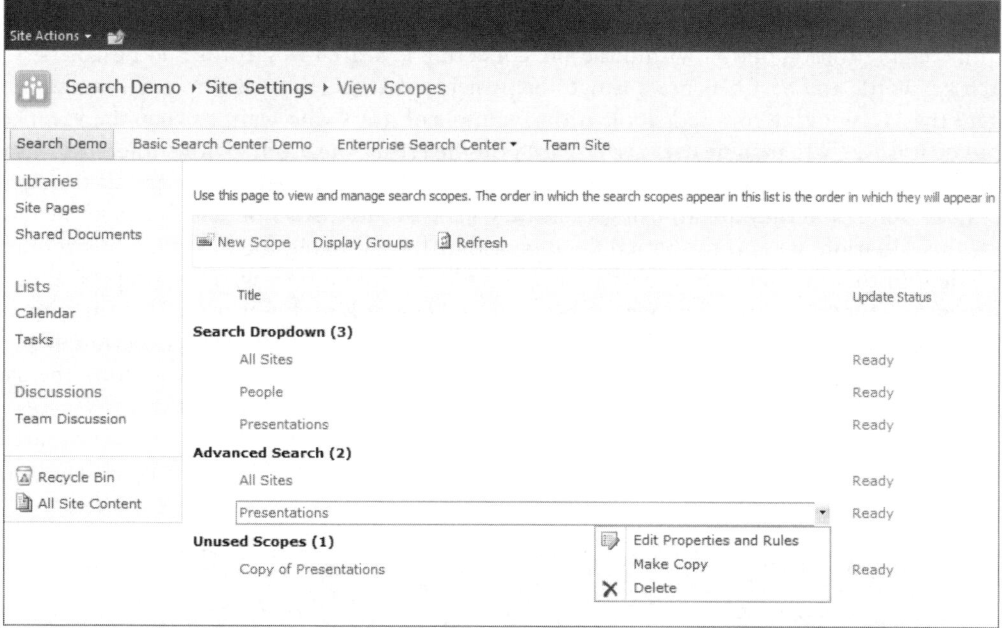

FIGURE 17-42

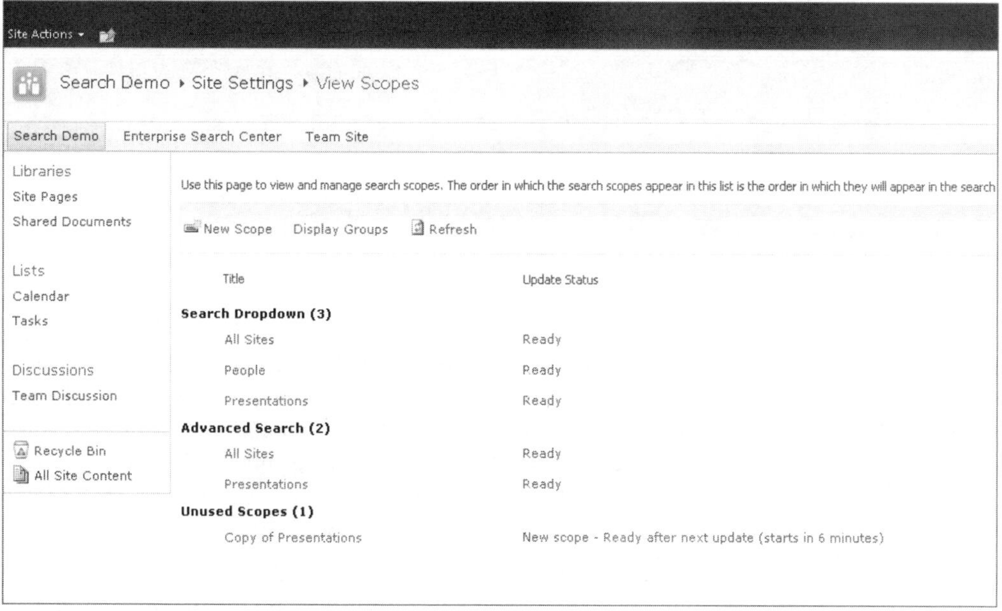

FIGURE 17-43

Search Keywords

The final configuration option within the site collection is Search Keywords and Best Bets. Search keywords and best bets are a way to help ensure that users are able to quickly find the content they are looking for. Let's look at the example of users who want to view the vacation calendar. It is likely that some users will search on the term "vacation," while others will use the term "holiday," and some others may use the phrase "office closed." They are all trying to access one thing, and they are all using what they view as the correct phrase to locate the data. Given this situation, what if the actual document they were looking for was titled "Corporate Schedule"? In this case, none of the users would find the content they were looking for. One way to ensure that this doesn't happen is by creating keywords and best bets. This functionality would allow you to provide a best bet link whenever a user searched using a collection of synonyms that you provide. This way, you can think ahead and, based on what you think the user will be using for search terms, you can create the matching keywords and best bets. Whenever a user searches with one of the keywords you identified, the best bet is returned on the search results page formatted with a star. Figure 17-44 is an example of a search that is returning a best bet based on a keyword.

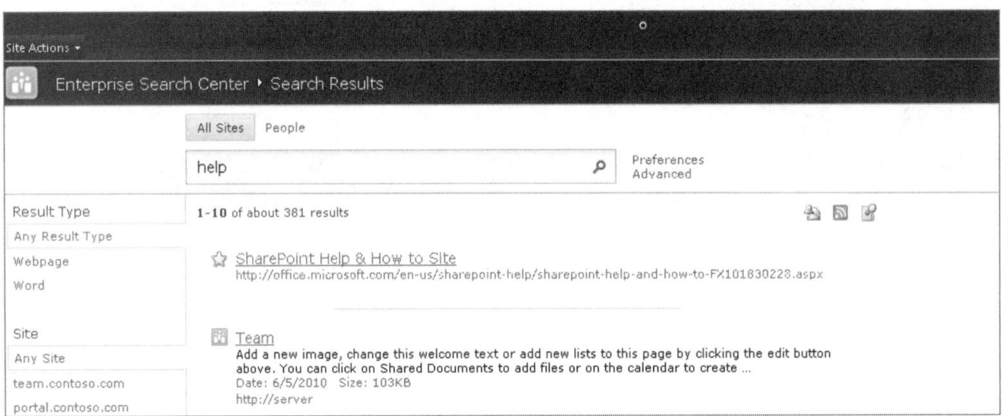

FIGURE 17-44

The great thing about keywords is that they are easy to create and maintain. As part of their configuration, you can specify a start date, an expiration date, and a review date. Whomever you assign as the owner of the keyword will get notifications when the keyword review data arrives. With the expiration dates, you can also push content during seasons of high demand. An example of this could be the end of each year, when you are working on benefits reenrollment. During that time of the year, it is likely that you will want to help users navigate directly to the content they are likely searching for.

Best bets and keywords are a great way for you to help narrow the users' search results to the content they are likely looking for, but what if you don't know what they are looking for? SharePoint provides tools to help you analyze what searches your users are generating, and based on those searches, these tools will recommend best bets for the site collection. All of these reports can be easily accessed from the Keywords Management screen.

TRY IT OUT Create a Search Keyword with Best Bets

In this exercise, you will be creating a search keyword and best bets. We know that users will be accessing search quite a bit, and since most of them are new to SharePoint, you want to be sure that, if they search on anything having to do with getting help, they get the links they are looking for. You are going to start by creating a best bet with a link to the online Microsoft SharePoint help information. Over time, you will watch the reports and suggested keywords and then update your best bets as needed.

1. Within your site collection, access the site settings page and access the Search Keywords Settings page (see Figure 17-45).

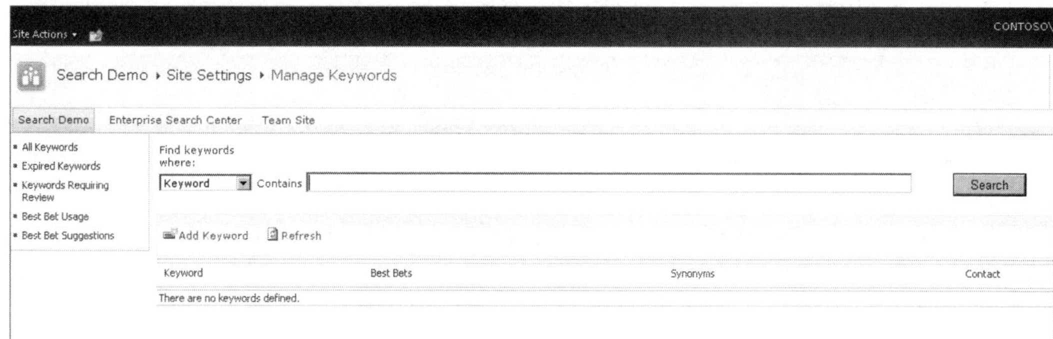

FIGURE 17-45

2. Click the Add Keyword link, and enter the following information for the properties (see Figure 17-46):

PROPERTIES	VALUE
Keyword Phrase	SharePoint Help
Synonyms	SharePoint; Help; User Support; Helpdesk
Keyword Definition	Follow these links to find helpful SharePoint End User Resources.
Contact	Your Username
Start Date	Today's Date
End Date	A Year from Today
Review Date	Six Months from Today

3. Once you have entered the Keyword data, click the Add Best Bet link in the Best Bets section of the form and enter the following properties:

PROPERTY	VALUE
URL	http://office.microsoft.com/en-us/sharepoint-help/sharepoint-help-and-how-to-FX101830228.aspx

continues

(continued)

PROPERTY	VALUE
Title	SharePoint Help & How To Site
Description	This site contains demos and feature listings for the SharePoint toolset.

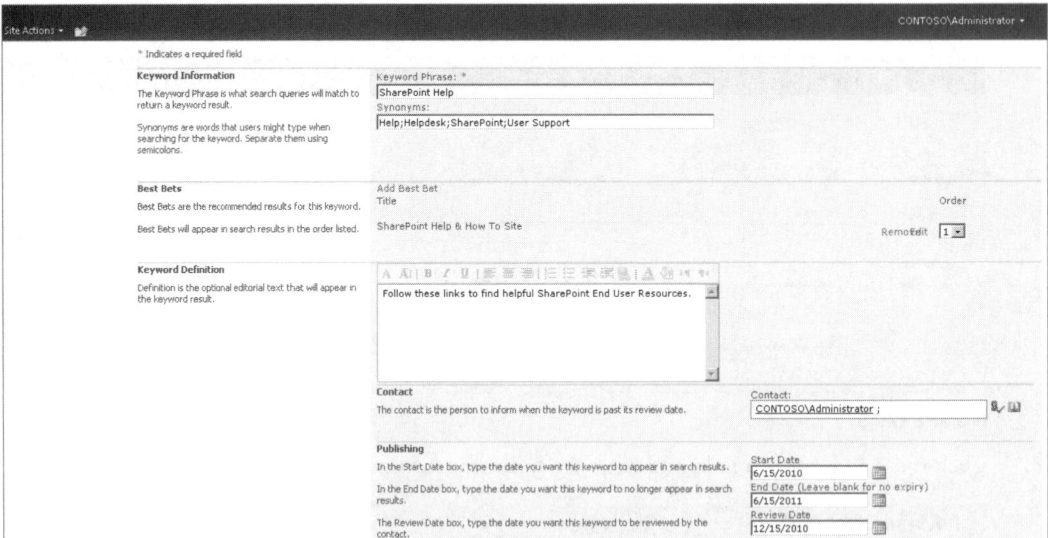

FIGURE 17-46

4. Click OK, and then navigate back to the home page for the site collection.
5. In the Search box, enter the search term **helpdesk** and press Enter. The search results will be returned and the first results provided to the user will be the best bets that you configured (see Figure 17-47).

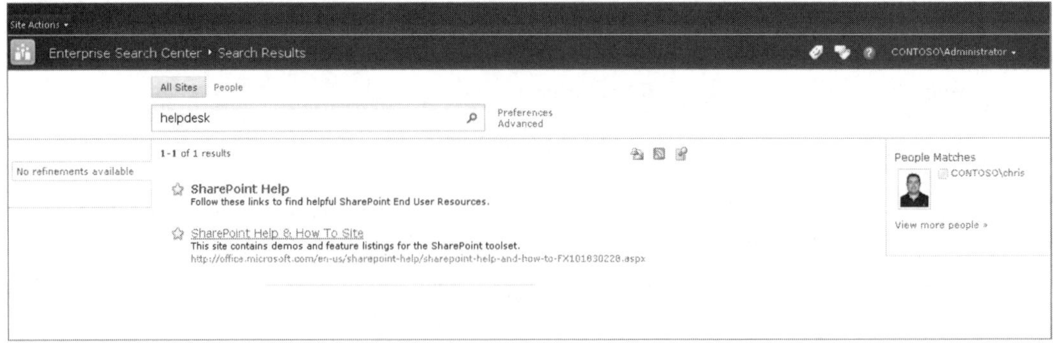

FIGURE 17-47

How It Works

In this example, you created a keyword and a best bet. Whenever the keyword or a synonym is included in the search query, your results will be displayed as a best bet. This allows you to easily direct users to relevant content based on their specific search terms.

Customizing Search Center

To this point in the chapter, you have customized the behavior of search only within the site collection. You have looked at how to create new scopes and add them to the drop-downs; you have also looked at how to add best bets and keywords to help improve the search experience for the end users. Now, you are going to be switching gears slightly and looking at ways to customize the search results that the users see. One of the first tasks you worked through was creating a Search Center site. You learned early in the chapter that the first step in customizing any search behaviors was to create a Search Center. You are now going to look at all the customizations you can make to the Search Center site.

Search Center

A Search Center is a type of site template that is included when SharePoint is installed. There are several different templates that are available, based on the level of licensing you have installed, including:

- Basic Search Center
- Enterprise Search Center
- FAST Search Center (not covered in detail in this book)

The Basic Search Center, shown in Figure 17-48, comes preconfigured for everything that you need to get started with Search. As you see, there is a search entry box, options for Advanced search, and even a link for users to configure preferences. The Enterprise Search Center, shown in Figure 17-49, comes preconfigured with all of the options in the Basic Search Center and several additional features, including the ability to create a tabbed search interface so that users can easily switch between tabs to conduct different search types, such as People and All Sites.

When people first start working with the Search Center templates, it is easy to get confused and overwhelmed. There are a lot of working parts, and sometimes, it can be hard to tell what pieces connect and keep things all together. The best thing to do is to start with the basics. As you learned earlier in the book, a site template is nothing more than a blank site with preconfigured lists, libraries, pages, and web parts. The Search Center is no different. In the following sections, we are going to review all of the different Search web parts, and then, once you know what you are working with, you will look at how they are combined to create such a rich search experience for users.

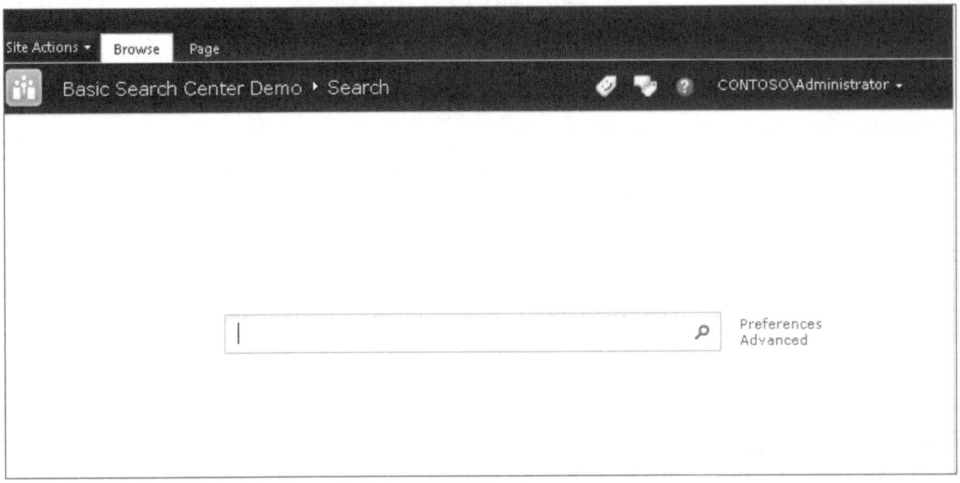

FIGURE 17-48

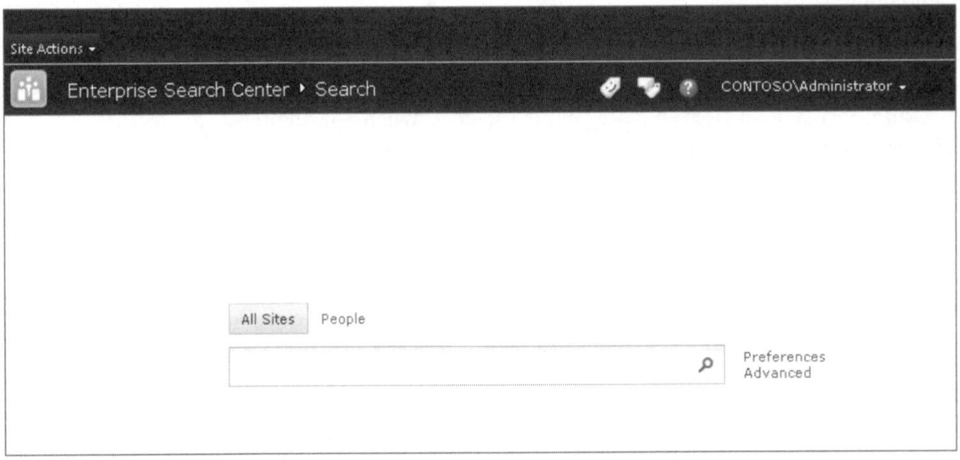

FIGURE 17-49

Search Web Parts

Each page that is created within the Search Center is built using preconfigured web parts. This means that the template is created ready to go, with all the needed parts and pieces connected and configured. These web parts, while they come preconfigured, are simply web parts. This means that they can be added to pages and then configured to behave using the parameters we configured in the Web Part tool pane. This also means that you can modify the behavior of the preconfigured web parts within each of the pages.

Advanced Search Box

This web part provides users an interface for building a search query that uses multiple properties and phrase combinations (see Figure 17-50). Within this web part, you can configure what elements are included on the page and what elements are excluded. Each of the elements within the box is configurable, for example the image below shows the option to search by language. This option, along with others, is configurable within the web part so that you can completely remove it from the advanced search box.

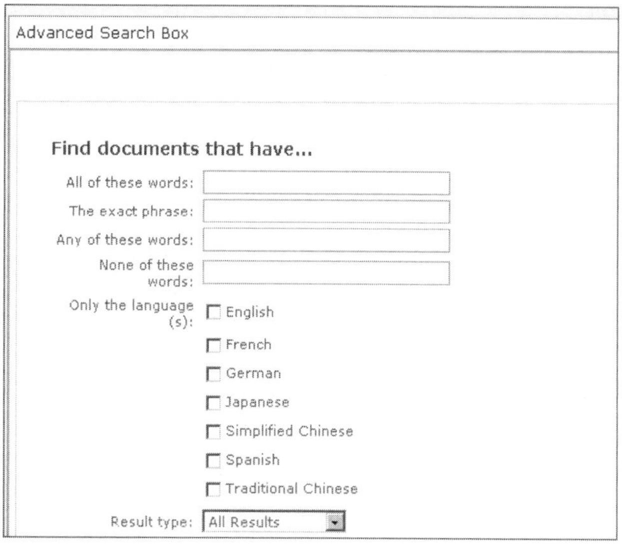

Advanced Search Box

Find documents that have...

All of these words:

The exact phrase:

Any of these words:

None of these words:

Only the language (s): English

French

German

Japanese

Simplified Chinese

Spanish

Traditional Chinese

Result type: All Results

FIGURE 17-50

Dual Chinese Search

This is a web part that is used to configure the display of Chinese search results. You would use this web part only if you had the Chinese language pack installed. Once configured, this web part would allow you to search in the Dual Chinese language.

Federated Results

When this web part is connected to a search box web part, the web part will return search results from the federated location for the provided search query (see Figure 17-51). This web part can be configured with the location of the federated search location, such as the Internet, and with different properties around how the data is displayed, such as limiting the items to only three.

People Refinement Panel

This web part will be used by users who want to further refine a people search (see Figure 17-52). Common properties from the people within the search results will be displayed for the users so that they can use those common properties to filter the results.

People Search Box

This is the search box that users will use when they are searching for a person (see Figure 17-53). This web part can be configured to include the scopes drop-down, to suggest search terms, and to append additional search terms to the user query.

FIGURE 17-51

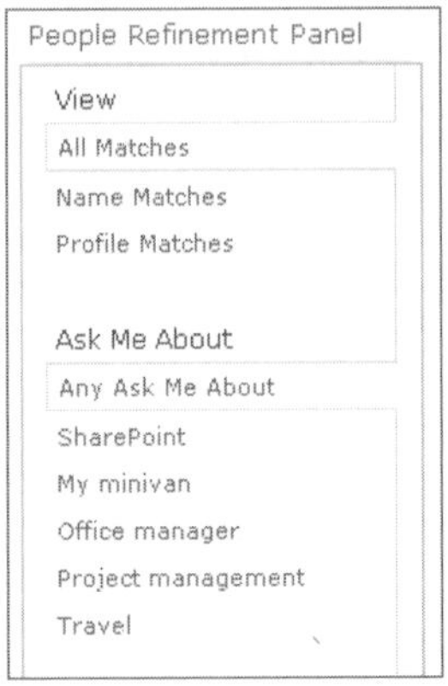

People Refinement Panel

View

All Matches

Name Matches

Profile Matches

Ask Me About

Any Ask Me About

SharePoint

My minivan

Office manager

Project management

Travel

FIGURE 17-52

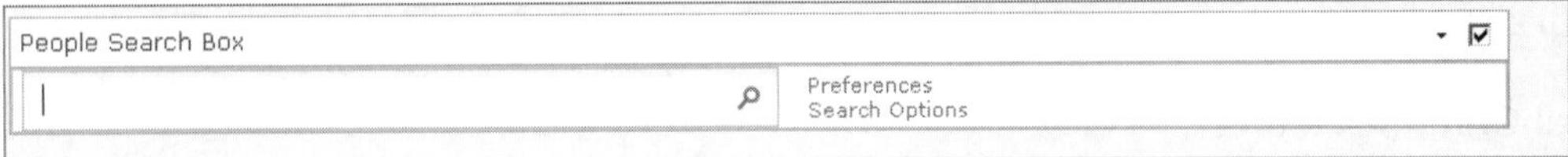

FIGURE 17-53

People Search Core Results

This search box connects to the People Search Box web part and displays the search results (see Figure 17-54).

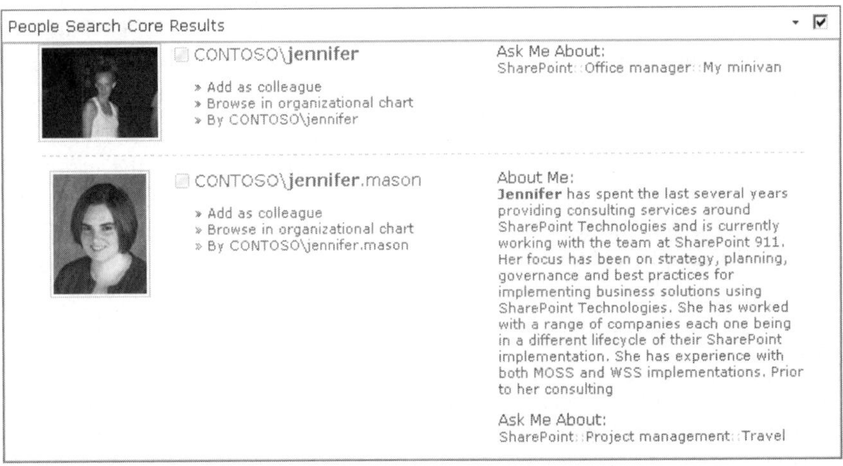

FIGURE 17-54

Refinement Panel

This web part looks for common properties within the search results and then displays them for users, so that users can select the common properties and further refine the search results (see Figure 17-55). The links within the refinement panel are dynamic and change based on the search results within the core search results web part.

Search Action Links

This web part provides users with links to the actions that can be activated for the search results, including sort order, search alerts, RSS feeds, and Window Explorer Search (see Figure 17-56). This web part is configurable so that you can select which actions you want to have displayed.

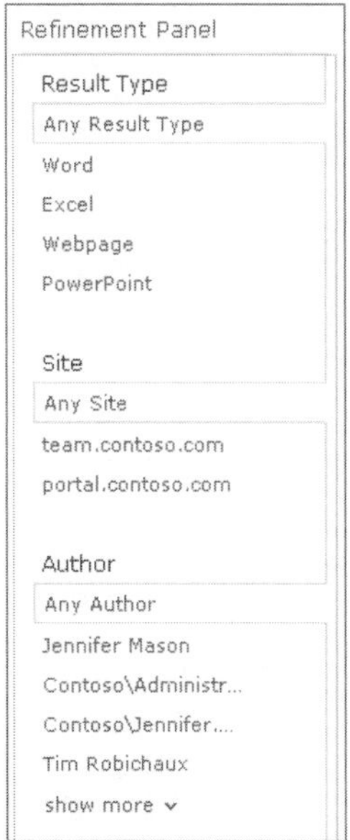

FIGURE 17-55

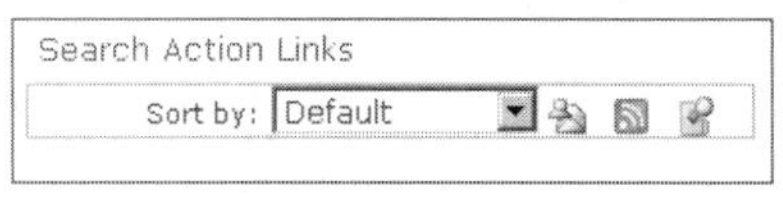

FIGURE 17-56

Search Best Bets

This web part will return all of the best bests for the search query (see Figure 17-57). The best bets are configured and stored within the site collection search settings and then, based on the user query, returned within this web part. This web part can be configured to display only certain information, such as the link or the description, as well as to limit the number of best bets displayed.

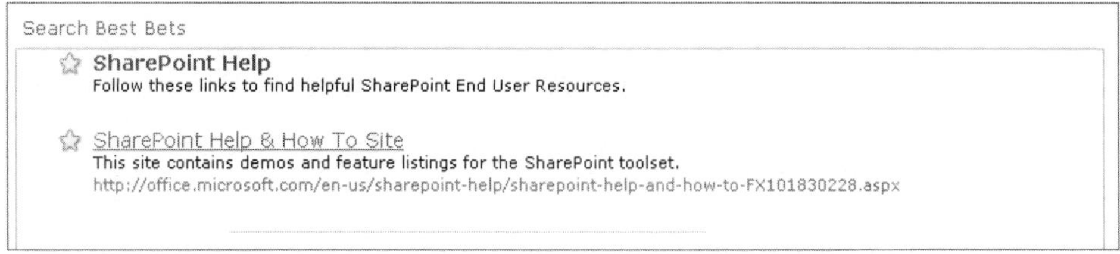

FIGURE 17-57

Search Box

This is the search box that users will use when they are entering a general query (see Figure 17-58). This web part can be configured to include the scopes drop-down, to suggest search terms, and to append additional search terms to the user query.

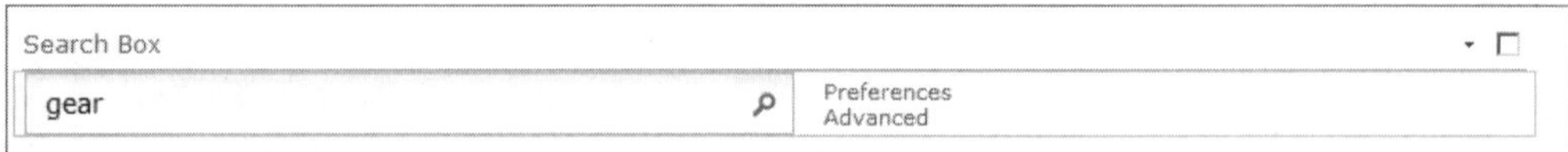

FIGURE 17-58

Search Core Results

This search box connects to the Search Box web part and displays the search results (see Figure 17-59).

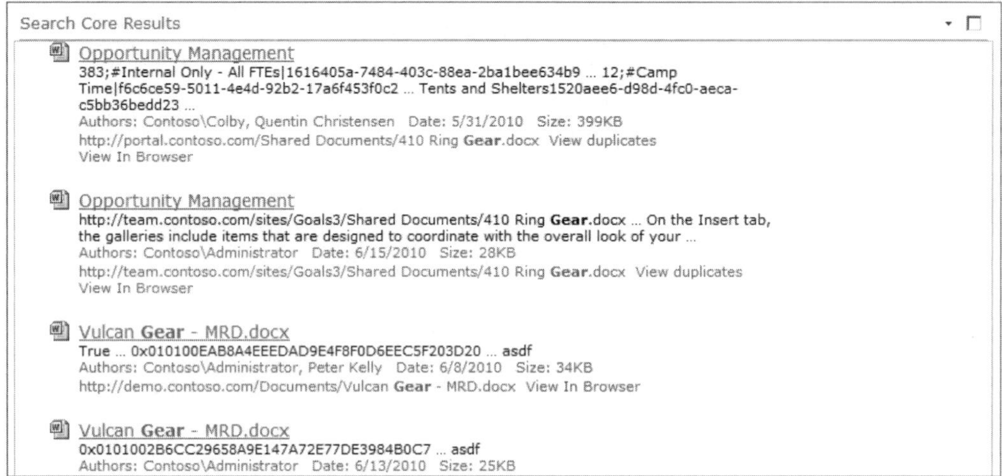

FIGURE 17-59

Search Paging

This web part is used to configure the way that the search results will be paged (see Figure 17-60). Within this web part, you can configure the number of pages to be displayed, as well as the images used to denote the next and previous options.

FIGURE 17-60

Search Statistics

This web part displays the summary information about the search, including the number of hits and the number

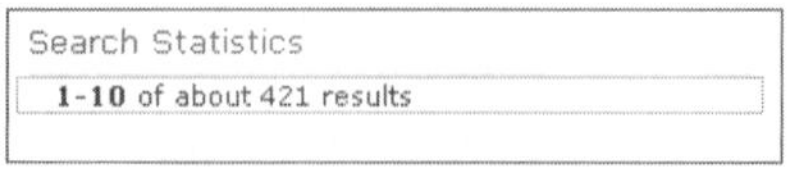

FIGURE 17-61

displayed on the current page (see Figure 17-61). You can configure this web part to display information on multiple lines and to display additional information, such as the search response time.

Search Summary

This web part is also known as the "Did you mean?" web part (see Figure 17-62). When queries are entered and a misspelling or alternate spelling is identified, the web part will provide that information to users, allowing them to update their search query.

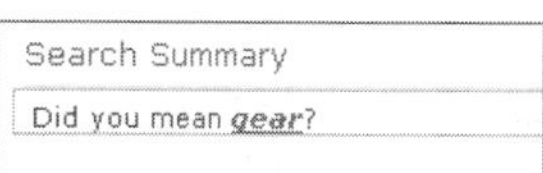

FIGURE 17-62

Top Federated Search Results

This web part will return a specified number of results from a federated search location (see Figure 17-63). This would allow you to show the top one or two results in one location on the page, with the remainder in the federated search results web part. This web part can be configured to display a specific number of results as well as configuration settings, such as the description and URL length.

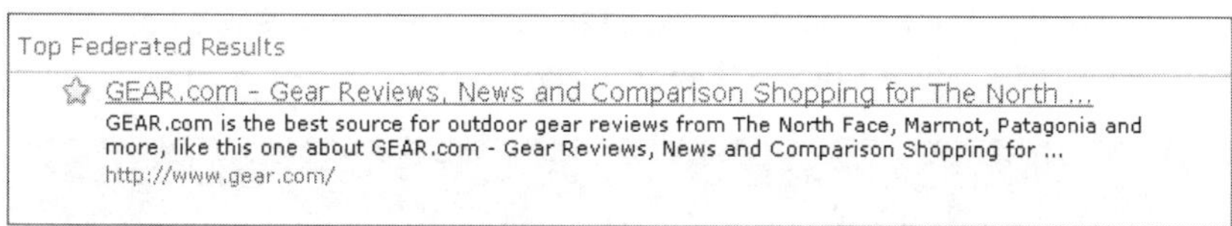

FIGURE 17-63

TRY IT OUT Customizing the Search Results Page

Now that you have reviewed all of the web parts available for search configuration, let's take a few minutes and customize some of the web parts. You will start by configuring the search entry page, and then, you will modify the search results page.

1. Navigate to the Enterprise Search Center that you created earlier in the chapter and select Site Actions ➪ Edit Page. You will notice that the page is preconfigured with the Search Box web part (see Figure 17-64).

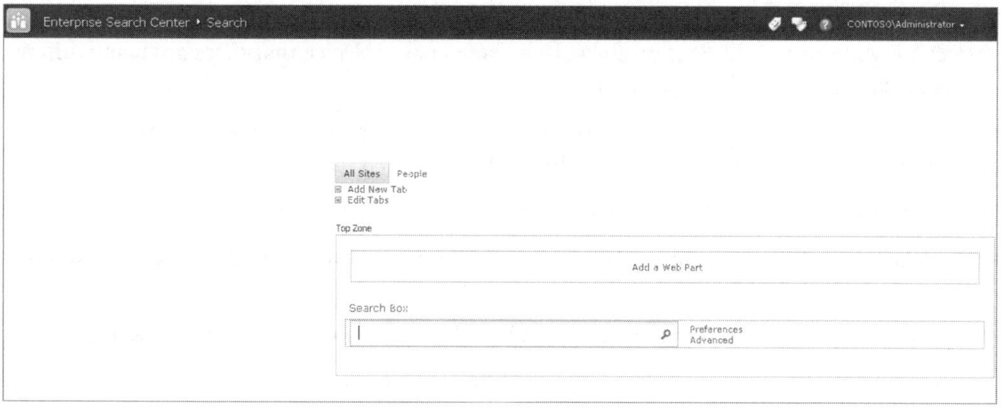

FIGURE 17-64

NOTE *In this Try It Out, you are going to focus on the search web parts and ignore the search tabs. You will work with the search tabs in the next section.*

2. Edit the Properties for the Search web part to include the scopes drop-down by configuring the tool pane with the following properties:

PROPERTY	VALUE
Dropdown Mode	Show, do not include contextual scopes, and default to "s" URL parameter.
Dropdown Label	Scope
All Other Fields	Accept the defaults.

3. Click Apply, and you will see that the web part is updated to reflect the changes you applied. Save and Close the current page to exit Edit Mode (see Figure 17-65).

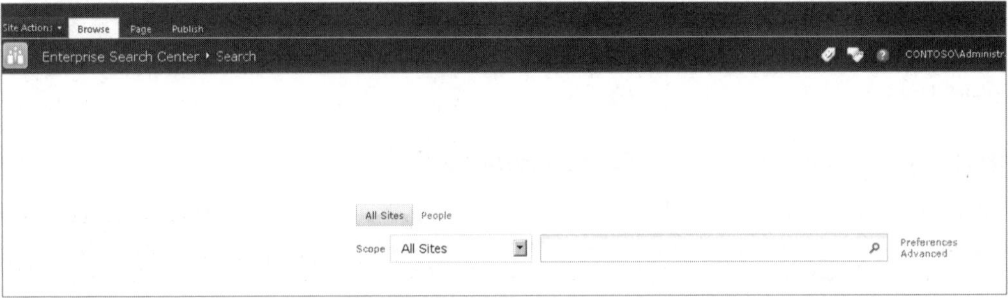

FIGURE 17-65

4. Enter the search term **gear** into the search box, and press Enter. This is the quickest way to open the search results page. Once the page is opened, we will be able to switch to edit mode and then modify the web parts.
5. Select Site Actions ➪ Edit Page on the search results page. Notice that there are many different web parts preconfigured on the page (see Figure 17-66).
6. Take a few minutes and explore each of the Web Part tool panes. This will allow you to see all of the different configurations you can use for each of the web parts.
7. Click the Add a Web Part link in the Right Zone.
8. Select the Search Categories in the Web Parts selection pane and select the Federated Results web part in the Web Parts Category, and then click Add.
9. Once the web part is added to the page, select the link to edit the web part properties.
10. Within the Web Part tool pane, configure the following options:
    - **Location:** Internet Search Results
    - For all other fields, accept the defaults.

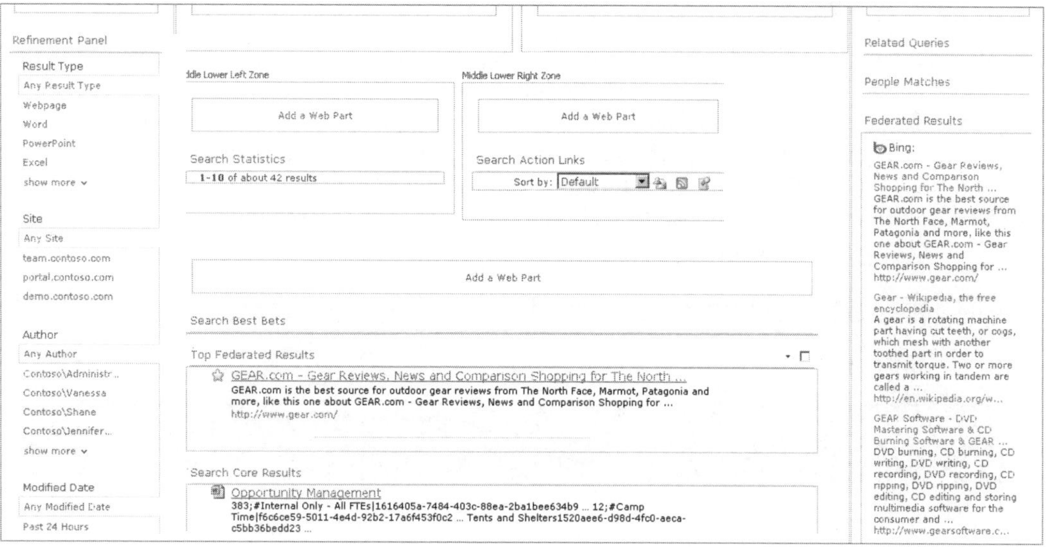

FIGURE 17-66

11. Click Apply, and you will see that the web part is updated to reflect the changes we applied. Save and Close the current page to exit edit mode.

12. Enter the search term **active directory** into the search box and press Enter. Notice that even though we had no results from the SharePoint index, we still are able to return the federated search results (see Figure 17-67).

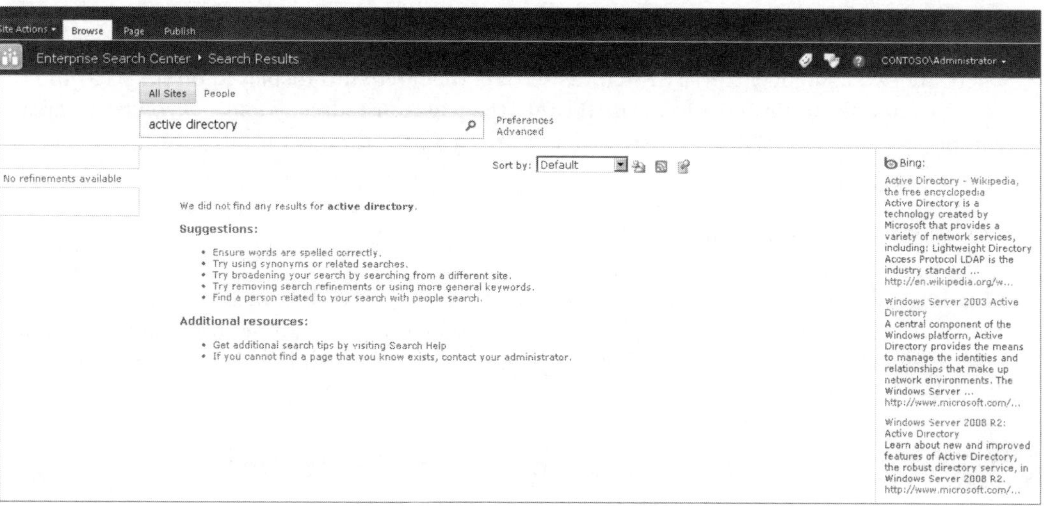

FIGURE 17-67

How It Works

Search results are delivered through configurable web parts. In this example, you modified the configuration of several different web parts, thus changing the way the information is displayed to the end user.

Search Center Tabs

Now that you have a good idea on the configuration of the Search web parts within the Search Center, let's loop our way back to the concept of the Search Center tabs. Tabs are a way within the Search Center to create an interface that allows users to quickly select and conduct searches. These tabs are really just links to a special page layout that contains the tab control. You will notice that, if you click the People tab on the Enterprise Search Center home page, you are actually being redirected to a new page. This is also true of the People tab on the search results page. Figure 17-68 shows this concept in action.

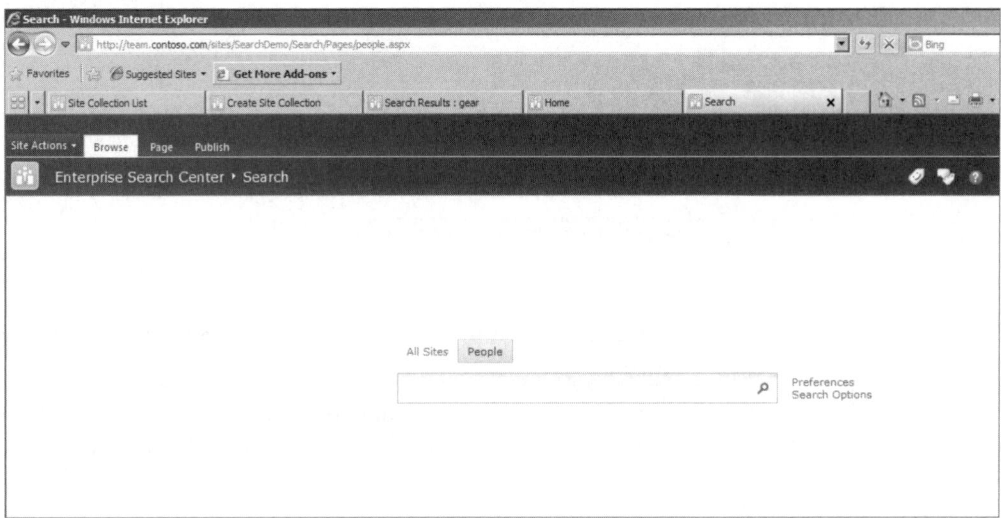

FIGURE 17-68

There are two components to a Search Center tab: the tab that is displayed on the page and the page that the tab links to. In order to create the tab, the page must already exist. If you try to create a tab without the page, you will get an error. There are two page layouts for tab pages:

- (Welcome Page) Search box
- (Welcome Page) Search results

Each of these page layouts comes preconfigured with the search box or the search results web parts, which gives you a great template to get started with. Tabs can be stored in two locations, the search box and the search results. Out of the box, the All Sites and the People tab are configured for both locations.

TRY IT OUT Creating a Search Center Tab for a Search Scope

In this Try It Out, you will be creating a new search tab for your presentation's scope. You will start by creating the two search pages in the pages library, and then you will configure your tabs for both the search box and the search results page. Creating tabs and pages can get a little tricky because some of the normal shortcuts you will take, such as creating a page from the Site Actions menu, will create content using defaults. Since the defaults may not be exactly what you want, it is easier to go directly to the list and create the content from this list. This will ensure that you get to make choices about your page layouts.

1. Navigate to the Enterprise Search Center that you created earlier in the chapter, and select Site Actions ➪ View All Site Content (see Figure 17-69). There are three specific lists that you will be making additions to:
   - Pages
   - Tabs in Search Pages
   - Tabs in Search Results

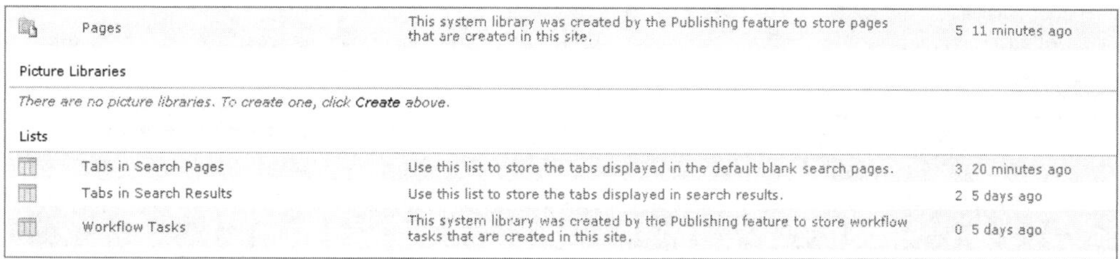

	Name	Description	Items	Last Modified
	Pages	This system library was created by the Publishing feature to store pages that are created in this site.	5	11 minutes ago
Picture Libraries				
There are no picture libraries. To create one, click ***Create*** *above.*				
Lists				
	Tabs in Search Pages	Use this list to store the tabs displayed in the default blank search pages.	3	20 minutes ago
	Tabs in Search Results	Use this list to store the tabs displayed in search results.	2	5 days ago
	Workflow Tasks	This system library was created by the Publishing feature to store workflow tasks that are created in this site.	0	5 days ago

FIGURE 17-69

2. Open the pages library and activate the Documents Ribbon. Under the New Document option, select the Page option. This is an important step because it will allow you to select the page layout you want to create (see Figure 17-70).

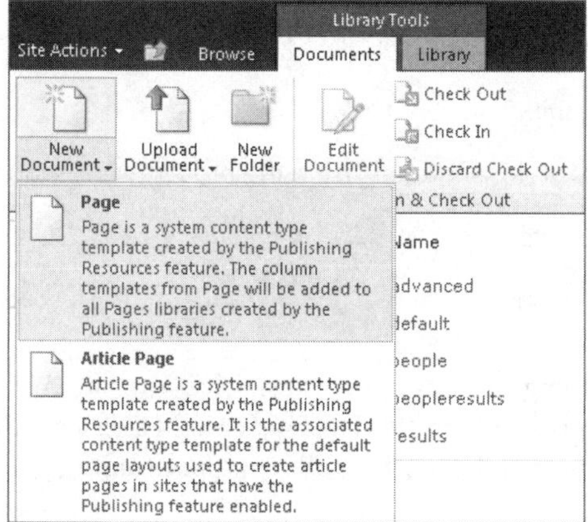

FIGURE 17-70

3. Enter the following properties for the new page, and click Create (see Figure 17-71).

PROPERTY	VALUE
Title	Presentations
Description	Search page to create searches within the presentations scope.

continues

(continued)

PROPERTY	VALUE
URL Name	Presentations
Page Layout	(Welcome Page) Search box

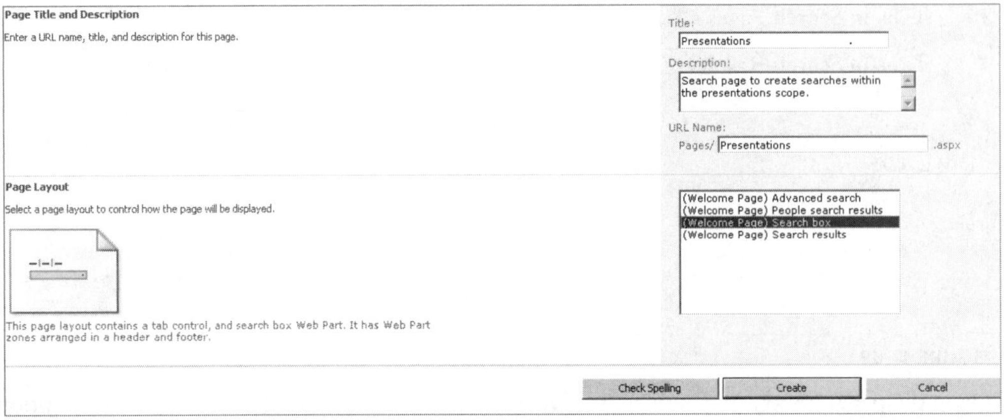

FIGURE 17-71

4. Repeat steps 2 and 3, this time entering the following properties:

PROPERTY	VALUE
Title	PresentationsResults
Description	Search results page for searches using the presentation scope.
URL Name	PresentationsResults
Page Layout	(Welcome Page) Search results

5. Now that your pages have been created, you are going to create your tabs. Select the Site Actions menu, and then select the View All Site Content option. Open the Tabs in Search Pages list, and then select the Add new item link within the web part and enter the following information (see Figure 17-72):

PROPERTY	VALUE
Tab Name	Presentations
Page	Presentations.aspx
Tooltip	Use this tab if you want to limit your search results to the presentation's search scope.

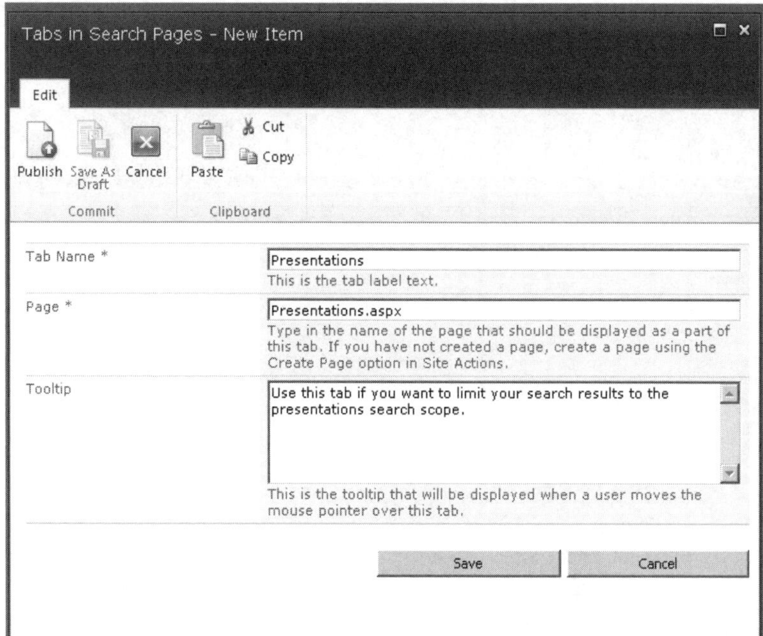

FIGURE 17-72

6. Select Save, select the Site Actions menu, and then select the View All Site Content option. Open the Tabs in Search Results list, and then, click the Add new item link within the web part and enter the following information:

PROPERTY	VALUE
Tab Name	Presentations
Page	PresentationsResults.aspx
Tooltip	Use this tab if you want to limit your search results to the presentations search scope.

7. Navigate back to the home page of the Search Center, and you should see a tab called Presentations. If you select this tab, you should notice that the URL changes to the page you associated with the tab (see Figure 17-73).

8. Now that you have configured your tabs and pages, you need to configure the web parts on the pages. In this example, you are creating the tabs so that users can use those tabs' pages to search within the Presentations scope. To accomplish this, you need to make two additional changes:

   - Configure the Search box web part to send results to the `PresentationsResults.aspx` page.
   - Configure the Search results web part to limit the results to the Presentations scope.

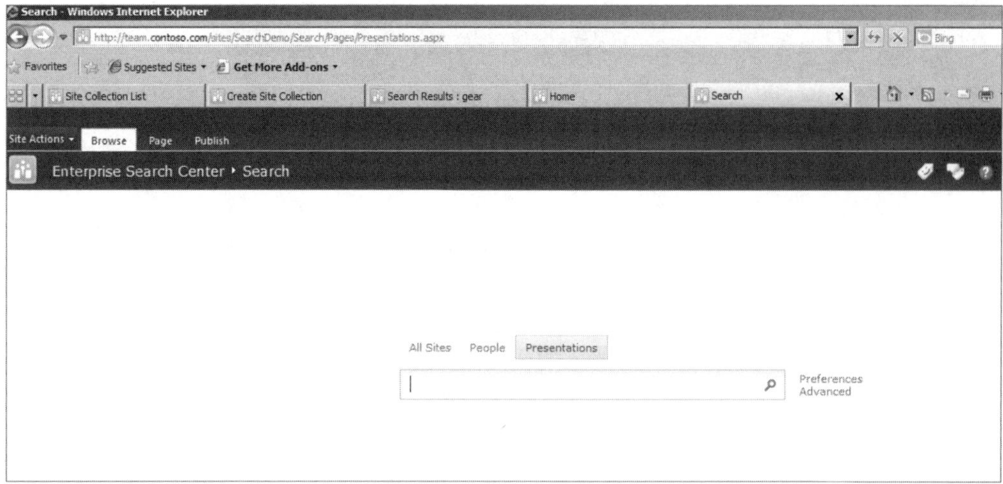

FIGURE 17-73

9. On the `presentations.aspx` page, select Site Actions, Edit Page. Choose the Modify the Search Box Web Part option. Within the Miscellaneous settings, change the value of the Target Results Page from `results.aspx` to `presentationsresults.aspx` and click Apply.
10. Enter the search term **gear** into the search box and click Enter. You should be redirected to the `presentationsresults.aspx` page that you created earlier in this example.
11. On the `presentations.aspx` page, select Site Actions, Edit Page. Choose the Modify the Search Core Results Web Part. In the Locations section, enter **Presentations** as the scope value. Select apply and then Save and Close the page. When the page reloads, you should see that the search results are filtered to the Presentations scope.

How It Works

In this example, you created a several pages and then associated them with the tab configuration within the Enterprise Search Center. Once the pages are associated with the tabs, users can click on a tab and generate different search results based on the configuration of that specific tab.

WHY DOESN'T THE SEARCH CENTER BEHAVE LIKE MY OTHER SITES?

As you are working with the Search Center site, keep in mind that this site has been preconfigured and designed with specific things in mind. This means that there are certain features and functionality that may be available on other sites that don't work the same way within this site. A good example of this is navigation. If you open the navigation settings of the Search Center site and make changes and then navigate back to the home page, you will notice that your navigation links are not displayed. This is actually by design. If you wanted to change this behavior, you would need to look at developing a custom master page for the search site that handled the navigation controls differently. This warning is not to keep you from using this powerful site template, but instead, to warn you that, if something seems different in this site collection compared with others, it is likely that the feature is not supported in the same context within this site definition.

SEARCH SERVICES CONFIGURATION

So far, everything covered in this chapter has been focused on the configuration of search within a site collection. These configurations within site collections are great, but sometimes, there is a need to configure things at a global level so that they can apply to all site collections. To do this, you need to make configurations within the Search Services application. While many of those settings are not within the scope of this book, it is important to at least be familiar with the locations of the settings and the different configurations that can be made.

Search Service Application Configurations

Search is configured through a Service Application on the farm. Each SharePoint Farm consumes many different service applications in order to provide the functionality available for the farm, including search, user profiles, and managed metadata. These different services are configured at the Central Administration level and can be accessed through the Service Applications Management pages. The Search Service application is typically created when the farm is first configured. By default, the Search Service application is configured with one content source and two search scopes. The default content source is called Local SharePoint Sites and contains all SharePoint content within the farm. The two search scopes are People and All Sites. All Sites will allow you to search across the entire index, and People will allow you to limit your search to only users from the profile database.

NOTE *All of the Try It Outs to this point have been completed within a site collection. The following Try It Out will be completed within the Central Administration site. If you do not have access to Central Administration, you will need to refer to your Server Administrator. If, within your environment, you only have access to a site collection, then you can benefit from reviewing the Try It Outs for Central Administration and then working through the Try It Outs once we move within the site collection.*

TRY IT OUT Accessing the Search Service Application

Let's take a few minutes and get familiar with the layout of the Search Service application.

1. Open the Central Administration Site for your farm. To do this, you will need to know the URL from your server administrator. A screenshot of the page is displayed in Figure 17-74.

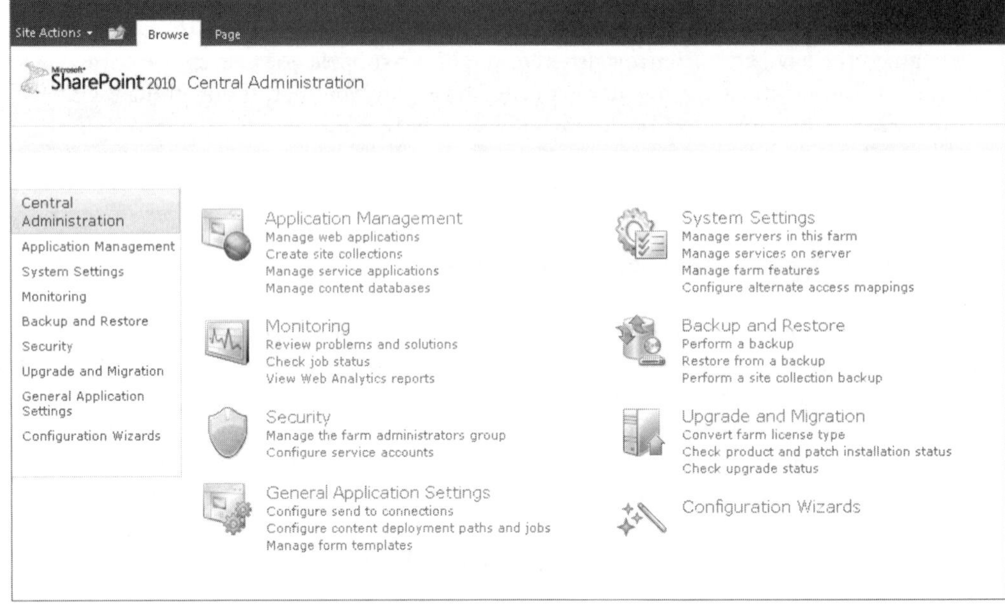

FIGURE 17-74

2. In the Application Management section of the home page, click the Manage Service Applications link. This will display all of the different service applications that are configured within your farm. An example screenshot is displayed in Figure 17-75. Keep in mind that each farm can be configured differently, so what you see on your screen may vary from what is shown in the figure.

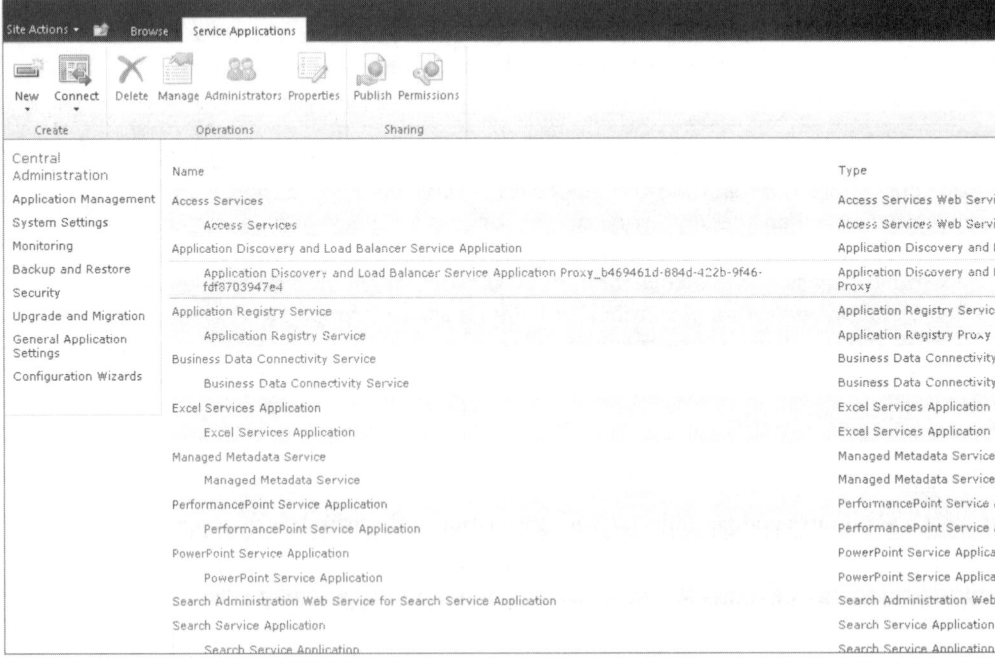

FIGURE 17-75

3. Locate and click on the Search Service Application link, and a configuration screen like the one in Figure 17-76 will be displayed. This is where we will be able to configure the various search features.

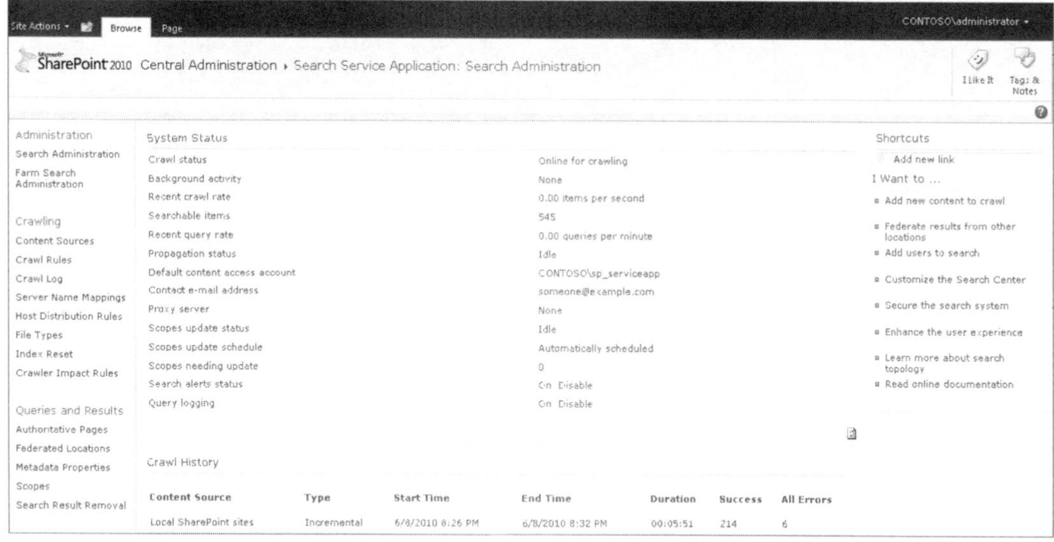

FIGURE 17-76

4. As you look around on the page, notice the page layout (see Figure 17-77). On the far-right side of the page, there are many different links, grouped by categories. These links will take you into the different configuration pages for each of the search features. In the middle of the page, you can see a summary of the different search processes that have been running. On the far left, you are given some links to help you quickly get to common search configuration tasks and to Microsoft help for configuring search.

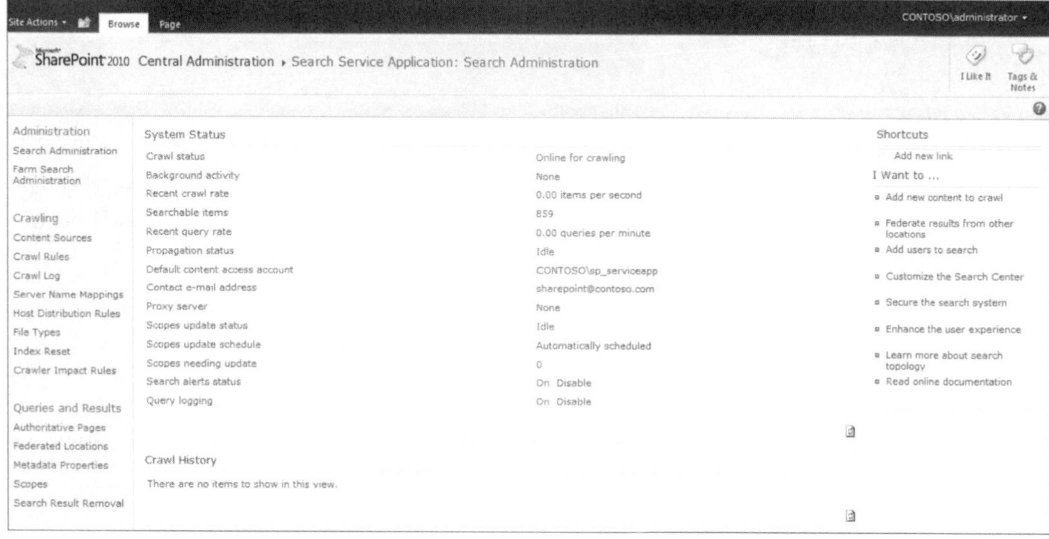

FIGURE 17-77

How It Works

From within this site, you will be able to manage all of the global search configurations, including the content sources, global search scopes, and the various crawl rules and schedules.

SEARCH ANALYTICS

The final area to cover in this chapter on search is the search analytics features. Reports that detail the usage of search within your environment are generated at both the site collection and the service application levels. At the application level, you can access reports that provide you information on the Number of Queries, the Top Queries, and the No Results Queries. At the site collection level, the reports generated include the following:

- Number of Queries
- Top Queries
- Failed Queries
- Best Bet Usage
- Best Bet Suggestions
- Best Bet Suggestions Action History
- Search Keywords

These reports are accessed from the Site Settings page through the Site Collection Web Analytics reports in the Site Actions section. These reports can be very helpful to monitor your usage of search over time. If you review these reports on a regular basis, you will have a good understanding of how users are interacting with search and how you can use the tools discussed in this chapter to help you improve their user experience.

SUMMARY

In this chapter, we have reviewed many of the key aspects of search and have worked through some of the key configurations. After reading this chapter, you should be familiar with and able to configure the different search components within the site, including:

- Using the default search features within a site.
- Creating a custom Search Center.
- Creating custom Search Scopes.
- Adding tabs to a Search Center and configuring them to return results from a single scope.
- Modifying the Search web parts to customize the search experience for your users.

- Understanding the difference between site collection search settings and global search settings.
- Working with your site administrator for global search configurations.
- Reviewing the search analytics to determine how effective your users' searches have been over time.

The most important lesson that you can take away from this chapter is understanding that search is simply a query that is passed to a collection of web parts. These web parts are configurable and can be customized to meet your specific needs. Once you have this understanding, you will really be able to customize your users' search experience and build organization-specific search solutions that will provide great benefit for everyone who uses it.

EXERCISES

1. What are the limits to configurations made at the site collection level?
2. Where do you need to make configurations if they need to be accessed by every site within the farm?
3. You have a group of users who want to be able to quickly search within all documents of a certain type. How would you help them configure this?
4. What is a best bet?
5. True or false: SharePoint supports the use of Boolean operations within a search query.

▶ WHAT YOU LEARNED IN THIS CHAPTER

TOPIC	KEY CONCEPTS
Building search queries	Out of the box, SharePoint provides the ability to search directly from any site collection. Users are able to enter search queries into the search box, and their results are displayed using the standard out-of-the-box search results page **(/_layouts/OSSSearchResults.aspx)**.
Customizing the search experience	If you would like to customize the search experience, then SharePoint provides several templates and various web parts that can be configured to customize your search experience.
Search Service application configurations	SharePoint search is managed at the farm level as a Service Application. Changes made at the Service Application level are global changes that apply to all site collections that are consuming that service.

18

Implementing a Governance Framework

WHAT YOU WILL LEARN IN THIS CHAPTER:

- Defining governance
- Reviewing the governance pillars
- Developing the governance team structure
- Reviewing best practices for implementing governance

By this point in the book, you have learned many things about SharePoint 2010, including how to create lists and libraries, how to build workflows, and even how to work with the personalization features. It is likely that your head is spinning with all the new information you have gathered as you read through all of the new and powerful things that SharePoint 2010 brings to the table. Now, as we are nearing the end of our journey together, we will be introducing the concept of *governance*. This topic is so central to the SharePoint implementation, that we have dedicated an entire chapter to help you identify and implement a strategy that works for your organization.

GOVERNANCE OVERVIEW

The dictionary defines governance as the act of maintaining control and order. When the definition is applied to SharePoint, we develop the concept of SharePoint governance as being the processes and procedures in place to help maintain control of the environment. Because of the breadth and depth of SharePoint, many different things need to be taken into consideration when developing your governance strategy. As you have seen throughout this book, SharePoint is a tool that will cross many different aspects of the organization. Some things, such as search settings, will most likely be configured and maintained by system administrators; however, things like site workflows are likely to be built and maintained by the business units. The governance that is put in place will need to support and sustain both of these scenarios, without inhibiting them from the end goal. At first thought, this might seem like a rather daunting task. How do you provide the policies, procedures, and processes so that SharePoint can be everything to everyone? This chapter is designed to show you just that. But before we get into the specific components of governance, there are a few things we should review together.

Your Role in Governance

There is probably a large range of readers who have made it this far into the book. You may be an end user who is getting up to speed on SharePoint features so that you can manage and maintain sites or you may be a IT professional who is learning the basic features of SharePoint so that you can best support your users, or you may fall anywhere in between. With that being said, it is important to point out the information in this chapter is about governance in general. If you are responsible for managing and maintaining SharePoint, this chapter will help you get started. If you are responsible for simply managing and maintaining specific SharePoint sites, then this chapter will help you see all the work and effort that goes into the system. You may find that you are part of the SharePoint governance team that is built or you may find that you just interact with them as needed. Either way, this chapter will help give you a good understanding of what is included within SharePoint governance and best practices for implementing governance. Even if you aren't responsible for managing the governance, it is still very valuable to understand all the pieces.

Unique Organizations

One of the most important things to remember when building your governance plan is that your organization is unique. Yes, your organization will be similar to other organizations, but no two organizations are the same. What works for one, may fail miserably in another. When building your governance plan, it is important that you pay attention to the uniqueness of your organization and plan accordingly. If you simply take "best practices" and apply them directly to your organization, then you are in danger of creating future issues. Instead, you should be evaluating the implementation of the best practices and then tweaking them to match your organization's unique culture and environment. Let's take training as an example. As a best practice, it is important that users who are given administrative control over site collections complete training so that they are prepared for their role as an administrator. The type, style, and implementation of the training should be such that it brings the most value to the organization. If you simply copy the same approach that others have used, you may not end up with the same results. Instead, you should take the best from everyone else and then apply what will work best for your organization. Using this approach will allow you to think of governance differently. You will be able to identify the key areas that need to have policies and procedures and then you will complete a process of answering the question "What does this mean specifically to my environment?" This means that your governance policies may look different from others', but at the end of the day, you will have developed policies and procedures that will work for you internally. At the other end of this spectrum is trying to change the organization to work with predefined policies and procedures that have been identified as "best practices." Keep in mind that it is better to modify policies to match the organization before trying to change the organization through policies.

Realistic Expectations

One piece of encouragement that I would like to give you before you read the rest of this chapter is to remember that no one starts with the perfect team or the perfect set of governance standards. The whole concept of SharePoint governance should be based on the fact that it is meant to change and to evolve based on your organization's lifecycle. If you are just getting started with SharePoint, then it is not likely that you are going to have a full team of people to support the effort. It is more likely that you will be working alone or working with a small team to get things started. In this case, it is important to identify the long-term needs and develop a strategy to "grow into" a full-scale support system. But the point is that you have to start somewhere, and you have to know where you are ultimately going. The biggest mistake you could make is to ignore the need for governance and take the approach of "we will work through this later, as we need it" because I promise that, once you realize you need it, you will wish you had started earlier on in your project.

Understanding the Vision

The last thing I want to look at before we dive into the specifics is the need to understand the vision of SharePoint within your organization. Governance is going to be put in place to help ensure that you are tracking toward a vision effectively, using sustainable and reliable systems. Without having a clearly defined vision, it will be hard to use governance to help you get somewhere. It may help you keep the system reliable and sustainable, but it won't assist in getting you to the next level as an organization. Having a clear vision will help keep your team on track and will help you decide what projects and functionality should be the focus of your efforts. Following are some examples of different goals and vision statements for SharePoint implementations:

- Provide a gateway to all systems and services provided by the organization.
- Use a strategic approach for implementation that allows for a consistent and gradual release of new functionality, allowing for the portal to be developed over time to meet the expanding organization's needs.
- Develop a framework that can be used for the release of future organization products and services.
- Whenever possible, use the out-of-the-box capabilities to build solutions.
- Improve communications by providing dynamic updates for both internal and external communications.
- Provide employees a centralized location to share and collaborate on internal and external content.
- Provide organization with tools that allow for departments to easily take ownership and provide dynamic updates for their content.
- Provide a tool to the organization that allows for structure to be added to the day-to-day operations and procedures through the use of standardized procedures and workflows.

As you can see from the list, there are many different things that can drive the vision of the implementation. Based on the vision, it is likely that you will want to have a concentrated effort in one area of functionality before another. Remember, your organization is unique, so your goals and vision will likely differ from the previously-listed examples.

UNDERSTANDING THE PILLARS OF A GOVERNANCE FRAMEWORK

Now that we have covered some of the general areas of governance, let's dive into the details. Throughout the rest of the chapter, we are going to be diving into the specifics of setting up governance. By the time you have completed the chapter, you should be ready to participate within your organizations governance team. Your role may differ according to your level within the organization, but after reading this chapter you should have a better understanding of what should be in place to support the SharePoint environment. Specifically, the key pillars you will review are:

- Key Roles
- Project and Change Management
- Information Architecture and Taxonomy
- Operations and Infrastructure
- Communications
- Training
- Development

Key Roles

There are several key roles that are included in most SharePoint implementations. Keep in mind, however, that it is more important to pay attention to the specific functions of the roles than to the exact titles. As long as you have each of the key areas accounted for, the titles don't matter as much. Figure 18-1 shows an example of the various roles that show up within SharePoint implementations. In the remainder of this section, we will describe, in greater detail, each of the roles and the specific functions they contribute to the team.

SharePoint Owner

The SharePoint owner is the person who is responsible for the overall implementation of SharePoint. This person is typically the person who is responsible for bringing SharePoint into the organization and also the person who is responsible for building the team that will provide the support for the implementation. This user is typically a strong project manager who is responsible for determining the best way to implement SharePoint in order to provide the greatest return on investment. The person who fills this role doesn't have to be a technical user; however, he or she should have a very strong understanding of how SharePoint works and should be able to clearly set the vision for how SharePoint should be used within the organization.

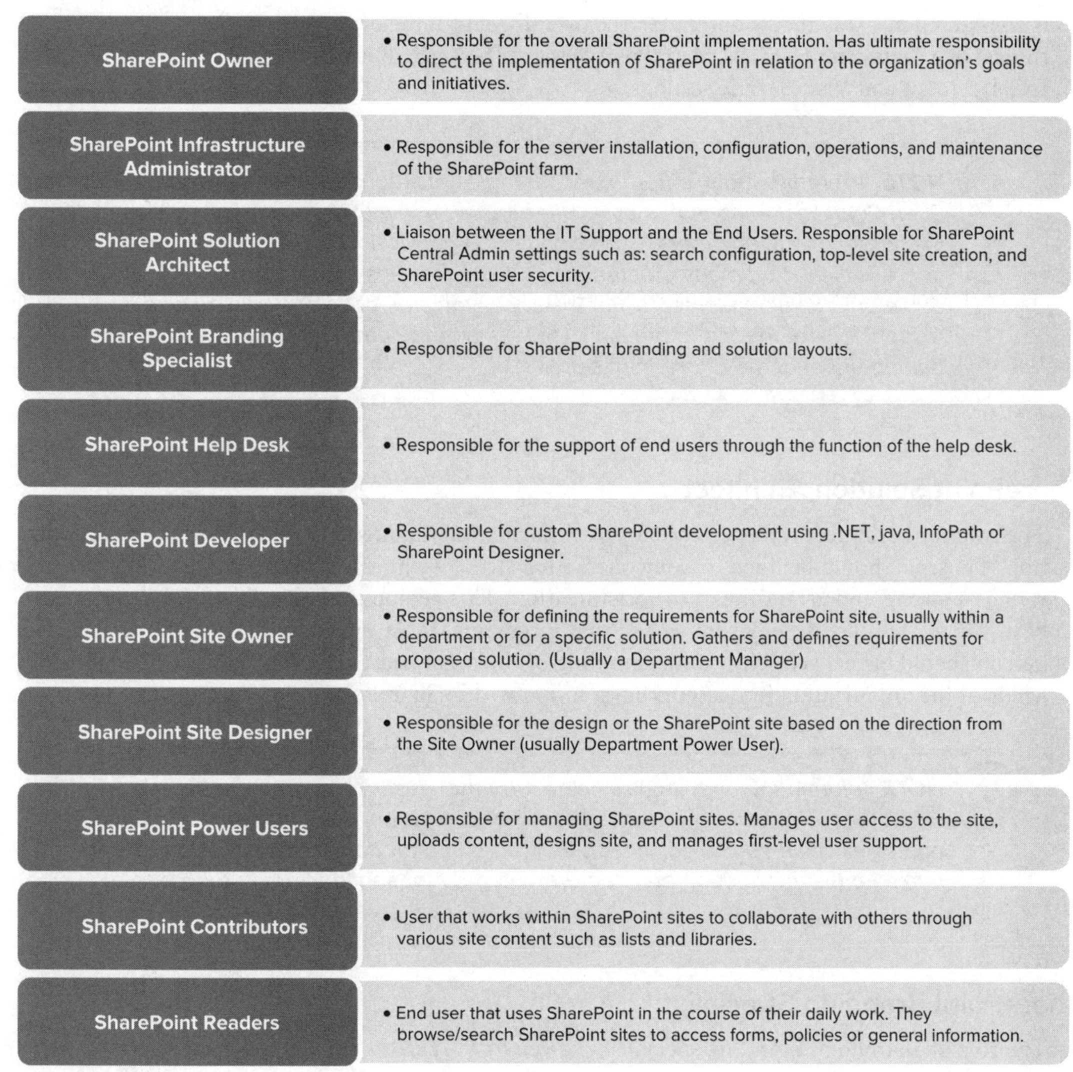

SharePoint Owner
• Responsible for the overall SharePoint implementation. Has ultimate responsibility to direct the implementation of SharePoint in relation to the organization's goals and initiatives.
SharePoint Infrastructure Administrator
• Responsible for the server installation, configuration, operations, and maintenance of the SharePoint farm.
SharePoint Solution Architect
• Liaison between the IT Support and the End Users. Responsible for SharePoint Central Admin settings such as: search configuration, top-level site creation, and SharePoint user security.
SharePoint Branding Specialist
• Responsible for SharePoint branding and solution layouts.
SharePoint Help Desk
• Responsible for the support of end users through the function of the help desk.
SharePoint Developer
• Responsible for custom SharePoint development using .NET, java, InfoPath or SharePoint Designer.
SharePoint Site Owner
• Responsible for defining the requirements for SharePoint site, usually within a department or for a specific solution. Gathers and defines requirements for proposed solution. (Usually a Department Manager)
SharePoint Site Designer
• Responsible for the design or the SharePoint site based on the direction from the Site Owner (usually Department Power User).
SharePoint Power Users
• Responsible for managing SharePoint sites. Manages user access to the site, uploads content, designs site, and manages first-level user support.
SharePoint Contributors
• User that works within SharePoint sites to collaborate with others through various site content such as lists and libraries.
SharePoint Readers
• End user that uses SharePoint in the course of their daily work. They browse/search SharePoint sites to access forms, policies or general information.

FIGURE 18-1

SharePoint Infrastructure Administrator

The SharePoint infrastructure administrator is the user that is responsible for the day-to-day management of the SharePoint servers. These servers are part of what is called the *SharePoint farm*. This farm is created when SharePoint is initially installed and consists of all the servers that are used to create the SharePoint environment. SharePoint farms are scalable, meaning that, as user demand increases, additional servers can be added to the farm to help increase the farm's capacity. The person who fills this role is responsible for configuring, managing, and maintaining the farm. This includes all regular server maintenance, as well as any service packs or hotfixes. This also includes ensuring that the server is configured in a way that is optimal to the overall goals of the organization. Configuration includes things such as disaster recovery, SharePoint Designer Settings, Business Connectivity Settings, and Excel, Access, and Visio Service settings.

NOTE *There are many different technologies and services that are part of SharePoint, including SQL, Active Directory, Windows Server, and possibly Exchange and even others. Based on your organization and your implementation, it is likely that many different people are responsible for maintaining all of the environment elements. For instance, you may have one person who is responsible for the management of SQL and yet another user responsible for the management of the SharePoint servers.*

SharePoint Solution Architect

The solutions architect is responsible for the information architecture design within the organization. This role should be filled by someone with a strong technical understanding of SharePoint, as well as a strong understanding of the organization. This person is responsible for determining the best way to architect the environment so that it remains stable, supportable and sustainable. This person should have a very clear understanding of the organization so that they can translate the needs of the organization into a working solution within SharePoint.

NOTE *Information architecture is the term that describes your farm's hierarchy and layout. This usually includes the different web applications, site collections, and sites within your organization. For more information on the components that make up the information architecture, refer to that section later in this chapter.*

SharePoint Branding Specialist

The role of SharePoint branding specialist is given to the person who controls the overall "look and feel" of the SharePoint sites. This "look and feel" is considered the site *branding*. Chapter 9 was dedicated entirely to branding and went through the process required to create a custom branding solution. This role corresponds to that chapter in that the person who fills this role is responsible for determining the branding guides for the organization. Will the organization use only one master page; will each site be able to create a custom master page, or will they have to use the one created by the organization? These are the areas that this role will be responsible for determining the guidelines and standards that all sites must follow.

SharePoint Help Desk

The role of the SharePoint help desk is to answer the various levels of SharePoint questions from the organization. It is the person/team that provides support when users run into issues using SharePoint. This function could be included with the organization's existing help desk, or an organization could have a user or team dedicated to supporting users as they work with SharePoint.

SharePoint Developer

A SharePoint developer is someone who is responsible for creating custom solutions that can be added to SharePoint. These custom solutions are typically created when SharePoint is needed to do something that cannot be easily done using the out-of-the-box configurations or when there are no third-party solutions that can be purchased to provide the required functionality.

SharePoint Power Users

These are the users within the organization that have been through advanced SharePoint training and are familiar with all of the tasks required to create, manage, and maintain SharePoint sites within the organization. They are responsible for working with the organization and then creating and managing the sites and are typically focused on creating and managing the following within sites or site collections:

- Sites
- Lists
- Workflows
- Forms
- Page layout and web parts

This group of users will play a key part in helping with the release and roll out of future SharePoint solutions. Once they have developed the skills needed to become effective Power Users, you will able to rely on them to provide meaningful input and assistance with future solution releases.

SharePoint Contributors

Contributors are the users who have been trained to add content to existing SharePoint sites. They are familiar with how SharePoint works and are able to navigate through sites, adding content as needed. Typically, they are familiar with the following tasks:

- Adding documents to libraries
- Office integration with libraries and lists
- Adding list content
- Starting workflows
- Creating alerts
- Managing personalization features (such as My Sites)
- Search

SharePoint Readers

These are the users within the organization that have been trained to navigate through SharePoint sites to find content they may need. Typically, these users haven't received a great deal of training and are able to navigate through the sites based on the sites' design and layout. Typically, they spend most of their time accessing sites where they are consuming information, such as an intranet or extranet site. At any point where they are required to do more than consume information, they would need additional training so that they could understand the value available when using SharePoint as a contributor.

Project and Change Management

Next up on our tour of governance are the concepts of project and change management. Project management is going to be the tool that helps you get somewhere, and change management is going to be the tool that allows users to make changes once you are there. Throughout the remainder of this section, we will be walking through some of the primary concepts related to each of these areas. In theory, these concepts apply to any area of business, but speaking from experience, when these are ignored or overlooked, some very interesting and complex issues can arise.

Project Management

In theory, there is nothing unique or special about SharePoint that requires you to do anything different when managing projects. In reality, however, when this aspect is ignored, you end up with many different and unique issues all related to the project fundamentals' time, scope, and budget. It would be impossible for us to cover all the basics of project management in this small section of the chapter, so instead we will look at and highlight some of the key issues that will repeatedly pop up as you are working through various SharePoint projects.

Defining the Project

The first thing to start with is defining your project. What is it that you are trying to accomplish? Following are some very common projects that can be completed in SharePoint. Reviewing the list will give you an idea of the different types of things we are referring to within this section of the chapter:

- Team collaboration site
- Document management solution
- Project site
- Intranet site
- Goals management site
- Time-tracking solutions
- Forms center

When defining your project, it is important that you develop clear requirements. You can start out by looking at the project in terms of what will be done and who will be doing it. In some projects, it is easier to start with the what and work your way back to the who. Either way, this entire process should occur apart from the technology. In other words, when defining the project, this should be done in nontechnical terms. You should be taking the time to define what needs to be done and setting all technology aside. Once the requirements are clear, you will map those requirements to the technologies available. This approach ensures that you remain focused on the requirements first and the technology second.

Time + Scope + Budget

When thinking about project management, there are three key areas that you should focus on: time, scope, and budget. Time is defined as the duration of the project, scope is the requirements that you must satisfy to complete the project, and budget is what it will cost you, which includes both hard (expenses) and soft (overhead) costs. Each of these three elements act together to define the project and if any of these elements changes, it will have an effect on the other two elements. The easiest way to envision this is by thinking of the project as a triangle, with the three sides each representing an element. If any one of the elements increases, then the others will also have to increase. If any elements decrease, then the same is also true of the other elements. This can clearly be seen when looking at the scope. If your requirements increase, then so will the time it takes you to complete it and the cost. Figure 18-2 provides a visual that can be used to represent this concept.

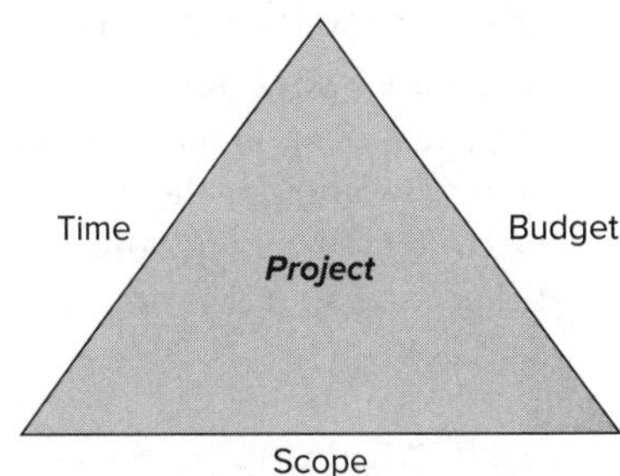

FIGURE 18-2

Change Management

Change management is a key concept in any type of project. Some of the key aspects covered are what types of changes will be allowed, who will approve the changes, and what is the process to get the approval and then release the changes to the organization? The difference with SharePoint is that changes can be made very easily and often without any thought to how it will affect the audience. Consider the example of navigation. What if every time a user accessed the corporate intranet the tabs were in a different location or order? It would not take long for a user to become frustrated and unwilling to access the site to gather information. With change management in place, it is likely that a request would be submitted to move the tabs, it would be tested, and then once all the stakeholders approved it, it would be communicated to the users and then the site would be updated. There would be a process in place to handle the changes to the site. Within SharePoint there will likely be many different sites, and it is likely that there will be many different site owners. The important thing is that each of the site owners implements processes within their sites that manage how the changes should be made. If you are working on an intranet site, it is likely that corporate communications or marketing will own the overall design and layout of the site, and they will probably also own the process for which changes are requested. But what about if you are an owner of a team or collaboration site? How will you manage changes within that site? It is important that, as the site collection's owner, you have an approach that will manage the changes and that this is communicated to the site's users. This way, they will know what to look out for and what to do if they want to make a change or a suggestion.

Content Approvals

Out of the box, there are a few ways that I can manage the approval process for managing content changes. Keep in mind that content is limited to list content such as list items or pages. For each library, I can configure the approval settings that allow me to require that all content be approved before it is made available for all site users. This means that, if I am using pages, I can create a page and approve it and it will be visible to all site owners. If I then need to update that page, I can make updates and they will only be visible to a set number of users (those with approval rights, or those configured with permissions to see drafts), who will be able to see the content. This will allow for the content to be updated directly on the production site but still ensures that it is not displayed to all site users until it has been approved by the designated approver.

Customizations

The one thing to remember when working with changes in SharePoint is that all changes to the site structure and layout done through the browser or through SharePoint Designer are considered *customizations*. Customizations are changes that are made and stored within the database. When the site loads, it basically loads the original and then applies your changes, or customizations. All customizations done to SharePoint are done against the live site and are not meant to be completed in a staging environment and then moved to production. This means that any customizations you make will be made against the live site. You may choose to first test the customizations in a test site, but in order to move them to the production site, you would need to complete the configuration again in the production environment. As an example, you may have a test intranet site, and you may restructure the navigation in that site and get approval from all the stakeholders on the changes. It may actually take you several iterations to end up with the solution that everyone approves. Once you have the final solution, you would then need to log on to the production site and go through the process of updating the navigation links. As you are making the changes, they will be immediately displayed on the site.

NOTE *Keep in mind that SharePoint supports many scenarios for custom development that can be deployed to the server and don't require making changes directly to the production environment. These changes, however, are done through custom development and are not within the scope of this chapter or this book. There are many great resources available to help you get started with custom development, so if you decide that customizations is not the route for you, there is no reason that custom development won't work. It is all about knowing the tools available and then picking the tools that will work best for your needs.*

Information Architecture and Taxonomy

Information architecture defines the layout of content within the SharePoint farm. There are several different levels included, and in this section of the chapter, we will define each of these areas, as well as provide two different examples of common information architectures. Figure 18-3 shows part of the SharePoint containment hierarchy. The containment hierarchy starts with the base servers and continues through to list content and is used to map out the entire SharePoint environment. For simplicity, we are going to start at the web application level and not the server farm level. Figure 18-3 should be read so that the lower levels are included in their parent item. For instance, lists are contained in webs, which are part of sites that are part of a content database that is part of a web application.

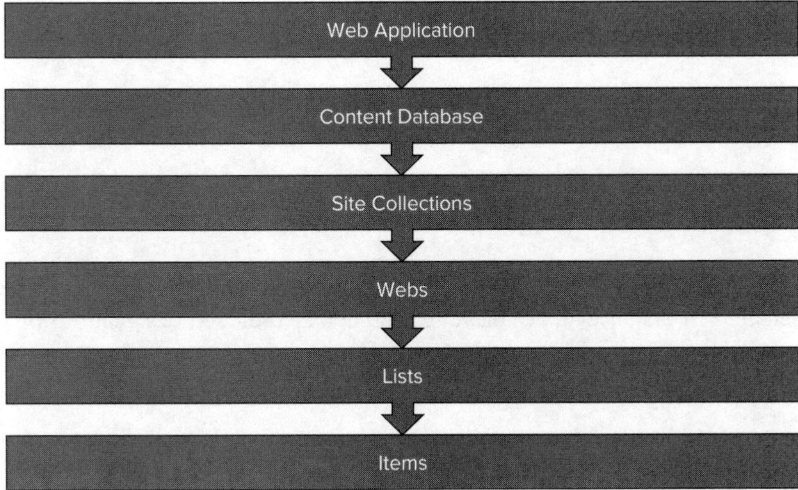

FIGURE 18-3

Web Applications

Web applications are created within SharePoint to provide a location for creating and storing sites. Web applications correspond to websites within IIS and can be easily identified by their unique URLs. Each web application created within SharePoint will have a corresponding, unique URL, such as `http://intranet.company.com` or `http://teams.company.com`. Web applications are created by the SharePoint Infrastructure Administrators, typically when the farm is first configured. There are usually 3–5 web applications per farm, and they are usually defined and managed by the governance team. Consider the following example for a company that is going to use SharePoint for internal department collaboration, for cross-departmental collaboration, and also for their intranet. In this example, there could be three separate web applications, one for each of the different types of content.

Content Databases

Content databases are the databases stored within SQL that contain the content from the site collections. Each site collection can be associated with a single content database; however, many content databases can be associated with a web application. Content databases are managed by the SharePoint Infrastructure Administrator and they are never accessed directly by the end users, but instead are accessed indirectly through the browser. For the purpose of this chapter, it is just good for you to understand that each site you are working with will have its content stored within a content database.

Sites

Sites, also referred to as site collections, consist of a top-level site and any webs (subsites). Within a top-level site collection, you can configure settings that will apply to all webs within the site collection. Some of these settings include:

- Site templates
- Web part gallery
- List templates
- Master page settings
- Site collection features
- Site collection policies

These settings are settings that will apply for each web created within the site collection. Only users who have been given site ownership permissions will be able to see and update these settings. Figure 18-4 shows the menu options available for site collections on the Site Settings page.

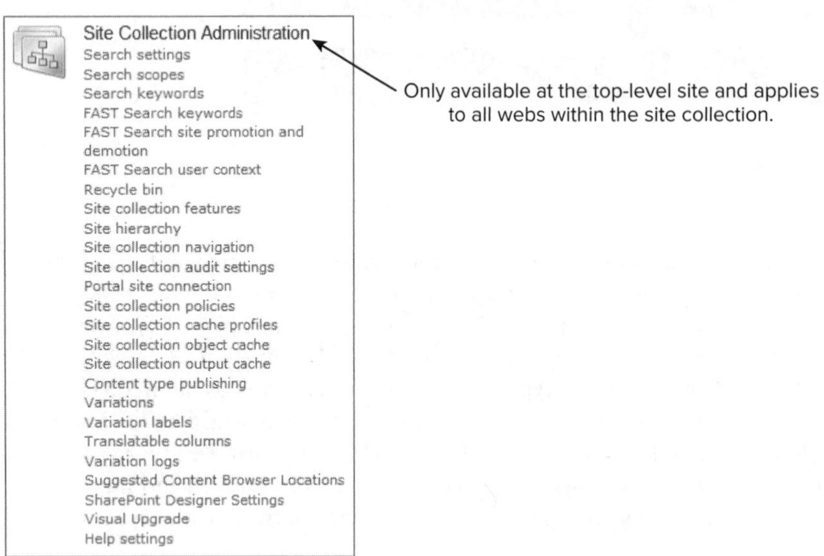

FIGURE 18-4

In addition to the configuration settings that make up a site collection, each site contains one root web, called the root site. This is the top-level site in the site collection where you go to access the site collection settings. Remember, this is also a web, so any settings that apply at the web level can also apply at this level.

Webs

Webs are subsites that are created within site collections that contain content, such as lists, libraries, pages, and web parts. Like site collections, webs also have different items that can be configured for the web. Figure 18-5 displays the Site Settings page for the web. Notice that in addition to all of the settings you can configure for the web, you also have a link to the site collection administration. Keep in mind that this link is security trimmed and is only available if you have rights to access these settings.

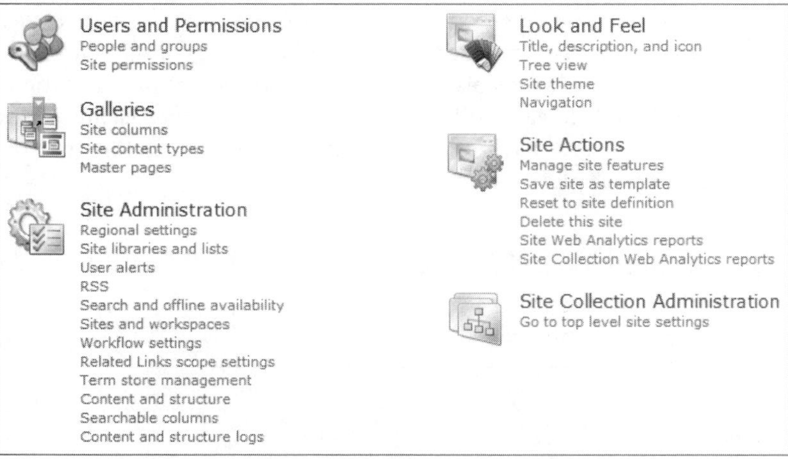

FIGURE 18-5

Lists

Lists are containers within webs that contain content. Chapter 2 is dedicated to working with lists, so if you have any questions, refer to that chapter.

Items

Items are the content store within SharePoint and the associated metadata. Examples could include documents, tasks, issues, or discussion threads.

Information Architecture Planning

As you begin building out your SharePoint environment, information architecture planning is typically one of the first tasks completed. This task includes looking at the content that will be added to SharePoint and determining how to best organize the content. The first and most important step in this process is to have a clear idea of the types of content that will be added to the environment and a clear understanding of how users will be interacting with the environment. If you proceed with the design of the site without understanding the content, it is almost guaranteed that you will need to adjust your design at a later date. If you have a clear understanding of what the overall vision for SharePoint is, then you can design a structure that allows for growth over time as you implement your vision. Once you know the content, you can then start mapping things to SharePoint. Typically, the web applications will equate to high-level types of communication, such as intranet or collaboration.

Once the web applications have been determined, the next step is to determine how sites and webs will be created within those web applications. For instance, take the intranet, since the content is mostly static and generally small, you might decide to put the intranet within one site collection. This would allow you to easily create a consistent look, feel, and navigation throughout the entire intranet for your users. On the other hand, collaboration is very different. Each group that wants to create a collaboration site is likely going to want to manage and control their settings for the site. They also will likely have content that is dynamic and large. Based on these factors, you may want to create our sites in separate site collections. This would allow you to segregate the sites from each other, and apply quotas so that you could easily manage the amount of space each site is using in SQL. Since the collaboration teams are separate teams, it is not as important that the navigation be consistent between the different sites. In fact, each collaboration team might want to configure and create a navigation structure that makes sense based on their specific needs. Figures 18-6 and 18-7 show diagrams of the preceding two examples.

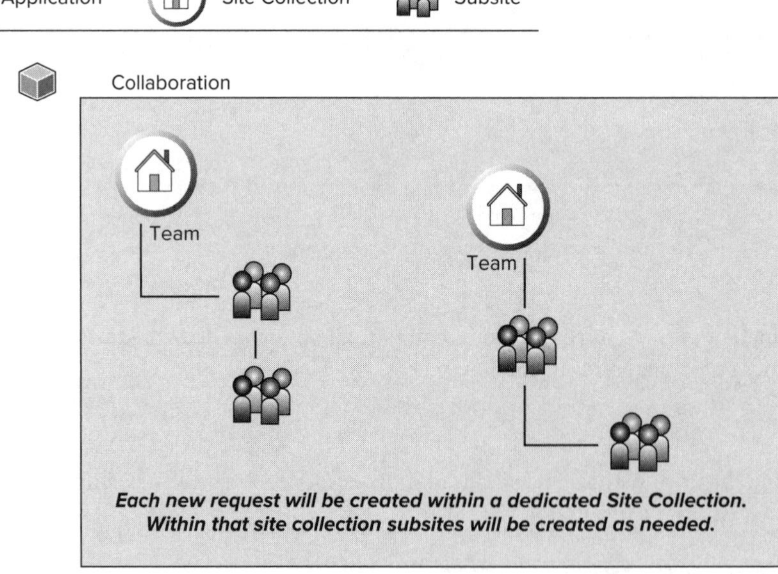

FIGURE 18-6

NOTE *Keep in mind, as we have said earlier in the chapter, that your organization is unique and may differ from the examples we have described.*

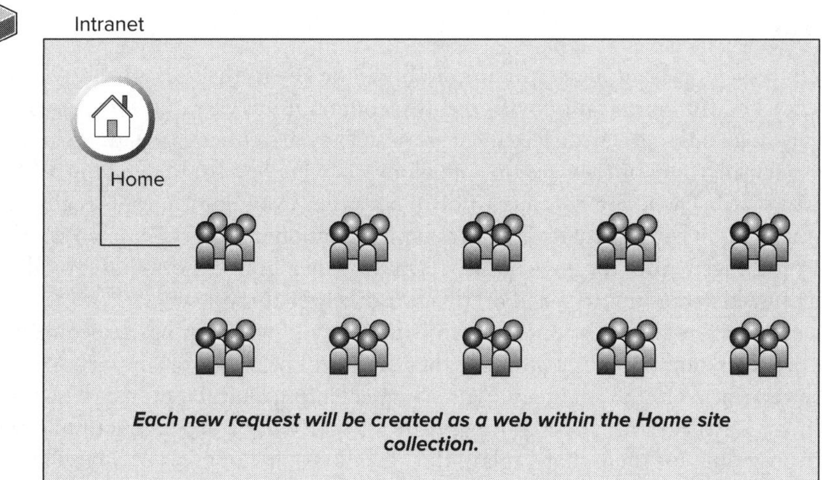
Intranet
Home
Each new request will be created as a web within the Home site collection.

FIGURE 18-7

Operations and Infrastructure

You can think of operations and infrastructure as all of the pieces that are part of the puzzle that keeps the environment up and running. This includes all of the servers, the network, and the applications that are required to run SharePoint. The list of included components can vary greatly depending on your environment; however, following is a list of several different technologies that could be in place within your SharePoint environment:

- SQL
- Windows Server
- Active Directory
- Exchange

When thinking of this list and how it applies to governance, you should be thinking of how you can keep all components working together for the good of the environment. This means that, in addition to applying SharePoint patches, it is also necessary to maintain patches for the other systems such as Windows Server and SQL. Just seeing this list, it should be evident that there are many different components, and keeping up with the management of all of them could become quite the chore for a server administrator. Governance policies should be put in place that can help reduce the level of complexity related to the management of these different components. Some common examples of governance in this area include having a standard downtime window to apply patches and having a test environment that allows administrators to fully test all patches prior to rolling them out to production. Also, keep in mind that sometimes patches can be released because of known security issues. These are typically released as needed and they do not have a specific schedule, so it is important that your governance plans also support this type of scenario.

Communications

Like most things within the organization, communication will be key to the success of any SharePoint implementation. Communication with the user community is essential for many reasons. Users can typically be divided into a few different categories. They are either early adopters who want to be the first to try anything or they are the late bloomers who want to understand all the facts before moving forward. Then, you have everyone in between. Communication is really just the glue that keeps them all on the same page. If your communication plan is articulated well, it can accomplish many great things within the environment. On the other side of the coin, if you don't put effort into an organized communications plan, then it is likely that there will be confusion and chaos throughout the implementation. No one will really understand where things are going and, since there is a lack of understanding, it is also likely that there will be a lack of support. Most users of the system will be very far from the core team that is implementing SharePoint, meaning they will not be part of the day-to-day decisions and planning. Instead, they will be depending on the communications you are providing for them that explain the overall vision and goals of SharePoint. The clearer and more articulate you are able to make the communications, the more likely you are to have support from those on the outside looking in.

When communicating with the user community, there are four questions that should be answered with each communication:

- Why is this good for the organization?
- What is it exactly that we are doing?
- How will this affect me and what I do on a regular basis?
- What training will I receive so that I can perform within the new environment?

These questions will directly impact each person who receives the communication. They will be able to immediately relate to the reasons behind what is being implemented as well as information on how it will directly impact how they work. They will also have all the information pertaining to how the organization is planning to get them ready for the changes. Since they are given all of this information up front, much of the fear and uncertainty is removed, and they are likely to participate more willingly with all of the new changes that are being introduced.

Keeping these things in mind, you should be able to start to see how there should be guidelines in place that outline how the SharePoint team will communicate with the user community. Having this plan in place prior to any major releases will help ensure that nothing is missed during each of the major rollouts. In fact, the governance policies on communication with end users will ultimately end up acting as a checklist outlining what needs to be done with each major project release. And, by following a set of guidelines, users will become used to the consistency in the message and over time they will know exactly what to expect from your team with each rollout.

Training

You can spend months or even years building a complex solution that solves many business problems; however, no matter how great the solution is, if users are not able to easily use the system, then the system cannot be considered a success. This is where training comes into play.

Your approach to training within the organization could have a large impact on the success of SharePoint within the implementation and should definitely not be overlooked during the planning stages. If you are able to train your users on how to use SharePoint, then the SharePoint implementation will have a high likelihood of being successful. Training should be considered at the earliest stages of a SharePoint implementation. By looking at training approaches early on, you will be able to match the training approach with the overall vision of SharePoint within the organization. Think of it this way, SharePoint is a tool that will likely be used by many different users in many different ways. In one SharePoint solution I may simply be a reader, in another I may be an active contributor of site content, and finally in another solution I may be responsible for the administration of the solution. If I am trained on the administrative items when I am only a reader it is likely that I will not be able to retain the information because I was not required to use it at the time of the training. At the same time, if I am expected to be a site administrator and then I am only given basic SharePoint training, then it is likely that I will manage my site incorrectly or in ways that don't align with best practices. This would not be because I purposely went against best practices but simply because I didn't receive the training I needed based on the tasks I would be required to complete. All of this leads us to several key things that should be incorporated into the training plans within the organization.

Current Needs

Training should be based on what users will need to be doing within the environment. Each user should be trained based on the role they will be filling within the environment. These roles should also be separated so that users are only trained in areas that pertain to them. They can however easily be staggered so that a user who will be an administrator first completes reader training, followed by contributor training, and then finally would complete administrator training. In this model a user who would only be contributing to the site would participate in the reader and contributor training but not the administrator training.

Time Sensitivity

Training delivery should be sensitive to when users will need to apply their learning to the solution. When training occurs 3–6 months prior to the system being released, then it is likely that the information learned in the training will be forgotten and users will struggle with the system as if they had not received training. The closer the training can be to the go-live needs of the users, the more effective the training will be.

Development

The final pillar in SharePoint governance is the area of development. This area can have a huge impact to your environment, so it is essential that governance policies are created that help define how development will be used within your environment. Development is anything that is done through a custom solution that changes the way that SharePoint behaves out of the box. This can be anything from a third-party management tool to a custom application developed within SharePoint. Custom code is typically deployed to the environment using a solution. A solution is a `.wsp` file that is similar to a `.cab` file. This `.wsp` file is added to the server and then deployed to the server through the Central Administration site. Essentially, when the file is deployed, all of the changes or custom solutions are added to the server. Whenever the solution is retracted, the changes are undone.

In some cases, custom development can be the snowball that starts at the top of the mountain and then quickly gets out of control as it is rolling down the hill. One thing leads to another and, before you know it, custom development is the solution for everything! This is definitely not a situation you want to find yourself in, and one way to ensure that is to develop some governance policies that help you define when you will use custom development. These policies are not meant to be an end all decision when a request comes in, but instead guidelines that should be followed. If at any point a request comes in for custom development, it should be evaluated based against your governance criteria and then a decision should be made on how to best support the request. Listed below are some guidelines that can be incorporated into your governance for development.

Out of the Box vs. Development

Whenever a request is made for custom development, it is likely that the requestor has tried to do something with SharePoint and was unable to complete the tasks using the tools available to them. Since they were unable to complete the request, then the next step is to request custom development. When the request is made, a team of experienced users should review the request and ensure that no solutions are available out of the box. If no solutions are available out of the box, then the team should review the process or custom solution to see if there might be a different process that can be followed to achieve the same results. Often, if you can simply modify part of your requirements, then you may be able to complete your solution using out-of-the-box tools and remove the need for the custom development. If during the review no alternate solutions are identified, then a cost analysis should be completed that looks at the cost to create and maintain the custom solution. This cost analysis can then be used to help determine if you should proceed with the custom development.

Third Party Solutions vs. Development

If it is determined that a custom solution needs to be developed, prior to development a search for third-party tools should be conducted to ensure that you are not developing a solution that can be purchased. There are many different vendors that specialize in developing add-ons for SharePoint environments, that often fill the gap between what users need and what is available out of the box within SharePoint. Whenever possible, these solutions should be purchased and incorporated into your environment. By taking this approach, you will be greatly reducing the cost that would be required for you to build and maintain the custom solution.

Solutions

If it is determined that custom developed solutions will be needed within your environment, then it is important that these custom-developed components be developed according to best practices and supported approaches. In most cases, this means that any custom code should be created within features and deployed to the server using solutions. Since this book is end-user focused, we will not go into detail on these components. However, as a member of the governance team, it is important that you understand that a solution is the primary method used for deploying custom development to the server.

BEST PRACTICES FOR EFFECTIVENESS

Now that we have worked through the key elements of governance, we will move into some practical examples of how you can implement these areas in your organization. Remember that it is never too late to start implementing governance. If you are several years into your implementation or if you are just getting started, then governance can help you. If you are just getting started, you can start with a clean slate and implement policies from the start. If you are trying to employ governance in an existing implementation, then it may take a little more effort, but just keep in mind that every step towards implementing governance is a step in the right direction. In this section, we will cover some different strategies and best practices that can be incorporated into your governance strategy to help ensure that governance is working for you and is not just another layer or red tape.

Working as a Team

In the first section of this chapter, we outlined several different roles that are common within SharePoint teams. These different roles all play a vital part in keeping the environment stable, and it is essential that each of these roles be represented when planning for building your governance strategies. As you get started with your team, it is important that each team member be represented in the development of the governance standards. Ideally, each role should be responsible for creating the different policies that should be included for their specific area of expertise. An example would be the help desk. The person filling the role of the SharePoint help desk would be the ideal person to manage and maintain the processes that need to be defined for how users go about receiving help with SharePoint. Using this approach allows each team member to really focus on the areas that they know best and not get tied down into being responsible for areas that don't fall into their realm of expertise.

Communication Is Key

As you have learned, it takes many different roles pulling together to build and develop a SharePoint environment. As the team is built and starts working together, it is likely that smaller subteams will be formed so that each role doesn't have to have an equal presence in each project. This allows for the key players to be brought on as needed, limiting their need to be fully committed to the SharePoint implementation. This approach is common; however, in order for it to be truly effective it is essential that all team members are able to get information about all current SharePoint initiatives. This will allow for the entire team to remain up to speed on all efforts, even if they are not actively participating in each roll out. This is important because so much information will be learned along the way and each new project or initiative is likely going to incorporate the lessons learned from the last project or initiative. If all the team members are up to speed along the way, then new projects can kick off and there is no need to spend time bringing everyone up to speed on what has happened on previous projects. Also, this approach helps in creating a quick decision process. Since everyone is up to speed on the project events, it will be easy to rely on team members to make decisions. Since everyone is aware of all that is happening, there will be no time wasted in bringing everyone up to speed so a team decision can be made.

Small Steps Are Better Than No Steps

One of the best pieces of advice that I can give you concerning governance is that it is important to get started. Even if you are only able to outline the plan and fill in the details later, at least you have a map of where you are going! Often I have seen organizations who decided to ignore the time required for governance planning simply because the project timeline didn't allow for development of the policies and procedures needed. This is a common scenario across organizations that should be avoided at all costs. However, if it must be done this way, then at a minimum, review the project and identify if there are any governance policies that would need to be created for this particular project. If so, create those policies within this project. Once the project is completed, you can then go back and create the additional policies and guidelines for the environment. If you simply forgo the governance planning, thinking you will come back to it, when you do, you will likely have to adjust the way you are currently doing things based on the policies you want to put in place. Overall, it would have been better to just start with those policies from the beginning. It is also likely that governance planning will become the key task that always needs to get done but that there is never time to complete. It would be infinitely better to build your governance policies as you go, based on need, than to keep putting the whole governance development on the back burner until you have time to dedicate to the planning effort.

Work from a Written Plan

As you begin to work through the required areas of governance you may be tempted to create the policies and keep them loosely recorded in meeting notes and emails between team members. I would encourage you to avoid this approach as much as possible and instead work from a documented and approved governance document. By taking the time to formalize and seek approval for the governance policies, you are laying the foundation for a solid implementation. Since all the policies are documented and approved, you will be able to fall back on these policies when things come up that clearly go against what was agreed upon. This will then allow you to either adjust the created policies to match the latest requirements or cause you to rework the requirements to match the stated policies. By having everything documented and approved, you are basically creating a road map for the implementation that will guide how you do things moving forward. If the information has been created but not formalized into a document, it is very hard to then use that information to identify when things are requested that go against your policies and would ultimately take your implementation way off track.

Avoiding the Jack of All Trades

The final warning that I would like to leave you with is that the most dangerous role to your implementation is the "jack of all trades." This is the person who can fill multiple levels within the team and who is solely responsible for many aspects of the environment. This is usually the person who would be voted MVP on the team because without them, who knows where your implementation would be! The problem with this approach is that once that person moves on and is no longer available to the team, there will be a huge skill set and experience gap within the team. This gap could end up being the difference between a team that is continually building solutions to solve business problems and a team that is trying to revamp their skill set so that they can create solutions within SharePoint. There will always be one or two team members that carry a large load on the team and it is crazy to think that you could have a team where everyone did equal amounts of work. The point is not to tell you that the ideal team is one that is impossible to have, but instead to encourage you to always be building your team in such a way to mitigate the risks of one team member leaving. If you can build this into your team strategy, then you will not be caught off guard with team changes when they occur.

SUMMARY

We have covered a lot of ground in this chapter! If you are just getting started with governance, you should now have a good understanding of everything that it takes to build a good governance plan. If you have already been working on SharePoint projects but don't have governance in place, it is likely that, as you read through this chapter, you identified with a lot of the warnings we gave about what can go wrong if you don't take the time to create a good governance strategy. I wanted to close out with a few simple reminders as you work through your implementation. First, remember that each organization is completely unique, and while best practices are good guidelines, they need to be incorporated into your organization based on how they will best work for you. Second, keep in mind that governance isn't developed overnight. In the ideal world, you will plan for governance before you implement your first SharePoint project; however, the real world doesn't always allow for such luxuries. The important thing to remember is that it is never too late to implement governance. If you are just getting started, simply pick your biggest pain points and identify what policies and procedures you could put in place to help reduce the pain and manage the environment more effectively. Over time you will begin to build the governance policies, and each new project will be created based on the policies you have in place. You can simply learn from the past and create policies that will keep you from committing the same mistakes again.

EXERCISES

1. True or false: The only time you can develop an effective governance policy is during the initial planning stages of a SharePoint implementation.

2. People within the organization are complaining that they don't understand SharePoint and how they can use it. What can you do to address these issues?

3. You just found out a key team member is going to be moving to be closer to his family. What impact should this have on your team?

▶ WHAT YOU LEARNED IN THIS CHAPTER

TOPIC	KEY CONCEPTS
Defining Governance	Understanding the value and need for creating a SharePoint Governance Policy.
Reviewing the Governance Pillars	Reviewing the key components that should be included in the governance plan.
Developing the Governance Team Structure	Understanding the key roles required for creating an effective governance team.
Reviewing best practices for implementing governance	Looking at principles that you can incorporate to help ensure the creation of an effective governance team.

Installing SharePoint Server 2010

In this appendix, you will learn how to install SharePoint Server 2010 for the purposes of establishing a test environment for the completion of exercises available within this book. It is recommended that prior to completing this exercise, you review the following resources:

- Hardware and Software Requirements for SharePoint Server 2010

  `http://technet.microsoft.com/en-us/library/cc262485.aspx`

- Administrative and Service Accounts Required for Initial Deployment of SharePoint Server 2010

  `http://technet.microsoft.com/en-us/library/ee662513.aspx`

- Deployment Scenarios for SharePoint Server 2010

  `http://technet.microsoft.com/en-us/library/cc303424.aspx`

- SharePoint Server 2010 Resource Center

  `http://technet.microsoft.com/en-us/sharepoint/ee263917.aspx#tab=1`

CHOOSING YOUR INSTALLATION TYPE

When installing SharePoint Server 2010, you have a choice between installing a standalone server and a complete server.

The standalone server will automatically deploy all configurations to your environment, including the installation of a SQL Server 2008 Express database. You will have very little choice in how specific services are configured, and the entire farm will be deployed to a single server. This option is only recommended for product evaluation or demonstration scenarios and is not advisable for use in production environments.

For details on how to create a standalone server-type installation, please review the following article from Microsoft:

```
http://technet.microsoft.com/en-us/library/cc263202.aspx
```

The complete installation type is most commonly chosen by system administrators and provides greater flexibility and control over the configuration of specific SharePoint components. It is the recommended installation for long term use of a system and will be the installation type we review as part of this exercise.

To complete the following exercise, you should have already installed Windows Server 2008 or Windows Server 2008 R2 on the server you wish to install SharePoint on. In addition, you should have already installed and configured SQL Server 2008 or SQL Server 2008 R2 so that it is available for use by your SharePoint Farm. For more information on this, please refer to the Hardware and Software requirements resource listed previously in this Appendix.

TRY IT OUT Installing SharePoint Server 2010

1. Open the install media location for SharePoint Server 2010.
2. Locate the splash.hta file as shown in Figure A-1.
3. Run the splash.hta file. The SharePoint Server 2010 Installation Options window will appear as shown in Figure A-2.

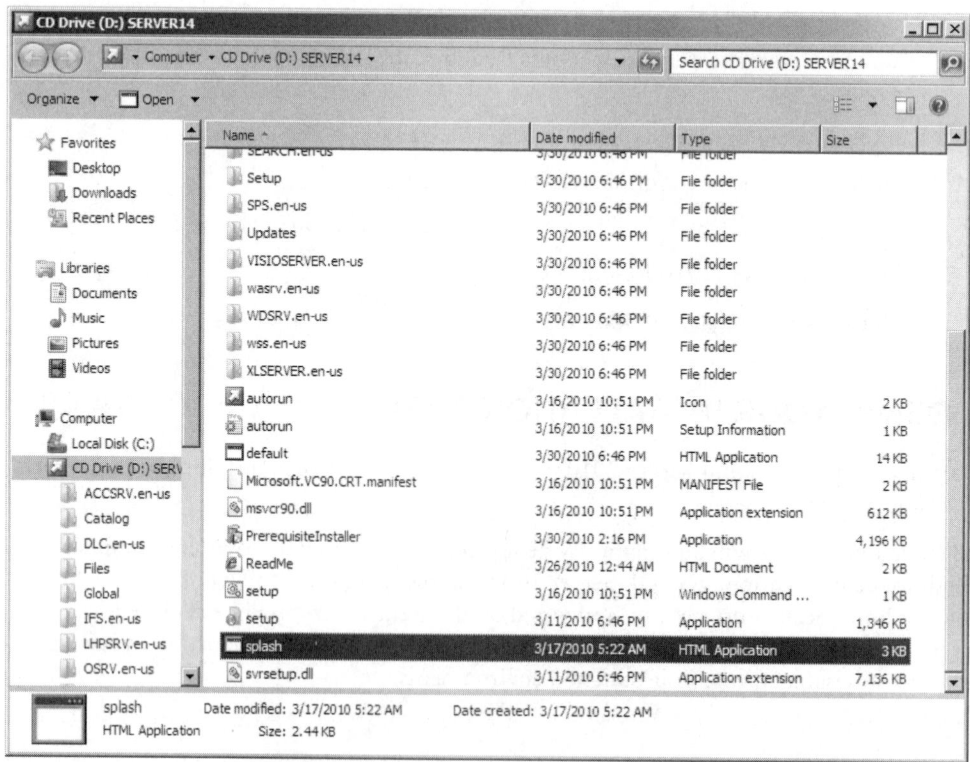

FIGURE A-1

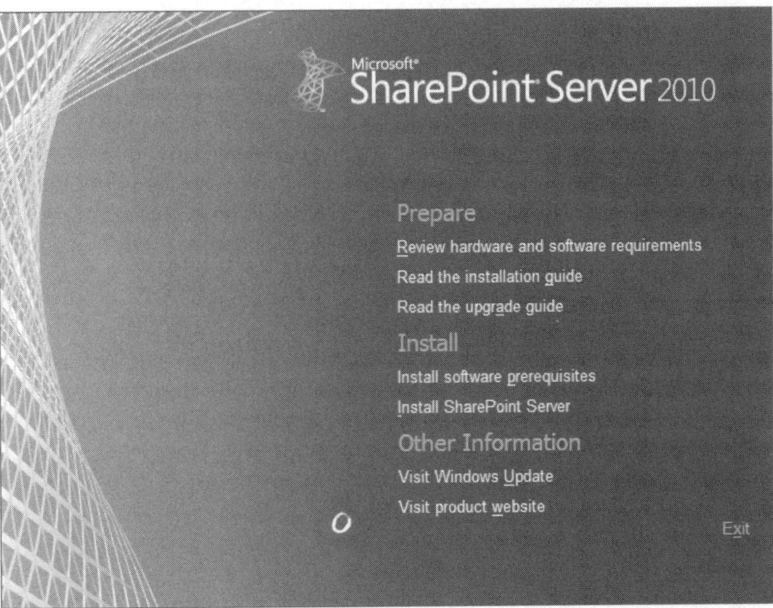

FIGURE A-2

4. Select the Install Software Prerequisites option. The SharePoint 2010 Products Preparation Tool will appear, listing the products that are about to be installed on your server. Please note that you must have an active Internet connection in order to download the prerequisite software on your server.
5. Click Next.
6. Review and accept the terms of the License Agreement.
7. Click Next to download and install the prerequisite software on your server. This process may take several minutes depending on a number of factors, such as the speed of your network connection and server. Once all components have been successfully installed, the Installation Complete window will appear.
8. Click Finish.
9. Return to the SharePoint Server 2010 Installation Options window and select the Install SharePoint Server option.
10. The product key window will appear. Enter the SharePoint Server 2010 Standard or Enterprise key Microsoft provided to you based on your licensing agreement and click Continue.
11. Review and accept the Microsoft Software License Terms.
12. Click Continue.
13. The Choose a File Location window will appear. Depending on your corporate guidelines, you may select an alternate location for the installation of the SharePoint 2010 software and search index files. Once you have selected the appropriate file locations, click the Install Now button.
14. Once the core software installation is finished, you will be required to run the SharePoint Products Configuration Wizard. Ensure the checkbox is selected and click Close.

15. The SharePoint Products Configuration Wizard will launch. Click Next.

16. You will receive a warning message that certain key services will be started or reset during the process. Click Yes to continue.

17. The Connect to a Server Farm window will appear. If this is the first server of a multiple server farm or you are installing on a single server, select the Create a New Server Farm option as shown in Figure A-3 and click Next. If you are adding new servers to an existing SharePoint farm, then select the Connect to an Existing Server Farm option.

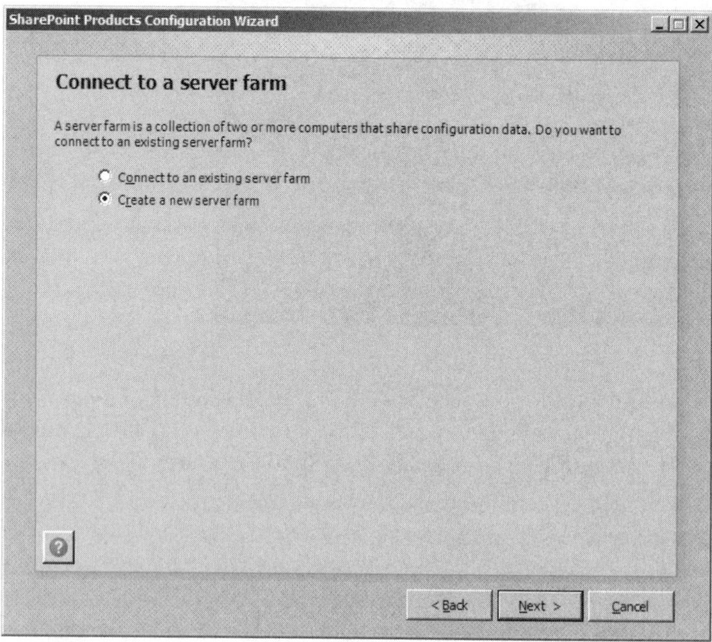

FIGURE A-3

18. The Configuration Database Settings window will appear. Enter the name of your database server as well as the credentials for your database access account and click Next.

19. You will then be asked to provide a passphrase for the farm, which is required when joining additional servers to the farm. Enter your passphrase in the required fields and click Next. It will be important to make note of this passphrase in case it is required at a later time.

20. You will then be redirected to the Configure SharePoint Central Administration Web Application step. For this step you must specify a port number for your web application. Ideally it would be best to enter something that will be memorable. Next select an authentication provider. In this example we will select NTLM, as shown in Figure A-4.

21. The Completing the SharePoint Products Configuration Wizard screen will appear with all the selected settings displayed for your review. Click Next.

22. The SharePoint Configuration Wizard will run. This process may take several minutes to complete. Once this process has finished, a successful configuration message will appear. Click Finish.

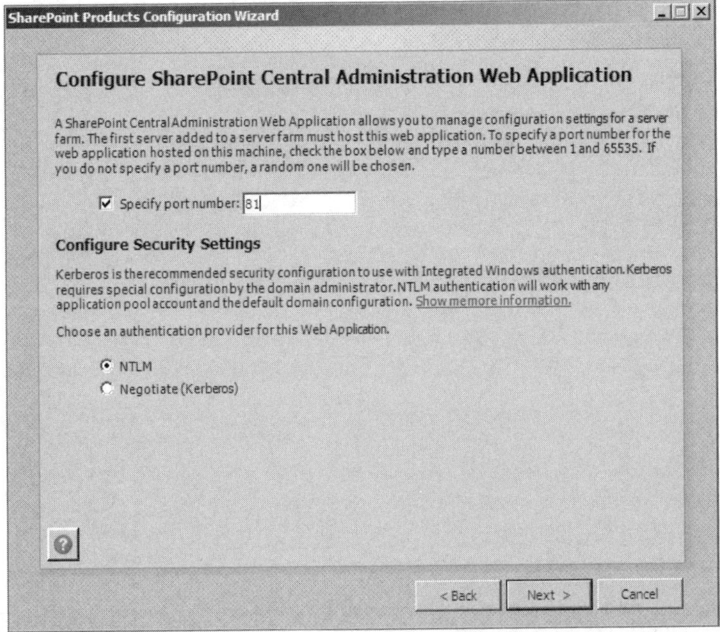

FIGURE A-4

23. The Central Administration Site will appear. The next step will be to configure the various services for your SharePoint farm, as shown in Figure A-5. You may select to configure the services via the Farm Configuration Wizard or manually. For this example, we will run the Farm Configuration Wizard by selecting the Start the Wizard button. However for production scenarios, you should consider configuring these services manually to allow for greater control and flexibility.

24. Specify the Service Account that you wish to run each of the services with.

25. Ensure each of the services is selected.

26. Click Next. The Farm Configuration Wizard will create and configure each of the services. This may take several minutes.

27. Once the services are configured, you will be redirected to a page, as shown in Figure A-6, where you can create the first site collection for your SharePoint farm.

28. Enter **Beginning SharePoint 2010** for the Title field.

29. For the Template Selection, select the Publishing tab and select the Publishing Portal.

30. Click OK. Your new site collection will be created and the Farm Configuration Wizard will complete, as shown in Figure A-7.

31. Click Finish.

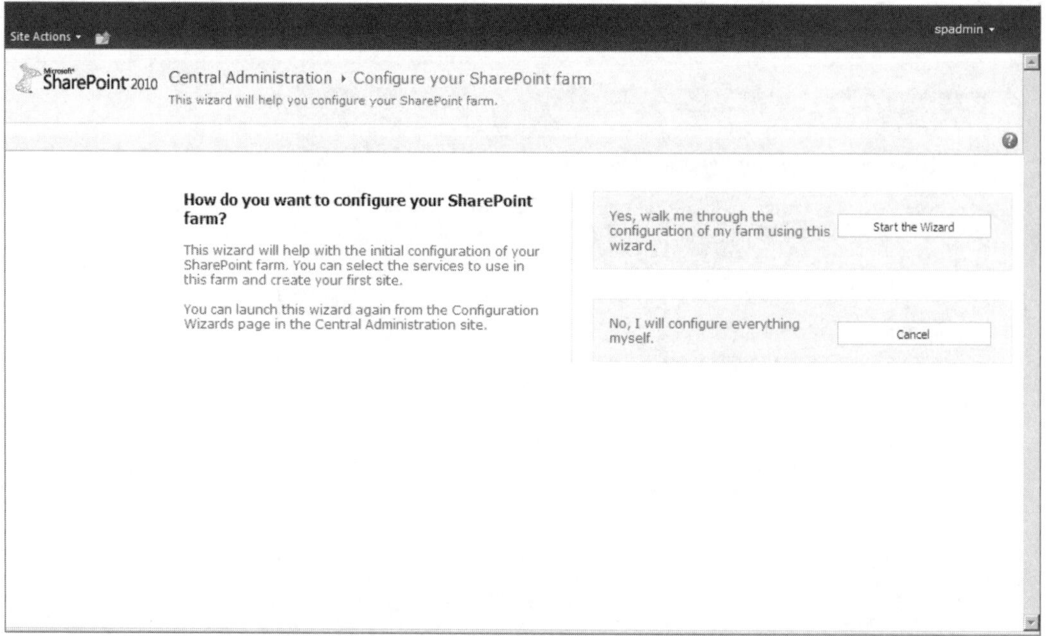

FIGURE A-5

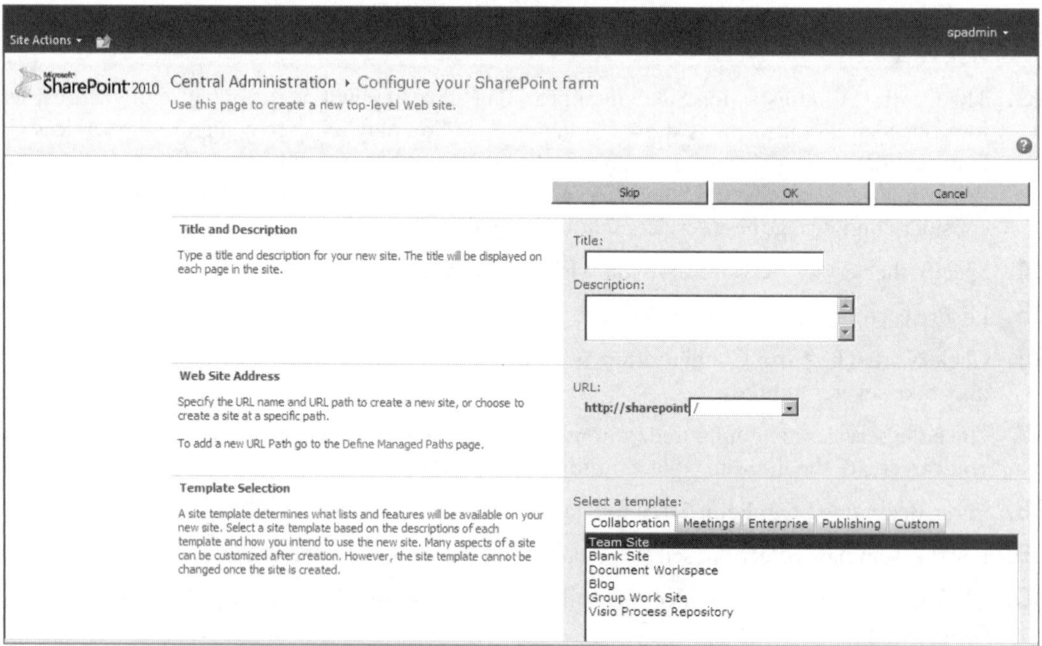

FIGURE A-6

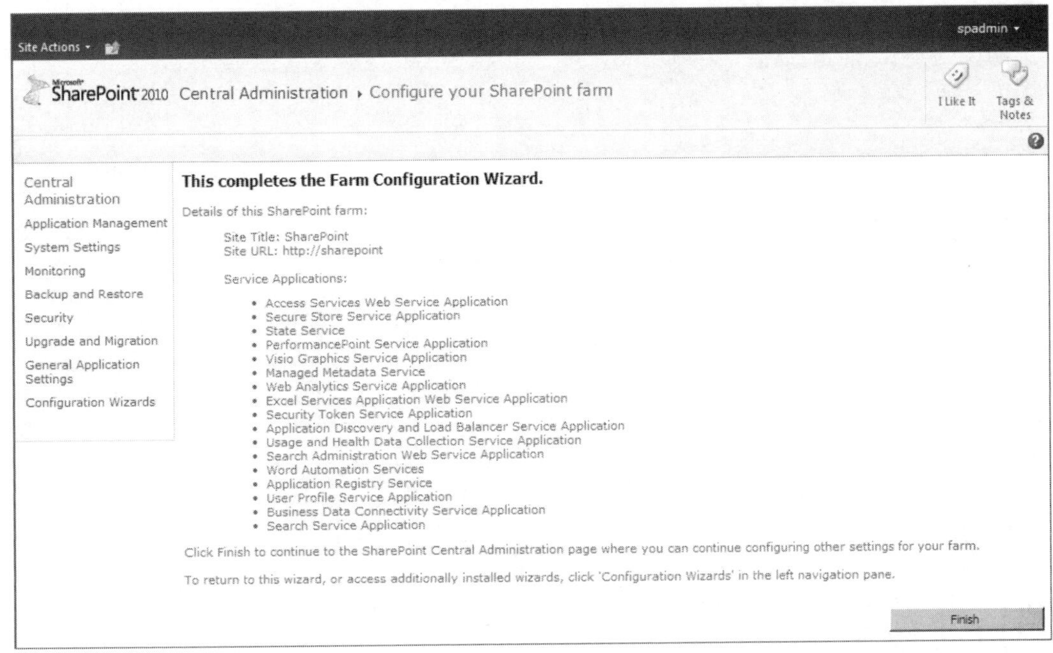
Site Actions
spadmin
SharePoint 2010 Central Administration ▸ Configure your SharePoint farm
I Like It
Tags & Notes
Central Administration
Application Management
System Settings
Monitoring
Backup and Restore
Security
Upgrade and Migration
General Application Settings
Configuration Wizards
This completes the Farm Configuration Wizard.
Details of this SharePoint farm:
Site Title: SharePoint
Site URL: http://sharepoint
Service Applications:
Access Services Web Service Application
Secure Store Service Application
State Service
PerformancePoint Service Application
Visio Graphics Service Application
Managed Metadata Service
Web Analytics Service Application
Excel Services Application Web Service Application
Security Token Service Application
Application Discovery and Load Balancer Service Application
Usage and Health Data Collection Service Application
Search Administration Web Service Application
Word Automation Services
Application Registry Service
User Profile Service Application
Business Data Connectivity Service Application
Search Service Application
Click Finish to continue to the SharePoint Central Administration page where you can continue configuring other settings for your farm.
To return to this wizard, or access additionally installed wizards, click 'Configuration Wizards' in the left navigation pane.
Finish

FIGURE A-7

B

Exercise Solutions

CHAPTER 1 EXERCISE SOLUTIONS

1. What is the difference between a site and a site collection?

   A site is a single location that stores lists and libraries related to a common subject. A site collection represents a group of sites.

2. Your manager informs you that the organization is currently reviewing the need for a corporate portal. List two reasons that justify why organizations invest in portal technologies.

   There are many reasons that organizations invest in portal technologies. Two major reasons are:

   People need to connect with information that will help them make informed business decisions regardless of their physical location. Because portals are web-based and are available via the browser, large numbers of users can access information from a centralized location.

   Portal technologies scale with an organization as it grows and can accommodate business processes and information management.

3. True or false: You must deploy Microsoft SharePoint Foundation 2010 and Microsoft SharePoint Server 2010 together.

   False. When installing SharePoint 2010 you may choose between two versions of the software. SharePoint Foundation provides the core collaborative and file sharing capabilities available within the platform and is most suitable for smaller deployments and teams. SharePoint Server includes all the capabilities of SharePoint Foundation along with more Enterprise-suitable features such as content management, business intelligence, records management, and forms management.

CHAPTER 2 EXERCISE SOLUTIONS

1. If you wanted to receive an email notification every time a new item was added to a list, how would you do that?

   To receive an email notification every time a new item is added to a list, you would create an alert. You create an alert by selecting Alert Me from the List tab of the Ribbon.

2. Describe the difference between a lookup column and a choice column.

   A choice column features a value list, from which you can select options that a site manager has manually entered into the column. A lookup column displays a value list based on the contents of an existing column from another list on the site.

3. Describe how you would send a report of information stored in a list to a partner outside your organization who did not have access to your SharePoint list.

   You can export SharePoint list views to an Excel spreadsheet from the Actions menu. This means you can take information from the SharePoint site, customize it, and send it to team members or partners who do not have direct access to the SharePoint list.

4. What are the differences between a tasks list and a projects task list?

   A projects task list is created with a Gantt chart view by default. Also, you can associate a tasks list with a workflow activity template whereas you can't do this with a projects task.

5. True or false: You can allow users to skip specific questions based on their responses to specific survey questions.

   True. SharePoint includes a concept known as *branching logic* in surveys that define what the next question is that a user should answer based on his response to a specific question.

CHAPTER 3 EXERCISE SOLUTIONS

1. Your project manager informs you that the version of the document you submitted for approval was not correct and that the version that was sent earlier in the week is more appropriate. How do you remedy the situation?

   In this situation, you would browse the available versions of your document to find the version submitted earlier in the week. Once you have found the correct version, you would restore the previous version and finally resubmit the newly restored version to the project manager.

2. Your manager assigns your team a series of presentations for an upcoming conference. How can your team most efficiently collaborate on various slides?

   In this case, you would browse to the View All site content page, select Create, and then select the Slide Library option to create a slide library where your team can collaborate and share slides.

3. You've been given the task of archiving an old document. Currently, these documents are stored in a common file share. What is the best method of mass-copying these documents to a document library?

Browse to the library that you want to use to archive your documents. Select Open with Explorer from the Library tab of the Ribbon menu. Copy and paste your documents into the Explorer view.

4. You need to change the metadata information for multiple documents. What is the fastest way to change the metadata of a particular column for multiple documents?

   In this situation, you could open your library in Datasheet mode (available from the Library tab of the Ribbon). While in Datasheet mode, you can update a particular column for multiple documents, and change them all at the same time.

CHAPTER 4 EXERCISE SOLUTIONS

You've just been assigned the task of customizing the SharePoint site for your company's sales team. The team has struggled with having a central location in which to store all information related to its various opportunities, contacts, meetings, and tasks. It has had a SharePoint site for a few months; however, the team has expressed some concerns that information is too difficult to find. The following exercises focus on ways in which you need to develop the site to become a more useful tool for the sales team.

1. After conducting a planning workshop with some members of the sales team, you determine that, while the sales manager wants to see all information stored in a single location, the actual sales team members struggle with seeing too much information. As a result, it takes sales team members longer than necessary to look up contact phone numbers. The sales team prefers to only see contacts from their own region. What can you do to make both groups happy?

   By creating a site column for Region, lists, such as the contact list, can feature custom views that filter items to only show items for a specific region. The sales manager can use a list view that shows items across all regions, and each regional office can have its own view that filters out information from regions other than its own. A list-centric column for Region would work specifically for this scenario as well. However, because you can assume this type of behavior is desired for other content lists on the site, a site column may be a better implementation choice.

2. Whenever a salesperson views the central list of contacts, he/she wants to see specific contacts that he/she has added. How would you accomplish that?

   You can accomplish this by creating a custom view that has a filter to only show items where Created By is equal to [me]. It may also be beneficial to make the custom personalized view the default view so that users can see that view first when they enter a list.

3. The sales manager wants to see a list of all opportunities that are in the pipeline for his staff. Because he has some concerns about the length of time certain sales staff members are taking to close their leads, he wants to visually identify leads that have the longest duration from initial point of contact to the expected date of sale. What can you suggest to help address this situation?

   By creating a Gantt view on the list, you can display visual indicators of items based on the date of initial contact and expected date of sale. The sales manager can easily identify the ones that are taking the longest to close.

CHAPTER 5 EXERCISE SOLUTIONS

1. The marketing department has a custom picture library approval status workflow. They would like to see a Visio diagram of a live flowchart that shows the steps of the workflow, and what activity has taken place. What setting do you recommend that they use?

   In the workflow in SharePoint Designer, go to the Workflow Settings page. Put a checkmark next to "Allow this workflow to be manually started," and publish the workflow again.

2. Each document in the company policies library needs to go through a strenuous collaboration and approval process. When the workflow is kicked off, it first needs to be sent to everyone in the taxation department for review and feedback. After the feedback is collected, the approval process should automatically begin. How do you recommend they configure the out-of-box Approval workflow in the browser?

   When adding the new Approval workflow in the browser, put the Taxation group of people in the Assign To box, with the order as Parallel. Click the Add a New Stage button. Add the same group of people, this time with the order as Serial. Save the workflow.

3. The personnel department has an approval workflow that needs to be strictly locked down so that members of the process cannot see each other's assigned tasks. Which action do you recommend that they use in their custom SharePoint Designer workflow?

   Each of the three task process actions has its own settings screen, which has a checkbox to "Only allow task recipients and process owners to read and edit workflow tasks." They should use the Start Approval Process action, since it is an Approval workflow.

4. Sue Ellen has added the Content Approval Status action to her custom workflow, but she is baffled at why this action does not seem to be doing its job. What list setting do you recommend that Sue Ellen modify?

   In the list settings, click on Versioning settings. Change the setting called "Require content approval for submitted items" to Yes. Click OK. The workflow will now be tied to the list's own content approval. Without this setting, the action called Content Approval Status does not work.

5. Bob is attempting to manually start his workflow called Policy Approval, but he does not see it in the Start a New Workflow section of the workflows page for that item. He has verified that the workflow is allowed to be manually started, and it has been published. Where can you look to troubleshoot his problem?

   Bob should click on the item name in the list, and click Workflows. The workflow he needs is not displayed in the Start a New Workflow section because it is already in the Running Workflows section. The status is Error Occurred. Click on this running workflow's name, and click Terminate This Workflow.

CHAPTER 6 EXERCISE SOLUTIONS

1. True or false: You can only associate one document template with a document library.

   This is somewhat of a trick question so the answer is both true and false. Prior to enabling content type management via the Advanced settings of a document library, you may only associate a single document template with a document library. However, if you enable content type management on your library, you can then manage multiple content types from that single location and have more than one document template associated with the library.

2. Imagine you are responsible for ensuring that all documents created and printed within your organization have the words Private and Confidential on them. What are your options for making this happen, and which would provide the best results?

   You have two primary methods for accomplishing this.

   - Your first method is to add the words Private and Confidential to all the standard document templates within the organization. This method is tedious and requires you to constantly add these words to all new document templates. Also it's difficult to prevent users from removing the text directly from their document themselves.
   - The second method involves creating an information management policy on the base document content type so that all child document content types inherit the policy. This method also supports the creation of new content types that maintain the same information management policy setting. There is a setting on the label configuration that allows you to enter custom text such as Private and Confidential, and you can select a checkbox option to prevent users from removing the label or changing it after it's been added.

3. People in your company have complained that recent job postings are being published on the corporate intranet website with typos and grammatical errors. Your management team demands a certain level of professionalism in any content that the division posts. What are some steps you can take to ensure that future job postings are reviewed prior to publishing them?

   To manage approval processes around specific types of information such as job postings, you associate an Approval workflow template with the Job Postings content type. You can define the workflow activity to launch whenever an item is either created or modified. You can also select who needs to provide the approval for new content. Because the workflow is configured on the content type level, no matter how many location job postings exist throughout the portal, you can apply the same business process.

CHAPTER 7 EXERCISE SOLUTIONS

1. Some users visit one particular document library on a regular basis, and they claim that it is very important that they are aware as soon as a change is made in the library. They have set up email alerts to be notified but would also like the document library on the page to also automatically stay updated, so that they don't have to refresh the browser to see changes. How can you make this happen?

   The answer is AJAX. Go to the document library and click Site Actions and Edit Page. Open the document library's Web Part tool pane, and expand the AJAX Options. Put checkmarks next to Show Manual Refresh Button and Enable Asynchronous Automatic Refresh. Set the interval in seconds per the site users' requirements. With these AJAX settings, the users will not only have a refresh button that they can click, but the document library will also refresh automatically.

2. The marketing manager has spent a lot of time configuring a Chart web part that is based on data in an external content type. He would like to save this web part and put a copy of it on a site in another site collection. How would he accomplish this?

   The answer is to export the web part and import it to the other site, and this is mentioned at the end of the "Chart Web Part" section of Chapter 7. By default, the Export option won't show, so this entails a quick edit to the Web Part properties.

3. The Human Resources department has its own Team Site for collaboration. Members of the site would like to quickly see a list of all documents that they are working on, no matter which library the files exist in. Which web part can accomplish this most easily?

   The Relevant Documents web part not only accomplishes this goal but is also the easiest to set up. Simply add this web part to the home page of the HR Team Site.

4. The company picnic happened last week, and the picnic photos have been uploaded to a picture library on the site, along with all of the pictures from other past events. How can you display only the picnic pictures in a pretty slideshow view on your site?

   You will use The Picture Library Slideshow web part for this task. Notice in the Web Part properties that there is an option to select a view from the list. The trick here is to create a filtered view in the library that only shows the picnic pictures and call it Picnic. One easy way would be to filter by date, so that the Created column is equal to *the date that the picnic pictures were uploaded*. In the Web Part properties view drop-down box, and select Picnic.

5. There is an announcement list on the site that really only pertains to IT managers. Without involving security or permissions, how do you display these announcements on a page so that only the SharePoint group of IT Managers can see the web part?

   The answer is to use audiences. Insert the manager-only announcements list on the home page. In the Web Part properties, expand the Advanced section, at the bottom of which you will see a Target Audiences box. Pick the IT Managers SharePoint group, and click OK. This web part can now only be seen by that particular group of people, although anyone will be able to access it via the View All Site Content button on the site.

CHAPTER 8 EXERCISE SOLUTIONS

1. Describe the differences between a site collection and site.

   A site collection is a container that holds many different types of content, including sites. Site collections have galleries associated with them that store content that can be used for all sites within the site collection. A site is created within a site collection. Sites are used to store different lists and libraries.

2. You have been asked to create a site to manage the collaboration of a small committee that meets on a regular basis. What template would be appropriate for managing this content?

   An appropriate template for this scenario would be one of the Meeting Workspace templates.

3. What options do you have for working with your site offline?

   You can work with your data offline when you use the SharePoint Workspace client.

CHAPTER 9 EXERCISE SOLUTIONS

1. Explain the importance of user experience to the user adoption process.

   A number of factors can impact the experience of a user when using a technology solution, such as usability, navigation, and intuitive interfaces. All of these factors improve the ability of users to locate the information they seek and subsequently improve how they do their job. When users view a technology tool as an aid in how they work, they are more likely to adopt it.

2. True or false: Themes and master pages require an understanding of CSS in order to apply branding changes to a SharePoint site.

   False. It is not necessary to have an understanding of CSS to make modifications to a SharePoint 2010 Theme. However, you should have an understanding of CSS for Master Page customizations.

3. True or false: A master page defines the chrome on a website.

   True. The master page defines how the outer portion of the website will look. It does not impact the look and feel of the content areas of the page.

4. According to best practices, where should you store your style sheets?

   Style sheets should be stored in a single location within a site collection. The optimal location is the Style Library located at the top level site of the site collection.

5. Why is it important to create and modify copies of existing versions of files rather than modifying the default files when branding SharePoint?

   It is critical not to change default files when branding SharePoint for two primary reasons:

   - By changing the default files, you will impact the look and feel of all locations associated with those files. This makes it difficult to contain specific changes to certain areas of the site collection or SharePoint environment.
   - Changing default files may have adverse impacts to future software updates or version releases which can cause difficulty for maintenance, operations, or migration activities.

CHAPTER 10 EXERCISE SOLUTIONS

1. Explain the difference between a SharePoint site group and an audience.

   A SharePoint site group is a role in SharePoint to which users can be assigned. It can be associated with a specific set of permissions to perform tasks and duties. An audience is a membership group that helps target relevant content to users based on personal profile properties or memberships within Windows or SharePoint groups.

2. True or false: By targeting content to users, you can ensure that only the right people have access to view items.

   False. Targeting content to users via audiences has no impact on the user's access to an item. Instead, audiences filter through large amounts of data and target specific items as those to which a member will most likely have an interest.

3. What are the three different types of audiences that you can create?

   You can create audiences in SharePoint based on Windows Group Memberships (distribution list or security groups), Profile Properties, or SharePoint Site Group Membership.

4. What are the different levels of access that you can control in SharePoint?

   There are several levels of access to information including:

   - Site Level Access
   - List or Library Level Access
   - Item Level Access

5. Explain from what source you can import user profile information.

   Users can update their profile information directly within the SharePoint application. They can also import it from external systems such as Active Directory, LDAP servers, or Business Connectivity Services applications.

CHAPTER 11 EXERCISE SOLUTIONS

1. You need to see where in the organizational chart a person named Christa Gellar fits in. How can you find that information about her?

   Click your name at the top right and choose My Site. In the Find People box at the top of the page, type Christa Gellar's name and click the magnifying glass. On the search results page, under Christa's name, click Browse in Organizational Chart.

2. Bob complains that the activity feed on his My Site has too much information, especially about ratings. What changes do you recommend for his settings?

   Here are the instructions to give Bob: At the top right, click My Site. Click Newsfeed Settings. In the Activities I am following section, uncheck "Rating," and click Save and Close.

3. Sally uses the Projects library on the Marketing site quite frequently. She would like it to be more readily available to her within the Office applications. How can she add this shortcut?

   When Sally is on the Projects library page, she can click the Library tab in the contextual Ribbon. Then, she can click Connect to Office and Add to SharePoint Sites.

4. Todd has added the Tag Cloud web part to his team site. He wants to know if he can configure it to display the number of times each tag was used. What is the answer?

   In the Tag Cloud web part properties, Todd can check the box next to Show Count. This will display a number in parentheses next to each tag in the cloud.

5. Management has decided that the link to My Links should be displayed in the top navigation of My Site. How can this be accomplished?

   In the User Profile Service Application in Central Administration, the SharePoint administrator can add a new Personalization Site Link. This URL is to the My Links page, and as long as no audience is applied, then everyone will see it.

CHAPTER 12 EXERCISE SOLUTIONS

1. Explain the reasons why you would decide to create a form that supports editing in the browser.

   Because not all users have access to the InfoPath application, creating a form template that is supported by the browser can expose the form to a wider audience. In addition, because the browser removes some of the interface elements that the InfoPath form itself offers, such as a view switcher or formatting controls, it may be a more controlled environment to have users complete and review form data. Finally, by using Forms Services to present the form to users, they see the form as a standard web-based form and can spend less time focusing on the technology and more time thinking about the information they are supplying and the decisions they are required to make as part of a business process.

2. Explain the different scenarios by which you can publish a form template.

   A form template can be published to SharePoint directly from a document library. This is suitable for scenarios where the form is only required to be hosted in a single location. Another alternative is to publish the form as a content type to a SharePoint Server. This method is most appropriate when there is a requirement to publish the form to multiple locations within a single site collection. Finally, there is an option to upload the form template via the Central Administration site as a server administrator. This method is most appropriate for complex forms featuring advanced customizations or custom code. It is also suitable for situations where a form template needs to be accessible across multiple site collections within a single server farm.

3. Describe a template part.

   A template is a reusable component that is comprised of form fields, controls, and customizations that can be saved as a single control and added to other form templates. An example of a template part might be a group of fields for entering contact information within a form. Because these fields are often exactly the same across all forms, it would be advantageous to save them once as a template part for reuse in other form templates.

4. Explain the difference between a control and a data source element.

   A data source element represents information and data that can be collected within a form. However, a control is the mechanism by which the data will be entered or viewed within the form. One single data source element may use multiple controls across different views depending on the requirements for data entry or viewing. However, each instance of a control that is added to a form can only be mapped to a single data source.

5. True or false: InfoPath cannot submit to a data connection. It can only retrieve information.

   False. InfoPath can submit data to an external data source as well as receive data.

CHAPTER 13 EXERCISE SOLUTIONS

1. Your manager informs you that you have been selected to create a website for the communications department on the new SharePoint Server. The main requirement is to have the site allow non-technical employees in the communications division to publish product information that can be viewed as a web page. What do you do?

In this situation, you begin by creating a Collaboration Portal. You would first create a Newsletter content type to have columns that represent such things as a title, body text, and a picture. Next, you create a page layout based on this content type. You would call the page layout "Newsletter," and the types of content you can create on this page would be the columns title, body text, and picture.

You can email communications to notify them that users with appropriate permissions can create newsletters by selecting Site Actions ➪ Create Page, and selecting the Newsletter Page Layout before finally inputting the title, body text, and picture.

2. True or false: You can enable the Publishing feature after you create a team site.

   True. Although initially you can create a website using a template, such as the Team Site, you can make it publishing-capable at a later date using the power of Features. You enable Features from the Site Collection Features and Site Features pages which you access from the Site Settings page. After enabling the Publishing feature on a team site, all publishing lists, libraries, and functionality are made available on your team site.

3. The sales manager says a recent sale requires the implementation of an externally facing customer support portal in two languages, English and French. How do you proceed?

   In this situation, you first create a Publishing Portal, the standard template for Internet-facing sites. To make your site accessible in two languages, you first enable and set up Variations on your site. You then create labels for your languages, one named English and one named French. You must specify one of the sites as the source site. The source site is where users initially create content. As content is created, it's automatically replicated on the other sites where it remains in the source sites language until someone translates it.

4. True or false: You only add controls to your page layouts that support text and rich text. You must use web parts for the display of rich media.

   False. A variety of controls exist that may be added to a page layout including controls for rich media, images, and hyperlinks.

CHAPTER 14 EXERCISE SOLUTIONS

1. What is the difference between a file plan and a classification plan?

   A file plan outlines the types of documents and information that exists within your organization as well as the rules that exist related to where the files must be stored and for how long. The classification plan focuses more specifically on the data that must be tracked related to each document type and is typically completed as a secondary step to the creation of the file plan.

2. How is In Place Records Management different than Archive-Based Records Management?

   In Place Records Management focuses on the declaration and storage of records within the contextual location from which they are created and collaborated on whereas Archive-Based Records Management focuses on the copy or movement of a file to a Records Repository where it will be stored outside of its original context.

3. True or false: A file cannot be deleted if it has been declared a record.

   Either. This is determined based on the Records Declaration Settings for the site collection as outlined in Chapter 14.

4. Can retentions schedules be applied to Folders or Content Types?

   Both. When defining retention schedules, you must determine whether they are applied to the content type or the folder that the file is stored within.

CHAPTER 15 EXERCISE SOLUTIONS

1. Chris is in the company's marketing department. He has created a custom list on the departmental SharePoint site. He would like to create a lookup column in this list to show the list of the company's products. This data already exists in a SQL database. How can he go about creating this lookup?

   Chris can create an external content type consisting of the SQL table he wants to reference. Then, in his custom list, he can create a new column of the type "External Data," and set it to look up that ECT.

2. Lori is a project manager and has created two external content types in SharePoint Designer. One ECT is a list of projects, and the other is a list of all tasks. Each task is related to one project. How can Lori create the relationship between the two lists in SharePoint?

   Lori can create an association between the two ECTs. This is done from within SharePoint Designer, in the Tasks ECT, on the Operations Design View. Right-click on the Tasks table in the data source explorer, and choose New Association. This is where the Project ID in the Tasks table can be mapped to the Project ID in the Project table.

3. Charlotte would like to use a query string in a URL and pass this information to several Business Data web parts on a page. Which out-of-the-box web part will allow her to do this?

   Charlotte would use the Business Data Item Builder web part. This out-of-the-box web part allows you to define the name of the query string parameter, and then you can add other web parts to the page. This creates web part connections between the Business Data Item Builder and each of the other web parts.

4. The project managers have a list of project tasks in a database. They would like to be able to view and work on these tasks from within Outlook, in the familiar interface. How can they accomplish this?

   They can create an external content type and external list for the tasks table. When they first create the ECT, they will need to set the Office Item Type drop-down box to Task. Then, when they create the external list, it will contain the Connect to Outlook button in the List tab in the Ribbon.

5. The IT department would like to allow users to create change requests in a help desk ticketing system that exists in a SQL database. Each change request should go through an approval process before it can be entered in the database. What is a method that can be used to accomplish this?

   IT can create the change request form as a custom list in SharePoint and create a workflow on this change request list. Insert a Start Approval Process action in the workflow, set to run when an item is created. Add a Create List Item action that runs when items have been approved. Set up the workflow to create a new item in the help desk ticket external list.

CHAPTER 16 EXERCISE SOLUTIONS

1. What site template comes preconfigured to support business intelligence content?

   Business Intelligence Center.

2. True or false: In SharePoint 2010 Excel services content can be edited through the browser.

   True. Content can be edited through the browser when the server is configured with the Office Web Applications.

3. What permission level would you need to apply so that users would only be able to open a snapshot of an Excel Services document?

   If you grant someone the View Item permission to an Excel Services document then they will only be able to access the snapshot.

4. What type of content can be configured within a KPI indicator?

   KPIs can be configured for the following types of data:

   - SharePoint List
   - Excel Services
   - SQL Analysis Services
   - Fixed Value based on Manual Entry

CHAPTER 17 EXERCISE SOLUTIONS

1 What are the limits to configurations made at the site collection level?

   These configurations are only available within the current site collection and cannot be used within another site collection.

2. Where do you need to make configurations if they need to be accessed by every site within the farm?

   Changes that are global in nature and need to be referenced by the entire farm should be made in Central Administration.

3. You have a group of users that wants to be able to quickly search within all documents of a certain type. How would you help them configure this?

   A search scope could be created that would limit their search to only a specific type of document, such as presentations (PowerPoint) or spreadsheets (Excel).

4. What is a Best Bet?

   A Best Bet is a keyword search result that is displayed whenever a user completes a search with the keyword in the query.

5. True or false: SharePoint supports the use of Boolean operations within a search query.

   True. SharePoint search supports Boolean search queries.

INDEX

Symbols

A

B

C

D

E

F

G

H

I

J

K

M

N

T

W

X